Algebra 2

HOLT, RINEHART AND WINSTON

A Harcourt Education Company

Austin • Orlando • Chicago • New York • Toronto • London • San Diego

Acknowledgments appear on pages 1093-1094, which are extensions of the copyright page.

Printed in the United States of America

ISBN: 0-03-070044-2

3 4 5 6 7   032   07 06 05 04

James E. Schultz, *Senior Series Author*

Dr. Schultz has over 30 years of experience teaching at the high school and college levels and is the Robert L. Morton Professor of Mathematics Education at Ohio University. He helped to establish standards for mathematics instruction as a co-author of the NCTM *Curriculum and Evaluation Standards for School Mathematics* and *A Core Curriculum: Making Mathematics Count for Everyone.*

Wade Ellis, Jr., *Senior Author*

Professor Ellis has co-authored numerous books and articles on how to integrate technology realistically and meaningfully into the mathematics curriculum. He was a key contributor to the landmark study *Everybody Counts: A Report to the Nation on the Future of Mathematics Education.*

Kathleen A. Hollowell

Dr. Hollowell is an experienced high school mathematics and computer science teacher who currently serves as Director of the Mathematics & Science Education Resource Center, University of Delaware. Dr. Hollowell is particularly well versed in the special challenge of motivating students and making the classroom a more dynamic place to learn.

Paul A. Kennedy

A professor in the Department of Mathematics at Colorado State University, Dr. Kennedy is a leader in mathematics education reform. His research focuses on developing algebraic thinking by using multiple representations and technology. He has been the author of numerous publications and he is often invited to speak and conduct workshops on the teaching of secondary mathematics.

CONTRIBUTING AUTHOR

Martin Engelbrecht
A mathematics teacher at Culver Academies, Culver, Indiana, Mr. Engelbrecht also teaches statistics at Purdue University, North Central. An innovative teacher and writer, he integrates applied mathematics with technology to make mathematics accessible to all students.

TECHNOLOGY WRITER AND CONSULTANT

Betty Mayberry
Ms. Mayberry is the mathematics department chair at Gallatin High School, Gallatin, Tennessee. She has received the Presidential Award for Excellence in Teaching Mathematics and the Tandy Technology Scholar award. She is a Teachers Teaching with Technology instructor and a popular speaker for the effective use of technology in mathematics instruction.

Table of Contents

1 DATA AND LINEAR REPRESENTATIONS   2

MATH CONNECTIONS

Coordinate Geometry 23, 27, 34   **Statistics** 38, 39, 60, 74
Geometry 31, 35, 47, 49, 75, 76, 79

APPLICATIONS

Science
Agriculture 19, 44
Anatomy 42, 79
Health 37, 43, 59, 68
Medicine 48
Meteorology 10, 19, 69
Physics 19, 32, 33, 35, 36
Temperature 46

Social Studies
Demographics 10, 40
Government 43, 60
Psychology 72

Language Arts
Communicate 7, 17,
   25, 33, 40, 48, 57, 67
Etymology 42, 69

Business and Economics
Business 10, 60, 75
Communications 12
Construction 19, 77
Consumer Economics 50, 75
Economics 10
Manufacturing 61, 66
Marketing 42
Real Estate 69
Sales Tax 7
Taxes 18, 40, 50, 54

Life Skills
Academics 28, 56, 58
Banking 50
Freight Charges 74
Fund-raising 59
Income 4, 5, 8, 9, 28, 33, 50, 51
Personal Finance 76

Sports and Leisure
Entertainment 68
Recreation 29, 30, 50, 51, 67, 69
Sports 39, 41, 69, 77
Travel 21, 22, 25, 27, 60

MATH CONNECTIONS

Geometry 99, 102, 104, 109   Transformations 126, 127, 130, 132
Statistics 91, 149

APPLICATIONS

Science
Chemistry 100, 121, 147
Engineering 100
Health 133
Medicine 97, 98
Meteorology 86
Physics 94, 98, 100, 141
Space Science 93, 101, 110, 117, 132
Temperature 116, 118

Social Studies
Current Events 92
Demographics 92, 116

Language Arts
Communicate 90, 98, 107, 114, 121, 128, 139
Etymology 90

Business and Economics
Business 90, 92, 116, 123
Manufacturing 116, 128, 129, 130
Real Estate 123
Taxes 88

Life Skills
Consumer Economics 106, 109, 114, 115, 117, 123, 126, 129, 131, 132, 146, 149
Income 107, 108, 124, 131
Transportation 107, 111

Sports and Leisure
Entertainment 102
Puzzles 123
Sports 146

Other
Genealogy 101

SYSTEMS OF LINEAR EQUATIONS & INEQUALITIES 154

MATH CONNECTIONS

Coordinate Geometry 169
Geometry 162, 177, 184, 192

Maximum/Minimum 188, 189, 190, 191, 192
Transformations 197, 200, 201

APPLICATIONS

Science
Agriculture 187, 188, 191, 193
Aviation 195, 201
Chemistry 156, 158, 163
Engineering 209
Health 182, 193, 201
Nutrition 170

Language Arts
Communicate 160, 168, 176, 182, 191, 199
Synonyms 186

Business and Economics
Broadcasting 206
Business 164, 165, 168, 170, 171, 185, 186, 193, 194
Economics 207
Fuel Economy 172, 174, 176
Investments 170
Landscaping 171
Manufacturing 184, 192, 206, 209
Small Business 161, 178, 194

Life Skills
Consumer Economics 163, 178
Fund-raising 177
Income 162, 170, 185, 209
Transportation 193

Sports and Leisure
Drama 179
Entertainment 185
Recreation 177
Sports 163, 170, 177, 198, 199, 200, 206

Other
Criminology 184

MATH CONNECTIONS

Coordinate Geometry 219, 221, 227, 230, 241
Geometry 249, 255
Probability 258
Transformations 220, 221, 222, 230, 265

APPLICATIONS

Science
Anatomy 267
Chemistry 250
Cryptography 234, 237, 239, 241
Networks 228, 229, 232, 233
Nutrition 227, 229, 230, 231

Social Studies
Geography 222

Language Arts
Communicate 220, 229, 239, 248, 256

Business and Economics
Business 259
Inventory 216, 218, 221, 223, 232
Investments 244, 245, 248, 250
Manufacturing 256, 258
Rentals 233
Small Business 251, 253, 267

Life Skills
Academics 223
Consumer Economics 223
Fund-raising 264

Sports and Leisure
Entertainment 249
Sports 225, 231, 232, 267
Travel 259

Other
Jewelry 263

Ancient clay tablet believed to contain Pythagorean triples

MATH CONNECTIONS

Coordinate Geometry 318, 321
Geometry 284, 285, 286, 287, 288, 296, 297, 305, 345
Maximum/Minimum 276, 277, 278, 312, 335

Patterns in Data 328
Statistics 323, 325
Transformations 279, 289, 302, 304, 306, 321, 345

APPLICATIONS

Science
Architecture 290, 295
Aviation 286, 344
Chemistry 347
Engineering 285, 288, 299, 303, 314, 345
Navigation 288
Physics 274, 288, 305, 328, 329, 336, 337, 345, 347
Rescue 281, 283

Language Arts
Communicate 277, 286, 295, 303, 310, 319, 326, 334

Business and Economics
Advertising 298
Business 312, 321, 328, 336, 347
Construction 279, 286, 289, 307, 309, 311
Manufacturing 312
Small Business 330, 332, 336, 337
Telecommunications 288

Life Skills
Fund-raising 279, 305

Highway Safety 322, 325, 327
Recycling 321

Sports and Leisure
Art 312
Recreation 288, 344
Sports 280, 288, 289, 297, 298, 304, 306, 313, 329, 336, 337

EXPONENTIAL AND LOGARITHMIC FUNCTIONS   352

MATH CONNECTIONS

Geometry 415
Patterns in Data 355, 359

Statistics 366, 368
Transformations 363, 364, 368, 373, 375, 386, 398

APPLICATIONS

Science
Agriculture 399
Archeology 396, 397, 398, 408
Biology 354, 408, 414
Chemistry 360, 373, 374, 375, 391, 413
Earth Science 415
Geology 402, 403, 407, 408
Health 357, 358, 359, 383, 414
Physical Science 360

Physics 376, 383, 386, 387, 389, 390, 398, 405, 407, 414
Space Science 360

Social Studies
Demographics 356, 358, 359, 360, 408, 415
Psychology 408

Language Arts
Communicate 358, 366, 374, 381, 389, 396, 406

Business and Economics
Business 399, 417
Depreciation 412
Economics 398
Investments 361, 365, 367, 368, 384, 392, 394, 396, 397, 398, 399, 409, 412, 414, 415, 417

7 POLYNOMIAL FUNCTIONS 422

MATH CONNECTIONS

Geometry 430, 448   **Transformations** 462
Statistics 436, 438

APPLICATIONS

Science
Agriculture 453
Archaeology 473
Medicine 454
Thermodynamics 465

Social Studies
Education 432
Geography 464

Language Arts
Communicate 429, 437,
  445, 452, 463

**Business and
Economics**
Business 430
Investments 424, 426, 458,
  470, 473

Manufacturing 447, 454,
  461, 470
Packaging 447, 471
Real Estate 438

Sports and Leisure
Travel 439

MATH CONNECTIONS

Coordinate Geometry 527
Geometry 482, 483, 485, 496, 503, 510, 518, 526, 534

Maximum/Minimum 553
Statistics 487
Transformations 481, 493, 521, 526

APPLICATIONS

Science
Aviation 487
Chemistry 489, 495, 496
Electricity 510
Engineering 536, 538, 541
Machines 484
Ornithology 487
Physical Science 511
Physics 487, 497, 504, 518, 520, 523, 525, 527, 542, 550

Language Arts
Communicate 485, 495, 502, 508, 517, 525, 532, 541

Business and Economics
Business 480, 533
Economics 496, 501, 503

Life Skills
Fund-raising 498
Transportation 535
Packaging 528, 530

Sports and Leisure
Entertainment 553
Photography 487
Recreation 485
Sightseeing 543
Sports 512, 517, 518
Travel 505, 508, 509, 510, 553

CONIC SECTIONS

560

MATH CONNECTIONS

Coordinate Geometry 563, 564, 568, 569, 577, 584

Geometry 566, 568, 569, 612
Transformations 577, 584, 593, 602

APPLICATIONS

Science
Architecture 593
Astronomy 588, 591, 593, 618
Biology 618
Forestry 610
Geology 585, 618
Lighting 577, 593
Physics 618
Radio Navigation 595
Space Science 585

Language Arts
Communicate 566, 576, 582, 591, 600, 610

Business and Economics
Business 608, 612, 613
Communications 570, 573, 577, 579, 581, 582, 585

Sports and Leisure
Sports 576, 577, 621

Other
Emergency Services 564, 567
Law Enforcement 602

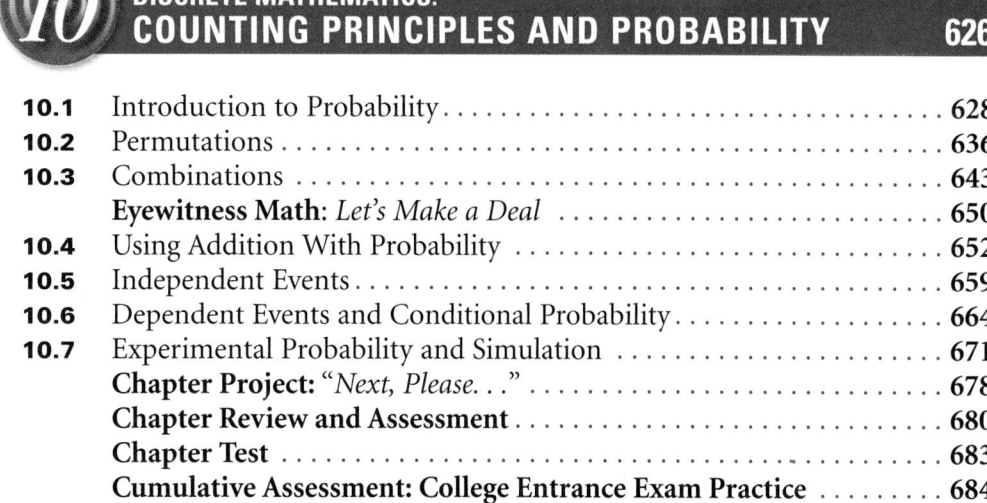

10 DISCRETE MATHEMATICS: COUNTING PRINCIPLES AND PROBABILITY 626

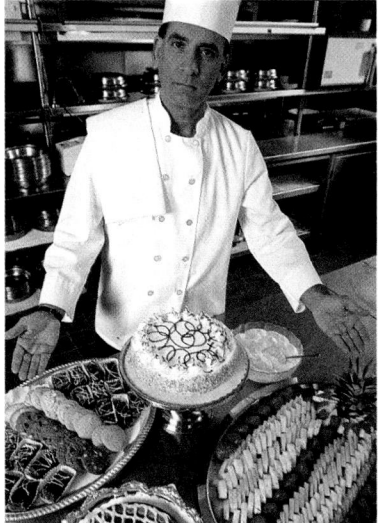

MATH CONNECTIONS

Geometry 630, 634, 641, 657, 669, 674, 675, 677   **Maximum/Minimum** 642

APPLICATIONS

Science
Computers 630, 632
Health 648, 664, 667, 668, 670, 682
Nutrition 642
Security 635, 663

Language Arts
Communicate 632, 640, 647, 655, 661, 667, 675

Social Studies
Demographics 634, 669
Politics 657
Surveys 646, 654
Voting 645, 670

Business and Economics
Advertising 670
Business 649
Catering 639
Management 673, 675
Production 658
Publishing 634
Quality Control 658
Small Business 641, 642

Life Skills
Academics 634
Education 656
Shopping 644, 645
Transportation 632, 634, 672, 675

Sports and Leisure
Entertainment 661
Extracurricular Activities 652, 655, 660, 665, 685
Lottery 649
Music 637
Sports 641, 642, 671
Travel 663

MATH CONNECTIONS

Geometry 697, 705, 725, 726, 733, 744, 745, 746
Maximum/Minimum 747
Patterns in Data 707, 708
Probability 735, 738, 739

APPLICATIONS

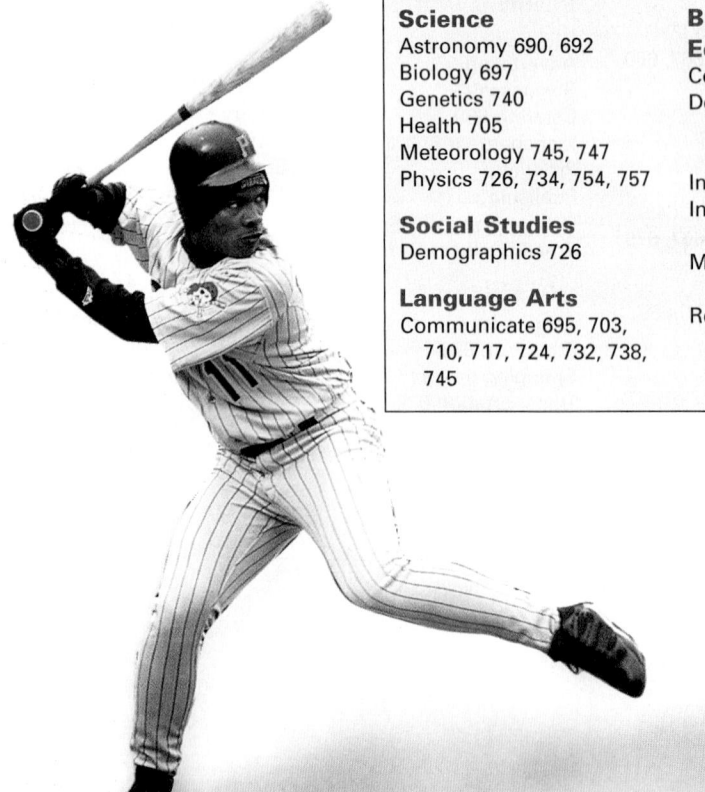

Science
Astronomy 690, 692
Biology 697
Genetics 740
Health 705
Meteorology 745, 747
Physics 726, 734, 754, 757

Social Studies
Demographics 726

Language Arts
Communicate 695, 703, 710, 717, 724, 732, 738, 745

Business and Economics
Construction 734
Depreciation 699, 701, 703, 705, 713, 714, 717, 726
Inventory 711
Investments 721, 724, 726, 733, 754
Merchandising 710, 712, 754
Real Estate 718, 754

Life Skills
Academics 740
Income 697, 705

Sports and Leisure
Art 728
Entertainment 712, 747, 754
Music 719, 727
Recreation 698
Sports 719, 741, 743, 746, 747

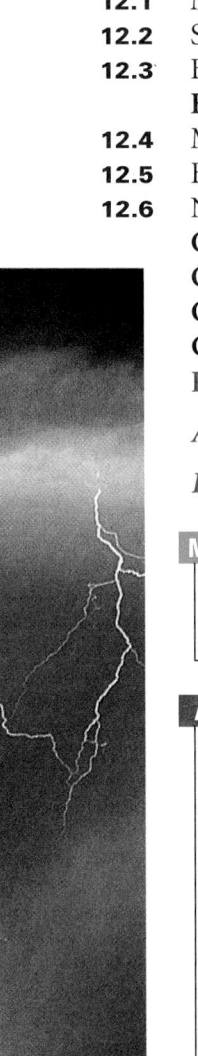

MATH CONNECTIONS

Patterns in Data 779, 786   **Transformations** 780, 795, 797
Probability 775, 777

APPLICATIONS

Science
Aviation 805
Climate 781, 784, 785, 792
Ecology 766, 767, 785
Meteorology 806
Veterinary Medicine 803

Social Studies
Demographics 786, 787, 819
Geography 787
Government 788
Social Services 782
Surveys 797, 804
Workforce 770

Language Arts
Communicate 768, 777, 785, 796, 803, 811

Business and Economics
Accounting 771
Automobile Distribution 818
Broadcasting 764, 765
Business 765, 770, 774, 777, 778, 779, 797
Inventory 770
Manufacturing 793, 794, 797, 811
Marketing 769, 772, 779
Quality Control 812, 813

Life Skills
Academics 771, 809
Awards 804
Education 778, 796, 805, 813

Income 779
Mortgage 812
Transportation 811, 812

Sports and Leisure
Entertainment 821
Gardening 800
Music 768
Recreation 773
Sports 784, 797
Travel 810

Other
Armed Forces 779
Emergency Services 799, 801
Hospital Statistics 804
Law Enforcement 778
Public Safety 776, 803
Security 789

13 TRIGONOMETRIC FUNCTIONS   826

MATH CONNECTIONS

Coordinate Geometry 850   Probability 842, 881
Geometry 832, 834, 843, 849, 851, 856   Transformations 860, 861, 862, 863

APPLICATIONS

Science
Acoustics 858, 862
Architecture 872
Astronomy 872
Aviation 834, 836, 837,
   841, 867, 871
Bicycle Design 849
Engineering 842, 856
Forestry 872
Machinery 857
Meteorology 851, 854
Navigation 842, 879
Robotics 843, 845, 848,
   849

Surveying 833
Technology 856
Temperature 865
Wildlife 828, 831

Language Arts
Communicate 832, 840,
   847, 854, 864, 871

Social Studies
Employment 865
Map Making 878
Public Safety 873

**Business and
Economics**
Carpentry 872
Construction 834, 849

Life Skills
Home Improvement 834
Income 866

Sports and Leisure
Auto Racing 856
Entertainment 855
Hiking 873

MATH CONNECTIONS

APPLICATIONS

INFO BANK 940

Data and Linear Representations

COLLECTING, ORGANIZING, AND REPRESENTING data are important skills in the real world. One example is the research of the annual migration of millions of monarch butterflies. Observers across North America collect data and share their information over the World Wide Web.

Lessons

Tagging a monarch butterfly

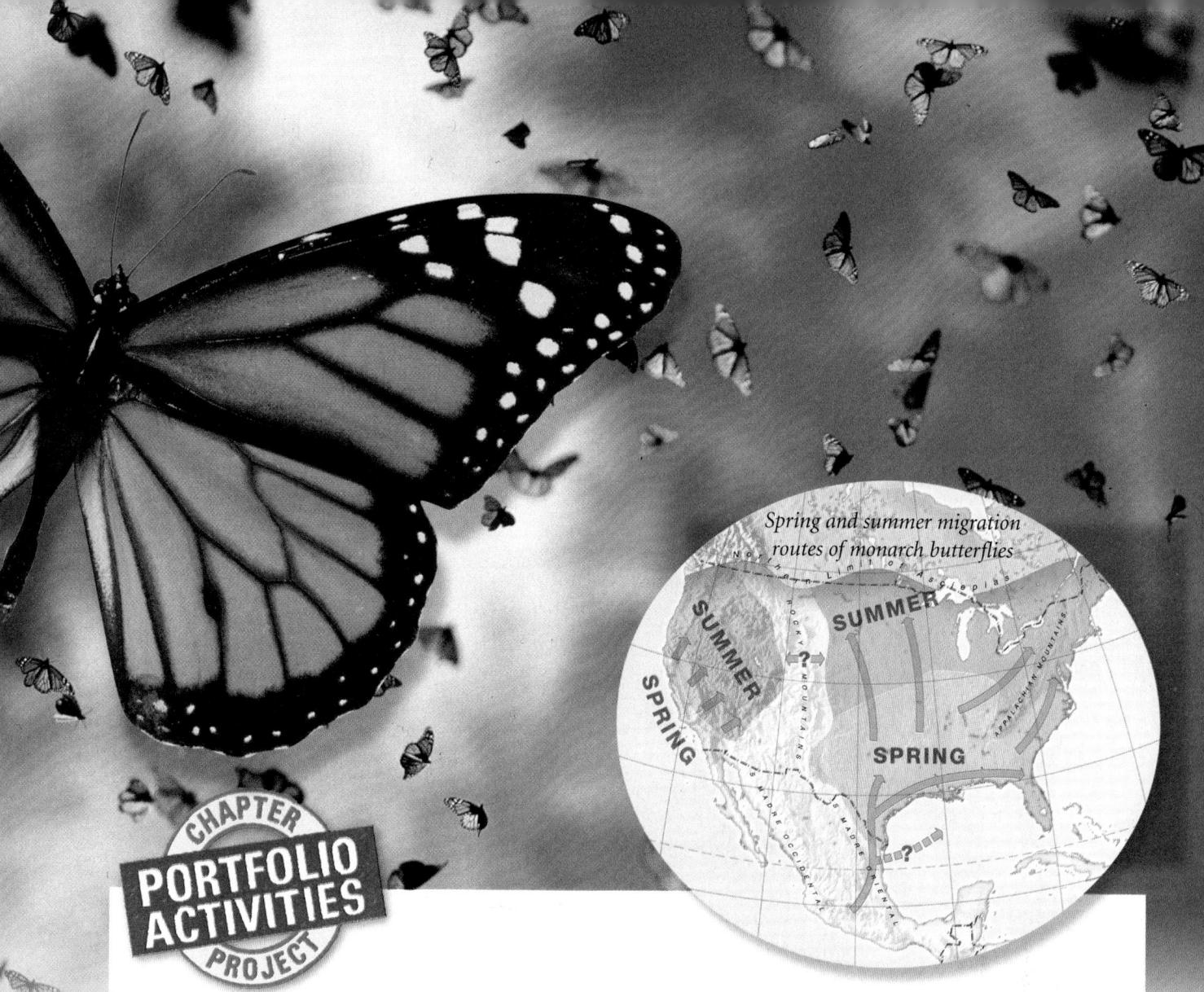

Spring and summer migration routes of monarch butterflies

PORTFOLIO ACTIVITIES PROJECT

About the Chapter Project

Algebra provides the power to model real-world data. In the Chapter Project, *Correlation Exploration*, you will investigate the correlations between many common variables. Throughout this book, you will learn about different types of algebraic models that can be used to investigate trends and make predictions. In this chapter, you will focus on linear models.

After completing the Chapter Project, you will be able to do the following:

- Represent real-world data by using scatter plots.
- Find and use linear models to predict other possible data values.

About the Portfolio Activities

Throughout the chapter, you will be given opportunities to complete Portfolio Activities that are designed to support your work on the Chapter Project.

- Creating a graph to represent your data is included in the Portfolio Activity on page 11.
- Estimating a linear model for your data is included in the Portfolio Activity on page 20.
- Using your linear model to predict other possible data values is included in the Portfolio Activity on page 36.
- Using technology to find a least-squares regression line for your data set is included in the Portfolio Activity on page 44.
- Using the least-squares regression line to predict other data values is included in the Portfolio Activity on page 51.

Tables and Graphs of Linear Equations

Why Linear relationships between two variables occur in a wide variety of situations. For example, the wages of a salesperson who earns a commission are often linearly related to the dollar amount of his or her sales.

A salesperson in a music store usually earns commission.

Objectives

● Represent a real-world linear relationship in a table, graph, or equation.

● Identify linear equations and linear relationships between variables in a table.

Activity

Investigating Commission

You will need: graph paper and a straightedge

Suppose that you work part-time in a music store. You earn $40 per week plus a 10% commission on all of the sales you make.

1. Discuss what it means to earn commission.

PROBLEM SOLVING

2. You can represent this relationship between weekly sales and weekly wages by **making a table.** Copy and complete the table below.

Weekly sales, s (in dollars)	Weekly wages, w (in dollars)
100	$40 + 0.10(100) = 50$
200	?
300	?
400	?
500	?

3. What observations can you make about successive entries in the weekly sales column? in the weekly wages column?

4. You can represent each row in the table as an ordered pair (s, w). Plot each ordered pair, and connect the first and last points with a straightedge. Does each point that you plotted appear to be contained in this line segment?

CHECKPOINT ✔

5. Write an equation to represent the relationship between s and w.

In the Activity on page 4, a linear relationship that can be modeled by a linear equation is described. Example 1 provides another instance of a linear relationship.

EXAMPLE 1

An attorney charges a fixed fee of $250 for an initial meeting and $150 per hour for all hours worked after that.

a. Make a table of the total charge for 1, 2, 3, and 4 hours worked.
b. Graph the points represented by your table and connect them.
c. Write a linear equation to model this situation.
d. Find the charge for 25 hours of work.

APPLICATION
INCOME

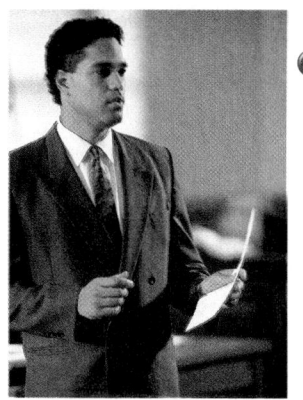

A lawyer, or attorney, in court

SOLUTION

a.

Hours worked	1	2	3	4
Total charge	$400	$550	$700	$850

b.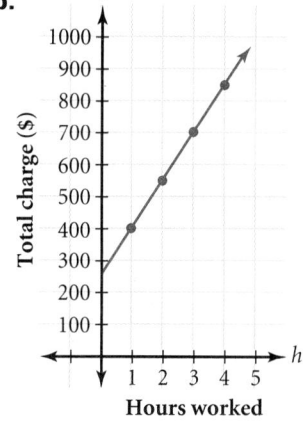

c. Translate the verbal description into an equation involving c and h.

$$\underset{\text{charge}}{\text{total}} = \underset{\text{charge}}{\text{variable}} + \underset{\text{fee}}{\text{fixed}}$$

$$c = 150h + 250$$

Thus, $c = 150h + 250$.

d. Use the equation. Substitute 25 for h in the equation.

$$c = 150h + 250$$
$$c = 150(25) + 250$$
$$c = 4000$$

CHECK

From the graph of $y = 150x + 250$, you can see that when $x = 25$, $y = 4000$.

Thus, the attorney charges $4000 for 25 hours of work.

TECHNOLOGY
GRAPHICS CALCULATOR

Keystroke Guide, page 80

TRY THIS

A water tank already contains 55 gallons of water when Darius begins to fill it. Water flows into the tank at a rate of 9 gallons per minute.

a. Make a table for the volume of water in the tank after 1, 2, 3, and 4 minutes.
b. Graph the points represented by your table and connect them.
c. Write a linear equation to model this situation.
d. Find the volume of water in the tank 20 minutes after Darius begins filling the tank.

The equations in Example 1 and the Try This exercise above have a characteristic in common. Each has the form shown below.

total amount = variable amount + fixed amount

In general, if a relationship between x and y can be written as $y = mx + b$, where m and b are real numbers, then x and y are **linearly related**. The equation $y = mx + b$ is called a **linear equation**. The graph of a linear equation is a straight line.

CHECKPOINT ✔ What are the values of m and b in the equation $c = 150h + 250$ from Example 1?

E X A M P L E ② Graph $y = \frac{2}{3}x - 1$.

● **SOLUTION**

Because $y = \frac{2}{3}x - 1$ is of the form $y = mx + b$, where $m = \frac{2}{3}$ and $b = -1$, its graph is a straight line. A line is determined by two points, so you need to plot only two ordered pairs that satisfy $y = \frac{2}{3}x - 1$ and draw the line through them.

x	0	3
y	$y = \frac{2}{3}(0) - 1 = -1$	$y = \frac{2}{3}(3) - 1 = 1$

Plot $(0, -1)$ and $(3, 1)$, and draw a line through them.

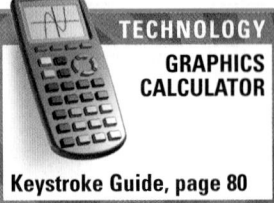

TECHNOLOGY

GRAPHICS CALCULATOR

Keystroke Guide, page 80

CHECK

Graph $y = \frac{2}{3}x - 1$ on a graphics calculator, and verify that the points $(0, -1)$ and $(3, 1)$ are on the line.

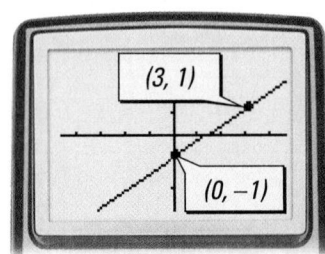

TRY THIS Graph $y = \frac{5}{4}x + 3$.

When variables represented in a table of values are linearly related and there is a constant difference in the x-values, there is also a constant difference in the y-values. For example, consider the linear equation $y = -2x + 5$.

Make a table of values by choosing x-values that have a constant difference, such as 1, 2, 3, 4, and so on.

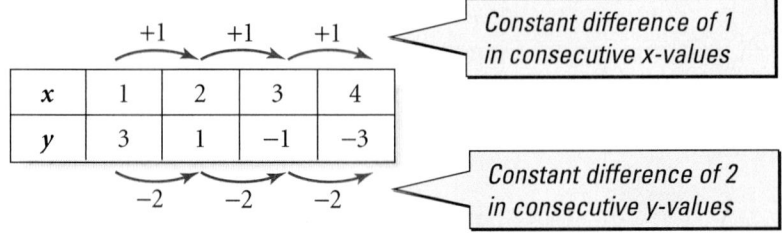

In a linear relationship, a constant difference in consecutive x-values results in a constant difference in consecutive y-values.

CHECKPOINT ✔ Suppose that you are making a table of values to determine whether the variables are linearly related. Describe the relationship. What must exist between the x-values that you choose?

E X A M P L E ❸ Does the table of values at right represent a linear relationship between *x* and *y*? Explain. If the relationship is linear, write the next ordered pair that would appear in the table.

x	7	12	17	22	27	32
y	11	8	5	2	−1	−4

● **SOLUTION**

Find differences in consecutive *x*-values and consecutive *y*-values.

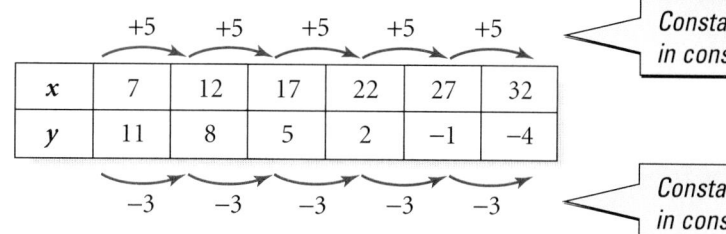

PROBLEM SOLVING **Look for a pattern.** Because there is a constant difference in the *x*-values and a constant difference in the *y*-values, the relationship between *x* and *y* is linear.

The next table entry for *x* is 32 + 5, or 7.
The next table entry for *y* is −4 + (−3), or −7.

TRY THIS Does the table of values at right represent a linear relationship between *x* and *y*? Explain. If the relationship is linear, write the next ordered pair that would appear in the table.

x	−2	2	6	10	14	18
y	1	2	4	8	16	32

CRITICAL THINKING Does the table at right represent a linear relationship between *x* and *y*? Explain.

x	9	6	3	0	−3	−6
y	5	5	5	5	5	5

Exercises

● Communicate

1. Discuss the relationships among the table, equation, and graph shown here.

x	−4	−2	0	2	4
y	−7	−4	−1	2	5

$y = \frac{3}{2}x - 1$

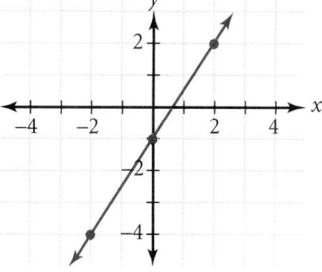

APPLICATION

2. SALES TAX Suppose that a state sales tax is 7%. Make a table showing the amount of tax on items with prices of \$6, \$8, \$10, and \$12. How can you find whether the price and amount of sales tax are linearly related?

3. Explain how to verify that the points (−1, 7), (0, 4), and (2, −2) are all on the same line.

Guided Skills Practice

APPLICATION

4. INCOME Suppose that you work part-time at a department store, earning a base salary of $50 per week plus a 15% commission on all sales that you make.
(EXAMPLE 1)

Weekly sales, x	Weekly income, y
100	$50 + (0.15)(100) = 65$
200	?
300	?
400	?
x	?

  a. Copy and complete the table.
  b. Graph the points represented in the table and connect them.
  c. Write a linear equation to represent the relationship between the weekly sales, x, and the weekly income y.
  d. Find the weekly income, y, for weekly sales of $1200.

5. Graph $y = 3x - 2$. *(EXAMPLE 2)*

6. Does the table below represent a linear relationship between x and y? If the relationship is linear, write the next ordered pair that would appear in the table. *(EXAMPLE 3)*

x	-4	1	6	11	16	21
y	13	19	25	31	37	43

internet connect

Activities Online

Go To: **go.hrw.com**
Keyword:
MB1 Paycheck

Practice and Apply

State whether each equation is a linear equation.

7. $y = -3x$ **8.** $y = -x$ **9.** $y = 12 + 2x$

10. $y = 5 - 4x$ **11.** $y = \frac{1}{2}x - 3$ **12.** $y = -\frac{2}{3}x$

13. $y = \frac{1}{x}$ **14.** $y = \frac{-4}{x}$ **15.** $y = -x^2 + 1$

16. $y = 2 + 5x^2$ **17.** $y = 5.5x - 2$ **18.** $y = 11 - 1.2x$

internet connect

Homework Help Online

Go To: **go.hrw.com**
Keyword:
MB1 Homework Help
 for Exercises 19–30

Graph each linear equation.

19. $y = 2x + 1$ **20.** $y = 4x + 3$ **21.** $y = 3x - 6$

22. $y = 6x - 3$ **23.** $y = 5 - 2x$ **24.** $y = 3 - 5x$

25. $y = -x + 5$ **26.** $y = -x - 2$ **27.** $y = \frac{2}{3}x + 4$

28. $y = \frac{1}{3}x - 5$ **29.** $y + 3 = x + 6$ **30.** $y + 4 = x - 3$

For Exercises 31–38, determine whether each table represents a linear relationship between *x* and *y*. If the relationship is linear, write the next ordered pair that would appear in the table.

31.

x	y
0	10
1	22
2	34
3	46

32.

x	y
0	-5
3	-1
6	3
9	7

33.

x	y
3	-5
4	1
5	6
6	11

34.

x	y
-2	1
-3	2
-4	4
-5	8

35.

x	y
8	28
6	22
4	16
2	10

36.

x	y
12	−3
9	−8
6	−13
3	−18

37.

x	y
6	115
9	100
12	85
15	75

38.

x	y
−6	58
−9	44
−12	32
−15	20

For each graph, make a table of values to represent the points. Does the table represent a linear relationship? Explain.

39.

40.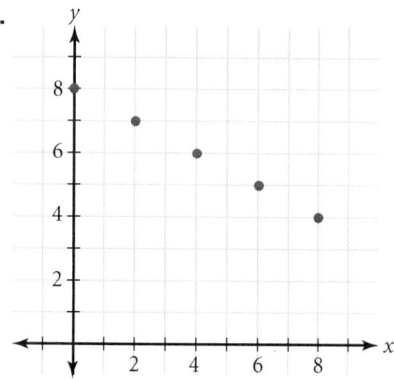

41. Make a table of values for the equation $y = 4x − 1$, and graph the line. Is the point $(2, 6)$ on this line? Explain how to answer this question by using the table, the graph, and the equation.

> Calculator button indicates that a graphics calculator is recommended.

Use a graphics calculator to graph each equation. Then sketch the graph on graph paper.

42 $y = −3x + 1.5$

43 $y = −x − 2.5$

44 $y = 12 − 2.5x$

45 $y = 4 − 0.5x$

46 $y = \frac{1}{2}x − \frac{3}{5}$

47 $y = −\frac{2}{3}x + \frac{1}{2}$

CHALLENGE

48. What can you determine about the graph of $y = mx + b$ when $x = 0$? What can you determine about the graph of $y = mx + b$ when $y = 0$?

APPLICATION

49. INCOME A video rental store charges a $6 membership fee and $3 for each video rented. In the graph at right, the x-axis represents the number of videos rented by a customer and the y-axis represents the store's revenue from that customer.

a. Make a table for the data points on the graph.

b. If 15 videos are rented, what is the revenue?

c. If a new member paid the store a total of $27, how many videos were rented?

d. Explain how to find answers to parts **b** and **c** by using an extended table and an extended graph.

Registration day at a community college

50. DEMOGRAPHICS City Community College plans to increase its enrollment capacity to keep up with an increasing number of student applicants. The college currently has an enrollment capacity of 2200 students and plans to increase its capacity by 70 students each year.

   a. Let x represent the number of years from now, and let y represent the enrollment capacity. Make a table of values for x and y with x-values of 0, 1, 2, 3, and 4.

   b. What will the enrollment capacity be 3 years from now?

   c. Write a linear equation that could be used to find the enrollment capacity, y, after x years.

51. BUSINESS An airport parking lot charges a basic fee of $2 plus $1 per half-hour parked.

   a. Copy and complete the table.

   b. Graph the points represented in the table. Label each axis, and indicate your scale.

   c. Write an equation for the total charge, c, in terms of the number of half-hours parked, h.

   d. How many half-hours is 72 hours? What is the total charge for parking in the lot for 72 hours?

Half-hours	Total charge ($)
0	$2 + (1)(0) = 2$
1	?
2	?
3	?
?	12

52. METEOROLOGY At 6:00 A.M., the temperature was 67°F. As a cold front passed, the temperature began to drop at a steady rate of 4°F per hour.

   a. Write a linear equation relating the temperature in degrees Fahrenheit, t, to the number of hours, h, after the initial temperature reading.

   b. Estimate, to the nearest 15 minutes, how long it would take to reach freezing (32°F) if the drop in temperature continued at the same rate.

> **Supply** is the amount that manufacturers are willing to produce at a certain price.
> **Demand** is the amount that consumers are willing to buy at a certain price.

53. ECONOMICS This table gives the price, the *supply*, and the *demand* for a video game.

   a. Graph the points representing price and supply and the points representing price and demand on the same coordinate plane.

   b. Estimate the price at which the supply of video games meets the demand. Estimate the supply and demand at this price.

   c. What happens to the supply and to the demand when the price of the video game is higher than the price in part **b**? lower than the price in part **b**?

Price ($)	Supply	Demand
20	150	500
30	250	400
50	450	200

54. BUSINESS Casey has a small business making dessert baskets. She estimates that her fixed weekly costs for rent, electricity, and salaries are $200. The ingredients for one dessert basket cost $2.50.

   a. If Casey makes 40 dessert baskets in a given week, what will her total weekly costs be?

   b. Casey's total costs for last week were $500. How many dessert baskets did she make?

Look Back

The following *Rules of Divisibility* are useful in finding factors of numbers. If a number is

- divisible by 3, the sum of the digits of the number is divisible by 3.
- divisible by 6, the number is divisible by 3 and is even.
- divisible by 9, the sum of the digits of the number is divisible by 9.
- divisible by 4, the number formed by the last two digits is divisible by 4.

Find numbers *a* and *b* that meet the following conditions:

55. $ab = 36$ and $a + b = 13$ **56.** $ab = 51$ and $a + b = 20$

57. $ab = 82$ and $a + b = 43$ **58.** $ab = 72$ and $a + b = 22$

59. $ab = 128$ and $a + b = 24$ **60.** $ab = 56$ and $a + b = 15$

61. $ab = 48$ and $a + b = 19$ **62.** $ab = 52$ and $a + b = 17$

Evaluate each expression. Write your answer in simplest form.

63. $\frac{1}{2} \times \frac{4}{7}$ **64.** $\frac{2}{3} \times \frac{6}{11}$ **65.** $3 \times \frac{2}{3}$ **66.** $\frac{13}{14} \times 7$

67. $7 \div \frac{7}{8}$ **68.** $5 \div \frac{5}{6}$ **69.** $21 \div \frac{7}{8}$ **70.** $10 \div \frac{5}{6}$

internet connect

Portfolio Extension

Go To: **go.hrw.com**
Keyword:
MB1 Linear

 Look Beyond

71. Graph the equations $y = 2x$, $y = 2x + 3$, and $y = 2x - 4$ on the same coordinate plane. How are the graphs alike? How are they different?

PORTFOLIO ACTIVITY

1. Describe three real-world situations in which a distance changes at a fairly constant rate over time. For example, the distance driven on an interstate highway or the distance walked in a walkathon changes at a fairly constant rate.

2. Choose one of your three real-world situations from Step 1, and determine a suitable way to collect some time and distance data. Collect and record a minimum of seven data values. This data will become your **portfolio data set**.

3. Organize the data from your portfolio data set in a table of values.

4. Use graph paper to graph your portfolio data set. Label the *x*-axis with units of time, and label the *y*-axis with units of distance. The point that represents the first distance measure that you took should have an *x*-coordinate of 0.

WORKING ON THE CHAPTER PROJECT

You should now be able to complete Activity 1 of the Chapter Project.

Slopes and Intercepts

Trends in the real world, such as the increase in cellular phone use, can often be modeled by a linear equation, in which the slope indicates a rate of change.

Objectives

- Graph a linear equation.
- Write a linear equation for a given line in the coordinate plane.

APPLICATION

COMMUNICATIONS

Every year more and more people in the United States become cellular phone subscribers. The table below represents the recent trend in cellular phone subscriptions. The third column in the table gives the change in the number of subscribers from one year to the next.

Year	Number of subscribers (in millions, rounded to the nearest 100,000)	Yearly change (in millions, rounded to the nearest 100,000)	
1990	5.3		
1991	7.6	1990–1991	2.3
1992	11.0	1991–1992	3.4
1993	16.0	1992–1993	5.0
1994	24.0	1993–1994	8.0
1995	33.8	1994–1995	9.8

U.S. Cellular Subscribers

Notice in the highlighted row above that the number of new subscribers from 1990 to 1991 is 7.6 − 5.3, or 2.3. This difference can also be represented by the ratio shown below.

$$\frac{\text{Change in subscribers}}{\text{Change in years}} = \frac{7.6 - 5.3}{1991 - 1990} = \frac{2.3}{1} = 2.3$$

All entries in the third column can be found by using a ratio. Each of the ratios gives the *rate of change* from one year to the next.

You can also find the *average rate of change* from 1990 to 1995. On average, from 1990 to 1995, there were about 5.7 million new subscribers per year. This average rate of change is indicated by the red dashed line on the graph at left.

$$\frac{\text{Total change in subscribers}}{\text{Total change in years}} = \frac{33.8 - 5.3}{1995 - 1990} = \frac{28.5}{5} = 5.7$$

CHECKPOINT ✔ Estimate the average rate of change from 1990 to 1993 and from 1993 to 1995.

In a graph, the *slope* of a line is the change in vertical units divided by the corresponding change in horizontal units.

Slope of a Line

If points (x_1, y_1) and (x_2, y_2) lie on a line, then the slope, *m*, of the line is given by the ratio below.

$$m = \frac{\text{change in } y}{\text{corresponding change in } x} = \frac{y_2 - y_1}{x_2 - x_1}$$

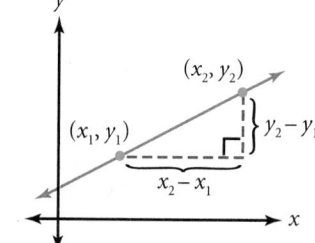

> The slope of a line is sometimes referred to as $m = \frac{rise}{run}$.

You can find the slope of a line if you know the coordinates of two points on the line. This is shown in Example 1.

E X A M P L E ❶ Find the slope of the line containing the points **(0, 4)** and **(3, 1)**.

● SOLUTION

PROBLEM SOLVING **Use a formula.** Let $(x_1, y_1) = (0, 4)$ and $(x_2, y_2) = (3, 1)$. Apply the definition of slope.

$$m = \frac{y_2 - y_1}{x_2 - x_1} = \frac{1 - 4}{3 - 0} = \frac{-3}{3} = -1$$

The line containing (0, 4) and (3, 1) has a slope of −1.

TRY THIS Find the slope of the line containing the points (−5, 3) and (3, −4).

Activity
Exploring Slopes

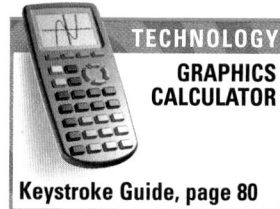

TECHNOLOGY

GRAPHICS CALCULATOR

Keystroke Guide, page 80

You will need: a graphics calculator

1. Each equation below has the form $y = mx$, where *m* is the slope. Graph each pair of equations. Describe how the slopes for each pair of lines are alike and how they are different.

   a. $y = \frac{1}{5}x$ and $y = -\frac{1}{5}x$

   b. $y = \frac{2}{3}x$ and $y = -\frac{2}{3}x$

   c. $y = x$ and $y = -x$

   d. $y = \frac{3}{2}x$ and $y = -\frac{3}{2}x$

   e. $y = 5x$ and $y = -5x$

2. Make a conjecture about the slopes of $y = mx$ when $m < 0$ and when $m > 0$. Explain how the graphs of these lines are related.

CHECKPOINT ✔ 3. Verify your conjecture from Step 2 by writing and graphing another pair of equations with the relationship that you described in Step 2.

Intercepts

The *y*-coordinate of the point where the graph of a linear equation crosses the *y*-axis is called the **y-intercept** of the line. In the graph below, the *y*-intercept of **line r** is 3 and the *y*-intercept of **line s** is −2.

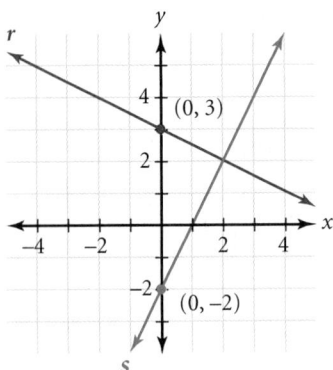

To find the *y*-intercept of a line, substitute 0 for *x* in an equation for the line.

Line s

$y = 2x - 2$

$y = 2(0) - 2$

$y = -2$ — *The y-intercept of $y = 2x - 2$ is −2.*

Line r

$y = -\frac{1}{2}x + 3$

$y = -\frac{1}{2}(0) + 3$

$y = 3$ — *The y-intercept of $y = -\frac{1}{2}x + 3$ is 3.*

Slope-Intercept Form

The **slope-intercept form** of a line is $y = mx + b$, where *m* is the slope and *b* is the *y*-intercept.

The slope of a line tells you about the steepness and direction of the line. The *y*-intercept tells you where the line crosses the *y*-axis.

Varying the slope
$y = mx + 1$

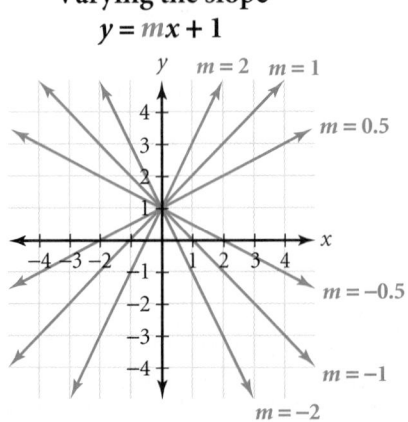

Varying the y intercept
$y = 2x + b$

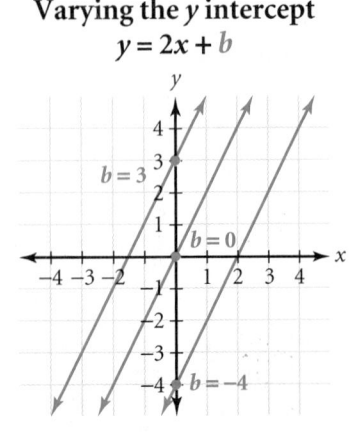

E X A M P L E **2** Use the slope and *y*-intercept to graph the equation $-2x + y = -3$.

● **SOLUTION**

1. Write the equation in slope-intercept form, $y = mx + b$.

$$-2x + y = -3$$
$$y = 2x - 3$$

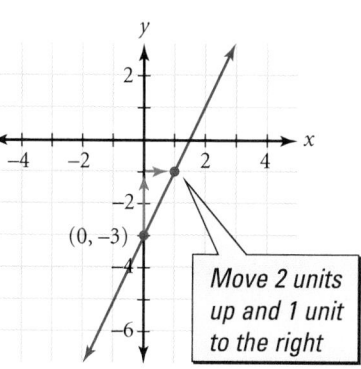

slope ⟶ y-intercept

The slope is 2 and the *y*-intercept is -3.

2. Plot the point $(0, -3)$, and use the slope to find a second point.

$$m = \frac{\text{change in } y}{\text{corresponding change in } x} = \frac{2}{1}$$

(0, –3)

Move 2 units up and 1 unit to the right

3. Connect the two points to graph the line.

TRY THIS Use the slope and *y*-intercept to graph the equation $2x + y = 3$.

Example 3 shows you how to write an equation for a line that is graphed.

E X A M P L E **3** Write the equation, in slope-intercept form, for the line graphed.

● **SOLUTION**

Because the point $(0, 2)$ is on the graph, the *y*-intercept is 2. Use another convenient point on the line, such as $(3, 0)$, to find the slope.

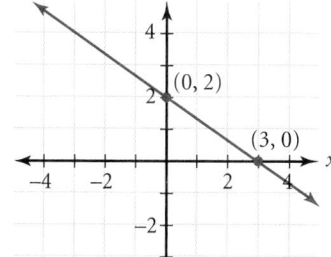

(0, 2)

(3, 0)

The same result occurs when $(x_1, y_1) = (3, 0)$ *and when* $(x_2, y_2) = (0, 2)$.

Let $(x_1, y_1) = (0, 2)$ and $(x_2, y_2) = (3, 0)$.

$$m = \frac{y_2 - y_1}{x_2 - x_1} = \frac{0 - 2}{3 - 0} = -\frac{2}{3}$$

The equation in slope-intercept form is $y = -\frac{2}{3}x + 2$.

TRY THIS Write the equation, in slope-intercept form, for the line that passes through $(1, 4)$ and has a *y*-intercept of 3.

Standard Form

The **standard form** of a linear equation is $Ax + By = C$, where A, B, and C are real numbers and A and B are not *both* 0.

Example 4 on page 16 shows you how to use the *x*- and *y*-intercepts to sketch the graph of a linear equation. The **x-intercept** of a graph is the *x*-coordinate of the point where the graph crosses the *x*-axis.

E X A M P L E ④ Use intercepts to graph the equation $2x - 3y = 6$.

● **SOLUTION**

To find the *x*-intercept, let $y = 0$.
$$2x - 3y = 6$$
$$2x - 3(0) = 6$$
$$x = 3$$

To find the *y*-intercept, let $x = 0$.
$$2x - 3y = 6$$
$$2(0) - 3y = 6$$
$$y = -2$$

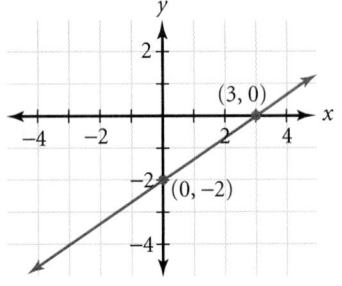

Graph the points $(3, 0)$ and $(0, -2)$. Draw the line through these two points.

TRY THIS Use intercepts to graph the equation $5x + 3y = 15$.

Horizontal and Vertical Lines

For the **horizontal line** at right, the formula for slope gives $\frac{3 - 3}{2 - (-3)} = \frac{0}{5}$, which is 0.

A **horizontal line** is a line that has a slope of 0.

For the **vertical line** at right, the formula for slope gives $\frac{1 - (-3)}{-2 - (-2)} = \frac{4}{0}$, which is undefined.

A **vertical line** is a line that has an undefined slope.

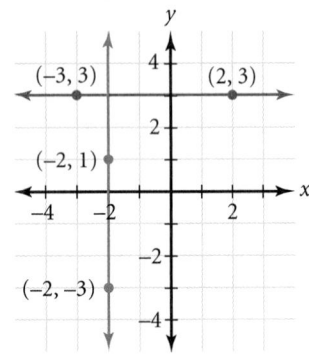

CHECKPOINT ✔ Which type of line has a *y*-intercept but no *x*-intercept? Which type of line has an *x*-intercept but no *y*-intercept?

E X A M P L E ⑤ Graph each equation.
  a. $y = -2$ **b.** $x = -3$

● **SOLUTION**

a.

Graph the horizontal line that crosses the y-axis at −2.

$y = -2$

b.

$x = -3$

Graph the vertical line that crosses the x-axis at −3.

CRITICAL THINKING Verify that every line of the form $By = C$ is horizontal and that every line of the form $Ax = C$ is vertical.

Exercises

Communicate

1. Explain how to arrange the linear equations given below in ascending order of steepness, that is, from least steep to most steep.

   a. $y = 3x - 5$　　　**b.** $y = \frac{1}{3}x + 5$　　　**c.** $y = \frac{1}{2}x + 5$

   d. $y = 5x + 5$　　　**e.** $y = 5$　　　**f.** $y = 3x + 5$

2. Describe how to sketch the graph of the line $3x + 2y = 4$.

3. Explain how to find the y-intercept for the graph of $2x - 5y = 10$.

4. Describe how to write the equation $x - y = 2$ in slope-intercept form.

Guided Skills Practice

5. Find the slope of the line containing the points $(-2, 4)$ and $(8, -3)$. **(EXAMPLE 1)**

6. Use the slope and y-intercept to graph the equation $\frac{1}{2}x + y = -4$. **(EXAMPLE 2)**

7. Write the equation in slope-intercept form for the line graphed at right. **(EXAMPLE 3)**

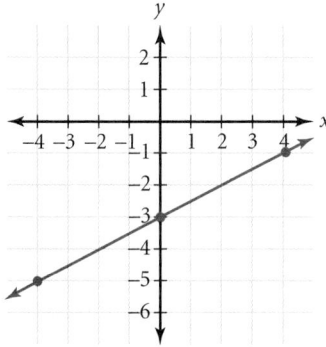

8. Use intercepts to graph $-2x - 4y = 8$. **(EXAMPLE 4)**

Graph each equation. **(EXAMPLE 5)**

9. $x = \frac{1}{2}$　　　　　　10. $y = \frac{3}{2}$

Practice and Apply

Write the equation in slope-intercept form for the line that has the indicated slope, m, and y-intercept, b.

11. $m = 2, b = 0.75$ 　　　　　　12. $m = -5, b = 0$

13. $m = 0, b = -3$ 　　　　　　14. $m = -\frac{1}{8}, b = 2$

15. $m = -3, b = 7$ 　　　　　　16. $m = -\frac{2}{3}, b = -1$

17. $m = \frac{1}{4}, b = -\frac{3}{4}$ 　　　　　　18. $m = 0.08, b = -2.91$

Find the slope of the line containing the indicated points.

19. $(0, 0)$ and $(3, 30)$ 　　　　　　20. $(1, -3)$ and $(3, -5)$

21. $(3, -2)$ and $(4, 5)$ 　　　　　　22. $(-10, -4)$ and $(-3, -3)$

23. $(-6, -6)$ and $(-3, 1)$ 　　　　　　24. $(-2, 8)$ and $(-2, -1)$

25. $\left(\frac{1}{2}, -3\right)$ and $\left(3, -\frac{1}{2}\right)$ 　　　　　　26. $(-4, 8)$ and $(-3, -6)$

Identify the slope, *m*, and the *y*-intercept, *b*, for each line. Then graph.

27. $y + 2x = 0$ **28.** $y = 2$ **29.** $-\frac{1}{3}x + y = -7$

30. $x + y = 6$ **31.** $y = x$ **32.** $-2x = 8 + 4y$

33. $-0.6x + y = -4$ **34.** $2x + y = 1$ **35.** $x = -3$

Write an equation in slope-intercept form for each line.

36.

37.

38.

39.

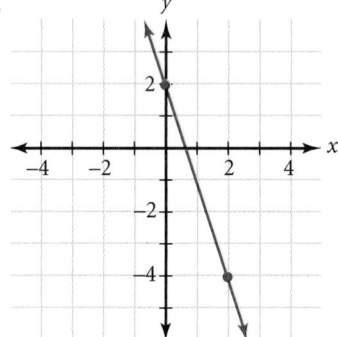

Use intercepts to graph each equation.

40. $4x + y = -4$ **41.** $x + 3y = 12$ **42.** $2x - y = 8$

43. $-x + 2y = 5$ **44.** $7x + 3y = 2$ **45.** $-x + 8y = -6$

46. $-3x + y = -9$ **47.** $-x - 7y = 3$ **48.** $x - y = -1$

49. $-\frac{1}{2}x + 3y = 7$ **50.** $5x - 8y = 16$ **51.** $x + \frac{1}{2}y = -2$

Find the slope of each line. Then graph.

52. $x = 5$ **53.** $x = -2$ **54.** $y = 8$

55. $y = -5$ **56.** $x = -1$ **57.** $x = 9$

58. $y = -8$ **59.** $y = 7$ **60.** $x = -\frac{1}{3}$

61. $x = -\frac{1}{4}$ **62.** $y = \frac{3}{4}$ **63.** $y = \frac{2}{3}$

CHALLENGE

64. The points $(-2, 4)$, $(0, 2)$, and $(3, a - 1)$ are on one line. Find *a*.

APPLICATION

65. TAXES Tristan buys a computer for $3600. For tax purposes, he declares a linear depreciation (loss of value) of $600 per year. Let *y* be the declared value of the computer after *x* years.
  a. What is the slope of the line that models this depreciation?
  b. Find the *y*-intercept of the line.
  c. Write a linear equation in slope-intercept form to model the value of the computer over time.
  d. Find the value of Tristan's computer after 4.5 years.

66. PHYSICS The graph at right shows data for the distance of an object from a motion detector.

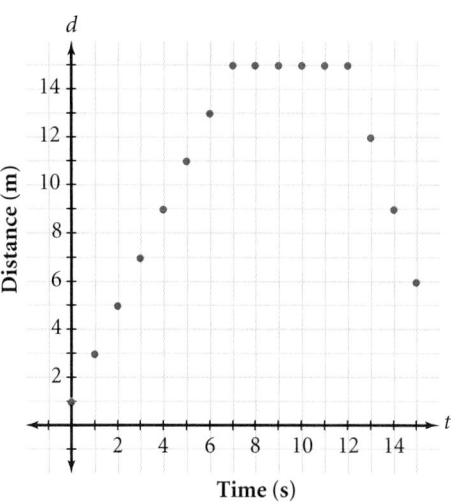

  a. Describe how the motion of the object changes with time in the graph.

  b. Model the distance of the object from the detector by using three linear equations.

  c. For what times is each equation valid?

  d. During which time interval is the object moving the fastest?

  e. Is the slope of the segment representing the fastest movement positive or negative? Explain what the sign of the slope indicates about the motion of the object.

67. METEOROLOGY The thermometer at left shows temperatures in degrees Fahrenheit, F, and in degrees Celsius, C. Room temperature is 20°C, or 68°F.

  a. Choose two other Fahrenheit temperatures, and use the thermometer at left to estimate the Celsius equivalents.

  b. Let the temperature equivalents from part **a** represent points of the form (F, C). Graph the three points and draw a line through the points.

  c. Find the slope and y-intercept of the line.

  d. Write the equation of the line in slope-intercept form.

68. CONSTRUCTION The slope of a roof is called the pitch and is defined as follows:

$$\text{pitch} = \frac{\text{rise of roof}}{\frac{1}{2} \times \text{span of roof}}$$

  a. Find the pitch of a roof if the rise is 12 feet and the span is 30 feet.

  b. Find the pitch of a roof if the rise is 18 feet and the span is 60 feet.

  c. Find the pitch of a roof if the rise is 4 feet and the span is 50 feet.

  d. If the pitch is constant, is the relationship between the rise and span linear? Explain.

69. AGRICULTURE The table at right shows the average milk production of dairy cows in the United States for the years from 1993 to 1996.

   a. Let $x = 0$ represent 1990. Make a line graph with years on the horizontal axis and pounds of milk on the vertical axis.

   b. In what year did the average milk production increase the most? What is the slope of the graph for that year?

   c. In what year did the average milk production increase the least? What is the slope of the graph for that year?

Year	Pounds of milk per day
1993	42.7
1994	44.3
1995	45.2
1996	45.2

[Source: U.S. Dept. of Agriculture]

Shown above is a Jersey cow, one type of dairy cow.

 Look Back

70. Find the value of V in the equation $V = lwh$ when $l = 2$, $w = 3$, and $h = 5$.

71. Use the formula $I = prt$ to find the interest, I, in dollars when the principal, p, is $1000; the annual interest rate, r, is 8%; and the time, t, is 2 years.

72. Use the formula $P = 4s$ to find the perimeter of a square, P, in feet when the length of a side, s, is 16 feet.

Portfolio Extension
Go To: **go.hrw.com**
Keyword:
MB1 Rate

73. Does the table of values at right represent a linear relationship between x and y? Explain. If the relationship is linear, write the next ordered pair that would appear in the table. **(LESSON 1.1)**

x	-8	-5	-2	1	4	7
y	9	7	5	3	1	-1

74. Make a table of values for the equation $y = -3x + 7$, and graph the line. Is the point $(4, -4)$ on this line? Explain how to answer this question by using the table, the graph, and the equation. **(LESSON 1.1)**

Calculator button indicates that a graphics calculator is recommended.

Look Beyond

75 Graph the equations $y = 2.12x - 3.7$ and $y = x + 5.4$ on the same screen. Find the coordinates of any points of intersection.

PORTFOLIO ACTIVITY

Refer to your portfolio data set from the Portfolio Activity on page 11.

   1. Choose two data points from your portfolio data set. Choose points that seem to fit the overall trend of your portfolio data set, not data points that contains values which may be far higher or lower than the others.

   2. Use a straightedge to draw a line through the points on your graph. This line will be your linear model for your portfolio data set. Find the equation of your linear model.

   3. What rate of change is indicated by your linear model? Include the appropriate units of measurement.

WORKING ON THE CHAPTER PROJECT

You should now be able to complete Activity 2 of the Chapter Project.

Linear Equations in Two Variables

1.3

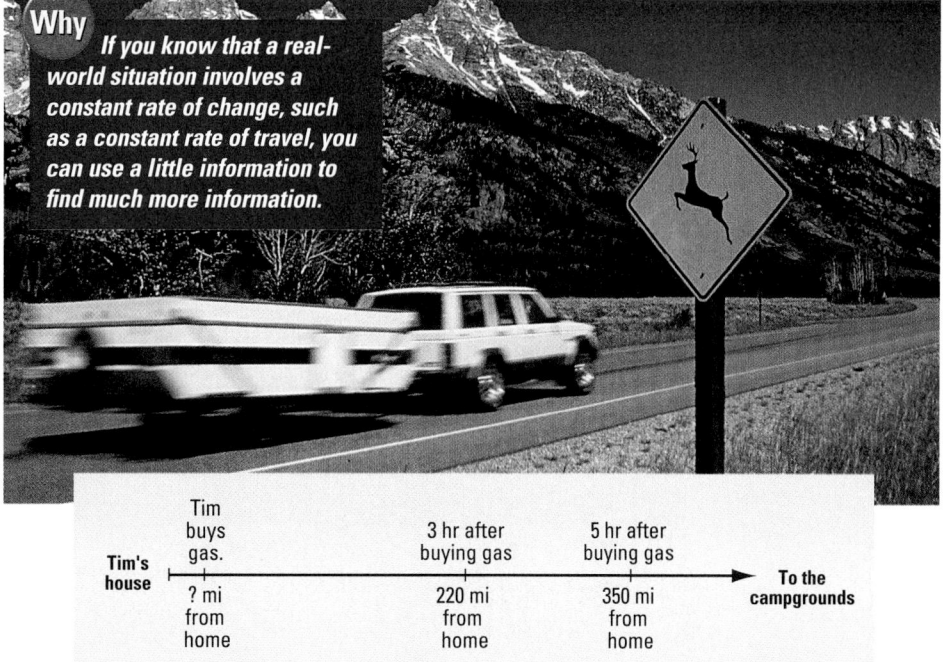

Why *If you know that a real-world situation involves a constant rate of change, such as a constant rate of travel, you can use a little information to find much more information.*

Objectives

* Write a linear equation in two variables given sufficient information.

* Write an equation for a line that is parallel or perpendicular to a given line.

Tim's house	Tim buys gas.		3 hr after buying gas	5 hr after buying gas	To the campgrounds
	? mi from home		220 mi from home	350 mi from home	

APPLICATION

TRAVEL

Tim leaves his house and drives at a constant speed to go camping. On his way to the campgrounds, he stops to buy gasoline. Three hours after buying gas, Tim has traveled 220 miles from home, and 5 hours after buying gas he has traveled 350 miles from home. How far from home was Tim when he bought gas? To answer this question, you can use the information given to write a linear equation in two variables. *You will solve this problem in Example 3.*

Example 1 shows you how to write a linear equation given two points on the line.

EXAMPLE ❶ Write an equation in slope-intercept form for the line containing the points (4, −3) and (2, 1).

● **SOLUTION**

1. Find the slope of the line.

$$m = \frac{1 - (-3)}{2 - 4} = \frac{4}{-2} = -2$$

2. Find the y-intercept of the line.

Substitute −2 for m and the coordinates of either point into $y = mx + b$.

$$y = mx + b$$
$$1 = -2(2) + b \qquad \boxed{\text{The point (2, 1) is used.}}$$
$$1 = -4 + b$$
$$5 = b$$

3. Write an equation.

$$y = mx + b$$
$$y = -2x + 5$$

You can use the *point-slope form* to write an equation of a line if you are given the slope and the coordinates of any point on the line.

Point-Slope Form

If a line has a slope of m and contains the point (x_1, y_1), then the **point-slope form** of its equation is $y - y_1 = m(x - x_1)$.

E X A M P L E **2** Write an equation in slope-intercept form for the line that has a slope of $\frac{1}{2}$ and contains the point $(-8, 3)$.

● **SOLUTION**

$$y - y_1 = m(x - x_1) \qquad \textit{Begin with point-slope form.}$$

$$y - 3 = \frac{1}{2}[x - (-8)] \qquad \textit{Substitute } \tfrac{1}{2} \textit{ for m, 3 for } y_1, \textit{ and } -8 \textit{ for } x_1.$$

$$y - 3 = \frac{1}{2}x + 4$$

$$y = \frac{1}{2}x + 7 \qquad \textit{Write the equation in slope-intercept form.}$$

The distance traveled by a motorist driving at a constant speed can be modeled by a linear equation.

E X A M P L E **3** Refer to the travel problem described at the beginning of the lesson.

How far from home was Tim when he bought gas?

● **SOLUTION**

Write a linear equation to model Tim's distance, y, in terms of time, x. Three hours after buying gas, Tim has traveled 220 miles, and 5 hours after buying gas, he has traveled 350 miles.

The line contains $(3, 220)$ and $(5, 350)$.

Find the slope. $m = \dfrac{350 - 220}{5 - 3} = 65$

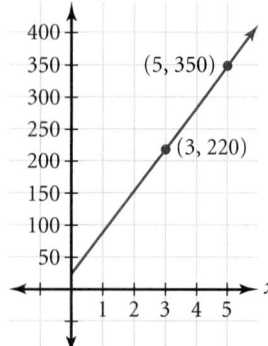

Write an equation. Begin with point-slope form.

$$y - y_1 = m(x - x_1)$$
$$y - 220 = 65(x - 3) \qquad \textit{Use either point. The point (3, 220) is used here.}$$
$$y - 220 = 65x - 195$$
$$y = 65x + 25 \qquad \textit{Write the equation in slope-intercept form.}$$

Thus, $y = 65x + 25$ models Tim's distance from home with respect to time. Since x represents the number of hours he traveled *after* he bought gas, he bought gas when $x = 0$. Thus, he bought gas when he was 25 miles from home.

CHECKPOINT ✔ What does the slope of the line $y = 65x + 25$ in Example 3 represent?

Parallel and Perpendicular Lines

The graph at right shows line ℓ_2 parallel to ℓ_1 and ℓ_3 perpendicular to ℓ_1 at point P.

In the Activity below, you can explore how parallel lines and perpendicular lines are related.

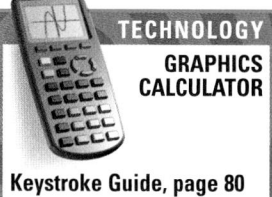
TECHNOLOGY
GRAPHICS CALCULATOR

Keystroke Guide, page 80

Activity
Exploring Parallel and Perpendicular Lines

You will need: a graphics calculator

1. Graph $y = 2x + 1$. On the same screen, graph $y = 2x$, $y = 2x - 2.5$, and $y = 3x + 1$. Which equations have graphs that appear to be parallel to that of $y = 2x + 1$? What do these equations have in common?

CHECKPOINT ✔ 2. Write an equation in slope-intercept form for a line whose graph you think will be parallel to that of $y = 2x + 1$. Verify by graphing.

3. Graph $y = 2x + 1$. On the same screen, graph $y = -\frac{1}{2}x + 2$, $y = \frac{1}{2}x + 2$, and $y = -\frac{1}{2}x + 3$. Which equations have graphs that appear to be perpendicular to that of $y = 2x + 1$? What do these equations have in common?

CHECKPOINT ✔ 4. Write an equation in slope-intercept form whose graph you think will be perpendicular to that of $y = 2x + 1$. Verify by graphing.

The relationships between the slopes of parallel lines are stated below.

Parallel Lines

If two lines have the same slope, they are parallel.

If two lines are parallel, they have the same slope.

All vertical lines have an undefined slope and are parallel to one another.

All horizontal lines have a slope of 0 and are parallel to one another.

The graphs of three parallel lines are shown at right.

$$y = 2x + 3$$
$$y = 2x - 1$$
$$y = 2x - 4$$

Notice that the lines do not intersect.

Because they are parallel, the lines will *never* intersect.

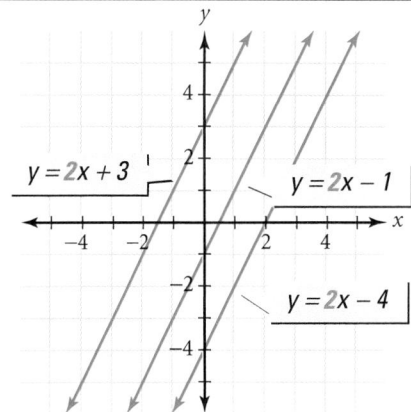

EXAMPLE ④ Write an equation in slope-intercept form for the line that contains the point $(-1, 3)$ and is parallel to the graph of $y = -2x + 4$.

● **SOLUTION**

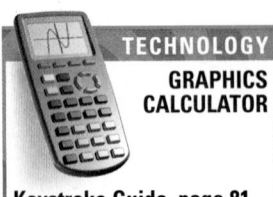

TECHNOLOGY

GRAPHICS CALCULATOR

Keystroke Guide, page 81

Because the line is parallel to the graph of $y = -2x + 4$, the slope is also -2.

$$y - y_1 = m(x - x_1)$$
$$y - 3 = -2[x - (-1)]$$
$$y - 3 = -2x - 2$$
$$y = -2x + 1$$

CHECK

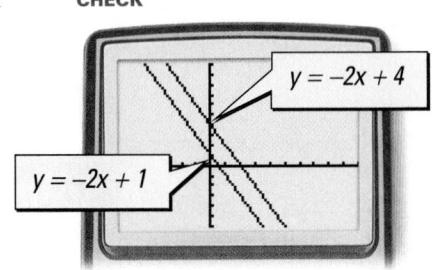

$y = -2x + 4$

$y = -2x + 1$

TRY THIS Write an equation in slope-intercept form for the line that contains the point $(-3, -4)$ and is parallel to the graph of $y = -4x - 2$.

The relationships between the slopes of perpendicular lines are stated below.

Perpendicular Lines

If a nonvertical line is perpendicular to another line, the slopes of the lines are negative reciprocals of one another.

All vertical lines are perpendicular to all horizontal lines.

All horizontal lines are perpendicular to all vertical lines.

The graphs of two perpendicular lines are shown at right.

$$y = 2x + 1 \text{ and } y = -\frac{1}{2}x - 3$$

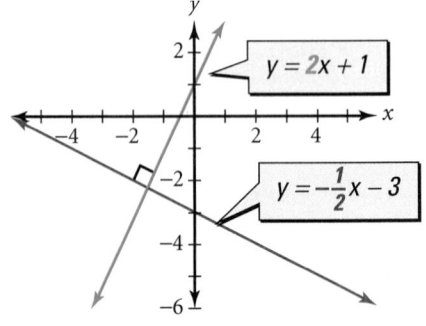

$y = 2x + 1$

$y = -\frac{1}{2}x - 3$

EXAMPLE ⑤ Write an equation in slope-intercept form for the line that contains the point $(4, -3)$ and is perpendicular to the graph of $y = 4x + 5$.

● **SOLUTION**

Use a square viewing window.

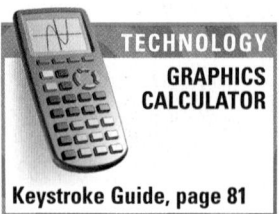

TECHNOLOGY

GRAPHICS CALCULATOR

Keystroke Guide, page 81

Because the line is perpendicular to the graph of $y = 4x + 5$, the slope is $-\frac{1}{4}$.

$$y - y_1 = m(x - x_1)$$
$$y - (-3) = -\frac{1}{4}(x - 4)$$
$$y + 3 = -\frac{1}{4}x + 1$$
$$y = -\frac{1}{4}x - 2$$

CHECK

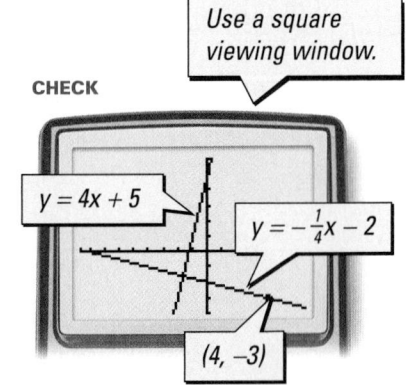

$y = 4x + 5$

$y = -\frac{1}{4}x - 2$

$(4, -3)$

TRY THIS Write an equation in slope-intercept form for the line that contains the point $(-1, 5)$ and is perpendicular to the graph of $y = -4x - 2$.

CRITICAL THINKING The graph of $3x - y = 4$ is perpendicular to the graph of $Ax + 2y = 8$ for some value of A. Find A.

Exercises

Communicate

1. Describe how to write an equation in slope-intercept form for the line containing two given points, such as $(1, 3)$ and $(4, -2)$.

2. Explain how to use the different forms of a linear equation to write the equation of the line graphed at right.

3. Describe how to determine whether the lines $5x + 6y = 12$ and $6x - 5y = 15$ are parallel, perpendicular, or neither.

4. Explain how to write the equation for the line that contains the point $(3, -1)$ and is perpendicular to the line $x + 2y = 4$.

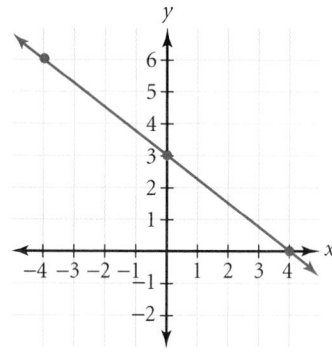

Guided Skills Practice

5. Write an equation in slope-intercept form for the line containing the points $(3, 3)$ and $(-5, -1)$. *(EXAMPLE 1)*

6. Write an equation in slope-intercept form for the line that has a slope of 3 and contains the point $(4, 7)$. *(EXAMPLE 2)*

APPLICATIONS

7. **TRAVEL** Tina leaves home and drives at a constant speed to college. On her way to the campus, she stops at a restaurant to have lunch. Two hours after leaving the restaurant, Tina has traveled 130 miles, and 4 hours after leaving the restaurant, she has traveled 240 miles. How far from home was Tina when she had lunch? *(EXAMPLE 3)*

8. Write an equation in slope-intercept form for the line that contains the point $(6, -5)$ and is parallel to the line $2x - 5y = -3$. *(EXAMPLE 4)*

9. Write an equation in slope-intercept form for the line that contains the point $(-7, 3)$ and is perpendicular to the line $2x + 5y = 3$. *(EXAMPLE 5)*

Practice and Apply

internet connect

**Homework
Help Online**

Go To: **go.hrw.com**
Keyword:
MB1 Homework Help
for Exercises 10–21

Write an equation for the line containing the indicated points.

10. $(0, 0)$ and $(3, 30)$

11. $(1, -3)$ and $(3, -5)$

12. $(-4, -4)$ and $(-3, -3)$

13. $(-10, -4)$ and $(-3, -3)$

14. $(-6, -6)$ and $(-3, 1)$

15. $(-2, 8)$ and $(-2, -1)$

16. $(4, -8)$ and $(3, -6)$

17. $(8, -3)$ and $(-8, 3)$

18. $\left(-\frac{1}{2}, 7\right)$ and $\left(-4, \frac{1}{2}\right)$

19. $\left(\frac{1}{2}, -3\right)$ and $\left(3, -\frac{1}{2}\right)$

20. $(-9, 1)$ and $\left(-\frac{1}{2}, 1\right)$

21. $(-5, 4)$ and $\left(-5, -\frac{2}{3}\right)$

Write an equation in slope-intercept form for the line that has the indicated slope, *m*, and contains the given point.

22. $m = -\frac{1}{2}, (8, 1)$

23. $m = -\frac{2}{3}, (6, -5)$

24. $m = -4, (5, -3)$

25. $m = 5, (-1, -3)$

26. $m = 0, (2, 3)$

27. $m = 0, (-7, 8)$

28. $m = 4, (9, -3)$

29. $m = 3, (-4, 9)$

30. $m = -\frac{1}{5}, (8, -2)$

31. $m = -\frac{2}{3}, (5, -4)$

Write a linear equation to model each table of values. For each equation, state what the slope represents.

32.

Hours	Miles
3	135
5	225

33.

Items	Cost ($)
4	14.00
7	21.50

34.

Hours	Parking fee ($)
3	6.50
7	12.50

Write an equation in slope-intercept form for the line that contains the given point and is parallel to the given line.

35. $(-2, 3), y = -3x + 2$

36. $(5, -3), y = 4x + 2$

37. $(0, -4), y = \frac{1}{2}x - 1$

38. $(-6, 2), y = -\frac{2}{3}x - 3$

39. $(-1, -3), 2x + 5y = 15$

40. $(4, -3), 3x + 4y = 8$

41. $(3, 0), -x + 2y = 17$

42. $(4, -3), -4x + y = -7$

Write an equation in slope-intercept form for the line that contains the given point and is perpendicular to the given line.

43. $(-2, 5), y = -2x + 4$

44. $(1, -4), y = 3x - 2$

45. $(8, 5), y = -x + 2$

46. $(0, -5), y = x - 5$

47. $(2, 5), 6x + 2y = 24$

48. $(3, -1), 12x + 4y = 8$

49. $(-2, 4), x - 6y = 15$

50. $(5, -2), 2x - 5y = 15$

51. Write an equation for the line that is perpendicular to the line $2x + 5y = 15$ at the *y*-intercept.

52. Write an equation for the line that is perpendicular to the line $x - 3y = 9$ at the *x*-intercept.

COORDINATE GEOMETRY **For Exercises 53–58, refer to the lines graphed on the coordinate plane below.**

53. Use slopes to determine whether ℓ_1 is parallel to ℓ_2.

54. Use slopes to determine whether ℓ_3 is parallel to ℓ_4.

55. Use slopes to determine whether ℓ_1 is perpendicular to ℓ_3.

56. Use slopes to determine whether ℓ_2 is perpendicular to ℓ_3.

57. Use slopes to determine whether ℓ_2 is perpendicular to ℓ_4.

58. Use slopes to determine whether ℓ_1 is perpendicular to ℓ_4.

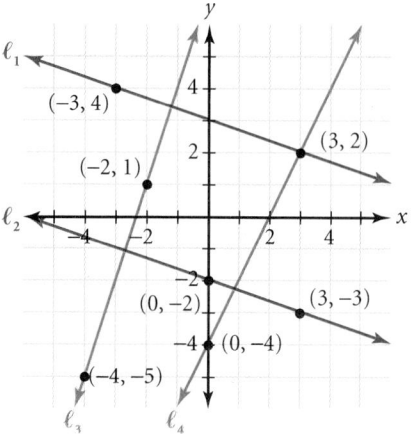

59. COORDINATE GEOMETRY Opposite sides of a parallelogram are parallel. Use slopes to determine whether the quadrilateral graphed in the coordinate plane at right is a parallelogram.

60. COORDINATE GEOMETRY A rectangle has opposite sides that are parallel and four right angles. Use slopes to determine whether the quadrilateral graphed in the coordinate plane at right is a rectangle.

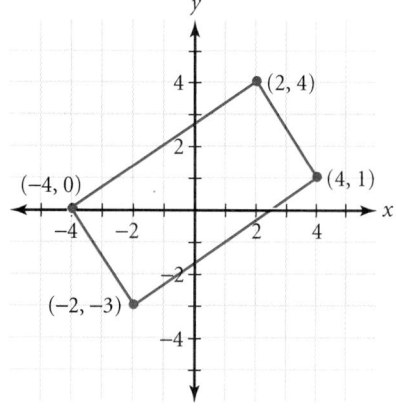

61. Use the diagram at right to prove that the diagonals of any square are perpendicular.

62. TRAVEL Mac bikes at a nonconstant rate of speed from home through town. He then begins his training ride at a constant speed of 25 miles per hour. After 3 hours of biking at a constant speed, his odometer shows that he has traveled 83 miles since he left home.

  a. Write a linear equation in slope-intercept form for the distance, d, in miles that Mac has traveled in terms of the time, t, in hours since he began his training ride.

  b. When Mac began his training ride, how far from home was he?

63. ACADEMICS A professor gives a test, and the scores range from 40 to 80. The professor decides to *scale* the test in order to make the scores range from 60 to 90. Let x represent an original score, and let y represent a converted score.

   a. Use the ordered pairs (40, 60) and (80, 90) to write the equation that the professor will use to scale the test scores.
   b. What will an original score of 45 become?
   c. If a converted score is 84, what was the original score?

64. INCOME Trevor is a salesperson who earns a weekly salary and a commission that is 7% of his weekly sales. In one week Trevor's sales were $952.00 and his weekly income was $466.64. In another week his sales were $2515.00 and his weekly income was $576.05.

   a. Write a linear equation in slope-intercept form for Trevor's weekly income, y, in terms of his weekly sales, x.
   b. What is Trevor's weekly salary?

 Look Back

Copy and complete the table. Write the fractions in simplest form.

	Fraction	Decimal	Percent
65.		$0.\overline{33}$	$33\frac{1}{3}\%$
66.		0.875	
67.			2%
68.	$\frac{1}{20}$		
69.			$12\frac{1}{2}\%$
70.	$\frac{2}{3}$		
71.	$\frac{1}{6}$		
72.			0.01%
73.		0.80	
74.	$\frac{2}{5}$		
75.		0.45	
76.	$\frac{5}{6}$		

77. Use the formula $d = rt$ to find the distance, d, in meters when the rate, r, is 50 meters per second and the time, t, is 4 seconds.

78. Use the formula $C = \pi d$ to find the circumference, C, in centimeters when the diameter, d, is 8 centimeters. Use 3.14 for π.

 Look Beyond

79. Let $y = 4x$.

   a. $\dfrac{y}{x} = $ ___?___
   b. If $y = 3$, then $x = $ ___?___ .

80. Let $y = mx$. If $y = 4$ and $x = 2$, then $m = $ ___?___ .

Direct Variation and Proportion

Why *Many events in the real world have a direct-variation relationship. For example, the distance you travel when bicycling can have a direct-variation relationship with time.*

Objectives

• Write and apply direct-variation equations.

• Write and solve proportions.

APPLICATION

RECREATION

Each day Johnathon rides his bicycle for exercise. When traveling at a constant rate, he rides 4 miles in about 20 minutes. At this rate, how long would it take Johnathon to travel 7 miles? To answer this question, you can use a *direct-variation equation* or a *proportion.* *You will solve this problem in Example 2.*

Recall that distance, d, rate, r, and elapsed time, t, are related by the equation $d = rt$. You can say that *d varies directly as t* because as time increases, the distance traveled increases proportionally.

Direct Variation

The variable y varies directly as x if there is a nonzero constant k such that $y = kx$. The equation $y = kx$ is called a **direct-variation equation** and the number k is called the **constant of variation**.

EXAMPLE ❶ Find the constant of variation, k, and the direct-variation equation if y varies directly as x and $y = -24$ when $x = 4$.

SOLUTION

$$y = kx \qquad \text{\textit{Use the direct-variation equation.}}$$
$$-24 = k \cdot 4 \qquad \text{\textit{Substitute 24 for y and 4 for x.}}$$
$$\frac{-24}{4} = k \qquad \text{\textit{Solve for k.}}$$
$$-6 = k$$

The direct-variation equation is $y = -6x$.

TRY THIS Find the constant of variation, k, and the direct-variation equation if y varies directly as x and $y = 15$ when $x = 3$.

At the constant rate that Johnathon bikes, how long would it take him to travel 7 miles?

● **SOLUTION**

1. Write a direct-variation equation, $d = rt$, that models Johnathon's distance as it varies with time.

Find the constant of variation, r.

$$r = \frac{4 \text{ mi}}{20 \text{ min}} = \frac{1}{5} \text{ mile per minute}$$

Write the direct-variation equation.

distance in miles   *time in minutes*

$$d = \frac{1}{5}t$$

2. Use the direct-variation equation to solve the problem.

$$d = \frac{1}{5}t$$

$$7 = \frac{1}{5}t \quad \text{\textit{Substitute 7 for d.}}$$

$$35 = t \quad \text{\textit{Solve for t.}}$$

CHECK

Graph the equation $y = \frac{1}{5}x$, and check to see that the point $(35, 7)$ is on the line.

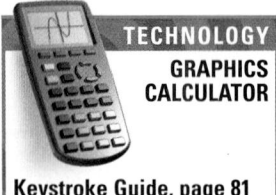

TECHNOLOGY
GRAPHICS
CALCULATOR

Keystroke Guide, page 81

Notice that the constant of variation, $\frac{1}{5}$, is the slope of the direct-variation equation, $y = \frac{1}{5}x$.

Thus, at the rate given it will take Johnathon 35 minutes to travel 7 miles.

TRY THIS   Suppose that when Johnathon is riding, he travels 5 miles in about 30 minutes. At this rate, how long would it take Johnathon to travel 12 miles?

The *Proportion Property* given below applies to all direct-variation relationships.

Proportion Property of Direct Variation

For $x_1 \neq 0$ and $x_2 \neq 0$:

If (x_1, y_1) and (x_2, y_2) satisfy $y = kx$, then $\frac{y_1}{x_1} = k = \frac{y_2}{x_2}$.

In the Activity below, you can see a connection between the concepts of geometric similarity, proportion, and direct variation.

Exploring Similarity and Direct Variation

You will need: a calculator

Recall from geometry that *similar* figures have the same shape. This means that the corresponding angles of similar polygons are congruent, and their corresponding sides are proportional.

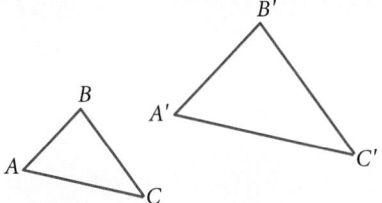

1. Copy and complete the table below to compare the lengths of the sides in $\triangle A'B'C'$ with the corresponding lengths in $\triangle ABC$.

Length in $\triangle ABC$	Length in $\triangle A'B'C'$	Ratio of $\triangle A'B'C'$ to $\triangle ABC$
$AB = 16$	$A'B' = 24$	$\frac{A'B'}{AB} = ?$
$BC = 20$	$B'C' = 30$	$\frac{B'C'}{BC} = ?$
$AC = 24$	$A'C' = 36$	$\frac{A'C'}{AC} = ?$

CHECKPOINT ✔ 2. Do your calculations in the third column indicate a direct-variation relationship between the lengths of the sides of $\triangle A'B'C'$ and those of $\triangle ABC$? Explain your response.

It is said that if y varies directly as x, then y is *proportional* to x.

A **proportion** is a statement that two *ratios* are equal. A ratio is the comparison of two quantities by division. A proportion of the form $\frac{a}{b} = \frac{c}{d}$ can be rearranged as follows:

$$\frac{a}{b} = \frac{c}{d}$$
$$\frac{a}{b} \cdot bd = \frac{c}{d} \cdot bd$$
$$ad = bc$$

The result is called the *Cross-Product Property of Proportions.*

Cross-Product Property of Proportions

For $b \neq 0$ and $d \neq 0$:

If $\frac{a}{b} = \frac{c}{d}$, then $ad = bc$.

In a proportion of the form $\frac{a}{b} = \frac{c}{d}$, a and d are the *extremes* and b and c are the *means*. By the Cross-Product Property, the product of the extremes equals the product of the means.

Using Newton's law of universal gravitation, ratios that compare the weight of an object on Earth with its weight on another planet can be calculated. For Mars and Earth, the ratio is shown below.

$$\text{weight on Mars} \rightarrow \frac{W_M}{W_E} \approx \frac{38}{100}$$
$$\text{weight on Earth} \rightarrow$$

E X A M P L E ③ *Sojourner* is the name of the first rover (robotic roving vehicle) that was sent to Mars. *Sojourner* weighs 24.3 pounds on Earth and is about the size of a child's small wagon.

   a. Find the weight of *Sojourner* on Mars to the nearest tenth of a pound.
   b. Write a direct-variation equation that gives the weight of an object on Mars, W_M, in terms of its weight on Earth, W_E.

● SOLUTION

a. Solve the proportion for the weight of *Sojourner* on Mars.

$$\frac{W_M}{24.3} \approx \frac{38}{100}$$

$(W_M)(100) \approx (24.3)(38)$ *Use the Cross-Product Property.*

$$W_M \approx \frac{(24.3)(38)}{100} \quad \leftarrow \text{weight on Mars}$$
$$\quad\quad\quad\quad\quad\quad \leftarrow \text{weight on Earth}$$

$$W_M \approx 9.2$$

On Mars, Sojourner would weigh about 9.2 pounds.

The Sojourner

b.
$$\frac{W_M}{W_E} \approx \frac{38}{100}$$
$$W_M \approx \frac{38 W_E}{100} \quad \leftarrow \text{weight on Mars}$$
$$\quad\quad\quad\quad\quad \leftarrow \text{weight on Earth}$$
$$W_M \approx 0.38 W_E$$

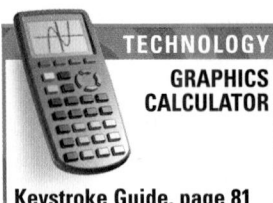

TECHNOLOGY
GRAPHICS
CALCULATOR

Keystroke Guide, page 81

CHECK
Graph $y = 0.38x$, and confirm that a weight of 24.3 pounds on Earth, x, corresponds to a weight of about 9.2 pounds on Mars, y.

Y1=.38X
(24.3, 9.234)
X=24.3   Y=9.234

E X A M P L E ④ Solve $\frac{3x-1}{5} = \frac{x}{2}$. **Check your answer.**

● SOLUTION

$$\frac{3x-1}{5} = \frac{x}{2}$$
$$(3x-1)(2) = (5)(x) \quad \textit{Use the Cross-Product Property.}$$
$$6x - 2 = 5x$$
$$x - 2 = 0$$
$$x = 2$$

CHECK

$$\frac{3x-1}{5} = \frac{x}{2}$$
$$\frac{3(2)-1}{5} \stackrel{?}{=} \frac{2}{2}$$
$$1 = 1 \quad \textbf{True}$$

TRY THIS Solve $\frac{3x+2}{7} = \frac{x}{2}$. Check your answer.

CRITICAL THINKING Let $a > 0$. How many solutions does $\frac{x}{a} = \frac{a}{x}$ have? Find the solutions. Justify your answer.

Exercises

Communicate

1. Suppose that y varies directly as x and that $y = 18$ when $x = 9$. Describe how you would find an equation of direct variation that relates these two variables.

2. When are linear equations *not* direct variations? How do their graphs differ from those of direct variations?

3. Describe two methods for solving the following problem:

   If y varies directly as x and $y = 8$ when $x = -2$, what is the value of x when $y = 12$?

Determine whether each equation describes a direct variation. Explain your reasoning.

4. $y = x + 5$ 5. $y = x - 5$ 6. $y = 5x$ 7. $y = \frac{x}{5}$

Guided Skills Practice

8. Find the constant of variation, k, and the direct-variation equation if y varies directly as x and $y = 1000$ when $x = 200$. *(EXAMPLE 1)*

APPLICATIONS

9. **PHYSICS** The speed of sound in air is about 335 feet per second. At this rate, how far would sound travel in 25 seconds? *(EXAMPLE 2)*

10. **INCOME** Workers at a particular store earn hourly wages. A person who worked 18 hours earned $114.30. *(EXAMPLE 3)*
    a. How many hours must this person work to earn $127?
    b. Write a direct-variation equation that gives the income of this person in terms of the hours worked. What does the constant of variation represent?

Solve each equation for x. Check your answers. *(EXAMPLE 4)*

11. $\frac{4x - 1}{21} = \frac{x}{6}$ 12. $\frac{x + 4}{-4} = \frac{3x}{36}$ 13. $\frac{2x}{8} = \frac{x + 3}{7}$

Practice and Apply

In Exercises 14–29, y varies directly as x. Find the constant of variation, and write an equation of direct variation that relates the two variables.

14. $y = 21$ when $x = 7$ 15. $y = 2$ when $x = 1$

16. $y = -16$ when $x = 2$ 17. $y = 1$ when $x = \frac{1}{3}$

18. $y = \frac{4}{5}$ when $x = \frac{1}{5}$ 19. $y = -\frac{6}{7}$ when $x = -\frac{18}{35}$

20. $y = -2$ when $x = 9$ 21. $y = 5$ when $x = -0.1$

22. $y = 1.8$ when $x = 30$ 23. $y = 0.4$ when $x = -1$

24. $y = 24$ when $x = 8$ 25. $y = 12$ when $x = \frac{1}{4}$

26. $y = -\frac{5}{8}$ when $x = -1$ **27.** $y = 4$ when $x = 0.2$

28. $y = 0.6$ when $x = -3$ **29.** $y = -1.2$ when $x = 4$

Write an equation that describes each direct variation.

30. p varies directly as q.   **31.** a is directly proportional to b.

For Exercises 32–36, *a* varies directly as *b*.

32. If a is 2.8 when b is 7, find a when b is −4.

33. If a is 6.3 when b is 70, find b when a is 5.4.

34. If a is −5 when b is 2.5, find b when a is 6.

35. If b is $-\frac{3}{5}$ when a is $-\frac{9}{10}$, find a when b is $\frac{1}{3}$.

36. If b is $-\frac{1}{2}$ when a is $-\frac{3}{10}$, find a when b is $-\frac{5}{9}$.

Homework Help Online

Go To: **go.hrw.com**
Keyword:
MB1 Homework Help
for Exercises 37–51

Solve each proportion for the variable. Check your answers.

37. $\frac{w}{4} = \frac{10}{12}$ **38.** $\frac{5}{q} = \frac{7}{8}$ **39.** $\frac{1}{8} = \frac{x}{100}$

40. $\frac{9}{10} = \frac{6}{r}$ **41.** $\frac{x}{3} = \frac{-7}{10}$ **42.** $\frac{3}{5} = \frac{x}{2}$

43. $\frac{7}{x} = \frac{3}{4}$ **44.** $\frac{x+5}{2} = \frac{4}{3}$ **45.** $\frac{x}{-5} = x - 6$

46. $\frac{x-1}{56} = \frac{x}{64}$ **47.** $\frac{3x+1}{5} = \frac{x}{2}$ **48.** $\frac{-4x}{-7} = x - 3$

49. $\frac{x+1}{9} = \frac{5x}{40}$ **50.** $\frac{6x-3}{9} = \frac{8x}{8}$ **51.** $\frac{5x}{-30} = \frac{x-5}{4}$

Determine whether the values in each table represent a direct variation. If so, write an equation for the variation. If not, explain.

52.

x	2	3	4	5	6
y	−4	−9	−16	−25	−36

53.

x	5	6	7	8	9
y	0.10	0.12	0.14	0.16	0.18

54.

x	−1	0	1	2	3
y	8	10	12	14	16

55.

x	−2	−1	0	1	2
y	1	0.5	0	−0.5	−1

56.

x	−7	−3	1	5	9
y	133	57	−19	−95	−171

57.

x	1	−5	−11	−17	−23
y	−6	42	90	138	186

58. Show that if x varies directly as y, then y varies directly as x.

CHALLENGE

59. If a varies directly as c and b varies directly as c, show that $a + b$ varies directly as c.

CONNECTION

60. **COORDINATE GEOMETRY** Which of the lines shown in the graph at right represents a direct variation? Explain your reasoning.

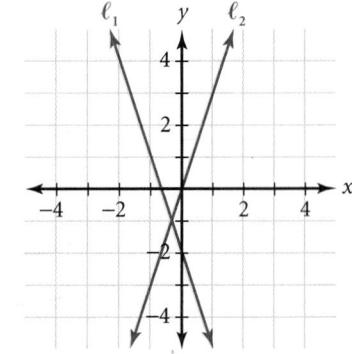

CULTURAL CONNECTION: ASIA The Harappan civilization flourished in an area near present-day Pakistan around 2500 B.C.E. They used balancing stones in their system of weights and measures. The Vedic civilization, which followed the Harappan civilization, used gunja seeds to weigh precious metals. The smallest Harappan stone has the same mass as 8 gunja seeds.

The scale is balanced with 16 gunja seeds on the left and the second smallest Harappan stone on the right.

61. The mass of a Harappan stone, *m*, varies directly as the number of gunja seeds, *g*. Find the constant of variation and the direct-variation equation for this relationship.

62. How many gunja seeds are equivalent to a Harappan stone whose mass is 3.52 grams?

63. The largest Harappan stone is equivalent to 320 gunja seeds. What is the mass of this stone?

Smallest Harappan stone

0.88 gram

1.76 grams

3.52 grams

320 gunja seeds Largest Harappan stone

CONNECTIONS

64. GEOMETRY In the figure at right, the height of each object is directly proportional to the length of its shadow. The person is $5\frac{1}{2}$ feet tall and casts an 8-foot shadow, while the tree casts a 33-foot shadow. How tall is the tree?

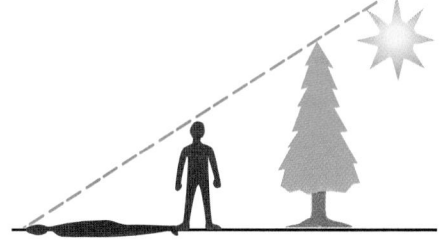

65. GEOMETRY In an aerial photograph, a triangular plot of land has the dimensions given in the figure at right. If the actual length of the longest side of the plot is 50 kilometers, find the actual lengths of the two shorter sides.

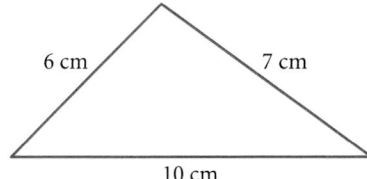

APPLICATIONS

PHYSICS In an electric circuit, Ohm's law states that the voltage, *V*, measured in volts varies directly as the electric current, *I*, measured in amperes according to the equation $V = IR$. The constant of variation is the electrical resistance of the circuit, *R*, measured in ohms.

66. An iron is plugged into a 110-volt electrical outlet, creating a current of 5.5 amperes in the iron. Find the electrical resistance of the iron.

67. A heater is plugged into a 110-volt outlet. If the resistance of the heater is 11 ohms, find the current in the heater.

68. Find the current, to the nearest hundredth of an ampere, in a night light with a resistance of 300 ohms that is plugged into a 110-volt outlet.

69. Find the current, to the nearest hundredth of an ampere, in a lamp that has a resistance of 385 ohms and is plugged into a 110-volt outlet.

70. PHYSICS As a scuba diver descends, the increase in water pressure varies directly as the increase in depth below the water's surface. However, the constant of variation is smaller in fresh water than in salt water. For example, at 80 feet below the surface of a typical freshwater lake, the pressure is 34.64 pounds per square inch greater than the pressure at the surface. In a typical ocean, where the water is salty, the pressure at 80 feet is 35.6 pounds per square inch greater than the pressure at the surface.

  a. Find the constant of variation and the equation of direct variation for the increase in pressure in a typical freshwater lake.

  b. Find the increase in pressure at 100 feet below the surface of a lake.

  c. Find the constant of variation and the equation of direct variation for the increase in pressure in a typical ocean.

  d. Find the increase in pressure at 100 feet below the surface of an ocean.

71. PHYSICS The distance a spring stretches varies directly as the amount of weight that is hanging on it. A weight of 32 pounds stretches the spring 6 inches, and a weight of 48 pounds stretches it 9 inches.

  a. Find the constant of variation and the equation of direct variation for the stretch of the spring. What does the constant of variation represent?

  b. How heavy is the weight hanging on the spring when it is stretched 3 inches?

  c. Find the stretch of the spring when a weight of 40 pounds is hanging on it.

 Look Back

Write the prime factorization for each number.

72. 261   **73.** 860   **74.** 315   **75.** 180   **76.** 154   **77.** 490

Evaluate.

78. $\dfrac{\frac{11}{13}}{\frac{11}{26}}$ **79.** $\dfrac{\frac{5}{6}}{\frac{15}{12}}$ **80.** $\dfrac{-\frac{1}{3}}{-\frac{4}{21}}$ **81.** $\dfrac{-\frac{2}{5}}{\frac{28}{25}}$

internet connect

Activities Online

Go To: **go.hrw.com**
Keyword:
MB1 Metrics

Calculator button indicates that a graphics calculator is recommended.

 Look Beyond

82 An equation of the form $xy = k$, where k is a constant greater than zero, is called an *inverse-variation equation*. Choose a positive value for k, and graph the equation. Describe the graph.

Refer to your portfolio data set from the Portfolio Activity on page 11.

  1. In your portfolio data set, does one variable vary directly as the other variable? Explain.

  2. Using data values from your portfolio data set, write a proportion of the form $\frac{y_1}{x_1} = \frac{y_2}{x_2}$. Is the proportion true for some values? Is the proportion true for all values? Explain.

  3. Using points on your linear model from the Portfolio Activity on page 20, write a proportion of the form $\frac{y_1}{x_1} = \frac{y_2}{x_2}$. Is the proportion true for some values? Is the proportion true for all values? Explain.

Scatter Plots and Least-Squares Lines

Why *Scatter plots and least-squares lines can be used to analyze trends in society. For example, from a scatter plot you can see an overall trend which shows that the number of reported cases of chicken pox is decreasing in the United States.*

Objectives

- Create a scatter plot and draw an informal inference about any correlation between the variables.

- Use a graphics calculator to find an equation for the least-squares line and use it to make predictions or estimates.

APPLICATION

HEALTH

In many real-world problems, you will find data that relate two variables such as time and distance or age and height. You can view the relationship between two variables with a **scatter plot**.

The following data on the number of reported cases of chicken pox in thousands in the United States is graphed in a scatter plot. The variable x represents the number of years after 1988 ($x = 0$ represents 1988) and y represents the number of cases in thousands.

Chicken Pox in the United States	
Year	Reported cases (in the thousands)
1989	185.4
1990	173.1
1991	147.1
1992	158.4
1993	134.7
1994	151.2

[*Source: Centers for Disease Control and Prevention*]

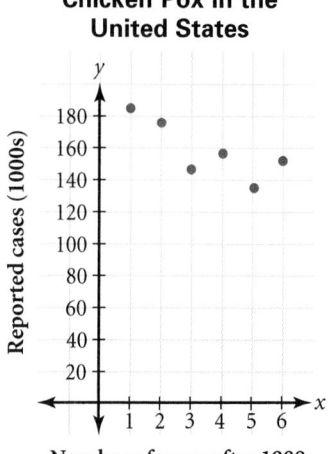

Chicken Pox in the United States

Number of years after 1988

Activity

Investigating a Scatter Plot

TECHNOLOGY

GRAPHICS CALCULATOR

Keystroke Guide, page 81

You will need: a graphics calculator

1. Create a scatter plot for the data on reported cases of chicken pox in the United States from 1989 to 1994. Let $x = 1$ represent the year 1989.

2. Write a linear equation in slope-intercept form that closely fits the data points. Graph your equation along with the data points.

3. Adjust the slope and *y*-intercept of your equation until you think the graph best fits the data points. Record your *best-fit* equation.

CHECKPOINT ✔ **4.** What rate of change is indicated by the slope of your linear equation? Write a sentence that states what the slope indicates about the reported cases of chicken pox.

The chicken-pox data in the Activity involves a two-variable data set that has a *negative correlation*. In general, there is a *correlation* between two variables when there appears to be a line about which the data points cluster. The diagrams below show the three possible correlations.

Positive correlation

Negative correlation

No reliable correlation

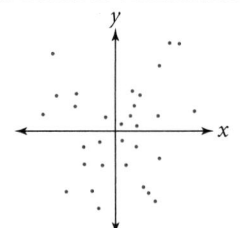

Finding the Least-Squares Line

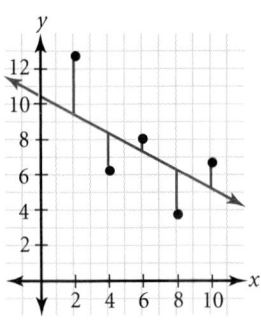

A scatter plot can help you see patterns in data involving two variables. If you think there may be a linear correlation between the variables, you can use a calculator to find a *linear-regression line*, also called the *least-squares line*, that best fits the data.

The graph at left shows the vertical distance from each point in a scatter plot to a fitted line. The fit of a **least-squares line** is based on *minimizing* these vertical distances for a data set. A least-squares line is one type of linear model for a data set.

E X A M P L E ❶ Create a scatter plot for the data shown at right. Describe the correlation. Then find and graph an equation for the least-squares line.

CONNECTION

STATISTICS

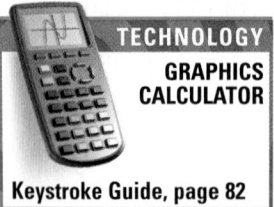

TECHNOLOGY

GRAPHICS CALCULATOR

Keystroke Guide, page 82

x	y
0	−3.2
2	1.2
4	5.0
6	8.8
7	11.6
8	13.0
10	17.5

SOLUTION

1. Create the scatter plot.

2. Describe the correlation.

Because the points rise from left to right, the correlation is positive.

3. Find and graph the least-squares line.

The equation of the least-squares line is $y \approx 2.05x - 3.13$.

Graph the least-squares line on the scatter plot with the data points.

CONNECTION

STATISTICS

Examine the graphics calculator display at left, which shows the linear-regression equation for Example 1. Notice that the display also shows a value of about 0.9993 for r. The **correlation coefficient,** denoted by r, indicates how closely the data points cluster around the least-squares line.

The correlation coefficient can vary from -1, which is a perfect fit for a negative correlation, to $+1$, which is a perfect fit for a positive correlation.

Perfect negative correlation

No correlation

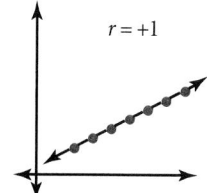

Perfect positive correlation

The closer the correlation coefficient is to -1 or $+1$, the better the least-squares line fits the data.

CHECKPOINT ✔ Refer to the data and the least-squares line found in Example 1. What is the correlation coefficient for this least-squares line? Is the correlation strong?

E X A M P L E ❷

APPLICATION

SPORTS

The winning times for the men's Olympic 1500-meter freestyle swimming event are given in the table. Notice that there is not a winning time recorded for the year 1940 (the Olympic games were not held during World War II).

Estimate what the winning time for this event could have been in 1940.

● **SOLUTION**

Let x represent the number of years after 1900. Let y represent the winning time in minutes. Enter the data into your calculator, and make a scatter plot.

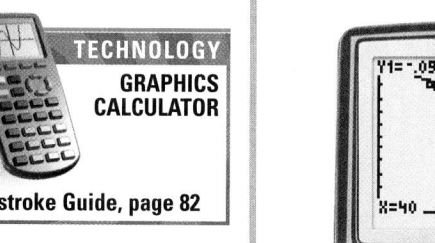

TECHNOLOGY

GRAPHICS CALCULATOR

Keystroke Guide, page 82

Year	Time (min:sec)	Time (min)
1908	22:48.4	22.81
1912	22:00.0	22.00
1920	22:23.2	22.39
1924	20:06.6	20.11
1928	19:51.8	19.86
1932	19:12.4	19.21
1936	19:13.7	19.23
1948	19:18.5	19.31
1952	18:30.3	18.51
1956	17:58.9	17.98
1960	17:19.6	17.33
1964	17:01.7	17.03
1968	16:38.9	16.65
1972	15:52.58	15.88
1976	15:02.40	15.04
1980	14:58.27	14.97
1984	15:05.20	15.09
1988	15:00.40	15.00
1992	14:43.48	14.72
1996	14:56.40	14.94

Using the equation for the least-squares line calculated from columns 1 and 2, the y-value that corresponds to $x = 40$ is about 19.29. Thus, for the men's Olympic 1500-meter freestyle in 1940, the winning time might have been about 19.29 minutes, or about 19:17.42.

TRY THIS   Use the least-squares line in Example 2 to estimate the winning time in this Olympic event in the year 2000.

CRITICAL THINKING   What assumption is made by using the least-squares line in the Try This exercise above?

Exercises

● Communicate

For Exercises 1–3, decide whether each statement is true or false. If it is false, explain why.

1. A correlation coefficient can be equal to 3.

2. For a given data set, if the slope of the least-squares line is positive, then the correlation coefficient is positive.

3. A data set with a correlation coefficient of 0.2 has a stronger linear relationship than a data set with a correlation coefficient of −0.9.

4. **DEMOGRAPHICS** As a population increases, the area available per person decreases. Give another example of a situation that you would expect to have a strong negative correlation with population.

5. **TAXES** As a population increases, the government revenue from taxes tends to increase. Give another example of a situation that you would expect to have a strong positive correlation with population.

Describe the correlation among data that have the given correlation coefficient.

6. $r = 0.02$ 7. $r = -0.61$ 8. $r = 0.96$

● Guided Skills Practice

Create a scatter plot of the data in each table. Describe the correlation. Then find an equation for the least-squares line. *(EXAMPLE 1)*

Calculator button indicates that a graphics calculator is recommended.

9

x	5	0	2	6	9	4	5	3	6	4	2	6	1	7	5	2
y	6	8	7	5	2	5	7	8	3	6	8	4	9	3	5	8

10

x	4	4	0	5	2	9	7	6	1	8	2	7	8	3	9	5
y	2	6	1	6	1	7	5	7	2	7	2	9	9	5	8	7

11

x	1	6	9	8	2	7	4	9	1	3	6	5	0	5	8	3
y	2	5	8	2	8	1	7	9	9	1	9	4	9	5	1	2

Ray Harroun, 1911

Jim Rathman, 1960

Arie Luyendyk, 1990

12 **SPORTS** The Indianapolis 500 auto race is held each year on Memorial Day. The table below gives the average speed, in miles per hour, of the winner for selected years from 1911 to 1996. In 1945, the race was not held. Estimate what could have been the average winning speed in 1945. Let $x = 0$ represent the year 1900. *(EXAMPLE 2)*

Year	Winner	Average speed	Year	Winner	Average speed
1911	Ray Harroun	74.602	1960	Jim Rathman	138.767
1915	Ralph DePalma	89.010	1965	Jimmy Clark	150.686
1920	Gaston Chevrolet	88.618	1970	Al Unser, Sr.	155.749
1925	Peter DePaolo	101.127	1975	Bobby Unser	149.213
1930	Billy Arnold	100.448	1980	Johnny Rutherford	142.862
1935	Kelly Petillo	106.240	1985	Danny Sullivan	152.982
1940	Wilbur Shaw	114.277	1990	Arie Luyendyk	185.984
1946	George Robson	114.820	1994	Al Unser, Jr.	160.872
1950	Johnnie Parsons	124.002	1995	Jacques Villenueve	153.616
1955	Bob Sweikert	128.209	1996	Buddy Lazier	147.956

[*Source: Sportsline USA, Inc., 1997*]

Practice and Apply

13 Create a scatter plot of the data in the table below. Describe the correlation. Then find an equation for the least-squares line.

x	8	4	1	5	4	4	9	8	5	2	7	1	6	3	2	4
y	7	6	2	5	6	4	8	8	6	3	8	3	6	4	1	3

14 *Find an equation* for the least-squares line of the data below. Use the equation to predict the x-value that corresponds to a y-value of 7.

x	9	5	8	6	2	4	7	3	1	2	6	5	7	2	4	6
y	8	4	9	5	1	4	8	3	2	1	5	5	6	2	5	6

Match each correlation coefficient with one of the data sets graphed.

$r = 1$ $r \approx 0.87$ $r \approx 0.63$ $r = -1$ $r \approx -0.91$ $r \approx -0.84$

15.

16.

17.

18.

19.

20.
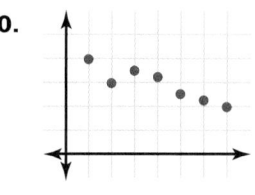

21. ETYMOLOGY Look for the words *interpolate* and *extrapolate* in a dictionary. For each word, write a definition that you think best applies to using a least-squares regression line to make predictions.

22 MARKETING Sixteen people of various ages were polled and asked to estimate the number of CDs they had bought in the previous year. The following table contains the collected data:

Age	18	20	20	22	24	25	25	26	28	30	30	31	32	33	35	45
CDs	12	15	18	12	10	8	6	6	4	4	4	2	2	3	6	1

a. Let x represent age, and let y represent the number of CDs purchased. Enter the data in a graphics calculator, and find the equation of the least-squares line.

b. Find the correlation coefficient, r, to the nearest tenth. Explain how the value of r describes the data.

c. Use the least-squares line to predict the number of CDs purchased by a person who is 27 years old.

d. Use the least-squares line to predict the age of a person who purchased 15 CDs in the previous year.

23 ANATOMY The following tables give the height and shoe size of some adults. Let x represent height, in inches, and let y represent shoe size.

WOMEN

MEN

a. Enter the data for women, and find the equation of the least-squares line.

b. Enter the data for men, and find the equation of the least-squares line.

c. Find the correlation coefficients for the women's data and for the men's data. Explain how the different correlation coefficients describe the two data sets.

d. Use the appropriate least-squares line to predict the shoe size of a woman who is 5'1" tall.

e. Use the appropriate least-squares line to predict the shoe size of a man who is 6'2" tall.

f. Use the appropriate least-squares line to predict the height of a man who wears size 12 shoes.

g. Use the appropriate least-squares line to predict the height of a woman who wears size 8 shoes.

L. Douglas Wilder served as governor of Virginia from 1990 to 1994. He was the first elected African American governor in U.S. history.

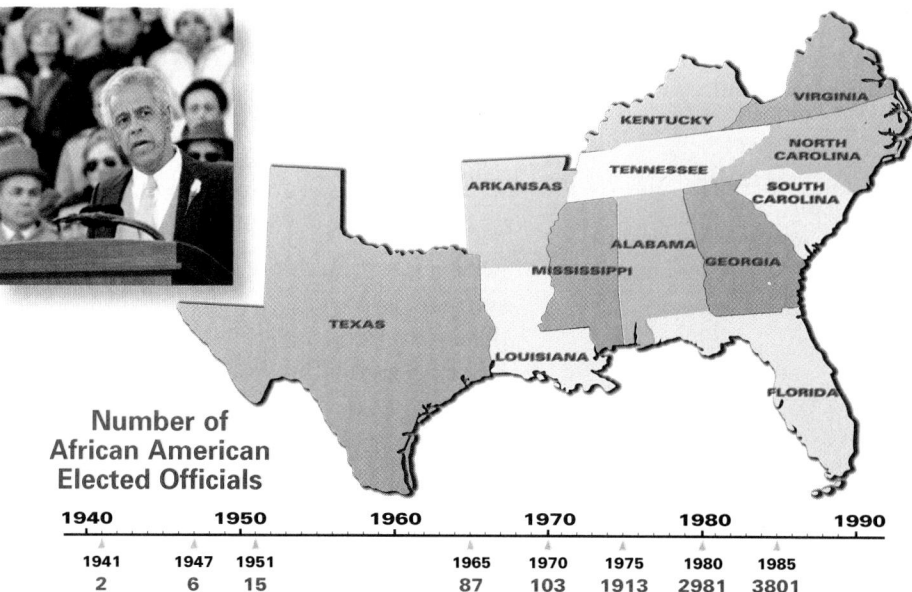

Number of African American Elected Officials

1940	1950	1960	1970	1980	1990

1941	1947	1951		1965	1970	1975	1980	1985
2	6	15		87	103	1913	2981	3801

APPLICATIONS

24 **GOVERNMENT** The time line above shows the number of African American elected officials in Southern states from 1941 to 1985.
   a. Create a scatter plot for this information, with the years on the x-axis. Let $x = 0$ represent 1900.
   b. Find the least-squares line for the data from 1941 to 1965.
   c. Find the least-squares line for the data from 1965 to 1985.
   d. Explain how the slopes of the two lines are different. What happened in the 1960s that might explain the extreme change?

25 **HEALTH** The table below gives information about cigarette smokers between the ages of 18 and 24 in the United States for selected years from 1965 to 1993.
   a. Enter the data for females, and find the equation of the least-squares line. Let $x = 0$ represent 1900.
   b. Enter the data for males, and find the equation of the least-squares line.
   c. Find the correlation coefficients for the female's data and for the male's data. Explain what the different correlation coefficients tell you about the two data sets.

Percent of Population That Are Cigarette Smokers in the United States

Year	Female (18–24)	Male (18–24)
1965	38.1	54.1
1974	34.1	42.1
1979	33.8	35.0
1983	35.5	32.9
1985	30.4	28.0
1987	26.1	28.2
1990	22.5	26.6
1992	24.9	28.0
1993	22.9	28.8

[*Source: Statistical Abstract of the United States, 1996*]

   d. Use the appropriate least-squares line to estimate the percent of females between the ages of 18 and 24 who were smokers in 1980.
   e. Use the appropriate least-squares line to estimate the percent of males between the ages of 18 and 24 who were smokers in 1970.
   f. Use the appropriate least-squares line to estimate the year in which 50% of males between the ages of 18 and 24 were smokers.
   g. Use the appropriate least-squares line to estimate the year in which 22% of males between the ages of 18 and 24 were smokers.

26 **AGRICULTURE** The table below gives the number of acres in an average farm in the United States from 1940 to 1995.

Year	1940	1950	1960	1970	1980	1995
Number of acres	174	213	297	374	426	469

[*Source: The World Almanac, 1997*]

   a. Let $x = 0$ represent the year 1900, and let y represent the number of acres in an average farm in the United States. Enter the data, and find the equation of the least-squares line.
   b. Find the correlation coefficient, r, to the nearest tenth. Explain what the value of r tells you about the data.
   c. Use the least-squares line to estimate the number of acres in an average farm in 1955.
   d. Use the least-squares line to predict the year in which there were about 325 acres in an average farm.

Look Back

Without using a calculator, write an equivalent decimal for each fraction.

27. $\frac{1}{3}$ **28.** $-\frac{3}{5}$ **29.** $\frac{17}{4}$ **30.** $\frac{5}{3}$ **31.** $\frac{7}{20}$

Without using a calculator, evaluate each expression. Write your answer as a decimal.

32. $5 \div 2$ **33.** $5 \div 0.2$ **34.** $5 \div 0.02$

35. The line whose equation is $y = -1.6x + 1$ is parallel to another line whose equation is $y = mx - 4$. Find m. **(LESSON 1.3)**

internet connect

Portfolio Extension
Go To: **go.hrw.com**
Keyword:
MB1 Regression

Look Beyond

Determine whether each equation is true when *a*, *b*, and *x* are real numbers.

36. $ax + bx = bx + ax$ **37.** $ax - bx = bx - ax$

38. $ax \cdot bx = bx \cdot ax$ **39.** $ax \div bx = bx \div ax$

PORTFOLIO ACTIVITY

   1. Use a graphics calculator to find the equation of the least-squares line for your portfolio data set.

   2. Plot the least-squares line on the same coordinate plane as your portfolio data points and with the linear model that you created in the Portfolio Activity on page 36.

   3. Compare the slope of the least-squares line with the slope of your linear model.

   4. What is the correlation coefficient for your least-squares line?

WORKING ON THE CHAPTER PROJECT

You should now be able to complete Activity 3 of the Chapter Project.

Introduction to Solving Equations

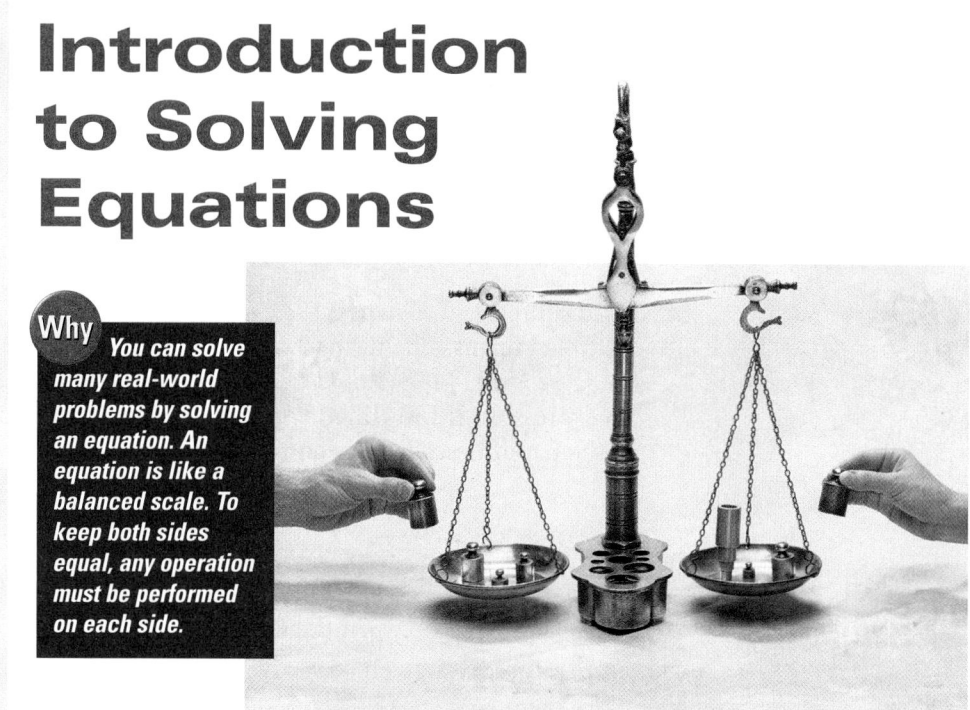

Why *You can solve many real-world problems by solving an equation. An equation is like a balanced scale. To keep both sides equal, any operation must be performed on each side.*

Objectives

● Write and solve a linear equation in one variable.

● Solve a literal equation for a specified variable.

An **equation** is a statement that two expressions are equal. An equation usually contains one or more variables. A **variable** is a symbol that represents many different numbers in a set of numbers.

> Equation in *one* variable, w:　　$12w = 10$
> Equation in *two* variables, x and y:　$2x + 3y = 12$

Any value of a variable that makes an equation true is called a **solution of the equation.** For example, $12w = 10$ is an equation in one variable, w. Because $\frac{5}{6}$ satisfies the equation, $\frac{5}{6}$ is a solution.

$$12w = 10$$
$$12\left(\frac{5}{6}\right) \stackrel{?}{=} 10$$
$$10 = 10 \quad \textbf{True}$$

To solve equations, the *Properties of Equality,* shown below, or the *Substitution Property,* shown on page 46, may be used.

Properties of Equality

For real numbers a, b, and c:

Reflexive Property	$a = a$
Symmetric Property	If $a = b$, then $b = a$.
Transitive Property	If $a = b$ and $b = c$, then $a = c$.
Addition Property	If $a = b$, then $a + c = b + c$.
Subtraction Property	If $a = b$, then $a - c = b - c$.
Multiplication Property	If $a = b$, then $ac = bc$.
Division Property	If $a = b$, then $\frac{a}{c} = \frac{b}{c}$, where $c \neq 0$.

Substitution Property

If $a = b$, you may replace a with b in any true statement containing a and the resulting statement will still be true.

In an expression, such as $5 + 3x - x - 1$, the parts that are added or subtracted are called **terms**. The terms $3x$ and x are called **like terms** because they contain the *same form of the variable x*. The constant terms, 5 and 1, are also like terms. An expression is **simplified** when all the like terms have been combined and all the parentheses have been removed.

$$5 + 3x - x - 1$$
$$= 2x + 4 \quad \textit{simplified}$$

E X A M P L E ① The relationship between the Celsius temperature, C, and the Fahrenheit temperature, F, is given by $F = \frac{9}{5}C + 32$.

APPLICATION
TEMPERATURE

Find the Celsius temperature that is equivalent to 86°F.

● **SOLUTION**

$$F = \frac{9}{5}C + 32$$
$$86 = \frac{9}{5}C + 32 \qquad \textit{Substitute 86 for F.}$$
$$86 - 32 = \frac{9}{5}C + 32 - 32 \qquad \textit{Use the Subtraction Property.}$$
$$54 = \frac{9}{5}C \qquad \textit{Simplify.}$$
$$\left(\frac{5}{9}\right)54 = \left(\frac{5}{9}\right)\left(\frac{9}{5}C\right) \qquad \textit{Use the Multiplication Property.}$$
$$30 = C \qquad \textit{Simplify.}$$

Thus, 30°C is equivalent to 86°F.

E X A M P L E ② **Solve $2x + 7 = 5x - 9$. Check your solution by using substitution.**

● **SOLUTION**

$$2x + 7 = 5x - 9$$
$$2x + 7 - 7 = 5x - 9 - 7 \qquad \textit{Use the Subtraction Property.}$$
$$2x = 5x - 16 \qquad \textit{Simplify.}$$

> **Combine $2x$ and $5x$.**

$$2x - 5x = 5x - 16 - 5x \qquad \textit{Use the Subtraction Property.}$$
$$-3x = -16 \qquad \textit{Simplify.}$$
$$x = \frac{-16}{-3} = \frac{16}{3}, \text{ or } 5\frac{1}{3} \qquad \textit{Use the Division Property.}$$

CHECK
$$2x + 7 = 5x - 9$$
$$2\left(\frac{16}{3}\right) + 7 \overset{?}{=} 5\left(\frac{16}{3}\right) - 9$$
$$17\frac{2}{3} = 17\frac{2}{3} \qquad \textbf{True}$$

TRY THIS Solve $3x + 12 = -5x + 24$. Check your solution by using substitution.

An algebraic solution method was shown in Example 2. In the Activity below, you can explore a graphic solution method for solving equations.

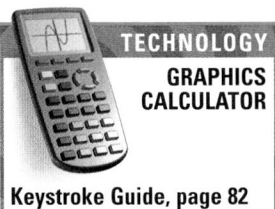

TECHNOLOGY
GRAPHICS
CALCULATOR

Keystroke Guide, page 82

Exploring Graphic Solution Methods

You will need: a graphics calculator

1. In the equation $x + 3 = 9 - 2x$, what two expressions are equal?

2. Use a graphics calculator to graph $y = x + 3$ and $y = 9 - 2x$ on the same screen. For what value of x do $x + 3$ and $9 - 2x$ have the same value?

3. Check to see if this value is the solution to the original equation.

CHECKPOINT ✔ 4. Describe how to solve $2x - 1 = 2 - x$ by using a graphics calculator.

E X A M P L E ❸ Solve $3.24x - 4.09 = -0.72x + 3.65$ by graphing.

● **SOLUTION**

Write the original equation as the pair of equations below.

$$3.24x - 4.09 = -0.72x + 3.65$$
$$y = 3.24x - 4.09 \quad \text{and} \quad y = -0.72x + 3.65$$

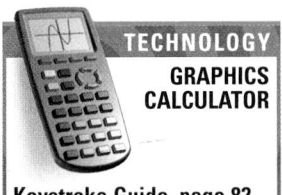

TECHNOLOGY
GRAPHICS
CALCULATOR

Keystroke Guide, page 82

Graph the two equations on the same screen, and find the point of intersection.

Read the x-coordinate of the point where the graphs intersect.

From the calculator display, the solution is $x \approx 1.95$.

TRY THIS Solve $2.24x - 6.24 = 4.26x - 8.76$ by graphing.

Literal Equations

A **literal equation** is an equation that contains two or more variables.

CONNECTION
GEOMETRY

Formulas are examples of literal equations. The following examples of literal equations are from geometry:

Volume of a cube, V:

$V = s^3$, where s is the side length

Area of a circle, A:

$A = \pi r^2$, where r is the radius

Volume of a square pyramid, V:

$V = \frac{1}{3}s^2h$, where s is the side length and h is the altitude

Young's formula is used to relate a child's dose of a medication to an adult's dose of the same medication. The formula applies to children from 1 to 12 years old.

$$\frac{a}{a+12} \times d = c, \text{ where } \begin{cases} a \text{ represents the child's age} \\ d \text{ represents the adult's dose} \\ c \text{ represents the child's dose} \end{cases}$$

E X A M P L E ④ Solve $\frac{a}{a+12} \times d = c$ for d.

● **SOLUTION**

$$\frac{a}{a+12} \times d = c$$

$$(a+12)\frac{a}{a+12} \times d = (a+12)c \qquad \textit{Use the Multiplication Property.}$$

$$ad = c(a+12) \qquad \textit{Simplify and use the Commutative Property.}$$

$$d = \frac{c(a+12)}{a} \qquad \textit{Use the Division Property.}$$

CRITICAL THINKING   Solve $\frac{a}{a+12} \times d = c$ for a.

CHECKPOINT ✔ Two equations are **equivalent** if they have the same solution.

Use substitution to verify that the following equations are equivalent:
$$86 = \frac{9}{5}C + 32 \qquad\qquad 54 = \frac{9}{5}C \qquad\qquad C = 30$$

Exercises

● *Communicate*

Tell which Properties of Equality you would use to solve each equation.

1. $52 = -2.7x - 3$ **2.** $\frac{x}{5} = x + 2.2$ **3.** $x - 5 = -2x - 2$

4. Describe one way to obtain an equation that is equivalent to $4x - 7 = 14$.

5. Describe how to solve $\frac{2(x+3)}{7} = \frac{9(x-3)}{5}$ by graphing.

● *Guided Skills Practice*

Solve each equation. Check your solution. *(EXAMPLES 1 AND 2)*

6. $4x + 12 = 20$ **7.** $\frac{x}{5} + 3 = 4$

8. $-\frac{5}{2}x + \frac{5}{2} = 2 - 3x$ **9.** $7 - 6x = 2x - 9$

Calculator button indicates that a graphics calculator is recommended.

10 Solve $\frac{4(x+5)}{3} = \frac{-3(x-7)}{5}$ by graphing. *(EXAMPLE 3)*

11. Solve $Ax + By = C$ for y. *(EXAMPLE 4)*

Practice and Apply

Solve each equation.

12. $1 = 2x - 5$ **13.** $-2x - 7 = 9$ **14.** $2x - 1 = -5$

15. $3x - 3 = 5$ **16.** $2x - 5 = 19$ **17.** $5x - 3 = 12$

18. $20 = 6x - 10$ **19.** $4 - 5x = 19$ **20.** $3x + 1 = \frac{1}{2}$

21. $4x + 80 = -6x$ **22.** $5x + 15 = 2x$ **23.** $7x = -2x + 5$

24. $5x + 3 = 2x + 18$ **25.** $-4x - 3 = x + 7$ **26.** $3x - 8 = 2x + 2$

27. $\frac{1}{5}x + 3 = 2$ **28.** $\frac{1}{4}x - \frac{5}{2} = -2$ **29.** $\frac{1}{6}x + \frac{3}{2} = 2$

30. $0 = \frac{1}{2}x + 2$ **31.** $-\frac{3}{5}x + 12 = 4$ **32.** $-5 = \frac{3}{2}x - 2$

33. $\frac{1}{3}x = -x + 4$ **34.** $x - 5 = -\frac{3}{2}x + \frac{5}{2}$

35. $-\frac{1}{3}x + 1 = \frac{3}{2}x - 1$ **36.** $-2x + 5 = -\frac{1}{3}x - 6$

37. $\frac{2}{3}x - 9 = -\frac{1}{2}x + 4$ **38.** $\frac{1}{4}x - 3 = 6x$

39. $\frac{1}{3}x - \frac{4}{3} = -\frac{1}{6}x - 1$ **40.** $\frac{2}{5}x + \frac{6}{5} = x - 3$

Solve each equation by graphing. Give your answers to the nearest hundredth.

41 $0.24x + 1.1 = 2.56x - 1.5$ **42** $1.05x - 4.28 = -2.65x + 4.1$

43 $-0.75x + 12.42 = 4.36$ **44** $0.35x - 2.72 = 5.83x$

45 $0.67x - 8.75 = -0.48x + 3.99$ **46** $5.9(0.33x - 1.33) = -1.03x - 5.72$

Solve each literal equation for the indicated variable.

47. $\frac{1}{2}bh = A$ for b **48.** $P = 2l + 2w$ for w

49. $\frac{1}{R} = \frac{1}{r_1} + \frac{1}{r_2}$ for r_2 **50.** $A = \frac{1}{2}h(b_1 + b_2)$ for b_2

51. $A = \frac{1}{2}h(b_1 + b_2)$ for h **52.** $y = \frac{u + 1}{u + 2}$ for u

53. $ax + b = cx + d$ for x **54.** $ax + b = cx + d$ for d

55. $I = P(1 + rt)$ for r **56.** $I = P(1 + rt)$ for t

Solve each literal equation for *v*.

57. $x = vt$ **58.** $x = vt + \frac{1}{2}at^2$ **59.** $y = \frac{1}{2}xv$

60. Given the equation $y = 4x + 7$, use substitution to solve $-2x + y = 19$ for x.

61. Given the equation $x = -y + 9$, use substitution to solve $3x - 5y = 59$ for x.

CONNECTIONS

62. GEOMETRY The measure of one supplementary angle is 45° more than twice the measure of the other. Write an equation and find the measure of each angle. Recall that two angles are supplementary if the sum of their measures is equal to 180°.

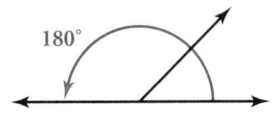

CHALLENGE

63. GEOMETRY The formula for the area of a cone in terms of the slant height, *s*, and the radius of the base, *r*, is $A = \pi rs + \pi r^2$. Write a formula for the slant height of a cone in terms of its area and the radius of its base.

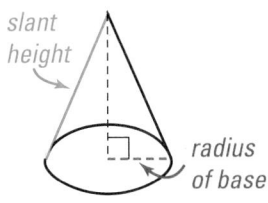

Write and solve an appropriate equation for each situation.

64. RECREATION A summer carnival charges a $2 admission fee and $0.50 for each ride. If Tamara has $10 to spend, how many rides can she go on?

65. TAXES Aaron's mother purchases a new computer for $1750. If she claims a linear depreciation (loss of value) on the computer at a rate of $250 per year, how long will it take for the value of the computer to be $0?

66. CONSUMER ECONOMICS The receipt for repairs on Victor's car is shown at right.
  a. Write an equation to model the total bill in terms of parts and labor.
  b. What hourly rate does the repair shop charge for labor?

AUTO REPAIR
#111 Auto Lane
Lana, TX 78787
INVOICE

Date: July 7

ITEM	AMOUNT
Parts:	
Brake Fluid	$6.00
Wheel Cylinder	$28.50
Rear Brake Shoes	$20.00
Front Brake Pads	$15.00
Shop Supplies	$2.50
Labor	3.5 hours
TOTAL	$272.00

67. INCOME Louis has two different job offers for a position in shoe sales. One pays $25 per week plus a $2 commission for each pair of shoes sold. The second job pays $40 per week plus a $1.50 commission for each pair of shoes sold. How many shoes would Louis have to sell to make the same total salary in either job?

68. BANKING Carmen has taken out a loan for $800 to buy a car. She plans to pay back the loan at a rate of $40 per month. Ramona has borrowed $500 to buy a car, which she plans to pay back at a rate of $20 per month.
  a. How long will it take Carmen to pay back her loan?
  b. How long will it take Ramona to pay back her loan?
  c. If Carmen and Ramona take out their loans at the same time, how long will it take for their remaining balances to be equal? What are their remaining balances after this amount of time?

69. INCOME Amelia has a job baby-sitting for a neighbor. She is paid $20 plus $2.50 for each hour on the job. If Amelia wants to earn $40 to buy a new sweater, how many hours would she need to work?

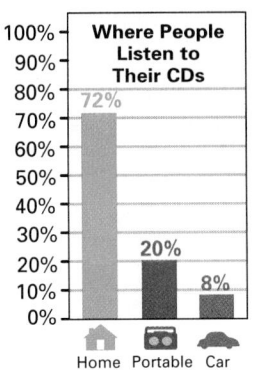

Where People Listen to Their CDs

100%
90%
80% 72%
70%
60%
50%
40%
30%
20%   20%
10%   8%
0%
Home Portable Car

70. RECREATION The results of a survey of CD listeners in 1993 show that 72% usually listen to CDs at home, 20% usually listen to CDs on a portable player, and 8% usually listen to CDs in a car. If 180 of the respondents say that they usually listen to CDs on a portable player, how many people were surveyed?

71. INCOME Anthony wants to buy a used car that will cost $185.00 per month. If Anthony earns $5.35 per hour, how many hours must Anthony work each month in order to pay for the car?

 Look Back

Identify the slope, *m*, and *y*-intercept, *b*, for each line. Then graph the equation. (LESSON 1.2)

72. $y = 2x - 6$ **73.** $3x + 4y = 9$ **74.** $y = 2$

Write each number in decimal notation.

75. 5.736×10^4 **76.** 7.4609×10^3

77. 46.72×10^6 **78.** 6.72×10^{-6}

Write each number in scientific notation.

79. 25,000   **80.** 720,000   **81.** 260.07

82. 5.7002   **83.** 0.05   **84.** 0.0002046

 Look Beyond

Explain what each expression means.

85. $y > -5$ **86.** $-3 < x < 3$ **87.** $-1 \leq y \leq 1$ **88.** $x \leq -3$

1. Choose a *y*-value (distance) that is different from those in your portfolio data set. Substitute this *y*-value into the equation for the least-squares line, and make a prediction about the corresponding time.

2. Show your results from Step 1 on your graph.

WORKING ON THE CHAPTER PROJECT

You should now be able to complete the Chapter Project.

A Man & A Method

Predicting eclipses and planetary motions seems complicated, but imagine having no formal education and teaching yourself the mathematics needed to make such calculations. Imagine publishing an almanac of your results for farmers and astronomers across the nation. That is exactly what an African American named Benjamin Banneker did over 200 years ago. The almanac impressed Thomas Jefferson so much that he asked Banneker to help survey the land for the new nation's capital, Washington, D.C.

Benjamin Banneker also published math puzzles. Some he made up. Others, like the one below, were sent to him. He published the puzzle shown below in his *Manuscript Journal*.

> Divide 60 into four Such parts, that the first being increased by 4, the Second decreased by 4, the third multiplyed by 4, the fourth part divided by 4, that the Sum, the difference, the product, and the Quotient shall be one and the Same Number—

Banneker gave the answer but not his method for finding it. He may have used a method called *false position*. In the false position method, you guess the answer, see how far off your guess is, and then use that information in a proportion to get the correct answer.

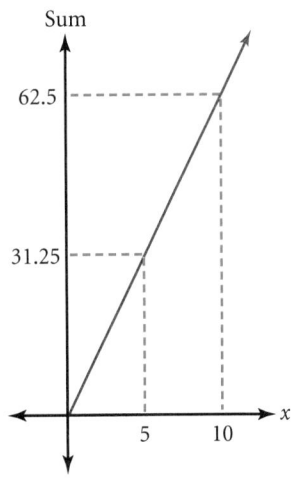

Cooperative Learning

1. Try the method of false position for yourself. Use it to solve Bannecker's puzzle, shown on the previous page, by following the steps below.

   a. Let x represent the answer, "one and the same number."

   first part $+ 4 = x$
   second part $- 4 = x$
   third part $\times 4 = x$
   fourth part $\div 4 = x$

   Choose any number to be the answer, x. For instance, you can choose 5 or 10 or any other number you like.

   b. Substitute the number you chose for the answer, x, into each equation above, and solve for each of the four parts. For example, if you chose 5 for x, then the first part can be found as shown below.

   first part $+ 4 = 5$
   first part $= 1$ *Solve for the "first part."*

   c. Find the sum of the four parts.

   d. Use a proportion to find the correct answer, x, for the "one and the same number."

   $$\frac{\text{Correct "one and the same number"}}{\text{Correct sum} = 60} = \frac{\text{Trial "one and the same number"}}{\text{Trial sum}}$$

   e. Use the correct answer for x, "one and the same number," from the proportion above to find the four parts. Is the sum of these parts really 60?

2. Now use algebra to solve the same puzzle. Follow the steps below.

   a. Write each of the four parts in terms of x, and represent the puzzle with one equation in one variable.

   b. Show that the solution to this equation gives the correct first, second, third, and fourth parts of the puzzle.

3. Use the graph at right to explain why the method of false position works for this puzzle.

Introduction to Solving Inequalities

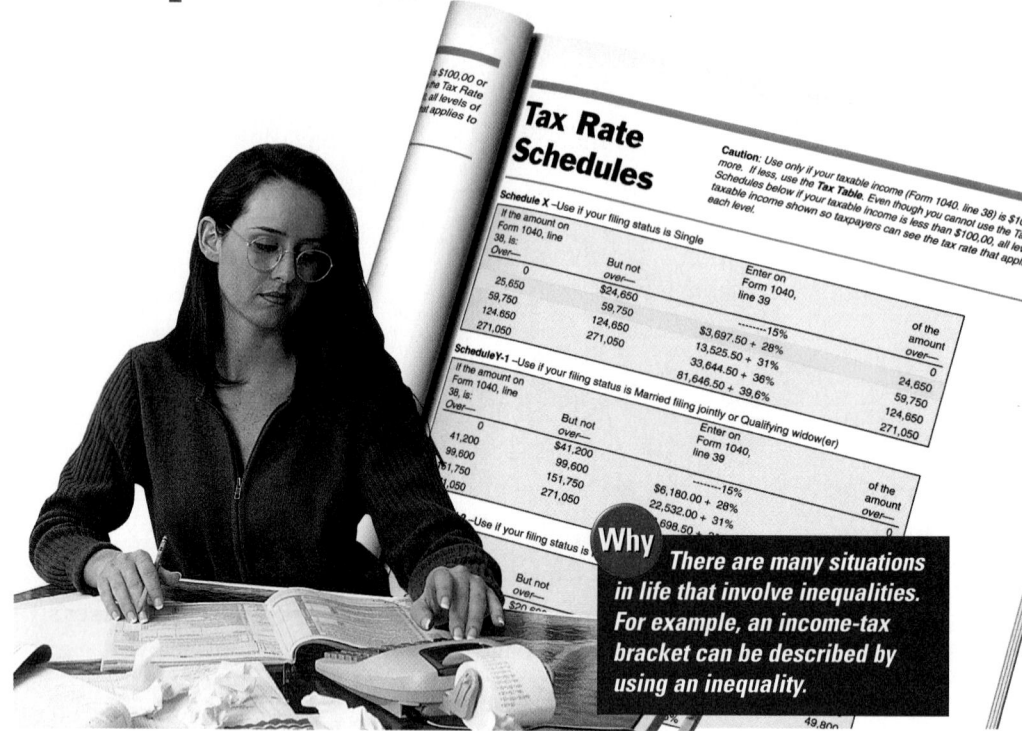

Why *There are many situations in life that involve inequalities. For example, an income-tax bracket can be described by using an inequality.*

Objectives

- Write, solve, and graph linear inequalities in one variable.

- Solve and graph compound linear inequalities in one variable.

APPLICATION

TAXES

The federal tax calculation table above applies to single people filing a tax return in 1998 for the tax year 1997.

Suppose, for example, that your taxable income is x dollars and the tax due is t dollars. You can read the second row as follows:

If $x > 24{,}650$ *and* $x \le 59{,}750$, then $t = 3697.50 + 0.28(x - 24{,}650)$.

The statements $x > 24{,}650$ *and* $x \le 59{,}750$ are examples of *linear inequalities in one variable*. In general, an **inequality** is a mathematical statement involving $<, >, \le, \ge,$ or $\ne$.

Just as there are Properties of Equality that you can use to solve equations, there are *Properties of Inequality* that you can use to solve inequalities.

Properties of Inequality

For all real numbers a, b, and c, where $a \le b$:

Addition Property	$a + c \le b + c$
Subtraction Property	$a - c \le b - c$
Multiplication Property	If $c \ge 0$, then $ac \le bc$.
	If $c \le 0$, then $ac \ge bc$.
Division Property	If $c > 0$, then $\dfrac{a}{c} \le \dfrac{b}{c}$.
	If $c < 0$, then $\dfrac{a}{c} \ge \dfrac{b}{c}$.

Similar statements can be written for $a < b$, $a \ge b$, and $a > b$.

Any value of a variable that makes an inequality true is called a **solution of the inequality.** For example, $6x + 1 < 13$ is an inequality in one variable, x. Values such as $\frac{1}{2}$ and -1 are solutions of the inequality, as shown below.

$$6x + 1 < 13 \qquad\qquad\qquad 6x + 1 < 13$$
$$6\left(\frac{1}{2}\right) + 1 \overset{?}{<} 13 \qquad\qquad 6(-1) + 1 \overset{?}{<} 13$$
$$4 < 13 \quad \textbf{True} \qquad\qquad -5 < 13 \quad \textbf{True}$$

CHECKPOINT ✔ Find two or more solutions of $6x + 1 < 13$, and show that they are solutions.

E X A M P L E **1** Solve $4x - 5 \geq 13$.

● **SOLUTION**

Because you are dividing by a positive number, the inequality sign remains the same.

$$4x - 5 \geq 13$$
$$4x - 5 + 5 \geq 13 + 5 \quad \textit{Use the Addition Property of Inequality.}$$
$$4x \geq 18$$
$$\frac{4x}{4} \geq \frac{18}{4} \qquad\qquad \textit{Use the Division Property of Inequality.}$$
$$x \geq 4.5$$

TRY THIS Solve $-4 < 7 - 3x$.

You can represent the solution of an inequality in one variable on a number line. The number line shown below is the graph of $x \geq 4.5$.

Because the inequality symbol is $\geq$, a solid dot is used.

E X A M P L E **2** Solve $4 - 3p > 16 - p$. Graph the solution on a number line.

● **SOLUTION**

$$4 - 3p > 16 - p$$
$$4 - 3p + p > 16 - p + p \quad \textit{Use the Addition Property of Inequality.}$$
$$4 - 2p > 16$$
$$4 - 2p - 4 > 16 - 4 \qquad\quad \textit{Use the Subtraction Property of Inequality.}$$
$$-2p > 12$$
$$\frac{-2p}{-2} < \frac{12}{-2} \qquad\qquad\quad \textit{Use the Division Property of Inequality.}$$
$$p < -6$$

Because you are dividing by a negative number, the inequality sign is reversed.

Because the inequality symbol is $<$, an open circle is used.

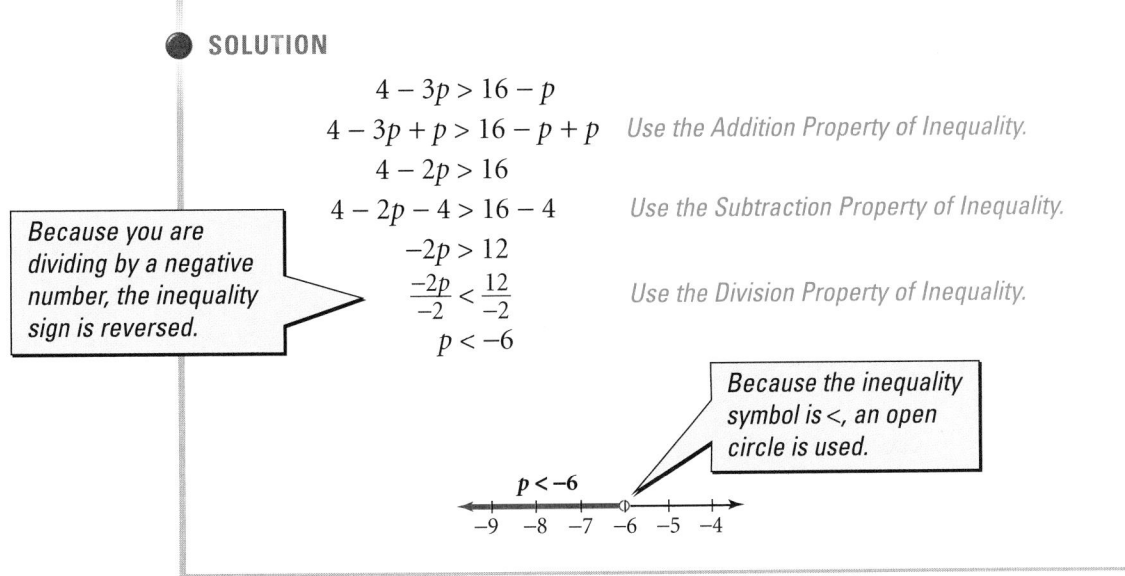

TRY THIS Solve $5 - 7t > 8 - 4t$. Graph the solution on a number line.

EXAMPLE ❸

APPLICATION
ACADEMICS

Claire's test average in her world history class is 90. The test average is $\frac{2}{3}$ of the final grade and the homework average is $\frac{1}{3}$ of the final grade.

What homework average does Claire need in order to have a final grade of at least 93?

● **SOLUTION**

PROBLEM SOLVING

Write an equation.

$$\text{Final grade} = \frac{2}{3}\left(\text{Test average}\right) + \frac{1}{3}\left(\text{Homework average}\right)$$

$$f = \frac{2}{3}(90) + \frac{1}{3}h$$

Claire wants a final grade of at least 93, or $f \geq 93$.

$$f \geq 93$$

$$\frac{2}{3}(90) + \frac{1}{3}h \geq 93 \qquad \textit{Substitute } \frac{2}{3}(90) + \frac{1}{3}h \textit{ for f.}$$

$$60 + \frac{1}{3}h \geq 93 \qquad \textit{Simplify.}$$

$$\frac{1}{3}h \geq 33 \qquad \textit{Use the Subtraction Property of Inequality.}$$

$$h \geq 99 \qquad \textit{Use the Multiplication Property of Inequality.}$$

Claire's homework average must be at least 99 in order for her to have a final grade of at least 93.

Exploring Inequalities Graphically

TECHNOLOGY

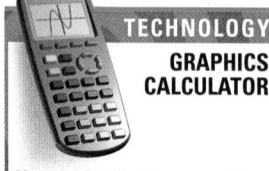

GRAPHICS CALCULATOR

Keystroke Guide, page 83

You will need: a graphics calculator

1. Solve $2x - 3 < 3$ for x.

2. Use a graphics calculator to graph $y = 2x - 3$ and $y = 3$ on the same screen.

3. For what values of x is the graph of $y = 2x - 3$ below the graph of $y = 3$?

4. Explain how the answer to Step 3 helps you to solve $2x - 3 < 3$.

CHECKPOINT ✔

5. How would you use graphs to solve $3x + 2 > 5$? List and explain your steps.

CRITICAL THINKING

Does the method you explored in the Activity above apply to solving inequalities such as $2x - 3 < x + 4$ and $4 \geq 3x + 1$? Justify your response.

The inequalities $x > 24{,}650$ *and* $x \leq 59{,}750$, which describe the income-tax bracket stated at the beginning of this lesson, form a compound inequality. A **compound inequality** is a pair of inequalities joined by *and* or *or*.

To solve an inequality involving *and*, find the values of the variable that satisfy *both* inequalities. This is shown in Example 4.

E X A M P L E **4** Solve $2x + 1 \geq 3$ *and* $3x - 4 \leq 17$. **Graph the solution.**

● **SOLUTION**

$$2x + 1 \geq 3 \quad and \quad 3x - 4 \leq 17$$
$$2x \geq 2 \qquad\qquad 3x \leq 21$$
$$x \geq 1 \qquad\qquad x \leq 7$$

The solution is all values of x between 1 and 7 inclusive.

$x \geq 1$ *and* $x \leq 7$

```
←+──+──+──+──+──+──+──+──+──→
  0  1  2  3  4  5  6  7  8
```

TRY THIS Solve $-2x + 5 \geq 3$ *and* $x - 5 > -12$. Graph the solution.

The solution $x \geq 1$ *and* $x \leq 7$ in Example 4 can also be written as $1 \leq x \leq 7$. In general, the compound statement $x > a$ *and* $x < b$, where $a < b$, can be written as $a < x < b$.

CHECKPOINT ✔ What is another way to express the statement $x < 3$ *and* $x > -4$?

When you solve a compound inequality involving *or*, find those values of the variable that satisfy *at least one* of the inequalities. This is shown in Example 5.

E X A M P L E **5** Solve $5x + 1 > 21$ *or* $3x + 2 < -1$. **Graph the solution.**

● **SOLUTION**

$$5x + 1 > 21 \quad or \quad 3x + 2 < -1$$
$$5x > 20 \qquad\qquad 3x < -3$$
$$x > 4 \qquad\qquad x < -1$$

The solution is all values of x less than -1 or greater than 4.

$x < -1$ *or* $x > 4$

```
←+──○──+──+──+──+──○──+──→
 -2 -1  0  1  2  3  4  5
```

TRY THIS Solve $2x \leq 5$ *or* $7x + 1 > 36$. Graph the solution.

Exercises

● *Communicate*

1. Describe the steps you would take to graph $7x - 7 > 0$ on a number line.

2. How does the graph of $7x - 7 > 0$ differ from the graph of $7x - 7 \geq 0$? from the graph of $7x - 7 < 0$?

3. Is $x < 16$ equivalent to $-x < -16$? Explain.

4. How can you express "x is nonnegative" by using an inequality?

5. Solve $3x + 1 < 13$. **(EXAMPLE 1)**

6. Solve $q + 4 < 4q - 11$. Graph the solution on a number line. **(EXAMPLE 2)**

APPLICATION

7. ACADEMICS Connor's homework average in English class is 92. The test average is $\frac{3}{4}$ of the final grade, and the homework average is $\frac{1}{4}$ of the final grade. What test average does Connor need in order to have a final grade of at least 80? **(EXAMPLE 3)**

8. Solve $3x - 7 \geq -13$ *and* $2x + 3 < 15$. Graph the solution. **(EXAMPLE 4)**

9. Solve $2x + 4 \geq -10$ *or* $4x - 6 > 14$. Graph the solution. **(EXAMPLE 5)**

● *Practice and Apply*

Write an inequality that describes each graph.

10.

11.

12.

13.

14.

15.

16.

17.

18.

19.

☐ internet connect

Homework Help Online

Go To: **go.hrw.com**
Keyword:
MB1 Homework Help
for Exercises 20–49

Solve each inequality, and graph the solution on a number line.

20. $5x > 10$

21. $35x > 70$

22. $-5x > 10$

23. $-35x > 70$

24. $-5x > -10$

25. $-35x > -70$

26. $s - 2 > 10$

27. $y + 5 < -3$

28. $3x + 7 < 31$

29. $2x - 3 \geq 19$

30. $\frac{1}{2}d - 1 \geq -15$

31. $\frac{1}{5}x - 2 \leq 28$

32. $-2x > 14$

33. $-5x \leq 30$

34. $-x + 8 < 41$

35. $-5x - 15 > 60$

36. $-10 < -5x$

37. $-81 \leq -9x$

38. $\frac{-x}{3} \geq 10$

39. $\frac{-t}{32} < 2$

40. $-6(p + 4) < 12$

41. $6 - (4x - 3) \geq 8$

42. $4y - 12 > 7y - 15$

43. $8a - 11 < 4a + 9$

44. $3(4x - 5) < 8x + 3$

45. $6(x - 9) \geq 21 + x$

46. $-4x - 3 < -6x - 17$

47. $-x + 5 \geq -4x - 7$

48. $2(x - 5) < -4(3x + 2)$

49. $-5(3x + 2) \geq 4(x - 1)$

50. Graph each compound inequality on a number line.

    a. $x > -4$ *and* $x < 2$

    b. $x > -4$ *and* $x > 2$

    c. $x > -4$ *or* $x < 2$

    d. $x > -4$ *or* $x > 2$

51. Graph each compound inequality on a number line.

    a. $x < -4$ *and* $x < 2$

    b. $x < -4$ *and* $x > 2$

    c. $x < -4$ *or* $x < 2$

    d. $x < -4$ *or* $x > 2$

Graph the solution of each compound inequality on a number line.

52. $n + 4 < 16$ *and* $n - 3 > 12$

53. $y - 2 < 4$ *and* $y + 4 > 7$

54. $s + 7 > 4$ *or* $s - 2 < 2$

55. $x + 8 < 5$ *or* $x - 1 > 3$

56. $x + 9 \le 5$ *and* $4x \ge 12$

57. $5y \ge 15$ *and* $y + 8 \ge 2$

58. $c - 8 \le 2$ *or* $6c \ge -18$

59. $x + 9 \le 5$ *or* $4x \ge 12$

60. $5a + 12 < 2$ *and* $5a - 12 < 3$

61. $3t + 5 > 11$ *and* $4t - 1 < 15$

62. $-9x > -81$ *and* $2(x + 6) > -4$

63. $-5d < 40$ *and* $4(d - 3) < -8$

64. $20 - 3x \ge 11$ *or* $-4x \le -20$

65. $14 - 3x \le 2$ *or* $5 - 4x \ge 17$

66. $5 - 2b > -3$ *or* $-3(b - 3) < -6$

67. $-6x - 11 < 13$ *or* $3(x + 2) \le -9$

68. $\frac{1}{2}(x + 9) \le -3$ *and* $-10 < -5x$

69. $\frac{4m}{3} + 5 > 2$ *and* $4 \le -2(m - 3) - 7$

70. $2x < 7x - 10$ *or* $8x \le 3x - 15$

71. $2x - 7 < 5x + 8$ *or* $\frac{1}{2}(16 - 4x) \ge 0$

CHALLENGE

72. Solve $-2a \le 3x + a < 10a$ for x.

APPLICATIONS

73. FUND-RAISING A charity is planning to raffle off a new car donated by a local car dealer. The charity wants to raise at least $70,000. It expects to sell at least 1250 tickets and to spend $5000 promoting the raffle. Find the possible ticket prices, p, by solving the inequality below.

$$1250p - 5000 \ge 70{,}000$$

HEALTH One study has found that people who reduced their fat intake to less than 20% of their total calories suffered fewer headaches. [*Source: Loma Linda University School of Public Health, CA*]

74. Write and solve an inequality to find the total number of calories consumed by people in this study before they reduced their fat intake to 324 fat calories.

75. Write and solve an inequality to find the number of fat calories consumed by someone in this study who consumed a total of 1850 calories before reducing the fat intake.

Hamburger with french fries: about 46 grams of fat

Grilled chicken with rice and carrots: about 10 grams of fat

76. BUSINESS The money earned, or *revenue R*, from selling x units of a product is $R = 54x$. The cost of producing x units is $C = 40x + 868$. In order to make a profit, the revenue must be greater than the cost.
  a. Write and solve an inequality in one variable that describes this relationship between revenue and cost.
  b. How many units of the product must be sold in order to make a profit?
  c. Graph the solution on a number line.

 Look Back

Find the slope of each line. *(LESSON 1.2)*

77. $y + 2x = 3$ **78.** $3x - y = 6$

79. $x - 3y = -8$ **80.** $2x - 4y = 3(x - y) + 7$

Write the equation in slope-intercept form of a line that passes through the given points. *(LESSON 1.3)*

81. $(1, 2)$ and $(3, -1)$ **82.** $(5, -2)$ and $(-4, -9)$ **83.** $(8, -30)$ and $(-1, -6)$

84. TRAVEL Michelle finds that after 4 hours of driving at a constant speed, she is 220 miles from her starting point. After 6 more hours, she is 550 miles from her starting point. Write an equation in slope-intercept form for the distance traveled, d, in miles in terms of the elapsed time, t, in hours. *(LESSON 1.3)*

85. GOVERNMENT In order to determine how people feel about a school-bond proposal, a public opinion poll is taken. Of a sample of 300 registered voters, 240 favor the bond proposal. If the number of people who favor the bond proposal is directly proportional to the number of registered voters, how many of the 75,000 registered voters favor the bond proposal? *(LESSON 1.4)*

Calculator button indicates that a graphics calculator is recommended.

86 STATISTICS **Enter the data from the table below in a graphics calculator.** *(LESSON 1.5)*

x	1.0	1.3	1.5	1.6	1.8	1.9	2.0	2.2	2.3	2.5
y	58	47	50	39	40	35	41	31	34	36

  a. Create a scatter plot, identify the correlation as positive or negative, and find the equation of the least-squares line.
  b. Use the equation of the least-squares line that you found in part **a** to predict the value of y when x is 2.8.

Solve each literal equation for the indicated variable. *(LESSON 1.6)*

87. $A = p + prt$ for t **88.** $SA = 2ab + 2ac + 2bc$ for a

 Look Beyond

89. What two real numbers have an absolute value of 4?

Solving Absolute-Value Equations and Inequalities

Objective

● Write, solve, and graph absolute-value equations and inequalities in mathematical and real-world situations.

Why *Measurement usually involves an allowable amount of error, called measurement tolerance, which can be expressed by using absolute-value notation. Measurement tolerance is important in many fields, including manufacturing.*

APPLICATION
MANUFACTURING

A company manufactures a small gear for a car according to design specifications. If the gear is made too large, it will not fit. If it is made too small, the car will not run properly. What measurement tolerance is close enough for this gear? *You will solve this problem in Example 5.*

Definition of Absolute Value

$$|-3| = 3$$ $$|3| = 3$$

The absolute value of a negative number is its opposite.

The absolute value of a nonnegative number is itself.

Notice that both 3 and −3 are 3 units from 0 on the number line.

The algebraic and geometric definitions of absolute value are given below.

Absolute Value

Let x be any real number.

Algebraic definition:

The **absolute value** of x, denoted by $|x|$, is given by the following:

If $x \geq 0$, then $|x| = x$.

If $x < 0$, then $|x| = -x$.

Geometric definition:

The **absolute value** of x is the distance from x to 0 on the number line.

CHECKPOINT ✔ Verify for the following values of x that the algebraic definition and the geometric definition of absolute value give the same result:

$$\{-2, -1, 0, 1, 2\}$$

Absolute-Value Equations

You can use a graph to better understand absolute-value equations. Examine the graphs below.

$y = |x|$ and $y = 2$ $y = |x|$ and $y = 3$ $y = |x|$ and $y = 4$

If $|x| = 2$, then   If $|x| = 3$, then   If $|x| = 4$, then
$x = -2$ or $x = 2$. $x = -3$ or $x = 3$. $x = -4$ or $x = 4$.

The graphs suggest the following fact:

Absolute-Value Equations

If $a > 0$ and $|x| = a$, then $x = a$ or $x = -a$.

By definition, $|x|$ is a distance and is therefore always nonnegative. Notice, however, that the solution to an absolute-value equation can be negative.

CHECKPOINT ✔ Solve the absolute-value equation $|x| = 5$.

EXAMPLE **1** Solve $|2x + 3| = 4$. Graph the solution on a number line.

SOLUTION

Solve the two related equations.

$$2x + 3 = 4 \qquad or \qquad 2x + 3 = -4$$
$$2x = 1 \qquad\qquad\qquad 2x = -7$$
$$x = 0.5 \qquad\qquad\qquad x = -\frac{7}{2}, \text{ or } -3.5$$

CHECK

Let $x = 0.5$.
$$|2x + 3| = 4$$
$$|2(0.5) + 3| \overset{?}{=} 4$$
$$|4| = 4 \quad \textbf{True}$$

Let $x = -3.5$.
$$|2x + 3| = 4$$
$$|2(-3.5) + 3| \overset{?}{=} 4$$
$$|-4| = 4 \quad \textbf{True}$$

You can also check your solutions by graphing $y = |2x + 3|$ and $y = 4$ on the same screen.

The graph shows that if $|2x + 3| = 4$, then $x = -3.5$ or $x = 0.5$.

The solution is graphed on the number line at right.

(−3.5, 4)   (0.5, 4)

$x = -3.5$ or $x = 0.5$

TECHNOLOGY
GRAPHICS CALCULATOR

Keystroke Guide, page 83

TRY THIS Solve $|3x + 5| = 7$. Graph the solution on a number line.

Activity
Exploring Solution Possibilities

TECHNOLOGY
GRAPHICS CALCULATOR

Keystroke Guide, page 83

You will need: a graphics calculator

The display at right shows the graphs of $y = |x|$ and $y = 2x - 2$. These equations model $|x| = mx + b$, where $m = 2$ and $b = -2$.

1. Graph these equations on the same screen. At how many points do the graphs intersect? From the graph, find the solution of $|x| = 2x - 2$.

PROBLEM SOLVING

2. **Guess and check.** Modify $y = 2x - 2$ so that the graph of the modified equation intersects the graph of $y = |x|$ at two points. Graph the equations to check. What are the solutions of $|x| = mx + b$ for your modified values of m and b?

3. Find values of m and b such that the graphs of $y = |x|$ and $y = mx + b$ have no points in common. Graph the equations to check.

4. Find values of m and b such that the graphs of $y = |x|$ and $y = mx + b$ have infinitely many points in common. Graph the equations to check.

CHECKPOINT ✓ 5. Summarize the possible solutions of $|x| = mx + b$.

E X A M P L E ❷ Solve $|x - 3| = 3x + 5$. Check your solution.

● **SOLUTION**

Solve the two related equations.

$$x - 3 = 3x + 5 \qquad or \qquad x - 3 = -(3x + 5)$$
$$-2x = 8 \qquad\qquad\qquad x - 3 = -3x - 5$$
$$x = -4 \qquad\qquad\qquad\qquad 4x = -2$$
$$\qquad\qquad\qquad\qquad\qquad\qquad x = -\frac{1}{2}, \text{ or } -0.5$$

CHECK

Let $x = -4$.

$$|x - 3| = 3x + 5$$
$$|(-4) - 3| \overset{?}{=} 3(-4) + 5$$
$$|-7| = -7 \quad \textbf{False}$$

Let $x = -0.5$.

$$|x - 3| = 3x + 5$$
$$|(-0.5) - 3| \overset{?}{=} 3(-0.5) + 5$$
$$|-3.5| = 3.5 \quad \textbf{True}$$

Since −4 does not satisfy the given equation and −0.5 does satisfy the given equation, the only solution is −0.5.

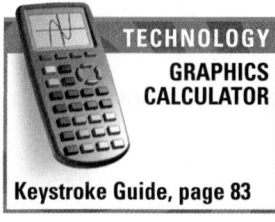

TECHNOLOGY
GRAPHICS CALCULATOR

Keystroke Guide, page 83

You can also check your solution by graphing $y = |x - 3|$ and $y = 3x + 5$ on the same screen and looking for any points of intersection.

The graph shows that $|x - 3| = 3x + 5$ is true only when $x = -0.5$.

(−0.5, 3.5)

Intersection
X=-.5   Y=3.5

TRY THIS   Solve $|x - 4| = x + 1$. Check your solution.

Absolute-Value Inequalities

The red dots on the number line below illustrate the solution of $|x| = 3$. Notice that these solutions divide the number line into three distinct regions.

This suggests a fact that will help you solve absolute-value inequalities.

points left of −3   points between −3 and 3   points right of 3

Absolute-Value Inequalities

If $a > 0$ and $|x| < a$, then $x > -a$ *and* $x < a$.

If $a > 0$ and $|x| > a$, then $x < -a$ *or* $x > a$.

You can write similar statements for $|x| \le a$ and $|x| \ge a$.

E X A M P L E 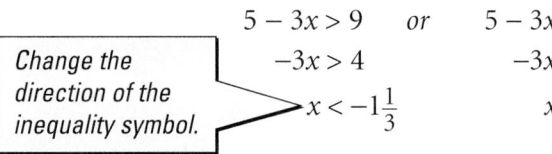 **Solve $|5 - 3x| > 9$. Graph the solution on a number line.**

● **SOLUTION**

The inequality is of the form $|x| > a$, so solve an *or* statement.

$$5 - 3x > 9 \quad or \quad 5 - 3x < -9$$

Change the direction of the inequality symbol.
$$-3x > 4 \qquad\qquad -3x < -14$$
$$x < -1\tfrac{1}{3} \qquad\qquad x > 4\tfrac{2}{3}$$
Change the direction of the inequality symbol.

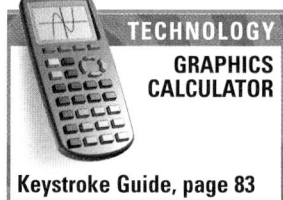
TECHNOLOGY
GRAPHICS CALCULATOR

Keystroke Guide, page 83

CHECK
Check your solution by graphing $y = |5 - 3x|$ and $y = 9$ on the same screen.

The graph shows that if $|5 - 3x| > 9$, then $x < -1\tfrac{1}{3}$ or $x > 4\tfrac{2}{3}$.

The solution is graphed on the number line at right.

$(\approx -1.33, 9)$ $(\approx 4.67, 9)$

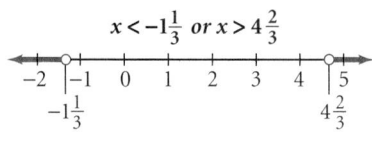
$x < -1\tfrac{1}{3}$ or $x > 4\tfrac{2}{3}$

TRY THIS   Solve $|3x - 7| > 1$. Graph the solution on a number line.

E X A M P L E **Solve $|5 - 3x| < 9$. Graph the solution on a number line.**

● **SOLUTION**

The inequality is of the form $|x| < a$, so solve an *and* statement.

$$5 - 3x < 9 \quad and \quad 5 - 3x > -9$$

Change the direction of the inequality symbol.
$$-3x < 4 \qquad\qquad -3x > -14$$
$$x > -1\tfrac{1}{3} \qquad\qquad x < 4\tfrac{2}{3}$$
Change the direction of the inequality symbol.

TECHNOLOGY
GRAPHICS CALCULATOR

Keystroke Guide, page 83

CHECK
Check your solution by graphing $y = |5 - 3x|$ and $y = 9$ on the same screen.

The graph shows that if $|5 - 3x| < 9$, then $x > -1\tfrac{1}{3}$ and $x < 4\tfrac{2}{3}$, or $-1\tfrac{1}{3} < x < 4\tfrac{2}{3}$.

The solution is graphed on the number line at right.

$(\approx -1.33, 9)$ $(\approx 4.67, 9)$

$x > -1\tfrac{1}{3}$ and $x < 4\tfrac{2}{3}$

TRY THIS   Solve $|5x - 3| < 7$. Graph the solution on a number line.

CHECKPOINT ✓ Compare and contrast the problems in Examples 3 and 4.

You can write an absolute-value inequality to describe the measurement tolerance for a machine part.

E X A M P L E ⑤ A gear is designed with a specification of 3.50 centimeters for the diameter. It will work if it is no more than ±0.01 centimeter of the specified measurement.

Write an absolute-value inequality to represent the measurement tolerance for the diameter of this gear.

Gear No. 40508 a & b – CNC Spec. 1 / Depai...nt R

● **SOLUTION**

Let d represent an acceptable gear diameter.
$$d \geq 3.50 - 0.01 \text{ and } d \leq 3.50 + 0.01$$
Write this compound inequality as follows:
$$3.50 - 0.01 \leq d \leq 3.50 + 0.01$$
Solve the compound inequality.
$$3.50 - 0.01 \leq \quad d \quad \leq 3.50 + 0.01$$
$$3.50 - 0.01 - \mathbf{3.50} \leq d - \mathbf{3.50} \leq 3.50 + 0.01 - \mathbf{3.50}$$
$$-0.01 \leq d - 3.50 \leq 0.01$$

Thus, $|d - 3.50| \leq 0.01$ represents the tolerance for the diameter of this gear.

TRY THIS   Write $12.00 - 0.01 \leq t \leq 12.00 + 0.01$ as an absolute-value inequality.

An absolute-value inequality may have no solution, or any real number may be a solution. Examine the graphs of $y = |2x - 1|$ and $y = -3$ below.

Notice that the graph of $y = |2x - 1|$ is never below the graph of $y = -3$. Thus, $|2x - 1| < -3$ has no solution. There is no value of x for which the absolute value, $|2x - 1|$, is less than -3.

Notice also that the graph of $y = |2x - 1|$ is always above the graph of $y = -3$. Thus, any real number is a solution to $|2x - 1| > -3$. The absolute value of any real number is greater than -3.

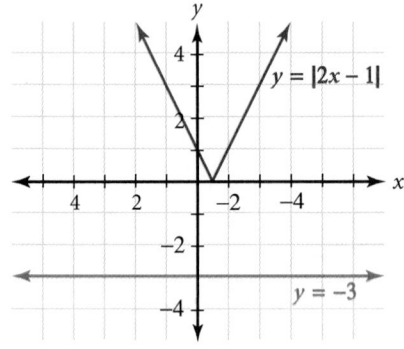

CHECKPOINT ✔ Write an absolute-value inequality that contains $\leq$ and has no solution. Write an absolute-value inequality that contains $\geq$ and has all real numbers as its solution.

CRITICAL THINKING   If $|x| \leq a$ has no solution, what can you conclude about the possible values of a and about the solution to $|x| > a$?

Exercises

 Communicate

1. Explain why the equation $|3x - 5| + 4 = 3$ has no solution.

2. Discuss why it is necessary to always check your solution when solving absolute-value equations.

3. Explain why an absolute-value equation can have two solutions.

4. Discuss the meanings of the words *and* and *or*. Compare the mathematical meanings of these words with their common meanings.

5. Use a graph to describe the type of absolute-value inequality whose solution is any real number.

Guided Skills Practice

Solve each equation. Check your solution. *(EXAMPLES 1 AND 2)*

6. $|x - 10| = 4$

7. $|2x - 5| = 3$

8. $10 = |7 - 3x|$

9. $x + 4 = |x - 2|$

10. $\frac{1}{2}x + 1 = |x - 2| - 1$

11. $\frac{1}{2}x + 1 = |x + 3|$

Solve each inequality. Graph the solution on a number line.
(EXAMPLES 3 AND 4)

12. $2 < |4 - x|$

13. $|2x + 1| \geq 5$

14. $|5 + x| < \frac{1}{2}$

15. $\frac{1}{2}|2x + 1| \geq 2$

16. $3|x + 1| \leq 2$

17. $3|x + 1| + 3 > 2$

18. **RECREATION** Ashley tosses a horseshoe at a stake 25 feet away. The horseshoe lands no more than 2 feet from the stake.
(EXAMPLE 5)
   a. Write an absolute-value inequality that represents the range of distances that the horseshoe traveled.
   b. Solve this inequality and graph it on a number line.

 Practice and Apply

Match each statement on the left with a statement or sentence on the right.

19. $|x + 2| = 4$

20. $|x + 2| < 4$

21. $|x + 2| < -4$

22. $|x + 2| > -4$

23. $|x + 2| > 4$

24. $|x + 2| = -4$

a. $x < 2 \text{ and } x > -6$

b. $x = 2 \text{ or } x = -6$

c. $x > 2 \text{ or } x < -6$

d. There is no solution.

e. The solution is all real numbers.

f. none of the above

Solve each equation.

25. $|x + 4| = 8$ **26.** $|x - 5| = 12$ **27.** $|2 + x| = 10$

28. $|8 - x| = 1$ **29.** $|x - 2| = 9$ **30.** $|x + 5| = 11$

31. $|2x - 15| = 11$ **32.** $|3x + 12| = 18$ **33.** $|10 - 4x| = 28$

34. $|5 + 4x| = 17$ **35.** $|5x - 6| = 2$ **36.** $|10 - 3x| + 5 = 2$

37. $|10x + 2| - 18 = -12$ **38.** $|4 - 3x| - 9 = 3$ **39.** $|2x - 8| + 2 = 1$

Solve each inequality. Graph the solution on a number line. If the equation has no solution, write *no solution*.

40. $|x - 4| > 1$ **41.** $|x + 5| \leq 7$ **42.** $|3x| > 15$

43. $|-2x| \leq 12$ **44.** $|4x| \leq -8$ **45.** $|3 - x| \geq -5$

46. $|2 + 5x| \leq 3$ **47.** $|2x - 3| < 11$ **48.** $|4x + 6| \leq 14$

49. $\left|\dfrac{2x + 3}{-5}\right| < 3$ **50.** $|4x - 5| \geq 15$ **51.** $|2x - 1| \geq -5$

52. $|5x + 3| > -2$ **53.** $|7 - 6x| < -4$ **54.** $|9x + 4| \leq -11$

55. $-2|4x + 1| \leq -4$ **56.** $-2|4x + 1| \geq -4$ **57.** $\left|\dfrac{3}{2} - \dfrac{5}{2}x\right| < -\dfrac{7}{2}$

SUMMARY		
Three different representations of an inequality are given below.		
Verbal	**Algebraic**	**Graphic**

The distance between x and 3 is less than 5.	$|x - 3| < 5$	◄—┼─┼─○─┼─┼─┼─┼─○─►
		  -4 -2 0 2 4 6 8
		             3

Examine the summary box above. For Exercises 58–60, write the two missing representations for each inequality.

58. The distance between x and 7 is less than 4.

59. $|x - 4| < 1$

60. ◄—┼─┼─┼─┼─●─┼─┼─┼─●─┼─►
    2   4   6   8 10 12 14

CHALLENGE

61. Solve the inequality $\left|\dfrac{4x}{3}\right| \leq 2x + 5$.

For Exercises 62–65, write and solve an absolute-value inequality.

APPLICATIONS

62. HEALTH Antonio weighs 120 pounds, and his doctor said that his weight differs from his ideal body weight by less than 5 percent. What are the possible values, to the nearest pound, for Antonio's ideal body weight?

63. ENTERTAINMENT A tightrope walker is 10 feet from one end of the rope. If he then takes 3 steps and each step is 11 inches long, how far is he now from the same end of the rope? Give both possible answers.

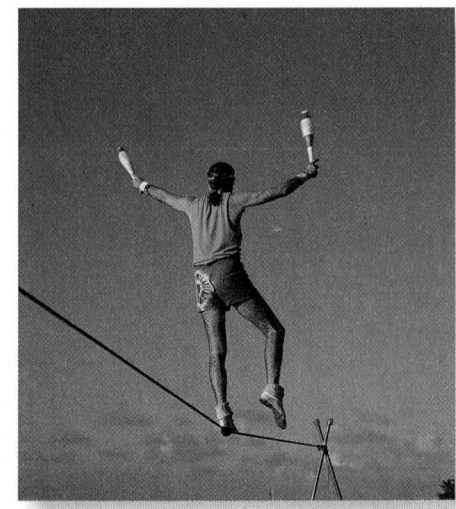

64. METEOROLOGY An instrument called an *anemometer* measures a wind speed of 30 feet per second. The true wind speed is within 2 feet per second (inclusive) of the measured wind speed. What range is possible for the true wind speed?

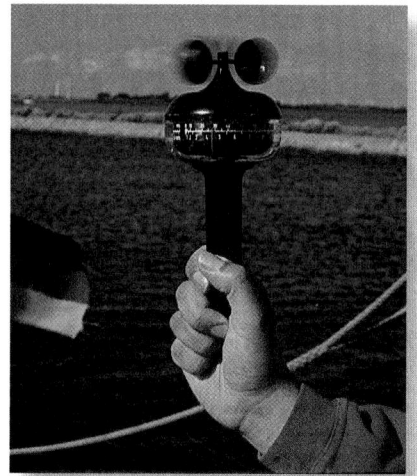

65. RECREATION A recent poll reported that 68 percent of moviegoers eat popcorn during the movie. The margin of error for the poll was 3%. What are the minimum and maximum possible percents according to this poll?

An anemometer is used to measure wind speed.

 Look Back

66. REAL ESTATE A rental property is purchased for $90,000. For tax purposes, a depreciation of 5% of property's initial value, or $4500, is assumed per year. *(LESSON 1.1)*
  a. Make a table of values for the value of the property, *v*, after *t* years.
  b. Write a linear equation for the value of the property, *v*, after *t* years.
  c. What is the value of the property after 15 years?

67. SPORTS A baseball pitcher allows 10 runs in 15 innings. At this rate, how many runs would you expect the pitcher to allow in a 9-inning game? *(LESSON 1.4)*

Solve each proportion for x. *(LESSON 1.4)*

68. $\frac{2}{x} = \frac{5}{8}$

69. $\frac{x-3}{4} = \frac{2x}{16}$

70. $\frac{10x}{-60} = \frac{2x-10}{8}$

71. Solve $\frac{1}{2}bh = A$ for *h*. *(LESSON 1.6)*

72. Solve $P = 2l + 2w$ for *l*. *(LESSON 1.6)*

Solve each inequality, and graph the solution on a number line. *(LESSON 1.7)*

73. $4x - 5 < \frac{1}{3}(8x + 3)$

74. $x - 9 \geq \frac{1}{6}(21 + x)$

Graph each compound inequality on a number line. *(LESSON 1.7)*

75. $x > -1$ *and* $x < 5$

76. $x < 3$ *and* $x > -3$

77. $x \leq -2$ *or* $x > 4$

78. $x > 2$ *or* $x \leq -1$

 Look Beyond

79. ETYMOLOGY Look up the word *rational* in the dictionary. Write the definition that is related to math. What is the meaning of the root word, *ratio,* that relates to the math usage?

CORRELATION EXPLORATION

Activity 1

Discuss the questions below, and record your hypotheses.

1. Do you think taller people have longer arm spans? Explain.

2. Do you think taller people have bigger hand spans? Explain.

3. Do you think the distance from the top of a person's head to the ceiling is related to his or her height? Explain.

4. Do you think the value of one's pocket change is related to his or her height? Explain.

Person	Height	Arm span	Hand span	Distance from head to ceiling	Value of change
1					
2					
3					
⋮					

5. Collect the information indicated in the table above for each student in the classroom. Record your data in a table like the one shown above. Create a scatter plot for the data identified below. Label the *x*-axis with units for height and the *y*-axis with units for the other variable in each case.
   a. height and arm span
   b. height and hand span
   c. height and distance from the top of one's head to the ceiling
   d. height and value of pocket change

Activity ②

1. Use a straightedge to estimate a linear model for each scatter plot.

2. Write an equation for each of your linear models.

3. Identify the slope and y-intercept for each of your linear models.

4. For each linear model, what does the slope tell you about the relationship between the variables?

5. For each linear model, what does the y-intercept tell you about the relationship between the variables?

Activity ③

1. Describe the correlation between the variables represented in each scatter plot.

2. Find the correlation coefficient for each scatter plot.

3. For each scatter plot, find and graph an equation for the least-squares line.

4. For each scatter plot, was your linear model reasonably close to the least-squares line? Explain.

5. Use the equations of the least-squares lines to make each prediction below.
   a. the arm span of a person who is 5 feet tall
   b. the hand span of a person who is 5 feet tall
   c. the distance to the ceiling from the head of a person who is 5 feet tall
   d. the value of the pocket change of a person who is 5 feet tall

Activity ④

Solve the equation of the appropriate least-squares line to make each prediction below. Name the Properties of Equality that you use to solve each equation.

1. the height of a person with an arm span of 62 inches

2. the height of a person with a hand span of $8\frac{1}{2}$ inches

3. the height of a person whose head is 28 inches from the ceiling

4. the height of a person with $1.26 in pocket change

Chapter Review and Assessment

VOCABULARY

Key Skills & Exercises

LESSON 1.1

Key Skills

Identify linear equations and linear relationships between variables in a table.

$y = 8x + 4$ is a linear equation in the form $y = mx + b$, where $m = 8$ and $b = 4$.

x	-2	0	2	4
$y = 8x + 4$	-12	4	20	36

(+2 +2 +2 across top; +8 +8 +8 across bottom)

Represent a real-world linear relationship in a table, graph, or equation.

Projected college enrollments are given below.

Year	Enrollment (in millions)
1998	14.3
2000	14.8
2002	15.3
2004	15.8

[Source: U.S. Department of Education]

The equation is $y = 0.5x + 14.3$, where $x = 0$ represents 1998 and y is the projected enrollment.

Exercises

State whether each relationship is linear; if so, write the next ordered pair that would appear in the table.

1.
x	3	6	9	12
y	3	6	12	24

2.
x	1	2	3	4
y	2	4	6	8

3.
x	7	14	21	28
y	5	10	15	20

PSYCHOLOGY Psychologists define intelligence quotient (IQ) as 100 times a person's mental age divided by his or her chronological age. The result is rounded to the nearest integer.

4. Find the IQ for an individual whose chronological age is 15 and whose mental age is the following: 10, 14, 15, 19, and 25.

5. Represent the linear relationship from Exercise 4 in a table, a graph, and an equation.

Key Skills

Graph a linear equation by using the slope and *y*-intercept.

Graph $y = -3x + 4$.

The *y*-intercept is 4.

The slope is −3.

$m = -3 = \dfrac{-3}{1} \text{ or } \dfrac{3}{-1}$

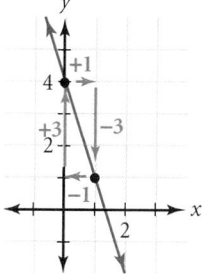

Exercises

Graph each equation.

6. $y = -\dfrac{1}{2}x$

7. $y = \dfrac{4}{5}x + 1$

8. $y = 3x - 1$

9. $y = -2x$

10. $2x + y = 3$

11. $3y - x = 1$

12. $y = 1$

13. $x = -2$

Key Skills

Write a linear equation in two variables given sufficient information.

slope of $\dfrac{2}{3}$ and contains the point $(6, 9)$

$$y - y_1 = m(x - x_1)$$
$$y - 9 = \tfrac{2}{3}(x - 6)$$
$$y = \tfrac{2}{3}x - 5$$

contains the points $(2, 500)$ and $(3, 1500)$

  Find *m*.

$$m = \dfrac{1500 - 500}{3 - 2} = 1000$$

  Find *b*.

$$y = 1000x + b$$
$$500 = 1000(2) + b$$
$$b = -1500$$

Thus, $y = 1000x - 1500$.

Write an equation in slope-intercept form for the line that contains a given point and is perpendicular or parallel to a given line.

perpendicular to $y = 4x + 10$ and contains $(60, 40)$

$$y - y_1 = m(x - x_1)$$
$$y - 40 = -\tfrac{1}{4}(x - 60)$$
$$y = -\tfrac{1}{4}x + 55$$

Substitute the negative reciprocal of 4 for m.

parallel to $y = 4x + 10$ and contains $(60, 40)$

$$y - y_1 = m(x - x_1)$$
$$y - 40 = 4(x - 60)$$
$$y = 4x - 200$$

Substitute 4 for m.

Exercises

Write an equation in slope-intercept form for the line that has the indicated slope, *m*, and contains the given point.

14. $m = -3$, $(5, 8)$

15. $m = 100$, $(-2, 198)$

16. $m = \dfrac{1}{20}$, $(0, 5)$

17. $m = 0$, $(-5, 4)$

Write an equation for the line that contains the indicated points.

18. $(3, 4)$ and $(5, 4)$

19. $(-2, 8)$ and $(-2, -1)$

20. $\left(-5\tfrac{3}{4}, 2\right)$ and $\left(-3\tfrac{1}{4}, 3\tfrac{1}{2}\right)$

21. $(6.8, 2)$ and $(3.6, 6)$

Write an equation for the line that contains the given point and is perpendicular or parallel to the given line.

22. $(3, 0)$, $y = -2x - 5$, perpendicular

23. $(-3, -2)$, $y = \tfrac{1}{3}x - 5$, parallel

24. $(4, -1)$, $y = -\tfrac{2}{3}x + 7$, parallel

25. $(4, -1)$, $y = -8$, perpendicular

Key Skills

Write a direct-variation equation for given variables.

Find the constant of variation and the direct-variation equation if y varies directly as x and $y = 2.25$ when $x = 9$.

$$k = \frac{2.25}{9} = 0.25$$
$$y = 0.25x$$

Write and solve proportions.

$$\frac{10}{12} = \frac{x}{24}$$
$$12x = 240$$
$$x = 20$$

Exercises

For Exercises 26–28, y varies directly as x. Find the constant of variation and the direct-variation equation.

26. $y = 750$ when $x = 25$

27. $y = 0.05$ when $x = 10$

28. $y = -2$ when $x = 14$

PHYSICS The bending of a beam varies directly as the mass of the load it supports. Suppose that a beam is bent 20 millimeters by a mass of 40 kilograms.

29. How much will the beam bend when it supports a mass of 100 kilograms?

30. If the beam bends 25 millimeters, what load is the beam supporting?

Key Skills

Make a scatter plot, and describe the correlation.

x	y
1	-6
2	-3
3	-4
4	0
5	-6
6	3
7	5
8	4
9	12
10	7

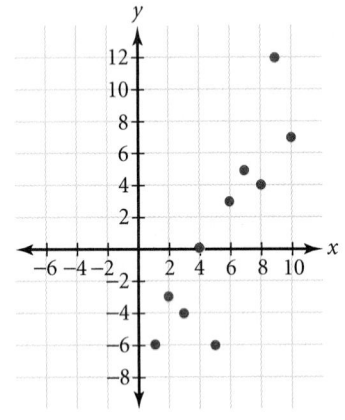

Because the data points go upward from left to right, the correlation is positive.

Find an equation for the least-squares line, and use it to make predictions.

The least-squares line for the data above is $y \approx 1.73x - 83$.

Exercises

31. STATISTICS Make a scatter plot of the data below. Describe the correlation.

x	-4	-3	-2	-1	0	1	2	3	4
y	30	25	24	25	17	10	13	5	-1

32. FREIGHT CHARGES A statistician for the Civil Aeronautics Board wants to be able to predict the freight charge for a standard-sized crate. The statistician takes a sample of 10 freight invoices from different companies. Let d represent the distance in miles and let c represent the freight charge in dollars. Make a scatter plot of the data below. Describe the correlation. Then find an equation for the least-squares line.

d	500	600	900	1000	1200	1400	1600	1700	2200
c	41	55	50	70	60	78	75	89	105

Key Skills

Write and solve a linear equation in one variable.

INCOME Johanna works as a waitress. Her wages are $2.50 per hour plus tips, which average $50 for each 4-hour shift. How many 4-hour shifts does she have to work to earn $300?

Let n represent the number of shifts.

(hourly rate × no. of hours + tips)$n = 300$

$$[2.5(4) + 50]n = 300$$
$$n = 5$$

Johanna must work 5 shifts to earn $300.

Solve each literal equation for the indicated variable.

Solve $A = \pi rs + \pi r^2$ for s.

$$A = \pi rs + \pi r^2$$
$$A - \pi r^2 = \pi rs$$
$$\frac{A - \pi r^2}{\pi r} = s$$
$$\frac{A}{\pi r} - r = s$$

Exercises

CONSUMER ECONOMICS Jorge's monthly bill from his Internet service provider was $25. The service provider charges a base rate of $15 per month plus $1 for each hour that the service is used.

33. Write a linear equation to represent the total monthly charges.

34. Find the number of hours that Jorge was charged for that month.

Solve each literal equation for the indicated variable.

35. $F = \frac{9}{5}C + 32$ for C

36. $S = s_0 + v_0 + \frac{1}{2}gt^2$ for v_0

37. $\frac{1}{f} = \frac{1}{f_1} + \frac{1}{f_2}$ for f

38. $A = \frac{h}{2}(b_1 + b_2)$ for b_2

Key Skills

Write, solve and graph linear inequalities in one variable.

Notice that the inequality sign is reversed.

$$14 - 6t \geq 16$$
$$-6t \geq 2$$
$$t \leq -\frac{2}{6}$$

Solve and graph compound linear equalities in one variable.

$$5x + 7(x - 2) > 6 \quad or \quad 4x + 6 \leq -6$$
$$x > \frac{5}{3} \qquad\qquad x \leq -3$$

$x > \frac{5}{3}$ or $x \leq -3$

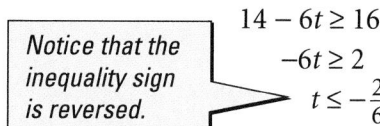

$$5x + 7(x - 2) < 6 \quad and \quad 4x + 6 \geq -6$$
$$x < \frac{5}{3} \qquad\qquad x \geq -3$$

$-3 \leq x < \frac{5}{3}$

Exercises

Write an inequality for each situation. Graph the solution.

39. GEOMETRY If the width of a rectangle is 10 meters and the perimeter is not to exceed 140 meters, how long can the length be?

40. BUSINESS An organization wants to sell tickets to a concert. It plans on selling 300 reserved-seat tickets and 150 general-admission tickets. The price of a reserved-seat ticket is $2 more than a general-admission ticket. If the organization wants to collect at least $3750, what is the minimum price it can charge for a reserved-seat ticket?

Solve and graph.

41. $4x - 3 < 29$ and $4 - 3x < -5$

42. $-3x - 8 \leq 7$ and $-4x > -18$

43. $4x - 3 < 29$ or $4 - 3x < -5$

44. $-3x - 8 \leq 7$ or $-4x > -18$

Key Skills

Solve and graph absolute-value equations.

a.
$$|5x| = 45$$
$$5x = 45 \quad or \quad 5x = -45$$
$$x = 9 \qquad\qquad x = -9$$

b.
$$\frac{1}{2}|5x| + 5 = 45$$
$$\frac{1}{2}|5x| = 40$$
$$5x = 80 \ ' \ or \quad x = -80$$
$$x = 16 \qquad\qquad x = -16$$

Solve and graph absolute-value inequalities.

a.
$$|x + 5| \geq 45$$
$$x + 5 \geq 45 \quad or \quad x + 5 \leq -45$$
$$x \geq 40 \qquad\qquad x \leq -50$$

$x \leq -50 \text{ or } x \geq 40$

b.
$$|x + 5| \leq 45$$
$$x + 5 \leq 45 \quad and \quad x + 5 \geq -45$$
$$x \leq 40 \qquad\qquad x \geq -50$$

$-50 \leq x \leq 40$

Exercises

Solve and graph on a number line.

45. $\left|\frac{1}{2}x\right| = 20$

46. $\left|\frac{4}{5}x\right| = 16$

47. $12|2x| = 108$

48. $\frac{2}{3}\left|x + 4\right| - 5 = 7$

Solve and graph on a number line.

49. $\left|\frac{1}{2}x\right| > 20$

50. $-\frac{1}{2}\left|\frac{1}{2}x\right| - 4 > 20$

51. $-5|6x - 7| \leq 35$

52. $|6x - 7| \leq -35$

Applications

GEOMETRY The length of the hypotenuse of a 30-60-90 triangle varies directly as the length of the side opposite the 30° angle. The length of the hypotenuse, h, is 45 units when the side opposite the 30° angle, s, is 22.5 units.

53. Find the constant of variation and the direct-variation equation.

54. Find the length of the side opposite the 30° angle when the hypotenuse is 13 inches long.

PERSONAL FINANCE The majority of American families save less than $\frac{1}{10}$ of their income. Suppose that an average American family saves $2850.

55. Write and solve an inequality that models this situation.

56. Graph the solution on a number line.

Chapter Test

State whether each relationship is linear. If so, write the next ordered pair that would appear in the table.

1.

x	2	4	6	8	10
y	4	16	36	64	100

2.

x	1	4	7	10	13
y	5	12	19	26	33

3. BUSINESS For automobile repairs Wayne charges $50 plus $30 per hour. Write a linear equation to model this situation and find the charge for 8.5 hours of work.

Graph each equation.

4. $y = 2x$

5. $3x - 5y = 15$

6. $2x + 5 = y$

7. $x = 2$

Write an equation in slope-intercept form for the line that

8. has slope $= 2$ and contains point $(-1, 4)$

9. has slope 0 and contains point $(-5, 7)$

10. contains points $(3, 5)$ and $(4, -7)$

11. contains $(1, 2)$ and is parallel to $y = 4x + 3$.

12. contains $(-5, 9)$ and is perpendicular to $2x + 3y = 4$.

Solve each variation problem.

13. If y varies directly as x and $y = 3$ when $x = 7$, find y when $x = 63$.

14. If $y = 25$ when $x = 2125$, find the constant of variation and the direct variation equation.

15. GEOGRAPHY A California map shows a scale indicating that 1 inch = 50 miles. The distance on the map between Sacramento and Los Angeles is $8\frac{1}{2}$ inches. What is the actual distance between the two cities?

Create a scatter plot for the data in the table below. Describe the correlation, and then find an equation for the least squares line.

16.

x	2	5	3	8	6
y	4	6	5	7	6

Solve each equation.

17. $4x - 3 = 17$

18. $\frac{x}{3} - 2 = 16$

19. $2x - 0.8 = -2.4$

20. $8x + 4 = 2x - 32$

21. GEOMETRY Complementary angles equal 90°. If the measure of one complementary angle is 30° more than twice the other angle measure, write an equation and find the measure of each angle.

22. Solve the equation $A = \frac{1}{2} r^2 \, \theta$ for θ.

Solve and graph each inequality on a number line.

23. $-3x - 6 > 15$

24. $2(4x - 5) < 6x - 6$

Solve and graph each compound inequality on a number line.

25. $3x + 4 > 7 \; and \; 2x - 3 < 5$

26. $5 - x \geq 3 \; or \; -2 + 4x \geq 10$

27. ENTERTAINMENT Three adults and 5 children want to see a movie. They have $40 between them. Write and solve an inequality to find the price a child's ticket cannot exceed, if an adult ticket costs $7.

Solve and graph on a number line.

28. $\left| \frac{1}{2}x - 4 \right| = 3$

29. $\left| 5x + 3 \right| \geq -2$

30. $\left| 2x + 13 \right| \leq -3$

31. $\left| \frac{3}{5}x + 6 \right| \geq 9$

College Entrance Exam Practice

 internet connect

**Standardized
Test Prep Online**
Go To: **go.hrw.com**
Keyword: **MM1 Test Prep**

MULTIPLE-CHOICE For Questions 1–13, write the letter that indicates the best answer.

1. Find the slope and y-intercept of the graph of the equation $2y - 3x = 4$. **(LESSON 1.2)**

  a. $m = \frac{3}{2}, b = 4$ **b.** $m = \frac{3}{2}, b = 2$

  c. $m = -3, b = 4$ **d.** $m = -3, b = 2$

2. Find the slope of the line graphed.
(LESSON 1.2)

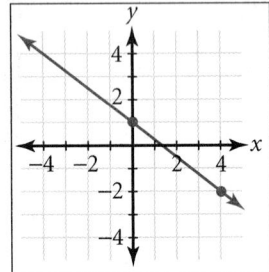

  a. $m = -\frac{4}{3}$ **b.** $m = -\frac{3}{4}$

  c. $m = -\frac{2}{3}$ **d.** $m = -\frac{1}{4}$

3. For which set of points does the graph of the line containing them have a slope of zero?
(LESSON 1.2)

  a. $(4, 3), (4, -3)$ **b.** $(4, -3), (4, 3)$
  c. $(4, 3), (-4, 3)$ **d.** $(-4, 3), (3, 4)$

4. Solve $\frac{1 - 2x}{5} = \frac{x}{6}$. **(LESSON 1.4)**

  a. $x = \frac{6}{7}$ **b.** $x = \frac{6}{17}$

  c. $x = -\frac{6}{7}$ **d.** $x = \frac{17}{6}$

5. For which absolute value equation is the distance between the values of x equal to 4?
(LESSON 1.8)

  a. $|x - 6| = 4$ **b.** $|4x + 3| = 4$

  c. $|4x| = 6$ **d.** $|5x| - 3 = 7$

6. Which one of the following equations is not a linear equation? **(LESSON 1.1)**

  a. $2x + 3y = 11$

  b. $y = \frac{3 - 4x}{7}$

  c. $y = \frac{7}{3 - 4x}$

  d. $x = 3 - y$

7. Which gives the slope and y-intercept for the graph of $2x + 3y = 2$? **(LESSON 1.2)**

  a. $m = -\frac{2}{3}, b = \frac{2}{3}$

  b. $m = \frac{2}{3}, b = -\frac{2}{3}$

  c. $m = 2, b = -2$

  d. $m = -2, b = 2$

8. Find the slope of the line containing the points $(2, -1)$ and $(-5, 0)$. **(LESSON 1.2)**

  a. -7 **b.** -3
  c. $\frac{1}{7}$ **d.** $-\frac{1}{7}$

9. Which equation represents a line with no y-intercept? **(LESSON 1.2)**

  a. $y = 4$ **b.** $x = -\frac{1}{4}$
  c. $x + y = 2$ **d.** $y = 3x$

10. Which statement is *not* true? **(LESSON 1.2)**

  a. All horizontal lines are perpendicular to vertical lines.

  b. The slopes of two nonvertical lines that are perpendicular to each other are reciprocals.

  c. The slope of any horizontal line is 0.

  d. The slope of any vertical line is undefined.

11. Which equation contains the point $(-4, 6)$ and is parallel to the graph of $y = -2x - \frac{1}{4}$? *(LESSON 1.3)*

   a. $y = -2x + 2$

   b. $y = 2x - 2$

   c. $y = 2x + 2$

   d. $y = -2x - 2$

12. If x varies directly as y and $x = 4$ when $y = -5$, what is x when $y = 2.5$? *(LESSON 1.4)*

   a. $-\frac{1}{2}$ **b.** $\frac{1}{2}$

   c. 2 **d.** -2

13. Solve $T = \dfrac{24I}{B(n+1)}$ for I. *(LESSON 1.6)*

   a. $I = \dfrac{24T}{B(n+1)}$

   b. $I = \dfrac{24B}{T(n+1)}$

   c. $I = \dfrac{T(n+1)}{24B}$

   d. $I = \dfrac{TB(n+1)}{24}$

14. Graph the equation $y = -5x - 12$. *(LESSON 1.1)*

15. Does the information in the table below represent a linear relationship between x and y? Explain your response. *(LESSON 1.1)*

x	0	1	2	3
y	13	17	21	25

16. Find the equation of the line containing the points $(-3, 6)$ and $(-5, 8)$. *(LESSON 1.3)*

17. Write the equation in slope-intercept form for the line that contains the point $(5, -8)$ and is perpendicular to the graph of $y = \frac{1}{3}x - 4$. *(LESSON 1.3)*

18. Write an equation in slope-intercept form for the line that contains the points $(2, -4)$ and $(3, -1)$. *(LESSON 1.3)*

ANATOMY The following table lists the heights and weights for 10 randomly selected young adult males with medium frames. The heights are in inches, and the weights are in pounds. *(LESSON 1.5)*

Heights, x	67	66	70	67	67	68	69	66	70	71
Weights, y	146	145	157	148	145	149	151	141	154	159

19 Create a scatter plot for this data. Is the correlation positive, negative, or none?

20 Find the correlation coefficient, r.

21 Graph the least-squares line with the scatter plot. Predict the weight (to the nearest pound) of a young adult male selected at random from this group who is 63 inches tall.

22. Solve and graph the inequality $5x - 6(x + 9) < 1$. *(LESSON 1.7)*

23. Solve $|2 + 3x| \geq 14$. *(LESSON 1.8)*

FREE RESPONSE GRID The following questions may be answered by using a free-response grid such as that commonly used by standardized-test services.

24. Find the slope of the line containing $(11, -3)$ and $(-3, 10)$. *(LESSON 1.2)*

25. Find the y-intercept of the graph of $3x - 5y = 2$. *(LESSON 1.2)*

26. Find the slope of the graph of $3x - 5y = 2$. *(LESSON 1.2)*

GEOMETRY The perimeter, p, of a square varies directly as the length, l, of a side. *(LESSON 1.4)*

27. What is the constant of variation that relates the perimeter to the length of a side?

28. If a square has a side length of 3.5 centimeters, how many centimeters long is its perimeter?

Keystroke Guide for Chapter 1

Essential keystroke sequences (using the model TI-82 or TI-83 graphics calculator) are presented below for all Activities and Examples found in this chapter that require or recommend the use of a graphics calculator.

☑ internet connect

For Keystrokes of other graphing calculator models, visit the HRW web site at **go.hrw.com** and enter the keyword **MB1 CALC**.

LESSON 1.1

E X A M P L E **❶** Graph $y = 150x + 250$, and find the value of y when $x = 25$.

Page 5

Use viewing window [0, 30] by [−500, 5000].

Graph the equation:

| Y= | 150 | X,T,θ,n | + | 250 | GRAPH |

Evaluate for $x = 25$:

| 2nd | TRACE (CALC) | 1:value | ENTER | $(x =)$ 25 | ENTER |

E X A M P L E **❷** Graph $y = \frac{2}{3}x - 1$, and verify that $(0, -1)$ and $(3, 1)$ are on the line.

Page 6

(3, 1)

(0, −1)

Use viewing window [−4, 4] by [−3, 3].

Graph the equation:

| Y= | (| 2 | ÷ | 3 |) | X,T,θ,n | − | 1 | GRAPH |

Evaluate for $x = 0$ and $x = 3$:
Use a keystroke sequence similar to that used in Example 1.

LESSON 1.2

Activity

Page 13

Graph each pair of equations in Step 1.

Use the standard viewing window [−10, 10] by [−10, 10]. Use a keystroke sequence similar to that used in Example 2 of Lesson 1.1.

LESSON 1.3

Activity

Page 23

For Steps 1 and 3, graph the given equations on the same screen.

Use viewing window [−3, 3] by [−3, 3].

Use a keystroke sequence similar to that used in Example 1 of Lesson 1.1.
Use keystrokes ZOOM 5:ZSquare ENTER to obtain a square viewing window.

E X A M P L E S ④ and ⑤ For Example 4, graph $y = -2x + 4$ and $y = -2x + 1$ on the same screen.

Page 24

Use viewing window [−6, 10] by [−6, 10].

[Y=] [(−)] 2 [X,T,θ,n] [+] 4 [ENTER] (Y2=) [(−)] 2 [X,T,θ,n] [+] 1 [GRAPH]

For Example 5, use viewing window [−6, 10] by [−6, 10].

Use a keystroke sequence similar to that used in Example 2 of Lesson 1.1. Use keystrokes [ZOOM] **5:ZSquare** [ENTER] to obtain a square viewing window.

LESSON 1.4

E X A M P L E ② Graph $y = \frac{1}{5}x$, and verify that the point (35, 7) is on the line.

Page 30

Use viewing window [0, 50] by [−4, 25].

Graph the equation:

[Y=] [( ] 1 [÷] 5 [ )] [X,T,θ,n] [GRAPH]

Evaluate for $x = 35$:

Use a keystroke sequence similar to that used in Example 1 of Lesson 1.1.

E X A M P L E ③ Graph the equation $y = 0.38x$, and confirm that an x-value of 24.3 corresponds to a y-value of about 9.2 kilograms.

Page 32

Use viewing window [0, 30] by [0, 15].

To graph the equation and evaluate for $x = 24.3$, use a keystroke sequence similar to that used in Example 1 of Lesson 1.1.

LESSON 1.5

Activity

Page 37

For Step 1, create a scatter plot of the data.

Use viewing window [0, 10] by [100, 200].

First clear old data and equations.

Enter the data:

[STAT] [EDIT] **1:EDIT** [ENTER] **L1** 1 [ENTER] 2 [ENTER] 3 [ENTER] 4 [ENTER] 5 [ENTER] 6
[ENTER] [▶] **L2** 185.4 [ENTER] 173.1 [ENTER] 147.1 [ENTER] 158.4 [ENTER] 134.7
[ENTER] 151.2 [ENTER]

Create a scatter plot:

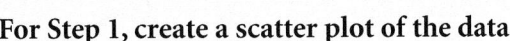

[2nd] [Y=] **STAT** **1:Plot 1** [ENTER] **On** [ENTER] [▼] (Type:) ⠠⠤⠄ [ENTER]

[▼] (Xlist:) [2nd] 1 [▼] (Ylist:) [2nd] 2 [▼] (Mark:) ▫
⇑ TI-82: **L1** [ENTER]   ⇑ TI-82: **L2** [ENTER]

[ENTER] [GRAPH]

E X A M P L E **1** Create a scatter plot for the data. Then graph the least-squares line.

Page 38

Use viewing window $[-1, 11]$ by $[-10, 24]$.

Create a scatter plot:

Use a keystroke sequence similar to that in the Activity for this lesson.

Graph the least-squares line:

| STAT | | CALC | | 4:LinReg(ax+b) | | ENTER | | Y= |

⇧ TI-82: 5:LinReg(ax+b)

| VARS | | VARS | | 5:Statistics | | ENTER | | EQ | | 1:RegEQ | | ENTER | | GRAPH |

⇧ TI-82: 7:RegEQ

E X A M P L E **2** Create a scatter plot for the data, graph the least-squares line, and find the *y*-value that corresponds to $x = 40$.

Page 39

Use viewing window $[0, 100]$ by $[0, 24]$.

Create a scatter plot, and graph the least-squares line:
Use a keystroke sequence similar to that in the Activity for this lesson and in Example 1 above.

Evaluate for $x = 40$:

| 2nd | | TRACE (CALC) | | 1: value | | ENTER | (X=) 40 | ENTER |

LESSON 1.6

Activity

Page 47

For Step 2, graph $y = x + 3$ and $y = 9 - 2x$ on the same screen. Find the value of *x* for which $y = x + 3$ and $y = 9 - 2x$ are equal.

Use the friendly viewing window $[-4.7, 4.7]$ by $[-10, 10]$.

| Y= | | X,T,θ,n | | + | 3 | ENTER | (Y2=) 9 | − | 2 | X,T,θ,n | | GRAPH |

Press | TRACE | and move the cursor toward the point of intersection.

Use | ▲ | and | ▼ | to move the cursor from one line to the other.

E X A M P L E **3** Graph $y = 3.24x - 4.09$ and $y = -0.72x + 3.65$ on the same screen, and find any points of intersection.

Page 47

Use viewing window $[-5, 5]$ by $[-5, 5]$.

Graph the equations:

Use a keystroke sequence similar to that in the Activity for this lesson.

Find any points of intersection:

> Move your cursor as indicated.

| 2nd | | TRACE (CALC) | | 5: intersect | | ENTER | (First curve?) | ENTER | (Second curve?) | ENTER |

(Guess?) | ENTER |

Page 56

For Step 2, graph $y = 2x - 3$ and $y = 3$ on the same screen.

Use the friendly viewing window $[-4.7, 4.7]$ by $[-5, 5]$. Use a keystroke sequence similar to that in the Activity for Lesson 1.6.

LESSON 1.8

Activity
Page 63

For Step 1, graph $y = |x|$ and $y = 2x - 2$, and find any points of intersection.

Use viewing window $[-5, 5]$ by $[-5, 5]$.

Graph the equations:

Find the point of intersection:
Use a keystroke sequence similar to that in
Example 3 of Lesson 1.6.

E X A M P L E S ❶ and ❷ **Graph the two equations on the same screen, and find any**
Pages 63 and 64 **points of intersection.**

For Example 1, use viewing window $[-7, 3]$ by $[-1, 5]$.
For Example 2, use viewing window $[-3, 7]$ by $[-3, 7]$.

Use a keystroke sequence similar to that in the Activity for this lesson.

E X A M P L E S ❸ and ❹ **For Examples 3 and 4, graph $y = |5 - 3x|$ and $y = 9$ on the same**
Page 65 **screen, and find any points of intersection.**

Use viewing window $[-11, 17]$ by $[-3, 15]$.

Use a keystroke sequence similar to that in
the Activity for this lesson.

Numbers and Functions

FUNCTIONS ARE USED IN THE REAL WORLD to quantify trends and relationships between two variables. For example, the relationship between the *speed* at which an amusement park ride rotates and the *force* that holds riders in their seat can be described by a function.

About the Chapter Project

Real-world situations are often very complex, with changing or unknown factors. Mathematical models can be used to represent such real-world situations and to predict probable outcomes. In the Chapter Project, *Space Trash,* you will use functions to model data related to the growing problem of space debris orbiting the Earth.

After completing the Chapter Project, you will be able to do the following:

- Use a table to represent the relationship between time in years and the number of space debris objects, and show that an appropriate function models this relationship.

- Find and discuss models for the accumulation of space debris.

- Determine the piecewise function that describes the relationship between altitude and number of orbital debris objects.

About the Portfolio Activities

Throughout the chapter, you will be given opportunities to complete Portfolio Activities that are designed to support your work on the Chapter Project.

- Finding the projected number of space debris objects at the end of each year through the year 2010 is included in the Portfolio Activity on page 93.

- Using exponents to project the number of space debris objects in a given year is included in the Portfolio Activity on page 101.

- Comparing regression models for the space debris data is included in the Portfolio Activity on page 110.

- Operating on function models is included in the Portfolio Activity on page 117.

- Using piecewise functions to model trends that change over time is included in the Portfolio Activity on page 132.

Operations With Numbers

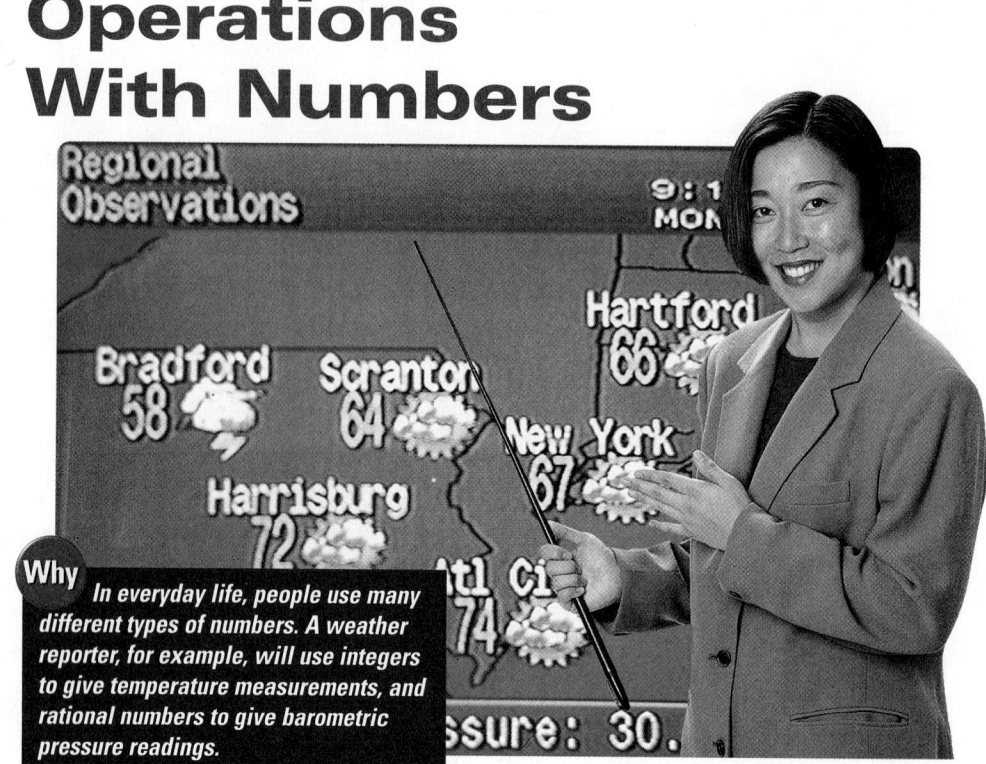

Objectives

● Identify and use Properties of Real Numbers.

● Evaluate expressions by using the order of operations.

Why *In everyday life, people use many different types of numbers. A weather reporter, for example, will use integers to give temperature measurements, and rational numbers to give barometric pressure readings.*

A typical weather report might say that the temperature is 82°F, which is an integer, and that the barometric pressure is 29.98 inches of mercury, which is a positive rational number written as a decimal. These, as well as other types of numbers, typically belong to more than one *number set*.

Number Sets

Natural numbers	$1, 2, 3, \ldots$
Whole numbers	$0, 1, 2, 3, \ldots$
Integers	$\ldots, -3, -2, -1, 0, 1, 2, 3, \ldots$
Rational numbers	$\frac{p}{q}$, where p and q are integers and $q \neq 0$
Irrational numbers	numbers whose decimal part does not terminate or repeat
Real numbers	all rational and all irrational numbers

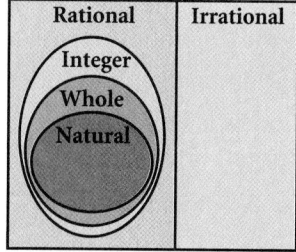

The *Venn diagram* at left shows the relationship between the various number sets. An important fact about rational numbers is stated in the following theorem, which will help you differentiate between rational and irrational numbers:

Every rational number can be written as a terminating or repeating decimal. Every terminating or repeating decimal represents a rational number.

When a repeating decimal is written, a bar is used to indicate the digit or digits that repeat. For example, $0.\overline{3}$ represents the repeating rational number $0.333333\ldots$

EXAMPLE **1** Classify each number in as many ways as possible.
   a. −2.77   **b.** 178,000   **c.** 12.020002000002 . . .

SOLUTION

a. Since −2.77 is a terminating decimal, it is a rational and a real number.
b. Since 178,000 is positive and has no decimal part, it is a natural number, a whole number, an integer, a rational number, and a real number.
c. The pattern of digits in the decimal part of 12.020002000002 . . . suggests that the decimal part does not terminate and does not repeat. This number is irrational and real.

Every real number corresponds to a point on the real-number line. Conversely, for every point on the number line, you can assign a real-number coordinate.

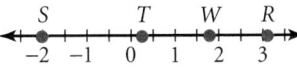

On the number line at left, point S corresponds to −2, point T corresponds to 0.5, point W corresponds to $1\frac{2}{3}$, and point R corresponds to the irrational number π, which is about 3.14.

Properties of Real Numbers

Properties for the fundamental operations of addition and multiplication with real numbers are listed below. Addition and multiplication are linked by the *Distributive Property*.

Properties of Addition and Multiplication

For all real numbers a, b, and c:

	Addition	**Multiplication**
Closure	$a + b$ is a real number.	ab is a real number.
Commutative	$a + b = b + a$	$ab = ba$
Associative	$(a + b) + c = a + (b + c)$	$(ab)c = a(bc)$
Identity	There is a number 0 such that $a + 0 = a$ and $0 + a = a$.	There is a number 1 such that $1 \cdot a = a$ and $a \cdot 1 = a$.
Inverse	For every real number a, there is a real number $-a$ such that $a + (-a) = 0$.	For every nonzero real number a, there is a real number $\frac{1}{a}$ such that $a\left(\frac{1}{a}\right) = 1$.

The Distributive Property

For all real numbers a, b, and c:

$$a(b + c) = ab + ac \text{ and } (b + c)a = ba + ca$$

Example 2 shows you how to use Properties of Real Numbers to rewrite an expression.

EXAMPLE ② Write and justify each step in the simplification of $(z + x)(2 + w)$.

● **SOLUTION**

$$\begin{aligned}
(z + x)(2 + w) &= (z + x)(2) + (z + x)(w) & \textit{Use the Distributive Property.} \\
&= z \cdot 2 + x \cdot 2 + zw + xw & \textit{Use the Distributive Property.} \\
&= 2z + 2x + wz + wx & \textit{Use the Commutative Property.}
\end{aligned}$$

TRY THIS Write and justify each step in the simplification of $(a + b)(c - d)$.

EXAMPLE ③ When you purchase an item costing c dollars in a state that has a sales tax of 5%, the total cost, T, is given by $T = c + 0.05c$.

APPLICATION
TAXES

Show that $T = 1.05c$. Justify each step.

● **SOLUTION**

$$\begin{aligned}
T &= c + 0.05c & \\
T &= 1c + 0.05c & \textit{Use the Identity Property.} \\
T &= (1 + 0.05)c & \textit{Use the Distributive Property.} \\
T &= 1.05c & \textit{Add.}
\end{aligned}$$

TRY THIS If the sales tax is 6%, then $T = c + 0.06c$. Show that $T = 1.06c$. Justify each step.

CRITICAL THINKING When you purchase an item costing c dollars in a state that has a sales tax of $r\%$, show that $T = \left(1 + \dfrac{r}{100}\right)c$. Justify each step.

Order of Operations

If an expression involves only numbers and operations, you can evaluate the expression by using the *order of operations*.

Order of Operations

1. Perform operations within the innermost grouping symbols according to Steps 2–4 below.
2. Perform operations indicated by exponents (powers).
3. Perform multiplication and division in order from left to right.
4. Perform addition and subtraction in order from left to right.

Example 4 shows you how to evaluate an expression by using the order of operations.

EXAMPLE **4** Evaluate $\dfrac{2^2(12+8)}{5}$ by using the order of operations.

● **SOLUTION**

$$\dfrac{2^2(12+8)}{5} = \dfrac{2^2(20)}{5}$$ *Evaluate within grouping symbols.*

$$= \dfrac{4(20)}{5}$$ *Evaluate powers.*

A fraction bar is a grouping symbol. $$= \dfrac{80}{5}$$ *Multiply within grouping symbols.*

$$= 16$$

TRY THIS Evaluate $\dfrac{18 - 2 \cdot 5}{15 + 3(-3)}$ by using the order of operations.

In the Activity below, you can explore how calculators use the order of operations.

Activity
Exploring the Order of Operations

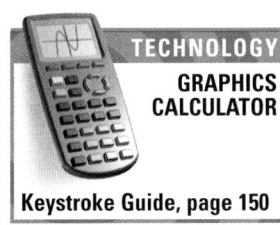

Keystroke Guide, page 150

You will need: a scientific or graphics calculator

1. Evaluate $\dfrac{12+8}{5}$ on a calculator as follows:

    a. without any parentheses for grouping

        12 [+] 8 [÷] 5

    b. with parentheses to group the numerator

        [( ] 12 [+] 8 [ )] [÷] 5

CHECKPOINT ✔ **2.** Explain why your results in parts **a** and **b** in Step 1 are not equal. Which result is correct?

3. The slope of the line containing the points (2, 3) and (5, 8) is $\dfrac{8-3}{5-2}$. Evaluate this expression on a calculator as follows:

    a. without any parentheses for grouping

        8 [-] 3 [÷] 5 [-] 2

    b. with parentheses to group the numerator but not the denominator

        [( ] 8 [-] 3 [ )] [÷] 5 [-] 2

    c. with parentheses to group the numerator and the denominator

        [( ] 8 [-] 3 [ )] [÷] [( ] 5 [-] 2 [ )]

CHECKPOINT ✔ **4.** Discuss why there are three different results to Step 3. Which result is correct?

When you use a calculator to evaluate expressions such as $\dfrac{9-4}{7-5}$, you need to enclose the numerator and the denominator in separate sets of parentheses.

CHECKPOINT ✔ What keystrokes will give the correct answer for $\dfrac{9-4}{7-5}$?

Communicate

1. Discuss two times in the past week when you added numbers. What type of numbers did you add? Can you think of occasions when you used any of the other types of numbers?

APPLICATIONS

2. ETYMOLOGY Explain what the Commutative Properties of Addition and Multiplication are. Why is the word *commutative* appropriate for these properties?

3. ETYMOLOGY Explain what the Associative Properties of Addition and Multiplication are. Why is the word *associative* appropriate for this property?

Guided Skills Practice

4. Classify $\frac{3}{2}$ and $-2.101001000\ldots$ in as many ways as possible. *(EXAMPLE 1)*

Write and justify each step in the simplification of each expression.
(EXAMPLE 2)

5. $2(b + d)$ **6.** $-3a + 3a$ **7.** $\frac{3(8 + 2)}{2}$

8. $\frac{7 - 1}{5 - 2}$ **9.** $\frac{1}{4}(4 \cdot 5)$ **10.** $-5(4t^2)$

APPLICATION

11. BUSINESS A monthly automotive insurance payment, m, is given by $m = \frac{p}{12} + \frac{0.06p}{12}$, where p is the yearly premium and $0.06p$ represents the annual processing fee. Show that $m = \frac{1.06p}{12}$. Justify each step. *(EXAMPLE 3)*

Evaluate each expression by using the order of operations. *(EXAMPLE 4)*

12. $5^2 + 8 \div 4 - 2$ **13.** $(7 - 3^2)2$

14. $\frac{5 \cdot 6 \div 3 \cdot 7}{12}$ **15.** $2[14 - 3(6 - 1)^2]$

An insurance adjuster evaluates the damage to a car after an accident.

Practice and Apply

internet connect

Homework Help Online

Go To: **go.hrw.com**
Keyword:
MB1 Homework Help
for Exercises 16–31

Classify each number in as many ways as possible.

16. -23 **17.** -5.1 **18.** $\sqrt{3}$ **19.** $\sqrt{2}$

20. $\frac{2}{3}$ **21.** $\frac{3}{9}$ **22.** $-0.\overline{85}$ **23.** $-1.0\overline{63}$

24. $-\frac{5}{7}$ **25.** $\sqrt{25}$ **26.** $\frac{\sqrt{36}}{2}$ **27.** 1

28. 0 **29.** $-\pi$ **30.** $5.010010001\ldots$ **31.** $\sqrt{28}$

Graph each pair of numbers on a number line.

32. -3 and -2.5 **33.** -1.5 and -4 **34.** $\frac{13}{2}$ and 7

35. $4\frac{3}{8}$ and 2 **36.** $-3.\overline{6}$ and -4 **37.** $\sqrt{7}$ and 3

State the property that is illustrated in each statement. All variables represent real numbers.

38. $v(3t) = (3t)v$

39. $(25x)y = 25(xy)$

40. $4x + 13y = 13y + 4x$

41. $2.3 + x = x + 2.3$

42. $(2 + 3) + 5 = 2 + (3 + 5)$

43. $(3 + a) + b = 3 + (a + b)$

44. $x\left(\dfrac{1}{x}\right) = 1$, where $x \neq 0$

45. $\dfrac{x}{3} \cdot \dfrac{3}{x} = 1$, where $x \neq 0$

46. $-7 + 7 = 0$

47. $0 = 2x + (-2x)$

48. $1 \cdot (3x) = 3x$

49. $63 \cdot 1 = 63$

50. $-5x + 0 = -5x$

51. $x + y = 0 + x + y$

52. $m(x^2 + x) = mx^2 + mx$

53. $2(3 - y) = 2 \cdot 3 - 2y$

54. $4yw = 4wy$

55. $5(127) = 127(5)$

Evaluate each expression by using the order of operations.

56. $3 \cdot 2^2 + 3$

57. $6 \div 3 \cdot 2$

58. $2^2(2 + 3) + 5$

59. $6 \div (3 - 1) \cdot 5$

60. $-3 \cdot 5^2 + 16$

61. $5(2 - 3)^2$

62. $(3 - 2) + (5 - 4) - 2$

63. $30 - 3 \times 2 + 6 \div 3$

64. $16 \div 2 \times 6 - 1$

65. $(2^2 + 1) + 4 \div 2$

66. $6 \div 3 - (10 - 3^2)$

67. $2^{(3-1)} + (3 - 1)$

68. $3 \cdot 4 - 2^{(4-1)}$

69. $\dfrac{8 - 2}{3} + (2 + 1)$

70. $2 \cdot 4 + \dfrac{14}{5 + 2}$

71. Complete the following investigation:
  a. Count the number of items in your home that display numbers.
  b. What types of numbers are represented?
  c. Name two examples of integers and two examples of rational numbers that you found.

CHALLENGE

CONNECTION

72. Can a number be both rational and irrational? Explain your reasoning.

73. STATISTICS While trying to find the average of 8, 10, 14, and 16, Ron entered 8 [+] 10 [+] 14 [+] 16 [÷] 4 [=] into a calculator and got 36 for an answer.
  a. Did Ron get the correct average of 8, 10, 14, and 16? Explain.
  b. What keystrokes should Ron have used?

74. CULTURAL CONNECTION: ASIA Ancient Babylonians used rational numbers as approximations of irrational numbers. For example, the Babylonians knew that the diagonal of a square was $\sqrt{2}$ times the length of a side. For the value of $\sqrt{2}$, the Babylonians used 1.4142. They thought this value was close enough for their practical purposes.

A Babylonian cuneiform tablet showing the calculation of areas

Use a calculator for the following exercises:
  a. Show that $\sqrt{2}$ does not equal exactly 1.4142.
  b. Find $\sqrt{2}$ on your calculator. Write down the result. Enter this number in your calculator, and square it. Is the result equal to 2? Explain why or why not.

75. **BUSINESS** A small business contributes $224 per month per worker for health insurance. This amount is half of the worker's monthly insurance premium and can be represented by $\frac{0.5p}{12} = 224$, where p is the yearly premium. Solve for p and justify each step.

76. **CURRENT EVENTS** Use your local newspaper to answer the following questions:
   a. Find three articles that include numerical data.
   b. Summarize each article. Include the reason that the article depends on numbers and the possible effect that each article may have on daily life.
   c. What types of numbers were included in each article? What units, if any, were used with the numbers?

DEMOGRAPHICS Read the article below and answer the questions that follow.

U. S. Birth Rate at a Record Low

The U. S. birth rate has fallen to a historic low, tying a record set in the mid-1970's.

The birth rate is falling because baby boomers are moving out of their childbearing years (ages 15 to 44) and older generations are living longer, demographers say.

For the 12 months that ended June 30, preliminary figures show the birth rate was 14.6 births per 1,000 people. That tied averages set in 1975 and 1976, according to the National Center for Health Statistics.

The birth rate has fallen 13% since 1990 and 38% since 1960. Baby boomers, who make up the largest generation in recent U. S. history, were born from 1946 to 1964. The generation that follows has less influence on the birth rate because it is much smaller in number.

Copyright © 1998, USA Today. Reprinted with permission.

77. Explain how rates such as 14.6 per 1000 can be considered rational numbers.

78. Explain how percents such as 13% can be considered rational numbers.

79. How much had the birth rate fallen since 1990 at the time of this article? Write this percent as a fraction, and classify it in as many ways as possible.

80. For the 12 months that ended June 30, 1998, what was the birth rate? Write this rate as a fraction, and classify it in as many ways as possible.

Look Back

Find the slope of each line. *(LESSON 1.2)*

81. $y = -3x$

82. $y = 2x - 1$

83. $y = \dfrac{3x - 1}{4}$

84. $y = -\dfrac{x}{2} + 1$

85. $4y = 3x + 21$

86. $5x - 2y = 6$

Solve each equation. *(LESSON 1.6)*

87. $3(x - 5) = 4$

88. $-\dfrac{x}{3} + 9 = 2$

89. $-3x - 5 = x + 12$

90. $\dfrac{1}{5}x - 4 = 3(x - 5)$

Solve each absolute-value equation or inequality. Graph the solution on a number line. *(LESSON 1.8)*

91. $|5x| = 12$

92. $\left|\dfrac{4}{5}x\right| = 12$

93. $|4x + 2| > x + 3$

94. $|4x + 2| > 5x + 5$

 Look Beyond

95. The solutions to equations illustrate the need for different kinds of numbers. The equation $x + 7 = 5$ has the solution $x = -2$, which is a negative number, even though only nonnegative numbers appear in the equation. Similarly, only integers appear in the equation $2x = 5$, but the solution is $x = 2.5$, which is not an integer.

   a. Find another example of an equation that includes only nonnegative numbers and that has a negative-number solution.

   b. Find another example of an equation that includes only integers and that has a non-integer solution.

SPACE SCIENCE Scientists catalog only the space debris objects large enough to be repeatedly tracked by ground-based radar. At the end of 1993, the Air Force Space Command cataloged a total of 7000 debris objects in Earth orbit. At that time, it was projected that the number of cataloged space debris objects would grow at a rate of 3% per year.

Start with 7000 objects, the total number of space debris objects tracked at the end of 1993.

Using the annual growth rate of 3% (1.03 × the previous year's total), find the projected number of space debris objects at the end of each successive year through the year 2010. Round all results to the nearest whole number. Record your results in a table. Throughout the Portfolio Activities in this chapter, this will be your **Space Debris Table.**

Properties of Exponents

2.2

Objectives

- Evaluate expressions involving exponents.
- Simplify expressions involving exponents.

Why *Exponential expressions can be found in a wide variety of fields, including physics. For example, the centripetal acceleration of a rider who is traveling in a circle at a high speed on an amusement park ride can be described by using exponents.*

In an amusement park ride, a compartment with a rider travels in a circle at a high speed. The centripetal acceleration acting on the rider can be calculated by using the equation below. *You will use this equation in Example 1.*

$$A_c = 4\pi^2 r T^{-2}, \text{ where } \begin{cases} A_c \text{ represents the centripetal acceleration in feet per} \\ \quad \text{second squared} \\ r \text{ represents the radius of the circle in feet} \\ T \text{ represents the time for a full rotation in seconds} \end{cases}$$

Recall that the expression a^n is called a **power** of a. In the expression, a is called the **base** and n is called the **exponent**.

Definition of Integer Exponents

Let a be a real number.

If n is a natural number, then $a^n = a \times a \times a \times \cdots \times a$, n times.

If a is nonzero, then $a^0 = 1$.

If n is a natural number, then $a^{-n} = \dfrac{1}{a^n}$.

In the expression a^0, a must be nonzero because 0^0 is undefined.

Example 1 shows how you can use the definition $a^{-n} = \frac{1}{a^n}$.

EXAMPLE ❶ Refer to the equation for centripetal acceleration given at the beginning of the lesson.

● **Find the centripetal acceleration in feet per second squared of a rider who makes one rotation in 2 seconds and whose radius of rotation is 6 feet.**

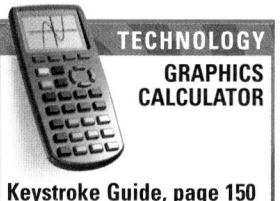

TECHNOLOGY
GRAPHICS CALCULATOR

Keystroke Guide, page 150

SOLUTION

Evaluate $A_c = 4\pi^2 r T^{-2}$ for $T = 2$ and $r = 6$.

$$A_c = 4\pi^2 r T^{-2}$$
$$= 4\pi^2(6)(2)^{-2}$$
$$= \frac{24\pi^2}{2^2} \qquad \textit{Use } a^{-n} = \frac{1}{a^n}.$$
$$= 6\pi^2 \approx 59.2$$

The centripetal acceleration is about 59 feet per second squared.

CHECK

```
4π²*6*(2^-2)
          59.21762641
```

TRY THIS Find the centripetal acceleration of a rider that makes one rotation in 5 seconds and whose radius of rotation is 6 feet.

Exploring Properties of Exponents

You will need: no special materials

1. Rewrite $a^3 \cdot a^5$ by writing out all of the factors of a, counting them, and simplifying them as a power with a single exponent. What operation could you perform on the exponents in $a^3 \cdot a^5$ to obtain an equivalent expression with a single exponent?

2. Rewrite $(a^3)^5$ by writing out five sets of three factors of a, counting the factors of a, and simplifying them as a power with a single exponent. What operation could you perform on the exponents in $(a^3)^5$ to obtain an equivalent expression with a single exponent?

CHECKPOINT ✔ 3. Explain how to simplify $(a^7 \cdot a^3)^2$ by using addition and multiplication.

The results of the Activity suggest some *Properties of Exponents*.

Properties of Exponents

Let a and b be nonzero real numbers. Let m and n be integers.

Product of Powers	$(a)^m(a)^n = a^{m+n}$
Quotient of Powers	$\dfrac{a^m}{a^n} = a^{m-n}$
Power of a Power	$(a^m)^n = a^{mn}$
Power of a Product	$(ab)^n = a^n b^n$
Power of a Quotient	$\left(\dfrac{a}{b}\right)^n = \dfrac{a^n}{b^n}$

In this lesson, you may assume that variables with negative exponents represent nonzero numbers.

E X A M P L E **2** **Simplify $3x^2y^{-2}(-2x^3y^{-4})$. Write your answer with positive exponents only.**

● **SOLUTION**

$$3x^2y^{-2}(-2x^3y^{-4}) = (3)(-2)x^2x^3y^{-2}y^{-4} \quad \textit{Use the Commutative Property.}$$

$$= (3)(-2)x^{(2+3)}y^{[-2+(-4)]} \quad \textit{Use the Product of Powers Property.}$$

$$= -6x^5y^{-6} \quad \textit{Simplify.}$$

$$= -\frac{6x^5}{y^6} \quad \textit{Use } a^{-n} = \frac{1}{a^n}.$$

TRY THIS   Simplify $2z(3x^2)(5z^{-3})$. Write your answer with positive exponents only.

PROBLEM SOLVING   **Look for a pattern.** Examine what happens to powers with a *negative* base:

$$(-2)^2 = (-2)(-2) = 4$$
$$(-2)^3 = (-2)(-2)(-2) = -8$$
$$(-2)^4 = (-2)(-2)(-2)(-2) = 16$$
$$(-2)^5 = (-2)(-2)(-2)(-2)(-2) = -32$$

When the exponent of a negative base is *even*, the result is positive. When the exponent of a negative base is *odd*, the result is **negative**.

When simplifying an expression, be careful not to confuse the results of a negative base with the results of a negative exponent.

Even Exponent

$$(-2x)^{-2}$$

$$= \frac{1}{(-2x)^2}$$

$$= \frac{1}{(-2)^2x^2}$$

$$= \frac{1}{4x^2}$$

Odd Exponent

$$(-2x)^{-3}$$

$$= \frac{1}{(-2x)^3}$$

$$= \frac{1}{(-2)^3x^3}$$

$$= \frac{1}{-8x^3}, \text{ or } -\frac{1}{8x^3}$$

E X A M P L E **3** **Simplify $\left(\dfrac{-y^7}{2z^{12}y^3}\right)^4$. Write your answer with positive exponents only.**

● **SOLUTION**

$$\left(\frac{-y^7}{2z^{12}y^3}\right)^4 = \frac{(-y^7)^4}{(2z^{12}y^3)^4} \quad \textit{Use the Power of a Quotient Property.}$$

$$= \frac{y^{28}}{16z^{48}y^{12}} \quad \textit{Use the Power of a Power Property.}$$

$$= \frac{y^{28-12}}{16z^{48}} \quad \textit{Use the Quotient of Powers Property.}$$

$$= \frac{y^{16}}{16z^{48}}$$

TRY THIS   Simplify $\left(\dfrac{-3b^2c^5}{c^2b^7}\right)^3$. Write your answer with positive exponents only.

CRITICAL THINKING   Find a, b, and c such that $(x^{-2}y^3z^2)(y^az^bx^c) = x^{-3}y^4$ for all nonzero values of x, y, and z.

Rational Exponents

An expression with rational exponents can be represented in an equivalent form that involves the radical symbol, $\sqrt{}$.

For example, $a^{\frac{1}{3}}$ equals $\sqrt[3]{a}$ because when $a^{\frac{1}{3}}$ is cubed, the result is a, as shown at right. This is the definition of $\sqrt[3]{a}$.

$$\left(a^{\frac{1}{3}}\right)^3 = a^{\frac{1}{3} \cdot 3} = a$$

This relationship is true for all rational exponents. An expression with an exponent of $\frac{2}{3}$ is rewritten at right.

$$a^{\frac{2}{3}} = a^{\frac{1}{3} \cdot 2} = \left(a^{\frac{1}{3}}\right)^2 = \left(\sqrt[3]{a}\right)^2$$

Definition of Rational Exponents

For all positive real numbers a:

If n is a nonzero integer, then $a^{\frac{1}{n}} = \sqrt[n]{a}$.

If m and n are integers and $n \neq 0$, then $a^{\frac{m}{n}} = \left(a^{\frac{1}{n}}\right)^m = \left(\sqrt[n]{a}\right)^m = \sqrt[n]{a^m}$.

Example 4 shows how you can use the definition of rational exponents.

E X A M P L E **4** Evaluate each expression.

a. $16^{\frac{1}{4}}$

b. $27^{\frac{4}{3}}$

SOLUTION

a. $16^{\frac{1}{4}} = (2^4)^{\frac{1}{4}}$

$= 2^{4 \cdot \frac{1}{4}}$

$= 2^1 = 2$

b. $27^{\frac{4}{3}} = (3^3)^{\frac{4}{3}}$

$= 3^{3 \cdot \frac{4}{3}}$

$= 3^4 = 81$

CHECK

```
16^(1/4)
              2
```

CHECK

```
27^(4/3)
             81
```

TECHNOLOGY

GRAPHICS CALCULATOR

Keystroke Guide, page 150

TRY THIS Evaluate $64^{\frac{1}{3}}$ and $36^{\frac{3}{2}}$.

APPLICATION

MEDICINE

The formula below is used to estimate a person's surface area based on his or her weight and height. This formula is used to calculate dosages for certain medications.

$$S = 0.007184 \times W^{0.425} \times H^{0.725},$$

where $\begin{cases} S \text{ is the surface area in square meters} \\ W \text{ is the weight in kilograms} \\ H \text{ is the height in centimeters} \end{cases}$

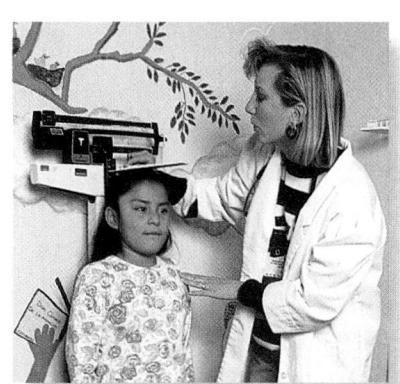

E X A M P L E **5** Estimate to the nearest tenth of a square meter the surface area of a person who stands 152.5 centimeters tall and weighs 57.2 kilograms.

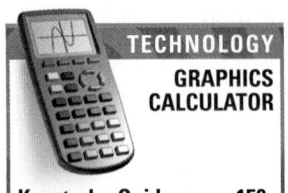

TECHNOLOGY

GRAPHICS
CALCULATOR

Keystroke Guide, page 150

● **SOLUTION**

Evaluate $S = 0.007184 \times W^{0.425} \times H^{0.725}$ for $W = 57.2$ and $H = 152.5$.

$$S = 0.007184 \times W^{0.425} \times H^{0.725}$$
$$= 0.007184 \times (57.2)^{0.425} \times (152.5)^{0.725}$$
$$\approx 1.54$$

The estimated surface area is about 1.5 square meters.

TRY THIS Estimate to the nearest tenth of a square meter the surface area of a person who stands 180 centimeters tall and weighs 62.3 kilograms.

Exercises

● *Communicate*

1. Explain why x^5x^3 and $(x^5)^3$ are not equivalent expressions.

2. Explain why ax^2 and $(ax)^2$ are not equivalent expressions.

3. Describe how to evaluate 5^{-2}.

4. Describe how to evaluate $4^{\frac{3}{2}}$ by using the definition of rational exponents.

● *Guided Skills Practice*

APPLICATION

5. **PHYSICS** Find the centripetal acceleration in feet per second squared of a model airplane that makes one rotation in 1.5 seconds and whose radius of rotation is 8 feet. *(EXAMPLE 1)*

Simplify each expression, assuming that no variable equals zero. Write your answers with positive exponents only. (EXAMPLES 2 AND 3)

6. x^4x^2 7. $\dfrac{z^9}{z^3}$ 8. $(y^3)^6$ 9. $(a^3b^7)^4$

10. $(y^5y^{-2})^4$ 11. $\left(\dfrac{-2x^3y}{5x^7}\right)^2$ 12. $\left(\dfrac{a^3b^{-1}}{a^{-2}b^2}\right)^{-2}$ 13. $\left(\dfrac{1}{x^{-1}y^3z^0}\right)^{-1}$

Evaluate each expression. (EXAMPLE 4)

14. $100^{\frac{1}{2}}$ 15. $9^{\frac{3}{2}}$ 16. $27^{\frac{1}{3}}$ 17. $64^{\frac{2}{3}}$

APPLICATION

18. **MEDICINE** Estimate to the nearest hundredth of a square meter the surface area of a person who stands 167.64 centimeters tall and weighs 53.64 kilograms. *(EXAMPLE 5)*

Practice and Apply

Evaluate each expression.

19. 3^0
20. 9^0
21. $(5a)^0$
22. $(2^5 \cdot 2^3)^0$

23. 6^{-1}
24. 4^{-2}
25. $\left(\dfrac{3}{5}\right)^4$
26. $\left(\dfrac{4}{5}\right)^2$

27. $\left(\dfrac{1}{4}\right)^{-1}$
28. $\left(\dfrac{2}{5}\right)^{-2}$
29. $\left(-\dfrac{1}{3}\right)^{-3}$
30. $\left(-\dfrac{2}{3}\right)^{-3}$

31. $49^{\frac{1}{2}}$
32. $27^{\frac{2}{3}}$
33. $64^{\frac{4}{3}}$
34. $25^{\frac{3}{2}}$

35. $36^{\frac{6}{4}}$
36. $8^{\frac{2}{6}}$
37. $-64^{\frac{2}{3}}$
38. $81^{-\frac{3}{2}}$

Simplify each expression, assuming that no variable equals zero. Write your answer with positive exponents only.

39. $y^5 y^2$
40. $-2z^3 z^5$
41. $-2y^3(5xy^4)$
42. $6x^5 \cdot 3x^5 \cdot x^0$

43. $\dfrac{m^9}{m^5}$
44. $\dfrac{bb^4}{b^2}$
45. $\dfrac{x^2 x^{-5}}{x^4}$
46. $\dfrac{s^5 t^2}{st^{-4}}$

47. $(2x^4 y)^3$
48. $(3st^{12})^3$
49. $(-5w^4 v^5)^2$
50. $(-3x^2 y^7)^3$

51. $\left(\dfrac{-2z^2}{x^3}\right)^7$
52. $\left(\dfrac{2b^4}{-a^2}\right)^3$
53. $\left(\dfrac{-2p^5 q^{-4}}{q^3}\right)^3$
54. $\left(\dfrac{3m^2 n^3}{m^{-1}}\right)^5$

55. $\left(\dfrac{3x^4}{y^{-2}}\right)^5$
56. $\left(\dfrac{-7y^{-2}}{-x^5}\right)^6$
57. $\left(\dfrac{5r^2 s^{-2}}{s^{-3}}\right)^{-1}$
58. $\left(\dfrac{x^{-2} y}{y^{-1}}\right)^{-3}$

Simplify each expression, assuming that no variable equals zero. Write your answer with positive exponents only.

59. $\left(\dfrac{15xy^3}{3y^2}\right)^{-1}$
60. $\left[\dfrac{2x^{-3}}{(2x)^3}\right]^{-1}$
61. $\left(\dfrac{4a^3 b^{-3}}{a^{-1} b^2}\right)^{-2}$

62. $\left(\dfrac{15a^2 b^{-2}}{-3ab^{-3}}\right)^{-2}$
63. $(x^{-3} y^{-1})^{-1}(x^{-3} y^0)^2$
64. $(a^{-3} b^2)^4 (-2a^3 b^7)^{-3}$

65. $\left[\dfrac{(a^3 b^5)^2}{a^5 b^2}\right]^{-1}$
66. $\left(\dfrac{s^{-3}}{4t}\right)^{-3}\left(\dfrac{5t}{s^{-7}}\right)^{-2}$
67. $\left(\dfrac{3z}{x^{-4}}\right)^2\left(\dfrac{3x^{-12} yz^{-3}}{2xy^7}\right)^{-3}$

68. $\left[\left(\dfrac{x^5 y^2}{x^{-3} y}\right)^{-2}\left(\dfrac{y^{-3}}{2x^5}\right)^3\right]^{-1}$
69. $\left[\dfrac{(a^{-5} b^2)^{-1}}{(-a^1 b^4 c^{-1})^2}\right]^{-3}$
70. $\left[\dfrac{(2s^{3x} t^{2y})^2}{(s^{3x} t^{-4})^{-1}}\right]^2$

Use a calculator to evaluate each expression to the nearest tenth.

71. $12^{6.05} + 8.8^{3.24}$
72. $3.3^{2.7} - 5^{1.9} + 0.63^{0.95}$

73. $0.005^{21.53} + 9.05^{0.034}$
74. $71.33^{0.44} + 478.2^{0.4}$

75. $11.7^{0.6} + 29.3^{1.23} - 6^{-2.2}$
76. $89^{3.5} - 5.25^{9.25} + 324^{0.05}$

CHALLENGES

77. Show that if $y \neq 0$, then $y^{a-b} = \dfrac{1}{y^{b-a}}$.

78. Show that $\dfrac{x^{-1} - y^{-1}}{x - y} = -\dfrac{1}{xy}$.

CONNECTION

79. GEOMETRY The height, h, of a right circular cone can be calculated from the equation $h = \dfrac{3}{\pi} V r^{-2}$, where V is the volume of the cone and r is the radius of the circular base.

a. Find the height to the nearest tenth of a right circular cone whose volume is 200 cubic centimeters and whose radius is 4 centimeters.

b. Write the equation for the height of a right circular cone with positive exponents only.

80. ENGINEERING The maximum load in tons that a foundation column can withstand is represented by the equation $F_{max} = \frac{9}{4}d^4l^{-2}$, where d is the diameter of the column in inches and l is the length of the column in feet.

  a. Find the maximum load for a column that is 5 feet long and 10 inches in diameter.

  b. Write the equation $F_{max} = \frac{9}{4}d^4l^{-2}$ with positive exponents only.

Foundation columns are cylindrical weight-bearing supports for structures such as the bridge shown above.

81. PHYSICS The resistance caused by friction between blood and the vessels that carry it can be modeled by the equation $R = \frac{2}{3}lr^{-4}$, where R is the resistance, l is the length of the blood vessel, and r is the radius of the blood vessel.

  a. Find the resistance to the nearest tenth for a 0.2-meter long vessel with a 0.015-meter radius.

  b. Write the resistance equation, $R = \frac{2}{3}lr^{-4}$, with positive exponents only.

82. PHYSICS The rate at which an object emits radiant energy can be expressed as $P = 5 \times 10^{-8}\left(\frac{A}{T^{-4}}\right)$, where P is the power radiated by the object in watts, A is the surface area of the object in square meters, and T is the temperature of the object in kelvins.

  a. Write the equation $P = 5 \times 10^{-8}\left(\frac{A}{T^{-4}}\right)$ with positive exponents only.

  b. Find the power radiated by a heater with a surface area of 0.25 square meters and a temperature of 300 K.

CHEMISTRY Radioactive plutonium decays very slowly. The percent of plutonium remaining after x years can be represented by $A = 100\left(0.5^{\frac{x}{24,360}}\right)$. Find the percent of plutonium remaining after each number of years.

83. $x = 100$ **84.** $x = 500$ **85.** $x = 1000$ **86.** $x = 5000$

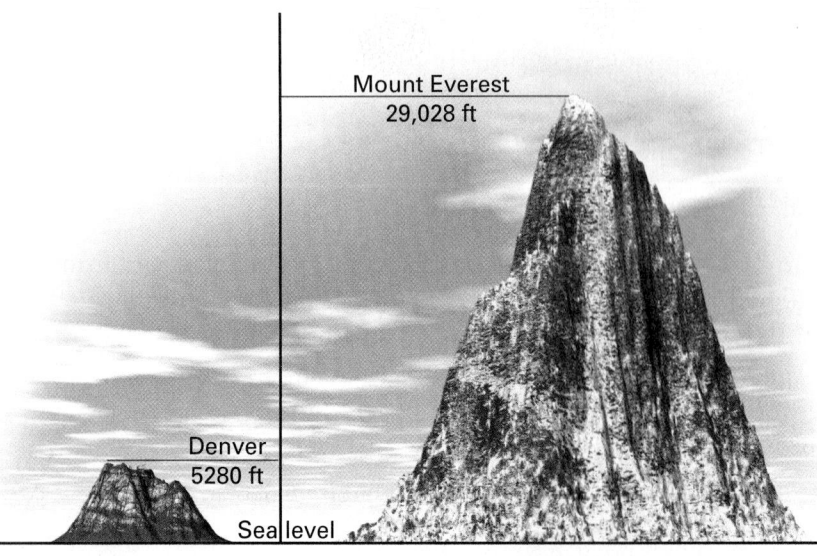

Mount Everest
29,028 ft

Denver
5280 ft

Sea level

PHYSICS Air pressure decreases with altitude according to the formula $P = 14.7(10)^{-0.000014a}$, where P is the air pressure in pounds per square inch and a is the altitude measured in feet above sea level.

87. Find the air pressure for Denver, Colorado, where the altitude is 1 mile (5280 feet) above sea level.

88. Find the air pressure at the top of Mount Everest, where the altitude is 29,028 feet above sea level.

internet connect

**Activities
Online**

Go To: **go.hrw.com**
Keyword:
MB1 Athletes

Graph the solution to each compound inequality on a number line.
(LESSON 1.7)

89. $x > -3$ *and* $x < 1$

90. $x > -\frac{1}{4}$ *and* $x > \frac{1}{2}$

91. $x > -3$ *or* $x < 1$

92. $x > -\frac{1}{4}$ *or* $x > \frac{1}{2}$

Classify each number in as many ways as possible. *(LESSON 2.1)*

93. $9.373737\ldots$

94. $13\frac{1}{2}$

95. $5.38388388838888\ldots$

96. -7.9

Evaluate each expression by using the order of operations. *(LESSON 2.1)*

97. $2(3 - 1) + 6 \div 3 \div 2$

98. $-3(9 - 12) - 2(7 - 3) - 1$

99. $3 \cdot 5^2 - 4(5 - 8)^2 \div 3$

100. $(5 - 3)^{\frac{(10-8)}{(13-12)}}$

Look Beyond

APPLICATION

101. GENEALOGY Your two parents are your first-generation ancestors, your four grandparents are your second-generation ancestors, and your eight great-grandparents are your third-generation ancestors. Make a table that represents these generations and the corresponding number of ancestors in each generation. Write an expression that represents the number of ancestors in the nth generation. (Hint: Use exponents in your expression.)

On January 22, 1997, the second-stage propellant tank of a Delta II launch vehicle landed near Georgetown, Texas, after spending nine months in Earth orbit.

SPACE SCIENCE Refer to the Space Debris Table from the Portfolio Activity on page 93.

1. For data in the table, let the years be represented by t (where $t = 0$ represents 1993) and let the total projected number of debris objects in orbit be represented by d.

Show that the data in the table can be modeled by the equation $d = 7000(1.03)^t$.

2. Use the equation in Step 1 to calculate the total projected number of debris objects in space at the end of the year 2020.

Introduction to Functions

Objectives

- State the domain and range of a relation, and tell whether it is a function.

- Write a function in function notation and evaluate it.

Why *Functions and relations are commonly used to represent a variety of real-world relationships.*

APPLICATION
ENTERTAINMENT

The table at right gives the number of theater screens in operation during each of the years from 1992 to 1996. You can represent this data as a collection of ordered pairs.

{(**1992, 25,105**), (**1993, 25,737**), (**1994, 26,586**), (**1995, 27,805**), (**1996, 29,690**)}

Theater Screens in Operation

Year	Total number of screens
1992	25,105
1993	25,737
1994	26,586
1995	27,805
1996	29,690

[*Source: Motion Picture Association of America, Inc.*]

Notice that for each year, there is exactly one total number of screens. This relationship between years and the total number of screens is one example of a *function*.

CONNECTION
GEOMETRY

Recall from geometry the formulas for the perimeter and the area of a square.

$$\text{Perimeter: } P = 4s \quad \text{Area: } A = s^2$$

Each value for *s* defines exactly one perimeter and exactly one area. These relationships are also examples of *functions*.

Definition of Function

A **function** is a relationship between two variables such that each value of the first variable is paired with exactly one value of the second variable.

The **domain** of a function is the set of all possible values of the first variable. The **range** of a function is the set of all possible values of the second variable.

A function may also be represented by data in a table, as shown in Example 1.

EXAMPLE ❶ **State whether the data in each table represents a function. Explain.**

a.

Domain, x	Range, y
1	−3.6
2	−3.6
3	4.2
4	4.2
5	10.7
6	12.1
52	52

b.

Domain, x	Range, y
3	7
3	8
3	10
4	42
10	34
11	18
52	52

● **SOLUTION**

a. For each value of x in the table, there is exactly one value of y. The data set represents a function.

b. The data set does not represent a function because three different y-values 7, 8, and 10, are paired with one x-value, 3.

You can use the *vertical-line test* to determine if a graph represents a function.

Vertical-Line Test

If every vertical line intersects a given graph at no more than one point, then the graph represents a function.

Example 2 shows how you can use the vertical-line test to determine whether a graph represents a function.

EXAMPLE ❷ **State whether each graph represents a function. Explain.**

a.

b.
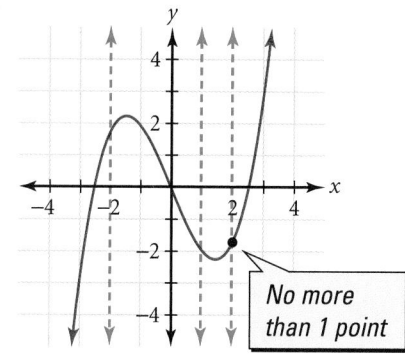

● **SOLUTION**

a. The graph does not represent a function. There are many vertical lines that intersect the graph at two points.

b. The graph represents a function. Every vertical line intersects the graph at no more than one point.

Exploring Functions

CONNECTION
GEOMETRY

You will need: no special tools

1. What variables influence how much water can be held in a cylindrical container? Discuss your responses.

2. Describe a real-world situation in which cost is a function of one or two variables. State the domain and range of your function.

3. The graph at right represents the volume, V, of water in a bathtub in gallons as a function of time, t, in minutes. Describe how V changes as t varies from 0 minutes to 16 minutes.

CHECKPOINT ✔ 4. Make up your own function like the one in Step 3. Describe your variables, and sketch a reasonable graph.

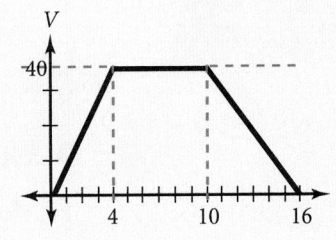

A function is a special type of *relation*.

Definition of Relation

A relationship between two variables such that each value of the first variable is paired with one or more values of the second variable is called a **relation**.

The **domain** is the set of all possible values of the first variable. The **range** is the set of all possible values of the second variable.

Example 3 gives an example of a real-world relation.

EXAMPLE ③ Let the first variable, R, represent residents in Brownsville, Texas, who have telephone service. Let the second variable, T, represent telephone numbers of residents in Brownsville, Texas.

Is the relationship between R and T a relation? a function? Explain.

● **SOLUTION**

A resident with telephone service has at least one telephone number and may have more. Thus, the relationship is a relation.

Because some residents may have more than one telephone number, the relation is not a function.

TRY THIS Let the first variable, R, represent checking and savings account customers at a local bank. Let the second variable, N, represent checking and savings account numbers. Is the relationship between R and N a relation? a function? Explain.

CHECKPOINT ✔ Give two sets of ordered pairs that form a relation but not a function.

Example 4 shows you how to determine the domain and range of a function or relation from a graph.

E X A M P L E ④ **State the domain and range of each function graphed.**

a.

b.

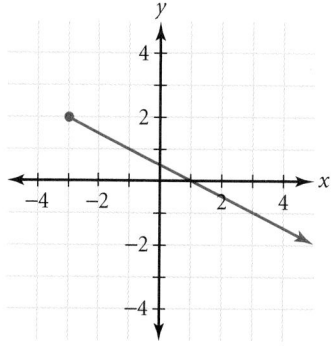

● **SOLUTION**

The domain consists of the *x*-values, and the range consists of the *y*-values.

a. domain: {−4, −1, 2, 5}
   range: {−2, 0, 2, 4}

b. domain: $x \geq -3$
   range: $y \leq 2$

TRY THIS State the domain and range of each function graphed.

a.

b.

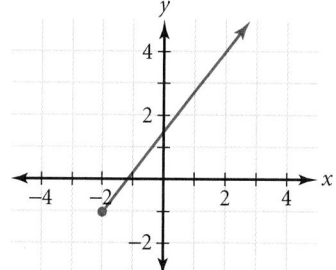

You can tell from a graph whether the function is *discrete* or *continuous*. The graph in part **a** of Example 4 illustrates a **discrete function**, whose graph is a set of individual points. The graph in part **b** of Example 4 illustrates a **continuous function**, whose graph is a line, ray, segment, or smooth curve.

CHECKPOINT ✔ Suppose that *x* is any real number. Is $y = 3x + 2$ a continuous function or a discrete function? Explain.

Functions and Function Notation

An equation can represent a function. The equation $y = 2x + 5$ represents a function. To express this equation as a function, use *function notation* and write $y = 2x + 5$ as $f(x) = 2x + 5$.

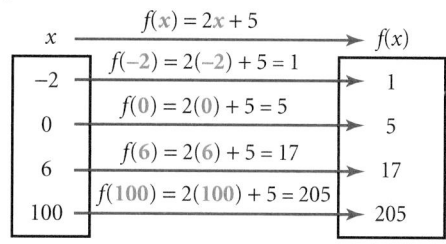

Function Notation

If there is a correspondence between values of the domain, x, and values of the range, y, that is a function, then $y = f(x)$, and (x, y) can be written as $(x, f(x))$. The notation $f(x)$ is read "f of x." The number represented by $f(x)$ is the value of the function f at x.

The variable x is called the **independent variable.**

The variable y, or $f(x)$, is called the **dependent variable**.

E X A M P L E ⑤ Evaluate $f(x) = 0.5x^2 - 3x + 2$ for $x = 4$ and $x = 2.5$.

● SOLUTION

$$f(x) = 0.5x^2 - 3x + 2 \qquad\qquad f(x) = 0.5x^2 - 3x + 2$$
$$f(4) = 0.5(4)^2 - 3(4) + 2 \qquad f(2.5) = 0.5(2.5)^2 - 3(2.5) + 2$$
$$f(4) = -2 \qquad\qquad\qquad\qquad f(2.5) = -2.375$$

TECHNOLOGY
GRAPHICS
CALCULATOR

Keystroke Guide, page 150

CHECK

E X A M P L E ⑥ **Monthly residential electric charges, c, are determined by adding a fixed fee of \$6.00 to the product of the amount of electricity consumed each month, x, in kilowatt-hours and a rate factor of 0.035 cents per kilowatt-hour.**

APPLICATION
CONSUMER ECONOMICS

a. Write a linear function to model the monthly electric charge, c, as a function of the amount of electricity consumed each month, x.

b. If a household uses 712 kilowatt-hours of electricity in a given month, how much is the monthly electric charge?

● SOLUTION

a. $c(x) =$ **electricity used + fixed fee**
$$c(x) = \quad 0.035x \quad + \quad 6.00$$

The linear function is $c(x) = 0.035x + 6.00$.

b. Evaluate the function for $x = 712$.

$$c(x) = 0.035x + 6.00$$
$$c(712) = 0.035(712) + 6.00$$
$$c(712) = 30.92$$

For 712 kilowatt-hours of electricity, the monthly charge is \$30.92.

CHECKPOINT ✔ State the independent and dependent variables in Example 6. Explain your response.

Exercises

Communicate

1. Explain how functions are different from relations. Sketch a graph of a relation that is not a function to illustrate your explanation.

2. Describe three ways to represent a function.

3. Explain how to find the domain and range of a set of ordered pairs such as $\{(4, 2), (3, 5), (-2, 0), (2, 5)\}$.

4. **INCOME** Cleo wants to graph the relationship between the dollar value of the meals she served and the amount of tips she received. Identify a real-world domain and range for this relationship and draw a sample graph for Cleo.

Guided Skills Practice

State whether the data in each table represents *y* as a function of *x*. Explain. *(EXAMPLE 1)*

5.

x	y
5	3
8	4
5	7
9	2

6.

x	y
0	3
1	8
2	8
3	-7

7.

x	y
10	7
20	11
30	9
40	7

8.

x	y
3	9
2	2
8	-3
2	1

State whether each graph represents a function. Explain. *(EXAMPLE 2)*

9.

10.

11. **TRANSPORTATION** If the first variable, R, represents registered automobiles in your state that may be legally driven and the second variable, L, represents license plate numbers for these automobiles, is the relationship between R and L a relation? a function? Explain. *(EXAMPLE 3)*

State the domain and range of each function graphed. *(EXAMPLE 4)*

12.

13.

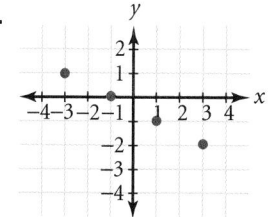

14. Evaluate $f(x) = x^2 + 2x - 1$ for $x = 3$ and $x = 1.5$. *(EXAMPLE 5)*

15. INCOME A plumber charges $24 per hour of work plus $20.00 to make a service call. *(EXAMPLE 6)*
  a. Write a linear function to model the plumber's wages, w, for the number of hours worked, h.
  b. Find the plumber's wages for 5.5 hours of work.

Practice and Apply

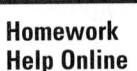

Homework Help Online
Go To: **go.hrw.com**
Keyword:
MB1 Homework Help
 for Exercises 16–30

State whether each relation represents a function.

16. $\{(0, 0), (1, 1)\}$

17. $\{(1, 2), (2, 2), (3, 2)\}$

18. $\{(1, -1), (1, -2), (1, -3)\}$

19. $\{(4, 1), (5, 2), (6, 3)\}$

20. $\left\{\left(\frac{1}{2}, 1\right), \left(\frac{2}{5}, 2\right), \left(\frac{1}{3}, 1\right)\right\}$

21. $\left\{\left(\frac{1}{3}, \frac{1}{4}\right), \left(\frac{1}{5}, \frac{1}{5}\right), \left(\frac{1}{4}, \frac{3}{4}\right)\right\}$

22. $\{(11, 0), (12, -1), (21, -2)\}$

23. $\{(0, 0), (2, 5), (3, 3)\}$

24. $\{(1, 7), (-1, 7), (1, -7)\}$

25. $\{(-1, 8), (-1, 7), (0, 9)\}$

26.

x	y
0	3
2	-5
2	1
4	7

27.

x	y
1	6
2	6
3	9
4	9

28.

x	y
4	-2
4	2
6	-3
6	3

29.

x	y
-5	8
-3	8
-1	-2
1	-2

30.

x	y
-2	-5
-2	-3
0	4
2	6

State whether each relation graphed below is a function. Explain.

31.

32.

33.

34.

35.

36.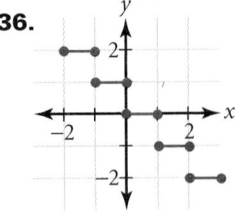

State the domain and range of each function.

37. $\{(0, 2), (3, 4)\}$

38. $\{(1, 5), (2, 5), (3, 5)\}$

39. $\{(9, -1), (8, -2), (7, -3)\}$

40. $\{(4, 1), (5, 2), (6, 3)\}$

41. $\{(6, -6), (5, -5), (4, -4)\}$

42. $\{(0, 0), (1.5, 0), (2.5, 0)\}$

Evaluate each function for the given values of *x*.

43. $f(x) = 2x - 6$ for $x = 1$ and $x = 3$

44. $f(x) = 5 - 3x$ for $x = 1$ and $x = 3$

45. $g(x) = \frac{2x - 1}{3}$ for $x = -1$ and $x = 1$

46. $g(x) = \frac{x - 4}{5}$ for $x = -9$ and $x = 9$

47. $f(x) = 2x^2 - 3x$ for $x = 3$ and $x = -2.5$

48. $f(x) = -x^2 + 4x - 1$ for $x = 2$ and $x = 1.5$

49. $f(x) = \frac{1}{3}x^2$ for $x = -1$ and $x = \frac{3}{4}$

50. $f(x) = -4x^2$ for $x = \frac{3}{2}$ and $x = -2$

Graph each function, and state the domain and range.

51 $y = -\frac{x}{2}$

52 $y = \frac{2}{3}x - 5$

53 $y = -2x^2$

54 $y = x^2 + 2$

55 $y = 4$

56 $y = -6$

57 $y = x^3$

58 $y = \left(\frac{x}{2}\right)^3$

59. Graph a function with a domain of $-3 \le x \le 3$ and a range of $-5 \le y \le 5$.

60. Graph a function with a domain of $-2 \le x \le 5$ and a range of $0 \le y \le 4$.

CHALLENGE

Given $f(t) = t^2 - 3$, find the indicated function value.

61. $f(\sqrt{2})$

62. $f(\sqrt{2} - 1)$

63. $f(a + \sqrt{2})$

CONNECTION

GEOMETRY The cube shown has volume *V*.

64. Express the volume of the cube as a function of *s*, the length of each side.

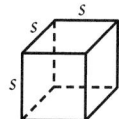

65. If the volume of the cube is 27 cubic meters, find the area of one face of the cube.

APPLICATIONS

66. CONSUMER ECONOMICS Computer equipment can depreciate very rapidly. Suppose a business assumes that a computer will depreciate linearly at a rate of 15% of its original price each year.
  a. If a computer is purchased for $3200, write an equation in which the value for the computer is a function of its age in years.
  b. Find the value of a computer after 3 years.

CONSUMER ECONOMICS A clothing store is selling all out-of-season clothing at 30% off the original price.

67. Write a function that gives the discounted price as a function of the original price.

68. Jason spent $47.25 on out-of-season items. Find the original cost of the items.

69. Helena purchased out-of-season items that originally cost $52. Find the sale price of these items.

Look Back

Write the equation in slope-intercept form for the line that has the indicated slope, *m*, and contains the given point. *(LESSON 1.3)*

70. $m = 5, (2, 3)$ **71.** $m = -3, (4, 1)$

72. $m = \frac{1}{5}, (4, -11)$ **73.** $m = -\frac{2}{3}, (-8, -3)$

Write an equation in slope-intercept form of the line containing the indicated points. *(LESSON 1.3)*

74. $(1, 4)$ and $(-3, 0)$ **75.** $(0, 2)$ and $(-1, 1)$

76. $(2, 3)$ and $(0, 0)$ **77.** $(-2, -5)$ and $(5, -1)$

Write an equation in slope-intercept form of the line that contains the given point and is perpendicular to a line with the given slope. *(LESSON 1.3)*

78. $P(6, -1), m = \frac{4}{3}$ **79.** $P(-5, 3), m = -\frac{1}{2}$

Evaluate each expression by using the order of operations. *(LESSON 2.1)*

80. $3[2 - (5 - 3) - 7] \div 2$ **81.** $-(-5^2)^3$

internet connect

Portfolio Extension

Go To: **go.hrw.com**
Keyword:
MB1 Exponential

 Look Beyond

82 Graph $y = x^2 - 3x - 10$. Explain why this is a function. Give the domain and range of this function.

83 Graph $y = 2^x$. Explain why this is a function. Give the domain and range of this function.

SPACE SCIENCE Refer to the Space Debris Table from the Portfolio Activity on page 93.

1. Graph the ordered pairs in the Space Debris Table that you created in the Portfolio Activity on page 93. Let the years be represented by x (where $x = 0$ represents 1993) and the total number of debris objects by y. Describe how your graph illustrates that the total number of debris objects in space, y, is a function of time, x.

2. Give the domain and range of the function you described in Step 1. Then state the independent and dependent variables for this function.

3. Using the linear regression feature on your calculator, find a linear function that models this data. Next, using the exponential regression feature, find an exponential function that models this data.

4. Graph your linear model and your exponential model, and compare how well or how poorly the models appear to fit the data.

WORKING ON THE CHAPTER PROJECT

You should now be able to complete Activities 1 and 2 of the Chapter Project.

Operations With Functions

Why *Many real-world relationships can be described by operations with functions. For example, the distance traveled by a vehicle before coming to a complete stop is the sum of the distance that it travels while the driver reacts and the distance that it travels while the brakes are applied.*

Objectives

● Perform operations with functions to write new functions.

● Find the composition of two functions.

←— Total stopping distance —→

| Reaction distance | Braking distance |

APPLICATION

TRANSPORTATION

Common sense tells you that the faster you drive, the farther you will travel while reacting to an obstacle and while braking to a complete stop. In other words, the reaction distance and braking distance depend on the speed of the car at the moment the obstacle is observed.

Stopping Distance Data

Speed (mph)	Reaction distance (ft)	Braking distance (ft)	Stopping distance (ft)
10	11	5	16
20	22	21	43
30	33	47	80
40	44	84	128
50	55	132	187
60	66	189	255
70	77	258	335

Investigating Braking Distance

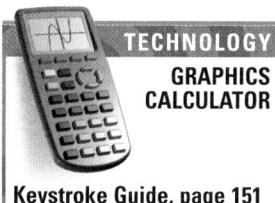

TECHNOLOGY

GRAPHICS CALCULATOR

Keystroke Guide, page 151

You will need: a graphics calculator

1. Using a graphics calculator, make a scatter plot of the data for speed and reaction distance. What type of function is represented by this data?

2. Using a graphics calculator, make a scatter plot of the data for speed and braking distance. What trend do you see in the graph?

3. Using the table above, identify a relationship between the stopping distance and the reaction and braking distances. Use this relationship to make predictions about the scatter plot of the data for speed and stopping distance.

CHECKPOINT ✔ 4. Using a graphics calculator, make a scatter plot of the data for speed and stopping distance. What trend do you see in the graph?

The functions at right relate speed, x, in miles per hour to the reaction distance, r, and to braking distance, b, both in feet.

$$r(x) = \tfrac{11}{10}x \qquad b(x) = \tfrac{1}{19}x^2$$

$$s(x) = r(x) + b(x)$$

You can relate speed, x, to the total stopping distance, s, as a *sum* of r and b.

$$s(x) = \tfrac{11}{10}x + \tfrac{1}{19}x^2$$

Functions can also be combined by subtraction, multiplication, and division.

Operations With Functions

For all functions f and g:

Sum	$(f + g)(x) = f(x) + g(x)$
Difference	$(f - g)(x) = f(x) - g(x)$
Product	$(f \cdot g)(x) = f(x) \cdot g(x)$
Quotient	$\left(\dfrac{f}{g}\right)(x) = \dfrac{f(x)}{g(x)}$, where $g(x) \neq 0$

E X A M P L E ① Let $f(x) = 5x^2 - 2x + 3$ and $g(x) = 4x^2 + 7x - 5$.
    a. Find $f + g$.   **b.** Find $f - g$.

● **SOLUTION**

    a. $(f + g)(x) = f(x) + g(x)$
              $= (5x^2 - 2x + 3) + (4x^2 + 7x - 5)$
              $= 5x^2 + 4x^2 - 2x + 7x + 3 - 5$ *Use the Commutative Property.*
              $= 9x^2 + 5x - 2$ *Combine like terms.*

    b. $(f - g)(x) = f(x) - g(x)$
              $= (5x^2 - 2x + 3) - (4x^2 + 7x - 5)$
              $= 5x^2 - 4x^2 - 2x - 7x + 3 - (-5)$ *Use the Commutative Property.*
              $= x^2 - 9x + 8$ *Combine like terms.*

TRY THIS   Let $f(x) = -7x^2 + 12x + 2.5$ and $g(x) = 7x^2 - 5$. Find $f + g$ and $f - g$.

E X A M P L E ② Let $f(x) = 5x^2$ and $g(x) = 3x - 1$.
    a. Find $f \cdot g$.   **b.** Find $\dfrac{f}{g}$, and state any domain restrictions.

● **SOLUTION**

    a. $(f \cdot g)(x) = f(x) \cdot g(x)$ **b.** $\left(\dfrac{f}{g}\right)(x) = \dfrac{f(x)}{g(x)}$, where $g(x) \neq 0$
              $= 5x^2(3x - 1)$
              $= 5x^2(3x) - 5x^2(1)$ $= \dfrac{5x^2}{3x - 1}$, where $x \neq \dfrac{1}{3}$
              $= 15x^3 - 5x^2$

$$3x - 1 \neq 0$$
$$3x \neq 1$$
$$x \neq \tfrac{1}{3}$$

CHECKPOINT ✔   Which property of real numbers is used in part **a** of Example 2?

TRY THIS   Let $f(x) = 3x^2 + 1$ and $g(x) = 5x - 2$. Find $f \cdot g$ and $\dfrac{f}{g}$.

Composition of Functions

When you apply a function rule on the result of another function rule, you *compose* the functions. The illustration below shows how the composition $f \circ g$, or $f(g(x))$, read "f of g of x," works.

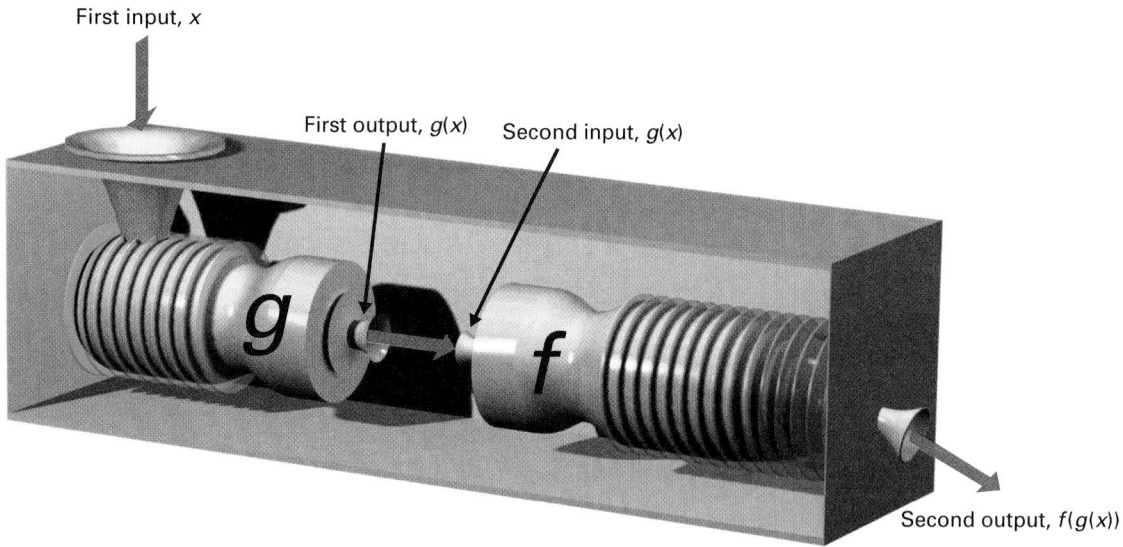

First input, x

First output, $g(x)$ Second input, $g(x)$

Second output, $f(g(x))$

Composition of Functions

Let f and g be functions of x.

The composition of f with g, denoted $f \circ g$, is defined by $f(g(x))$.

The domain of $y = f(g(x))$ is the set of domain values of g whose range values are in the domain of f. The function $f \circ g$ is called the **composite** function of f with g.

Example 3 shows you how to form the composition of two functions.

E X A M P L E ③ Let $f(x) = x^2 - 1$ and $g(x) = 3x$.

  a. Find $f \circ g$.   **b.** Find $g \circ f$.

● SOLUTION

  a. $(f \circ g)(x) = f(g(x))$ **b.** $(g \circ f)(x) = g(f(x))$
$$= f(3x)$$
$$= (3x)^2 - 1$$
$$= 9x^2 - 1$$

                                                   $= g(x^2 - 1)$
$$= 3(x^2 - 1)$$
$$= 3x^2 - 3 \quad \textit{Distributive Property}$$

TRY THIS   Let $f(x) = -2x^2 + 3$ and $g(x) = -2x$. Find $f \circ g$ and $g \circ f$.

In Example 3 and in most cases, $f \circ g$ and $g \circ f$ are not equivalent. That is, the composition of functions is not commutative.

CRITICAL THINKING   Write two functions, f and g, whose composite functions $f \circ g$ and $g \circ f$ are equivalent. Justify your response.

Example 4 shows you how composite functions can model problems that involve a series of actions.

E X A M P L E ④ A local electronics store is offering a $100.00 rebate along with a 10% discount. Let x represent the original price of an item in the store.

   a. Write the function D that represents the sale price after a 10% discount and the function R that represents the sale price after a $100 rebate.
   b. Find the composite functions $(R \circ D)(x)$ and $(D \circ R)(x)$, and explain what they represent.

● **SOLUTION**

   a. Since a 10% discount on the original price is the same as paying 90% of the original price, $D(x) = x - 0.1x = 0.9x$.

   The rebate function is $R(x) = x - 100$.

   b. 10% discount first

   $$(R \circ D)(x) = R(D(x)) = R(0.9x)$$
   $$= (0.9x) - 100$$
   $$= 0.9x - 100$$

   $100 rebate first

   $$(D \circ R)(x) = D(R(x)) = D(x - 100)$$
   $$= 0.9(x - 100)$$
   $$= 0.9x - 90$$

   Notice that taking the 10% discount first results in a lower sale price.

Exercises

● *Communicate*

   1. Explain how to write a function for reaction distance, r, in terms of the function for braking distance, b, and the function for stopping distance, s.

   2. Explain how to find $f \circ g$ given $f(x) = 4x - 7$ and $g(x) = 2x^2 + 4$.

   3. Show that $f \circ g$ and $g \circ f$ are not equivalent functions given $f(x) = 3x + 1$ and $g(x) = 2x$.

internet connect

Activities Online
Go To: **go.hrw.com**
Keyword:
MB1 UV

● *Guided Skills Practice*

Let $f(x) = \frac{x}{2}$ and $g(x) = 3x + 1$. Perform each function operation. State any domain restrictions. *(EXAMPLES 1, 2, AND 3)*

   4. $f + g$ **5.** $f - g$ **6.** $f \cdot g$

   7. $\dfrac{f}{g}$ **8.** $f \circ g$ **9.** $g \circ f$

10. **CONSUMER ECONOMICS** A coupon for $5 off any meal states that a 15% tip will be added to the total check before the $5 is subtracted. Let x represent the total check amount. Write a function, R, for the price reduction and a function, T, for the tip. Find the composite functions $(R \circ T)(x)$ and $(T \circ R)(x)$, and explain which composite function represents the conditions of the coupon. *(EXAMPLE 4)*

Practice and Apply

Find $f + g$ and $f - g$.

11. $f(x) = 4x + 3$; $g(x) = 5$ 12. $f(x) = 20x + 7$; $g(x) = -3x$

13. $f(x) = x^2 + 2x - 1$; $g(x) = 3x - 5$ 14. $f(x) = -x^2 - 3x$; $g(x) = 6x^2 - 3$

15. $f(x) = x - 2$; $g(x) = 4 - 3x^2$ 16. $f(x) = 3x^2 - x$; $g(x) = 6 - x^2$

Find $f \cdot g$ and $\frac{f}{g}$. State any domain restrictions.

17. $f(x) = 3x^2$; $g(x) = x - 8$ 18. $f(x) = 2x^2$; $g(x) = 7 - x$

19. $f(x) = -x^2$; $g(x) = 3x$ 20. $f(x) = 4x^2 - 2x + 1$; $g(x) = -5x$

21. $f(x) = 2x^2$; $g(x) = 7 - x$ 22. $f(x) = 7x^2$; $g(x) = 2x - 6$

23. $f(x) = -3x^2 - x$; $g(x) = 5 - x$ 24. $f(x) = 4x^2 + 3$; $g(x) = 3x - 9$

Let $f(x) = x^2 - 1$ and $g(x) = 2x - 3$. Find each new function and write it in simplest form. Justify each step in the simplification, and state any domain restrictions.

25. $f + g$ 26. $f - g$ 27. $g - f$ 28. $f \cdot g$ 29. $\frac{f}{g}$

Let $f(x) = x - 3$ and $g(x) = x^2 - 9$. Find each new function and write it in simplest form. Justify each step in the simplification, and state any domain restrictions.

30. $f + g$ 31. $f - g$ 32. $g - f$ 33. $f \cdot g$ 34. $\frac{g}{f}$

Find $f \circ g$ and $g \circ f$.

35. $f(x) = x + 1$; $g(x) = 2x$ 36. $f(x) = 3x$; $g(x) = 2x + 3$

37. $f(x) = 3x - 2$; $g(x) = x + 2$ 38. $f(x) = 2x - 3$; $g(x) = x + 4$

39. $f(x) = -3x^2 - 1$; $g(x) = -5x$ 40. $f(x) = -2x$; $g(x) = -2x^2 + 3$

41. $f(x) = -4x^2 + 3x - 1$; $g(x) = 3$ 42. $f(x) = 2x^2 + 3x - 5$; $g(x) = 4$

Let $f(x) = 3x - 4$ and $g(x) = -x^2$. Evaluate each composite function.

43. $(f \circ g)(2)$ 44. $(f \circ g)(-2)$ 45. $(f \circ f)(2)$ 46. $(f \circ f)(-2)$

47. $(g \circ g)(2)$ 48. $(g \circ g)(-2)$ 49. $(g \circ f)(0)$ 50. $(f \circ g)(0)$

Let $f(x) = 2x$, $g(x) = x^2 + 2$, and $h(x) = -4x + 3$. Find each composite function.

51. $f \circ g$ 52. $g \circ f$ 53. $f \circ h$ 54. $h \circ g$

55. $f \circ f$ 56. $h \circ f$ 57. $h \circ (h \circ g)$ 58. $(h \circ f) \circ g$

59. Let $h(x) = x^2 - 9$. Find two functions f and g such that $f \circ g = h$.

60. DEMOGRAPHICS College enrollments in the United States are projected to increase from 1995 to 2005 for public and private schools. The models below give the total projected college enrollments in thousands, where $t = 0$ represents the year 1995. [*Source: U.S. National Center for Education Statistics*]

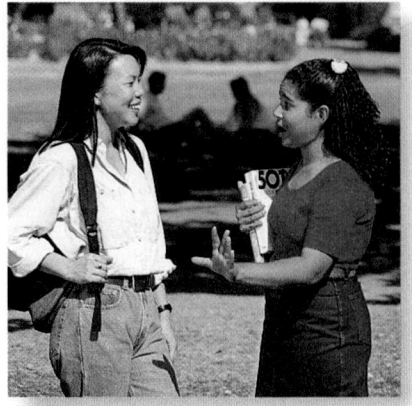

Public: $f(t) = 160t + 11{,}157$
Private: $g(t) = 50t + 3114$

  a. Find $f + g$.
  b. Evaluate $f + g$ for the year 2000.

61. MANUFACTURING The function $C(x) = 4x + 850$ closely approximates the cost of a daily production run of x picture frames. The number of picture frames produced is represented by the function $x(t) = 90t$, where t is the time in hours since the beginning of the production run.
  a. Give the cost of a daily production run, C, as a function of time, t.
  b. Find the cost of the production run that lasts 5 hours.
  c. How many picture frames are produced in 5 hours?

62. TEMPERATURE A temperature given in kelvins is equivalent to the temperature given in degrees Celsius plus 273. A temperature given in degrees Celsius is equivalent to $\frac{5}{9}$ times the quantity given by the temperature in degrees Fahrenheit minus 32.
  a. Write a function expressing kelvins in terms of degrees Celsius.
  b. Write a function expressing degrees Celsius in terms of degrees Fahrenheit.
  c. Write a function expressing kelvins in terms of degrees Fahrenheit.
  d. Water freezes at 32°F. At what Kelvin temperature does water freeze?
  e. Are kelvins and degrees Fahrenheit linearly related? Explain.

63. BUSINESS Jovante decides to start a business by making buttons and selling them for 25 cents each. The button machine costs $125 dollars, and the materials for each button cost 10 cents.
  a. Write a cost function, C, that represents the cost in dollars of making n buttons.
  b. Write an income function, I, that represents the income in dollars generated by selling n buttons.
  c. Write a profit function, P, that represents the income, I, minus the cost, C.
  d. Find the number of buttons that Jovante must sell in order to make a $100 profit.

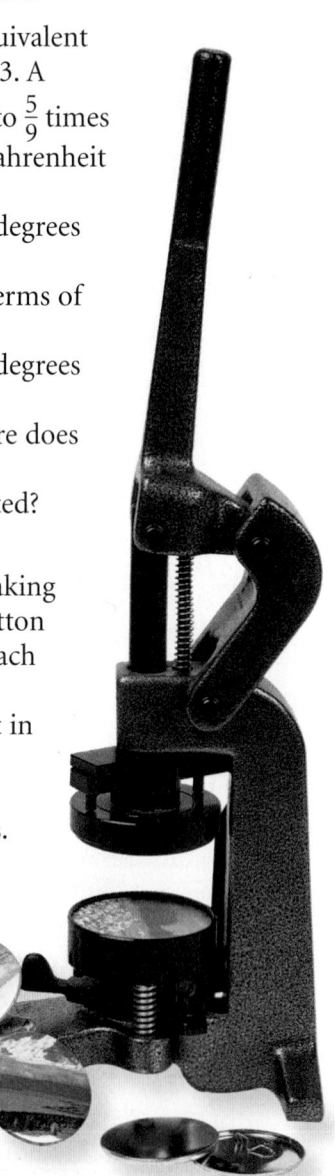

64. CONSUMER ECONOMICS A store is offering a discount of 30% on a suit. There is a sales tax of 6%.

   a. Using a composition of functions, represent the situation in which the discount is taken before the sales tax is applied.

   b. Using a composition of functions, represent the situation in which the sales tax is applied before the discount is taken.

   c. Compare the composite functions from parts **a** and **b.** Does one of them result in a lower final cost? Explain why or why not.

 Look Back

Write an equation in slope-intercept form for each line described. *(LESSON 1.2)*

65. contains $(3, -2)$ and has a slope of $-\frac{1}{2}$

66. contains $(-1, 4)$ and $(-3, 8)$

Describe the correlation among data that have the given correlation coefficient. *(LESSON 1.5)*

67. $r = 0.09$ **68.** $r = -0.95$ **69.** $r = 0.52$

State the domain and range of each function. *(LESSON 2.3)*

70. $\{(1, 3), (2, 5), (3, 7)\}$ **71.** $y = -4x + 2$

 Look Beyond

72. Given $f(x) = 2x + 5$ and $g(x) = \frac{x - 5}{2}$, find $f \circ g$ and $g \circ f$. Compare your results.

SPACE SCIENCE One source of space debris is nonfunctional spacecraft components. At the end of 1993, scientists tracked 1550 nonfunctional components in orbit and projected that 42 such objects are added each year. Suppose that an average of 15 of these are brought back to Earth each year.

   1. Let t represent time in years. Write the function D that models the total number of cataloged nonfunctional components in orbit at the end of the year if 42 such objects are added each year to the initial 1550 objects in orbit.

   2. Write the function R that models the total number of components that are brought back to Earth each year.

   3. Write a function relating time, t, in years and the total number of nonfunctional components in orbit as a difference of D and R.

   4. Graph the function from Step 3 on a graphics calculator. Examine the table of values for the function. Are there constant first differences in the x-values and in the y-values?

   5. Identify the type of function that you graphed in Step 4 and justify your answer.

Inverses of Functions

Boiling point
of water

Freezing point
of water

Why *Many real-world relationships can be represented with a pair of inverse functions. For example, the equations used to convert degrees Fahrenheit to degrees Celsius and vice versa are inverse fractions.*

Objectives

- Find the inverse of a relation or function.

- Determine whether the inverse of a function is a function.

APPLICATION

TEMPERATURE

In Lesson 1.6, you used the equation $F = \frac{9}{5}C + 32$ to find the Celsius temperature corresponding to 86°F. How can you find the Celsius temperatures that correspond to Fahrenheit temperatures? To answer this question, you need a function that gives C in terms of F. You will need to find the *inverse of a function*.

EXAMPLE ❶ Solve $F = \frac{9}{5}C + 32$ for C.

● **SOLUTION**

$$F = \frac{9}{5}C + 32$$

$$F - 32 = \frac{9}{5}C + 32 - 32$$

$$\frac{5}{9}(F - 32) = \frac{5}{9}\left(\frac{9}{5}C\right)$$

$$\frac{5}{9}(F - 32) = C$$

Thus, $C = \frac{5}{9}(F - 32)$.

> *Notice that subtraction of 32 and multiplication by $\frac{5}{9}$ are the inverse operations of those in $F = \frac{9}{5}C + 32$.*

Example 1 indicates that finding the inverse of a function involves changing an ordered pair of the form (C, F) to an ordered pair of the form (F, C).

Inverse of a Relation

The **inverse of a relation** consisting of the ordered pairs (x, y) is the set of all ordered pairs (y, x).

The domain of the inverse is the range of the original relation.

The range of the inverse is the domain of the original relation.

E X A M P L E **2** Find the inverse of each relation. State whether the relation is a function. State whether the inverse is a function.

a. $\{(1, 2), (2, 4), (3, 6), (4, 8)\}$ **b.** $\{(1, 5), (1, 6), (3, 6), (4, 9)\}$

● **SOLUTION**

a. relation: $\{(1, 2), (2, 4), (3, 6), (4, 8)\}$
inverse: $\{(2, 1), (4, 2), (6, 3), (8, 4)\}$

The given relation is a function because each domain value is paired with exactly one range value. The inverse is also a function because each domain value is paired with exactly one range value.

b. relation: $\{(1, 5), (1, 6), (3, 6), (4, 9)\}$
inverse: $\{(6, 1), (5, 1), (6, 3), (9, 4)\}$

The given relation is not a function because the domain value 1 is paired with two range values, 5 and 6. The inverse is not a function because the domain value 6 is paired with two range values, 1 and 3.

Example 3 shows you how to find the inverse of a function by interchanging x and y and then solving for y.

E X A M P L E **3** Find an equation for the inverse of $y = 3x - 2$.

● **SOLUTION**

In $y = 3x - 2$, interchange x and y. Then solve for y.

$$x = 3y - 2$$
$$x + 2 = 3y$$
$$\frac{x + 2}{3} = y$$
$$y = \frac{1}{3}x + \frac{2}{3}$$

TRY THIS   Find an equation for the inverse of $y = 4x - 5$.

In the Activity below, you can explore the relationship between the graph of a function and the graph of its inverse.

Activity
Exploring Functions and Their Inverses

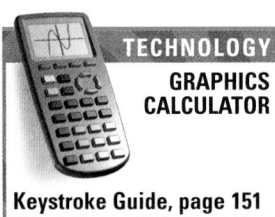

TECHNOLOGY
GRAPHICS CALCULATOR

Keystroke Guide, page 151

You will need: a graphics calculator

1. Graph $y = 2x - 1$, its inverse, and $y = x$ in a square viewing window. Use the inverse feature of the calculator. How do the graphs of these functions relate to one another? Consider symmetry in your response.

2. Repeat Step 1 for each function listed at right.

CHECKPOINT ✔ 3. Write a generalization about the relationship between the graph of a function and the graph of its inverse.

Function
$y = 3x - 2$
$y = 3x + 2$
$y = -2x + 5$
$y = x^2$

If a function f and its inverse are both functions, the inverse of f is denoted by f^{-1}.

The graph of $f(x) = 3x - 2$ and its inverse, $f^{-1}(x) = \frac{1}{3}x + \frac{2}{3}$, from Example 3 are shown at right. Notice that the ordered pairs $(-2, 0)$ and $(0, -2)$ are "mirror images" or *reflections* of one another across the line $y = x$. This means every point (a, b) on the graph of f corresponds to a point (b, a) on the graph of f^{-1}. This is true for any two relations that are inverses of each other.

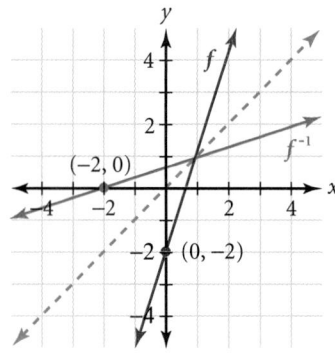

You can use the *horizontal-line test* to determine from a graph whether the inverse of a given function is a function.

Horizontal-Line Test

The inverse of a function is a function if and only if every horizontal line intersects the graph of the given function at no more than one point.

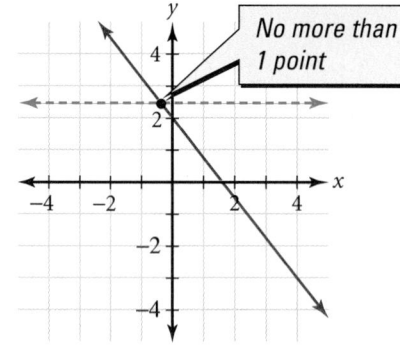

The horizontal-line test above shows that the inverse of this function is not a function.

The horizontal-line test above shows that the inverse of this function is a function.

If a function has an inverse that is also a function, then the function is **one-to-one**. Every one-to-one function passes the horizontal-line test and has an inverse that is a function.

Just as the graphs of f and f^{-1} are reflections of one another across the line $y = x$, the composition of a function and its inverse are related to the *identity function*. The **identity function**, I, is defined as $I(x) = x$.

Composition and Inverses

If f and g are functions and $(f \circ g)(x) = (g \circ f)(x) = I(x) = x$, then f and g are inverses of one another.

E X A M P L E ④ Show that $f(x) = 7x - 2$ and $g(x) = \frac{1}{7}x + \frac{2}{7}$ are inverses of each other.

SOLUTION

$(f \circ g)(x) = f(g(x)) = f\left(\frac{1}{7}x + \frac{2}{7}\right)$ $(g \circ f)(x) = g(f(x)) = g(7x - 2)$

$\qquad\qquad\qquad\quad = 7\left(\frac{1}{7}x + \frac{2}{7}\right) - 2 \qquad\qquad\qquad = \frac{1}{7}(7x - 2) + \frac{2}{7}$

$\qquad\qquad\qquad\quad = x + 2 - 2 \qquad\qquad\qquad\qquad = x - \frac{2}{7} + \frac{2}{7}$

$\qquad\qquad\qquad\quad = x \qquad\qquad\qquad\qquad\qquad\quad = x$

CHECK

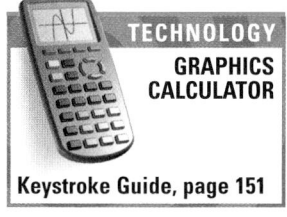

TECHNOLOGY

GRAPHICS CALCULATOR

Keystroke Guide, page 151

Graph $f \circ g$ and $g \circ f$ to check that the two functions are inverses.

Because $(f \circ g)(x) = x$ and $(g \circ f)(x) = x$, the two functions are inverses of each other.

The identity function $y = x$

TRY THIS

Show that $f(x) = -5x + 7$ and $g(x) = -\frac{1}{5}x + \frac{7}{5}$ are inverses of each another.

CRITICAL THINKING

Let $f(x) = mx + b$, where $m \neq 0$. Find f^{-1}. Using composition, verify that f and f^{-1} are inverses of one another.

Exercises

● Communicate

1. Explain what it means for a function to be a one-to-one function.

2. Describe when and why you would use the vertical-line test and the horizontal-line test.

3. Describe the procedure for finding the inverse of $y = 4x - 1$.

4. Explain how the graphs of a function and its inverse are related.

● Guided Skills Practice

APPLICATION

5. **CHEMISTRY** A chemical reaction takes place at temperatures between 290 K and 300 K. The Fahrenheit and Kelvin temperature scales are related by the formula $K = \frac{5}{9}(F - 32) + 273$. Solve this equation for F. **(EXAMPLE 1)**

Find the inverse of each relation. State whether the relation is a function. State whether the inverse is a function. *(EXAMPLE 2)*

6. $\{(8, 3), (2, 2), (4, 3)\}$ 7. $\{(3, 2), (9, 5), (2, 3), (4, 7)\}$

Find an equation for the inverse of each function. *(EXAMPLE 3)*

8. $y = 3x + 9$

9. $y = 5 - 3x$

10. Verify that $f(x) = 6x - 5$ and $g(x) = \frac{1}{6}x + \frac{5}{6}$ are inverses of each other. *(EXAMPLE 4)*

Practice and Apply

Find the inverse of each relation. State whether the relation is a function. State whether the inverse is a function.

11. $\{(3, 5), (6, 10), (9, 15)\}$

12. $\{(2, -3), (3, -4), (4, -2)\}$

13. $\{(5, 2), (4, 3), (3, 4), (2, 5)\}$

14. $\{(-1, -6), (0, 2), (1, 2), (3, 6)\}$

15. $\{(-3, -6), (-1, 2), (1, 2), (3, 6)\}$

16. $\{(2, 1), (4, 2), (2, 3), (8, 4)\}$

17. $\{(1, 2), (3, 4), (-3, 4), (-1, 2)\}$

18. $\{(9, -2), (4, -1), (1, 0), (3, 1), (7, 2)\}$

Find the inverse of each function. State whether the inverse is a function.

19. $\{(-1, 0), (-2, 1), (4, 3), (3, 4)\}$

20. $\{(1, 4), (2, 3), (3, 2), (4, 1)\}$

21. $\{(1, 2), (2, 3), (3, 2), (4, 1)\}$

22. $\{(3, -2), (2, -3), (1, -2), (0, -1)\}$

23. $\{(5, 2), (4, 3), (3, 5), (2, 3)\}$

24. $\{(3, 0), (2, -1), (1, 2), (0, 1), (-1, 2)\}$

25. $\{(0, 2), (2, 3), (3, 4), (1, 1)\}$

26. $\{(-1, 2), (-2, 3), (-3, 4), (0, 0)\}$

Determine whether the inverse of each function graphed is also a function.

27.

28.

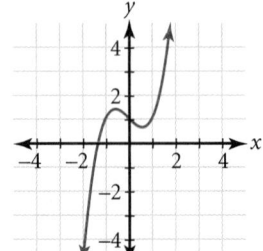

For each function, find an equation for the inverse. Then use composition to verify that the equation you wrote is the inverse.

29. $f(x) = 5x + 1$

30. $g(x) = -2x - 7$

31. $h(x) = -\frac{1}{2}x + 3$

32. $g(x) = \frac{x - 1}{4}$

33. $h(x) = \frac{x + 8}{3}$

34. $f(x) = \frac{x - 3}{2}$

35. $f(x) = \frac{2x - 3}{4}$

36. $f(x) = \frac{1}{3}x - 1$

37. $g(x) = 2x - \frac{3x}{4}$

38. $h(x) = \frac{1}{4}(x - 1)$

39. $g(x) = \frac{1}{2}(x + 2) - 3$

40. $h(x) = \frac{3}{2}(x - 3) + 2$

Graph each function, and use the horizontal-line test to determine whether the inverse is a function.

41 $f(x) = 1 - x^2$

42 $h(x) = -\frac{1}{3}x + 5$

43 $g(x) = \frac{7 - 2x}{5}$

44 $f(x) = 2x^3$

45 $g(x) = 3$

46 $h(x) = \frac{3}{x}$

47 $g(x) = x^4$

48 $f(x) = x^2 - 2x$

49 $f(x) = x^5$

CHALLENGE

50. If a relation is not a function, can its inverse be a function? Explain and give examples.

APPLICATIONS

51. CONSUMER ECONOMICS New carpeting can be purchased and installed for $17.50 per square yard plus a $50 delivery fee.
  a. Write an equation that gives the cost, *c*, of carpeting *s* square yards of a house.
  b. Find the inverse of the cost function.
  c. How many square yards can be carpeted for $1485?

52. REAL ESTATE New house prices depend on the cost of the property, or lot, and the size of the house. Suppose that a lot costs $60,000 and a builder charges $84 per square foot of living area in a house.
  a. Write the function *p* that represents the price of a house with *x* square feet of living area.
  b. Find the inverse of the price function, and discuss what it represents.
  c. How big, to the nearest square foot, is a house that can be purchased for $180,000?

53. PUZZLES In a number puzzle, you are told to add 4 to your age, then multiply by 2, subtract 6, and finally divide by 2. You give the result, and you are immediately told your age. Use an inverse function to explain how the puzzle works.

 Look Back

APPLICATION

54. BUSINESS The total revenue, *R*, is directly proportional to the number of cameras, *x*, sold. When 500 cameras are sold, the revenue is $3800. *(LESSON 1.4)*
  a. Find the revenue when 600 cameras are sold.
  a. What is the constant of variation?
  c. In this situation, what does the constant of variation represent?

Evaluate each expression. *(LESSON 2.2)*

55. $2^3 \cdot 2^5$ **56.** $25^{-\frac{1}{2}}$ **57.** $(3^2)^3$

Let $f(x) = 3x - 2$ **and** $g(x) = 5x + 2$. *(LESSON 2.4)*

58. Find $f + g$.   **59.** Find $f \cdot g$.
60. Evaluate $(f + g)(-1)$.   **61.** Evaluate $(f \cdot g)(-3)$.

Look Beyond

62 Graph $f(x) = 2^x$. Why would you expect this function to have an inverse that is a function? Graph the inverse and state its domain.

Special Functions

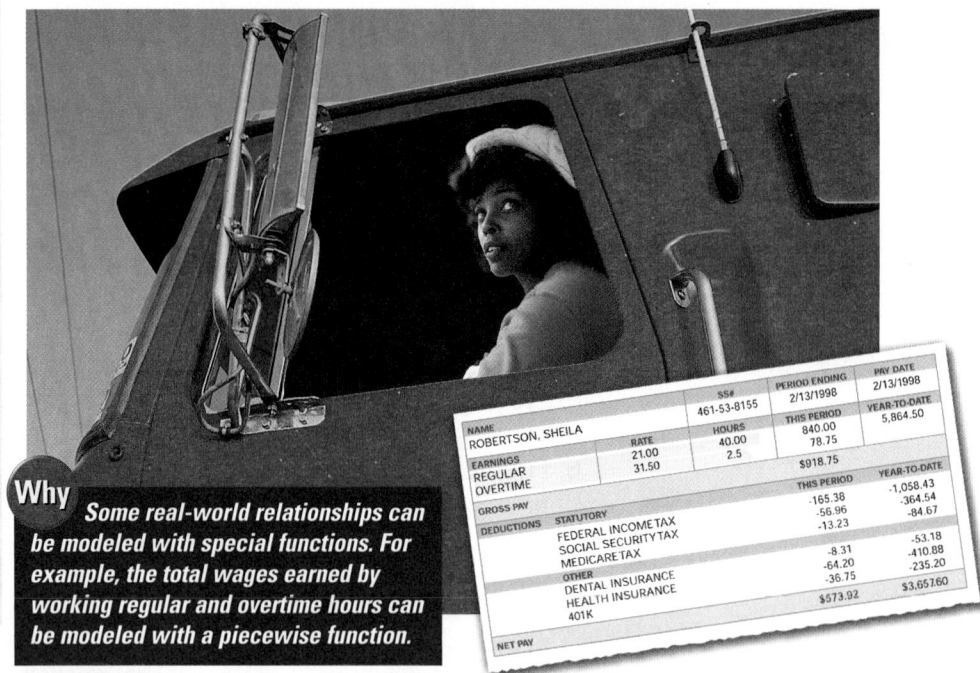

Objective

- Write, graph, and apply special functions: piecewise, step, and absolute value.

Why *Some real-world relationships can be modeled with special functions. For example, the total wages earned by working regular and overtime hours can be modeled with a piecewise function.*

Piecewise Functions

APPLICATION

INCOME

A truck driver earns $21.00 per hour for the first 40 hours worked in one week. The driver earns time-and-a-half, or $31.50, for each hour worked in excess of 40. The pair of function rules below represent the driver's wage, $w(h)$, as a function of the hours worked in one week, h.

$$w(h) = \begin{cases} 21h & \text{if } 0 < h \le 40 \\ 31.5h - 420 & \text{if } h > 40 \end{cases}$$

This function is an example of a *piecewise function*. A **piecewise function** consists of different function rules for different parts of the domain.

CRITICAL THINKING

Where does the number -420 in the piecewise function w come from?

Exploring Piecewise Functions

You will need: graph paper

1. Copy and complete the table below, using the function for the truck driver's wages given above.

Hours worked, h	10.0	30.0	35.0	40.0	52.5
Wage, $w(h)$					

2. Extend your table by choosing other values of h in the interval $0 < h \le 60$.

3. Plot the ordered pairs from your table and make a scatter plot.

CHECKPOINT ✔ 4. If you connect the consecutive points in the scatter plot, what observations can you make about the graph?

Example 1 shows you how to use the appropriate function rule for each domain of a piecewise function when graphing it.

EXAMPLE ① Graph: $f(x) = \begin{cases} 2x & \text{if } 0 \le x < 2 \\ 4 & \text{if } 2 < x < 4 \\ -\frac{1}{4}x + 5 & \text{if } 4 \le x \le 6 \end{cases}$

● **SOLUTION**

1. Graph $y = 2x$ for $0 \le x < 2$.
$0 = 2(0)$ and $4 = 2(2)$
Connect $(0, 0)$ and $(2, 4)$. Use an open circle at $(2, 4)$.

2. Graph $y = 4$ for $2 < x < 4$.
Connect $(2, 4)$ and $(4, 4)$. Use an open circle at $(2, 4)$.

3. Graph $y = -\frac{1}{4}x + 5$ for $4 \le x \le 6$.
$4 = -\frac{1}{4}(4) + 5$ and $3\frac{1}{2} = -\frac{1}{4}(6) + 5$

Notice that an open circle is graphed at (2, 4) because 2 is not included in the domain.

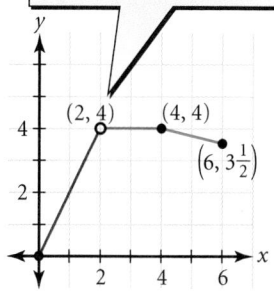

Connect $(4, 4)$ and $\left(6, 3\frac{1}{2}\right)$.

TRY THIS Graph: $f(x) = \begin{cases} -2x + 3 & \text{if } 0 \le x < 5 \\ -3x + 8 & \text{if } 5 \le x \le 10 \end{cases}$

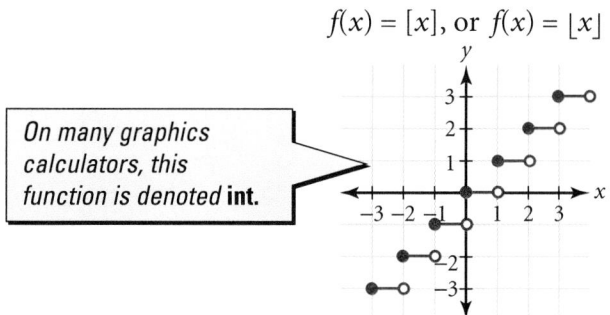

Step Functions

The graph of a linear function with a slope of 0 is a horizontal line. This type of function is called a **constant function** because every function value is the same number.

A **step function** is a piecewise function that consists of different constant range values for different intervals of the domain of the function. The two basic step functions are shown below.

Greatest-integer function, or rounding-down function

$f(x) = [x]$, or $f(x) = \lfloor x \rfloor$

On many graphics calculators, this function is denoted **int.**

x	-3	-1.5	0	2.8
$f(x) = [x]$	-3	-2	0	2

Rounding-up function

$f(x) = \lceil x \rceil$

x	-3	-1.5	0	2.8
$f(x) = \lceil x \rceil$	-3	-1	0	3

The domain of both $f(x) = [x]$ and $f(x) = \lceil x \rceil$ is the set of all real numbers, and the range of both functions is the set of all integers.

CHECKPOINT ✔ Evaluate $[5]$, $[3.2]$, and $[-4.4]$. Evaluate $\lceil 5 \rceil$, $\lceil 3.2 \rceil$, and $\lceil -4.4 \rceil$.

Example 2 shows how first-class postage can be modeled with a rounding-up function.

E X A M P L E ② The cost of mailing a first-class letter (up to 11 ounces inclusive) in 1998 is given by the function $p(w) = 32 + 23\lceil w - 1 \rceil$, where w represents the weight in ounces and p represents the postage in cents.

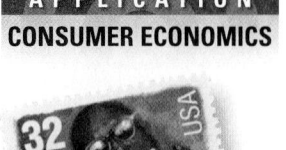

APPLICATION
CONSUMER ECONOMICS

Find the cost of mailing a first-class letter given each weight.
 a. 2.2 ounces **b.** 4.8 ounces

● **SOLUTION**

a. $p(2.2) = 32 + 23\lceil 2.2 - 1 \rceil$

$= 32 + 23\lceil 1.2 \rceil$

$= 32 + 23(2)$

$= 78$

The cost is \$0.78.

b. $p(4.8) = 32 + 23\lceil 4.8 - 1 \rceil$

$= 32 + 23\lceil 3.8 \rceil$

$= 32 + 23(4)$

$= 124$

The cost is \$1.24.

TRY THIS Find the cost of mailing an 0.8-ounce and a 2.9-ounce first-class letter.

Example 3 shows you how to graph a variation, or transformation, of a basic step function.

E X A M P L E ③ **Graph $g(x) = 2\lceil x \rceil$.**

● **SOLUTION**

PROBLEM SOLVING

CONNECTION
TRANSFORMATIONS

Make a table to compare values of $f(x) = \lceil x \rceil$ with values of $g(x)$.

Interval of x	$f(x) = \lceil x \rceil$	$g(x) = 2\lceil x \rceil$
$-4 < x \le -3$	-3	-6
$-3 < x \le -2$	-2	-4
$-2 < x \le -1$	-1	-2
$-1 < x \le 0$	0	0
$0 < x \le 1$	1	2
$1 < x \le 2$	2	4
$2 < x \le 3$	3	6

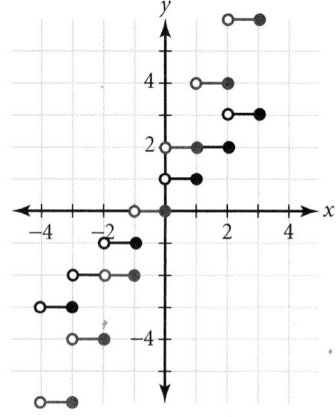

TRY THIS Graph $g(x) = \lceil x \rceil - 1$.

CRITICAL THINKING Let $f(x) = [x]$ and $g(x) = \lceil x \rceil$. Compare and contrast $f - g$ with $g - f$.

Absolute-Value Functions

The **absolute-value function**, denoted by $f(x) = |x|$, can be defined as a piecewise function as follows:

$$f(x) = \begin{cases} |x| = x & \text{if } x \geq 0 \\ |x| = -x & \text{if } x < 0 \end{cases}$$

The graph of the absolute-value function has a characteristic **V**-shape, as shown. The domain of $f(x) = |x|$ is the set of all real numbers, and the range is the set of all nonnegative real numbers.

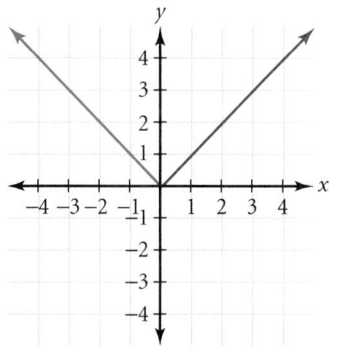

Example 4 involves a transformation of the absolute-value function.

E X A M P L E **4** Graph $g(x) = 3|x| - 1$ by making a table of values. Then graph the inverse of g on the same coordinate plane.

PROBLEM SOLVING

CONNECTION
TRANSFORMATIONS

SOLUTION

Make a table of values to compare values of g with values of $f(x) = |x|$.

x	$f(x) = |x|$	$g(x) = 3|x| - 1$
-2	2	$3|-2| - 1 = 5$
-1	1	$3|-1| - 1 = 2$
0	0	$3|0| - 1 = -1$
1	1	$3|1| - 1 = 2$
2	2	$3|2| - 1 = 5$

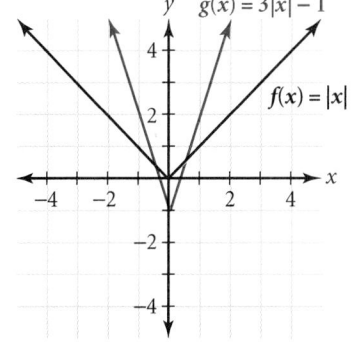

To graph the inverse of g, interchange the values of x and $g(x)$ given in the table above.

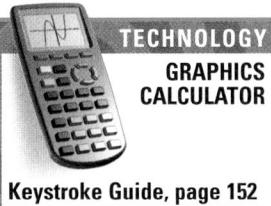

TECHNOLOGY
GRAPHICS CALCULATOR

Keystroke Guide, page 152

x	Inverse of g
5	-2
2	-1
-1	0
2	1
5	2

CHECK

TRY THIS Graph $f(x) = \frac{1}{2}|x| + 1$ by making a table of values. Then graph the inverse of f on the same coordinate plane.

When a measurement is performed on an object, the measured value and the true value may be slightly different. This difference may be due to factors such as the quality of the measuring device or the skill of the individual using the measuring device.

The *relative error* in a measurement of an object gives the amount of error in the measurement relative to the *true measure* of the object. If an object's true measure is x_t units, then the **relative error**, r, in the measurement, x, is given by $r(x) = \left| \frac{x_t - x}{x_t} \right|$.

E X A M P L E ⑤ A certain machine part's true length is 25.50 centimeters. Its length is measured as 25.55 centimeters.

Find the relative error in the measurement.

● **SOLUTION**

$$r(x) = \left| \frac{x_t - x}{x_t} \right|$$

$$r(25.55) = \left| \frac{25.50 - 25.55}{25.50} \right|$$

$$= \left| \frac{-0.05}{25.50} \right|$$

$$\approx 0.002$$

The relative error in the measurement, 25.55 centimeters, is about 0.002, or 0.2%.

TRY THIS   The true length of a second machine part is 40.00 centimeters. Its length is measured as 40.05 centimeters. Find the relative error in this measurement.

Exercises

● *Communicate*

1. Describe the defining characteristics of piecewise functions.

2. Explain why $[1.5] = 1$ but $[-1.5] \neq -1$.

3. Compare and contrast the greatest-integer and rounding-up functions.

4. Is the inverse of $y = |x|$ a function? Explain.

● *Guided Skills Practice*

Graph each piecewise function. *(EXAMPLE 1)*

5. $f(x) = \begin{cases} 3x + 5 & \text{if } -1 \leq x < 2 \\ -x + 9 & \text{if } 2 \leq x < 5 \end{cases}$ **6.** $g(x) = \begin{cases} x + 3 & \text{if } -3 \leq x < 3 \\ 2x & \text{if } x \geq 3 \end{cases}$

CONSUMER ECONOMICS Darren and Joel called their grandmother during winter break. In 1998, this daytime call from Austin, Texas, to Denver, Colorado, was charged at a rate of $0.14 per minute or fraction of a minute. The cost of this phone call can be modeled by $c(x) = 0.14\lceil x \rceil$, where c is the cost in dollars and x is the length of the call in minutes. Find the cost for each call. *(EXAMPLE 2)*

7. 21.25 minutes   **8.** 10 minutes
9. 33.5 minutes   **10.** 0.1 minutes

Graph each step function by making a table of values. *(EXAMPLE 3)*

11. $f(x) = 3\lceil x \rceil$ **12.** $g(x) = -4\lfloor x \rfloor$

Graph each absolute-value function by making a table of values. Then graph the inverse on the same coordinate plane. *(EXAMPLE 4)*

13. $f(x) = |x| + 2$ **14.** $g(x) = 2|x| - 1$

15. MANUFACTURING A certain machine part's true length is 16.000 centimeters. Its length is measured as 16.035 centimeters. Find the relative error in this measurement. *(EXAMPLE 5)*

Practice and Apply

Graph each piecewise function.

16. $f(x) = \begin{cases} x + 1 & \text{if } 0 \le x < 5 \\ 2x - 4 & \text{if } 5 \le x < 10 \end{cases}$ **17.** $g(x) = \begin{cases} 3x - 4 & \text{if } 0 \le x < 6 \\ 20 - x & \text{if } 6 \le x < 12 \end{cases}$

18. $m(x) = \begin{cases} 20 & \text{if } 0 \le x < 10 \\ \frac{x}{2} + 15 & \text{if } 10 \le x < 20 \end{cases}$ **19.** $f(x) = \begin{cases} 4x & \text{if } 0 \le x < 2 \\ -2x + 10 & \text{if } 2 \le x < 5 \\ 2 & \text{if } 5 \le x < 10 \end{cases}$

20. $h(x) = \begin{cases} -2 & \text{if } x < 0 \\ x + 1 & \text{if } 0 \le x \le 10 \\ -\frac{1}{2}x + 16 & \text{if } x > 10 \end{cases}$ **21.** $b(x) = \begin{cases} 2 & \text{if } x < 1 \\ 2x & \text{if } 1 \le x \le 3 \\ 7 - \frac{1}{3}x & \text{if } x > 3 \end{cases}$

22. $k(x) = \begin{cases} 2x + 3 & \text{if } x < 4 \\ x - 1 & \text{if } 4 \le x \le 9 \end{cases}$ **23.** $f(x) = \begin{cases} 5 - x & \text{if } x < 2 \\ x - 1 & \text{if } 2 \le x \le 10 \end{cases}$

Write the piecewise function represented by each graph.

24.

25.

26.

27.

internet connect

Homework Help Online

Go To: **go.hrw.com**
Keyword:
MB1 Homework Help
for Exercises 28–51

Evaluate.

28. $[3.9]$

29. $[-6.105]$

30. $\lceil 3.9 \rceil$

31. $\lceil -6.105 \rceil$

32. $[-4.1] - [-3.25]$

33. $[5.1] + [-2.01]$

34. $\lceil -4.1 \rceil - \lceil -3.25 \rceil$

35. $\lceil 5.1 \rceil + \lceil -2.01 \rceil$

36. $[-2.5] + [1.999]$

37. $[-2.99] + [2.99]$

38. $[-5.1] - [5.1]$

39. $\lceil -2.5 \rceil - \lceil 1.999 \rceil$

40. $[-2.3] - \lceil 5.6 \rceil$

41. $-\lceil 0.9 \rceil + [-8.7]$

42. $[6.2] - \lceil -4.7 \rceil$

43. $\lceil -8.99 \rceil - [-5.1]$

44. $-[0.25] - \lceil 0.25 \rceil$

45. $\lceil 2.75 \rceil - [2.75]$

46. $|4| - |-5|$

47. $|-7| - |2.2|$

48. $|3| + |-4|$

49. $-|-1| - |1|$

50. $|-1| - |3|$

51. $|6| - |-2.67|$

Graph each function.

52. $f(x) = 2\lceil x \rceil$

53. $f(x) = 3\lceil x \rceil$

54. $g(x) = [x] + 3$

55. $g(x) = [x] - 3$

56. $g(x) = 2 - \lceil x \rceil$

57. $h(x) = 4 + \lceil x \rceil$

Graph each function and its inverse together on a coordinate plane.

58. $f(x) = 4|x| - 1$

59. $g(x) = \frac{1}{2}|x|$

60. $h(x) = 5|x| + 10$

Determine whether each statement is true or false. Explain.

61. $|x + y| = |x| + |y|$

62. $|x - y| = |x| - |y|$

63. $|xy| = |x| \cdot |y|$

64. $\left|\frac{x}{y}\right| = \frac{|x|}{|y|}$

65 Let $S(x) = \left| x - [x] - \frac{1}{2} \right|$ for $x \geq 0$. Graph S for $x \geq 0$. Describe the shape of the graph of S.

CHALLENGES

66. Compare and contrast $y = |[x]|$ with $y = [|x|]$. Include a discussion of the graphs of these functions.

67. Write a function f that rounds x up to the nearest tenth. Write another function g that rounds x down to the nearest hundredth.

CONNECTION

68. TRANSFORMATIONS The absolute-value function can be used to reflect a portion of the graph of g across the x-axis by using composition. Given $f(x) = |x|$ and $g(x) = x^2 - 2$, find and graph $f \circ g$. Compare the graphs of g and $f \circ g$.

APPLICATION

MANUFACTURING Find the relative error for each measurement of a machine part whose true length is 6.000 centimeters.

69. 6.035 centimeters

70. 6.025 centimeters

71. 6.150 centimeters

72. 6.300 centimeters

73. CONSUMER ECONOMICS A gourmet coffee store sells the house blend of coffee beans at $9.89 per pound for quantities up to and including 5 pounds. For each additional pound, the price is $7.98 per pound.

   a. Construct a table to represent the cost for the domain $0 < x \le 10$, where x is the number of pounds of coffee beans purchased.

   b. Graph the data in your table.

   c. Write a function that relates the cost and the number of pounds of coffee beans purchased.

   d. Determine the cost for 5.5 pounds of coffee beans.

74. INCOME An air-conditioning salesperson receives a base salary of $2850 per month plus a commission. The commission is 2% of the sales up to and including $25,000 for the month and 5% of the sales over $25,000 for the month.

   a. Construct a table to represent the salesperson's total monthly income for the domain $0 < s \le 50,000$, where s is the sales for the month.

   b. Graph the data in your table.

   c. Write a function that relates the salesperson's total monthly income with his or her sales for the month.

   d. Determine the salesperson's total monthly income if his or her sales were $43,000 for the month.

75. CONSUMER ECONOMICS The Break-n-Fix Repair Store charges $45 for a service call that involves up to and including one hour of labor. For each additional half-hour of labor or fraction thereof, the store charges $20.

   a. Construct a table to represent the charges for the domain $0 < t \le 5$, where t is the labor measured in hours.

   b. Graph the data in your table.

   c. Write a function that relates the cost and the amount of labor involved in the service call.

   d. Determine the cost of a service call that takes 3.75 hours.

76. CONSUMER ECONOMICS Residential water charges, c, are based on the monthly consumption of water, x, in thousands of gallons. Graph the piecewise function given below, which represents the rate schedule for monthly charges.

$$c(x) = \begin{cases} 1.25x + 4.50 & \text{if } 0 < x \le 3 \\ 2x + 2.25 & \text{if } 3 < x \le 7 \\ 2.60x - 7.25 & \text{if } 7 < x \le 15 \\ 3.80x - 22.75 & \text{if } x > 15 \end{cases}$$

APPLICATION

77. CONSUMER ECONOMICS A valet parking lot charges a fixed fee of $2.00 to park a car plus $1.50 per hour for covered parking. *(LESSON 2.3)*
  a. Write a linear function, c, to model the valet parking charge for h hours of covered parking.
  b. If a car is parked in covered parking for 3.5 hours, what is the charge?

Let $f(x) = x + 2$ and $g(x) = 3x$. Perform each function operation. State any domain restrictions. *(LESSON 2.4)*

78. Find $f \circ g$.

79. Find $g \circ f$.

80. Find $f \circ f$.

81. Find $g \circ g$.

82. Find $f - g$.

83. Find $f + g$.

84. Find $f \cdot g$.

85. Find $\dfrac{f}{g}$.

Find an equation for the inverse of each function. Then use composition to verify that the equation you wrote is the inverse. *(LESSON 2.5)*

86. $f(x) = 3x - \dfrac{1}{2}$

87. $a(x) = \dfrac{3}{4}(x - 2)$

88. $h(x) = -2(x - 4) + 1$

89. $g(x) = -x + 8$

Portfolio Extension
Go To: **go.hrw.com**
Keyword:
MB1 Piecewise

 Look Beyond

90 **TRANSFORMATIONS** Graph $f(x) = \dfrac{|x|}{x}$, $g(x) = \dfrac{2|x|}{x}$, and $h(x) = \dfrac{-2|x|}{x}$. State the domain and range for each function.

SPACE SCIENCE In future years, space technology is expected to improve to a point where many of the components presently left orbiting in space can be returned to Earth. This will greatly reduce the current rate of space debris accumulation.

1. Your Space Debris Table specified an initial 7000 objects and an annual rate of increase of 3%. Now assume that the projected annual increase becomes a constant 200 objects each year, beginning in 2001. Write and graph a piecewise function that models the total number of debris objects at the end of t years.

2. Determine the total number of debris objects in 2005 by using the function you wrote in Step 1.

3. Using your piecewise function from Step 1, calculate how many years it would take for the number of debris objects to be double the number found at the end of 1993. (Refer to the table that you created in the Portfolio Activity on page 93.) Compare this with the number of years it would take to double without the change in Step 1. (Refer to the Portfolio Activity on page 110.)

4. Using the piecewise function you wrote in Step 1, model the number of debris objects in space in 2010. Compare this with the number for the same year in the table that you created in the Portfolio Activity on page 93.

A Preview of Transformations

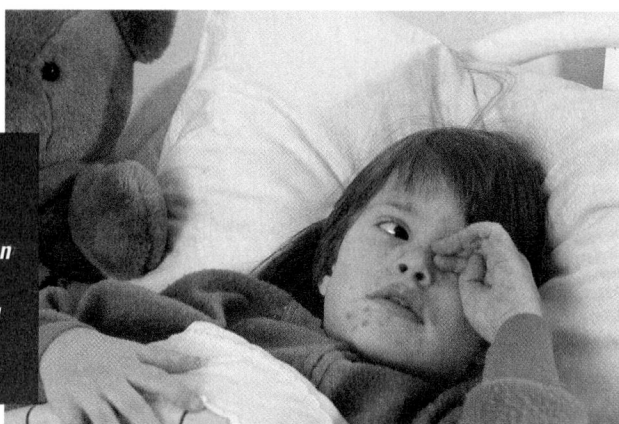

Why *Many real-world situations are represented by using transformations. For example, translations are often used to graph data involving trends such as the decreasing number of reported cases of chickenpox over time.*

Objective

• Identify the transformation(s) from one function to another.

APPLICATION
HEALTH

The table of data below gives the number of reported cases of chickenpox in the United States in thousands from 1989 to 1994. In Lesson 1.5, this data was used to create a scatter plot by *translating* the x-values from the actual year to the number of years after 1988. Columns 2 and 3 in the table below show two other possible translations.

Year	Number of years after 1960	Number of years after 1970	Cases reported (in thousands)
1989	29	19	185.4
1990	30	20	173.1
1991	31	21	147.1
1992	32	22	158.4
1993	33	23	134.7
1994	34	24	151.2

[*Source: U.S. Centers for Disease Control and Prevention*]

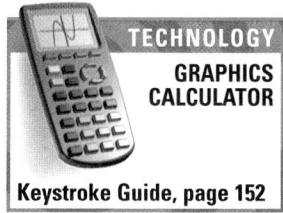

TECHNOLOGY
GRAPHICS CALCULATOR

Keystroke Guide, page 152

Exploring Translations of Data

You will need: a graphics calculator

1. Enter the data from columns 2 and 4 into your graphics calculator. Make a scatter plot. Then use linear regression to find an equation for the least-squares line.

2. Enter the data from columns 3 and 4 into your graphics calculator. Make a scatter plot. Then find an equation for the least-squares line.

CHECKPOINT ✔ 3. How are the equations for the least-squares lines different? How are the graphs of the least-squares lines similar?

Just as you translate data, you can translate a function. A translation is one type of *transformation*. A **transformation** of a function is an alteration of the function rule that results in an alteration of its graph.

Translation

Example 1 illustrates a *vertical translation* and a *horizontal translation*.

E X A M P L E **1** **Graph each pair of functions, and identify the transformation from f to g.**
   a. $f(x) = x^2$ and $g(x) = x^2 + 3$ **b.** $f(x) = |x|$ and $g(x) = |x + 4|$

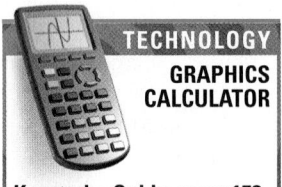

TECHNOLOGY

GRAPHICS CALCULATOR

Keystroke Guide, page 153

● **SOLUTION**

a.

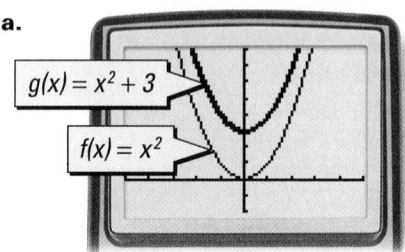

$g(x) = x^2 + 3$

$f(x) = x^2$

Notice that $g(x) = f(x) + 3$. The function $g(x) = x^2 + 3$ is a vertical translation of the graph of f 3 units up.

b.

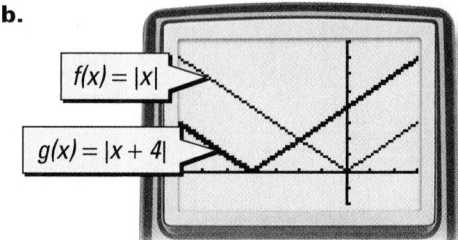

$f(x) = |x|$

$g(x) = |x + 4|$

Notice that $g(x) = f(x + 4)$. The function $g(x) = |x + 4|$ is a horizontal translation of the graph of f 4 units to the left.

TRY THIS Graph each pair of functions, and identify the transformation from f to g.
   a. $f(x) = x^2$ and $g(x) = x^2 - 2$ **b.** $f(x) = |x|$ and $g(x) = |x - 3|$

Notice that the shape of the transformed graphs in Example 1 do not change. Only the position of the graphs with respect to the coordinate axes changes.

Vertical and horizontal translations are generalized as follows:

Vertical and Horizontal Translations

If $y = f(x)$, then $y = f(x) + k$ gives a **vertical translation** of the graph of f. The translation is k units up for $k > 0$ and $|k|$ units down for $k < 0$.

If $y = f(x)$, then $y = f(x - h)$ gives a **horizontal translation** of the graph of f. The translation is h units to the right for $h > 0$ and $|h|$ units to the left for $h < 0$.

Vertical Translation

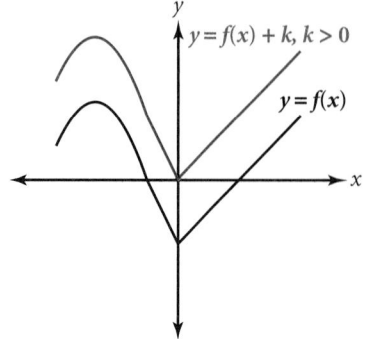

$y = f(x) + k, k > 0$

$y = f(x)$

Horizontal Translation

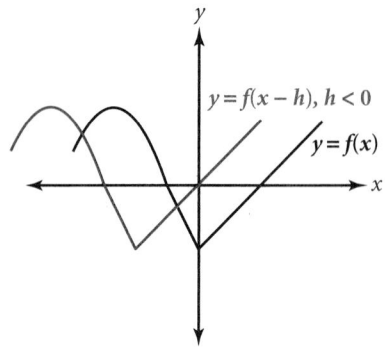

$y = f(x - h), h < 0$

$y = f(x)$

CHECKPOINT ✔ How does writing the function $j(x) = |x + 4|$ as $j(x) = |x - (-4)|$ help you to recognize that the translation is to the left?

Vertical Stretch and Compression

Example 2 illustrates a *vertical stretch* and a *vertical compression*.

EXAMPLE ❷ Graph each pair of functions, and identify the transformation from *f* to *g*.

a. $f(x) = \sqrt{16 - x^2}$ and
$g(x) = 2\sqrt{16 - x^2}$

b. $f(x) = \sqrt{16 - x^2}$ and
$g(x) = \frac{1}{2}\sqrt{16 - x^2}$

● **SOLUTION**

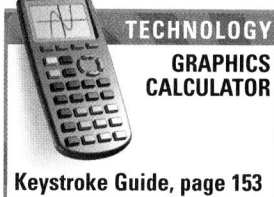
TECHNOLOGY
GRAPHICS CALCULATOR

Keystroke Guide, page 153

a.

$g(x) = 2\sqrt{16 - x^2}$

$f(x) = \sqrt{16 - x^2}$

b.

$f(x) = \sqrt{16 - x^2}$

$g(x) = \frac{1}{2}\sqrt{16 - x^2}$

Notice that $g(x) = 2 \cdot f(x)$.
The function $g(x) = 2\sqrt{16 - x^2}$ is a vertical stretch of the graph of *f* by a factor of 2.

Notice that $g(x) = \frac{1}{2} \cdot f(x)$.
The function $g(x) = \frac{1}{2}\sqrt{16 - x^2}$ is a vertical compression of the graph of *f* by a by a factor of $\frac{1}{2}$.

TRY THIS   Graph each pair of functions, and identify the transformation from *f* to *g*.

a. $f(x) = \sqrt{25 - x^2}$ and $g(x) = 3\sqrt{25 - x^2}$

b. $f(x) = \sqrt{25 - x^2}$ and $g(x) = \frac{1}{3}\sqrt{25 - x^2}$

A vertical stretch or compression moves the graph away from or toward the *x*-axis, respectively. It can be generalized as follows:

Vertical Stretch and Vertical Compression

If $y = f(x)$, then $y = af(x)$ gives a **vertical stretch** or **vertical compression** of the graph of *f*.

- If $a > 1$, the graph is stretched vertically by a factor of *a*.
- If $0 < a < 1$, the graph is compressed vertically by a factor of *a*.

Vertical Stretch

$y = af(x), a > 1$

$y = f(x)$

Vertical Compression

$y = f(x)$

$y = af(x), 0 < a < 1$

CRITICAL THINKING   Let $0 < r < 1$ and $s > 1$. Compare the graphs of $f(x) = r|x|$ and $g(x) = s|x|$.

Horizontal Stretch and Compression

Example 3 illustrates a *horizontal stretch* and a *horizontal compression*.

EXAMPLE ③ Graph each pair of functions, and identify the transformation from *f* to *g*.

a. $f(x) = \sqrt{16 - x^2}$ and $g(x) = \sqrt{16 - (2x)^2}$

b. $f(x) = \sqrt{16 - x^2}$ and $g(x) = \sqrt{16 - \left(\frac{1}{2}x\right)^2}$

● **SOLUTION**

a.

$g(x) = \sqrt{16 - (2x)^2}$

$f(x) = \sqrt{16 - x^2}$

b.

$g(x) = \sqrt{16 - \left(\frac{1}{2}x\right)^2}$

$f(x) = \sqrt{16 - x^2}$

Notice that $g(x) = f(2x)$. The function $g(x) = \sqrt{16 - (2x)^2}$ is a horizontal compression of the graph of *f* by a factor of $\frac{1}{2}$.

Notice that $g(x) = f\left(\frac{1}{2}x\right)$. The function $g(x) = \sqrt{16 - \left(\frac{1}{2}x\right)^2}$ is a horizontal stretch of the graph of *f* by a factor of 2.

TRY THIS Graph each pair of functions, and identify the transformation from *f* to *g*.

a. $f(x) = \sqrt{25 - x^2}$ and $g(x) = \sqrt{25 - (3x)^2}$

b. $f(x) = \sqrt{25 - x^2}$ and $g(x) = \sqrt{25 - \left(\frac{1}{4}x\right)^2}$

A horizontal stretch or compression moves the graph away from or toward the *y*-axis, respectively. It can be generalized as follows:

Horizontal Stretch and Horizontal Compression

If $y = f(x)$, then $y = f(bx)$ gives a **horizontal stretch** or **horizontal compression** of the graph of *f*.

- If $b > 1$, the graph is compressed horizontally by a factor of $\frac{1}{b}$.
- If $0 < b < 1$, the graph is stretched horizontally by a factor of $\frac{1}{b}$.

Horizontal Stretch

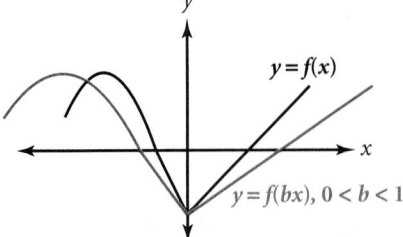

$y = f(x)$

$y = f(bx),\ 0 < b < 1$

Horizontal Compression

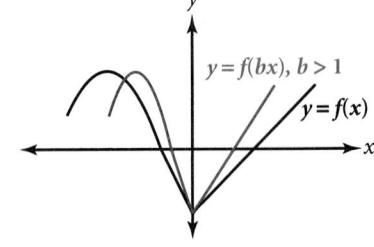

$y = f(bx),\ b > 1$

$y = f(x)$

Reflection

Example 4 illustrates reflections across the *x*-axis and across the *y*-axis.

E X A M P L E **4** **Graph each pair of functions, and identify the transformation from *f* to *g*.**

    a. $f(x) = x^2$ and $g(x) = -(x^2)$ **b.** $f(x) = 2x + 3$ and $g(x) = 2(-x) + 3$

● **SOLUTION**

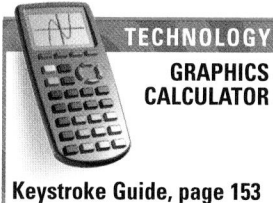

TECHNOLOGY

GRAPHICS CALCULATOR

Keystroke Guide, page 153

a.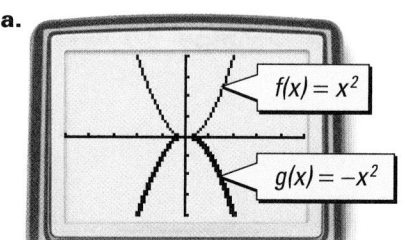

Notice that $g(x) = -f(x)$. The function $g(x) = -(x^2)$ is a reflection of the graph of *f* across the *x*-axis.

b.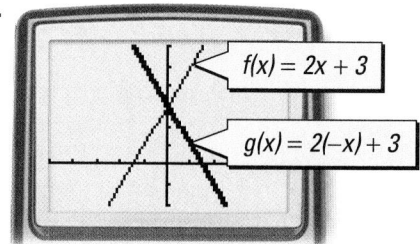

Notice that $g(x) = f(-x)$. The function $g(x) = 2(-x) + 3$, or $g(x) = -2x + 3$, is a reflection of the graph of *f* across the *y*-axis.

TRY THIS   Graph each pair of functions, and identify the transformation from *f* to *g*.

    a. $f(x) = |x|$ and $g(x) = -|x|$ **b.** $f(x) = 2x - 1$ and $g(x) = 2(-x) - 1$

CRITICAL THINKING   Can the graph of a function be reflected across both the *x*- and *y*-axes simultaneously? Explain and give an example.

Reflections can be generalized as follows:

Reflections

If $y = f(x)$, then $y = -f(x)$ gives a **reflection** of the graph of *f* across the *x*-axis.

If $y = f(x)$, then $y = f(-x)$ gives a **reflection** of the graph of *f* across the *y*-axis.

Reflection Across the *x*-axis

Reflection Across the *y*-axis

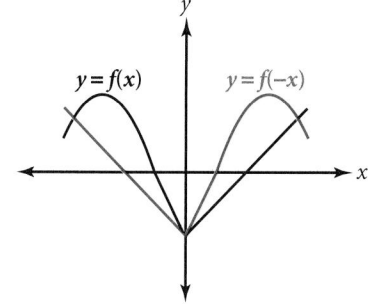

CRITICAL THINKING   Let $f(x) = x^2$. What does $f(-x) = (-x)^2 = x^2$ tell you about the graph of $f(-x)$? Justify your response.

Combining Transformations

The functions $f(x) = x^2$ and $h(x) = |x|$ are examples of *parent functions* because other functions are related to them by one or more transformations. Example 5 illustrates a combination of transformations.

EXAMPLE ⑤ Graph each pair of functions, and identify the transformations from f to g.

　a. $f(x) = x^2$ and $g(x) = (x + 2)^2 - 1$　　**b.** $f(x) = |x|$ and $g(x) = -4|x| + 3$

● **SOLUTION**

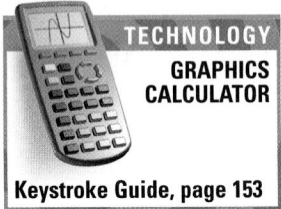

TECHNOLOGY
GRAPHICS CALCULATOR

Keystroke Guide, page 153

a.

$f(x) = x^2$

$g(x) = (x + 2)^2 - 1$

Notice that $g(x) = f(x + 2) - 1$, or $g(x) = f(x - (-2)) - 1$.
There are two transformations of the parent function $f(x) = x^2$: a translation of 2 units to the left and a translation of 1 unit down.

$$g(x) = [x - (-2)]^2 - 1$$

horizontal　　　　vertical
translation　　　　translation

b.

$f(x) = |x|$

$g(x) = -4|x| + 3$

Notice that $g(x) = -4 \cdot f(x) + 3$.
There are three transformations of the parent function $f(x) = |x|$: a vertical stretch by a factor of 4, a reflection across the x-axis, and a vertical translation of 3 units up.

reflection

$$g(x) = -4|x| + 3$$

vertical　　　vertical
stretch　　　translation

TRY THIS　Graph each pair of functions, and identify the transformations from f to g.

　a. $f(x) = x^2$ and $g(x) = 3(x - 1)^2$　　**b.** $f(x) = |x|$ and $g(x) = \frac{1}{2}|x| - 2$

A summary of the transformations in this lesson is given below.

SUMMARY OF TRANSFORMATIONS	
Transformations of $y = f(x)$	**Transformed function**
Vertical translation of k units up	$y = f(x) + k$, where $k > 0$
Vertical translation of $|k|$ units down	$y = f(x) + k$, where $k < 0$
Horizontal translation of h units to the right	$y = f(x - h)$, where $h > 0$
Horizontal translation of $|h|$ units to the left	$y = f(x - h)$, where $h < 0$
Vertical stretch by a factor of a	$y = af(x)$, where $a > 1$
Vertical compression by a factor of a	$y = af(x)$, where $0 < a < 1$
Horizontal stretch by a factor of $\frac{1}{b}$	$y = f(bx)$, where $0 < b < 1$
Horizontal compression by a factor of $\frac{1}{b}$	$y = f(bx)$, where $b > 1$
Reflection across the x-axis	$y = -f(x)$
Reflection across the y-axis	$y = f(-x)$

● Communicate

1. Describe each transformation of $f(x) = x^2$.

a.

b.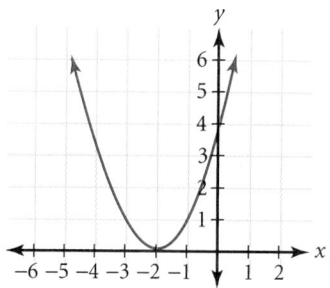

2. Describe the range of possible values of $\frac{1}{b}$ when $0 < b < 1$.

3. Compare and contrast reflections and translations.

4. For what values of h will the graph of $f(x - h)$ be translated to the right? to the left? Explain.

5. Differentiate between the effects of a vertical stretch and a horizontal stretch on the graph of a function.

● Guided Skills Practice

Identify the transformations from _f_ to _g_.

6. $f(x) = x^2$ and $g(x) = x^2 - 3$ *(EXAMPLE 1)*

7. $f(x) = \sqrt{9 - x^2}$ and $g(x) = \frac{4}{3}\sqrt{9 - x^2}$ *(EXAMPLE 2)*

8. $f(x) = \sqrt{36 - x^2}$ and $g(x) = \sqrt{36 - (2x)^2}$ *(EXAMPLE 3)*

9. $f(x) = -3x + 1$ and $g(x) = -3(-x) + 1$ *(EXAMPLE 4)*

10. $f(x) = x^2$ and $g(x) = (x - 3)^2 + 1$ *(EXAMPLE 5)*

● Practice and Apply

Identify each transformation from the parent function $f(x) = x^2$ to g.

11. $g(x) = 4x^2$

12. $g(x) = 5x^2$

13. $g(x) = (4x)^2$

14. $g(x) = (-5x)^2$

15. $g(x) = -\frac{1}{2}x^2$

16. $g(x) = -\frac{1}{5}x^2$

17. $g(x) = x^2 - 2$

18. $g(x) = x^2 + 3$

19. $g(x) = (x - 2)^2$

20. $g(x) = (x + 3)^2$

21. $g(x) = (-5x)^2 + 2$

22. $g(x) = 3(x - 1)^2$

23. $g(x) = \frac{1}{3}x^2 - 1$

24. $g(x) = -\frac{1}{4}x^2 + 3$

25. $g(x) = -2(x + 4)^2 + 1$

26. $g(x) = -5(x - 2)^2 - 4$

Identify each transformation from the parent function $f(x) = \sqrt{x}$ to g.

27. $g(x) = 4\sqrt{x}$ **28.** $g(x) = 3\sqrt{x}$ **29.** $g(x) = -\frac{1}{4}\sqrt{x}$

30. $g(x) = -\frac{1}{3}\sqrt{x}$ **31.** $g(x) = \sqrt{-4x}$ **32.** $g(x) = \sqrt{-3x}$

33. $g(x) = \sqrt{x} + 4$ **34.** $g(x) = \sqrt{x} - 3$ **35.** $g(x) = \sqrt{x+4}$

36. $g(x) = \sqrt{x-3}$ **37.** $g(x) = \sqrt{-2x} + 1$ **38.** $g(x) = -\sqrt{x+3}$

39. $g(x) = -\sqrt{x-4} + 3$ **40.** $g(x) = -\sqrt{3x} - 1$ **41.** $g(x) = -\sqrt{-x}$

internet connect

Homework Help Online

Go To: **go.hrw.com**
Keyword:
MB1 Homework Help
for Exercises 42–57

Write the function for each graph described below.

42. the graph of $f(x) = |x|$ translated 4 units to the left

43. the graph of $f(x) = x^2$ translated 2 units to the right

44. the graph of $f(x) = |x|$ translated 5 units up

45. the graph of $f(x) = x^2$ translated 6 units down

46. the graph of $f(x) = x^2$ vertically stretched by a factor of 3

47. the graph of $f(x) = \sqrt{x}$ vertically compressed by a factor of $\frac{1}{3}$

48. the graph of $f(x) = x^2$ horizontally compressed by a factor of $\frac{1}{5}$

49. the graph of $f(x) = \sqrt{x}$ horizontally stretched by a factor of 4

50. the graph of $f(x) = 3x + 1$ reflected across the x-axis

51. the graph of $f(x) = 2x - 1$ reflected across the y-axis

52. the graph of $f(x) = x^2$ vertically stretched by a factor of 2 and translated 1 unit to the right

53. the graph of $f(x) = |x|$ horizontally compressed by a factor of $\frac{1}{3}$, reflected across the x-axis, and translated 3 units down

54. the graph of $f(x) = x^2$ translated 7 units to the left

55. the graph of $f(x) = x^2$ translated 5 units up

56. the graph of $f(x) = x^2$ stretched vertically by a factor of 2

57. the graph of $f(x) = x^2$ reflected across the y-axis and stretched horizontally by a factor of 2

CHALLENGES

58. How are the domain and range of a function affected by a reflection across the y-axis? across the x-axis? Include examples in your explanation.

59. Show that a vertical compression can have the same effect on a graph as a horizontal stretch.

At right is the graph of the function f. Draw a careful sketch of each transformation of f.

60. $g(x) = f(2x)$ **61.** $g(x) = 2f(x)$

62. $g(x) = -f(x)$ **63.** $g(x) = f(x+2)$

64. $g(x) = f(x) + 3$ **65.** $g(x) = f\left(\frac{1}{2}x\right)$

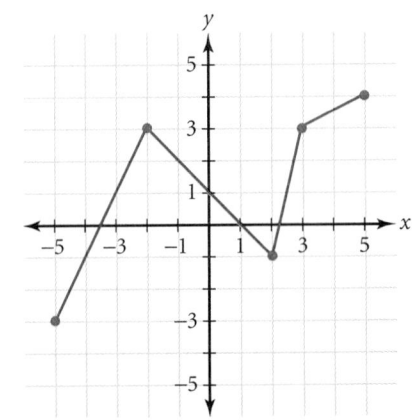

66. PHYSICS Let the function $h(t) = -16t^2 + 100$ model the altitude of an eagle in free fall when it dives from an initial altitude of 100 feet to catch a fish.

a. Describe the transformations from the graph of $f(t) = t^2$ to the graph of h.

b. Write a transformed function, g, that represents the altitude of an eagle diving from an initial altitude of 25 feet.

c. Graph f and h on the same coordinate plane, and describe the transformation from f to h by following the transformation of a point.

A bald eagle, the national bird of the United States

Look Back

67. Write an equation in slope-intercept form for the line that contains $(-3, 4)$ and is perpendicular to the graph of $y = -\frac{1}{2}x + 10$. *(LESSON 1.3)*

68. Solve $\frac{3}{5} = \frac{5}{x}$. *(LESSON 1.4)*

69. Solve the literal equation $D = \pi\left(\frac{b}{2}\right)^2 sn$ for s. *(LESSON 1.6)*

Classify each number in as many ways as possible. *(LESSON 2.1)*

70. 15.3849 **71.** $14.393939\ldots$ **72.** $17.1012012301234\ldots$

Find the inverse of each relation. State whether the relation is a function. State whether the inverse is a function. *(LESSON 2.5)*

73. $\{(1, 100), (2, 200), (3, 300), (4, 400)\}$

74. $\{(1, 5), (2, 10), (3, 10), (4, 15)\}$

75. Graph the piecewise function below. *(LESSON 2.6)*

$$f(x) = \begin{cases} x & \text{if } -4 \leq x \leq -1 \\ x + 2 & \text{if } -1 < x < 3 \\ -3x + 18 & \text{if } 3 \leq x \leq 5 \end{cases}$$

Look Beyond

76 Graph the linear functions $x - 2y = -4$ and $3x + 2y = -4$ together. Find the coordinates of the point of intersection. Then add the corresponding sides of the two equations and solve the resulting equation for x. Is this x-value close to the x-value at the intersection of the two graphs?

Space Trash

More than 3600 space missions since 1957 have left thousands of large and millions of smaller debris objects in near-Earth space. Information about the orbital debris is needed to determine the current and future hazards that this debris may pose to space operations. Only the largest objects can be repeatedly tracked and cataloged.

The table at right shows the estimated number of cataloged rocket bodies and fragmentation debris from 1965 to 1990 in five-year periods.

Space Debris Table		
Year	Rocket bodies	Fragmentation debris
1965	175	900
1970	350	1850
1975	525	2250
1980	700	2600
1985	875	3200
1990	1050	2900

Activity ❶

1. Use the data from the Space Debris Table on the previous page, which shows the estimated number of cataloged rocket bodies and fragmentation debris for the years 1965 to 1990. Find the average annual rate of change in the number of rocket bodies and debris from 1965 to 1990. Then find the rate of change for each five-year interval. Compare the individual five-year rates with the average rate.

2. Find a linear model for all of the rocket body data from Step 1. Let the years be represented by x (where $x = 0$ represents 1965 and $x = 5$ represents 1970). Verify your equation by using data from the table.

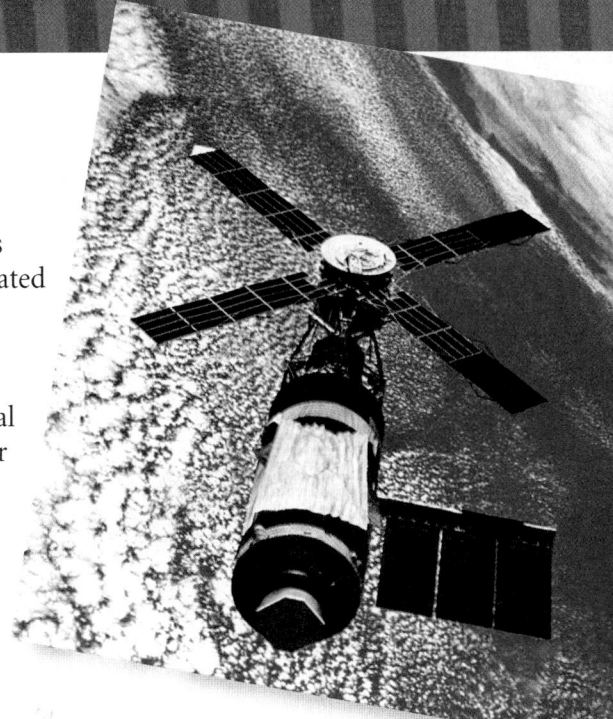

Skylab, *the United States' first space station*

Activity ❷

1. Create a scatter plot for the number of other cataloged debris objects for the given years from 1965 to 1990 from the Space Debris Table on the previous page. Plot the years on the horizontal axis (where $x = 0$ represents 1965) and number of other debris objects on the vertical axis.

2. Sketch the curve on your scatter plot that you think best models your data. Describe the trend you see in the scatter plot. Do you think you can make reliable predictions by using the model you sketched? Explain.

3. Using a graphics calculator, find linear, quadratic, and exponential regression equations for this data. Discuss which model best approximates the data.

Cataloged Space Debris

Activity ❸

1. Using the Cataloged Space Debris graph at left, which shows the distribution of cataloged debris objects by altitude, describe what happens to the number of debris objects as the altitude increases. Write an approximate step function that models the data in the graph.

2. Using the step function that you wrote in Step 1, estimate the number of objects at an altitude of 725 kilometers, 1450 kilometers, and 1900 kilometers. Discuss the usefulness of your model.

Chapter Review and Assessment

Key Skills & Exercises

LESSON 2.1

Key Skills

Identify and use Properties of Real Numbers.

The real numbers have the Closure, Commutative, Associative, Identity, Inverse, and Distributive Properties for addition and multiplication.

Evaluate expressions by using the order of operations.

$$\frac{-3 \times (6-4)^2}{6} = \frac{-3 \times 2^2}{6}$$
$$= \frac{-3 \times 4}{6}$$
$$= \frac{-12}{6}$$
$$= -2$$

Exercises

State the property that is illustrated in each statement. All variables represent real numbers.

1. $a(2b) = (2b)a$ **2.** $2 \times 1 = 2$

3. $a\left(\frac{1}{a}\right) = 1$ **4.** $(2s)t = 2(st)$

5. $4x + 0 = 4x$ **6.** $-2a + 2a = 0$

7. $(x + y) + 5 = 5 + (x + y)$

8. $5(2 - x) = 5(2) + 5(-x)$

Evaluate each expression.

9. $-1(5 + 3)^2 - 11$ **10.** $\frac{(11-5)^2}{3 \times 2}$

11. $\frac{(6-12)5}{3^3}$ **12.** $\frac{2^3 - (13 + 4)}{(-3)^2}$

LESSON 2.2

Key Skills

Simplify and evaluate expressions by using the Properties of Exponents.

$$\left(\frac{(5^3)(5^{-2})}{5^2}\right)^2 = \left(\frac{5^{3-2}}{5^2}\right)^2 = \left(\frac{5^1}{5^2}\right)^2 = (5^{1-2})^2$$
$$= (5^{-1})^2 = 5^{-2} = \frac{1}{5^2} = \frac{1}{25}$$

Exercises

Evaluate or simplify each expression. Assume that no variable equals zero.

13. $x^4(3x)^2$ **14.** $2a(5a^3b^5)^2$ **15.** $\frac{(u^2v)^3}{v^2}$

16. $\left(\frac{p^{-1}q^2}{p^{-1}}\right)^{-4}\left(\frac{-p^5q^{-3}}{p^{-3}q^{-1}}\right)^{-3}$ **17.** $\frac{(2x)^3}{y^2}\left(\frac{x^2}{3}\right)^3$

Key Skills

State the domain and range of a relation, and state whether it is a function.

The relation $\{(1, 2), (2, 4), (3, 6), (4, 8)\}$ is a function because each x-coordinate is paired with one and only one y-coordinate.

domain: $\{1, 2, 3, 4\}$ range: $\{2, 4, 6, 8\}$

Evaluate functions.

Evaluate $f(x) = 2x^2 - x + 3$ for $x = 5$.

$$f(5) = 2(5)^2 - 5 + 3$$
$$f(5) = 50 - 5 + 3$$
$$f(5) = 48$$

Exercises

State whether each relation is a function.

18. $\{(1, 2), (2, 3), (3, 5), (4, 7), (5, 11)\}$

19. $\{(1, -1), (2, -2), (3, -3)\}$

20. $\{(1, -1), (1, 1), (2, -3)\}$

21. $\{(1, 1), (1, -1), (2, 2), (2, -2)\}$

State the domain and range for each function.

22. $\{(-1, -6), (5, 8), (9, -1), (2, 3)\}$

23. $\{(-1, 2), (0, 6), (2, 7), (4, -7)\}$

Evaluate each function for $x = 1$ and $x = -1$.

24. $f(x) = 3x^2 - 2x + 1$ **25.** $g(x) = 11x - 2$

26. $f(x) = 3x^2 - 2$ **27.** $h(x) = 2 - 3x$

Key Skills

Add, subtract, multiply, and divide functions.

The sum, difference, product, and quotient of functions f and g are defined as follows:

$$(f + g)(x) = f(x) + g(x)$$

$$(f - g)(x) = f(x) - g(x)$$

$$(f \cdot g)(x) = f(x) \cdot g(x)$$

$$\left(\frac{f}{g}\right)(x) = \frac{f(x)}{g(x)}, \text{ where } g(x) \neq 0$$

Compose functions.

If f and g are functions with appropriate domains and ranges, then the composition of f with g, $f \circ g$, is defined by $f(g(x))$.

Exercises

Let $f(x) = 3x - 4$ and $g(x) = \frac{x}{2} - 5$. Find each new function, and state any domain restrictions.

28. $f + g$ **29.** $f - g$ **30.** $g - f$

31. $f \circ g$ **32.** $\frac{f}{g}$ **33.** $\frac{g}{f}$

Let $f(x) = 2x$ and $g(x) = -x + 2$. Find each composite function.

34. $f \circ g$ **35.** $g \circ f$

36. $f \circ f$ **37.** $g \circ g$

Let $f(x) = -3x - 5$ and $g(x) = 4x - 1$. Evaluate each composite function.

38. $(f \circ g)(3)$ **39.** $(g \circ f)(2)$ **40.** $(g \circ g)(-1)$

Key Skills

Find the inverse of a function.

To find the inverse of the function $f = \{(1, 2), (2, 4), (3, 8), (4, 16)\}$, reverse the order of the coordinates in each ordered pair. The inverse of f is $\{(2, 1), (4, 2), (8, 3), (16, 4)\}$.

To find the inverse of a function f defined by a function rule, replace $f(x)$ with y, interchange x and y, and solve for y.

Exercises

Find the inverse of each function.

41. $f = \{(-2, 0), (-1, 1), (0, 0), (1, 1), (2, 0)\}$

42. $f = \{(1, 2), (2, 3), (3, 4), (4, 5)\}$

Find an equation for the inverse of each function. Then use composition to verify that the equation you wrote is the inverse.

43. $f(x) = -\frac{2}{3}x + 4$ **44.** $f(x) = \frac{2 - x}{3}$

Use the horizontal-line test to determine whether the inverse relation is a function.

If a function, f, has an inverse that is a function, then any horizontal line that intersects the graph of f will do so at only one point.

Graph each function, and use the horizontal-line test to determine whether the inverse is a function.

45 $f(x) = \dfrac{3x + 3}{2}$

46 $f(x) = x^2 - 1$

47 $f(x) = 2\left(\dfrac{2x}{3} + 1\right)$

48 $f(x) = 3x + 5$

LESSON 2.6

Key Skills

Define and graph piecewise functions, step functions, and absolute-value functions.

The piecewise function $f(x) = \begin{cases} 2x + 1 & \text{if } x < 0 \\ 5x & \text{if } x \geq 0 \end{cases}$
is the function that assigns the function value $2x + 1$ to negative values of x and the function value $5x$ to nonnegative values of x.

A step function consists of different constant range values, and its graph resembles stair steps.

The absolute-value function $f(x) = |x|$ gives the distance from x to 0 on a number line and has a v-shaped graph.

Exercises

Graph each function.

49. $f(x) = \begin{cases} x & \text{if } x < 1 \\ -2x + 3 & \text{if } x \geq 1 \end{cases}$

50. $f(x) = \begin{cases} x^2 + 1 & \text{if } x < 0 \\ 1 & \text{if } x \geq 0 \end{cases}$

51. $f(x) = 3[x]$

52. $f(x) = \frac{1}{2}|x| - 1$

Evaluate.

53. $[-77.99]$

54. $[4] - [-7.1]$

55. $\lceil 3.5 \rceil$

56. $\lceil 4.0 \rceil - \lceil -7.001 \rceil$

57. $|-7| + [1.09]$

58. $|3.5| - \lceil 2.9 \rceil$

LESSON 2.7

Key Skills

Identify transformations of functions.

The graph of $g(x) = 2[3(x - 1)]^2 + 4$ is formed by the following transformations of the graph of $f(x) = x^2$:

- a horizontal translation of 1 unit to the right
- a horizontal compression by a factor of $\frac{1}{3}$
- a vertical stretch by a factor of 2
- a vertical translation of 4 units up

Exercises

Identify the transformations from f to g.

59. $f(x) = x^2, g(x) = (x - 2)^2$

60. $f(x) = \sqrt{x}, g(x) = \sqrt{-x} + 3$

61. $f(x) = |x|, g(x) = -|x + 3|$

Applications

62. CONSUMER ECONOMICS Hardwood flooring costs $4.75 per square foot for amounts up to and including 500 square feet and $4.50 for amounts of more than 500 square feet. Write and graph a function that describes the cost, c, of x square feet of hardwood flooring.

63. SPORTS The function $h(t) = -9.8t^2 + 1.5$ gives the height in meters of a basketball thrown from an initial height of 1.5 meters. Describe the transformations from $f(t) = t^2$ to h.

Chapter Test

Evaluate each expression by using the order of operations.

1. $5 + 2(7 - 4)^2$

2. $12 - 9 \div 3 + 2 \cdot 5$

3. $\frac{4 + 6}{2} + 2 \cdot 5$

4. $5 \cdot 4 \div 2 + 3^{(4 - 1)}$

State the property that is used in each statement. All variables represent real numbers.

5. $5x \cdot 1 = 5x$

6. $7d - 14 = 7(d - 2)$

7. $\left(\frac{2}{r}\right)\left(\frac{r}{2}\right) = 1$

8. $4(yz) = (yz)4$

Simplify each expression. Assume that no variable equals zero.

9. $y^3(x^2y)$

10. $(9rt)^2(3rst)^{-3}$

11. $\frac{14r^2s^{-3}t^4}{35r^{-2}s^5t^3}$

12. $\left(\frac{3p^4q^{-1}}{8p^{-2}q^3}\right)^{-2}$

13. PHYSICS Kinetic energy can be measured in joules and is given by the formula $k = \frac{1}{2}mv^2$. What is the kinetic energy in joules of an object with mass $m = 100$ kg and velocity $v = 5$ meters per second?

State whether the following are functions, and if so give the domain and range.

14. $\{(5, 7), (7, 12), (9, 7), (11, 12), (13, 7)\}$

15. $\{(-2, 4), (0, 6), (-2, 8), (0, 10), (-2, 12)\}$

Evaluate each function for $x = -2$, $x = 0$, and $x = 2$.

16. $f(x) = 5x^2 - 4x + 7$ **17.** $f(x) = \frac{x^2}{2} + x - 4$

18. CONSUMER ECONOMICS The cost of enrollment at a community college is $120 plus $75 per credit, c, taken. Express the college costs as a function of c and find the cost when 12 credits are taken.

For Items 19–23, let $f(x) = 2x + 7$ and $g(x) = x - 9$. Find new functions and state any domain restrictions, if appropriate.

19. $f + g$

20. $\frac{g}{f}$

21. $f \cdot g$

Evaluate each composite function.

22. $(g \circ f)(3)$

23. $(f \circ g)(2)$

24. BIOLOGY The number of times a cricket chirps per minute can be predicted using the formula $n = 4(F - 40)$, where n is the number of chirps per minute and F is the Fahrenheit temperature. The Celsius scale for temperature can be converted to Fahrenheit using $F = \frac{9}{5}C + 32$. Find the number of cricket chirps per minute as a function of Celsius temperature.

Find the inverse of each function. State whether the inverse is a function.

25. $\{(3, 4), (4, 3), (5, 6), (6, 5), (7, 8), (8, 7)\}$

26. $\{(1, 2), (5, 6), (2, 2), (6, 6), (3, 4)\}$

Find an equation for the inverse and state whether the inverse is a function.

27. $f(x) = \frac{3x - 8}{4}$

28. $f(x) = x^4 - 3$

Graph each function.

29. $f(x) = \begin{cases} 2x + 5 & \text{if } x \le 0 \\ -\frac{1}{3}x + 3 & \text{if } x > 0 \end{cases}$

30. $f(x) = 2[x] - 1$

Evaluate.

31. $[4.5] + 3.5$

32. $[-1.7] + [1.7]$

Identify each transformation from the parent function f to g.

33. $f(x) = \sqrt{x}, g(x) = \sqrt{x} - 3$

34. $f(x) = x^2, g(x) = (x + 3)^2 - 4$

College Entrance Exam Practice

MULTIPLE-CHOICE For Questions 1–14, write the letter that indicates the best answer.

1. Solve $x - 2 = 3 + 4x$. *(LESSON 1.6)*

   a. $x = -\frac{1}{5}$ **b.** $x = -\frac{5}{3}$

   c. $x = -\frac{1}{3}$ **d.** $x = -\frac{3}{5}$

2. Find an equation for the inverse of $f(x) = \frac{1}{2}x + 3$. *(LESSON 2.5)*

   a. $f^{-1}(x) = 2x - 6$

   b. $f^{-1}(x) = x + 6$

   c. $f^{-1}(x) = 2x - 3$

   d. $f^{-1}(x) = 2x + 6$

3. Simplify $\frac{x^3}{x} \cdot x^{-2}$, where $x \neq 0$. *(LESSON 2.2)*

   a. x^2 **b.** 1

   c. 0 **d.** x^4

4. Evaluate $f(x) = x^2 - 2x + 3$ for $x = -1$. *(LESSON 2.3)*

   a. 4 **b.** 0

   c. 6 **d.** 3

5. Which is the equation for the line whose graph is parallel to the graph of $y = -\frac{1}{6}x + 5$? *(LESSON 1.3)*

   a. $x + 6y = -12$

   b. $x - 6y = -30$

   c. $6x + y = 5$

   d. $6x + y = 30$

6. Which is the equation for the line whose slope, m, is -5 and y-intercept, b, is $-\frac{1}{2}$? *(LESSON 1.2)*

   a. $y = -\frac{1}{2}x - 5$ **b.** $y = -\frac{1}{2}x + 5$

   c. $y = -5x - \frac{1}{2}$ **d.** $y = -5x + \frac{1}{2}$

7. Solve $|2 + 3x| = 14$. *(LESSON 1.7)*

   a. $x = -4$ **b.** $x = -\frac{16}{3}$

   c. $x = -4$ or $x = \frac{16}{3}$ **d.** $x = 4$ or $x = -\frac{16}{3}$

8. Let $f(x) = -3x^2$ and $g(x) = 2 - x$. Which of the following function operations gives the new function $h(x) = 3x^3 - 6x^2$? *(LESSON 2.4)*

   a. $f - g$ **b.** $f \cdot g$

   c. $f \div g$ **d.** $f \circ g$

9. Solve $S = \frac{1780Ad}{r}$ for A. *(LESSON 1.6)*

   a. $A = \frac{1780Sd}{r}$ **b.** $A = \frac{Sd}{1780r}$

   c. $A = \frac{1780dr}{S}$ **d.** $A = \frac{Sr}{1780d}$

10. Which linear equation contains the points $(-1, -4)$ and $(3, 8)$? *(LESSON 1.3)*

    a. $y = \frac{1}{3}x + 7$ **b.** $y = -\frac{1}{3}x + 9$

    c. $y = 3x - 1$ **d.** $y = -3x - 7$

11. Which number is irrational? *(LESSON 2.1)*

    a. -3 **b.** $\frac{1}{3}$

    c. $0.\overline{5}$ **d.** π

12. Which is an equation for the line that contains the point $(10, 3)$ and is perpendicular to the graph of $y = 5x - 3$? *(LESSON 1.3)*

    a. $y = -\frac{1}{5}x + 5$ **b.** $y = -\frac{1}{5}x - 3$

    c. $y = -5x - 3$ **d.** $y = -5x + 5$

13. Which is the inverse of the function $y = -3x + 12$? *(LESSON 2.5)*

    a. $y = -3x + 12$

    b. $y = \frac{1}{3}x + 12$

    c. $y = -\frac{1}{3}x + 4$

    d. $y = -3x + 4$

14. Which description below identifies the transformations from $f(x)$ to $y = 3f(x - 2)$? *(LESSON 2.7)*
   a. a horizontal translation of 2 units to the right and a vertical stretch by a factor of 3
   b. a horizontal translation of 2 units to the left and a vertical stretch by a factor of 3
   c. a vertical translation of 2 units up and a vertical stretch by a factor of 3
   d. a vertical translation of 2 units down and a vertical stretch by a factor of 3

STATISTICS The following data set gives the resale price of a certain computer at monthly intervals. *(LESSON 1.5)*

Months	Price ($)	Months	Price ($)
1	3250	6	2700
2	3150	7	2700
3	3100	8	2450
4	2850	9	2350
5	2800	10	2300

15 Find the equation of the least-squares line.

16 Use the least-squares line to predict the price after 12 months.

17 Find the correlation coefficient, and explain how it describes the data.

Find the inverse of each function. State whether the inverse is a function. *(LESSON 2.5)*

18. $\{(3, 4)), (8, 4),(13, -4), (4, 0)\}$

19. $f(x) = \frac{x - 2}{4}$

20. Solve and graph the inequality $2(1 - 2x) \geq -x + 4$. *(LESSON 1.7)*

21. Write a relation that is not a function, and explain why it is not a function. *(LESSON 2.3)*

Let $f(x) = 2x - 2$ and $g(x) = 3x$. Perform each operation below, and write your answer in simplest form. *(LESSON 2.4)*

22. $f + g$ **23.** $f - g$ **24.** $f \cdot g$
25. $f \div g$ **26.** $f \circ g$ **27.** $g \circ f$

CONSUMER ECONOMICS Residential wastewater rates are based on a monthly customer charge of $4.00 plus $1.75 per 1000 gallons of water used up to and including 6900 gallons and $3.50 for each additional 1000 gallons of water. *(LESSON 2.6)*

28. Write a piecewise function to represent the monthly cost, c, in dollars for x gallons of water used.

29. Graph the function from Item 28. What is the monthly cost for using 8400 gallons of water in a month?

30. If the monthly wastewater bill is $25.00, how much water was used?

FREE RESPONSE GRID
The following questions may be answered by using a free-response grid such as that commonly used by standardized-test services.

31. What value should replace the "?" in the table below in order for x and y to be linearly related? *(LESSON 1.1)*

x	3	5	7	9	11
y	2	?	-4	-7	-10

32. Evaluate $27^{\frac{2}{3}}$. *(LESSON 2.2)*

33. If a varies directly as b and $a = -3$ when $b = 12$, what is b when $a = 1.5$? *(LESSON 1.4)*

34. Evaluate $-[-32.90]$. *(LESSON 2.6)*

35. Evaluate $75 - \frac{3(4 + 12 \div 2)^2}{2 + 3}$. *(LESSON 2.1)*

36. Evaluate $\frac{6^2 \cdot 6^{-3}}{6^{-1}}$. *(LESSON 2.2)*

37. Find the slope of the line represented by $2x + 3y = 7$. *(LESSON 1.2)*

38. Find $f(0)$ for $f(x) = 5x^2 - x + 12$. *(LESSON 2.3)*

39. What value of x is the solution to the equation $\frac{3x - 15}{2} = 9 - 4x$? *(LESSON 1.5)*

40. Evaluate $\lceil -0.75 \rceil$. *(LESSON 2.6)*

Keystroke Guide for Chapter 2

Essential keystroke sequences (using the model TI-82 or TI-83 graphics calculator) are presented below for all Activities and Examples found in this chapter that require or recommend the use of a graphics calculator.

☑ internet connect
For Keystrokes of other graphing calculator models, visit the HRW web site at **go.hrw.com** and enter the keyword **MB1 CALC**.

LESSON 2.1

Page 89

For Step 1, evaluate $\frac{12+8}{5}$ without and with parentheses.

12 [+] 8 [÷] 5 [ENTER] [( ] 12 [+] 8 [ )] [÷] 5 [ENTER]

Use a similar keystroke sequence for Step 3.

LESSON 2.2

E X A M P L E **1** Evaluate $A_c = 4\pi^2 r T^{-2}$ for $T = 2$ and $r = 6$.
Page 95

4 [2nd] [$\overset{\pi}{\wedge}$] [x^2] [×] 6 [×] [( ] 2 [^] [(-)] 2 [ )] [ENTER]

E X A M P L E S **4** and **5** For Example 4, part a, evaluate the expression $16^{\frac{1}{4}}$.
Pages 97 and 98

16 [^] [( ] 1 [÷] 4 [ )] [ENTER]

Use a similar keystroke sequence for part **b** and for Example 5.

LESSON 2.3

E X A M P L E **5** Evaluate $f(x) = 0.5x^2 - 3x + 2$ for $x = 4$ and $x = 2.5$.
Page 106

Use viewing window $[-7, 12]$ by $[-7, 12]$.

Graph the function:

[Y=] 0.5 [X,T,θ,n] [x^2] [−] 3 [X,T,θ,n]

[+] 2 [GRAPH]

First clear all equations and statplots.

Evaluate for $x = 4$ and $x = 2.5$:

[2nd] [TRACE]^{CALC} [1: value] [ENTER] (X=) 4 [ENTER]

[2nd] [TRACE]^{CALC} [1: value] [ENTER] (X=) 2.5 [ENTER]

Activity

Page 111

First clear all data.

First clear all equations.

For Step 1, enter the data for the speed and the reaction distance, and create a scatter plot.

Use viewing window [0, 75] by [−15, 95].

Enter the data:

STAT EDIT 1:EDIT ENTER L1 10 ENTER 20 ENTER 30 ENTER 40 ENTER 50

ENTER 60 ENTER 70 ENTER ▶ L2 11 ENTER 22 ENTER 33 ENTER 44 ENTER

55 ENTER 66 ENTER 77 ENTER

Create the scatter plot:

STAT PLOT

2nd Y= STAT PLOT 1:PLOT 1 ENTER ON ENTER ▼ (Type:) [::::] ENTER

▼ (Xlist:) L1 2nd 1 ▼ (Ylist:) L2 2nd 2nd ▼ (Mark:) ▪

⇑TI-82: L1 ENTER   ⇑TI-82: L2 ENTER

ENTER GRAPH

Use a similar keystroke sequence for Steps 2 and 4.

Activity

Page 119

First clear all equations and statplots.

For Step 1, graph $y = 2x − 1$, its inverse, and $y = x$ on the same screen.

Begin with viewing window [−10, 10] by [−10, 10].

Graph the given functions:

Y= 2 X,T,θ,n − 1 ENTER (Y2=) X,T,θ,n ZOOM 5:ZSquare ENTER

Graph the inverse of $y = 2x − 1$:

DRAW

2nd PRGM 8:DrawInv ENTER VARS Y-VARS 1:Function ENTER 1:Y1

Y-VARS

⇑TI-82: 2nd VARS

ENTER ENTER

Use a similar keystroke sequence for Step 2.

E X A M P L E ④ Let $f(x) = 7x − 2$ and $g(x) = \frac{1}{7}x + \frac{2}{7}$. Graph $f \circ g$.

Page 121

Use friendly viewing window [−4.7, 4.7] by [−3.1, 3.1].

Graph $f \circ g$:

Y= ◀ ▬ ENTER ▶ (1 ÷ 7) X,T,θ,n + (2 ÷

7) ENTER (Y2=) 7 VARS Y-VARS 1:Function ENTER 1:Y1 ENTER −

Y-VARS

⇑TI-82: 2nd VARS

2 GRAPH

To graph $g \circ f$, change x in Y1 to Y2, and change Y1 in Y2 to x. Turn off Y2, turn on Y1, and graph.

EXAMPLE 4 Graph $y = 3|x| - 1$ and its inverse on the same screen.

Page 127

Use friendly viewing window $[-4.7, 4.7]$ by $[-3.1, 3.1]$.

Activity

Page 133

For Step 1, enter the data from columns 2 and 4, create a scatter plot, and graph the least-squares line for the data.

Use viewing window $[25, 35]$ by $[120, 200]$.

Enter the data:

STAT EDIT 1:Edit ENTER L1 29 ENTER 30 ENTER 31 ENTER 32 ENTER 33 ENTER 34 ENTER ▶ L2 185.4 ENTER 173.1 ENTER 147.1 ENTER 158.4 ENTER 134.7 ENTER 151.2 ENTER

Create the scatter plot:

Graph the regression line for the data:

STAT CALC 4:LinReg(ax+b) ENTER 2nd L1 1 , 2nd L2 2 ,
VARS Y-VARS 1:Function ENTER 1:Y1 ENTER ENTER GRAPH

TI-82:

Use a similar keystroke sequence for Step 2.

E X A M P L E **1** For part a, graph $y = x^2$ and $y = x^2 + 3$ on the same screen.

Page 134

Use friendly viewing window $[-4.7, 4.7]$ by $[-2, 8]$.

> The TI-82 model does not draw thick lines. Omit cursor keys and ENTER key in Y2.

For part b, graph $y = |x|$ and $y = |x + 4|$ on the same screen.

Use friendly viewing window $[-4.7, 4.7]$ by $[-2, 8]$.

E X A M P L E **2** For part a, graph $y = \sqrt{16 - x^2}$ and $y = 2\sqrt{16 - x^2}$ on the same screen.

Page 135

Use friendly viewing window $[-4.7, 4.7]$ by $[0, 8]$.

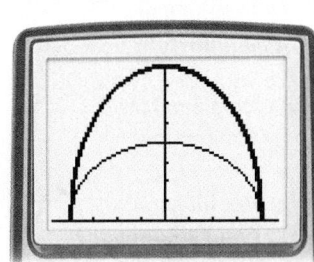

E X A M P L E S **3**, **4**, and **5** For Example 3, part a, graph $y = \sqrt{(16 - x^2)}$ and $y = \sqrt{16 - (2x)^2}$ on the same screen.

Pages 136–138

Use friendly viewing window $[-9.4, 9.4]$ by $[0, 6.2]$.

Use a similar keystroke sequence for part **b**.

Use a similar keystroke sequence for Examples 4 and 5.

Systems of Linear Equations and Inequalities

SYSTEMS OF LINEAR EQUATIONS AND INEQUALITIES are used to find optimal solutions to problems in business, finance, manufacturing, agriculture, and other fields such as photography.

For instance, the time required to develop a photograph involves both the *concentration* and the *temperature* of the developer fluid. Situations in which variables are related in more than one way can be represented with a system of equations.

Lessons

Supplies used to develop photographs.

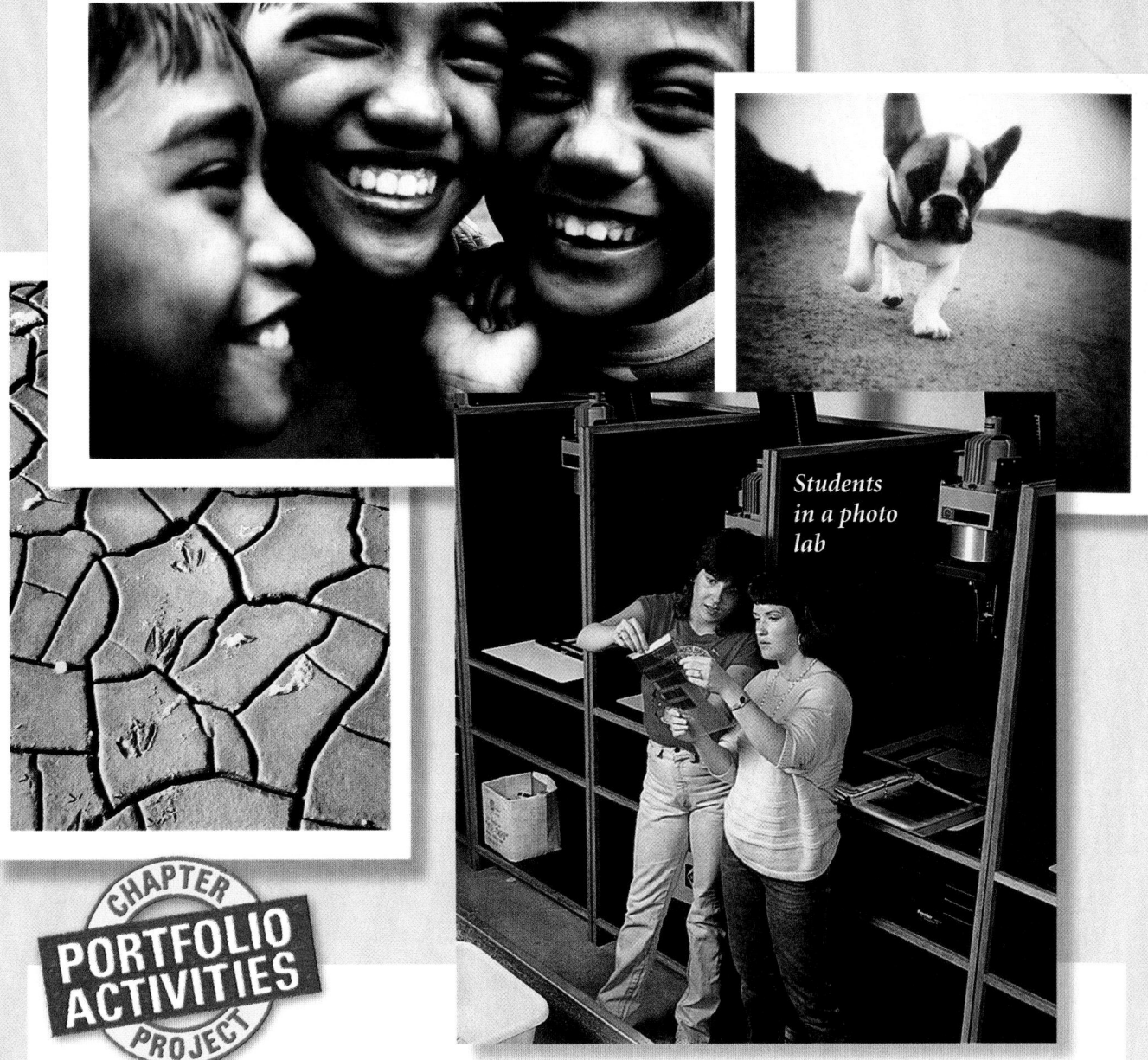

Students in a photo lab

PORTFOLIO
ACTIVITIES
CHAPTER
PROJECT

About the Chapter Project

The Chapter Project, *Maximum Profit/Minimum Cost,* consists of two linear-programming problems. In one, you will be faced with a limited number of resources and will be asked to maximize profit. In the second, you will be asked to complete a job while minimizing the costs of labor. You will have an opportunity to use mathematics as it is often used in the real world to solve problems and make decisions.

After completing the Chapter Project, you will be able to do the following:

• Set up and solve linear-programming problems that involve finding maximums or minimums.

• Investigate how changes in the objective function or in the constraint inequalities affect the outcomes.

About the Portfolio Activities

Throughout the chapter, you will be given opportunities to complete Portfolio Activities that are designed to support your work on the Chapter Project.

• Writing and solving a system of equations to solve a production problem is included in the Portfolio Activity on page 171.

• Using a system of linear inequalities to find production limits and possibilities is included in the Portfolio Activity on page 186.

• Using linear programming to maximize the profits of a production company are included in the Portfolio Activity on page 194.

Solving Systems by Graphing or Substitution

Objectives

- Solve a system of linear equations in two variables by graphing.

- Solve a system of linear equations by substitution.

APPLICATION

CHEMISTRY

A laboratory technician is mixing a 10% saline solution with a 4% saline solution. How much of each solution is needed to make 500 milliliters of a 6% saline solution? *You will solve this problem in Example 3.*

A **system of equations** is a collection of equations in the same variables.

The solution of a system of two linear equations in x and y is any ordered pair, (x, y), that satisfies both equations. The solution (x, y) is also the point of intersection for the graphs of the lines in the system. For example, the ordered pair $(2, -1)$ is the solution of the system below.

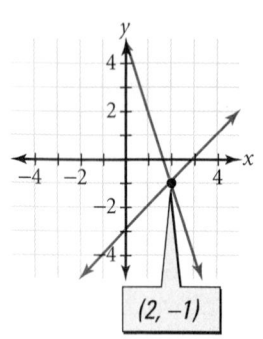

$(2, -1)$

$$\begin{cases} y = x - 3 \\ y = 5 - 3x \end{cases} \rightarrow \begin{cases} (-1) = (2) - 3 \\ (-1) = 5 - 3(2) \end{cases} \begin{matrix} \textbf{True} \\ \textbf{True} \end{matrix}$$

Activity

Exploring Graphs of Systems

TECHNOLOGY

GRAPHICS CALCULATOR

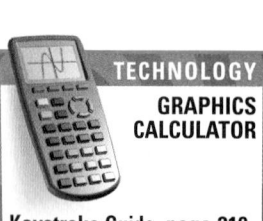

Keystroke Guide, page 210

You will need: graph paper or a graphics calculator

1. Graph system I at right.

   a. Are there any points of intersection?

   b. Can you find exactly one solution to the system? If so, what is it? If not, modify the system so that it has exactly one solution and state that solution.

2. Repeat Step 1 for systems II and III.

CHECKPOINT ✔ 3. Describe the slopes of the lines whose equations form a system with no solution, with infinitely many solutions, and with exactly one solution.

System
I. $\begin{cases} y = 2x - 1 \\ y = -x + 5 \end{cases}$
II. $\begin{cases} y = 2x - 1 \\ y = 2x + 1 \end{cases}$
III. $\begin{cases} y = \dfrac{8 - 3x}{4} \\ y = -\dfrac{3}{4}x + 2 \end{cases}$

You can graph a system of equations in two variables to find whether a solution for the system exists. The systems and graphs below illustrate the three possibilities for a system of two linear equations in two variables.

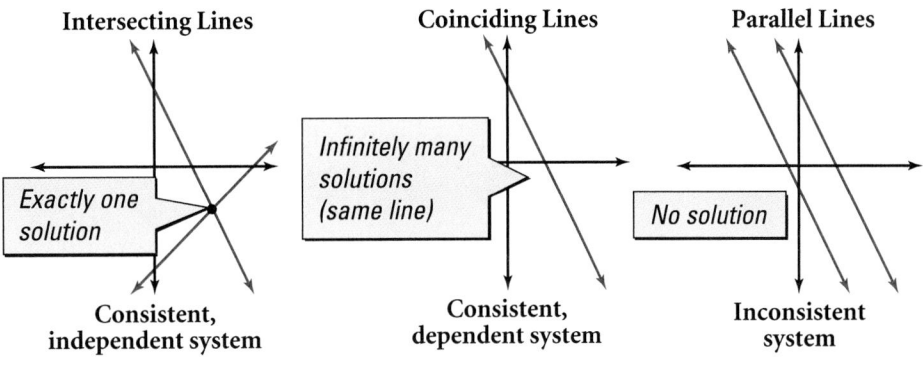

Intersecting Lines — Exactly one solution — Consistent, independent system

Coinciding Lines — Infinitely many solutions (same line) — Consistent, dependent system

Parallel Lines — No solution — Inconsistent system

Classifying Systems of Equations

If a system of equations has at least one solution, it is called **consistent**.
  • If a system has exactly one solution, it is called **independent**.
  • If a system has infinitely many solutions, it is called **dependent**.
If a system does not have a solution, it is called **inconsistent**.

E X A M P L E ❶ Graph and classify each system. Then find the solution from the graph.

a. $\begin{cases} x + y = 5 \\ x - 5y = -7 \end{cases}$

b. $\begin{cases} x - 2y = 3 \\ x + 5 = 2y \end{cases}$

● **SOLUTION**

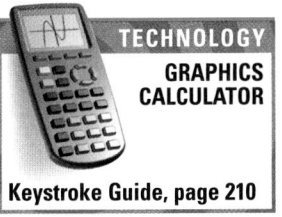

TECHNOLOGY
GRAPHICS CALCULATOR

Keystroke Guide, page 210

Solve each equation for y.

a. $\begin{cases} x + y = 5 \\ x - 5y = -7 \end{cases}$ → $\begin{cases} y = -x + 5 \\ y = \dfrac{x + 7}{5} \end{cases}$

b. $\begin{cases} x - 2y = 3 \\ x + 5 = 2y \end{cases}$ → $\begin{cases} y = \dfrac{x - 3}{2} \\ y = \dfrac{x + 5}{2} \end{cases}$

Intersecting lines have different slopes.

Intersection
X=3   Y=2

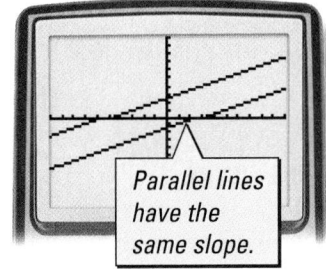

Parallel lines have the same slope.

Because the lines intersect at exactly one point, the system is consistent and independent. The solution is (3, 2).

The lines appear to be parallel. You can verify this by examining the slopes of the lines—both are $\frac{1}{2}$. Thus, the system is inconsistent, and there is no solution.

TRY THIS Graph and classify $\begin{cases} y = 3x + 4 \\ y = -2x + 4 \end{cases}$. Then find the solution from the graph.

CRITICAL THINKING Classify $\begin{cases} y = mx \\ y = nx \end{cases}$, where $m \neq 0$ and $n \neq 0$, as thoroughly as possible.

Example 2 shows you how to use substitution to solve a system in which a variable has a coefficient of 1.

EXAMPLE **2** Use substitution to solve the system. Check your solution. $\begin{cases} 2x + y = 3 \\ 3x - 2y = 8 \end{cases}$

● **SOLUTION**

Solve the first equation for y because it has a coefficient of 1.

$$2x + y = 3$$
$$y = 3 - 2x$$

Substitute $3 - 2x$ for y in the second equation.

$$3x - 2y = 8$$
$$3x - 2(3 - 2x) = 8 \quad \longleftarrow \boxed{\textit{This equation has only one variable.}}$$
$$3x - 6 + 4x = 8 \quad \textit{Use the Distributive Property.}$$
$$7x = 14$$
$$x = 2$$

Substitute 2 for x in either original equation to find y.

First equation: $\quad 2x + y = 3$ | Second equation: $\quad 3x - 2y = 8$
$\qquad\qquad 2(2) + y = 3$ | $\qquad\qquad 3(2) - 2y = 8$
$\qquad\qquad\qquad y = -1$ | $\qquad\qquad\qquad -2y = 8 - 6$
| $\qquad\qquad\qquad\qquad y = -1$

The solution is $(2, -1)$.

CHECK

$$\begin{cases} 2x + y = 3 \\ 3x - 2y = 8 \end{cases} \quad \rightarrow \quad \begin{cases} 2(2) + (-1) = 3 \quad \textbf{True} \\ 3(2) - 2(-1) = 8 \quad \textbf{True} \end{cases}$$

$\boxed{\textit{Always check your answers by substituting them into both original equations.}}$

TRY THIS   Use substitution to solve the system. Check your solution. $\begin{cases} 3x + y = 8 \\ 18x + 2y = 4 \end{cases}$

EXAMPLE **3** Refer to the saline solution mixture described at the beginning of the lesson.

How much of each solution, to the nearest milliliter, is needed to make 500 milliliters of a 6% saline solution?

● **SOLUTION**

PROBLEM SOLVING

Write two equations in x and y. Let x and y represent the amounts of the 10% and 4% solutions, respectively.

Solution A $\quad$ Solution B $\quad$ Solution C

$\boxed{x} \quad + \quad \boxed{y} \quad = \quad \boxed{\begin{array}{c} 500 \\ mL \end{array}}$

10% saline $\qquad$ 4% saline $\qquad$ 6% saline

amount of 10% solution	+	amount of 4% solution	=	amount of 6% solution
x	+	y	=	500

saline in 10% solution	+	saline in 4% solution	=	saline in 6% solution
$0.10x$	+	$0.04y$	=	$0.06(500)$

Method 1 Use the substitution method.

1. Solve the first equation for y.

$$x + y = 500$$
$$y = 500 - x$$

> The first equation can be solved for either x or y.

2. Substitute $500 - x$ for y into the second equation, and solve for x.

$$0.10x + 0.04y = 0.06(500)$$
$$0.10x + 0.04(500 - x) = 0.06(500) \qquad \textit{Substitute.}$$
$$0.10x + 20 - 0.04x = 30 \qquad \textit{Simplify.}$$
$$0.06x = 10$$
$$x \approx 167$$

3. Substitute 167 for x into the first equation.

$$x + y = 500$$
$$167 + y \approx 500$$
$$y \approx 333$$

> You can use either original equation for this step.

TECHNOLOGY

GRAPHICS CALCULATOR

Keystroke Guide, page 210

Method 2 Use the graphing method.

Graph the equations, and find any points of intersection.

To graph the system with a graphics calculator, solve for y and rewrite the system as shown below.

$$\begin{cases} y = 500 - x \\ y = \dfrac{0.06(500) - 0.10x}{0.04} \end{cases}$$

Intersection
X=166.66667 Y=333.33333

The technician needs to combine 167 milliliters of the 10% solution and 333 milliliters of the 4% solution.

TRY THIS If a 7% saline solution and a 4% saline solution are mixed to make 500 milliliters of a 5% saline solution, how much of each solution, to the nearest milliliter, is needed?

The solution of a system in three variables, such as in x, y, and z, is an *ordered triple* (x, y, z) that satisfies all three equations.

E X A M P L E **4** Use substitution to solve the system. Check your solution.

$$\begin{cases} x + y + z = 5 \\ 2x - 3y + z = -2 \\ 4z = 8 \end{cases}$$

SOLUTION

1. Solve the third equation for z.

$$4z = 8$$
$$z = 2$$

2. Substitute 2 for z in the first and second equations. Then simplify.

$$\begin{cases} x + y + z = 5 \\ 2x - 3y + z = -2 \\ z = 2 \end{cases} \rightarrow \begin{cases} x + y + 2 = 5 \\ 2x - 3y + 2 = -2 \end{cases} \rightarrow \begin{cases} x + y = 3 \\ 2x - 3y = -4 \end{cases}$$

3. Use substitution to solve the resulting system. $\begin{cases} x + y = 3 \\ 2x - 3y = -4 \end{cases}$

$$x + y = 3 \qquad\qquad 2x - 3y = -4$$
$$y = 3 - x \quad \rightarrow \quad 2x - 3(3 - x) = -4$$

> Substitute $3 - x$ for y in $2x - 3y = -4$.

$$2x - 9 + 3x = -4$$
$$5x = 5$$
$$x = 1$$

4. Now substitute 1 for x and 2 for z to find y.

$$x + y + z = 5$$
$$1 + y + 2 = 5$$
$$y = 2$$

> You can use either the first or second equation of the original system.

Thus, the solution for the system is $(1, 2, 2)$.

CHECK

$$\begin{cases} x + y + z = 5 \\ 2x - 3y + z = -2 \\ 4z = 8 \end{cases} \rightarrow \begin{cases} 1 + 2 + 2 = 5 \\ 2(1) - 3(2) + 2 = -2 \\ 4(2) = 8 \end{cases} \begin{array}{l} \textbf{True} \\ \textbf{True} \\ \textbf{True} \end{array}$$

TRY THIS Use substitution to solve the system. $\begin{cases} x + y + z = 5 \\ 2x - 3y + z = -2 \\ 4z = -12 \end{cases}$
Check your solution.

Exercises

Communicate

1. Describe the graphs of the three types of systems of linear equations.

2. Create three systems of linear equations, one to demonstrate each type of system: inconsistent, dependent, and independent.

3. Explain how to solve the system $\begin{cases} y = 2x - 5 \\ x + y = 13 \end{cases}$ by graphing.

4. Explain how to use substitution to solve the system. $\begin{cases} p - q = -7 \\ 2p + q = 17 \end{cases}$

Guided Skills Practice

Graph and classify each system. Then find the solution from the graph. (EXAMPLE 1)

5. $\begin{cases} x - y = -4 \\ 3x + y = 8 \end{cases}$

6. $\begin{cases} 3x + 4y = 12 \\ 4y - 12 = -3x \end{cases}$

7. Use substitution to solve the system. Check your solution. *(EXAMPLE 2)* $\begin{cases} 2x + y = 8 \\ 6x + 2y = -8 \end{cases}$

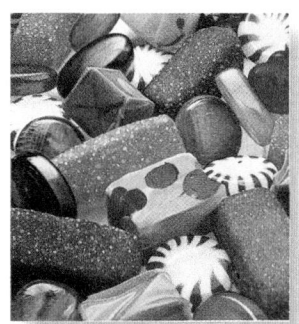
8. SMALL BUSINESS A candy manufacturer wishes to mix two candies as a sales promotion. One candy sells for $2.00 per pound and the other candy sells for $0.75 per pound. The manufacturer wishes to have 1000 pounds of the mixture and to sell the mixture for $1.35 per pound. How many pounds of each type of candy should be used in the mixture? *(EXAMPLE 3)*

9. Use substitution to solve the system. Check your solution. *(EXAMPLE 4)*

$$\begin{cases} x + 6y + 2z = 1 \\ -2x + 3y - z = 4 \\ -1 = z + 2 \end{cases}$$

Practice and Apply

Classify the type of system of equations represented by each graph below. If the system has exactly one solution, write it.

10.

11.

12.
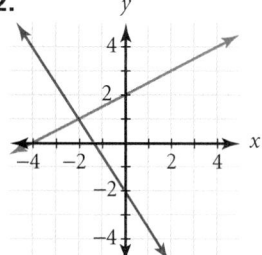

Graph and classify each system. Then find the solution from the graph.

13. $\begin{cases} 6x + 4y = 12 \\ 2y = 6 - 3x \end{cases}$

14. $\begin{cases} 2x + 3y = 1 \\ -3x + 4y = -10 \end{cases}$

15. $\begin{cases} y = 2x - 1 \\ 6x - y = 13 \end{cases}$

16. $\begin{cases} x + 3y = 13 \\ 2x - y = -9 \end{cases}$

17. $\begin{cases} y = -2x - 7 \\ 4x + 2y = 6 \end{cases}$

18. $\begin{cases} 2x + y = 5 \\ 4x + 2y = 6 \end{cases}$

19. $\begin{cases} -\frac{1}{2}x + y = 4 \\ x + 2y = 8 \end{cases}$

20. $\begin{cases} 3x - 6y = 9 \\ \frac{1}{2}x = y + \frac{3}{2} \end{cases}$

21. $\begin{cases} 4x + 5y = -7 \\ 3x - 6y = 24 \end{cases}$

22. $\begin{cases} -x + 2y = 3 \\ 2x - 4y = -6 \end{cases}$

23. $\begin{cases} 3x - y = 2 \\ -3x + y = 1 \end{cases}$

24. $\begin{cases} 6x - 3y = 9 \\ 3x + 7y = 47 \end{cases}$

Use substitution to solve each system of equations. Check your solution.

25. $\begin{cases} y = x + 3 \\ y = 2x - 4 \end{cases}$

26. $\begin{cases} x = y + 4 \\ 2x + 3y = 43 \end{cases}$

27. $\begin{cases} 4x + 2y = 20 \\ y = x - 2 \end{cases}$

28. $\begin{cases} x - y = 3 \\ 2x + 2y = 2 \end{cases}$

29. $\begin{cases} x - 2y = 0 \\ 2x - y = 6 \end{cases}$

30. $\begin{cases} x + y = 0 \\ y + 2x = 4 \end{cases}$

31. $\begin{cases} 2x + y = 8 \\ x - y = 3 \end{cases}$

32. $\begin{cases} x + 5y = 2 \\ x - 1 = 2y \end{cases}$

33. $\begin{cases} a = b + 2 \\ a = 5b - 6 \end{cases}$

34. $\begin{cases} p = 3q - 3 \\ 2p + 5q = -17 \end{cases}$

35. $\begin{cases} 3t - r = 9 \\ r = 2t + 8 \end{cases}$

36. $\begin{cases} 2x + y = -9 \\ 3x + y = 11 \end{cases}$

37. $\begin{cases} x - 5y = 2 \\ 9x + 8 = 15y \end{cases}$

38. $\begin{cases} s = 10 + 5t \\ 2s = 40 + 4t \end{cases}$

39. $\begin{cases} -3x - y = 2 \\ -6x + 2y = -2 \end{cases}$

40. Determine whether the given ordered pair is a solution of the given system.

a. $(1, 3)$ $\begin{cases} 5x + 2y = 11 \\ x - y = 7 \end{cases}$

b. $(5, -2)$ $\begin{cases} 4x - 3y = 26 \\ 2x + y = 8 \end{cases}$

c. $(2, 1)$ $\begin{cases} 2x - y = 8 \\ x + 3y = 5 \end{cases}$

d. $(5, 2)$ $\begin{cases} 4x - 2y = 16 \\ -8x + 4y = -32 \end{cases}$

e. Of the four systems given above, one is dependent. Identify that system and give three additional ordered pairs that satisfy the system.

Use substitution to solve each system of equations.

41. $\begin{cases} 2x - 3y - z = 12 \\ y + 3z = 10 \\ z = 4 \end{cases}$

42. $\begin{cases} 2x - 3y + 4z = 8 \\ 3x + 2y = 7 \\ x = 1 \end{cases}$

43. $\begin{cases} x + 3y - z = 8 \\ 2x - y + 2z = -9 \\ 3y = 9 \end{cases}$

44. $\begin{cases} 2x + 3y - 2z = 4 \\ 3x - 3y + 2z = 16 \\ 2z = -5 \end{cases}$

45. $\begin{cases} 3x + 5y = -3 \\ 10y - 2z = 2 \\ x = -z \end{cases}$

46. $\begin{cases} a + b + c = 6 \\ 3a - b + c = 8 \\ 2b = c \end{cases}$

Graph and classify each system. Then find the solution from the graph. Round your answers to the nearest hundredth when necessary.

47 $\begin{cases} y = 5x + 2.72 \\ y = 3.6x + 3.126 \end{cases}$

48 $\begin{cases} y = 4.3x - 0.44 \\ y = -2x + 4.6 \end{cases}$

49 $\begin{cases} -\frac{2}{5}x + y = -\frac{1}{10} \\ 3y - 2x = -\frac{5}{6} \end{cases}$

50 $\begin{cases} \frac{1}{7} = \frac{1}{14}x + 5\frac{1}{2}y \\ y = 4x + 14 \end{cases}$

51 $\begin{cases} 0.7y = 0.8x + 0.78 \\ -\frac{1}{5}x + \frac{1}{2}y = 2.1 \end{cases}$

52 $\begin{cases} 0.001y + \frac{4}{5}x = 0.2014 \\ 0.8x - 0.02y = 0.172 \end{cases}$

CHALLENGE

53. Solve $\begin{cases} ax + by = c \\ y = dx + e \end{cases}$ for x and y. Use the resulting expressions for x and y to solve a system in the same form, such as $\begin{cases} 2x + 3y = 21 \\ y = x + 2 \end{cases}$.

CONNECTION

GEOMETRY The perimeter of a rectangular swimming pool is 130 yards. Three times the length is equal to 10 times the width.
54. Find the length and the width of the pool.
55. Find the area of the pool.

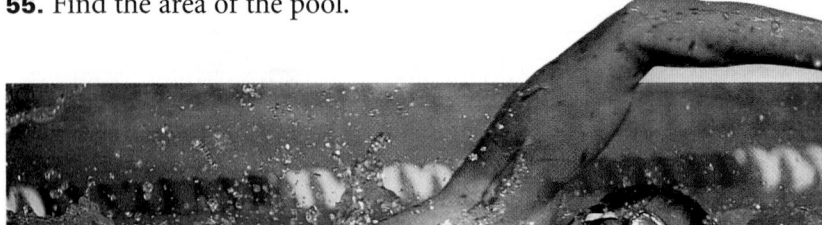

For Exercises 56–59, solve by writing a system of equations and using substitution. Check your answers.

APPLICATION

56. INCOME To earn money for college, Susan is making and selling earrings. Her weekly costs for advertising and phone calls are $36, and each pair of earrings costs $1.50 to produce. If Susan sells the earrings at $6 per pair, how many pairs must she sell per week to break even?

57. CONSUMER ECONOMICS Armando is comparing parking prices at a local concert. One option is a $7 entry fee plus $2 per hour. A second option is a $5 entry fee plus $3 per hour. What is the break-even point (intersection) for the two options? Which option do you think is better? Explain your reasoning.

58. CHEMISTRY To conduct a scientific experiment, students need to mix 90 milliliters of a 3% acid solution. They have a 1% and a 10% solution available. How many milliliters of the 1% solution and of the 10% solution should be combined to produce 90 milliliters of the 3% solution?

59. SPORTS Rebecca is the star forward on her high-school basketball team. In one game, her field-goal total was 23 points, made up of 2-point and 3-point baskets. If she made 4 more 2-point baskets than 3-point baskets, how many of each type of basket did she make?

 Look Back

Solve each equation or inequality, and graph the solution on a number line. *(LESSON 1.8)*

60. $|x - 4| = 9$ **61.** $|x - 2| \le 5$ **62.** $|x + 3| \le -1$

State the property that is illustrated in each statement. All variables represent real numbers. *(LESSON 2.1)*

63. $\frac{2}{3}(6x + 12) = \frac{2}{3} \cdot 6x + \frac{2}{3} \cdot 12$ **64.** $5a + (3a + 6) = (5a + 3a) + 6$

65. $-4a + 4a = 0$ **66.** $5x \cdot 9y = 9y \cdot 5x$

Evaluate each expression. *(LESSON 2.2)*

67. $5a^0$ **68.** $36^{\frac{1}{2}}$ **69.** $25^{-\frac{1}{2}}$ **70.** $9^{\frac{3}{2}}$

Simplify each expression, assuming that no variable equals zero. *(LESSON 2.2)*

71. $\left(\frac{2x^3}{x^{-2}}\right)^2$ **72.** $\left(\frac{m^{-1}n^2}{n^{-3}}\right)^{-3}$ **73.** $\left(\frac{2a^3b^{-2}}{-a^2b^{-3}}\right)^{-1}$ **74.** $\frac{(2y^2y)^{-2}}{3xy^{-4}}$

Find the inverse of each function and state whether the inverse is a function. *(LESSON 2.5)*

75. $\{(1, 4), (-3, 4), (2, 0)\}$ **76.** $\{(7, 8), (6, 4), (5, 0), (4, 4)\}$

77. $\{(3, 4), (4, 3), (3, -1), (11, -3)\}$ **78.** $\{(8, 6), (9, 4), (-8, 6), (0, 0)\}$

 Look Beyond

Use a graph to solve each nonlinear system of equations. Round your answers to the nearest hundredth when necessary.

79. $\begin{cases} y = x^2 + 3 \\ y = 4x \end{cases}$ **80.** $\begin{cases} x + y = 19 \\ y = 2^x \end{cases}$

internet connect

Activities Online

Go To: go.hrw.com
Keyword:
MB1 WBB

Solving Systems by Elimination

Objective

- Solve a system of two linear equations in two variables by elimination.

Why *You can model real-world situations involving two variables, such as business cost and revenue, with a system of two equations in two variables.*

In business, makers and sellers of goods must relate the cost of making goods to their selling price. They must also keep production costs within budget and maintain realistic expectations of revenue.

This table gives production costs and selling prices per frame for two sizes of picture frames. How many of each size should be made and sold if the production budget is $930 and the expected revenue is $1920? *You will solve this problem in Example 2.*

	Small	Large
Production cost	$5.50	$7.50
Selling price	$12.00	$15.00

You have learned to solve systems of linear equations by graphing and by using substitution. Some systems are more easily solved by another method called the *elimination method*. The **elimination method** involves multiplying and combining the equations in a system in order to eliminate a variable.

Independent Systems

EXAMPLE **1** Use elimination to solve the system. Check your solution.
$$\begin{cases} 2x + 5y = 15 \\ -4x + 7y = -13 \end{cases}$$

● **SOLUTION**

1. To eliminate x, multiply each side of the first equation by 2, and combine the resulting equations.

$$\begin{cases} 2x + 5y = 15 \\ -4x + 7y = -13 \end{cases} \rightarrow \begin{cases} 2(2x + 5y) = 2(15) \\ -4x + 7y = -13 \end{cases} \rightarrow \begin{cases} 4x + 10y = 30 \\ -4x + 7y = -13 \end{cases}$$

$$\begin{array}{r} 4x + 10y = 30 \\ -4x + 7y = -13 \\ \hline 17y = 17 \\ y = 1 \end{array}$$

Use the Addition Property of Equality.

Solve for y.

2. Substitute 1 for y in either original equation to find x.

First equation:

$$2x + 5y = 15$$
$$2x + 5(1) = 15$$
$$x = 5$$

Second equation:

$$-4x + 7y = -13$$
$$-4x + 7(1) = -13$$
$$x = 5$$

The solution of the system is $x = 5$ and $y = 1$, or $(5, 1)$.

CHECK

$$\begin{cases} 2x + 5y = 15 \\ -4x + 7y = -13 \end{cases} \rightarrow \begin{cases} 2(5) + 5(1) = 15 & \textbf{True} \\ -4(5) + 7(1) = -13 & \textbf{True} \end{cases}$$

TRY THIS

Use elimination to solve the system. Check your solution. $\begin{cases} 6r + 7s = -15 \\ -3r + s = -6 \end{cases}$

E X A M P L E ② Refer to the picture-frame problem described at the beginning of the lesson.

How many small frames and how many large frames can be made and sold if the production budget is \$930 and the expected revenue is \$1920?

● **SOLUTION**

1. Write a system of equations to represent the problem.

Let x represent the number of small picture frames, and let y represent the number of large picture frames.

	Small	Large	Total
Production cost	$5.5x$	$7.5y$	930
Selling price	$12x$	$15y$	1920

From the data in the table, write the system. $\begin{cases} 5.5x + 7.5y = 930 \\ 12x + 15y = 1920 \end{cases}$

2. To eliminate y, multiply each side of the first equation by -2, and combine the resulting equations.

$$\begin{cases} -2(5.5x + 7.5y) = -2(930) \\ 12x + 15y = 1920 \end{cases} \rightarrow \begin{cases} -11x - 15y = -1860 \\ 12x + 15y = 1920 \end{cases}$$

$$\begin{array}{r} -11x - 15y = -1860 \\ 12x + 15y = 1920 \\ \hline x \qquad\quad = 60 \end{array}$$

Use the Addition Property of Equality.

3. Substitute 60 for x in either original equation to find y.

First equation:

$$5.5x + 7.5y = 930$$
$$5.5(60) + 7.5y = 930$$
$$7.5y = 600$$
$$y = 80$$

Second equation:

$$12x + 15y = 1920$$
$$12(60) + 15y = 1920$$
$$15y = 1200$$
$$y = 80$$

Thus, the solution is $(60, 80)$. To meet the required goals, 60 small picture frames and 80 large ones should be made.

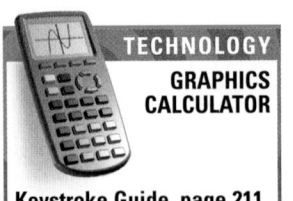
CHECK

You can use a graph, a table, or substitution to verify the solution.

To use a graphics calculator, solve each equation for y.

$$\begin{cases} 5.5x + 7.5y = 930 \\ 12x + 15y = 1920 \end{cases} \rightarrow \begin{cases} y = \dfrac{930 - 5.5x}{7.5} \\ y = \dfrac{1920 - 12x}{15} \end{cases}$$

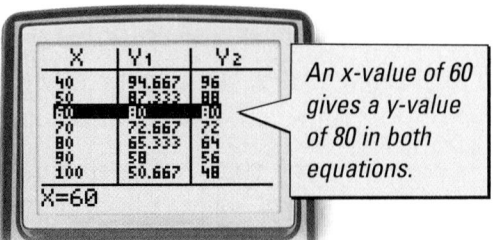

An x-value of 60 gives a y-value of 80 in both equations.

TRY THIS How does the solution to Example 2 change if the production budget is $1245 and the revenue goal is $2580?

CHECKPOINT ✔ Explain how you know that $5.5x + 7.5y$ and $12x + 15y$ are expressions that represent dollar amounts in Example 2.

CRITICAL THINKING The graph for the production budget and the graph for the revenue goal in Example 2 are quite similar. Describe what this means in terms of the number of small and large picture frames made and sold and in terms of the production budget and revenue goal.

Dependent and Inconsistent Systems

Investigating Systems

You will need: graph paper or a graphics calculator

1. Refer to system I in the first row.
   a. Graph the system and classify it as independent, dependent, or inconsistent.
   b. Solve the system by using elimination. Interpret the resulting mathematical statement.

System
I. $\begin{cases} x - y = -2 \\ -5x + 5y = 10 \end{cases}$
II. $\begin{cases} 3x + 3y = -5 \\ 2x + 2y = 7 \end{cases}$

2. Repeat parts **a** and **b** in Step 1 for system II.

CHECKPOINT ✔ 3. If an attempt to solve a system of equations results in the mathematical statement $0 = -3$, what can you say about this system?

CHECKPOINT ✔ 4. If an attempt to solve a system of equations results in the mathematical statement $0 = 0$, what can you say about this system?

You can use the elimination method to solve any system of two linear equations in two variables. Examples 3 and 4 show you how to interpret your results when the system is inconsistent or dependent.

EXAMPLE ③ Use elimination to solve the system. Check your solution.
$$\begin{cases} 2x + 5y = 12 \\ 2x + 5y = 15 \end{cases}$$

● **SOLUTION**

Combine the equations to eliminate a variable.

$$2x + 5y = 12$$

This is a false statement. → $2x + 5y = 15$

$$0 = -3$$ *Use the Subtraction Property of Equality.*

Because the result is a contradiction, the system is inconsistent. This means that the system has no solution.

CHECK

Graph the system. $\begin{cases} y = \dfrac{12 - 2x}{5} \\ y = \dfrac{15 - 2x}{5} \end{cases}$

The graph indicates that the system is inconsistent. The slopes are equal.

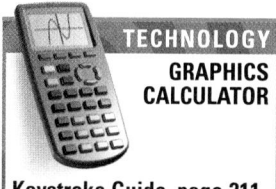
TECHNOLOGY
GRAPHICS CALCULATOR

Keystroke Guide, page 211

TRY THIS Use elimination to solve the system. Check your solution.
$$\begin{cases} 6x - 2y = 9 \\ 6x - 2y = 7 \end{cases}$$

CHECKPOINT ✔ Find the slope of each equation in the system in Example 3. How do the slopes of those equations confirm the conclusion reached in Example 3?

EXAMPLE ④ Use elimination to solve the system. Check your solution.
$$\begin{cases} 2x + 5y = 15 \\ -3x - 7.5y = -22.5 \end{cases}$$

● **SOLUTION**

Multiply each side of the first equation by 3, and multiply each side of the second equation by 2. Then combine the resulting equations to eliminate x.

$$\begin{cases} 3(2x + 5y) = 3(15) \\ 2(-3x - 7.5y) = 2(-22.5) \end{cases} \rightarrow \begin{cases} 6x + 15y = 45 \\ -6x - 15y = -45 \end{cases}$$

$$6x + 15y = 45$$

This is a true statement. → $-6x - 15y = -45$

$$0 = 0$$ *Use the Addition Property of Equality.*

Because the result is true regardless of the values of the variables in the system, the system is consistent and dependent. This means that the solution of the system is all points on the graph of either equation.

CHECK

Graph the system. $\begin{cases} y = \dfrac{15 - 2x}{5} \\ y = \dfrac{-22.5 + 3x}{-7.5} \end{cases}$

The two equations describe the same line.

The graph indicates that the system is dependent.

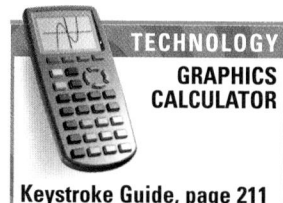
TECHNOLOGY
GRAPHICS CALCULATOR

Keystroke Guide, page 211

TRY THIS　Use elimination to solve the system. Check your solution. $\begin{cases} 8x + 4y = -16 \\ 2x + y = -4 \end{cases}$

CHECKPOINT ✔ Find the slope and y-intercept of each line represented in the system in Example 4. How do the slopes and y-intercepts of those lines confirm the conclusion reached in Example 4?

SUMMARY

THE ELIMINATION METHOD

1. Arrange each equation in standard form, $Ax + By = C$.

2. If the coefficients of x (or y) are the same number, use subtraction to eliminate the variable.

3. If the coefficients of x (or y) are opposites, use addition to eliminate the variable.

4. If the coefficients of x (or y) are different, multiply one or both equations by constants so that the coefficients of x (or y) are the same or opposite numbers. Then use Step 2 or 3 to eliminate the variable.

5. Use substitution to solve for the remaining variable.

Exercises

Communicate

1. Explain how to solve $\begin{cases} 3x - 4y = 3 \\ 2x + y = -5 \end{cases}$ by elimination.

2. When attempting to solve a system by elimination, what are the results for an inconsistent system? for a dependent system?

3. What property justifies adding the corresponding sides of two equations to create a new equation?

4. Compare the elimination method with the substitution method for solving systems of linear equations. What type of system is most easily solved by using substitution, and what type of system is most easily solved by using elimination?

Guided Skills Practice

5. Use elimination to solve the system. Check your solution. **(EXAMPLE 1)** $\begin{cases} 2x - 3y = 1 \\ 5x + 6y = 16 \end{cases}$

APPLICATION

6. BUSINESS How does the solution to Example 2 change if the production costs for large and small picture frames are $7 and $6, respectively? **(EXAMPLE 2)**

Use elimination to solve each system of equations. Check your solution.
(EXAMPLES 3 AND 4)

7. $\begin{cases} 3x - y = -2 \\ 9x - 3y = 3 \end{cases}$

8. $\begin{cases} 3x + 2y = 5 \\ -6x - 4y = -10 \end{cases}$

Practice and Apply

Use elimination to solve each system of equations. Check your solution.

9. $\begin{cases} 2x + y = 8 \\ x - y = 10 \end{cases}$

10. $\begin{cases} 3x + 4y = 23 \\ -3x + y = 2 \end{cases}$

11. $\begin{cases} -2x + 3y = -14 \\ 2x + 2y = 4 \end{cases}$

12. $\begin{cases} 2p + 5q = 13 \\ p - q = -4 \end{cases}$

13. $\begin{cases} 2s - 5t = 22 \\ 2s - 3t = 6 \end{cases}$

14. $\begin{cases} 12y - 5z = 19 \\ 12y + 16z = 40 \end{cases}$

15. $\begin{cases} x + y = 4 \\ 2x + 3y = 9 \end{cases}$

16. $\begin{cases} 3a + 2b = 2 \\ a + 6b = 18 \end{cases}$

17. $\begin{cases} 2x - 7y = 3 \\ 5x - 4y = -6 \end{cases}$

18. $\begin{cases} 5x + 3y = 2 \\ 2x + 20 = 4y \end{cases}$

19. $\begin{cases} 7b - 5c = 11 \\ -4c - 2b = -14 \end{cases}$

20. $\begin{cases} 2y - 4x = 18 \\ -5x + 3y = 23 \end{cases}$

21. $\begin{cases} 5x - 8 = 3y \\ 10x - 6y = 18 \end{cases}$

22. $\begin{cases} 2x = 5 + 4y \\ 2y = 8 + x \end{cases}$

23. $\begin{cases} -8x + 4y = -2 \\ 4x - 2y = 1 \end{cases}$

24. $\begin{cases} 4y + 30 = 10x \\ 5x - 2y = 15 \end{cases}$

25. $\begin{cases} 3x - 4y = -1 \\ -10 + 8y = -6x \end{cases}$

26. $\begin{cases} 3x + 7y = 10 \\ 5x = 7 - 2y \end{cases}$

Use any method to solve each system of linear equations. Check your solution.

27. $\begin{cases} -4.5x + 7.5y = -9 \\ 3x - 5y = 6 \end{cases}$

28. $\begin{cases} 5x - 3y = 8 \\ x + 0.6y = 1.8 \end{cases}$

29. $\begin{cases} 3y = 5 - x \\ x + 4y = 8 \end{cases}$

30. $\begin{cases} 7y - \frac{1}{2}x = 2 \\ -2y = x + 4 \end{cases}$

31. $\begin{cases} \frac{5}{2}x - y = 5 \\ 4y = 3x - 6 \end{cases}$

32. $\begin{cases} 5x + 4y = 2 \\ 2x + 3y = 5 \end{cases}$

33. $\begin{cases} -2x + 5y = -23 \\ 24 + 4y = 3x \end{cases}$

34. $\begin{cases} \frac{x + 3}{2} = x + 4y \\ x = 5y \end{cases}$

35. $\begin{cases} 16x - 6y = -1 + 6y \\ \frac{2}{3}x = 4y + 3 \end{cases}$

CHALLENGE

Find the value(s) of *k* that satisfy the given condition for each system.

36. The system $\begin{cases} kx - 5y = 8 \\ 7x + 5y = 10 \end{cases}$ is consistent.

37. The system $\begin{cases} kx - 5y = 8 \\ 7x + 5y = 10 \end{cases}$ has infinitely many solutions.

CONNECTION

38. COORDINATE GEOMETRY The ordered pairs (2, 9) and (6, 17) satisfy the linear equation $Ax + By = 5$, with coefficients *A* and *B*.
   a. Substitute each ordered pair into the equation to obtain two new equations in two variables, *A* and *B*.
   b. Solve the system of equations obtained in part **a** for *A* and *B*.
   c. Rewrite the linear equation $Ax + By = C$ with the values for *A* and *B* from part **b**.
   d. Solve the linear equation for *y* and identify the slope and *y*-intercept.
   e. Use the two ordered pairs and the slope formula to find the slope.
   f. Do your slopes from parts **d** and **e** agree?

39. CULTURAL CONNECTION: CHINA The *Jiuzhang*, or *Nine Chapters on the Mathematical Art*, was written around 250 B.C.E. in China. It includes problems with systems of linear equations, such as the one below. Solve the problem.

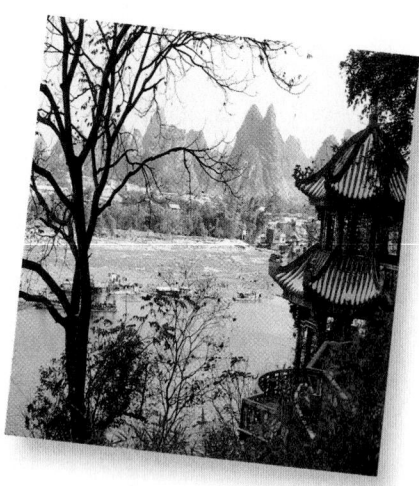

A family bought 100 acres of land and paid 10,000 pieces of gold. The price of good land is 300 pieces of gold per acre and the price of bad land is 500 pieces of gold for 7 acres. How many acres of good land and how many acres of bad land were purchased?

APPLICATIONS

40. SPORTS Greg is a star player on the basketball team. In one game, his field-goal total was 20 points, made up of 2-point and 3-point baskets. If Greg made a total of 9 baskets, how many of each type did he make?

INVESTMENTS Beth has saved $4500. She would like to earn $250 per year by investing her money. She received advice about two different investments: a low-risk investment that pays a 5% annual interest and a high-risk investment that pays a 9% annual interest.

41. How much should Beth invest in each type of investment to earn her annual goal?

42. How much should Beth invest in each type of investment if she wishes to earn $325 per year?

43. BUSINESS A mail-order company charges for postage and handling according to the weight of the package. A package that weighs less than 3 pounds costs $2.00 for shipping and handling, and a package that weighs 3 pounds or more costs $3.00. An order of 12 packages had a total shipping and handling cost of $29.00. Find the number of packages that weighed less than 3 pounds and the number of packages that weighed 3 pounds or more.

NUTRITION One unit of whole-wheat flour has 13.6 grams of protein and 2.5 grams of fat. One unit of whole milk has 3.4 grams of protein and 3.7 grams of fat.

44. Write a system of equations that can be used to find the number of units of whole-wheat flour and the number of units of whole milk that must be mixed to make a dough that has 75 grams of protein and 15 grams of fat.

45. Solve the system and give the number of units, to the nearest tenth, of flour and of milk in the dough.

46. INCOME When Dale baby-sat for 8 hours and worked at a restaurant for 3 hours, he made a total of $58. When he baby-sat for 2 hours and worked at a restaurant for 5 hours, he made a total of $40. How much does Dale get paid for each type of work?

Look Back

47. LANDSCAPING The cost of plants is directly proportional to the area to be planted. Suppose that a nursery charges $78 for enough plants to cover an area of 50 square feet. How much would it cost to cover an area of 80 square feet? *(LESSON 1.4)*

Create a scatter plot of the data in each table. Then describe the correlation as positive or negative. *(LESSON 1.5)*

48.

x	3	5	6	0	8	5
y	9	4	3	11	1	3

49.

x	1	3	5	2	9	4
y	2	5	5	1	12	4

Solve each equation. *(LESSON 1.6)*

50. $3x - 12 = 24$ **51.** $\frac{1}{5}x - 3 = x + 3$ **52.** $5x - 2(3x - 1) = x - 10$

Solve each inequality, and graph the solution on a number line. *(LESSON 1.7)*

53. $4x > 6$ **54.** $8x \leq 24$ **55.** $-\frac{1}{2}x \leq 5$

Solve each compound inequality, and graph the solution on a number line. *(LESSON 1.7)*

56. $n + 1 < 9$ *and* $n - 3 > 1$ **57.** $2y - 10 \leq -6$ *and* $y + 8 \geq 2$

58. $x + 11 \geq 7$ *or* $x - 4 \leq 4$ **59.** $-2a - 8 < 4$ *or* $3a - 9 < 21$

Evaluate each expression by using the order of operations. *(LESSON 2.1)*

60. $7(6 - 5^2)$ **61.** $-(-3)^2 - 4^2$ **62.** $21 - 7 \times 3 + 8 \div 3$

 Look Beyond

Solve each system of nonlinear equations by elimination.

63. $\begin{cases} x^2 + y^2 = 3 \\ x^2 + y^2 = 9 \end{cases}$ **64.** $\begin{cases} y^2 = 1 - x^2 \\ x^2 + y^2 = 1 \end{cases}$

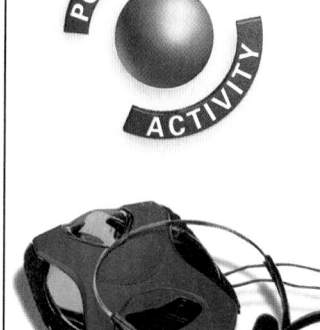

BUSINESS A company manufactures two different models of portable CD players: a regular model and a sport model.

Each model requires production time on two different machines, as shown at right.

	Regular model	Sport model
Machine A	2 minutes	1 minute
Machine B	1 minute	1 minute

Each machine is used for manufacturing many different items. In a given hour, machine A is used for CD-player production for 18 minutes and machine B is used for 10 minutes. How many CD players of each model are produced per hour?

Linear Inequalities in Two Variables

Why Linear inequalities can be used to model real-world situations, such as the distance that a car with given fuel-economy ratio can be driven using no more than 20 gallons of gasoline.

Objectives

● Solve and graph a linear inequality in two variables.

● Use a linear inequality in two variables to solve real-world problems.

The fuel-economy test results for three different automobiles are shown below.

EPA 1997 Fuel-Economy Program

Automobile	Fuel Economy (mpg)	
	City	Highway
Automobile A	28.1	33.3
Automobile B	25.6	31.5
Automobile C	20.2	31.7

[*Source: Environmental Protection Agency*]

Consider automobile A. If you let x represent miles driven in the city and y represent the miles driven on the highway, then $\frac{x}{28.1} + \frac{y}{33.3}$ represents the number of gallons of gasoline consumed. Solve $\frac{x}{28.1} + \frac{y}{33.3} \leq 20$ to find how far you can drive using no more than 20 gallons of gasoline. *You will solve this problem in Example 3.*

The inequality $\frac{x}{28.1} + \frac{y}{33.3} \leq 20$ is an example of a *linear inequality in two variables.*

Linear Inequality in Two Variables

A **linear inequality in two variables**, x and y, is any inequality that can be written in one of the forms below, where $A \neq 0$ and $B \neq 0$.

$$Ax + By \geq C \qquad Ax + By > C \qquad Ax + By \leq C \qquad Ax + By < C$$

A solution of a linear inequality in two variables, x and y, is an ordered pair (x, y) that satisfies the inequality. The solution to a linear inequality is a region of the coordinate plane and is called a *half-plane* bounded by a *boundary line*.

EXAMPLE ❶ Graph each linear inequality.

    a. $y < x + 2$ **b.** $y \geq -2x + 3$

● **SOLUTION**

a. Graph the boundary line $y = x + 2$. Use a dashed line because the values on this line are not included in the solution.

Choose a point such as $(0, 0)$ to test.

$$y \overset{?}{<} x + 2$$
$$0 < 0 + 2 \quad \textbf{True}$$

Since $(0, 0)$ satisfies the inequality, shade the region that contains this point.

b. Graph the boundary line $y = -2x + 3$. Use a solid line because the values on this line are included in the solution.

Choose a point such as $(0, 0)$ to test.

$$y \overset{?}{\geq} -2x + 3$$
$$0 \geq -2(0) + 3 \quad \textbf{False}$$

Since $(0, 0)$ does *not* satisfy the inequality, shade the region that does *not* contain this point.

Notice that (2, 2) satisfies the inequality and is in the solution region.

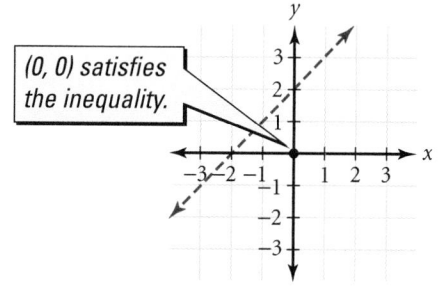

(0, 0) satisfies the inequality.

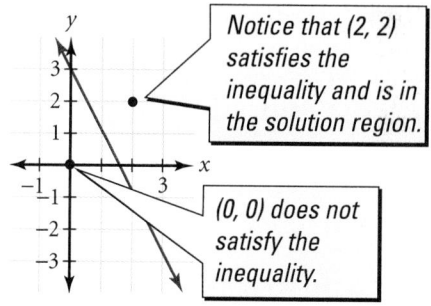

(0, 0) does not satisfy the inequality.

TRY THIS   Graph each linear inequality.

    a. $y > -2x - 2$ **b.** $y \leq 2x + 5$

Sometimes you may need to solve for y before graphing a linear inequality, as shown in Example 2.

EXAMPLE ❷ Graph $-2x - 3y \leq 3$.

● **SOLUTION**

Solve for y in terms of x.

$$-2x - 3y \leq 3$$
$$-3y \leq 2x + 3$$
$$y \geq -\frac{2}{3}x - 1 \quad \textit{Change} \leq \textit{to} \geq.$$

Then graph $y \geq -\frac{2}{3}x - 1$.

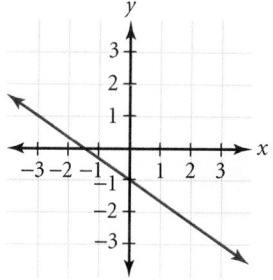

TRY THIS   Graph $3x - 4y \geq 4$.

CHECKPOINT ✔ Is the solution to $y < mx + b$ above or below the boundary line?
                       Is the solution to $y > mx + b$ above or below the boundary line?

EXAMPLE ③ **Refer to the fuel-economy test results given at the beginning of the lesson.**

    a. Represent in a graph the possible distances that automobile A can travel using no more than 20 gallons of gasoline.

    b. Can you drive 25 miles in the city and 400 miles on the highway in automobile A and use no more than 20 gallons of gasoline?

TECHNOLOGY

GRAPHICS CALCULATOR

Keystroke Guide, page 212

● **SOLUTION**

    a. Solve for y, and graph.

$$\frac{x}{28.1} + \frac{y}{33.3} \le 20$$

$$y \le -\frac{33.3}{28.1}x + 20(33.3)$$

Distance cannot be negative, so both $x \ge 0$ and $y \ge 0$.

    b. Test $(25, 400)$ to see if the inequality is true.

$$\frac{25}{28.1} + \frac{400}{33.3} \overset{?}{\le} 20 \quad \rightarrow \quad 12.9 \le 20 \quad \textbf{True}$$

You can also plot the point $(25, 400)$ to see whether the point is in the solution region.

Thus, you can drive 25 miles in the city and 400 miles on the highway and use no more than 20 gallons of gasoline in automobile A.

The solution to a linear inequality in only one variable is also a half-plane when graphed in the coordinate plane.

EXAMPLE ④ **Graph each linear inequality.**

    a. $x > -2$ **b.** $y \le -1$

● **SOLUTION**

    a. Any ordered pair whose x-coordinate is greater than -2 is a solution. Graph the boundary line $x = -2$, using a dashed line, and shade the half-plane to the right of the line.

    b. Any ordered pair whose y-coordinate is less than or equal to -1 is a solution. Graph the boundary line $y = -1$, using a solid line, and shade the half-plane below the line.

TRY THIS   Graph $x \le 4$ and $y > 3$ separately.

On which side of the boundary line is the solution region for $x > c$ (or $x \geq c$)?
On which side of the boundary line is the solution region for $x < c$ (or $x \leq c$)?

As you will notice in the Activity below, sometimes the solution to a linear inequality is a set of *discrete* points in a region instead of the entire region.

Activity

Exploring Discrete Solutions

You will need: no special materials

Daryll wants to buy some cassette tapes and CDs. A tape costs $8 and a CD costs $15. He can spend no more than $90 on tapes and CDs.

PROBLEM SOLVING
1. Let x represent the number of tapes he can buy. Let y represent the number of CDs he can buy. **Write a linear inequality** in x and y to represent his possible purchases.

CHECKPOINT ✔
2. Explain why x and y must be whole numbers.

3. List four ordered pairs (x, y) that satisfy your inequality from Step 1.

4. How many tapes can Daryll buy if he chooses not to buy any CDs? How many CDs can Daryll buy if he chooses not to buy any tapes?

5. Graph all possible solutions to your inequality in Step 1 on a coordinate plane.

CHECKPOINT ✔
6. Describe other situations that can be modeled by a linear inequality that has only nonnegative integer solutions.

The procedure for graphing linear inequalities is summarized below.

SUMMARY

GRAPHING LINEAR INEQUALITIES

1. Given a linear inequality in two variables, graph its related linear equation.
- For inequalities involving $\leq$ or $\geq$, use a solid boundary line.
- For inequalities involving $<$ or $>$, use a dashed boundary line.

2. Shade the appropriate region.
- For inequalities of the form $y \leq mx + b$ or $y < mx + b$, shade below boundary line.
- For inequalities of the form $y \geq mx + b$ or $y > mx + b$, shade above boundary line.
- For inequalities of the form $x \leq c$ or $x < c$, shade to the left of the boundary line.
- For inequalities of the form $x \geq c$ or $x > c$, shade to the right of the boundary line.

CRITICAL THINKING
Let $Ax + By \geq C$, where $A \neq 0$ and $B \neq 0$. Under what conditions is the solution region of the inequality above the boundary line? Under what conditions is the solution region below the boundary line?

Exercises

Communicate

1. Describe how to graph $7x - 5y > 0$ on graph paper.

2. When graphing a linear inequality, what determines whether the boundary line is dashed or solid?

3. Describe two ways to determine which region of the plane should be shaded for the different types of linear inequalities.

Guided Skills Practice

Graph each linear inequality. *(EXAMPLES 1 AND 2)*

4. $y < 2x + 6$ **5.** $y \geq -\frac{1}{3}x + 6$ **6.** $2y + 3x \geq 12$ **7.** $4y - 5x < -8$

APPLICATION

8. FUEL ECONOMY Refer to the fuel-economy test results given on page 172. Can you drive 25 miles in the city and 400 miles on the highway in automobile B using no more than 20 gallons of gasoline? *(EXAMPLE 3)*

Graph each linear inequality. *(EXAMPLE 4)*

9. $x \leq 2$ **10.** $y > -3$

Practice and Apply

internet connect

Homework Help Online
Go To: **go.hrw.com**
Keyword:
MB1 Homework Help
for Exercises 11–28, 32–44

Graph each linear inequality.

11. $y \geq 3x + 1$ **12.** $y > 5x + 2$ **13.** $y < 6x + 2$

14. $y \leq \frac{3}{2}x + 1$ **15.** $y \geq -\frac{1}{2}x + \frac{2}{3}$ **16.** $y > -3x - 4$

17. $y < -2x + \frac{1}{2}$ **18.** $y \leq -10x + 3$ **19.** $y - 5x \geq 2$

20. $2x + y > -2$ **21.** $x + 3y < 1$ **22.** $5x + 3y \leq 4$

23. $5x - y \geq 1$ **24.** $-2x - y > 0$ **25.** $6x - 4y > -2$

26. $3x - 2y > 5$ **27.** $\frac{3}{2}x - \frac{5}{4}y - 1 \leq 0$ **28.** $\frac{2}{3}x - \frac{1}{2}y \leq -2$

Write an inequality for each graph.

29.   **30.**   **31.**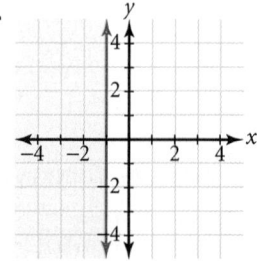

Graph each linear inequality.

32. $x < -1$ **33.** $x \leq 2$ **34.** $y \geq 3$ **35.** $y > -2$

36. $2y < 5$ **37.** $2y \leq -1$ **38.** $-x \leq 4$ **39.** $-\frac{5}{4}x < -2$

40. $-7y < 21$ **41.** $\frac{3 - 12y}{7} < 0$ **42.** $\frac{6x + 5}{3} \geq 8$ **43.** $3(4 - 2x) \leq -7$

44. Graph the inequality $y \geq \frac{1}{2}x + 5$.

    a. Does the ordered pair $(4, 1)$ satisfy the inequality? Support your answer by using both the inequality and the graph.

    b. Identify three ordered pairs that have an x-coordinate of 6 and satisfy the inequality.

    c. Identify three ordered pairs that have a y-coordinate of 8 and satisfy the inequality.

CHALLENGE

Describe the graphs in each *family* of inequalities for *n*-values of 1, 2, 3, and 4.

45. $x < n$ **46.** $y > (-1)^n x$ **47.** $ny \leq 2x$

CONNECTION

48. GEOMETRY The perimeter of a rectangle with a length of x feet and a width of y feet cannot exceed 200 feet.

    a. Write three linear inequalities to describe the restrictions on the values of the perimeter, of x, and of y.

    b. Graph the solution region of the three inequalities from part **a**.

APPLICATIONS

SPORTS Michael is close to breaking his high-school record for field-goal points in a basketball game, needing 24 points to tie the record and 25 points to break the record. A field goal can be worth either 2 or 3 points. Michael will play in a game tonight. Write an equation or inequality for each situation below.

49. He fails to tie or break the record.

50. He ties the record.

51. He breaks the record.

52. FUND-RAISING The junior class is sponsoring a refreshment booth at home football games. They will earn a $0.25 profit on each soft drink sold and a $0.20 profit on each ice-cream bar sold. Their goal is to earn a profit of at least $50.

    a. Write an inequality that describes the profit goal.

    b. Graph the inequality.

    c. Give four ordered pairs that represent a profit of exactly $50.

    d. Give three ordered pairs that represent a profit more than $50.

    e. Give three ordered pairs that represent a profit less than $50.

53. RECREATION Amanda is planning a cookout. She has budgeted a maximum of $60 for hamburgers and turkey dogs. Hamburgers cost $3 per pound, and turkey dogs cost $2 per pound.

    a. Write an inequality to describe the possible number of pounds of hamburgers and of turkey dogs that she can purchase.

    b. Graph the inequality.

    c. What is the maximum number of pounds of hamburgers that she can purchase?

    d. What is the maximum number of pounds of turkey dogs that she can purchase?

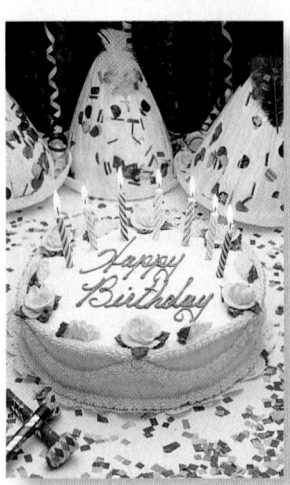

54. SMALL BUSINESS A local bakery makes cakes for two special occasions: birthdays and holidays. A birthday cake requires 2 pounds of flour, and a holiday cake requires 1 pound of flour. The bakery currently has 20 pounds of flour available for making the two types of cakes.
   a. Write an inequality to show the possible numbers of birthday and holiday cakes that the bakery can make.
   b. Graph the inequality.
   c. Give three specific ordered pairs that satisfy the inequality.

55. CONSUMER ECONOMICS At the corner store, bags of popcorn cost $0.95 and bags of peanuts cost $1.25. Suppose that you want to buy x bags of popcorn and y bags of peanuts and that you have $5.75.
   a. Write an inequality to describe the number of bags of popcorn and the number of bags of peanuts you could buy.
   b. Solve the inequality for y.
   c. Graph the inequality.

 Look Back

For Exercises 56–59, y varies directly as x. Find the constant of variation and the direct-variation equation that relates the two variable. *(LESSON 1.4)*

56. $x = 55$ when $y = 11$ **57.** $x = 4$ when $y = 32$

58. $x = -68$ when $y = \frac{1}{2}$ **59.** $x = \frac{1}{6}$ when $y = -45$

Solve each equation. *(LESSON 1.6)*

60. $3x - 5 = 1 - 4x$ **61.** $\frac{3}{2}x + 2 = 4 - 3x$ **62.** $-3(x - 2) = -x$

Graph and classify each system as independent, dependent, or inconsistent. Then find the solution from the graph. *(LESSON 3.1)*

63. $\begin{cases} x + 2y = -1 \\ 3x + 2y = 1 \end{cases}$ **64.** $\begin{cases} 2x - y = 3 \\ 3x + y = 7 \end{cases}$ **65.** $\begin{cases} 5x - 2y = 10 \\ x + 2y = 14 \end{cases}$

Use substitution to solve each system. *(LESSON 3.1)*

66. $\begin{cases} y = -2x - 4 \\ y = 2x + 5 \end{cases}$ **67.** $\begin{cases} y = 8 - x \\ \frac{1}{2}y - x = \frac{5}{2} \end{cases}$ **68.** $\begin{cases} y = 3x - 2 \\ 2y = 6x - 4 \end{cases}$

Use elimination to solve each system. *(LESSON 3.2)*

69. $\begin{cases} 8x + 5y = 22 \\ 6x + 2y = 13 \end{cases}$ **70.** $\begin{cases} 2x + 2y = 12 \\ 7x - 4y = -13 \end{cases}$ **71.** $\begin{cases} 2x - 3y = 3 \\ 4x + 2y = 14 \end{cases}$

 Look Beyond

Graph each inequality.

72. $|x + y| \leq 5$ **73.** $|x - y| \leq 5$ **74.** $|x| + |y| \leq 5$ **75.** $2|x| + |y| \leq 5$

Systems of Linear Inequalities

Why *Systems of linear inequalities can be used to represent real-world situations such as the height and weight criteria that are needed for an actor.*

Objectives

● Write and graph a system of linear inequalities in two variables.

● Write a system of linear inequalities in two variables for a given solution region.

Suppose that an actor is needed for the lead character in a play. The search is on for a male actor between the ages of 25 and 35, standing between 5' 8" and 5' 10" tall, with a medium build, and within the weight ranges given below for males with medium builds.

Height (in.)	Weight (lb)
66	139–151
67	142–154
68	145–157
69	148–160
70	151–163

[*Source: Taber's Cyclopedic Medical Dictionary, 15th Edition*]

You can represent the height and weight criteria for this actor with the *system of linear inequalities* below.

$$\begin{cases} 68 \leq h \leq 70 \\ w \geq 3h - 59 \\ w \leq 3h - 47 \end{cases}$$

The system of linear inequalities can be graphed as shown at right. The dark blue shaded region indicates the range of acceptable heights and weights for the lead actor.

A **system of linear inequalities** is a collection of linear inequalities in the same variables. The solution is any ordered pair that satisfies each of the inequalities in the system.

To graph a system of linear inequalities, shade the part of the plane that is the intersection of all of the individual solution regions.

EXAMPLE **1** Graph the system.
$$\begin{cases} x \geq 0 \\ y \geq 0 \\ y > -2x + 5 \\ y \leq 3x + 1 \end{cases}$$

● **SOLUTION**

The inequalities $x \geq 0$ and $y \geq 0$ tell you that the final solution region is in the first quadrant of a coordinate plane and may include points on the positive axes.

Graph $y > -2x + 5$ in the first quadrant. Use a dashed boundary line.

Graph $y \leq 3x + 1$ in the first quadrant. Use a solid boundary line.

The solution is the intersection of these two regions.

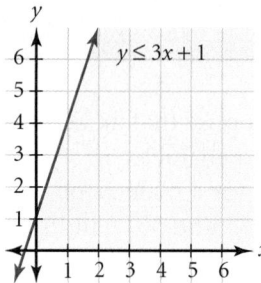

TRY THIS Graph the system.
$$\begin{cases} x \geq 0 \\ y \geq 0 \\ y < -x + 2 \\ y \geq -2x + 3 \end{cases}$$

EXAMPLE **2** Graph the system.
$$\begin{cases} y \geq -x - 1 \\ y \leq 2x + 1 \\ x < 1 \end{cases}$$

● **SOLUTION**

Graph $y \geq -x - 1$. Use a solid boundary line.

Graph $y \leq 2x + 1$. Use a solid boundary line.

Graph the intersection of $y \geq -x - 1$ and $y \leq 2x + 1$ with $x < 1$.

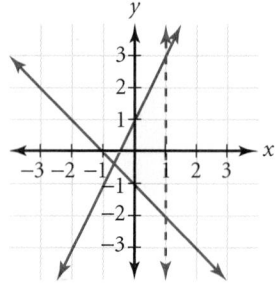

TRY THIS Graph the system.
$$\begin{cases} y > -x - 2 \\ y > x + 3 \\ y \leq 3 \end{cases}$$

CRITICAL THINKING Find the coordinates of the vertices of the triangle graphed in Example 2. Do the coordinates of all three vertices satisfy the system? Justify your response.

In a coordinate plane, the graph of a compound inequality in one variable can be a vertical or horizontal strip, as shown in Example 3.

E X A M P L E ③ **Graph each inequality in a coordinate plane.**
   a. $-3 \leq x \leq 2$ **b.** $-1 < y < 3$

● **SOLUTION**

a. The solution is the set of all ordered pairs whose x-coordinate is between -3 and 2 inclusive. The solution is a vertical strip.

b. The solution is the set of all ordered pairs whose y-coordinate is between -1 and 3. The solution is a horizontal strip.

 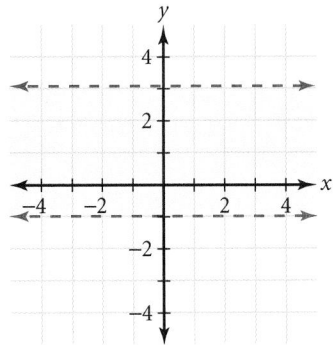

TRY THIS   Graph each inequality in a coordinate plane.
     a. $1 \leq y < 4$ **b.** $0 < x \leq 4$

CRITICAL THINKING   In a coordinate plane, is the graph of a compound inequality in one variable always a vertical or horizontal strip? Explain.

E X A M P L E ④ **Write the system of inequalities graphed at right.**

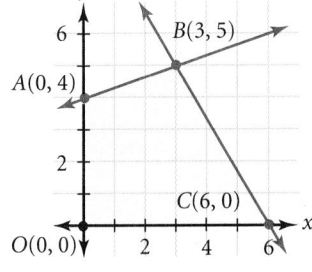

● **SOLUTION**

1. First find equations for the boundary lines.
   $\overleftrightarrow{AB}$: $m = \frac{5-4}{3-0} = \frac{1}{3}$ and $b = 4$ → $y = \frac{1}{3}x + 4$
   $\overleftrightarrow{BC}$: $m = \frac{0-5}{6-3} = -\frac{5}{3}$ → $y - 0 = -\frac{5}{3}(x-6)$
   $\overleftrightarrow{OA}$: $x = 0$ $y = -\frac{5}{3}x + 10$
   $\overleftrightarrow{OC}$: $y = 0$

2. Give each boundary line the appropriate inequality symbol. Because each boundary is solid, use $\geq$ or $\leq$.

below $\overleftrightarrow{AB}$: $y \leq \frac{1}{3}x + 4$ right of $\overleftrightarrow{OA}$: $x \geq 0$

below $\overleftrightarrow{BC}$: $y \leq -\frac{5}{3}x + 10$ above $\overleftrightarrow{OC}$: $y \geq 0$

The system of inequalities is $\begin{cases} y \leq \frac{1}{3}x + 4 \\ y \leq -\frac{5}{3}x + 10 \\ x \geq 0 \\ y \geq 0 \end{cases}$.

Exploring the Comfort Zone

APPLICATION
HEALTH

You will need: no special materials

The region labeled "Comfort Zone" in the graph at right shows the temperatures and relative humidity levels at which the average person feels comfortable.

1. What do $\overleftrightarrow{WX}$ and $\overleftrightarrow{ZY}$ represent? What do $\overleftrightarrow{WZ}$ and $\overleftrightarrow{XY}$ represent?

2. Record the coordinates of *W*, *X*, *Y*, and *Z*. Estimate the temperature at these points to the nearest one-half of a degree.

3. Write a system of linear inequalities that represents the comfort zone.

CHECKPOINT ✔ 4. What can you say about the temperature in the comfort zone as the relative humidity increases? Explain how this relates to the slope of one of the boundary lines.

[*Source: Concepts in Thermal Comfort*]

Exercises

● Communicate

1. Describe when to use a solid line and when to use a dashed line to graph of a system of linear inequalities.

2. If the coordinates of a point above a boundary line make the inequality false, which side of the boundary line should be shaded?

3. Describe a system of linear inequalities that has no solution.

● Guided Skills Practice

Graph each system. (EXAMPLES 1 AND 2)

4. $\begin{cases} x \geq 0 \\ y \geq 0 \\ y \geq -x + 4 \\ y > x \end{cases}$

5. $\begin{cases} y \geq x \\ y \geq -x + 1 \\ y < 2 \end{cases}$

Activities Online
Go To: **go.hrw.com**
Keyword:
MB1 Investments

Graph each inequality in a coordinate plane. *(EXAMPLE 3)*

6. $2 < x < 4$

7. $-1 \le y \le 5$

8. Write the system of inequalities graphed at right.
(EXAMPLE 4)

Practice and Apply

Homework Help Online
Go To: **go.hrw.com**
Keyword:
MB1 Homework Help
 for Exercises 9–20

Graph each system of linear inequalities.

9. $\begin{cases} y \ge 2 \\ y < x + 1 \end{cases}$

10. $\begin{cases} x < 3 \\ y \le 2x + 2 \end{cases}$

11. $\begin{cases} y < 3x - 4 \\ y \ge 6 - x \end{cases}$

12. $\begin{cases} y \le 3 - x \\ y \ge x - 5 \end{cases}$

13. $\begin{cases} x \ge 0 \\ y \ge 0 \\ y > 2x + 1 \end{cases}$

14. $\begin{cases} x \ge 0 \\ y \le 0 \\ y < -x \end{cases}$

15. $\begin{cases} x \ge 0 \\ y \le 0 \\ y > 2x - 5 \end{cases}$

16. $\begin{cases} x \ge 0 \\ y \ge -1 \\ y < -2x + 3 \end{cases}$

17. $\begin{cases} y \ge 2x - 1 \\ x > 1 \\ y < 5 \end{cases}$

18. $\begin{cases} x \ge 0 \\ y \ge 1 \\ y \le 5 - x \end{cases}$

19. $\begin{cases} y < x - 1 \\ y + 2x < 3 \\ y \ge -1 \end{cases}$

20. $\begin{cases} y + 2x \ge 0 \\ y \ge 2x - 4 \\ y \le 3 \end{cases}$

Graph each compound inequality in a coordinate plane.

21. $-5 < y < 1$

22. $-1 \le y \le 3$

23. $2 \le x \le 8$

24. $-2 < x < 3$

25. $0 < y < 4$

26. $-6 \le y \le -2$

27. $-5 \le x < -1$

28. $-\frac{2}{3} < x \le \frac{1}{3}$

29. $-\frac{1}{4} \le y < -\frac{1}{5}$

30. $-4.4 < y \le -4$

31. $-1.5 \le x < -0.5$

32. $-5.5 < x \le -5.1$

Write the system of inequalities whose solution is graphed. Assume that each vertex has integer coordinates.

33.

34.

35.

36.
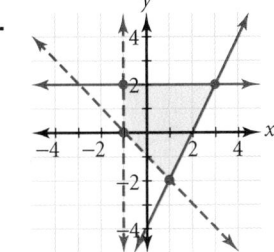

Graph each system of linear inequalities.

37. $\begin{cases} 3x + 2y \geq 1 \\ 2x + 3y < 2 \\ x < 3 \end{cases}$

38. $\begin{cases} x + y < 1 \\ 2x + 3y > 2 \\ x \geq -5 \end{cases}$

39. $\begin{cases} x + \frac{1}{2}y \leq 2 \\ 2x + 3y < 2 \end{cases}$

40. $\begin{cases} 2x + y \geq 2 \\ y \geq 3x + 2 \end{cases}$

41. $\begin{cases} x + y \leq 4 \\ 2x \leq y \end{cases}$

42. $\begin{cases} 2x - 2y < 1 \\ x + 2y \geq 2 \end{cases}$

43. $\begin{cases} 2x - y \leq 16 \\ x + y \leq 10 \\ x \geq 0 \\ y \geq 0 \end{cases}$

44. $\begin{cases} 3x - y \leq 15 \\ x + 2y \leq 10 \\ x \geq 0 \\ y \geq 0 \end{cases}$

45. $\begin{cases} 3x - 2y \geq 4 \\ x + y > 4 \\ x - y \leq 7 \\ x \geq 0 \\ y \geq 0 \end{cases}$

CONNECTIONS

46. GEOMETRY A parallelogram is a quadrilateral whose opposite sides are parallel. Create a graph of a parallelogram on a coordinate plane. Write a system of inequalities that represents the parallelogram and its interior.

CHALLENGE

47. GEOMETRY Classify the solution to $\begin{cases} y \leq a \\ y \geq |x| \end{cases}$, for $a > 0$, as a geometric figure.

APPLICATIONS

48. MANUFACTURING A small-appliance manufacturing company makes standard and deluxe models of a toaster oven. The company can make up to 200 ovens per week. The standard model costs $20 to produce, and the deluxe model costs $30 to produce. The company has budgeted no more than $3600 per week to produce the ovens.

a. Let x represent the number of standard models, and let y represent the number of deluxe models. Write a system of linear inequalities to represent the possible combinations of standard and deluxe models that the company can make in one week.

b. Graph the system of inequalities.

c. Due to an increase in the rental costs for the company's factory, the company can budget no more that $3000 per week to make the toaster ovens. Explain how this changes the possible combinations of standard and deluxe models that the company can make in one week.

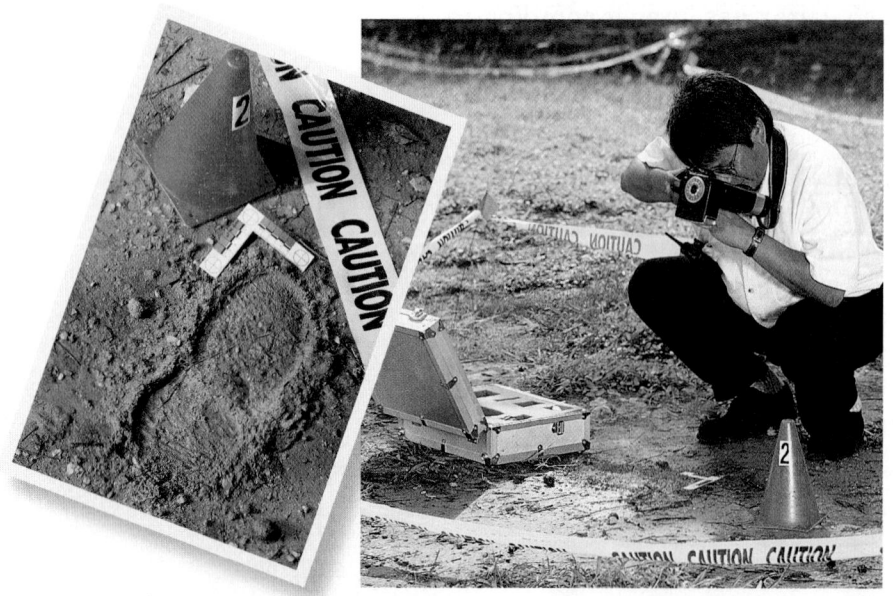

49. CRIMINOLOGY Officer Cheek is trying to solve a crime that was committed by a man with a shoe size from 9 to 10. According to witnesses, the man's height is between 5 feet and 5 feet 6 inches inclusive.

a. Let x represent the shoe size, and let y represent the height. Write a system of inequalities to represent the given information.

b. Graph the system of inequalities.

50. INCOME Angela works 40 hours or fewer per week programming computers and tutoring. She earns $20 per hour programming and $10 per hour tutoring. Angela needs to earn at least $500 per week.

  a. Write a system of linear inequalities that represents the possible combinations of hours spent tutoring and hours spent programming that will meet Angela's needs.

  b. Graph the system of linear inequalities. Is the solution a polygon?

  c. Find a point that is a solution to the system of linear inequalities. What are the coordinates of this point and what do the coordinates of this point represent?

  d. Which point in the solution region represents the best way for Angela to spend her time? Explain why you think this is the best solution.

51. ENTERTAINMENT A ticket office sells reserved tickets and general-admission tickets to a rock concert. The auditorium normally holds no more than 5000 people. There can be no more than 3000 reserved tickets and no more than 4000 general-admission tickets sold.

  a. Let x represent the number of reserved tickets, and let y represent the number of general-admission tickets. Write a system of three linear inequalities to represent the possible combinations of reserved and general-admission tickets that can be sold. (Note that x and y must be non-negative integers.)

  b. Graph the system of inequalities.

  c. In order to increase the number of people that come to the concert, the auditorium increases its seating capacity to 5500. Explain how this addition changes the possible ticket combinations.

52. BUSINESS A lawn and garden store sells gas-powered and electric hedge clippers. The store wants to sell at least 45 hedge clippers per month. The profit on each electric model is $50, and the profit on each gas-powered model is $40. The shop wants to earn at least $2000 per month on the sale of hedge clippers.

  a. Let x represent the number of electric hedge clippers, and let y represent the number of gas-powered hedge clippers. Write a system of linear inequalities to represent the possible combinations of each model sold.

  b. Graph the system of inequalities.

  c. If the shop sells 16 electric hedge clippers in one month, what is the minimum number of gas-powered hedge clippers that must be sold that month in order to meet their goals?

Look Back

53. Use intercepts to graph $5x - 3y = 7$. *(LESSON 1.2)*

54. Write the equation in slope-intercept form for the line that contains the point $(4, -3)$ and is parallel to $2x - 4y = 26$. *(LESSON 1.3)*

Solve each proportion for the variable. Check your answers. *(LESSON 1.4)*

55. $\dfrac{3x}{2} = \dfrac{15}{12}$ **56.** $\dfrac{1-2x}{8} = \dfrac{7}{4}$ **57.** $\dfrac{3x+5}{6} = \dfrac{x-2}{5}$

Solve each equation. *(LESSON 1.6)*

58. $5x = 15 + 3x$ **59.** $7x - 13 = -2x$

Let $f(x) = 3x + 2$ and $g(x) = 5 - x$. Find each new function, and state any domain restrictions. *(LESSON 2.4)*

60. $f + g$ **61.** $f - g$ **62.** $f \cdot g$ **63.** $\dfrac{f}{g}$

Use any method to solve each system of equations. Then classify each system as independent, dependent, or inconsistent. *(LESSONS 3.1 AND 3.2)*

64. $\begin{cases} 4x - 2y = 3 \\ 8y - 6x = 24 \end{cases}$ **65.** $\begin{cases} 5x + y = -1 \\ 10x - y = 3 \end{cases}$

66. $\begin{cases} 2x + 5y = 10 \\ 2x - 5y = 0 \end{cases}$ **67.** $\begin{cases} 3x + y = 6 \\ 6x + 2y = 12 \end{cases}$

 Look Beyond

68. Evaluate $P = 20x + 30y$ for $(3, 5)$, $(4, 7)$, and $(5, 8)$. As x- and y-values increase, does the value of P increase or decrease?

69. Evaluate $C = 400p + 500q$ for $(1, 2)$, $(2, 5)$, and $(3, 8)$. As p- and q-values increase, does the value of C increase or decrease?

70. SYNONYMS Define the word *feasible*. Use a dictionary or write your own definition. What is a synonym for *feasible*?

internet connect

Portfolio Extension
Go To: **go.hrw.com**
Keyword:
MB1 Diet

BUSINESS Another company also manufactures two different models of portable CD players: a regular model and a sport model. Each model requires time on three different machines, as shown below.

	Regular model	Sport model
Machine A	2 minutes	1 minute
Machine B	1 minute	3 minutes
Machine C	1 minute	1 minute

Each machine is used for manufacturing many different items, so in a given hour, machine A is available for CD-player production a maximum of 18 minutes, machine B for a maximum of 24 minutes, and machine C for a maximum of 10 minutes.

1. Is it possible for the company to produce 4 regular models and 5 sport models in one hour? Explain your reasoning.

2. Is it possible for the company to produce 6 regular models and 5 sport models in one hour? Explain your reasoning.

WORKING ON THE CHAPTER PROJECT
You should now be able to complete Activities 1 and 3 of the Chapter Project.

Linear Programming

Why *Linear programming is widely used in the management of business and agriculture to find optimal solutions to complex problems.*

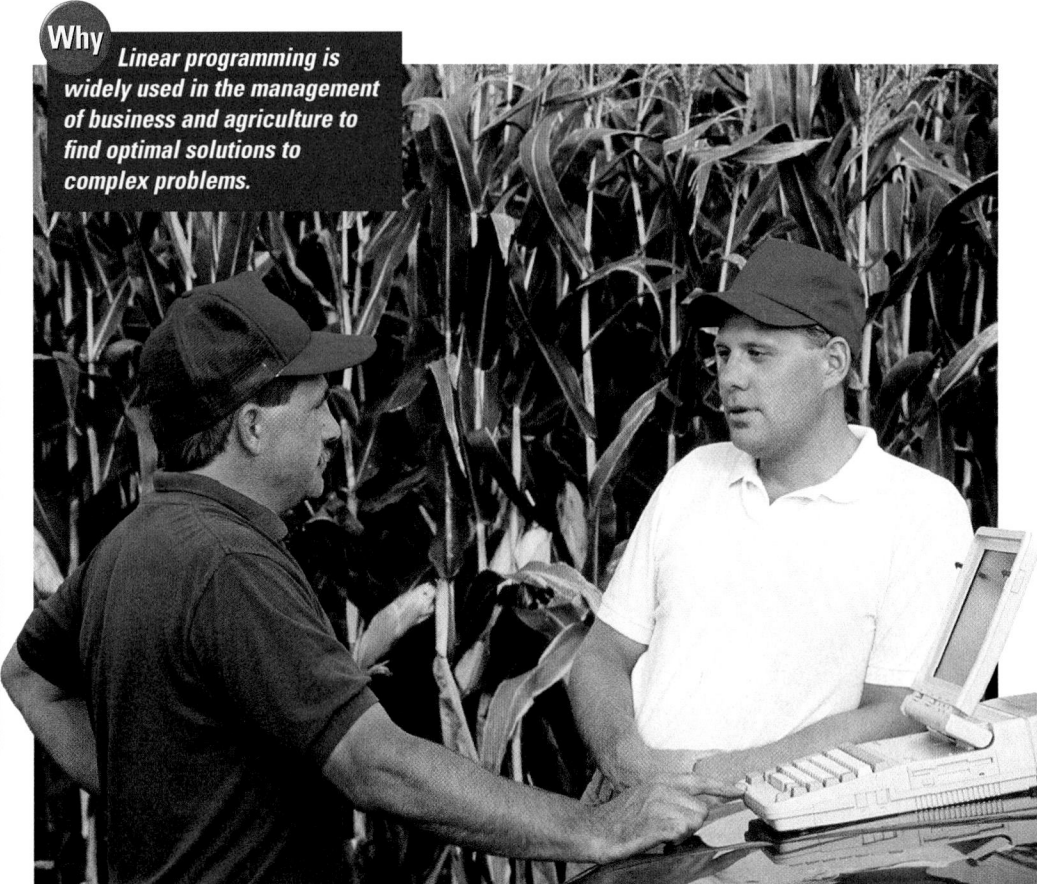

Objectives

● Write and graph a set of constraints for a linear-programming problem.

● Use linear programming to find the maximum or minimum value of an objective function.

Max Desmond is a farmer who plants corn and wheat. In making planting decisions, he used the 1996 statistics at right from the United States Bureau of the Census.

Crop	Yield per acre	Average price
corn	113.5 bu	$3.15/bu
soybeans	34.9 bu	$6.80/bu
wheat	35.8 bu	$4.45/bu
cotton	540 lb	$0.759/lb
rice, rough	5621 lb	$0.0865/lb

(The abbreviation for bushel is bu.)

Mr. Desmond wants to plant according to the following *constraints*:
• no more than 120 acres of corn and wheat
• at least 20 and no more than 80 acres of corn
• at least 30 acres of wheat

How many acres of each crop should Mr. Desmond plant to maximize the revenue from his harvest? *You will answer this question in Example 2.*

A method called **linear programming** is used to find optimal solutions such as the maximum revenue from Mr. Desmond's harvest. Linear-programming problems have the following characteristics:
• The inequalities contained in the problem are called **constraints**.
• The solution to the set of constraints is called the **feasible region**.
• The function to be maximized or minimized is called the **objective function**.

Example 1 illustrates how to begin the method of linear programming.

EXAMPLE ❶ **Refer to the planting problem described at the beginning of the lesson.**

    a. Write a system of inequalities to represent the constraints.
    b. Graph the feasible region.
    c. Write an objective function for the revenue from Mr. Desmond's harvest.

● **SOLUTION**

a. Let x represent the number of acres of corn. Let y represent the number of acres of wheat. Since x and y must be positive, $x \geq 0$ and $y \geq 0$.

b. The graph is shown below.

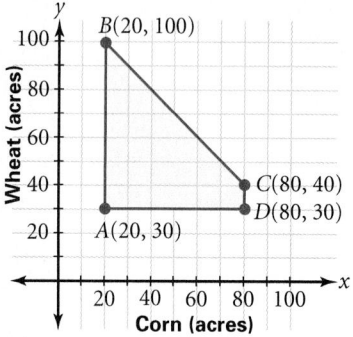

Corn constraint: $20 \leq x \leq 80$
Wheat constraint: $y \geq 30$
Total acreage: $x + y \leq 120$

The system is: $\begin{cases} 20 \leq x \leq 80 \\ y \geq 30 \\ x + y \leq 120 \end{cases}$

c. The objective function for the revenue is as follows:

$$R = \begin{pmatrix} \text{yield} \\ \text{per} \\ \text{acre} \end{pmatrix} \begin{pmatrix} \text{average} \\ \text{price} \end{pmatrix} x + \begin{pmatrix} \text{yield} \\ \text{per} \\ \text{acre} \end{pmatrix} \begin{pmatrix} \text{average} \\ \text{price} \end{pmatrix} y$$

$$R = (113.5)(3.15)x + (35.8)(4.45)y$$
$$R = 357.525x + 159.31y$$

For each point in the feasible region of a linear-programming problem, the objective function has a value. This value depends on both variables in the system that represents the feasible region.

In the Activity below, you will explore values in the feasible region for the objective function from Example 1.

Exploring the Objective Function

You will need: no special materials

1. Copy and complete the table to find the revenue at each of the four vertices of the feasible region from Example 1.

Vertex	Objective function
$A(20, 30)$	$R = 357.525(20) + 159.31(30) = 11{,}929.80$
$B(20, 100)$	?
$C(80, 40)$	?
$D(80, 30)$	?

2. Which vertex represents the greatest revenue? What do the coordinates of this vertex represent?

3. **Guess and check.** Choose points on the boundary lines of the feasible region. Find the corresponding revenues for these points. Can you find a point that gives a greater revenue than the vertex you chose in Step 2?

4. **Guess and check.** Choose points inside the feasible region. Find the corresponding revenues for these points. Can you find a point that gives a greater revenue than the vertex you chose in Step 2?

5. Do your investigations suggest that the maximum value of the objective function occurs at a vertex? Justify your response.

6. **Look for a pattern.** Repeat Steps 2–5 for the minimum revenue instead of the maximum revenue. Explain how the points that correspond to the maximum and minimum revenues are related.

In the Activity, you may have examined several points in the feasible region and found that the maximum and minimum revenues occur at vertices of the feasible region. The *Corner-Point Principle* confirms that you need to examine only the vertices of the feasible region to find the maximum or minimum value of the objective function.

Corner-Point Principle

In linear programming, the maximum and minimum values of the objective function each occur at one of the vertices of the feasible region.

Using the information in Example 1, maximize the objective function. Then graph the objective function that represents the maximum revenues along with the feasible region.

● **SOLUTION**

Make a table containing the coordinates of the vertices of the feasible region. Evaluate $R = 357.525x + 159.31y$ for each ordered pair.

Vertex	Objective function
$A(20, 30)$	$R = 357.525(20) + 159.31(30) = 11{,}929.80$
$B(20, 100)$	$R = 357.525(20) + 159.31(100) = 23{,}081.50$
$C(80, 40)$	$R = 357.525(80) + 159.31(40) = 34{,}974.40$
$D(80, 30)$	$R = 357.525(80) + 159.31(30) = 33{,}381.30$

The maximum revenue of \$34,974.40 occurs at $C(80, 40)$. Thus, Mr. Desmond should plant 80 acres of corn and 40 acres of wheat.

Write $357.525x + 159.31y = 34{,}974.4$ as $y = \dfrac{34{,}974.4 - 357.525x}{159.31}$, and graph it along with the boundaries of the feasible region.

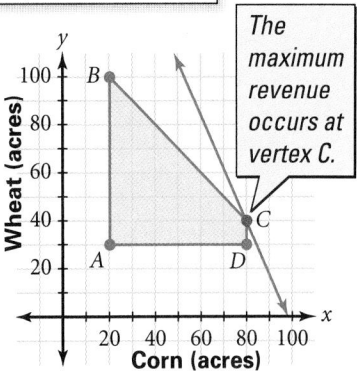

The maximum revenue occurs at vertex C.

EXAMPLE ③ Find the maximum and minimum values, if they exist, of the objective function $S = 2x + 3y$ given the set of constraints provided at right.

$$\begin{cases} x \geq 0, y \geq 0 \\ 5x + y \geq 20 \\ x + y \geq 12 \\ x + 2y \geq 16 \end{cases}$$

CONNECTION

MAXIMUM/MINIMUM

● **SOLUTION**

1. Graph the feasible region as shown.

2. The objective function is $S = 2x + 3y$.

3. Find the coordinates of each vertex by solving the appropriate system.

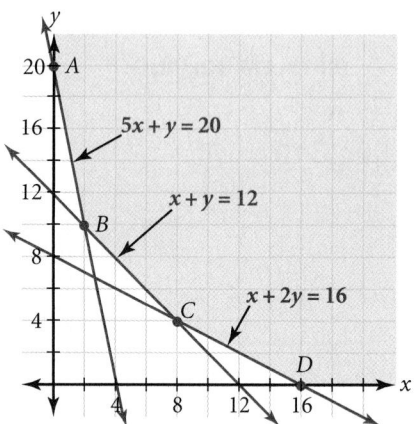

$$\begin{cases} 5x + y = 20 \\ x = 0 \end{cases}$$ gives $A(0, 20)$

$$\begin{cases} 5x + y = 20 \\ x + y = 12 \end{cases}$$ gives $B(2, 10)$

$$\begin{cases} x + y = 12 \\ x + 2y = 16 \end{cases}$$ gives $C(8, 4)$

$$\begin{cases} y = 0 \\ x + 2y = 16 \end{cases}$$ gives $D(16, 0)$

4. Evaluate $S = 2x + 3y$ for the coordinates of each vertex.

Vertex	Objective function
$A(0, 20)$	$S = 2(0) + 3(20) = 60$
$B(2, 10)$	$S = 2(2) + 3(10) = 34$
$C(8, 4)$	$S = 2(8) + 3(4) = 28$
$D(16, 0)$	$S = 2(16) + 3(0) = 32$

The feasible region is unbounded on the right of the vertices. Thus, there is no maximum value. The minimum value, 28, of $S = 2x + 3y$ occurs at $(8, 4)$.

CHECKPOINT ✔ Describe a real-world situation in which the feasible region would be unbounded on the right.

CRITICAL THINKING Can there be a real-world situation in which the feasible region would be unbounded on the left? Explain.

SUMMARY

LINEAR-PROGRAMMING PROCEDURE

Step 1. Write a system of inequalities, and graph the feasible region.

Step 2. Write the objective function to be maximized or minimized.

Step 3. Find the coordinates of the vertices of the feasible region.

Step 4. Evaluate the objective function for the coordinates of the vertices of the feasible region. Then identify the coordinates that give the required maximum or minimum.

Exercises

internet connect

Activities Online

Go To: **go.hrw.com**
Keyword:
MB1 Nutrition

Communicate

1. What is a *constraint* on a variable, such as *x*?

2. Discuss what the term *feasible* means when it is used to describe the possible solution region of a linear-programming problem.

3. In your own words, explain how to solve a linear-programming problem.

Guided Skills Practice

APPLICATION

AGRICULTURE Use the table of statistics at the beginning of the lesson to determine the constraints and to graph the feasible region for each situation below. Then write the corresponding objective function for the revenue. *(EXAMPLE 1)*

4. A farmer wants to plant corn and soybeans on 150 acres of land. The farmer wants to plant between 40 and 120 acres of corn and no more than 100 acres of soybeans.

5. A farmer wants to plant wheat and soybeans on 220 acres of land. The farmer wants to plant between 100 and 200 acres of wheat and no more than 75 acres of soybeans.

Find the number of acres of each crop that the farmer should plant to maximize the revenue for each situation. *(EXAMPLE 2)*

6. See Exercise 4.   7. See Exercise 5.

CONNECTION

MAXIMUM/MINIMUM **Find the maximum and minimum values, if they exist, of $C = 3x + 4y$ for each set of constraints.** *(EXAMPLE 3)*

8. $\begin{cases} 3 \le x \le 8 \\ 2 \le y \le 6 \\ 2x + y \ge 12 \end{cases}$

9. $\begin{cases} 2 \le x \\ 4 \le y \le 8 \\ x + 2y \ge 16 \end{cases}$

Practice and Apply

Graph the feasible region for each set of constraints.

10. $\begin{cases} x + 2y \le 8 \\ 2x + y \ge 10 \\ x \ge 0, y \ge 0 \end{cases}$

11. $\begin{cases} 3x + 2y \le 12 \\ \frac{1}{2}x - y \le -2 \\ x \ge 0, y \ge 0 \end{cases}$

12. $\begin{cases} x + 2y \le 6 \\ 2x - y \le 7 \\ x \ge 2, y \ge 0 \end{cases}$

13. $\begin{cases} 3x + y \le 12 \\ 2x - 3y \ge -3 \\ x \le 0, y \le 6 \end{cases}$

Identify the vertices of the feasible region in

14. Exercise 10.   15. Exercise 11.

16. Exercise 12.   17. Exercise 13.

The feasible region for a set of constraints has vertices at (–2, 0), (3, 3), (6, 2), and (5, 1). Given this feasible region, find the maximum and minimum values of each objective function.

18. $C = 2x - y$

19. $M = 3y - x$

20. $I = 100x + 200y$

21. $P = 3x + 2.5y$

Find the maximum and minimum values, if they exist, of each objective function for the given constraints.

22. $P = 5y + 3x$
Constraints:
$$\begin{cases} x + y \le 6 \\ x - y \le 4 \\ x \ge 0 \\ y \ge 0 \end{cases}$$

23. $P = 3x + y$
Constraints:
$$\begin{cases} x + y \ge 3 \\ 3x + 4y \le 12 \\ x \ge 0 \\ y \ge 0 \end{cases}$$

24. $P = 4x + 7y$
Constraints:
$$\begin{cases} x + y \le 8 \\ y - x \le 2 \\ x \ge 0 \\ y \ge 0 \end{cases}$$

25. $P = 2x + 7y$
Constraints:
$$\begin{cases} 4x - 2y \le 8 \\ x \ge 1 \\ 0 \le y \le 4 \end{cases}$$

26. $E = 2x + y$
Constraints:
$$\begin{cases} x + y \ge 6 \\ x - y \le 4 \\ x \ge 0 \\ y \ge 0 \end{cases}$$

27. $E = x + y$
Constraints:
$$\begin{cases} x + 2y \ge 3 \\ 3x + 4y \ge 8 \\ x \ge 0 \\ y \ge 0 \end{cases}$$

28. $E = 3x + 5y$
Constraints:
$$\begin{cases} x - 2y \ge 0 \\ x + 2y \ge 8 \\ 1 \le x \le 6 \\ y \ge 0 \end{cases}$$

29. $E = 3x + 2y$
Constraints:
$$\begin{cases} x + y \le 5 \\ y - x \ge 5 \\ 4x + y \ge -10 \end{cases}$$

CONNECTIONS

30. GEOMETRY If the feasible region for a linear-programming problem is bounded, it must form a *convex polygon*. Convex polygons cannot have "dents" and are defined as polygons in which any line segment connecting two points of the polygon has no part outside the polygon. Sketch two examples of convex polygons and two examples of polygons that are not convex (that is, concave).

CHALLENGE

31. MAXIMUM/MINIMUM An objective function can have a maximum (or minimum) value at two vertices if the graph of the objective function, equal to a constant function value, contains both vertices.
a. Draw the graph of a feasible region that has maximum values of 6 at two vertices for the objective function $P = 2x + 3y$.
b. Draw the graph of a feasible region that has minimum values of 6 at two vertices for the objective function $P = 2x + 3y$.

internet connect

Homework Help Online
Go To: **go.hrw.com**
Keyword:
MB1 Homework Help
for Exercises 32–37

32. MANUFACTURING A ski manufacturer makes two types of skis and has a fabricating department and a finishing department. A pair of downhill skis requires 6 hours to fabricate and 1 hour to finish. A pair of cross-country skis requires 4 hours to fabricate and 1 hour to finish. The fabricating department has 108 hours of labor available per day. The finishing department has 24 hours of labor available per day. The company makes a profit of $40 on each pair of downhill skis and a profit of $30 on each pair of cross-country skis.
a. Write a system of linear inequalities to represent the constraints.
b. Graph the feasible region.
c. Write the objective function for the profit, and find the maximum profit for the given constraints.

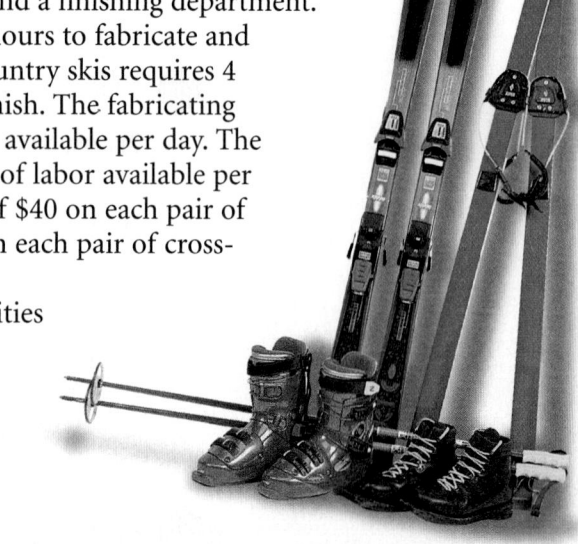

33. TRANSPORTATION Trenton, Michigan, a small community, is trying to establish a public transportation system of large and small vans. It can spend no more than $100,000 for both sizes of vehicles and no more than $500 per month for maintenance. The community can purchase a small van for $10,000 and maintain it for $100 per month. The large vans cost $20,000 each and can be maintained for $75 per month. Each large van carries a maximum of 15 passengers, and each small van carries a maximum of 7 passengers.
a. Write a system of linear inequalities to represent the constraints.
b. Graph the feasible region.
c. Write the objective function for the number of passengers, and find the maximum number of passengers for the given constraints.

34. BUSINESS A tourist agency can sell up to 1200 travel packages for a football game. The package includes airfare, weekend accommodations, and the choice of two types of flights: a nonstop flight or a two-stop flight. The nonstop flight can carry up to 150 passengers, and the two-stop flight can carry up to 100 passengers. The agency can locate no more than 10 planes for the travel packages. Each package with a nonstop flight sells for $1200, and each package with a two-stop flight sells for $900. Assume that each plane will carry the maximum number of passengers.
a. Write a system of linear inequalities to represent the constraints.
b. Graph the feasible region.
c. Write an objective function that maximizes the revenue for the tourist agency, and find the maximum revenue for the given constraints.

35. HEALTH A school dietitian wants to prepare a meal of meat and vegetables that has the lowest possible fat and that meets the Food and Drug Administration recommended daily allowances (RDA) of iron and protein. The RDA minimums are 20 milligrams of iron and 45 grams of protein. Each 3-ounce serving of meat contains 45 grams of protein, 10 milligrams of iron, and 4 grams of fat. Each 1-cup serving of vegetables contains 9 grams of protein, 6 milligrams of iron, and 2 grams of fat. Let x represent the number of 3-ounce servings of meat, and let y represent the number of 1-cup servings of vegetables.
a. Write a system of linear inequalities to represent the constraints.
b. Graph the feasible region.
c. Write the objective function for the number of grams of fat, and find the minimum number of grams of fat for the given constraints.

36. AGRICULTURE A farmer has 90 acres available for planting millet and alfalfa. Seed costs $4 per acre for millet and $6 per acre for alfalfa. Labor costs are $20 per acre for millet and $10 per acre for alfalfa. The expected income is $110 per acre for millet and $150 per acre for alfalfa. The farmer intends to spend no more than $480 for seed and $1400 for labor.
a. Write a system of linear inequalities to represent the constraints.
b. Graph the feasible region.
c. Write the objective function that maximizes the income, and find the maximum income for the given constraints.

37. SMALL BUSINESS A carpenter makes bookcases in two sizes, large and small. It takes 6 hours to make a large bookcase and 2 hours to make a small one. The profit on a large bookcase is $50, and the profit on a small bookcase is $20. The carpenter can spend only 24 hours per week making bookcases and must make at least 2 of each size per week.
   a. Write a system of linear inequalities to represent the constraints.
   b. Graph the feasible region.
   c. Write the objective function for the profit, and find the maximum profit for the given constraints.

 Look Back

Determine whether each table represents a linear relationship between *x* and *y*. If the relationship is linear, write the next ordered pair that would appear in the table. *(LESSON 1.1)*

38.

x	0	2	4	6
y	5	10	20	40

39.

x	−1	−2	−3	−4
y	2	4	6	8

Graph each function, and state the domain and the range. *(LESSON 2.3)*

40. $f(x) = 2x + 5$

41. $g(x) = 2x^2 - 3$

Find an equation for the inverse of each function. *(LESSON 2.5)*

42. $f(x) = 4x + 1$

43. $g(x) = -2x + \frac{1}{4}$

44. $f(x) = 5 - 2x$

45. $g(x) = \frac{1}{4}x - 6$

internet connect

Portfolio Extension
Go To: **go.hrw.com**
Keyword:
MB1 Simplex

 Look Beyond

Find the *x*-intercepts for the graph of each function. Compare the factors of each function rule with the *x*-intercepts of the graph.

46 $f(x) = (x - 3)(x + 2)$

47 $f(x) = (x + 4)(x - 9)$

48 $f(x) = x(x + 12)$

PORTFOLIO ACTIVITY

BUSINESS Refer to the second company's CD-player production described in the Portfolio Activity on page 186.

1. Determine the coordinates of the vertices of the feasible region.

2. The second company estimates that it makes a $20 profit for every regular model produced and a $30 profit for every sport model produced. Write the objective function for the profit.

3. How many regular models and sport models should the second company produce per hour in order to maximize their profit? What is the maximum profit?

WORKING ON THE CHAPTER PROJECT
You should now be able to complete the Chapter Project.

Parametric Equations

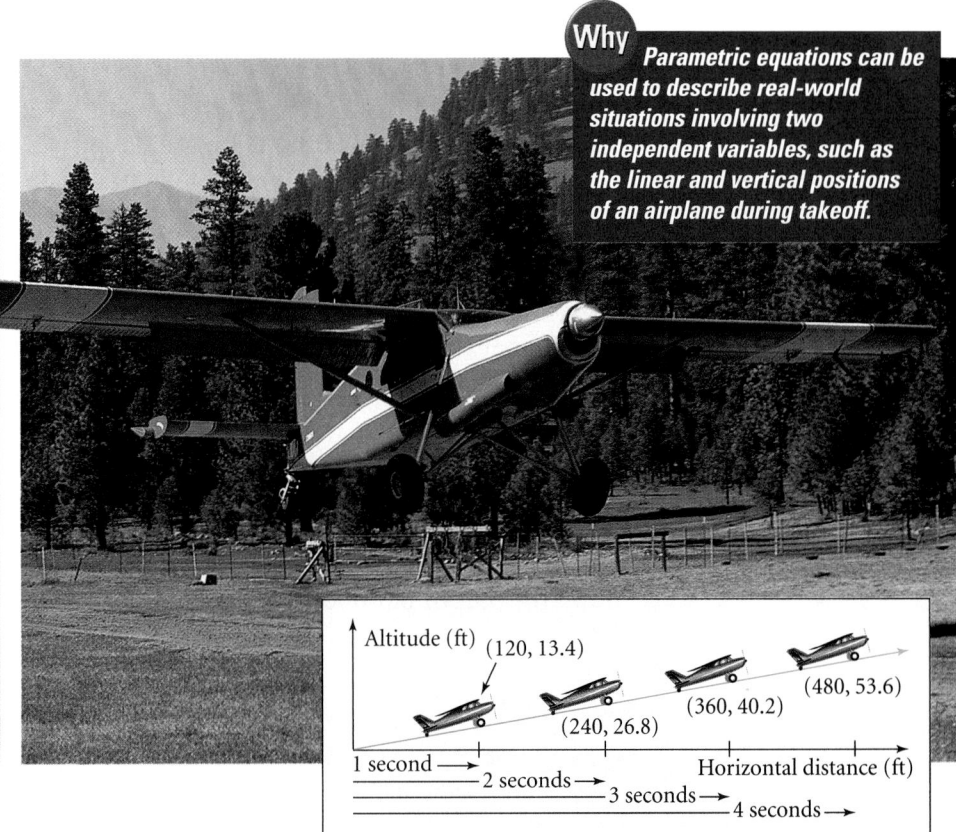

Why *Parametric equations can be used to describe real-world situations involving two independent variables, such as the linear and vertical positions of an airplane during takeoff.*

Objectives

- Graph a pair of parametric equations, and use them to model real-world applications.

- Write the function represented by a pair of parametric equations.

A small airplane takes off from a field. One second after takeoff, the airplane is 120 feet down the runway and 13.4 feet above it. The airplane's ascent continues at a constant rate. To analyze the position of the airplane as a function of time, you can represent the horizontal and vertical distances traveled in terms of a third variable, the time after takeoff.

For the Activity below, use the information in the diagram above.

Activity

Exploring the Position of an Airplane

You will need: a graphics calculator

Refer to the airplane described above. Let t represent the time in seconds after takeoff, let x represent the horizontal distance in feet traveled in t seconds, and let y represent the vertical distance, or altitude, in feet traveled in t seconds.

1. Copy and complete each table of values below.

t	0	1	2	3	4
x					

t	0	1	2	3	4
y					

2. Verify that the relationships between x and t and between y and t are linear. Write a pair of *parametric equations*: an equation for x in terms of t and an equation for y in terms of t. Then write a linear function for the altitude, y, in terms of horizontal distance traveled, x.

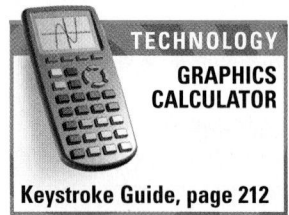

TECHNOLOGY

GRAPHICS CALCULATOR

Keystroke Guide, page 212

CHECKPOINT ✔

3. Use a graphics calculator in parametric mode to find how many seconds it will take for the airplane to achieve an altitude of 1500 feet. What is the horizontal distance that the airplane will have traveled from the point of takeoff when it reaches this altitude (assuming that the airplane continues along a straight path)?

4. Can you use the linear function that you wrote in Step 2 to answer the questions in Step 3? What additional information does the pair of parametric equations give you that the linear function does not?

In general, a pair of **parametric equations** is a pair of continuous functions that define the *x*- and *y*-coordinates of a point in a coordinate plane in terms of a third variable, such as *t*, called the **parameter**.

To graph a pair of parametric equations, you can make a table of values or use a graphics calculator, as shown in Example 1.

E X A M P L E ❶ Graph the pair of parametric equations for $-3 \le t \le 3$. $\begin{cases} x(t) = 2t - 1 \\ y(t) = -t + 2 \end{cases}$

● **SOLUTION**

Method 1 Use graph paper.

PROBLEM SOLVING

Make a table of values, and graph each ordered pair (x, y) in the table. Draw a line segment through the points graphed.

t	x	y
−3	$2(-3) - 1 = -7$	$-(-3) + 2 = 5$
−2	$2(-2) - 1 = -5$	$-(-2) + 2 = 4$
−1	$2(-1) - 1 = -3$	$-(-1) + 2 = 3$
0	$2(0) - 1 = -1$	$-(0) + 2 = 2$
1	$2(1) - 1 = 1$	$-(1) + 2 = 1$
2	$2(2) - 1 = 3$	$-(2) + 2 = 0$
3	$2(3) - 1 = 5$	$-(3) + 2 = -1$

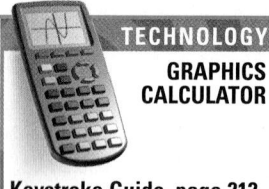

TECHNOLOGY

GRAPHICS CALCULATOR

Keystroke Guide, page 212

Method 2 Use a graphics calculator.

In parametric mode, enter the functions for *x* and for *y* in terms of *t*.

Define your viewing window, including minimum and maximum values for *t*. Then graph.

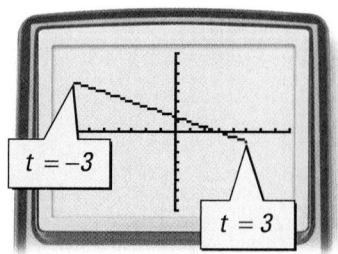

t = −3

t = 3

TRY THIS   Graph the pair of parametric equations $\begin{cases} x(t) = -2t + 2 \\ y(t) = -t - 2 \end{cases}$ for $-4 \le t \le 4$.

196 CHAPTER 3

CRITICAL THINKING   Let *r* and *s* be real numbers. Describe the line defined by each pair of parametric equations.

a. $\begin{cases} x(t) = r \\ y(t) = t \end{cases}$

b. $\begin{cases} x(t) = t \\ y(t) = s \end{cases}$

Example 2 shows how to describe a pair of parametric equations as an equation in two variables by eliminating the parameter.

E X A M P L E ② **Write the pair of parametric equations as a single equation in *x* and *y*.** $\begin{cases} x(t) = 2t + 4 \\ y(t) = 5t - 2 \end{cases}$

● **SOLUTION**

Method 1

1. Solve either equation for *t*.

$$x(t) = 2t + 4 \quad \rightarrow \quad x = 2t + 4$$

$$\frac{x - 4}{2} = t$$

2. Substitute the expression for *t* in the other equation, and simplify.

$$y(t) = 5t - 2 \quad \rightarrow \quad y = 5t - 2$$

$$y = 5\left(\frac{x - 4}{2}\right) - 2$$

$$y = \frac{5}{2}x - 10 - 2$$

$$y = \frac{5}{2}x - 12$$

Method 2

1. Solve both equations for *t*.

$$x(t) = 2t + 4 \quad \rightarrow \quad x = 2t + 4$$

$$\frac{x - 4}{2} = t$$

$$y(t) = 5t - 2 \quad \rightarrow \quad y = 5t - 2$$

$$\frac{y + 2}{5} = t$$

2. Set the resulting expressions for *t* equal to each other.

$$\frac{x - 4}{2} = \frac{y + 2}{5}$$

$$5(x - 4) = 2(y + 2)$$

$$5x - 20 = 2y + 4$$

$$y = \frac{5}{2}x - 12$$

TRY THIS   Write the pair of parametric equations as a single equation in *x* and *y*. $\begin{cases} x(t) = -2t - 6 \\ y(t) = 3t - 1 \end{cases}$

TECHNOLOGY
GRAPHICS CALCULATOR

Keystroke Guide, page 213

You can graph functions and their inverses by using parametric equations. If *f* is a function containing the point (x, y), then its inverse contains the point (y, x).

For example, $f(x) = x^2$ can be represented by $\begin{cases} x_1(t) = t \\ y_1(t) = t^2 \end{cases}$. The inverse of $f(x) = x^2$ can be represented by $\begin{cases} x_2(t) = t^2 \\ y_2(t) = t \end{cases}$.

C O N N E C T I O N

TRANSFORMATIONS

Graph these two pairs of parametric equations for *t*-values from −5 to 5. Notice that the graphs are reflections of one another across the line $y = x$.

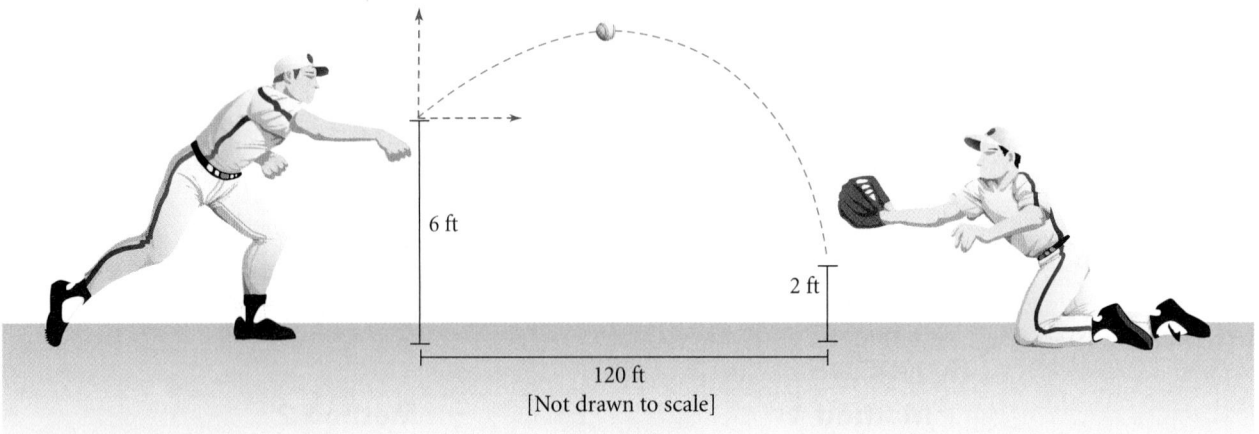

6 ft

2 ft

120 ft
[Not drawn to scale]

An outfielder throws a baseball to the catcher 120 feet away to prevent a runner from scoring. The ball is released 6 feet above the ground with a horizontal speed of 70 feet per second and a vertical speed of 25 feet per second. The catcher holds his mitt 2 feet off the ground. The following parametric equations describe the path of the ball:

$$\begin{cases} x(t) = 70t \\ y(t) = 6 + 25t - 16t^2 \end{cases}$$

x(t) gives the horizontal distance in feet after t seconds.
y(t) gives the vertical distance in feet after t seconds.

a. When does the ball reach its greatest altitude?
b. Can the catcher catch the ball?

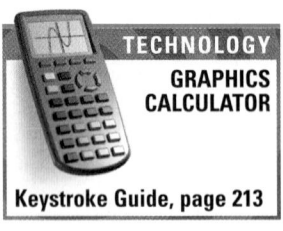
TECHNOLOGY
GRAPHICS
CALCULATOR

Keystroke Guide, page 213

SOLUTION

a. Graph the pair of parametric equations. Using the trace feature, you can find that the ball reaches its maximum altitude of about 16 feet after about 0.8 second.

```
T=.8
X=56        Y=15.76
```

b. When the ball has traveled about 120 feet, the ball will be about 2.3 feet off the ground (and directly in front of the catcher). The catcher should be able to catch the ball.

```
T=1.7
X=119       Y=2.26
```

TRY THIS   Suppose that an outfielder throws the ball to the catcher 100 feet away. The ball is released 6 feet above the ground, and the catcher holds his mitt 2 feet off the ground. The following parametric equations describe the path of the ball:

$$\begin{cases} x(t) = 60t \\ y(t) = 6 + 30t - 16t^2 \end{cases}$$

x(t) gives the horizontal distance in feet after t seconds.
y(t) gives the vertical distance in feet after t seconds.

a. When does the ball reach its greatest altitude?
b. Can the catcher catch the ball?

Exercises

Communicate

1. Describe the procedure for eliminating the parameter t in the pair of parametric equations $x(t) = 2t + 3$ and $y(t) = -t + 1$.

2. Explain what is lost when a pair of parametric equations are rewritten as a function in two variables.

3. Describe what each variable in the parametric equations in Example 3 represents.

Guided Skills Practice

Graph each pair of parametric equations for the given interval of t.
(EXAMPLE 1)

4. $\begin{cases} x(t) = t \\ y(t) = 3t + 2 \end{cases}$ for $-3 \le t \le 3$

5. $\begin{cases} x(t) = t + 7 \\ y(t) = 8 - t \end{cases}$ for $-4 \le t \le 4$

Write each pair of parametric equations as a single equation in x and y.
(EXAMPLE 2)

6. $\begin{cases} x(t) = 5t - 6 \\ y(t) = 3t + 1 \end{cases}$

7. $\begin{cases} x(t) = 2t + 5 \\ y(t) = 3 - 2t \end{cases}$

APPLICATION

8. SPORTS A batter hits a ball 3 feet above the ground with a horizontal speed of 98 feet per second and a vertical speed of 45 feet per second toward the outfield fence. The fence is 250 feet from the batter and 10 feet high. If $x(t)$ gives the horizontal distance in feet after t seconds and $y(t)$ gives the vertical distance in feet after t seconds, the following parametric equations describe the path of the ball. **(EXAMPLE 3)**

$$\begin{cases} x(t) = 98t \\ y(t) = 3 + 45t - 16t^2 \end{cases}$$

a. How long will it take the ball to reach the fence?
b. Will the ball go over the fence?

Practice and Apply

Graph each pair of parametric equations for the given interval of t.

9. $\begin{cases} x(t) = 3t \\ y(t) = t - 2 \end{cases}$ for $-4 \le t \le 4$

10. $\begin{cases} x(t) = t + 5 \\ y(t) = 4t \end{cases}$ for $-3 \le t \le 3$

11. $\begin{cases} x(t) = 2t \\ y(t) = 6 - t \end{cases}$ for $-3 \le t \le 3$

12. $\begin{cases} x(t) = 5 - 2t \\ y(t) = \dfrac{t}{2} \end{cases}$ for $-4 \le t \le 4$

13. $\begin{cases} x(t) = 2t + 3 \\ y(t) = t^2 \end{cases}$ for $-3 \le t \le 3$

14. $\begin{cases} x(t) = t^2 \\ y(t) = 3t - 5 \end{cases}$ for $-4 \le t \le 4$

Write each pair of parametric equations as a single equation in *x* and *y*.

15. $\begin{cases} x(t) = 2t \\ y(t) = t - 1 \end{cases}$

16. $\begin{cases} x(t) = t + 3 \\ y(t) = 3t \end{cases}$

17. $\begin{cases} x(t) = 2t + 1 \\ y(t) = t + 5 \end{cases}$

18. $\begin{cases} x(t) = t - 2 \\ y(t) = t + 7 \end{cases}$

19. $\begin{cases} x(t) = 3t \\ y(t) = 1 - t \end{cases}$

20. $\begin{cases} x(t) = t \\ y(t) = 3 - 2t \end{cases}$

21. $\begin{cases} x(t) = 2t \\ y(t) = t^2 - 1 \end{cases}$

22. $\begin{cases} x(t) = t^2 \\ y(t) = \frac{t}{2} \end{cases}$

23. $\begin{cases} x(t) = \frac{1}{3}t \\ y(t) = t^2 \end{cases}$

24. $\begin{cases} x(t) = t^2 + 2t \\ y(t) = 2t \end{cases}$

25. $\begin{cases} x(t) = 5 - t^2 \\ y(t) = \frac{3}{2}t \end{cases}$

26. $\begin{cases} x(t) = 2 - 3t^2 \\ y(t) = -\frac{1}{3}t \end{cases}$

internet connect

**Homework
Help Online**

Go To: **go.hrw.com**
Keyword:
MB1 Homework Help
for Exercises 27–32

Graph the function represented by each pair of parametric equations. Then graph its inverse on the same coordinate plane.

27 $\begin{cases} x(t) = t^2 - 2 \\ y(t) = t \end{cases}$

28 $\begin{cases} x(t) = t^2 \\ y(t) = t + 3 \end{cases}$

29 $\begin{cases} x(t) = t \\ y(t) = 6 - t^2 \end{cases}$

30 $\begin{cases} x(t) = 4 - t \\ y(t) = t^2 - 1 \end{cases}$

31 $\begin{cases} x(t) = t^2 + 5t - 1 \\ y(t) = t + 1 \end{cases}$

32 $\begin{cases} x(t) = 4 + 5t - t^2 \\ y(t) = t - 1 \end{cases}$

CHALLENGE

33. Write a pair of parametric equations to represent a line that has a slope of 3 and contains the point (4, −5).

CONNECTION

34. TRANSFORMATIONS Write the pair of parametric equations that represent a transformation of $\begin{cases} x(t) = t \\ y(t) = t^2 \end{cases}$ 1 unit down and 2 units to the right.

APPLICATION

35 SPORTS Frannie throws a softball from one end of a 200-foot field. The ball leaves her hand at a height of 6.5 feet with an initial velocity of 60 feet per second in the horizontal direction and 40 feet per second in the vertical direction. If $x(t)$ gives the horizontal distance in feet after t seconds and $y(t)$ gives the vertical distance in feet after t seconds, the following parametric equations describe the ball's path:

$$\begin{cases} x(t) = 60t \\ y(t) = 6.5 + 40t - 16t^2 \end{cases}$$

a. How high does the ball get? How long does it take for the ball to reach this height?

b. What horizontal distance will the ball travel before it hits the ground? How long does it take for the ball to reach this point?

36 SPORTS The server in a volleyball game serves the ball at an angle of 35° with the ground and from a height of 2 meters. The server is 9 meters from the 2.2-meter high net. The ball must not touch the net when served and must land within 9 meters of the other side of the net. If $x(t)$ gives the horizontal distance in meters after t seconds and $y(t)$ gives the vertical distance in meters after t seconds, the following parametric equations describe the ball's path:

$$\begin{cases} x(t) = 8.2t \\ y(t) = 2 + 5.7t - 4.9t^2 \end{cases}$$

a. How high above the net will the ball travel?

b. According to the parametric equations, what horizontal distance will the ball travel before hitting the ground?

c. Will the ball land within the area described? Explain.

37 **AVIATION** An airplane at an altitude of 2000 feet is descending at a constant rate of 160 feet per second horizontally and 15 feet per second vertically.

   a. Write the pair of parametric equations that represent the airplane's flight path.

   b. After how many seconds will the airplane touch down?

   c. What horizontal distance will the airplane have traveled when it touches down on the runway?

38 **HEALTH** A newborn baby weighs 7 pounds and is 21 inches long. During each of the first 6 months, the baby grows $\frac{1}{2}$ inch in length and gains 2 pounds.

   a. Write the parametric equations describing the height and weight for t months, where $0 < t < 6$.

   b. How many months will it take for the baby to weigh 14 pounds? How long is the baby at this time?

   c. How many months will it take for the baby to reach 23 inches? How much does the baby weigh at this time?

Look Back

Let $f(x) = x + 2$ and $g(x) = 1 - x$. *(LESSON 2.4)*

39. Find $f \circ g$.   **40.** Find $g \circ f$.

41. Find $f \circ f$.   **42.** Find $g \circ g$.

TRANSFORMATIONS Identify each transformation from the parent function $f(x) = x^2$ to g. *(LESSON 2.7)*

43. $g(x) = 12x^2 + 3$ **44.** $g(x) = -\left(\frac{1}{3}x\right)^2$

45. $g(x) = -\frac{1}{2}x^2 + 4$ **46.** $g(x) = -0.25(4x - 1)^2$

TRANSFORMATIONS Write the function for each graph described below. *(LESSON 2.7)*

47. the graph of $f(x) = |x|$ translated 2 units to the right

48. the graph of $f(x) = |x|$ translated 1.5 units up

49. the graph of $f(x) = x^2$ compressed vertically by a factor of $\frac{1}{5}$

50. the graph of $f(x) = x^2$ reflected across the x-axis and stretched horizontally by a factor of 4

Look Beyond

51 Graph the parametric equations $x(t) = \cos(t)$ and $y(t) = \sin(t)$ by using the ⌊ SIN ⌋ and ⌊ COS ⌋ keys on your calculator. Make sure your calculator is in radian and parametric modes. Use the following viewing window:

    Tmin = 0   Tmax = 10   Tstep = 0.01
    Xmin = −4.7   Xmax = 4.8   Xscl = 1
    Ymin = −3.1   Ymax = 3.2   Yscl = 1

Did the calculator draw the figure in a clockwise or counterclockwise direction? What is the shape of the graph?

MAXIMUM PROFIT/ MINIMUM COST

FLORAL ARRANGEMENTS FOR MAXIMUM PROFITS

A local florist is making two types of floral arrangements for Thanksgiving: regular and special. Each regular arrangement requires 3 mums, 3 daisies, and 2 roses, and each special arrangement requires 4 mums, 2 daisies, and 4 roses. The florist has set aside 60 mums, 54 daisies, and 52 roses for the two types of arrangements.

Activity 1

Let x represent the number of regular arrangements, and let y represent the number of special arrangements. Write a system of three equations to represent the florist's situation.

Activity 2

The florist will make a profit of $2 on each regular arrangement and $3 on each special arrangement.

1. Write an objective function for the profit.

2. Create a system of inequalities to represent the constraints. Graph the feasible region.

3. Identify the vertices of the feasible region.

4. How many of each type of arrangement should the florist make in order to maximize the profit? What is the maximum profit?

5. If the maximum profit is achieved, will there be any flowers left over? Explain your reasoning.

TILING AT MINIMUM LABOR COST

A construction firm employs two levels of tile installers: craftsmen and apprentices. Craftsmen install 500 square feet of specialty tile, 100 square feet of plain tile, and 100 linear feet of trim in one day. An apprentice installs 100 square feet of specialty tile, 200 square feet of plain tile, and 100 linear feet of trim in one day. The firm has a one-day job that requires 2000 square feet of specialty tile, 1600 square feet of plain tile, and 1200 linear feet of trim.

Activity 3

Let x represent the number of craftsmen, and let y represent the number of apprentices. Write a system of three equations to represent the construction firm's situation with this job.

Activity 4

The construction firm pays craftsmen $200 per day and pays apprentices $120 per day.

1. Write an objective function for the labor costs.

2. Create a system of inequalities to represent the constraints. Graph the feasible region.

3. Identify the vertices of the feasible region.

4. How many craftsmen and how many apprentices should be assigned to this job so that it can be completed in one day with the minimum labor cost? What is the minimum labor cost?

Activity 5

Suppose that each apprentice's wages are increased to $150 per day.

1. In this case, how many craftsmen and how many apprentices should be assigned to the job so that it can be completed in one day with the minimum labor cost? What is the minimum labor cost?

2. Do any points in the feasible region call for apprentices but no craftsmen? If so, is this a realistic scenario for the construction firm? What constraint could you add to ensure that every job has at least one craftsman assigned to it?

Activity 6

Suppose that union regulations require at least 1 craftsman for every 3 apprentices on a job.

1. Which of the vertices of the original feasible region (from Activity 4) satisfy this new constraint?

2. Write an inequality to represent the new constraint. Modify the feasible region on your graph by adding the boundary line for the new constraint.

3. Using the new constraints and the original labor cost of $120 per day for an apprentice, how many craftsmen and how many apprentices should be assigned to the job so that it can be completed in one day with the minimum labor cost? What is the minimum labor cost?

Key Skills & Exercises

LESSON 3.1

Key Skills

Solve a system of two linear equations in two variables graphically.

Classification of Systems of Equations	
Number of solutions	Type
0	inconsistent
1	consistent, independent
infinite	consistent, dependent

The solution to a consistent, independent system is given by the point of intersection of the graphs.

Use substitution to solve a system of linear equations.

Solve $\begin{cases} 3x - 5y = 28 \\ x + y = 4 \end{cases}$ by using substitution.

First solve $x + y = 4$ for one variable.
$$y = -x + 4$$

Then substitute $-x + 4$ for y in the other equation.
$$3x - 5y = 28$$
$$3x - 5(-x + 4) = 28$$
$$8x = 48$$
$$x = 6$$

Substitute 6 for x to find y.
$$x + y = 4$$
$$6 + y = 4$$
$$y = -2$$

Thus, the solution is $(6, -2)$.

Exercises

Graph and classify each system. Then find the solution from the graph.

1. $\begin{cases} x + y = 6 \\ 3x - 4y = 4 \end{cases}$

2. $\begin{cases} 3x + y = 11 \\ x - 2y = 6 \end{cases}$

3. $\begin{cases} y = 2x - 3 \\ -6x + 3y = -9 \end{cases}$

4. $\begin{cases} x + 2y = 4 \\ -3x - 6y = 12 \end{cases}$

5. $\begin{cases} 2x + 10y = -2 \\ 6x + 4y = 20 \end{cases}$

6. $\begin{cases} 5x + 6y = 14 \\ 3x + 5y = 7 \end{cases}$

Use substitution to solve each system. Check your solution.

7. $\begin{cases} y = 2x - 4 \\ 7x - 5y = 14 \end{cases}$

8. $\begin{cases} y = 3x - 12 \\ 2x + 3y = -3 \end{cases}$

9. $\begin{cases} 2x + 8y = 1 \\ x = 2y \end{cases}$

10. $\begin{cases} 4x + 3y = 13 \\ x + y = 4 \end{cases}$

11. $\begin{cases} 6y = x + 18 \\ 2y - x = 6 \end{cases}$

12. $\begin{cases} x + y = 7 \\ 2x + y = 5 \end{cases}$

Key Skills

Use elimination to solve a system of linear equations.

Solve $\begin{cases} 2x - 3y = -17 \\ 5x = 15 - 4y \end{cases}$ by using elimination.

Write each equation in standard form.

$$\begin{cases} 2x - 3y = -17 \\ 5x + 4y = 15 \end{cases}$$

Multiply the equations as needed, and then combine to eliminate one of the variables.

$$\begin{cases} 5(2x - 3y) = 5(-17) \\ -2(5x + 4y) = -2(15) \end{cases} \rightarrow \begin{array}{r} 10x - 15y = -85 \\ -10x - 8y = -30 \\ \hline -23y = -115 \\ y = 5 \end{array}$$

Then use substitution to solve for the other variable.

$$5x = 15 - 4y$$
$$5x = 15 - 4(5)$$
$$x = -1$$

Thus, the solution is $(-1, 5)$.

Exercises

Use elimination to solve each system. Check your solution.

13. $\begin{cases} 2x - 5y = 1 \\ 3x - 4y = -2 \end{cases}$ 14. $\begin{cases} 9x + 2y = 2 \\ 21x + 6y = 4 \end{cases}$

15. $\begin{cases} -x + 2y = 12 \\ x + 6y = 20 \end{cases}$ 16. $\begin{cases} 2x + 3y = 18 \\ 5x - y = 11 \end{cases}$

17. $\begin{cases} 3y = 3x - 6 \\ y = x - 2 \end{cases}$ 18. $\begin{cases} y = \frac{3}{2}x + 4 \\ 2y - 8 = 3x \end{cases}$

19. $\begin{cases} y = \frac{1}{2}x + 9 \\ 2y - x = 1 \end{cases}$ 20. $\begin{cases} y = -2x - 4 \\ 2x + y = 6 \end{cases}$

Key Skills

Graph a linear inequality in two variables.

Solve the inequality for y, reversing the inequality symbol if multiplying or dividing by a negative number. Graph the boundary line, using a dashed line for $<$ or $>$ and a solid line for $\le$ or $\ge$. Substitute a point into the inequality to determine whether to shade above or below the boundary line.

Exercises

Graph each linear inequality.

21. $y > 2x - 3$ 22. $y - 3x < 4$

23. $2x - y \le 5$ 24. $4x - 2y \le -3$

25. $\frac{y}{4} \ge -\frac{x}{3} + 1$ 26. $\frac{3}{2}x \le \frac{1}{4}y - 3$

27. $y > -2$ 28. $x \le 7$

Key Skills

Graph the system of linear inequalities.

Graph. $\begin{cases} y \ge -1 \\ y \le \frac{4}{3}x + \frac{1}{3} \\ y < -4x + 11 \end{cases}$

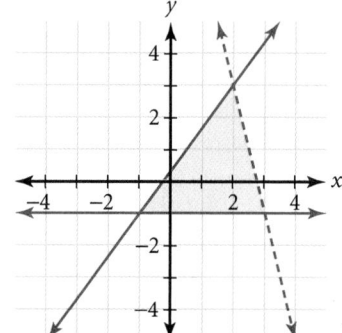

Graph each boundary line, using a solid line or a dashed line. The solution is the shaded region shown.

Exercises

Graph each system of linear inequalities.

29. $\begin{cases} y \ge 0 \\ x \ge 0 \\ y > -2x + 3 \\ y < 4x \end{cases}$ 30. $\begin{cases} y \ge 0 \\ x \ge 0 \\ y \le x + 8 \\ y \ge -2x + 3 \end{cases}$

31. $\begin{cases} y < 2x + 3 \\ y \ge 3x - 1 \\ x > 1 \end{cases}$ 32. $\begin{cases} y \ge -x - 3 \\ y < 4x + 2 \\ x > -2 \end{cases}$

Key Skills

Use linear programming to find the maximum or minimum value of an objective function.

Step 1 Write a system of inequalities, and graph the feasible region.

Step 2 Write the objective function to be maximized or minimized.

Step 3 Find the coordinates of the vertices of the feasible region.

Step 4 Evaluate the objective function for the coordinates of the vertices of the feasible region. Then identify the coordinates that give the required maximum or minimum.

Exercises

33. BROADCASTING At a radio station, 6 minutes of each hour are devoted to news, and the remaining 54 minutes are devoted to music and commercials. Station policy requires at least 30 minutes of music per hour and at least 3 minutes of music for each minute of commercials. Use linear programming to find the maximum number of minutes available for commercials each hour.

Key Skills

Graph a pair of parametric equations for a given interval of t.

Make a table, plot the ordered pairs (x, y), and draw a line or curve through the points. Or use a graphics calculator in parametric mode.

Write a pair of parametric equations as a single equation in x and y.

Given the parametric equations $\begin{cases} x(t) = 3t + 1 \\ y(t) = t - 5 \end{cases}$, solve either equation for t and substitute the expression for t in the other equation.

$$y = t - 5 \quad \rightarrow \quad t = y + 5$$
$$x = 3t + 1$$
$$x = 3(y + 5) + 1$$
$$x = 3y + 16, \text{ or } y = \frac{x - 16}{3}$$

Exercises

Write each pair of parametric equations as a single equation in x and y.

34. $\begin{cases} x(t) = 2t \\ y(t) = t - 1 \end{cases}$ **35.** $\begin{cases} x(t) = t + 3 \\ y(t) = 3t - 1 \end{cases}$

36. $\begin{cases} x(t) = t \\ y(t) = 3 - 2t \end{cases}$ **37.** $\begin{cases} x(t) = t + 5 \\ y(t) = 4t - 3 \end{cases}$

38. SPORTS A goalie kicks a soccer ball from a height of 2 feet above the ground toward the center of the field. The ball is kicked with a horizontal speed of 40 feet per second and a vertical speed of 65 feet per second. If $x(t)$ gives the horizontal distance in feet after t seconds and $y(t)$ gives the vertical distance in feet after t seconds, then the ball's path can be described by the parametric equations

$\begin{cases} x(t) = 40t \\ y(t) = 2 + 65t - 16t^2 \end{cases}$. What horizontal distance does the ball travel before striking the ground?

Applications

39. MANUFACTURING A tire manufacturer has 1000 units of raw rubber to use for car and truck tires. Each car tire requires 5 units of rubber and each truck tire requires 12 units of rubber. Labor costs are $8 for a car tire and $12 for a truck tire. The manufacturer does not want to pay more than $1500 in labor costs. Write and graph a system of inequalities to represent this situation.

Chapter Test

Classify the type of system represented by each graph as independent, dependent, or inconsistent. If the system has exactly one solution, write it.

1.

2.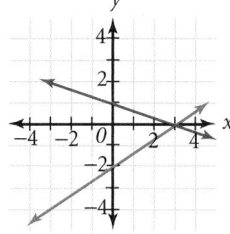

Use substitution to solve each system. Check your solution.

3. $\begin{cases} 2x - 3y = 1 \\ y = x - 2 \end{cases}$

4. $\begin{cases} x + y + z = 7 \\ 2x + 3y = 3 \\ x = -2y \end{cases}$

5. NUMBER The sum of two numbers is 7. Four times the first number is one more than five times the second. Find the two numbers by setting up a system of equations and solving by substitution.

Use elimination to solve each system. Check your solution.

6. $\begin{cases} x + y = 1 \\ x - 2y = -8 \end{cases}$

7. $\begin{cases} 5x + 2y = 24 \\ 2x - 12 = 4y \end{cases}$

8. $\begin{cases} \frac{1}{3}x - y = 4 \\ 2x - 6y = 12 \end{cases}$

9. $\begin{cases} 4x + 3y = 0 \\ y - x = -7 \end{cases}$

10. CONSUMER ECONOMICS Three blouses and four skirts are on sale for $72.50. Five blouses and two skirts would cost $66.00. Find the cost of one blouse and one skirt by setting up a system of equations and solving by elimination.

Graph each linear inequality.

11. $y < 3x - 4$

12. $2x + 3y \geq 6$

13. $x \leq 3$

14. $\frac{2}{3}x - \frac{3}{4}y > -1$

15. RECREATION Misha has a 2500-meter spool of rope that he must cut into 50-meter and 75-meter lengths for his rock-climbing class. Write an inequality that will express the possible numbers of each length he can cut from this spool of rope.

Graph each system of linear inequalities.

16. $\begin{cases} x \geq 0 \\ y \geq 0 \\ x + y \leq 4 \\ x - y \leq 2 \end{cases}$

17. $\begin{cases} y > -2 \\ 2x - y > -2 \\ y \leq -2x + 6 \end{cases}$

18. MANUFACTURING A company produces windows and doors. A profit of $5 is realized on each window, and profit is $3 on each door. The company has 18 hours available for manufacturing in Plant A. Each window requires 3 hours, and each door 2 hours to manufacture. Plant B has 7.5 hours available for assembly. Each window requires 1.5 hours to assemble, and each door requires 0.75 hour. Use linear programming to determine how many windows and doors the manufacturer should produce to maximize profit.

Write each pair of parametric equations as a single equation in x and y.

19. $\begin{cases} x(t) = t - 4 \\ y(t) = 2t - 11 \end{cases}$

20. $\begin{cases} x(t) = 5t \\ y(t) = -2t + 3 \end{cases}$

21. AGRICULTURE A farmer recently planted a new crop of cherry trees in his orchard. The first year, the trees grow to 10 feet tall and produce $3\frac{1}{2}$ pounds of cherries each. The trees grow at the rate of $1\frac{1}{2}$ feet per year and increase their production of cherries by $\frac{3}{4}$ pounds each year. Write a system of parametric equations to determine the height $h(t)$ of a tree in t years and its cherry production $c(t)$ in t years. Then express the cherry production, c, as a function of height, h.

☑ **internet** connect

Standardized Test Prep Online
Go To: **go.hrw.com**
Keyword: **MM1 Test Prep**

MULTIPLE-CHOICE For Questions 1–13, write the letter that indicates the best answer.

1. Which of the following is an example of the Associative Property of Multiplication? **(LESSON 2.1)**

a. $(-21x)y = -21(xy)$
b. $(-4x)y = -4x - 4y$
c. $x(3y) = (3y)x$
d. $3x(47y) = 141xy$

2. Which of the following relations represents a function? **(LESSON 2.3)**

a. $\{(0, -4), (0, -3), (1, -2)\}$
b. $\{(1, 1), (1, 2), (1, 3)\}$
c. $\{(2, -1), (2, 1), (2, 3)\}$
d. $\{(-1, 2), (1, 2), (3, 2)\}$

3. Solve $\frac{x}{4} = \frac{x+2}{5}$. **(LESSON 1.4)**

a. $x = 8$
b. $x = \frac{7}{2}$
c. $x = 2$
d. $x = -10$

4. Which graph is the solution of $|x - 2| < 5$? **(LESSON 1.8)**

a. ![number line from -8 to 8, open circle at 7]
b. ![number line from -8 to 8, open circles at -3 and 7]
c. ![number line from -8 to 8, open circle at -3]
d. ![number line from -8 to 8, open circles at -3 and 7]

5. Let $f(x) = -3x$ and $g(x) = x - 4$. Find $(f \circ g)(-5)$. **(LESSON 2.4)**

a. 27
b. 11
c. -135
d. -45

6. Which is a solution of the system?
$\begin{cases} -2x + y \leq 8 \\ x - 3y > 9 \end{cases}$ **(LESSON 3.4)**

a. $(0, -3)$
b. $(0, 9)$
c. both **a** and **b**
d. neither **a** nor **b**

7. Which equation in x and y represents $\begin{cases} x(t) = 3t - 1 \\ y(t) = 2 - 3t \end{cases}$? **(LESSON 3.6)**

a. $y = x - 1$
b. $y = 3x - 1$
c. $y = 1 - x$
d. $y = -3x - 1$

8. Evaluate $[3(2 + 1) + 3](2^2)$. **(LESSON 2.1)**

a. 36
b. 20
c. 32
d. 48

9. How many solutions does the system have?
$\begin{cases} 2x - 3y = 11 \\ 6x - 9y = 33 \end{cases}$ **(LESSON 3.1)**

a. 0
b. 1
c. 2
d. infinite

10. Which function represents the graph of $f(x) = x^2$ translated 5 units down? **(LESSON 2.7)**

a. $f(x) = x^2 + 5$
b. $f(x) = x^2 - 5$
c. $f(x) = (x - 5)^2$
d. $f(x) = (x + 5)^2$

11. Which is the range of $f(x) = -\left(\frac{x}{3}\right)^2$? **(LESSON 2.3)**

a. $f(x) \geq 0$
b. $f(x) \geq 3$
c. $f(x) \leq 3$
d. $f(x) \leq 0$

12. Simplify $\left(\frac{2x^{-2}y^3}{x^2y^{-3}}\right)^{-1}$. **(LESSON 2.2)**

a. 2
b. $\frac{2x^4}{y^6}$
c. $\frac{1}{2}$
d. $\frac{x^4}{2y^6}$

13. Which is the equation of the line that contains the point $(0, -2)$ and is parallel to the graph of $y = -\frac{1}{2}x - 1$? **(LESSON 1.3)**

a. $y = -\frac{1}{2}x - 2$
b. $y = -\frac{1}{2}x + 2$
c. $y = 2x - 2$
d. $y = 2x + 2$

Match each statement on the left with a solution on the right. *(LESSON 1.8)*

14. $|a - 5| < 3$ **a.** $a = 2$ *or* $a = 8$

15. $|a - 5| > 3$ **b.** $a < 2$ *or* $a > 8$

16. $|a - 5| = 3$ **c.** $a > 2$ *and* $a < 8$

17. $|a - 5| < -3$ **d.** There is no solution.

18. Graph $2y > -1$. *(LESSON 3.3)*

19. Write the pair of parametric equations
$$\begin{cases} x(t) = 2 + t \\ y(t) = 3 + t \end{cases}$$
as a single equation in x and y.
(LESSON 3.6)

20. Classify
$$\begin{cases} 3y = 4x - 1 \\ x = \frac{4}{3}y \end{cases}$$
as inconsistent, dependent, or independent. *(LESSON 3.1)*

21. Write the function for the graph of $f(x) = x^2$ translated 2 units up. *(LESSON 2.7)*

22. Solve.
$$\begin{cases} 3x - 3y = 1 \\ x + y = 4 \end{cases}$$
(LESSON 3.1)

23. Graph the system.
$$\begin{cases} y \leq x + 1 \\ y \geq 2x - 1 \end{cases}$$
(LESSON 3.4)

24. Find the inverse of the function $f(x) = 3x - 2$.
(LESSON 2.5)

25. Graph the ordered pairs below, and describe the correlation for the data as positive, negative, or none. *(LESSON 1.5)*

    (10, 6), (20, 8), (20, 12), (30, 16), (40, 18), (50, 21), (60, 32), (80, 41), (100, 46), (110, 60), (120, 58)

26. Solve the literal equation $\frac{ax - b}{2} = c$ for x.
(LESSON 1.6)

27. Graph the parametric equations for $-3 \leq t \leq 3$.
$$\begin{cases} x(t) = t + 1 \\ y(t) = 2t - 1 \end{cases}$$
(LESSON 3.6)

28. Let $f(x) = 2x + 1$ and $g(x) = 3x^2$. Find $f \circ g$.
(LESSON 2.4)

Solve each inequality, and graph the solution on a number line. *(LESSON 1.7)*

29. $6(x - 4) \geq 6 + x$ 30. $\frac{-x}{4} > 3$

Solve each equation. *(LESSON 1.8)*

31. $|x - 4| = 9$ 32. $|3x + 12| = 18$

FREE-RESPONSE GRID The following questions may be answered by using a free-response grid such as that commonly used by standardized-test services.

33. If a varies directly as b and $a = 16$ when $b = -8$, what is b when $a = 4$? *(LESSON 1.4)*

34. For what value of t does the graph of
$$\begin{cases} x(t) = t^2 + 1 \\ y(t) = t - 1 \end{cases}$$
pass through the point (7.25, 1.5)? *(LESSON 3.6)*

35. The graph of $g(x) = x + 1$ can be formed by translating the graph of $f(x) = x + 3$ how many units to the right? *(LESSON 2.7)*

36. Evaluate $|-2| - |-2|$. *(LESSON 2.6)*

37. Let $f(x) = |x| + 2x$. Find $f(-2)$. *(LESSON 2.3)*

38. Find the slope of a line that contains the points $(-3, 4)$ and $(-1, -8)$. *(LESSON 1.2)*

39. **ENGINEERING** The equation $F = \frac{9}{4}d^4l^{-2}$, where d is the diameter in inches and l is the length in feet, gives the maximum load in tons that a foundation column can support. Find the maximum load, in tons, for a column that is 6 feet long and 12 inches in diameter.
(LESSON 2.2)

40. **MANUFACTURING** The true diameter of a pipe is 7.25 inches. Its diameter is measured as 7.29 inches. Find the relative error in the measurement to the nearest thousandth.
(LESSON 2.6)

41. **INCOME** Becky wants to buy a computer that costs $1590. If Becky earns $6.25 per hour, what is the minimum number of whole hours that she must work to earn enough money to buy the computer? *(LESSON 1.7)*

Keystroke Guide for Chapter 3

Essential keystroke sequences (using the model TI-82 or TI-83 graphics calculator) are presented below for all Activities and Examples found in this chapter that require or recommend the use of a graphics calculator.

☑ internet connect

For Keystrokes of other graphing calculator models, visit the HRW web site at **go.hrw.com** and enter the keyword **MB1 CALC**.

LESSON 3.1

Page 156

For Step 1, graph $y = 2x - 1$ and $y = -x + 5$ on the same screen, and find any points of intersection.

Use friendly viewing window [−9.4, 9.4] by [−6.2, 6.2].

Graph the equations:

| Y= | 2 | X,T,θ,n | − | 1 | ENTER | (Y2=) | (−) | X,T,θ,n | + | 5 | GRAPH |

> *Move the cursor as indicated.*

Find any points of intersection:

| 2nd | TRACE (CALC) | 5:intersect | ENTER | (First curve?) | ENTER | (Second curve?)

| ENTER | (Guess?) | ENTER |

Use a similar keystroke sequence for Step 2.

E X A M P L E ❶

Page 157

For part a, graph $y = -x + 5$ and $y = \dfrac{x + 7}{5}$ on the same screen, and find any points of intersection.

Use standard viewing window [−10, 10] by [−10, 10].

Graph the equations:

| Y= | (−) | X,T,θ,n | + | 5 | ENTER | (Y2=) | (| X,T,θ,n | + | 7 |) |

| ÷ | 5 | GRAPH |

Find any points of intersection:
Use a keystroke sequence similar to that in the previous Activity.

Use a similar keystroke sequence for part **b**.

E X A M P L E ❸

Page 159

Graph $y = 500 - x$ and $y = \dfrac{0.06(500) - 0.10x}{0.04}$ on the same screen, and find any points of intersection.

Use viewing window [0, 400] by [0, 500].

Graph the equations:

Y= 500 − X,T,Θ,n ENTER (Y2=) (.06 (500) − .10
X,T,Θ,n) ÷ .04)

Find any points of intersection:
Use a keystroke sequence similar to that in the previous Activity.

LESSON 3.2

E X A M P L E ② *Page 166*

Graph $y = \dfrac{930 - 5.5x}{7.5}$ and $y = \dfrac{1920 - 12x}{15}$ on the same screen, and find any points of intersection. Then verify with a table.

Use viewing window [0, 200] by [0, 150].

Graph the equations, and find any points of intersection:

Use a keystroke sequence similar to that in the Activity and Examples 1 and 3 in Lesson 3.1.

Verify the solution with a table:

TBLSET
2nd WINDOW (TblStart =) 40 ENTER

⇑ TI-82: (Tbl Min =)

(ΔTbl =) 10 ENTER (Indpnt:) Auto ▼

TABLE
(Depend:) Auto 2nd GRAPH

Enter the equations before using the table.

Activity *Page 166*

For Step 1, graph $y = x + 2$ and $y = \dfrac{10 + 5x}{5}$ on the same screen.

Use standard viewing window [−10, 10] by [−10, 10].

Use a keystroke sequence similar to that in the Activity in Lesson 3.1.

For Step 2, use a keystroke sequence similar to that in the Activity in Lesson 3.1. Use standard viewing window [−10, 10] by [−10, 10].

E X A M P L E S ③ and ④ *Page 167*

For Example 3, graph $y = \dfrac{12 - 2x}{5}$ and $y = \dfrac{15 - 2x}{5}$ on the same screen.

Use viewing window [−5, 5] by [−1, 5].

Y= (12 − 2 X,T,Θ,n) ÷ 5

ENTER (Y2=) (15 − 2 X,T,Θ,n)

÷ 5 GRAPH

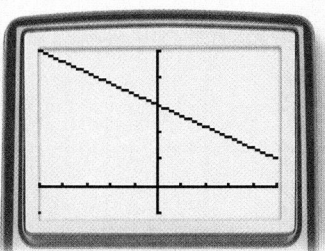

For Example 4, use a similar keystroke sequence. Use viewing window [−5, 5] by [−1, 5].

EXAMPLE ❸
Page 174

Graph $y \leq \dfrac{-33.3}{28.1}x + 20(33.3)$, and see whether (25, 400) satisfies the inequality.

Use viewing window [0, 800] by [0, 800].

Graph the inequality:

Y= ◄ ◄ ENTER ENTER ENTER

(◣ Y1=) ► ► ((−)

33.3 ÷ 28.1) X,T,Θ,n +

20 (33.3) GRAPH

TI-82: Graph the line and use the shade feature.

First clear old data from L1 and L2.

Plot the point:

STAT EDIT 1:Edit ENTER L1 25 ENTER ► L2

STAT PLOT
400 ENTER 2nd Y= 1:Plot 1 ENTER ON

ENTER ▼ (Type:) ⠿ ENTER ▼

L1   L2
(Xlist:) 2nd 1 ▼ (Ylist:) 2nd 2

▼ (Mark:) + ENTER GRAPH

You can also move the cursor to find approximate coordinates.

Activity
Page 196

For Step 3, graph the parametric equations for the horizontal and vertical distances, and find the values of t and x for $y = 1500$.

MODE Par ENTER

Use viewing window [0, 120, 1] by [0, 15,000] by [0, 1600].

Y= (X1T=) 120 X,T,Θ,n ENTER (Y1T=) 13.4 X,T,Θ,n ENTER TRACE

Move the cursor to the desired point.

EXAMPLE ❶
Page 196

Graph the parametric equations $x(t) = 2t - 1$ and $y(t) = -t + 2$.

Use viewing window [−3, 3, 0.1] by [−8, 8] by [−8, 8].

Y= (X1T=) 2 X,T,Θ,n − 1 ENTER

(Y1T=) (−) X,T,Θ,n + 2 GRAPH

Be sure that the calculator is in parametric mode.

Graph the parametric equations $x(t) = t$ and $y(t) = t^2$ and the inverse on the same screen with $y = x$.

Use square viewing window [−5, 5, 0.3] by [−4.7, 4.7] by [−3.1, 3.1].

Graph the function:

| Y= | $(X_1T=)$ | X,T,θ,n | ENTER | $(Y_1T=)$ | X,T,θ,n | x^2 | ENTER |

Be sure that the calculator is in parametric mode.

Graph the inverse:

$(X_2T=)$ X,T,θ,n x^2 ENTER $(Y_2T=)$

X,T,θ,n ENTER

Graph the line $y = x$:

The TI-82 cannot graph a dashed line.

$(X_3T=)$ ◄ ◄ ENTER ENTER ENTER

ENTER ($\because X_3T=$) ► ► X,T,θ,n

ENTER $(Y_3T=)$ X,T,θ,n GRAPH

TI-82: $(X_3T=)$ X,T,θ ENTER $(Y_3T=)$ X,T,θ ENTER

EXAMPLE **3**

Page 198

Graph the parametric equations $x(t) = 70t$ and $y(t) = 6 + 25t − 16t^2$.

Use viewing window [0, 10, 0.1] by [0, 150] by [0, 20].

| Y= | $(X_1T=)$ 70 | X,T,θ,n | ENTER | $(Y_1T=)$ 6 | + | 25 | X,T,θ,n | − | 16 |

X,T,θ,n x^2 GRAPH

Be sure that the calculator is in parametric mode.

a. Find the maximum y-value on the graph.

Use the TRACE feature.

Move the cursor to the desired point.

b. Find the y-value when x is near 120.

Use the TRACE feature.

Move the cursor to the desired point.

Matrices

MATRICES CAN CONVENIENTLY ORGANIZE AND store data represented in tables. For example, an inventory of the number and types of plants in a large garden can be stored in a matrix.

Matrices are also used to manipulate data. For example, an updated inventory matrix can be obtained by combining the original inventory matrix with a matrix that represents the number and types of plants added to and removed from the garden.

PLANT LIST

Flowering Dogwood	4. Marigolds	7. Lily
alea	5. Hybrid Tea Rose	8. Rosemary
ese Juniper	6. Coneflower	9. Lilac

About the Chapter Project

Mathematical models can apply to our everyday world in ways we rarely think about. By ordering seemingly random data into an organized format, models allow us to see underlying relations and to use them in fascinating ways.

In the Chapter Project, *Spell Check*, you will use the modeling process to examine spell-checking software.

After completing the Chapter Project, you will be able to do the following:

- Create a directed network and corresponding adjacency matrix to represent associated words in a spell-checking directory.

- Interpret powers of adjacency matrices.

About the Portfolio Activities

Throughout the chapter, you will be given opportunities to complete Portfolio Activities that are designed to support your work on the Chapter Project.

- Interpreting a directed network that represents paths between exhibits in the New York Museum of Natural History is included in the Portfolio Activity on page 224.

- Finding and interpreting powers of adjacency matrices that represent multistep paths between exhibits is included in the Portfolio Activity on page 233.

215

Using Matrices to Represent Data

Why *Matrices can be used to organize data. For example, information about picnic tables and barbeque grills can be organized into matrices.*

Objectives

● Represent mathematical and real-world data in a matrix.

● Find sums and differences of matrices and the scalar product of a number and a matrix.

APPLICATION
INVENTORY

The table below shows business activity for one month in a home-improvement store. The table shows stock (inventory on June 1), sales (during June), and receipt of new goods (deliveries in June).

	Inventory (June 1)		Sales (June)		Deliveries (June)	
	Small	Large	Small	Large	Small	Large
Picnic tables	8	10	7	9	15	20
Barbeque grills	15	12	15	12	18	24

You can represent the inventory data in a *matrix*.

$$\text{Inventory matrix} \rightarrow \quad \begin{matrix} & \text{Small} & \text{Large} \\ \text{Picnic tables} \\ \text{Barbeque grills} \end{matrix} \begin{bmatrix} 8 & 10 \\ 15 & 12 \end{bmatrix} = M = \begin{bmatrix} m_{11} & m_{12} \\ m_{21} & m_{22} \end{bmatrix}$$

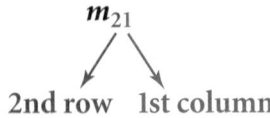

m_{21}

2nd row   1st column

A **matrix** (plural, *matrices*) is a rectangular array of numbers enclosed in a single set of brackets. The **dimensions** of a matrix are the number of horizontal rows and the number of vertical columns it has. For example, if a matrix has 2 rows and 3 columns, its dimensions are 2×3, read as "2 by 3." The inventory matrix above, M, is a matrix with dimensions of 2×2.

Each number in the matrix is called an **entry**, or element. You can denote the *address* of the entry in row 2 and column 1 of the inventory matrix, M, as m_{21} and state that $m_{21} = 15$. This entry represents 15 small barbeque grills in stock on June 1.

EXAMPLE ① Represent the June sales data in matrix S. Interpret the entry at s_{12}.

● **SOLUTION**

$$\text{Sales matrix} \rightarrow \quad \begin{matrix} & \text{Small} & \text{Large} \\ \text{Picnic tables} \\ \text{Barbeque grills} \end{matrix} \begin{bmatrix} 7 & 9 \\ 15 & 12 \end{bmatrix} = S$$

In matrix S, $s_{12} = 9$. In June, 9 large picnic tables were sold.

TRY THIS Represent the delivery data in matrix D. Interpret the entry at d_{21}.

Two matrices are *equal* if they have the same dimensions and if corresponding entries are equivalent.

E X A M P L E ② Solve $\begin{bmatrix} 2x+4 & 5 & 1 \\ -2 & -3y+5 & -4 \end{bmatrix} = \begin{bmatrix} 12 & 5 & 1 \\ -2 & 5y-3 & -4 \end{bmatrix}$ for *x* and *y*.

● **SOLUTION**

Because the matrices are equal, $2x + 4 = 12$ and $-3y + 5 = 5y - 3$.

$$2x + 4 = 12 \qquad\qquad -3y + 5 = 5y - 3$$
$$2x = 8 \qquad\qquad\qquad -8y = -8$$
$$x = 4 \qquad\qquad\qquad\qquad y = 1$$

Thus, $x = 4$ and $y = 1$.

TRY THIS Solve $\begin{bmatrix} -3 & -2x-3 \\ -2 & 3y-12 \end{bmatrix} = \begin{bmatrix} -3 & -15 \\ -2 & -2y+13 \end{bmatrix}$ for *x* and *y*.

Addition and Scalar Multiplication

To find the sum (or difference) of matrices *A* and *B* with the same dimensions, find the sums (or differences) of *corresponding* entries in *A* and *B*.

E X A M P L E ③ Let $A = \begin{bmatrix} -2 & 0 & 1 \\ 5 & -7 & 8 \end{bmatrix}$ and $B = \begin{bmatrix} 5 & 7 & -1 \\ 0 & 2 & -8 \end{bmatrix}$.

   a. Find *A* + *B*.   **b.** Find *A* − *B*.

● **SOLUTION**

TECHNOLOGY
GRAPHICS CALCULATOR

Keystroke Guide, page 268

a.

$$A + B = \begin{bmatrix} -2 & 0 & 1 \\ 5 & -7 & 8 \end{bmatrix} + \begin{bmatrix} 5 & 7 & -1 \\ 0 & 2 & -8 \end{bmatrix}$$
$$= \begin{bmatrix} -2+5 & 0+7 & 1+(-1) \\ 5+0 & -7+2 & 8+(-8) \end{bmatrix}$$
$$= \begin{bmatrix} 3 & 7 & 0 \\ 5 & -5 & 0 \end{bmatrix}$$

CHECK

```
[A]+[B]
        [[3 7  0]
         [5 -5 0]]
```

b.
$$A - B = \begin{bmatrix} -2 & 0 & 1 \\ 5 & -7 & 8 \end{bmatrix} - \begin{bmatrix} 5 & 7 & -1 \\ 0 & 2 & -8 \end{bmatrix}$$
$$= \begin{bmatrix} -2-5 & 0-7 & 1-(-1) \\ 5-0 & -7-2 & 8-(-8) \end{bmatrix}$$
$$= \begin{bmatrix} -7 & -7 & 2 \\ 5 & -9 & 16 \end{bmatrix}$$

CHECK

```
[A]-[B]
        [[-7 -7 2 ]
         [5  -9 16]]
```

TRY THIS

Let $A = \begin{bmatrix} 0 & 0 \\ 4 & 1 \\ -3 & -5 \end{bmatrix}$ and $B = \begin{bmatrix} -10 & 5 \\ 0 & 4 \\ -7 & 3 \end{bmatrix}$.

   a. Find *A* − *B*.   **b.** Find *A* + *B*.

CHECKPOINT ✔ Is it possible to find the sum $\begin{bmatrix} -2 & 5 & 6 \\ 1 & -8 & 0 \end{bmatrix} + \begin{bmatrix} 1 & -5 \\ 8 & -6 \\ -3 & 0 \end{bmatrix}$? Explain.

Example 4 below shows how matrix addition and subtraction can be used in inventory calculations. You can perform matrix addition and subtraction in one step.

E X A M P L E ④ Refer to the table of business activity at the beginning of the lesson. Let matrices M, S, and D represent the inventory, sales, and delivery data, respectively.

APPLICATION
INVENTORY

Find $M - S + D$. Interpret the final matrix.

● **SOLUTION**

$$M - S + D = \begin{bmatrix} 8 & 10 \\ 15 & 12 \end{bmatrix} - \begin{bmatrix} 7 & 9 \\ 15 & 12 \end{bmatrix} + \begin{bmatrix} 15 & 20 \\ 18 & 24 \end{bmatrix}$$

$$= \begin{bmatrix} 8 - 7 + 15 & 10 - 9 + 20 \\ 15 - 15 + 18 & 12 - 12 + 24 \end{bmatrix}$$

$$= \begin{matrix} & \text{Small} & \text{Large} \\ & \begin{bmatrix} 16 & 21 \\ 18 & 24 \end{bmatrix} & \begin{matrix} \textbf{Picnic tables} \\ \textbf{Barbeque grills} \end{matrix} \end{matrix}$$

At the end of June, the store has 16 small and 21 large picnic tables in stock. It also has 18 small and 24 large barbeque grills.

TRY THIS Find $\begin{bmatrix} 3 & 6 \\ -3 & -6 \end{bmatrix} + \begin{bmatrix} -4 & 5 \\ -7 & 8 \end{bmatrix} - \begin{bmatrix} 0 & 2 \\ -10 & 11 \end{bmatrix}$.

To multiply a matrix, A, by a real number, k, write a matrix whose entries are k times each of the entries in matrix A. This operation is called **scalar multiplication**.

E X A M P L E ⑤ Let $A = \begin{bmatrix} 3 & 2 & 0 \\ -1 & -3 & 6 \\ 2 & 0 & -10 \end{bmatrix}$. **Find $-2A$.**

● **SOLUTION**

$$-2A = \begin{bmatrix} -2(3) & -2(2) & -2(0) \\ -2(-1) & -2(-3) & -2(6) \\ -2(2) & -2(0) & -2(-10) \end{bmatrix} = \begin{bmatrix} -6 & -4 & 0 \\ 2 & 6 & -12 \\ -4 & 0 & 20 \end{bmatrix}$$

CHECKPOINT ✔ What are the entries in matrix kA if A is a 2×3 matrix and $k = 0$?

When $k = -1$, the scalar product kA is $-1A$, or simply $-A$, and is called the **additive inverse**, or *opposite*, of matrix A. For example,

if $A = \begin{bmatrix} 3 & -4 & 0 \\ 2 & -8 & 6 \\ 7 & 1 & -5 \end{bmatrix}$, then $-A = \begin{bmatrix} -3 & 4 & 0 \\ -2 & 8 & -6 \\ -7 & -1 & 5 \end{bmatrix}$ is the additive inverse of A.

CHECKPOINT ✔ Let $T = \begin{bmatrix} 3 & -5 \\ 0 & 2 \end{bmatrix}$. Write the sum of T and its additive inverse.

CRITICAL THINKING Let $k = 3$ and $A = \begin{bmatrix} 10 & -4 \\ -3 & 5 \end{bmatrix}$. Use matrix addition and scalar multiplication to show that $A + A + A = 3A$.

Properties of Matrix Addition

For matrices A, B, and C, each with dimensions of $m \times n$:

Commutative $A + B = B + A$

Associative $(A + B) + C = A + (B + C)$

Additive Identity The $m \times n$ matrix having 0 as all of its entries is the $m \times n$ identity matrix for addition.

Additive Inverse For every $m \times n$ matrix A, the matrix whose entries are the opposite of those in A is the additive inverse of A.

Geometric Transformations

Example 6 shows you how to represent a polygon in the coordinate plane as a matrix.

EXAMPLE 6 **Represent quadrilateral $ABCD$ as matrix P.**

● **SOLUTION**

Because each point has 2 coordinates and there are 4 points, create a 2×4 matrix.

$$P = \begin{matrix} A & B & C & D \\ \begin{bmatrix} -3 & 3 & 3 & -2 \\ 3 & 2 & -2 & -1 \end{bmatrix} & & & \end{matrix} \begin{matrix} x\text{-coordinates} \\ y\text{-coordinates} \end{matrix}$$

CONNECTION
COORDINATE GEOMETRY

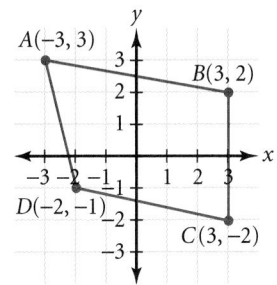

When you perform a *transformation* on one geometric figure to get another geometric figure, the original figure is called the **pre-image** and the resulting figure is the **image.** When you apply scalar multiplication to a matrix that represents a polygon, the product represents either an enlarged image or a reduced image of the pre-image polygon. This is shown in Example 7 on page 220.

EXAMPLE

7 Refer to quadrilateral *ABCD* and matrix *P* in Example 6.

Graph the polygon that is represented by each matrix.

a. $2P$ **b.** $\frac{1}{2}P$

CONNECTION
TRANSFORMATIONS

SOLUTION

a. Let quadrilateral $A'B'C'D'$ represent the image.

$$2P = \begin{matrix} A' & B' & C' & D' \\ \begin{bmatrix} -6 & 6 & 6 & -4 \\ 6 & 4 & -4 & -2 \end{bmatrix} \end{matrix}$$

Graph $A'B'C'D'$.

b. Let quadrilateral $A''B''C''D''$ represent the image.

$$\frac{1}{2}P = \begin{matrix} A'' & B'' & C'' & D'' \\ \begin{bmatrix} -\frac{3}{2} & \frac{3}{2} & \frac{3}{2} & -1 \\ \frac{3}{2} & 1 & -1 & -\frac{1}{2} \end{bmatrix} \end{matrix}$$

Graph $A''B''C''D''$.

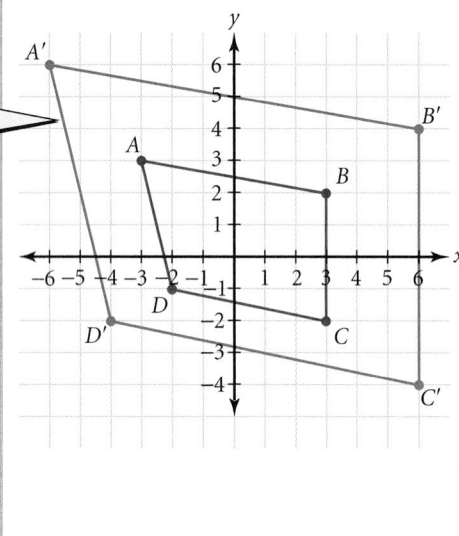

Quadrilateral $A'B'C'D'$ is an enlarged image, or dilation, of quadrilateral *ABCD* by a scale factor of 2.

Quadrilateral $A''B''C''D''$ is a reduced image of quadrilateral *ABCD* by a scale factor of $\frac{1}{2}$.

TRY THIS
Refer to quadrilateral *ABCD* and matrix *P* in Example 6. Sketch the polygon that is represented by each matrix.

a. $4P$ **b.** $\frac{1}{4}P$

Exercises

Communicate

1. Describe the location of entry m_{52} in a matrix called *M*.

2. Describe the location of entries b_{21}, b_{22}, b_{23}, and b_{24} in a matrix called *B*. What are the smallest possible dimensions of matrix *B*?

3. Explain how to represent a polygon in the coordinate plane as a matrix.

4. Explain how to use scalar multiplication to transform a polygon (pre-image) in the coordinate plane into another polygon (image).

Guided Skills Practice

APPLICATION

5. INVENTORY Represent the inventory data at right in a matrix, M. Interpret the entry at m_{23}. *(EXAMPLE 1)*

	Inventory		
	Small	**Medium**	**Large**
Jerseys	12	28	17
T-shirts	15	32	45
Sweatshirts	6	20	30

6. Solve $\begin{bmatrix} 6 & 5 \\ x+8 & 4 \\ 0 & 2y-1 \end{bmatrix} = \begin{bmatrix} 6 & 5 \\ 14-x & 4 \\ 0 & -13-y \end{bmatrix}$ for x and y. *(EXAMPLE 2)*

7. Let $R = \begin{bmatrix} 3 & 2 \\ -5 & -1 \\ -7 & 9 \end{bmatrix}$ and $S = \begin{bmatrix} 8 & -9 \\ -2 & 6 \\ 7 & -3 \end{bmatrix}$. *(EXAMPLE 3)*

    a. Find $R + S$.   **b.** Find $R - S$.

8. Find $\begin{bmatrix} 2 & -9 & -5 \\ -6 & 1 & 3 \end{bmatrix} - \begin{bmatrix} 5 & -2 & 12 \\ 2 & -4 & -5 \end{bmatrix} + \begin{bmatrix} 0 & -2 & 8 \\ -4 & -6 & 7 \end{bmatrix}$. *(EXAMPLE 4)*

9. Let $A = \begin{bmatrix} -1 & 0 & 8 \\ 6 & -4 & 5 \end{bmatrix}$. Find $-\frac{1}{2}A$. *(EXAMPLE 5)*

CONNECTIONS

10. COORDINATE GEOMETRY Represent quadrilateral $ABCD$ at right as a matrix, Q. *(EXAMPLE 6)*

11. TRANSFORMATIONS Refer to quadrilateral $ABCD$ at right and matrix Q in Exercise 10. Graph the polygon that is represented by each matrix below. *(EXAMPLE 7)*

    a. $3Q$ **b.** $\frac{1}{3}Q$

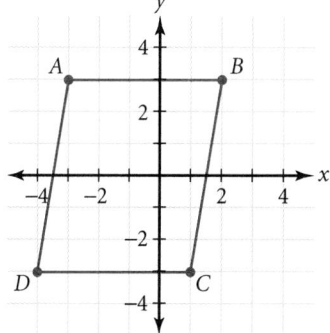

Practice and Apply

For Exercises 12–23,

let $A = \begin{bmatrix} 5 & 7 & -3 & 0 \\ -2 & 1 & 8 & 11 \end{bmatrix}$, $B = \begin{bmatrix} 8 & -5 & 2 \\ -1 & 4 & -2 \\ 0 & -5 & 3 \\ 5 & 7 & -6 \end{bmatrix}$, and $C = \begin{bmatrix} 7 \\ 2 \\ 6 \end{bmatrix}$.

internet connect

Homework Help Online

Go To: **go.hrw.com**
Keyword:
MB1 Homework Help
for Exercises 12-17,
50-52, 55-59

Give the dimensions of each matrix.

12. A **13.** B **14.** C

Give the entry at the indicated address in matrix A, B, or C.

15. a_{23} **16.** b_{12} **17.** c_{31}

Find the indicated matrix.

18. $-A$ **19.** $-4C$ **20.** $-2B$

21. $-B$ **22.** $3A$ **23.** $\frac{1}{2}B$

Solve for *x* and *y*.

24. $\begin{bmatrix} 3 & 4y \\ 5 & 8 \end{bmatrix} = \begin{bmatrix} 3 & 2 \\ 2x-1 & 8 \end{bmatrix}$

25. $\begin{bmatrix} -6 & 5 \\ -1 & 0 \end{bmatrix} = \begin{bmatrix} y+12 & 5 \\ -1 & x+7 \end{bmatrix}$

26. $\begin{bmatrix} 18 & \frac{1}{24}x \\ -\frac{2}{9}y & 15 \end{bmatrix} = \begin{bmatrix} 2x+6 & \frac{1}{4} \\ \frac{2}{3} & -5y \end{bmatrix}$

27. $\begin{bmatrix} \frac{2}{3}x & 12 \\ -4 & \frac{1}{2}y+5 \end{bmatrix} = \begin{bmatrix} 6 & x+3 \\ -4 & y+1 \end{bmatrix}$

28. $\begin{bmatrix} 2.5x & 3y+5 \\ 4 & y \end{bmatrix} = \begin{bmatrix} -10 & 2 \\ -x & y \end{bmatrix}$

29. $\begin{bmatrix} 4.1x & x \\ -100 & -3.7y \end{bmatrix} = \begin{bmatrix} 16.4 & x \\ -25x & -11.1 \end{bmatrix}$

For Exercises 30–45, let $A = \begin{bmatrix} 7 & 3 & -1 & 5 \\ -2 & 8 & 0 & -4 \end{bmatrix}$ **and** $B = \begin{bmatrix} 6 & 0 & 11 & -3 \\ -5 & 2 & -8 & 9 \end{bmatrix}$.

Perform the indicated operations.

30. $A + B$

31. $A - B$

32. $2A$

33. $-3B$

34. $B - A$

35. $A + B - A$

36. $4(B - A)$

37. $(B + A) - (-A)$

38. $-(A - B)$

39. $2A - (-B - A)$

40. $-\left(\frac{1}{2}B - A\right)$

41. $-3(B + A) - A$

42. $-\frac{1}{2}A + (B - A)$

43. $3B + 2A$

44. $\frac{1}{4}(B - 2A)$

45. $4\left(\frac{1}{2}A + \frac{2}{3}A\right)$

CHALLENGE

46. Construct a 3×3 square matrix, A, where $a_{ij} = i^2 + 2j - 3$.

CONNECTION

TRANSFORMATIONS For Exercises 47–49, refer to the coordinate plane at left.

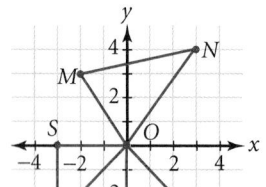

47. a. Represent $\triangle MNO$ as matrix A.
  b. Graph the polygon that is represented by $\frac{1}{2}A$.
  c. Graph the polygon that is represented by $-\frac{1}{2}A$.
  d. Graph the polygon that is represented by $4A$.

48. a. Represent $\triangle OPQ$ as matrix B.
  b. Graph the polygon that is represented by $2B$.
  c. Graph the polygon that is represented by $-4B$.
  d. Graph the polygon that is represented by $\frac{1}{4}B$.

49. a. Represent $\triangle ORS$ as matrix C.
  b. Graph the polygon that is represented by $2C$.
  c. Graph the polygon that is represented by $-C$.
  d. Graph the polygon that is represented by $-\frac{1}{2}C$.

APPLICATION

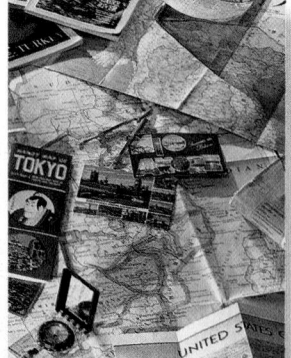

GEOGRAPHY Tracy and Renaldo both collect maps. Together they have a variety of maps from the 1960s to the 1990s. Matrix M shows the number of each type of map they have.

	'60s	'70s	'80s	'90s	
Europe	3	1	4	2	
Asia	5	3	6	3	$= M$
North America	2	7	9	5	
Africa	8	5	4	6	

50. What are the dimensions of matrix M?

51. Describe the entry at m_{42}.

52. Describe the entry at m_{21}.

53. What is the total number of maps of Africa that Renaldo and Tracy have?

54. What is the total number of maps from the 1960s that Tracy and Renaldo have?

CONSUMER ECONOMICS At a local farmer's market, Jane sold 27 squash, 31 tomatoes, 24 peppers, and 18 melons. Jose sold 48 squash, 72 tomatoes, 61 peppers, and 25 melons.

55. Create a 2 × 4 matrix of this data. Name this matrix *P*.

56. What is the address of the number of peppers that Jane sold?

57. What is the address of the data stored in the second row and first column. What does this entry represent?

58. Could you have created a matrix with different dimensions from the one you created in Exercise 55?

ACADEMICS The matrix below shows the number of events during the fall semester for three extracurricular activities.

	Aug.	Sept.	Oct.	Nov.	Dec.
Drama productions	0	1	2	1	2
Soccer games	1	4	3	3	0
Journalism publications	1	2	3	3	2

59. What are the dimensions of this matrix?

60. Find the total number of events that occurred in September.

61. Find the total number of drama productions during the fall semester.

62. During which month did the most events occur?

INVENTORY A music store manager wishes to organize information about his inventory. The store carries records, tapes, and compact discs of country, jazz, rock, blues, and classical music.

63. Give possible numbers for each type of music in each type of format.

64. Create a matrix to store this information. Name this matrix *M*.

65. Indicate what the entry at m_{23} of the matrix you created in Exercise 64 represents.

Look Back

Write an equation in slope-intercept form for the line containing the indicated points. *(LESSON 1.3)*

66. $(4, 0)$ and $(-9, 11)$

67. $(10, 3)$ and $(8, -5)$

68. If y varies directly as x and y is 49 when x is 14, find x when y is 63. *(LESSON 1.4)*

69. Find the inverse of $f(x) = 2x - 1$. *(LESSON 2.5)*

Write each pair of parametric equations as a single equation in x and y. *(LESSON 3.6)*

70. $\begin{cases} x(t) = 3t - 1 \\ y(t) = 2t \end{cases}$

71. $\begin{cases} x(t) = 5 - t \\ y(t) = 3t \end{cases}$

72. $\begin{cases} x(t) = -6t \\ y(t) = t^2 \end{cases}$

☑ internet connect

Portfolio Extension

Go To: **go.hrw.com**
Keyword:
MB1 Matrix

Look Beyond

73. Write the system of linear equations represented by these equivalent matrices: $\begin{bmatrix} 5x - 2y \\ x + 4y \end{bmatrix} = \begin{bmatrix} 3 \\ 7 \end{bmatrix}$.

Finding your way around the exhibits in museums may appear to be a random process. However, to calculate the number of paths to and from exhibits requires a mathematical approach.

The exhibits on the fourth floor of the Museum of Natural History can be modeled by the network diagram below. The address n_{23} of matrix N below represents a path from the Evolution of Horses, H, to the Dinosaur Mummy, D.

Fourth Floor, NY Museum of Natural History

G: Glen Rose Trackway
T: Tyrannosaurus
D: Dinosaur Mummy
H: Evolution of Horses
M: Warren Mastodon

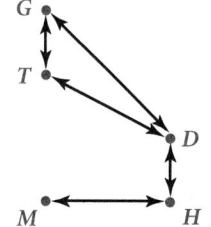

$$\begin{array}{c} \qquad\qquad\qquad \textbf{To:} \\ \qquad\quad M \;\; H \;\; D \;\; T \;\; G \\ \text{From: } \begin{array}{c} M \\ H \\ D \\ T \\ G \end{array} \begin{bmatrix} 0 & 1 & 0 & 0 & 0 \\ 1 & 0 & 1 & 0 & 0 \\ 0 & 1 & 0 & 1 & 1 \\ 0 & 0 & 1 & 0 & 1 \\ 0 & 0 & 1 & 1 & 0 \end{bmatrix} = N \end{array}$$

1. Describe the difference between locations n_{34} and n_{43} in matrix N.

2. Explain the meaning of the 1 at n_{54} and 0 at n_{14}.

3. Describe how to use matrix N to determine whether it is possible to reach Tyrannosaurus, T, directly from the Glen Rose Trackway, G.

4. Explain why each element of the main diagonal is 0.

5. Explain how to find the number of paths leading to each exhibit by using the matrix.

6. Explain how to find the number of paths going from each exhibit by using the matrix.

WORKING ON THE CHAPTER PROJECT

You should now be able to complete Activity 1 of the Chapter Project.

Matrix Multiplication

Why *Many simple calculations, such as keeping track of the score of a football game, involve a process of calculation that is very similar to matrix multiplication. Matrix multiplication can also be used for more complicated calculations.*

Objectives

● Multiply two matrices.

● Use matrix multiplication to solve mathematical and real-world problems.

APPLICATION

SPORTS

Matrix multiplication involves multiplication and addition. The process of matrix multiplication can be demonstrated by using football scores.

A football team scores 5 touchdowns, 4 extra points, and 2 field goals. A touchdown is worth 6 points, an extra point is 1 point, and a field goal is 3 points. The final score is evaluated as follows:

(5 touchdowns)(6 pts) + (4 extra points)(1 pt) + (2 field goals)(3 pts)
= 30 points + 4 points + 6 points
= 40 points total

Matrix multiplication is performed in the same way.

$$\begin{array}{cccccc} \text{Touch-} & \text{Extra} & \text{Field} & \text{Point} & & \text{Total} \\ \text{downs} & \text{points} & \text{goals} & \text{values} & & \text{score} \end{array}$$

$$[5 \quad 4 \quad 2] \quad \times \quad \begin{bmatrix} 6 \\ 1 \\ 3 \end{bmatrix} = [(5)(6) + (4)(1) + (2)(3)] = [40]$$

Notice that a 1×3 matrix multiplied by a 3×1 matrix results in a 1×1 matrix. To multiply any two matrices, the *inner dimensions* must be the same. Then the *outer dimensions* become the dimensions of the resulting product matrix.

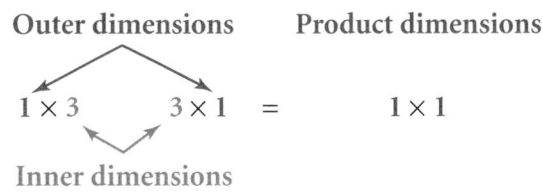

Outer dimensions   **Product dimensions**

$1 \times 3 \qquad 3 \times 1 \quad = \qquad 1 \times 1$

Inner dimensions

CHECKPOINT ✔ Let $A = \begin{bmatrix} 2 & -1 & 3 \\ 0 & 5 & 1 \end{bmatrix}$ and $B = \begin{bmatrix} 1 & 0 \\ 2 & -1 \end{bmatrix}$. Is it possible to find the product AB? Is it possible to find the product BA? Explain.

The procedure for finding the product of two matrices is given below.

Matrix Multiplication

If matrix A has dimensions $m \times n$ and matrix B has dimensions $n \times r$, then the product AB has dimensions $m \times r$.

Find the entry in row i and column j of AB by finding the sum of the products of the corresponding entries in row i of A and column j of B.

E X A M P L E 1 Let $H = \begin{bmatrix} 2 & -3 \\ 1 & 5 \end{bmatrix}$ and $G = \begin{bmatrix} 6 & 0 \\ 4 & 7 \end{bmatrix}$.

a. Find HG, if it exists. **b.** Find GH, if it exists.

SOLUTION

a. The product HG has dimensions of 2×2.

$$\begin{bmatrix} 2 & -3 \\ 1 & 5 \end{bmatrix} \begin{bmatrix} 6 & 0 \\ 4 & 7 \end{bmatrix} = \begin{bmatrix} (2)(6) + (-3)(4) & (2)(0) + (-3)(7) \\ (1)(6) + (5)(4) & (1)(0) + (5)(7) \end{bmatrix} = \begin{bmatrix} 0 & -21 \\ 26 & 35 \end{bmatrix}$$

b. The product GH has dimensions of 2×2.

$$\begin{bmatrix} 6 & 0 \\ 4 & 7 \end{bmatrix} \begin{bmatrix} 2 & -3 \\ 1 & 5 \end{bmatrix} = \begin{bmatrix} (6)(2) + (0)(1) & (6)(-3) + (0)(5) \\ (4)(2) + (7)(1) & (4)(-3) + (7)(5) \end{bmatrix} = \begin{bmatrix} 12 & -18 \\ 15 & 23 \end{bmatrix}$$

In Example 1, notice that although both HG and GH exist, the products are not equal; that is, $HG \neq GH$. Thus, matrix multiplication is *not* commutative.

TRY THIS Let $R = \begin{bmatrix} 2 & -3 \\ 0 & 5 \\ -2 & 0 \end{bmatrix}$ and $W = \begin{bmatrix} 5 & 0 \\ 4 & 7 \end{bmatrix}$.

a. Find RW, if it exists. **b.** Find WR, if it exists.

CRITICAL THINKING Find any matrices A and B such that $AB = A + B$. What can you say about the dimensions of any matrices A and B for which $AB = A + B$ is true?

Karl and Kayla are making two snack mixes by mixing dried fruit and nuts. The amounts of protein, carbohydrates, and fat, in grams per serving, for the dried fruit and nuts are given in Table 1. The number of servings of dried fruit and nuts in each mix is given in Table 2.

Table 1

	Dried fruit	Nuts
Protein	3	20
Carbohydrates	65	21
Fat	1	52

Table 2

	Sports mix	Camp mix
Dried fruit	4	3
Nuts	2	3

a. Represent the information from Table 1 in a matrix called *N*. Represent the information from Table 2 in a matrix called *G*.

b. Find the product *NG*, and determine which mix has more protein and which mix has less fat.

● **SOLUTION**

Notice that three distinct categories are represented: nutrients, ingredients, and type of mix. The categories that correspond to the *inner* dimensions of the matrices must be the same. The categories that correspond to the outer dimensions are different from one another and will become the labels of the product matrix.

a.

$$N = \begin{array}{c} \text{Protein} \\ \text{Carbohydrates} \\ \text{Fat} \end{array} \begin{bmatrix} 3 & 20 \\ 65 & 21 \\ 1 & 52 \end{bmatrix}$$

$$G = \begin{array}{c} \text{Dried fruit} \\ \text{Nuts} \end{array} \begin{bmatrix} 4 & 3 \\ 2 & 3 \end{bmatrix}$$

b.

$$NG = \begin{bmatrix} 3 & 20 \\ 65 & 21 \\ 1 & 52 \end{bmatrix} \begin{bmatrix} 4 & 3 \\ 2 & 3 \end{bmatrix} = \begin{bmatrix} 3(4) + 20(2) & 3(3) + 20(3) \\ 65(4) + 21(2) & 65(3) + 21(3) \\ 1(4) + 52(2) & 1(3) + 52(3) \end{bmatrix}$$

$$= \begin{bmatrix} 52 & 69 \\ 302 & 258 \\ 108 & 159 \end{bmatrix} \begin{array}{l} \text{Protein} \\ \text{Carbohydrates} \\ \text{Fat} \end{array}$$

The camp mix has more protein, 69 grams. The sport mix has less fat, 108 grams.

Activity
Exploring Rotations in the Plane

You will need: no special tools

You are given △*KLM* with vertices $K(0, 0)$, $L(4, 0)$, and $M(4, 3)$.

Let $A = \begin{bmatrix} 0 & -1 \\ 1 & 0 \end{bmatrix}$ and $B = \begin{bmatrix} 0 & 1 \\ -1 & 0 \end{bmatrix}$.

1. Sketch △*KLM* on graph paper. Then represent △*KLM* as matrix *C*.

2. Find *AC*. Graph the triangle represented by *AC*, △*K′L′M′*, on the coordinate plane with △*KLM*. How are △*KLM* and △*K′L′M′* related?

3. Find *BC*. Graph triangle △*K″L″M″*, represented by *BC*, on the coordinate plane with △*KLM*. How are △*KLM* and △*K″L″M″* related?

CHECKPOINT ✔ 4. Make and verify a conjecture about the effect of matrix *A* on a geometric figure in the coordinate plane.

CHECKPOINT ✔ 5. Make and verify a conjecture about the effect of matrix *B* on a geometric figure in the coordinate plane.

APPLICATION

NETWORKS

Computer network connections

A *network* is a finite set of connected points. Each point is called a **vertex** (plural, *vertices*). A **directed network** is a network in which permissible directions of travel between the vertices are indicated.

You can represent a network in an **adjacency matrix**, which indicates how many one-stage (direct) paths are possible from one vertex to another. A directed network and corresponding adjacency matrix are shown below.

Directed network   **Adjacency matrix**

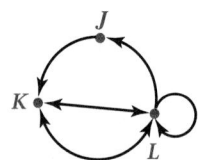

$$\text{From: } \begin{matrix} \\ J \\ K \\ L \end{matrix} \begin{matrix} J & K & L \\ \end{matrix} \begin{bmatrix} 0 & 1 & 0 \\ 0 & 0 & 2 \\ 1 & 2 & 1 \end{bmatrix} = A$$

With the points traveled from naming the rows and the points traveled to naming the columns, the matrix shows that there is no path from *J* to itself (a_{11}), but there is a path from *L* to itself (a_{33}). There are two paths from *K* to *L* (a_{23}).

If *A* is the adjacency matrix of a network, then the product $A \times A = A^2$ gives the number of two-stage paths from one vertex to another vertex by means of one intermediate vertex, such as from *L* to *K* by means of *J*.

EXAMPLE ③ **Refer to the directed network and adjacency matrix *A* above.**
  a. Find the matrix that gives the number of two-stage paths.
  b. Interpret a_{32} in matrix A^2. List the corresponding paths.

TECHNOLOGY
GRAPHICS
CALCULATOR

Keystroke Guide, page 268

● **SOLUTION**

  a. The matrix product A^2 gives the number of two-stage paths. Find A^2 or $A \times A$.
  b. The entry in row 3 column 2 is 3.

$$\text{From: } \begin{matrix} \\ J \\ K \\ L \end{matrix} \begin{matrix} J & K & L \\ \end{matrix} \begin{bmatrix} 0 & 0 & 2 \\ 2 & 4 & 2 \\ 1 & ③ & 5 \end{bmatrix} = A^2$$

This number 3 represents the number of two-stage paths from *L* to *K*. From the directed network above you can see that these paths are as follows:

$L \rightarrow L \rightarrow K$ (using one path to *K*)
$L \rightarrow L \rightarrow K$ (using another path to *K*)
$L \rightarrow J \rightarrow K$

Exercises

Communicate

1. What is necessary in order for two matrices to be multiplied?

2. Explain the steps you would use to multiply $\begin{bmatrix} 3 & -2 \\ 5 & 7 \end{bmatrix}$ and $\begin{bmatrix} 5 & -3 & 1 \\ -2 & -1 & 4 \end{bmatrix}$.

3. Explain how to represent a directed network with an adjacency matrix.

Guided Skills Practice

4. Let $A = [-1 \quad 3 \quad 5]$ and $B = \begin{bmatrix} -4 \\ 2 \\ -5 \end{bmatrix}$. *(EXAMPLE 1)*

    a. Find AB, if it exists.   **b.** Find BA, if it exists.

5. **NUTRITION** Refer to Example 2 on page 227. Add a third kind of snack mix called trail mix, to matrix G. Let the trail mix contain 2 servings of dried fruit and 4 servings of nuts. *(EXAMPLE 2)*
    a. What will be the entries in the new version of matrix G?
    b. Find the new product NG.
    c. Which of the three mixes has the greatest amount of protein? Which has the greatest amount of carbohydrates?

6. **NETWORKS** Represent the directed network at right in an adjacency matrix, M. *(EXAMPLE 3)*
    a. Find the matrix that gives the number of two-stage paths.
    b. Interpret m_{22} in the resulting matrix, and list the corresponding paths.

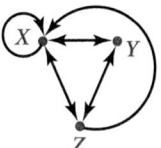

Practice and Apply

Find each product, if it exists.

7. $\begin{bmatrix} 2 \\ 0 \\ 6 \end{bmatrix} \begin{bmatrix} 1 & -3 & 4 \end{bmatrix}$

8. $\begin{bmatrix} 2 & 5 & 0 \end{bmatrix} \begin{bmatrix} 8 & 1 \\ 0 & 4 \\ 2 & 5 \end{bmatrix}$

9. $\begin{bmatrix} 5 & 3 \\ 0 & 1 \end{bmatrix} \begin{bmatrix} 4 & 2 & -1 \\ 0 & 1 & 3 \end{bmatrix}$

10. $\begin{bmatrix} 1 & 5 \\ -3 & 0 \end{bmatrix} \begin{bmatrix} 3 & -2 \\ -4 & 6 \end{bmatrix}$

11. $\begin{bmatrix} 3 & 9 \\ 2 & -1 \end{bmatrix} \begin{bmatrix} 7 & 0 \\ 1 & 3 \end{bmatrix}$

12. $\begin{bmatrix} -1 & 4 & 3 & 5 \\ 2 & 0 & -6 & 1 \end{bmatrix} \begin{bmatrix} 2 & 0 \\ 1 & 4 \\ 3 & -2 \\ -5 & 1 \end{bmatrix}$

13. $\begin{bmatrix} 4 & -6 & 5 \\ 2 & 4 & -1 \end{bmatrix} \begin{bmatrix} 2 & 7 & 1 \\ -1 & 5 & 2 \\ 1 & 4 & 1 \end{bmatrix}$

14. $\begin{bmatrix} 1 & 1 & -1 \\ 2 & 1 & 1 \\ 1 & -2 & 3 \end{bmatrix} \begin{bmatrix} 1 & -0.2 & 0.4 \\ -1 & 0.8 & -0.6 \\ -1 & 0.6 & -0.2 \end{bmatrix}$

Let $A = \begin{bmatrix} 4 & -2 & 8 & 0 \\ 1 & 3 & -6 & 9 \\ -5 & 7 & 2 & 1 \end{bmatrix}$, $B = \begin{bmatrix} 7 & 6 \\ 2 & -3 \\ -1 & 8 \\ 9 & 5 \end{bmatrix}$, and $C = \begin{bmatrix} 0 & 8 \\ -2 & 1 \end{bmatrix}$. Find each

product, if it exists.

15. BC

16. CB

17. BA

18. CA

19. $A(BC)$

20. $(AB)C$

CONNECTIONS

21. TRANSFORMATIONS Matrix $\begin{bmatrix} -2 & 3 & 0 \\ 0 & 0 & -4 \end{bmatrix}$ represents $\triangle ABC$ graphed at left.

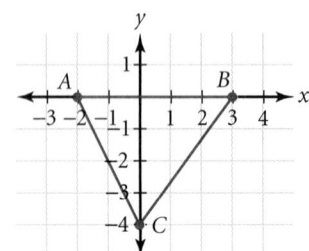

a. Find the coordinates of the vertices of the image, $\triangle A'B'C'$, after

multiplying the matrix above by the transformation matrix $\begin{bmatrix} \frac{1}{2} & 0 \\ 0 & \frac{1}{2} \end{bmatrix}$.

b. Sketch the image, $\triangle A'B'C'$, on the same plane as the pre-image, $\triangle ABC$.

c. Compare this transformation with the transformation resulting in an enlarged image or reduced image, which you learned in Lesson 4.1.

CHALLENGE

COORDINATE GEOMETRY For Exercises 22 and 23, let $A = \begin{bmatrix} -1 & 0 \\ 0 & 1 \end{bmatrix}$ **and**

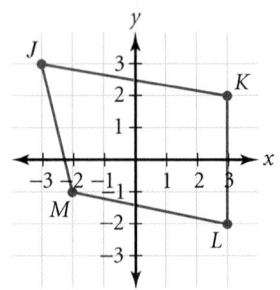

$B = \begin{bmatrix} 1 & 0 \\ 0 & -1 \end{bmatrix}$. **Matrix** $Q = \begin{bmatrix} -3 & 3 & 3 & -2 \\ 3 & 2 & -2 & -1 \end{bmatrix}$ **represents the vertices of**

quadrilateral *JKLM* at left.

22. a. Find the product AQ.
  b. Graph $J'K'L'M'$, the quadrilateral represented by AQ, on a coordinate plane with $JKLM$.
  c. Make and verify a conjecture about the effect of matrix A on a geometric figure in the plane. (Hint: Describe the movement of the vertices from $JKLM$ to $J'K'L'M'$.)

23. a. Find the product BQ.
  b. Graph $J''K''L''M''$, the quadrilateral represented by BQ.
  c. Make and verify a conjecture about the effect of matrix B on a geometric figure in the coordinate plane.

APPLICATION

24. NUTRITION Jackson High School serves breakfast and lunch, each in two shifts. The cafeteria manager needs to estimate the number of meals needed during the first week of school. Table 1 gives the percentage of students who prefer meals with meat and of those who prefer meals with no meat at the first and second shifts. Table 2 shows the average number of students who come to first and second shifts of breakfast and of lunch.

Table 1

	1st shift	2nd shift
With meat	55%	62%
Without meat	45%	38%

Table 2

	Breakfast	Lunch
1st shift	72	102
2nd shift	85	130

a. Put the information from the tables into matrices.
b. Use matrix multiplication to find how many meals without meat are needed for breakfast and for lunch.

25. SPORTS A high-school football team has played four games this season. Matrix S shows the number of touchdowns, extra points, and field goals scored in each game. Use matrix S and the point-values matrix, P, to answer parts **a–c**.

$$
\begin{array}{c c}
& \begin{array}{c c c}
\text{Touchdowns} & \text{Extra} \atop \text{points} & \text{Field} \atop \text{goals}
\end{array} \\
\begin{array}{c}
\text{Game 1} \\ \text{Game 2} \\ \text{Game 3} \\ \text{Game 4}
\end{array}
&
\left[\begin{array}{c c c}
2 & 2 & 1 \\
4 & 4 & 3 \\
3 & 1 & 3 \\
5 & 4 & 2
\end{array}\right] = S
\end{array}
$$

$$
\begin{array}{c}
\text{Point} \\ \text{values}
\end{array} \qquad
\begin{array}{c}
\text{Touchdowns} \\ \text{Extra points} \\ \text{Field goals}
\end{array}
\left[\begin{array}{c} 6 \\ 1 \\ 3 \end{array}\right] = P
$$

a. Find the product SP. What is the total number of points scored in game 3? in all four games?

b. Find the difference between the number of points scored in games 2 and 3. In which of these two games were the most points scored?

c. Suppose that matrix S included the information for all nine games of the season. How many rows and columns would the new product SP have?

26. NUTRITION A veterinarian has created formulas for producing her own mixtures of pet food. Using these formulas, she produces 3 mixtures from the 3 varieties of brand A food (regular, lite, and growth). She does the same for brand B. These mixtures are numbered 1, 2, and 3.

- The amounts of protein, fiber, and fat (in percent per serving) are given in matrix G for brand A and in matrix H for brand B.
- The three formulas that she is using, with the ingredients given in parts per serving, are stated in matrix J.

Brand A

$$
\begin{array}{c c}
& \begin{array}{c c c} \text{Regular} & \text{Lite} & \text{Growth} \end{array} \\
\begin{array}{c} \text{Protein} \\ \text{Fiber} \\ \text{Fat} \end{array}
&
\left[\begin{array}{c c c}
22 & 14 & 26 \\
3 & 15 & 3 \\
13 & 4 & 17
\end{array}\right] = G
\end{array}
$$

Brand B

$$
\begin{array}{c c}
& \begin{array}{c c c} \text{Regular} & \text{Lite} & \text{Growth} \end{array} \\
\begin{array}{c} \text{Protein} \\ \text{Fiber} \\ \text{Fat} \end{array}
&
\left[\begin{array}{c c c}
26 & 22 & 17 \\
5 & 5 & 4 \\
15 & 12 & 28
\end{array}\right] = H
\end{array}
$$

Formulas for mixtures

$$
\begin{array}{c c}
& \begin{array}{c c c} \mathbf{1} & \mathbf{2} & \mathbf{3} \end{array} \\
\begin{array}{c} \text{Regular} \\ \text{Lite} \\ \text{Growth} \end{array}
&
\left[\begin{array}{c c c}
1 & 2 & 1 \\
2 & 1 & 1 \\
1 & 1 & 2
\end{array}\right] = J
\end{array}
$$

a. Which two matrices must be multiplied to determine the nutritional content of mixtures 1, 2, and 3 from brand A? Find the product.

b. Which two matrices would be multiplied to determine the nutritional content of mixtures 1, 2, and 3 from brand B? Find the product.

c. The veterinarian wants mixture 3 to have the highest percentage of protein and fiber per serving. Should she use brand A or brand B for the mixture?

d. The veterinarian wants mixture 1 to have the lowest percentage of fat per serving. Determine whether brand A or brand B should be used in this mixture.

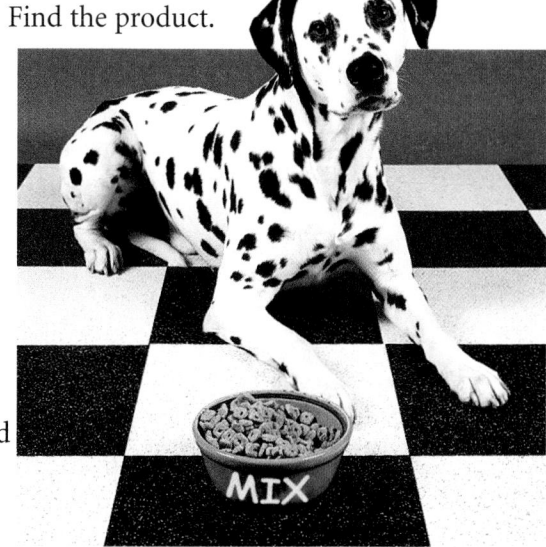

27. INVENTORY A car rental agency has offices in New York and Los Angeles. Each month, $\frac{1}{2}$ of the cars in New York go to Los Angeles and $\frac{1}{3}$ of the cars in Los Angeles go to New York. If the company starts with 1000 cars at each office, how many cars are at each office n months later?

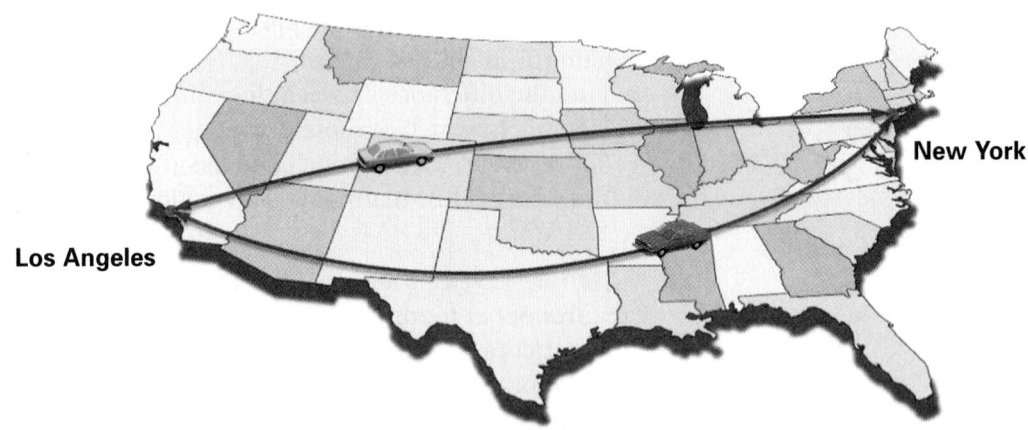

$$\text{Number of cars} \begin{array}{cc} \text{NY} & \text{LA} \end{array} [1000 \quad 1000] = N \qquad \text{Origin:} \begin{array}{c} \\ \text{NY} \\ \text{LA} \end{array} \overset{\begin{array}{cc} \text{NY} & \text{LA} \end{array}}{\begin{bmatrix} \frac{1}{2} & \frac{1}{2} \\ \frac{1}{3} & \frac{2}{3} \end{bmatrix}} = P$$

Destination:

New York

Los Angeles

a. The product NP represents the number of cars in each location after one month. Find NP. How many rental cars are in each location after 1 month?

b. Multiply matrix NP by P to find the number of cars in each location after 2 months. (Hint: Round up the entry in column one, and round down the entry in column two of the product.)

c. Continue to multiply each new product matrix by P until the product (with entries rounded to the nearest whole number) no longer changes. What is the final distribution of cars? How many months have passed?

NETWORKS **For Exercises 28 and 29, refer to the directed network at left.**

28. a. Create an adjacency matrix that represents the number of one-stage paths between the vertices.
 b. How many one-stage paths does this directed network contain?
 c. List the one-stage paths.

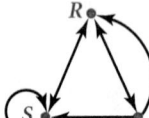

29. a. Create an adjacency matrix for the two-stage paths between the vertices.
 b. How many two-stage paths does this directed network contain?
 c. List the two-stage paths.

30. SPORTS Suppose that a football team scores 5 touchdowns, 4 extra points, and 2 field goals in one game. A touchdown is worth 6 points, an extra point is 1 point, and a field goal is 3 points.
 a. Construct a matrix, S, to represent the team's scoring events and a matrix, P, to represent the point values for each scoring event.
 b. Multiply the two matrices to determine the team's total score for the game.

Look Back

Find the slope and the *y*-intercept for each line. *(LESSON 1.2)*

31. $4(2x - 7) = -6$ **32.** $y = -2\left(\frac{1}{3}x + 5\right)$ **33.** $6 - \frac{2}{3}(y + 9) = 12x$

Which of the following are true for all nonzero real numbers *a* and *b*? *(LESSON 2.1)*

34. $a \div b = b \div a$ **35.** $a + b = b + a$

36. $a - b = b - a$ **37.** $a \cdot b = b \cdot a$

Let *f(x)* = 2*x* + 3 and *g(x)* = 5*x* – 2. *(LESSON 2.4)*

38. Find $f \circ g$.   **39.** Find $g \circ f$.

40. Is $f \circ g$ equal to $g \circ f$?   **41.** Find $(f \circ g)(6)$.

APPLICATION

42. RENTALS An apartment building contains 200 apartments. Some apartments have only one bedroom and rent for $435 per month. The rest have two bedrooms and rent for $575 per month. When all the units are rented, the total monthly income is $97,500. How many one- and two-bedroom apartments are there? *(LESSON 3.2)*

Portfolio Extension

Go To: **go.hrw.com**
Keyword:
MB1 Matrix Multiply

Look Beyond

43. Write the system of two equations represented by this matrix equation.

$$\begin{bmatrix} -3 & 4 \\ -6 & 8 \end{bmatrix} \begin{bmatrix} x \\ y \end{bmatrix} = \begin{bmatrix} 3 \\ 6 \end{bmatrix}$$

NETWORKS Refer to the adjacency matrix *N* below, taken from the Portfolio Activity on page 224.

Matrix powers can be used to give the number of *n*-stage paths from one vertex to another. Matrix powers can also be used to locate circuits, which are paths that start and end at the same vertex.

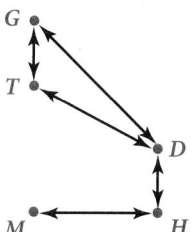

Matrix N^3 gives the number of three-stage paths from one vertex to another.

1. Find N^3. Interpret n_{54} in matrix N^3. List the corresponding paths.

2. Interpret n_{43} in matrix N^3. List the corresponding paths.

3. Find the sums of the rows of N^3. Use the sums to determine which exhibits have the greatest number of three-stage paths to themselves or other exhibits.

4. Find N^4. Interpret n_{13} in matrix N^4.

5. Find the number of four-stage paths from vertex *D* to itself. List the corresponding paths.

WORKING ON THE CHAPTER PROJECT

You should now be able to complete the Chapter Project.

The Inverse of a Matrix

Objectives

● Find and use the inverse of a matrix, if it exists.

● Find and use the determinant of a matrix.

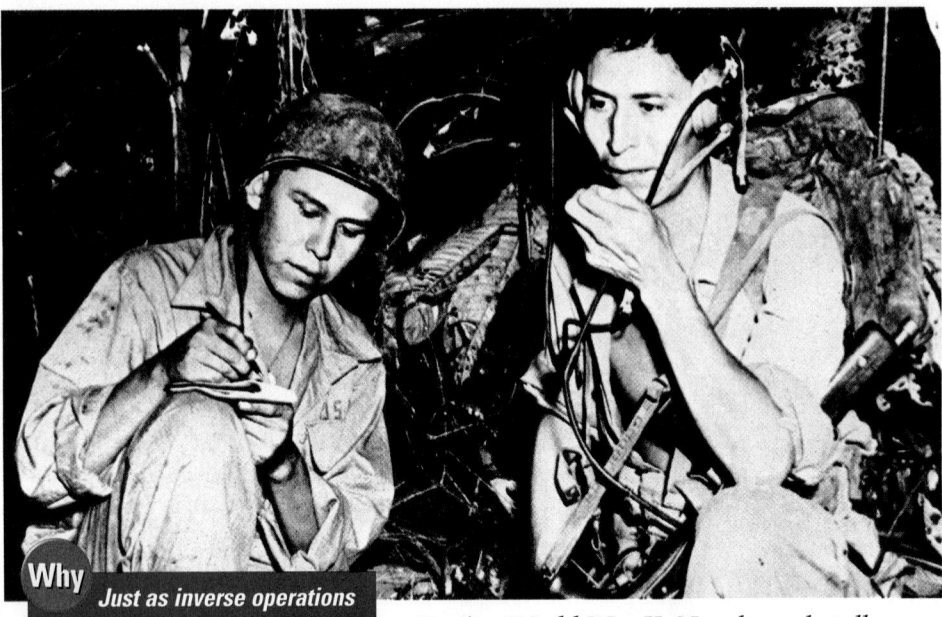

Why *Just as inverse operations can be used to solve equations, inverse matrices can be used to decode messages.*

During World War II, Navaho code talkers, 29 members of the Navaho Nation, developed a code that was used by the United States Armed Forces.

APPLICATION

CRYPTOGRAPHY

The table at right is an assignment table for a code. Each letter of the alphabet is assigned a number. For example, the letter **A** is assigned the number 1 and **Z** is assigned the number 26. The dash, which represents the space between words in a message, is assigned the number 0. The question mark is assigned the number 27. For example, the phrase **HELP ME** would be encoded as 8 | 5 | 12 | 16 | 0 | 13 | 5.

– 0	G 7	N 14	U 21
A 1	H 8	O 15	V 22
B 2	I 9	P 16	W 23
C 3	J 10	Q 17	X 24
D 4	K 11	R 18	Y 25
E 5	L 12	S 19	Z 26
F 6	M 13	T 20	? 27

A matrix can be used to encode a message and another matrix, its inverse, is used to decode the message once it is received. *You will use a matrix to decode a message in Example 3.*

A **square matrix** is a matrix that has the same number of columns and rows. The following matrices are examples of square matrices:

$$\begin{bmatrix} 2 & -3 \\ \frac{1}{2} & 4 \end{bmatrix} \quad \begin{bmatrix} -1 & 5 & 3 \\ 4 & -8 & 1 \\ 3 & 7 & 0 \end{bmatrix} \quad \begin{bmatrix} -2 & -8 & 4 & 11 \\ 1 & -4 & 3 & -15 \\ 3 & 5 & 2 & 6 \\ 7 & 1 & 8 & 3 \end{bmatrix}$$

2×2 $\qquad\qquad$ 3×3 $\qquad\qquad$ 4×4

The *identity matrix for multiplication* for all 2×2 square matrices is $\begin{bmatrix} 1 & 0 \\ 0 & 1 \end{bmatrix}$.

An identity matrix, called I, has 1s on its *main diagonal* and 0s elsewhere.

$$I_{2 \times 2} = \begin{bmatrix} 1 & 0 \\ 0 & 1 \end{bmatrix} \qquad I_{3 \times 3} = \begin{bmatrix} 1 & 0 & 0 \\ 0 & 1 & 0 \\ 0 & 0 & 1 \end{bmatrix} \qquad I_{4 \times 4} = \begin{bmatrix} 1 & 0 & 0 & 0 \\ 0 & 1 & 0 & 0 \\ 0 & 0 & 1 & 0 \\ 0 & 0 & 0 & 1 \end{bmatrix}$$

234 CHAPTER 4

The Identity Matrix for Multiplication

Let A be a square matrix with n rows and n columns. Let I be a matrix with the same dimensions and with 1s on the main diagonal and 0s elsewhere. Then $AI = IA = A$.

The product of a real number and 1 is the same number. The product of a square matrix, A, and I is the same matrix, A.

$$\underbrace{\begin{bmatrix} 3 & 1 \\ 2 & 1 \end{bmatrix}}_{A} \times \underbrace{\begin{bmatrix} 1 & 0 \\ 0 & 1 \end{bmatrix}}_{I} = \begin{bmatrix} 3(1) + 1(0) & 3(0) + 1(1) \\ 2(1) + 1(0) & 2(0) + 1(1) \end{bmatrix} = \underbrace{\begin{bmatrix} 3 & 1 \\ 2 & 1 \end{bmatrix}}_{A}$$

CHECKPOINT ✔ What is the product of $\begin{bmatrix} a & b \\ c & d \end{bmatrix}$ and $\begin{bmatrix} 1 & 0 \\ 0 & 1 \end{bmatrix}$?

The product of a real number and its multiplicative inverse is 1. The product of a square matrix and its *inverse* is the identity matrix I.

$$\underbrace{\begin{bmatrix} 3 & 1 \\ 2 & 1 \end{bmatrix}}_{A} \times \underbrace{\begin{bmatrix} 1 & -1 \\ -2 & 3 \end{bmatrix}}_{\substack{\text{inverse} \\ \text{of } A}} = \begin{bmatrix} 3(1) + 1(-2) & 3(-1) + 1(3) \\ 2(1) + 1(-2) & 2(-1) + 1(3) \end{bmatrix} = \underbrace{\begin{bmatrix} 1 & 0 \\ 0 & 1 \end{bmatrix}}_{I}$$

The Inverse of a Matrix

Let A be a square matrix with n rows and n columns. If there is an $n \times n$ matrix B such that $AB = I$ and $BA = I$, then A and B are inverses of one another. The inverse of matrix A is denoted by A^{-1}. $\left(\text{Note: } A^{-1} \neq \dfrac{1}{A}\right)$

In general, to show that matrices are inverses of one another, you need to show that the multiplication of the matrices is commutative and results in the identity matrix.

E X A M P L E ① Let $A = \begin{bmatrix} 2 & 3 \\ 3 & 5 \end{bmatrix}$ and $B = \begin{bmatrix} 5 & -3 \\ -3 & 2 \end{bmatrix}$.

Show that A and B are inverses of one another.

● **SOLUTION**

$$AB = \begin{bmatrix} 2 & 3 \\ 3 & 5 \end{bmatrix} \begin{bmatrix} 5 & -3 \\ -3 & 2 \end{bmatrix} \qquad\qquad BA = \begin{bmatrix} 5 & -3 \\ -3 & 2 \end{bmatrix} \begin{bmatrix} 2 & 3 \\ 3 & 5 \end{bmatrix}$$

$$= \begin{bmatrix} 2(5) + 3(-3) & 2(-3) + 3(2) \\ 3(5) + 5(-3) & 3(-3) + 5(2) \end{bmatrix} \qquad = \begin{bmatrix} 5(2) + (-3)(3) & 5(3) + (-3)(5) \\ -3(2) + 2(3) & -3(3) + 2(5) \end{bmatrix}$$

$$= \begin{bmatrix} 1 & 0 \\ 0 & 1 \end{bmatrix} \qquad\qquad\qquad\qquad\quad = \begin{bmatrix} 1 & 0 \\ 0 & 1 \end{bmatrix}$$

Since both product matrices are the 2×2 identity matrix for multiplication, A and B are inverses of one another.

You can use the equation $AB = I$ to find the inverse of a matrix. For example, let $A = \begin{bmatrix} 1 & 2 \\ 3 & 5 \end{bmatrix}$ and $B = \begin{bmatrix} a & b \\ c & d \end{bmatrix}$. Then write the equation $AB = I$, and proceed as follows:

$$\begin{bmatrix} 1 & 2 \\ 3 & 5 \end{bmatrix} \begin{bmatrix} a & b \\ c & d \end{bmatrix} = \begin{bmatrix} 1 & 0 \\ 0 & 1 \end{bmatrix}$$

$$\begin{bmatrix} a + 2c & b + 2d \\ 3a + 5c & 3b + 5d \end{bmatrix} = \begin{bmatrix} 1 & 0 \\ 0 & 1 \end{bmatrix}$$

Set the corresponding entries equal to each other, and solve the two resulting systems.

$$\begin{cases} a + 2c = 1 \\ 3a + 5c = 0 \end{cases} \qquad\qquad \begin{cases} b + 2d = 0 \\ 3b + 5d = 1 \end{cases}$$

$$a = -5 \text{ and } c = 3 \qquad\qquad b = 2 \text{ and } d = -1$$

Thus, the inverse of matrix A does exist. $B = A^{-1} = \begin{bmatrix} -5 & 2 \\ 3 & -1 \end{bmatrix}$.

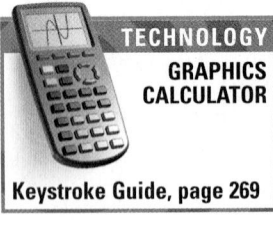

TECHNOLOGY
GRAPHICS CALCULATOR
Keystroke Guide, page 269

You can find the inverse of $A = \begin{bmatrix} 1 & 2 \\ 3 & 5 \end{bmatrix}$ on most graphics calculators. Enter the matrix, and use the $\boxed{x^{-1}}$ key. The display at right shows matrices A and A^{-1}, the inverse of A.

Finding the inverse of a 3×3 matrix or verifying that there is one is a very lengthy process. For matrices larger than 2×2, you will find that a graphics calculator especially useful.

E X A M P L E ❷ Use a graphics calculator to find the inverse of each matrix.

a. $A = \begin{bmatrix} 6 & 8 \\ 5 & 7 \end{bmatrix}$ **b.** $B = \begin{bmatrix} 2 & -1 & 1 \\ -1 & 3 & 4 \\ -2 & 1 & 0 \end{bmatrix}$ **c.** $C = \begin{bmatrix} 8 & 4 \\ 6 & 3 \end{bmatrix}$

● **SOLUTION**

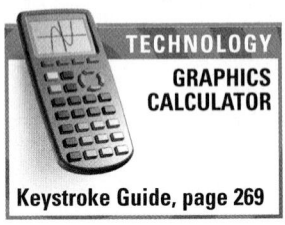

TECHNOLOGY
GRAPHICS CALCULATOR
Keystroke Guide, page 269

To find each inverse, enter the matrix and use the $\boxed{x^{-1}}$ key.

a. **b.** **c.**

$A^{-1} = \begin{bmatrix} 3.5 & -4 \\ -2.5 & 3 \end{bmatrix}$ $B^{-1} = \begin{bmatrix} -0.8 & 0.2 & -1.4 \\ -1.6 & 0.4 & -1.8 \\ 1 & 0 & 1 \end{bmatrix}$ Matrix C does not have an inverse.

Matrix C in Example 2 is called *non-invertible* because it *does not* have an inverse. An *invertible* matrix *does* have an inverse.

CRITICAL THINKING If $A^{-1} = \begin{bmatrix} 2 & 3 \\ 5 & 7 \end{bmatrix}$, find A. Then find $(A^{-1})^{-1}$. Explain how the three matrices are related.

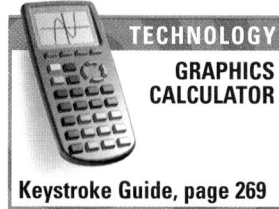
APPLICATION
CRYPTOGRAPHY

Using the table at the beginning of the lesson, assign a number to each letter and space in a message. If the message has an uneven number of characters, then add a zero to the end. Then choose an invertible matrix, A, that can multiply B to encode the message. A^{-1} can then be used to decode the message.

For example, the message GO BOB, represented by 7 | 15 | 0 | 2 | 15 | 2, would be translated into the 2×3 matrix B shown below:

$$B = \begin{bmatrix} 7 & 15 & 0 \\ 2 & 15 & 2 \end{bmatrix}$$

TECHNOLOGY
GRAPHICS CALCULATOR

Keystroke Guide, page 269

You can use an invertible matrix, such as $A = \begin{bmatrix} 6 & 5 \\ 7 & 6 \end{bmatrix}$, to encode the message by multiplying A and B.

During World War II, the United States used a rotor machine called the ECM Mark II, also known as SIGABA, to encrypt messages. The SIGABA was so well designed that its codes were never broken.

Example 3 shows how you can then use A^{-1} to decode a message that was encoded by A.

EXAMPLE 3 Use A^{-1} to decode the message 52 | 165 | 10 | 61 | 195 | 12 which was encoded by matrix $A = \begin{bmatrix} 6 & 5 \\ 7 & 6 \end{bmatrix}$.

APPLICATION
CRYPTOGRAPHY

PROBLEM SOLVING

● **SOLUTION**

Work backward. To decode the message, insert the code numbers into a 2×3 matrix C. Multiply this matrix by A^{-1}.

$$C = \begin{bmatrix} 52 & 165 & 10 \\ 61 & 195 & 12 \end{bmatrix}$$

Enter the coding matrix A. Then find $A^{-1}C$.

$$A^{-1}C = \begin{bmatrix} 7 & 15 & 0 \\ 2 & 15 & 2 \end{bmatrix}$$

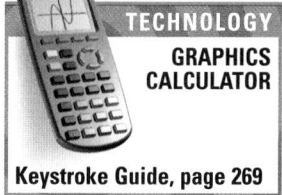
TECHNOLOGY
GRAPHICS CALCULATOR

Keystroke Guide, page 269

The matrix product gives the decoded message 7 | 15 | 0 | 2 | 15 | 2. These numbers translate to the original message, GO BOB.

Determinants

Each square matrix can be assigned a real number called the *determinant of the matrix*. The determinant of a 2 × 2 matrix is defined below.

Determinant of a 2 × 2 Matrix

Let $A = \begin{bmatrix} a & b \\ c & d \end{bmatrix}$. The **determinant** of A, denoted by $\det(A)$ or $\begin{vmatrix} a & b \\ c & d \end{vmatrix}$,

is defined as $\det(A) = \begin{vmatrix} a & b \\ c & d \end{vmatrix} = ad - bc$.

Matrix A has an inverse if and only if $\det(A) \neq 0$.

E X A M P L E ④ Find the determinant, and tell whether each matrix has an inverse.

a. $G = \begin{bmatrix} 7 & 8 \\ 6 & 7 \end{bmatrix}$

b. $H = \begin{bmatrix} 1 & 1 \\ 2 & 2 \end{bmatrix}$

TECHNOLOGY
GRAPHICS CALCULATOR
Keystroke Guide, page 270

SOLUTION

a. $\det(G) = (7)(7) - (8)(6)$
$= 1$
Since $\det(G) \neq 0$, matrix G has an inverse.

b. $\det(H) = (1)(2) - (1)(2)$
$= 0$
Since $\det(H) = 0$, matrix H has no inverse.

TRY THIS Find the determinant, and tell whether each matrix has an inverse.

a. $S = \begin{bmatrix} -3 & 4 \\ -2 & 9 \end{bmatrix}$

b. $T = \begin{bmatrix} -6 & 12 \\ 2 & -4 \end{bmatrix}$

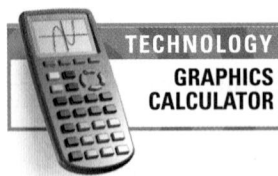

TECHNOLOGY
GRAPHICS CALCULATOR

PROBLEM SOLVING

Activity
Exploring Codes

You will need: a graphics calculator

1. Create a 2 × 2 matrix that you would like to use to encode messages.

2. **Guess and check.** Use your calculator to verify that your matrix has an inverse. If it does not, modify your matrix so that it does. (Hint: Create your matrix so that its determinant does not equal 0.)

3. Write a brief message. Use the assignment table from page 234 to translate it into numbers.

4. Use your matrix to encode the message. Write the coded message.

CHECKPOINT ✔ 5. Use your inverse to decode your message.

6. Explain why a matrix must be square and invertible in order to be an encoding matrix.

Communicate

1. Look up the words *encryption* and *decryption* in a dictionary, and explain how matrices are used to encrypt and decrypt messages.

2. Describe each product matrix without multiplying.

   a. $\begin{bmatrix} 1 & 3 \\ 2 & -1 \end{bmatrix} \begin{bmatrix} 1 & 0 \\ 0 & 1 \end{bmatrix}$ b. $\begin{bmatrix} 1 & 0 \\ 0 & 1 \end{bmatrix} \begin{bmatrix} -2 & 1 \\ 5 & 3 \end{bmatrix}$

3. How do you find the inverse of a matrix with a graphics calculator?

4. Explain one way in which determinants can be used.

Guided Skills Practice

5. Show that the matrices $\begin{bmatrix} 2 & 1 \\ 1 & 1 \end{bmatrix}$ and $\begin{bmatrix} 1 & -1 \\ -1 & 2 \end{bmatrix}$ are inverses. **(EXAMPLE 1)**

6. Find the inverse of $\begin{bmatrix} 9 & 5 \\ 7 & 4 \end{bmatrix}$. **(EXAMPLE 2)**

APPLICATION

7. **CRYPTOGRAPHY** Use the inverse matrix you found in Exercise 6 to decode the message 282 | 9 | 260 | 75 | 180 | 221 | 7 | 203 | 60 | 140. **(EXAMPLE 3)**

Find the determinant, and tell whether each matrix has an inverse. (EXAMPLE 4)

8. $\begin{bmatrix} 2 & 1 \\ 6 & 3 \end{bmatrix}$ 9. $\begin{bmatrix} -5 & 2 \\ 3 & -2 \end{bmatrix}$

Practice and Apply

Determine whether each pair of matrices are inverses of each other.

10. $\begin{bmatrix} 4 & 0 \\ 0 & 3 \end{bmatrix}, \begin{bmatrix} \frac{1}{4} & 0 \\ 0 & \frac{1}{3} \end{bmatrix}$ 11. $\begin{bmatrix} 1 & 2 \\ 3 & 4 \end{bmatrix}, \begin{bmatrix} -2 & 1 \\ \frac{3}{2} & -\frac{1}{2} \end{bmatrix}$ 12. $\begin{bmatrix} 4 & 3 \\ 4 & 2 \end{bmatrix}, \begin{bmatrix} 2 & -3 \\ -4 & 6 \end{bmatrix}$

Find the determinant, and tell whether each matrix has an inverse.

13. $\begin{bmatrix} 2 & -5 \\ -1 & 3 \end{bmatrix}$ 14. $\begin{bmatrix} 1 & 2 \\ 1 & 3 \end{bmatrix}$ 15. $\begin{bmatrix} 2 & 3 \\ 4 & 6 \end{bmatrix}$ 16. $\begin{bmatrix} -3 & 2 \\ 9 & -6 \end{bmatrix}$

17. $\begin{bmatrix} 3 & 4 \\ 6 & 8 \end{bmatrix}$ 18. $\begin{bmatrix} 5 & 6 \\ 2 & 2 \end{bmatrix}$ 19. $\begin{bmatrix} 2 & 2 \\ 3 & 4 \end{bmatrix}$ 20. $\begin{bmatrix} 7 & 6 \\ 9 & 8 \end{bmatrix}$

internet connect

Homework Help Online
Go To: go.hrw.com
Keyword:
MB1 Homework Help
for Exercises 13–20

Find the inverse matrix, if it exists. If the inverse matrix does not exist, write *no inverse*.

21. $\begin{bmatrix} -2 & 2 & -1 \\ 3 & -5 & 4 \\ 5 & -6 & 4 \end{bmatrix}$ 22. $\begin{bmatrix} 1 & 6 & 2 \\ -2 & 3 & 5 \\ 7 & 12 & -4 \end{bmatrix}$ 23. $\begin{bmatrix} 1 & -2 & 1 \\ -2 & 4 & -2 \\ 3 & 5 & 3 \end{bmatrix}$

If $A = \begin{bmatrix} a & b \\ c & d \end{bmatrix}$ and $\det(A) \neq 0$, then A^{-1} is given by the formula

$A^{-1} = \dfrac{1}{\det(A)} \begin{bmatrix} d & -b \\ -c & a \end{bmatrix}$. Use this formula to find the inverse of each

matrix, if it exists. If the inverse does not exist, write *no inverse*.

24. $\begin{bmatrix} 1 & 3 \\ 1 & 1 \end{bmatrix}$ **25.** $\begin{bmatrix} 2 & 1 \\ 0 & 3 \end{bmatrix}$ **26.** $\begin{bmatrix} -4 & 8 \\ 2 & -4 \end{bmatrix}$ **27.** $\begin{bmatrix} 6 & 3 \\ 9 & 10 \end{bmatrix}$

28. $\begin{bmatrix} 2 & 3 \\ 1 & 2 \end{bmatrix}$ **29.** $\begin{bmatrix} 3 & 7 \\ 2 & 5 \end{bmatrix}$ **30.** $\begin{bmatrix} 2 & -6 \\ 1 & -2 \end{bmatrix}$ **31.** $\begin{bmatrix} 2 & 1 \\ 1 & 1 \end{bmatrix}$

32. $\begin{bmatrix} 1 & 3 \\ 2 & 7 \end{bmatrix}$ **33.** $\begin{bmatrix} 5 & -7 \\ -2 & 3 \end{bmatrix}$ **34.** $\begin{bmatrix} \frac{1}{2} & \frac{3}{8} \\ 1 & \frac{1}{4} \end{bmatrix}$ **35.** $\begin{bmatrix} \frac{1}{3} & \frac{1}{6} \\ \frac{5}{6} & \frac{2}{3} \end{bmatrix}$

Find the inverse matrix, if it exists. Round entries to the nearest hundredth. If the inverse matrix does not exist, write *no inverse*.

36 $\begin{bmatrix} 2 & -4 \\ -3 & 6 \end{bmatrix}$ **37** $\begin{bmatrix} \frac{1}{2} & 0 \\ 1 & \frac{1}{4} \end{bmatrix}$ **38** $\begin{bmatrix} \frac{1}{2} & \frac{1}{10} \\ \frac{3}{2} & \frac{1}{5} \end{bmatrix}$

39 $\begin{bmatrix} \frac{1}{3} & \frac{1}{2} \\ \frac{1}{2} & \frac{1}{6} \end{bmatrix}$ **40** $\begin{bmatrix} 2 & -10 \\ -1 & 10 \end{bmatrix}$ **41** $\begin{bmatrix} -2 & -1 & 1 \\ 1 & -2 & 3 \\ 4 & 1 & 2 \end{bmatrix}$

42 $\begin{bmatrix} 2 & 0 & 5 \\ -3 & 1 & -5 \\ 0 & 2 & 4 \end{bmatrix}$ **43** $\begin{bmatrix} \pi & 2 & -1 \\ 1 & 5 & \pi \\ 2 & -3 & 4 \end{bmatrix}$ **44** $\begin{bmatrix} 2\pi & 3 & -1 \\ 0 & -2 & \pi \\ 3 & 0 & -5 \end{bmatrix}$

45. The determinant of a 3×3 matrix, $A = \begin{bmatrix} a & b & c \\ d & e & f \\ g & h & i \end{bmatrix}$, can be found by using the formula shown below.

$$\det(A) = \begin{vmatrix} a & b & c \\ d & e & f \\ g & h & i \end{vmatrix} = a\begin{vmatrix} e & f \\ h & i \end{vmatrix} - b\begin{vmatrix} d & f \\ g & i \end{vmatrix} + c\begin{vmatrix} d & e \\ g & h \end{vmatrix}$$

Use this formula to find the determinant of each 3×3 matrix.

a. $\begin{bmatrix} 2 & -1 & 3 \\ 4 & 0 & 1 \\ 2 & 0 & 3 \end{bmatrix}$ **b.** $\begin{bmatrix} 3 & 1 & -6 \\ -5 & 2 & 10 \\ 4 & 2 & -8 \end{bmatrix}$ **c.** $\begin{bmatrix} 1 & 2 & 0 \\ -3 & 7 & -2 \\ 2 & 1 & 5 \end{bmatrix}$

CHALLENGE

46. a. Find x, y, u, and v in terms of a, b, c, and d such that

$$\begin{bmatrix} a & b \\ c & d \end{bmatrix}\begin{bmatrix} x & u \\ y & v \end{bmatrix} = I.$$

b. Substitute the values of x, y, u, and v from part **a** in $\begin{bmatrix} x & u \\ y & v \end{bmatrix}$.

Divide out the common factor (a rational expression) from each term, and place it in front of the matrix as a scalar multiplier. How does this expression compare with the formula for A^{-1} given for Exercises 24–35?

47. COORDINATE GEOMETRY The matrix $A = \begin{bmatrix} 2 & 0 \\ 0 & 1 \end{bmatrix}$ horizontally stretches an object in the coordinate plane by a factor of 2. Find A^{-1}. Verify that A^{-1} horizontally compresses an object in the coordinate plane by a factor of $\frac{1}{2}$ by applying A^{-1} to the square with vertices at the points $(2, 2)$, $(2, -2)$, $(-2, -2)$, and $(-2, 2)$. Graph your results.

CRYPTOGRAPHY Let $A = \begin{bmatrix} 5 & 3 \\ 3 & 2 \end{bmatrix}$. Use matrix A to encode each message.

48. MOVE OUT   **49.** HEAD NORTH

50. FALL IN   **51.** CEASE FIRE

Given $A = \begin{bmatrix} 5 & 3 \\ 3 & 2 \end{bmatrix}$, find A^{-1} and decode each message.

52. 97 | 70 | 68 | 80 | 24 | 62 | 45 | 45 | 52 | 16

53. 77 | 50 | 139 | 42 | 47 | 33 | 88 | 28

54. 8 | 160 | 100 | 17 | 18 | 124 | 42 | 5 | 100 | 60 | 11 | 11 | 79 | 28

55. 18 |100 | 5 | 132 | 80 | 70 | 42 | 11 | 64 | 3 | 82 | 51 | 45 | 28

 Look Back

Write an equation in slope-intercept form for the line containing the indicated points. *(LESSON 1.3)*

56. $(2, -2)$ and $(0, -1)$ **57.** $(0, 3)$ and $(-2, -6)$

Solve each equation. *(LESSON 1.6)*

58. $8.91 + x = 11.09$ **59.** $\frac{1}{4} = \frac{3}{4} + x$ **60.** $5\frac{1}{2}x = -62$

61. $\frac{1}{5}x = 0.3$ **62.** $\frac{2}{3}x + 1 = x + 3$ **63.** $\frac{1}{2}x + \frac{1}{4} = 2\frac{3}{4} - \frac{1}{3}x$

64. Evaluate $f(x) = 2 - 5x + x^2$ for $x = 3$ and $x = -4$.
(LESSON 2.3)

65. Use any method to solve the system. $\begin{cases} 5x + 7y = 32 \\ 2x - 14y = 6 \end{cases}$
(LESSONS 3.1 AND 3.2)

Graph the solution to each system of linear inequalities. *(LESSON 3.4)*

66. $\begin{cases} 2x + y \geq 2 \\ y \geq 3x + 2 \end{cases}$ **67.** $\begin{cases} x + \frac{1}{2}y \leq 2 \\ 2x + 3y < 2 \end{cases}$ **68.** $\begin{cases} 3x + 2y \geq 1 \\ 2x + 3y < 2 \\ x < 3 \end{cases}$

 Look Beyond

69. a. Write the system of equations $\begin{cases} 3x + 7y = 4 \\ 2x + 5y = 1 \end{cases}$ in matrix form.

$\left(\text{Hint: } \begin{bmatrix} ? & ? \\ ? & ? \end{bmatrix} \begin{bmatrix} x \\ y \end{bmatrix} = \begin{bmatrix} 4 \\ 1 \end{bmatrix}.\right)$

b. Let $A = \begin{bmatrix} 3 & 7 \\ 2 & 5 \end{bmatrix}$. Find A^{-1}. Find the product on each side of the

equation $A^{-1} \begin{bmatrix} 3 & 7 \\ 2 & 5 \end{bmatrix} \begin{bmatrix} x \\ y \end{bmatrix} = A^{-1} \begin{bmatrix} 4 \\ 1 \end{bmatrix}$. What is the resulting equation?

c. Explain the connection between parts **a** and **b** of this exercise.

HOW SECRET IS SECRET?

Biggest Division a Giant Leap in Math

BY GINA KOLATA

In a mathematical feat that seemed impossible a year ago, a group of several hundred researchers using about 1,000 computers has broken a 155-digit number down into three smaller numbers that cannot be further divided.

The latest finding could be the first serious threat to systems used by banks and other organizations to encode secret data before transmission, cryptography experts said yesterday.

These systems are based on huge numbers that cannot be easily factored, or divided into two numbers that cannot be divided further.

In 1977, a group of three mathematicians devised a way of making secret codes that involves scrambling messages according to a mathematical formula based on factoring. Now, such codes are used in banking, for secure telephone lines and by the Defense Department.

In making these codes, engineers have to strike a delicate balance when they select the numbers used to scramble messages. If they choose a number that is easy to factor, the code can be broken. If they make the number much larger, and much harder to

factor, it takes much longer for the calculations used to scramble a message.

For most applications outside the realm of national security, cryptographers have settled on numbers that are about 150 digits long.

Dr. Mark Manasse of the Digital Equipment Corporation's Systems Research Center in Palo Alto, Calif., calculates that if a computer could perform a billion divisions a second, it would take 10 to the 60th years, or 1 with 60 zeros after it, to factor the number simply by trying out every smaller number that might divide into it easily. But with a newly discovered factoring method and with a world-wide collaborative effort, the number was cracked in a few months.

Connection Machine® is one of the most powerful high-performance computers in the world.

Factoring a 155-Digit
Number:
13,407,807,929,942,
597,099,574,024,998,
205,846,127,479,365,
820,592,393,377,723,
561,443,721,764,030,
073,546,976,801,874,
298,166,903,427,690,
031,858,186,486,050,
853,753,882,811,946,
569,946,433,649,006,
084,097

equals

2,424,833

times

7,455,602,825,647,
884,208,337,395,736,
200,454,918,783,366,
342,657

times

741,640,062,627,530,
801,524,787,141,901,
937,474,059,940,781,
097,519,023,905,821,
306,144,415,759,504,
705,008,092,818,711,
693,940,737

[*Source:* New York Times, *June 20, 1990*]

You can use small numbers to get an idea of how code systems like the one described in the article work. Before you begin, you need a key (a number, p, that is not prime). You will use p to encode a secret message and then use p and its factors to decode the message.

| X secret message | → | Sender uses *p* to encode the secret message. | → | Y coded message | → | Receiver uses *p* and its factors to decode the message. | → | X secret message |

Cooperative Learning

For this activity, use 55 for *p*. You will use a special algorithm to encode and decode the message. To keep things simple, let your secret message, *X*, be a two-digit number between 11 and 50.

1. To encode a secret message, *X*, follow the steps below.

a. Calculate X^3.

b. Divide X^3 by 55. Multiply the whole-number part of the quotient by 55. Subtract that product from X^3. The difference is the remainder. Use the remainder as the coded message *Y*.

Let *X* be 42. → $X^3 = 74{,}088$

$74{,}088 \div 55 = 1347.054545\ldots$

$1347 \times 55 = 74{,}085$

$74{,}088 - 74{,}085 = 3 \rightarrow Y = 3$

c. If your calculator can display only 8 digits, then *Y* cannot be greater than 13. If it can display 10 digits, then *Y* cannot be greater than 26. If *Y* is too large, start over at part **a** with a different value for *X*.

2. To decode your secret message, use the factors of 55. Follow these steps.

a. Find Y^3. Divide Y^3 by 5. Multiply the whole-number part of the quotient by 5, and subtract this product from Y^3. Call the remainder *a*.

Y is 3. → $Y^3 = 27$

$27 \div 5 = 5.4$

$5 \times 5 = 25$

$27 - 25 = 2 \rightarrow a = 2$

b. Find Y^7. Divide Y^7 by 11. Multiply the whole-number part of the quotient by 11, and subtract this product from Y^7. Call the remainder *b*.

Y is 3. → $Y^7 = 2187$

$2187 \div 11 = 198.8181\ldots$

$198 \times 11 = 2178$

$2187 - 2178 = 9 \rightarrow b = 9$

c. Evaluate $11a + 45b$, and divide the result by 55. Multiply the whole-number part of the quotient by 55, and subtract this product from the value of $11a + 45b$. How does the remainder compare with *X*, the secret message?

$11a + 45b = 11(2) + 45(9) = 427$

$427 \div 55 = 7.763\ldots$

$7 \times 55 = 385$

$427 - 385 = 42$

3. Explain how you used the factors of *p* to encode or decode the message. Why would it be important for the factors of *p* to be secret?

4. How do you think coding systems may be affected if efficient methods for factoring very large numbers are found?

The enigma machine was used in World War II for breaking coded messages.

Solving Systems With Matrix Equations

Objective

- Use matrices to solve systems of linear equations in mathematical and real-world situations.

Why *Many real-world situations, such as investment options, can be represented by a system of linear equations that can be solved quite efficiently by solving a matrix equation.*

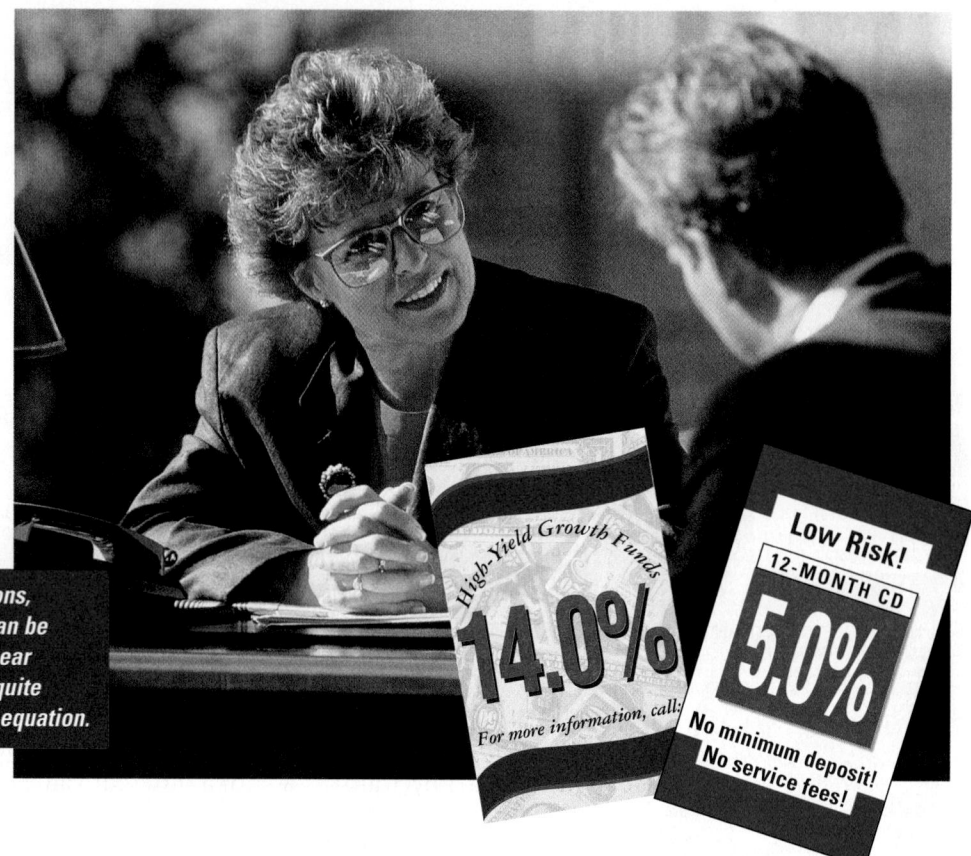

APPLICATION

INVESTMENTS

A financial manager wants to invest $50,000 for a client by putting some of the money in a low-risk investment that earns 5% per year and some of the money in a high-risk investment that earns 14% per year. How much money should be invested at each interest rate to earn $5000 in interest per year?
You will answer this question in Example 1.

PROBLEM SOLVING

Let x represent the amount invested at 5%, and let y represent the amount invested at 14%. **Write a system of linear equations** to represent the situation.

$$\begin{cases} x + y = 50{,}000 \\ 0.05x + 0.14y = 5000 \end{cases}$$

The system $\begin{cases} x + y = 50{,}000 \\ 0.05x + 0.14y = 5000 \end{cases}$ can be written as a **matrix equation**, $AX = B$.

Coefficient matrix, A	Variable matrix, X	Constant matrix, B

Let $A = \begin{bmatrix} 1 & 1 \\ 0.05 & 0.14 \end{bmatrix}$, $X = \begin{bmatrix} x \\ y \end{bmatrix}$, and $B = \begin{bmatrix} 50{,}000 \\ 5000 \end{bmatrix}$.

Then $AX = B$ is $\begin{bmatrix} 1 & 1 \\ 0.05 & 0.14 \end{bmatrix} \begin{bmatrix} x \\ y \end{bmatrix} = \begin{bmatrix} 50{,}000 \\ 5000 \end{bmatrix}$.

CHECKPOINT ✔ Use the interest rates mentioned above. If the client wants to invest $100,000 and earn $10,000 in interest, what system of linear equations and corresponding matrix equation represent this investment?

Solving a matrix equation of the form $AX = B$, where $X = \begin{bmatrix} x \\ y \end{bmatrix}$, is similar to solving a linear equation of the form $ax = b$, where a, b, and x are real numbers and $a \neq 0$.

Real Numbers	Matrices
$ax = b$	$AX = B$
$\frac{1}{a}(ax) = \frac{1}{a}(b)$	$A^{-1}(AX) = A^{-1}B$
$\left(\frac{1}{a} \cdot a\right)x = \frac{b}{a}$	$(A^{-1}A)\,X = A^{-1}B$
	$IX = A^{-1}B$
$x = \frac{b}{a}$	$X = A^{-1}B$

Just as $\frac{1}{a}$ must exist in order to solve $ax = b$ (where $a \neq 0$), A^{-1} must exist to solve $AX = B$.

CHECKPOINT ✔ When solving the matrix equation $AX = B$, does it matter whether you calculate $A^{-1}B$ or BA^{-1}? Explain.

E X A M P L E ❶ Refer to the investment options described at the beginning of the lesson.

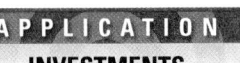
APPLICATION
INVESTMENTS

How much money should the manager invest at each interest rate to earn $5000 in interest per year?

● **SOLUTION**

Solve $\begin{bmatrix} 1 & 1 \\ 0.05 & 0.14 \end{bmatrix} \begin{bmatrix} x \\ y \end{bmatrix} = \begin{bmatrix} 50{,}000 \\ 5000 \end{bmatrix}$ for $\begin{bmatrix} x \\ y \end{bmatrix}$.

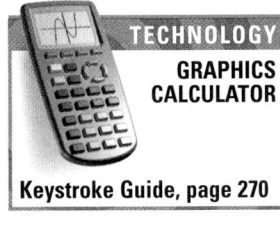
TECHNOLOGY
GRAPHICS CALCULATOR

Keystroke Guide, page 270

Enter the coefficient matrix, $A = \begin{bmatrix} 1 & 1 \\ 0.05 & 0.14 \end{bmatrix}$, and the constant matrix,

$B = \begin{bmatrix} 50{,}000 \\ 5000 \end{bmatrix}$, into your calculator. Solve for the variable matrix, X, by finding the product $A^{-1}B$.

$$X = A^{-1}B$$
$$\begin{bmatrix} x \\ y \end{bmatrix} = \begin{bmatrix} \$22{,}222.22 \\ \$27{,}777.78 \end{bmatrix}$$

```
[A]-1[B]
 [[22222.22222]
  [27777.77778]]
```

The manager should invest $22,222.22 at 5% and $27,777.78 at 14% to achieve the earned interest goal of $5000 per year.

TRY THIS How much money should the manager invest at each interest rate to earn $4000 in interest per year?

CRITICAL THINKING Suppose that the earned interest goal is $10,000 per year for an investment of $50,000. What happens when you try to find how much to invest at 5% and how much to invest at 14%? Explain your response.

Just as you can use a 2×2 matrix and its inverse to solve a system of two linear equations in two variables, you can use a 3×3 matrix and its inverse to solve a system of three equations in three variables, as shown in Example 2.

E X A M P L E 2 **Refer to the system of equations at right.**
 a. Write the system as a matrix equation.
 b. Solve the matrix equation.

$$\begin{cases} 2y - z = -7 - 5x \\ x - 2y + 2z = 0 \\ 3y = 17 - z \end{cases}$$

● SOLUTION

a. First write the equations of the system in *standard form*.

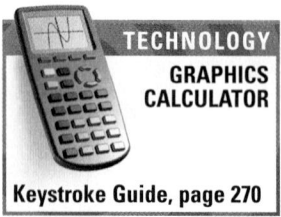
In the third equation, use 0 as the coefficient of x.

$$\begin{cases} 5x + 2y - z = -7 \\ x - 2y + 2z = 0 \\ 3y + z = 17 \end{cases} \rightarrow \begin{bmatrix} 5 & 2 & -1 \\ 1 & -2 & 2 \\ 0 & 3 & 1 \end{bmatrix} \begin{bmatrix} x \\ y \\ z \end{bmatrix} = \begin{bmatrix} -7 \\ 0 \\ 17 \end{bmatrix}$$

b. $\begin{bmatrix} 5 & 2 & -1 \\ 1 & -2 & 2 \\ 0 & 3 & 1 \end{bmatrix} \begin{bmatrix} x \\ y \\ z \end{bmatrix} = \begin{bmatrix} -7 \\ 0 \\ 17 \end{bmatrix}$

$\begin{bmatrix} x \\ y \\ z \end{bmatrix} = \begin{bmatrix} 5 & 2 & -1 \\ 1 & -2 & 2 \\ 0 & 3 & 1 \end{bmatrix}^{-1} \begin{bmatrix} -7 \\ 0 \\ 17 \end{bmatrix}$

$\begin{bmatrix} x \\ y \\ z \end{bmatrix} = \begin{bmatrix} -2 \\ 4 \\ 5 \end{bmatrix}$

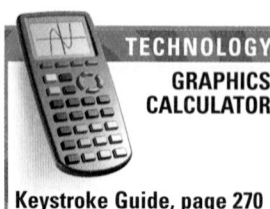
TECHNOLOGY
GRAPHICS CALCULATOR
Keystroke Guide, page 270

Thus, the solution is $x = -2$, $y = 4$, and $z = 5$.

TRY THIS Refer to the system at right.
 a. Write the system as a matrix equation.
 b. Solve the matrix equation.

$$\begin{cases} 2y - z = 4x - 3 \\ 2x + 3z = y - 6 \\ 3y - 1 = 2x + 2z \end{cases}$$

Exploring Slopes and Solutions

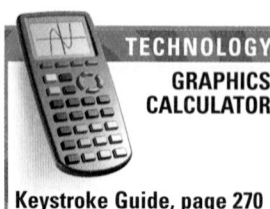
TECHNOLOGY
GRAPHICS CALCULATOR
Keystroke Guide, page 270

You will need: a graphics calculator

Let $A = \begin{bmatrix} 4 & 9 \\ 2 & 5 \end{bmatrix}$ be the coefficient matrix for the system $\begin{cases} 4x + 9y = r \\ 2x + 5y = s \end{cases}$.

1. Find the determinant of matrix A. Does the matrix have an inverse? Justify your response.

2. Choose values for r and s. Write a matrix equation and use the inverse of matrix A to find x and y.

3. Find the slopes of the lines represented by the equations with your values for r and s. Do the slopes depend on the values of r and s?

4. Graph these lines. Based on the slopes and graphs, what can you conclude about any solution(s) of the system?

PROBLEM SOLVING **5. Guess and check.** Choose other values for r and s, and graph the new equation. Do you think that this system will have a unique solution regardless of the values for r and s?

CHECKPOINT ✔ **6.** Summarize what you know about the solutions of this system.

As you have learned, not all systems of linear equations have solutions. In matrix equation of the form $AX = B$, if the coefficient matrix, A, does not have an inverse, then the system represented by the matrix equation does not have a unique solution. This is shown in Example 3.

E X A M P L E **3** Solve $\begin{cases} -3x + 4y = 3 \\ -6x + 8y = 18 \end{cases}$, if possible, by using a matrix equation. If not possible, classify the system.

● **SOLUTION**

The given system is represented by $\begin{bmatrix} -3 & 4 \\ -6 & 8 \end{bmatrix} \begin{bmatrix} x \\ y \end{bmatrix} = \begin{bmatrix} 3 \\ 18 \end{bmatrix}$.

$\qquad\qquad\qquad\qquad\quad A \qquad X \qquad B$

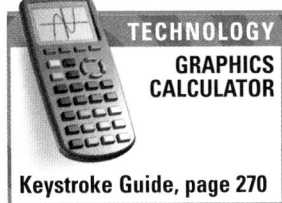

TECHNOLOGY

GRAPHICS CALCULATOR

Keystroke Guide, page 270

When you try to find $A^{-1}B$ on a graphics calculator, you will get an error. The inverse of A does not exist. Notice that $\det(A) = (-3)(8) - (4)(-6) = 0$, which also indicates that the inverse of A does not exist.

Therefore, there is no *unique* solution for the system, and the system is either dependent or inconsistent.

In this case, the system is inconsistent because the lines are parallel.

$$\begin{cases} -3x + 4y = 3 \\ -6x + 8y = 18 \end{cases} \rightarrow \begin{cases} y = \frac{3}{4}x + \frac{3}{4} \\ y = \frac{3}{4}x + 3 \end{cases}$$

TRY THIS Solve $\begin{bmatrix} -3 & 4 \\ -6 & 8 \end{bmatrix} \begin{bmatrix} x \\ y \end{bmatrix} = \begin{bmatrix} 3 \\ 6 \end{bmatrix}$, if possible, by using a matrix equation. If not possible, classify the system.

CRITICAL THINKING Consider the system $\begin{cases} ax + by = e \\ (na)x + (nb)y = f \end{cases}$, where b and n are nonzero. Find the slope of each equation. Find the determinant of the coefficient matrix. How are the slopes and the determinant related?

Communicate

1. Explain how to write a system of equations as a matrix equation.

2. Describe how to represent the system at right by using a matrix equation.

$$\begin{cases} x - y = 5 \\ -z + y = -6 \\ 2x - z = 2 \end{cases}$$

3. Discuss how solving the matrix equation $AX = B$ is similar to solving the linear equation $ax = b$, where a, b, and x are real numbers and $a \neq 0$.

4. Describe the steps involved in using a matrix equation to solve a system of linear equations such as $\begin{cases} 2x - 5y = 0 \\ x + y = -2 \end{cases}$.

5. How can you verify that $\begin{bmatrix} -1 \\ -3 \\ 2 \end{bmatrix}$ is a solution of $\begin{bmatrix} 1 & 1 & 3 \\ 2 & -1 & -2 \\ 3 & 2 & -2 \end{bmatrix} \begin{bmatrix} x \\ y \\ z \end{bmatrix} = \begin{bmatrix} 2 \\ -3 \\ -13 \end{bmatrix}$?

6. If coefficient matrix A in the matrix equation $AX = B$ does not have an inverse, what do you know about the related system of equations?

Guided Skills Practice

APPLICATION

7 **INVESTMENTS** A total of $10,000 was invested in two certificates of deposit that earned 6% per year and 8% per year. If the investments earned $750 in interest each year, find the amount invested at each rate. *(EXAMPLE 1)*

Write each system of equations as a matrix equation. Then solve the system, if possible, by using a matrix equation. If not possible, classify the system. *(EXAMPLES 2 AND 3)*

8 $\begin{cases} x + y = 8 \\ 2x + y = 1 \end{cases}$

9 $\begin{cases} x + 3y = 7 \\ x + 3y = -2 \end{cases}$

10 $\begin{cases} 3x - 2y = 11 \\ 6x - 4y = 5 \end{cases}$

Practice and Apply

Write the matrix equation that represents each system.

11. $\begin{cases} 3x - 5y = 1 \\ 2x + y = -2 \end{cases}$

12. $\begin{cases} -3x + y = -3 \\ 6x - 12y = 6 \end{cases}$

13. $\begin{cases} 2a + 4b = -3 \\ a - b = 9 \end{cases}$

14. $\begin{cases} 4x + y - 2z = 10 \\ 3x + 5z = 14 \\ 8x + 3y - z = 23 \end{cases}$

15. $\begin{cases} y + 5z = -14 \\ -2x + 3y - z = 2 \\ 6x - 3z = 21 \end{cases}$

16. $\begin{cases} 12x + y - z = -7 \\ 11x + 2y = -2 \\ -x + 9y = -9 \end{cases}$

Write the system of equations represented by each matrix equation.

17. $\begin{bmatrix} 2 & -1 & 3 \\ -3 & 0 & -1 \\ 1 & -3 & 1 \end{bmatrix} \begin{bmatrix} x \\ y \\ z \end{bmatrix} = \begin{bmatrix} 4 \\ 1 \\ 5 \end{bmatrix}$

18. $\begin{bmatrix} -2 & 2 & 8 \\ 4 & 3 & 5 \\ 5 & 1 & 0 \end{bmatrix} \begin{bmatrix} x \\ y \\ z \end{bmatrix} = \begin{bmatrix} 3 \\ -2 \\ 1 \end{bmatrix}$

Write the matrix equation that represents each system, and solve system, if possible, by using a matrix equation.

19 $\begin{cases} x + y - z = 14 \\ 4x - y + 5z = -22 \\ 2x + 2y - 3z = 35 \end{cases}$

20 $\begin{cases} -2x + y + 6z = 18 \\ 5x + 8z = -16 \\ 3x + 2y - 10z = -3 \end{cases}$

21 $\begin{cases} 3x + 6y - 6z = 9 \\ 2x - 5y + 4z = 6 \\ -x + 16y + 14z = -3 \end{cases}$

22 $\begin{cases} x + 3y - 2z = 4 \\ 4x - y + z = -1 \\ 3x - 4y + 3z = -5 \end{cases}$

23 $\begin{cases} x - 2y + 3z = 11 \\ 4x - z = 4 \\ 2x - y + 3z = 10 \end{cases}$

24 $\begin{cases} x + 2y - z = 5 \\ 3x + 9y - z = 8 \\ 2x + 10y - 2z = -2 \end{cases}$

25 $\begin{cases} x + y - 2z = -2 \\ 2x - 3y + z = 1 \\ 2x + y - 3z = -2 \end{cases}$

26 $\begin{cases} x - \frac{1}{2}y - 3z = -9 \\ 8z = -16 - 5x \\ \frac{3}{5}x + \frac{2}{5}y - 2z = -\frac{3}{5} \end{cases}$

27 $\begin{cases} 2.5x + y - z = -6 \\ -3.5y + 2.5z = 2.5 \\ 5x + 4y - 2z = -12 \end{cases}$

28 $\begin{cases} x + 2y = -6 \\ y + 2z = 11 \\ 2x + z = 16 \end{cases}$

Write the matrix equation that represents each system, and solve the system, if possible, by using a matrix equation.

29 $\begin{cases} x + y + z + w = 10 \\ 2x - y + z - 3w = -9 \\ 3x + y - z - w = -2 \\ 2x - 3y + z - w = -5 \end{cases}$

30 $\begin{cases} x + 2y - 6z + w = 12 \\ -2x - 3y + 9z + w = -19 \\ x + 2y - 5z + 2w = 15 \\ 2x + 4y - 12z + 3w = 24 \end{cases}$

CHALLENGE

31. The matrix $\begin{bmatrix} -1 & 0 \\ 0 & 1 \end{bmatrix}$ is its own inverse. Find another matrix, other than the identity matrix, which is its own inverse.

CONNECTION

32 GEOMETRY The measure of the largest angle of a certain triangle is 3 times the measure of the smallest angle. The measure of the remaining angle of the triangle is the average of the measures of the largest and smallest angles. Write the system of equations that describes the measure of each angle of the triangle. Then solve the system by using a matrix equation.

APPLICATION

33 ENTERTAINMENT One hundred and twenty people attended a musical. The total amount of money collected for tickets was $1515. Prices were $15 for regular adult admission, $12 for children, and $10 for senior citizens. Twice as many children's tickets as regular adult tickets were sold. Write a system of equations to find the number of children, adults, and senior citizens that attended the musical. Then solve the system by using a matrix equation and the inverse matrix.

34 **CHEMISTRY** A nurse is mixing a 3% saline solution and an 8% saline solution to get 2 liters of a 5% saline solution. How many liters of each solution must be combined?

35 **CHEMISTRY** A solution of 4% acid and a solution of 7% acid are to be mixed to create 3 liters of a 6% acid solution. How many liters of the 3% solution and 7% solution must be combined?

36 **INVESTMENTS** A brokerage firm invested in three mutual-fund companies, A, B, and C. The firm invested $16,110 in low-risk funds, $9016.25 in medium-risk funds, and $5698.75 in high-risk funds, distributed among the three companies as shown below.

☐ Low-risk funds
☐ Medium-risk funds
☐ High-risk funds

Company A Company B Company C

a. Write a system of equations to find the amount that the firm invested in each company.
b. Write the matrix equation that represents this system.
c. Solve the matrix equation by using the inverse matrix.

 Look Back

37. State the domain and range of $f(x) = |x - 5| + 2$. *(LESSON 2.3)*

Let $f(x) = 2x + 3$ and $g(x) = x^2 - 3x + 1$. *(LESSONS 2.3 AND 2.4)*

38. Find $g(-3)$. **39.** Find $g \circ f$. **40.** Find $f \circ g$.

Graph each function. *(LESSON 2.6)*

41. $f(x) = 3[x]$ **42.** $f(x) = 2\lceil x \rceil - 3$

Look Beyond

A method called *Cramer's rule* allows you to solve systems of equations by using determinants. Cramer's rule states that if $\begin{cases} ax + by = e \\ cx + dy = f \end{cases}$ is a system of equations and $\begin{vmatrix} a & b \\ c & d \end{vmatrix} \neq 0$, then the solution of the system can be found as follows:

$$x = \frac{\begin{vmatrix} e & b \\ f & d \end{vmatrix}}{\begin{vmatrix} a & b \\ c & d \end{vmatrix}} \quad \text{and} \quad y = \frac{\begin{vmatrix} a & e \\ c & f \end{vmatrix}}{\begin{vmatrix} a & b \\ c & d \end{vmatrix}}$$

Use Cramer's rule to solve each system.

43. $\begin{cases} 2x + y = 6 \\ x + 2y = 9 \end{cases}$ **44.** $\begin{cases} x + y = 3 \\ 3x + 2y = 4 \end{cases}$ **45.** $\begin{cases} x - 2y = 5 \\ 2x + 2y = 4 \end{cases}$ **46.** $\begin{cases} 2x + y = 10 \\ 3x + 3y = 21 \end{cases}$

Using Matrix Row Operations

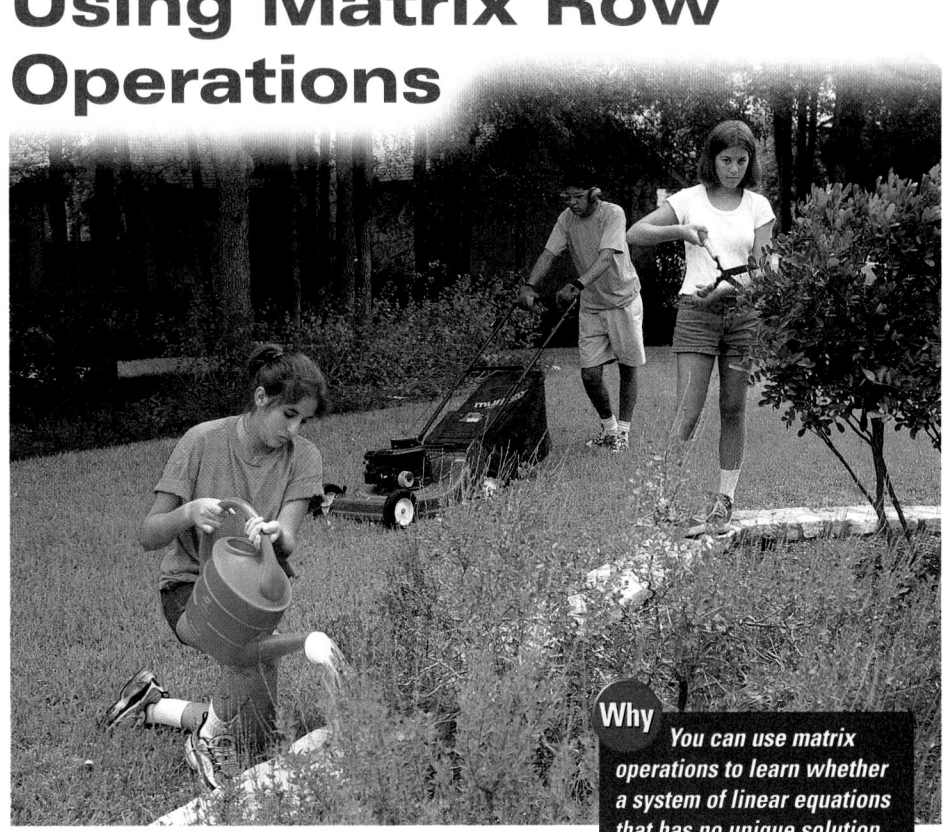

Objectives

- Represent a system of equations as an augmented matrix.

- Solve a system of linear equations by using elementary row operations.

Maya and her friends Amit and Nina have a lawn care business offering three services:

- lawn mowing and edging
- fertilizing and weeding
- trimming shrubs and small trees

They charge a flat rate for each service. The three partners divide up the work for a particular customer as shown below.

Service	Workers and Hours	Cost
Mowing	Maya—1 hr Amit—1 hr Nina—1 hr	$21
Fertilizing	Maya—2 hr Amit—1 hr	$23
Trimming	Amit—1 hr Nina—3 hr	$25

How much does each partner earn per hour and how much will each partner earn in total for his or her work for this customer? *You will solve this problem in Example 1.*

Recall from Lesson 4.4 that if the coefficient matrix of a matrix equation has an inverse, the system represented by the matrix equation is consistent and independent. If there is no inverse, the system is either dependent or inconsistent, but you cannot determine which one.

The **row-reduction method** of solving a system allows you to determine whether the system is independent, dependent, or inconsistent.

The row-reduction method is performed on an *augmented matrix*. An **augmented matrix** consists of the coefficients and constant terms in the system of equations.

The system of equations and the corresponding augmented matrix that represent the lawn-care problem are shown below. Let m, a, and n represent the hourly wages for Maya, Amit, and Nina, respectively.

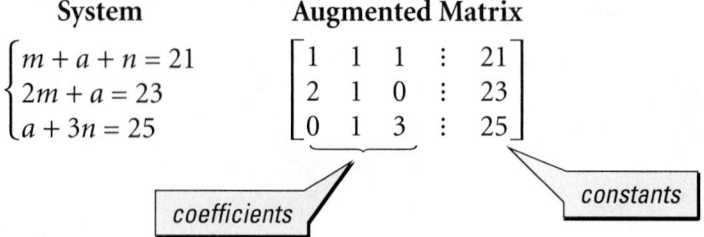

System

$$\begin{cases} m + a + n = 21 \\ 2m + a = 23 \\ a + 3n = 25 \end{cases}$$

Augmented Matrix

$$\left[\begin{array}{ccc:c} 1 & 1 & 1 & 21 \\ 2 & 1 & 0 & 23 \\ 0 & 1 & 3 & 25 \end{array}\right]$$

coefficients

constants

The goal of the row-reduction method is to transform, if possible, the coefficient columns into columns that form an identity matrix. This is called the **reduced row-echelon form** of an augmented matrix if the matrix represents an independent system. If the identity matrix can be formed, then the resulting constants will represent the unique solution to the system.

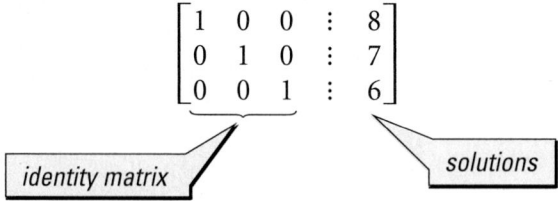

$$\left[\begin{array}{ccc:c} 1 & 0 & 0 & 8 \\ 0 & 1 & 0 & 7 \\ 0 & 0 & 1 & 6 \end{array}\right]$$

identity matrix

solutions

This final matrix is said to be in *reduced row-echelon* form.

To transform an augmented matrix into reduced row-echelon form, use the elementary row operations described below.

Elementary Row Operations

The following operations produce equivalent matrices, and may be used in any order and as many times as necessary to obtain reduced row-echelon form.

- Interchange two rows.
- Multiply all entries in one row by a nonzero number.
- Add a multiple of one row to another row.

You may use *row operation notation* to keep a record of the row operations that you perform.

ROW OPERATION	NOTATION
• Interchange rows 1 and 2.	$R_1 \leftrightarrow R_2$
• Multiply each entry in row 3 by –2.	$-2R_3 \rightarrow R_3$
• Replace row 1 with the sum of row 1 and 4 times each entry in row 2.	$4R_2 + R_1 \rightarrow R_1$

CRITICAL THINKING   Explain why the row operation $R_2 - 4R_1 \rightarrow R_1$ results in an equivalent matrix.

1 **Refer to the lawn-care problem described at the beginning of the le⌐ .**
   a. Use the row-reduction method to solve the system.
   b. Find the hourly wages for Maya, Amit, and Nina. Then find the total amount that each partner earns for this job.

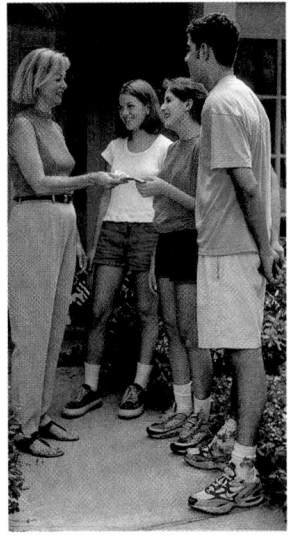

APPLICATION
SMALL BUSINESS

● **SOLUTION**

System	Augmented Matrix

$$\begin{cases} m + a + n = 21 \\ 2m + a = 23 \\ a + 3n = 25 \end{cases} \qquad \begin{bmatrix} 1 & 1 & 1 & \vdots & 21 \\ 2 & 1 & 0 & \vdots & 23 \\ 0 & 1 & 3 & \vdots & 25 \end{bmatrix}$$

a. Perform row operations.

• Inspect column 1.

The first row begins with 1, but the 2 in the second row needs to become 0.

$$-2R_1 + R_2 \rightarrow R_2$$

> Replace row 2 with the sum of row 2 and –2 times row 1.

$$\begin{bmatrix} 1 & 1 & 1 & \vdots & 21 \\ ⓪ & -1 & -2 & \vdots & -19 \\ 0 & 1 & 3 & \vdots & 25 \end{bmatrix}$$

• Inspect column 2.

Row 1:   Row 2:   Row 3:
Change the entry to 0.   Change the entry to 1.   Change the entry to 0.

$$R_2 + R_1 \rightarrow R_1 \qquad\qquad -1R_2 \rightarrow R_2 \qquad\qquad -1R_2 + R_3 \rightarrow R_3$$

$$\begin{bmatrix} 1 & ⓪ & -1 & \vdots & 2 \\ 0 & -1 & -2 & \vdots & -19 \\ 0 & 1 & 3 & \vdots & 25 \end{bmatrix} \begin{bmatrix} 1 & 0 & -1 & \vdots & 2 \\ 0 & ① & 2 & \vdots & 19 \\ 0 & 1 & 3 & \vdots & 25 \end{bmatrix} \begin{bmatrix} 1 & 0 & -1 & \vdots & 2 \\ 0 & 1 & 2 & \vdots & 19 \\ 0 & ⓪ & 1 & \vdots & 6 \end{bmatrix}$$

• Inspect column 3.

Row 1:   Row 2:
Change the entry to 0.   Change the entry to 0.

$$R_3 + R_1 \rightarrow R_1 \qquad\qquad -2R_3 + R_2 \rightarrow R_2$$

$$\begin{bmatrix} 1 & 0 & ⓪ & \vdots & 8 \\ 0 & 1 & 2 & \vdots & 19 \\ 0 & 0 & 1 & \vdots & 6 \end{bmatrix} \begin{bmatrix} 1 & 0 & 0 & \vdots & 8 \\ 0 & 1 & ⓪ & \vdots & 7 \\ 0 & 0 & 1 & \vdots & 6 \end{bmatrix}$$

The matrix is now in reduced row-echelon form.

$$\begin{bmatrix} 1 & 0 & 0 & \vdots & 8 \\ 0 & 1 & 0 & \vdots & 7 \\ 0 & 0 & 1 & \vdots & 6 \end{bmatrix} \quad \begin{matrix} m = 8 \\ a = 7 \\ n = 6 \end{matrix}$$

b. Maya receives $8 an hour; since she works 3 hours, she will earn $24.
Amit receives $7 an hour and works 3 hours, so he will earn $21.
Nina receives $6 an hour and works 4 hours, so she will earn $24.

CHECKPOINT ✔ Check the solution to Example 1 by using substitution.

On many graphics calculators, you can enter an augmented matrix, and the calculator will give you the reduced row-echelon form. The displays below show the augmented matrix and the reduced row-echelon form for the system in Example 1.

, page 271

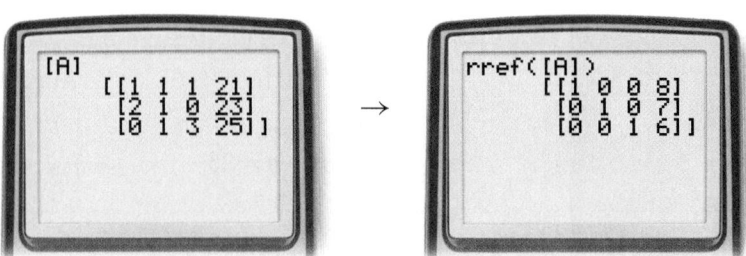

Sometimes row operations do not result in an identity matrix in the coefficient columns. Examples 2 and 3 illustrate two possible alternative results and how they show that the system is inconsistent or dependent.

EXAMPLE 2 **Use the row-reduction method to solve the system below. Then classify the system as independent, dependent, or inconsistent.**

$$\begin{cases} x - 2y - 2z = 6 \\ 3x - 4y + z = -1 \\ 5x - 8y - 3z = 11 \end{cases}$$

● **SOLUTION**

For the given system, the augmented matrix is shown below.

$$\begin{bmatrix} 1 & -2 & -2 & \vdots & 6 \\ 3 & -4 & 1 & \vdots & -1 \\ 5 & -8 & -3 & \vdots & 11 \end{bmatrix}$$

The reduced row-echelon form of the matrix and the corresponding simplified system of equations are shown below.

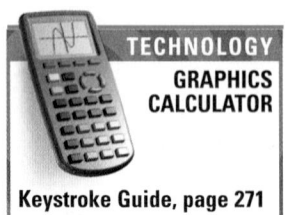

TECHNOLOGY
GRAPHICS
CALCULATOR

Keystroke Guide, page 271

$$\rightarrow \begin{cases} x + 5z = -13 \\ y + 3.5z = -9.5 \\ 0z = 0 \end{cases} \rightarrow \begin{cases} x = -13 - 5z \\ y = -9.5 - 3.5z \\ 0z = 0 \end{cases}$$

> This equation tells you that z can be any real number.

The system is dependent because it has infinitely many solutions. You can describe the solution as $(-13 - 5z, -9.5 - 3.5z, z)$, where z can be any real number.

TRY THIS Use the row-reduction method to solve the system below. Then classify the system as independent, dependent, or inconsistent.

$$\begin{cases} 2x + 3y - z = -2 \\ x + 2y + 2z = 8 \\ 5x + 9y + 5z = 22 \end{cases}$$

EXAMPLE ③ Use the row-reduction method to solve the system below. Then classify the system as independent, dependent, or inconsistent.

$$\begin{cases} 2x + 6y - 4z = 1 \\ x + 3y - 2z = 4 \\ 2x + y - 3z = -7 \end{cases}$$

● SOLUTION

Write the augmented matrix.

$$\begin{bmatrix} 2 & 6 & -4 & \vdots & 1 \\ 1 & 3 & -2 & \vdots & 4 \\ 2 & 1 & -3 & \vdots & -7 \end{bmatrix}$$

Find the reduced row-echelon form and the simplified system as shown below.

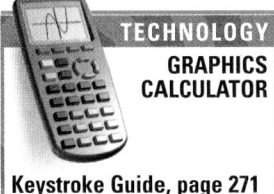

TECHNOLOGY

GRAPHICS
CALCULATOR

Keystroke Guide, page 271

```
rref([A])
    [[1 0 -1.4 0]
     [0 1 -.2  0]
     [0 0 0    1]]
```

$\rightarrow \begin{cases} x - 1.4z = 0 \\ y - 0.2z = 0 \\ 0 = 1 \end{cases}$ This false statement tells you that there is no solution.

The system is inconsistent.

TRY THIS   Use the row-reduction method to solve the system below. Then classify the system as independent, dependent, or inconsistent.

$$\begin{cases} 4x - 4y - 3z = 2 \\ 4x + 3z = 3 \\ 4y + 6z = 3 \end{cases}$$

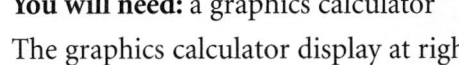

Activity
Exploring Systems of Three Equations

TECHNOLOGY

GRAPHICS
CALCULATOR

Keystroke Guide, page 271

CONNECTION

GEOMETRY

You will need: a graphics calculator

The graphics calculator display at right shows the graph of the system below.

$$\begin{cases} -5x + 2y = 6 \\ x + 2y = -8 \\ x + 2y = 8 \end{cases}$$

1. How can you tell from the system of equations that two of the lines are parallel?

2. Modify the equations in the system so that the intersections of the graphs form the vertices of a triangle. Graph the new system on a graphics calculator. What must be true of the system you wrote in order for the vertices of a triangle to be formed?

CHECKPOINT ✔ 3. Modify the equations in the original system so that the intersections of the graphs form the vertices of a right triangle. Graph the new system on a graphics calculator. Explain your strategy for changing the equations.

Exercises

● *Communicate*

1. Describe how the second and third elementary row operations listed on page 252 may correspond to the operations you perform on equations in a system when using the elimination method.

2. Explain how to write the augmented matrix for the system of equations at right.

$$\begin{cases} x - 4y + 7z = 17 \\ 2x + y - z = -5 \\ x + 4z = 13 \end{cases}$$

3. Write the system of equations represented by the augmented matrix at right.

$$\begin{bmatrix} -3 & -4 & 0 & \vdots & 2 \\ 4 & 2 & -3 & \vdots & 6 \\ -2 & 0 & 1 & \vdots & -6 \end{bmatrix}$$

4. State which row operations were applied to the first matrix to obtain the second matrix.

$$\begin{bmatrix} 1 & 2 & 3 & \vdots & 1 \\ 2 & 5 & 7 & \vdots & 3 \\ 3 & 2 & 1 & \vdots & 1 \end{bmatrix} \rightarrow \begin{bmatrix} 2 & 4 & 6 & \vdots & 2 \\ 2 & 5 & 7 & \vdots & 3 \\ 5 & 7 & 8 & \vdots & 4 \end{bmatrix}$$

 Guided Skills Practice

APPLICATION

5. MANUFACTURING A company makes a total of 120 leather and imitation-leather jackets per week. The leather jackets cost the company $200 each to produce and the imitation-leather cost the company $50 each to produce. The company spends $12,750 per week on costs for producing jackets. *(EXAMPLE 1)*

a. Let x represent the number of leather jackets and y represent the number of imitation-leather jackets. Write a system of linear equations to represent this situation.

b. Write an augmented matrix and use the row-reduction method to solve the system and find the number of each type of jacket made each week.

Use the row-reduction method to solve each system. Then classify each system as independent, dependent, or inconsistent. *(EXAMPLES 2 AND 3)*

6. $\begin{cases} x + 2y + z = 3 \\ y + 2z = 3 \\ y + 2z = 5 \end{cases}$

7. $\begin{cases} x + y = 3 \\ 3x + y = 15 \\ 5x + y + z = 25 \end{cases}$

☑ internet connect

Homework Help Online

Go To: **go.hrw.com**
Keyword:
MB1 Homework Help
for Exercises 8–10, 19–30

● *Practice and Apply*

Write the augmented matrix for each system of equations.

8. $\begin{cases} x + 3y = 23 \\ 4x - 2y = -6 \end{cases}$

9. $\begin{cases} -x + 2y - 5z = 23 \\ 2x + 7z = 19 \\ 5x - 2y + z = -10 \end{cases}$

10. $\begin{cases} 2x - 5y - z = -32 \\ -x + 4y + 2z = 34 \\ 3x + 7y - 3z = -2 \end{cases}$

Perform the indicated row operations on matrix _A_.

11. $3R_1 + R_2 \to R_2$

12. $-8R_1 + R_3 \to R_3$

$$A = \begin{bmatrix} -1 & 2 & -5 & \vdots & 4 \\ 3 & 7 & -2 & \vdots & 3 \\ -8 & 4 & 1 & \vdots & -7 \end{bmatrix}$$

Find the reduced row-echelon form of each matrix.

13. $\begin{bmatrix} 2 & -2 & \vdots & -2 \\ 0 & 1 & \vdots & 3 \end{bmatrix}$

14. $\begin{bmatrix} 3 & 3 & 6 & \vdots & 30 \\ 0 & 1 & 0 & \vdots & 3 \\ 0 & 0 & 2 & \vdots & 2 \end{bmatrix}$

15. $\begin{bmatrix} 4 & 4 & \vdots & 32 \\ 1 & 3 & \vdots & 16 \end{bmatrix}$

16. $\begin{bmatrix} 3 & 0 & 3 & \vdots & 24 \\ 1 & 2 & 3 & \vdots & 28 \\ 0 & 0 & 2 & \vdots & 12 \end{bmatrix}$

17. $\begin{bmatrix} 5 & 2 & 1 & \vdots & -4 \\ 7 & 4 & 1 & \vdots & -4 \\ 3 & 2 & 1 & \vdots & 0 \end{bmatrix}$

18. $\begin{bmatrix} 2 & 1 & 2 & \vdots & 19 \\ 3 & 3 & 3 & \vdots & 33 \\ 2 & 2 & 4 & \vdots & 30 \end{bmatrix}$

Solve each system of equations by using the row-reduction method. Show each step.

19. $\begin{cases} 4x + 3y = 1 \\ 3x - 2y = 5 \end{cases}$

20. $\begin{cases} x + 2y = 16 \\ 2x + y = 11 \end{cases}$

21. $\begin{cases} 3x - y = 4 \\ x + 4y = -3 \end{cases}$

22. $\begin{cases} x + 4y - 3z = -13 \\ -2y + z = 1 \\ -6z = -30 \end{cases}$

23. $\begin{cases} 4x - 7y + 5z = -52 \\ 3y + 8z = 7 \\ -z = 1 \end{cases}$

24. $\begin{cases} 2x - 3y + z = 2 \\ x - y + 2z = 2 \\ x + 2y - 3z = 4 \end{cases}$

25. $\begin{cases} 2x + y + 3z = 2 \\ x + y + 8z = 2 \\ x + y + z = 3 \end{cases}$

26. $\begin{cases} 2x - y + z = 1 \\ 2x + 2z = 4 \\ x + y + z = 4 \end{cases}$

27. $\begin{cases} 2x + 5z = 5 \\ x - 3y + 2z = 2 \\ 3x + y + 3z = 3 \end{cases}$

28. $\begin{cases} y + 2z = \frac{3}{2} \\ 2x + 2y + 2z = 4 \\ x + y = 2 \end{cases}$

29. $\begin{cases} 3x + 3y = -2 \\ x + z = 4 \\ 2x + y = 0 \end{cases}$

30. $\begin{cases} 2x + y + 4z = 4 \\ x - 3y + 2z = 2 \\ 3x + y + 6z = 6 \end{cases}$

Classify each system as inconsistent, dependent, or independent.

31 $\begin{cases} x + y = 3 \\ 2x + 2y = 6 \end{cases}$

32 $\begin{cases} x + y = 0 \\ x + y = 1 \end{cases}$

33 $\begin{cases} 2x + 3y = 8 \\ 3x + 2y = 7 \end{cases}$

34 $\begin{cases} 2x + y + 4z = 1 \\ 3x - y + z = 2 \\ x + 2y - z = -1 \end{cases}$

35 $\begin{cases} x + y + z = 2 \\ 3x + 2y + z = 3 \\ 6x + 4y + 2z = 6 \end{cases}$

36 $\begin{cases} 3x + 2y + z = 1 \\ x - y - z = -5 \\ 6x + 4y + 2z = 2 \end{cases}$

CHALLENGE

37. To perform a row operation on an $n \times n$ matrix A, you can perform the row operations on the identity matrix I_n to obtain a matrix E. The product EA is same as the product obtained by performing the row operations on A directly.

Let $A = \begin{bmatrix} 1 & 2 \\ 3 & 4 \end{bmatrix}$. Perform each operation below by using this technique.

First find matrix E. Then find EA. Verify that EA is equivalent to the matrix that results from performing the operations on A directly.

a. Multiply the entries in row 1 by 2.

b. Interchange rows 1 and 2.

c. Replace row 2 with the sum of 2 times the entries in row 1 and the entries in row 2.

38. CULTURAL CONNECTION: CHINA Over 2000 years ago, the Chinese used a counting board to solve systems of equations. The counting board later evolved into the abacus.

The sticks, or rod numerals, arranged on the counting board at right represent the system of equations below.

$$\begin{cases} 3x + 2y + z = 39 \\ 2x + 3y + z = 34 \\ x + 2y + 3z = 26 \end{cases}$$

a. How are numbers greater than 5 represented?

b. How are the numerals in the tens place represented?

c. How is the Chinese counting board similar to an augmented matrix?

d. Write the system of equations represented on the Chinese counting board at right.

e. Write the system of equations represented on the Chinese counting board at right.

CONNECTION

39. PROBABILITY Suppose that a certain experiment has three possible outcomes with probabilities p_1, p_2, and p_3. The sum of p_1, p_2, and p_3 is 1. If $3p_1 + 18p_2 - 12p_3 = 3$ and $p_1 - 2p_2 - 2p_3 = 0$, find the probabilities of the three outcomes by solving a system of 3 equations.

APPLICATION

40. MANUFACTURING A tool company manufactures pliers and scissors. In one hour the company uses 140 units of steel and 290 units of aluminum. Each pair of scissors requires 1 unit of steel and 3 units of aluminum. Each pair of pliers contains 2 units of steel and 4 units of aluminum. How many scissors and how many pliers can the tool company make in one hour?

41. TRAVEL A traveler is going south along the west coast of South America through the Andes mountain range. While in Peru, the traveler spent $20 per day on housing and $30 per day on food and travel. Passing through Bolivia, the traveler spent $30 per day on housing and $20 per day on food and travel. Finally, while following the long coast of Chile, the traveler spent $20 per day both for housing and for food and travel. In each country, the traveler spent $10 per day on miscellaneous items. The traveler spent a total of $220 on housing, $230 on food and travel, and $100 on miscellaneous items. Write and solve a system of linear equations in three variables to find the number of days the traveler spent in each country.

Look Back

Tell whether each equation is linear. *(LESSON 1.1)*

42. $y + 1 = 5$ **43.** $y + x^2 = 6$ **44.** $y + x = 5$

State whether each relation represents a function. Explain. *(LESSON 2.3)*

45. $\{(-1, 6), (0, 6), (1, 6), (2, 6)\}$ **46.** $\{(0, 14), (1, 12), (2, 10), (3, 8)\}$

47. $\{(-2, 0), (0, 0), (2, 0), (4, 0)\}$ **48.** $\{(-1, 0), (0, -1), (0, 1), (1, 0)\}$

49. Graph the piecewise function $f(x) = \begin{cases} x^2 - 1 & \text{if } 0 \le x < 5 \\ 3x + 9 & \text{if } 5 \le x < 10 \end{cases}$. *(LESSON 2.6)*

BUSINESS A movie theater charges $5 for an adult ticket and $3 for a child's ticket. The theater needs to sell at least $2500 worth of tickets to cover its expenses. Graph the solution to each scenario. *(LESSON 3.3)*

50. The theater sells less than $2500 worth of tickets.

51. The theater breaks even, selling exactly $2500 worth of tickets.

52. The theater makes a profit, selling more than $2500 worth of tickets.

53. Let $A = \begin{bmatrix} 3 & 2 & -2 \\ 1 & 1 & 4 \\ -1 & 2 & 3 \end{bmatrix}$ and $B = \begin{bmatrix} 2 & 3 & 1 \\ -1 & -2 & 2 \\ 4 & 1 & -4 \end{bmatrix}$. *(LESSON 4.2)*

    a. Find AB.   **b.** Find BA.   **c.** Is AB equal to BA?

Look Beyond

54. Let the points $(0, 0)$, $(1, 4)$ and $(2, 12)$ be on the graph of the function $f(x) = ax^2 + bx + c$. Write a system of three equations in terms of a, b, and c. Solve the system and use the values to write the function f.

PROJECT CHAPTER FOUR

SPELL CHECK

When you write a term paper on your word processor or computer, how do you make sure that your spelling is correct? Do you use spell-checker software? Have you ever wondered how it works? The basis for a spell-checker is a modeling process that uses a directed network.

Spelling

Not in Dictionary: classs

Change To: class

Suggestions:
- class
- clasps
- classes
- claps

Add Words To: Custom Dictionary ▼

[Ignore] [Ignore All]
[Change] [Change All]
[Add] [Close]
[Suggest] [Options...]

Activity ①

1. Place the six words below in a circular arrangement. Each word will represent a vertex in a directed network.

   glass   clams   class   clays   clasp   claps

2. With a double-headed arrow, connect the words in which 4 of the 5 letter positions match exactly, while 1 of the 5 positions contains a non-matching letter. For example, *clays* and *claps* can be joined with a double-headed arrow, but *clays* and *clasp* cannot be.

   3. Represent the directed network in an adjacency matrix, W. Record a 1 if there is an arrow joining two words, or vertices. Otherwise record a 0.

   4. Which row or column in W represents the paths leading to the word *clasp*?

   5. Which row or column in W represents the paths going from the word *clays*?

Activity 2

1. Using your results from Activity 1, find the number of two-stage paths from *class* to *clams*. List these paths.

2. Find the number of two-stage paths from *clams* to *clams*. List these paths.

Activity 3

The matrix $W + W^2$ gives the total number of one-stage and two-stage paths from one word to another.

1. Find $W + W^2$.

2. In how many ways can *clays* be connected to *claps* by using only a one-stage or a two-stage path? Which entry in the matrix gives this number? List the paths.

Chapter Review and Assessment

Key Skills & Exercises

LESSON 4.1

Key Skills

Add and subtract matrices, and find the scalar product of a number and a matrix.

$$\begin{bmatrix} 0 & 7 \\ 1 & 2 \end{bmatrix} - \begin{bmatrix} -2 & 1 \\ 3 & 9 \end{bmatrix} + 2\begin{bmatrix} 2 & 8 \\ 0 & -1 \end{bmatrix}$$

$$= \begin{bmatrix} 0 - (-2) & 7 - 1 \\ 1 - 3 & 2 - 9 \end{bmatrix} + \begin{bmatrix} 2(2) & 2(8) \\ 2(0) & 2(-1) \end{bmatrix}$$

$$= \begin{bmatrix} 2 & 6 \\ -2 & -7 \end{bmatrix} + \begin{bmatrix} 4 & 16 \\ 0 & -2 \end{bmatrix}$$

$$= \begin{bmatrix} 2 + 4 & 6 + 16 \\ -2 + 0 & -7 - 2 \end{bmatrix}$$

$$= \begin{bmatrix} 6 & 22 \\ -2 & -9 \end{bmatrix}$$

Exercises

Let $A = \begin{bmatrix} -1 & 2 & 1 \\ 0 & 5 & 3 \end{bmatrix}$, $B = \begin{bmatrix} 6 & -9 & 4 \\ 1 & 0 & 7 \end{bmatrix}$, and

$C = \begin{bmatrix} 0 & -1 & -2 \\ 2 & 4 & 7 \end{bmatrix}$. **Perform the indicated operations.**

1. $A + B$
2. $B - A$
3. $C - C$
4. $B + A - C$
5. $11C$
6. $-3B$
7. $C - 3A$
8. $0.5A - 3B$
9. $-C - 2B$
10. $A + 2C - B$

LESSON 4.2

Key Skills

Multiply matrices.

In order to multiply matrices, the inner dimensions must be the same. The dimensions of the product matrix are the result of the outer dimensions. For example, the product of a 3×2 matrix and a 2×1 matrix is a 3×1 matrix.

$$\begin{bmatrix} 4 & 0 \\ -1 & 3 \\ 2 & -5 \end{bmatrix} \begin{bmatrix} 1 \\ -3 \end{bmatrix} = \begin{bmatrix} 4(1) + 0(-3) \\ -1(1) + 3(-3) \\ 2(1) + (-5)(-3) \end{bmatrix}$$

$$= \begin{bmatrix} 4 \\ -10 \\ 17 \end{bmatrix}$$

Exercises

Let $A = \begin{bmatrix} -9 & 2 \\ 4 & 1 \end{bmatrix}$, $B = \begin{bmatrix} 4 & 5 \\ -2 & 1 \\ 3 & 0 \end{bmatrix}$, and

$C = \begin{bmatrix} 1 & -2 & 1 \\ 0 & 3 & -4 \end{bmatrix}$. **Find each product, if possible.**

11. AB
12. BC
13. BA
14. AC
15. CA
16. CB

Key Skills

Find the inverse and the determinant of a matrix.

Let $C = \begin{bmatrix} 4 & 2 \\ -1 & -3 \end{bmatrix}$. Find the determinant and the inverse of the matrix, if it exists.

$$\det(C) = (4)(-3) - (2)(-1) = -10$$

If $\det(C) \neq 0$, then C^{-1} exists.

Use a graphics calculator to find the inverse of the matrix.

$$C^{-1} = \begin{bmatrix} 0.3 & 0.2 \\ -0.1 & -0.4 \end{bmatrix}$$

Exercises

Find the determinant and inverse of each matrix. If the inverse matrix does not exist, write *no inverse*.

17. $\begin{bmatrix} -2 & 3 \\ 5 & 0 \end{bmatrix}$ **18.** $\begin{bmatrix} 3 & 1 \\ 7 & 9 \end{bmatrix}$ **19.** $\begin{bmatrix} 2 & 2 \\ 2 & 2 \end{bmatrix}$

20. $\begin{bmatrix} 3 & 3 \\ 1 & 1 \end{bmatrix}$ **21.** $\begin{bmatrix} 5 & -1 \\ -1 & 5 \end{bmatrix}$ **22.** $\begin{bmatrix} 0 & 7 \\ -2 & 0 \end{bmatrix}$

23. $\begin{bmatrix} -3 & -4 \\ -1 & -3 \end{bmatrix}$ **24.** $\begin{bmatrix} 5 & 6 \\ 7 & 8 \end{bmatrix}$ **25.** $\begin{bmatrix} -9 & 12 \\ 3 & -4 \end{bmatrix}$

26. Let $A = \begin{bmatrix} 5 & 7 \\ 7 & 10 \end{bmatrix}$ and $B = \begin{bmatrix} 10 & -7 \\ -7 & 5 \end{bmatrix}$. Show that A and B are inverses of one another.

Key Skills

Use matrices to solve systems of linear equations.

Write the system as a matrix equation, $AX = B$. Insert 0 for any missing variables in an equation.

$$\begin{cases} x + 2y - z = -3 \\ -2x + y - 3z = -9 \\ y + 2z = 3 \end{cases} \rightarrow \overset{A}{\begin{bmatrix} 1 & 2 & -1 \\ -2 & 1 & -3 \\ 0 & 1 & 2 \end{bmatrix}} \overset{\times X}{\begin{bmatrix} x \\ y \\ z \end{bmatrix}} = \overset{B}{\begin{bmatrix} -3 \\ -9 \\ 3 \end{bmatrix}}$$

Solve the matrix equation by using an inverse matrix.

$$X = A^{-1}B \rightarrow \begin{bmatrix} x \\ y \\ z \end{bmatrix} = \begin{bmatrix} 1 \\ -1 \\ 2 \end{bmatrix}$$

$x = 1$, $y = -1$, and $z = 2$

Exercises

Use a matrix equation to solve each system of linear equations, if possible.

27. $\begin{cases} 6x + 4y = 12 \\ 3x + 2y = 6 \end{cases}$

28. $\begin{cases} 2x + y = 3 \\ 3x - 2y = 8 \end{cases}$

29. $\begin{cases} 3x - y = -1 \\ 2x - y + z = -6 \\ x + 4y - z = 9 \end{cases}$

30. $\begin{cases} 2x - 3y + 5z = 5 \\ x - y - 2z = 2 \\ -3x + 3y + 6z = 5 \end{cases}$

31. $\begin{cases} -\frac{1}{6}y = -\frac{1}{6} - \frac{1}{3}x \\ x + \frac{1}{2}z = -3 + \frac{1}{2}y \\ \frac{1}{5}x + \frac{4}{5}y = \frac{9}{5} + \frac{1}{5}z \end{cases}$

32. JEWELRY A jeweler plans to combine two silver alloys to make 50 grams of a new alloy that is 75% silver and contains 37.5 grams of pure silver (75% of 50 grams). If one silver alloy is 80% silver and the other is 60% silver, how many grams of each are needed?

Key Skills

Solve a system of linear equations by using elementary row operations.

Write the system as an augmented matrix.

$$\begin{cases} 2x + 3y - z = -7 \\ x + y - z = -4 \\ 3x - 2y - 3z = -7 \end{cases} \rightarrow \begin{bmatrix} 2 & 3 & -1 & : & -7 \\ 1 & 1 & -1 & : & -4 \\ 3 & -2 & -3 & : & -7 \end{bmatrix}$$

Use a calculator to obtain the reduced row-echelon form.

The solution for this independent system is $x = -1$, $y = -1$, and $z = 2$.

From the reduced row-echelon form of an augmented matrix, you can classify the system as dependent or inconsistent.

Dependent system

$$\begin{bmatrix} 1 & 0 & 5 & : & -13 \\ 0 & 1 & 3.5 & : & -9.5 \\ 0 & 0 & 0 & : & 0 \end{bmatrix}$$

$0 = 0$ is always a true statement.

Inconsistent system

$$\begin{bmatrix} 1 & 0 & 1 & : & 0 \\ 0 & 1 & 3 & : & 0 \\ 0 & 0 & 0 & : & 1 \end{bmatrix}$$

$0 = 1$ is always a false statement.

Exercises

Use the row-reduction method to solve each system, if possible. Then classify each system as independent, dependent, or inconsistent.

33. $\begin{cases} 3x - 2y + z = -5 \\ -2x + 3y - 3z = 12 \\ 3x - 2y - 2z = 4 \end{cases}$

34. $\begin{cases} 3x - y + 2z = 9 \\ x - 2y - 3z = -1 \\ 2x - 3y + z = 10 \end{cases}$

35. $\begin{cases} x - 2y + z = -2 \\ 2x + 6y = 12 \\ 3x - y + 2z = 4 \end{cases}$

36. $\begin{cases} 3x - y - 2z = 0 \\ x + 2y - 4z = 0 \\ 2x - 10y + 12z = 0 \end{cases}$

37. $\begin{cases} x - 3y - z = 0 \\ 2x - y - 4z = 0 \\ -2x + 6y - 4z = 0 \end{cases}$

38. $\begin{cases} 4x + 6y - 2z = 10 \\ 4x - 5y + 5z = -3 \\ 3x - y + 2z = 1 \end{cases}$

Application

39. **FUND-RAISING** Two hundred and ten people attended a school carnival. The total amount of money collected for tickets was $710. Prices were $5 for regular admission, $3 for students, and $1 for children. The number of regular tickets sold was 10 more than twice the number of child tickets sold. Write a system of equations to find the number of regular tickets, student tickets, and child tickets sold. Solve the system by using a matrix equation.

Chapter Test

For Items 1–4,

let $A = \begin{bmatrix} 2 & 5 & -3 \\ 4 & -1 & 7 \end{bmatrix}$, $B = \begin{bmatrix} -4 & 1 & 0 \\ 2 & -5 & -1 \end{bmatrix}$, and

$C = \begin{bmatrix} 0 & -2 & 1 \\ 1 & 0 & 3 \end{bmatrix}$. Perform the indicated operations.

1. $A + B$

2. $2C - B$

3. $A - B + 3C$

4. $-2C$

5. COORDINATE GEOMETRY Represent the quadrilateral $ABCD$ as a matrix P.

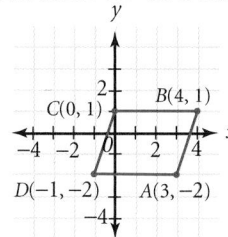

For Items 6–11,

let $A = \begin{bmatrix} 2 & 3 & -1 \\ 0 & -5 & 4 \end{bmatrix}$, $B = \begin{bmatrix} 1 & 0 \\ 2 & -1 \end{bmatrix}$, and

$C = \begin{bmatrix} 1 & -3 \\ 0 & 2 \\ -2 & -1 \end{bmatrix}$. Find each product, if possible.

6. AB

7. BA

8. AC

9. CB

10. CA

11. CBA

Find the determinant and inverse of each matrix. If the inverse matrix does not exist, write *no inverse*.

12. $\begin{bmatrix} 1 & 2 \\ 3 & 4 \end{bmatrix}$

13. $\begin{bmatrix} -5 & 4 \\ 10 & -8 \end{bmatrix}$

14. $\begin{bmatrix} 1 & 0 & -3 \\ 0 & 2 & -1 \\ 1 & 3 & 0 \end{bmatrix}$

15. $\begin{bmatrix} 2 & 0 & 3 \\ 4 & 0 & 1 \\ 2 & -1 & 3 \end{bmatrix}$

Use matrices to solve each system of linear equations, if possible.

16. $\begin{cases} 3x + 4y = -1 \\ 4x - 3y = 32 \end{cases}$

17. $\begin{cases} 7x + 3y = 25 \\ 9x - 2y = -3 \end{cases}$

18. $\begin{cases} x + y + z = 6 \\ x + y - z = 0 \\ 3x + 2y + z = 10 \end{cases}$

19. CHEMISTRY A radiator in a large truck has a capacity of 10 gallons. Currently the radiator fluid is 20% antifreeze. How much fluid should be drained out and replaced with a 75% antifreeze solution to bring the solution in the radiator to 50% antifreeze? Set up and solve a system of equations to answer this question.

Use the row-reduction method to solve each system, if possible. Then classify each system as independent, dependent, or inconsistent.

20. $\begin{cases} 5x - 7y + 4z = -3 \\ 3x - y + 2z = 1 \\ -2x - 3y + 5z = 2 \end{cases}$

21. $\begin{cases} x + 6y + 2z = 4 \\ -2x + 3y + 5z = 9 \\ 7x + 12y - 4z = 0 \end{cases}$

22. $\begin{cases} 2x - y + 3z = -5 \\ x + 3y - 4z = 9 \\ 3x + 2y - z = 4 \end{cases}$

23. ENTERTAINMENT Concert tickets are $24 for adults, $15 for children and $12 for seniors. The revenue from the concert was $5670. Five times as many adults attended as seniors. Twice as many children attended as seniors. Set up and solve a system of equations to determine how many of each ticket were sold.

1–4

College Entrance Exam Practice

MULTIPLE-CHOICE For Questions 1–11, write the letter that indicates the best answer.

1. Solve $\begin{bmatrix} 2 & 3x+1 \\ 2y-1 & 5 \end{bmatrix} = \begin{bmatrix} 2 & -3y+1 \\ -5 & 5 \end{bmatrix}$ for

x and y. **(LESSON 4.1)**
 a. $x = 2, y = -2$
 b. $x = -2, y = -2$
 c. $x = -3, y = 3$
 d. $x = 3, y = -3$

2. Evaluate $\lfloor 5.001 \rfloor - \lceil 3.125 \rceil$. **(LESSON 2.6)**
 a. 2
 b. 1
 c. 3
 d. 0

3. Solve $\frac{x}{2} - 1 = 3$. **(LESSON 1.6)**
 a. 8 **b.** 4
 c. 5 **d.** 7

4. Solve. $\begin{cases} 3x + y = 10 \\ 2x + 3y = -5 \end{cases}$ **(LESSON 3.1)**

 a. $(5, -5)$
 b. $(5, 5)$
 c. $(15, -35)$
 d. $(35, -95)$

5. Find the slope of the line containing the points $(4, 5)$ and $(6, 3)$. **(LESSON 1.3)**
 a. -2 **b.** 2
 c. 1 **d.** -1

6. Simplify $\left(\frac{-2x^4 y^{-1}}{5x^{-2} y^4} \right)^3$. **(LESSON 2.2)**

 a. $\frac{8}{5} x^{14} y^{-7}$

 b. $-\frac{8}{125} x^{18} y^{-15}$

 c. $\frac{8}{125} x^{-18} y^{15}$

 d. $\frac{8}{5} x^{18} y^{-9}$

7. If $A = \begin{bmatrix} 3 & 0 & -2 \\ -1 & 2 & 1 \\ 1 & 5 & -1 \end{bmatrix}$ and $B = \begin{bmatrix} 0 & -3 & -1 \\ -1 & 4 & 3 \\ 2 & 2 & 2 \end{bmatrix}$,

what is $A - B$? **(LESSON 4.1)**

 a. $\begin{bmatrix} 3 & 3 & -1 \\ 0 & -2 & -2 \\ -1 & 3 & -3 \end{bmatrix}$ **b.** $\begin{bmatrix} 3 & -3 & -3 \\ -2 & 6 & 4 \\ 3 & 7 & 1 \end{bmatrix}$

 c. $\begin{bmatrix} 3 & -3 & -3 \\ 0 & -2 & 4 \\ -1 & 7 & 1 \end{bmatrix}$ **d.** $\begin{bmatrix} 3 & 3 & -1 \\ -2 & -2 & -2 \\ 3 & 3 & -3 \end{bmatrix}$

8. Which equation in x and y represents this system of parametric equations? **(LESSON 3.6)**
$$\begin{cases} x(t) = 2t + 1 \\ y(t) = t - 2 \end{cases}$$
 a. $y = x - 5$
 b. $y = \frac{1}{2}x - \frac{5}{2}$
 c. $y = x - t - 3$
 d. $y = \frac{1}{2}x + 3$

9. Which set of ordered pairs represents a function? **(LESSON 2.3)**
 a. $\{(8, -9), (-9, 8), (8, 9)\}$
 b. $\{(0.1, 5), (0.2, 5), (0.1, 0)\}$
 c. $\{(-1, 4), (3, -2), (3, 2), (4, -1)\}$
 d. $\{(0, 1), (2, -2), (-2, 2), (1, 0)\}$

10. What is the inverse of $\{(0, 1), (2, -1), (3, 2),$ $(4, -1)\}$? Is the inverse a function? **(LESSON 2.5)**
 a. $\{(0, 1), (2, -1), (3, 2), (4, -1)\}$; yes
 b. $\{(0, 1), (2, -1), (3, 2), (4, -1)\}$; no
 c. $\{(1, 0), (-1, 2), (2, 3), (-1, 4)\}$; yes
 d. $\{(1, 0), (-1, 2), (2, 3), (-1, 4)\}$; no

11 Let $A = \begin{bmatrix} 3 & -1 \\ -4 & 2 \end{bmatrix}$. Find A^{-1}. *(LESSON 4.3)*

a. $\begin{bmatrix} 3 & 1 \\ 4 & 2 \end{bmatrix}$ **b.** $\begin{bmatrix} 1 & 0.5 \\ 2 & 1.5 \end{bmatrix}$

c. $\begin{bmatrix} 2 & 1 \\ 4 & 3 \end{bmatrix}$ **d.** $\begin{bmatrix} 1.5 & 0.5 \\ 2 & 1 \end{bmatrix}$

ANATOMY The table below lists the height and weight of 10 young adult males with medium frames. The heights are in inches, and the weights are in pounds. *(LESSON 1.5)*

Height	65	66	70	69	67	68	67	66	68	71
Weight	146	145	157	158	145	149	155	141	154	159

12. Create a scatter plot, and identify the correlation as positive, negative, or none.

13 Use the least-squares line to estimate the weight of a 74-inch-tall male with a medium frame.

14. Solve $3 - 2x \geq -x + 2$, and graph the solution on a number line. *(LESSON 1.7)*

For Items 15 and 16, find $f \circ g$ and $g \circ f$.
(LESSON 2.4)

15. $f(x) = 3x, g(x) = 2x - 1$

16. $f(x) = 2 - x, g(x) = x + 3$

17. Find the inverse of $f(x) = -5x + 3$. Is the inverse a function? *(LESSON 2.5)*

18. Graph the piecewise function below.
$$f(x) = \begin{cases} x - 6 & \text{if } 0 \leq x < 4 \\ -2x & \text{if } 4 \leq x < 10 \end{cases}$$ *(LESSON 2.6)*

19. Identify the transformation from the parent function $f(x) = |x|$ to $g(x) = -2|x - 4|$.
(LESSON 2.7)

20. Graph the solution to $2(1 - 2x) \geq -y + 4$.
(LESSON 3.3)

21. Graph the solution to the system of linear inequalities below. *(LESSON 3.4)*
$$\begin{cases} x + 2y \leq 4 \\ -2x + 3y \geq 6 \end{cases}$$

22. Solve the system below, if possible, by using a matrix equation. *(LESSON 4.4)*
$$\begin{cases} x + y - 2z = -1 \\ 2x + 2y + z = 3 \\ -3x - 2y - 3z = -4 \end{cases}$$

FREE-RESPONSE GRID The following questions may be answered by using a free-response grid such as that commonly used by standardized test services.

23. If the inverse function for $f(x) = \frac{2}{3}x - 7$ is written in the form $g(x) = ax + b$, what is the value of a? *(LESSON 2.5)*

24. Find the maximum value of the objective function $P = 2x + 3y$ given the constraints below. *(LESSON 3.5)*
$$\begin{cases} x + y \leq 4 \\ 2x + y \geq 2 \\ x \geq 0, y \geq 0 \end{cases}$$

25. Find the constant of variation, k, if y varies directly as x and $y = 102$ when $x = 3$.
(LESSON 1.4)

SMALL BUSINESS Joshua wants to mix two types of candy. Candy A costs $2.50 per pound and candy B costs $4.50 per pound. Ten pounds of the combined candy mixture cost $37.00.
(LESSON 3.1)

26. How many pounds of candy A are in the mixture?

27. How many pounds of candy B are in the mixture?

SPORTS The cost of an adult ticket to a football game is $4.00, and a student ticket is $2.50. The total amount received from 600 tickets was $1830.
(LESSON 3.2)

28. How many adult tickets were sold?

29. How many student tickets were sold?

Keystroke Guide for Chapter 4

Essential keystroke sequences (using the model TI-82 or TI-83 graphics calculator) are presented below for all Activities and Examples found in this chapter that require or recommend the use of a graphics calculator.

☑ internet connect

For Keystrokes of other graphing calculator models, visit the HRW web site at **go.hrw.com** and enter the keyword **MB1 CALC**.

LESSON 4.1

E X A M P L E **3** Let $A = \begin{bmatrix} -2 & 0 & 1 \\ 5 & -7 & 8 \end{bmatrix}$ and $B = \begin{bmatrix} 5 & 7 & -1 \\ 0 & 2 & -8 \end{bmatrix}$. For part a, find $A + B$.

Page 217

For TI-83 Plus, press [2nd] [x^{-1}] **MATRX** to access the matrix menu.

Enter the matrices:

Matrix A has dimensions of 2×3.

[MATRX] [EDIT] [1:[A]] [ENTER] (Matrix[A]) 2 [ENTER] 3 [ENTER] [(–)] 2 [ENTER] 0 [ENTER] 1 [ENTER] 5 [ENTER] [(–)] 7 [ENTER] 8 [ENTER] [MATRX] [EDIT] [2:[B]] [ENTER] (Matrix[B]) 2 [ENTER] 3 [ENTER] 5 [ENTER] 7 [ENTER] [(–)] 1 [ENTER] 0 [ENTER] 2 [ENTER] [(–)] 8 [ENTER] [2nd] [MODE] (QUIT)

Add the matrices:

[MATRX] [NAMES] [1:[A]] [ENTER] [+] [MATRX]

[NAMES] [2:[B]] [ENTER] [ENTER]

For part **b**, find $A - B$ by using a similar keystroke sequence to subtract the matrices.

LESSON 4.2

E X A M P L E **3** Enter matrix A, and find A^2.

Page 228

Enter the matrix:

Use a keystroke sequence similar to that in Example 3 of Lesson 4.1.

Square the matrix:

[MATRX] [NAMES] [1:[A]] [ENTER] [x^2] [ENTER]

TECHNOLOGY
Page 236

Enter matrix $A = \begin{bmatrix} 1 & 2 \\ 3 & 5 \end{bmatrix}$, and find its inverse.

Enter the matrix:

Use a keystroke sequence similar to that in Example 3 of Lesson 4.1.

Find the inverse of matrix A:

MATRX | NAMES | 1:[A] | ENTER | x^{-1} | ENTER

E X A M P L E ② For part a, enter matrix $A = \begin{bmatrix} 6 & 8 \\ 5 & 7 \end{bmatrix}$, and find its inverse.

Page 236

Enter the matrix:

Use a keystroke sequence similar to that in Example 3 of Lesson 4.1.

Find the inverse of matrix A:

MATRX | NAMES | 1:[A] | ENTER | x^{-1} | ENTER

For parts **b** and **c**, use a similar keystroke sequence.

TECHNOLOGY
Page 237

Let $A = \begin{bmatrix} 6 & 5 \\ 7 & 6 \end{bmatrix}$ and $B = \begin{bmatrix} 7 & 15 & 0 \\ 2 & 15 & 2 \end{bmatrix}$. Find the product AB.

Enter the matrices:

Use a keystroke sequence similar to that in Example 3 of Lesson 4.1.

Find the product AB:

MATRX | NAMES | 1:[A] | ENTER | X | MATRX | NAMES

2:[B] | ENTER | ENTER

E X A M P L E ③ Let $A = \begin{bmatrix} 6 & 5 \\ 7 & 6 \end{bmatrix}$ and $C = \begin{bmatrix} 52 & 165 & 10 \\ 61 & 195 & 12 \end{bmatrix}$. Find $A^{-1}C$.

Page 237

Enter the matrices:

Use a keystroke sequence similar to that in Example 3 of Lesson 4.1.

Find the product $A^{-1}C$:

MATRX | NAMES | 1:[A] | ENTER | x^{-1} | X | MATRX | NAMES | 2:[C] | ENTER | ENTER

E X A M P L E **4** For part a, find the determinant of $\begin{bmatrix} 7 & 8 \\ 6 & 7 \end{bmatrix}$.

Page 238

Enter the matrix:

Use a keystroke sequence similar to that in Example 3 of Lesson 4.1.

Find the determinant:

[MATRX] [MATH] [1:det(] [ENTER] [MATRX] [NAMES] [1:[A]] [ENTER] [ENTER]

LESSON 4.4

E X A M P L E **1** Solve $\begin{bmatrix} 1 & 1 \\ 0.05 & 0.14 \end{bmatrix}\begin{bmatrix} x \\ y \end{bmatrix} = \begin{bmatrix} 50{,}000 \\ 5000 \end{bmatrix}$ for $\begin{bmatrix} x \\ y \end{bmatrix}$.

Page 245

Enter the matrices:

Enter the coefficient matrix, $A = \begin{bmatrix} 1 & 1 \\ 0.05 & 0.14 \end{bmatrix}$, and the constant matrix,

$B = \begin{bmatrix} 50{,}000 \\ 5000 \end{bmatrix}$. Use a keystroke sequence

> Do not enter the comma when you enter the number 50,000.

similar to that in Example 3 of Lesson 4.1.

Find the product $A^{-1}B$:

[MATRX] [NAMES] [1:[A]] [ENTER] [x^{-1}] [X]

[MATRX] [NAMES] [2:[B]] [ENTER] [ENTER]

```
[A]⁻¹[B]
    [[22222.22222]
     [27777.77778]]
```

E X A M P L E **2** Solve $\begin{bmatrix} 5 & 2 & -1 \\ 1 & -2 & 2 \\ 0 & 3 & 1 \end{bmatrix}\begin{bmatrix} x \\ y \\ z \end{bmatrix} = \begin{bmatrix} -7 \\ 0 \\ 17 \end{bmatrix}$ for $\begin{bmatrix} x \\ y \\ z \end{bmatrix}$.

Page 246

Enter the matrices:

Enter matrix $A = \begin{bmatrix} 5 & 2 & -1 \\ 1 & -2 & 2 \\ 0 & 3 & 1 \end{bmatrix}$ and matrix $B = \begin{bmatrix} -7 \\ 0 \\ 17 \end{bmatrix}$.

Use a keystroke sequence similar to that in Example 3 of Lesson 4.1.

Find the product $A^{-1}B$:

Use a keystroke sequence similar to that in Example 1 of Lesson 4.4.

```
[A]⁻¹[B]
    [[-2]
     [4 ]
     [5 ]]
```

Activity

Page 246

For Step 1, find the determinant of matrix $A = \begin{bmatrix} 4 & 9 \\ 2 & 5 \end{bmatrix}$.

Enter the matrix:

Use a keystroke sequence similar to that in Example 3 of Lesson 4.1.

Find the determinant:

[MATRX] [MATH] [1:det(] [ENTER] [MATRX] [NAMES] [1:[A]] [ENTER] [ENTER]

EXAMPLE 3

Page 247

Solve $\begin{bmatrix} -3 & 4 \\ -6 & 8 \end{bmatrix}\begin{bmatrix} x \\ y \end{bmatrix} = \begin{bmatrix} 3 \\ 18 \end{bmatrix}$ for $\begin{bmatrix} x \\ y \end{bmatrix}$.

Enter matrix $A = \begin{bmatrix} -3 & 4 \\ -6 & 8 \end{bmatrix}$ and matrix

$B = \begin{bmatrix} 3 \\ 18 \end{bmatrix}$, and find $A^{-1}B$. Use a keystroke

sequence similar to that in Example 1 of Lesson 4.4.

Solve $-3x + 4y = 3$ and $-6x + 8y = 18$ for y, and graph the lines:

Use viewing window $[-5, 5]$ by $[-5, 5]$.

Y=	(	3	÷	4	)	X,T,θ,n	+
(	3	÷	4	)	ENTER	(Y2=)
(	3	÷	4	)	X,T,θ,n	+	(	9
÷	4	)	GRAPH

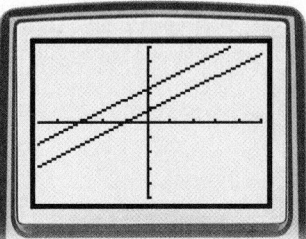

LESSON 4.5

TECHNOLOGY
Page 254

Find the reduced row-echelon form of the matrix $\begin{bmatrix} 1 & 1 & 1 & \vdots & 21 \\ 2 & 1 & 0 & \vdots & 23 \\ 0 & 1 & 3 & \vdots & 25 \end{bmatrix}$.

Enter the matrix:

Enter the augmented matrix as a 3×4 matrix without the column of dots. Use a keystroke sequence similar to that in Example 3 of Lesson 4.1.

> The reduced row-echelon form can not be computed with one command on the TI-82.

Find the reduced row-echelon form:

| MATRX | MATH | B:rref(| ENTER | MATRX |
| NAMES | 1:[A] | ENTER |) | ENTER |

EXAMPLES 2 and 3

Pages 254 and 255

Find the reduced row-echelon form of the augmented matrix in each example.

Use a keystroke sequence similar to that in the Technology example above.

Activity
Page 255

Graph the system of equations $\begin{cases} -5x + 2y = 6 \\ x + 2y = -8 \\ x + 2y = 8 \end{cases}$.

Use square viewing window $[-9.4, 9.4]$ by $[-6.2, 6.2]$.

Solve each equation for y, and use a keystroke sequence similar to that in Example 3 of Lesson 4.4.

Quadratic Functions

QUADRATIC FUNCTIONS HAVE IMPORTANT applications in science and engineering. For example, the parabolic path of a bouncing ball is described by a quadratic function. In fact, the motion of all falling objects can be described by quadratic functions. In this chapter, various techniques for solving quadratic equations are included, such as factoring and the quadratic formula.

Lessons

A basketball game is about to begin. The referee tosses the ball vertically into the air. A video camera follows the motion of the ball as it rises to its maximum height and then begins to fall.

The following table and graph represent the height of the ball in feet at 0.1-second intervals. After 1.1 seconds, one of the players makes contact with the ball by tapping it out of its vertical path to a teammate.

Time, x	Height, y
0.0	6.00
0.1	7.84
0.2	9.36
0.3	10.61
0.4	11.47
0.5	12.00
0.6	12.30
0.7	12.19
0.8	11.83
0.9	11.12
1.0	9.98
1.1	8.64

About the Chapter Project

The Chapter Project, *Out of This World*, extends the idea presented in the Portfolio Activities. By using different accelerations caused by the gravity on other planets, the height of the ball after a vertical toss on different planets can be compared with its height after a similar toss on Earth.

After completing the Chapter Project, you will be able to do the following:

- Use the function $h(t) = \frac{1}{2}gt^2 + v_0t + h_0$ to model the vertical motion of a basketball.
- Compare and contrast algebraic models of the form $h(t) = \frac{1}{2}gt^2 + v_0t + h_0$ for the vertical motion of the basketball on different planets.

About the Portfolio Activities

Throughout the chapter, you will be given opportunities to complete Portfolio Activities that are designed to support your work on the Chapter Project.

- Finding a reasonable model for the basketball data is included in the Portfolio Activity on page 280.

- Using various algebraic methods to answer questions about the height of the basketball along its path is in the Portfolio Activities on pages 298, 306, and 313.

- Comparing the algebraic model from physics with the quadratic regression model for the basketball data is included in the Portfolio Activity on page 329.

- Solving quadratic inequalities to answer questions about the height of the basketball along its path is in the Portfolio Activity on page 337.

Introduction to Quadratic Functions

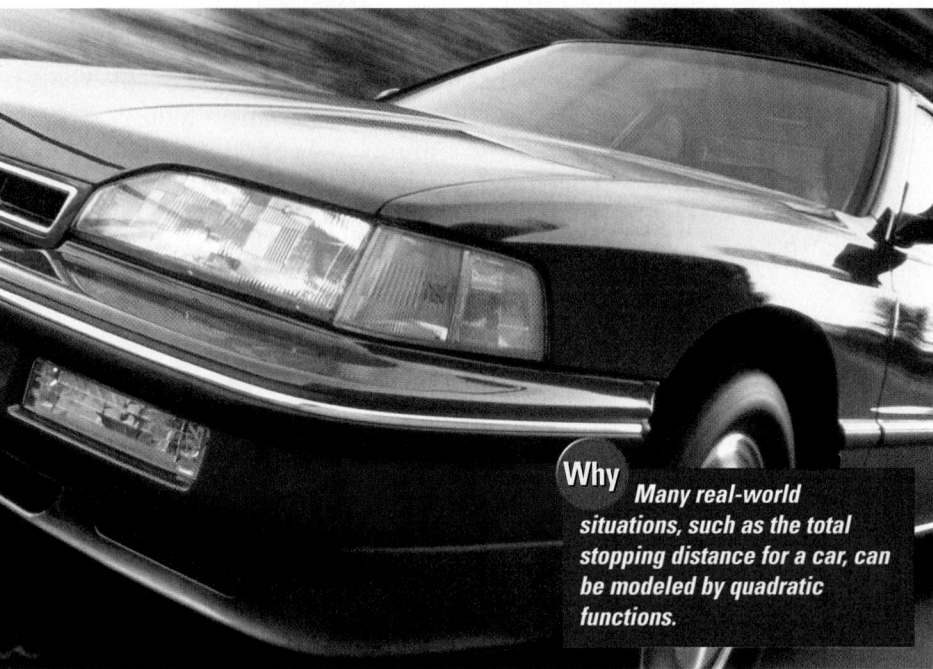

Objectives

- Define, identify, and graph quadratic functions.

- Multiply linear binomials to produce a quadratic expression.

Why *Many real-world situations, such as the total stopping distance for a car, can be modeled by quadratic functions.*

Recall from Lesson 2.4 that the total stopping distance of a car on certain types of road surfaces is modeled by the function

$$d(x) = \frac{11}{10}x + \frac{1}{19}x^2,$$

where x is the speed of the car in miles per hour at the moment the hazard is observed and $d(x)$ is the distance in feet required to bring the car to a complete stop.

Observe hazard. Apply brakes. Come to a complete stop.

reaction distance · braking distance

stopping distance

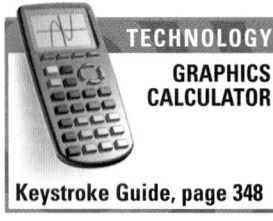

TECHNOLOGY

GRAPHICS CALCULATOR

Keystroke Guide, page 348

A table of values for the function d shows that a motorist driving at 20 miles per hour requires about 43 feet to come to a complete stop. However, a motorist traveling at 60 miles per hour requires over 255 feet to stop. Although the speed tripled, the total stopping distance increased by about 6 times. Clearly, the function for stopping distance is not a linear function.

X	Y1
0	0
10	16.263
20	43.053
30	80.368
40	128.21
50	186.58
60	255.47

X=0

Investigating Quadratic Functions

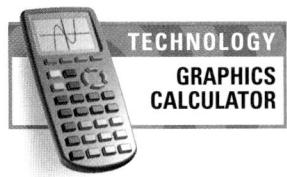
TECHNOLOGY
GRAPHICS CALCULATOR

You will need: a graphics calculator

1. Graph functions f and g from the first row of the table below on the same screen. Describe f and g and their graphs.

2. Graph $f \cdot g$ with f and g from the first row of the table on the same screen. Describe $f \cdot g$ and its graph. Then clear all three functions.

f	g	$f \cdot g$
$f(x) = 2x - 2$	$g(x) = 2x + 1$	$(f \cdot g)(x) = (2x - 2)(2x + 1)$
$f(x) = x + 1$	$g(x) = x + 1$	$(f \cdot g)(x) = (x + 1)(x + 1)$
$f(x) = 2x$	$g(x) = -2x + 1$	$(f \cdot g)(x) = 2x(-2x + 1)$
$f(x) = -x + 2$	$g(x) = 0.5x + 1$	$(f \cdot g)(x) = (-x + 2)(0.5x + 1)$

3. Repeat Steps 1 and 2 for the functions in the other rows of the table.

CHECKPOINT ✔ 4. In what ways do the graphs of f and g differ from the graph of $f \cdot g$?

CHECKPOINT ✔ 5. How are the x-intercepts of the graphs of f and g related to the x-intercepts of the graph of $f \cdot g$? Explain.

As the Activity suggests, when you multiply two linear functions with nonzero slopes, the result is a *quadratic function*.

In general, a **quadratic function** is any function that can be written in the form $f(x) = ax^2 + bx + c$, where $a \neq 0$. It is defined by a **quadratic expression**, which is an expression of the form $ax^2 + bx + c$, where $a \neq 0$. The stopping-distance function $d(x) = \frac{11}{10}x + \frac{1}{19}x^2$, or $d(x) = \frac{1}{19}x^2 + \frac{11}{10}x$, is an example of a quadratic function.

CHECKPOINT ✔ Identify a, b, and c for the stopping-distance function, d, on page 274.

E X A M P L E ❶ Let $f(x) = (2x - 1)(3x + 5)$. **Show that f represents a quadratic function. Identify a, b, and c when the function is written in the form $f(x) = ax^2 + bx + c$.**

● **SOLUTION**

Method 1

$f(x) = (2x - 1)(3x + 5)$
$= (2x - 1)3x + (2x - 1)5$
$= 6x^2 - 3x + 10x - 5$
$= 6x^2 + 7x - 5$

Method 2

$f(x) = (2x - 1)(3x + 5)$
$= 2x(3x + 5) + (-1)(3x + 5)$
$= 6x^2 + 10x - 3x - 5$
$= 6x^2 + 7x - 5$

Since $f(x) = 6x^2 + 7x - 5$ has the form $f(x) = ax^2 + bx + c$, f is a quadratic function with $a = 6$, $b = 7$, and $c = -5$.

TRY THIS Let $g(x) = (2x - 5)(x - 2)$. Show that g represents a quadratic function. Identify a, b, and c when the function is written in the form $g(x) = ax^2 + bx + c$.

The graph of a quadratic function is called a **parabola.** Two types of parabolas are graphed below. Notice that each parabola has an **axis of symmetry,** a line that divides the parabola into two parts that are mirror images of each other. The **vertex of a parabola** is either the lowest point on the graph or the highest point on the graph.

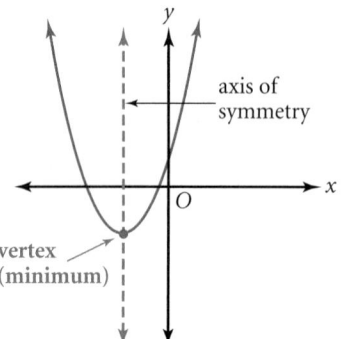

Notice that the axis of symmetry passes through the vertex of the parabola.

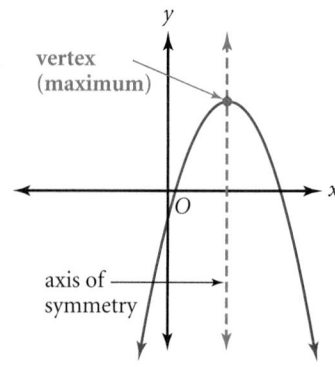

The domain of any quadratic function is the set of all real numbers. The range is either the set of all real numbers greater than or equal to the minimum value of the function (when the graph opens up) or the set of all real numbers less than or equal to the maximum value of the function (when the graph opens down).

E X A M P L E ❷ Identify whether $f(x) = x^2 - x + 1$ has a maximum value or a minimum value at the vertex. Then give the approximate coordinates of the vertex.

SOLUTION

Method 1 Use a graph.
From the graph, you can see that the function has a minimum value.

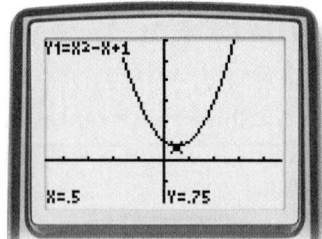

Tracing the graph, the coordinates of the vertex appear to be $(0.5, 0.75)$.

Method 2 Use a table.
From a table of values you can see that an x-value between 0 and 1 gives the minimum value of the function.

The coordinates of the vertex appear to be $(0.5, 0.75)$.

TRY THIS Identify whether $f(x) = -2x^2 - 4x + 1$ has a maximum value or a minimum value at the vertex. Then give the approximate coordinates of the vertex.

CRITICAL THINKING Refer to solution Methods 1 and 2 in Example 2. If you know that $f(0) = f(1)$ for $f(x) = x^2 - x + 1$, describe how you can find the equation for the axis of symmetry.

By examining a in $f(x) = ax^2 + bx + c$, you can identify whether the function has a maximum or a minimum value.

Minimum and Maximum Values

Let $f(x) = ax^2 + bx + c$, where $a \neq 0$. The graph of f is a parabola.

If $a > 0$, the parabola opens up and the vertex is the lowest point. The y-coordinate of the vertex is the **minimum value** of f.

If $a < 0$, the parabola opens down and the vertex is the highest point. The y-coordinate of the vertex is the **maximum value** of f.

EXAMPLE ③

CONNECTION

MAXIMUM/MINIMUM

State whether the parabola opens up or down and whether the y-coordinate of the vertex is the minimum value or the maximum value of the function. Then check by graphing.

a. $f(x) = x^2 + x - 6$

b. $g(x) = 5 + 4x - x^2$

● **SOLUTION**

a. In $f(x) = x^2 + x - 6$, the coefficient of x^2 is 1. Because $a > 0$, the parabola opens up and the function has a minimum value at the vertex.

b. In $g(x) = 5 + 4x - x^2$, the coefficient of x^2 is -1. Because $a < 0$, the parabola opens down and the function has a maximum value at the vertex.

TECHNOLOGY

GRAPHICS CALCULATOR

Keystroke Guide, page 348

CHECK

CHECK

Exercises

● *Communicate*

1. Describe differences between the graphs of linear and quadratic functions.

2. Explain the difference between the expressions that define linear and quadratic functions.

3. How can you determine whether a quadratic function has a minimum value or a maximum value?

Guided Skills Practice

Show that each function is a quadratic function by writing it in the form $f(x) = ax^2 + bx + c$ and identifying a, b, and c. (EXAMPLE 1)

4. $f(x) = (x + 1)(x - 7)$ **5.** $g(x) = (x + 2)(x + 5)$ **6.** $f(x) = (2x + 5)(3x + 1)$

CONNECTIONS

MAXIMUM/MINIMUM Identify whether each function has a maximum or minimum value. Then give the approximate coordinates of the vertex. (EXAMPLE 2)

7 $g(x) = x^2 - 3x + 5$ **8** $f(x) = 2 - 3x - x^2$ **9** $g(x) = x^2 + 5x + 3$

MAXIMUM/MINIMUM State whether the parabola opens up or down and whether the y-coordinate of the vertex is the maximum value or the minimum value of the function. Then check by graphing. (EXAMPLE 3)

10. $f(x) = x^2 - 2x + 7$ **11.** $g(x) = -x^2 + 8x + 14$ **12.** $g(x) = -2x^2 - 5x + 1$

Practice and Apply

internet connect

Homework Help Online

Go To: go.hrw.com
Keyword:
MB1 Homework Help
for Exercises 13–26

Show that each function is a quadratic function by writing it in the form $f(x) = ax^2 + bx + c$ and identifying a, b, and c.

13. $f(x) = (x - 3)(x + 8)$ **14.** $k(x) = (x + 3)(x - 5)$

15. $g(x) = (4 - x)(7 + x)$ **16.** $g(x) = (10 - x)(x + 4)$

17. $g(x) = -(x - 2)(x + 6)$ **18.** $f(x) = -(x + 3)(x - 9)$

19. $f(x) = 3(x - 2)(x + 1)$ **20.** $h(x) = 2(x + 1)(3x - 4)$

21. $h(x) = x(x - 3)$ **22.** $f(x) = 2x(x + 5)$

23. $g(x) = (2x + 3)(4 - x)$ **24.** $f(x) = (4x + 1)(4 - x)$

25. $h(x) = (x - 4)(x + 4)$ **26.** $f(x) = (x - 6)(x + 6)$

Identify whether each function is a quadratic function. Use a graph to check your answers.

27. $f(x) = 3 - x^2$ **28.** $g(s) = 3 - s$

29. $f(t) = \frac{1}{4}t^2 + \frac{1}{2}t - \frac{2}{3}$ **30.** $h(x) = \frac{3x^2 + 4x + 1}{x + 1}$

31. $g(t) = t^2 - t^2(t + 7)$ **32.** $h(x) = |x^2 + 5x - 2|$

State whether the parabola opens up or down and whether the y-coordinate of the vertex is the minimum value or the maximum value of the function.

33. $f(x) = -2x^2 - 2x$ **34.** $f(x) = 8x^2 - x$

35. $g(x) = -(3x^2 - x + 3)$ **36.** $f(x) = 2 + 3x - 5x^2$

37. $h(x) = 1 - 9x - x^2$ **38.** $g(x) = -(x^2 + x - 12)$

39. $g(x) = 3(x + 8)(-x + 9)$ **40.** $h(x) = -(4x + 1)(x + 4)$

Graph each function and give the approximate coordinates of the vertex.

41 $f(x) = x^2 - x + 9$ **42** $g(x) = 9 - 2x - x^2$

43 $g(x) = 4x^2 - 2x + 2$ **44** $f(x) = -0.5(x + 4)^2$

45 $f(x) = (x - 2)^2 - 1$ **46** $f(x) = -(x - 2)(x + 6)$

CHALLENGE

CONNECTION

APPLICATIONS

47. Describe a way to find the exact coordinates of the vertex of a parabola given by $f(x) = (x + a)(x - a)$.

48. TRANSFORMATIONS Graph each function.

$$f(x) = (x + 2)(x - 4) \qquad g(x) = 2(x + 2)(x - 4) \qquad h(x) = \tfrac{1}{2}(x + 2)(x - 4)$$

$$i(x) = -(x + 2)(x - 4) \qquad j(x) = -2(x + 2)(x - 4) \qquad k(x) = -\tfrac{1}{2}(x + 2)(x - 4)$$

a. What do all of the graphs have in common?
b. Which of the functions have a maximum value?
c. Which of the functions have a minimum value?

49. CONSTRUCTION Carly plans to build a rectangular pen against an existing fence for her dog. She will buy 20 yards of fence material.
  a. The table at left shows some different widths, lengths, and resulting areas that are possible with 20 yards of fence material. Complete the table.
  b. Let w be the width function. Graph $w(x) = x$. What domain for w is possible in this situation?
  c. Based on the completed table, write and graph a linear function, l, for the length. What domain for l is possible in this situation?
  d. Let $A(x) = w(x) \cdot l(x)$ be the area function. Show that the area function is quadratic.
  e. What domain for A is possible in this situation? What range is possible?
  f. What is the maximum area possible for the pen? What width and length will produce the maximum area?

Width (yd)	Length (yd)	Area (yd²)
1	18	18
2	16	32
3	14	
4		
⋮	⋮	⋮
x		

fence

width

length

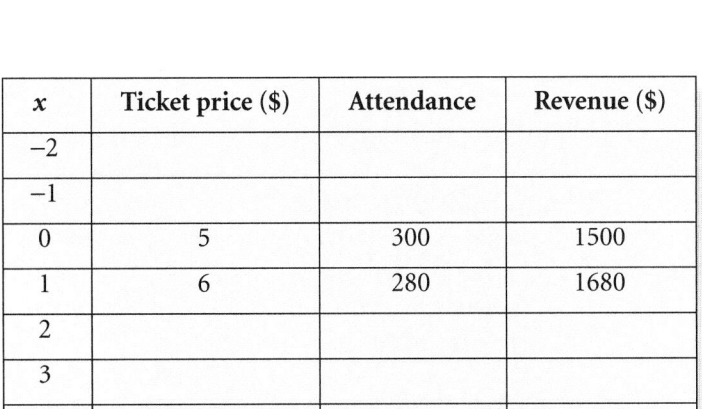

50. FUND-RAISING The student council plans to run a talent show to raise money. Last year tickets sold for $5 each and 300 people attended. This year, the student council wants to make an even bigger profit than last year. They estimate that for each $1 increase in the ticket price, attendance will drop by 20 people, and for each $1 decrease in the ticket price, attendance will increase by 20 people.

a. Let x be the change in the ticket price, in dollars. Copy and complete the table at left.

x	Ticket price ($)	Attendance	Revenue ($)
−2			
−1			
0	5	300	1500
1	6	280	1680
2			
3			
4			
⋮			
x			

b. Write the function for the ticket price, $t(x)$. What type of function is t? What domain for t is possible in this situation?

c. Write the function for the attendance, $a(x)$. What type of function is a? What domain for a is possible in this situation?

d. Let $R(x) = t(x) \cdot a(x)$ be the function for the revenue. Show that this function is quadratic.

e. What domain for R is possible in this situation?

f. What is the maximum revenue possible for the talent show? What ticket price and attendance will produce the maximum revenue?

 Look Back

For Exercises 51–54, let $y = -4x + 11$. *(LESSON 1.2)*

51. Identify the slope m.

52. What is the x-intercept?

53. What is the y-intercept?

54. Graph the line.

 Look Beyond

55 Graph $y = x^2 - 3x + 5$, $y = x^2 + 7x + 6$, and $y = x^2 - 14x + 49$ on the same screen. How many x-intercepts are possible for the graph of a quadratic function?

SPORTS Refer to the basketball toss described on page 273.

1. Create a scatter plot of the data.

2. The height of a basketball thrown vertically into the air can be modeled by the function $h(t) = \frac{1}{2}gt^2 + v_0t + h_0$, where g is the acceleration due to gravity (-32 feet per second squared), v_0 is the initial velocity in feet per second, and h_0 is the initial height in feet of the ball. Thus, $h(t) = -16t^2 + v_0t + h_0$. Substitute 6 for the initial height, h_0, of the ball into $h(t) = -16t^2 + v_0t + h_0$. Then graph the function on the same screen as the scatter plot, using different values for the initial velocity, v_0, until you find a model that provides a reasonably good fit for the data.

3. Use your best model to answer the questions below.

a. What is the value of v_0?

b. What is the maximum height achieved by the basketball?

c. At what time does the basketball reach its maximum height?

4. Solve for v_0 algebraically by substituting the coordinates of one of the data points into $h(t) = -16t^2 + v_0t + h_0$. Graph the resulting function on the same screen as the scatter plot. Use this model to answer the questions below.

a. What is the value of v_0?

b. What is the maximum height achieved by the basketball?

c. At what time does the basketball reach its maximum height?

WORKING ON THE CHAPTER PROJECT

You should now be able to complete Activity 1 of the Chapter Project.

Introduction to Solving Quadratic Equations

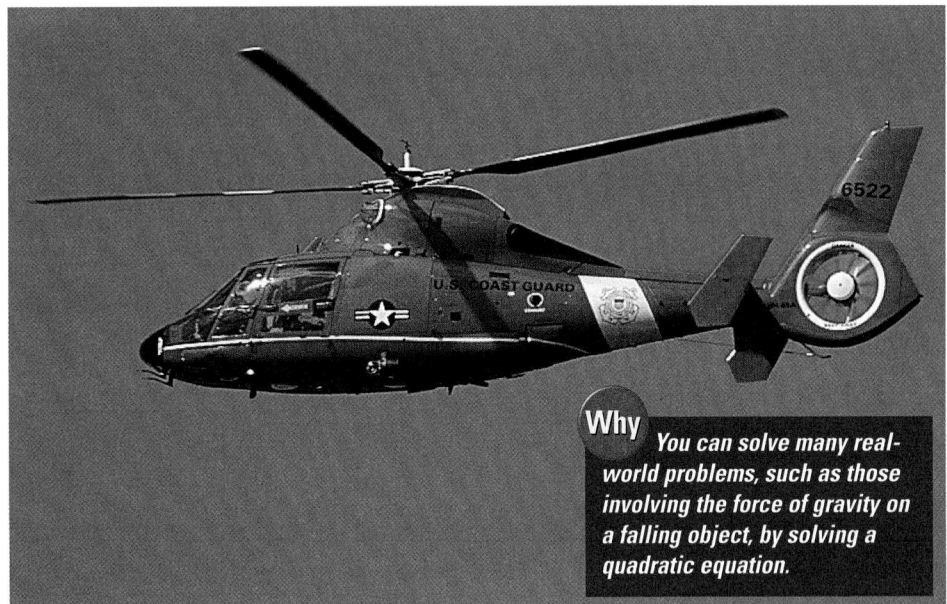

6522

U.S. COAST GUARD

Objectives

● Solve quadratic equations by taking square roots.

● Use the Pythagorean Theorem to solve problems involving right triangles.

Why *You can solve many real-world problems, such as those involving the force of gravity on a falling object, by solving a quadratic equation.*

APPLICATION

RESCUE

A rescue helicopter hovering 68 feet above a boat in distress drops a life raft. The height in feet of the raft above the water can be modeled by $h(t) = -16t^2 + 68$, where t is the time in seconds after it is dropped. How many seconds after the raft is dropped will it hit the water? Solving this problem involves finding square roots. *You will answer this question in Example 3.*

If $x^2 = a$ and $a \geq 0$, then x is called a square root of a. If $a > 0$, the number a has two square roots, $\sqrt{a}$ and $-\sqrt{a}$. The positive square root of a, $\sqrt{a}$, is called the **principal square root** of a. If $a = 0$, then $\sqrt{0} = 0$. When you solve a quadratic equation of the form $x^2 = a$, you can use the rule below.

Solving Equations of the Form $x^2 = a$

If $x^2 = a$ and $a \geq 0$, then $x = \sqrt{a}$ or $x = -\sqrt{a}$, or simply $x = \pm\sqrt{a}$.

The expression $\pm\sqrt{a}$ is read as "plus or minus the square root of a." To use the rule above, you may need to transform a given equation so that it is in the form $x^2 = a$. You can also use the *Properties of Square Roots* below to simplify the resulting square root.

Properties of Square Roots

Product Property of Square Roots   If $a \geq 0$ and $b \geq 0$: $\sqrt{ab} = \sqrt{a} \cdot \sqrt{b}$

Quotient Property of Square Roots   If $a \geq 0$ and $b > 0$: $\sqrt{\dfrac{a}{b}} = \dfrac{\sqrt{a}}{\sqrt{b}}$

EXAMPLE ❶ Solve $4x^2 + 13 = 253$. **Give exact solutions. Then approximate the solutions to the nearest hundredth.**

● **SOLUTION**

$$4x^2 + 13 = 253$$
$$4x^2 = 240 \qquad \text{Subtract 13 from each side.}$$
$$x^2 = 60 \qquad \text{Divide each side by 4.}$$
$$x = \pm\sqrt{60} \qquad \text{Take the square root of each side.}$$

$x = \sqrt{60} \quad or \quad x = -\sqrt{60}$ *Exact solution*

$x \approx 7.75 \qquad\quad x \approx -7.75$ *Approximate solution*

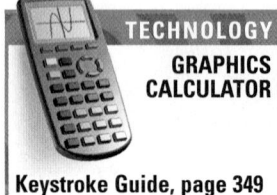

TECHNOLOGY
GRAPHICS CALCULATOR
Keystroke Guide, page 349

CHECK

Graph $y = 4x^2 + 13$ and $y = 253$ on the same screen, and find any points of intersection.

$(\approx -7.75, 253)$ $(\approx 7.75, 253)$

TRY THIS   Solve $5x^2 - 19 = 231$. Give exact solutions. Then approximate the solutions to the nearest hundredth.

CHECKPOINT ✔ Use the Product Property of Square Roots to show that $\sqrt{60} = 2\sqrt{15}$. Then use a calculator to approximate $2\sqrt{15}$.

EXAMPLE ❷ Solve $9(x - 2)^2 = 121$.

● **SOLUTION**

$$9(x - 2)^2 = 121$$

$$(x - 2)^2 = \frac{121}{9} \qquad\qquad \text{Divide each side by 9.}$$

$$x - 2 = \pm\sqrt{\frac{121}{9}} \qquad\qquad \text{Take the square root of each side.}$$

$$x = 2 + \sqrt{\frac{121}{9}} \quad or \quad x = 2 - \sqrt{\frac{121}{9}}$$

$$x = 2 + \frac{\sqrt{121}}{\sqrt{9}} \qquad\qquad x = 2 - \frac{\sqrt{121}}{\sqrt{9}} \qquad\qquad \text{Use the Quotient Property of Square Roots.}$$

$$x = 2 + \frac{11}{3} \qquad\qquad x = 2 - \frac{11}{3}$$

$$x = \frac{17}{3}, \text{ or } 5\frac{2}{3} \qquad x = -\frac{5}{3}, \text{ or } -1\frac{2}{3}$$

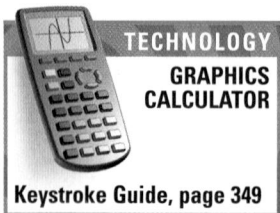

TECHNOLOGY
GRAPHICS CALCULATOR
Keystroke Guide, page 349

CHECK

Graph $y = 9(x - 2)^2$ and $y = 121$ on the same screen, and find any points of intersection.

$(\approx -1.67, 121)$ $(\approx 5.67, 121)$

TRY THIS   Solve $4(x + 2)^2 = 49$.

Exploring Solutions to Quadratic Equations

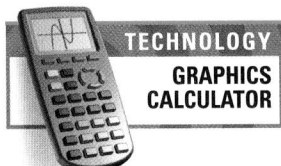

TECHNOLOGY
GRAPHICS CALCULATOR

You will need: a graphics calculator or graph paper

1. Copy and complete the second and third columns of the table below.

Equation	Exact solution(s)	Number of solutions	Related function	Number of x-intercepts
$x^2 - 7 = 0$	$x = \pm\sqrt{7}$	2	$f(x) = x^2 - 7$	2
$x^2 - 2 = 0$			$f(x) = x^2 - 2$	
$x^2 = 0$			$f(x) = x^2$	
$-x^2 + 2 = 0$			$f(x) = -x^2 + 2$	
$-x^2 + 7 = 0$			$f(x) = -x^2 + 7$	
$-x^2 = 0$			$f(x) = -x^2$	

2. Graph the related quadratic function for each equation, and complete the last column of the table.

CHECKPOINT ✔ **3.** What is the relationship between the number of solutions to a quadratic equation and the number of x-intercepts of the related function?

E X A M P L E ③ Refer to the rescue-helicopter problem described at the beginning of the lesson.

After how many seconds will the raft dropped from the helicopter hit the water?

APPLICATION
RESCUE

● **SOLUTION**

The raft will hit the water when its height above the water is 0 feet, or when $h(t) = 0$.

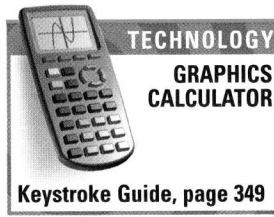

TECHNOLOGY
GRAPHICS CALCULATOR

Keystroke Guide, page 349

Method 1 Use algebra.
Let $h(t) = 0$.
$$-16t^2 + 68 = 0$$
$$-16t^2 = -68$$
$$t^2 = \frac{-68}{-16}$$
$$t^2 = \frac{17}{4}$$
$$t = \pm\sqrt{\frac{17}{4}}$$
$$t \approx \pm 2.1$$

Method 2 Use the graph.
Graph $h(t) = -16t^2 + 68$, and find the reasonable t-value for which $h(t) = 0$.

The graph of h for t < 0 is not reasonable in this context.

$x \approx 2.06$

Since t must be greater than 0, the raft will hit the water about 2.1 seconds after it is dropped.

TRY THIS How many seconds will it take the raft to hit the water if the helicopter drops the raft from a height of 34 feet?

Using the Pythagorean Theorem

Greek mathematician Pythagoras (around 580–500 B.C.E.)

CULTURAL CONNECTION: ASIA

Sometime between 1900 B.C.E. and 1600 B.C.E. in ancient Babylonia (now Iraq), a table of numbers was inscribed on a clay tablet. When archeologists discovered the tablet, part of it was missing, so the meaning of the numbers on it remained a mystery. The sets of numbers on the tablet are believed to be triples, called *Pythagorean triples*, that form a special right-triangle relationship. This relationship, named after the Greek mathematician Pythagoras, is commonly called the *Pythagorean Theorem*.

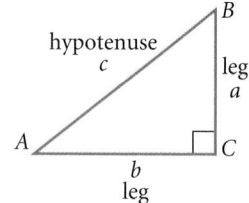

Ancient tablet believed to contain Pythagorean triples

When you sketch a right triangle, use capital letters to name the angles and corresponding lowercase letters to name the lengths of the sides opposite the angles. For example, $\overline{BC}$ is labeled a because it is opposite angle A.

Pythagorean Theorem

If $\triangle ABC$ is a right triangle with the right angle at C, then $a^2 + b^2 = c^2$.

When you apply the Pythagorean Theorem, use the principal square root because distance and length cannot be negative.

EXAMPLE ④

CONNECTION

GEOMETRY

Find the unknown length in each right triangle. Give answers to the nearest tenth.

a.

b.
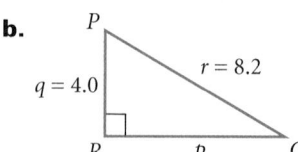

● **SOLUTION**

PROBLEM SOLVING

Use a formula.

a.
$$x^2 + y^2 = z^2$$
$$2.5^2 + 5.1^2 = z^2$$
$$z^2 = 5.1^2 + 2.5^2$$
$$z = \sqrt{5.1^2 + 2.5^2}$$
$$z \approx 5.68$$

z is about 5.7 units.

b.
$$p^2 + q^2 = r^2$$
$$p^2 + 4.0^2 = 8.2^2$$
$$p^2 = 8.2^2 - 4.0^2$$
$$p = \sqrt{8.2^2 - 4.0^2}$$
$$p \approx 7.16$$

p is about 7.2 units.

Find the unknown length in each right triangle. Give answers to the nearest tenth.

a.

b.

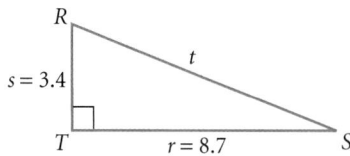

CRITICAL THINKING

Suppose that $\triangle ABC$ is a right triangle with the right angle at C. Write a formula for b in terms of a and c, assuming that a and c are known. Then write a formula for a in terms of b and c, assuming that b and c are known.

Sometimes you may need to apply the Pythagorean Theorem twice in order to find the solution to a problem. This is shown in Example 5.

E X A M P L E **5** The diagram shows support wires $\overline{AD}$ and $\overline{BD}$ for a tower.

APPLICATION
ENGINEERING

How far apart are the support wires where they contact the ground? Give your answer to the nearest whole foot.

[Not drawn to scale]

● **SOLUTION**

The distance between the support wires where they contact the ground is AB.

1. Apply the Pythagorean Theorem to $\triangle ADC$ to find AC.

$$(AC)^2 + (CD)^2 = (AD)^2$$
$$(AC)^2 + 760^2 = 900^2$$
$$(AC)^2 = 900^2 - 760^2$$
$$AC = \sqrt{900^2 - 760^2}$$
$$AC \approx 482.08$$

CONNECTION
GEOMETRY

2. Apply the Pythagorean Theorem to $\triangle BDC$ to find BC.

$$(BC)^2 + (CD)^2 = (BD)^2$$
$$(BC)^2 + 760^2 = 850^2$$
$$(BC)^2 = 850^2 - 760^2$$
$$BC = \sqrt{850^2 - 760^2}$$
$$BC \approx 380.66$$

TECHNOLOGY
SCIENTIFIC
CALCULATOR

You can edit the previous entry by replacing 900 with 850.

3. Find $AC - BC = AB$.

$$482.08 - 380.66 = 101.42$$

The wires are about 101 feet apart at ground level.

TRY THIS

In the diagram below, find PQ. Give your answer to the nearest whole meter.

Exercises

 Communicate

1. Describe the procedure you would use to solve $5(x + 3)^2 = 12$.

2. Describe three situations in which it makes sense to consider only the principal root as a solution.

3. How can you find the length of the hypotenuse of a right triangle with legs that are 3 and 4 units long?

Guided Skills Practice

Solve each equation. Give exact solutions. Then approximate each solution to the nearest hundredth, if necessary. *(EXAMPLES 1 AND 2)*

4. $x^2 = 29$ **5.** $2x^2 - 4 = 18$ **6.** $(x + 1)^2 = 9$

7. $3(x - 2)^2 = 21$ **8.** $2(x^2 - 4) + 3 = 15$ **9.** $\frac{1}{2}(x^2 + 6) - 5 = 10$

APPLICATION

10. AVIATION A crate of blankets and clothing is dropped without a parachute from a helicopter hovering at an altitude of 110 feet. The crate's height in feet above the ground is modeled by $h(t) = -16t^2 + 110$, where t is the time in seconds after it is dropped. How long will it take for the crate to reach the ground? *(EXAMPLE 3)*

CONNECTION

GEOMETRY **Find the unknown length in each right triangle. Give your answer to the nearest tenth.** *(EXAMPLE 4)*

11.

12.
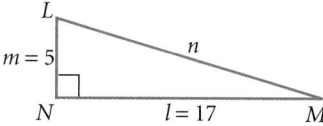

APPLICATION

13. CONSTRUCTION Two support wires and their lengths are shown in the diagram below. What is the distance in meters between the wires, represented by $\overline{CD}$, where they are attached to the ground? Give your answer to the nearest tenth of a meter. *(EXAMPLE 5)*

internet connect

Homework Help Online
Go To: **go.hrw.com**
Keyword:
MB1 Homework Help
for Exercises 14–31

Practice and Apply

Solve each equation. Give exact solutions. Then approximate each solution to the nearest hundredth, if necessary.

14. $x^2 = 121$ **15.** $x^2 = 32$ **16.** $3x^2 = 49$

17. $4x^2 = 20$ **18.** $4t^2 = 1$ **19.** $\frac{1}{2}x^2 = 6$

20. $\frac{2}{3}a^2 = 13$ **21.** $x^2 + 5 = 41$ **22.** $x^2 - 37 = 0$

23. $2t^2 - 5 = 6$ **24.** $4x^2 + 5 = 20$ **25.** $10 - 3x^2 = 4$

26. $8 - 2x^2 = -3$ **27.** $(x - 5)^2 = 16$ **28.** $(t + 2)^2 = 7$

29. $\frac{1}{3}(t^2 - 15) = 37$ **30.** $4(s^2 + 7) - 9 = 39$ **31.** $7 = 2(r + 1)^2 - 3$

Find the unknown length in each right triangle. Give answers to the nearest tenth.

32.

33.

34.

35.

36.

37.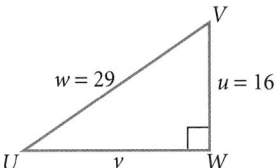

Find the missing side length in right triangle *ABC*. Give answers to the nearest tenth, if necessary.

38. *a* is 9 and *b* is 2.   **39.** *a* is 8 and *b* is 4.

40. *c* is 5 and *b* is 3.   **41.** *c* is $\sqrt{29}$ and *b* is 5.

42. *a* is 9 and *c* is $\sqrt{90}$.   **43.** *a* is 7 and *c* is $\sqrt{74}$.

CHALLENGE **Write a quadratic equation for each pair of solutions.**

44. 7 and -7 **45.** $\sqrt{17}$ and $-\sqrt{17}$ **46.** $\sqrt{2001}$ and $-\sqrt{2001}$

CONNECTIONS **47.** GEOMETRY The area of a circle is 20π square inches. Find the radius of the circle. (Hint: The area of a circle is given by $A = \pi r^2$.)

48. GEOMETRY Copy and complete the table.

Area of square	4	5	6	7	8	...	A
Side of square	2					...	
Diagonal of square	$\sqrt{8}$					...	

49. GEOMETRY A cube measures 3 feet on each edge.
  a. What is the length of a diagonal, such as *a*, along one of the faces of the cube?
  b. What is the length of a diagonal, such as *b*, that passes through the interior of the cube?

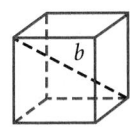

50. GEOMETRY A right pyramid that is 12 feet tall has a square base whose side length is 5 feet.
   a. What is its slant height?
   b. What is the length of its lateral edges?

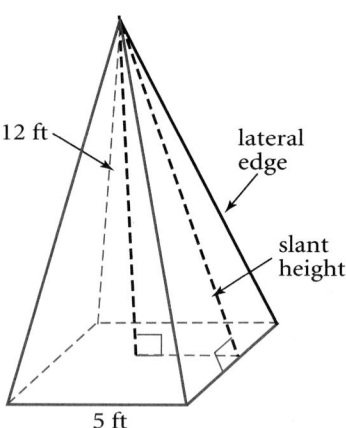

12 ft

lateral edge

slant height

5 ft

APPLICATIONS

51. PHYSICS A worker drops a hammer from a second-story roof that is 10 meters above the ground. If the hammer's height in meters above the ground is modeled by $h(t) = -4.9t^2 + 10$, where t represents time in seconds after the hammer is dropped, about how long will it take the hammer to reach the ground?

52. RECREATION A child at a swimming pool jumps off a 12-foot platform into the pool. The child's height in feet above the water is modeled by $h(t) = -16t^2 + 12$, where t is the time in seconds after the child jumps. How long will it take the child to reach the water?

53. SPORTS A baseball diamond is a square with sides of 90 feet. To the nearest foot, how long is a throw to first base from third base?

54. NAVIGATION A hiker leaves camp and walks 5 miles east. Then he walks 10 miles south. How far from camp is the hiker?

55. TELECOMMUNICATIONS The cable company buries a line diagonally across a rectangular lot. The lot measures 105 feet by 60 feet. How long is the cable line?

56. ENGINEERING The velocity, v, in centimeters per second, of a fluid flowing in a pipe varies with respect to the radius, x, of the pipe according to the equation $v(x) = 16 - x^2$.
   a. Find x for $v = 7$.
   b. Find x for $v = 12$.

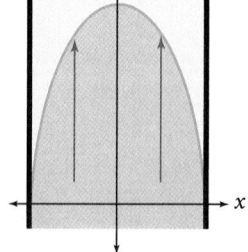

57. CONSTRUCTION The bottom of a 20-foot ladder is placed $4\frac{1}{2}$ feet from the base of a house, as shown at right. At what height does the ladder touch the house?

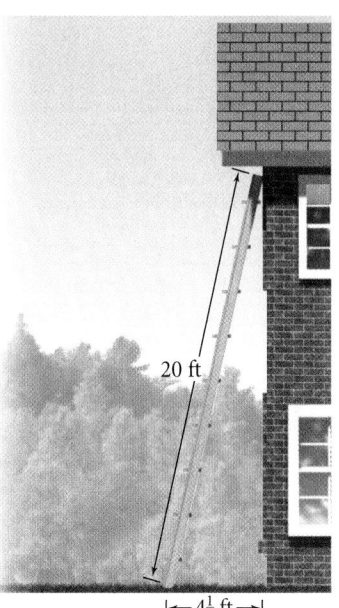

20 ft

$|\leftarrow 4\frac{1}{2}\, \text{ft} \rightarrow|$

internet connect

Activities Online

Go To: **go.hrw.com**
Keyword:
MB1 Tallest

58. SPORTS A cliff diver stands on a cliff overlooking water. To approximate his height above the water, he drops a pebble and times its fall. If the pebble takes about 3 seconds to strike the water, approximately how high is the diver above the water? Use the model $h(t) = -4.9t^2 + h_0$, where h is the pebble's height in meters above the ground, t is the time in seconds after the pebble is dropped, and h_0 is the height of the cliff in meters.

59. CONSTRUCTION Find the length of the rafter that provides for a rise of 5 feet over a run of 24 feet. Allow for a 1-foot overhang in the length of the rafter.

1-ft overhang   rafter

5 ft

24 ft

 Look Back

Determine whether each table represents a linear relationship between *x* and *y*. If the relationship is linear, write the next ordered pair that would appear in the table. **(LESSON 1.1)**

60.

x	−5	−3	−1	0	2	4
y	2	1	0	−1	−2	−3

61.

x	−3	−1	1	3	5	7
y	−9	−5	−1	3	7	11

Find the slope of the line passing through the given points, and write the equation of the line in slope-intercept form. **(LESSON 1.2)**

62. $(-4, -2)$ and $(6, -7)$ **63.** $(3, 5)$ and $(-6, 1)$

Evaluate each expression. **(LESSON 2.2)**

64. $4^5 \cdot 4^{-3}$ **65.** $\left(5^4\right)^{-\frac{1}{2}}$ **66.** $\left(6^4 \cdot 6\right)^0$

Give the domain and range of each function. **(LESSON 2.3)**

67. $f(x) = 3x^2 - 7$ **68.** $f(x) = \dfrac{x - 6}{5}$ **69.** $f(x) = 3\left(\dfrac{x}{2}\right)^2$

 Look Beyond

TRANSFORMATIONS Graph each pair of functions, find the vertices, and describe how the graphs are related.

70 $f(x) = (x - 3)^2 - 5$ and $g(x) = (x - 3)^2 + 5$

71 $f(x) = (x + 5)^2 - 4$ and $g(x) = (x - 2)^2 - 4$

72 $f(x) = x^2$ and $g(x) = (x - 3)^2 - 4$

Factoring Quadratic Expressions

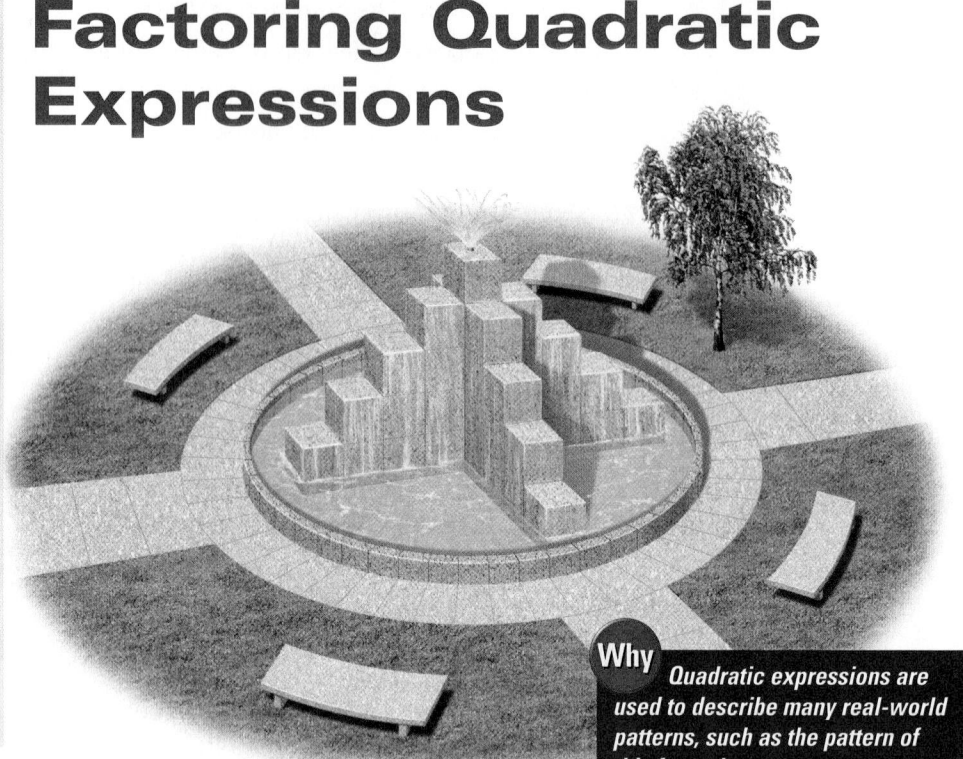

Why *Quadratic expressions are used to describe many real-world patterns, such as the pattern of this fountain.*

Objectives

- Factor a quadratic expression.

- Use factoring to solve a quadratic equation and find the zeros of a quadratic function.

APPLICATION

ARCHITECTURE

An architect created a proposal for the fountain shown above. Each level (except the top one) is an **X** formed by cubes. The number of cubes in each of the four parts of the **X** is one less than the number on the level below. A formula for the total number of cubes, c, in the fountain is given by $c = 2n^2 - n$, where n is the number of levels in the fountain. How many levels would a fountain consisting of 66 cubes have? *You will answer this question in Example 7.*

Factoring Quadratic Expressions

Multiplying

$$2x(x + 3) = 2x^2 + 6x$$

Factoring

When you learned to multiply two expressions like $2x$ and $x + 3$, you learned how to write a product as a sum. **Factoring** reverses the process, allowing you to write a sum as a product.

To factor an expression containing two or more terms, factor out the *greatest common factor* (GCF) of the two expressions, as shown in Example 1.

EXAMPLE ❶ Factor each quadratic expression.

    a. $3a^2 - 12a$ **b.** $3x(4x + 5) - 5(4x + 5)$

● **SOLUTION**

Factor out the GCF for all of the terms.

    a. $3a^2 = 3a \cdot a$ and $12a = 3a \cdot 4$ **b.** The GCF is $4x + 5$.
        The GCF is $3a$. $3x(4x + 5) - 5(4x + 5)$
        $3a^2 - 12a = 3a(a) - 3a(4)$ $= (3x - 5)(4x + 5)$
                    $= (3a)(a - 4)$

TRY THIS   Factor $5x^2 + 15x$ and $(2x - 1)4 + (2x - 1)x$.

An expression of the form $ax^2 + bx + c$, where $a \neq 0$, is often called a quadratic *trinomial*. In the Activity below, you will investigate how to factor this type of expression.

Activity

Factoring With Algebra Tiles

You will need: algebra tiles

You can model a quadratic expression that can be factored with algebra tiles, as shown below.

The rectangular region formed by algebra tiles above illustrates that the total area, $x^2 + 7x + 10$, can be represented as the product $(x + 5)(x + 2)$.

1. Use tiles to determine whether $x^2 + 4x + 4$ can be represented as the product of two linear factors. Justify and illustrate your response.

2. Use tiles to determine whether $x^2 + 6x + 8$ can be represented as the product of two linear factors. Justify and illustrate your response.

3. Use tiles to determine whether $x^2 + 7x + 12$ can be represented as the product of two linear factors. Justify and illustrate your response.

CHECKPOINT ✔ 4. Describe how algebra tiles can be used to factor a quadratic trinomial.

Many quadratic expressions can be factored algebraically. Examine the factored expressions below.

PROBLEM SOLVING **Look for a pattern.** Notice how the sums and products of the constants in the *binomial* factors are related to the last two terms in the unfactored expression.

$x^2 + 7x + 10 = (x + 5)(x + 2)$
| $5 + 2 = 7$ | $5 \times 2 = 10$ |

$x^2 - 7x + 10 = (x - 5)(x - 2)$
| $-5 - 2 = -7$ | $-5 \times (-2) = 10$ |

$x^2 + 3x - 10 = (x + 5)(x - 2)$
| $5 - 2 = 3$ | $5 \times (-2) = -10$ |

$x^2 - 3x - 10 = (x - 5)(x + 2)$
| $-5 + 2 = -3$ | $-5 \times 2 = -10$ |

The patterns shown above suggest a rule for factoring quadratic expressions of the form $x^2 + bx + c$.

Factoring $x^2 + bx + c$

To factor an expression of the form $ax^2 + bx + c$ where $a = 1$, look for integers r and s such that $r \cdot s = c$ and $r + s = b$. Then factor the expression.
$$x^2 + bx + c = (x + r)(x + s)$$

When c is positive in $x^2 + bx + c$ ($c > 0$), test factors with the same sign.

E X A M P L E ❷ **Factor $x^2 + 5x + 6$.**

● SOLUTION

PROBLEM SOLVING

Guess and check. Begin with $(x\quad)(x\quad)$. Find the factors of 6 that result in $5x$ for the bx-term.

$(x + 1)(x + 6)$	$(x + 2)(x + 3)$	$(x - 1)(x - 6)$	$(x - 2)(x - 3)$
$1x + 6x = 5x$	$2x + 3x = 5x$	$-1x + (-6x) = 5x$	$-2x + (-3x) = 5x$
False	**True**	**False**	**False**

Thus, $x^2 + 5x + 6 = (x + 2)(x + 3)$.

TRY THIS   Factor $x^2 + 9x + 20$.

When c is negative in $x^2 + bx + c$ ($c < 0$), test factors with opposite signs.

E X A M P L E ❸ **Factor $x^2 - 7x - 30$.**

● SOLUTION

PROBLEM SOLVING

Guess and check. Begin with $(x\quad)(x\quad)$. Find the factors of -30 that result in $-7x$ for the bx-term.

$(x - 1)(x + 30)$	$(x + 1)(x - 30)$	$(x - 2)(x + 15)$
$-1x + 30x = -7x$	$1x + (-30x) = -7x$	$-2x + 15x = -7x$
False	**False**	**False**

$(x + 2)(x - 15)$	$(x - 3)(x + 10)$	$(x + 3)(x - 10)$
$2x + (-15x) = -7x$	$-3x + 10x = -7x$	$3x + (-10x) = -7x$
False	**False**	**True**

Thus, $x^2 - 7x - 30 = (x + 3)(x - 10)$.

TRY THIS   Factor $x^2 - 10x - 11$.

You can use guess-and-check to factor an expression of the form $ax^2 + bx + c$, where $a \neq 1$.

E X A M P L E ❹ **Factor $6x^2 + 11x + 3$. Check by graphing.**

● SOLUTION

PROBLEM SOLVING

Guess and check. The positive factors of a, are 1, 6, 3, and 2. Begin with $(6x\quad)(x\quad)$ or $(3x\quad)(2x\quad)$. Find the factors of 3 that produce $11x$ for the bx-term.

$(6x + 3)(x + 1)$	$(6x + 1)(x + 3)$	$(3x + 3)(2x + 1)$	$(3x + 1)(2x + 3)$
$3x + 6x = 11x$	$1x + 18x = 11x$	$6x + 3x = 11x$	$2x + 9x = 11x$
False	**False**	**False**	**True**

Thus, $6x^2 + 11x + 3 = (3x + 1)(2x + 3)$.

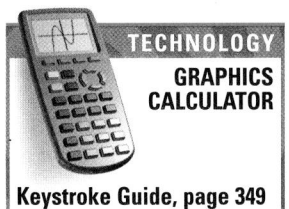
CHECK

Graph $y = 6x^2 + 11x + 3$ and $y = (3x + 1)(2x + 3)$.

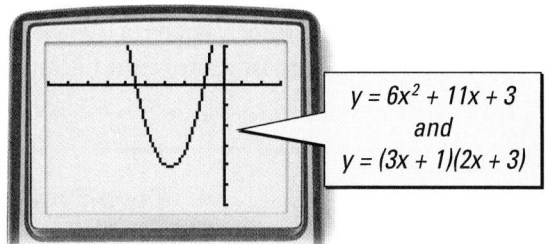

$y = 6x^2 + 11x + 3$
and
$y = (3x + 1)(2x + 3)$

The graphs appear to coincide. Thus, $6x^2 + 11x + 3 = (3x + 1)(2x + 3)$.

TRY THIS Factor $3x^2 + 11x - 20$. Check by graphing.

Examine the product when $x + 3$ and $x - 3$ are multiplied.

$$(x + 3)(x - 3) = x^2 + 3x - 3x + 9$$
$$= x^2 - 9$$
$$= x^2 - 3^2 \quad \text{difference of two squares}$$

Factoring the Difference of Two Squares

$$a^2 - b^2 = (a + b)(a - b)$$

Examine the products when $x + 3$ and $x - 3$ are squared.

$$(x + 3)^2 = (x + 3)(x + 3)$$
$$= x^2 + 3x + 3x + 9$$
$$= x^2 + 2(3x) + 9$$

perfect-square trinomials

$$(x - 3)^2 = (x - 3)(x - 3)$$
$$= x^2 - 3x - 3x + 9$$
$$= x^2 - 2(3x) + 9$$

Factoring Perfect-Square Trinomials

$$a^2 + 2ab + b^2 = (a + b)^2 \qquad a^2 - 2ab + b^2 = (a - b)^2$$

E X A M P L E ⑤ Factor each expression.

a. $x^4 - 16$ **b.** $4x^2 - 24x + 36$

SOLUTION

a. $x^4 - 16 = (x^2 + 4)(x^2 - 4)$
$= (x^2 + 4)(x + 2)(x - 2)$

b. $4x^2 - 24x + 36 = 4(x^2 - 6x + 9)$
$= 4[x^2 - 2(3)x + 3^2]$
$= 4(x - 3)^2$

TRY THIS Factor $9x^2 - 49$ and $3x^2 + 6x + 3$.

Using Factoring to Solve Quadratic Equations

You can sometimes use factoring to solve an equation and to find zeros of a function. A **zero of a function** f is any number r such that $f(r) = 0$.

Zero-Product Property

If $pq = 0$, then $p = 0$ *or* $q = 0$.

An equation of the form $ax^2 + bx + c = 0$ is called the **general form of a quadratic equation**. If a quadratic equation is in standard form and the expression $ax^2 + bx + c$ can be factored, then the Zero-Product Property can be applied to solve the equation. To apply the Zero-Product Property, write the equation as a factored expression equal to zero. For example, $x^2 + 6x = -5$ must first be rewritten in standard form as $x^2 + 6x + 5 = 0$ and then factored as $(x + 5)(x + 1) = 0$.

CHECKPOINT ✔ What is the solution to the equation $(x + 5)(x + 1) = 0$?

Example 6 shows you how to use the Zero-Product Property to find the zeros of a quadratic function.

E X A M P L E ⑥ Use the Zero-Product Property to find the zeros of each quadratic function.
   a. $f(x) = 2x^2 - 11x$
   b. $g(x) = x^2 - 14x + 45$

● **SOLUTION**

Set each function equal to zero, and use the Zero-Product Property to solve the resulting equation.

a.
$$2x^2 - 11x = 0$$
$$x(2x - 11) = 0$$
$$x = 0 \quad or \quad 2x - 11 = 0$$
$$x = 0 \qquad\qquad x = \frac{11}{2}$$

b.
$$x^2 - 14x + 45 = 0$$
$$(x - 5)(x - 9) = 0$$
$$x - 5 = 0 \quad or \quad x - 9 = 0$$
$$x = 5 \qquad\qquad x = 9$$

CHECK

CHECK

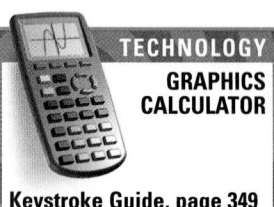

TECHNOLOGY
GRAPHICS CALCULATOR

Keystroke Guide, page 349

TRY THIS Use the Zero-Product Property to find the zeros of each function.
   a. $h(x) = 3x^2 + 12x$
   b. $j(x) = x^2 + 4x - 21$

CRITICAL THINKING Show that $f(x) = ax^2 + bx$, where $a \neq 0$, has two zeros, namely 0 and $-\frac{b}{a}$.

EXAMPLE **7** Refer to the fountain problem discussed at the beginning of the lesson.

Keystroke Guide, page 349

APPLICATION
ARCHITECTURE

How many levels would a fountain consisting of 66 cubes have?

SOLUTION

Method 1 Use algebra.
Solve $2n^2 - n = 66$ by factoring.

$2n^2 - n - 66 = 0$ *Write in standard form.*

$(2n + 11)(n - 6) = 0$ *Factor $2n^2 - n - 66$.*

$2n + 11 = 0$ *or* $n - 6 = 0$

$n = -5.5$ $n = 6$

Because the number of levels must be a positive integer, -5.5 cannot be a solution. The fountain would have 6 levels.

TECHNOLOGY
GRAPHICS CALCULATOR

Method 2 Use a table.
Make a table of values for $y = 2x^2 - x - 66$. From the table at right you can see that the function has a zero at $x = 6$.

Therefore, the fountain would have 6 levels.

Exercises

Communicate

1. If $x^2 + 34x + 285$ is factored as $(x + q)(x + s)$, how do you find q and s?

2. What do you know about the factors of $x^2 + bx + c$ when c is positive? when c is negative? What information does the sign of b give you in each case?

3. State what must be true about the numbers p and q if $pq = 0$.

Guided Skills Practice

Factor each quadratic expression. *(EXAMPLE 1)*

4. $2x^2 - 8x$

5. $2y^2 - 6y$

6. $5ax^2 - 15a^2x$

7. $4x(x + 3) - 7(x + 3)$

8. $(4r + 7)3 - (4r + 7)2r$

9. $(9s - 5)8s + 3(9s - 5)$

Factor each quadratic expression. *(EXAMPLES 2, 3, AND 4)*

10. $x^2 + 5x + 6$

11. $x^2 + 8x + 7$

12. $y^2 - 5y + 4$

13. $x^2 - 4x - 12$

14. $y^2 - 9y - 36$

15. $x^2 + 10x - 24$

16. $2x^2 + 9x + 10$

17. $3x^2 + 5x + 2$

18. $5x^2 + 13x - 6$

19. $8x^2 + 24x - 14x - 42$

20. $12r^2 + 21r - 8r - 14$

21. $72s^2 - 56s - 36s + 28$

Factor each quadratic expression. *(EXAMPLE 5)*

22. $x^4 - 81$ **23.** $2x^2 - 8$ **24.** $16x^2 - 25$ **25.** $x^2 + 8x + 16$

Use the Zero-Product Property to find the zeros of each quadratic function. *(EXAMPLE 6)*

26. $f(x) = x^2 + 7x$ **27.** $g(x) = x^2 + 6x + 9$ **28.** $f(t) = t^2 + 3t - 10$

CONNECTION

29. **GEOMETRY** Line segments are drawn to connect n points with one another. The number of connecting segments is described by the function $h(n) = \dfrac{n(n-1)}{2}$. If 36 connecting segments are drawn, how many points are there? *(EXAMPLE 7)*

Practice and Apply

Factor each expression.

30. $3x + 6$

31. $3x^2 + 18$

32. $10n - n^2$

33. $x - 4x^2$

34. $6x - 2x^2$

35. $-3y^2 - 15y$

36. $5x(x - 2) - 3(x - 2)$

37. $(x + 3)(2x) + (x + 3)(7)$

38. $a^2x + 5a^2x^2 - 2ax$

39. $4ab^2 - 6a^2b$

Factor each quadratic expression.

40. $x^2 - 16x + 15$

41. $x^2 + 8x + 16$

42. $x^2 - 26x + 48$

43. $x^2 + 4x - 32$

44. $x^2 + 7x - 30$

45. $x^2 - 10x - 24$

46. $-22x - 48 + x^2$

47. $2x + x^2 - 24$

48. $x^2 - 56 - 10x$

49. $56 + 10x - x^2$

50. $30 + x - x^2$

51. $24 + 10x - x^2$

52. $3x^2 + 10x + 3$

53. $2x^2 + 5x + 2$

54. $2x^2 + 3x + 1$

55. $3x^2 + 7x + 2$

56. $12x^2 - 3x - 9$

57. $3x^2 - 5x - 2$

internet connect

**Homework
Help Online**

Go To: **go.hrw.com**
Keyword:
MB1 Homework Help
for Exercises 58–87

Solve each equation by factoring and applying the Zero-Product Property.

58. $15x^2 = 7x + 2$

59. $3x^2 - 5x = 2$

60. $4x - 4 = -15x^2$

61. $3x^2 + 3 = 10x$

62. $2x^2 - 15 = -7x$

63. $6x^2 - 17x = -12$

64. $x^2 - 36 = 0$

65. $t^2 - 9 = 0$

66. $x^4 - 81 = 0$

67. $x^4 - 1 = 0$

68. $4x^2 - 9 = 0$

69. $25x^2 - 16 = 0$

70. $x^2 - 2x + 1 = 0$

71. $x^2 + 4x + 4 = 0$

72. $9x^2 = -6x - 1$

73. $4x^2 + 1 = 4x$

74. $-4 + 20x - 25x^2 = 0$

75. $40x + 25 = -16x^2$

76. $64 + 16x + x^2 = 0$

77. $9 - 6x + x^2 = 0$

Use factoring and the Zero-Product Property to find the zeros of each quadratic function.

78. $f(x) = x^2 - 7x + 10$

79. $g(t) = t^2 - 2t - 15$

80. $f(x) = 4x^2 + 4x - 24$

81. $g(x) = 6x^2 + 3x - 9$

82. $f(t) = t^2 + 7t - 60$

83. $h(x) = x^2 - 15x + 56$

84. $f(x) = x^2 + 8x + 12$

85. $g(x) = x^2 - 3x - 40$

86. $g(x) = 6x^2 + 20x - 16$

87. $h(x) = 4x^2 - 8x + 3$

Use graphing to find the zeros of each function.

88. $f(n) = n^2 - n - 30$

89. $g(t) = 24 + 8t - 2t^2$

90. $f(x) = 2x^2 + 13x + 15$

91. $f(x) = 5x^2 + 30x + 40$

92. $g(a) = 24a^2 + 36a - 24$

93. $h(x) = 6x^2 - 33x - 18$

CHALLENGE

Factor each expression.

94. $(a + b)^4 - (a - b)^4$

95. $x^{2n} - 1$

96. $x^{2n} - 2x^n + 1$

CONNECTIONS

GEOMETRY The area of a triangle is $A = \frac{1}{2}bh$, where b is the base and h is the altitude. Use this information for Exercises 97 and 98.

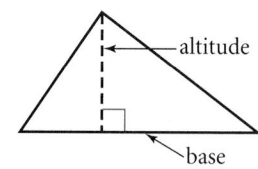

97. The base of a triangle is 5 centimeters longer than its altitude. If the area of the triangle is 42 square centimeters, what is its altitude?

98. The altitude of a triangle is 5 centimeters shorter than its base. If the area of the triangle is 12 square centimeters, what is its base?

99. GEOMETRY The area of a circle is given by $A = \pi r^2$, where r is the radius. If the radius of a circle is increased by 4 inches, the area of the resulting circle is 100π square inches. Find the radius of the original circle.

100. GEOMETRY The length of one leg of a right triangle is 7 centimeters longer than the other leg, and the hypotenuse is 13 centimeters. Find the lengths of the two legs.

APPLICATIONS

101. SPORTS A soccer ball is kicked from the ground, and its height in meters above ground is modeled by the function $h(t) = -4.9t^2 + 19.6t$, where t represents the time in seconds after the ball is kicked. How long is the ball in the air?

102. SPORTS A golf ball is hit from the ground, and its height in feet above the ground is modeled by the function $h(t) = -16t^2 + 180t$, where t represents the time in seconds after the ball is hit. How long is the ball in the air?

Solve each inequality, and graph the solution on a number line.
(LESSON 1.7)

103. $2x - 4 > 12 + 5x$

104. $2x - \frac{3}{4} \geq 7$

105. $3(3x + 7) - 12 \leq 8 - \left(\frac{1}{2}x + 9\right)$

106. $-2\left(\frac{2}{3}x + 5\right) - 13 < -6$

APPLICATION

107. **ADVERTISING** An advertising agency can spend no more than $1,270,000 for television advertising. The two available time slots for commercials cost $40,000 and $25,000, and at least 40 commercials are desired. *(LESSON 3.4)*

a. Write a system of linear inequalities to represent how many commercials at each price can be purchased.

b. Graph the region in which the solution to the system of inequalities can be found.

c. Find the coordinates of a point that is a solution to the system. What do the coordinates represent?

For Exercises 108–111, let $A = \begin{bmatrix} -3 & 1 & 0 \\ 2 & 6 & -4 \\ 5 & -2 & 1 \end{bmatrix}$ and $B = \begin{bmatrix} 0 & 2 & 8 \\ 1 & 4 & 3 \\ -2 & 0 & -1 \end{bmatrix}$.

Evaluate each expression. *(LESSON 4.1)*

108. $3A$

109. $-\frac{1}{2}B$

110. $A - B$

111. $2B + A$

Find each product. *(LESSON 5.1)*

112. $(3x + 4)(-x - 5)$

113. $(-2x + 9)(-4x + 7)$

114. $\left(\frac{1}{3}x + \frac{1}{4}\right)(-5x - 2)$

 Look Beyond

Factor each quadratic expression, if possible.

115. $(x + 2)^2 - 4$

116. $(x + 9)^2 + 36$

117. $(x - 1)^2 - 16$

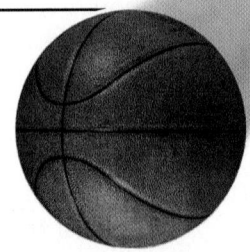

SPORTS Refer to the height function given in the Portfolio Activity on page 280.

1. Find the time when the basketball will return to a height of 6 feet by solving the related quadratic equation for $h(t) = 6$.

2. Use the data on page 273 to estimate the equation of the axis of symmetry of the

function. Using symmetry, estimate when the basketball will return to a height of 6 feet.

3. Compare your answers to Steps 1 and 2 above. Explain any difference you find.

Completing the Square

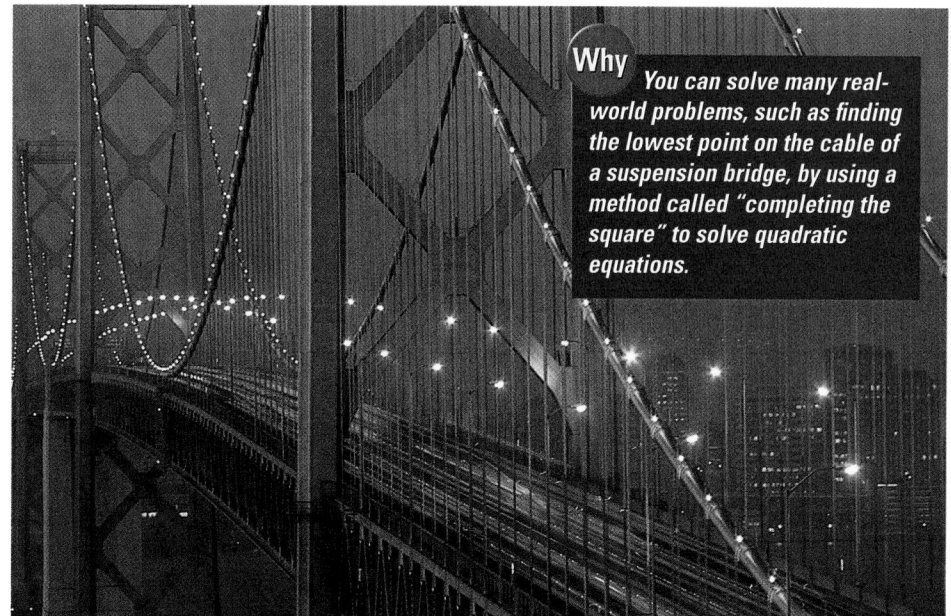

Objectives

- Use completing the square to solve a quadratic equation.

- Use the vertex form of a quadratic function to locate the axis of symmetry of its graph.

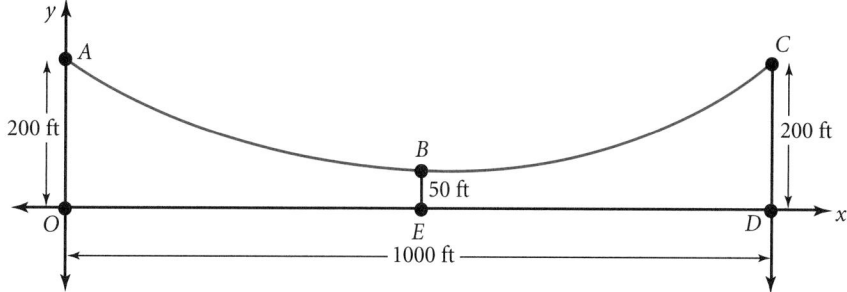

APPLICATION

ENGINEERING

Engineers are planning to build a cable suspension bridge like the one shown in the diagram above. The cable forms a *catenary* curve, which can be approximated by the quadratic function $f(x) = \frac{3}{5000}x^2 - \frac{3}{5}x + 200$, where $0 \le x \le 1000$. Write this quadratic function in a form that allows the coordinates of the lowest point on the cable to be easily identified. *You will solve this problem in Example 5.*

Completing the Square

Activity
Completing the Square With Tiles

You will need: algebra tiles

1. Can you arrange 1 x^2-tile and 4 x-tiles to form a square? Explain your response.

2. What is the smallest number of unit tiles you need to add to your tiles to form a square?

3. Write an expression in both standard and factored form for the complete set of tiles that form the square.

CHECKPOINT ✔   **6.** Explain how to find the smallest number of unit tiles needed to complete a square with 1 x^2-tile and 8 x-tiles.

Recall from Lesson 5.2 that you can solve equations of the form $x^2 = k$ by taking the square root of each side.

$$x^2 = 9$$
$$\sqrt{x^2} = \pm\sqrt{9}$$
$$x = \pm 3$$

The same is true for equations of the form $(x + a)^2 = k$.

$$(x + 3)^2 = 16$$
$$\sqrt{(x + 3)^2} = \pm\sqrt{16}$$
$$x + 3 = \pm 4$$
$$x = 1 \quad or \quad x = -7$$

When a quadratic equation does not contain a perfect square, you can create a perfect square in the equation by *completing the square*. **Completing the square** is a process by which you can force a quadratic expression to factor.

Examine the relationship between terms in a perfect-square trinomial.

Specific case

$$x^2 + 8x + 16 = (x + 4)^2$$
$$\tfrac{1}{2}(8) = 4 \rightarrow 4^2 = 16$$

General case

$$x^2 + bx + \left(\frac{b}{2}\right)^2 = \left(x + \frac{b}{2}\right)^2$$
$$\tfrac{1}{2}(b) = \frac{b}{2} \rightarrow \left(\frac{b}{2}\right)^2$$

In general, the constant term in a perfect square trinomial is the square of one-half the coefficient of the second term.

E X A M P L E **①** Complete the square for each quadratic expression to form a perfect-square trinomial. Then write the new expression as a binomial squared.
 a. $x^2 - 6x$ **b.** $x^2 + 15x$

● **SOLUTION**

a. The coefficient of x is -6.

$$\tfrac{1}{2}(-6) = -3 \rightarrow (-3)^2 = \mathbf{9}$$

Thus, the perfect-square trinomial is $x^2 - 6x + \mathbf{9}$.

$$x^2 - 6x + 9 = (x - 3)^2$$

b. The coefficient of x is 15.

$$\tfrac{1}{2}(15) = \frac{15}{2} \rightarrow \left(\frac{15}{2}\right)^2$$

Thus, the perfect-square trinomial is $x^2 + 15x + \left(\frac{15}{2}\right)^2$.

$$x^2 + 15x + \left(\frac{15}{2}\right)^2 = \left(x + \frac{15}{2}\right)^2$$

TRY THIS   Complete the square for each quadratic expression to form a perfect-square trinomial. Then write the new expression as a binomial squared.
 a. $x^2 - 7x$ **b.** $x^2 + 16x$

Solving Equations by Completing the Square

Examples 2 and 3 show you how to solve a quadratic equation by completing the square and by using square roots.

E X A M P L E ② Solve $x^2 + 6x - 16 = 0$ by completing the square.

● **SOLUTION**

$$x^2 + 6x - 16 = 0$$
$$x^2 + 6x = 16$$
$$x^2 + 6x + \left(\frac{6}{2}\right)^2 = 16 + \left(\frac{6}{2}\right)^2 \quad \text{Add } \left(\frac{6}{2}\right)^2 \text{ to each side of the equation.}$$
$$x^2 + 6x + 9 = 25$$
$$(x + 3)^2 = 25$$
$$x + 3 = \pm\sqrt{25} \quad \text{Take the square root of each side.}$$
$$x + 3 = \pm 5$$
$$x = 5 - 3 \quad or \quad x = -5 - 3$$
$$x = 2 \qquad\qquad x = -8$$

TRY THIS   Solve $x^2 + 10x - 24 = 0$ by completing the square.

E X A M P L E ③ Solve $2x^2 + 6x = 7$.

● **SOLUTION**

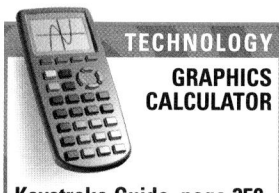

TECHNOLOGY
GRAPHICS CALCULATOR

Keystroke Guide, page 350

Method 1 Use algebra.
Solve by completing the square.
$$2x^2 + 6x = 7$$
$$2(x^2 + 3x) = 7$$
$$x^2 + 3x = \frac{7}{2}$$
$$x^2 + 3x + \left(\frac{3}{2}\right)^2 = \frac{7}{2} + \left(\frac{3}{2}\right)^2$$
$$\left(x + \frac{3}{2}\right)^2 = \frac{7}{2} + \frac{9}{4}$$
$$x + \frac{3}{2} = \pm\sqrt{\frac{23}{4}}$$
$$x = -\frac{3}{2} + \sqrt{\frac{23}{4}} \quad or \quad x = -\frac{3}{2} - \sqrt{\frac{23}{4}}$$
$$x \approx 0.90 \qquad\qquad\qquad x \approx -3.90$$

Thus, the exact solution is
$$x = -\frac{3}{2} + \sqrt{\frac{23}{4}} \ or \ x = -\frac{3}{2} - \sqrt{\frac{23}{4}}.$$

Method 2 Use a graph.
Graph $y = 2x^2 + 6x$ and $y = 7$, and find the x-coordinates of any points of intersection.

Or graph $y = 2x^2 + 6x - 7$, and find any zeros.

TRY THIS   Solve $2x^2 + 10x = 6$.

Vertex Form

You know that the graph of $y = ax^2 + bx + c$, where $a \neq 0$, is a parabola. Using the method of completing the square, you can write the quadratic function in a form that contains the coordinates (h, k) of the vertex of the parabola.

Vertex Form

If the coordinates of the vertex of the graph of $y = ax^2 + bx + c$, where $a \neq 0$, are (h, k), then you can represent the parabola as $y = a(x - h)^2 + k$, which is the **vertex form** of a quadratic function.

CONNECTION

TRANSFORMATIONS

Recall from Lesson 2.7 that if $y = f(x)$, then
- $y = af(x)$ gives a vertical stretch or compression of f,
- $y = f(bx)$ gives a horizontal stretch or compression of f,
- $y = f(x) + k$ gives a vertical translation of f, and
- $y = f(x - h)$ gives a horizontal translation of f.

E X A M P L E ④ Given $g(x) = 2x^2 + 12x + 13$, write the function in vertex form, and give the coordinates of the vertex and the equation of the axis of symmetry. Then describe the transformations from $f(x) = x^2$ to g.

● **SOLUTION**

$$g(x) = 2x^2 + 12x + 13$$
$$= 2(x^2 + 6x) + 13 \qquad \textit{Factor 2 from the } x^2\textit{- and x-terms.}$$
$$= 2(x^2 + 6x + 9) + 13 - 2(9) \qquad \textit{Complete the square.}$$
$$= 2(x + 3)^2 - 5 \qquad \textit{Simplify.}$$
$$= 2[x - (-3)]^2 + (-5) \qquad \textit{Write in vertex form.}$$

The coordinates (h, k) of the vertex are $(-3, -5)$, and the equation for the axis of symmetry is $x = -3$.

Notice from the vertex form of the function that $g(x) = 2f(x + 3) - 5$. There are three transformations from f to g:
- a vertical stretch by a factor of 2
- a horizontal translation of 3 units to the left
- a vertical translation of 5 units down

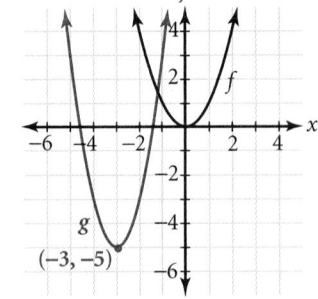

TRY THIS Given $g(x) = 3x^2 - 9x - 2$, write the function in vertex form, and give the coordinates of the vertex and the equation of the axis of symmetry. Then describe the transformations from $f(x) = x^2$ to g.

EXAMPLE ⑤ Refer to the suspension bridge described at the beginning of the lesson.

Complete the square, and write $f(x) = \frac{3}{5000}x^2 - \frac{3}{5}x + 200$ in vertex form. Then find the coordinates of the lowest point on the cable.

● SOLUTION

Method 1 Use algebra.

$$f(x) = \frac{3}{5000}x^2 - \frac{3}{5}x + 200$$

$$= \frac{3}{5000}(x^2 - 1000x) + 200$$

$$= \frac{3}{5000}\left[x^2 - 1000x + \left(\frac{1000}{2}\right)^2\right] + 200 - \frac{3}{5000}\left(\frac{1000}{2}\right)^2$$

$$= \frac{3}{5000}(x^2 - 1000x + 500^2) + 200 - \frac{3}{5000}(500^2)$$

$$= \frac{3}{5000}(x - 500)^2 + 50$$

Thus, $f(x) = \frac{3}{5000}(x - 500)^2 + 50$ is a function containing a perfect square.

The lowest point on the cable is represented by the vertex (500, 50).

Method 2 Use a graph.

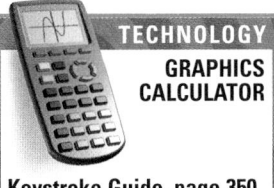

Graph $y = \frac{3}{5000}x^2 - \frac{3}{5}x + 200$, and find the coordinates of the lowest point.

From the graph of the function, the lowest point on the cable appears to be (500, 50).

Minimum
X=500.00006 Y=50

CRITICAL THINKING Explain why you cannot write an equation for a parabola when given only the coordinates of the vertex.

● *Communicate*

1. Explain how to solve the equation $x^2 + 4x - 13 = 0$ by completing the square.

2. Explain how to solve the equation $2x^2 + 4x = 15$ by completing the square.

3. Refer to Example 3. Describe two ways of solving $2x^2 + 4x = 15$ by graphing.

4. Explain what h and k represent in the vertex form of a parabola.

Guided Skills Practice

Complete the square for each quadratic expression to form a perfect-square trinomial. Then write the new expression as a binomial squared. *(EXAMPLE 1)*

5. $x^2 - 12x$ **6.** $x^2 + 5x$

7. Solve $x^2 - 4x - 21 = 0$ by completing the square. *(EXAMPLE 2)*

8. Solve $2x^2 + 5x = 3$. *(EXAMPLE 3)*

CONNECTION

9. TRANSFORMATIONS Given $g(x) = x^2 + 12x + 20$, write the function in vertex form, and give the coordinates of the vertex and the equation of the axis of symmetry. Then describe the transformations from $f(x) = x^2$ to g. *(EXAMPLE 4)*

APPLICATION

10. SPORTS A softball is thrown upward with an initial velocity of 32 feet per second from 5 feet above ground. The ball's height in feet above the ground is modeled by $h(t) = -16t^2 + 32t + 5$, where t is the time in seconds after the ball is released. Complete the square and rewrite h in vertex form. Then find the the maximum height of the ball. *(EXAMPLE 5)*

Practice and Apply

internet connect

**Homework
Help Online**

Go To: **go.hrw.com**
Keyword:
MB1 Homework Help
for Exercises 17–37

Complete the square for each quadratic expression to form a perfect-square trinomial. Then write the new expression as a binomial squared.

11. $x^2 + 10x$ **12.** $x^2 - 14x$ **13.** $x^2 - 8x$

14. $x^2 + 2x$ **15.** $x^2 + 13x$ **16.** $x^2 + 7x$

Solve each equation by completing the square. Give exact solutions.

17. $x^2 - 8x = 3$ **18.** $x^2 + 2x = 13$ **19.** $x^2 - 5x - 1 = 4 - 3x$

20. $0 = x^2 - 6x + 3$ **21.** $0 = x^2 + 7x - 26$ **22.** $0 = x^2 - 3x - 6$

23. $x^2 + 7x + 10 = 0$ **24.** $x^2 + 10x + 16 = 0$ **25.** $x^2 - x = 30$

26. $0 = 3x^2 - 2x - 12$ **27.** $-2x^2 + 14x + 60 = 0$ **28.** $0 = 3x^2 - 11x + 6$

29. $-10 = x^2 - 8x + 2$ **30.** $x^2 + 16x = 2$ **31.** $4 - x^2 = 10x$

32. $x^2 = 23 - 15x$ **33.** $8x - 2 = x^2 + 15x$ **34.** $-32x = 16 - x^2$

35. $2x^2 = 22x - 11$ **36.** $4x^2 - 8 = -13x$ **37.** $2x^2 - 12 = 3x$

Write each quadratic function in vertex form. Give the coordinates of the vertex and the equation of the axis of symmetry. Then describe the transformations from $f(x) = x^2$ to g.

38. $g(x) = 3x^2$ **39.** $g(x) = -x^2 + 2$ **40.** $g(x) = x^2 - 5x$

41. $g(x) = x^2 + 8x + 11$ **42.** $g(x) = x^2 - 6x - 2$ **43.** $g(x) = -x^2 + 4x + 2$

44. $g(x) = x^2 + 7x + 3$ **45.** $g(x) = -3x^2 + 6x - 9$ **46.** $g(x) = -2x^2 + 12x + 13$

47. Write three different quadratic functions that each have a vertex at $(2, 5)$.

48. Write an equation for the quadratic function that has a vertex at $(2, 5)$ and contains the point $(1, 8)$.

For Exercises 49 and 50, give both an exact answer and an approximate answer rounded to the nearest tenth.

49. GEOMETRY Each side of a square is increased by 2 centimeters, producing a new square whose area is 30 square centimeters. Find the length of the sides of the original square. width:

50. GEOMETRY The length of a rectangle is 6 feet longer than its width. If the area is 50 square feet, find the length and the width of the rectangle.

51. PHYSICS The power, in megawatts, produced between midnight and noon by a power plant is given by $P = h^2 - 12h + 210$, where h is the hour of the day.
   a. At what time does the minimum power production occur?
   b. What is the minimum power production?
   c. During what hour(s) is the power production 187 megawatts?

52. FUND-RAISING Each year a school's booster club holds a dance to raise funds. In the past, the profit the club made after paying for the band and other costs has been modeled by the function $P(t) = -16t^2 + 800t - 4000$, where t represents the ticket price in dollars.
   a. What ticket price gives the maximum profit?
   b. What is the maximum profit?
   c. What ticket price(s) would generate a profit of $5424?

Look Back

Solve each equation. (LESSON 1.6)

53. $5x + 3 = 2x + 18$ **54.** $\frac{2(x+3)}{5} = x - 3$ **55.** $20 = 6x - 10$

For Exercises 56–59, determine whether each set of ordered pairs represents a function. (LESSON 2.3)

56. $\{(11, 0), (12, -1), (21, -2)\}$ **57.** $\{(0, 0), (2, 5), (3, 3)\}$

58. $\{(1, -1), (1, -2), (1, -3)\}$ **59.** $\{(4, 1), (5, 2), (6, 3)\}$

60. Evaluate $f(x) = \frac{1}{3}x - 2$ for $x = 2$ and $x = -3$. (LESSON 2.3)

61. Evaluate $g(x) = 7 - 4x$ for $x = 2$ and $x = -3$. (LESSON 2.3)

TRANSFORMATIONS **For Exercises 62–65, write the equation for the graph described.** *(LESSON 2.7)*

62. the graph of $f(x) = |x|$ translated 7 units to the left
63. the graph of $f(x) = x^2$ translated 6 units down
64. the graph of $f(x) = x^2$ stretched vertically by a factor of 8
65. the graph of $f(x) = |x|$ reflected through the x-axis and stretched horizontally by a factor of 3

66. Write a quadratic function whose zeros are -2 and 6. *(LESSON 5.1)*

Look Beyond

CULTURAL CONNECTION: AFRICA One of the first algebra books was written in Arabic by al-Khowarizmi around 800 C.E. This book used a method similar to algebra tiles to complete the square and solve for x.

To complete the square for the equation $x^2 + 12x = 45$, the al-Khowarizmi method begins with one square that is x units long on each side and 12 rectangles that are 1 unit wide and x units long.

Step 1 Divide the **12 rectangles** into 4 groups, and arrange them on the sides of the **square**. From the equation $x^2 + 12x = 45$, you know that the area of this shape is still 45 square units.

Step 2 To complete the square, add 3×3, or 9 units to each of the 4 corners:

$$9 \text{ units} \times 4 = 36 \text{ units}$$

The new area is $45 + 36 = 81$. If the area is 81, then the side length is 9. To find the length of x, solve $3 + x + 3 = 9$. Thus, $x = 3$.

67. Solve $x^2 + 20x = 125$ by using the al-Khowarizmi method.

68. Solve $x^2 + 32x = 33$ by using the al-Khowarizmi method.

69. Solve $x^2 + 56x = 116$ by using the al-Khowarizmi method.

internet connect

Portfolio Extension

Go To: **go.hrw.com**
Keyword:
MB1 CompleteSq

SPORTS Refer to the height function in the Portfolio Activity on page 280.

Complete the square for the height function and answer the questions below.

1. What is the maximum height achieved by the basketball?

2. How long does it take the basketball to reach its maximum height?

3. What is the equation of the axis of symmetry for the height function?

4. How long would it take the basketball to drop to the ground if it were not tapped by a player?

5. Compare your answers to the questions above with those obtained in Portfolio Activities on page 280 and 298.

The Quadratic Formula

Objectives

● Use the quadratic formula to find real roots of quadratic equations.

● Use the roots of a quadratic equation to locate the axis of symmetry of a parabola.

Why *You can solve many real-world problems, such as finding the dimensions of this patio, by using the quadratic formula to solve quadratic equations.*

After watching a home-improvement show, the Wilkersons decided to build a patio along two sides of their home, as shown here. The patio will have the same width along both sides.

Find the width of the patio if the Wilkersons have enough material to cover a surface area of 650 square feet. You can use the *quadratic formula* to solve this problem. *You will solve this problem in Example 3.*

Using the method of completing the square, you can derive a formula that can be used to solve any quadratic equation in standard form.

$$ax^2 + bx + c = 0 \qquad \text{\textit{Assume that } a \neq 0.}$$

$$x^2 + \frac{b}{a}x + \frac{c}{a} = 0 \qquad \text{\textit{Divide each side by a.}}$$

$$x^2 + \frac{b}{a}x = -\frac{c}{a} \qquad \text{\textit{Subtract } } \frac{c}{a} \text{ \textit{from each side.}}$$

$$x^2 + \frac{b}{a}x + \left(\frac{b}{2a}\right)^2 = -\frac{c}{a} + \left(\frac{b}{2a}\right)^2 \qquad \text{\textit{Complete the square.}}$$

$$\left(x + \frac{b}{2a}\right)^2 = \frac{-4ac + b^2}{4a^2} \qquad \text{\textit{Simplify.}}$$

$$\sqrt{\left(x + \frac{b}{2a}\right)^2} = \pm\sqrt{\frac{b^2 - 4ac}{4a^2}} \qquad \text{\textit{Take the square root of each side.}}$$

$$x + \frac{b}{2a} = \pm\frac{\sqrt{b^2 - 4ac}}{2a} \qquad \text{\textit{Simplify.}}$$

$$x = -\frac{b}{2a} \pm \frac{\sqrt{b^2 - 4ac}}{2a} \qquad \text{\textit{Subtract } } \frac{b}{2a} \text{ \textit{from each side.}}$$

$$x = \frac{-b \pm \sqrt{b^2 - 4ac}}{2a} \qquad \text{\textit{Simplify.}}$$

Quadratic Formula

If $ax^2 + bx + c = 0$ and $a \neq 0$, then the solutions, or roots, are

$$x = \frac{-b \pm \sqrt{b^2 - 4ac}}{2a}.$$

Example 1 shows how to use the quadratic formula to solve a quadratic equation that is in standard form.

E X A M P L E ① **Use the quadratic formula to find the roots of $x^2 + 5x - 14 = 0$.**

● **SOLUTION**

In $x^2 + 5x - 14 = 0$, $a = 1$, $b = 5$, and $c = -14$.

$$x = \frac{-b \pm \sqrt{b^2 - 4ac}}{2a}$$

$$x = \frac{-5 \pm \sqrt{5^2 - 4(1)(-14)}}{2(1)}$$ *Use the quadratic formula.*

$$x = \frac{-5 + \sqrt{81}}{2} \quad or \quad x = \frac{-5 - \sqrt{81}}{2}$$

$$x = \frac{-5 + 9}{2} \qquad\qquad x = \frac{-5 - 9}{2}$$ *Substitute 9 for $\sqrt{81}$.*

$$x = 2 \qquad\qquad\qquad x = -7$$

TRY THIS Use the quadratic formula to solve $x^2 - 7x + 6 = 0$.

CHECKPOINT ✔ Solve $x^2 + 5x - 14 = 0$ by factoring to check the solution to Example 1.

The solutions to a quadratic equation can be irrational numbers. This is shown in Example 2.

E X A M P L E ② **Use the quadratic formula to solve $4x^2 = 8 - 3x$. Give exact solutions and approximate solutions to the nearest tenth.**

● **SOLUTION**

PROBLEM SOLVING

Use a formula. Write the equation in standard form. Then use the quadratic formula.

$$4x^2 = 8 - 3x$$

$$4x^2 + 3x - 8 = 0$$

$$x = \frac{-3 \pm \sqrt{3^2 - 4(4)(-8)}}{2(4)}$$

$$x = \frac{-3 \pm \sqrt{137}}{8}$$

$$x = \frac{-3 + \sqrt{137}}{8} \quad or \quad x = \frac{-3 - \sqrt{137}}{8}$$ *Exact solution*

$$x \approx 1.1 \qquad\qquad\qquad x \approx -1.8$$ *Approximate solution*

TRY THIS Use the quadratic formula to solve $2x^2 - 6x = -3$. Give exact solutions and approximate solutions to the nearest tenth.

EXAMPLE ③ Refer to the patio described at the beginning of the lesson.

APPLICATION
CONSTRUCTION

Find the width of the patio if there is enough material to cover a surface area of 650 square feet.

● **SOLUTION**

PROBLEM SOLVING

Write an equation.

$$A(x) = 25x + 30x + x^2$$
$$= x^2 + 55x$$

Solve $x^2 + 55x = 650$ for x.

TECHNOLOGY
SCIENTIFIC CALCULATOR

$$x^2 + 55x = 650$$
$$x^2 + 55x - 650 = 0$$
$$x = \frac{-55 \pm \sqrt{55^2 - 4(1)(-650)}}{2(1)}$$
$$x = \frac{-55 \pm 75}{2}$$
$$x = 10 \quad or \quad x = -65$$

Since the width must be positive, −65 cannot be a solution. The patio should be 10 feet wide.

A shortcut on a graphics calculator is to edit the previous entry by changing the plus to a minus.

TRY THIS Find the width of the patio described at the beginning of the lesson if there is enough cement to cover a surface area of 500 square feet.

Recall from Lesson 5.3 that real-number solutions of a quadratic equation $ax^2 + bx + c = 0$ are also the x-intercepts of the related quadratic function $f(x) = ax^2 + bx + c$. You can examine this in the Activity below.

Activity
Exploring Roots of Equations

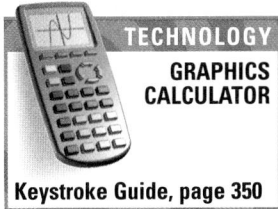

TECHNOLOGY
GRAPHICS CALCULATOR

Keystroke Guide, page 350

You will need: a graphics calculator

1. Copy the table below. Complete the second and third columns of the table by using any method to find the roots of each equation.

2. Graph each related function and find the x-coordinate of the vertex. Then complete the last two columns of the table.

Equation	Roots	Average of roots	Related function	x-coordinate of vertex
$x^2 + 2x = 0$	0, −2	−1	$f(x) = x^2 + 2x$	−1
$-x^2 + 4 = 0$				
$x^2 + 4x + 4 = 0$				
$2x^2 + 5x - 3 = 0$				
$-x^2 - 3x + 4 = 0$				

CHECKPOINT ✔ 3. Write a brief explanation that tells how to find the x-coordinate of the vertex for the graph of a quadratic function.

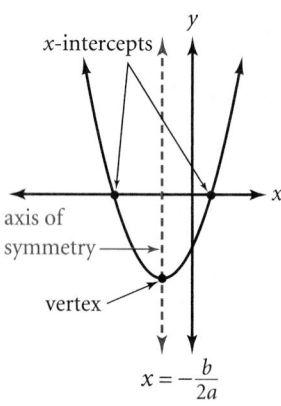

x-intercepts

y

axis of symmetry

vertex

$x = -\dfrac{b}{2a}$

Recall from Lesson 5.1 that the equation of the axis of symmetry of a parabola is obtained from the x-coordinate of the vertex of the parabola. Using the symmetry of the parabola, an equation for the axis of symmetry can be found by taking the average of the two roots found with the quadratic formula.

$$\dfrac{\left(\dfrac{-b + \sqrt{b^2 - 4ac}}{2a}\right) + \left(\dfrac{-b - \sqrt{b^2 - 4ac}}{2a}\right)}{2} = -\dfrac{b}{2a}$$

Axis of Symmetry of a Parabola

If $y = ax^2 + bx + c$, where $a \neq 0$, then the equation for the axis of symmetry of the parabola is $x = -\dfrac{b}{2a}$.

E X A M P L E ❹ Let $f(x) = 19 + 8x + 2x^2$. Write the equation for the axis of symmetry of the graph, and find the coordinates of the vertex.

● **SOLUTION**

To find a and b, rewrite the function as $f(x) = 2x^2 + 8x + 19$. Then $a = 2$ and $b = 8$.

PROBLEM SOLVING

Use a formula. The axis of symmetry is $x = -\dfrac{b}{2a}$.

$x = -\dfrac{8}{2(2)} = -2$ ⌐ $f(x) = 19 + 8x + 2x^2$

└→ $f(-2) = 19 + 8(-2) + 2(-2)^2$ *Substitute −2 for x.*

$f(-2) = 11$

Thus, the equation for the axis of symmetry is $x = -2$, and the coordinates of the vertex are $(-2, 11)$.

TRY THIS   Let $g(x) = x^2 - 4x + 1$. Write the equation for the axis of symmetry of the graph, and find the coordinates of the vertex.

CRITICAL THINKING   What do you know about an equation that has integer solutions when it is solved by using the quadratic formula?

Exercises

● *Communicate*

1. Describe at least three methods you can use to find the x-intercepts of the parabola described by $f(x) = x^2 + 2x - 3$.

2. Describe two ways to find the vertex of a parabola.

3. How is the axis of symmetry related to the vertex of a parabola?

Guided Skills Practice

Use the quadratic formula to find the roots of each equation.
(EXAMPLE 1)

4. $x^2 - 5x + 4 = 0$ **5.** $2x^2 - 5x = 3$

6. Use the quadratic formula to solve $3x^2 - 3x = 4$. Give exact solutions and approximate solutions to the nearest tenth. *(EXAMPLE 2)*

APPLICATION

7. CONSTRUCTION If the Wilkersons have enough material to cover a surface area of 700 square feet, then the equation becomes $x^2 + 55x = 700$. Find the width of the patio, to the nearest tenth of a foot, from this equation. *(EXAMPLE 3)*

For each function, write the equation for the axis of symmetry of the graph, and find the coordinates of the vertex. *(EXAMPLE 4)*

8. $f(x) = x^2 - x - 2$ **9.** $f(x) = 2x^2 - 12x + 11$

Practice and Apply

internet connect

**Homework
Help Online**
Go To: **go.hrw.com**
Keyword:
MB1 Homework Help
for Exercises 10–27

Use the quadratic formula to solve each equation. Give exact solutions.

10. $x^2 + 7x + 9 = 0$ **11.** $x^2 + 6x = 0$

12. $(x + 1)(x - 2) = 5$ **13.** $(x - 4)(x + 5) = 7$

14. $t^2 - 9t + 5 = 0$ **15.** $x^2 - 3x - 1 = 0$

16. $x^2 + 9x - 2 = -16$ **17.** $x^2 - 5x - 6 = 18$

18. $5x^2 + 16x - 6 = 3$ **19.** $4x^2 = -8x - 3$

20. $3x^2 - 3 = -5x - 1$ **21.** $x^2 + 3x = 2 - 2x$

22. $x^2 + 6x + 5 = 0$ **23.** $x^2 + 10x = 5$

24. $-2x^2 + 4x = -2$ **25.** $5x^2 - 2x - 3 = 0$

26. $-6x^2 + 3x + 19 = 0$ **27.** $-x^2 - 3x + 1 = 0$

For each quadratic function, write the equation for the axis of symmetry, and find the coordinates of the vertex.

28. $y = 7x^2 + 6x - 5$ **29.** $y = x^2 + 9x + 14$

internet connect

**Activities
Online**
Go To: **go.hrw.com**
Keyword:
MB1 QuadFormula

30. $y = 3 + 7x + 2x^2$ **31.** $y = 10 - 5x^2 - 15x$

32. $y = 3x^2 + 6x - 18$ **33.** $y = 14 + 8x - 2x^2$

34. $y = 4 - 10x + 5x^2$ **35.** $y = -x^2 - 6x + 2$

36. $y = 3x^2 + 21x - 4$ **37.** $y = -2x^2 + 3x - 1$

38. $y = 3x^2 - 18x + 22$ **39.** $y = -2x^2 + 8x + 13$

40. $y = 3x - 2x^2 + 2$ **41.** $y = -1 - 8x + 12x^2$

42. $y = 7x^2 - 12x + 2$ **43.** $y = 2x - 2 + x^2$

44. $y = 4x^2 - 3x - 8$ **45.** $y = 9 - 3x^2$

46. $y = 5x - x^2$ **47.** $y = 5x^2 + 2x - 3$

CHALLENGE

48. Prove that if the roots of $ax^2 + bx + c = 0$, where $a \neq 0$, are reciprocals, then $a = c$.

MAXIMUM/MINIMUM A professional pyrotechnician shoots fireworks vertically into the air from the ground with an initial velocity of 192 feet per second. The height in feet of the fireworks is given by $h(t) = -16t^2 + 192t$.

49. How long does it take for the fireworks to reach the maximum height?

50. What is the maximum height reached by the fireworks?

51. Certain fireworks shoot sparks for 2.5 seconds, leaving a trail. After how many seconds might the pyrotechnician want the fireworks to begin firing in order for the sparks to be at the maximum height? Explain.

APPLICATIONS

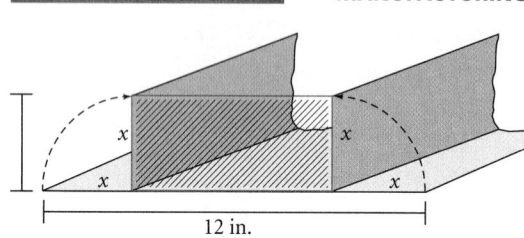

12 in.

MANUFACTURING To form a rectangular rain gutter from a flat sheet of aluminum that is 12 inches wide, an equal amount of aluminum, x, is bent up on each side, as shown at left. The area of the cross section is 18 square inches.

52. Write a quadratic equation to model the area of the cross section.

53. Find the depth of the gutter.

BUSINESS The owner of a company that produces handcrafted music stands hires a consultant to help set the selling price for the product. The consultant analyzes the production costs and consumer demand for the stands and arrives at a function for the profit, $P(x) = -0.3x^2 + 75x - 2000$, where x represents the selling price of the stands.

54. At what price should the stands be sold to earn the maximum profit?

55. According to the function given, what is the maximum profit that the company can make?

56. What are the break-even points (the selling prices for which the profit is 0)? Give your answers to the nearest cent.

57. For what values of x does the company make a profit?

58. For what values of x does the company suffer a loss?

CHALLENGE

59. ART In the art of many cultures, a ratio called the *golden ratio*, or *golden mean*, has been used as an organizing principle because it produces designs that are deemed naturally pleasing to the eye. The golden mean is based on the division of a line segment into two parts, a and b, such that the ratio of the longer segment, a, to the shorter segment, b, equals the ratio of the whole segment, $a + b$, to the longer segment, a.
  a. Solve the golden ratio for a in terms of b.
  b. Find the value of the golden ratio. Give the exact value and the approximate value to the nearest hundredth. (Hint: Divide each side of the equation from part **a** by b, and simplify.)

Write an equation in slope-intercept form for the line that contains the given point and is perpendicular to the given line. *(LESSON 1.3)*

60. $(-2, 3), y = x - 5$

61. $(4, -6), 2x - y = 1$

Write an equation in slope-intercept form for the line that contains the given point and is parallel to the given line. *(LESSON 1.3)*

62. $(8, -1), y = -3x + 12$

63. $(-4, -2), 5x = 4 - y$

Solve each absolute-value inequality. Graph the solution on a number line. *(LESSON 1.8)*

64. $|x + 6| > 2$ **65.** $|x - 3| < 5$ **66.** $|-4x| \le 8$ **67.** $|8 - 2x| \ge 6$

Find the inverse of each matrix, if it exists. Round numbers to the nearest hundredth. Indicate if the matrix does not have an inverse. *(LESSON 4.3)*

68. $\begin{bmatrix} -3 & 2 \\ 12 & 9 \end{bmatrix}$

69. $\begin{bmatrix} -1 & 8 \\ 4 & -7 \end{bmatrix}$

70. $\begin{bmatrix} 6 & -4 & 18 \\ 21 & -3 & 19 \\ 4 & 5 & -2 \end{bmatrix}$

Solve each equation. *(LESSON 5.2)*

71. $-2x^2 = -16$ **72.** $-3x^2 + 15 = -6$ **73.** $32 = 2x^2 - 4$

 Look Beyond

74. Use the quadratic formula to solve $2x^2 + 5x + 6 = 0$. Can you find a real-number solution? Explain.

SPORTS Use the quadratic formula and the formula for the axis of symmetry of a parabola to answer the questions below based on the height function from the Portfolio Activity on page 280.

1. What is the equation of the axis of symmetry for the model?

2. What is the maximum height achieved by the basketball?

3. How long does it take the basketball to reach its maximum height?

4. How much time would it take the basketball to drop to the ground if it were not tapped?

5. Compare your answers to the questions above with those obtained in the Portfolio Activities on pages 280, 298, and 306.

WORKING ON THE CHAPTER PROJECT

You should now be able to complete Activity 2 of the Chapter Project.

Quadratic Equations and Complex Numbers

Why *Solutions to many real-world problems, such as classifying a shock absorber spring system, involve complex numbers.*

Objectives

- Classify and find all roots of a quadratic equation.
- Graph and perform operations on complex numbers.

Overdamped	Critically damped	Underdamped

2 real roots	1 real root	0 real roots

Each diagram represents the motion of a shock absorber spring over a period of 2 seconds from left to right.

APPLICATION

ENGINEERING

Carlos and Keiko are mechanical engineers who are analyzing car shock absorbers. They know that the motion of the spring is affected by a damping force. Three situations are possible depending on how the mass of the car, the spring, and the damping force are related. The roots of $x^2 + mx + n = 0$, where m and n depend on the car's mass, the spring, and the damping force, help them to classify a spring system. *You will classify a spring system after Example 1.*

The Discriminant

When you apply the quadratic formula to any quadratic equation, you will find that the value of $b^2 - 4ac$ is either positive, negative, or 0. The expression $b^2 - 4ac$ is called the **discriminant** of a quadratic equation.

You can see from the quadratic formula that if $b^2 - 4ac > 0$, the formula will give two different answers. If $b^2 - 4ac = 0$, there will be one answer, called a **double root**. If $b^2 - 4ac < 0$, the radical will be undefined for real numbers, so the formula gives no real solutions.

Solutions of a Quadratic Equation

Let $ax^2 + bx + c = 0$, where $a \neq 0$.

- If $b^2 - 4ac > 0$, then the quadratic equation has 2 distinct real solutions.
- If $b^2 - 4ac = 0$, then the equation has 1 real solution, a double root.
- If $b^2 - 4ac < 0$, then the equation has 0 real solutions.

EXAMPLE **1** Find the discriminant for each equation. Then determine the number of real solutions for each equation by using the discriminant.

a. $2x^2 + 4x + 1 = 0$ **b.** $2x^2 + 4x + 2 = 0$ **c.** $2x^2 + 4x + 3 = 0$

SOLUTION

a. $2x^2 + 4x + 1 = 0$
$b^2 - 4ac$
$= 4^2 - 4(2)(1)$
$= 8$

Because $b^2 - 4ac > 0$, the equation has 2 real solutions.

b. $2x^2 + 4x + 2 = 0$
$b^2 - 4ac$
$= 4^2 - 4(2)(2)$
$= 0$

Because $b^2 - 4ac = 0$, the equation has 1 real solution.

c. $2x^2 + 4x + 3 = 0$
$b^2 - 4ac$
$= 4^2 - 4(2)(3)$
$= -8$

Because $b^2 - 4ac < 0$, the equation has no real solutions.

CHECK

Graph the related functions to check.

TECHNOLOGY
GRAPHICS
CALCULATOR

The graph of $y = 2x^2 + 4x + 1$ shows that $2x^2 + 4x + 1 = 0$ for two different values of x.

The graph of $y = 2x^2 + 4x + 2$ shows that $2x^2 + 4x + 2 = 0$ for one value of x.

The graph of $y = 2x^2 + 4x + 3$ shows that $2x^2 + 4x + 3 = 0$ for no real x.

TRY THIS   Identify the number of real solutions to $-3x^2 - 6x + 15 = 0$.

CHECKPOINT ✔ Refer to the shock-absorber situation described on page 314. Classify a spring system in which $m = 8$ and $n = 24$.

Complex Numbers

CULTURAL CONNECTION: EUROPE Whether it is possible to take the square root of a negative number is a question that puzzled mathematicians for a long time. In the sixteenth century, Italian mathematician Girolamo Cardano (1501–1576) was the first to use complex numbers to solve quadratic equations. Leonhard Euler (1707–1783) defined the **imaginary unit**, *i*, such that $i = \sqrt{-1}$ and $i^2 = -1$. In the nineteenth century, the theoretical basis of complex numbers was rigorously developed.

Leonhard Euler

Girolamo Cardano

Imaginary Numbers

If $r > 0$, then the **imaginary number** $\sqrt{-r}$ is defined as follows:
$$\sqrt{-r} = \sqrt{-1} \cdot \sqrt{r} = i\sqrt{r}$$

For example, $\sqrt{-4} = \sqrt{-1} \cdot \sqrt{4} = 2i$ and $\sqrt{-6} = \sqrt{-1} \cdot \sqrt{6} = i\sqrt{6}$.

With the quadratic formula and the imaginary unit, i, you can find solutions to any quadratic equation. This is shown in Example 2.

EXAMPLE ❷ Use the quadratic formula to solve $3x^2 - 7x + 5 = 0$.

● **SOLUTION**

$$x = \frac{-(-7) \pm \sqrt{(-7)^2 - 4(3)(5)}}{2(3)}$$ *Substitute $a = 3$, $b = -7$, and $c = 5$.*

$$x = \frac{7 \pm \sqrt{-11}}{6}$$

$$x = \frac{7}{6} + \frac{\sqrt{-11}}{6} \quad or \quad x = \frac{7}{6} - \frac{\sqrt{-11}}{6}$$

$$x = \frac{7}{6} + \frac{i\sqrt{11}}{6} \qquad\qquad x = \frac{7}{6} - \frac{i\sqrt{11}}{6}$$ *Replace $\sqrt{-11}$ with $i\sqrt{11}$.*

> The numbers $\frac{7}{6} + \frac{i\sqrt{11}}{6}$ and $\frac{7}{6} - \frac{i\sqrt{11}}{6}$ are complex numbers.

TRY THIS Use the quadratic formula to solve $-4x^2 + 5x - 3 = 0$.

Complex Numbers

A **complex number** is any number that can be written as $a + bi$, where a and b are real numbers and $i = \sqrt{-1}$; a is called the **real part** and b is called the **imaginary part**.

The form $a + bi$ is called the *standard form* of a complex number. Real numbers are complex numbers for which $b = 0$. A complex number is called a *pure* imaginary number if its real part, a, is 0.

EXAMPLE ❸ Find x and y such that $7x - 2iy = 14 + 6i$.

● **SOLUTION**

Two complex numbers are equal if their real parts are equal and their imaginary parts are equal.

Real parts	Imaginary parts
$7x = 14$	$-2y = 6$
$x = 2$	$y = -3$

Thus, $x = 2$ and $y = -3$.

TRY THIS Find x and y such that $2x + 3iy = -8 + 10i$.

EXAMPLE **4** **Find each sum or difference.**

    a. $(-3 + 5i) + (7 - 6i)$ **b.** $(-3 - 8i) - (-2 - 9i)$

SOLUTION

Add or subtract the corresponding real parts and imaginary parts.

    a. $(-3 + 5i) + (7 - 6i)$ **b.** $(-3 - 8i) - (-2 - 9i)$

        $= (-3 + 7) + (5i - 6i)$ $= (-3 + 2) - (8i - 9i)$

        $= 4 - 1i$ $= -1 + 1i$

        $= 4 - i$ $= -1 + i$

Two complex numbers whose real parts are opposites and whose imaginary parts are opposites are called *additive inverses*.

$$(4 + 3i) + (-4 - 3i) = 0 + 0i = 0$$

CHECKPOINT ✔ What is the additive inverse of $2i - 12$?

EXAMPLE **5** **Multiply $(2 + i)(-5 - 3i)$.**

SOLUTION

$(2 + i)(-5 - 3i) = 2(-5 - 3i) + i(-5 - 3i)$ *Apply the Distributive Property.*

               $= -10 - 6i - 5i - 3i^2$

               $= -10 - 11i - 3(-1)$ *Replace i^2 with -1.*

               $= -7 - 11i$

TRY THIS   Multiply $(6 - 4i)(5 - 4i)$.

Exploring Powers of i

You will need: no special materials

1. Copy and complete the table below. (Hint: Recall that $i^2 = -1$.)

i	$i^2 =$	$i^3 =$	$i^4 =$
$i^5 =$	$i^6 =$	$i^7 =$	$i^8 =$

2. Observe the patterns in the table above. Use your observations to complete the table below.

$i^9 =$	$i^{10} =$	$i^{11} =$	$i^{12} =$
$i^{13} =$	$i^{14} =$	$i^{15} =$	$i^{16} =$

CHECKPOINT ✔   **3.** Describe the pattern that occurs in the powers of i. Explain how to use the pattern to evaluate i^{41}, i^{66}, i^{75}, and i^{100}.

In order to simplify a fraction containing complex numbers, you often need to use the *conjugate of a complex number*. For example, the conjugate of $2 + 5i$ is $2 - 5i$ and the conjugate of $1 - 3i$ is $1 + 3i$.

Conjugate of a Complex Number

The **conjugate** of a complex number $a + bi$ is $a - bi$. The conjugate of $a + bi$ is denoted $\overline{a + bi}$.

To simplify a quotient with an imaginary number in the denominator, multiply by a fraction equal to 1, using the conjugate of the denominator, as shown in Example 6. This process is called **rationalizing the denominator.**

E X A M P L E **6** Simplify $\frac{2 + 5i}{2 - 3i}$. **Write your answer in standard form.**

● **SOLUTION**

$\frac{2 + 5i}{2 - 3i} = \frac{2 + 5i}{2 - 3i} \cdot \frac{2 + 3i}{2 + 3i}$ *Multiply by 1, using the conjugate of the denominator.*

$= \frac{(2 + 5i)(2 + 3i)}{(2 - 3i)(2 + 3i)}$

$= \frac{4 + 10i + 6i + 15i^2}{4 - 6i + 6i - 9i^2}$

$= \frac{-11 + 16i}{13}$

$= -\frac{11}{13} + \frac{16}{13}i$

CHECK

In complex mode, enter the expression. Then express the answer with fractions.

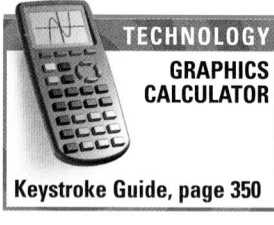
TECHNOLOGY

GRAPHICS CALCULATOR

Keystroke Guide, page 350

Note that the last term is $\frac{16}{13}i$, not $\frac{16}{13i}$.

```
(2+5i)/(2-3i)
-.8461538462+1....
Ans▶Frac
    -11/13+(16/13)i
```

TRY THIS

Simplify $\frac{3 - 4i}{2 + i}$. Write your answer in standard form.

CRITICAL THINKING

Show that if a complex number is equal to its conjugate, the number is real.

C O N N E C T I O N

COORDINATE GEOMETRY

Complex numbers are graphed in the *complex plane*. In the **complex plane**, the horizontal axis is called the **real axis** and the vertical axis is called the **imaginary axis.** To graph the complex number $a + bi$, plot the point (a, b). For example, the point $(3, 2)$ represents the complex number $3 + 2i$ and the point $(-3, -4)$ represents the complex number $-3 - 4i$.

The absolute value of a real number is its distance from zero on the number line. Likewise, the **absolute value of a complex number** $a + bi$, denoted by $|a + bi|$, is its distance from the origin in the complex plane. By the Pythagorean Theorem, $|a + bi| = \sqrt{a^2 + b^2}$. For example, $|3 + 2i| = \sqrt{3^2 + 2^2} = \sqrt{13}$ and $|-3 - 4i| = \sqrt{(-3)^2 + (-4)^2} = 5$.

EXAMPLE **7** Evaluate $|-2 - 3i|$. Sketch a diagram that shows $-2 - 3i$ and $|-2 - 3i|$.

● **SOLUTION**

$$|-2 - 3i| = \sqrt{(-2)^2 + (-3)^2}$$
$$= \sqrt{4 + 9}$$
$$= \sqrt{13}$$

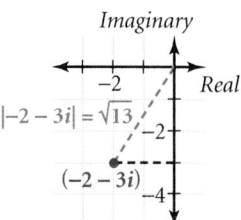

TRY THIS   Evaluate $|-3 + 5i|$. Sketch a diagram that shows $-3 + 5i$ and $|-3 + 5i|$.

CRITICAL THINKING   The real numbers are said to be "well-ordered," meaning that any real number is either larger or smaller than any other given real number. Are the complex numbers well-ordered? Explain.

Exercises

● *Communicate*

1. What can the discriminant tell you about the solutions of a quadratic equation?

2. How do you simplify a rational expression that contains a complex number in the denominator?

3. How do you graph a real number in the complex plane? a pure imaginary number?

● *Guided Skills Practice*

Determine the number of real solutions for each equation. *(EXAMPLE 1)*

4. $x^2 + 2x + 1 = 0$ 5. $2x^2 + 4x + 5 = 0$ 6. $x^2 + 3x + 1 = 0$

7. Solve the equation $2x^2 + 5x + 4 = 0$. *(EXAMPLE 2)*

8. Find x and y such that $-2x + 3yi = 2 + 6i$. *(EXAMPLE 3)*

Simplify each expression.

9. $(2 + 3i) + (4 + 7i)$ *(EXAMPLE 4)*

10. $(8 + 4i) - (3 + 2i)$ *(EXAMPLE 4)*

11. $(-1 + 2i)(3 + 4i)$ *(EXAMPLE 5)*

12. $\dfrac{-1 + 4i}{2 + 3i}$ *(EXAMPLE 6)*

13. Evaluate $|3 + 4i|$. Sketch a diagram that shows $3 + 4i$ and $|3 + 4i|$. *(EXAMPLE 7)*

Practice and Apply

Identify the real and imaginary parts of each complex number.

14. $-5 + 6i$ **15.** $2 + i$ **16.** 6 **17.** $4i$

Simplify.

18. $\sqrt{-36}$ **19.** $\sqrt{-100}$ **20.** $\sqrt{-13}$

21. $\sqrt{-17}$ **22.** $(-3i)^2$ **23.** $(-7i)^2$

Find the discriminant, and determine the number of real solutions. Then solve.

24. $x^2 + 5x + 8 = 0$ **25.** $3x^2 - 5x + 4 = 0$ **26.** $x^2 - 7x = -10$

27. $5x^2 - 5x + 2 = 0$ **28.** $-x^2 + 8x - 19 = 0$ **29.** $x^2 - 3x = 7$

30. $-2x^2 + 10x = 15$ **31.** $2x^2 - 6x = -5$ **32.** $4x^2 + x - 2 = 0$

33. $2x^2 + 3x = 0$ **34.** $5x^2 + 4x = -5$ **35.** $2x^2 + 2x + 2 = 0$

36. $16 - 8x = -x^2$ **37.** $x^2 + 49 = 14x$ **38.** $-x^2 + 4x - 5 = 0$

39. $8x^2 + 5x + 2 = 0$ **40.** $4x^2 + 9 = 12x$ **41.** $1 + 9x^2 = 6x$

Find x and y.

42. $6x + 7iy = 18 - 21i$ **43.** $3x - 4iy = 4 + 4i$ **44.** $2x + 5i = 8 + 20yi$

Perform the indicated addition or subtraction.

45. $(-2 + 3i) + (-1 - 4i)$ **46.** $(1 + 2i) - (1 + 5i)$ **47.** $\left(\frac{1}{2} + \frac{2}{5}i\right) + \left(\frac{1}{2} - \frac{1}{5}i\right)$

48. $\left(\frac{3}{8} + \frac{2}{3}i\right) - \left(\frac{1}{4} - \frac{1}{3}i\right)$ **49.** $(3 + i) + (6 - 2i)$ **50.** $(8 - 6i) - (4 - 3i)$

Multiply.

51. $i(2 + i)$ **52.** $(1 + i)(1 - i)$ **53.** $(-5 - i)(-2 + 2i)$

54. $(-5 + 3i)(2 - 3i)$ **55.** $(6 - 7i)^2$ **56.** $(2 - 4i)^2$

57. $(-1 + i\sqrt{5})^2$ **58.** $(2 + i\sqrt{3})^2$ **59.** $(2 - 3i\sqrt{2})^2$

Write the conjugate of each complex number.

60. $2 + 3i$ **61.** 8 **62.** $-4 - i$ **63.** $8 - 3i$

Simplify.

64. $\frac{4 + 2i}{2 + i}$ **65.** $\frac{3 + 2i}{5 + i}$ **66.** $\left(\frac{1}{2} + i\right)\left(\frac{2}{3} + \frac{1}{4}i\right)$

67. $\frac{4 + 2i}{\frac{2}{3} + \frac{1}{2}i}$ **68.** $2(3 - 2i) + 5(1 + i)$ **69.** $\frac{1}{4}(1 + i\sqrt{3})(1 - i\sqrt{3})$

70. $(1 + i)^2 + \frac{2 + 2i}{2 + i}$ **71.** $\frac{3 + i}{4 + i} + 1 + i$ **72.** $(-3i)(3i) - (2 + 2i)$

73. $i(1 + i) - (3 + i)$ **74.** $i^3(5 + i) + 7i$ **75.** $\left(\frac{\sqrt{2}}{2} + \frac{\sqrt{2}}{2}i\right)^2$

Graph each number and its conjugate in the complex plane.

76. $5 + 3i$ **77.** $-2 + 4i$ **78.** $-3 - 5i$ **79.** $2 - 3i$

80. $-2i$ **81.** $6i$ **82.** $-2 + 7i$ **83.** $-7 - 2i$

84. -4 **85.** $5 + i$ **86.** $3 - 5i$ **87.** 3

Evaluate. Then sketch a diagram that shows the absolute value.

88. $|1 + i|$ **89.** $|i|$ **90.** $\left|\frac{3}{5} + \frac{4}{5}i\right|$ **91.** $\left|1 + 0.01i\right|$

92. $|2i|$ **93.** $|2 + 3i|$ **94.** $\left|\frac{1}{\sqrt{2}} + \frac{1}{\sqrt{2}}i\right|$ **95.** $\left|\frac{1}{\sqrt{3}} + \frac{\sqrt{2}}{\sqrt{3}}i\right|$

96. Identify the complex numbers graphed on the complex plane at right.

97. Identify the coordinates of the conjugate of each complex number graphed at right.

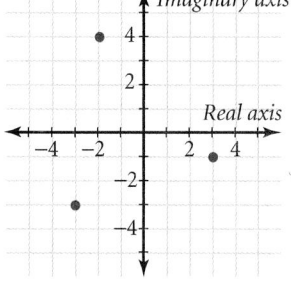

CHALLENGES

98. If $\overline{c + di} = -(c + di)$, what can you say about the complex number $c + di$? (Hint: Solve for c.)

99. Let $a > 0$ and $b > 0$. Plot $a + bi$, $a - bi$, $-(a + bi)$, and $-a + bi$ in the complex plane. Connect the points with vertical and horizontal lines. What is the result?

CONNECTION

100. **TRANSFORMATIONS** Describe the relationship between the graph of a complex number and the graph of its conjugate as a translation, rotation, or reflection.

 Look Back

Graph each function and its inverse on the same coordinate plane. *(LESSON 2.5)*

101. $f(x) = 2x - 3$ **102.** $f(x) = -3x + 5$ **103.** $f(x) = 2x$

Let $f(x) = 3x - 5$. Find the indicated function. *(LESSONS 2.4 AND 2.5)*

104. $f^{-1}(x)$ **105.** $(f \circ f^{-1})(x)$ **106.** $(f^{-1} \circ f)(x)$

APPLICATIONS

107. **BUSINESS** Gene ordered 8 prints for his new restaurant. Each unframed print cost $50, and each framed print cost $98. The total cost of the prints was $640. How many framed prints did Gene buy? *(LESSONS 3.1 AND 3.2)*

108. **RECYCLING** A recycling center pays $1.25 for 100 pounds of newspaper and $0.40 for 1 pound of aluminum. Linda took a 460-pound load of aluminum and newspaper to the recycling center and was paid $21.82. How many pounds of aluminum and how many pounds of newspaper did Linda have? *(LESSONS 3.1 AND 3.2)*

 Look Beyond

Predict the zeros and verify by graphing.

109 $f(x) = (x - 2)(x + 3)(x + 5)$ **110** $f(x) = x(x - 6)(x + 1)$

111 $f(x) = x^3 + x^2 - 2x$ **112** $f(x) = x^3 + 2x^2 + x$

Curve Fitting With Quadratic Models

Objectives

● Find a quadratic function that exactly fits three data points.

● Find a quadratic model to represent a data set.

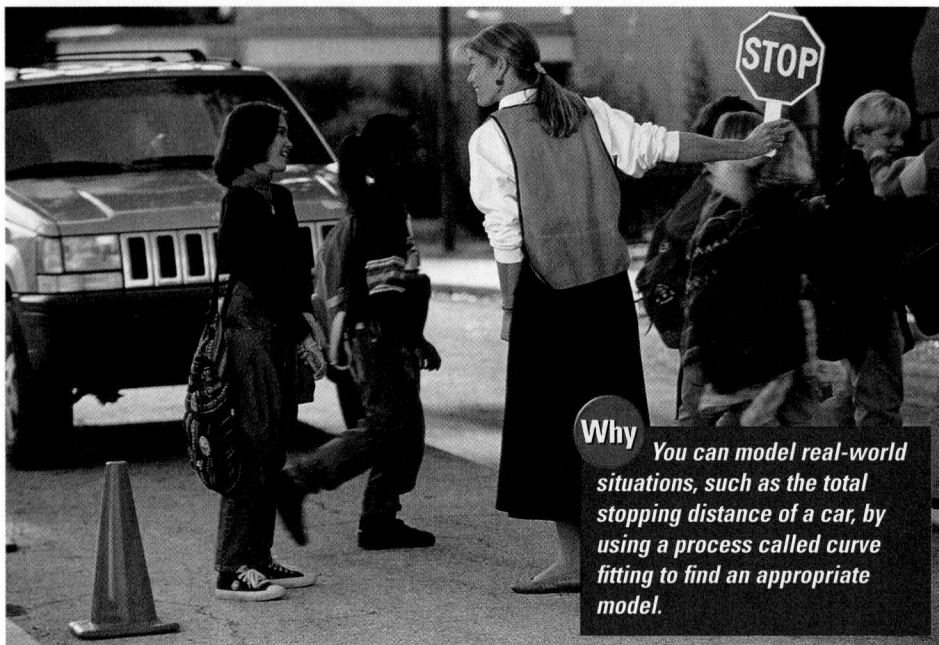

Why *You can model real-world situations, such as the total stopping distance of a car, by using a process called curve fitting to find an appropriate model.*

Traffic speeds are reduced in school zones for improved safety of students.

Fitting a set of data with a quadratic model is an example of *curve fitting*. In Lesson 5.1, you examined a quadratic model for the total stopping distance, d, in feet as a function of a car's speed, x, in miles per hour.

$$d(x) = \frac{11}{10}x + \frac{1}{19}x^2$$

This function models actual data that is provided in Lesson 2.4. Another set of data for speed and stopping distance is shown at right. How can you find a quadratic model for this data? *You will answer this question in Example 3.*

Speed (mph)	Stopping distance (ft)
10	12.5
20	36.0
30	69.5
40	114.0
50	169.5
60	249.0
70	325.5

Some graphics calculators can fit a parabola to three noncollinear points. Example 1 illustrates another method that you can use.

EXAMPLE ① Find a quadratic function whose graph contains the points $(1, 3)$, $(2, -3)$, and $(6, 13)$.

● **SOLUTION**

1. To find a, b, and c in $f(x) = ax^2 + bx + c$, write and solve a system of three linear equations in three variables, a, b, and c.

Point	Substitution	Equation
$(1, 3)$	$a(1)^2 + b(1) + c = 3$	$a + b + c = 3$
$(2, -3)$	$a(2)^2 + b(2) + c = -3$	$4a + 2b + c = -3$
$(6, 13)$	$a(6)^2 + b(6) + c = 13$	$36a + 6b + c = 13$

$$\begin{cases} a + b + c = 3 \\ 4a + 2b + c = -3 \\ 36a + 6b + c = 13 \end{cases}$$

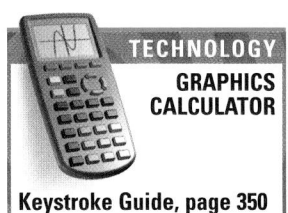
2. Use a matrix equation to solve the system.

$$\begin{bmatrix} 1 & 1 & 1 \\ 4 & 2 & 1 \\ 36 & 6 & 1 \end{bmatrix} \begin{bmatrix} a \\ b \\ c \end{bmatrix} = \begin{bmatrix} 3 \\ -3 \\ 13 \end{bmatrix} \rightarrow \begin{bmatrix} a \\ b \\ c \end{bmatrix} = \begin{bmatrix} 2 \\ -12 \\ 13 \end{bmatrix}$$

The solution is $a = 2$, $b = -12$, and $c = 13$.

3. Write the quadratic function.

$$f(x) = ax^2 + bx + c$$
$$f(x) = 2x^2 - 12x + 13$$

CHECK

Create a scatter plot of the three data points. Graph $f(x) = 2x^2 - 12x + 13$ on the same screen. The graph should contain the data points.

TRY THIS Find a quadratic function whose graph contains the points $(2, -3)$, $(4, 3)$, and $(6, 1)$.

When variables in a table represent a quadratic relationship, a constant difference in the consecutive x-values results in a constant *second difference* in the respective y-values. This fact is used in Example 2 to help determine whether a quadratic model is appropriate for a set of data.

E X A M P L E ② Refer to the pattern of dots below, in which each set of dots except the first is formed by adding a bottom row containing 1 more dot than the previous bottom row.

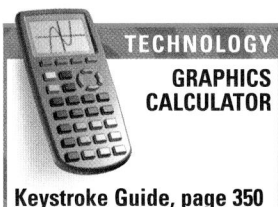
$$d = 1 \qquad d = 3 \qquad d = 6 \qquad d = 10 \qquad d = 15$$
$$n = 1 \qquad n = 2 \qquad n = 3 \qquad n = 4 \qquad n = 5 \qquad \text{and so on...}$$

a. Explain why a quadratic model is suitable for relating the number of dots, d, in the triangle to the number of dots, n, on each side of the triangle.
b. Find a quadratic function for d in terms of n.
c. Use the model to predict the number of dots in a triangle with 10 dots on each side.

SOLUTION

a. Make a scatter plot of points, (n, d). Use $(1, 1)$, $(2, 3)$, $(3, 6)$, $(4, 10)$, and $(5, 15)$. It appears that a curve rather than a straight line will fit the data.

CONNECTION
STATISTICS

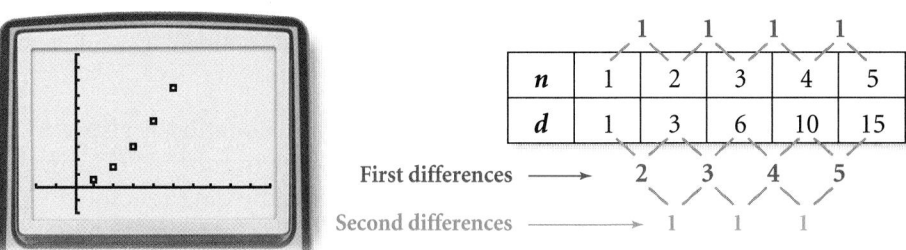

n	1	2	3	4	5
d	1	3	6	10	15

First differences ⟶ 2 3 4 5

Second differences ⟶ 1 1 1

PROBLEM SOLVING

Look for a pattern. Because the second differences are constant, there will be a quadratic equation that models the data exactly.

b. To find a, b, and c in $d = an^2 + bn + c$, write and solve a system of three linear equations in three variables a, b, and c.

Point	Evaluation	Equation
$(1, 1)$	$a(1)^2 + b(1) + c = 1$	$a + b + c = 1$
$(2, 3)$	$a(2)^2 + b(2) + c = 3$	$4a + 2b + c = 3$
$(3, 6)$	$a(3)^2 + b(3) + c = 6$	$9a + 3b + c = 6$

$$\begin{cases} a + b + c = 1 \\ 4a + 2b + c = 3 \\ 9a + 3b + c = 6 \end{cases}$$

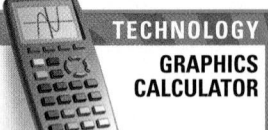

Keystroke Guide, page 351

Use a matrix equation to solve the system.

$$\begin{bmatrix} 1 & 1 & 1 \\ 4 & 2 & 1 \\ 9 & 3 & 1 \end{bmatrix} \begin{bmatrix} a \\ b \\ c \end{bmatrix} = \begin{bmatrix} 1 \\ 3 \\ 6 \end{bmatrix} \rightarrow \begin{bmatrix} a \\ b \\ c \end{bmatrix} = \begin{bmatrix} 0.5 \\ 0.5 \\ 0 \end{bmatrix}$$

The solution is $a = 0.5$, $b = 0.5$, and $c = 0$.

Write the quadratic function.

$$d(n) = 0.5n^2 + 0.5n$$

CHECK

Check that the fourth and fifth data points satisfy $d(n) = 0.5n^2 + 0.5n$.

$d(n) = 0.5n^2 + 0.5n$	$d(n) = 0.5n^2 + 0.5n$
$10 \stackrel{?}{=} 0.5(4)^2 + 0.5(4)$	$15 \stackrel{?}{=} 0.5(5)^2 + 0.5(5)$
$10 = 8 + 2$ **True**	$15 = 12.5 + 2.5$ **True**

Thus, $d(n) = 0.5n^2 + 0.5n$ models the pattern of dots.

c. Evaluate d for $n = 10$.

$$d(n) = 0.5n^2 + 0.5n$$
$$d(10) = 0.5(10)^2 + 0.5(10)$$
$$= 55$$

Thus, a triangle with 10 dots on each side would contain a total of 55 dots.

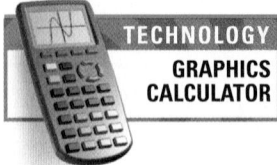

In Example 1, part **b**, you can also use a statistical model to find a quadratic function for d in terms of n. Enter the data, and use the keystrokes below to find a quadratic regression model for the dot pattern.

The quadratic regression equation is also $d(n) = 0.5n^2 + 0.5n$. Because the second differences for the number of dots in the triangle pattern are constant, this quadratic model fits the data exactly.

CRITICAL THINKING

Explain why you can always find a quadratic function to fit any three noncollinear points in the coordinate plane.

Modeling Real-World Data

Real-world data typically do not conform perfectly to a particular mathematical model. Just as you can use a linear function to represent data that show a linear pattern, you can use a quadratic function to model data that follow a parabolic pattern. In Example 3, you find a quadratic regression model to represent real-world data.

EXAMPLE ③ Make a scatter plot of the data below. Find a quadratic model to represent this data.

APPLICATION
HIGHWAY SAFETY

Speed (mph)	Stopping distance (ft)
10	12.5
20	36.0
30	69.5
40	114.0
50	169.5
60	249.0
70	325.5

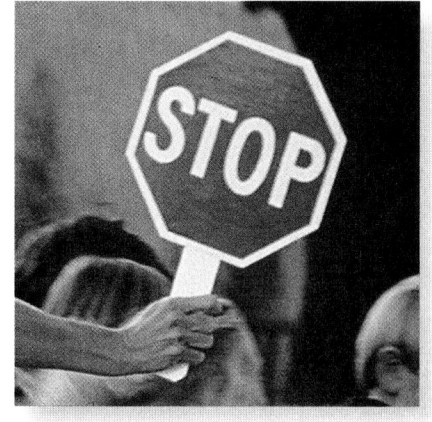

● **SOLUTION**

The scatter plot is shown at right.

The data appear to follow a parabolic pattern. Use the quadratic regression feature of a graphics calculator to find a quadratic model.

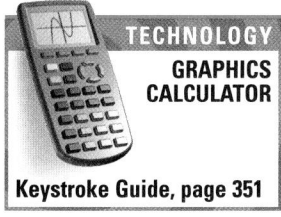

TECHNOLOGY

GRAPHICS CALCULATOR

Keystroke Guide, page 351

Notice that the regression equation fits the data points very closely, but not exactly.

According to this data, the quadratic model for the stopping distance, y, in terms of the car's speed, x, is $y \approx 0.06x^2 + 0.31x + 4$.

CHECKPOINT ✔ Explain why a quadratic model for stopping distance depends on the actual data from which it is obtained. Discuss the circumstances of the situation, such as the road conditions, the reaction time of the driver, and the condition of the brakes.

Collecting and Modeling Data Electronically

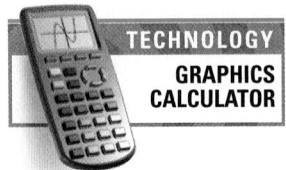

TECHNOLOGY

GRAPHICS CALCULATOR

You will need: a graphics calculator and a motion detector

This Activity involves tossing a ball vertically into the air, using a motion detector to measure its height over the elapsed time, using a graph to represent the data, and finding a quadratic model for the data.

1. Using a graphics calculator with a motion detector, collect data (elapsed time and height) for the vertical toss of a ball, such as a beach ball.

2. Make a scatter plot for the data. Do the data indicate a linear or quadratic relationship? Explain your response.

CHECKPOINT ✔   3. Find a quadratic model for the data. Give values of a, b, and c to the nearest hundredth.

4. Acceleration due to gravity is about 32 feet per second squared. The value of a in your model represents half of the ball's acceleration due to gravity. Is the value of a in your model reasonable? Explain.

Exercises

Communicate

1. Let the points $(1, 6)$, $(-3, 8)$, and $(5, -2)$ be on a parabola.
   a. Explain how to write a system of equations representing these points.
   b. Explain how to find a quadratic function that fits these points.

2. Describe how to find first and second differences of a data set. What type of function is indicated by a constant first difference? a constant second difference?

Guided Skills Practice

3. Find a quadratic function whose graph contains the points $(2, -8)$, $(5, 1)$, and $(0, 6)$. *(EXAMPLE 1)*

4. Suppose that everyone in a room is required to shake hands with everyone else in the room. *(EXAMPLE 2)*

Number of people, n	Number of handshakes, h
2	1
3	3
4	6
5	
6	

a. Copy and complete the table at left. Explain why a quadratic model is suitable for relating the number of handshakes, h, to the number of people, n.
b. Find a quadratic function for h in terms of n.
c. Use the model to predict the number of handshakes when there are 10 people in the room.

5. HIGHWAY SAFETY The table below appears in a driver's manual.
(EXAMPLE 3)

Stopping Distance on Dry Concrete

Speed (mph)	Reaction distance before applying brakes (ft)*	Braking distance (ft)	Stopping distance (ft)
20	22	22	44
30	33	50	83
40	44	88	132
50	55	138	193
60	66	198	264
70	77	270	347

Safety tests can be used to find a car's stopping distance.

*Assume that perception time is zero seconds and reaction time is $\frac{3}{4}$ seconds. This is optimistic.

a. Make a scatter plot for stopping distance versus speed.
b. Does it appear that a quadratic function would fit the data? If so, find a quadratic function for the stopping distance, d, in terms of the speed, x.

Practice and Apply

6. If the point (2, 3) is on a parabola whose equation is in the form $y = ax^2 + bx + c$, which linear equation in three variables represents the parabola?

$$y = 2x^2 + 3x + c \qquad y = 4a + 2b + c \qquad 2 = 9a + 3b + c$$
$$3 = 4x^2 + 2x + c \qquad 3 = 4a + 2b + c$$

Solve a system of equations in order to find a quadratic function that fits each set of data points exactly.

7. $(1, -1), (2, 5), (3, 13)$ **8.** $(1, 13), (4, 7), (5, -3)$

9. $(2, 18), (6, 10), (8, -6)$ **10.** $(-2, -7), (1, 8), (2, 21)$

11. $(0, 4), (1, 5), (3, 25)$ **12.** $(-3, 7), (-1, -5), (6, 16)$

13. $(0, 15), (2, 5), (3, 6)$ **14.** $(1, 7), (-2, 4), (3, 19)$

15. $(5, 9), (2, 21), (4, 9)$ **16.** $(-1, 5), (4, 5), (8, -13)$

17. $(0, 7), (-2, -3), (2, 13)$ **18.** $(0, 4), (2, 1), (-2, 3)$

19. $(-2, 7), (4, 10), (1, 4)$ **20.** $(4, -4), (-2, 5), (0, 6)$

21. Find a quadratic model for the data points (1, 4), (2, 5), and (3, 10) by using two methods: (1) writing a system of three equations in three variables and solving it and (2) using a graphics calculator to find a quadratic regression equation.

22. **PATTERNS IN DATA** Cubes of various sizes are to be built from unit cubes. The surfaces of the resulting figures are to be painted green.

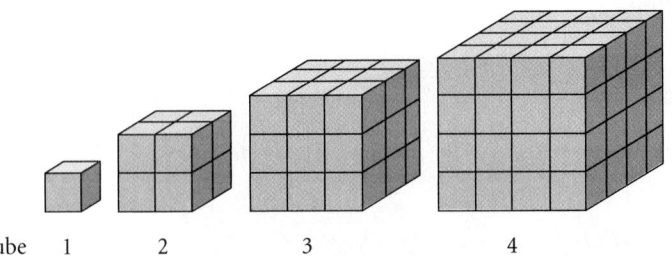

Cube   1   2   3   4

a. Copy and complete the table below.

Cube	Unit cubes with exactly 3 green faces	Unit cubes with exactly 2 green faces	Unit cubes with exactly 1 green face
2	8	0	0
3	8	12	6
4			
5			
6			

b. Find an appropriate model for the data in each column.

c. Use your models to add rows to the table for cubes 7, 8, and 20.

PHYSICS Imagine that an experiment is conducted on Mars in which an object is launched vertically from a height of h_0 above the surface of the planet and with an initial velocity of v_0 in feet per second. The height of the object is measured at three different points in time, and the data are recorded in the table shown at right.

Time (s)	Height (ft)
1	19
2	21
3	11

23. Find a quadratic function that fits the data by solving a system.

24. Find the initial height and the initial velocity of the object.

25. How long will it take for the object to reach its maximum height?

26. What is the maximum height reached by the object?

27. How long after the object is launched will it return to the surface of Mars?

28. Use your function to predict the height of the object when t is 2.5 seconds.

29. Use your function to predict the time(s) when the object is 16 feet above the surface of Mars.

30. **BUSINESS** A small computer company keeps track of its monthly production and profit over three months. The data are shown in the table at left.

a. Use the data in the table to find a quadratic function that describes the profit as a function of the number of computers produced.

b. Use your function to predict the level of production that will maximize the profit.

c. Use your function to predict the maximum profit, assuming that all business conditions stay the same.

Number of computers produced	Profit
50	$5100
100	$5600
150	$1100

APPLICATION

31. PHYSICS With the use of a regulation-size girls' basketball, a graphics calculator, a CBL, and a motion detector, the data below was collected and rounded to the nearest hundredth. Find a quadratic model to represent the data.

Time (s)	0.01	0.11	0.21	0.31	0.41	0.51	0.61	0.71	0.81	0.91
Height (ft)	1.88	3.05	4.13	4.91	5.37	5.50	5.31	4.82	4.00	2.97

 Look Back

Determine whether the inverse of each function below is also a function. (LESSON 2.5)

32. $f(x) = 1 - 2x^2$ **33.** $g(x) = x - 2$ **34.** $h(x) = -\frac{1}{2}x + 3$

35. $f(x) = \frac{1}{3}x - 3$ **36.** $g(x) = \frac{3-x}{2}$ **37.** $h(x) = \frac{2}{x}$

Evaluate. (LESSON 2.6)

38. $[-0.99] + [1.99]$ **39.** $[-2.1 - 1.1]$ **40.** $[-0.3] - [3.7]$

Find the determinant and tell whether each matrix has an inverse. (LESSON 4.3)

41. $\begin{bmatrix} 6 & -4 \\ -1 & 2 \end{bmatrix}$ **42.** $\begin{bmatrix} \frac{1}{3} & 0 \\ 1 & \frac{1}{2} \end{bmatrix}$ **43.** $\begin{bmatrix} \frac{1}{2} & \frac{1}{5} \\ \frac{2}{3} & \frac{1}{10} \end{bmatrix}$ **44.** $\begin{bmatrix} 1 & 0 \\ 0 & 1 \end{bmatrix}$

 Look Beyond

45. Which is the solution to the inequality $x^2 - 16 < 0$?
 a. $x < 4$ **b.** $x > -4$
 c. $-4 < x < 4$ **d.** $x > 4$ or $x < -4$

46. Which is the solution to the inequality $x^2 - 2x - 15 < 0$?
 a. $-3 < x < 5$ **b.** $x < -3$ or $x > 5$
 c. $-5 < x < 3$ **d.** $x < -5$ or $x > 3$

PORTFOLIO ACTIVITY

SPORTS Refer to the basketball data given on page 273 to answer the questions below.

 1. Write and solve a system of equations to find a quadratic function whose graph contains any three points from the basketball data.

 2. Use your calculator to find a quadratic regression model for the three data points.

 3. Do your quadratic models from Steps 1 and 2 agree? How do these models compare with the models used in the Portfolio Activities on pages 280, 298, 306, and 313? Explain.

WORKING ON THE CHAPTER PROJECT

You should now be able to complete the Chapter Project.

Internet connect

Activities Online

Go To: **go.hrw.com**
Keyword:
MB1 Schools

Solving Quadratic Inequalities

Why *You can solve many real-world problems, such as those involving business profits related to revenue and cost, by solving quadratic inequalities.*

Objectives

● Write, solve, and graph a quadratic inequality in one variable.

● Write, solve, and graph a quadratic inequality in two variables.

Katie makes and sells T-shirts. A consultant found that her monthly costs, C, are related to the selling price, p, of the shirts by the function $C(p) = 75p + 2500$. The revenue, R, from the sale of the shirts is represented by $R(p) = -25p^2 + 700p$. Her profit, P, is the difference between the revenue and the costs each month.

$$P(p) = R(p) - C(p)$$
$$= -25p^2 + 700p - (75p + 2500)$$
$$= -25p^2 + 625p - 2500$$

For what range of prices can Katie sell the shirts in order to make a profit? That is, for what values of p will $-25p^2 + 625p - 2500 > 0$? *You will answer this question in Example 2.*

One-Variable Quadratic Inequalities

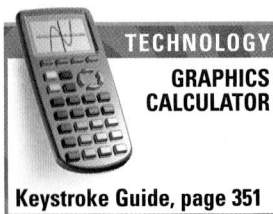

Activity

Exploring Quadratic Inequalities

You will need: a graphics calculator

The display at right shows the values of $f(x) = x^2 - 2x - 3$ for integer values of x between -2 and 4 inclusive.

The table suggests the following three cases:
• When $x = -1$ or $x = 3$, $f(x) = 0$.
• When $x < -1$ or $x > 3$, $f(x) > 0$.
• When $-1 < x < 3$, $f(x) < 0$.

1. Copy and complete the table below. What values of x satisfy each equation or inequality?

Function	Number of x-intercepts	$f(x) = 0$	$f(x) > 0$	$f(x) < 0$
$f(x) = x^2 - 4$	2			
$f(x) = -x^2 + 2x + 3$				

2. Repeat Step 1 for the functions in the table below.

Function	Number of x-intercepts	$f(x) = 0$	$f(x) > 0$	$f(x) < 0$
$f(x) = x^2$	1			
$f(x) = -x^2$				

3. Repeat Step 1 for the functions in the table below.

Function	Number of x-intercepts	$f(x) = 0$	$f(x) > 0$	$f(x) < 0$
$f(x) = -x^2 + x - 1$	0			
$f(x) = x^2 + x + 3$				

CHECKPOINT ✔ **4. a.** If the graph of a quadratic function crosses the x-axis at 2 distinct points, the graph separates the x-axis into __?__ distinct interval(s).
b. If the graph of a quadratic function crosses or touches the x-axis at 1 point, the graph separates the x-axis into __?__ distinct interval(s).
c. If the graph of a quadratic function does not cross the x-axis, the graph separates the x-axis into __?__ distinct interval(s).

You can determine the solution to a given inequality by finding the roots of the related quadratic equation or by using the graph of the related quadratic equation.

E X A M P L E ❶ Solve $x^2 - 2x - 15 \geq 0$. Graph the solution on a number line.

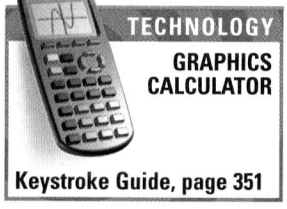

TECHNOLOGY
GRAPHICS CALCULATOR
Keystroke Guide, page 351

● **SOLUTION**

The graph of $y = x^2 - 2x - 15$ indicates that the solution has two parts.

$$x \leq \text{smaller root} \quad or \quad x \geq \text{larger root}$$

$$x^2 - 2x - 15 = 0$$
$$(x + 3)(x - 5) = 0$$
$$x = -3 \quad or \quad x = 5$$

Therefore, the solution to the given inequality is $x \leq -3$ or $x \geq 5$.

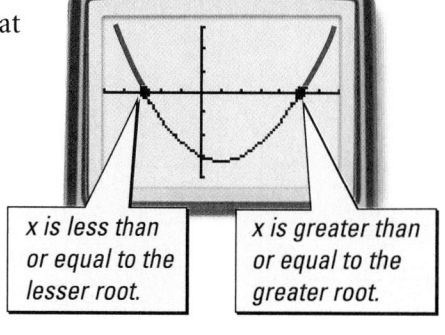

x is less than or equal to the lesser root.

x is greater than or equal to the greater root.

```
 ◄─┼──┼──●──┼──┼──┼──┼──┼──┼──●──┼──►
  -5 -4 -3 -2 -1  0  1  2  3  4  5  6  7
```

TRY THIS Solve $x^2 - 8x + 12 \leq 0$. Graph the solution on a number line.

E X A M P L E ❷ Refer to Katie's T-shirt business from the beginning of the lesson.

APPLICATION

SMALL BUSINESS

TECHNOLOGY

GRAPHICS CALCULATOR

Keystroke Guide, page 351

At what price range can Katie sell her T-shirts in order to make a profit?

● SOLUTION

Use the quadratic formula to find the roots of $-25x^2 + 625x - 2500 = 0$.

$$p = \frac{-b \pm \sqrt{b^2 - 4ac}}{2a}$$

$$p = \frac{-625 \pm \sqrt{625^2 - 4(-25)(-2500)}}{2(-25)}$$

$$p = 5 \quad or \quad p = 20$$

(5, 0)   (20, 0)

The graph of $y = -25x^2 + 625x - 2500$ indicates that the profit is positive *between* the roots of the related equation. If Katie sells her shirts at a price between \$5 and \$20, she will make a profit.

Special types of solutions to quadratic inequalities are shown in Example 3.

E X A M P L E ❸ Solve each inequality.

a. $(x - 2)^2 \geq 0$ **b.** $(x + 3)^2 < 0$ **c.** $2(x + 1)^2 > 0$

● SOLUTION

a. The square of every real number is greater than or equal to 0. Therefore, the solution is all real numbers.

b. The square of a real number cannot be negative. Therefore, there is no solution.

c. The square of any *nonzero* real number is greater than 0. Thus, $2(x + 1)^2 > 0$ is always true unless $x + 1 = 0$, or $x = -1$.

$y = (x - 2)^2$

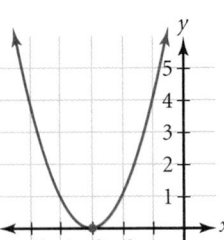

$y = (x + 3)^2$

$y = 2(x + 1)^2$

(−1, 0)

The graph of $y = (x - 2)^2$ indicates that all y-values of $y = (x - 2)^2$ are greater than or equal to zero for all real numbers x.

The graph of $y = (x + 3)^2$ indicates that no y-values of $y = (x + 3)^2$ are less than zero.

The graph of $y = 2(x + 1)^2$ indicates that the y-values of $y = 2(x + 1)^2$ are greater than zero for all real numbers x except $x = -1$.

TRY THIS   Find all solutions of $-(x + 1)^2 > 0$, if any exist.

332 CHAPTER 5

Two-Variable Quadratic Inequalities

A **quadratic inequality in two variables** is an inequality that can be written in one of the forms below, where a, b, and c are real numbers and $a \neq 0$.

$$y \geq ax^2 + bx + c \qquad y > ax^2 + bx + c$$
$$y \leq ax^2 + bx + c \qquad y < ax^2 + bx + c$$

Example 4 shows how to graph a quadratic inequality in two variables.

EXAMPLE ④ Graph the solution to $y \geq (x-2)^2 + 1$.

● **SOLUTION**

1. Graph the related equation, $y = (x-2)^2 + 1$. Use a solid curve because the inequality symbol is $\geq$.

2. Test $(0, 0)$ to see if this point satisfies the given inequality.

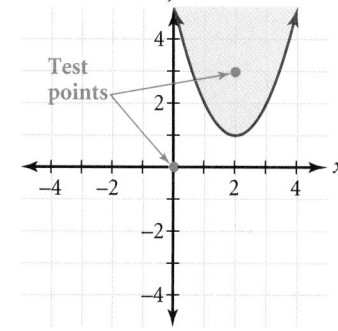

$$y \geq (x-2)^2 + 1$$
$$0 \stackrel{?}{\geq} (0-2)^2 + 1$$
$$0 \geq 5 \quad \textbf{False}$$

Test a point inside the parabola, such as $(2, 3)$.

$$y \geq (x-2)^2 + 1$$
$$3 \stackrel{?}{\geq} (2-2)^2 + 1$$
$$3 \geq 1 \quad \textbf{True}$$

3. Shade the region *inside* the graph of $y = (x-2)^2 + 1$ because this region contains the test point that satisfies $y \geq (x-2)^2 + 1$.

TRY THIS   Graph the solution to $y < (x+2)^2 - 3$.

CRITICAL THINKING   Explain why you should not use $(0, 0)$ as a test point when graphing the solution to an inequality such as $y > x^2 + 2x$.

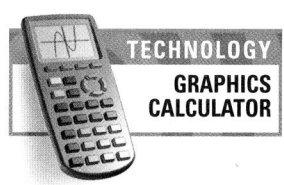
TECHNOLOGY
GRAPHICS CALCULATOR

On most graphics calculators, you can graph a quadratic inequality in two variables. The graph of $y \geq (x-2)^2 + 1$ from Example 4 is shown below. The keystrokes for a TI-83 model are also given.

Use viewing window $[-2, 6]$ by $[-2, 6]$.

Exercises

■ internet connect

Activities Online

Go To: **go.hrw.com**
Keyword:
MB1 Videos

Communicate

1. Explain how to solve $x^2 - 2x - 8 > 0$.

2. Explain how a graph can assist you when solving $x^2 - 2x - 8 > 0$.

3. Explain how to graph an inequality such as $y < (x-2)^2 + 2$.

4. Explain how to test whether the correct area has been shaded in the graph of an inequality.

5. Explain how to determine the possible solutions to $(x+7)^2 < 0$ without solving the inequality.

Guided Skills Practice

6. Solve $x^2 - 7x + 12 \geq 0$. Graph the solution on a number line. **(EXAMPLE 1)**

7. For what integer values of x is $-2x^2 + 25x - 72 > 0$ true? **(EXAMPLE 2)**

Solve each inequality. (EXAMPLE 3)

8. $(x-3)^2 < 0$ **9.** $(x-5)^2 > 0$ **10.** $(x-1)^2 < 0$

11. Graph the solution to $y \leq 2(x-3)^2 - 2$. **(EXAMPLE 4)**

Practice and Apply

Solve each inequality. Graph the solution on a number line.

12. $x^2 - 1 \geq 0$ **13.** $-x^2 + 5x - 6 > 0$ **14.** $x^2 - 8x + 12 \leq 0$

15. $x^2 - 4x - 5 < 0$ **16.** $x^2 - 7x + 10 \leq 0$ **17.** $50 - 15x > -x^2$

18. $x^2 \leq \frac{3}{4} + x$ **19.** $x^2 - x - 12 \leq 0$ **20.** $-x^2 + \frac{4}{3}x - \frac{5}{9} > 0$

21. $x^2 - 4x - 12 > 0$ **22.** $x^2 - 2x - 99 > 0$ **23.** $x^2 + x - 6 \leq 0$

24. $-x^2 - x + 20 < 0$ **25.** $x^2 \leq 7x - 6$ **26.** $x^2 + 35 > -12x$

27. $10 - x^2 \geq 9x$ **28.** $x^2 + 10x + 25 > 0$ **29.** $x^2 + 3x - 18 > 0$

30. $x^2 - 2 > x$ **31.** $x^2 + 6x \geq 7$ **32.** $15 - 8x \leq -x^2$

33. $-x^2 + 3x + 6 < 0$ **34.** $4x - 1 > 8 - x^2$ **35.** $x^2 + 5x - 7 < 4x$

Sketch the graph of each inequality. Then decide which of the given points are in the solution region.

36. $y \geq (x-1)^2 + 5$; $A(4, 1)$, $B(4, 14)$, $C(4, 20)$

37. $y > -(x-3)^2 + 8$; $A(5, 1)$, $B(5, 4)$, $C(5, 6)$

38. $y < (x-2)^2 + 6$; $A(3, 1)$, $B(3, 7)$, $C(3, 10)$

39. $y \leq -(x-4)^2 + 7$; $A(6, 1)$, $B(6, 3)$, $C(6, 5)$

internet connect

**Homework
Help Online**

Go To: **go.hrw.com**
Keyword:
MB1 Homework Help
for Exercises 40–57

Graph each inequality.

40. $y \le (x - 2)^2 + 2$ **41.** $y \ge (x + 2)^2$ **42.** $y < (x - 5)^2 + 1$

43. $y > 2(x + 3)^2 - 5$ **44.** $y \le \left(x - \frac{1}{2}\right)^2 + 1$ **45.** $y \ge (x + 1)^2 + 2$

46. $y \le x^2 + 2x + 1$ **47.** $y < x^2 - 3x + 2$ **48.** $y \ge 2x^2 + 5x + 1$

49. $y > x^2 + 4x + 2$ **50.** $y - 3 \le x^2 - 6x$ **51.** $y - 1 < x^2 - 4x$

52. $y \le (x - \pi)^2 + 1$ **53.** $y \le -\left(x - \frac{5}{7}\right)^2 + 2$ **54.** $y + 3 < (x - 1)^2$

55. $y > x^2 + 12x + 35$ **56.** $x + y > x^2 - 6$ **57.** $y - 2x \le x^2 - 8$

CHALLENGES

58. Create a quadratic function in which $f(x) \ge 0$ for values of x between 2 and 6 inclusive.

59. Write a quadratic inequality whose solution is $x < 3 \text{ or } x > 7$.

CONNECTION

60. MAXIMUM/MINIMUM Jon is a sales representative for a winter sports equipment wholesaler. The price per snowboard varies based on the number of snowboards purchased in each order. Beginning with a price of $124 for one snowboard, the price for each snowboard is reduced by $1 when additional snowboards are purchased.

  a. Copy and complete the table.
  b. What is the function for the revenue?
  c. What is the maximum revenue per order?
  d. How many snowboards must be sold per order to attain the maximum revenue?
  e. Assume that it costs the wholesaler $68 to produce each snowboard and that John spends an average of $128 in fixed costs (travel expenses, phone calls, and so on) per order. Based on these two factors alone, what is the function for the costs? Is the function linear or quadratic?

Number of snowboards purchased	Price per board ($)	Revenue per order ($)
1	124	124
2	123	246
3	122	366
4	121	484
5	120	600
⋮	⋮	⋮
x		

  f. Graph the revenue and cost functions on the same coordinate plane. In order for the revenue to be greater than the costs, how many snowboards does Jon need to sell?
  g. What is the function for profit per order?
  h. Graph the profit function on the same coordinate plane as the functions for revenue per order and cost per order. How many snowboards does Jon need to sell per order to make a profit?
  i. What is the maximum profit per order? How many snowboards must be sold to earn the maximum profit per order?

61. SPORTS At the beginning of a basketball game, the referee tosses the ball vertically into the air. Its height, h, in feet after t seconds is given by $h(t) = -16t^2 + 24t + 5$. During what time interval (to the nearest tenth of a second) is the height of the ball greater than 9 feet?

62. SMALL BUSINESS Suppose that the profit, p, for selling x bumper stickers is given by $p(x) = -0.1x^2 + 8x - 50$.
   a. What is the minimum number of bumper stickers that must be sold to make a profit?
   b. Is it possible for the profit to be greater than $100? Justify your answer algebraically and graphically.

63. BUSINESS A camping supplies company has determined cost and revenue information for the production of their backpacks.

The cost is given by $C(x) = 50 + 30x$, and the revenue is given by $R(x) = 5x(40 - x)$, where x is the number of backpacks sold in thousands. Both the cost and revenue are given in thousands of dollars.

The profit is given by $P(x) = R(x) - C(x)$.

Use the graph at right to give approximate answers to the questions below.

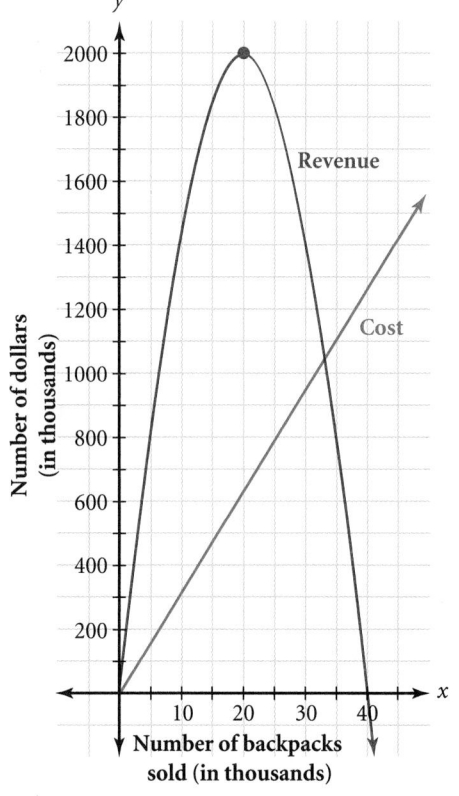

   a. To make a profit, revenue must be greater than cost. What is the range for the quantity of backpacks that the company must sell in order to make a profit?
   b. At what number of backpacks sold is the revenue maximized?
   c. Is there a greatest cost? Why or why not?
   d. Graph the profit function.
   e. What is the range for the quantity of backpacks that the company must sell to make a profit? Compare this answer to your answer from part **a.** Would you expect the answers to be the same? Why or why not?
   f. For what number of backpacks sold is the profit maximized? Compare this answer to your answer from part **b.** Would you expect the answers to be the same? Why or why not?
   g. At what point will the company start to lose money by producing too many backpacks?

PHYSICS The approximate length of a pendulum, l, in feet is related to the time, t, in seconds required for one complete swing as given by the formula $l \approx 0.81t^2$.

64. For what values of t is $l > 2$?   **65.** For what values of t is $l < 5$?

PHYSICS An object is dropped from a height of 1000 feet. Its height, h, in feet after t seconds is given by the function $h(t) = -16t^2 + 1000$.

66. For approximately how long, to the nearest hundredth of a second, will the height of the object be above 500 feet?

67. About how long, to the nearest hundredth of a second, does it take the object to fall from 500 feet to the ground?

SMALL BUSINESS A small company can produce up to 200 handmade sandals a month. The monthly cost, C, of producing x sandals is $C(x) = 1000 + 5x$. The monthly revenue, R, is given by $R(x) = 75x - 0.4x^2$.

68. For what values of x is the revenue greater than the cost?

69. At what production levels will the company make a profit?

70. At what production levels will the company lose money?

 Look Back

Graph each equation, and state whether _y_ is a function of _x_. *(LESSON 2.3)*

71. $y = |x|$ **72.** $x = |y|$ **73.** $y = -|x|$ **74.** $x = y^2$

Solve each equation. Give exact solutions. *(LESSON 5.2)*

75. $-2x^2 = -16$ **76.** $-3x^2 + 15 = -6$ **77.** $32 = 2x^2 - 4$

Simplify each expression, where $i = \sqrt{-1}$. *(LESSON 5.6)*

78. $(8 - 2i)(6 + 3i)$ **79.** $(1 + 5i) - (2 + i)$

80. $\dfrac{2 + i}{2 + 3i}$ **81.** $(3 + 2i) + (3 - i)$

Portfolio Extension
Go To: **go.hrw.com**
Keyword:
MB1 QInequalities

 Look Beyond

82 Let $f(x) = x^3 - 2x^2 + 3x + d$. If the graph of f contains the point $(1, 9)$, find the value of d. Verify your answer by substituting this value for d in the function and graphing it.

PORTFOLIO ACTIVITY

SPORTS Refer to the basketball data on page 273.

1. At what point(s) in time is the basketball at a height of 10 feet?

2. During what period(s) of time is the height of the basketball above 10 feet?

3. During what period(s) of time is the height of the basketball below 10 feet?

4. Use a graph to show that your answers to Steps 1–3 are correct.

CHAPTER PROJECT

FIVE

OUT OF THIS WORLD!

The vertical motion of a basketball at the beginning of a game was described on page 273. The referee holds the ball at a height of 3 feet above the floor. He tosses the ball upward with a velocity of 24 feet per second. The ball is subject to the acceleration due to gravity at the Earth's surface, which is approximately 32 feet per second squared.

The vertical motion of the basketball can be described by the quadratic model below.

$$h(t) = -\frac{1}{2}gt^2 + v_0 t + h_0$$

In this project, you will compare the vertical motion of the basketball on Earth with its vertical motion on each of the other 8 planets. On each planet, assume that the initial vertical height of the ball is 3 feet and that the initial velocity of the ball is 24 feet per second. However, the acceleration due to gravity near the surface of each planet is different from that on Earth.

The table below contains the acceleration due to gravity near the surface of each planet as a fraction of that on Earth.

Activity 1

Complete the table.

Planet	Gravity at surface (as a fraction of Earth's)	Gravity at surface, g (ft/s^2)	Vertical height model: $h(t) = -\frac{1}{2}gt^2 + v_0 t + h_0$
Mercury	0.37		
Venus	0.88		
Earth	1.00	32	$h(t) = -16t^2 + 24t + 3$
Mars	0.38		
Jupiter	2.64		
Saturn	1.15		
Uranus	1.15		
Neptune	1.12		
Pluto	0.04		

Activity 2

1. Complete the table below by using the quadratic functions obtained in Activity 1. Use a graphics calculator to obtain approximate values.

Planet	Maximum height of basketball	Time required to reach maximum height	Time required to return to planet's surface	Time required to reach a height of 10 feet
Mercury				
Venus				
Earth				
Mars				
Jupiter				
Saturn				
Uranus				
Neptune				
Pluto				

2. Are there any planets on which the ball would never reach a height of 10 feet? If so, name them.

Refer to the table from Activity 2.

1. On which planet would the basketball achieve the highest maximum height?

2. On which planet would the basketball achieve the lowest maximum height?

3. Make a generalization about the relationship between the acceleration due to gravity, g, and the maximum height, h, that is reached.

5 Chapter Review and Assessment

Key Skills & Exercises

LESSON 5.1

Key Skills

Multiply linear binomials, and identify and graph a quadratic function.

$$f(x) = (x + 4)(x - 1)$$
$$= x(x - 1) + 4(x - 1)$$
$$= x^2 + 3x - 4$$

The function f is a quadratic function because it can be written in the form $f(x) = ax^2 + bx + c$, where $a = 1$, $b = 3$, and $c = -4$.

Since $a > 0$ in $f(x) = x^2 + 3x - 4$, the parabola opens up and the vertex contains the minimum value of the function.

The coordinates of the vertex are $(-1.5, -6.25)$.

The equation of the axis of symmetry is $x = -1.5$.

Exercises

Show that each function is a quadratic function by writing it in the form $f(x) = ax^2 + bx + c$ and identifying a, b, and c.

1. $f(x) = -(x + 1)(x - 4)$

2. $f(x) = 5(2x - 1)(3x + 2)$

Graph each function and give the approximate coordinates of the vertex.

3 $f(x) = -x^2 + 3x - 1$

4 $f(x) = 5x^2 - x - 12$

State whether the parabola opens up or down and whether the y-coordinate of the vertex is the maximum or the minimum value of the function.

5. $f(x) = -x^2 - x - 1$

6. $f(x) = (x - 3)(x + 2)$

Key Skills

Solve quadratic equations by taking square roots.

$$16(x + 3)^2 = 81$$
$$(x + 3)^2 = \frac{81}{16}$$
$$x + 3 = \pm\sqrt{\frac{81}{16}}$$
$$x = -3 + \frac{9}{4} \quad or \quad x = -3 - \frac{9}{4}$$
$$x = -\frac{3}{4} \qquad\qquad x = -5\frac{1}{4}$$

Use the Pythagorean Theorem to solve problems involving right triangles.

Find the unknown length, b, in right triangle ABC.

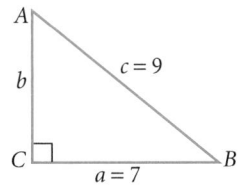

$$a^2 + b^2 = c^2$$
$$7^2 + b^2 = 9^2$$
$$b = \sqrt{9^2 - 7^2}$$
$$b = \sqrt{32}$$
$$b \approx 5.66$$

Exercises

Solve each equation, giving both exact solutions and approximate solutions to the nearest hundredth.

7. $x^2 = 8$ **8.** $3x^2 = 60$

9. $x^2 - 3 = 46$ **10.** $x^2 + 4 = 9$

11. $(x - 3)^2 = 64$ **12.** $(x - 5)^2 = 48$

13. $7(x + 1)^2 = 54$ **14.** $6(x + 2)^2 = 30$

Find the unknown length in right triangle *ABC*. Give your answers to the nearest tenth.

15. $a = 4, b = 5$

16. $c = 4, a = 1$

17. $b = 7, c = 12$

18. $a = 12, c = 15$

19. $c = 25, b = 5$

20. $b = 6, a = 6$

21. $a = 0.2, c = 0.75$

22. $b = 3.2, c = 5.8$

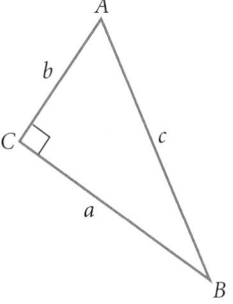

Key Skills

Use factoring to solve a quadratic equation and to find the zeros of a quadratic function.

$$6x^2 + 9x = 6$$
$$6x^2 + 9x - 6 = 0$$
$$3(2x^2 + 3x - 2) = 0$$
$$3(2x - 1)(x + 2) = 0$$
$$x = \frac{1}{2} \quad or \quad x = -2$$

The zeros of the related quadratic function, $f(x) = 6x^2 + 9x - 6$, are $\frac{1}{2}$ and -2.

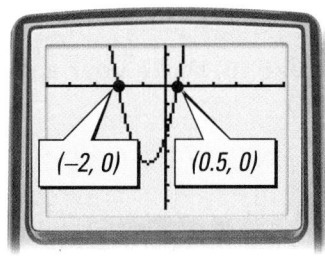

Exercises

Factor each expression.

23. $7x^2 - 21x$ **24.** $6n - 4n^2$

25. $x^2 + 7x + 10$ **26.** $x^2 + 11x + 28$

27. $t^2 - 5t - 24$ **28.** $x^2 - 7x + 12$

29. $x^2 - 8x - 20$ **30.** $y^2 - 6y - 27$

31. $x^2 + x - 20$ **32.** $x^2 + 4x - 21$

33. $3y^2 - y - 2$ **34.** $2x^2 - 5x - 25$

35. $16 - 9x^2$ **36.** $4x^2 - 49$

37. $x^2 - 16x + 64$ **38.** $4a^2 + 4a + 1$

Use the Zero-Product Property to find the zeros of each function.

39. $f(x) = x^2 - 10x + 24$

40. $g(x) = 2x^2 - 3x - 2$

41. $h(t) = 6t^2 + 11t - 10$

Key Skills

Use completing the square to solve a quadratic equation.

$$3x^2 - 8x = 48$$
$$x^2 - \frac{8}{3}x = 16$$
$$x^2 - \frac{8}{3}x + \left(\frac{8}{6}\right)^2 = 16 + \left(\frac{8}{6}\right)^2$$
$$\left(x - \frac{8}{6}\right)^2 = \frac{160}{9}$$
$$x = \frac{8}{6} \pm \frac{\sqrt{160}}{3}$$
$$x = \frac{4 + \sqrt{160}}{3} \quad or \quad x = \frac{4 - \sqrt{160}}{3}$$

The coordinates of the vertex of the graph of a quadratic function in vertex form, $y = a(x - h)^2 + k$, are (h, k).

Exercises

Solve each quadratic equation by completing the square.

42. $x^2 - 6x = 27$ **43.** $5x^2 = 2x + 1$

44. $x^2 - 10x + 21 = 0$ **45.** $x^2 + 5x = 84$

46. $x^2 - 7x - 8 = 0$ **47.** $2x^2 + 7x = 4$

48. $4x^2 + 4 = 17x$ **49.** $2x + 8 = 3x^2$

Write each function in vertex form, and identify the coordinates of the vertex.

50. $y = 2x^2 - 16x + 33$ **51.** $y = -3x^2 - 6x - 7$

52. $y = -x^2 - 5x - 2$ **53.** $y = 4x^2 - 9x + 2$

Key Skills

Use the quadratic formula to find the real roots of quadratic equations.

Solve $2x^2 + x = 10$.
$2x^2 + x - 10 = 0 \rightarrow a = 2, b = 1, c = -10$
$$x = \frac{-b \pm \sqrt{b^2 - 4ac}}{2a}$$
$$x = \frac{-1 \pm \sqrt{1^2 - 4(2)(-10)}}{2(2)}$$
$$x = \frac{-1 \pm \sqrt{81}}{4}$$
$$x = 2 \quad or \quad x = -\frac{10}{4}$$

The coordinates of the vertex of the graph of $f(x) = ax^2 + bx + c$ are $\left(-\frac{b}{2a}, f\left(-\frac{b}{2a}\right)\right)$.

Exercises

Use the quadratic formula to solve each equation.

54. $2x + 1 = 2x^2$ **55.** $6x = 2 - 5x^2$

56. $x^2 - 7x = -10$ **57.** $x^2 + 6x = -8$

58. $11x = 5x^2 - 3$ **59.** $x = 6x^2 - 3$

60. $3 = x^2 + 5x$ **61.** $x^2 = 1 - x$

For each function, find the coordinates of the vertex of the graph.

62. $f(x) = x^2 + 7x + 6$ **63.** $f(x) = x^2 - x - 12$

64. $g(x) = x^2 + 2x - 3$ **65.** $f(n) = n^2 + 12n + 5$

Key Skills

Find and classify all roots of a quadratic equation.

Solve $x^2 + 8 = 0$. $a = 1, b = 0,$ and $c = 8$

$$b^2 - 4ac = 0^2 - 4(1)(8) = -32$$

Because the discriminant is less than zero, the solutions are imaginary.

$$x^2 + 8 = 0$$
$$x = \pm\sqrt{-8}$$
$$x = \pm i\sqrt{8}, \text{ or } \pm 2i\sqrt{2}$$

Exercises

Determine the number of real solutions for each equation by using the discriminant.

66. $4x^2 - 20x = -25$ **67.** $9x^2 + 12x = -2$

68. $x^2 = 21x - 110$ **69.** $-x^2 + 6x = 10$

Solve each equation. Write your answers in the form $a + bi$.

70. $x^2 - 6x + 25 = 0$ **71.** $x^2 + 10x + 34 = 0$

72. $x^2 + 8x + 20 = 0$ **73.** $x^2 - 6x + 11 = 0$

74. $4x^2 = 2x - 1$ **75.** $3x^2 + 2 = 2x$

Graph and perform operations on complex numbers.

a. $(3 + 2i) + (-4 + i)$
$= -1 + 3i$

b. $(3 + 2i) - (-4 + i)$
$= 7 + i$

c. $(3 + 2i)(-4 + i)$
$= -12 - 8i + 3i + 2i^2$
$= -14 - 5i - 2$
$= -16 - 5i$

d. $\dfrac{(3 + 2i)}{-4 + i} = \dfrac{(3 + 2i)(-4 - i)}{(-4 + i)(-4 - i)}$
$= -\dfrac{10}{17} - \dfrac{11}{17}i$

e. $|3 - 3i| = \sqrt{3^2 + (-3)^2}$
$= \sqrt{18}$

The graph of $|3 - 3i|$ is shown at right.

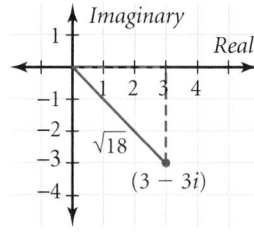

Perform the indicated operation.

76. $(3 - 4i) + (-1 - 8i)$ **77.** $(-2 - i)(1 + 3i)$

78. $\dfrac{5 - 2i}{-4 + i}$ **79.** $\dfrac{-3 + 3i}{3 - 3i}$

80. $(2 + 7i) - (-2 - 6i)$ **81.** $(9 - 3i) + (-3 - 6i)$

82. $(2 + i)(4 - 8i)$ **83.** $(8 - 2i) - (6 + 2i)$

Find each value. Then sketch a diagram that shows the absolute value.

84. $|4 - 2i|$ **85.** $|-3 - i|$

86. $|5 - 2i|$ **87.** $|1 + i|$

LESSON 5.7

Key Skills

Find a quadratic function that exactly fits three data points.

Find a quadratic function whose graph contains the points $(-1, 2)$, $(0, 3)$, and $(3, -6)$.

$$
\begin{aligned}
a(-1)^2 + b(-1) + c &= 2 \\
a(0)^2 + b(0) + c &= 3 \\
a(3)^2 + b(3) + c &= -6
\end{aligned}
\rightarrow
\begin{cases}
a - b + c = 2 \\
c = 3 \\
9a + 3b + c = -6
\end{cases}
$$

$$
\begin{bmatrix} 1 & -1 & 1 \\ 0 & 0 & 1 \\ 9 & 3 & 1 \end{bmatrix}
\begin{bmatrix} a \\ b \\ c \end{bmatrix}
=
\begin{bmatrix} 2 \\ 3 \\ -6 \end{bmatrix}
\rightarrow
\begin{bmatrix} a \\ b \\ c \end{bmatrix}
=
\begin{bmatrix} -1 \\ 0 \\ 3 \end{bmatrix}
$$

The quadratic function is $f(x) = -x^2 + 3$.

Find a quadratic model to represent a data set.

If the points of a given data set form an approximately parabolic shape, find the quadratic regression equation.

The quadratic regression equation shown above is $f(x) \approx 0.8x^2 + 2.3x - 3.1$.

Exercises

Find a quadratic function that fits each set of data points exactly.

88. $(-10, 185)$, $(-5, 70)$, $(1, -2)$

89. $(0, -9)$, $(3, 42)$, $(-5, 106)$

90. $(-2, -7)$, $(1, 2)$, $(-1, -2)$

91. $(0, 6)$, $(1, 0)$, $(-2, -12)$

92. $(-1, 4)$, $(0, 4)$, $(4, 84)$

93. $(-1, 3)$, $(1, -3)$, $(0, -3)$

94. $(-2, -1)$, $(3, -6)$, $(0, 9)$

95. $(-1, 6)$, $(1, 6)$, $(0, -1)$

Find a quadratic model to represent each data set.

96.

x	-3	-2	-1	0	1	2	3
y	50	28	10	-2	20	33	80

97.

x	-3	-2	-1	0	1	2	3
y	-12	-10	-8	-2	-1	-1	-6

98.

x	-25	-10	0	15	30
y	1500	275	49	800	2015

Key Skills

Solve and graph quadratic inequalities in one variable.

$$x^2 - x < 12$$
$$x^2 - x - 12 < 0$$
$$(x + 3)(x - 4) < 0$$

The roots of the related equation, $x^2 - x - 12 = 0$, are -3 and 4.

(−3, 0)   (4, 0)

The graph of $y = x^2 - x - 12$ indicates that $x^2 - x - 12$ is negative when x is between the roots. The solution is $-3 < x < 4$.

Solve and graph quadratic inequalities in two variables.

To graph $y \leq x^2 - 2x - 3$, graph $y = x^2 - 2x - 3$, and test a point, such as $(0, 0)$.

$$y \leq x^2 - 2x - 3$$
$$0 \overset{?}{\leq} 0^2 - 2(0) - 3$$

$$0 \leq -3 \quad \textbf{False}$$

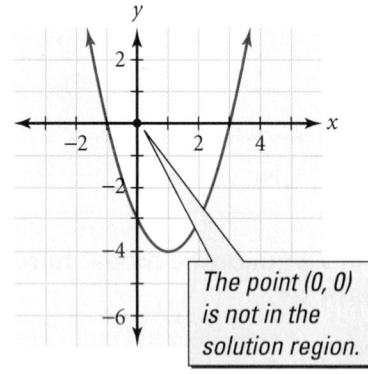

The point (0, 0) is not in the solution region.

Exercises

Solve each quadratic inequality, and graph the solution on a number line.

99. $x^2 - 8x + 12 > 0$

100. $x^2 - 3x - 10 < 0$

101. $x^2 + 7x + 10 \geq 0$

102. $2x^2 + x < 15$

103. $4x^2 > 9x + 9$

104. $2x^2 \geq 9x$

105. $4x^2 \leq 10x$

106. $-x^2 + 6x \geq 8$

Graph each quadratic inequality on a coordinate plane.

107. $y > x^2 - 6x + 8$

108. $y \leq x^2 + 3x - 10$

109. $y - 2x^2 < -x - 1$

110. $y - 5x \leq 2x^2 - 3$

111. $y + 4x + 21 \geq x^2$

112. $y - 5x > 6x^2 + 1$

Applications

113. AVIATION A crate of blankets and clothing is dropped without a parachute from a helicopter hovering at a height of 125 feet. The altitude of the crate, a, in feet, is modeled by $a(t) = -16t^2 + 125$, where t is the time, in seconds, after it is released. How long will it take for the crate to reach the ground?

114. RECREATION Students are designing an archery target with one ring around the bull's-eye. The bull's-eye has a radius of 6 inches. The area of the outer ring should be 5 times that of the bull's-eye. What should be the radius of the outer circle?

Chapter Test

Write each function in the form
$f(x) = ax^2 + bx + c$ **and identify** *a, b,* **and** *c.*
State whether the parabola opens up or down and whether the *y*-coordinate of the vertex is the maximum or the minimum.

1. $f(x) = (x + 3)(x - 4)$

2. $f(x) = -5(x + 1)(x - 7)$

3. $f(x) = -2(x + 3)(3x)$

Solve each equation giving both exact and approximate solutions to the nearest hundredth.

4. $3x^2 = 81$ **5.** $(x - 7)^2 = 12$

Find the unknown length in the right triangle ABC to the nearest tenth.

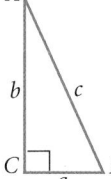

6. $a = 7, b = 9$

7. $a = 2, c = 4$

8. $b = 8.4, c = 9.2$

Use factoring and the Zero-Product Property to find the zeros of each quadratic function.

9. $f(x) = x^2 - 9x$

10. $f(x) = 4x^2 - 64$

11. $f(x) = 4x^2 - 4x + 1$

12. $f(x) = x^2 - 3x - 10$

13. NUMBER THEORY The product of two numbers is 90. One number is 3 more than twice the other number. Model these numbers with a quadratic equation. Solve the equation by factoring and using the Zero-Product Property.

Solve each quadratic equation by completing the square.

14. $x^2 - 8x + 4 = 0$

15. $2x^2 - 11x + 5 = 0$

16. GEOMETRY The area of a triangle is 24 square inches. The height is 4 inches shorter than the

base. Find the height and the base of the triangle.

Use the quadratic formula to solve each equation.

17. $x^2 + 2x - 5 = 0$

18. $-3x^2 + 15 = 12x$

For each quadratic function, write the equation for the axis of symmetry, and find the coordinates of the vertex.

19. $y = x^2 - 7x + 10$

20. $y = 3x^2 + 18x + 6$

Use the discriminant to determine the number of real solutions.

21. $x^2 + 2x + 5 = 0$

22. $-3x^2 = 5 + 3x$

23. $4x^2 = 27$

Perform the indicated operations.

24. $(3 + 2i) + (5 - 7i)$ **25.** $(2 + i) - (6 - 3i)$

26. $3i(7 + 3i)$ **27.** $(-2 + i)(3 - 4i)$

28. $\dfrac{2 + 3i}{1 - i}$ **29.** $\left| 5 + 12i \right|$

Find a quadratic function that fits each set of data points exactly.

30. $(-1, -6), (2, 3), (1, -2)$

31. $(2, -11), (3, 9), (-1, -23)$

Solve each quadratic inequality. Graph the solution on a number line.

32. $x^2 - x - 12 > 0$

33. $15x^2 - 2x - 8 \geq 0$

Graph each quadratic inequality on a coordinate plane.

34. $y \leq x^2 + 4x - 5$

35. $y + 1 > x^2 - 2x - 7$

College Entrance Exam Practice

MULTIPLE-CHOICE For Questions 1–14, write the letter that indicates the best answer.

1. Evaluate $27^{\frac{1}{3}}$. *(LESSON 2.2)*
   a. 9
   b. 3
   c. $\frac{1}{9}$
   d. $\frac{1}{3}$

2. Evaluate $|-3i|$. *(LESSON 5.6)*
   a. -3
   b. 3
   c. 3i
   d. $i\sqrt{3}$

3. Simplify $\left(\frac{1}{2}\right)^{-2}$. *(LESSON 2.2)*
   a. -4
   b. $\frac{1}{4}$
   c. 4
   d. $-\frac{1}{4}$

4. Let $A = \begin{bmatrix} 2 & 3 \\ 3 & 2 \end{bmatrix}$ and $B = \begin{bmatrix} 1 & 2 \\ 3 & 5 \end{bmatrix}$ Find AB.
   (LESSON 4.2)
   a. $\begin{bmatrix} 8 & 7 \\ 21 & 19 \end{bmatrix}$
   b. $\begin{bmatrix} 11 & 19 \\ 9 & 16 \end{bmatrix}$
   c. $\begin{bmatrix} 8 & 7 \\ 19 & 14 \end{bmatrix}$
   d. $\begin{bmatrix} 2 & 6 \\ 9 & 10 \end{bmatrix}$

5. Solve the equation $x^2 - 3x = -2$.
   (LESSON 5.3)
   a. $-1, -2$
   b. $1, 2$
   c. $-3, 1$
   d. $3, -1$

6. Find the value of n that completes the square for $x^2 + 16x + n$. *(LESSON 5.4)*
   a. 64
   b. 32
   c. 16
   d. 256

7. Find $2R - N$ given $R = \begin{bmatrix} 3 & 5 \\ -2 & 0 \end{bmatrix}$ and
   $N = \begin{bmatrix} 1 & -1 \\ 3 & 1 \end{bmatrix}$. *(LESSON 4.1)*
   a. $\begin{bmatrix} -2 & 6 \\ -5 & -1 \end{bmatrix}$
   b. $\begin{bmatrix} 2 & 4 \\ 1 & -1 \end{bmatrix}$
   c. $\begin{bmatrix} 2 & 6 \\ -5 & -1 \end{bmatrix}$
   d. $\begin{bmatrix} 5 & 11 \\ -7 & -1 \end{bmatrix}$

8. How many roots does the equation $5x^2 + 2x + 1 = 0$ have? *(LESSON 5.6)*
   a. 2 real roots
   b. no real roots
   c. 1 real root
   d. 2 complex roots

9. Which is the value of i^{13}? *(LESSON 5.6)*
   a. 1
   b. -1
   c. i
   d. $-i$

10. Simplify: $\frac{a^2 b^{-1}}{a^{-3} b^2}$. *(LESSON 2.2)*
    a. $\frac{a}{b}$
    b. $\frac{a^5}{b^3}$
    c. $\frac{b^2}{a}$
    d. $\frac{b^3}{a^5}$

11. Which is the solution of the system?
    $\begin{cases} 5x + y = 11 \\ 3x + 2y = 8 \end{cases}$ *(LESSON 3.2)*
    a. $(3, 2)$
    b. $(2, 1)$
    c. $(-1, 2)$
    d. $(5, 6)$

12. Which is a correct factorization of $x^2 + 5x + 6$?
    (LESSON 5.3)
    a. $(x + 1)(x + 6)$
    b. $(x + 2)(x + 3)$
    c. $(x - 1)(x - 6)$
    d. $(x - 2)(x - 3)$

13. Which term describes the system?
    $\begin{cases} 2x + 5y = 3 \\ 4x + 10y = 6 \end{cases}$ *(LESSON 3.1)*
    a. inconsistent
    b. dependent
    c. independent
    d. incompatible

14. Which is the inverse of the function $f(x) = 3x + 2$? *(LESSON 2.5)*

   a. $g(x) = 6x$

   b. $g(x) = \dfrac{x-3}{2}$

   c. $g(x) = 3 + \dfrac{x}{2}$

   d. $g(x) = \dfrac{x-2}{3}$

15. Graph $-\dfrac{1}{3}x \le 6$. *(LESSON 3.3)*

16. Find $(2 + i)(3 + 2i)$. *(LESSON 5.6)*

17. Solve $\begin{cases} 3x - 2y = 2 \\ x + y = 4 \end{cases}$. *(LESSON 3.1)*

18. Let $A = \begin{bmatrix} 3 & 2 \\ 1 & 4 \end{bmatrix}$ and $B = \begin{bmatrix} 1 & 4 \\ 2 & 3 \end{bmatrix}$. Find $A + B$.

   (LESSON 4.1)

19. Solve $x^2 + 3x + 1 = 0$. *(LESSON 5.5)*

20. Let $A = \begin{bmatrix} 1 & 4 \\ 3 & 1 \end{bmatrix}$ and $B = \begin{bmatrix} 0 & 1 \\ 2 & 3 \end{bmatrix}$. Find $A + B$.

   (LESSON 4.1)

21. Write the pair of parametric equations

   $\begin{cases} x(t) = 1 - t \\ y(t) = 2 - t \end{cases}$ as a single equation in x and y.

   (LESSON 3.6)

22. Write the function for the graph of $f(x) = x^2$ translated 3 units to the left. *(LESSON 2.7)*

23. Let $f(x) = 3x + 1$ and $g(x) = x^2$. Find $(f \cdot g)(x)$.

   (LESSON 2.4)

24. Find the product $\begin{bmatrix} 2 & 3 \\ 2 & 1 \end{bmatrix}\begin{bmatrix} 3 & 2 \\ 1 & 0 \end{bmatrix}$. *(LESSON 4.2)*

25. Find the value of $i^2 + i^4$. *(LESSON 5.6)*

26. Evaluate $h(x) = 11 - \dfrac{1}{2}x$ for $x = -6$.

   (LESSON 2.3)

27. Given $5\begin{bmatrix} 1 & x \\ x-y & 5 \end{bmatrix} = \begin{bmatrix} 5 & 15 \\ 20 & 25 \end{bmatrix}$, find x and y.

   (LESSON 4.1)

28. CHEMISTRY A scientist wants to create 60 milliliters of a 5% salt solution from a 2% salt solution and a 12% salt solution. How much of each should be used? *(LESSON 3.1)*

FREE RESPONSE GRID The following questions may be answered by using a free-response grid such as that commonly used by standardized test services.

29. Evaluate $8^{\frac{2}{3}}$. *(LESSON 2.2)*

30. Simplify $\dfrac{(3^2 - 7)^2}{3^{(2^2 - 2)}}$.

   (LESSON 2.1)

31. Find $\left| \dfrac{\sqrt{2}}{4} + \dfrac{\sqrt{2}}{4}i \right|$.

   (LESSON 5.6)

32. Find the discriminant for $x^2 + 4x + 1 = 0$.

   (LESSON 5.6)

33. What is the maximum value of $f(x) = -x^2 + 2x + 1$? *(LESSON 5.1)*

34. Let $A = \begin{bmatrix} 3 & 2 \\ 4 & 1 \end{bmatrix}$ and $B = \begin{bmatrix} 2x & 2 \\ 4 & 1 \end{bmatrix}$. For what value of x does $A = B$? *(LESSON 4.1)*

35. Find the maximum value of the objective function $P = 2x + 3y$ that satisfies the given constraints. *(LESSON 3.5)*

   $\begin{cases} x \ge 0, y \ge 0 \\ x + y \le 4 \\ 2x + y \ge 2 \end{cases}$

36. PHYSICS A ball is dropped from a height of 10 feet. If the ball's height is modeled by $h(t) = -16t^2 + 10$, where h represents the height of the ball in feet and t represents time in seconds, how many seconds, to the nearest tenth, will it take the ball to reach the ground? *(LESSON 5.2)*

37. BUSINESS A company's profit on sales of digital pagers is modeled by the function $P(x) = -x^2 + 90x + 497{,}975$, where x represents the price of a pager in dollars. To the nearest dollar, what price gives the maximum profit? *(LESSON 5.4)*

Keystroke Guide for Chapter 5

Essential keystroke sequences (using the model TI-82 or TI-83 graphics calculator) are presented below for Activities and Examples found in this chapter that require or recommend the use of a graphics calculator.

internet connect

For Keystrokes of other graphing calculator models, visit the HRW web site at **go.hrw.com** and enter the keyword **MB1 CALC**.

LESSON 5.1

TECHNOLOGY
Page 274

Create a table of values for $y = \frac{11}{10}x + \frac{1}{19}x^2$.

Enter the function:

| Y= | (| 11 | ÷ | 10 |) | X,T,θ,n | + | (| 1 | ÷ | 19 |) |

| X,T,θ,n | x^2 |

Create a table of values:

| 2nd | WINDOW | (TblStart=) 0 | ENTER | (ΔTbl=) 10 | ENTER | (Indpnt:) **AUTO** | ENTER |

TBLSET (above WINDOW)

⇑ TI-82: (TblMin=)   TABLE

| ▼ | (Depend:) **AUTO** | ENTER | 2nd | GRAPH |

EXAMPLES ② and ③

Pages 276 and 277

For Example 2, graph $y = x^2 - x + 1$, and find the maximum or minimum value at the vertex.

Use friendly viewing window [–4.7, 4.7] by [–2, 6].

Graph the function:

| Y= | X,T,θ,n | x^2 | – | X,T,θ,n | + | 1 | GRAPH |

Find the minimum value:
Press TRACE , and use your cursor.

Create a table of values:
Use a keystroke sequence similar to that used in the Technology example above. First use TblStart = –2 and ΔTbl = 1. Then refine the table by using TblStart = 0 and ΔTbl = 0.1.

For Example 3, use a keystroke sequence similar to that above to graph each function. Use viewing window [–10, 10] by [–10, 10].

E X A M P L E S ① and ② For Example 1, graph $y = 4x^2 + 13$ and $y = 253$ on the same
Page 282   screen, and find any points of intersection.

Use viewing window $[-10, 10]$ by $[-150, 400]$.

Graph the functions:
Use a keystroke sequence similar to that in Example 2 of Lesson 5.1.

Find any points of intersection:

Move your cursor as indicated.

 CALC
[2nd] [TRACE] **5:intersect** **(First curve?)**

[ENTER] **(Second curve?)** [ENTER]

(Guess?) [ENTER]

For Example 2, use viewing window $[-5, 10]$ by $[-25, 150]$. Use a keystroke sequence similar to that above.

$(\approx -7.75, 253)$ $(\approx 7.75, 253)$

E X A M P L E ③ Graph $y = -16x^2 + 68$, and find the reasonable x-intercept.
Page 283

Use viewing window $[-5, 5]$ by $[-10, 80]$.

Graph the functions:
Use a keystroke sequence similar to that in Example 2 of Lesson 5.1.

Find the x-intercepts:

Move your cursor as indicated.

 CALC
[2nd] [TRACE] **2:zero** **(Left Bound?)** [ENTER]

⇧ TI-82: **2:root**

(Right Bound?) [ENTER] **(Guess?)** [ENTER]

$x \approx 2.06$

E X A M P L E S ④ and ⑥ For Example 4, use viewing window $[-9, 3]$ by $[-7, 2]$.
Pages 293 and 294   For part **a** of Example 6, use viewing window $[-2, 7]$ by $[-20, 8]$.
For part **b** of Example 6, use viewing window $[0, 12]$ by $[-6, 6]$.

To graph the functions, use a keystroke sequence similar to that in Example 2 of Lesson 5.1. To find the zeros for Example 6, use a keystroke sequence similar to finding the x-intercepts in Example 3 of Lesson 5.2. Repeat for each zero.

E X A M P L E ⑦ Make a table of values for $y = 2x^2 - x - 66$.
Page 295

Use a keystroke sequence similar to that used in the Technology example of Lesson 5.1. Use TblStart = 3 and ΔTbl = 1.

E X A M P L E **3** Solve $2x^2 + 6x = 7$ by graphing.

Page 301

Use viewing window [–5, 5] by [–12, 12].

To graph $y = 2x^2 - 6x$ and $y = 7$ and find the x-coordinates of any points of intersection, use keystroke sequences similar to those in Example 2 of Lesson 5.1 and Example 1 of Lesson 5.2.

To graph $y = 2x^2 - 6x - 7$ and find any zeros, use keystroke sequences similar to those in Example 2 of Lesson 5.1 and Example 6 of Lesson 5.3.

E X A M P L E **5** Graph $y = \frac{3}{5000}x^2 - \frac{3}{5}x + 200$, and find the coordinates of the lowest point.

Page 303

Use viewing window [–100, 1000] by [–150, 40].

Minimum
X=500.00006 Y=50

Find the minimum value:

CALC

[2nd] [TRACE] [3:minimum] (Left Bound?) [ENTER] (Right Bound?) [ENTER]

⇑ TI-82: (Lower Bound?)   ⇑ TI-82: (Upper Bound?)

(Guess)? [ENTER]

Activity

Page 309

For Step 2, use friendly viewing window [–9.4, 9.4] by [–7, 7]. Press [TRACE], and use your cursor to find the coordinates of each vertex.

E X A M P L E **6** Evaluate the expression $\frac{2 + 5i}{2 - 3i}$, and express the answer with fractions.

Page 318

First put your calculator in complex mode.

QUIT
[MODE] [a+bi] [ENTER] [2nd] [MODE] (2 + 5 [2nd] [.]) ÷

i

(2 – 3 [2nd] [.]) [ENTER] [MATH] [1:▸Frac] [ENTER] [ENTER]

The TI-82 does not have a complex mode.

E X A M P L E S **1** and **2** For Step 2 of Example 1, solve $\begin{bmatrix} 1 & 1 & 1 \\ 4 & 2 & 1 \\ 36 & 6 & 1 \end{bmatrix} \begin{bmatrix} a \\ b \\ c \end{bmatrix} = \begin{bmatrix} 3 \\ -3 \\ 13 \end{bmatrix}$.

Pages 323 and 324

Enter the coefficient matrix and the constant matrix:

[MATRX] [EDIT] [1:[A]] [ENTER] (MATRIX[A]) 3 [ENTER] 3 [ENTER] 1 [ENTER] 1 [ENTER] 1 [ENTER]

4 [ENTER] 2 [ENTER] 1 [ENTER] 36 [ENTER] 6 [ENTER] 1 [ENTER] [MATRX] [EDIT] [2:[B]] [ENTER]

QUIT
(MATRIX[B]) 3 [ENTER] 1 [ENTER] 3 [ENTER] [(-)] 3 [ENTER] 13 [ENTER] [2nd] [MODE]

Find the product $A^{-1}B$:

MATRX **NAMES** **1:[A]** ENTER x^{-1} ✕ MATRX **NAMES** **2:[B]** ENTER ENTER

Plot points (1, 3), (2, −3), and (6, 13), and make a scatter plot:

Use viewing window [−5, 10] by [−10, 20].

STAT **EDIT** **1:EDIT** ENTER **L1** 1 ENTER 2 ENTER 6 ENTER ► **L2** 3

ENTER (−) 3 ENTER 13 ENTER 2nd Y= **STAT PLOT** **1:Plot 1**

ENTER **ON** ENTER ▼ (Type:) ⣿ ENTER ▼ (Xlist:) 2nd **L1** 1

⇑ TI-82: **L1** ENTER

▼ (Ylist:) 2nd **L2** 2 ▼ (Mark:) ▢ ENTER GRAPH

⇑ TI-82: **L2** ENTER

To graph $f(x) = 2x^2 - 12x + 13$, use a keystroke sequence similar to that in Example 2 of Lesson 5.1.

For Example 2, use a similar keystroke sequence. Use viewing window [−2, 10] by [−5, 20].

E X A M P L E ❸ **Create a scatter plot of the given data, and find a quadratic model to represent the data.**

Page 325

Create the scatter plot:
Use a keystroke sequence similar to that in Example 2 of this lesson.

Find a quadratic model:
Use a keystroke sequence similar to that given on page 324.

LESSON 5.8

Page 330

For Step 2, use a keystroke sequence similar to that used in the Technology example of Lesson 5.1. Use TblStart = −2 and ΔTbl = 1.

E X A M P L E S ❶ **and** ❷ **For Example 1, graph $y = x^2 - 2x - 15$ and find the zeros of the function.**

Pages 331 and 332

Use viewing window [−5, 7] by [−20, 15].

Graph the function:
Use a keystroke sequence similar to that in Example 2 of Lesson 5.1.

Find the zeros of the function:
Use a keystroke sequence similar to that used to find the *x*-intercepts in Example 3 of Lesson 5.2.

For Example 2, use a similar keystroke sequence. Use viewing window [0, 25] by [−100, 1500].

6 Exponential and Logarithmic Functions

EXPONENTIAL AND LOGARITHMIC FUNCTIONS model many scientific phenomena. Some applications of exponential functions include population growth, compound interest, and radioactive decay. Radioactive decay is used in dating ancient objects found at archeological sites. Applications of logarithmic functions include the pH scale in chemistry, sound intensity, and Newton's law of cooling.

Lessons

CHAPTER
PORTFOLIO
ACTIVITIES
PROJECT

About the Chapter Project

The heating and cooling of objects can be modeled by functions. Throughout this chapter and in the Chapter Project, *Warm Ups*, you will model the heating and cooling of a temperature probe over several temperature ranges in order to find an appropriate general model for these phenomena.

After completing the Chapter Project, you will be able to do the following:

- Collect real-world data on the heating and cooling of an object, and determine an appropriate exponential function to model the heating and cooling of an object.

- Make predictions about the temperature of an object that is heating or cooling to a constant surrounding temperature.

- Verify Newton's law of cooling.

In the Portfolio Activities for Lessons 6.1 and 6.4 and in the Chapter Project, you will need to use a program like the one shown on the calculator screen at right to collect temperature data with a CBL.

About the Portfolio Activities

Throughout the chapter, you will be given opportunities to complete Portfolio Activities that are designed to support your work on the Chapter Project.

- Using a CBL to collect cooling temperature data in a laboratory setting is included in the Portfolio Activity on page 361.

- Comparing different models for the cooling temperature data is included in the Portfolio Activity on page 369.

- Using a CBL to collect warming temperature data and performing appropriate transformations on regression equations are included in the Portfolio Activity on page 384.

- Comparing Newton's law of cooling with regression models from empirical data is included in the Portfolio Activity on page 409.

```
PROGRAM:CBLTEMP
:ClrHome:(1,0)→L
1:Send(L1):(1,1,
1)→L1:Send(L1):3
0→dim(L2):(3,1,-
1,0)→L1:Send(L1)
:For(I,1,30,1)
:Get(L2(I)):End
```

Exponential Growth and Decay

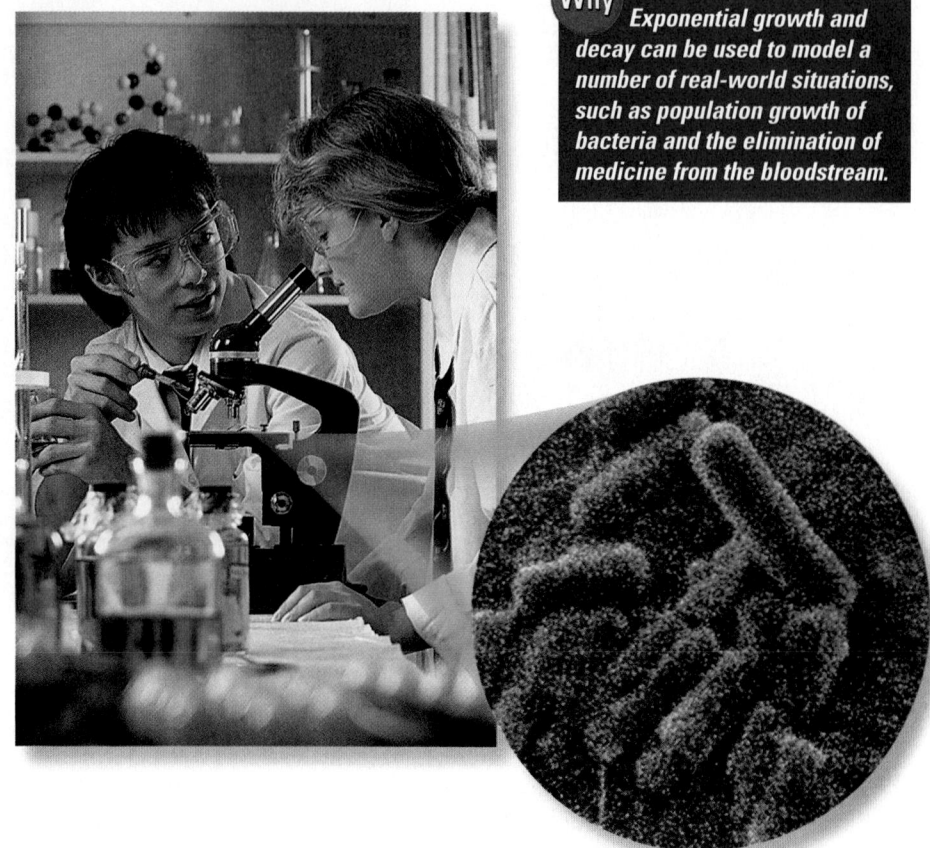

Objectives

● Determine the multiplier for exponential growth and decay.

● Write and evaluate exponential expressions to model growth and decay situations.

APPLICATION
BIOLOGY

Bacteria are very small single-celled organisms that live almost everywhere on Earth. Most bacteria are not harmful to humans, and some are helpful, such as the bacteria in yogurt.

Bacteria reproduce, or grow in number, by dividing. The total number of bacteria at a given time is referred to as the population of bacteria. When each bacterium in a population of bacteria divides, the population doubles.

Activity
Modeling Bacterial Growth

TECHNOLOGY
GRAPHICS CALCULATOR

Keystroke Guide, page 418

You will need: a calculator

You can use a calculator to model the growth of 25 bacteria, assuming that the entire population doubles every hour.

First enter 25. Then multiply this number by 2 to find the population of bacteria after 1 hour. Repeat this doubling procedure to find the population after 2 hours.

1. Copy and complete the table below.

Time (hr)	0	1	2	3	4	5	6
Population	25	50	100				

2. Write an algebraic expression that represents the population of bacteria after n hours. (Hint: Factor out 25 from each population figure.)

3. Use your algebraic expression to find the population of bacteria after 10 hours and after 20 hours.

CHECKPOINT ✔ **4.** Suppose that the initial population of bacteria was 75 instead of 25. Find the population after 10 hours and after 20 hours.

You can represent the growth of an initial population of 100 bacteria that doubles every hour by creating a table.

$\xrightarrow{+1}\xrightarrow{+1}\xrightarrow{+1}\xrightarrow{+1}$

Time (hr)	0	1	2	3	4	$\cdots$	n
Population	100	200	400	800	1600	$\cdots$	$100(2)^n$

$\xrightarrow{\times 2}\xrightarrow{\times 2}\xrightarrow{\times 2}\xrightarrow{\times 2}$

CONNECTION

PATTERNS IN DATA

The bar chart at right illustrates how the doubling pattern of growth quickly leads to large numbers.

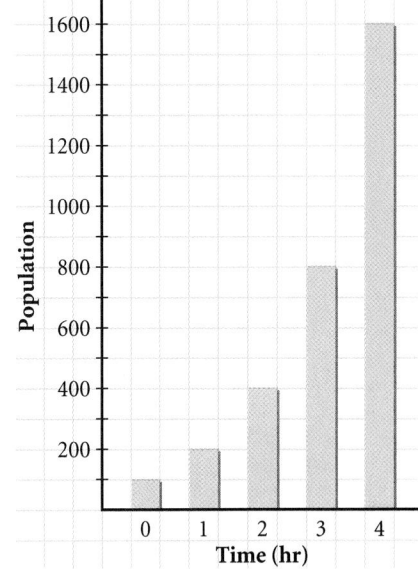

CHECKPOINT ✔ Assuming an initial population of 100 bacteria, predict the population of bacteria after 5 hours and after 6 hours.

The population after n hours can be represented by the following *exponential expression*:

$$100 \times \overbrace{2 \times 2 \times 2 \times \cdots \times 2}^{n \text{ times}} = 100 \times 2^n$$

This expression, $100 \cdot 2^n$, is called an **exponential expression** because the exponent, n, is a variable and the base, 2, is a fixed number. The base of an exponential expression is commonly referred to as the **multiplier**.

Modeling Human Population Growth

Human populations grow much more slowly than bacterial populations. Bacterial populations that double each hour have a growth rate of 100% per hour. The population of the United States in 1990 was growing at a rate of about 8% per decade.

In Example 1, you will use this growth rate to make predictions.

EXAMPLE ① The population of the United States was 248,718,301 in 1990 and was projected to grow at a rate of about 8% per decade. [*Source: U.S. Census Bureau*]

Predict the population, to the nearest hundred thousand, for the years 2010 and 2025.

● **SOLUTION**

1. To obtain the multiplier for exponential growth, add the growth rate to 100%.

$$100\% + 8\% = 108\%, \text{ or } 1.08$$

2. Write the expression for the population n decades after 1990.

$$248,718,301 \cdot (1.08)^n$$

TECHNOLOGY
SCIENTIFIC CALCULATOR

3. Since the year 2010 is 2 decades after 1990, substitute 2 for n.

$$248,718,301(1.08)^n$$
$$= 248,718,301(1.08)^2$$
$$= 290,105,026.3$$

To the nearest hundred thousand, the predicted population for 2010 is 290,100,000.

Since the year 2025 is 3.5 decades after 1990, substitute 3.5 for n.

$$248,718,301(1.08)^n$$
$$= 248,718,301(1.08)^{3.5}$$
$$= 325,604,866$$

To the nearest hundred thousand, the predicted population for 2025 is 325,600,000.

These predictions are based on the assumption that the growth rate remains a constant 8% per decade.

TRY THIS The population of Brazil was about 162,661,000 in 1996 and was projected to grow at a rate of about 7.7% per decade. Predict the population, to the nearest hundred thousand, of Brazil for 2016 and 2020. [*Source: U.S. Census Bureau*]

CRITICAL THINKING If a population's growth rate is 1% per *year*, what is the population's growth rate per *decade*?

Modeling Biological Decay

APPLICATION

HEALTH

Caffeine is eliminated from the bloodstream of a child at a rate of about 25% per hour. This exponential decrease in caffeine in a child's bloodstream is shown in the bar chart.

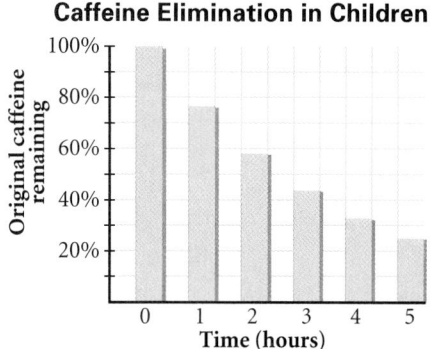

Caffeine Elimination in Children

A *rate of decay* can be thought of as a negative growth rate. To obtain the multiplier for the decrease in caffeine in the bloodstream of a child, subtract the rate of decay from 100%. Thus, the multiplier is 0.75, as calculated below.

$$100\% - 25\% = 75\%, \text{ or } 0.75$$

E X A M P L E **2** The rate at which caffeine is eliminated from the bloodstream of an adult is about 15% per hour. An adult drinks a caffeinated soda, and the caffeine in his or her bloodstream reaches a peak level of 30 milligrams.

Predict the amount, to the nearest tenth of a milligram, of caffeine remaining 1 hour after the peak level and 4 hours after the peak level.

Caffeine is an ingredient in coffee, tea, chocolate, and some soft drinks.

● **SOLUTION**

1. To obtain the multiplier for exponential decay, subtract the rate of decay from 100%. The multiplier is found as follows:

$$100\% - 15\% = 85\%, \text{ or } 0.85$$

2. Write the expression for the caffeine level x hours after the peak level.

$$30(0.85)^x$$

3. Substitute 1 for x.

$$30(0.85)^x$$
$$= 30(0.85)^1$$
$$= 25.5$$

The amount of caffeine remaining 1 hour after the peak level is 25.5 milligrams.

Substitute 4 for x.

$$30(0.85)^x$$
$$= 30(0.85)^4$$
$$\approx 15.7$$

The amount of caffeine remaining 4 hours after the peak level is about 15.7 milligrams.

TECHNOLOGY

SCIENTIFIC CALCULATOR

TRY THIS A vitamin is eliminated from the bloodstream at a rate of about 20% per hour. The vitamin reaches a peak level in the bloodstream of 300 milligrams. Predict the amount, to the nearest tenth of a milligram, of the vitamin remaining 2 hours after the peak level and 7 hours after the peak level.

Exercises

● *Communicate*

1. What type of values of n are possible in the bacterial growth expression $25 \cdot 2^n$ and in the United States population growth expression $248,718,301 \cdot (1.08)^n$?

2. Explain how the United States population growth expression $248,718,301 \cdot (1.08)^n$ incorporates the growth rate of 8% per decade.

3. What assumption(s) do you make about a population's growth when you make predictions by using an exponential expression?

4. Describe the difference between the procedures for finding the multiplier for a growth rate of 5% and for a decay rate of 5%.

● *Guided Skills Practice*

Find the multiplier for each rate of exponential growth or decay.
(EXAMPLES 1 AND 2)

5. 5.5% growth   **6.** 0.25% growth   **7.** 3% decay   **8.** 0.5% decay

Evaluate each expression for $x = 3$. (EXAMPLES 1 AND 2)

9. 2^x **10.** $50(3)^x$ **11.** 0.8^x **12.** $100(0.75)^x$

APPLICATIONS

13. DEMOGRAPHICS The population of Tokyo-Yokohama, Japan, was about 28,447,000 in 1995 and was projected to grow at an annual rate of 1.1%. Predict the population, to the nearest hundred thousand, for the year 2004. [*Source: U.S. Census Bureau*] **(EXAMPLE 1)**

14. HEALTH A certain medication is eliminated from the bloodstream at a rate of about 12% per hour. The medication reaches a peak level in the bloodstream of 40 milligrams. Predict the amount, to the nearest tenth of a milligram, of the medication remaining 2 hours after the peak level and 3 hours after the peak level. **(EXAMPLE 2)**

● *Practice and Apply*

Find the multiplier for each rate of exponential growth or decay.

15. 7% growth   **16.** 9% growth   **17.** 6% decay

18. 2% decay   **19.** 6.5% growth   **20.** 8.2% decay

21. 0.05% decay   **22.** 0.08% growth   **23.** 0.075% growth

Given $x = 5$, $y = \frac{3}{5}$, and $z = 3.3$, evaluate each expression.

24. 2^x **25.** 3^y **26.** 2^{2x}

27. $50(2)^{3x}$ **28.** $25(2)^z$ **29.** $25(2)^y$

30. $100(3)^{x-1}$ **31.** $10(2)^{z+2}$ **32.** 2^{2y-1}

33. $100(2)^{4z}$ **34.** $100(0.5)^{3z}$ **35.** $75(0.5)^{2y}$

Z internet connect

**Homework
Help Online**
Go To: **go.hrw.com**
Keyword:
MB1 Homework Help
for Exercises 24–35

Predict the population of bacteria for each situation and time period.

36. 55 bacteria that double every hour
   a. after 3 hours   **b.** after 5 hours

37. 125 bacteria that double every hour
   a. after 6 hours   **b.** after 8 hours

38. 33 *E. coli* bacteria that double every 30 minutes
   a. after 1 hour   **b.** after 6 hours

39. 75 *E. coli* bacteria that double every 30 minutes
   a. after 2 hours   **b.** after 3 hours

40. 225 bacteria that triple every hour
   a. after 1 hour   **b.** after 3 hours

41. 775 bacteria that triple every hour
   a. after 2 hours   **b.** after 4 hours

CHALLENGE

42. Suppose that you put $2500 into a retirement account that grows with an interest rate of 5.25% compounded once each year. After how many years will the balance of the account be at least $15,000?

CONNECTION

PATTERNS IN DATA Determine whether each table represents a linear, quadratic, or exponential relationship between *x* and *y*.

43.

x	y
0	2
1	4
2	8
3	16

44.

x	y
1	1
2	3
3	9
4	27

45.

x	y
0	6
2	10
4	14
6	18

46.

x	y
0	−2
3	7
6	34
9	79

APPLICATIONS

47. DEMOGRAPHICS The population of Indonesia was 191,256,000 in 1990 and was growing at a rate of 1.9% per year. Predict the population, to the nearest hundred thousand, of Indonesia in 2010. [*Source: U.S. Census Bureau*]

Bali, Indonesia

48. HEALTH A dye is injected into the pancreas during a certain medical procedure. A physician injects 0.3 grams of the dye, and a healthy pancreas will secrete 4% of the dye each minute. Predict the amount of dye remaining, to the nearest hundredth of a gram, in a healthy pancreas 30 minutes after the injection.

49. DEMOGRAPHICS The population of China was 1,210,005,000 in 1996 and was growing at a rate of about 6% per decade. Predict the population, to the nearest hundred thousand, of China in 2016 and in 2021. [*Source: U.S. Census Bureau*]

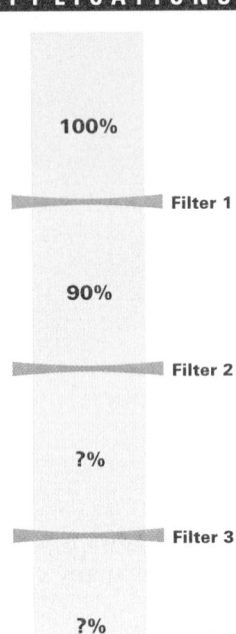

100%

Filter 1

90%

Filter 2

?%

Filter 3

?%

50. PHYSICAL SCIENCE Suppose that a camera filter transmits 90% of the light striking it, as illustrated at left.
  a. If a second filter of the same type is added, what portion of light is transmitted through the combination of the two filters?
  b. Write an expression to model the portion of light that is transmitted through n filters.
  c. Calculate the portion of light transmitted through 4, 5, and 6 filters.

51. DEMOGRAPHICS The population of India was 952,108,000 in 1996 and was growing at a rate of about 1.3% per year. [*Source: U.S. Census Bureau*]
  a. Predict the population, to the nearest hundred thousand, of India in 2000 and in 2010.
  b. Find the growth rate per decade that corresponds to the growth rate of 1.3% per year.
  c. Suppose that the population growth rate of India slows to 1% per year after the year 2000. What is the predicted population, to the nearest hundred thousand, of India in 2010?

52. CHEMISTRY A dilution is commonly used to obtain the desired concentration of a sample. For example, suppose that 1 milliliter of hydrochloric acid, or HCl, is combined with 9 milliliters of a buffer. The concentration of the resulting mixture is $\frac{1}{10}$ of the original concentration of HCl.
  a. Suppose that this dilution is performed again with 1 millimeter of the already diluted mixture and 9 milliliters of buffer. What is the concentration of the resulting mixture (compared with the original concentration)?
  b. Write an expression to model the concentration of HCl in the resulting mixture after repeated dilutions as described in part **a**.
  c. What is the concentration of the resulting mixture (compared to the original concentration) after 5 repeated dilutions?

53. SPACE SCIENCE The first stage of the *Saturn 5* rocket that propelled astronauts to the moon burned about 8% of its remaining fuel every 15 seconds and carried about 600,000 gallons of fuel at liftoff. Estimate the amount of fuel remaining, to the nearest ten thousand gallons, in the first stage 2 minutes after liftoff.

Look Back

Evaluate each expression. *(LESSON 2.2)*

54. 4^{-2} **55.** $\left(\dfrac{1}{2}\right)^{-1}$ **56.** $25^{\frac{3}{2}}$ **57.** $49^{\frac{1}{2}}$

Simplify each expression, assuming that no variable equals zero. Write your answer with positive exponents only. *(LESSON 2.2)*

58. $\left(\dfrac{2x^3}{x^{-2}}\right)^2$ **59.** $\left(\dfrac{m^{-1}n^2}{n^{-3}}\right)^{-3}$ **60.** $\left(\dfrac{2a^3b^{-2}}{-a^2b^{-3}}\right)^{-1}$ **61.** $\dfrac{(2y^2y)^{-2}}{3xy^{-4}}$

Identify each transformation from the graph of $f(x) = x^2$ to the graph of g. *(LESSON 2.7)*

62. $g(x) = 6x^2$ **63.** $g(x) = (-2x)^2$ **64.** $g(x) = -\dfrac{1}{2}x^2 + 1$

65. $g(x) = -(0.5x)^2 + 3$ **66.** $g(x) = (x - 3)^2 + 2$ **67.** $g(x) = -5(x - 2)^2 - 4$

State whether each parabola opens up or down and whether the y-coordinate of the vertex is the maximum or minimum value of the function. *(LESSON 5.1)*

68. $f(x) = \dfrac{1}{2}x^2$ **69.** $f(x) = -2x^2 - x + 1$ **70.** $f(x) = 3 - 5x - x^2$

Look Beyond

APPLICATION

71. INVESTMENTS Suppose that you want to invest $100 in a bank account that earns 5% interest *compounded once* at the end of each year. Determine the balance after 10 years.

Refer to the discussions of the Portfolio Activities and Chapter Project on page 353 for background on this activity.

You will need a CBL with a temperature probe, a glass of ice water, and a graphics calculator.

1. First use the CBL to find the temperature of the air. Then place the probe in the ice water for 2 minutes. Record 30 CBL readings taken at 2-second intervals. Take a final reading at the end of the 2 minutes.

2. a. Use the linear regression feature on your calculator to find a linear function that models your first 30 readings. (Use the variable t for the time in seconds).

b. Use your linear function to predict the temperature of the probe after 2 minutes, or 120 seconds. Compare this

prediction with your actual 2-minute reading.

c. Discuss the usefulness of your linear function for modeling the cooling process. (You may want to illustrate your answer with graphs.)

Save your data and results for use in the remaining Portfolio Activities.

WORKING ON THE CHAPTER PROJECT

You should now be able to complete Activity 1 of the Chapter Project.

Exponential Functions

Why *You can use exponential functions to calculate the value of investments that earn compound interest and to compare different investments by calculating effective yields.*

Objectives

- Classify an exponential function as representing exponential growth or exponential decay.

- Calculate the growth of investments under various conditions.

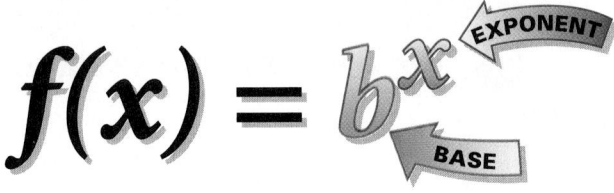

$$f(x) = b^x$$

EXPONENT

BASE

Consider the function $y = x^2$ and $y = 2^x$. Both functions have a base and an exponent. However, $y = x^2$ is a quadratic function, and $y = 2^x$ is an *exponential function.* In an exponential function, the base is fixed and the exponent is variable.

Exponential Function

The function $f(x) = b^x$ is an **exponential function** with **base** b, where b is a positive real number other than 1 and x is any real number.

---

x	$y = 2^x$
-3	$2^{-3} = \frac{1}{8}$
-2	$2^{-2} = \frac{1}{4}$
-1	$2^{-1} = \frac{1}{2}$
0	$2^0 = 1$
1	$2^1 = 2$
$\sqrt{2}$	$2^{\sqrt{2}} \approx 2.67$
2	$2^2 = 4$
3	$2^3 = 8$

Examine the table at left and the graph at right of the exponential function $y = 2^x$.

Notice that as x-values decrease, the y-values for $y = 2^x$ get closer and closer to 0, approaching the x-axis as an *asymptote.* An **asymptote** is a line that a graph approaches (but does not reach) as its x- or y-values become very large or very small.

The graph of $y = 2^x$ approaches the x-axis but never reaches it.

Notice that the domain of $y = 2^x$ includes irrational numbers, such as $\sqrt{2}$.

Investigating Exponential Functions

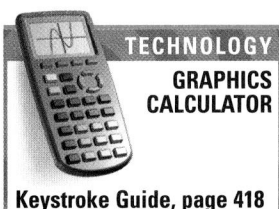
You will need: a graphics calculator

1. Graph $y_1 = 3^x$, $y_2 = 2^x$, and $y_3 = (1.5)^x$ on the same screen.

2. For what value of x is $y_1 = y_2 = y_3$ true? For what values of x is $y_1 > y_2 > y_3$ true? For what values of x is $y_1 < y_2 < y_3$ true?

3. Graph $y_4 = \left(\frac{1}{3}\right)^x$, $y_5 = \left(\frac{1}{2}\right)^x$, and $y_6 = \left(\frac{1}{1.5}\right)^x$ on the same screen as y_1, y_2, and y_3.

PROBLEM SOLVING

4. **Look for a pattern.** Examine each corresponding pair of functions.

$$y_1 = 3 \text{ and } y_4 = \left(\frac{1}{3}\right)^x \qquad y_2 = 2^x \text{ and } y_5 = \left(\frac{1}{2}\right)^x$$

$$y_3 = (1.5)^x \text{ and } y_6 = \left(\frac{1}{1.5}\right)^x$$

How are the graphs of each corresponding pair of functions related? How are the bases of each corresponding pair of functions related?

CHECKPOINT ✔

5. For what values of b does the graph of $y = b^x$ rise from left to right? For what values of b does the graph of $y = b^x$ fall from left to right?

The graphs of $f(x) = 2^x$ and $g(x) = \left(\frac{1}{2}\right)^x$ exhibit the two typical behaviors for exponential functions.

$g(x) = \left(\frac{1}{2}\right)^x$ is a decreasing exponential function because its base is a positive number less than 1.

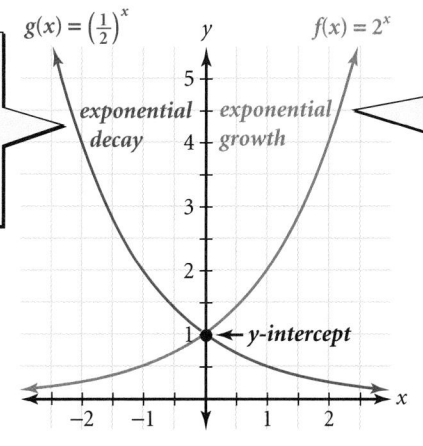

$f(x) = 2^x$ is an increasing exponential function because its base is a positive number greater than 1.

CONNECTION

TRANSFORMATIONS

Recall from Lesson 2.7 that the graphs of f and g are reflections of one another across the y-axis because $g(x) = f(-x) = 2^{-x} = \left(\frac{1}{2}\right)^x$.

Exponential Growth and Decay

When $b > 1$, the function $f(x) = b^x$ represents **exponential growth**.

When $0 < b < 1$, the function $f(x) = b^x$ represents **exponential decay**.

Exponential growth functions and exponential decay functions of the form $y = b^x$ have the same domain, range, and y-intercept. For example:

Function	Domain	Range	y-intercept
$f(x) = 2^x$	all real numbers	all positive real numbers	1
$g(x) = \left(\frac{1}{2}\right)^x$	all real numbers	all positive real numbers	1

Recall from Lesson 2.7 that $y = a \cdot f(x)$ represents a vertical stretch or compression of the graph of $y = f(x)$. This transformation is applied to exponential functions in Example 1.

E X A M P L E ❶ Graph $f(x) = 2^x$ along with each function below. Tell whether each function represents exponential growth or exponential decay. Then give the y-intercept.

    a. $y = 3 \cdot f(x)$ **b.** $y = 5 \cdot f(-x)$

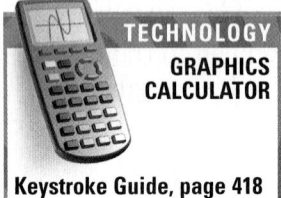

TECHNOLOGY
GRAPHICS CALCULATOR

Keystroke Guide, page 418

CONNECTION
TRANSFORMATIONS

● **SOLUTION**

    a. $y = 3 \cdot f(x) = 3 \cdot 2^x$

        The function $y = 3 \cdot 2^x$ represents exponential growth because the base, 2, is greater than 1.

        The y-intercept is 3 because the graph of $f(x) = 2^x$, which has a y-intercept of 1, is stretched by a factor of 3.

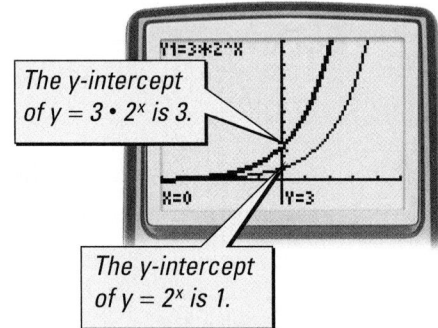

The y-intercept of $y = 3 \cdot 2^x$ is 3.

The y-intercept of $y = 2^x$ is 1.

    b. $y = 5 \cdot f(-x) = 5 \cdot 2^{-x} = 5 \cdot \left(\frac{1}{2}\right)^x$

        The function $y = 5 \cdot \left(\frac{1}{2}\right)^x$ represents exponential decay because the base, $\frac{1}{2}$, is less than 1.

        The y-intercept is 5 because the graph of $f(x) = 2^x$, which has a y-intercept of 1, is stretched by a factor of 5.

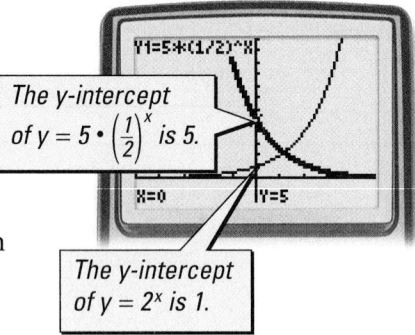

The y-intercept of $y = 5 \cdot \left(\frac{1}{2}\right)^x$ is 5.

The y-intercept of $y = 2^x$ is 1.

TRY THIS   Graph $f(x) = 2^x$ along with each function below. Tell whether each function represents exponential growth or exponential decay. Then give the y-intercept.

    a. $y = \frac{1}{3} \cdot f(x)$ **b.** $y = \frac{1}{4} \cdot f(-x)$

CHECKPOINT ✔   What transformation of f occurs when $a < 0$ in $y = a \cdot f(x)$?

CRITICAL THINKING   Describe the effect on the graph of $f(x) = b^x$ when $b > 1$ and b increases. Describe the effect on the graph of $f(x) = b^x$ when $0 < b < 1$ and b decreases.

Compound Interest

APPLICATION

INVESTMENTS

The growth in the value of investments earning compound interest is modeled by an exponential function.

Compound Interest Formula

The total amount of an investment, A, earning compound interest is

$$A(t) = P\left(1 + \frac{r}{n}\right)^{nt},$$

where P is the principal, r is the annual interest rate, n is the number of times interest is compounded per year, and t is the time in years.

E X A M P L E ② Find the final amount of a $100 investment after 10 years at 5% interest compounded annually, quarterly, and daily.

● **SOLUTION**

In this situation, the principal is $100, the annual interest rate is 5%, and the time period is 10 years. Thus, $P = 100$, $r = 0.05$, and $t = 10$. The table shows calculations for $n = 1$, $n = 4$, and $n = 365$.

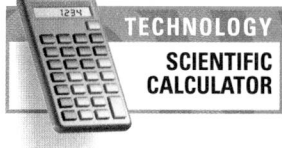

TECHNOLOGY

SCIENTIFIC CALCULATOR

Compounding period	n	$A(10) = 100\left(1 + \frac{0.05}{n}\right)^{n \cdot 10}$	Final amount
annually	1	$A(10) = 100\left(1 + \frac{0.05}{1}\right)^{1 \cdot 10}$	$162.89
quarterly	4	$A(10) = 100\left(1 + \frac{0.05}{4}\right)^{4 \cdot 10}$	$164.36
daily	365	$A(10) = 100\left(1 + \frac{0.05}{365}\right)^{365 \cdot 10}$	$164.87

CHECKPOINT ✔ Describe what happens to the final amount as the number of compounding periods increases.

Effective Yield

APPLICATION

INVESTMENTS

Suppose that you buy an item for $100 and sell the item one year later for $105. In this case, the *effective yield* of your investment is 5%. The **effective yield** is the annually compounded interest rate that yields the final amount of an investment. You can determine the effective yield by fitting an exponential regression equation to two points.

EXAMPLE ❸ A collector buys a painting for $100,000 at the beginning of 1995 and sells it for $150,000 at the beginning of 2000.

Use an exponential regression equation to find the effective yield.

SOLUTION

1. Find the exponential equation that represents this situation.

   To find effective yield, the interest is compounded annually, so $n = 1$.

   From 1995 to 2000 is 5 years, so $t = 5$.

   $$A(t) = P\left(1 + \frac{r}{n}\right)^{nt}$$

   $$150,000 = 100,000\left(1 + \frac{r}{1}\right)^{1 \cdot 5}$$

   $$150,000 = 100,000(1 + r)^5$$

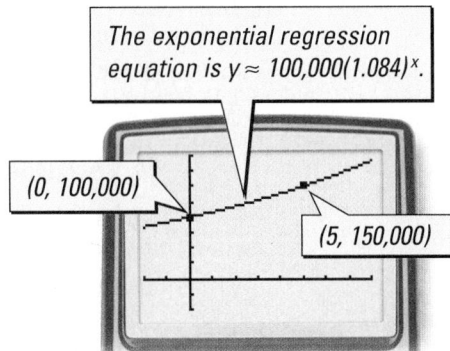

The exponential regression equation is $y \approx 100,000(1.084)^x$.

(0, 100,000)

(5, 150,000)

2. Enter the two points that represent the given information, (0, 100,000) and (5, 150,000). Find and graph the exponential regression equation that fits the points.

3. The multiplier is about 1.084, so the effective yield, is about $1.084 - 1 = 0.084$, or 8.4%.

TECHNOLOGY
GRAPHICS CALCULATOR

Keystroke Guide, page 419

TRY THIS Find the effective yield for a painting bought for $100,000 at the end of 1994 and sold for $200,000 at the end of 2004.

Exercises

internet connect

Activities Online

Go To: go.hrw.com
Keyword:
MB1 Medicine

Communicate

1. If $b > 0$ and the graph of $y = b^x$ falls from left to right, describe the possible values of b.

2. Compare the domain and range of $y = 3^x$ with the domain and range of $y = \left(\frac{1}{3}\right)^x$.

3. Describe how the y-intercept of the graph of $f(x) = 2(5)^x$ is related to the value of a in $f(x) = ab^x$.

4. How are the functions $y = x^2$ and $y = 2^x$ similar, and how are they different?

Tell whether each function represents exponential growth or exponential decay, and give the *y*-intercept. *(EXAMPLE 1)*

5. $f(x) = \left(\frac{1}{2}\right)^x$ **6.** $g(x) = 3(2)^x$ **7.** $k(x) = 5(0.5)^x$

APPLICATIONS

8. INVESTMENTS Find the final amount of a $250 investment after 5 years at 6% interest compounded annually, quarterly, and daily. *(EXAMPLE 2)*

9. INVESTMENTS Find the effective yield for a $2000 investment that is worth $4000 after 15 years. *(EXAMPLE 3)*

● *Practice and Apply*

Identify each function as linear, quadratic, or exponential.

10. $g(x) = 10x + 3$ **11.** $k(x) = (77 - x)x$.   **12.** $f(x) = 12(2.5)^x$

13. $k(x) = 0.5^x - 3.5$ **14.** $g(x) = (2200)^{3.5x}$ **15.** $h(x) = 0.5x^2 + 7.5$

Tell whether each function represents exponential growth or decay.

16. $y(x) = 12(2.5)^x$ **17.** $k(x) = 500(1.5)^x$ **18.** $y(t) = 45\left(\frac{1}{4}\right)^t$

19. $d(x) = 0.125\left(\frac{1}{2}\right)^x$ **20.** $g(x) = 0.25(0.8)^x$ **21.** $s(k) = 0.5(0.5)^k$

22. $m(x) = 222(0.9)^x$ **23.** $f(k) = 722^{-k}$ **24.** $g(x) = 0.5(787)^{-x}$

Match each function with its graph.

25. $y = 2^x$ **26.** $y = 2(3)^x$

27. $y = 2\left(\frac{1}{3}\right)^x$ **28.** $y = \left(\frac{1}{2}\right)^x$

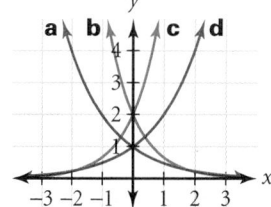

Find the final amount for each investment.

29. $1000 at 6% interest compounded annually for 20 years

30. $1000 at 6% interest compounded semiannually for 20 years

31. $750 at 10% interest compounded quarterly for 10 years

32. $750 at 5% interest compounded quarterly for 10 years

33. $1800 at 5.65% interest compounded daily for 3 years

34. $1800 at 5.65% interest compounded daily for 6 years

35. Graph $f(x) = 2^x$, $g(x) = 5^x$, and $h(x) = 8^x$.
     a. Which function exhibits the fastest growth? the slowest growth?
     b. What is the *y*-intercept of each function?
     c. State the domain and range of each function.

36. Graph $a(x) = \left(\frac{1}{2}\right)^x$, $b(x) = \left(\frac{1}{5}\right)^x$, and $c(x) = \left(\frac{1}{8}\right)^x$.
     a. Which function exhibits the fastest decay? the slowest decay?
     b. What is the *y*-intercept of each function?
     c. State the domain and range of each function.

CHALLENGE

37. Describe when the graph of $f(x) = ab^x$ is a horizontal line.

TRANSFORMATIONS **Graph each pair of functions and describe the transformations from *f* to *g*.**

38. $f(x) = \left(\frac{1}{2}\right)^x$ and $g(x) = 5\left(\frac{1}{2}\right)^x$

39. $f(x) = \left(\frac{1}{10}\right)^x$ and $g(x) = 0.5\left(\frac{1}{10}\right)^x$

40. $f(x) = 2^x$ and $g(x) = 3(2)^x + 1$

41. $f(x) = 10^x$ and $g(x) = 2(10)^x - 3$

42. $f(x) = 10^x$ and $g(x) = 3(10)^{x+2}$

43. $f(x) = 2^x$ and $g(x) = 5(2)^{x-1}$

44. $f(x) = 3\left(\frac{1}{2}\right)^x$ and $g(x) = 3(2^x)$

45. $f(x) = \left(\frac{1}{3}\right)^x$ and $g(x) = 2(3)^{-x}$

46. TRANSFORMATIONS Describe how each transformation of $f(x) = b^x$ affects the domain and range, the asymptotes, and the intercepts.
  a. a vertical stretch
  b. a vertical compression
  c. a horizontal translation
  d. a vertical translation
  e. a reflection across the *y*-axis

STATISTICS **Use an exponential regression equation to find the effective yield for each investment. Assume that interest is compounded only once each year.**

47 a $1000 mutual fund investment made at the beginning of 1990 that is worth $1450 at the beginning of 2000

48 a house that is bought for $75,000 at the end of 1995 and that is worth $95,000 at the end of 2005

STATISTICS **Use an exponential regression equation to model the annual rate of inflation, or percent increase in price, for each item described.**

49 a half-gallon of milk cost $1.37 in 1989 and $1.48 in 1995 [*Source: U.S. Bureau of Labor Statistics*]

50 a gallon of regular unleaded gasoline cost $0.93 in 1986 and $1.11 in 1993 [*Source: U.S. Bureau of Labor Statistics*]

APPLICATIONS

51. INVESTMENTS Find the final amount of a $2000 certificate of deposit (CD) after 5 years at an annual interest rate of 5.51% compounded annually.

Certificate of Deposit

5.51%

Annual Percentage Yield*

$2,000 Minimum

52. INVESTMENTS Consider a $1000 investment that is compounded annually at three different interest rates: 5%, 5.5%, and 6%.
  a. Write and graph a function for each interest rate over a time period from 0 to 60 years.
  b. Compare the graphs of the three functions.
  c. Compare the shapes of the graphs for the first 10 years with the shapes of the graphs between 50 and 60 years.

53. INVESTMENTS The final amount for $5000 invested for 25 years at 10% annual interest compounded semiannually is $57,337.
  a. What is the effect of doubling the amount invested?
  b. What is the effect of doubling the annual interest rate?
  c. What is the effect of doubling the investment period?
  d. Which of the above has the greatest effect on the final amount of the investment?

Find the inverse of each function. State whether the inverse is a function. *(LESSON 2.5)*

54. $\{(-2, 4), (-3, -1), (2, 2), (3, 4)\}$

55. $\{(7, 2), (3, -1), (2, 2), (0, 0)\}$

56. $y = 2(x + 3)$ **57.** $y = 3x^2$ **58.** $y = x^2 + 2$ **59.** $y = -x^2$

Graph each piecewise function. *(LESSON 2.6)*

60. $f(x) = \begin{cases} 9 & \text{if } 0 \le x < 5 \\ 2x - 1 & \text{if } 5 \le x < 10 \end{cases}$ **61.** $g(x) = \begin{cases} x & \text{if } 0 \le x < 2 \\ -3x + 8 & \text{if } 2 \le x < 5 \\ -5 & \text{if } 5 \le x < 10 \end{cases}$

Let $A = \begin{bmatrix} 3 & 4 & -1 \\ -2 & -8 & 6 \\ 10 & 8 & 0 \end{bmatrix}$, $B = \begin{bmatrix} 0 & 2 \\ 7 & -2 \\ -5 & 1 \end{bmatrix}$, and $C = \begin{bmatrix} 2 & -6 & -2 \\ 3 & -1 & 4 \end{bmatrix}$. **Find each**

product matrix, if it exists. *(LESSON 4.2)*

62. AB **63.** BA **64.** AC **65.** CA **66.** BC **67.** CB

Find a quadratic function to fit each set of points exactly. *(LESSON 5.7)*

68. $(1, -1), (2, -5), (3, 13)$ **69.** $(0, 4), (1, 5), (3, 25)$

70. Use guess-and-check to find x such that $10^x = 50$.

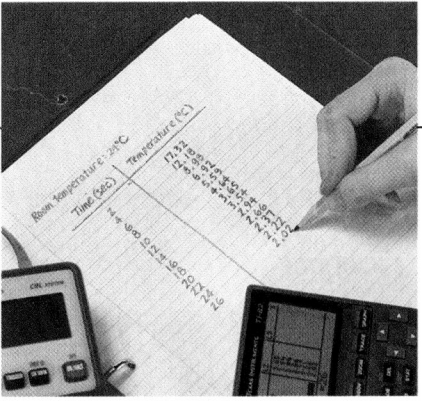

For this activity, use the data collected in the Portfolio Activity on page 361.

1. a. Use the quadratic regression feature on your calculator to find a quadratic function that models your first 30 readings.

    b. Use your linear function to predict the temperature of the probe after 2 minutes. Compare this prediction with your actual 2-minute reading.

    c. Discuss the usefulness of your quadratic function for modeling the cooling process.

2. Now use the exponential regression feature on your calculator to find an exponential function that models your first 30 readings, and repeat parts **b** and **c** of Step 1.

Save your data and results to use in the remaining Portfolio Activities.

WORKING ON THE CHAPTER PROJECT

You should now be able to complete Activity 2 of the Chapter Project.

Logarithmic Functions

Substance	pH
gastric fluid	1.8
lemon juice	2.2–2.4
vinegar	2.4–3.4
banana	4.8
saliva	6.5–7.5
water	7
egg white	7.6–8.0
Rolaids, Tums	9.9
milk of magnesia	10.5

The pH of an acidic solution is less than 7, the pH of a basic solution is greater than 7, and the pH of a neutral solution is 7.

Objectives

- Write equivalent forms for exponential and logarithmic equations.

- Use the definitions of exponential and logarithmic functions to solve equations.

Why *Logarithmic functions are widely used in measurement scales such as the pH scale, which ranges from 0 to 14.*

Logarithms are used to find unknown exponents in exponential models.

Logarithmic functions define many measurement scales in the sciences, including the pH, decibel, and Richter scales.

Activity
Approximating Exponents

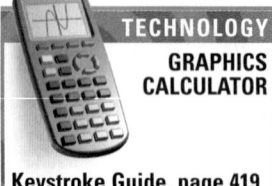

TECHNOLOGY
GRAPHICS CALCULATOR
Keystroke Guide, page 419

You will need: a graphics calculator

Use the table below to complete this Activity.

x	-3	-2	-1	0	1	2	3
$y = 10^x$	$\frac{1}{1000}$	$\frac{1}{100}$	$\frac{1}{10}$	1	10	100	1000

1. How are the x-values in the table related to the y-values?

CHECKPOINT ✔ 2. Use the table above to find the value of x in each equation below.

    a. $10^x = 1000$ **b.** $10^x = \frac{1}{100}$ **c.** $10^x = \frac{1}{1000}$ **d.** $10^x = 1$

PROBLEM SOLVING 3. **Make a table** of values for $y = 10^x$. Use the table to approximate the solution to $10^x = 7$ to the nearest hundredth.

CHECKPOINT ✔ 4. Use a table of values to approximate the solution to $10^x = 85$ to the nearest hundredth.

A table of values for $y = 10^x$ can be used to solve equations such as $10^x = 1000$ and $10^x = \frac{1}{100}$. However, to solve equations such as $10^x = 85$ or $10^x = 2.3$, a *logarithm* is needed. With logarithms, you can write an exponential equation in an equivalent logarithmic form.

Exponential form   **Logarithmic form**

Equivalent Exponential and Logarithmic Forms

For any positive base b, where $b \neq 1$:
$b^x = y$ if and only if $x = \log_b y$

EXAMPLE 1
a. Write $5^3 = 125$ in logarithmic form.
b. Write $\log_3 81 = 4$ in exponential form.

● **SOLUTION**

a. $5^3 = 125 \rightarrow 3 = \log_5 125$ *3 is the exponent and 5 is the base.*
b. $\log_3 81 = 4 \rightarrow 3^4 = 81$ *3 is the base and 4 is the exponent.*

TRY THIS   Copy and complete each column in the table below.

Exponential form	$2^5 = 32$	?	$3^{-2} = \frac{1}{9}$	?
Logarithmic form	?	$\log_{10} 1000 = 3$	?	$\log_{16} 4 = \frac{1}{2}$

You can evaluate logarithms with a base of 10 by using the [LOG] key on a calculator.

EXAMPLE 2 Solve for $10^x = 85$ for x. Round your answer to the nearest thousandth.

● **SOLUTION**

TECHNOLOGY
SCIENTIFIC CALCULATOR

Write $10^x = 85$ in logarithmic form, and use the [LOG] key.

> *Because $10^1 = 10$ and $10^2 = 100$, $x \approx 1.9294$ is a reasonable answer.*

$10^x = 85$
$x = \log_{10} 85$
$x \approx 1.9294$ *Use a calculator.*

TRY THIS   Solve $10^x = \frac{1}{109}$ for x. Round your answer to the nearest thousandth.

Definition of Logarithmic Function

The inverse of the exponential function $y = 10^x$ is $x = 10^y$. To rewrite $x = 10^y$ in terms of y, use the equivalent logarithmic form, $y = \log_{10} x$.

Examine the tables and graphs below to see the inverse relationship between $y = 10^x$ and $y = \log_{10} x$.

x	$y = 10^x$	x	$y = \log_{10} x$
-3	$\frac{1}{1000}$	$\frac{1}{1000}$	-3
-2	$\frac{1}{100}$	$\frac{1}{100}$	-2
-1	$\frac{1}{10}$	$\frac{1}{10}$	-1
0	1	1	0
1	10	10	1
2	100	100	2
3	1000	1000	3

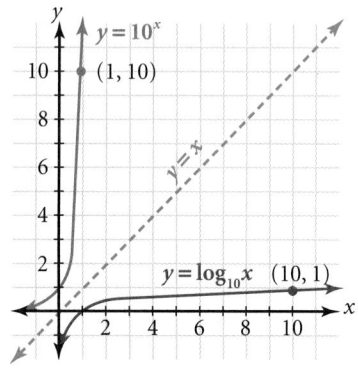

The table below summarizes the relationship between the domain and range of $y = 10^x$ and of $y = \log_{10} x$.

Function	Domain	Range
$y = 10^x$	all real numbers	all positive real numbers
$y = \log_{10} x$	all positive real numbers	all real numbers

Logarithmic Functions

The **logarithmic function** $y = \log_b x$ with base b, or $x = b^y$, is the inverse of the exponential function $y = b^x$, where $b \neq 1$ and $b > 0$.

CRITICAL THINKING   Describe the graph that results if $b = 1$ in $y = \log_b x$. Is $y = \log_1 x$ a function?

Because $y = \log_b x$ is the inverse of the exponential function $y = b^x$ and $y = \log_b x$ is a function, the exponential function $y = b^x$ is a one-to-one function. This means that for each element in the domain of an exponential function, there is exactly one corresponding element in the range. For example, if $3^x = 3^2$, then $x = 2$. This is called the *One-to-One Property of Exponents*.

One-to-One Property of Exponents

If $b^x = b^y$, then $x = y$.

EXAMPLE ③ Find the value of v in each equation.

  a. $v = \log_{125} 5$ **b.** $5 = \log_v 32$ **c.** $4 = \log_3 v$

● **SOLUTION**

Write the equivalent exponential form, and solve for v.

  a. $v = \log_{125} 5$
     $125^v = 5$
     $(5^3)^v = 5$
     $5^{3v} = 5^1$
     $3v = 1$
     $v = \dfrac{1}{3}$

  Apply the One-to-One Property.

  b. $5 = \log_v 32$
     $v^5 = 32$
     $v^5 = 2^5$
     $v = 2$

  c. $4 = \log_3 v$
     $3^4 = v$
     $81 = v$

TRY THIS Find the value of v in each equation.

  a. $v = \log_4 64$ **b.** $2 = \log_v 25$ **c.** $6 = \log_3 v$

CONNECTION

TRANSFORMATIONS

Recall from Lesson 2.7 that the graph of $y = -f(x)$ is the graph of $y = f(x)$ reflected across the x-axis. The graph of $y = \log_{10} x$ and of its reflection across the x-axis, $y = -\log_{10} x$, are shown at right.

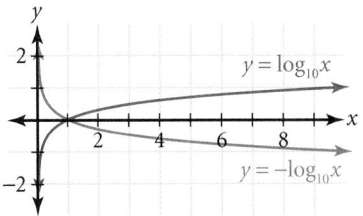

The function $y = -\log_{10} x$ is used in chemistry to measure pH levels. The pH of a solution describes its acidity. Substances that are more acidic have a lower pH, while substances that are less acidic, or basic, have a higher pH. The pH of a substance is defined as $\text{pH} = -\log_{10}[\text{H}^+]$, where $[\text{H}^+]$ is the hydrogen ion concentration of a solution in moles per liter.

EXAMPLE ④ The pH of a carbonated soda is 3.

What is $[\text{H}^+]$ for this soda?

APPLICATION

CHEMISTRY

● **SOLUTION**

$\text{pH} = -\log_{10}[\text{H}^+]$
$3 = -\log_{10}[\text{H}^+]$ *Substitute 3 for pH.*
$-3 = \log_{10}[\text{H}^+]$
$10^{-3} = [\text{H}^+]$ *Write the equivalent exponential equation.*

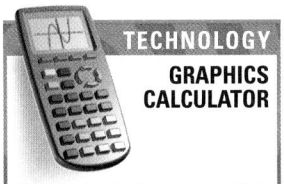

TECHNOLOGY

GRAPHICS CALCULATOR

Keystroke Guide, page 419

CHECK

Graph $y = -\log_{10} x$ and $y = 3$ on the same screen, and find the point of intersection. The window at right shows x-values between 0 and 0.01.

Thus, there is $\dfrac{1}{1000}$, or 0.001, moles of hydrogen ions in a liter of carbonated soda that has a pH of 3.

TRY THIS Find $[\text{H}^+]$ for orange juice that has a pH of 3.75.

Exercises

Communicate

1. Describe the relationship between logarithmic functions and exponential functions.

2. State the domain and range of logarithmic functions. How are they related to the domain and range of exponential functions?

3. Explain how to approximate the value of x in $2^x = 58$ by using the table feature of a graphics calculator.

Guided Skills Practice

4. Write $4^2 = 16$ in logarithmic form. *(EXAMPLE 1)*

5. Write $\log_5 25 = 2$ in exponential form. *(EXAMPLE 1)*

Solve each equation for x. Round your answers to the nearest thousandth. *(EXAMPLE 2)*

6. $10^x = 568$

7. $10^x = \dfrac{1}{500}$

Find the value of v in each equation. *(EXAMPLE 3)*

8. $v = \log_7 49$

9. $2 = \log_v 144$

10. $2 = \log_4 v$

APPLICATION

11. **CHEMISTRY** The pH of black coffee is 5. What is $[H^+]$ for this coffee? *(EXAMPLE 4)*

Practice and Apply

Write each equation in logarithmic form.

12. $11^2 = 121$

13. $5^4 = 625$

14. $3^5 = 243$

15. $6^3 = 216$

16. $6^{-2} = \dfrac{1}{36}$

17. $7^{-2} = \dfrac{1}{49}$

18. $27^{\frac{1}{3}} = 3$

19. $16^{\frac{1}{4}} = 2$

20. $\left(\dfrac{1}{4}\right)^{-3} = 64$

21. $\left(\dfrac{1}{9}\right)^{-2} = 81$

22. $\left(\dfrac{1}{3}\right)^{2} = \dfrac{1}{9}$

23. $\left(\dfrac{1}{2}\right)^{3} = \dfrac{1}{8}$

Write each equation in exponential form.

24. $\log_6 36 = 2$

25. $\log_{10} 1000 = 3$

26. $\log_{10} 0.001 = -3$

27. $\log_{10} 0.1 = -1$

28. $3 = \log_9 729$

29. $3 = \log_7 343$

30. $\log_3 \dfrac{1}{81} = -4$

31. $\log_2 \dfrac{1}{32} = -5$

32. $-2 = \log_2 \dfrac{1}{4}$

33. $-3 = \log_3 \dfrac{1}{27}$

34. $\log_{121} 11 = \dfrac{1}{2}$

35. $\log_{144} 12 = \dfrac{1}{2}$

Find the approximate value of each logarithmic expression.

36. $\log_{10} 1026$

37. $\log_{10} 79$

38. $\log_{10} 8$

39. $\log_{10} 21,050$

40. $\log_{10} 0.08$

41. $\log_{10} 0.9$

42. $\log_{10} 0.002$

43. $\log_{10} 0.00013$

Solve each equation for *x*. Round your answers to the nearest hundredth.

44. $10^x = 31$

45. $10^x = 12$

46. $10^x = 7210$

47. $10^x = 3588$

48. $10^x = 1.498$

49. $10^x = 1.89$

50. $10^x = 0.0054$

51. $10^x = 0.035$

52. $10^x = \dfrac{3}{49}$

53. $10^x = \dfrac{1}{1085}$

54. $10^x = \sqrt{7.4}$

55. $10^x = \dfrac{1}{\sqrt{500}}$

Find the value of *v* in each equation.

56. $v = \log_{10} 1000$

57. $v = \log_4 64$

58. $v = \log_7 343$

59. $v = \log_{17} 289$

60. $v = \log_3 3$

61. $v = \log_7 7$

62. $v = \log_{10} 0.001$

63. $v = \log_{10} 0.01$

64. $v = \log_2 \dfrac{1}{4}$

65. $v = \log_{10} \dfrac{1}{100}$

66. $v = \log_4 1$

67. $v = \log_9 1$

68. $3 = \log_6 v$

69. $2 = \log_7 v$

70. $1 = \log_5 v$

71. $1 = \log_3 v$

72. $\dfrac{1}{2} = \log_9 v$

73. $\dfrac{1}{3} = \log_8 v$

74. $-2 = \log_6 v$

75. $-3 = \log_4 v$

76. $0 = \log_{13} v$

77. $0 = \log_2 v$

78. $\log_v 16 = 2$

79. $\log_v 125 = 3$

80. $\log_v 9 = \dfrac{1}{2}$

81. $\log_v 4 = \dfrac{1}{3}$

82. $\log_v \dfrac{1}{16} = -4$

83. $\log_v \dfrac{1}{8} = -3$

84. $\log_v 216 = 3$

85. $\log_v 243 = 5$

86. Graph $f(x) = 3^x$ along with f^{-1}. Make a table of values that illustrates the relationship between f and f^{-1}.

87. Graph $f(x) = 3^{-x}$ along with f^{-1}. Make a table of values that illustrates the relationship between f and f^{-1}.

CHALLENGES

Find the value of each expression.

88. $\log_{27} \sqrt{3}$

89. $\log_2 16\sqrt{2}$

90. $\log_{\frac{1}{2}} 8$

internet connect

Homework Help Online

Go To: **go.hrw.com**
Keyword:
MB1 Homework Help
for Exercises 91–96

TRANSFORMATIONS Let $f(x) = \log_{10} x$. For each function, identify the transformations from f to g.

91. $g(x) = 3 \log_{10} x$

92. $g(x) = -5 \log_{10} x$

93. $g(x) = \dfrac{1}{2} \log_{10} x + 1$

94. $g(x) = 0.25 \log_{10} x - 2$

95. $g(x) = -\log_{10}(x - 2)$

96. $g(x) = \log_{10}(x + 5) - 3$

CHEMISTRY Calculate [H$^+$] for each of the following:

97. household ammonia with a pH of about 10

98. distilled water with a pH of 7

99. human blood with a pH of about 7.4

100. **CHEMISTRY** How much greater is [H$^+$] for lemon juice, which has a pH of 2.1, than [H$^+$] for water, which has a pH of 7.0?

pH paper turns red in an acidic solution, $0 < pH < 7$; the paper turns green in a neutral solution, indicating a pH of 7; and the paper turns blue in a basic solution, $7 < pH < 14$.

| Battery acid | Stomach acid, lemons | Tomatoes, bananas | Black coffee | Pure water | Baking soda | Hand soap | Household ammonia | Lye (drain cleaner) |

101. PHYSICS Earth's atmosphere is like an "ocean" of air with the upper layers of air pressing down on the lower layers of air. The weight of the layers of air creates atmospheric air pressure. At sea level (altitude of zero), the average air pressure is about 14.7 pounds per square inch. The air pressure, P, decreases with altitude, a, in feet according to the function $P = 14.7(10)^{-0.000018a}$. Find the altitude that corresponds to the air pressure commonly found in commercial airplanes, 11.82 pounds per square inch.

Look Back

102. Write a linear equation for a line with a slope of 4 and a y-intercept of 3. *(LESSON 1.2)*

State the property that is illustrated in each statement. All variables represent real numbers. *(LESSON 2.1)*

103. $1 \cdot (5xy) = 5xy$

104. $(2 + z) + y = 2 + (z + y)$

105. $2(3x) = 3x(2)$

106. $-x + 0 = -x$

107. $\frac{a}{2} \cdot \frac{2}{a} = 1$, where $a \neq 0$

108. $-3 + x = x + (-3)$

109 Find the inverse of the matrix $\begin{bmatrix} 2 & 3 \\ 1 & -4 \end{bmatrix}$. *(LESSON 4.3)*

110. Solve the quadratic equation $x^2 - 6x + 9 = 0$. *(LESSONS 5.2 AND 5.4)*

111. State the two solutions of the equation $x^2 + 1 = 0$. *(LESSON 5.6)*

112. If an interest rate is 7.3%, what is the multiplier? *(LESSON 6.1)*

Look Beyond

113. Calculate $\log_2 2 + \log_2 8$ and $\log_2 32 - \log_2 2$. Then compare these values with the value of $\log_2 16$.

Properties of Logarithmic Functions

Why *The properties of logarithms allow you to simplify logarithmic expressions, which makes evaluating the expressions easier.*

Objectives

- Simplify and evaluate expressions involving logarithms.

- Solve equations involving logarithms.

John Napier
(1550–1617)

MIRIFICI

Logarithmorum
Canonis defcriptio,

Ejufque ufus, in utraque
Trigonòmetria; ut etiam in
omni Logiftica Mathematica,
Ampliffimi, Facillimi, &
expeditiffimi explicatio.

Authore ac Inventore,
IOANNE NEPERO,
Barone Merchiftonii,
&c. Scoto.

EDINBURGI,
Ex officinâ ANDREÆ HART
Bibliopolæ. CIↃ. Ɔ C. XIV.

*Title page and calculations from
Napier's* Mirifici Logarithmorum
Canonis Descriptio

In the seventeenth century, a Scottish mathematician named John Napier developed methods for efficiently performing calculations with large numbers. He found a method for finding the *product* of two numbers by *adding* two corresponding numbers, which he called logarithms.

John Napier's contributions to mathematics are contained in two essays: *Mirifici Logarithmorum Canonis Descriptio* (Description of the Marvelous Canon of Logarithms), published in 1614, and *Mirifici Logarithmorum Canonis Constructio* (Construction of the Marvelous Canon of Logarithms), published in 1619, two years after his death.

Product and Quotient Properties of Logarithms

The Product, Quotient, and Power Properties of Exponents are as follows:

$$a^m \cdot a^n = a^{m+n} \qquad \text{Product Property}$$
$$\frac{a^m}{a^n} = a^{m-n} \qquad \text{Quotient Property}$$
$$(a^m)^n = a^{m \cdot n} \qquad \text{Power Property}$$

Each property of exponents has a corresponding property of logarithms.

Activity
Exploring Properties of Logarithms

You will need: no special tools

Use the following table to complete the activity:

x	2	4	8	16	32	64	128
$y = \log_2 x$	1	2	3	4	5	6	7

1. The expression $\log_2 (2 \cdot 4)$ can be written as $\log_2 8$. Use this fact and the table above to evaluate each expression below.

   a. $\log_2(2 \cdot 4) = $? and $\log_2 2 + \log_2 4 = $?

   b. $\log_2(2 \cdot 8) = $? and $\log_2 2 + \log_2 8 = $?

   c. $\log_2(2 \cdot 16) = $? and $\log_2 2 + \log_2 16 = $?

   d. $\log_2(2 \cdot 32) = $? and $\log_2 2 + \log_2 32 = $?

CHECKPOINT ✔ 2. In Step 1, how is the first expression in each pair related to the second expression? Use this pattern to make a conjecture about $\log_2 (a \cdot b)$.

3. The expression $\log_2 \frac{16}{2}$ can be written as $\log_2 8$. Use this fact and the table above to evaluate each expression below.

   a. $\log_2 \frac{16}{2} = $? and $\log_2 16 - \log_2 2 = $?

   b. $\log_2 \frac{64}{32} = $? and $\log_2 64 - \log_2 32 = $?

   c. $\log_2 \frac{32}{8} = $? and $\log_2 32 - \log_2 8 = $?

   d. $\log_2 \frac{8}{4} = $? and $\log_2 8 - \log_2 4 = $?

CHECKPOINT ✔ 4. In Step 3, how is the first expression in each pair related to the second expression? Use this pattern to make a conjecture about $\log_2 \frac{a}{b}$.

The patterns explored in the Activity illustrate the *Product and Quotient Properties of Logarithms* given below.

Product and Quotient Properties of Logarithms

For $m > 0$, $n > 0$, $b > 0$, and $b \neq 1$:

Product Property $\log_b(mn) = \log_b m + \log_b n$

Quotient Property $\log_b \frac{m}{n} = \log_b m - \log_b n$

You can use the Product and Quotient Properties of Logarithms to evaluate logarithmic expressions. This is shown in Example 1.

E X A M P L E ❶ Given $\log_2 3 \approx 1.5850$, approximate the value of each expression below by using the Product and Quotient Properties of Logarithms.

a. $\log_2 12$ **b.** $\log_2 1.5$

● **SOLUTION**

a. $\log_2 12 = \log_2 (2 \cdot 2 \cdot 3)$ **b.** $\log_2 1.5 = \log_2 \frac{3}{2}$

$= \log_2 2 + \log_2 2 + \log_2 3$ $= \log_2 3 - \log_2 2$

$\approx 1 + 1 + 1.5850$ $\approx 1.5850 - 1$

≈ 3.5850 ≈ 0.5850

TRY THIS Given that $\log_2 3 = 1.5850$, approximate each expression below by using the Product and Quotient Properties of Logarithms.

a. $\log_2 18$ **b.** $\log_2 \frac{3}{4}$

Example 2 demonstrates how to use the properties of logarithms to rewrite a logarithmic expression as a single logarithm.

E X A M P L E ❷ Write each expression as a single logarithm. Then simplify, if possible.

a. $\log_3 10 - \log_3 5$ **b.** $\log_b u + \log_b v - \log_b uw$

● **SOLUTION**

a. $\log_3 10 - \log_3 5 = \log_3 \frac{10}{5}$ **b.** $\log_b u + \log_b v - \log_b uw = \log_b uv - \log_b uw$

$= \log_3 2$ $= \log_b \frac{uv}{uw}$

$= \log_b \frac{v}{w}$

TRY THIS Write each expression as a single logarithm. Then simplify if possible.

a. $\log_4 18 - \log_4 6$ **b.** $\log_b 4x - \log_b 3y + \log_b y$

The Power Property of Logarithms

Examine the process of rewriting the expression $\log_b(a^4)$.

$$\log_b(a^4) = \log_b(a \cdot a \cdot a \cdot a)$$

$$= \log_b a + \log_b a + \log_b a + \log_b a$$

$$= 4 \cdot \log_b a$$

This illustrates the *Power Property of Logarithms* given below.

Power Property of Logarithms

For $m > 0$, $b > 0$, $b \neq 1$, and any real number p:

$$\log_b m^p = p \log_b m$$

In Example 3, the Power Property of Logarithms is used to simplify powers.

EXAMPLE ③ Evaluate $\log_5 25^4$.

● SOLUTION

$$\log_5 25^4 = 4 \log_5 25 \quad \textit{Use the Power Property of Logarithms.}$$
$$= 4 \cdot 2$$
$$= 8$$

TRY THIS Evaluate $\log_3 27^{100}$.

Exponential-Logarithmic Inverse Properties

Recall from Lesson 2.5 that functions f and g are inverse functions if and only if $(f \circ g)(x) = x$ and $(g \circ f)(x) = x$. The functions $f(x) = \log_b x$ and $g(x) = b^x$ are inverses, so $(f \circ g)(x) = \log_b b^x = x$ and $(g \circ f)(x) = b^{\log_b x} = x$.

Exponential-Logarithmic Inverse Properties

For $b > 0$ and $b \neq 1$:
$$\log_b b^x = x \quad \text{and} \quad b^{\log_b x} = x \text{ for } x > 0$$

EXAMPLE ④ Evaluate each expression.

a. $3^{\log_3 4} + \log_5 25$

b. $\log_2 32 - 5^{\log_5 3}$

● SOLUTION

a. $3^{\log_3 4} + \log_5 25$
$= 4 + \log_5 5^2$
$= 4 + 2$
$= 6$

b. $\log_2 32 - 5^{\log_5 3}$
$= \log_2 2^5 - 3$
$= 5 - 3$
$= 2$

TRY THIS Evaluate each expression.

a. $7^{\log_7 11} - \log_3 81$

b. $\log_8 8^5 + 3^{\log_3 8}$

CRITICAL THINKING Verify the Exponential-Logarithmic Inverse Properties by using only the equivalent exponential and logarithmic forms given on page 371.

Because exponential functions and logarithmic functions are one-to-one functions, for each element in the domain of $y = \log x$, there is exactly one corresponding element in the range of $y = \log x$.

One-to-One Property of Logarithms

If $\log_b x = \log_b y$, then $x = y$.

E X A M P L E **5** Solve $\log_3(x^2 + 7x - 5) = \log_3(6x + 1)$ for x. Check your answers.

SOLUTION

$$\log_3(x^2 + 7x - 5) = \log_3(6x + 1)$$
$$x^2 + 7x - 5 = 6x + 1 \qquad \textit{Use the One-to-One Property of Logarithms.}$$
$$x^2 + x - 6 = 0$$
$$(x - 2)(x + 3) = 0$$
$$x = 2 \quad or \quad x = -3 \qquad \textit{Use the Zero Product Property.}$$

CHECK

Let $x = 2$.

$$\log_3(x^2 + 7x - 5) \overset{?}{=} \log_3(6x + 1)$$
$$\log_3 13 = \log_3 13$$

True

Let $x = -3$.

$$\log_3(x^2 + 7x - 5) \overset{?}{=} \log_3(6x + 1)$$
$$\log_3(-17) = \log_3(-17)$$

Undefined

Since the domain of a logarithmic function excludes negative numbers, the solution cannot be -3. Therefore, the solution is 2.

Exercises

Communicate

1. Given that $\log_{10} 5 \approx 0.6990$, explain how to approximate the values of $\log_{10} 0.005$ and $\log_{10} 500$.

2. Explain how to write an expression such as $\log_7 32 - \log_7 4$ as a single logarithm.

3. Explain how to evaluate $4^{\log_4 8}$ and $\log_2 2^7$. Include the names of the properties you would use.

4. Explain why you must check your answers when solving an equation such as $\log_2 3x = \log_2(x + 4)$ for x.

Guided Skills Practice

Given $\log_3 7 \approx 1.7712$, approximate the value for each logarithm by using the Product and Quotient Properties of Logarithms. *(EXAMPLE 1)*

5. $\log_3 49$

6. $\log_3 \frac{3}{7}$

Write each expression as a single logarithm. Then simplify, if possible. *(EXAMPLE 2)*

7. $\log_3 x - \log_3 y + \log_3 z$

8. $\log_2 3 + \log_2 6 - \log_2 10$

Evaluate each expression. *(EXAMPLES 3 AND 4)*

9. $\log_4 16^8$

10. $3^{\log_3 12}$

11. $\log_7 7^3$

12. Solve $\log_3 x = \log_3(2x - 4)$ for x, and check your answers. *(EXAMPLE 5)*

**Homework
Help Online**

Go To: **go.hrw.com**
Keyword:
MB1 Homework Help
 for Exercises 13–16,
 29–42

Practice and Apply

Write each expression as a sum or difference of logarithms. Then simplify, if possible.

13. $\log_8(5 \cdot 8)$ **14.** $\log_2 8xy$ **15.** $\log_3 \frac{x}{9}$ **16.** $\log_4 \frac{x}{32}$

Use the values given below to approximate the value of each logarithmic expression in Exercises 17–28.

$\log_2 7 \approx 2.8074$	$\log_2 5 \approx 2.3219$	$\log_4 5 \approx 1.1610$
$\log_4 3 \approx 0.7925$	$\log_2 3 \approx 1.5850$	$\log_{10} 8.3 \approx 0.9191$

17. $\log_4 15$ **18.** $\log_2 35$ **19.** $\log_2 28$

20. $\log_4 12$ **21.** $\log_4 60$ **22.** $\log_2 105$

23. $\log_{10} 830$ **24.** $\log_{10} 0.0083$ **25.** $\log_4 \frac{3}{5}$

26. $\log_2 \frac{7}{10}$ **27.** $\log_4 \frac{5}{4}$ **28.** $\log_2 \frac{2}{7}$

Write each expression as a single logarithm. Then simplify, if possible.

29. $\log_2 5 + \log_2 7$ **30.** $\log_4 8 + \log_4 2$

31. $\log_3 45 - \log_3 9$ **32.** $\log_2 14 - \log_2 7$

33. $\log_2 5 + \log_2 x - \log_2 10$ **34.** $\log_3 x + \log_3 4 - \log_3 2$

35. $\log_7 3x - \log_7 9x + \log_7 6y$ **36.** $\log_5 6s - \log_5 s + \log_5 4t$

37. $5 \log_2 m - 2 \log_2 n$ **38.** $7 \log_3 y - 4 \log_3 x$

39. $4 \log_b m + \frac{1}{2} \log_b n - 3 \log_b 2p$ **40.** $\frac{1}{2} \log_b 3c + \frac{1}{2} \log_b 4d - 2 \log_b 5e$

41. $1 - 2 \log_7 x$ **42.** $2 + 4 \log_3 x$

Evaluate each expression.

43. $3^{\log_3 8}$ **44.** $9^{\log_9 2}$ **45.** $\log_4 4^5$

46. $\log_{10} 10^2$ **47.** $7^{\log_7 9} + \log_2 8$ **48.** $5^{\log_5 7} + \log_3 9$

49. $\log_9 9^{11} - \log_4 64$ **50.** $\log_3 3^5 + \log_5 125$ **51.** $6^{\log_6 3} - \log_5 \frac{1}{25}$

52. $2^{\log_2 3} + \log_6 \frac{1}{36}$ **53.** $\log_3 \frac{1}{9} - 2^{\log_2 3}$ **54.** $\log_2 \frac{1}{8} - 4^{\log_4 7}$

Solve for x, and check your answers. Justify each step in the solution process.

55. $\log_2 7x = \log_2(x^2 + 12)$ **56.** $\log_5(3x^2 - 1) = \log_5 2x$

57. $\log_b(x^2 - 15) = \log_b(6x + 1)$ **58.** $\log_{10}(5x - 3) - \log_{10}(x^2 + 1) = 0$

59. $2 \log_a x + \log_a 2 = \log_a(5x + 3)$ **60.** $\log_b(x^2 - 2) + 2 \log_b 6 = \log_b 6x$

61. $2 \log_3 x + \log_3 5 = \log_3(14x + 3)$ **62.** $\log_5 2 + 2 \log_5 t = \log_5(3 - t)$

State whether each equation is always true, sometimes true, or never true. Assume that x is a positive real number.

63. $\log_3 9 = 2 \log_3 3$ **64.** $\log_2 8 - \log_2 2 = 2$ **65.** $\log x^2 = 2 \log x$

66. $\log x - \log 5 = \log \frac{x}{5}$ **67.** $\frac{\log 3}{\log x} = \log 3 - \log x$ **68.** $\log(x - 2) = \frac{\log x}{\log 2}$

69. $\frac{1}{2} \log x = \log \sqrt{x}$ **70.** $\log 12x = 12 \log x$ **71.** $\log_3 x + \log_3 x = \log_3 2x$

Solve each equation.

72. $\log_4(\log_3 x) = 0$

73. $\log_6[\log_5(\log_3 x)] = 0$

74. HEALTH The surface area of a person is commonly used to calculate dosages of medicines. The surface area of a child is often calculated with the following formula, where S is the surface area in square centimeters, W is the child's weight in kilograms, and H is the child's height in centimeters.

$$\log_{10} S = 0.425 \log_{10} W + 0.725 \log_{10} H + \log_{10} 71.84$$

Use the properties of logarithms to write a formula for S without logarithms.

75. PHYSICS Atmospheric air pressure, P, in pounds per square inch and altitude, a, in feet are related by the logarithmic equation $a = -55{,}555.56 \log_{10} \frac{P}{14.7}$. Use properties of logarithms to find how much greater the air pressure at the top of Mount Whitney in the United States is compared with the air pressure at the top of Mount Everest on the border of Tibet and Nepal. The altitude of Mount Everest is 29,028 feet, and the altitude of Mount Whitney is 14,495 feet. (*Hint:* Find the ratio of the air pressures.)

Mount Everest
29,028 feet

Mount Whitney
14, 495 feet

Sea level

Look Back

Minimize each objective function under the given constraints.
(LESSON 3.5)

76. Objective function: $C = 2x + 5y$

Constraints: $\begin{cases} x + 5y \geq 8 \\ y - 3x \leq 14 \\ x \geq 0 \\ y \geq 0 \end{cases}$

77. Objective function: $C = x + 4y$

Constraints: $\begin{cases} x - y \geq 12 \\ 7y - x \leq 12 \\ x \geq 0 \\ y \geq 0 \end{cases}$

Write the matrix equation that represents each system. *(LESSON 4.4)*

78. $\begin{cases} 2x - y = 5 \\ 3x + 4y = -3 \end{cases}$

79. $\begin{cases} 3x + 2y - z = 7 \\ 5x + 3y - 2z = -12 \\ 3y - z + 2x = -5 \end{cases}$

80. $\begin{cases} x + y + z = 18 \\ \frac{1}{4}x + \frac{1}{2}y + \frac{1}{3}z = 6 \\ 2y + 3z = 33 \end{cases}$

Write the augmented matrix for each system of equations. *(LESSON 4.5)*

81. $\begin{cases} -3x + 2y = 11 \\ 4x = 5 - y \end{cases}$

82. $\begin{cases} 3x - 6y + 3z = 4 \\ x - 2y = 1 - z \\ 2x - 4y + 2z = 5 \end{cases}$

83. $\begin{cases} 0.5x + 0.3y = 2.2 \\ -8.5y + 1.2z = -24.4 \\ 3.3z + 1.3x = 29 \end{cases}$

APPLICATIONS

84. **INVESTMENTS** An investment of $100 earns an annual interest rate of 5%. Find the amount after 10 years if the interest is compounded annually, quarterly, and daily. *(LESSON 6.2)*

85. **INVESTMENTS** Find the final amount after 8 years of a $500 investment that is compounded semiannually at 6%, 7%, and 8% annual interest. *(LESSON 6.2)*

 Look Beyond

86. e is an irrational number between 2 and 3. The expression $\log_e x$ is commonly written as $\ln x$. Use the ⌊ LN ⌋ key to solve $2e^{3x} = 5$ for x to the nearest hundredth.

 PORTFOLIO ACTIVITY

In this activity, you will use the CBL to collect data as a warm probe cools in air.

1. First record the air temperature for reference. Then place the temperature probe in hot water until it reaches a reading of at least 60°C. Remove the probe from the water and record the readings as in Step 1 of the Portfolio Activity on page 361.

2. **a.** Using the regression feature on your calculator, find linear, quadratic, and exponential functions that model this data. (Use the variable t for time in seconds.)

   b. Use each function to predict the temperature of the probe after 2 minutes (120 seconds). Compare the predictions with the actual 2-minute reading.

   c. Discuss the usefulness of each function for modeling the cooling process.

3. Create a new function to model the cooling process by performing the steps below.

   a. Subtract the air temperature from each temperature recorded in your data list. Store the resulting data values in a new list.

   b. Use the exponential regression feature on your calculator to find an exponential function of the form $y = a \cdot b^t$ that models this new data set.

   c. Add the air temperature to the function you found in part **b**. Graph the resulting function, $y = a \cdot b^t + c$, which will be called the approximating function.

   d. Repeat parts **b** and **c** from Step 2 with the approximating function.

Save your data and results to use in the last Portfolio Activity.

WORKING ON THE CHAPTER PROJECT

You should now be able to complete Activity 3 of the Chapter Project.

Applications of Common Logarithms

Objectives

- Define and use the common logarithmic function to solve exponential and logarithmic equations.

- Evaluate logarithmic expressions by using the change-of-base formula.

The human ear is sensitive to a wide range of sound intensities.

Type of sound	Relative intensity, R (in dB)
threshold of hearing	0
whisper	≈ 20
soft music	≈ 30
conversation	≈ 65
rock band	≈ 100
threshold of pain	120

The base-10 logarithm is called the *common logarithm*. The **common logarithm**, $\log_{10} x$, is usually written as $\log x$.

A table of values and a graph for $y = \log x$ are given below. Notice that the values in the domain increase quickly (by a factor of 10), while values in the range increase slowly (by adding 1). In general, logarithmic functions are used to assign large values in the domain to small values in the range.

x	10	100	1000	10,000	100,000	...
$y = \log x$	1	2	3	4	5	...

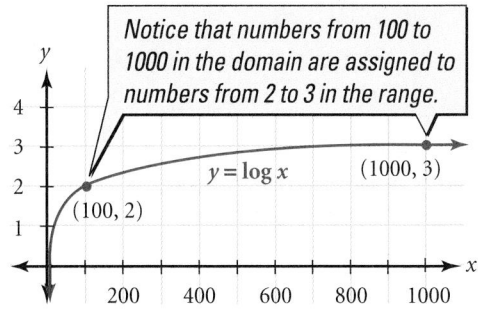

Notice that numbers from 100 to 1000 in the domain are assigned to numbers from 2 to 3 in the range.

$y = \log x$

$(1000, 3)$

$(100, 2)$

Recall from Lesson 2.7 that the graph of $y = a \cdot f(x)$ is the graph of $y = f(x)$ stretched by a factor of a. Therefore, the graph of $y = 10 \log x$ is the graph of $y = \log x$ stretched by a factor of 10.

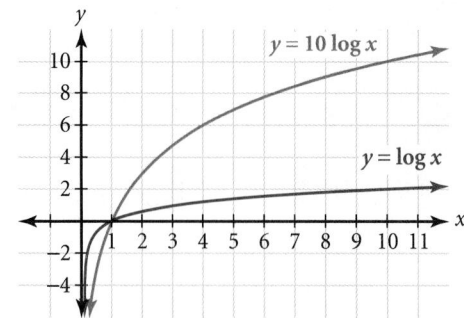

APPLICATION

PHYSICS

The function $y = 10 \log x$ models the relative intensities of sound. The intensity of the faintest sound audible to the human ear, called the *threshold of hearing*, is 10^{-12} watts per meters squared (W/m^2). Sound intensities, I, which are between 0 and 1, are often compared with the threshold of hearing, I_0, yielding a ratio of sound intensities, $\frac{I}{I_0}$, between 1 and 10^{12}. On the decibel scale, the relative intensity, R, of a sound in decibels (dB) is given by the function $R = 10 \log \frac{I}{I_0}$.

The bel, the unit of measure for the intensity of sound, was named after Alexander Graham Bell, 1847–1922.

I (in W/m^2)	$\frac{I}{I_0}$	$R = 10 \log \frac{I}{I_0}$ (in dB)
	Domain of R	**Range of R**
10^{-12}	1	0
10^{-11}	10	10
10^{-10}	100	20
$\vdots$	$\vdots$	$\vdots$
10^{-2}	10^{10}	100
10^{-1}	10^{11}	110
$10^0 = 1$	10^{12}	120

EXAMPLE ❶ The intensity of a whisper is about 300 times as loud as the threshold of hearing, I_0.

Find the relative intensity, R, of this whisper in decibels.

● SOLUTION

PROBLEM SOLVING

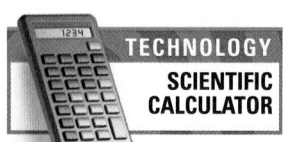
TECHNOLOGY
SCIENTIFIC
CALCULATOR

Identify the wanted, given, and unknown information. In this problem, the ratio of I to I_0 is given and you need to find R.

$$R = 10 \log \frac{I}{I_0}$$

$$R = 10 \log \frac{300 I_0}{I_0} \qquad \textit{Substitute } 300 I_0 \textit{ for the intensity, I.}$$

$$R = 10 \log 300$$

$$R \approx 25 \qquad \textit{Use the } \boxed{\text{LOG}} \textit{ key on a calculator.}$$

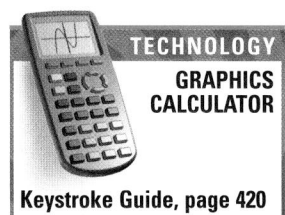

TECHNOLOGY
GRAPHICS
CALCULATOR

Keystroke Guide, page 420

CHECK

Use a graphics calculator to graph $y = 10 \log x$. You find that when x is 300, y is about 25.

The relative intensity of this whisper is about 25 decibels.

E X A M P L E ② The relative intensity, R, of a running vacuum cleaner is about 70 decibels.

Compare the intensity of this running vacuum cleaner with the threshold of hearing.

APPLICATION
PHYSICS

● **SOLUTION**

PROBLEM SOLVING

Identify the wanted, given, and unknown information. In this problem, R is given and you need to find the ratio of I to I_0.

$$R = 10 \log \frac{I}{I_0}$$

$$70 = 10 \log \frac{I}{I_0} \qquad \textit{Substitute 70 for the relative intensity, R.}$$

$$7 = \log \frac{I}{I_0}$$

$$10^7 = \frac{I}{I_0} \qquad \textit{Write the equivalent exponential equation.}$$

$$10^7 \cdot I_0 = I \qquad \textit{Write the intensity, I, in terms of } I_0.$$

This running vacuum cleaner is about 10^7, or 10,000,000, times as loud as the threshold of hearing.

If x and y are positive real numbers and $x = y$, then $\log x = \log y$ by substitution. This is used to solve an equation in Example 3.

E X A M P L E ③ Solve $5^x = 62$ for x. Round your answer to the nearest hundredth.

● **SOLUTION**

$$5^x = 62$$

$$\log 5^x = \log 62 \qquad \textit{Take the common logarithm of both sides.}$$

$$x \log 5 = \log 62 \qquad \textit{Apply the Power Property of Logarithms.}$$

$$x = \frac{\log 62}{\log 5}$$

$$x \approx 2.56 \qquad \textit{Use a calculator to evaluate.}$$

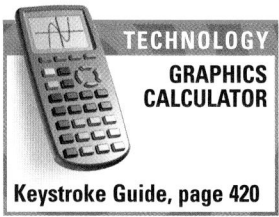

TECHNOLOGY
GRAPHICS
CALCULATOR

Keystroke Guide, page 420

CHECK

Graph $y = 5^x$ and $y = 62$ in the same window, and find the point of intersection.

Thus, the solution to $5^x = 62$ is approximately 2.56.

TRY THIS Solve $8^x = 792$ for x. Round your answer to the nearest hundredth.

The Activity below leads to a method for evaluating logarithmic expressions with bases other than 10.

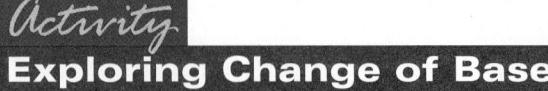

Exploring Change of Base

You will need: a scientific calculator

1. Write $3^x = 81$ as a logarithmic expression for x in base 3.

2. Write $3^x = 81$ as a logarithmic expression for x in base 10. (Hint: Refer to Example 3.)

3. Set your expressions for x from Steps 1 and 2 equal to each other.

CHECKPOINT ✔   4. Write $b^x = y$ in logarithmic form. Then solve $b^x = y$ for x, and give the result as a quotient of logarithms. Set your two resulting expressions equal to each other.

The answer to Step 4 in the Activity suggests a *change-of-base formula,* shown below, for writing equivalent logarithmic expressions with different bases.

Change-of-Base Formula

For any positive real numbers $a \neq 1$, $b \neq 1$, and $x > 0$:

$$\log_b x = \frac{\log_a x}{\log_a b}$$

CHECKPOINT ✔   Write $\log_9 27$ as a base 3 expression.

You can use the change-of-base formula to change a logarithmic expression of any base to base 10 so that you can use the ⎡ LOG ⎤ key on a calculator. This is shown in Example 4.

E X A M P L E ④ **Evaluate $\log_7 56$. Round your answer to the nearest hundredth.**

● **SOLUTION**

Use the change-of-base formula to change from base 7 to base 10.

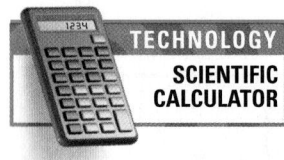

$$\log_7 56 = \frac{\log 56}{\log 7}$$

$$\approx \frac{1.748}{0.845}$$

$$\approx 2.07 \qquad \textit{Use a calculator to evaluate.}$$

TRY THIS   Evaluate $\log_8 36$. Round your answer to the nearest hundredth.

CRITICAL THINKING   Use the change-of-base formula to justify each formula below.

a. $(\log_a b)(\log_b c) = \log_a c$ **b.** $\log_a b = \dfrac{1}{\log_b a}$

Exercises

Communicate

1. Explain why a common logarithmic function is appropriate to use for the decibel scale of sound intensities.

2. Describe the steps you would take to solve $6^x = 39$ for x.

3. Explain how to evaluate $\log_4 29$ by using a calculator.

Guided Skills Practice

APPLICATIONS

4. **PHYSICS** Suppose that a soft whisper is about 75 times as loud as the threshold of hearing, I_0. Find the relative intensity, R, of this whisper in decibels. *(EXAMPLE 1)*

5. **PHYSICS** The relative intensity, R, of a loud siren is about 130 decibels. Compare the intensity of this siren with the threshold of hearing, I_0. *(EXAMPLE 2)*

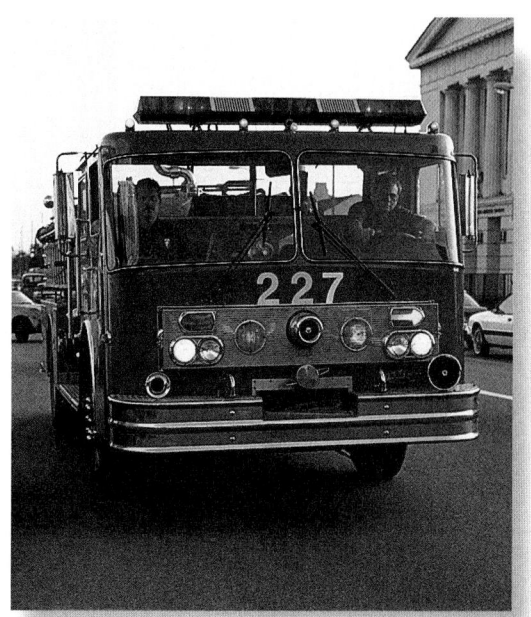

Solve each exponential equation for x. Round your answers to the nearest hundredth. *(EXAMPLE 3)*

6. $8^x = 4$

7. $4^x = 72$

Evaluate each logarithmic expression. Round your answers to the nearest hundredth. *(EXAMPLE 4)*

8. $\log_2 46$

9. $\log_5 2$

Practice and Apply

internet connect

Homework Help Online
Go To: go.hrw.com
Keyword:
MB1 Homework Help
for Exercises 10–27

Solve each equation. Round your answers to the nearest hundredth.

10. $4^x = 17$
11. $2^x = 49$
12. $7^x = 908$

13. $8^x = 240$
14. $3.5^x = 28$
15. $7.6^x = 64$

16. $25^x = 0.04$
17. $3^x = 0.26$
18. $2^{-x} = 0.045$

19. $7^{-x} = 0.022$
20. $3^x = 0.45$
21. $5^x = 1.29$

22. $2^{x+1} = 30$
23. $3^{x-6} = 81$
24. $11 - 6^x = 3$

25. $67 - 2^x = 39$
26. $8 + 3^x = 10$
27. $1 + 5^x = 360$

Evaluate each logarithmic expression to the nearest hundredth.

28. $\log_4 92$　　　　**29.** $\log_6 87$　　　　**30.** $\log_6 18$

31. $\log_3 15$　　　　**32.** $\log_6 3$　　　　**33.** $\log_5 2$

34. $\log_9 4$　　　　**35.** $\log_8 3$　　　　**36.** $\log_4 0.37$

37. $\log_9 1.43$　　　　**38.** $\log_{\frac{1}{3}} 9$　　　　**39.** $\log_{\frac{1}{2}} 8$

40. $\log_8 \frac{1}{4}$　　　　**41.** $\log_7 \frac{1}{50}$　　　　**42.** $8 - \log_2 64$

43. $1 - \log_5 21$　　　　**44.** $9 + \log_3 27$　　　　**45.** $4 + \log_5 125$

CHALLENGE
46. Prove that $\log_{(b^n)} x = \frac{1}{n} \log_b x$ is true.

APPLICATIONS
47. PHYSICS The sound of a leaf blower is about $10^{10.5}$ times the intensity of the threshold of hearing, I_0. Find the relative intensity, R, of this leaf blower in decibels.

48. PHYSICS The sound of a conversation is about 350,000 times the intensity of the threshold of hearing, I_0. Find the relative intensity, R, of this conversation in decibels.

49. PHYSICS Suppose that the relative intensity, R, of a rock band is about 115 decibels. Compare the intensity of this band with that of the threshold of hearing, I_0.

50. PHYSICS The relative intensity, R, of an automobile engine is about 55 decibels. Compare the intensity of this engine with that of the threshold of hearing, I_0.

51. PHYSICS Suppose that background music is adjusted to an intensity that is 1000 times as loud as the threshold of hearing. What is the relative intensity of the music in decibels?

52. PHYSICS Suppose that a burglar alarm has a rating of 120 decibels. Compare the intensity of this decibel rating with that of the threshold of hearing, I_0.

53. PHYSICS Simon Robinson set the world record for the loudest scream by producing a scream of 128 decibels at a distance of 8 feet and 2 inches. Compare the intensity of this decibel rating with that of the threshold of hearing, I_0. [*Source: The Guinness Book of World Records, 1997*]

54. PHYSICS A small jet engine produces a sound whose intensity is one billion times as loud as the threshold of hearing. What is the relative intensity of the engine's sound in decibels?

CHEMISTRY In chemistry, pH is defined as pH = $-\log$ [H$^+$], where [H$^+$] is the hydrogen ion concentration in moles per liter.

55. An alkaline solution has a pH in the range $7 < \text{pH} < 14$. Determine the corresponding range of [H$^+$] for alkaline substances.

56. An acidic solution has a pH in the range $0 < \text{pH} < 7$. Determine the corresponding range of [H$^+$] for acidic substances.

57. For hydrochloric acid, [H$^+$] is about 5×10^{-2} moles per liter. Find the pH for this strong acid to the nearest tenth.

58. For chicken eggs, [H$^+$] is about 1.6×10^{-8} moles per liter. Find the pH of chicken eggs to the nearest tenth.

59. For milk of magnesia, [H$^+$] is about 3.2×10^{-11} moles per liter. Find the pH of milk of magnesia to the nearest tenth.

60. CHEMISTRY Find the pH that corresponds to each hydrogen ion concentration.
   a. [H$^+$] is about 6.3×10^{-5} moles per liter for tomato juice.
   b. [H$^+$] is about 0.03 moles per liter for gastric juice.
   c. How much more concentrated is the gastric juice than the tomato juice? (Hint: Make a ratio of their hydrogen ion concentrations.)

 Look Back

Solve each system of equations. (LESSONS 3.1 AND 3.2)

61. $\begin{cases} x + y = 7 \\ 2x - 3y = 4 \end{cases}$

62. $\begin{cases} x + 3y = 23 \\ 4x - 2y = -6 \end{cases}$

63. $\begin{cases} -2x + 5y = -4 \\ 3x - y = -7 \end{cases}$

Show that each function is a quadratic function by writing it in the form $f(x) = ax^2 + bx + c$. (LESSON 5.1)

64. $h(x) = 11x(5 - x)$

65. $g(x) = (2x - 10)(x + 1)$

66. $k(x) = 4(x + 5)(x - 5)$

67. $f(x) = -(x + 1)(3x - 1)$

Solve each equation for x. (LESSON 5.6)

68. $x^2 + 5x = -6$

69. $x^2 + 2x - 15 = 0$

70. $(x - 2)(x + 3) = 5$

Identify each function as representing exponential growth or exponential decay. (LESSON 6.2)

71. $f(t) = 1000(2.5)^t$

72. $f(t) = 55(0.5)^t$

73. $f(t) = 0.005(8)^t$

 Look Beyond

74 Graph $y = 2^x$, $y = e^x$, and $y = 3^x$. Describe how the graph of e^x compares to the others. Use your calculator to find a value for e to four decimal places.

The Natural Base, *e*

The model below shows the embryo inside an 18-inch dinosaur egg, the largest known.

Objectives

● Evaluate natural exponential and natural logarithmic functions.

● Model exponential growth and decay processes.

Why *The exponential function with base e and its inverse, the natural logarithmic function, have a wide variety of real-world applications. For example, these functions are used to estimate the ages of artifacts found at archaeological digs.*

The natural base, *e*, is used to estimate the ages of artifacts and to calculate interest that is compounded continuously. Recall from Lesson 6.2 the compound interest formula, $A(t) = P\left(1 + \frac{r}{n}\right)^{nt}$, where *P* is the principal, *r* is the annual interest rate, *n* is the number of compounding periods per year, and *t* is the time in years. This formula is used in the Activity below.

Activity

Investigating the Growth of $1

You will need: a scientific calculator

1. Copy and complete the table below to investigate the growth of a $1 investment that earns 100% annual interest (*r* = 1) over 1 year (*t* = 1) as the number of compounding periods per year, *n*, increases. Use a calculator, and record the value of *A* to five places after the decimal point.

Compounding schedule	*n*	$1\left(1 + \frac{1}{n}\right)^n$	Value, *A*
annually	1	$1\left(1 + \frac{1}{1}\right)^1$	2.00000
semiannually	2	$1\left(1 + \frac{1}{2}\right)^2$	
quarterly	4		
monthly	12		
daily	365		
hourly			
every minute			
every second			

CHECKPOINT ✔ 2. Describe the behavior of the sequence of numbers in the *Value* column.

As *n* becomes very large, the value of $1\left(1 + \frac{1}{n}\right)^n$ approaches the number 2.71828 . . . , named *e*. Because *e* is an irrational number like π, its decimal expansion continues forever without repeating patterns.

The Natural Exponential Function

The exponential function with base e, $f(x) = e^x$, is called the **natural exponential function** and e is called the **natural base.** The function $f(x) = e^x$ is graphed at right. Notice that the domain is all real numbers and the range is all positive real numbers.

CHECKPOINT ✔ What is the y-intercept of the graph of $f(x) = e^x$?

Natural exponential functions model a variety of situations in which a quantity grows or decays continuously. Examples that you will solve in this lesson include continuous compounding interest and continuous radioactive decay.

E X A M P L E ❶ Evaluate $f(x) = e^x$ to the nearest thousandth for each value of x below.

  a. $x = 2$ **b.** $x = \dfrac{1}{2}$ **c.** $x = -1$

● SOLUTION

  a. $f(2) = e^2$ **b.** $f\left(\dfrac{1}{2}\right) = e^{\frac{1}{2}}$ **c.** $f(-1) = e^{-1}$

     ≈ 7.389 ≈ 1.649 ≈ 0.368

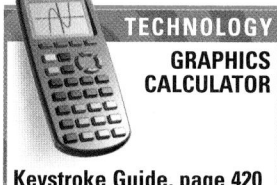

TECHNOLOGY
GRAPHICS CALCULATOR

Keystroke Guide, page 420

CHECK
Use a table of values for $y = e^x$ or a graph of $y = e^x$ to verify your answers.

TRY THIS   Evaluate $f(x) = e^x$ to the nearest thousandth for $x = 6$ and $x = -\dfrac{1}{3}$.

Many banks compound the interest on accounts daily or monthly. However, some banks compound interest continuously, or at every instant, by using the *continuous compounding formula*, which includes the number e.

Continuous Compounding Formula

If P dollars are invested at an interest rate, r, that is compounded continuously, then the amount, A, of the investment at time t is given by

$$A = Pe^{rt}.$$

EXAMPLE ② An investment of $1000 earns an annual interest rate of 7.6%.

Compare the final amounts after 8 years for interest compounded quarterly and for interest compounded continuously.

APPLICATION
INVESTMENTS

● **SOLUTION**

Substitute 1000 for P, 0.076 for r, and 8 for t in the appropriate formulas.

Compounded quarterly	Compounded continuously
$A = P\left(1 + \frac{r}{n}\right)^{nt}$	$A = Pe^{rt}$
$A = 1000\left(1 + \frac{0.076}{4}\right)^{4 \cdot 8}$	$A = 1000e^{0.076 \cdot 8}$
$A \approx 1826.31$	$A \approx 1836.75$

Interest that is compounded continuously results in a final amount that is about $10 more than that for the interest that is compounded quarterly.

TRY THIS Find the value of $500 after 4 years invested at an annual interest rate of 9% compounded continuously.

The Natural Logarithmic Function

The **natural logarithmic function**, $y = \log_e x$, abbreviated $y = \ln x$, is the inverse of the natural exponential function, $y = e^x$. The function $y = \ln x$ is graphed along with $y = e^x$ at right.

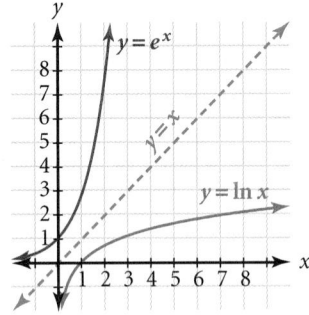

CHECKPOINT ✔ State the domain and range of $y = e^x$ and of $y = \ln x$.

EXAMPLE ③ **Evaluate $f(x) = \ln x$ to the nearest thousandth for each value of x below.**

  a. $x = 2$ **b.** $x = \frac{1}{2}$ **c.** $x = -1$

● **SOLUTION**

  a. $f(2) = \ln 2$
      ≈ 0.693

  b. $f\left(\frac{1}{2}\right) = \ln \frac{1}{2}$
      ≈ -0.693

  c. $f(-1) = \ln(-1)$ is undefined.

CHECK

Use a table of values for $y = \ln x$ or a graph of $y = \ln x$ to verify your answers.

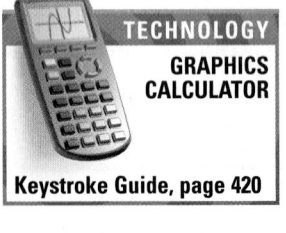

TECHNOLOGY
GRAPHICS CALCULATOR

Keystroke Guide, page 420

Nonpositive numbers are not in the domain of $y = \ln x$.

$(2, \approx 0.693)$

$(2, \approx -0.693)$

The natural logarithmic function can be used to solve an equation of the form $A = Pe^{rt}$ for the exponent t in order to find the time it takes for an investment that is compounded continuously to reach a specific amount. This is shown in Example 4.

E X A M P L E ④ **How long does it take for an investment to double at an annual interest rate of 8.5% compounded continuously?**

● **SOLUTION**

PROBLEM SOLVING

Use the formula $A = Pe^{rt}$ **with** $r = 0.085$.

$$A = Pe^{0.085t}$$
$$2 \cdot P = Pe^{0.085t} \qquad \textit{When the investment doubles, } A = 2 \cdot P.$$
$$2 = e^{0.085t}$$
$$\ln 2 = \ln e^{0.085t} \qquad \textit{Take the natural logarithm of both sides.}$$
$$\ln 2 = 0.085t \qquad \textit{Use the Exponential-Logarithmic Inverse Property.}$$
$$t = \frac{\ln 2}{0.085}$$
$$t \approx 8.15$$

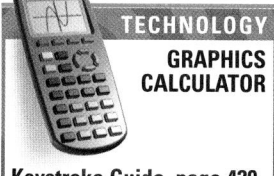

TECHNOLOGY

GRAPHICS CALCULATOR

Keystroke Guide, page 420

CHECK

Graph $y = e^{0.085x}$ and $y = 2$, and find the point of intersection.

Notice that the graph of $y = e^{0.085x}$ is a horizontal stretch of the function $y = e^x$ by a factor of $\frac{1}{0.085}$, or almost 12.

Thus, it takes about 8 years and 2 months to double an investment at an annual interest rate of 8.5% compounded continuously.

TRY THIS

How long does it take for an investment to triple at an annual interest rate of 7.2% compounded continuously?

CRITICAL THINKING

Explain why the time required for the value of an investment to double or triple does not depend on the amount of principal.

Radioactive Decay

Most of the carbon found in the Earth's atmosphere is the isotope carbon-12, but a small amount is the radioactive isotope carbon-14. Plants absorb carbon dioxide from the atmosphere, and animals obtain carbon from the plants they consume. When a plant or animal dies, the amount of carbon-14 it contains decays in such a way that exactly half of its initial amount is present after 5730 years. The function below models the decay of carbon-14, where N_0 is the initial amount of carbon-14 and $N(t)$ is the amount present t years after the plant or animal dies.

$$N(t) = N_0 e^{-0.00012t}$$

Example 5 shows how *radiocarbon dating* is used to estimate the age of an archaeological artifact.

E X A M P L E ⑤ Suppose that archaeologists find scrolls and claim that they are 2000 years old. Tests indicate that the scrolls contain 78% of their original carbon-14.

APPLICATION
ARCHAEOLOGY

Could the scrolls be 2000 years old?

SOLUTION

Since the scrolls contain 78% of their original carbon-14, substitute $0.78N_0$ for $N(t)$.

$$N(t) = N_0e^{-0.00012t}$$
$$0.78N_0 = N_0e^{-0.00012t} \quad \text{Substitute } 0.78N_0 \text{ for } N(t).$$
$$0.78 = e^{-0.00012t}$$
$$\ln 0.78 = -0.00012t \quad \text{Take the natural logarithm of each side.}$$
$$-0.00012t = \ln 0.78$$
$$t = \frac{\ln 0.78}{-0.00012}$$
$$t \approx 2070.5$$

Thus, it appears that the scrolls are about 2000 years old.

Exercises

● *Communicate*

1. Compare the natural and exponential logarithmic functions with the base-10 exponential and logarithmic functions.

2. Give a real-world example of an exponential growth function and of an exponential decay function that each have the base *e*.

3. State the continuous compounding formula, and describe what each variable represents.

4. Describe how the continuous compounding formula can represent continuous growth as well as continuous decay.

● *Guided Skills Practice*

APPLICATION

Evaluate $f(x) = e^x$ to the nearest thousandth for each value of *x*.
(EXAMPLE 1)

5. $x = 3$

6. $x = 3.5$

7. INVESTMENTS An investment of $1500 earns an annual interest rate of 8.2%. Compare the final amounts after 5 years for interest compounded quarterly and for interest compounded continuously. **(EXAMPLE 2)**

Evaluate $f(x) = \ln x$ to the nearest thousandth for each value of x.
(EXAMPLE 3)

8. $x = 5$ **9.** $x = 2.5$

APPLICATIONS

10. INVESTMENTS How long does it take an investment to double at an annual interest rate of 7.5% compounded continuously? *(EXAMPLE 4)*

11. ARCHAEOLOGY A piece of charcoal from an ancient campsite is found in an archaeological dig. It contains 9% of its original amount of carbon-14. Estimate the age of the charcoal. *(EXAMPLE 5)*

Practice and Apply

internet connect

Homework Help Online
Go To: go.hrw.com
Keyword:
MB1 Homework Help
for Exercises 12–31

Evaluate each expression to the nearest thousandth. If the expression is undefined, write *undefined*.

12. e^6 **13.** e^9 **14.** $e^{1.2}$ **15.** $e^{3.4}$

16. $2e^{0.3}$ **17.** $3e^{0.05}$ **18.** $2e^{-0.5}$ **19.** $3e^{-0.257}$

20. $e^{\sqrt{2}}$ **21.** $e^{\frac{1}{4}}$ **22.** $\ln 3$ **23.** $\ln 7$

24. $\ln 10{,}002$ **25.** $\ln 99{,}999$ **26.** $\ln 0.004$ **27.** $\ln 0.994$

28. $\ln \frac{1}{5}$ **29.** $\ln \sqrt{5}$ **30.** $\ln(-2)$ **31.** $\ln(-3)$

For Exercises 32–35, write the expressions in ascending order.

32. $e^2, e^5, \ln 2, \ln 5$ **33.** $e, e^0, \ln 1, \ln \frac{1}{2}$

34. $e^{2.5}, \ln 2.5, 10^{2.5}, \log 2.5$ **35.** $e^{1.3}, \ln 1.3, 10^{1.3}, \log 1.3$

State whether each equation is always true, sometimes true, or never true.

36. $e^{5x} \cdot e^3 = e^{15x}$ **37.** $\left(e^{4x}\right)^3 = e^{12x}$ **38.** $e^{6x-4} = e^{6x} \cdot e^{-4}$ **39.** $\dfrac{e^{8x}}{e^4} = e^{2x}$

Simplify each expression.

40. $e^{\ln 2}$ **41.** $e^{\ln 5}$ **42.** $e^{3\ln 2}$ **43.** $e^{2\ln 5}$

44. $\ln e^3$ **45.** $\ln e^4$ **46.** $3 \ln e^2$ **47.** $2 \ln e^4$

Write an equivalent exponential or logarithmic equation.

48. $e^x = 30$ **49.** $e^x = 1$ **50.** $\ln 2 \approx 0.69$

51. $\ln 5 \approx 1.61$ **52.** $e^{\frac{1}{3}} \approx 1.40$ **53.** $e^{0.69} \approx 1.99$

Solve each equation for x by using the natural logarithm function. Round your answers to the nearest hundredth.

54. $35^x = 30$ **55.** $1.3^x = 8$ **56.** $3^{-3x} = 17$

57. $36^{2x} = 20$ **58.** $0.42^{-x} = 7$ **59.** $2^{-\frac{1}{3}x} = 10$

CHALLENGE

60. Sketch $f(x) = e^x$ for $-1 \le x \le 2$. A line that intersects a curve at only one point is called a *tangent line* of the curve.
     a. Sketch lines that are tangent to the graph of $f(x) = e^x$ at $x = 0.5$, $x = 0$, $x = 1$, and $x = 2$.
     b. Find the approximate slope of each tangent line. Compare the slope of each tangent line with the corresponding y-coordinate of the point where the tangent line intersects the graph.
     c. Make a conjecture about the slope of $f(x) = e^x$ as x increases.

TRANSFORMATIONS **Let $f(x) = e^x$. For each function, describe the transformations from f to g.**

61. $g(x) = 6e^x + 1$

62. $g(x) = 0.75e^x - 4$

63. $g(x) = 0.25e^{(4x + 4)}$

64. $g(x) = 3e^{(2x - 4)}$

TRANSFORMATIONS **Let $f(x) = \ln x$. For each function, describe the transformations from f to g.**

65. $g(x) = 3\ln(x + 1)$

66. $g(x) = -2\ln(x - 1)$

67. $g(x) = 0.5\ln(5x) - 2$

68. $g(x) = 5\ln(0.25x) - 1$

$f(x) = e^{-2x}$ $i(x) = e^{2x}$
$g(x) = e^{-x}$ $h(x) = e^x$

69. TRANSFORMATIONS The graphs of $f(x) = e^{-2x}$, $g(x) = e^{-x}$, $h(x) = e^x$, and $i(x) = e^{2x}$ are shown on the same coordinate plane at left. What transformations relate each function, f, g, and i, to h?

70. TRANSFORMATIONS For $f(x) = e^x$, describe how each transformation affects the domain, range, asymptotes, and y-intercept.
a. a vertical stretch
b. a horizontal stretch
c. a vertical translation
d. a horizontal translation

71. TRANSFORMATIONS For $f(x) = \ln x$, describe how each transformation affects the domain, range, asymptotes, and x-intercept.
a. a vertical stretch
b. a horizontal stretch
c. a vertical translation
d. a horizontal translation

72. PHYSICS The amount of radioactive strontium-90 remaining after t years decreases according to the function $N(t) = N_0 e^{-0.0238t}$. How much of a 40-gram sample will remain after 25 years?

73. ECONOMICS The factory sales of pagers from 1990 through 1995 can be modeled by the function $S = 116e^{0.18t}$, where $t = 0$ in 1990 and S represents the sales in millions of dollars. [*Source: Electronic Market Data Book*]
a. According to this function, find the factory sales of pagers in 1995 to the nearest million.
b. If the sales of pagers continued to increase at the same rate, when would the sales be double the 1995 amount?

74. INVESTMENTS Compare the growth of an investment of $2000 in two different accounts. One account earns 3% annual interest, the other earns 5% annual interest, and both are compounded continuously over 20 years.

75. ARCHAEOLOGY A wooden chest is found and is said to be from the second century B.C.E. Tests on a sample of wood from the chest reveal that it contains 92% of its original carbon-14. Could the chest be from the second century B.C.E.?

Basketball Backboard Sales

Sales (in millions of $)

3.2
1.5
0.65

1986 1991 1996

76. BUSINESS Sales of home basketball backboards from 1986 to 1996 can be modeled by $S = 0.65e^{0.157t}$, where S is the sales in millions of dollars, t is time in years, and $t = 0$ in 1986. [*Source: Huffy Sports*]

    a. Use this model to estimate the sales of backboards in 1997 to the nearest thousand.

    b. If the sales of basketball backboards continued to increase at the same rate, when would the sales of basketball backboards be double the amount of 1996?

INVESTMENTS For Exercises 77–79, assume that all interest rates are compounded continuously.

77. How long will it take an investment of $5000 to double if the annual interest rate is 6%?

78. How long will it take an investment to double at 10% annual interest?

79. If it takes a certain amount of money 3.7 years to double, at what annual interest rate was the money invested?

80. AGRICULTURE The percentage of farmers in the United States workforce has declined since the turn of the century. The percent of farmers in the workforce, f, can be modeled by the function $f(t) = 29e^{-0.036t}$, where t is time in years and $t = 0$ in 1920. Find the percent of farmers in the workforce in 1995. [*Source: Bureau of Labor Statistics*]

Look Back

Solve each inequality, and graph the solution on a number line. (LESSON 1.8)

81. $|-3x| \geq 15$

82. $|3x - 4| \geq 12$

83. $\left| \dfrac{3x + 2}{-4} \right| \geq 5$

Graph each function. (LESSON 2.7)

84. $f(x) = \frac{1}{2}|x|$

85. $g(x) = -\lceil x \rceil$

86. $h(x) = [x - 3]$

Graph each system. (LESSON 3.4)

87. $\begin{cases} y > 2x - 1 \\ 4 - 3x \geq y \end{cases}$

88. $\begin{cases} 1 - 3x > y + 4 \\ 2x + 3y \leq 8 \end{cases}$

89. $\begin{cases} y + 2x \geq 0 \\ 4 - 2x > y \\ x \leq 3 \end{cases}$

Factor each expression. (LESSON 5.3)

90. $x^2 - 3x - 10$

91. $3x^2 - 6x + 3$

92. $x^2 - 49$

Look Beyond

93 Solve $\ln x + \ln(x + 2) = 5$ by graphing $y = \ln x + \ln(x + 2)$ and $y = 5$ and finding the x-coordinate of the point of intersection.

Meet "e" in St. Louis

How does a 630-foot-high arch stand up to the forces of nature? Will it last for its projected life of 1000 years? How does it withstand winds up to 150 miles per hour?

The secret is in the shape of the arch, which transfers forces downward through its legs into huge underground foundations. You can learn more about this remarkable shape, called a **catenary curve,** by looking at some of its simpler forms.

The general equation for a catenary curve is $y = \dfrac{a}{2}\left(e^{\frac{x}{a}} + e^{-\frac{x}{a}}\right)$, where a is a real nonzero constant.

ARCH COMPLETED

St. Louis Can Now Boast of the Nation's Highest Memorial

With the joining of the stainless steel legs of the Gateway Arch Thursday, St. Louis became the location of the tallest—630 feet—national memorial in the United States. More than 10,000 persons—including hundreds of school children who attended the "topping out" as a field trip—look upward as the leg-locking segment is hoisted off the ground and begins the long trip to the Arch.

[*Source:* St. Louis Globe-Democrat, *October 29, 1965*]

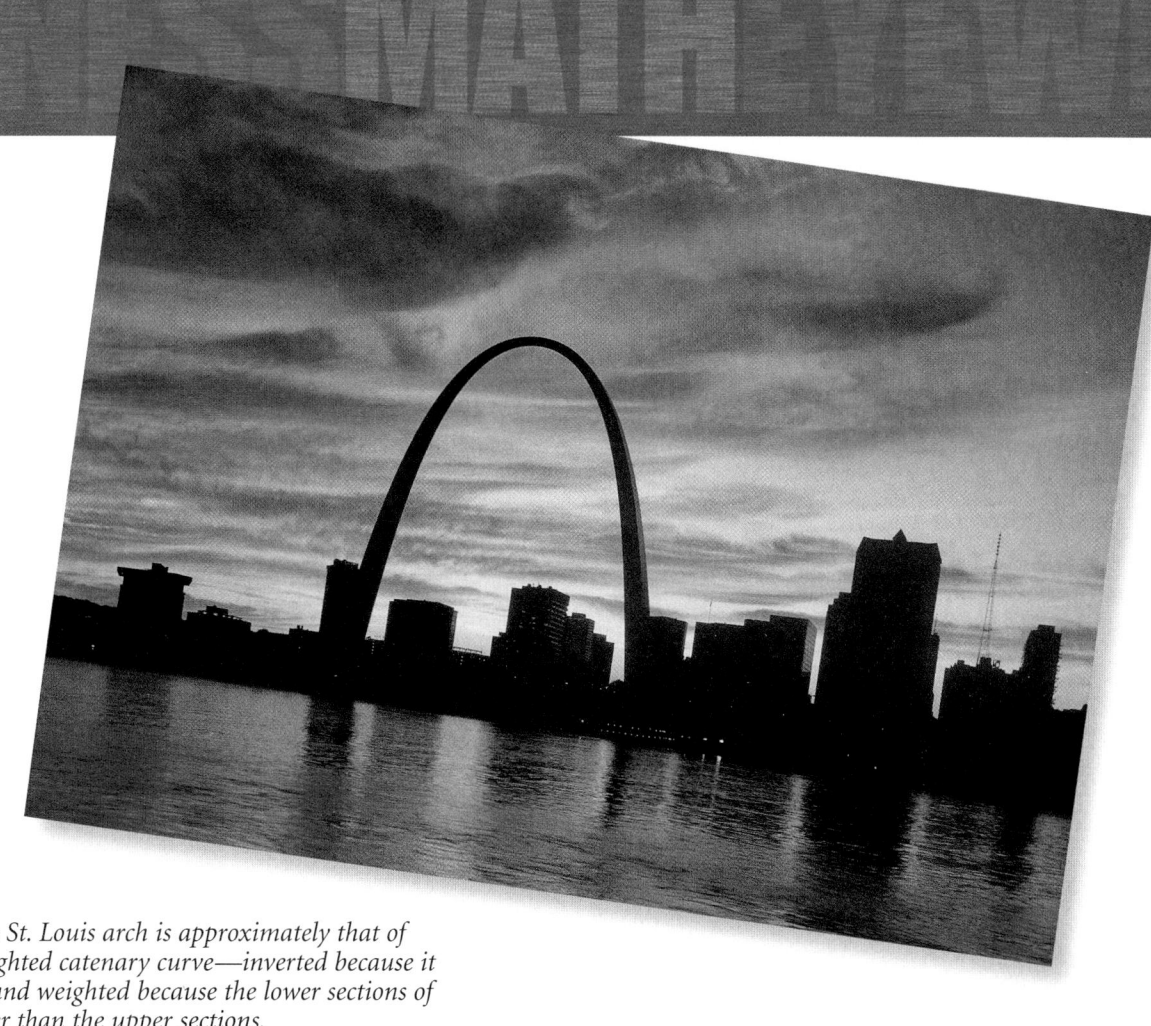

The shape of the St. Louis arch is approximately that of an inverted, weighted catenary curve—inverted because it is upside down and weighted because the lower sections of the legs are wider than the upper sections.

Cooperative Learning

1. Begin exploring the catenary by letting $a = 2$.
   a. Write the equation for a catenary curve with $a = 2$.
   b. Copy and complete the table below.

x	0	1	2	3	4	5
y						

   c. What is y when $x = -1$? Compare this value for y with the value of y when $x = 1$.
   d. Why will the y-values for $-x$ and x always be equal for this equation?

2. Now explore the graph of the equation for the curve with $a = 2$.
   a. Graph the equation for a catenary curve with $a = 2$. Describe the graph.
   b. Your graph should look like an upside-down arch. What can you do to the equation to invert the graph? (Hint: Think about how to invert, or reflect, a parabola.) Check your new equation by graphing it.

3. Your catenary curve may look similar to a parabola. To see how it is different, follow the steps below.
   a. Write an equation and draw the graph for a parabola that resembles your graph from part **a** of Step 2. (Hint: How do the values of a, h, and k in a quadratic equation of the form $y = a(x - h)^2 + k$ affect the location and shape of the parabola?)
   b. Compare the graph of your parabola with that of the catenary curve.

Solving Equations and Modeling

Objectives

- Solve logarithmic and exponential equations by using algebra and graphs.

- Model and solve real-world problems involving exponential and logarithmic relationships.

Why *Physicists, chemists, and geologists use exponential and logarithmic equations to model various phenomena, such as the magnitude of earthquakes.*

RICHTER SCALE RATINGS

Magnitude	Result near the epicenter	Approximate number of occurrences per year
8–9	near total damage	0.2
7.0–7.9	serious damage to buildings	14
6.0–6.9	moderate damage to buildings	185
5.0–5.9	slight damage to buildings	1000
4.0–4.9	felt by most people	2800
3.0–3.9	felt by some people	26,000
2.0–2.9	not felt but recorded	800,000

APPLICATION

GEOLOGY

On the Richter scale, the magnitude, M, of an earthquake depends on the amount of energy, E, released by the earthquake as follows:

$$M = \frac{2}{3} \log \frac{E}{10^{11.8}}$$

The amount of energy, measured in ergs, is based on the amount of ground motion recorded by a seismograph at a known distance from the epicenter of the quake.

The logarithmic function for the Richter scale assigns very large numbers for the amount of energy, E, to numbers that range from 1 to 9. A rating of 2 on the Richter scale indicates the smallest tremor that can be detected. Destructive earthquakes are those rated greater than 6 on the Richter scale.

1 One of the strongest earthquakes in recent history occurred in Mexico City in 1985 and measured 8.1 on the Richter scale.

Find the amount of energy, E, released by this earthquake.

● **SOLUTION**

PROBLEM SOLVING

Use a formula.

$$M = \frac{2}{3} \log \frac{E}{10^{11.8}}$$

A seismogram produced by a seismograph

$$8.1 = \frac{2}{3} \log \frac{E}{10^{11.8}}$$ *Substitute 8.1 for the magnitude, M.*

$$12.15 = \log \frac{E}{10^{11.8}}$$

$$10^{12.15} = \frac{E}{10^{11.8}}$$ *Use the definition of logarithm.*

$$10^{11.8} \cdot 10^{12.15} = E$$

$$8.91 \times 10^{23} \approx E$$ *Write the answer in scientific notation.*

The amount of energy, E, released by this earthquake was approximately 8.91×10^{23} ergs. *In physics, an erg is a unit of work or energy.*

To solve the logarithmic equation in Example 1, you must use the definition of a logarithm. However, solving exponential and logarithmic equations often requires a variety of the definitions and properties from this chapter. A summary of the definitions and properties that you have learned is given below.

Copy these properties and definitions into your notebook for reference.

SUMMARY	
Exponential and Logarithmic Definitions and Properties	
Definition of logarithm	$y = \log_b x$ if and only if $b^y = x$
Product Property	$\log_b mn = \log_b m + \log_b n$
Quotient Property	$\log_b\left(\dfrac{m}{n}\right) = \log_b m - \log_b n$
Power Property	$\log_b m^p = p \log_b m$
Exponential-Logarithmic Inverse Properties	$b^{\log_b x} = x$ for $x > 0$ $\log_b b^x = x$ for all x
One-to-One Property of Exponents	If $b^x = b^y$, then $x = y$.
One-to-One Property of Logarithms	If $\log_b x = \log_b y$, then $x = y$.
Change-of-base formula	$\log_c a = \dfrac{\log_b a}{\log_b c}$

CHECKPOINT ✔ Show how to solve $M = \frac{2}{3} \log \frac{E}{10^{11.8}}$ for E.

CRITICAL THINKING Use the properties of exponents and logarithms to show that $\log_a\left(\frac{1}{x}\right) = \log_{\frac{1}{a}} x$.

EXAMPLE ② Solve $\log x + \log(x - 3) = 1$ for x.

● **SOLUTION**

Method 1 Use algebra.

$\log x + \log(x - 3) = 1$

$\log[x(x - 3)] = 1$ *Apply the Product Property of Logarithms.*

$x(x - 3) = 10^1$ *Write the equivalent exponential equation.*

$x^2 - 3x - 10 = 0$

$(x - 5)(x + 2) = 0$

$x = 5 \quad or \quad x = -2$

CHECK

Let $x = 5$.

$\log x + \log(x - 3) = 1$

$\log 5 + \log 2 \stackrel{?}{=} 1$

$1 = 1$ **True**

Let $x = -2$.

$\log x + \log(x - 3) = 1$

$\log(-2) + \log(-5) = 1$ **Undefined**

Since the domain of a logarithmic function excludes negative numbers, the only solution is 5.

TECHNOLOGY

GRAPHICS CALCULATOR

Keystroke Guide, page 421

Method 2 Use a graph.

Graph $y = \log x + \log(x - 3)$ and $y = 1$, and find the point of intersection.

The coordinates of the point of intersection are $(5, 1)$, so the solution is 5.

TRY THIS

Solve $\log(x + 48) + \log x = 2$ by using algebra and a graph.

EXAMPLE ③ Solve $4e^{3x-5} = 72$ for x.

● **SOLUTION**

Method 1 Use algebra.

$4e^{3x-5} = 72$

$e^{3x-5} = 18$

$\ln e^{3x-5} = \ln 18$ *Take the natural logarithm of each side.*

$3x - 5 = \ln 18$ *Use Exponential-Logarithmic Inverse Properties.*

$x = \dfrac{\ln 18 + 5}{3}$ *Exact solution*

$x \approx 2.63$ *Approximate solution*

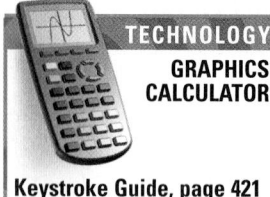

TECHNOLOGY

GRAPHICS CALCULATOR

Keystroke Guide, page 421

Method 2 Use a graph.

Graph $y = 4e^{3x-5}$ and $y = 72$, and find the point of intersection.

The coordinates of the point of intersection are approximately $(2.63, 72)$, so the solution is approximately 2.63.

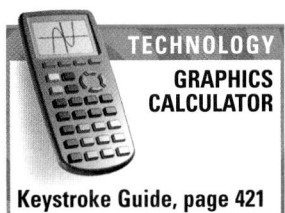

TECHNOLOGY

GRAPHICS CALCULATOR

Keystroke Guide, page 421

CHECKPOINT ✔

CHECKPOINT ✔

Solving Exponential Inequalities

You will need: a graphics calculator

1. Graph $y_1 = \log x + \log(x + 21)$ and $y_2 = 2$ on the same screen.

2. For what value(s) of x is $y_1 = y_2$? $y_1 < y_2$? $y_1 > y_2$?

3. Explain how you can use a graph to solve $\log x + \log(x + 21) > 2$.

4. Graph $y_1 = 2e^{4x-1}$ and $y_2 = 38$ on the same screen.

5. For what approximate value(s) of x is $y_1 = y_2$? $y_1 < y_2$? $y_1 > y_2$?

6. Explain how you can use a graph to solve $2e^{4x-1} < 38$.

Newton's Law of Cooling

An object that is hotter than its surroundings will cool off, and an object that is cooler than its surroundings will warm up. **Newton's law of cooling** states that the temperature difference between an object and its surroundings decreases exponentially as a function of time according to the following:

$$T(t) = T_s + (T_0 - T_s)e^{-kt}$$

T_0 is the initial temperature of the object, T_s is the temperature of the object's surroundings (assumed to be constant), t is the time, and $-k$ represents the constant rate of decrease in the temperature difference $(T_0 - T_s)$.

E X A M P L E ❹ When a container of milk is taken out of the refrigerator, its temperature is 40°F. An hour later, its temperature is 50°F. Assume that the temperature of the air is a constant 70°F.

APPLICATION

PHYSICS

a. Write the function for the temperature of this container of milk as a function of time, t.

b. What is the temperature of the milk after 2 hours?

c. After how many hours is the temperature of the milk 65°F?

● **SOLUTION**

a. First substitute 40 for T_0 and 70 for T_s, and simplify.

$$T(t) = T_s + (T_0 - T_s)e^{-kt}$$
$$T(t) = 70 + (40 - 70)e^{-kt}$$
$$T(t) = 70 + (-30)e^{-kt}$$

Since $T(1) = 50$, substitute 1 for t and 50 for $T(t)$, and solve for $-k$.

$$50 = 70 - 30e^{-k}$$
$$30e^{-k} = 20$$
$$e^{-k} = \frac{2}{3}$$
$$\ln e^{-k} = \ln \frac{2}{3}$$
$$-k = \ln \frac{2}{3}$$

Substitute $\ln \frac{2}{3}$ for $-k$ and simplify to get the function for the temperature of this container of milk.

$$T(t) = 70 - 30e^{-kt}$$

$$T(t) = 70 - 30e^{(\ln \frac{2}{3})t}$$

$$T(t) = 70 - 30\left(\frac{2}{3}\right)^t \quad \textit{Apply the Exponential-Logarithmic Inverse Property.}$$

The function for the temperature of this container of milk is
$$T(t) = 70 - 30\left(\frac{2}{3}\right)^t.$$

b. Find $T(2)$.

$$T(t) = 70 - 30\left(\frac{2}{3}\right)^t$$

$$T(2) = 70 - 30\left(\frac{2}{3}\right)^2 \approx 56.7$$

The temperature of the milk after 2 hours is approximately 56.7°F.

c. Substitute 65 for $T(t)$, and solve for t.

$$T(t) = 70 - 30\left(\frac{2}{3}\right)^t$$

$$65 = 70 - 30\left(\frac{2}{3}\right)^t$$

$$30\left(\frac{2}{3}\right)^t = 5$$

$$\left(\frac{2}{3}\right)^t = \frac{1}{6}$$

$$t \ln \frac{2}{3} = \ln \frac{1}{6}$$

$$t = \frac{\ln \frac{1}{6}}{\ln \frac{2}{3}} \approx 4.42$$

It will take approximately 4.42 hours, or about 4 hours and 25 minutes, for the milk to warm up to 65°F.

Exercises

Communicate

1. Explain how to solve the exponential equation $e^{x+7} = 98$ by algebraic methods.

2. How can you solve the logarithmic equation $\log_2 x + \log_2(x + 3) = 2$ by algebraic methods?

3. Explain how to solve exponential and logarithmic equations by graphing.

APPLICATIONS

4. GEOLOGY In 1989, an earthquake that measured 7.1 on the Richter scale occurred in San Francisco, California. Find the amount of energy, E, released by this earthquake. *(EXAMPLE 1)*

5. Solve $\log(x - 90) + \log x = 3$ for x. *(EXAMPLE 2)*

6. Solve $0.5e^{0.08t} = 40$ for x. *(EXAMPLE 3)*

7. PHYSICS When the air temperature is a constant 70°F, an object cools from 170°F to 140°F in one-half hour. *(EXAMPLE 4)*
   a. Write the function for the temperature of this object, T, as a function of time, t.
   b. What is the temperature of this object after 1 hour?
   c. After how many hours is the temperature of this object 90°F?

Practice and Apply

internet connect

Homework Help Online
Go To: **go.hrw.com**
Keyword:
MB1 Homework Help
for Exercises 8–25

Solve each equation for x. Write the exact solution and the approximate solution to the nearest hundredth, when appropriate.

8. $3^x = 3^4$ **9.** $3^{2x} = 81$ **10.** $5^{x-2} = 25$

11. $x = \log_3 \frac{1}{27}$ **12.** $x = \log_4 \frac{1}{64}$ **13.** $\log_x \frac{1}{16} = -2$

14. $4 = \log_x \frac{1}{16}$ **15.** $e^{2x} = 20$ **16.** $e^{-2(x+1)} = 2$

17. $\ln(2x - 3) = \ln 21$ **18.** $\ln(x + 3) = 2 \ln 4$ **19.** $10^{2x} + 75 = 150$

20. $e^{-4x} - 22 = 56$ **21.** $3 \ln x = \ln 4 + \ln 2$ **22.** $\ln x + \ln(x + 1) = \ln 2$

23. $2 \ln x + 2 = 1$ **24.** $3 \ln x + 3 = 1$ **25.** $3 \log x + 7 = 5$

CHALLENGE

Solve each equation for x. Write the exact solution and the approximate solution to the nearest hundredth, when appropriate.

26. $\ln(3\sqrt{x}) = \sqrt{\ln x}$ **27.** $\log x^3 = (\log x)^3$

APPLICATIONS

28. GEOLOGY On May 10, 1997, a light earthquake with a magnitude of 4.7 struck the Calaveras Fault 10 miles east of San Jose, California. Find the amount of energy, E, released by this earthquake.

29. GEOLOGY In 1976, an earthquake that released about 8×10^{19} ergs of energy occurred in San Salvador, El Salvador. Find the magnitude, M, of this earthquake to the nearest tenth.

30. PHYSICS A hot coal (at a temperature of 160°C) is immersed in ice water (at a temperature of 0°C). After 30 seconds, the temperature of the coal is 60°C. Assume that the ice water is kept at a constant temperature of 0°C.
   a. Write the function for the temperature, T, of this object as a function of time, t, in seconds.
   b. What will be the temperature of this coal after 2 minutes (120 seconds)?
   c. After how many minutes will the temperature of the coal be 1°C?

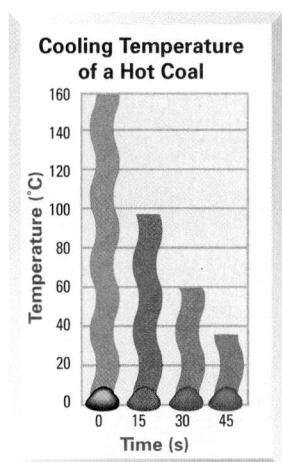

Cooling Temperature of a Hot Coal

31. GEOLOGY Compare the amounts of energy released by earthquakes that differ by 1 in magnitude. In other words, how much more energy is released by an earthquake of magnitude 6.8 than an earthquake of magnitude 5.8?

> 6.8 magnitude earthquake off the coast of northern California on February 19, 1995

The map shows the locations of the three strongest earthquakes in the United States in 1995.

> 5.8 magnitude earthquake in Ridgecrest, California, northeast of Los Angeles on September 20, 1995

> 5.7 magnitude earthquake in Brewster County, Texas, on April 14, 1995

32. PSYCHOLOGY Educational psychologists sometimes use mathematical models of memory. Suppose that some students take a chemistry test. After a time, t (in months), without a review of the material, they take an equivalent form of the same test. The mathematical model $a(t) = 82 - 12\log(t + 1)$, where a is the average score at time t, is a function that describes the students' retention of the material.
  a. What is the average score when the students first took the test ($t = 0$)?
  b. What is the average score after 6 months?
  c. After how many months is the average score 60?

33. BIOLOGY A population of bacteria grows exponentially. A population that initially consists of 10,000 bacteria grows to 25,000 bacteria after 2 hours.
  a. Use the exponential growth function, $P(t) = P_0e^{kt}$, to find the value of k. Then write a function for this population of bacteria in terms of time, t. Round the value of k to the nearest hundredth.
  b. How many bacteria will the population consist of after 12 hours, rounded to the nearest hundred thousand?
  c. How many bacteria will the population consist of after 24 hours?

34. DEMOGRAPHICS The population of India was estimated to be 574,220,000 in 1974 and 746,388,000 in 1984. Assume that this population growth is exponential. Let $t = 0$ represent 1974 and $t = 10$ represent 1984.
  a. Use the exponential growth function, $P(t) = P_0e^{kt}$, to find the value of k. Then write the function for this population as a function of time, t.
  b. Estimate the population in 2004, rounded to the nearest hundred thousand.
  c. Use the function you wrote in part **a** to estimate the year in which the population will reach 1.5 billion.

35. ARCHEOLOGY Refer to the discussion of radioactive decay on page 395. Suppose that an animal bone is unearthed and it is determined that the amount of carbon-14 it contains is 40% of the original amount.
  a. Use the decay function for carbon-14, $N(t) = N_0e^{-0.00012t}$, to write an equation using the percentage of carbon-14 given above.
  b. Use the equation you wrote in part **a** to find the approximate age, t, of the bone.

Look Back

Graph each system of linear inequalities. *(LESSON 4.8)*

36. $\begin{cases} 2x - 5y < 4 \\ -3x \geq 2y \end{cases}$

37. $\begin{cases} -x \leq -3 \\ y - 5 > -3 \end{cases}$

38. $\begin{cases} -y + 3 \leq 12 \\ -x < y + 8 \end{cases}$

Solve each equation for x. *(LESSON 5.2)*

39. $x^2 - 3 = 46$

40. $7 - x^2 = 4$

Solve for x, and check your answers. *(LESSON 6.4)*

41. $\log_b(x^2 - 11) = \log_b(2x + 4)$

42. $\log_{10}(8x + 1) = \log_{10}(x^2 - 8)$

43. $\log_a(x^2 + 1) + 2\log_a 4 = \log_a 40x$

44. $2\log_b x - \log_b 3 = \log_b(2x - 3)$

APPLICATION

INVESTMENTS Assume that all interest rates are compounded continuously in Exercises 45–47. *(LESSON 6.6)*

45. How long will it take an investment of $5000 to double if the annual interest rate is 5%?

46. How long will it take an investment to double at 8% annual interest?

47. If it takes a certain amount of money 3.2 years to double, at what annual interest rate was the money invested?

Portfolio Extension
Go To: go.hrw.com
Keyword:
MB1 Newton

 Look Beyond

48. Graph each function and compare the shapes of the graphs.
  a. $y = x^2$ **b.** $y = x^3 - 2x$ **c.** $y = x^4 - 2x^2$

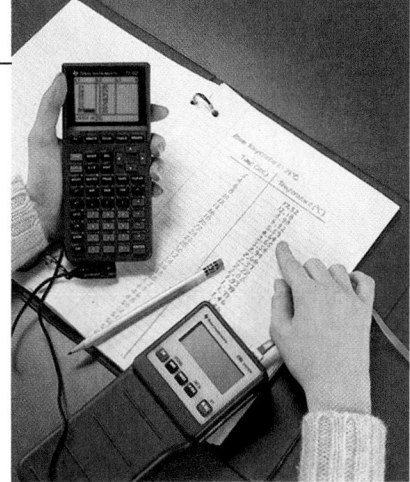

This activity requires the data collected for the Portfolio Activities on pages 361, 369, and 384.

1. Refer to your data from the Portfolio Activity on page 361.
  a. Use Newton's law of cooling, found in Example 4 on page 405, to write a function that models the temperature of the probe as it cooled to the temperature of ice water.
  b. Compare the graph of this function with the graph of the exponential function that you generated for the same data in the Portfolio Activity on page 369. (Hint: You can use the table function on your graphics calculator to compare the *y*-values of these functions with the original values.)

2. a. Repeat part **a** of Step 1, using the data collected in the Portfolio Activity on page 384.

  b. Repeat part **b** from Step 1, comparing your new graph with the graphs of both the exponential function and the approximating function from the Portfolio Activity on page 384.

WORKING ON THE PROJECT

You should now be able to complete the Chapter Project.

PROJECT CHAPTER SIX

WARM UPS

You will need a CBL with a temperature probe, a glass of ice water, and a graphics calculator. Refer to the discussion of the Chapter Project on page 358.

Step 1: First use the CBL to measure the air temperature. Record this temperature.

Step 2: Cool the temperature probe in the ice water to near 0°C.

Step 3: Remove the probe from the water. Record 30 CBL readings taken at 2-second intervals. These readings will be your data set.

Step 4: Take and record a final reading at 2 minutes.

Activity 1

1. Find the function that models the linear regression of your data set. Use the variable t for time in seconds.

2. Use the linear model to predict the temperature of the probe after 2 minutes. Compare the prediction to your actual 2-minute reading. Discuss the usefulness of a linear function for modeling the warming process.

Activity 2

1. Use the regression feature on your calculator to find a quadratic function and an exponential function that model your data set.

2. Predict the temperature of the probe after 2 minutes by using the quadratic and exponential models. Compare the predictions with your actual 2-minute reading. Discuss the usefulness of each function for modeling the warming process.

Activity 3

1. Transform your data by taking the opposite of each temperature in the data set and add the air temperature to it. Store this data in a new list.

2. Use the exponential regression feature on your calculator to find an exponential function to model this transformed data. Discuss the usefulness of this function for modeling the warming process.

3. Add the air temperature to the exponential function in Step 2. This new function will be called the "approximating function."

4. Use the approximating function to predict the temperature of the probe after 2 minutes. Discuss the usefulness of this function for modeling the warming process.

Activity 4

1. Use your data and Newton's law of cooling (from page 405) to write a function for the temperature of the probe as it warms to room temperature. Use this function to predict the temperature of the probe after 2 minutes.

2. Compare the accuracy of the prediction from Step 1 with the accuracy of the prediction obtained with the approximating function in Step 4 of Activity 3.

Chapter Review and Assessment

6

VOCABULARY

asymptote 362
base 362
change-of-base formula ... 388
common logarithm 385
compound interest formula .. 365
continuous compounding
    formula 393
effective yield 365
exponential decay 363
exponential expression ... 355

exponential function 362
exponential growth 363
Exponential-Logarithmic
    Inverse Properties 380
logarithmic function 372
multiplier 355
natural base 393
natural exponential
    function 393
natural logarithmic
    function 394

Newton's law of cooling ... 405
One-to-One Property of
    Exponents 372
One-to-One Property of
    Logarithms 380
Power Property of
    Logarithms 379
Product Property
    of Logarithms 378
Quotient Property
    of Logarithms 378

Key Skills & Exercises

LESSON 6.1

Key Skills

Write and evaluate exponential expressions.

The world population rose to about 5,734,000,000 in 1995. The world population was increasing at an annual rate of 1.6%. Write and evaluate an expression to predict the world population in 2020. [*Source: Worldbook Encyclopedia*]

$$5,734,000,000(1.016)^x$$
$$5,734,000,000(1.016)^{25} \approx 8,527,000,000$$

The projected world population for 2020 is about 8.5 billion people.

Exercises

1. **INVESTMENTS** The value of a painting is $12,000 in 1990 and increases by 8% of its value each year. Write and evaluate an expression to estimate the painting's value in 2005.

2. **DEPRECIATION** The value of a new car is $23,000 in 1998; it loses 15% of its value each year. Write and evaluate an expression to estimate the car's value in 2005.

LESSON 6.2

Key Skills

Classify an exponential function as exponential growth or exponential decay.

When $b > 1$, the function $f(x) = b^x$ represents exponential growth.

When $0 < b < 1$, the function $f(x) = b^x$ represents exponential decay.

Calculate the growth of investments.

The total amount of an investment, A, earning compound interest is $A(t) = P\left(1 + \frac{r}{n}\right)^{nt}$, where P is the principal, r is the annual interest rate, n is the number of times interest is compounded per year, and t is the time in years.

Exercises

Identify each function as representing exponential growth or decay.

3. $f(x) = 4(0.89)^x$ 4. $g(x) = \frac{1}{3}(1.06)^x$

5. $h(x) = 5(1.06)^x$ 6. $j(x) = 25\left(\frac{2}{5}\right)^x$

INVESTMENTS For each compounding period below, find the final amount of a $2400 investment after 12 years at an annual interest rate of 4.5%.

7. annually   8. quarterly

9. daily

LESSON 6.3

Key Skills

Write equivalent forms of exponential and logarithmic equations.

$3^4 = 81$ is $\log_3 81 = 4$ in logarithmic form.

$\log_2 64 = 6$ is $2^6 = 64$ in exponential form.

Use the definitions of exponential and logarithmic functions to solve equations.

$$
\begin{array}{lll}
v = \log_6 36 & 3 = \log_4 v & 4 = \log_v 81 \\
6^v = 36 & 4^3 = v & v^4 = 81 \\
6^v = 6^2 & 64 = v & v^4 = 3^4 \\
v = 2 & & v = 3
\end{array}
$$

Exercises

10. Write $5^2 = 25$ in logarithmic form.

11. Write $\log_3 27 = 3$ in exponential form.

12. Write $\log_3 \frac{1}{9} = -2$ in exponential form.

Find the value of v in each equation.

13. $v = \log_8 64$

14. $\log_v 4 = 2$

15. $2 = \log_{12} v$

16. $3 = \log_v 1000$

17. $\log_2 v = -3$

18. $\log_{27} 3 = v$

19. $\log_v 49 = 2$

20. $\log_4 \frac{1}{16} = v$

LESSON 6.4

Key Skills

Use the Product, Quotient, and Power Properties of Logarithms to simplify and evaluate expressions involving logarithms.

Given $\log_3 7 \approx 1.7712$, $\log_3 63$ can be approximated as shown below.

$$
\begin{aligned}
\log_3 63 &= \log_3 9 + \log_3 7 \\
&= 2 + 1.7712 \approx 3.7712
\end{aligned}
$$

$$\log_5 25^7 = 7 \log_5 25 = 7 \cdot 2 = 14$$

Exercises

Given $\log_7 5 \approx 0.8271$ and $\log_7 9 \approx 1.1292$, approximate the value of each logarithm.

21. $\log_7 45$ **22.** $\log_7 \frac{5}{9}$ **23.** $\log_7 35$

Write each expression as a single logarithm. Then simplify, if possible.

24. $\log_5 3 + \log_5 6 + \log_5 9$

25. $\log 6 - \log 3 + 2 \log 7$

Evaluate each expression.

26. $2^{\log_2 12}$ **27.** $\log_7 7^3$ **28.** $\log_6 36^7$

LESSON 6.5

Key Skills

Use the common logarithmic function to solve exponential and logarithmic equations.

$$
\begin{array}{ll}
4 = \log x & 2^x = 34 \\
10^4 = x & \log 2^x = \log 34 \\
10{,}000 = x & x \log 2 = \log 34 \\
& x = \dfrac{\log 34}{\log 2} \\
& x \approx 5.09
\end{array}
$$

Apply the change-of-base formula to evaluate logarithmic expressions.

The change-of-base formula is $\log_a x = \dfrac{\log_b x}{\log_b a}$,

where $a \neq 1$, $b \neq 1$, and $x > 0$.

$$\log_2 5 = \frac{\log 5}{\log 2} \approx 2.32$$

Exercises

Solve each equation. Give your answers to the nearest hundredth.

29. $\log x = 8$

30. $\log 0.01 = x - 5$

31. $5^x + 100 = 98$

32. $5 - 2^x = 40$

33. $7 + 3^{2x-1} = 154$

34. $3 + 7^{3x+1} = 346$

Evaluate each logarithmic expression to the nearest hundredth.

35. $\log_3 14$

36. $\log_{16} 3$

37. $\log_{0.5} 6$

38. $\log_{1.5} 10$

39. CHEMISTRY What is $[H^+]$ of a carbonated soda if its pH is 2.5?

Key Skills

Evaluate exponential functions of base *e* and natural logarithms.

Using a calculator and rounding to the nearest thousandth, $e^{2.5} \approx 12.182$ and $\ln 3.5 \approx 1.253$.

Model exponential growth and decay processes by using base *e*.

The continuous compounding formula is $A = Pe^{rt}$, where A is the final amount when the principal P is invested at an annual interest rate of r for t years.

Exercises

Evaluate each expression to the nearest thousandth.

40. $e^{0.5}$ **41.** e^{-5}

42. $\ln 5$ **43.** $\ln 0.05$

44. INVESTMENTS Sharon invests $2500 at an annual interest rate of 9%. How much is the investment worth after 10 years if the interest is compounded continuously?

Key Skills

Solve logarithmic and exponential equations.

$$\log_x \frac{1}{32} = -5 \qquad \ln x^3 + 5 = 1$$
$$x^{-5} = \frac{1}{32} \qquad 3 \ln x = -4$$
$$x^{-5} = 2^{-5} \qquad \ln x = -\frac{4}{3}$$
$$x = 2 \qquad x = e^{-\frac{4}{3}}$$
$$x \approx 0.264$$

$$\ln(x + 6) = 2 \ln 3$$
$$\ln(x + 6) = \ln 9$$
$$x + 6 = 9$$
$$x = 3$$

Exercises

Solve each equation for *x*. Write the exact solution and the approximate solution to the nearest hundredth, when appropriate.

45. $\log_x \frac{1}{128} = -7$

46. $\ln(2x) = 4 \ln 2$

47. $x \log \frac{1}{6} = \log 6$

48. $\ln \sqrt{x} - 3 = 1$

49. HEALTH The normal healing of a wound can be modeled by $A = A_0 e^{-0.35n}$, where A is the area of the wound in square centimeters after n days. After how many days is the area of the wound half of its original size, A_0?

Applications

50. BIOLOGY Given favorable living conditions, fruit fly populations can grow at the astounding rate of 28% per day. If a laboratory selects a population of 25 fruit flies to reproduce, about how big will the population be after 3 days? after 5 days? after 1 week?

51. PHYSICS Suppose that the sound of busy traffic on a four-lane street is about $10^{8.5}$ times the intensity of the threshold of hearing, I_0. Find the relative intensity, R, in decibels of the traffic on this street.

52. PHYSICS Radon is a radioactive gas that has a half-life of about 3.8 days. This means that only half of the original amount of radon gas will be present after about 3.8 days. Using the exponential decay function $A = Pe^{-kt}$, find the value of k to the nearest hundredth, and write the function for the amount of radon remaining after t days.

Fruit fly

Chapter Test

1. **DEMOGRAPHICS** The population of Petoskey, Michigan, was 6076 in 1990 and was growing at the rate of 3.7% per year. The city planners want to know what the population will be in the year 2025. Write and evaluate an expression to estimate this population.

2. **INCOME TAX** The government allows for linear depreciation of capital expenditures for income tax purposes at the rate of 10% per year. What will be the value of a $150,000 tool and die machine after 7 years of use?

Tell whether each function represents exponential growth or decay.

3. $f(x) = 3.6(1.01)^x$

4. $g(t) = 0.015(1.23)^t$

5. $h(t) = \left(7\frac{3}{4}\right)\left(\frac{5}{8}\right)^t$

6. $j(x) = 2500(0.25)^x$

INVESTMENTS For each compounding period below, find the final amount of a $5000 investment after 10 years at a 5.6% annual interest rate.

7. daily

8. monthly

9. quarterly

10. annually

Write each logarithmic equation in exponential form and each exponential equation in logarithmic form.

11. $\log_3 81 = 4$

12. $2^8 = 256$

13. $\left(\frac{1}{4}\right)^{-5} = 1024$

14. $\log_5\frac{1}{625} = -4$

Find the value of v in each equation.

15. $3 = \log_v 343$

16. $\log_9 729 = v$

17. $\log_6 v = 5$

Write each expression as a single logarithm. Then simplify, if possible.

18. $\log_2 5 - 3\log_2 3 + \log_2 6$

19. $\log_7\frac{1}{4} + 2\log_7 4 - \frac{1}{2}\log_7 16$

Evaluate each expression.

20. $5^{\log_5 32}$

21. $\log_6 36$

22. $\log_9 9^{\frac{2}{3}}$

23. $\log_b b^{(x-2)}$

Solve each equation. Give your answers to the nearest hundredth.

24. $\log_4 x = 6.2$

25. $3^{x+2} = 238$

26. $274 - 5^x = 198$

27. $\log_6 468 = x$

28. **SEISMOLOGY** The amount of energy E, in ergs, released by an earthquake of magnitude M is given by the formula $E = 10^{(1.5M + 11.8)}$. What is the difference in the amount of energy released by an earthquake of magnitude 6.5 and one of magnitude 8.7?

Evaluate each expression to the nearest thousandth.

29. $e^{3.4}$

30. $\ln\pi$

31. $e^{-3.25}$

32. $\ln(e^{1.618})$

33. **ARCHAEOLOGY** The age of an artifact can be determined using carbon-14 dating with the equation $N(t) = N_0 e^{-0.00012t}$. What is the approximate age of an artifact if a sample reveals that it contains 34% of its original carbon-14?

Solve each equation for x. Write the exact solution and the approximate solution to the nearest hundredth, when appropriate.

34. $3^x = 5^{2.3}$

35. $\ln(x+1) = 2\ln 4$

36. $\log x + \log(x+3) = 1$

1-6 College Entrance Exam Practice

MULTIPLE-CHOICE For Questions 1–12, write the letter that indicates the best answer.

1. Find the minimum value in the range of the function $f(x) = |x - 2|$. **(LESSON 2.6)**

  a. 0   **b.** −2

  c. 2   **d.** 1

2. Multiply $(5 - 2i)(5 + 2i)$. **(LESSON 5.6)**

  a. 20   **b.** 29

  c. 14   **d.** 21

3. Solve $\frac{1}{5}(x - 2)^2 = 1$. **(LESSON 5.2)**

  a. $x = 2 \pm \sqrt{5}$ **b.** $x = 2 \pm \sqrt{3}$

  c. $x = 4 \pm \sqrt{5}$ **d.** $x = 4 \pm \sqrt{3}$

4. Let $f(x) = 3x$ and $g(x) = x^2 + 2$. Find $(g \circ f)(-2)$. **(LESSON 2.4)**

  a. −6   **b.** 38

  c. −34   **d.** 18

5. Determine the number of real solutions for $2x^2 - 3x = 3$. **(LESSON 5.6)**

  a. 2   **b.** 1

  c. 0   **d.** undefined

6. What is the slope of the line that contains the points $(6, -8)$ and $(-2, -4)$? **(LESSON 1.2)**

  a. 2   **b.** −2

  c. $-\frac{1}{2}$ **d.** $\frac{1}{2}$

7. Which term describes the system of equations below? **(LESSON 3.1)**

$$\begin{cases} 2x - y = 7 \\ 2y - 4x = -14 \end{cases}$$

  a. inconsistent   **b.** dependent

  c. independent   **d.** incompatible

8. What are the coordinates of the vertex for the graph of $y = (x - 2)(x + 1)$? **(LESSON 5.5)**

  a. $(-0.5, -2.25)$ **b.** $(-1, 0)$

  c. $(0.5, -2.25)$ **d.** $(-0.5, 3.75)$

9. In triangle *ABC* below, what is the value of *a*? **(LESSON 5.2)**

  a. 28

  b. $2\sqrt{7}$

  c. 2

  d. 4

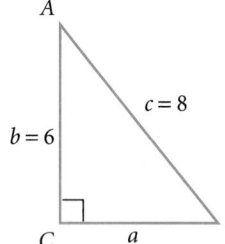

10. Which is a solution for the system below? **(LESSON 3.1)**

$$\begin{cases} y = x + 3 \\ y - x = 4 \end{cases}$$

  a. $(3, 7)$

  b. $(2, 5)$

  c. both **a** and **b**

  d. neither **a** nor **b**

11. Simplify $\left(\frac{-x^{-3}y^5}{2xy^{-2}}\right)^4$. **(LESSON 2.2)**

  a. $\dfrac{y^{28}}{8x^{16}}$

  b. $-\dfrac{y^{28}}{8x^{16}}$

  c. $\dfrac{y^{28}}{16x^{16}}$

  d. $\dfrac{1}{16}x^{11}y^{22}$

12. Determine which set of ordered pairs represents a function. *(LESSON 2.3)*
   a. {(1, −1), (−1, 1), (1, 1)}
   b. {(0, 1), (1, 0), (0, 0)}
   c. {(−1, 1), (1, −1), (1, 0), (0, −1)}
   d. {(0, 1), (1, 2), (2, 1), (−1, 0)}

13. Solve $\begin{cases} 2x + 8y = -10 \\ -3x + 12y = 3 \end{cases}$.
   (LESSONS 3.1 AND 3.2)

14. Solve $2x^2 - 7 = 121$ for x. *(LESSON 5.2)*

15. Write the equation in vertex form for the parabola described by $f(x) = 2x^2 - 3x + 7$. *(LESSON 5.4)*

16. If $f(x) = x^2 - 2x$, find the inverse of f. *(LESSON 2.5)*

17. Find the matrix product below. *(LESSON 4.2)*
$$\begin{bmatrix} 3 & -6 \\ 5 & 4 \end{bmatrix} \begin{bmatrix} 1 & 0 \\ 0 & 1 \end{bmatrix}$$

18. Factor to find the zeros of $f(x) = x^2 - x - 6$. *(LESSON 5.3)*

19. Let $f(x) = 2x - 3$ and $g(x) = -3x$. Find $(f \cdot g)(x)$. *(LESSON 2.4)*

20. Let $A = \begin{bmatrix} 2 & 3 & 8 \\ -4 & 5 & -8 \\ 0 & 6 & -5 \end{bmatrix}$ and let

$B = \begin{bmatrix} 0 & 3 & -1 \\ -1 & 4 & 3 \\ 2 & -7 & 2 \end{bmatrix}$. Find $A - B$.
   (LESSON 4.1)

FREE-RESPONSE GRID The following questions may be answered by using a free-response grid such as that commonly used by standardized-test services.

21. In the formula $F = \frac{9}{5}C + 32$, find the value of C if $F = 95$. *(LESSON 1.6)*

22. What is the value of $\log_2 \frac{1}{8}$? *(LESSON 6.3)*

23. What is the minimum value of $f(x) = x^2 - 5x + 8$? *(LESSON 5.1)*

24. Solve the equation $5e^{3-x} = 2$ for x. *(LESSON 6.6)*

25. INVESTMENTS If $2500 is invested at 6.9% compounded daily, determine the value of the investment after 12 years. *(LESSON 6.2)*

26. Simplify $\frac{(9 - 3)^2}{2(3 - 1)}$. *(LESSON 2.1)*

27. Evaluate $[3.2] - [4.99]$. *(LESSON 2.6)*

28. Find the determinant of $\begin{bmatrix} 3 & 6 \\ -1 & 4 \end{bmatrix}$.
   (LESSON 4.3)

BUSINESS A skate store makes two kinds of in-line skates: regular skates and those with custom boots. The store can make 90 pairs of skates per month and can spend, at most, no more than $11,400 per month to produce them. Each pair of regular skates costs $80 to make and brings a profit of $60. Each pair of skates with custom boots costs $150 to make and brings a profit of $70. *(LESSON 3.5)*

29. Find the number of regular in-line skates that the skate store needs to sell in order to maximize its profit.

30. Find the number of in-line skates with custom boots that the skate store needs to sell in order to maximize its profit.

Keystroke Guide for Chapter 6

Essential keystroke sequences (using the model TI-82 or TI-83 graphics calculator) are presented below for all Activities and Examples found in this chapter that require or recommend the use of a graphics calculator.

☑ internet connect

For Keystrokes of other graphing calculator models, visit the HRW web site at **go.hrw.com** and enter the keyword **MB1 CALC**.

LESSON 6.1

Activity
Page 354

Use a calculator to model the population growth of 25 bacteria that double every hour for 6 hours.

25 [ENTER] [X] 2 [ENTER] [ENTER] [ENTER] [ENTER] [ENTER] [ENTER]

LESSON 6.2

Activity
Page 363

For Step 1, graph $y_1 = 3^x$, $y_2 = 2^x$, and $y_3 = (1.5)^x$ on the same screen.

Use viewing window $[-3, 3]$ by $[0, 4]$.

[Y=] 3 [^] [X,T,θ,n] [ENTER] (Y2 =) 2 [^] [X,T,θ,n] [ENTER]
(Y3 =) 1.5 [^] [X,T,θ,n] [ENTER]

For Step 3, graph $y_4 = \left(\frac{1}{3}\right)^x$, $y_5 = \left(\frac{1}{2}\right)^x$, and $y_6 = \left(\frac{1}{1.5}\right)^x$ on the same screen as the graphs above.

[Y=] (Y4=) [(] 1 [D] 3 [)] [^] [X,T,θ,n] [ENTER]
(Y5=) [(] 1 [D] 2 [)] [^] [X,T,θ,n] [ENTER]
(Y6=) [(] 1 [D] 1.5 [)] [^] [X,T,θ,n] [ENTER]

EXAMPLE ①
Page 364

For part a, graph $y_1 = 2^x$ and $y_2 = 3 \cdot 2^x$ together, and find the y-intercepts.

Use viewing window $[-5, 5]$ by $[-2, 12]$.

To graph the functions, use a keystroke sequence similar to that in the Activity for this lesson.

Find the y-intercepts:

CALC
[2nd] [TRACE] [1: value] [ENTER] [ENTER] (X=) 0 [ENTER] [▼]

For part **b**, use a similar keystroke sequence.

EXAMPLE ❸

Page 366

Find the exponential regression equation that best fits the points (0, 100,000) and (5, 150,000).

Use viewing window [−2, 7] by [−20,000, 200,000] and Yscl: 20,000.

Enter the data:

[STAT] [EDIT] [1: edit] [ENTER] [L1] 0 [ENTER] 5 [ENTER] [▶] [L2] 100000 [ENTER]

150000 [ENTER]

Create the scatter plot:

[2nd] [Y=] (STATPLOT) [1:Plot 1] [ENTER] On [ENTER] [▼] (Type:) [···] [ENTER] [▼] (Xlist:)

[2nd] [1] (L1) [▼] (Ylist:) [2nd] [2] (L2) [▼] (Mark:) [▫] [ENTER] [2nd] [MODE] (QUIT)

Graph an exponential model for the data:

[STAT] [CALC] [0:ExpReg] [ENTER] [ENTER] [Y=] [VARS] [5:Statistics] [ENTER] [EQ] [1:RegEQ]

[ENTER] [GRAPH]

TI-82:

[STAT] [CALC] [A:ExpReg] [ENTER] [ENTER] [Y=] [VARS] [5:Statistics] [ENTER] [EQ] [7:RegEQ] [ENTER] [GRAPH]

LESSON 6.3

Activity

Page 370

Make a table of values for $y = 10^x$, and use the table to approximate the solution to $10^x = 7$ to the nearest hundredth.

[Y=] 10 [^] [X,T,Θ,n] [2nd] [WINDOW] (TBLSET)

(TblStart=) 0.83 [ENTER] (△Tbl=) 0.01 [ENTER]

(Indpnt:) [Auto] [ENTER] [▼]

(Depend:) [Auto] [ENTER] [2nd] [GRAPH] (TABLE)

X	Y₁
.83	6.7608
.84	6.9183
.85	7.0795
.86	7.2444
.87	7.4131
.88	7.5858
.89	7.7625

Y₁=7.07945784384

EXAMPLE ❹

Page 373

Solve $3 = -\log_{10} x$ for x by graphing

Use viewing window [0, 0.01] by [−2, 5].

Graph the related equations:

[Y=] [(−)] [LOG] [X,T,Θ,n] [ )] [ENTER]

⇑ TI-82: [( ]

(Y2=) 3 [GRAPH]

Intersection
X=1E⁻³   Y=3

Find any points of intersection:

[2nd] [TRACE] (CALC) [5:intersect] (First curve?)

[ENTER] (Second curve?) [ENTER] (Guess?) [ENTER]

Move your cursor as indicated.

EXAMPLE 1
Page 387

Graph $y = 10 \log x$, and evaluate y for $x = 300$.

Use viewing window $[-50, 350]$ by $[-10, 50]$.

Graph the function:

⇧TI-82: ◁

Find the point on the graph where $x = 300$:

CALC
2nd TRACE 1: value ENTER (X=) 300 ENTER

EXAMPLE 3
Page 387

Solve $5^x = 62$ by graphing.

Use viewing window $[-1, 5]$ by $[-40, 100]$.

Graph the related equations, and use a keystroke sequence similar to that in Example 4 of Lesson 6.3 to find any points of intersection.

EXAMPLES 1 and 3
Pages 393 and 394

For part a of Example 1, evaluate $y = e^x$ to the nearest thousandth for $x = 2$.

Use viewing window $[-2, 3]$ by $[-1, 10]$.

Enter the equation: Y= 2nd LN$^{e^x}$ X,T,θ,n) ENTER

⇧TI-82: ◁

Create a table of values:
Use a keystroke sequence similar to that in the Activity in Lesson 6.3. Use TblStart $= -1$ and $\triangle$Tbl $= 0.5$.

Find the point on the graph where $x = 2$:
Use a keystroke sequence similar to that in Example 1 of Lesson 6.5.

For parts **b** and **c** of Example 1, use a similar keystroke sequence.

For Example 3, use viewing window $[-2, 10]$ by $[-2, 4]$ and a similar keystroke sequence.

EXAMPLE 4
Page 395

Solve $2 = e^{0.085x}$ by graphing.

Use viewing window $[-20, 100]$ by $[-3, 10]$.

Graph the related equations:

Y= 2 ENTER (Y2=) 2nd LN$^{e^x}$ .085 X,T,θ,n) ENTER

⇧TI-82: ◁

Find the point of intersection:
Use a keystroke sequence similar to that in Example 4 of Lesson 6.3.

E X A M P L E Solve $\log x + \log(x - 3) = 1$ by graphing.

Page 404

Use viewing window $[-2, 8]$ by $[-1, 5]$.

Graph the related equations:

| Y= | LOG | X,T,Θ,n |) | + |

⇑ TI-82: (

| LOG | X,T,Θ,n | – | 3 |) | ENTER |

⇑ TI-82: (

(Y2=) 1 GRAPH

Find the point of intersection:
Use a keystroke sequence similar to that in Example 4 of Lesson 6.3.

E X A M P L E Solve $4e^{3x-5} = 72$ by graphing.

Page 404

Use viewing window $[-1, 4]$ by $[-30, 100]$.

Graph the related equations:

| Y= | 4 | 2nd | LN | 3 | X,T,Θ,n | – | 5 |) |

ENTER (Y2=) 72 GRAPH

Find the point of intersection:
Use a keystroke sequence similar to that in Example 4 of Lesson 6.3.

Activity

Page 405

For Step 1, graph $y_1 = \log x + \log(x + 21)$ and $y_2 = 2$ together, and find any points of intersection.

Use viewing window $[-1, 6]$ by $[-1, 3]$.

Use a keystroke sequence similar to that in Example 2 of Lesson 6.7.

For Step 4, use viewing window $[-1, 4]$ by $[-30, 100]$ and a keystroke sequence similar to that in Example 3 of Lesson 6.7.

E X A M P L E For part b, evaluate $y = 70 - 30\left(\frac{2}{3}\right)^x$ for $x = 2$.

Page 406

Use viewing window $[-1, 10]$ by $[-20, 100]$.

Graph the function:

| Y= | 70 | – | 30 | (| 2 | ÷ | 3 |) |

| ^ | X,T,Θ,n | GRAPH |

Find the y-value for $x = 2$:
Use a keystroke sequence similar to that in Example 1 of Lesson 6.2.

For part **c**, use a keystroke sequence similar to that in Example 4 of Lesson 6.3.

Polynomial Functions

POLYNOMIAL FUNCTIONS CAN BE USED TO model many real-world situations, including annuities and volumes. For example, the volumes of the irregularly shaped buildings shown here can be modeled by polynomial functions.

Polynomial functions are important in algebra. In this chapter, you will learn how to combine polynomial functions, how to graph them, and how to find their roots.

Atomium in
Brussels, Belgium

Montreal Expo Habitat in
Montreal, Canada

Lessons

The east wing of the National Gallery of Art in Washington, D.C.

PORTFOLIO ACTIVITIES
CHAPTER PROJECT

About the Chapter Project

In this chapter, you will use polynomial functions to model real-world data. A good model must consistently provide answers to the question or problem it was created to solve. In the Chapter Project, *Fill It Up!*, you will predict the shape of containers by using polynomial models that are created from the relationship between the volume of water contained and the height of water in the container.

After completing the Chapter Project, you will be able to do the following:

- Collect and organize data.
- Determine a polynomial model that best fits a data set.
- Test your polynomial model.

About the Portfolio Activities

Throughout the chapter, you will be given opportunities to complete Portfolio Activities that are designed to support your work on the Chapter Project.

- Creating a polynomial model for the volume of an irregularly shaped container is included in the Portfolio Activity on page 431.

- Analyzing the behavior of the polynomial model is included in the Portfolio Activity on page 439.

- Creating a polynomial model and using it to solve problems is included in the Portfolio Activity on page 455.

An Introduction to Polynomials

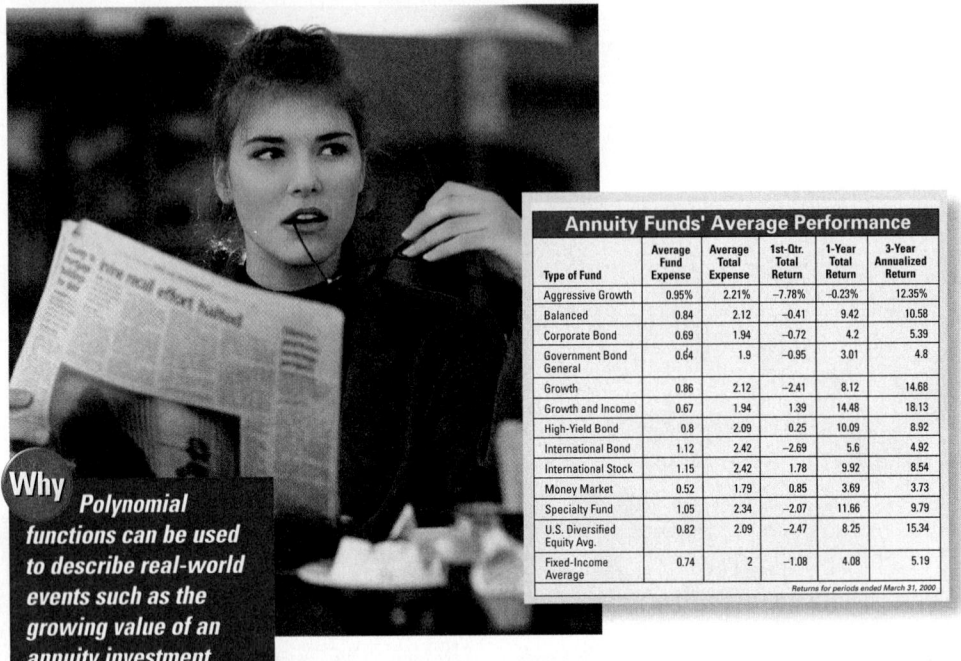

Objectives

- Identify, evaluate, add, and subtract polynomials.

- Classify polynomials, and describe the shapes of their graphs.

Why *Polynomial functions can be used to describe real-world events such as the growing value of an annuity investment.*

Annuity Funds' Average Performance

Type of Fund	Average Fund Expense	Average Total Expense	1st-Qtr. Total Return	1-Year Total Return	3-Year Annualized Return
Aggressive Growth	0.95%	2.21%	−7.78%	−0.23%	12.35%
Balanced	0.84	2.12	−0.41	9.42	10.58
Corporate Bond	0.69	1.94	−0.72	4.2	5.39
Government Bond General	0.64	1.9	−0.95	3.01	4.8
Growth	0.86	2.12	−2.41	8.12	14.68
Growth and Income	0.67	1.94	1.39	14.48	18.13
High-Yield Bond	0.8	2.09	0.25	10.09	8.92
International Bond	1.12	2.42	−2.69	5.6	4.92
International Stock	1.15	2.42	1.78	9.92	8.54
Money Market	0.52	1.79	0.85	3.69	3.73
Specialty Fund	1.05	2.34	−2.07	11.66	9.79
U.S. Diversified Equity Avg.	0.82	2.09	−2.47	8.25	15.34
Fixed-Income Average	0.74	2	−1.08	4.08	5.19

Returns for periods ended March 31, 2000

Periodically adding a fixed amount of money to an account that pays compound interest is an investment that people often use to prepare for the future. Such an investment option is called an *annuity*.

Consider an annuity of $1000 invested at the beginning of each year in an account that pays 5% interest compounded annually. The diagram below illustrates the growth of this investment over 4 years.

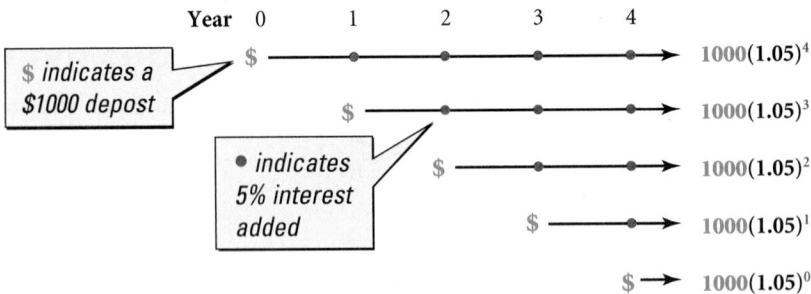

The total value of this investment after 4 years can be written as the sum below.

$$1000(1.05)^4 + 1000(1.05)^3 + 1000(1.05)^2 + 1000(1.05)^1 + 1000(1.05)^0$$

To consider different interest rates, replace 1.05 with 1.06 for 6%, 1.07 for 7%, and so on. In general, the value of this investment after 4 years can be represented by the *polynomial* expression $1000x^4 + 1000x^3 + 1000x^2 + 1000x + 1000$, where x is the multiplier determined by the annual interest rate.

How much will the investment be worth at the time the last payment is made if the interest rate is 6%? *You will answer this question in Example 2.*

A **monomial** is a numeral, a variable, or the product of a numeral and one or more variables. A monomial with no variables, such as -1 or $\frac{2}{3}$, is called a **constant**.

A **coefficient** is the numerical factor in a monomial. For example:

- x has a coefficient of 1.
- $-2t$ has a coefficient of -2.
- $\frac{-x^3y^2}{3}$ has a coefficient of $-\frac{1}{3}$ because it can be written as $-\frac{1}{3}x^3y^2$.
- $-ab$ has a coefficient of -1.

The **degree of a monomial** is the sum of the exponents of its variables. For example, x^2yz is of degree 4 because $x^2yz = x^2y^1z^1$ and $2 + 1 + 1 = 4$. A nonzero constant such as 3 is of degree 0 because it can be written as $3x^0$.

A **polynomial** is a monomial or a sum of terms that are monomials. In this chapter, you will study polynomials in one variable. Polynomials can be classified by the number of terms they contain. A polynomial with two terms is a **binomial**. A polynomial with three terms is a **trinomial**.

The **degree of a polynomial** is the same as that of its term with the greatest degree. Polynomials can also be classified by degree, as shown below.

CLASSIFICATION OF A POLYNOMIAL BY DEGREE		
Degree	Name	Example
$n = 0$	constant	3
$n = 1$	linear	$5x + 4$
$n = 2$	quadratic	$-x^2 + 11x - 5$
$n = 3$	cubic	$4x^3 - x^2 + 2x - 3$
$n = 4$	quartic	$9x^4 + 3x^3 + 4x^2 - x + 1$
$n = 5$	quintic	$-2x^5 + 3x^4 - x^3 + 3x^2 - 2x + 6$

E X A M P L E **1** Classify each polynomial by degree and by number of terms.

a. $2x^3 - 3x + 4x^5$ **b.** $-2x^3 + 3x^4 + 2x^3 + 5$

● **SOLUTION**

a. The greatest exponent of x is 5, so the degree is 5.

The polynomial has three terms, so it is a trinomial.

The polynomial is a quintic trinomial.

b. When simplified to $3x^4 + 5$, the greatest exponent of x is 4, so the degree is 4.

The simplified polynomial has two terms, so it is a binomial.

The polynomial is a quartic binomial.

TRY THIS Classify each polynomial by degree and by number of terms.

a. $x^2 + 4 - 8x - 2x^3$ **b.** $3x^3 + 2 - x^3 - 6x^5$

Evaluating Polynomials

Example 2 shows you how polynomials can be used for calculations in real-world situations.

E X A M P L E ② Refer to the annuity described at the beginning of the lesson.

APPLICATION
INVESTMENTS

How much will the investment be worth at the time the last payment is made if the annual interest rate is 6%?

● **SOLUTION**

Method 1 Use substitution.
$1000x^4 + 1000x^3 + 1000x^2 + 1000x + 1000$
$= 1000(1.06)^4 + 1000(1.06)^3 + 1000(1.06)^2 + 1000(1.06) + 1000$
$= 5637.09$

Method 2 Use a table or a graph.
Enter $y = 1000x^4 + 1000x^3 + 1000x^2 + 1000x + 1000$ into a graphics calculator.
Use a table of values or a graph to find the y-value for $x = 1.06$.

PROBLEM SOLVING

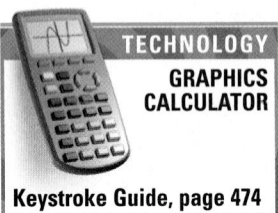

TECHNOLOGY
GRAPHICS CALCULATOR

Keystroke Guide, page 474

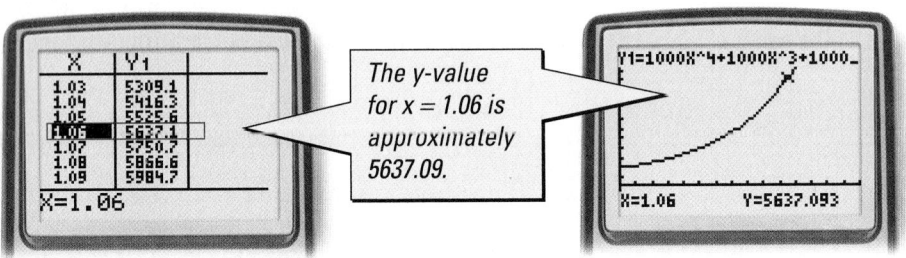

The y-value for x = 1.06 is approximately 5637.09.

The investment will be worth $5637.09.

TRY THIS Evaluate the polynomial $3x^4 + 2x^2 + 2x - 5$ for $x = 1.5$.

Adding and Subtracting Polynomials

To add and subtract polynomials, combine like terms. Recall that *like terms* have the same degree, or exponent, of the variable. When you write your answer, use *standard form*. The **standard form** of a polynomial expression is written with the exponents in *descending order* of degree.

E X A M P L E ③ **Find the sum.** $(-2x^2 - 3x^3 + 5x + 4) + (-2x^3 + 7x - 6)$

● **SOLUTION**

$(-2x^2 - 3x^3 + 5x + 4) + (-2x^3 + 7x - 6)$
$= (-3x^3 - 2x^3) + (-2x^2) + (5x + 7x) + (4 - 6)$ *Combine like terms.*
$= -5x^3 - 2x^2 + 12x - 2$ *Write in standard form.*

TRY THIS Find the sum. $(2x^4 + 4x^3 + 5x - 2) + (-2x^4 - 7x^2 + 8x - 10)$

CRITICAL THINKING Find a polynomial expression P such that $(2x^2 - 3x + 5) + P = 0$.

EXAMPLE Find the difference. $(-6x^3 - 6x^2 + 7x - 1) - (3x^3 - 5x^2 - 2x + 8)$

SOLUTION

$(-6x^3 - 6x^2 + 7x - 1) - (3x^3 - 5x^2 - 2x + 8)$
$= (-6x^3 - 3x^3) + (-6x^2 + 5x^2) + (7x + 2x) + (-1 - 8)$ *Combine like terms.*
$= -9x^3 - x^2 + 9x - 9$ *Write in standard form.*

TRY THIS   Find the difference. $(3x^3 - 12x^2 - 5x + 1) - (-x^2 + 5x + 8)$

Graphing Polynomial Functions

A **polynomial function** is a function that is defined by a polynomial expression. In the Activity below, you will explore the characteristic shapes of the graphs of some polynomial functions.

Activity
Exploring Graphs of Polynomial Functions

TECHNOLOGY

GRAPHICS CALCULATOR

Keystroke Guide, page 474

You will need: a graphics calculator

Graph each function below in a viewing window that shows all of the "U-turns" in the graph. Copy the table and record the degree and number of U-turns.

	Function	Degree	Number of U-turns in the graph
1.	$y = x^2 + x - 2$	2	1
2.	$y = 3x^3 - 12x + 4$		
3.	$y = -2x^3 + 4x^2 + x - 2$		
4.	$y = x^4 + 5x^3 + 5x^2 - x - 6$		
5.	$y = x^4 + 2x^3 - 5x^2 - 6x$		

PROBLEM SOLVING

6. **Look for a pattern.** Make a conjecture about the degree of a function and the number of U-turns in its graph.

Graph each function below in a viewing window that shows all of the U-turns in the graph. Copy the table and record the degree and number of U-turns.

	Function	Degree	Number of U-turns in the graph
7.	$y = x^3$		
8.	$y = x^3 - 3x^2 + 3x - 1$		
9.	$y = x^4$		

CHECKPOINT ✔

10. Now make another conjecture about the degree of a function and the number of U-turns in its graph. Is this conjecture different from the conjecture you made in Step 6? Explain.

EXAMPLE **⑤** **Graph each function. Describe its general shape.**

    a. $P(x) = 3x^3 - 5x^2 - 2x + 1$ **b.** $Q(x) = x^4 - 8x^2$

● SOLUTION

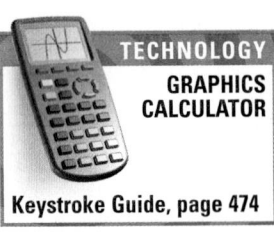

TECHNOLOGY

GRAPHICS CALCULATOR

Keystroke Guide, page 474

a.

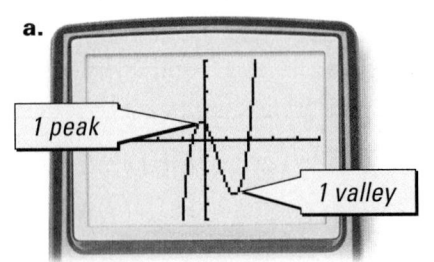

1 peak

1 valley

The graph of this cubic function has an **S**-shape with 2 U-turns.

b.

1 peak

2 valleys

The graph of this quartic function has a **W**-shape with 3 U-turns.

TRY THIS   Graph each function. Describe its general shape.

    a. $P(x) = -3x^3 - 2x^2 + 2x - 1$ **b.** $Q(x) = 2x^4 - 3x^2 - x + 2$

Examine the shapes of the linear, quadratic, cubic, and quartic functions shown below.

Linear

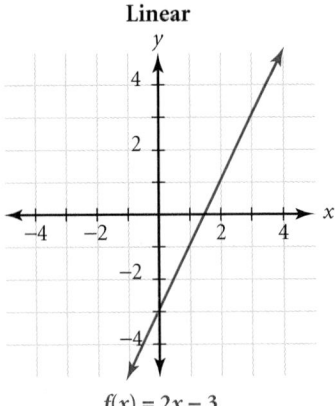

$f(x) = 2x - 3$

Quadratic

$g(x) = 2x^2 - 3$

Cubic

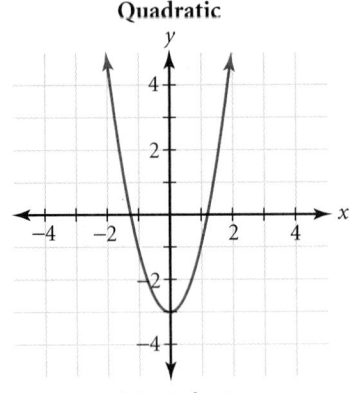

$h(x) = 2x^3 - 3x - 1$

Quartic

$j(x) = x^4 - 2x^3 + 2x + 1$

CHECKPOINT ✔ What is the range of the polynomial functions above that are of an odd degree? What can you say about the ranges of the polynomial functions above that are of an even degree?

In Lesson 7.2, you will learn more about the graphs of polynomial functions.

Exercises

Communicate

1. In your own words, define a *polynomial*.

2. Describe how to determine the degree of a polynomial function.

3. Use the definition of a polynomial function to explain how you know that a quadratic function is a polynomial function.

Guided Skills Practice

Classify each polynomial by degree and by number of terms. (EXAMPLE 1)

4. $x^4 + 3x^3 - x^2$

5. $x^5 + 3x^4 - 4x^2 + x - 1$

6. Evaluate the polynomial $x^3 + 2x^2 - x + 1$ for $x = 2$. (EXAMPLE 2)

7. Find the sum. $(2x^3 + 3x^2 - x + 2) + (-3x^2 + 4x + 5)$ (EXAMPLE 3)

8. Find the difference. $(6x^3 - 5x^2 + 14x + 3) - (3x^3 - 2x^2 + 7x - 2)$ (EXAMPLE 4)

Graph each function and describe the general shape. (EXAMPLE 5)

9. $f(x) = x^3 - x$

10. $f(x) = x^4 - x^2 + 1$

Practice and Apply

Write each polynomial in standard form.

11. $5x^3 + 4x + 2x^2 + 1$

12. $4x^4 + x^2 + x^3 + x + 1$

13. $2.7x^3 + 3.3x^8 + 4.1x^2$

14. $9.1x^2 + 5.4x^5 + 3.3x^2 + 2.1$

15. $\frac{x^7}{13} + \frac{x^9}{7} - \frac{2}{3}$

16. $\frac{13}{15}x^4 + \frac{5}{7}x^3 + \frac{3}{5}x^5 + \frac{1}{2}$

Determine whether each expression is a polynomial. If so, classify the polynomial by degree and by number of terms.

17. $7x^5 + 3x^3 - 2x + 4$

18. $-4x^2 + 3x^3 - 5x^6 + 4$

19. $3^x + 2^x - x - 7$

20. $4^{2x} + 5^x - x + 1$

21. $0.35x^4 + 2x^2 + 3.8x$

22. $7.81x^4 + 8.9x^3 + 2.5x^2$

23. $\frac{3}{x^2} + \frac{5}{x} + 6$

24. $\frac{8}{x^3} - \frac{7}{x^2} + x$

25. $\frac{5}{7}x^6 + \frac{2}{3}x^4 + 5$

26. $\frac{x^5}{5} - \frac{x^3}{3}$

27. $\sqrt{x} - 1$

28. $7\sqrt{x} + 4$

Evaluate each polynomial expression for the indicated value of x.

29. $x^3 + x^2 + 1$ for $x = -3$

30. $x^4 + 2x^3 + 2$ for $x = -2$

31. $-2x^3 - 3x + 2$ for $x = 4$

32. $-4x^3 + 1 + x$ for $x = 3$

33. $3x^3 + x^2 + 2x + 4$ for $x = 5$

34. $5x^3 + 2x^2 - 5x + 2$ for $x = 6$

35. $\frac{1}{4}x^4 + \frac{1}{8}x^3 + \frac{3}{8}x^2 + \frac{5}{8}x + \frac{7}{8}$ for $x = 2$

36. $\frac{3}{10}x^3 + \frac{7}{10}x^2 + \frac{1}{10}x + \frac{9}{10}$ for $x = 10$

37. $1 + x^2 - 3x^3$ for $x = 2.5$

38. $5x^3 + 4x + 2x^2 + 1$ for $x = 3.8$

Write each sum or difference as a polynomial in standard form. Then classify the polynomial by degree and by number of terms.

39. $(x^3 + x^2 + x + 1) + (2x^3 + 3x^2 + x + 3)$

40. $(x^5 + x^3 + x) + (x^4 + x^2 + 1)$

41. $(1 - 5x + x^3) - (2x^4 + 5x^3 - 10x^2)$

42. $(5x^3 + 3x^2 + 8x + 2) - (2x^2 + 4x + 7)$

43. $(2x^2 - 5x + 3) + (4x^3 + 6x^2 - 2x + 5)$

44. $(x^2 - 5x^3 + 7) + (6x + x^3 + 3x^2)$

45. $(x^4 + 5x^2 + x) - (x^4 + 2x^3 + x - 4)$

46. $(8x^2 + x^3 + 1 - 3x) + (2x^3 + 11x^4)$

47. $\left(\frac{2}{3}x + \frac{2}{3}x^3 + 1\right) + \left(\frac{2}{3} + \frac{1}{3}x^2 + \frac{1}{3}x\right)$

48. $\left(\frac{2}{7}x^2 + \frac{1}{7}x + \frac{3}{7}\right) - \left(\frac{4}{7}x^3 + \frac{6}{7}x^2 + \frac{2}{7}\right)$

49. $(-3.2x^2 + 2.7x^3 + 7.8x) + (4.9x^3 + 2.5x^4)$

50. $(4.1x^2 + 5.6x + 7.8) - (x^4 + 7.6x^2 + 9.8x)$

Graph each function. Describe its general shape.

51 $f(x) = x^3 - 3x^2 - 3x + 9$

52 $b(x) = x^3 - 4x^2 - 2x + 8$

53 $k(x) = x^4 - x^3 - x^2$

54 $m(x) = x^4 - 10x^2 + 9$

55 $r(x) = -4x^3 + 4x^2 + 19x - 10$

56 $s(x) = -2x^3 + x^2 + 10x - 5$

57 $j(x) = -x^4 + 7x^2 - 6$

58 $k(x) = -x^4 + 2x^3 + 13x^2 - 14x - 24$

CHALLENGES

59. When $4x^3 - 3ax + 5$ is subtracted from $11x^3 + ax^2 - x + b$, the result is $cx^3 - 2x^2 + dx - 1$. Find a, b, c, and d.

60. The expression $ax^3 + 2x^2 + cx + 1$ is $5x^3 - 3$ greater than $3x^3 + bx^2 + d - 7x$. Find a, b, c, and d.

CONNECTION

61. GEOMETRY Find the total area of the faces of the rectangular prism at right.

APPLICATIONS

62. BUSINESS Polynomials are used in business to express the cost of manufacturing products. If the cubic function $C(x) = x^3 - 15x + 15$ gives the cost of manufacturing x units (in thousands) of a product, what is the cost to manufacture 10,000 units of the product?

63. BUSINESS The cost of manufacturing a certain product can be represented by $C(x) = 3x^3 - 18x + 45$, where x is the number of units of the product in hundreds. What is the cost to manufacture 20,000 units of the product?

*CDs on a
conveyor belt*

Look Back

Let $A = \begin{bmatrix} 1 & -1 \\ 0 & 2 \end{bmatrix}$ and $B = \begin{bmatrix} -1 & 4 \\ 5 & 3 \end{bmatrix}$. **Perform each operation below.**

(LESSONS 4.1 AND 4.2)

64. $A - B$

65. $B - A$

66. $2A$

67. $2B$

68. AB

69. BA

70. $A - 4B$

71. $B - 3A$

Solve each equation by factoring. *(LESSON 5.2)*

72. $x^2 + 12x + 11 = 0$

73. $x^2 - 2x - 15 = 0$

74. $x^2 + 14x + 48 = 0$

75. $x^2 + 17x + 72 = 0$

76. Give an example of a perfect-square trinomial and then write it as a binomial squared. *(LESSON 5.3)*

Use the quadratic formula to solve each equation. *(LESSONS 5.5 AND 5.6)*

77. $3x^2 + 7x + 2 = 0$

78. $-2x^2 + 4x + 5 = 0$

79. $5x^2 + 2x + 4 = 0$

80. $-6x^2 + 5x - 4 = 0$

internet connect

Portfolio Extension
Go To: **go.hrw.com**
Keyword:
MB1 Polynomials

Look Beyond

81. Sketch the graph of a cubic polynomial that intersects the *x*-axis at exactly the number of points indicated. Write *impossible* if appropriate.

    a. 3 points   **b.** 2 points   **c.** 1 point   **d.** 0 points

PORTFOLIO ACTIVITY

The bottle below has a circular base, a flat bottom, and curved sides. There is no geometric formula for the volume of a solid with this shape. In this activity, you will find a polynomial function that models the volume of a solid with this shape.

1. Obtain a bottle with a circular base, a flat bottom, and curved sides. Measure the diameter of the circular base in centimeters. Calculate the radius and the area of the circular base ($A = \pi r^2$).

2. Pour water into the bottle until the bottle is approximately half full. Place a cap on the bottle, and measure the height, h_1, in centimeters of the water. The volume in milliliters of the part of the bottle containing water, W, can be approximated by $W(r) = \pi r^2 h_1$. Calculate the approximate volume of this part of the bottle.

3. Turn the bottle upside-down, and measure the height, h_2, in centimeters of the air space above the water. The volume of the air space, A, in milliliters can be approximated by $A(r) = \pi r^2 h_2$. Calculate the approximate volume of the air space.

4. The total volume in milliliters of the bottle, V, can be modeled by the function below. Find the total volume of the bottle.

$$V(r) = W(r) + A(r)$$
$$= \pi r^2 h_1 + \pi r^2 h_2$$

WORKING ON THE CHAPTER PROJECT

You should now be able to complete Activity 1 of the Chapter Project.

LESSON 7.1 AN INTRODUCTION TO POLYNOMIALS **431**

Polynomial Functions and Their Graphs

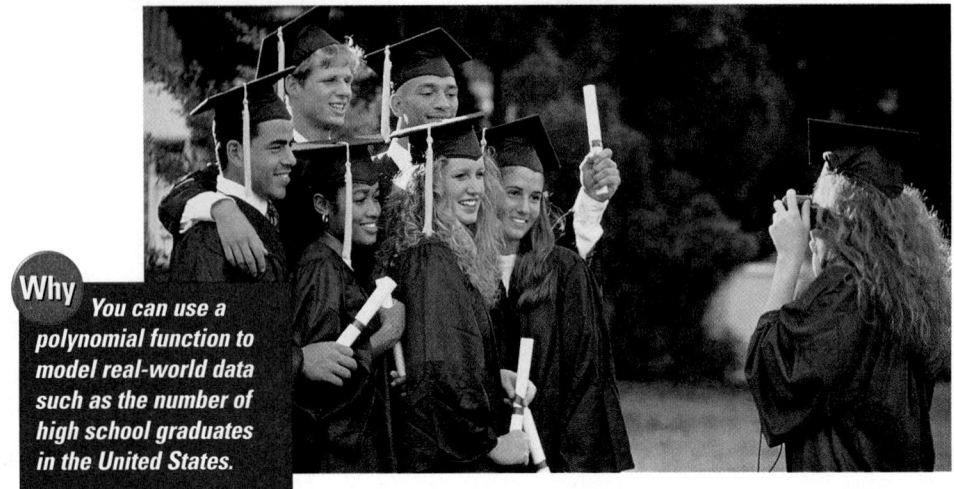

Objectives

- Identify and describe the important features of the graph of a polynomial function.

- Use a polynomial function to model real-world data.

Why *You can use a polynomial function to model real-world data such as the number of high school graduates in the United States.*

The table below gives the number of students who graduated from high school in the United States from 1960 to 1994. The scatter plot of the data indicates an increase and then a decrease in the number of graduates since 1960. Find a quartic regression model for the data in this table. *You will solve this problem in Example 3.*

Year	Graduates	Year	Graduates
1960	1679	1978	3161
1961	1763	1979	3160
1962	1838	1980	3089
1963	1741	1981	3053
1964	2145	1982	3100
1965	2659	1983	2964
1966	2612	1984	3012
1967	2525	1985	2666
1968	2606	1986	2786
1969	2842	1987	2647
1970	2757	1988	2673
1971	2872	1989	2454
1972	2961	1990	2355
1973	3059	1991	2276
1974	3101	1992	2398
1975	3186	1993	2338
1976	2987	1994	2517
1977	3140		

[*Source: Statistical Abstract of the United States, 1996*]

Number of High School Graduates in the United States

CHECKPOINT ✔ Explain why a quadratic model with a vertex near point C in the scatter plot would not be suitable for predicting the number of graduates after 1994.

Graphs of Polynomial Functions

When a function rises and then falls over an interval from left to right, the function has a *local maximum*. If the function falls and then rises over an interval from left to right, it has a *local minimum*.

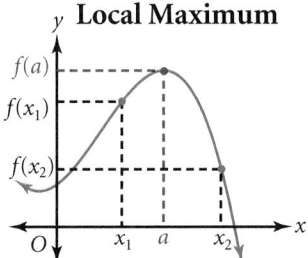

Local Maximum

For $x \neq a$ in the interval, $f(a) > f(x)$.

Local Minimum

For $x \neq a$ in the interval, $f(a) < f(x)$.

Local Maximum and Minimum

$f(a)$ is a **local maximum** (plural, *local maxima*) if there is an interval around a such that $f(a) > f(x)$ for all values of x in the interval, where $x \neq a$.

$f(a)$ is a **local minimum** (plural, *local minima*) if there is an interval around a such that $f(a) < f(x)$ for all values of x in the interval, where $x \neq a$.

The points on the graph of a polynomial function that correspond to local maxima and local minima are called **turning points**. Functions change from *increasing* to *decreasing* or from *decreasing* to *increasing* at turning points. A cubic function has at most 2 turning points, and a quartic function has at most 3 turning points. In general, a polynomial function of degree n has at most $n - 1$ turning points.

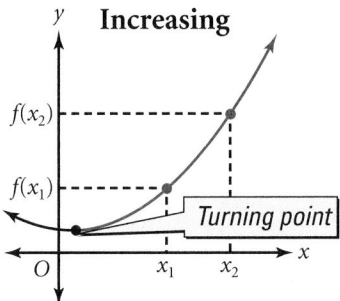

Increasing

For every $x_1 < x_2$ in the interval, $f(x_1) < f(x_2)$.

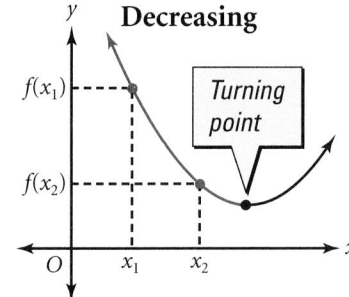

Decreasing

For every $x_1 < x_2$ in the interval, $f(x_1) > f(x_2)$.

Increasing and Decreasing Functions

Let x_1 and x_2 be numbers in the domain of a function, f.

The function f is **increasing** over an open interval if for every $x_1 < x_2$ in the interval, $f(x_1) < f(x_2)$.

The function f is **decreasing** over an open interval if for every $x_1 < x_2$ in the interval, $f(x_1) > f(x_2)$.

E X A M P L E **1** Graph $P(x) = x^3 + 3x^2 - x - 3$.

   a. Approximate any local maxima or minima to the nearest tenth.

   b. Find the intervals over which the function is increasing and decreasing.

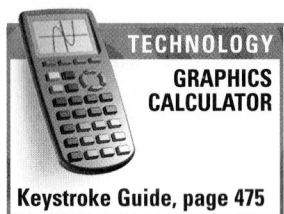

Keystroke Guide, page 475

● **SOLUTION**

   a. The graph of P has 2 turning points, a local maximum of about 3.1, and a local minimum of about −3.1.

   b. The function increases for all values of x except over the interval of approximately $-2.2 < x < 0.2$, where it decreases.

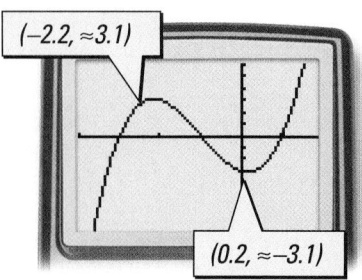

CHECK

You can use the table feature to verify the approximate coordinates of the turning points.

In the table above, when $x = -2$, the y-value, 3, is greater than the neighboring y-values. This indicates that the maximum point has an x-value between −3 and −1.

In the table above, the local maximum can be approximated more closely as 3.1, to the nearest tenth.

A similar procedure can be used to check the local minimum.

TRY THIS   Graph $Q(x) = -x^3 + 2x^2 + x + 4$.

   a. Approximate any local maxima or minima to the nearest tenth.

   b. Find the intervals over which the function is increasing and decreasing.

Recall from Lesson 5.3 that a zero of a function $P(x)$ is any number r such that $P(r) = 0$. The real zeros of a polynomial function correspond to the x-intercepts of the graph of the function. For example, the graph of $P(x) = x^3 + 3x^2 - x - 3$ in Example 1 above shows zeros of P at x-values of −3, −1, and 1.

Polynomial functions are one type of *continuous functions*. The graph of a **continuous function** is unbroken. The graph of a **discontinuous function** has breaks or holes in it.

Continuous Functions   **Discontinuous Functions**

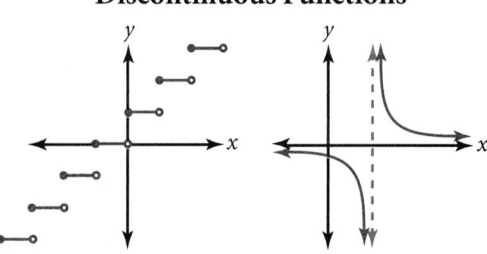

Continuity of a Polynomial Function

Every polynomial function $y = P(x)$ is continuous for all values of x.

The domain of every polynomial function is the set of all real numbers. As a result, the graph of a polynomial function extends infinitely. What happens to a polynomial function as its domain values get very small and very large is called the **end behavior** of a polynomial function.

Exploring the End Behavior of $f(x) = ax^n$

TECHNOLOGY
GRAPHICS CALCULATOR

Keystroke Guide, page 475

You will need: a graphics calculator

Graph each function separately. For each function, answer parts a–c.

1. $y = x^2$	**2.** $y = x^4$	**3.** $y = 2x^2$	**4.** $y = 2x^4$
5. $y = x^3$	**6.** $y = x^5$	**7.** $y = 2x^3$	**8.** $y = 2x^5$
9. $y = -x^2$	**10.** $y = -x^4$	**11.** $y = -2x^2$	**12.** $y = -2x^4$
13. $y = -x^3$	**14.** $y = -x^5$	**15.** $y = -2x^3$	**16.** $y = -2x^5$

    a. Is the degree of the function even or odd?
    b. Is the leading coefficient positive or negative?
    c. Does the graph rise or fall on the left? on the right?

CHECKPOINT ✔   **17.** Write a conjecture about the end behavior of a function of the form $f(x) = ax^n$ for each pair of conditions below. Then test each conjecture.
    a. when $a > 0$ and n is even   **b.** when $a < 0$ and n is even
    c. when $a > 0$ and n is odd   **d.** when $a < 0$ and n is odd

If a polynomial function is written in standard form,
$$f(x) = a_nx^n + a_{n-1}x^{n-1} + \cdots + a_1x + a_0,$$
the **leading coefficient** is a_n. That is, the leading coefficient is the coefficient of the term of greatest degree in the polynomial.

The end behavior of a polynomial function depends on the sign of its leading coefficient and whether the degree of the polynomial is odd or even. Let P be a polynomial function of degree n and with a leading coefficient of a. There are four possible end behaviors for P. The end behavior of P can rise on the left and rise on the right ($\nwarrow$ $\nearrow$), fall on the left and fall on the right ($\swarrow$ $\searrow$), fall on the left and rise on the right ($\swarrow$ $\nearrow$), or rise on the left and fall on the right ($\nwarrow$ $\searrow$). These four possible end behaviors are summarized below.

END BEHAVIOR OF A POLYNOMIAL FUNCTION, $f(x) = ax^n + \cdots$				
	$a > 0$		**$a < 0$**	
	left	right	left	right
n is even.	$\nwarrow$ rise	rise $\nearrow$	$\swarrow$ fall	fall $\searrow$
n is odd.	$\swarrow$ fall	rise $\nearrow$	$\nwarrow$ rise	fall $\searrow$

EXAMPLE **2** Describe the end behavior of each function.

a. $P(x) = -x^3 + x^2 + 3x - 1$
b. $Q(x) = -x + 3 - x^4 + 3x^2 + x^3$

● **SOLUTION**

a. $P(x)$ is written in standard form.

$$P(x) = -x^3 + x^2 + 3x - 1$$

The degree of P is 3, which is odd, so the graph will rise at one end and fall at the other end. The leading coefficient is negative, so the graph rises on the left and falls on the right.

b. Write $Q(x)$ in standard form.

$$Q(x) = -x^4 + x^3 + 3x^2 - x + 3$$

The degree of Q is 4, which is even, so its graph will either rise at both ends or fall at both ends. The leading coefficient is negative, so the graph falls on the left and the right.

TECHNOLOGY
GRAPHICS CALCULATOR

Keystroke Guide, page 475

CHECK
Graph $y = -x^3 + x^2 + 3x - 1$.

Rises on the left

Falls on the right

CHECK
Graph $y = -x^4 + x^3 + 3x^2 - x + 3$.

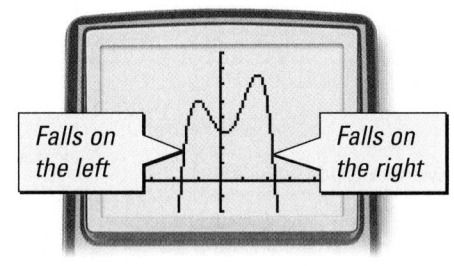

Falls on the left

Falls on the right

TRY THIS Describe the end behavior of each function.

a. $P(x) = -6x^2 + x^3 + 32$
b. $Q(x) = x^4 + x^3 - 2x^2 + 1$

Modeling With Polynomial Functions

You can use a polynomial of degree 3 or higher to fit a data set that has more than one local maximum and minimum.

EXAMPLE **3** Selected data from the table at the beginning of the lesson are given at right.

	A	B	C	D	E
x	10	18	30	41	44
y	1679	2606	3089	2276	2517

CONNECTION
STATISTICS

a. Find a quartic regression model for the number of high school graduates in the United States from 1960 to 1994.

b. Use your quartic regression model to estimate the number of high school graduates in 1970. Compare the value given by the regression model with the actual data value given for 1970.

TECHNOLOGY
GRAPHICS CALCULATOR

Keystroke Guide, page 475

● **SOLUTION**

a. Make a scatter plot of the selected data points, and find the quartic regression model. The calculator gives the following quartic regression model:

$$P(x) \approx 0.02x^4 - 1.94x^3 + 63.67x^2 - 723.74x + 4296.30$$

b. Because x represents the number of years since 1950, $x = 20$ represents the year 1970. Find $P(20)$.

The quartic model gives the number of high school graduates (in thousandths) in 1970 as 2850. The actual value given in the table is 2757, which differs by only 93 students.

TRY THIS   Find a quartic regression model for the data in the table below.

x	2	5	6	9	11
y	4	16	11	14	9

CRITICAL THINKING   The function in Example 3 models the number of high school graduates for the period from 1960 to 1994. Explain why this function may not be a good model for estimating the number of high school graduates after 1994.

Exercises

Communicate

internet connect

**Activities
Online**

Go To: **go.hrw.com**
Keyword:
MB1 Traffic

1. Describe the graph of $f(x) = 2x^2 + x^3 + 3x + 1$. Include any turning points, its continuity, and its end behavior.

2. Using your own words, define a local maximum and a local minimum.

3. Describe the four possibilities for the end behavior of the graph of a polynomial function.

4. Using your own words, define increasing and decreasing functions.

Guided Skills Practice

5 Graph $P(x) = x^3 + x^2 - 2x$. Approximate any local maxima or minima to the nearest tenth. Find the intervals over which the function is increasing and decreasing. *(EXAMPLE 1)*

Describe the end behavior of each function. *(EXAMPLE 2)*

6. $P(x) = x^6 + x^4 + x + 1$ **7.** $P(x) = x^4 + 1 + x^3 - x^5$

8 Find a quartic regression model for the data in the table below.
(EXAMPLE 3)

x	1	2	3	4	5
y	2	3	2	1	5

Graph each function and approximate any local maxima or minima to the nearest tenth.

9 $P(x) = 2x^3 - 5x$

10 $P(x) = x^3 - 3x + 1$

11 $P(x) = 2x^3 - 4x + 1$

12 $P(x) = 3x - 3 - 3x^3$

13 $P(x) = -2x + 3 + x^2$

14 $P(x) = -x^2 + 6x - 11$

15 $P(x) = x^4 - 5x^2 + 2$

16 $P(x) = -x^4 + x^3 + 4x^2 - 3$

17 $P(x) = -3x^3 + 3x + x^4 + 3$

18 $P(x) = 3x^3 - x^4 - 3x - 3$

Graph each function. Find any local maxima or minima to the nearest tenth. Find the intervals over which the function is increasing and decreasing.

19 $P(x) = x^3 - 4x; -8 \le x \le 8$

20 $P(x) = -2x^3 + 3x; -5 \le x \le 5$

21 $P(x) = x^4 - 2x^2 + 2; -5 \le x \le 5$

22 $P(x) = -x^4 + 3x^2 + 3; -5 \le x \le 5$

23 $P(x) = -x^2 + 4x - 1; -5 \le x \le 10$

24 $P(x) = x^2 - 6x + 7; -5 \le x \le 10$

25 $P(x) = x^4 - 3x^3 + 3x + 3; -2 \le x \le 5$

26 $P(x) = -x^4 + 3x^3 - 3x - 3; -2 \le x \le 5$

27 $P(x) = x^3 - 3x + 3; -3 \le x \le 4$

28 $P(x) = -x^3 + 4x - 2; -3 \le x \le 3$

Describe the end behavior of each function.

29. $P(x) = 2x^3 + x^2 + 3x + 2$

30. $P(x) = -3x^3 + 5x^2 + x + 2$

31. $P(x) = 6x + 1 - x^2$

32. $P(x) = x^2 - 8x + 3$

33. $P(x) = 4x^4 + x^5 + 1 + 3x^3$

34. $P(x) = x^6 + x^4 + 3x^2 + 2$

35. $P(x) = 7x^3 + 2 - 8x^5$

36. $P(x) = 5x^4 - 6x^6 + 3x + 2$

37 The function $y = 10x^3 - 25x^2 + x^4 - 10x + 24$ is graphed at left. Explain how you can tell that the viewing window chosen here does not show all of the important characteristics of the graph. Find a viewing window that does show all of the important characteristics of the graph.

CHALLENGE

38 Solve a system of equations by using a matrix equation to find the coefficients $a_3, a_2, a_1,$ and a_0 such that the polynomial function $P(x) = a_3x^3 + a_2x^2 + a_1x + a_0$ passes through the points $(0, 0), (1, 1), (2, 0),$ and $(3, 2)$.

STATISTICS Find a quartic regression model for each data set.

39

x	1	2	3	4	5
y	1	-2	3	0	1

40

x	1	2	3	4	5
y	0	4	3	1	4

41

x	2	4	6	8	10
y	3	-1	4	-3	4

42

x	-1	0	2	4	5
y	2	1	1	6	3

43 REAL ESTATE The median monthly rent (in dollars) in the United States for 1988 through 1996 is given in the table below. Find a quartic regression model for the data by using $x = 0$ for 1980. [*Source: U.S. Bureau of Census*]

1988	1989	1990	1991	1992	1993	1994	1995	1996
343	346	371	398	411	430	429	438	444

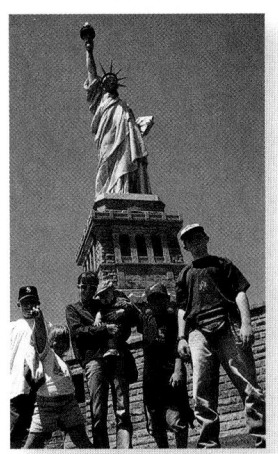

APPLICATION

44 TRAVEL The number of business and pleasure travelers (in thousands) to the United States from Canada is given in the table below for certain years. Find a quartic regression model for the data by using $x = 0$ for 1980. [*Source: U.S. Travel and Tourism Administration*]

1985	1989	1990	1991	1992	1993	1994	1995
10,721	15,325	17,263	19,113	18,596	17,293	14,970	13,668

 Look Back

Find the inverse of each matrix, if it exists. If the inverse does not exist, write *no inverse*. (LESSON 4.3)

45 $\begin{bmatrix} 1 & 1 \\ 1 & 1 \end{bmatrix}$ **46** $\begin{bmatrix} 1 & 3 \\ 1 & 2 \end{bmatrix}$ **47** $\begin{bmatrix} 2 & 5 \\ 4 & 11 \end{bmatrix}$ **48** $\begin{bmatrix} 2 & 2 \\ 4 & 4 \end{bmatrix}$

Solve each quadratic equation. Give exact solutions. (LESSON 5.2)

49. $x^2 - 50 = 0$ **50.** $(x + 3)^2 - 36 = 0$ **51.** $3(x - 1)^2 = 12$

Solve each logarithmic equation. (LESSON 6.3)

52. $\log 1000 = x$ **53.** $\log_x 8 = 3$ **54.** $\log_3 x = 2$ **55.** $\log_x 1 = 0$

 Look Beyond

56. Find $(x + y)(x^2 - xy + y^2)$. **57.** Find $(x - y)(x^2 + xy + y^2)$.

PORTFOLIO ACTIVITY

Examining the behavior of a polynomial function can often provide insight into the real-world situation that the function models.

1. Graph each function in a viewing window that includes all of the *x*- and *y*-intercepts. For each function, answer questions **a** and **b** below.
   $f(x) = x^2 - 2x + 1$ $g(x) = x^3 - 3x + 2$
   $h(x) = x^4 - 4x + 3$ $j(x) = x^5 - 5x + 4$

   a. Describe the shape of the graph, and state the number of local maxima and minima.
   b. Does the function have any zeros that are local maxima or minima?

2. Compare the graphs of the functions from Step 1. How are they alike? How are they different?

3. Refer to the bottle from the Portfolio Activity on page 431. If height h_1 is 1 unit less than the radius, r, and height h_2 is 2 units less than the radius, r, write a function for the total volume, V, in terms of r.

4. Graph the function you wrote in Step 3, and describe the graph. Explain how the graph relates to the real-world situation that it models.

WORKING ON THE CHAPTER PROJECT

You should now be able to complete Activity 2 of the Chapter Project.

Products and Factors of Polynomials

Why *You can use the factored form of a polynomial function to create a model for the volume of an open-top box.*

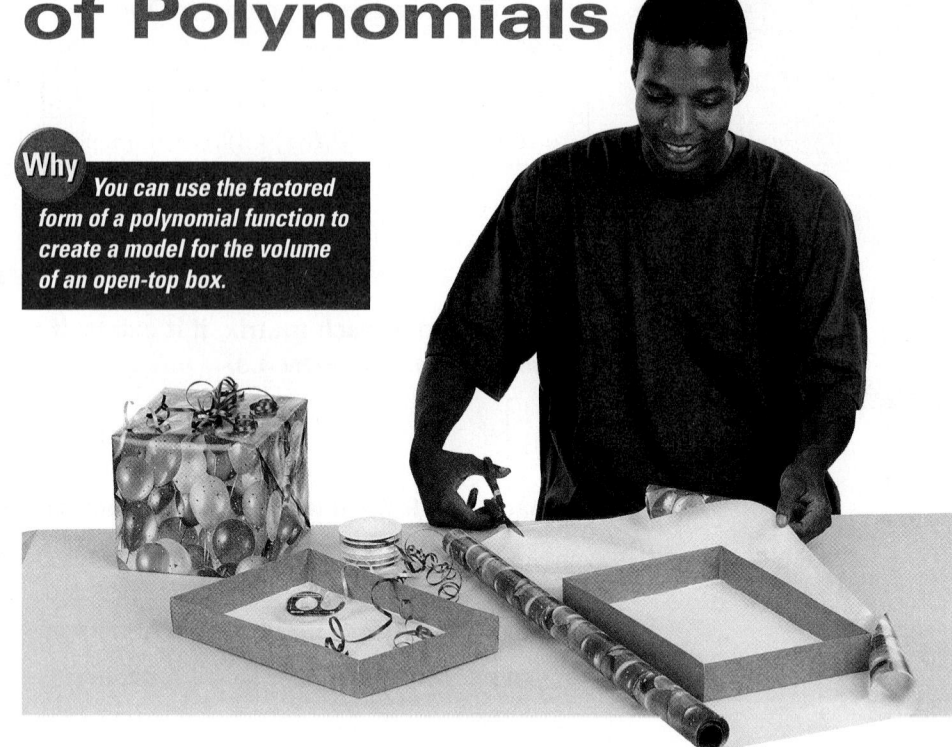

Objectives

● Multiply polynomials, and divide one polynomial by another by using long division and synthetic division.

● Use the Remainder and Factor Theorems to solve problems.

Making an open-top box out of a single rectangular sheet involves cutting and folding square flaps at each of the corners. These flaps are then pasted to the adjacent side to provide reinforcement for the corners.

The dimensions of the rectangular sheet and the square flaps determine the volume of the resulting box. For the 12-inch-by-16-inch sheet shown, the volume function is $V(x) = x(16 - 2x)(12 - 2x)$, where x is the side length in inches of the square flap.

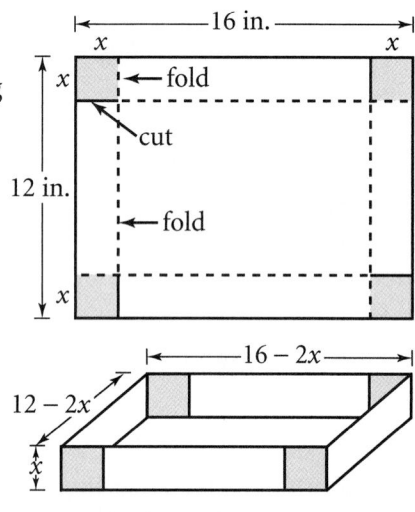

Multiplying Polynomials

E X A M P L E ① Write the volume function for the open-top box, $V(x) = x(16 - 2x)(12 - 2x)$, as a polynomial function in standard form.

● **SOLUTION**

$$
\begin{aligned}
x(16 - 2x)(12 - 2x) &= x[(16 - 2x)(12 - 2x)] \\
&= x[16(12 - 2x) - 2x(12 - 2x)] \\
&= x(192 - 32x - 24x + 4x^2) \\
&= x(192 - 56x + 4x^2) \\
&= 192x - 56x^2 + 4x^3 \\
&= 4x^3 - 56x^2 + 192x
\end{aligned}
$$

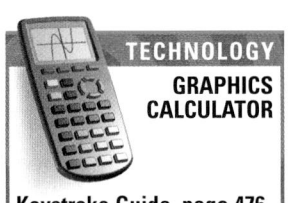

TECHNOLOGY

GRAPHICS CALCULATOR

Keystroke Guide, page 476

CHECK

You can check your multiplication by graphing the polynomial function in factored form and in standard form. If the graphs coincide, then the functions are equivalent.

The graphs of $Y1 = x(16 - 2x)(12 - 2x)$ and $Y2 = 4x^3 - 56x^2 + 192x$ appear to coincide.

TRY THIS   Write $f(x) = 2x^2(x^2 + 2)(x - 3)$ as a polynomial in standard form.

Factoring Polynomials

Just as a quadratic expression is factored by writing it as a product of two factors, a polynomial expression of a degree greater than 2 is factored by writing it as a product of more than two factors.

E X A M P L E **2** Factor each polynomial.

    a. $x^3 - 5x^2 - 6x$　　　　　　　　　　　　**b.** $x^3 + 4x^2 + 2x + 8$

● **SOLUTION**

    a. $x^3 - 5x^2 - 6x = x(x^2 - 5x - 6)$　　　　*Factor out the GCF, x.*
    　　　　　　　　　$= x(x - 6)(x + 1)$　　　*Factor the trinomial into binomials.*

    b. The polynomial $x^3 + 4x^2 + 2x + 8$ can be factored in pairs.

    　　$x^3 + 4x^2 + 2x + 8 = (x^3 + 4x^2) + (2x + 8)$　　*Group the terms in pairs.*
    　　　　　　　　　　　　$= x^2(x + 4) + 2(x + 4)$　　*Factor each pair of terms.*
    　　　　　　　　　　　　$= (x^2 + 2)(x + 4)$　　*Factor (x + 4) from each term.*

TRY THIS   Factor the polynomials $x^3 - 9x$ and $x^3 - x^2 + 2x - 2$.

Factoring the Sum and Difference of Two Cubes

$$a^3 + b^3 = (a + b)(a^2 - ab + b^2)　　　　　　a^3 - b^3 = (a - b)(a^2 + ab + b^2)$$

E X A M P L E **3** Factor each polynomial.

    a. $x^3 + 27$　　　　　　　　　　　　**b.** $x^3 - 1$

● **SOLUTION**

    a. $x^3 + 27 = x^3 + 3^3$　　　　　　**b.** $x^3 - 1 = x^3 - 1^3$
    　　　　　$= (x + 3)(x^2 - 3x + 9)$　　　　　　　$= (x - 1)(x^2 + x + 1)$

TRY THIS   Factor the polynomials $x^3 + 1000$ and $x^3 - 125$.

The *Factor Theorem*, given below, states the relationship between the linear factors of a polynomial expression and the zeros of the related polynomial function.

Factor Theorem

$x - r$ is a factor of the polynomial expression that defines the function P if and only if r is a solution of $P(x) = 0$, that is, if and only if $P(r) = 0$.

With the Factor Theorem, you can test for linear factors involving integers by using substitution.

E X A M P L E **4** Use substitution to determine whether $x + 2$ is a factor of $x^3 - 2x^2 - 5x + 6$.

TECHNOLOGY
GRAPHICS
CALCULATOR

Keystroke Guide, page 476

SOLUTION

Write the related function, $f(x) = x^3 - 2x^2 - 5x + 6$.

Write $x + 2$ as $x - (-2)$.

Find $f(-2)$.

$f(-2) = (-2)^3 - 2(-2)^2 - 5(-2) + 6$
$\quad = 0$

Because $f(-2) = 0$, the Factor Theorem states that $x + 2$ is a factor of $x^3 - 2x^2 - 5x + 6$.

CHECK

Graph $y = x^3 - 2x^2 - 5x + 6$.

(−2, 0)

The graph confirms that -2 is a zero of the related function.

TRY THIS Use substitution to determine whether $x + 3$ is a factor of $x^3 - 3x^2 - 6x + 8$.

Dividing Polynomials

A multiplication equation can be rewritten as two or more division equations.

$$x^3 + 3x^2 - 4x - 12 = (x^2 + 5x + 6)(x - 2)$$

$$\frac{x^3 + 3x^2 - 4x - 12}{x^2 + 5x + 6} = x - 2 \qquad \frac{x^3 + 3x^2 - 4x - 12}{x - 2} = x^2 + 5x + 6$$

A polynomial can be divided by a divisor of the form $x - r$ by using **long division** or a shortened form of long division called **synthetic division**.

Long division of polynomials is similar to long division of real numbers. Examine the division of $\frac{x^3 + 3x^2 - 4x - 12}{x - 2}$ shown at right.

Long Division

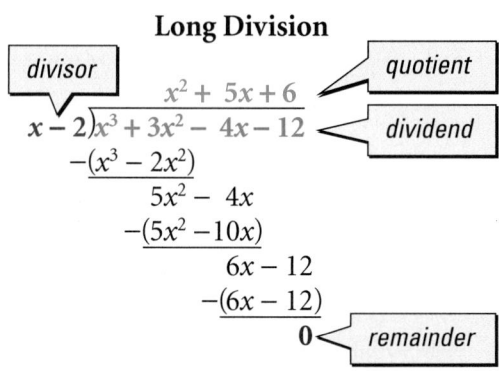

divisor

quotient

dividend

remainder

$$x - 2 \overline{\smash{)}\,x^3 + 3x^2 - 4x - 12}$$
quotient: $x^2 + 5x + 6$
$$-(x^3 - 2x^2)$$
$$5x^2 - 4x$$
$$-(5x^2 - 10x)$$
$$6x - 12$$
$$-(6x - 12)$$
$$0$$

In synthetic division, you do not write the variables.

Synthetic Division

Step 1: Write the coefficients of the polynomial $x^3 + 3x^2 - 4x - 12$, and then write the r-value, 2, of the divisor, $x - 2$, on the left. Write the first coefficient, 1, below the line.

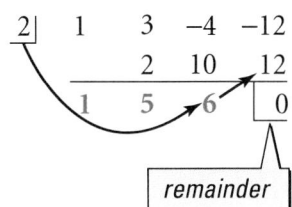

Step 2: Multiply the r-value, 2, by the number below the line, and write the product below the next coefficient.

$$2\rfloor \quad 1 \quad 3 \quad -4 \quad -12$$
$$\qquad\qquad 2 \quad 10$$
$$\overline{\quad 1 \quad 5}$$

Step 3: Write the *sum* (not the difference) of 3 and 2 below the line. Multiply 2 by the number below the line, and write the product below the next coefficient.

$$2\rfloor \quad 1 \quad 3 \quad -4 \quad -12$$
$$\qquad\qquad 2 \quad 10 \quad 12$$
$$\overline{\quad 1 \quad 5 \quad 6 \quad \boxed{0}}$$

remainder

Step 4: Write the sum of -4 and 10 below the line. Multiply 2 by the number below the line, and write the product below the next coefficient.

The remainder is 0, and the resulting numbers, 1, 5, and 6, are the coefficients of the quotient, $x^2 + 5x + 6$.

Synthetic division can be used to divide a polynomial only by a linear binomial of the form $x - r$. When dividing by nonlinear divisors, long division must be used. This is shown in Example 5.

EXAMPLE 5 Find the quotient. $(x^3 + 3x^2 + 3x + 2) \div (x^2 + x + 1)$

● **SOLUTION**

Step 1: Divide the first term of the **dividend** by the first term of the **divisor**:
$x^3 \div x^2 = x$.

Step 2: Write x in the **quotient** and use it to multiply the **divisor**:
$x(x^2 + x + 1)$.

Step 3: Subtract the product, $x^3 + x^2 + x$, from the **dividend**.

Step 4: Repeat Steps 1–3, using the difference from Step 3 as the new dividend.

$$
\begin{array}{r}
x + 2 \\
x^2 + x + 1 \overline{)\, x^3 + 3x^2 + 3x + 2} \\
-(x^3 + x^2 + x) \\
\hline
2x^2 + 2x + 2 \\
-(2x^2 + 2x + 2) \\
\hline
0
\end{array}
$$

quotient

dividend

divisor

remainder

$$(x^3 + 3x^2 + 3x + 2) \div (x^2 + x + 1) = x + 2$$

TRY THIS Find the quotient. $(x^3 + 3x^2 - 13x - 15) \div (x^2 - 2x - 3)$

If there is a nonzero remainder after dividing with either method, it is usually written as the numerator of a fraction, with the divisor as the denominator.

$$
\begin{array}{r|rrrr}
-3 & 1 & 0 & 0 & 48 \\
& & -3 & 9 & -27 \\
\hline
& 1 & -3 & 9 & \boxed{21}
\end{array}
\qquad
(x^3 + 48) \div (x + 3) = x^2 - 3x + 9 + \dfrac{21}{x + 3}
$$

EXAMPLE 6 Given that 2 is a zero of $P(x) = x^3 + x - 10$, use division to factor $x^3 + x - 10$.

● **SOLUTION**

Method 1 Use long division.

$$
\begin{array}{r}
x^2 + 2x + 5 \\
x - 2 \overline{\smash{\big)}\ x^3 + 0x^2 + \ x - 10} \\
\underline{-(x^3 - 2x^2)} \\
2x^2 + \ x \\
\underline{-(2x^2 - 4x)} \\
5x - 10 \\
\underline{-(5x - 10)} \\
0
\end{array}
$$

Method 2 Use synthetic division.

$$
\begin{array}{r|rrrr}
2 & 1 & 0 & 1 & -10 \\
& & 2 & 4 & 10 \\
\hline
& 1 & 2 & 5 & \boxed{0}
\end{array}
$$

Notice that zeros are used for the coefficients of terms that do not exist.

Quotient: $x^2 + 2x + 5$

Thus, $x^3 + x - 10 = (x - 2)(x^2 + 2x + 5)$.   *$x^2 + 2x + 5$ cannot be factored.*

TRY THIS Given that -3 is a zero of $P(x) = x^3 - 13x - 12$, use division to factor $x^3 - 13x - 12$.

CRITICAL THINKING Explain why you add the products in synthetic division instead of subtracting them as in long division.

Given $P(x) = 2x^3 + 7x^2 + 2x + 1$, the *Remainder Theorem* states that $P(-3)$ is the value of the remainder when $2x^3 + 7x^2 + 2x + 1$ is divided by $x + 3$.

synthetic division:
$$
\begin{array}{r|rrrr}
-3 & 2 & 7 & 2 & 1 \\
& & -6 & -3 & 3 \\
\hline
& 2 & 1 & -1 & \boxed{4}
\end{array}
$$

The remainder is 4.

substitution:
$$P(x) = 2x^3 + 7x^2 + 2x + 1$$
$$P(-3) = 2(-3)^3 + 7(-3)^2 + 2(-3) + 1 = 4$$

Remainder Theorem

If the polynomial expression that defines the function of P is divided by $x - a$, then the remainder is the number $P(a)$.

EXAMPLE 7 Given $P(x) = 2x^3 + 7x^2 + 2x + 1$, find $P(5)$.

● **SOLUTION**

Method 1 Use synthetic division.

$$
\begin{array}{r|rrrr}
5 & 2 & 7 & 2 & 1 \\
& & 10 & 85 & 435 \\
\hline
& 2 & 17 & 87 & \boxed{436}
\end{array}
$$

Thus, $P(5) = 436$.

Method 2 Use substitution.

$$P(x) = 2x^3 + 7x^2 + 2x + 1$$
$$P(5) = 2(5)^3 + 7(5)^2 + 2(5) + 1$$
$$= 250 + 175 + 10 + 1$$
$$= 436$$

TRY THIS Given $P(x) = 3x^3 + 2x^2 - 3x + 4$, find $P(3)$.

Exercises

internet connect

Activities Online

Go To: **go.hrw.com**
Keyword:
MB1 Ceramics

Communicate

1. Describe how the Factor Theorem can be used to determine whether $x + 1$ is a factor of $x^3 - 2x^2 - 8x - 5$.

2. Describe the condition necessary to use synthetic division to divide polynomials.

3. Explain how to use the Remainder Theorem to evaluate $P(5)$ if P is a polynomial function.

Guided Skills Practice

4. Write $P(x) = x(10 - x)(2 + x)$ as a polynomial function in standard form. *(EXAMPLE 1)*

Factor each polynomial. *(EXAMPLES 2 AND 3)*

5. $x^3 - 5x^2 + 6x$ **6.** $x^3 + 5x^2 + 3x + 15$ **7.** $x^3 - 216$

8. Use substitution to determine whether $x + 2$ is a factor of $x^3 + 4x^2 + 5x + 2$. *(EXAMPLE 4)*

9. Find the quotient. $(x^3 + 4x^2 + 4x + 3) \div (x^2 + x + 1)$ *(EXAMPLE 5)*

Given that –3 is a zero of $P(x) = x^3 - 14x - 15$, use each method below to factor $x^3 - 14x - 15$. *(EXAMPLE 6)*

10. long division   **11.** synthetic division

Given $P(x) = 2x^3 + 3x^2 + 4x + 1$, find $P(2)$ by using each method below. *(EXAMPLE 7)*

12. synthetic division   **13.** substitution

Practice and Apply

Write each product as a polynomial in standard form.

14. $3x^2(4x^3 - 2x^2 + 5x + 2)$ **15.** $2x^3(4x^3 - 2x^2 + x + 3)$

16. $(2x - 3)(x + 4)$ **17.** $(x + 7)(5x - 3)$

18. $(x + 2)(x^2 + 4x + 1)$ **19.** $(x + 3)(2x^3 + 3x^2 + 1)$

20. $(2x + 3)(x^3 - 5x^2 + 4)$ **21.** $(2x + 1)(x^2 - 4x - 3)$

22. $(x - 4)(2x^3 - 3x^2 + 2)$ **23.** $(x - 5)(-3x^3 - 4x - 1)$

24. $(x - 3)(2 - x)(x - 1)$ **25.** $(x - 2)(2x + 3)(3 - x)$

26. $(x + 1)^2(x - 2)$ **27.** $(2x - 4)(x + 1)^2$

28. $(2x + 1)^3$ **29.** $(3x + 2)^3$

30. $(x - 1)^2(x^2 - 3x + 2)$ **31.** $(-3x^2 - x + 2)(x + 1)^2$

32. $\left(x - \frac{5}{7}\right)\left(\frac{2}{5}x^2 - \frac{1}{5}x + \frac{3}{5}\right)$ **33.** $\left(x - \frac{1}{4}\right)\left(\frac{2}{3}x^2 + \frac{1}{3}x + \frac{2}{3}\right)$

Factor each polynomial.

34. $x^3 + 8x^2 + 15x$ **35.** $x^3 + 6x^2 + 8x$ **36.** $x^3 - 10x^2 + 24x$

37. $x^3 + 2x^2 - 3x$ **38.** $x^3 - x^2 - 30x$ **39.** $x^3 - 2x^2 - 3x$

40. $3x^3 - 300x$ **41.** $18x^3 - 60x^2 + 50x$ **42.** $x^3 + 3x^2 - 2x - 6$

43. $x^3 - 3x^2 + 4x - 12$ **44.** $x^3 + 3x^2 - x - 3$ **45.** $x^3 - 2x^2 - 5x + 10$

46. $x^3 + x^2 + x + 1$ **47.** $1 - x + x^2 - x^3$ **48.** $x^3 + 2x^2 + 14x + 7x^2$

49. $x^3 + x^2 + 2 + 2x$ **50.** $x^3 - 64$ **51.** $x^3 + 1000$

52. $x^6 + 125$ **53.** $x^6 + 27$ **54.** $x^3 - 8$

55. $x^3 - 216$ **56.** $8x^3 - 1$ **57.** $27x^3 - 125$

58. $x^6 - 1$ **59.** $64 - x^3$ **60.** $27 + 8x^3$

Use substitution to determine whether the given linear expression is a factor of the polynomial.

61. $x^2 + x + 1; x - 1$ **62.** $x^2 + 2x + 1; x + 2$

63. $x^3 + 3x^2 - 33x - 35; x + 1$ **64.** $x^3 + 5x^2 - 18x - 48; x + 6$

65. $x^3 + 3x^2 - 18x - 40; x - 4$ **66.** $x^3 - 8x^2 + 9x + 18; x - 6$

67. $x^3 + 6x^2 - x - 30; x - 2$ **68.** $x^3 - x^2 - 17x - 15; x + 3$

69. $2x^3 + 9x^2 + 6x + 8; x + 4$ **70.** $2x^3 - x^2 - 12x - 9; x - 3$

Divide by using long division.

71. $(x^2 + 4x + 4) \div (x + 2)$ **72.** $(x^2 - 3x + 2) \div (x - 1)$

73. $(x^3 - 7x - 6) \div (x + 1)$ **74.** $(x^3 + 11x^2 + 39x + 45) \div (x + 5)$

75. $(3x^2 - x + x^3 - 3) \div (x^2 + 4x + 3)$ **76.** $(x^3 + 6x^2 - x - 30) \div (x^2 + 8x + 15)$

77. $(x^3 - 43x + 42) \div (x^2 + 6x - 7)$ **78.** $(10x - 5x^2 + x^3 - 24) \div (x^2 - x + 6)$

79. $\left(x^2 - \frac{1}{6}x - \frac{1}{6}\right) \div \left(x - \frac{1}{2}\right)$ **80.** $\left(x^2 + \frac{1}{2}x - \frac{3}{16}\right) \div \left(x + \frac{3}{4}\right)$

Divide by using synthetic division.

81. $(x^2 - 4x - 12) \div (x - 4)$ **82.** $(x^2 - 3x + 2) \div (x - 1)$

83. $(x^3 + x^2 - 9x - 9) \div (x + 1)$ **84.** $(x^3 - 2x^2 - 22x + 40) \div (x - 4)$

85. $(x^3 + 5x^2 - 18) \div (x + 3)$ **86.** $(x^3 - 27) \div (x - 3)$

87. $(x^3 + 3) \div (x - 1)$ **88.** $(x^2 - 6) \div (x + 4)$

89. $(x^4 - 3x + 2x^3 - 6) \div (x - 2)$ **90.** $(x^5 + 6x^3 - 5x^4 + 5x - 15) \div (x - 3)$

For each function below, use synthetic division and substitution to find the indicated value.

91. $P(x) = x^2 + 1; P(1)$ **92.** $P(x) = x^2 + 1; P(2)$

93. $P(x) = x^2 + x; P(2)$ **94.** $P(x) = x^2 + x; P(1)$

95. $P(x) = 4x^2 - 2x + 3; P(3)$ **96.** $P(x) = 3x^3 + 2x^2 + 3x + 1; P(-2)$

97. $P(x) = 2x^4 + x^3 - 3x^2 + 2x; P(-4)$ **98.** $P(x) = 2x^3 - 3x^2 + 2x - 2; P(3)$

CHALLENGE

Find the value of k that makes the linear expression a factor of the cubic expression.

99. $x^3 + 3x^2 - x + k; x - 2$ **100.** $kx^3 - 2x^2 + x - 6; x + 3$

101. MANUFACTURING An open-top box is made from a 14-inch-by-32-inch piece of cardboard, as shown at right. The volume of the box is represented by $V(x) = x(14 - 2x)(32 - 2x)$, where x is the height of the box.

a. Write the volume of the box as a polynomial function in standard form.
b. Find the volume of the box if the height is 2 inches.

102. PACKAGING A pizza box with a lid is made from a 19-inch-by-40-inch piece of cardboard, as shown below. The volume of the pizza box is represented by $V(x) = \frac{1}{2}x(19 - 2x)(40 - 5x)$, where x is the height of the box.

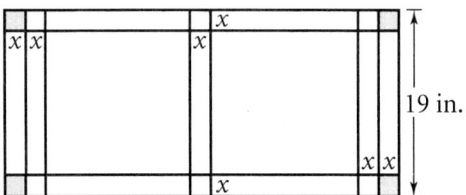

a. Write the volume of the box as a polynomial function in standard form.
b. Find the volume of the box if its height is 2 inches.
c. Find the volume of the box if its height is 2.5 inches.

Look Back

103. Solve $x + 3 \le 3(x - 1)$ for x. Graph the solution on a number line. *(LESSON 1.7)*

104. Does the set of ordered pairs $\{(2, 3), (3, 5), (4, 3)\}$ represent a function? Explain. *(LESSON 2.3)*

Factor each expression. *(LESSON 5.3)*

105. $5a^2 - 5b^2$ **106.** $2x^2 - 32y^2$ **107.** $n^2 + n - 12$

108. $5 - 6s + s^2$ **109.** $4x^2 + 4x + 1$ **110.** $2x^2 + 11x + 15$

Solve for x. Round your answers to the nearest hundredth. *(LESSONS 6.3 AND 6.6)*

111. $10^x = 32$ **112.** $3^x = 7$ **113.** $e^x = 5$ **114.** $e^{2x} = 7$

Look Beyond

115. If $f(x) = x^3 + 4x^2 - 3x - 18$ and $f(2) = 0$, how many other values of x are zeros of f? How many times does the graph of f cross the x-axis?

Solving Polynomial Equations

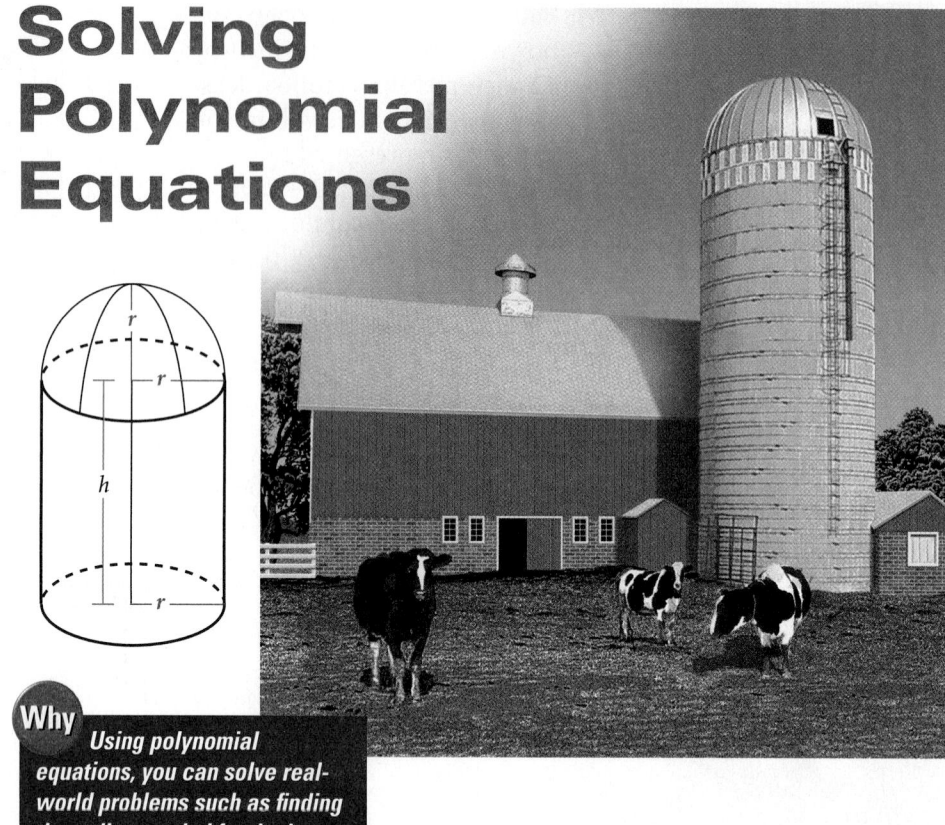

Objectives

● Solve polynomial equations.

● Find the real zeros of polynomial functions and state the multiplicity of each.

Why *Using polynomial equations, you can solve real-world problems such as finding the radius needed for the base of a grain silo in order to have a desired volume.*

CONNECTION

GEOMETRY

A silo that stores grain is often shaped as a cylinder with a hemispherical top (dome), as shown above. From geometry, you know that the volume of the cylinder, C, is represented by $C(r) = \pi r^2 h$ and that the volume of the hemispherical top, H, is represented by $H(r) = \left(\frac{1}{2}\right)\left(\frac{4}{3}\pi r^3\right)$, or $\frac{2}{3}\pi r^3$. Therefore, the total volume of the silo is given by the function T below.

$$T(r) = H(r) + C(r)$$
$$= \frac{2}{3}\pi r^3 + \pi r^2 h$$

A farmer wants to design a silo whose cylindrical part has a height of 20 feet. Approximately what radius of the cylinder and hemispherical top will give a total volume of 1830 cubic feet? To answer this question, you will solve a polynomial equation. *You will answer this question in Example 4.*

E X A M P L E **1** Use factoring to solve $2x^3 - 7x^2 + 3x = 0$.

SOLUTION

$$2x^3 - 7x^2 + 3x = 0$$
$$x(2x^2 - 7x + 3) = 0 \qquad \textit{Factor out the GCF.}$$
$$x(2x - 1)(x - 3) = 0 \qquad \textit{Factor the remaining trinomial.}$$
$$x = 0 \quad or \quad 2x - 1 = 0 \quad or \quad x - 3 = 0 \quad \textit{Use the Zero-Product Property.}$$
$$x = \frac{1}{2} \qquad\qquad x = 3$$

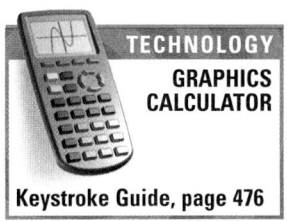

TECHNOLOGY
GRAPHICS
CALCULATOR
Keystroke Guide, page 476

CHECK

Graph $y = 2x^3 - 7x^2 + 3x$, and look for any zeros of the function.

The graph of $y = 2x^3 - 7x^2 + 3x$ confirms that the solutions of $2x^3 - 7x^2 + 3x = 0$ are $x = 0$, $x = \frac{1}{2}$, and $x = 3$.

$\left(\frac{1}{2}, 0\right)$

$(0, 0)$

$(3, 0)$

TRY THIS   Use factoring to solve $2x^3 + x^2 - 6x = 0$.

The polynomial equation in Example 1 has three linear factors and three distinct solutions, or **roots.** Some polynomial equations have factors (and roots) that occur more than once, as shown in Example 2.

E X A M P L E ❷ Use a graph, synthetic division, and factoring to find all of the roots of $x^3 - 7x^2 + 15x - 9 = 0$.

● **SOLUTION**

PROBLEM SOLVING

Use a graph of the related function to approximate the roots. Then use synthetic division to test your choices.

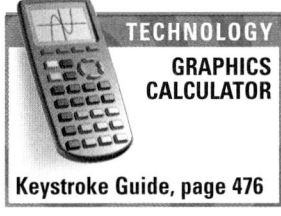

TECHNOLOGY
GRAPHICS
CALCULATOR
Keystroke Guide, page 476

The graph of $y = x^3 - 7x^2 + 15x - 9$

$(1, 0)$

$$\begin{array}{r|rrrr} \underline{1|} & 1 & -7 & 15 & -9 \\ & & 1 & -6 & 9 \\ \hline & 1 & -6 & 9 & \boxed{0} \end{array}$$

The remainder is 0.

The quotient is $x^2 - 6x + 9$.

Since the remainder is 0, $x - 1$ is a factor of $x^3 - 7x^2 + 15x - 9$.

$$x^3 - 7x^2 + 15x - 9 = 0$$
$$(x - 1)(x^2 - 6x + 9) = 0 \qquad \textit{Factor out } x - 1.$$
$$(x - 1)(x - 3)^2 = 0 \qquad \textit{Factor the remaining trinomial.}$$
$$x - 1 = 0 \quad or \quad x - 3 = 0 \quad or \quad x - 3 = 0 \qquad \textit{Use the Zero-Product Property.}$$
$$x = 1 \qquad\qquad x = 3 \qquad\qquad x = 3$$

The roots of $x^3 - 7x^2 + 15x - 9 = 0$ are 1 and 3, with the root 3 occurring twice.

TRY THIS   Use a graph, synthetic division, and factoring to find all of the roots of $x^3 + 2x^2 - 4x - 8 = 0$.

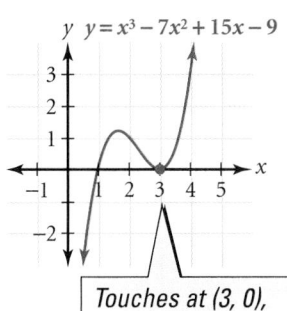

$y = x^3 - 7x^2 + 15x - 9$

Touches at (3, 0), but does not cross

If $x - r$ is a factor that occurs m times in the factorization of a polynomial expression, P, then r is a root with **multiplicity** m of the related polynomial equation, $P = 0$. In Example 2 above, 3 is a root with multiplicity 2 of the equation $x^3 - 7x^2 + 15x - 9 = 0$.

When r is a root with *even multiplicity*, then the graph of the related function *will touch but not cross* the x-axis at $(r, 0)$. This is shown at left for the related function from Example 2 above.

In general, you cannot tell the multiplicity of a root by a graph of the related function alone. The graph may appear to touch but actually cross the x-axis.

Sometimes polynomials can be factored by using *variable substitution*. This is shown in Example 3.

PROBLEM SOLVING

EXAMPLE ❸ **Use variable substitution and factoring to find all of the roots of**
$x^4 - 4x^2 + 3 = 0$.

● **SOLUTION**

1. **Solve a simpler problem.** The expression $x^4 - 4x^2 + 3$ can be put in the form of a factorable quadratic expression by substituting u for x^2. Solve the resulting equation for u.

$$x^4 - 4x^2 + 3 = 0$$
$$(x^2)^2 - 4(x^2) + 3 = 0$$
$$u^2 - 4u + 3 = 0$$
$$(u - 1)(u - 3) = 0$$
$$u = 1 \ or \ u = 3$$

2. Replace u with x^2, and solve for x by using the Zero-Product Property.

$$x^2 = 1 \qquad or \qquad x^2 = 3$$
$$x = \pm\sqrt{1} \qquad\qquad x = \pm\sqrt{3}$$

The roots of $x^4 - 4x^2 + 3 = 0$ are $\sqrt{1}, -\sqrt{1}, \sqrt{3},$ and $-\sqrt{3}$.

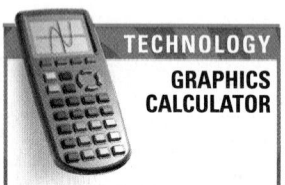

TECHNOLOGY

GRAPHICS CALCULATOR

Keystroke Guide, page 476

CHECK

Graph $y = x^4 - 4x^2 + 3$, and look for any zeros of the function.

Because $\sqrt{3} \approx 1.73$ and $\sqrt{1} = 1$, the graph of $y = x^4 - 4x^2 + 3$ confirms that the roots of the related equation are $-\sqrt{3}, -\sqrt{1}, \sqrt{1},$ and $\sqrt{3}$.

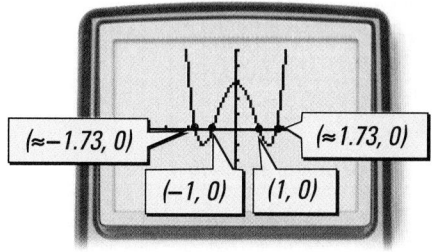

$(\approx -1.73, 0)$ $(\approx 1.73, 0)$

$(-1, 0)$ $(1, 0)$

TRY THIS

Use variable substitution and factoring to find all of the roots of $x^4 - 9x^2 + 14 = 0$.

CRITICAL THINKING

Let a, b, and c be real numbers. Find all roots of $ax^3 + bx^2 + cx = 0$, where $a \neq 0$. Classify the roots as real or complex.

Finding Real Zeros

The *Location Principle*, given below, can be used to find real zeros.

Location Principle

If P is a polynomial function and $P(x_1)$ and $P(x_2)$ have opposite signs, then there is a real number r between x_1 and x_2 that is a zero of P, that is, $P(r) = 0$.

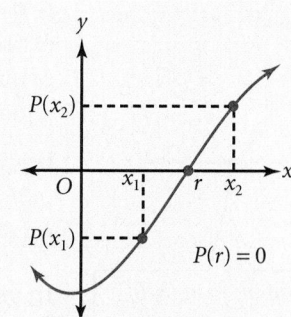

The graph of $P(x) = x^3 - 4x + 2$ at right shows that when x is 1, $P(x) < 0$, and when x is 2, $P(x) > 0$.

According to the Location Principle, there is a zero of $P(x) = x^3 - 4x + 2$ somewhere between 1 and 2. It is about 1.7.

When you use a graph to find a zero of a continuous function, you are actually using the Location Principle.

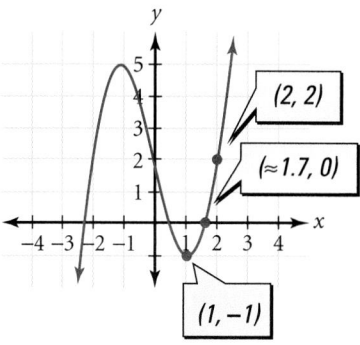

(2, 2)

(≈1.7, 0)

(1, −1)

CHECKPOINT ✔ Graph $y = x^2 + 2$. Use the graph and the Location Principle to explain why $y = x^2 + 2$ has no real zeros.

E X A M P L E ④ Refer to the silo described at the beginning of the lesson.

What radius of the cylinder and hemispherical top gives a total volume of 1830 cubic feet if the cylinder's height is 20 feet?

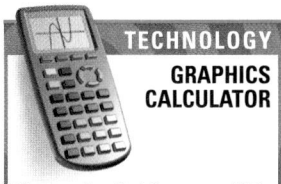

TECHNOLOGY

GRAPHICS CALCULATOR

Keystroke Guide, page 476

● **SOLUTION**

The total volume is represented by $T(r) = \frac{2}{3}\pi r^3 + \pi r^2 h$. Substituting 20 for the height and 1830 for the total volume gives $1830 = \frac{2}{3}\pi r^3 + 20\pi r^2$.

Solve for r by graphing the related function,
$y = \frac{2}{3}\pi x^3 + 20\pi x^2 - 1830$,
and approximating the real zeros.

The only reasonable radius is a positive x-value.

The y-values shown are from −5000 to 7000.

(≈5, 0)

The x-values shown are from −40 to 20.

Thus, a radius of about 5 feet gives a volume of approximately 1830 cubic feet.

The Activity below involves using a table of values and the Location Principle to find the zeros of a function.

Activity
Exploring With Tables

TECHNOLOGY

GRAPHICS CALCULATOR

Keystroke Guide, page 477

You will need: a graphics calculator

Let $P(x) = x^4 - 3x^3 - 5x^2 + 13x + 6$.

1. Use the table feature of a calculator to find $P(x)$ for each x-value listed in the table at right.

2. From the table, what integer zeros of P can you find?

3. Use the table feature of a graphics calculator and the Location Principle to locate another zero of P to the nearest hundredth.

x	P(x)
−3	
−2	
−1	
0	
1	
2	
3	

4. Now graph $P(x) = x^4 - 3x^3 - 5x^2 + 13x + 6$ in a viewing window that shows x-values from -5 to 5 and y-values from -15 to 15. Use the graph to locate a fourth zero.

CHECKPOINT ✔ **5.** Explain how to use a graph and a table to find the real zeros of a polynomial function. Explain how to use a graph and a table to find the real roots of a polynomial equation.

Below is a summary of what you have learned about real roots and zeros.

SUMMARY
Roots and Zeros

The real number r is a zero of $f(x)$ if and only if all of the following are true:
- r is a solution, or root, of $f(x) = 0$.
- $x - r$ is a factor of the expression that defines f (that is, $f(r) = 0$).
- When the expression that defines f is divided by $x - r$, the remainder is 0.
- r is an x-intercept of the graph of f.

Exercises

Communicate

1. If a polynomial has an even number of repeated factors, what do you know about its graph?

2. Describe how the Location Principle can help you to find the zeros of a polynomial function.

3. Explain how these terms are related: zeros, solutions, roots, factors, and x-intercepts.

Guided Skills Practice

Use factoring to solve each equation. *(EXAMPLE 1)*

4. $x^3 - x^2 - 12x = 0$

5. $y^3 + 15y^2 + 54y = 0$

Use a graph, synthetic division, and factoring to find all of the roots of each equation. *(EXAMPLE 2)*

6. $x^3 - 5x^2 + 3x = 0$

7. $x^3 - 3x - 2 = 0$

Use variable substitution and factoring to find all of the roots of each equation. *(EXAMPLE 3)*

8. $x^4 - 8x^2 + 16 = 0$

9. $x^4 - 2x^2 + 1 = 0$

10 **AGRICULTURE** The volume of a cylindrical silo with a cone-shaped top is represented by $V(x) = \frac{1}{3}\pi r^3 + 25\pi r^2$, where r is the radius of the silo in feet. Find the radius to the nearest tenth of a foot that gives a volume of 2042 cubic feet. *(EXAMPLE 4)*

25 ft

Practice and Apply

Use factoring to solve each equation.

11. $x^3 + 2x^2 - 35x = 0$ **12.** $x^3 + 2x^2 - 48x = 0$

13. $y^3 - 6y^2 - 27y = 0$ **14.** $a^3 - 8a^2 - 48a = 0$

15. $x^3 - 13x^2 + 40x = 0$ **16.** $x^3 - 7x^2 + 10x = 0$

17. $x^3 = 25x$ **18.** $y^3 = 49y$

19. $2x^3 - 10x^2 - 100x = 0$ **20.** $16x - 6x^2 - x^3 = 0$

21. $3y^3 + 9y^2 - 162y = 0$ **22.** $20a^2 + 5a^3 - 60a = 0$

23. $110x - 2x^3 = 12x^2$ **24.** $3y^3 + 36y^2 = 3y^4$

25. $28a - 5a^2 - 3a^3 = 0$ **26.** $15y - 4y^2 - 3y^3 = 0$

Use a graph, synthetic division, and factoring to find all of the roots of each equation.

27 $a^3 - a^2 - 5a - 3 = 0$ **28** $x^3 + 5x^2 + 7x + 3 = 0$

29 $x^3 + 5x^2 + 3x - 9 = 0$ **30** $x^3 - 4x^2 - 3x + 18 = 0$

31 $2b^3 + 16b^2 + 32b = 0$ **32** $5h^3 - 60h^2 + 180h = 0$

33 $x^3 - 3x - 2 = 0$ **34** $x^3 - 3x + 2 = 0$

35 $x^3 - 2x^2 - 9x + 18 = 0$ **36** $x^3 + 3x^2 - 4x - 12 = 0$

37 $n^3 + 8 = 2n^2 + 4n$ **38** $x^3 + 3x^2 = 27 + 9x$

Use variable substitution and factoring to find all of the roots of each equation.

39. $x^4 - 4x^2 + 4 = 0$ **40.** $x^4 - 6x^2 + 9 = 0$

41. $y^4 - 18y^2 + 81 = 0$ **42.** $a^4 - 24a^2 + 144 = 0$

43. $x^4 - 13x^2 + 36 = 0$ **44.** $x^4 - 9x^2 + 18 = 0$

45. $x^5 - 9x^3 + 8x = 0$ **46.** $z^5 - 28z^3 + 27z = 0$

47. $x^4 - 12x^2 = -36$ **48.** $x^4 - 14x^2 = -49$

49. $h^4 + 12 = 7h^2$ **50.** $t^4 + 14 = 9t^2$

Use a graph and the Location Principle to find the real zeros of each function. Give approximate values to the nearest hundredth, if necessary.

51 $f(x) = 9x^3 - x^4 - 23$ **52** $g(x) = x^3 - 3x - 2$

53 $f(a) = a^3 - a^2 - 8a + 12$ **54** $h(x) = x^3 - 36x^2 + 18x - 27$

55 $m(n) = n^3 - 6n^2 + 12n - 8$ **56** $f(t) = 64t^2 - 80t + 25$

57 $g(x) = 2x^4 - 2x^2 + 3x - 1$ **58** $h(x) = 13x^4 - 21x + 7$

59 $f(x) = x^2 - 5x^3 + 3x$ **60** $a(x) = x^2 + 12x^3 - 3x$

61. Find the range of values of c such that the function $f(x) = 2x^3 - x^2 - 6x + c$ has a zero between $x = 0$ and $x = 1$.

62 **CULTURAL CONNECTION: ASIA** Omar Khayyam, 1050–1122 C.E., of Persia (modern-day Iran) is usually remembered as a poet and the author of *The Rubaiyat*, although he was also a scientist and mathematician. Khayyam developed a method for finding the zeros of a cubic polynomial function of the form $f(x) = x^3 - bx - a$, where $a > 0$ and $b > 0$, by finding the x-coordinates of the intersection points of the graphs of familiar curves.

Omar Khayyam was a poet, author, scientist, and mathematician.

a. Given $f(x) = x^3 - 7x - 6$, identify the values of a and b.

b. Graph $y = -\dfrac{1}{\sqrt{b}}x^2$, $y = \sqrt{x^2 + \dfrac{a}{b}x}$, and $y = -\sqrt{x^2 + \dfrac{a}{b}x}$, using the values of a and b from part **a**.

c. Find all nonzero x-coordinates of the intersection points of these graphs. The x-coordinates represent the zeros of the original function, f.

d. Graph $f(x) = x^3 - 7x - 6$ and find all of its zeros to verify that the x-coordinates from part **c** are the zeros.

63. MANUFACTURING The volume of a cedar chest whose length is 3 times its width and whose height is 1 foot greater than its width is represented by $V(x) = 3x^3 + 3x^2$, where V is the volume in cubic feet and x is the width in feet. If the volume of the chest is 36 cubic feet, what are its dimensions?

64. MEDICINE The volume of a cylindrical vitamin with a hemispherical top and bottom can be represented by the function $V(x) = 10\pi r^2 + \dfrac{4}{3}\pi r^3$, where V is the volume in cubic millimeters and r is the radius in millimeters. What should be the radius of the cylinder and hemispherical ends (to the nearest thousandth) so that the total volume is 160 cubic millimeters?

Solve each equation by factoring and applying the Zero-Product Property. *(LESSON 5.3)*

65. $x^2 - 2x = 63$ **66.** $2x^2 - 5 = -9x$ **67.** $3x^2 + 60 = 27x$

Simplify. *(LESSON 5.6)*

68. $\sqrt{-49}$ **69.** $\sqrt{-81}$ **70.** $\sqrt{-11}$

Write the conjugate of each complex number. *(LESSON 5.6)*

71. $6 - 2i$ **72.** $4i - 2$ **73.** 5

Plot each number and its conjugate in the complex plane. *(LESSON 5.6)*

74. $-4 - 3i$ **75.** $-1 - 3i$ **76.** $2i - 4$

Use the quadratic formula to find the solutions to each equation. Write your answers in the form *a + bi*. *(LESSON 5.6)*

77. $x^2 + 2x + 7 = 0$ **78.** $4x^2 - 3x + 5 = 0$ **79.** $x^2 - 3x = -9$

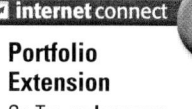

Portfolio Extension
Go To: **go.hrw.com**
Keyword:
MB1 PolySolve

 Look Beyond

80. Let $P(x) = x^3 - 2x^2 + 5x + 26$.
    a. Verify that $x - (2 + 3i)$ and $x - (2 - 3i)$ are factors of P.
    b. Find the third factor and write P in factored form.

In the Portfolio Activity on page 431, you took measurements and made calculations to find a polynomial model for a cylindrical container with a flat circular base. In this activity, you will find a model for the volume of a bottle with a different shape.

1. Obtain a bottle with a flat square base. Fill the bottle about halfway with water.

2. Write a function that approximates the volume, in milliliters, of the part of the bottle containing water, W.

3. Turn the bottle upside-down, and write a function that approximates the volume, in milliliters, of the air space in the bottle, A.

4. Write a function that models the total volume, in milliliters, of the bottle, V.

5. Suppose that the height of the water is equal to the length of each side of the square base. If the height of the air space above the water is 2 centimeters, what side length of the base will give a total volume of 96 milliliters?

WORKING ON THE CHAPTER PROJECT

You should now be able to complete Activity 3 of the Chapter Project.

THE EYEWITNESS MATH

SCREAM MACHINE!

'Highest, fastest, steepest' in the world

[Source: Sandusky Register, January 31, 1989]

Coasting to Records

On June 9, 1988, *Cedar Point's* Magnum XL-200 roller coaster was certified as the fastest roller coaster in the world, with the longest vertical drop. As a result, it was listed in the 1990 edition of the *Guinness Book of World Records*. To enter the record books, the coaster needed two witnesses: one was Lt. Gov. Paul Leonard, who observed the ride's 72 miles per hour top speed and vertical drop of 194 feet, 8 inches.

[Source: Sandusky Register, July 27, 1989]

In this activity, you will design your own *scream machine*. Picture your roller coaster climbing slowly up the first incline, slowing momentarily at the peak, and then, propelled only by gravity, plunging down one hill and up another. Will it have enough energy to reach the end? Or will it slow to an embarrassing stall part way up a slope?

Fortunately, roller coasters follow laws of motion. When a coaster glides up or down a hill, it slows down or speeds up, respectively. You can figure out in advance whether the ride will thrill or fizzle. Disregarding air resistance and friction, the speed is given by the following formula:

$$v = v_i \pm 8\sqrt{h}$$
$\begin{cases} \text{where } h \text{ is the vertical rise or drop of the hill in feet,} \\ v \text{ is the new speed in feet per second,} \\ v_i \text{ is the initial speed in feet per second, and} \\ + \text{ is for downhill calculations and } - \text{ is for uphill calculations} \end{cases}$

In real life, however, there is air resistance and friction. Take the Magnum XL-200, for example. Its first drop, h, is 195 feet. Assume that the initial speed, v_i, at the top of the hill is 0.

$$v = v_i \pm 8\sqrt{h}$$

$$v = 0 + 8\sqrt{195} \approx 112 \quad \textit{Use + for downhill calculations.}$$

According to the formula, the Magnum XL-200 will be traveling at a speed of about 112 feet per second, or about 76 miles per hour. Actually, the Magnum reaches a speed of only 72 miles per hour. Friction and air resistance on the first descent cause the coaster to lose about 4 miles per hour, or about 5%, of its *theoretical* speed.

Cooperative Learning

Design your own roller-coaster track. Include at least three hills. Assume that the coaster loses 5% of its theoretical speed each time it goes up or down a hill. Make sure your roller coaster doesn't stall going up a hill.

1. Determine the vertical rise of each hill.

2. Assuming that the speed at the top of the first hill is 0 feet per second, determine the actual speeds at the top and the bottom of each hill.

3. What would it mean if the speed at the top of a hill was negative? How would you change the design to fix this situation?

Zeros of Polynomial Functions

Investment Growth

Objectives

- Use the Rational Root Theorem and the Complex Conjugate Root Theorem to find the zeros of a polynomial function.

- Use the Fundamental Theorem to write a polynomial function given sufficient information about its zeros.

APPLICATION

INVESTMENTS

Why *Polynomial functions can be used to solve real-world problems such as finding an effective yield, or interest rate, for an investment.*

Polynomial functions can be used to solve problems in a variety of fields. Consider the following example from the field of finance:

$1000 is invested at the beginning of each year in a fund that earns a variable interest rate. At the end of 10 years, the account is worth $14,371.56. To find the *effective interest rate* of this investment over these 10 years, you can solve the polynomial equation

$$1000x^{10} + 1000x^9 + \cdots + 1000x^2 + 1000x = 14{,}371.56,$$

or find the roots of

$$1000x^{10} + 1000x^9 + \cdots + 1000x^2 + 1000x - 14{,}371.56 = 0.$$

The *Rational Root Theorem* can be used to identify possible roots of polynomial equations with integer coefficients. To see how this theorem can be used, examine the solution to the equation $3x^2 + 10x - 8 = 0$ below.

$$3x^2 + 10x - 8 = 0$$
$$(3x - 2)(x + 4) = 0$$
$$3x - 2 = 0 \quad or \quad x + 4 = 0$$
$$x = \frac{2}{3} \qquad x = -4, \text{ or } \frac{-4}{1}$$

Notice that the numerators, 2 and −4, are factors of the constant term, −8, in the polynomial. Also notice that the denominators, 3 and 1, are the factors of the leading coefficient, 3, in the polynomial.

Rational Root Theorem

Let P be a polynomial function with integer coefficients in standard form. If $\frac{p}{q}$ (in lowest terms) is a root of $P(x) = 0$, then

- p is a factor of the constant term of P and

- q is a factor of the leading coefficient of P.

E X A M P L E ❶ Find all of the rational roots of $10x^3 + 9x^2 - 19x + 6 = 0$.

● **SOLUTION**

Write the related function, $P(x) = 10x^3 + 9x^2 - 19x + 6$. According to the Rational Root Theorem, $\frac{p}{q}$ is a root of $10x^3 + 9x^2 - 19x + 6 = 0$ if p is a factor of the constant term, 6, and q is a factor of the leading coefficient, 10.

PROBLEM SOLVING

Make an organized list. Form all quotients that have factors of 6 in the numerator and factors of 10 in the denominator.

factors of 6: $\pm 1, \pm 2, \pm 3, \pm 6$
factors of 10: $\pm 1, \pm 2, \pm 5, \pm 10$

$\pm\frac{1}{1}, \pm\frac{1}{2}, \pm\frac{1}{5}, \pm\frac{1}{10}$	$\pm\frac{2}{1}, \pm\frac{2}{2}, \pm\frac{2}{5}, \pm\frac{2}{10}$	$\pm\frac{3}{1}, \pm\frac{3}{2}, \pm\frac{3}{5}, \pm\frac{3}{10}$	$\pm\frac{6}{1}, \pm\frac{6}{2}, \pm\frac{6}{5}, \pm\frac{6}{10}$

Notice that some rational numbers are repeated, such as $\frac{3}{1}$ and $\frac{6}{2}$.

PROBLEM SOLVING

Use a graph. Rather than testing each quotient to see which ones satisfy $10x^3 + 9x^2 - 19x + 6 = 0$, you can examine the graph of the related function, $P(x) = 10x^3 + 9x^2 - 19x + 6$, and use the process of elimination.

One root of $P(x) = 0$ appears to be -2. Test whether $P(-2) = 0$ is true.

```
-2 | 10    9   -19    6
   |      -20   22   -6
   ----------------------
     10  -11    3    |0|  ← remainder
```

Since the remainder is 0, $P(-2) = 0$ is true and -2 is a root of $P(x) = 0$.

(−2, 0)

2 real roots or
1 real root with
multiplicity 2?

From the graph of the related function, there appears to be two real zeros or one real zero with a multiplicity of 2 between 0 and 1.

A closer look between 0 and 1 on the graph of the related function shows two zeros at $\frac{1}{2}$ and $\frac{3}{5}$, which are possible roots of $P(x) = 0$ according to the Rational Root Theorem.

(0.5, 0)   (0.6, 0)

Test whether $P\left(\frac{1}{2}\right) = 0$ and $P\left(\frac{3}{5}\right) = 0$ are true.

```
1/2 | 10    9   -19    6               3/5 | 10    9   -19    6
    |       5    7    -6                   |       6    9    -6
    ----------------------                 ----------------------
      10   14   -12   |0|  ← remainder       10   15   -10   |0|  ← remainder
```

Thus, there are three rational roots: -2, $\frac{1}{2}$, and $\frac{3}{5}$.

TRY THIS   Find all of the rational roots of $3x^3 - 17x^2 + 59x - 65 = 0$.

You can often use the quadratic formula to solve a polynomial equation.

E X A M P L E **2** Find all of the zeros of $Q(x) = x^3 - 2x^2 - 2x + 1$.

● **SOLUTION**

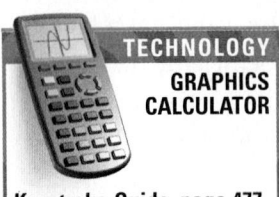
From the Rational Root Theorem and the graph of $Q(x) = x^3 - 2x^2 - 2x + 1$, you know that a zero may occur at -1. Test whether $Q(-1) = 0$ is true.

$(-1, 0)$

$$\begin{array}{r|rrrr} \underline{-1|} & 1 & -2 & -2 & 1 \\ & & -1 & 3 & -1 \\ \hline & 1 & -3 & 1 & \boxed{0} \end{array}$$

Because $Q(-1) = 0$, $x + 1$ is a factor of $x^3 - 2x^2 - 2x + 1$.

$$x^3 - 2x^2 - 2x + 1 = 0$$
$$(x + 1)(x^2 - 3x + 1) = 0 \qquad \textit{Factor out x + 1.}$$
$$x + 1 = 0 \quad or \quad x^2 - 3x + 1 = 0 \qquad \textit{Apply the Zero-Product Property.}$$
$$x = -1 \qquad x = \frac{3 \pm \sqrt{9 - 4}}{2} \qquad \textit{Use the quadratic formula.}$$

Notice that $\frac{3 + \sqrt{5}}{2}$ and $\frac{3 - \sqrt{5}}{2}$ are conjugates.

$$x = \frac{3 \pm \sqrt{5}}{2}$$

The zeros of $Q(x) = x^3 - 2x^2 - 2x + 1$ are -1, $\frac{3 + \sqrt{5}}{2}$, and $\frac{3 - \sqrt{5}}{2}$.

TRY THIS Find all of the zeros of $P(x) = x^3 - 6x^2 + 7x + 2$.

E X A M P L E **3** Find all of the zeros of $P(x) = 3x^3 - 10x^2 + 10x - 4$.

● **SOLUTION**

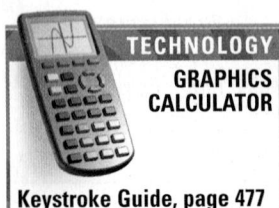
From the Rational Root Theorem and the graph of $P(x) = 3x^3 - 10x^2 + 10x - 4$, you know that a zero may occur at 2. Test whether $P(2) = 0$ is true.

$(2, 0)$

$$\begin{array}{r|rrrr} \underline{2|} & 3 & -10 & 10 & -4 \\ & & 6 & -8 & 4 \\ \hline & 3 & -4 & 2 & \boxed{0} \end{array}$$

Because $P(2) = 0$, $x - 2$ is a factor of $3x^3 - 10x^2 + 10x - 4$.

$$3x^3 - 10x^2 + 10x - 4 = 0$$
$$(x - 2)(3x^2 - 4x + 2) = 0 \qquad \textit{Factor out x - 2.}$$
$$x - 2 = 0 \quad or \quad 3x^2 - 4x + 2 = 0 \qquad \textit{Apply the Zero-Product Property.}$$
$$x = 2 \qquad x = \frac{4 \pm \sqrt{16 - 24}}{6} \qquad \textit{Use the quadratic formula.}$$

Notice that $\frac{2 + i\sqrt{2}}{3}$ and $\frac{2 - i\sqrt{2}}{3}$ are conjugates.

$$x = \frac{2 \pm i\sqrt{2}}{3}$$

The zeros of $P(x) = 3x^3 - 10x^2 + 10x - 4$ are 2, $\frac{2 + i\sqrt{2}}{3}$, and $\frac{2 - i\sqrt{2}}{3}$.

TRY THIS Find all of the zeros of $P(x) = x^3 - 9x^2 + 49x - 145$.

Complex Conjugate Root Theorem

If P is a polynomial function with real-number coefficients and $a + bi$ (where $b \neq 0$) is a root of $P(x) = 0$, then $a - bi$ is also a root of $P(x) = 0$.

Activity
Exploring Zeros of Cubic Functions

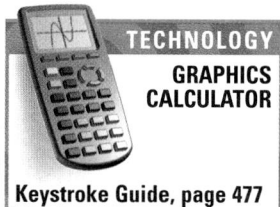

TECHNOLOGY
GRAPHICS CALCULATOR

Keystroke Guide, page 477

You will need: a graphics calculator

1. How many real zeros does the function in Example 2 have? How many real zeros does the function in Example 3 have?

2. Graph $R(x) = 2x^3 - x^2 - 4x$. How many real zeros does R have?

3. Graph $S(x) = 2x^3 - x^2 - 4x + 3$. How many real zeros does S have?

4. Graph $T(x) = 2x^3 - x^2 - 4x + 6$. How many real zeros does T have?

CHECKPOINT ✔ 5. Write a conjecture about the number of real zeros that a cubic function can have. How does the Complex Conjugate Root Theorem help you to determine whether your conjecture is true?

EXAMPLE ④ Jasmine is a manufacturing engineer who is trying to find out if she can use a 12-inch-by-20-inch sheet of cardboard and a 15-inch-by-16-inch sheet of cardboard to make boxes with the same height and volume.

APPLICATION
MANUFACTURING

Is such a pair of boxes possible?

● **SOLUTION**

Box 1: 12 inches by 20 inches
$$V_1(x) = x(12 - 2x)(20 - 2x)$$

Box 2: 15 inches by 16 inches
$$V_2(x) = x(15 - 2x)(16 - 2x)$$

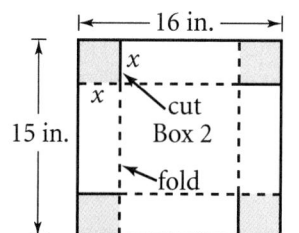

Find x such that $V_1(x) = V_2(x)$. Because x represents height, find $x > 0$ such that $x(20 - 2x)(12 - 2x) = x(16 - 2x)(15 - 2x)$.

Graph $y = x(20 - 2x)(12 - 2x)$ and $y = x(16 - 2x)(15 - 2x)$ on the same screen.

When you look for the intersection, you will find that the only solution is $x = 0$.

Since it is not possible to have a height of 0, it is not possible to make boxes with the same height and volume from the given materials.

TECHNOLOGY
GRAPHICS CALCULATOR

Keystroke Guide, page 477

In this chapter, you have learned several different methods of finding the zeros of polynomial functions. The following theorem, along with its important corollary, tells you how many zeros a function has.

Fundamental Theorem of Algebra

Every polynomial function of degree $n \geq 1$ has at least one complex zero.

Corollary: Every polynomial function of degree $n \geq 1$ has exactly n complex zeros, counting multiplicities.

CULTURAL CONNECTION: EUROPE At the age of 20, German mathematician Karl Frederick Gauss, 1777–1855, earned his Ph.D. by proving that every polynomial equation has at least one complex root. The proof is beyond the scope of this book, but it remains one of the outstanding accomplishments of modern mathematics.

Karl Frederick Gauss
1777–1855

When given enough information about a polynomial function, you can find and write the function. One possibility is shown in Example 5.

EXAMPLE 5 The zeros of a fourth-degree polynomial function, P, include 3, with a multiplicity of 2, and $5 + 3i$. Also, $P(0) = 1224$.

Write the function in factored form and in standard form.

● **SOLUTION**

The four factors of the polynomial are as follows:
$$(x - 3) \quad (x - 3) \quad [x - (5 + 3i)] \quad [x - (5 - 3i)]$$
The simplest possible polynomial is $(x - 3)^2[x - (5 + 3i)][x - (5 - 3i)]$.

Because the graph of P can be stretched vertically by any nonzero constant factor and retain the same zeros, let a represent the stretch factor for this polynomial.
$$P(x) = a(x - 3)^2[x - (5 + 3i)][x - (5 - 3i)], \text{ where } a \neq 0$$
$$P(x) = a(x - 3)^2(x^2 - 10x + 34)$$

Since $P(0) = 1224$, substitute 0 for x and 1224 for $P(x)$. Solve for a.
$$P(x) = a(x - 3)^2(x^2 - 10x + 34)$$
$$1224 = a(0 - 3)^2[0^2 - 10(0) + 34]$$
$$1224 = a(-3)^2(34)$$
$$1224 = 306a$$
$$4 = a$$
The function in factored form is $P(x) = 4(x - 3)^2(x^2 - 10x + 34)$.

Multiplying $4(x - 3)^2(x^2 - 10x + 34)$ gives the standard form,
$P(x) = 4x^4 - 64x^3 + 412x^2 - 1176x + 1224$.

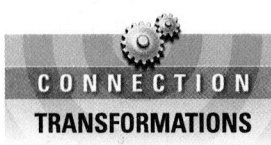

CONNECTION
TRANSFORMATIONS

TRY THIS　The zeros of a third-degree polynomial function, P, include 1 and $3 + 4i$. Also, $P(0) = 50$. Write the function in factored form and standard form.

Exercises

Communicate

1. What are the possible rational roots for the polynomial equation $2x^3 + a_2x^2 + a_1x + 3 = 0$, where a_2 and a_1 are integers?

2. If 0 and $3 - 2i$ are roots of a polynomial equation with rational coefficients, what other numbers must also be roots of the equation?

3. How many zeros does $P(x) = x^5 + x - 3$ have? Are all of the zeros distinct? Why or why not? How many are real zeros?

4. Let $P(x) = x(x - 1)(x - 2i)$ and $Q(x) = x(x - 1)(x - 2i)(x + 2i)$. Does P have real-number coefficients? Does Q have real-number coefficients? Multiply to verify your responses. How do your answers support the Complex Conjugate Root Theorem?

Guided Skills Practice

5. Find all of the rational roots of $12x^3 - 32x^2 - 145x + 25 = 0$. **(EXAMPLE 1)**

6. Find all of the zeros of $Q(x) = x^3 + 3x^2 - 8x - 4$. **(EXAMPLE 2)**

7. Find all of the zeros of $Q(x) = 2x^3 - 4x^2 - 5x - 3$. **(EXAMPLE 3)**

8. Let $P(x) = (x - 1)^3$ and $Q(x) = (x - 3)^2$. Find all real values of x such that $P(x) = Q(x)$. **(EXAMPLE 4)**

9. The zeros of a fourth-degree polynomial function P include 3, with a multiplicity of 2, and $3 + 4i$. Also, $P(0) = -6$. Write the function in factored form and in standard form. **(EXAMPLE 5)**

Practice and Apply

Find all of the rational roots of each polynomial equation.

10. $2x^2 + 3x + 1 = 0$

11. $6x^3 - 29x^2 - 45x + 18 = 0$

12. $4x^3 - 13x^2 + 11x - 2 = 0$

13. $3x^3 - 2x^2 - 12x + 8 = 0$

14. $3x^3 + 3x^2 - 4x + 4 = 0$

15. $4x^3 + 3x^2 + x + 2 = 0$

16. $15a^3 + 38a^2 + 17a + 2 = 0$

17. $10x^3 + 69x^2 - 9x - 14 = 0$

18. $18c^3 - 23c + 6 + 9c^2 = 0$

19. $50x^3 - 7x + 35x^2 - 6 = 0$

20. $18x^4 + 15x + 15x^3 - 34x^2 - 2 = 0$

21. $10x^4 - 103x^3 - 207x + 294x^2 - 54 = 0$

Find all zeros of each polynomial function.

22 $B(x) = x^3 - 4x^2 - 3x + 12$

23 $P(x) = 3x^3 - x^2 - 24x + 8$

24 $f(x) = 4x^3 - 20x^2 - 3x + 15$

25 $f(x) = 9x^3 + 72x^2 - 5x - 40$

26 $t(x) = x^3 - 2x^2 + 78 - 35x$

27 $g(x) = x^3 - 5x^2 + 144x - 720$

28 $N(x) = x^3 - 3x^2 + 4x - 12$

29 $f(b) = b^3 - 5b^2 + 9b - 45$

30 $G(x) = x^3 + 5x^2 + 10 + 2x$

31 $a(x) = x^3 - 3x^2 + 12x - 36$

32 $W(x) = x^3 + 2x^4 - 5x + 5 - 11x^2$

33 $H(x) = x^4 + 16x - x^2 + 4x^3 - 20$

Find all real values of x for which the functions are equal. Give your answers to the nearest hundredth.

34 $P(x) = x^2$, $Q(x) = x^3 + 3x^2 + 3x + 1$

35 $P(x) = x^2 - 2x + 1$, $Q(x) = -x^3 + 3x^2 - 3x + 3$

36 $P(x) = x^4 - 6x + 3$, $Q(x) = -0.2x^4$

37 $P(x) = x^3 - 5x$, $Q(x) = 0.5x^4$

38 $P(x) = x^4 - 4x^2 + 3$, $Q(x) = x^2$

39 $P(x) = x^4 - 5x^2 + 4$, $Q(x) = 2$

40 $P(x) = 0.25x^4$, $Q(x) = -x^2 + 2$

Write a polynomial function, P, in factored form and in standard form by using the given information.

41. P is of degree 2; $P(0) = 12$; zeros: 2, 3

42. P is of degree 2; $P(0) = 4$; zeros: -1, 4

43. P is of degree 3; $P(0) = 20$; zeros: -2, 1, 2

44. P is of degree 3; $P(0) = 24$; zeros: -1, 2, 4

45. P is of degree 4; $P(0) = 1$; zeros: 1 (multiplicity 2), 2 (multiplicity 2)

46. P is of degree 5; $P(0) = 2$; zeros: 1 (multiplicity 3), 2 (multiplicity 2)

47. P is of degree 3; $P(0) = -1$; zeros: 1, i

48. P is of degree 3; $P(0) = 4$; zeros: -1, $2i$

49. P is of degree 4; $P(0) = 3$; zeros: 1, 2, $5i$

50. P is of degree 4; $P(0) = -3$; zeros: 2, 5, $3i$

CHALLENGE

51. Use the Rational Root Theorem and the polynomial $P(x) = x^2 - 3$ to show that $\sqrt{3}$ is irrational.

APPLICATION

52 **GEOGRAPHY** A mountain ridge is drawn to scale on the wall of a visitors' center in West Virginia. The ridge has approximately the same shape as the graph of the function $f(x) = -x^4 + 3x^2 - 3x + 6$ between x-values of -2.5 and 2.0.

a. The zeros of the function represent sea level. What are the approximate zeros of f?

b. Find the approximate maximum value of f.

c. Find the vertical scale factor that would place the maximum height of the ridge at 3200 feet above sea level.

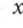

53. THERMODYNAMICS A hot-air balloon rises at an increasing rate as its altitude increases. Its altitude, in feet, can be modeled by the function $y = 0.025t^2 + 2t$, where t is time in seconds. How long will it take for the balloon to reach an altitude of 800 feet?

Look Back

Let $f(x) = 5x + 4$ and $g(x) = 2 - x$. Find or evaluate each composite function. *(LESSON 2.4)*

54. $f \circ g$ **55.** $g \circ f$ **56.** $f \circ f$

57. $(f \circ g)(-2)$ **58.** $(g \circ f)(5)$ **59.** $(f \circ f)(0.2)$

Write the equation for the axis of symmetry and find the coordinates of the vertex. *(LESSON 5.5)*

60. $y = 6x^2 - x - 12$ **61.** $y = 2x^2 + 5x + 2$ **62.** $y = x^2 + 3x - 2$

63 Graph $f(x) = x^3 - 3x^2 + 4x - 5$, and describe its end behavior. *(LESSON 7.2)*

64. Describe the end behavior of the function $f(x) = -3(x + 1)^2(x - 1)^3(x - 2)^4$. *(LESSON 7.2)*

In Exercises 65 and 66, divide by using synthetic division. *(LESSON 7.3)*

65. $\dfrac{3x^4 - 4x^2 + 2x - 1}{x - 1}$ **66.** $\dfrac{x^4 + 4x^3 + 5x^2 - 5x - 14}{x + 2}$

Look Beyond

67. Use factoring to simplify the expression $\dfrac{x^2 + 5x + 6}{x^2 + 7x} \cdot \dfrac{x^2 - 2x}{x^2 - 4}$.

68. Solve the equation $\sqrt{x + 1} = \sqrt{2x}$. Begin by squaring both sides. Check by substituting your solution(s) into the original equation.

FILL IT UP!

In this project you will find polynomial models to represent the shapes of various containers. You will perform experiments that involve adding water to a container in equal increments until the container is full. After each addition of water, the height of the water in the container is measured. The volume of water in the container and the height of the water are both recorded. Ordered pairs are formed from the data and displayed in a scatter plot. A polynomial regression model is selected to represent the data.

Materials:
- flat-bottomed, medium-size, clear container of irregular shape
- plastic beaker with measurements labeled in milliliters
- centimeter ruler
- water

Activity 1

1. Each student should have a flat-bottomed, clear container of irregular shape. First determine the total volume of the container. Divide the total volume by 10, and round to the nearest whole number. (For example, if the total volume is 347 milliliters, divide by 10 and round 34.7 to 35.)

2. Add water to the container in 10 equal increments based on your answer from Step 1. After each increment is added, measure the height of the water in the container. Record your data in a table like the one below. Continue this procedure until the container is full.

[Note: 1 cm³ = 1 mL]

	Volume (mL)	Height (cm)
1.		
2.		
3.		
4.		
5.		
6.		
7.		
8.		
9.		
10.		

Activity 2

1. Using the data in your table from Activity 1, let x represent the volume in milliliters, and let y represent the height in centimeters. Make a scatter plot of the data in the table.

2. Use the regression feature on your graphics calculator to find a cubic polynomial model and a quadratic polynomial model for the data you collected.

3. Compare the two models. Choose the model that appears to best fit the data.

4. Can you use this model to predict data points not plotted? Explain.

Activity 3

In this activity, you will test the validity of the polynomial model that you chose as the best fit in Activity 2.

1. In small groups, mix up the containers and graphs so that the graphs are not matched with the containers.

2. Trade containers and graphs with another group. Each group must match the containers they receive with the corresponding graphs.

3. Discuss how each group's matching choices were made.

7 Chapter Review and Assessment

VOCABULARY

Key Skills & Exercises

LESSON 7.1

Key Skills

Classify polynomials.

$5x - 4x^4 + -5x^3 - 9x + 4x + 1$

$\qquad = 4x^4 + 5x^3 + 1$ *Combine like terms.*

The polynomial is a quartic trinomial.

Evaluate, add, and subtract polynomial functions.

Evaluate $g(x) = x^3 - 2x^2 + 4x$ for $x = -5$.

$\quad g(-5) = (-5)^3 - 2(-5)^2 + 4(-5)$

$\qquad\quad = -125 - 50 - 20 = -195$

Simplify $(-2x^3 + 4x^2 - 9x + 5) - (5x^3 - x + 7)$.

$(-2x^3 + 4x^2 - 9x + 5) - (5x^3 - x + 7)$

$\quad = -2x^3 - 5x^3 + 4x^2 - 9x + x + 5 - 7$

$\quad = -7x^3 + 4x^2 - 8x - 2$

Exercises

Classify each polynomial by degree and by number of terms.

1. $3a^3 + 11a^2 - 2a + 1$ **2.** $8x^5 - 6x^2 + 10x^3$

3. $-b^2 + 8b - 5b^4 - 3$ **4.** $-2x^2 - x^3 + 7x^4$

Evaluate each polynomial for $x = 2$ and $x = -1$.

5. $-x^3 + 4x^2 - 2$ **6.** $x^3 + 2x^2 - 1$

7. $x^4 - 22$ **8.** $19 - x^2 - x^3$

Write each sum or difference as a polynomial in standard form. Then classify the polynomial by degree and by number of terms.

9. $(3x^3 - 5x^2 + 8x + 1) + (11x^3 - x^2 + 2x - 3)$

10. $(7x^3 - 8x^2 + 2x - 3) - (2x^3 + x^2 - 6)$

LESSON 7.2

Key Skills

Identify and describe the important features of the graph of a polynomial function.

Let $f(x) = -x^3 - 3x^2 + 10$. Because the leading coefficient of f is negative and the degree of f is odd, its graph rises on the left and falls on the right.

Exercises

Describe the end behavior of each function.

11. $c(a) = -a^2 - 2a + 22$

12. $d(x) = -2x^3 + 3x^2 - 7$

13. $f(x) = x^4 + 7x + 1$

14. $f(x) = 4x + x^3 - 6$

The graph of $f(x) = -x^3 - 3x^2 + 10$ below shows that f increases for $-2 < x < 0$ and f decreases for $x < -2$ and for $x > 0$.

local maximum of 10 at x = 0

local minimum of 6 at x = -2

Graph each function. Find any local maxima and minima to the nearest tenth and the intervals over which the function is increasing and decreasing.

15 $f(x) = x^2 - 2x + 9$

16 $g(x) = -x^2 + 5x - 4$

17 $f(a) = 2a^3 + 5a^2 - 1$

18 $m(x) = -2x^3 + x^2 - 9$

LESSON 7.3

Key Skills

Use long division and synthetic division to find factors and remainders of polynomials.

Use long division to find whether $x - 5$ is a factor of $x^3 - 2x^2 - 13x - 10$.	Use synthetic division to find whether $x - 2$ is a factor of $x^3 + 2x - 3$.

Use long division to find whether $x - 5$ is a factor of $x^3 - 2x^2 - 13x - 10$.

$$\begin{array}{r} x^2 + 3x + 2 \\ x - 5 \overline{) x^3 - 2x^2 - 13x - 10} \\ -(x^3 - 5x^2) \\ \hline 3x^2 - 13x \\ -(3x^2 - 15x) \\ \hline 2x - 10 \\ -(2x - 10) \\ \hline 0 \end{array}$$

The remainder is 0, so $x - 5$ is a factor and $x^3 - 2x^2 - 13x - 10 = (x - 5)(x^2 + 3x + 2)$.

Because $P(5) = 0$, $x - 5$ is a factor.

Use synthetic division to find whether $x - 2$ is a factor of $x^3 + 2x - 3$.

$$\begin{array}{r|rrrr} 2 & 1 & 0 & 2 & -3 \\ & & 2 & 4 & 12 \\ \hline & 1 & 2 & 6 & \boxed{9} \end{array}$$

The remainder is 9, so $x - 2$ is not a factor of $x^3 + 2x - 3$.

The Remainder Theorem states that if the expression that defines $P(x) = x^3 + 2x - 3$ is divided by $x - 2$, the remainder is the value of $P(2)$.

$P(2) = 2^3 + 2(2) - 3 = 9$

Exercises

Write each product as a polynomial in standard form.

19. $-2x^3(5x^4 - 3x + x^2 - 6 - x^3)$

20. $(x + 4)(x^3 - 7)(x + 1)$

Factor each polynomial.

21. $x^3 + 4x^2 - 5x$ **22.** $x^3 - 3x^2 - 10x$

23. $x^3 - 125$ **24.** $27x^3 + 1$

Use substitution to tell whether the given binomial is a factor of the polynomial.

25. $(x^3 - 7x^2 + 4x + 12); (x - 2)$

26. $(x^3 - 5x^2 - 2x + 24); (x + 2)$

Divide by using long division.

27. $(x^3 + 6x^2 - x - 30) \div (x - 2)$

28. $(x^3 - 2x^2 - 11x + 12) \div (x^2 - x - 12)$

Divide by using synthetic division.

29. $(x^3 + 3x^2 - 34x + 48) \div (x - 3)$

30. $(x^3 + x^2 - 22x - 40) \div (x + 4)$

LESSON 7.4

Key Skills

Find all of the roots of a polynomial equation.

Use variable substitution to find all of the roots of $x^4 - 7x^2 + 12 = 0$.

Substitute u for x^2: $(u)^2 - 7(u) + 12 = 0$
Factor and solve for u: $u = 3$ or $u = 4$
Substitute x^2 for u: $x^2 = 3$ or $x^2 = 4$

Thus, the roots are $\sqrt{3}$, $-\sqrt{3}$, 2, and -2.

Exercises

Find all of the real roots of each polynomial equation.

31. $x^4 - 8x^2 + 16 = 0$

32. $x^4 - 10x^2 + 24 = 0$

33. $x^4 - 10x^2 + 9 = 0$

34. $x^4 - 13x^2 + 12 = 0$

35. $x^3 - x^2 - 6x + 6 = 0$

Use factoring to find all of the roots of $x^3 - 4x^2 - 3x + 12 = 0$.

Factor by grouping:

$$(x^3 - 12x^2) - (3x - 12) = 0$$
$$x^2(x - 4) - 3(x - 4) = 0$$
$$(x^2 - 3)(x - 4) = 0$$

Thus, the roots are $\sqrt{3}$, $-\sqrt{3}$, and 4.

Given that one root of $x^3 - 3x - 2 = 0$ is 2, use synthetic division to find all of the other roots.

$$\begin{array}{r|rrrr} 2 & 1 & 0 & -3 & -2 \\ & & 2 & 4 & 2 \\ \hline & 1 & 2 & 1 & 0 \end{array}$$

$$x^3 - 3x - 2 = 0$$
$$\rightarrow (x - 2)(x^2 + 2x + 1) = 0$$
$$(x - 2)(x + 1)^2 = 0$$

Thus, the remaining root is -1 (multiplicity 2).

36. $x^5 - x^3 - 8x^2 + 8 = 0$

37. $x^4 + 2x^3 - x - 2 = 0$

38. $x^5 - 9x^3 - x^2 + 9 = 0$

Given the indicated root, find all of the other roots of the polynomial equation.

39. -3; $x^3 + 7x^2 + 16x + 12 = 0$

40. -3; $x^3 + 3x^2 - 16x - 48 = 0$

41. 4; $x^3 - 11x^2 + 38x - 40 = 0$

42. 6; $x^3 - 6x^2 - x + 6 = 0$

Key Skills

Find all rational roots of a polynomial equation.

Find all rational roots of $9x^2 - 9x + 2 = 0$. The possible values are $\pm\frac{1}{1}$, $\pm\frac{1}{3}$, $\pm\frac{1}{9}$, $\pm\frac{2}{1}$, $\pm\frac{2}{3}$, and $\pm\frac{2}{9}$. Checking each possibility reveals that the rational roots are $\frac{1}{3}$ and $\frac{2}{3}$.

Write a polynomial function given sufficient information.

The zeros of a fourth degree polynomial include 1 (multiplicity 2) and i. Also, $P(0) = 4$. Write the function in factored form and in standard form.

$$P(x) = a(x - 1)^2(x - i)(x + i)$$
$$4 = a(0 - 1)^2(0 - i)(0 + i)$$
$$4 = a$$

$$P(x) = 4(x - 1)^2(x - i)(x + i)$$
$$= 4x^4 - 8x^3 + 8x^2 - 8x + 4$$

Exercises

Find all of the rational roots of each polynomial equation.

43. $15x^2 + x - 2 = 0$

44. $9x^3 - 27x^2 - 34x - 8 = 0$

45. $9x^3 - 18x^2 + 2x - 4 = 0$

46. $x^3 - 3x^2 + 4x - 12 = 0$

Write a polynomial function of degree 4 in factored form and in standard form by using the given information.

47. $P(0) = 6$; zeros: 2, -1(multiplicity 2), and 3

48. $P(0) = -16$; zeros: -2 (multiplicity 3) and 1

49. $P(0) = -45$; zeros: 3 (multiplicity 2) and $2 + i$

50. $P(0) = -140$; zeros: 5, -7, and $-\frac{2}{3}i$

Applications

51. **INVESTMENTS** Suppose that $500 is invested at the end of every year for 5 years. One year after the last payment, the investment is worth $3200. Use the polynomial equation $500x^5 + 500x^4 + 500x^3 + 500x^2 + 500x = 3200$ to find the effective interest rate of this investment.

52. **MANUFACTURING** Using standard form, write the polynomial function that represents the volume of a crate with a length of x feet, a width of $8 - x$ feet, and a height of $x - 3$ feet. Then find the maximum volume of the crate and the dimensions for this volume.

Chapter Test

Evaluate each polynomial for $x = 3$ and $x = -2$.

1. $x^3 - 2x^2 + 5$

2. $x^4 - x^2 + 3x - 4$

3. $5x^2 - 3x + 1$

4. $7x^3 + 4x^2 - 3$

Write each sum or difference as a polynomial in standard form. Then classify the polynomial by degree and number of terms.

5. $(5x^3 - 3x^2 + x - 7) + (3x^2 - x + 6)$

6. $(2x^5 + 9x^3 - 7x + 4) - (9x^3 + 3x^2 + 4)$

7. FINANCE An annuity of $500 invested at the beginning of each year earns 7% interest, compounded annually. How much will the investment be worth at the time of the fifth payment?

Describe the end behavior of each function.

8. $P(x) = x^4 - 3x^2 + x$

9. $P(x) = 12x^3 - 7x^5$

10. $P(x) = 3x^3 - x^2 - 1$

11. $P(x) = 3 - 2x$

Use a graphing calculator to graph each function. Find any local maxima or minima to the nearest tenth and find the intervals over which the function is increasing and decreasing.

12. $P(x) = 3 - 2x - x^2$

13. $P(x) = x^3 + 3x^2 + 4$

14. $P(x) = x^4 - 3x^2 - 4$

15. $P(x) = 5 - 3x^2 - x^3$

Factor each polynomial.

16. $5x^4 - 180x^2$

17. $4x^3 - 5x^2 - 8x + 10$

18. $2x^3 + 128$

19. $x^4 - 7x^3 + 12x^2$

Divide by using long division.

20. $(2x^4 - 7x^3 - 15x^2 + 8x + 12) \div (2x + 3)$

21. $(x^3 + 3x^2 - 2x - 6) \div (x^2 - 2)$

Divide by using synthetic division.

22. $(-x^3 + 6x^2 - 11x + 6) \div (x - 3)$

23. $(x^3 + 6x^2 - 20) \div (x + 3)$

24. MANUFACTURING A box with an open top has a volume given by the formula $V(x) = x(14 - 2x)(32 - 2x)$. Write the volume of the box as a polynomial function in standard form. Then find the volume when $x = 3$.

Find all of the real roots of each polynomial.

25. $-2x^3 + 7x^2 + 3x - 18 = 0$

26. $x^4 + 2x^3 - 7x^2 - 14x = 0$

27. $x^4 - 6x^2 + 8 = 0$

28. $8x^3 + 1 = 0$

29. ENERGY A liquid propane tank has the shape of a cylinder with hemispherical ends. The volume of the tank is represented by the function $V(x) = 15\pi x^2 + \frac{4}{3}\pi x^3$, where x is the radius. If the volume is approximately 540 cubic feet, what is the radius?

Find all of the rational roots of each polynomial equation.

30. $6x^2 + 11x - 10 = 0$

31. $6x^3 - 13x^2 - 41x - 12 = 0$

Write a polynomial function P in factored form and in standard form by using the given information.

32. degree = 2; $P(0) = 3$; zeros: $1, \frac{3}{7}$

33. degree = 3; $P(0) = -18$; zeros: $-3, -1, 3$

34. degree = 3; $P(0) = 30$; zeros: $-3, -1, 2$

35. degree = 4; $P(0) = 15$; zeros: $-1 + i, -3, 5$

MULTIPLE-CHOICE For Questions 1–16, write the letter that indicates the best answer.

1. Classify $2x^3 + x^4 + x + 1$ by degree.
(LESSON 7.1)

  a. quartic
  b. quadratic
  c. cubic
  d. polynomial

2. Solve $x \log \frac{1}{6} = \log 6$ for x. **(LESSON 6.7)**

  a. 36
  b. -1
  c. -6
  d. undefined

3. Evaluate $e^{\ln 2}$, and round to the nearest tenth.
(LESSON 6.6)

  a. 0.7   **b.** 7.4
  c. 2.0   **d.** 1.9

4. Find the number of rational roots of $x^3 - 4x = 0$.   **(LESSON 7.5)**

  a. 2   **b.** 4
  c. 3   **d.** undefined

5. Identify which parabola has a maximum value at the vertex. **(LESSON 5.1)**

  a. $f(x) = x^2 + 1$
  b. $f(x) = (x-1)^2 + 1$
  c. $f(x) = 1 - 3x - x^2$
  d. $f(x) = 9 - x + x^2$

6. Which is a solution of the system below?
$\begin{cases} y \geq -x \\ y \geq 3x + 2 \end{cases}$ **(LESSON 3.4)**

  a. $(1, -5)$
  b. $(0, 5)$
  c. both **a** and **b**
  d. neither **a** nor **b**

7. Find the slope of the line $3x + 4y = 2$.
(LESSON 1.2)

  a. 3   **b.** $\frac{2}{3}$
  c. $-\frac{3}{4}$ **d.** 4

8. Which equation contains the point $(1, -3)$ and is perpendicular to $y = 2x - 2$?
(LESSON 1.3)

  a. $2y = -x + 5$
  b. $2y = -x - 5$
  c. $y = -\frac{1}{2}x + 6$
  d. $y = -\frac{1}{2}x + \frac{3}{2}$

9. Which is the solution of the system below?
$\begin{cases} x + 2y = 4 \\ 2x + y = 5 \end{cases}$ **(LESSON 3.1)**

  a. $(2, 3)$ **b.** $(2, 1)$
  c. $(-3, 2)$ **d.** $(0, 1)$

10. Which set of ordered pairs represents a function? **(LESSON 2.3)**

  a. $\{(0, 3), (1, 4), (1, 3)\}$
  b. $\{(2, 1), (4, -1), (6, 2)\}$
  c. $\{(3, 5), (2, 10), (3, 15)\}$
  d. $\{(10, 4), (10, 5), (20, 6)\}$

11. For which function does the vertex give a maximum value? **(LESSON 5.1)**

  a. $a(x) = 3x^2 + 5x$
  b. $b(x) = 7x + 5x - 3x^2$
  c. $c(x) = 3 + 5x + \frac{1}{3}x^2$
  d. $d(x) = \frac{1}{3}x^2$

12. How many solutions does a consistent system of linear equations have? *(LESSON 3.1)*
  a. 0
  b. 1
  c. at least 1
  d. infinitely many

13. What is the y-intercept for the graph of the equation $x - 5y = 15$? *(LESSON 1.2)*
  a. 15
  b. -1
  c. 3
  d. -3

14. Which is the solution of the inequality $4x + 2 < 2x + 1$? *(LESSON 1.7)*
  a. $x \geq 1$
  b. $x > 2$
  c. $x < \frac{1}{3}$
  d. $x < -\frac{1}{2}$

15. Which is the solution to the inequality $|x| \leq 5$? *(LESSON 1.8)*
  a. $-5 \leq x \leq 5$
  b. $-2 \leq x \leq 2$
  c. $-5 \geq x \geq 5$
  d. $-3 \leq x \leq 3$

16. Which is the factorization of $x^2 - 5x + 6$? *(LESSON 5.3)*
  a. $(x - 2)(x - 3)$
  b. $(x + 2)(x - 3)$
  c. $(x + 1)(x + 6)$
  d. $(x - 1)(x - 6)$

17. Write $(x + 1)(x + 2)(x - 4)$ in standard form. *(LESSON 7.3)*

18. Find the product. $\begin{bmatrix} 2 & 3 \\ 4 & 3 \end{bmatrix}\begin{bmatrix} 1 & 1 \\ 2 & 3 \end{bmatrix}$
  (LESSON 4.2)

19. Let $f(x) = 3x + 5$ and $g(x) = x^2 + x + 5$. Find $f + g$. *(LESSON 2.4)*

20. Solve $\ln x = 5$ for x. *(LESSONS 6.3 AND 6.6)*

21. Write the equation in vertex form for the parabola described by $f(x) = 2x^2 - 8x + 9$. *(LESSON 5.4)*

22. Find the sum. $(2x^3 + 3x^2 + 1) + (5x^2 - 2x + 2)$ *(LESSON 7.1)*

23. Find the difference below. *(LESSON 7.1)*
$(5x^3 + 4x^2 - x) - (x^3 + 2x^2 - 1)$

24. Let $f(x) = 3x + 2$. Find the inverse of f. *(LESSON 2.5)*

25. Find all rational roots of $3x^2 + 5x - 2 = 0$. *(LESSON 7.5)*

26. Multiply. $(4 - 2i)(4 + 2i)$ *(LESSON 5.6)*

Factor each quadratic expression, if possible. (LESSON 5.3)

27. $-3y^2 - 5y$
28. $x^2 - 5x - 36$
29. $24x^2 + 5x - 36$
30. $36x^2 - 46x - 12$

FREE-RESPONSE GRID The following questions may be answered by using a free-response grid such as that commonly used by standardized-test services.

31. Evaluate $\lceil 3.1 \rceil + \lceil 2.5 \rceil$. *(LESSON 2.6)*

32. Find the value of $\log_5 25$. *(LESSON 6.3)*

33. Solve the equation $\ln x + \ln(2 - x) = 0$ for x. *(LESSON 6.7)*

34. Simplify $5[3 - (3 - 2)]^2$. *(LESSON 2.1)*

35. Find the rational zeros of the polynomial function $f(x) = 2x^3 - x^2 - 4x + 2$. *(LESSON 7.5)*

36. Solve the proportion $\frac{x + 2}{2} = \frac{2x}{3}$ for x. *(LESSON 1.4)*

37. Evaluate $|-2.5| - |3.2|$. *(LESSON 2.6)*

38. Solve $-3x + 4 = 5 - x$ for x. *(LESSON 1.6)*

39. INVESTMENTS Find the final amount in dollars of a $1000 investment after 5 years at an interest rate of 8% compounded annually. *(LESSON 6.2)*

40. ARCHAEOLOGY A sample of wood found at an archaeological site contains 60% of its original carbon-14. Use the function $N(t) = N_0 e^{-0.00012t}$, which gives the amount of remaining carbon-14, to estimate the age of the sample of wood. *(LESSON 6.6)*

41. INVESTMENTS If $1000 is invested at 8% annual interest, compounded continuously, find the dollar amount of the investment after 5 years. *(LESSON 6.6)*

Keystroke Guide for Chapter 7

Essential keystroke sequences (using the model TI-82 or TI-83 graphics calculator) are presented below for all Activities and Examples found in this chapter that require or recommend the use of a graphics calculator.

☑ internet connect

For Keystrokes of other graphing calculator models, visit the HRW web site at **go.hrw.com** and enter the keyword **MB1 CALC**.

LESSON 7.1

E X A M P L E ②
Page 426

Graph $y = 1000x^4 + 1000x^3 + 1000x^2 + 1000x + 1000$, and evaluate for $x = 1.06$.

Use viewing window [0, 1.5] by [−1000, 7000].

Graph the function:

| Y= | 1000 | X,T,θ,n | ^ | 4 | + | 1000 | X,T,θ,n | ^ | 3 | + | 1000 | X,T,θ,n |

| x^2 | + | 1000 | X,T,θ,n | + | 1000 | GRAPH |

Use the graph:

| 2nd | TRACE | 1:valu | ENTER | (X=) 1.06 | ENTER |
(CALC above TRACE)

Use a table:

| 2nd | WINDOW | (TblStart=) 1.03 | ▼ | (△Tbl=) .01 | ▼ | (Indpt:) **Aut** | ENTER | ▼ |
(TBLSET above WINDOW)
⇑ TI-82: (TblMin=)

(Depend:) **Aut** | ENTER | ▼ | 2nd | GRAPH |
(TABLE above GRAPH)

𝒜𝒸𝓉𝒾𝓋𝒾𝓉𝓎
Page 427

For Step 1, graph $y = x^2 + x - 2$.

Use viewing window [−15, 15] by [−15, 15].

| Y= | X,T,θ,n | x^2 | + | X,T,θ,n | − | 2 | GRAPH |

Use a similar keystroke sequence for Steps 2–9. For Steps 7–9, use viewing window [−4, 4] by [−4, 4].

E X A M P L E ⑤
Page 428

For part a, graph $y = 3x^3 - 5x^2 - 2x + 1$.

Use viewing window [−5, 5] by [−5, 5].

| Y= | 3 | X,T,θ,n | ^ | 3 | − | 5 | X,T,θ,n | x^2 |

| − | 2 | X,T,θ,n | + | 1 | GRAPH |

For part **b**, use a similar keystroke sequence.
Use viewing window [−5, 5] by [−20, 5].

E X A M P L E ❶

Page 434

Graph $y = x^3 + 3x^2 - x - 3$, and approximate the coordinates of any local maxima or minima.

Use friendly viewing window $[-4.7, 4.7]$ by $[-10, 10]$.

Graph the function:

Find the coordinates of any local maxima or minima:

Press TRACE , and move the cursor.

Make a table of values:

⇑ TI-82: (TblMin=)

(**Depend:**) Aut ENTER ▼ 2nd GRAPH

To approximate more closely, change to TblStart= -2.5 and $\triangle$Tbl= 0.1.

Page 435

For Steps 1–16, graph each function by using a keystroke sequence similar to that in Example 2 of Lesson 7.1.

Use viewing window $[-5, 5]$ by $[-5, 5]$.

E X A M P L E ❷

Page 436

For part a, graph $y = -x^3 + x^2 + 3x - 1$.

Use viewing window $[-5, 5]$ by $[-5, 5]$.

Y= (−) X,T,θ,n ^ 3 + X,T,θ,n x^2 + 3 X,T,θ,n − 1 GRAPH

For part **b**, use a similar keystroke sequence to graph
$y = -x^4 + x^3 + 3x^2 - x + 3$. Use viewing window $[-5, 5]$ by $[-2, 8]$.

E X A M P L E ❸

Page 436

Enter the given data, and find a quartic regression model for the data. Then estimate y when x is 20.

Use viewing window $[0, 60]$ by $[0, 5000]$.

Enter the data:

STAT EDIT 1:Edit ENTER L1 10 ENTER 18 ENTER 30 ENTER 41 ENTER 44

ENTER ▶ L2 1679 ENTER 2606 ENTER 3089 ENTER 2276 ENTER 2517 ENTER

Graph the scatter plot:

⇑ TI-82: L1 ENTER   ⇑ TI-82: L2 ENTER

Find and graph the quartic regression model:

| STAT | CALC | 7:QuartReg | ENTER | ENTER | Y= |

⇑ TI-82: 8:QuartReg

| VARS | 5:Statistics EQ | 1:RegEQ | ENTER | GRAPH |

⇑ TI-82: 7:RegEQ

Evaluate y for x = 20:

CALC

| 2nd | TRACE | 1:value | ENTER | (X=) 20 | ENTER |

LESSON 7.3

E X A M P L E S ❶ **and** ❹ Graph $y = x(16 - 2x)(12 - 2x)$ and $y = 4x^3 - 56x^2 + 192x$ on the same screen.

Pages 441 and 442

Use viewing window $[-1, 10]$ by $[-30, 200]$.

| Y= | X,T,θ,n | (| 16 | − | 2 | X,T,θ,n |) | (| 12 | − | 2 | X,T,θ,n |) |

| ENTER | (Y2=) 4 | X,T,θ,n | ^ | 3 | − | 56 | X,T,θ,n | x^2 | + | 192 |

| X,T,θ,n | GRAPH |

For Example 4, use a similar keystroke sequence.

LESSON 7.4

E X A M P L E ❶ Graph $y = 2x^3 - 7x^2 + 3x$, and look for any zeros of the function.

Page 449

Use viewing window $[-2, 5]$ by $[-8, 4]$.

Graph the function:

| Y= | 2 | X,T,θ,n | ^ | 3 | − | 7 | X,T,θ,n | x^2 | + | 3 | X,T,θ,n | GRAPH |

> *Move your cursor as indicated.*

Find any zeros:

CALC

| 2nd | TRACE | 2:zero | ENTER | (Left Bound?) |

⇑ TI-82: 2:root

| ENTER | (Right Bound?) | ENTER | (Guess?) |

| ENTER |

(0, 0) $\left(\frac{1}{2}, 0\right)$ (3, 0)

E X A M P L E S ❷, ❸, **and** ❹ Graph each function, and find any zeros.

Pages 449–451

For Examples 2 and 3, use viewing window $[-5, 5]$ by $[-5, 5]$.
For Example 4, use viewing window $[-40, 20]$ by $[-5000, 7000]$.

Graph the function:

Use a keystroke sequence similar to that in Example 2 of Lesson 7.1.

Find any zeros:

Use a keystroke sequence similar to that in Example 1 of Lesson 7.4.

Activity
Page 451

For Step 1, enter $y = x^4 - 3x^3 - 5x^2 + 13x + 6$, and use a table of values to find the corresponding y-value for each x-value in the table.

Use viewing window $[-5, 5]$ by $[-15, 15]$.

Enter and graph the function:
Use a keystroke sequence similar to that in Example 2 of Lesson 7.1.

Make a table of values:
Use a keystroke sequence similar to that in Example 1 of Lesson 7.2.

LESSON 7.5

E X A M P L E S ❶, ❷, and ❸   For Example 1, graph $y = 10x^3 + 9x^2 - 19x + 6$, and verify
Pages 459 and 460   that -2, $\frac{1}{2}$, and $\frac{3}{5}$ are zeros.

Use viewing window $[-3, 3]$ by $[-30, 30]$.

(−2, 0)

Graph the function:
Use a keystroke sequence similar to that in Example 1 of Lesson 7.1.

Evaluate y for x-values of -2, $\frac{1}{2}$, and $\frac{3}{5}$:
Use a keystroke similar to that used in Example 2 of Lesson 7.2. For a closer look around $x = \frac{1}{2}$ and $x = \frac{3}{5}$, use viewing window $[0.3, 0.8]$ by $[-1, 1]$.

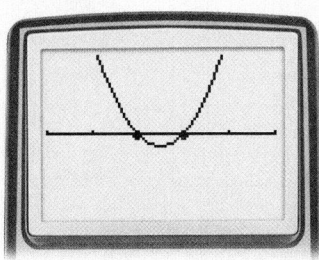

For Example 2, graph $y = x^3 - 2x^2 - 2x + 1$, and evaluate for $x = -1$. Use viewing window $[-5, 5]$ by $[-5, 5]$.

For Example 3, graph $y = 3x^3 - 10x^2 + 10x - 4$, and evaluate for $x = 2$. Use viewing window $[-3, 5]$ by $[-6, 4]$.

Activity
Page 461

For Step 2, graph $y = 2x^3 - x^2 - 4x$.

Use viewing window $[-5, 5]$ by $[-3, 8]$.

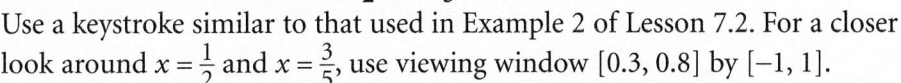

For Steps 3 and 4, use a similar keystroke sequence.

E X A M P L E ❹   Graph $y = x(20 - 2x)(12 - 2x)$ and $y = x(16 - 2x)(15 - 2x)$ on the same
Page 461   screen, and look for any points of intersection.

Use viewing window $[0, 6]$ by $[0, 350]$.

Graph the functions:
Use a keystroke sequence similar to that in Example 1 of Lesson 7.3.

Look for any points of intersection:

(Guess?) ENTER

8

Rational Functions and Radical Functions

IN THIS CHAPTER, YOU WILL STUDY RATIONAL functions and radical functions. Rational functions are ratios of polynomials. Radical functions are formed from the *n*th roots of numbers. The square-root function studied in Chapter 5 is an example of a radical function. Rational functions and radical functions have applications in physics, chemistry, engineering, business, economics, and many other fields.

Lessons

8.1 ● Inverse, Joint, and Combined Variation

8.2 ● Rational Functions and Their Graphs

8.3 ● Multiplying and Dividing Rational Expressions

8.4 ● Adding and Subtracting Rational Expressions

8.5 ● Solving Rational Equations and Inequalities

8.6 ● Radical Expressions and Radical Functions

8.7 ● Simplifying Radical Expressions

8.8 ● Solving Radical Equations and Inequalities

Chapter Project
Means to an End

The size of the pupil determines the amount of light that enters the eye. In the same way, a camera's aperture, or opening, determines the amount of light that enters the camera.

Galileo is credited as the first person to notice that the motion of a pendulum depends only upon its length.

CHAPTER PROJECT PORTFOLIO ACTIVITIES

About the Chapter Project

Finding an average is something that most people can do almost instinctively. Currency exchange, hourly wage, car mileage, and average speed are common daily topics of discussion. You can measure an average in various ways. Two common averages are the arithmetic mean and the harmonic mean. In the Chapter Project, *Means to an End*, you will use the data provided to determine the most appropriate average.

After completing the Chapter Project, you will be able to do the following:

- Find the arithmetic mean and the harmonic mean of a set of data.
- Determine the relationship between the arithmetic and harmonic mean.
- Determine which of the averages—arithmetic mean, harmonic mean, or weighted harmonic mean—best represents a data set.

About the Portfolio Activities

Throughout the chapter, you will be given opportunities to complete Portfolio Activities that are designed to support your work on the Chapter Project.

- Exploring a historical representation of harmonic means is included in the Portfolio Activity on page 488.
- Exploring a geometric representation of harmonic means is included in the Portfolio Activity on page 497.
- Extending the definition of harmonic mean to n numbers is included in the Portfolio Activity on page 511.
- Using harmonic means to find average speeds is included in the Portfolio Activity on page 519.

Inverse, Joint, and Combined Variation

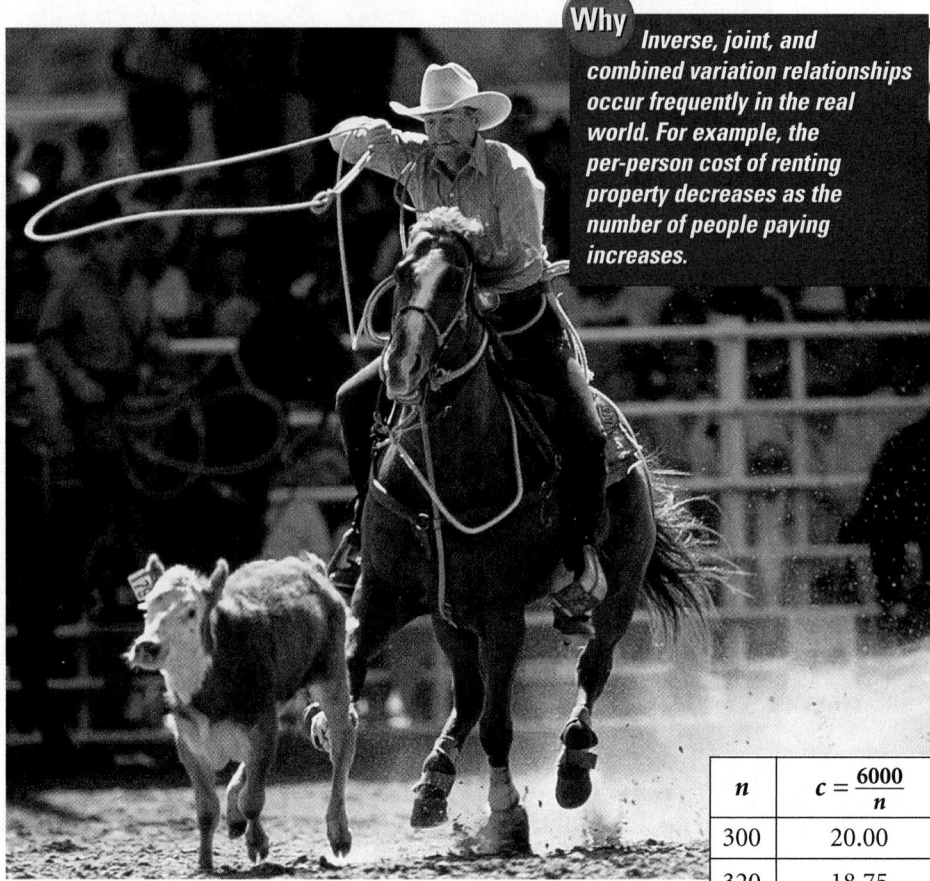

Why *Inverse, joint, and combined variation relationships occur frequently in the real world. For example, the per-person cost of renting property decreases as the number of people paying increases.*

Objectives

- Identify inverse, joint, and combined variations, find the constant of variation, and write an equation for the variation.

- Solve real-world problems involving inverse, joint, or combined variation.

A ranch can be rented for rodeos for a flat fee of $6000 per day. Janet Flores, a promoter, wants to rent the ranch for a 1-day rodeo. She knows that an admission price of $20 or less will be acceptable to the general public.

The table at right indicates what the per-person charge, c, would be if n people attend the rodeo. From the table, any number of attendees greater than 300 people will enable the promoter to cover the ranch's rental fee.

Notice that as the number of attendees increases, the per-person charge decreases. That is, as n increases, c decreases, which is characteristic of an *inverse-variation* relationship.

n	$c = \dfrac{6000}{n}$
300	20.00
320	18.75
340	≈17.65
360	≈16.67
380	≈15.79
400	15.00
420	≈14.29
440	≈13.64
460	≈13.04
480	12.50
500	12.00
520	≈11.54
540	≈11.11

Inverse Variation

Two variables, x and y, have an **inverse-variation** relationship if there is a nonzero number k such that $xy = k$, or $y = \frac{k}{x}$. The **constant of variation** is k.

You will need: no special materials

1. Copy and complete the table below for $y = \frac{1}{x}$.

x	$\frac{1}{10}$	$\frac{1}{4}$	$\frac{1}{2}$	1	2	3	4	5	6
y									
xy									

PROBLEM SOLVING

2. **Look for a pattern.** What can you say about the values of y as the values of x increase? What can you say about the values of y as the values of x decrease?

3. Repeat Step 1 for $y = \frac{2}{x}$ and $y = \frac{4}{x}$. Do you think that the pattern you identified in Step 2 will also be true for $y = \frac{3}{x}$? Repeat Step 1 for $y = \frac{3}{x}$.

CHECKPOINT ✔ 4. Describe the behavior of $y = \frac{k}{x}$, where $k > 0$, as x increases and as x decreases.

5. Let $y = \frac{k}{x}$, where $k > 0$. What happens when $x = 0$?

CONNECTION

TRANSFORMATIONS

The functions $y = \frac{1}{x}$, $y = \frac{2}{x}$, and $y = \frac{4}{x}$ all represent inverse-variation relationships. The typical graphical behavior of such a relationship can be observed at right.

Notice that the graphs of $y = \frac{2}{x}$ and $y = \frac{4}{x}$ are vertical stretches of the graph of the parent function $y = \frac{1}{x}$. That is, if $f(x) = \frac{1}{x}$, $g(x) = \frac{2}{x}$, and $h(x) = \frac{4}{x}$, then $g(x) = 2 \cdot f(x)$ and $h(x) = 4 \cdot f(x)$.

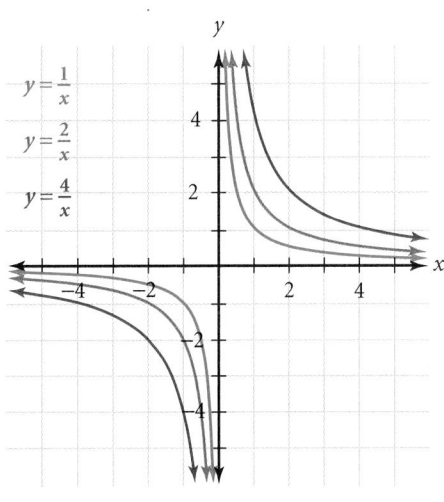

CHECKPOINT ✔ Describe where the graph of $y = \frac{3}{x}$ would lie in relation to the graphs shown above.

If you know one ordered pair (x, y) in a given inverse-variation relationship, you can find the constant of variation, k, and write the inverse-variation equation, $y = \frac{k}{x}$. In real-world situations, the x- and y-values are usually positive, and as the x-values increase, the y-values decrease. This is shown in Example 1 on the next page.

EXAMPLE ① The variable *y* varies inversely as *x*, and *y* = 13.5 when *x* = 4.5.

a. Find the constant of variation, and write an equation for the relationship.

b. Find *y* when *x* is 0.5, 1, 1.5, 2, and 2.5.

● **SOLUTION**

a.
$$xy = k$$
$$(4.5)(13.5) = k$$
$$k = 60.75$$

Thus, an equation for the relationship is $y = \frac{60.75}{x}$.

b. Enter $y = \frac{60.75}{x}$, and use the table feature with an *x*-increment of 0.5.

From the table, you can see that the *x*-values of 0.5, 1, 1.5, 2, and 2.5 have corresponding *y*-values of 121.5, 60.75, 40.5, 30.375, and 24.3, respectively.

Notice that when x is 0, the function is undefined.

TECHNOLOGY
GRAPHICS CALCULATOR

Keystroke Guide, page 554

TRY THIS The variable *y* varies inversely as *x*, and *y* = 120 when *x* = 6.5. Find the constant of variation, and write an equation for the relationship. Then find *y* when *x* is 1.5, 4.5, 8, 12.5, and 14.

Recall from Lesson 1.4 that in a direct-variation relationship, *y* varies directly as *x* for any nonzero value of *k* such that *y* = *kx*. In *joint variation*, one quantity varies directly as two quantities.

Joint Variation

If $y = kxz$, then *y* **varies jointly** as *x* and *z*, and the constant of variation is *k*.

EXAMPLE ② Refer to the rectangular prism shown at right.

a. Write an equation for the volume of the prism, and identify the type of variation and the constant of variation.

b. Find the volume of the prism if the length of the base is 4 inches and the width of the base is 2 inches.

CONNECTION
GEOMETRY

8 in.

● **SOLUTION**

a. The volume of a rectangular prism is $V = \ell wh$.
$$V = \ell wh$$
$$V = \ell w(8), \text{ or } 8\ell w$$
Volume varies jointly as the length, ℓ, and width, *w*. The constant of variation is 8.

b. $V = 8\ell w = 8(4)(2) = 64$ The volume is 64 cubic inches.

TRY THIS

a. Write an equation for the volume of a rectangular prism whose base has a length of 12 inches. Identify the type of variation and the constant of variation.

b. Find the volume of the prism if the width of the base is 2 inches and the height of the prism is 4 inches.

If $y = kx^2$, where k is a nonzero constant, then y varies directly as the square of x. Many geometric relationships involve this type of joint variation, as shown in Example 3.

E X A M P L E ❸

C O N N E C T I O N

GEOMETRY

a. Write an equation to represent the area, A, of the isosceles right triangle shown at right. Identify the type of variation and the constant of variation.

b. Find the area of the triangle when x is 1.5, 2.5, 3.5, and 4.5.

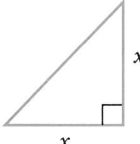

🔵 **SOLUTION**

a. The equation for the area is $A = \frac{1}{2}bh$, where b is the base and h is the height. Since the base is x and the height is x, A varies directly as the square of x. The constant of variation is $\frac{1}{2}$.

$$A = \frac{1}{2}bh$$
$$A = \frac{1}{2}(x)(x)$$
$$A = \frac{1}{2}x^2$$

TECHNOLOGY

**GRAPHICS
CALCULATOR**

Keystroke Guide, page 554

b. Enter $y = \frac{1}{2}x^2$ into a graphics calculator, and use the table feature. Begin with $x = 1.5$, and use an x-increment of 1.

From the table, you can read the areas.

x	Area
1.5	1.125 square units
2.5	3.125 square units
3.5	6.125 square units
4.5	10.125 square units

TRY THIS

a. Write the formula for the area, A, of a circle whose radius is r. Identify the type of variation and the constant of variation.

b. Find the area of the circle when r is 1.5, 2.5, 3.5, and 4.5.

CRITICAL THINKING

Let y vary as the square of x. How does y change when x is doubled, tripled, and quadrupled? Justify your response.

When more than one type of variation occurs in the same equation, the equation represents a **combined variation**.

The rotational speeds, s_A and s_B, of gear A with t_A teeth and gear B with t_B teeth are related as indicated below.

$$t_A s_A = t_B s_B$$

The combined-variation equation for the rotational speed of gear B in terms of t_A, s_A, and t_B is as follows:

$$s_B = \frac{t_A s_A}{t_B}$$

Gear B   **Gear A**

E X A M P L E ❹ A bicycle's pedal gear has 52 teeth and is rotating at 65 revolutions per minute. A chain links the pedal gear to a rear-wheel gear that has 18 teeth and is attached to a 26-inch wheel.

At what speed, in miles per hour, is the bicycle traveling?

● **SOLUTION**

Let the pedal gear be gear A and the rear-wheel gear be gear B.

1. Find the rotational speed in revolutions per minute for gear B.

$$s_B = \frac{t_A s_A}{t_B}$$

$$s_B = \frac{(52)(65)}{18}$$

$$s_B \approx 188$$

The rear-wheel gear is rotating at about 188 revolutions per minute.

2. Convert revolutions per minute to miles per hour to find the speed of the bicycle.

A 26-inch wheel (including tire) has a circumference of 26π inches. Therefore, the bicycle is traveling at about $26\pi \times 188$ inches per minute. To convert to miles per hour, multiply by fractions equal to 1.

$$\frac{(26\pi)(188)\ \text{in.}}{1\ \text{min}} \times \frac{1\ \text{ft}}{12\ \text{in.}} \times \frac{1\ \text{mi}}{5280\ \text{ft}} \times \frac{60\ \text{min}}{1\ \text{hr}} \approx 14.5\ \text{miles per hour}$$

TRY THIS   A bicycle's pedal gear has 46 teeth and is rotating at 55 revolutions per minute. If the pedal gear is linked to a rear-wheel gear that has 24 teeth and is attached to a 27-inch wheel, at what speed, in miles per hour, is the bicycle traveling?

CHECKPOINT ✔ Predict the effect of a rear-wheel gear with more teeth than the pedal gear. Verify your prediction by reworking Example 4 for a rear-wheel gear that has 60 teeth, 80 teeth, and 100 teeth.

CRITICAL THINKING   Suppose that the pedal gear in Example 4 has n teeth, the rear-wheel gear has m teeth, and $n > m$. What is the rotational speed of the rear-wheel gear relative to the speed of the pedal gear?

Exercises

● Communicate

1. Explain how direct variation and joint variation are related.

2. Let $xy = k$, where k is a constant greater than zero. Explain how you know that y must decrease when x increases.

CONNECTION

GEOMETRY Two formulas from geometry are shown below. Explain how to identify the type of variation found in each formula.

3. area, A, of a rhombus with diagonals of lengths p and q
$$A = \frac{1}{2}pq$$

4. area, A, of an equilateral triangle with sides of length s
$$A = \frac{\sqrt{3}}{4}s^2$$

5. Identify and explain how z varies as x, y, and d in the equation $z = \frac{2xy}{d^2}$.

6. Given the proportion $\frac{a}{b} = \frac{c}{d}$, write a related combined-variation equation. Explain how to form a different proportion from the combined-variation equation you wrote.

● Guided Skills Practice

7. The variable y varies inversely as x, and $y = 132$ when $x = 15$. Find the constant of variation, and write an equation for the relationship. Then find y when x is 1.5, 2.0, 2.5, 3.0, and 3.5. *(EXAMPLE 1)*

CONNECTIONS

GEOMETRY Refer to the rectangular prism at right. *(EXAMPLE 2)*

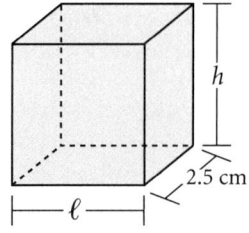

8. Write an equation for the volume of the prism, and identify the type of variation and the constant of variation.

9. Find the volume of the prism if the length of the base is 2 centimeters and the height is 8 centimeters.

GEOMETRY Refer to the figure at right, which consists of one square inside a larger square. *(EXAMPLE 3)*

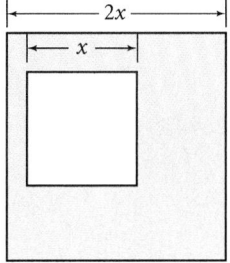

10. Write an equation to represent the area, A, of the shaded region. Identify the type of variation and the constant of variation.

11. Find the area of the shaded region for x-values of 1.5, 2.5, 3.5, 4.5, 5.5, and 6.5.

APPLICATION

12. RECREATION A bicycle's pedal gear has 52 teeth and is rotating at 145 revolutions per minute. At what speed, in miles per hour, is the bicycle traveling if the rear-wheel gear has 28 teeth and the wheels are 26 inches in diameter? *(EXAMPLE 4)*

Practice and Apply

internet connect

Homework Help Online

Go To: **go.hrw.com**
Keyword:
MB1 Homework Help
for Exercises 13–48

For Exercises 13–20, *y* varies inversely as *x*. Write the appropriate inverse-variation equation, and find *y* for the given values of *x*.

13. $y = 36$ when $x = 9$; x-values: 3, 4, 5, 6, and 7

14. $y = 10$ when $x = 5$; x-values: 2.5, 3, and 3.5

15. $y = 0.5$ when $x = 8$; x-values: 5, 4, 3, 2, and 1

16. $y = 0.25$ when $x = 0.3$; x-values: 0.1, 0.2, 0.3, and 0.4

17. $y = 14$ when $x = 8$; x-values: 10, 15, and 20

18. $y = 2.25$ when $x = 1.5$; x-values: 0.1, 0.2, 0.3, and 0.4

19. $y = 1000$ when $x = 0.2$; x-values: 10^2, 10^3, and 10^4

20. $y = 10^{-2}$ when $x = 50$; x-values: 10^2, 10^3, and 10^4

For Exercises 21–28, *y* varies jointly as *x* and *z*. Write the appropriate joint-variation equation, and find *y* for the given values of *x* and *z*.

21. $y = -108$ when $x = -4$ and $z = 3$; $x = 6$ and $z = -2$

22. $y = -315$ when $x = 5$ and $z = 9$; $x = -7$ and $z = 8$

23. $y = 15$ when $x = 9$ and $z = 1.5$; $x = 18$ and $z = 3$

24. $y = 0.5$ when $x = 10$ and $z = 3$; $x = 1.8$ and $z = 6$

25. $y = 120$ when $x = 8$ and $z = 20$; $x = 54$ and $z = 7$

26. $y = 0.1$ when $x = 0.1$ and $z = 5$; $x = 0.2$ and $z = 0.4$

27. $y = 10^4$ when $x = 10^2$ and $z = 10^1$; $x = 10^5$ and $z = 10^2$

28. $y = 2 \times 10^5$ when $x = 10^1$ and $z = 10^3$; $x = 3 \times 10^4$ and $z = 1.5 \times 10^3$

For Exercises 29–34, *z* varies jointly as *x* and *y* and inversely as *w*. Write the appropriate combined-variation equation, and find *z* for the given values of *x*, *y*, and *w*.

29. $z = 3$ when $x = 3$, $y = -2$, and $w = -4$; $x = 6$, $y = 7$, and $w = -4$

30. $z = 10$ when $x = 5$, $y = -2$, and $w = 3$; $x = 8$, $y = 6$, and $w = -12$

31. $z = 36$ when $x = 9$, $y = 10$, and $w = 15$; $x = 10$, $y = 18$, and $w = 5$

32. $z = 15$ when $x = 3$, $y = 4$, and $w = 9$; $x = 1.5$, $y = 20.5$, and $w = 5.4$

33. $z = 100$ when $x = 100$, $y = 7$, and $w = 2$; $x = 3.5$, $y = 24$, and $w = 27$

34. $z = 54$ when $x = 8$, $y = 10$, and $w = 1.5$; $x = 1.5$, $y = 2.4$, and $w = 3$

If (x_1, y_1) and (x_2, y_2) satisfy $xy = k$, then $x_1y_1 = x_2y_2$. Find *x* or *y* as indicated.

35. $(x, 2.5)$ and $(6, 4)$

36. $(4.5, y)$ and $(12, 6)$

37. $(3.6, 5)$ and $(7.2, y)$

38. $(3, y)$ and $(18, 6)$

39. $(18, 2)$ and (y, y)

40. (x, x) and $(5, 125)$

CHALLENGE

41. Show that if (x_1, y_1) and (x_2, y_2) satisfy the inverse-variation equation $xy = k$ and if $x_1, y_1, x_2,$ and y_2 are nonzero, then $\dfrac{x_1}{x_2} = \dfrac{y_2}{y_1}$ and $y_2 = y_1\left(\dfrac{x_1}{x_2}\right)$.

42 STATISTICS Refer to the table and scatter plot below.

x	0	1	2	3	4	5	6
y	0.00	0.25	1.00	2.25	4.00	6.25	9.00

a. Use a graphics calculator to find an equation of the form $y = kx^2$ to represent the data.

b. Find y for x-values of 24, 25, 26, 27, 28, 29, and 30.

43. PHOTOGRAPHY Under certain conditions of artificial light, the exposure time required to photograph an object varies directly as the candlepower of the light and varies inversely as the square of the object's distance from the light source. If the exposure time is 0.01 second when the light source is 6.00 feet from the object, how far from the object should the light source be when both the candlepower and the exposure time are doubled?

44. AVIATION The lifting force exerted by the atmosphere on the wings of an airplane in flight varies directly as the surface area of the wings and the square of the plane's airspeed. A small private plane has a cruising airspeed of 250 miles per hour. In order to obtain 3 times the lifting force, a new plane is designed with a wing surface area twice that of the older model. What cruising speed, to the nearest mile per hour, is planned for the new model?

45. PHYSICS Heat loss, h, in calories per hour through a glass window varies jointly as the difference, d, between the inside and outside temperatures and as the area, A, of the window and inversely as the thickness, t, of the pane of glass. If the temperature difference is 30°F, there is a heat loss of 9000 calories per hour through a window with an area of 1500 cubic centimeters and thickness of 0.25 centimeter. Find the heat loss through a window with the same area and a thickness of 0.2 centimeter when the temperature difference is 15°F.

46. ORNITHOLOGY There are many forces that work together to make both airplanes and birds fly. Although wingshape varies greatly among birds, the number of wing beats per second (one wing beat is considered to be one upward and downward motion) for any bird in flight is approximately inversely related to the length of its wing.

a. Find the approximate constant of variation, k, to the nearest tenth, if a herring gull flaps its wings at a rate of about 2.8 wing beats per second and has a wing length of about 24.1 centimeters.

b. Use the approximate value of k from part **a** to find the approximate number of wing beats per second for a starling that has a wing length of about 13.2 centimeters.

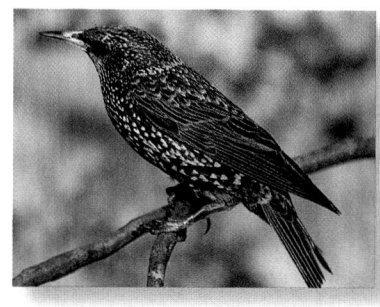

c. Use the approximate value of k from part **a** to find the approximate wing length of a cormorant who flaps its wings at a rate of about 1.9 wing beats per second.

Double-crested cormorant

Starling

Look Back

Rewrite each expression with positive exponents only. *(LESSON 2.2)*

47. x^{-1} **48.** ab^{-3} **49.** $\left(\dfrac{x}{y}\right)^{-2}$ **50.** $a^{-2}b^3c^{-5}d$ **51.** $[(x^{-3})^{-2}]^{-3}$

Identify the vertex and the axis of symmetry in the graph of each function. *(LESSON 5.4)*

52. $f(x) = -3x^2 + 5$ **53.** $h(x) = x^2 + 2x - 3$ **54.** $b(t) = -t^2 - 5t + 6$

55. $g(x) = x^2 + 2$ **56.** $d(t) = t^2 + t + 1$ **57.** $r(t) = 2t^2 - 3t + 2$

Give the degree of each polynomial. *(LESSON 7.1)*

58. $3x^5 - 2x^4 + x^2 - 1$ **59.** $2 - 5x + 7x^2 - x^3$ **60.** $-5x^3 - x^4 + 1$

Describe the end behavior of each function. *(LESSON 7.2)*

61. $f(x) = x^4 + 2x^3 - x^2 + 2$ **62.** $g(x) = -3x^3 - 2x^2 + x - 4$

Portfolio Extension
Go To: **go.hrw.com**
Keyword:
MB1 MeanMean

 Look Beyond

63. Make a table of values for $f(x) = \dfrac{1}{x + 2}$ for values of x near -2. Use this table to describe the values of f near $x = -2$.

As early as 300 C.E., Pappus of Alexandria represented the arithmetic mean and the harmonic mean geometrically by constructing the figure shown below. In the figure, arc ADC is a semicircle of circle O.

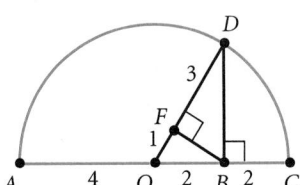

For any two numbers a and b, the arithmetic mean is $\dfrac{a + b}{2}$.

For any two nonzero numbers a and b, the harmonic mean is $\dfrac{2}{\frac{1}{a} + \frac{1}{b}}$.

1. Find the arithmetic mean and the harmonic mean of AB and BC.

2. Identify the side of a triangle in the figure whose length equals the arithmetic mean that you found in Step 1.

3. Identify the side of a triangle in the figure whose length equals the harmonic mean that you found in Step 1.

WORKING ON THE CHAPTER PROJECT

You should now be able to complete Activity 1 of the Chapter Project.

Rational Functions and Their Graphs

Objectives

● Identify and evaluate rational functions.

● Graph a rational function, find its domain, write equations for its asymptotes, and identify any holes in its graph.

Why *Rational functions are used to describe many real-world relationships. For example, rational functions are often used to solve mixture problems.*

Dane is a chemist who is varying the salt concentration of a solution. He can use a *rational function* to represent the salt concentration of the solution.

E X A M P L E ❶ Dane begins with 65 milliliters of a 10% saline solution. He adds x milliliters of distilled water to the container holding the saline solution.

a. Write a function, C, that represents the salt concentration of the solution.

b. What is the salt concentration of the solution if 100 millimeters of distilled water is added?

APPLICATION
CHEMISTRY

● **SOLUTION**

a. Original concentration of salt solution:

$$10\% \text{ of } 65 = 6.5 \quad \frac{6.5}{65} \quad \begin{array}{l} \leftarrow \textit{salt} \\ \leftarrow \textit{solution} \end{array}$$

New concentration of salt solution:

$$\text{Add } x \text{ millimeters of distilled water.} \quad \frac{6.5}{65+x} \quad \begin{array}{l} \leftarrow \textit{salt} \\ \leftarrow \textit{solution} \end{array}$$

Function for the salt concentration in this solution:

$$C(x) = \frac{6.5}{65+x}$$

b. Salt concentration when 100 milliliters of distilled water is added:

$$C(100) = \frac{6.5}{65+100} \approx 0.039, \text{ or } 3.9\%$$

A **rational expression** is the quotient of two polynomials. A **rational function** is a function defined by a rational expression. The function $C(x) = \frac{6.5}{65+x}$ from Example 1 is a rational function.

CHECKPOINT ✔ Explain why $y = \frac{e^x}{x-1}$ and $y = \frac{x^2+2}{|x|}$ are not rational functions.

The rational function $f(x) = \frac{1}{x}$ is undefined when $x = 0$. In general, the domain of a rational function is the set of all real numbers except those real numbers that make the denominator equal to zero.

E X A M P L E ② **Find the domain of $g(x) = \frac{x^2 - 7x + 12}{x^2 + 9x + 20}$.**

● **SOLUTION**

Find the values of x for which the denominator, $x^2 + 9x + 20$, equals 0.

$$x^2 + 9x + 20 = 0$$
$$(x + 4)(x + 5) = 0$$
$$x = -4 \ \ or \ \ x = -5$$

The domain is all real numbers except −4 and −5.

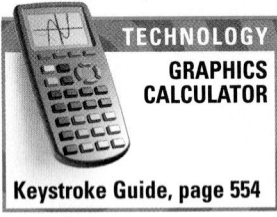

TECHNOLOGY
GRAPHICS CALCULATOR

Keystroke Guide, page 554

CHECK

Enter $y = \frac{x^2 - 7x + 12}{x^2 + 9x + 20}$ into a graphics calculator. Use the table feature to verify that −4 and −5 are not included in the domain.

TRY THIS   Find the domain of $j(x) = \frac{3x^2 + x - 2}{x^2 + 2x - 3}$.

Vertical Asymptotes

Recall from Lesson 6.2 that exponential functions, such as $y = 2^x$, have a horizontal asymptote. Rational functions can have horizontal *and* vertical asymptotes. In the Activity below, you will explore the vertical asymptotes of some rational functions.

Activity
Exploring Vertical Asymptotes

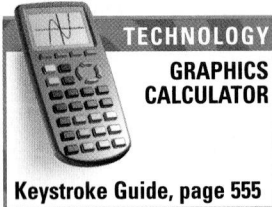

TECHNOLOGY
GRAPHICS CALCULATOR

Keystroke Guide, page 555

You will need: a graphics calculator

1. Enter the function $y = \frac{1}{x - 2}$ into a graphics calculator.

  a. Copy the table below. Use the table feature to complete it.

x	1.0	1.1	1.2	1.3	1.4	1.5	1.6	1.7	1.8	1.9
y										

  b. Copy the table below. Use the table feature to complete it.

x	3.0	2.9	2.8	2.7	2.6	2.5	2.4	2.3	2.2	2.1
y										

CHECKPOINT ✔ **2.** What can you say about y as x approaches 2 from values of x less than 2? What can you say about y as x approaches 2 from values of x greater than 2? What do you think is the value of y when $x = 2$?

CHECKPOINT ✔ **3.** Let $y = \dfrac{1}{x+3}$. Use the table feature of a graphics calculator to evaluate y for values of x a little less than -3 and for values of x a little greater than -3. What can you say about y as x approaches -3 from values of x less than -3? What can you say about y as x approaches -3 from values of x greater than -3? What do you think is the value of y when $x = -3$?

Real numbers for which a rational function is not defined are called **excluded values**.

CHECKPOINT ✔ Find the excluded values for the function $y = \dfrac{x+3}{x^2 - x - 6}$.

At an excluded value, a rational function *may* have a vertical asymptote. The necessary conditions for a vertical asymptote are given below.

Vertical Asymptote

If $x - a$ is a factor of the denominator of a rational function but not a factor of its numerator, then $x = a$ is a vertical asymptote of the graph of the function.

EXAMPLE ③ Identify all vertical asymptotes of the graph of $r(x) = \dfrac{2x}{x^2 - 1}$.

● **SOLUTION**

Factor the denominator: $\qquad r(x) = \dfrac{2x}{x^2 - 1} = \dfrac{2x}{(x-1)(x+1)}$

Since neither factor of the denominator is a factor of the numerator, equations for the vertical asymptotes are $x = -1$ and $x = 1$.

CHECK
Graph $y = \dfrac{2x}{x^2 - 1}$, and look for the vertical asymptotes, $x = -1$ and $x = 1$.

Note: Depending on the viewing window used, the calculator may display lines that look like vertical asymptotes but are actually lines that connect consecutive points on each side of the asymptotes.

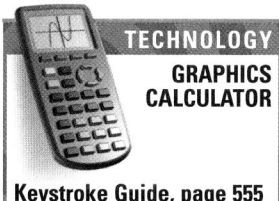

TECHNOLOGY
GRAPHICS
CALCULATOR

Keystroke Guide, page 555

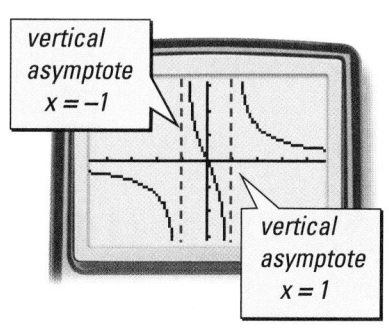

vertical asymptote $x = -1$

vertical asymptote $x = 1$

TRY THIS Identify all vertical asymptotes of the graph of $r(x) = \dfrac{x}{x^2 + 5x + 6}$.

CRITICAL THINKING Let P be a polynomial expression. Write a rational function of the form $R(x) = \dfrac{1}{P}$ that has vertical asymptotes at $x = -2$, $x = 0$, and $x = 2$.

Horizontal Asymptotes

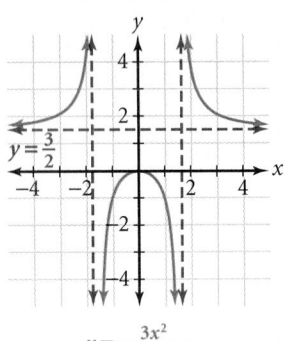

$$y = \frac{3x^2}{-5 + 2x^2}$$

To examine the *horizontal asymptotes* of rational functions, consider the graph of $y = \frac{3x^2}{-5 + 2x^2}$ shown at left. The graph shows a horizontal asymptote at $y = \frac{3}{2}$, or $y = 1.5$. The tables below confirm that as the x-values get farther away from 0, the y-values approach 1.5.

x-values are positive and increasing.

y-values approach 1.5.

x-values are negative and decreasing.

y-values approach 1.5.

Because both the numerator and the denominator of the function $y = \frac{3x^2}{-5 + 2x^2}$ have the same degree, you can use the leading coefficients, 3 and 2, of the numerator and denominator to write the equation for the horizontal asymptote of its graph, $y = \frac{3}{2}$.

Horizontal Asymptote

Let $R(x) = \frac{P}{Q}$ be a rational function, where P and Q are polynomials.

- If the degree of P is less than the degree of Q, then $y = 0$ is the equation of the horizontal asymptote of the graph of R.

- If the degree of P equals the degree of Q and a and b are the leading coefficients of P and Q, respectively, then $y = \frac{a}{b}$ is the equation of the horizontal asymptote of the graph of R.

- If the degree of P is greater than the degree of Q, then the graph of R has no horizontal asymptote.

E X A M P L E   **4** Let $R(x) = \frac{x}{x^2 - 2x - 3}$. Identify all vertical asymptotes and all horizontal asymptotes of the graph of R.

SOLUTION

1. To find the equations of all vertical asymptotes, factor the denominator, and look for excluded values of the domain.

$$R(x) = \frac{x}{(x-3)(x+1)}$$

Since neither factor of the denominator is a factor of the numerator, the equations for the vertical asymptotes are $x = 3$ and $x = -1$.

2. Because the degree of the numerator is less than the degree of the denominator, the equation for the horizontal asymptote is $y = 0$.

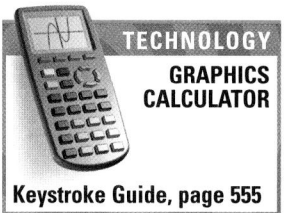
CHECK

Graph $y = \dfrac{x}{x^2 - 2x - 3}$, and look for the vertical and horizontal asymptotes.

vertical asymptotes at $x = -1$ and $x = 3$

horizontal asymptote at $y = 0$

TRY THIS

Let $R(x) = \dfrac{2x^2 - 2x + 1}{x^2 - x - 12}$. Find the equations of all vertical asymptotes and all horizontal asymptotes of the graph of R.

Using Asymptotes to Graph

You can graph a rational function by using the asymptotes, as shown in Example 5.

EXAMPLE ⑤ Graph $y = \dfrac{x + 2}{x - 2}$, showing all asymptotes.

● **SOLUTION**

Write equations for the asymptotes, and graph them as dashed lines.

vertical asymptote: $x = 2$

horizontal asymptote: $y = 1$

PROBLEM SOLVING

Use a table. To help obtain an accurate graph, plot some points on each branch of the graph, and sketch the curves through these points.

x	-1	0	1	3	4	5
y	$-\frac{1}{3}$	-1	-3	5	3	$2\frac{1}{3}$

CONNECTION
TRANSFORMATIONS

By dividing, you can rewrite $y = \dfrac{x + 2}{x - 2}$ from Example 5 as $y = 1 + \dfrac{4}{x - 2}$.

From this form, you can see the transformations of the graph of $y = \dfrac{1}{x}$.

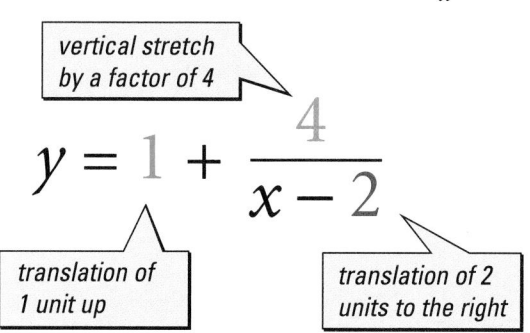

vertical stretch by a factor of 4

$$y = 1 + \dfrac{4}{x - 2}$$

translation of 1 unit up

translation of 2 units to the right

$y = 1 + \dfrac{4}{x - 2}$

$y = \dfrac{1}{x}$

Holes in Graphs

The graph of a rational function may have a *hole* in it. For example, $f(x) = \dfrac{x^2 - 9}{x - 3}$ can be written as $f(x) = \dfrac{(x - 3)(x + 3)}{x - 3}$. Because $x - 3$ is a factor of *both* the numerator *and* the denominator, the graph of f has a hole when $x = 3$.

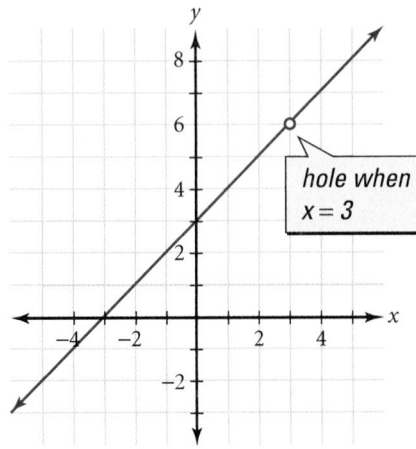

hole when $x = 3$

Hole in the Graph

If $x - b$ is a factor of the numerator and the denominator of a rational function, then there is a **hole in the graph** of the function when $x = b$ unless $x = b$ is a vertical asymptote.

EXAMPLE 6 Let $y = \dfrac{3 - 2x - x^2}{x^2 + x - 2}$. **Identify all asymptotes and holes in the graph.**

SOLUTION

Factor the numerator and denominator.

$$y = \frac{3 - 2x - x^2}{x^2 + x - 2} = \frac{-(x^2 + 2x - 3)}{(x - 1)(x + 2)} = \frac{-(x + 3)(x - 1)}{(x - 1)(x + 2)}$$

Because $x - 1$ is a factor of *both* the numerator and the denominator, the graph has a hole when $x = 1$.

Because $x + 2$ is a factor of *only* the denominator, there is a vertical asymptote at $x = -2$.

Because the degree of the numerator equals the degree of the denominator, there is a horizontal asymptote at $y = \dfrac{-1}{1} = -1$.

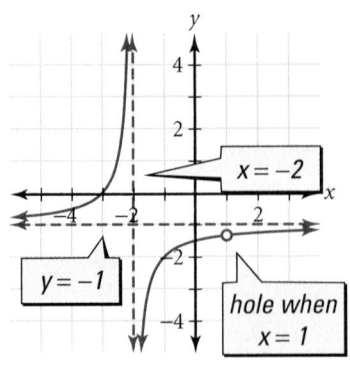

$x = -2$

$y = -1$

hole when $x = 1$

TRY THIS Let $y = \dfrac{3x^2 + x^3}{x^2 + 2x - 3}$. Identify all asymptotes and holes in the graph.

Exercises

Communicate

1. Why is the quotient of two polynomials described as "rational"?

2. Describe how to find the excluded values of a rational function.

3. Explain how to decide whether a linear factor of the denominator of a rational function is related to a vertical asymptote of the graph of the function or to a hole in the graph of the function.

4. Explain how to use the asymptotes of the graph of $g(x) = \frac{x-5}{x-3}$ to sketch the graph of the function.

Guided Skills Practice

APPLICATION

5. CHEMISTRY Refer to the salt-concentration problem at the beginning of the lesson. If Dane begins with 90 milliliters of a 15% saline solution and adds x milliliters of distilled water, what function represents the salt concentration of the new solution? What is the concentration of the solution if 150 milliliters of distilled water is added? *(EXAMPLE 1)*

6. Find the domain of $h(x) = \frac{2x^2 - 5}{x^2 - 7x + 12}$. *(EXAMPLE 2)*

Identify all asymptotes and holes in the graph of each rational function.
(EXAMPLES 3, 4, AND 6)

7. $r(x) = \frac{3x - 1}{4x^2 - 9}$　　　**8.** $R(x) = \frac{2x^2 - 1}{x^2 - 9}$　　　**9.** $f(x) = \frac{(x-3)^2}{x^2 - 5x + 6}$

10. Graph $f(x) = \frac{2x + 1}{x - 3}$, showing all asymptotes. *(EXAMPLE 5)*

Practice and Apply

Determine whether each function is a rational function. If so, find the domain. If the function is not rational, state why not.

11. $f(x) = \frac{x}{2x - 7}$　　　**12.** $g(x) = \frac{x + 2}{2x}$　　　**13.** $h(x) = \frac{x^{-\frac{1}{2}}}{x^2}$

14. $f(x) = \frac{x}{(2x - 7)(x + 3)}$　　**15.** $g(x) = \frac{5^x}{x^5}$　　**16.** $h(x) = \frac{|x^2 - 4|}{|x + 2|}$

Identify all asymptotes and holes in the graph of each rational function.

17. $f(x) = \frac{3x + 5}{x - 2}$　　　**18.** $g(x) = \frac{x + 2}{2x^2}$　　　**19.** $d(x) = \frac{x^2 - 4}{x^2 - 4x + 4}$

20. $g(x) = \frac{(x + 2)^2}{x^2 + 5x + 6}$　　**21.** $r(x) = \frac{x^2 - 16}{4 - 5x + x^2}$　　**22.** $b(x) = \frac{x^2 - 2x + 1}{x^2 + x - 2}$

Find the domain of each rational function. Identify all asymptotes and holes in the graph of each rational function. Then graph.

23. $h(x) = \dfrac{2x - 2}{2x + 2}$

24. $r(x) = \dfrac{2x}{2x(x - 5)}$

25. $w(x) = \dfrac{(3x - 1)(x + 2)}{x + 2}$

26. $a(x) = \dfrac{x + 1}{x^2 + 4x - 21}$

27. $d(x) = \dfrac{3x - 1}{9x^2 - 36}$

28. $d(x) = \dfrac{7x + 8}{x^2 - 10x + 25}$

29. $f(x) = \dfrac{7x + 1}{5x^2 + 3}$

30. $r(x) = \dfrac{x^2 - 4}{x^2 + 4}$

31. $m(x) = \dfrac{x(x^2 - 4)}{x^2 - 7x + 6}$

32. $t(x) = \dfrac{x^2 - 4x}{x^3 - x^2 - 20x}$

33. $g(x) = \dfrac{5x^2 - 3x}{x^3 - 8x^2 + 16x}$

34. $t(x) = \dfrac{2x + 1}{x^3 - 27}$

Write a rational function with the given asymptotes and holes.

35. $x = 2$ and $y = 3$

36. $x = -2$ and $y = 0$

37. $x = \pm 1$, $y = 1.5$, hole when $x = 0$

38. $x = 1$, $y = 3$, hole when $x = 2$

39. holes when $x = 0$ and $x = 2$

40. holes when $x = 0$, $x = 2$, and $x = 3$

CHALLENGE

41. Let $f(x) = \dfrac{1}{x^2 - 3x + c}$. Find c such that the graph of f has the given number of vertical asymptotes. Justify your responses.

    a. none   **b.** one   **c.** two

CONNECTIONS

42. GEOMETRY Refer to the rectangle at right.
    a. Write a rational function, R, to represent the ratio of the perimeter, P, to the area, A.
    b. For what values of x is P defined? is A defined? is R defined?

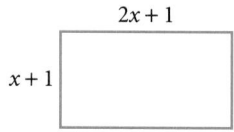

43. GEOMETRY Refer to the circle at right.
    a. Write a rational function, R, to represent the ratio of the circumference, C, to the area, A.
    b. For what values of x is C defined? is A defined? is R defined?

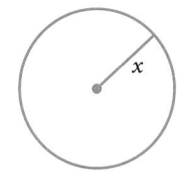

APPLICATIONS

44. CHEMISTRY Leon begins with 72 milliliters of an 8% saline solution. He adds x milliliters of distilled water to the saline solution.
    a. What function represents salt concentration, C, of the new solution?
    b. What is the approximate concentration if 720 milliliters of distilled water is added?

45. ECONOMICS Max owns a small florist shop. His fixed costs are $250 per week, and his average variable costs are $11.45 per arrangement.
    a. Write a function, T, that represents Max's total costs for one week if he makes x floral arrangements that week.
    b. Write a function in terms of T and x for the cost, C, per floral arrangement during that week.

46. PHYSICS An object weighing w_0 kilograms on Earth is h kilometers above the surface of the Earth. Then the function for the object's weight at that altitude is $w(h) = w_0 \left(\dfrac{6400}{6400 + h} \right)^2$.

  a. Explain why w is a rational function of h.

  b. Use a table to find w for h-values of 10, 20, and 100.

  c. At about what altitude will an object weigh half of what it weighs on Earth?

 Look Back

Solve. *(LESSON 1.8)*

47. $|5x - 6| > 2$ **48.** $|x + 5| \geq 7$ **49.** $\left| \dfrac{3}{2} - \dfrac{5}{2}x \right| \leq \dfrac{7}{2}$ **50.** $\left| \dfrac{3}{2} - \dfrac{5}{2}x \right| \leq -\dfrac{7}{2}$

Write each expression in standard form, $ax^2 + bx + c$. *(LESSON 5.1)*

51. $-12x(3x - 2)$ **52.** $(3x - 1)(6x - 7)$ **53.** $(4 - 5x)(x - 9)$

54. $(x - 5)(2x + 3)$ **55.** $(3x - 4)(3x + 4)$ **56.** $-4(x - 3)^2$

Factor each expression. *(LESSON 5.3)*

57. $3x^2 - 6x$ **58.** $1 - 25y^2$ **59.** $9x^2 - 49$

60. $t^2 - 5t - 24$ **61.** $x^2 + 12x + 36$ **62.** $x^2 - 16x + 64$

Look Beyond

Simplify.

63. $\dfrac{9}{3}$ **64.** $\dfrac{x^2}{x}$ **65.** $\dfrac{x^2 + 4x + 4}{x + 2}$

PORTFOLIO ACTIVITY

In this activity you will use rational functions to show that if a rectangle and a square have the same ratio of area to perimeter, then the side length of the square is the harmonic mean of the width and length of the rectangle.

Refer to the rectangle and square shown at left.

1. Write a rational function, R, to represent the ratio of the area, A, of the rectangle to its perimeter, P.

2. Find a value of x such that the ratio of the area to the perimeter is 2.

3. Use this value to find the length and width of the rectangle.

4. Write a rational function, S, to represent the ratio of the area, A, of the square to its perimeter, P.

5. Find a value of x such that the ratio of the area to the perimeter is 2.

6. Use this value to find the side length of the square.

7. Show that the side length of the square is the harmonic mean of the length and width of the rectangle.

Multiplying and Dividing Rational Expressions

8.3

Why Multiplying and dividing rational expressions are sometimes used to solve real-world problems, such as analyzing the revenue and cost for a fund-raising activity.

Objectives

- Multiply and divide rational expressions.

- Simplify rational expressions, including complex fractions.

APPLICATION
FUND-RAISING

To analyze the revenue and costs from the sale of school-spirit ribbons, members of the Jamesville High School Home Economics Club used the revenue-to-cost ratio below.

$$\frac{\text{revenue from the sale of each ribbon}}{\text{cost of making each ribbon}}$$

They represented the number of ribbons produced and sold by x and the total production cost in dollars by $0.8x + 25$. If the revenue for each ribbon was \$3, for how many ribbons was the revenue-to-cost ratio 1.5 or greater? Finding the answer to this question involves writing and simplifying a rational expression. *You will answer this question in Example 6.*

Simplifying Rational Expressions

To *simplify* a rational expression, divide the numerator and the denominator by a common factor. The expression is simplified when you can no longer divide the numerator and denominator by a common factor other than 1.

E X A M P L E ❶ Simplify $\dfrac{x^2 + 5x - 6}{x^2 - 36}$.

SOLUTION

$$\frac{x^2 + 5x - 6}{x^2 - 36} = \frac{(x + 6)(x - 1)}{(x - 6)(x + 6)} \qquad \textit{Factor the numerator and denominator.}$$

$$= \frac{\cancel{(x + 6)}(x - 1)}{(x - 6)\cancel{(x + 6)}} \qquad \textit{Divide out the common factor.}$$

$$= \frac{x - 1}{x - 6}$$

Note that 6 and −6 are excluded values of x in the original expression.

TRY THIS Simplify $\dfrac{b^2 - 49}{b^2 - 8b + 7}$.

Multiplying Rational Expressions

Multiplying rational expressions is similar to multiplying rational numbers.

Rational Numbers

$$\frac{15}{4} \cdot \frac{14}{9} = \frac{3 \cdot 5}{4} \cdot \frac{2 \cdot 7}{9} = \frac{35}{6}$$

Rational Expressions

$$\frac{15}{x^2} \cdot \frac{4x^4}{21} = \frac{3 \cdot 5}{x^2} \cdot \frac{4 \cdot x^4}{3 \cdot 7} = \frac{20x^2}{7}$$

E X A M P L E 2 Simplify $\dfrac{3}{4x^2} \cdot \dfrac{4x^3}{21} \cdot \dfrac{14}{4x^5}$.

● **SOLUTION**

$$\frac{3}{4x^2} \cdot \frac{4x^3}{21} \cdot \frac{14}{4x^5} = \frac{3 \cdot 4 \cdot 2 \cdot 7}{4 \cdot 3 \cdot 7 \cdot 2 \cdot 2} \cdot \frac{x^3}{x^7} = \frac{1}{2x^4}$$

TRY THIS Simplify $\dfrac{28}{4a^3} \cdot \dfrac{4a^5}{21} \cdot \dfrac{3}{49a^4}$.

To multiply one rational expression by another, multiply as with fractions.

$$\frac{a}{b} \cdot \frac{c}{d} = \frac{ac}{bd}, \text{ where } b \neq 0 \text{ and } d \neq 0$$

You can simplify the product by dividing out the common factors in the numerator and denominator before or after multiplying.

E X A M P L E 3 Simplify $\dfrac{x+1}{x^2 + 2x - 3} \cdot \dfrac{x^2 + x - 6}{x^2 - 2x - 3}$.

● **SOLUTION**

$$\frac{x+1}{x^2 + 2x - 3} \cdot \frac{x^2 + x - 6}{x^2 - 2x - 3} = \frac{x+1}{(x+3)(x-1)} \cdot \frac{(x+3)(x-2)}{(x-3)(x+1)}$$

$$= \frac{x-2}{(x-1)(x-3)}, \quad \text{or} \quad \frac{x-2}{x^2 - 4x + 3}$$

TRY THIS Simplify $\dfrac{x^2 - 25}{x^2 - 5x + 6} \cdot \dfrac{x^2 - 4}{x^2 + 2x - 15}$.

Dividing Rational Expressions

Dividing one rational expression by another is similar to dividing one rational number by another.

Rational Numbers

$$\frac{6}{8} \div \frac{12}{32} = \frac{6}{8} \cdot \frac{32}{12}$$

> *Multiply by the reciprocal of $\frac{12}{32}$.*

$$= \frac{6}{8} \cdot \frac{32}{12}$$

$$= \frac{4}{2}, \text{ or } 2$$

Rational Expressions

$$\frac{6}{x^3} \div \frac{12}{x^5} = \frac{6}{x^3} \cdot \frac{x^5}{12}$$

> *Multiply by the reciprocal of $\frac{12}{x^5}$.*

$$= \frac{6}{x^3} \cdot \frac{x^5}{12}$$

$$= \frac{x^2}{2}, \text{ or } \frac{1}{2}x^2$$

To divide one rational expression by another, multiply by the reciprocal of the divisor.

$$\frac{a}{b} \div \frac{c}{d} = \frac{a}{b} \cdot \frac{d}{c} = \frac{ad}{bc}, \text{ where } b \neq 0, c \neq 0, \text{ and } d \neq 0$$

Simplify by dividing out common factors in the numerator and denominator.

E X A M P L E ④ Simplify $\frac{x-4}{(x-2)^2} \div \frac{x^2-3x-4}{x^2-4}$.

● **SOLUTION**

$$\frac{x-4}{(x-2)^2} \div \frac{x^2-3x-4}{x^2-4} = \frac{x-4}{(x-2)^2} \cdot \frac{x^2-4}{x^2-3x-4} \qquad \textit{Multiply by the reciprocal.}$$

$$= \frac{\overset{1}{\cancel{x-4}}}{(x-2)\cancel{(x-2)}} \cdot \frac{\cancel{(x-2)}(x+2)}{\cancel{(x-4)}(x+1)} \qquad \textit{Divide out common factors.}$$

$$= \frac{x+2}{(x-2)(x+1)}, \quad \text{or} \quad \frac{x+2}{x^2-x-2}$$

TRY THIS   Simplify $\frac{(x+3)^2}{x-5} \div \frac{x^2-9}{x^2-8x+15}$.

PROBLEM SOLVING   You can **use a graph** to identify polynomials in a rational expression that cannot be factored with real numbers. For example, to determine whether $x^2 - x + 1$ in the rational expression $\frac{x-4}{x-1} \cdot \frac{x^2-x+1}{x^2}$ can be factored with real numbers, look for x-intercepts in the graph of $y = x^2 - x + 1$.

The graph of $y = x^2 - x + 1$ has no x-intercepts, so $y = x^2 - x + 1$ has no real zeros and $x^2 - x + 1$ cannot be factored with real numbers. Thus, the rational expression $\frac{x-4}{x-1} \cdot \frac{x^2-x+1}{x^2}$ cannot be simplified further.

Complex Fractions

A **complex fraction** is a quotient that contains one or more fractions in the numerator, the denominator, or both.

E X A M P L E ⑤ Simplify the complex fraction $\dfrac{\dfrac{4a^2-1}{a^2-4}}{\dfrac{2a-1}{a+2}}$.

● **SOLUTION**

$$\frac{\dfrac{4a^2-1}{a^2-4}}{\dfrac{2a-1}{a+2}} = \frac{4a^2-1}{a^2-4} \cdot \frac{a+2}{2a-1} \qquad \textit{Multiply by the reciprocal.}$$

$$= \frac{(2a-1)(2a+1)}{(a-2)(a+2)} \cdot \frac{a+2}{2a-1} \qquad \textit{Factor.}$$

$$= \frac{\cancel{(2a-1)}(2a+1)\cancel{(a+2)}}{(a-2)\cancel{(a+2)}\cancel{(2a-1)}} \qquad \textit{Divide out common factors.}$$

$$= \frac{2a+1}{a-2}$$

TRY THIS Simplify $\dfrac{\dfrac{(x+2)^2}{x-3}}{\dfrac{x^2-4}{(x-3)^2}}$.

CRITICAL THINKING Use mental math to simplify $\dfrac{\dfrac{x+y}{x-y}}{\dfrac{y+x}{y-x}}$.

E X A M P L E **6** Refer to the revenue-to-cost ratio given at the beginning of the lesson.

APPLICATION
ECONOMICS

For how many ribbons was the revenue-to-cost ratio 1.5 or greater?

SOLUTION

$$\dfrac{\text{revenue from the sale of each ribbon}}{\text{cost of making each ribbon}} = \dfrac{3}{\dfrac{0.8x+25}{x}}$$

Simplify the complex fraction.

$$\dfrac{3}{\dfrac{0.8x+25}{x}} = 3 \cdot \dfrac{x}{0.8x+25} = \dfrac{3x}{0.8x+25}$$

TECHNOLOGY
GRAPHICS CALCULATOR

Keystroke Guide, page 555

Enter $y = \dfrac{3x}{0.8x+25}$ into a graphics calculator, and examine a table of values.

Since x represents the number of ribbons, use an increment of 1.

X	Y1
18	1.3706
19	1.4179
20	1.4634
21	1.5072
22	1.5493
23	1.5899
24	1.629

Y1=1.50717703349

From the table, you can see that the revenue-to-cost ratio, y, is greater than 1.5 when 21 or more ribbons, x, were produced and sold.

Activity
Exploring Excluded Values in Quotients

TECHNOLOGY
GRAPHICS CALCULATOR

Keystroke Guide, page 555

You will need: a graphics calculator

1. Let $f(x) = \dfrac{\dfrac{x-3}{x+2}}{\dfrac{x-2}{x+2}}$. When the complex fraction that defines f is simplified, it becomes $\dfrac{x-3}{x-2}$. Let $g(x) = \dfrac{x-3}{x-2}$. Graph f and g on the same screen. What observations can you make about these graphs?

PROBLEM SOLVING

2. **Make a table** to evaluate f and g for x-values of $-3, -2, -1, 0, 1, 2,$ and 3. How do the entries in the table compare?

3. Repeat Steps 1 and 2 for the functions $f(x) = \dfrac{\dfrac{x^2-4}{x-1}}{\dfrac{x^2-9}{x-1}}$ and $g(x) = \dfrac{x^2-4}{x^2-9}$.

CHECKPOINT ✔ 4. Let $f(x) = \dfrac{\dfrac{P}{Q}}{\dfrac{R}{Q}}$ and $g(x) = \dfrac{P}{R}$, where $P, Q,$ and R are polynomials. Explain how to find the excluded values of f and why you should not try to find those values by examining g.

Exercises

Communicate

1. In what ways is the multiplication of two rational expressions similar to the multiplication of two rational numbers?

2. In what ways is the division of two rational expressions similar to the division of two rational numbers?

3. Explain how to simplify a complex fraction such as $\dfrac{\dfrac{x^2}{x^2-1}}{\dfrac{x}{x^2+2x-3}}$. Compare the excluded values of x in the complex fraction and in its simplified form.

Guided Skills Practice

Simplify each rational expression. *(EXAMPLES 1 AND 2)*

4. $\dfrac{x^2-25}{x^2-10x+25}$

5. $\dfrac{4x^2}{5} \cdot \dfrac{30}{x^4} \cdot \dfrac{20x^3}{60}$

Simplify each rational expression. *(EXAMPLES 3 AND 4)*

6. $\dfrac{x^2+8x+12}{x^2+2x-15} \cdot \dfrac{x^2+8x+15}{x^2+9x+18}$

7. $\dfrac{x^2-2x+1}{x^2+6x+8} \div \dfrac{x^2-1}{x^2+3x+2}$

8. Simplify the complex fraction $\dfrac{\dfrac{2x-6}{x^2+9x+20}}{\dfrac{x^2-9}{x^2+5x+4}}$. *(EXAMPLES 5 AND 6)*

Practice and Apply

internet connect

Homework Help Online

Go To: go.hrw.com
Keyword:
MB1 Homework Help
for Exercises 9–43

Simplify each rational expression.

9. $\dfrac{4x^2+8x+4}{x+1}$

10. $\dfrac{x^2-6x+9}{x^2-9}$

11. $\dfrac{15}{x^2} \cdot \dfrac{x^5}{12} \cdot \dfrac{4}{x}$

12. $\dfrac{36x}{9x^2} \cdot \dfrac{12x^7}{2x} \cdot \dfrac{5}{x^2}$

13. $\dfrac{x^2-10x+9}{x^2+2x-3}$

14. $\dfrac{-x^2-x+6}{x^2-5x+6}$

15. $\dfrac{x}{9x^8} \cdot \dfrac{x^7}{2x} \cdot \dfrac{45}{x^4}$

16. $\dfrac{-5}{x^3} \cdot \dfrac{-x^5}{3} \cdot \dfrac{-4}{x} \cdot \dfrac{20}{x^3}$

17. $\dfrac{x^2-4x-5}{x^2-3x+2} \cdot \dfrac{x^2-4}{x^2-3x-10}$

18. $\dfrac{x^2-9}{x^2-4x+4} \cdot \dfrac{x^2-4}{x^2-x-6}$

19. $\dfrac{2x^2-2x}{x^2-9} \div \dfrac{x^2+x-2}{x^2+2x-3}$

20. $\dfrac{4x^2+20x}{9+6x+x^2} \div \dfrac{x+5}{x^2-9}$

21. $\dfrac{x^4+2x^3+x^2}{x^2+x-6} \cdot \dfrac{x^2-x-2}{x^4-x^2}$

22. $\dfrac{x^5-4x^3}{x^2-x-2} \cdot \dfrac{x^2-1}{x^5-x^4-2x^3}$

23. $\dfrac{4x^3-9x}{2x-7} \div \dfrac{3x^3+2x^2}{4x^2-14x}$

24. $\dfrac{x^4-4x^2}{x^2-9} \div \dfrac{4x^2-4x^3+x^4}{x^2-6x+9}$

25. $\dfrac{ax-bx+ay-by}{ax+bx+ay+by}$

26. $\dfrac{x^2-y^2-4x+4y}{x^2-y^2+4x-4y}$

27. $\dfrac{x^2}{4} \cdot \left(\dfrac{xy}{6}\right)^{-1} \cdot \dfrac{2y^2}{x}$

28. $2rs \div \dfrac{2r^2}{s} \div \dfrac{2s^2}{r}$

Simplify each expression.

29. $\dfrac{\dfrac{(x+2)^2}{(x+3)^2}}{\dfrac{x+3}{x+2}}$

30. $\dfrac{\dfrac{x^2-4}{x^2-9}}{\dfrac{(x-2)^2}{(x-3)^2}}$

31. $\dfrac{\dfrac{x^2-9x+14}{x^2-6x+5}}{\dfrac{x^2-8x+7}{x^2-7x+10}}$

32. $\dfrac{\dfrac{x^2+4x+3}{x^2+6x+8}}{\dfrac{x^2+9x+18}{x^2+7x+10}}$

33. $\dfrac{x+2}{x+5} \cdot \dfrac{\dfrac{x^2}{x+2}}{\dfrac{x+1}{x+5}}$

34. $\dfrac{\dfrac{1}{x+3}}{\dfrac{x^2}{x-7}} \cdot \dfrac{x}{x-7}$

35. $\dfrac{2x+3}{x-1} \div \dfrac{\dfrac{x}{x-1}}{\dfrac{3x}{2x+3}}$

36. $\dfrac{x}{x^2-1} \div \dfrac{\dfrac{x+1}{x-1}}{\dfrac{x}{x+1}}$

37. $\dfrac{\dfrac{x+3}{x-1}}{x(x-1)^{-1}}$

38. $\dfrac{\dfrac{2y+6}{y-7}}{(y+2)(y+3)^{-1}}$

39. $\dfrac{\dfrac{(x+y)^2}{(x+y)^3}}{\dfrac{x+y}{x^2+2xy+y^2}}$

40. $\dfrac{\dfrac{x+2y}{2x^2+3xy+y^2}}{\dfrac{2x^2+5xy+2y^2}{x+y}}$

41. $\dfrac{1-7x^{-1}-18x^{-2}}{1-4x^{-2}}$

42. $\dfrac{1+12x^{-1}+27x^{-2}}{x^{-1}+9x^{-2}}$

43. $\dfrac{(x+y)y^{-1}-2x(x+y)^{-1}}{(x-y)y^{-1}+2x(x-y)^{-1}}$

CHALLENGE

44. Find the rational expression R whose numerator and denominator have degree 2 and leading coefficients of 1 such that $\dfrac{x^2+3x-10}{x^2-8x+15} \cdot R = \dfrac{x-2}{x-3}$.

CONNECTION

45. GEOMETRY An open-top box is to be made from a sheet of cardboard that is 20 inches by 16 inches. Squares with sides of x inches are to be cut on one side and creased on another to form tabs. When the sides are folded up, these tabs are glued to the adjacent sides to provide reinforcement.

a. Show that $x(20-2x)(16-2x)$ represents the volume of the box.

b. Show that $320-4x^2$ represents the surface area of the bottom and sides of the inside of the box.

c. Write and simplify an expression for the ratio of the volume of the box to the inside surface area of the box.

d. How does the ratio from part **c** change as x increases?

APPLICATION

46. ECONOMICS It costs Emilio and Maria Vianco $1200 to operate their sandwich shop for one month. The average cost of preparing one sandwich is $1.69.

a. Using the menu shown, find the average revenue per sandwich.

b. Let x represent the number of sandwiches sold in one month. Write a function for the total cost, C, of operating the business for one month by using the average cost of preparing one sandwich.

c. Write a function for the ratio, R, of average revenue per sandwich to the average cost per sandwich.

47. PHYSICS The diagram below illustrates an ambulance traveling a definite distance in a specific period of time. The average acceleration, *a*, is defined as the change in velocity over the corresponding change in time.

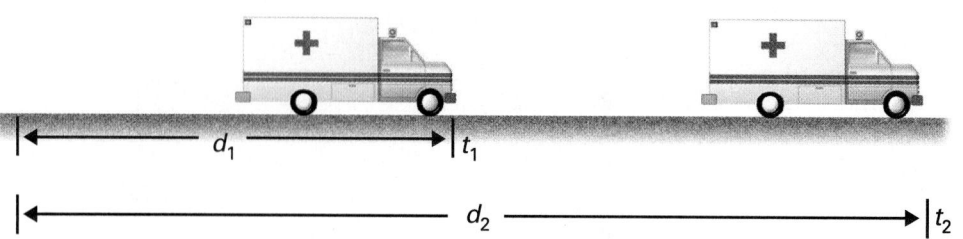

a. Simplify the expression at right that defines *a*.
b. If the distance, *d*, is measured in feet and the time, *t*, is measured in seconds, in what units is acceleration measured?

$$a = \dfrac{\dfrac{d_2}{t_2} - \dfrac{d_1}{t_1}}{t_2 - t_1}$$

 Look Back

Write an equation in slope-intercept form for the line that contains the given point and is perpendicular to the given line. *(LESSON 1.3)*

48. $(8, -4), y = -6x - 1$ **49.** $(3, 5), y = \frac{1}{5}x - 11$

Graph each piecewise function. *(LESSON 2.6)*

50. $f(x) = \begin{cases} x - 5 & \text{if } -1 < x \le 4 \\ 9 - 2x & \text{if } 4 < x \le 5 \end{cases}$
51. $g(x) = \begin{cases} -4 & \text{if } x < 0 \\ 2x - 4 & \text{if } 0 \le x \le 5 \\ -\frac{2}{5}x + 8 & \text{if } x > 5 \end{cases}$

Factor each expression. *(LESSON 5.3)*

52. $8x^2 - 4x$ **53.** $12x^2 - 3x + 6$ **54.** $12 - 4a - 22a^2$

Simplify each expression. Write your answer in the standard form for a complex number. *(LESSON 5.6)*

55. $\dfrac{2+i}{3+2i}$ **56.** $\dfrac{4-i}{6-3i}$ **57.** $\dfrac{3-2i}{5+i}$

Write each product as a polynomial expression in standard form. *(LESSON 7.3)*

58. $x^2(x^3 - x^2 - 6x + 2)$ **59.** $(x - 2)(3x^3 - 6x - x^2)$ **60.** $(x^2 + 1)(2x^3 - 9)$

Factor each polynomial expression. *(LESSON 7.3)*

61. $x^3 - 1$ **62.** $125x^3 + 27$ **63.** $x^3 - 6x^2 - 8x$

 Look Beyond

Simplify.

64. $\dfrac{5}{8} + \dfrac{1}{8}$ **65.** $\dfrac{3}{x} + \dfrac{1}{x}$ **66.** $\dfrac{3}{2x} + \dfrac{1}{x}$ **67.** $\dfrac{3}{2x} + \dfrac{1}{3x}$

Adding and Subtracting Rational Expressions

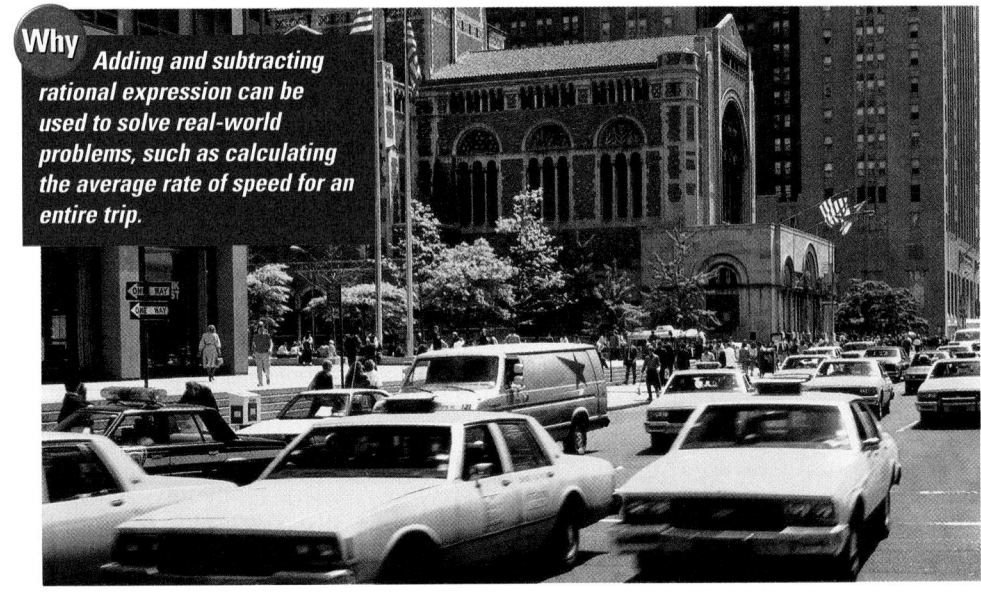

Why Adding and subtracting rational expression can be used to solve real-world problems, such as calculating the average rate of speed for an entire trip.

Objective

● Add and subtract rational expressions.

A cab driver drove from the airport to a passenger's home at an average speed of 55 miles per hour. He returned to the airport along the same highway at an average speed of 45 miles per hour. What was the cab driver's average speed over the entire trip? The answer is not the average of 45 and 55. To answer this question, you need to add two rational expressions. *You will answer this question in Example 5.*

Adding two rational expressions with the same denominator is similar to adding two rational numbers with the same denominator.

Rational Numbers

$$\frac{1}{7} + \frac{3}{7} = \frac{1+3}{7} = \frac{4}{7}$$

Common denominator

Rational Expressions

$$\frac{3}{x^2} + \frac{5}{x^2} = \frac{3+5}{x^2} = \frac{8}{x^2}$$

Common denominator

EXAMPLE ❶ Simplify.

a. $\dfrac{2x}{x+3} + \dfrac{5}{x+3}$

b. $\dfrac{x^2}{x-3} - \dfrac{9}{x-3}$

● **SOLUTION**

a. $\dfrac{2x}{x+3} + \dfrac{5}{x+3} = \dfrac{2x+5}{x+3}$

b. $\dfrac{x^2}{x-3} - \dfrac{9}{x-3} = \dfrac{x^2-9}{x-3}$

$$= \frac{(x+3)(x-3)^1}{x-3_1}$$

$$= x+3$$

Note that 3 is an excluded value of x in the original expression.

TRY THIS Simplify.

a. $\dfrac{3x-1}{2x-1} + \dfrac{5+2x}{2x-1}$

b. $\dfrac{2x}{x-5} - \dfrac{10}{x-5}$

To add two rational expressions with unlike denominators, you first need to find common denominators. The **least common denominator (LCD)** of two rational expressions is the *least common multiple* of the denominators. The **least common multiple (LCM)** of two polynomials is the polynomial of lowest degree that is divisible by each polynomial.

Finding the LCM for two rational expressions is similar to finding the LCM for two rational numbers. Compare the procedures for rational numbers and for rational expressions shown below.

Rational Numbers

$$\frac{7}{300} + \frac{1}{90} = \frac{7}{300}\left(\frac{3}{3}\right) + \frac{1}{90}\left(\frac{10}{10}\right)$$

$$= \frac{21 + 10}{900}$$

Least common denominator

$$= \frac{31}{900}$$

Rational Expressions

$$\frac{7}{3x^2} + \frac{1}{9x} = \frac{7}{3x^2}\left(\frac{3}{3}\right) + \frac{1}{9x}\left(\frac{x}{x}\right)$$

$$= \frac{21 + x}{9x^2}$$

Least common denominator

Adding and Subtracting Rational Expressions

To add or subtract two rational expressions, find a common denominator, rewrite each expression by using the common denominator, and then add or subtract. Simplify the resulting rational expression.

E X A M P L E ❷ Simplify $\dfrac{x}{x - 2} + \dfrac{-8}{x^2 - 4}$.

● **SOLUTION**

$$\frac{x}{x - 2} + \frac{-8}{x^2 - 4} = \frac{x}{x - 2} + \frac{-8}{(x - 2)(x + 2)}$$

$$= \frac{x}{x - 2}\left(\frac{x + 2}{x + 2}\right) + \frac{-8}{(x - 2)(x + 2)} \qquad \text{\textit{The LCD is } } (x - 2)(x + 2).$$

$$= \frac{x(x + 2) - 8}{(x - 2)(x + 2)} \qquad \text{\textit{Add the fractions.}}$$

$$= \frac{x^2 + 2x - 8}{(x - 2)(x + 2)} \qquad \text{\textit{Write the numerator in standard form.}}$$

$$= \frac{(x + 4)(x - 2)}{(x - 2)(x + 2)} \qquad \text{\textit{Factor the numerator.}}$$

$$= \frac{(x + 4)(x - 2)^{\,1}}{(x - 2)(x + 2)} \qquad \text{\textit{Divide out the common factors.}}$$

$$= \frac{x + 4}{x + 2} \qquad \boxed{\text{\textit{Note that 2 and } -2 \textit{ are excluded values of x in the original expression.}}}$$

TRY THIS Simplify $\dfrac{x}{x + 5} + \dfrac{-50}{x^2 - 25}$.

CHECKPOINT ✔ Explain how factoring a polynomial can help you to add two rational expressions. Illustrate your response by simplifying $\dfrac{x}{x - 3} + \dfrac{5}{x^2 - 6x + 9}$.

3 Simplify $\dfrac{6x}{3x-1} - \dfrac{4x}{2x+5}$.

● **SOLUTION**

$\dfrac{6x}{3x-1} - \dfrac{4x}{2x+5} = \dfrac{6x}{3x-1}\left(\dfrac{2x+5}{2x+5}\right) - \dfrac{4x}{2x+5}\left(\dfrac{3x-1}{3x-1}\right)$ *The LCD is $(3x-1)(2x+5)$.*

$= \dfrac{6x(2x+5) - 4x(3x-1)}{(3x-1)(2x+5)}$ *Subtract.*

$= \dfrac{12x^2 + 30x - 12x^2 + 4x}{(3x-1)(2x+5)}$

$= \dfrac{34x}{(3x-1)(2x+5)},$ or $\dfrac{34x}{6x^2 + 13x - 5}$

CHECK

Graph $y = \dfrac{6x}{3x-1} - \dfrac{4x}{2x+5}$ and $y = \dfrac{34x}{6x^2 + 13x - 5}$

together on the same screen to see if the graphs are the same.

You can also use a table of values to verify that the corresponding y-values are the same.

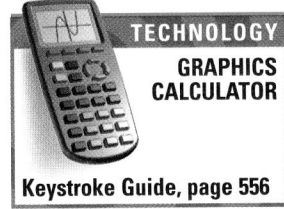

TECHNOLOGY

GRAPHICS CALCULATOR

Keystroke Guide, page 556

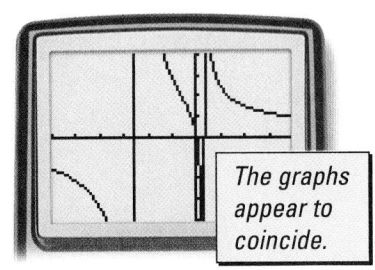

The graphs appear to coincide.

CHECKPOINT ✔ Identify the excluded values of x for the original expression and for the simplified expression in Example 3. Are they the same or different? Explain.

TRY THIS   Simplify $\dfrac{6}{x^2 - 2x} - \dfrac{1}{x^2 - 4}$.

Sometimes you need to rewrite complex fractions as rational expressions in order to add or subtract them, as shown in Example 4.

E X A M P L E **4** Simplify $\dfrac{1}{1+\dfrac{1}{a}} + \dfrac{1}{1-\dfrac{1}{a}}$.

● **SOLUTION**

$\dfrac{1}{1+\dfrac{1}{a}} + \dfrac{1}{1-\dfrac{1}{a}} = \dfrac{1}{\dfrac{a+1}{a}} + \dfrac{1}{\dfrac{a-1}{a}}$ *Add or subtract within the denominators.*

$= 1 \cdot \dfrac{a}{a+1} + 1 \cdot \dfrac{a}{a-1}$ *Multiply by the reciprocals.*

$= \dfrac{a}{a+1} + \dfrac{a}{a-1}$

$= \dfrac{a}{a+1}\left(\dfrac{a-1}{a-1}\right) + \dfrac{a}{a-1}\left(\dfrac{a+1}{a+1}\right)$ *The LCD is $(a+1)(a-1)$.*

$= \dfrac{a^2 - a + a^2 + a}{(a+1)(a-1)}$ *Multiply, and then add.*

$= \dfrac{2a^2}{a^2 - 1}$

TRY THIS   Simplify $\dfrac{a}{a-\dfrac{1}{a}} - \dfrac{a}{a+\dfrac{1}{a}}$.

EXAMPLE **5** Refer to the cab driver's round trip described at the beginning of the lesson.

What is the cab driver's average speed for the entire trip?

● **SOLUTION**

Let d represent the length of the trip one way, let t_1 represent the cab driver's travel time to the passenger's home, and let t_2 represent his travel time back to the airport.

$$d = r_1 t_1 \qquad \text{and} \qquad d = r_2 t_2$$

$$t_1 = \frac{d}{r_1} = \frac{d}{55} \qquad\qquad t_2 = \frac{d}{r_2} = \frac{d}{45}$$

$$\text{average speed} = \frac{\text{total distance}}{\text{total time}}$$

$$= \frac{d + d}{t_1 + t_2}$$

$$= \frac{d + d}{\frac{d}{55} + \frac{d}{45}} \qquad \textit{Substitute } \frac{d}{55} \textit{ for } t_1 \textit{ and } \frac{d}{45} \textit{ for } t_2.$$

$$= \frac{2d}{\frac{9d + 11d}{495}} \qquad \textit{The LCD for } \frac{d}{55} \textit{ and } \frac{d}{45} \textit{ is 495.}$$

$$= \frac{2d}{\frac{20d}{495}}$$

$$= 2d \times \frac{495}{20d} \qquad \textit{Multiply by the reciprocal.}$$

$$= 49.5$$

Thus, the cab driver's average speed was 49.5 miles per hour. The average speed was less than the average of 45 and 55 because he spent more time driving at 45 miles per hour than at 55 miles per hour.

CRITICAL THINKING

Suppose that the cab driver travels to the passenger's home at a miles per hour and returns along the same route at b miles per hour. Show that his average speed for the entire trip is not simply $\frac{a+b}{2}$.

Exercises

● *Communicate*

1. Explain how to find the least common denominator in order to add $\frac{x+5}{x^2-7x+6} + \frac{x-1}{x^2-36}$.

2. Explain how to use a graph to check your answer when you add two rational expressions.

3. Choose the two expressions below that are equivalent and explain why they are equivalent.

a. $\frac{3+7}{x^2+4}$ **b.** $\frac{10}{x^2} + \frac{10}{4}$ **c.** $\frac{3}{x^2} + \frac{7}{4}$ **d.** $\frac{3}{x^2+4} + \frac{7}{x^2+4}$

Simplify. *(EXAMPLES 1 AND 2)*

4. $\dfrac{3x}{x-1} + \dfrac{2}{x-1}$ **5.** $\dfrac{3x+5}{x+2} - \dfrac{x+1}{x+2}$ **6.** $\dfrac{12}{x^2-1} + \dfrac{4}{x+1}$

Simplify. *(EXAMPLES 3 AND 4)*

7. $\dfrac{x+1}{2x-1} - \dfrac{2x+1}{x-1}$ **8.** $\dfrac{1}{1-\frac{1}{t}}$

APPLICATION

9. TRAVEL Refer to the cab driver's round trip described at the beginning of the lesson. What is the average speed for the entire trip if he drives to the passenger's home at 52 miles per hour and returns to the airport along the same route at 38 miles per hour? *(EXAMPLE 5)*

✔ internet connect

Homework Help Online

Go To: **go.hrw.com**
Keyword:
MB1 Homework Help
for Exercises 13–15, 17-18, 21, 24, 34–41

Simplify.

10. $\dfrac{2x-3}{x+1} + \dfrac{6x+5}{x+1}$ **11.** $\dfrac{7x-13}{2x-1} + \dfrac{x+9}{2x-1}$ **12.** $\dfrac{r+9}{4} + \dfrac{r-3}{2}$

13. $\dfrac{x+7}{3} - \dfrac{4x+1}{9}$ **14.** $\dfrac{x}{x^2-4} - \dfrac{2}{x-2}$ **15.** $\dfrac{2x}{x+3} - \dfrac{x-3}{x^2+6x+9}$

16. $\dfrac{-4}{x-5} + \dfrac{5}{x+3}$ **17.** $\dfrac{2}{x+2} - \dfrac{6}{x-2}$ **18.** $\dfrac{3}{x-1} - \dfrac{2}{x+1}$

19. $\dfrac{8}{3x-5} + \dfrac{7}{2x+3}$ **20.** $\dfrac{2x+3}{x+3} + \dfrac{x}{x-2}$ **21.** $\dfrac{x+2}{2x-1} - \dfrac{2x}{x-1}$

22. $x^2 + \dfrac{2x}{3x-5}$ **23.** $\dfrac{x+1}{(x-1)^2} + \dfrac{x-2}{x-1}$ **24.** $2x^2 - 1 - \dfrac{x-1}{x+2}$

25. $\dfrac{3}{\frac{2x-1}{x}}$ **26.** $\dfrac{\frac{1}{3x+1}}{2}$ **27.** $\dfrac{\frac{4}{x-1}}{\frac{2}{x-1}} + \dfrac{3}{x-1}$

28. $\dfrac{\frac{4}{x+2}}{\frac{x+2}{3}} - \dfrac{3}{x+2}$ **29.** $\dfrac{\frac{x+2}{x+5}}{\frac{x-1}{x+5}} + \dfrac{1}{x+1}$ **30.** $\dfrac{\frac{2x+10}{x-1}}{\frac{x+5}{x^2-1}} - \dfrac{4}{x+1}$

31. $\dfrac{1-xy^{-1}}{x^{-1}-y^{-1}}$ **32.** $\dfrac{x-y}{x^{-1}-y^{-1}}$ **33.** $\dfrac{\frac{1}{a^2}-\frac{1}{b^2}}{a^{-2}+2(ab)^{-1}+b^{-2}}$

Write each expression as a single rational expression in simplest form.

34. $\dfrac{3x}{x-1} + \dfrac{5x+2}{x-1} - \dfrac{10}{x-1}$ **35.** $\dfrac{7x}{x^2-1} - \dfrac{x}{x^2-1} + \dfrac{6}{x^2-1}$

36. $\dfrac{7}{x+7} + \dfrac{-x}{x-7} + \dfrac{2x}{x^2-49}$ **37.** $\dfrac{x}{x-3} - \dfrac{3}{x+4} + \dfrac{7}{x^2+x-12}$

38. $(a-b)^{-1} - (a+b)^{-1}$ **39.** $(a-b)^{-2} - (a+b)^{-2}$

40. $\dfrac{x}{x-y} - \dfrac{x^2+y^2}{x^2-y^2} + \dfrac{y}{x+y}$ **41.** $\dfrac{3r}{2r-s} - \dfrac{2r}{2r+s} + \dfrac{2s^2}{4r^2-s^2}$

CHALLENGE

Find numbers *A*, *B*, *C*, and *D* such that the given rational expression equals the sum of the two simpler rational expressions, as indicated.

42. $\dfrac{3x+2}{x-5} = \dfrac{Ax}{x-5} + \dfrac{D}{x-5}$ **43.** $\dfrac{-x+1}{(x-2)(x-3)} = \dfrac{B}{x-2} + \dfrac{D}{x-3}$

44. $\dfrac{2x^2+5}{x^2+11x+30} = \dfrac{Ax}{x+5} + \dfrac{Cx+D}{x+6}$ **45.** $\dfrac{x^2-7}{x^2+2x-3} = \dfrac{Ax}{x+3} + \dfrac{Cx+D}{x-1}$

46. GEOMETRY In the diagram at right, square A is 1 unit on a side, square B is $\frac{1}{2}$ of a unit on a side, square C is $\frac{1}{4}$ of a unit on a side, and so on.

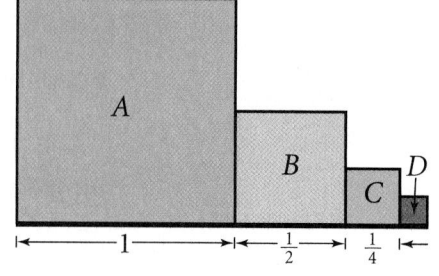

a. Write a sum for the total area of squares A, B, C, and D, using only powers of 2.

b. Rewrite the sum you wrote in part **a** as a single rational number.

c. Suppose that two more squares, E and F, are added to the set of squares, continuing the pattern. Write a single rational number for the total area of squares A through F.

d. Convert your answers from parts **b** and **c** to decimals rounded to the nearest ten-thousandth. What common fraction do the answers appear to be getting closer and closer to?

47. ELECTRICITY The effective resistance, R_T, of parallel resistors in an electric circuit equals the reciprocal of the sum of the reciprocals of the individual resistances.

$$R_T = \frac{1}{\dfrac{1}{R_A} + \dfrac{1}{R_B} + \dfrac{1}{R_C}}$$

Resistance in an electric circuit is measured in ohms.

a. A circuit has three parallel resistors, R_A, R_B, and R_C. Find R_T to the nearest hundredth, given $R_A = 5$ ohms, $R_B = 8$ ohms, and $R_C = 12$ ohms.

b. Write R_T as a rational expression with no fractions in the denominator.

TRAVEL The diagram below shows the parts of a trip that Justine recently took. The distances between A and B, B and C, and C and D are all equal. The speed in each direction is shown in the diagram. Find each average speed listed below to the nearest tenth of a mile per hour.

48. Justine's average speed for a trip from A to C and back to A

49. Justine's average speed for a trip from B to D and back to B

50. Justine's average speed for a trip from A to D and back to A

State the property that is illustrated in each statement. All variables represent real numbers. *(LESSON 2.1)*

51. $-8x(5x + 2) = -40x^2 - 16x$ **52.** $(3 - x)12x = 12x(3 - x)$

Find the discriminant, and determine the number of real solutions. Then solve. *(LESSON 5.6)*

53. $0 = x^2 - 3x + 4$ **54.** $x^2 - 2x + 1 = 0$ **55.** $-2x^2 - 5x + 12 = 0$

APPLICATION

56. PHYSICAL SCIENCE When sunlight strikes the surface of the ocean, the intensity of the light beneath the surface decreases exponentially with the depth of the water. If the intensity of the light is *reduced* by 75% for each meter of depth, what expression represents the intensity of light beneath the surface? *(LESSON 6.2)*

Write each expression as a single logarithm. Then evaluate. *(LESSON 6.4)*

57. $\log_2 32 - \log_2 8$ **58.** $\log_2 4^3 + \log_2 16$

Use a graph and the Location Principle to find the real zeros of each function. *(LESSON 7.4)*

59 $d(x) = x^3 - 6x^2 + 5x + 12$ **60** $f(x) = x^3 - 2x^2 - 11x + 12$

61 $f(x) = x^3 + 2x^2 - 5x - 6$ **62** $g(x) = x^3 + 8x^2 + 4x - 48$

 Look Beyond

63 Find all real solutions of the rational equation $1.4 = \dfrac{(x + 3)(x - 1)}{x^2 - 1}$. Be sure to check for excluded values.

The definition of a harmonic mean may be extended for 3, 4, or n numbers. For any three numbers a, b, and c, the harmonic mean is $\dfrac{3}{\frac{1}{a} + \frac{1}{b} + \frac{1}{c}}$.

1. Simplify this complex fraction.

2. Find the harmonic mean of the numbers 3, 4, and 5.

For any four numbers a, b, c, and d, the harmonic mean is $\dfrac{4}{\frac{1}{a} + \frac{1}{b} + \frac{1}{c} + \frac{1}{d}}$.

3. Simplify this complex fraction.

4. Find the harmonic mean of the numbers 2, 4, 6, and 8.

WORKING ON THE CHAPTER PROJECT

You should now be able to complete Activity 2 of the Chapter Project.

Solving Rational Equations and Inequalities

Objectives

● Solve a rational equation or inequality by using algebra, a table, or a graph.

● Solve problems by using a rational equation or inequality.

Why *There are many events in the real world that can be represented by a rational equation or inequality. For example, you can write a rational equation to represent speed and distance information for a triathlon.*

Rachel finished a triathlon involving swimming, bicycling, and running in 2.5 hours. Rachel's bicycling speed was about 6 times her swimming speed, and her running speed was about 5 miles per hour greater than her swimming speed. To find the speeds at which Rachel competed, you can solve a *rational equation*. A **rational equation** is an equation that contains at least one rational expression.

	Distance (mi)	Speed (mph)
Swimming	$d_s = 0.5$	s
Bicycling	$d_b = 25$	$6s$
Running	$d_r = 6$	$s + 5$

EXAMPLE  Find the speeds at which Rachel competed if she finished the triathlon in 2.5 hours.

● **SOLUTION**

1. Find the time for each part of the triathlon.

Swimming time	Bicycling time	Running time
$d_s = rt_s$	$d_b = rt_b$	$d_r = rt_r$
$0.5 = st_s$	$25 = (6s)t_b$	$6 = (s + 5)t_r$
$\dfrac{0.5}{s} = t_s$	$\dfrac{25}{6s} = t_b$	$\dfrac{6}{s + 5} = t_r$

TECHNOLOGY
GRAPHICS
CALCULATOR

Keystroke Guide, page 556

2. Write a rational function to represent the total time, T, in hours for the triathlon in terms of the swimming speed, s, in miles per hour.

$$T(s) = t_s + t_b + t_r$$

$$T(s) = \frac{0.5}{s} + \frac{25}{6s} + \frac{6}{s+5}$$

$$T(s) = \frac{0.5}{s}\left[\frac{6(s+5)}{6(s+5)}\right] + \frac{25}{6s}\left(\frac{s+5}{s+5}\right) + \frac{6}{s+5}\left(\frac{6s}{6s}\right) \quad \textit{The LCD is 6s(s + 5).}$$

$$T(s) = \frac{3s + 15 + 25s + 125 + 36s}{6s(s+5)}$$

$$T(s) = \frac{64s + 140}{6s(s+5)}$$

3. Solve the rational equation $2.5 = \frac{64s + 140}{6s(s+5)}$.
Graph $y = \frac{64x + 140}{6x(x+5)}$ and $y = 2.5$, and find the x-coordinate of the point of intersection.

Thus, Rachel swam at about 2.7 miles per hour, bicycled at about 6 · 2.7, or 16.2, miles per hour, and ran at about 5 + 2.7, or 7.7, miles per hour.

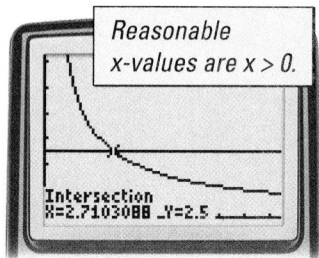

Reasonable
x-values are x > 0.

Intersection
X=2.7103088 _Y=2.5

CHECKPOINT ✔ Examine the table of values at right for $y = \frac{64x + 140}{6x(x + 5)}$. Describe Rachel's triathlon times if her swimming speed (x-value) were less than 2.7 miles per hour and if her swimming speed were greater than 2.7 miles per hour.

X	Y₁
2.4	2.7553
2.5	2.6667
2.6	2.5843
2.7	2.5076
2.8	2.4359
2.9	2.3687
3	2.3056

X=2.7

CRITICAL THINKING

How can you solve $2.5 = \frac{64x + 140}{6x(x + 5)}$ by using the quadratic formula?

E X A M P L E ➁ Solve $\frac{x}{x - 6} = \frac{1}{x - 4}$.

● **SOLUTION**

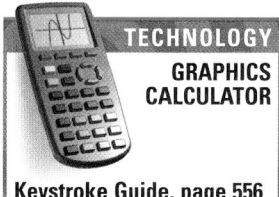

TECHNOLOGY
GRAPHICS
CALCULATOR

Keystroke Guide, page 556

Method 1 Use algebra.

$$\frac{x}{x-6} = \frac{1}{x-4} \quad x \neq 6, x \neq 4$$

$$x(x - 4) = 1(x - 6)$$

$$x^2 - 4x = x - 6$$

$$x^2 - 5x + 6 = 0$$

$$(x - 2)(x - 3) = 0$$

$$x = 2 \quad or \quad x = 3$$

CHECK

Let $x = 2$.

$$\frac{x}{x-6} = \frac{1}{x-4}$$

$$\frac{2}{2-6} \stackrel{?}{=} \frac{1}{2-4}$$

$$-\frac{1}{2} = -\frac{1}{2} \quad \textbf{True}$$

Let $x = 3$.

$$\frac{x}{x-6} = \frac{1}{x-4}$$

$$\frac{3}{3-6} \stackrel{?}{=} \frac{1}{3-4}$$

$$-1 = -1 \quad \textbf{True}$$

The solutions are 2 and 3.

Method 2 Use a graph.

Because it is not easy to see the intersection of $y = \frac{x}{x-6}$ and $y = \frac{1}{x-4}$, use another graphing method.

Write $\frac{x}{x-6} = \frac{1}{x-4}$ as $\frac{x}{x-6} - \frac{1}{x-4} = 0$.
Then graph $y = \frac{x}{x-6} - \frac{1}{x-4}$, and find the zeros of the function.

(2, 0)　(3, 0)

TRY THIS

Solve $\frac{x}{3} = \frac{1}{x-2}$.

Sometimes solving a rational equation introduces *extraneous solutions*. An **extraneous solution** is a solution to a resulting equation that is not a solution to the original equation. Therefore, it is important to check your answers, as shown in Example 3.

E X A M P L E ③ Solve $\frac{x}{x-3} + \frac{2x}{x+3} = \frac{18}{x^2-9}$.

● **SOLUTION**

Method 1 Use algebra.
Multiply each side of the equation by the LCD, $(x-3)(x+3)$, or x^2-9.

$$\frac{x}{x-3} + \frac{2x}{x+3} = \frac{18}{x^2-9}, \text{ where } x \neq 3 \text{ and } x \neq -3$$

$$\frac{x}{x-3}(x+3)(x-3) + \frac{2x}{x+3}(x+3)(x-3) = \frac{18}{x^2-9}(x+3)(x-3)$$

$$x(x+3) + 2x(x-3) = 18$$

$$x^2 + 3x + 2x^2 - 6x = 18$$

$$3x^2 - 3x - 18 = 0$$

$$3(x^2 - x - 6) = 0$$

$$3(x-3)(x+2) = 0$$

$$x = 3 \quad or \quad x = -2$$

CHECK
Since $x = 3$ is an excluded value of x in the original equation, it is an extraneous solution. Check $x = -2$.

$$\frac{x}{x-3} + \frac{2x}{x+3} = \frac{18}{x^2-9}$$

$$\frac{-2}{-2-3} + \frac{2(-2)}{-2} + 3 \stackrel{?}{=} \frac{18}{(-2)^2 - 9}$$

$$-3\frac{3}{5} = \frac{-18}{5} \quad \textbf{True}$$

Thus, the only solution is $x = -2$.

Method 2 Use a graph.
Because it is not easy to see the intersection of $y = \frac{x}{x-3} + \frac{2x}{x+3}$ and $y = \frac{18}{x^2-9}$, use another graphing method.

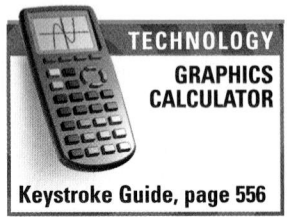

TECHNOLOGY
GRAPHICS CALCULATOR

Keystroke Guide, page 556

Write $\frac{x}{x-3} + \frac{2x}{x+3} = \frac{18}{x^2-9}$ as $\frac{x}{x-3} + \frac{2x}{x+3} - \frac{18}{x^2-9} = 0$. Then graph $y = \frac{x}{x-3} + \frac{2x}{x+3} - \frac{18}{x^2-9}$, and find any zeros of the function.

The only zero of the function is at (−2, 0).

The solution is −2.

TRY THIS Solve $\frac{x}{x-2} + \frac{x}{x-3} = \frac{3}{x^2-5x+6}$.

CRITICAL THINKING Explain why an extraneous solution is obtained in Example 3 above.

A **rational inequality** is an inequality that contains at least one rational expression.

Solving Rational Inequalities

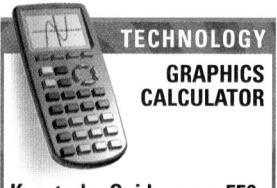

TECHNOLOGY

GRAPHICS CALCULATOR

Keystroke Guide, page 556

You will need: a graphics calculator

1. Graph $y_1 = \dfrac{x+2}{x-4}$.

2. Use the table feature and the graph to identify the values of x for which y_1 is 0, y_1 is undefined, y_1 is positive, and y_1 is negative.

3. On the same screen, graph $y_2 = 2x - 11$.

4. For what values of x is $y_1 = y_2$? $y_1 < y_2$? $y_1 > y_2$?

CHECKPOINT ✔ 5. Explain how to use a graph and a table of values to solve
$\dfrac{x+2}{x-4} < 2x - 11$ and $\dfrac{x+2}{x-4} > 2x - 11$.

E X A M P L E **4** Solve $\dfrac{x}{2x-1} \le 1$.

SOLUTION

Method 1 Use algebra.

To clear the inequality of fractions, multiply each side by $2x - 1$. You must consider both cases: $2x - 1$ is positive *or* $2x - 1$ is negative.

$\dfrac{x}{2x-1} \le 1$, where $2x - 1 > 0$	*or*	$\dfrac{x}{2x-1} \le 1$, where $2x - 1 < 0$
$\dfrac{x}{2x-1} \le 1$		$\dfrac{x}{2x-1} \le 1$
$x \le 2x - 1$		$x \ge 2x - 1$ *Change $\le$ to $\ge$.*
$-x \le -1$		$-x \ge -1$
$x \ge 1$ *Change $\le$ to $\ge$.*		$x \le 1$ *Change $\ge$ to $\le$.*

For this case, $x > \frac{1}{2}$ because $2x - 1 > 0$.
Therefore, the solution must satisfy
$x \ge 1$ *and* $x > \frac{1}{2}$.

For this case, $x < \frac{1}{2}$ because $2x - 1 < 0$.
Therefore, the solution must satisfy
$x \le 1$ *and* $x < \frac{1}{2}$.

For this case, $x \ge 1$.

For this case, $x < \frac{1}{2}$.

Thus, the solution is $x \ge 1$ *or* $x < \frac{1}{2}$.

Method 2 Use a graph.

Graph $y = \dfrac{x}{2x-1}$ and $y = 1$, and find the values of x for which the graph of $y = \dfrac{x}{2x-1}$ is below the graph of $y = 1$.

Thus, the solution is $x \ge 1$ *or* $x < \frac{1}{2}$.

vertical asymptote at $x = \frac{1}{2}$

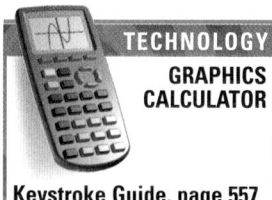

TECHNOLOGY

GRAPHICS CALCULATOR

Keystroke Guide, page 557

TRY THIS Solve $\dfrac{x-1}{x+2} < 3$.

EXAMPLE **5** Solve $\dfrac{x-2}{2(x-3)} > \dfrac{x}{x+3}$.

SOLUTION

In order to clear the inequality of fractions, you can multiply each side by the LCD, $2(x-3)(x+3)$. You must consider four possible cases:

Case 1: $x-3$ is positive *and* $x+3$ is positive,

or

Case 2: $x-3$ is positive *and* $x+3$ is negative,

or

Case 3: $x-3$ is negative *and* $x+3$ is positive,

or

Case 4: $x-3$ is negative *and* $x+3$ is negative.

The algebraic method of solution is beyond the scope of this textbook, but with a graphics calculator, the solution is much easier to find.

Rewrite $\dfrac{x-2}{2(x-3)} > \dfrac{x}{x+3}$ as $\dfrac{x-2}{2(x-3)} - \dfrac{x}{x+3} > 0$.

Graph $y = \dfrac{x-2}{2(x-3)} - \dfrac{x}{x+3}$, and find the values of x for which $y > 0$.

TECHNOLOGY
GRAPHICS CALCULATOR
Keystroke Guide, page 557

Any part of the graph that is above the x-axis indicates solutions to the inequality.

The graph shows that there are two intervals of x for which $y > 0$. These two intervals can be found by using a table of values.

One interval for which $y > 0$ is $-3 < x < 1$, as shown above. The other interval for which $y > 0$ is $3 < x < 6$, as shown below.

Thus, the solution is $-3 < x < 1$ *or* $3 < x < 6$.

TRY THIS   Solve $\dfrac{x+1}{x-1} < \dfrac{x}{x-1}$.

Exercises

Communicate

1. Explain what an extraneous solution is and how you can tell whether a solution to a rational equation is extraneous.

2. Explain how to use a graph to check the solutions to a rational equation that are obtained by using algebra.

3. Explain how to use the graphs of $y = \frac{x-1}{x+2}$ and $y = 3$, shown at right, to solve $\frac{x-1}{x+2} < 3$ and $\frac{x-1}{x+2} > 3$.

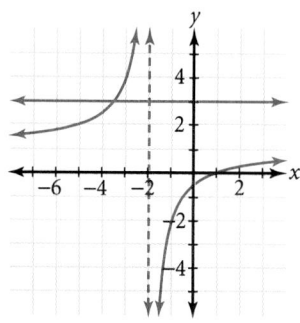

Guided Skills Practice

APPLICATION

4 **SPORTS** Refer to Rachel's triathlon information given at the beginning of the lesson. At what swimming, bicycling, and running speeds must Rachel compete in order to finish the triathlon in 2 hours? *(EXAMPLE 1)*

Solve each equation.

5. $\frac{2x-1}{x} = \frac{3}{x+2}$ *(EXAMPLE 2)*   **6.** $\frac{2}{x-1} + \frac{2}{x+1} = \frac{-4}{x^2-1}$ *(EXAMPLE 3)*

Solve each inequality.

7. $\frac{2x-3}{x} \geq 2$ *(EXAMPLE 4)*   **8** $\frac{1}{x+2} < \frac{1}{x+3}$ *(EXAMPLE 5)*

Practice and Apply

Solve each equation. Check your solution.

9. $\frac{x+3}{2x} = \frac{5}{8}$ **10.** $\frac{2y-1}{4y} = \frac{4}{6}$ **11.** $\frac{4}{n+4} = 1$

12. $\frac{-6}{m-3} = 1$ **13.** $\frac{1}{3z} + \frac{1}{8} = \frac{4}{3z}$ **14.** $\frac{1}{t} + \frac{1}{3} = \frac{8}{3t}$

15. $\frac{y+3}{y-1} = \frac{y+2}{y-3}$ **16.** $\frac{2n+1}{3n+4} = \frac{2n-8}{3n+8}$ **17.** $\frac{x+3}{x} + 1 = \frac{x+5}{x}$

18. $\frac{2x}{x+3} - 1 = \frac{x}{x+3}$ **19.** $\frac{x+1}{x-1} + \frac{2}{x} = \frac{x}{x+1}$ **20.** $\frac{3}{x+2} - \frac{x}{1} = \frac{4}{3}$

21. $\frac{1}{6} - \frac{1}{x} = \frac{4}{3x^2}$ **22.** $\frac{1}{1+c} - \frac{1}{2+c} = \frac{1}{4}$

23. $\frac{2x+3}{x-1} - \frac{2x-3}{x+1} = \frac{10}{x^2-1}$ **24.** $\frac{x-4}{x+2} + \frac{2}{x-2} = \frac{17}{x^2-4}$

25. $\frac{b}{b+3} - \frac{b}{b-2} = \frac{10}{b^2+b-6}$ **26.** $\frac{3z}{z-1} + \frac{2z}{z-6} = \frac{5z^2-15z+20}{z^2-7z+6}$

27. $\frac{3}{x+2} + \frac{12}{x^2-4} = \frac{-1}{x-2}$ **28.** $\frac{x+2}{2x-3} - \frac{x-2}{2x+3} = \frac{21}{4x^2-9}$

internet connect

**Homework
Help Online**

Go To: **go.hrw.com**
Keyword:
MB1 Homework Help
for Exercises 29–37

Solve each inequality. Check your solution.

29. $\dfrac{x+3}{3x} > 2$

30. $\dfrac{x+5}{4x} > 3$

31. $\dfrac{x-5}{3x} < -3$

32. $\dfrac{x-5}{3x} < 3$

33. $\dfrac{2x+1}{x-2} > 4$

34. $3 < \dfrac{3x+4}{2+1}$

35. $\dfrac{x+1}{x} \leq \dfrac{1}{2}$

36. $-\dfrac{1}{2} \geq \dfrac{1}{x-4}$

37. $\dfrac{7x}{3x+2} < 2$

Use a graphics calculator to solve each rational inequality. Round answers to the nearest tenth.

38 $\dfrac{1}{2} > x^2$

39 $\dfrac{1}{x} \leq x^2 - 1$

40 $\dfrac{x-2}{x-1} \geq 2x$

41 $x^2 - 4 \leq \dfrac{1}{x^2}$

42 $2x + 1 \geq \dfrac{1}{2x+1}$

43 $\dfrac{t}{t-1} - \dfrac{2}{t+1} \leq \dfrac{5}{t^2-1}$

44 $\dfrac{x+1}{x-1} + \dfrac{2}{x} \geq 1$

45 $\dfrac{a-3}{3a} \geq \dfrac{1}{3a^2+9a} + \dfrac{1}{a+3}$

46 $\dfrac{x^2+1}{(x-1)^2} > \dfrac{1}{x}$

State whether each equation is always true, sometimes true, or never true.

47. $\dfrac{2x+8}{x^2-16} = \dfrac{2}{x-4}, x \neq \pm 4$

48. $\dfrac{1 - 5x^{-1} + 4x^{-2}}{1 - 16x^{-2}} = \dfrac{x-1}{x+4}, x \neq 0 \text{ or } \pm 4$

49. $\dfrac{3}{x+2} + \dfrac{12}{x^2-4} = \dfrac{-1}{x-2}$

50. $\dfrac{2x+3}{x-1} - \dfrac{2x-3}{x+1} = \dfrac{10}{x^2-1}$

51. $\dfrac{x}{x+4} > 2x + 6$

52. $\dfrac{x-6}{x^2-2x-8} + \dfrac{3}{x-4} \leq \dfrac{2}{x+2}$

CHALLENGE

53. Solve $\dfrac{3}{(x-1)^2} > 0$ by using mental math.

54. CULTURAL CONNECTION: ASIA A ninth-century Indian mathematician, Mahavira, posed the following problem:

> *There are four pipes leading into a well. Individually, the four pipes can fill the well in $\frac{1}{2}$, $\frac{1}{3}$, $\frac{1}{4}$, and $\frac{1}{5}$ of a day. How long would it take for the pipes to fill the well if they were all working simultaneously, and what fraction of the well would be filled by each pipe?*

CONNECTION

55. GEOMETRY The length of a rectangle is 5 more than its width. Find the length and the width of the rectangle if the ratio of the length to the width is at least 1.5 and no more than 3.

APPLICATIONS

Satellite in orbit over Earth.

56. SPORTS Michael is training for a triathlon. He swims 0.6 miles, bicycles 15 miles, and runs 8 miles. Michael bicycles about 9 times as fast as he swims, and he runs about 6 miles per hour faster than he swims.
  a. Write a rational function, in terms of swimming speed, for the total time it takes Michael to complete his workout.
  b. Find the speeds at which Michael must swim, run, and bike to complete his workout in 1.5 hours.

57. PHYSICS An object weighing w_0 kilograms on Earth is h kilometers above Earth. The function that represents the object's weight at that altitude is $w(h) = w_0 \left(\dfrac{6400}{6400+h} \right)^2$. Find the approximate altitude of a satellite that weighs 3500 kilograms on Earth and 1200 kilograms in space.

Look Back

Evaluate each expression. *(LESSON 2.2)*

58. $81^{\frac{1}{2}}$ **59.** 13^0 **60.** $9^{\frac{3}{2}}$ **61.** $27^{\frac{1}{3}}$

Find the inverse of each function. State whether the inverse is a function. *(LESSON 2.5)*

62. $\{(3, 5), (2, 8), (1, 5), (0, 3)\}$ **63.** $\{(-1, -4), (-2, -3), (-3, -2), (0, -1)\}$

64. $g(x) = \frac{1}{4}x - 5$ **65.** $h(x) = \frac{5 - x}{2}$

Identify each transformation from the parent function $f(x) = x^2$ to g. *(LESSON 2.7)*

66. $g(x) = -2x^2$ **67.** $g(x) = (x - 2)^2$ **68.** $g(x) = \frac{1}{2}(x + 3)^2$

69. $g(x) = 3x^2 - 5$ **70.** $g(x) = (-2x)^2 + 1$ **71.** $g(x) = 2(4 - x)^2 - 6$

Look Beyond

72 Graph the functions $f(x) = \sqrt{x}$, $g(x) = \sqrt[3]{x}$, $h(x) = \sqrt[4]{x}$, and $k(x) = \sqrt[5]{x}$. How are they alike? How are they different? (Hint: Use the fact that $\sqrt[n]{x} = x^{\frac{1}{n}}$.)

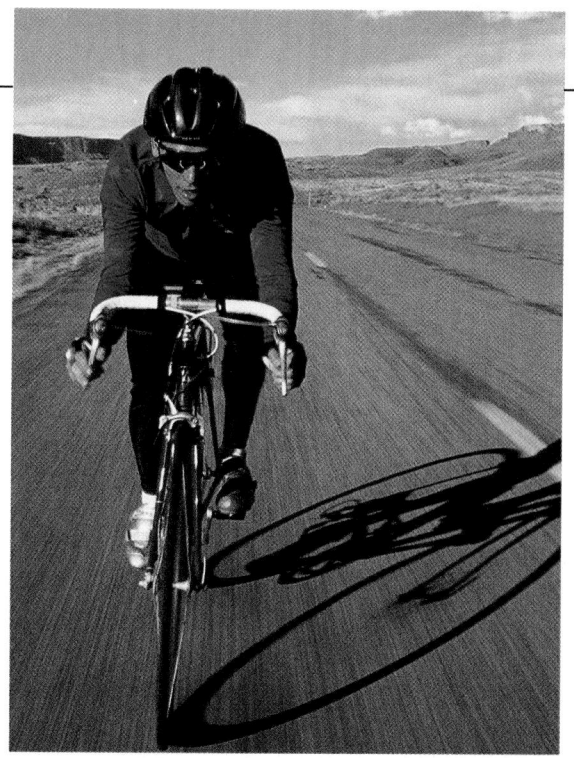

Refer to Example 5 on page 508. Notice that the cab driver's average speed is the total distance divided by the total time. The harmonic mean of the two speeds, 45 miles per hour and 55 miles per hour, gives the average speed for the entire trip.

1. Find the harmonic mean of 45 and 55.

2. How does your answer to Step 1 compare with the average speed found in Example 5?

Justin cycles for $4\frac{1}{2}$ hours. He cycles along a level road for 24 miles, and then he cycles up an incline for 24 miles more. Justin immediately turns around and cycles back to his starting point along the same route. Justin cycles on level ground at a rate of 24 miles per hour, uphill at a rate of 12 miles per hour, and downhill at a rate of 48 miles per hour.

3. Explain why Justin's average speed over the entire trip is the harmonic mean of 24, 12, 48, and 24.

4. Find Justin's average speed over the entire trip.

WORKING ON THE CHAPTER PROJECT

You should now be able to complete the Chapter Project.

Radical Expressions and Radical Functions

Objectives

- Analyze the graphs of radical functions, and evaluate radical expressions.

- Find the inverse of a quadratic function.

APPLICATION

PHYSICS

Nancy noticed that a long pendulum swings more slowly than a short pendulum. The time it takes for a pendulum to complete one full swing, or cycle, is called the *period*. The relationship between the period, *T*, (in seconds) of the pendulum and its length, *x*, (in meters) is given below.

$$T(x) = 2\pi\sqrt{\frac{x}{9.8}}$$

Find the period for pendulums whose lengths are 0.1 meter, 0.2 meter, and 0.3 meter. *You will do this in Example 4.*

Square-Root Functions

The **square root** of a number, $\sqrt{x}$, is a number that when multiplied by itself produces the given number, *x*. Recall from Lesson 5.6 that the expression $\sqrt{-4}$ is not a real number.

Since the domain of a function is the set of all real-number values of *x* for which a function, *f*, is defined, the domain of the square-root function, $f(x) = \sqrt{x}$, does not include negative numbers.

The domain of $f(x) = \sqrt{x}$ is all nonnegative real numbers, and the range of $f(x) = \sqrt{x}$ is all nonnegative real numbers.

The graph of $f(x) = \sqrt{x}$ is shown at right.

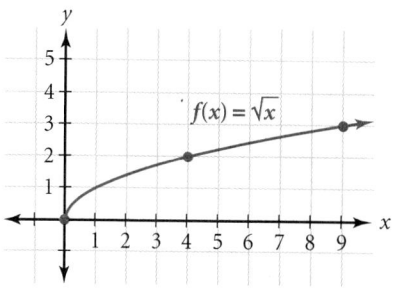

Example 1 shows you how to determine the domain of a square-root function.

E X A M P L E ① **Find the domain of $f(x) = \sqrt{2x - 5}$.**

● **SOLUTION**

The domain is all real numbers x that do not make $2x - 5$ negative. Solve $2x - 5 \geq 0$ to find the domain of $f(x) = \sqrt{2x - 5}$.

$$2x - 5 \geq 0$$
$$x \geq \frac{5}{2}, \text{ or } 2.5$$

CHECK

Graph $y = \sqrt{2x - 5}$.

(2.5, 0)

TECHNOLOGY
GRAPHICS CALCULATOR
Keystroke Guide, page 557

The domain of $f(x) = \sqrt{2x - 5}$ is $x \geq \frac{5}{2}$.

TRY THIS Find the domain of $g(x) = \sqrt{5x + 18}$.

CONNECTION
TRANSFORMATIONS

The transformations given in Lesson 2.7 are summarized below for the square-root parent function, $y = \sqrt{x}$.

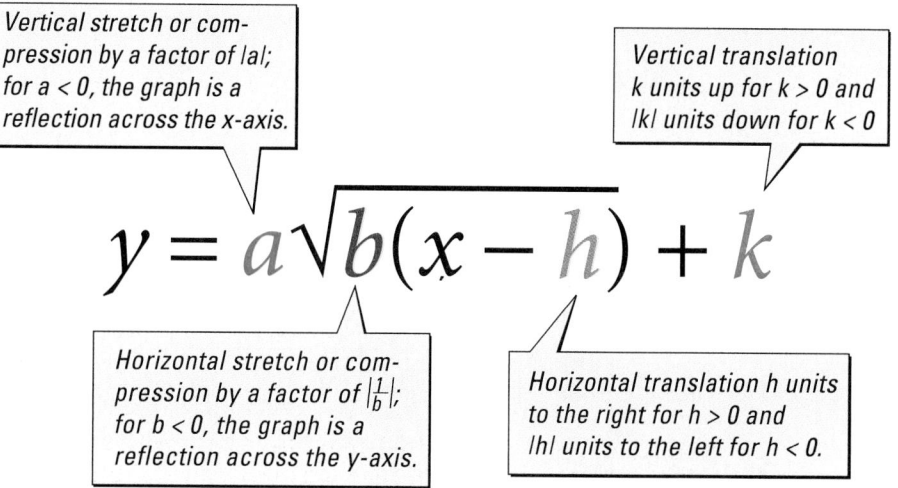

Vertical stretch or compression by a factor of |a|; for a < 0, the graph is a reflection across the x-axis.

Vertical translation k units up for k > 0 and |k| units down for k < 0

$$y = a\sqrt{b(x - h)} + k$$

Horizontal stretch or compression by a factor of $\left|\frac{1}{b}\right|$; for b < 0, the graph is a reflection across the y-axis.

Horizontal translation h units to the right for h > 0 and |h| units to the left for h < 0.

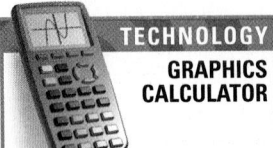

E X A M P L E ② For each function, describe the transformations applied to $y = \sqrt{x}$.

    a. $y = -2\sqrt{x + 1} + 4$ **b.** $y = \sqrt{4x - 3} - 1$

● **SOLUTION**

a. Use the form $y = a\sqrt{b(x - h)} + k$.   **b.** Use the form $y = a\sqrt{b(x - h)} + k$.

| vertical stretch by a factor of 2 and a reflection across the x-axis | vertical translation 4 units up | no vertical stretch or compression | vertical translation 1 unit down |

$$y = -2\sqrt{1[x - (-1)]} + 4 \qquad\qquad y = 1\sqrt{4\left[x - \left(\frac{3}{4}\right)\right]} - 1$$

| no horizontal stretch or compression | horizontal translation 1 unit to the left | horizontal compression by a factor of $\frac{1}{4}$ | horizontal translation $\frac{3}{4}$ unit to the right |

CHECK

Graph $y = -2\sqrt{x + 1} + 4$ and $y = \sqrt{x}$ on the same screen, and compare the graphs.

CHECK

Graph $y = \sqrt{4x - 3} - 1$ and $y = \sqrt{x}$ on the same screen, and compare the graphs.

$(-1, 4)$

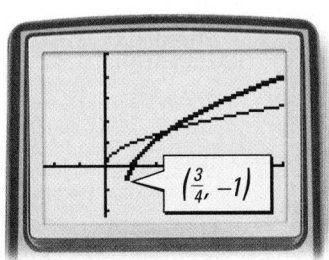

$\left(\frac{3}{4}, -1\right)$

TRY THIS   For each function, describe the transformations applied to $y = \sqrt{x}$.

    a. $y = 3\sqrt{x - 1} - 2$ **b.** $y = \sqrt{2x + 1} + 3$

Recall from Lesson 2.5 that you can find the inverse of a function by interchanging x and y and then solving for y. This is shown for a quadratic function in Example 3.

E X A M P L E ③ Find the inverse of $y = x^2 - 2x$. Then graph the function and its inverse together.

● **SOLUTION**

1. Interchange x and y.

$$y = x^2 - 2x \quad \rightarrow \quad x = y^2 - 2y$$

2. Solve $x = y^2 - 2y$ for y.

$$x = y^2 - 2y$$
$$y^2 - 2y - x = 0 \qquad\qquad \textit{Write as a quadratic equation in terms of y.}$$
$$y = \frac{-(-2) \pm \sqrt{(-2)^2 - 4(1)(-x)}}{2(1)} \qquad \textit{Apply the quadratic formula for } a = 1, b = -2, \textit{and } c = -x.$$
$$y = \frac{2 \pm \sqrt{4 + 4x}}{2}$$
$$y = 1 \pm \sqrt{1 + x}$$

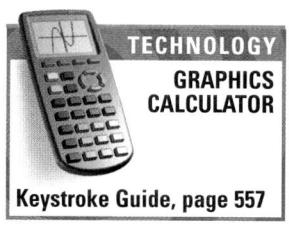
3. Graph $y = x^2 - 2x$ and its inverse, $y = 1 + \sqrt{1 + x}$ and $y = 1 - \sqrt{1 + x}$, along with $y = x$.

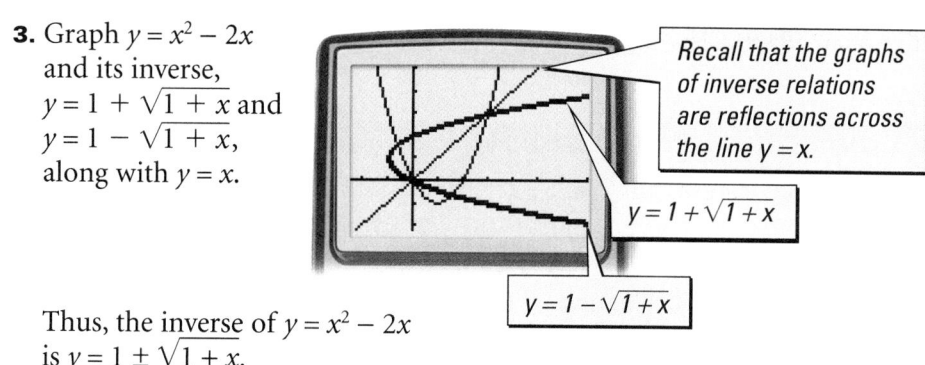

Recall that the graphs of inverse relations are reflections across the line $y = x$.

$y = 1 + \sqrt{1 + x}$

$y = 1 - \sqrt{1 + x}$

Thus, the inverse of $y = x^2 - 2x$ is $y = 1 \pm \sqrt{1 + x}$.

TRY THIS   Find the inverse of $y = x^2 + 3x - 4$. Then graph the function and its inverse together.

CRITICAL THINKING   Show that if $y = ax^2 + bx + c$, then $x = \dfrac{-b \pm \sqrt{b^2 - 4a(c - y)}}{2a}$.

E X A M P L E **4**   Recall the pendulum problem described at the beginning of the lesson. The relationship between the period, T, (in seconds) of a pendulum and its length, x, (in meters) is $T(x) = 2\pi\sqrt{\dfrac{x}{9.8}}$.

APPLICATION

PHYSICS

Find the period for pendulums whose lengths are 0.1 meter, 0.2 meter, and 0.3 meter.

SOLUTION

Enter the function $y = 2\pi\sqrt{\dfrac{x}{9.8}}$ into a graphics calculator, and use the table feature with an x-increment of 0.1.

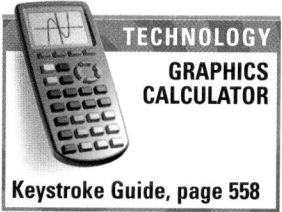
For a 0.1-meter pendulum, the period is about 0.6 second.

For a 0.2-meter pendulum, the period is about 0.9 second.

For a 0.3-meter pendulum, the period is about 1.1 seconds.

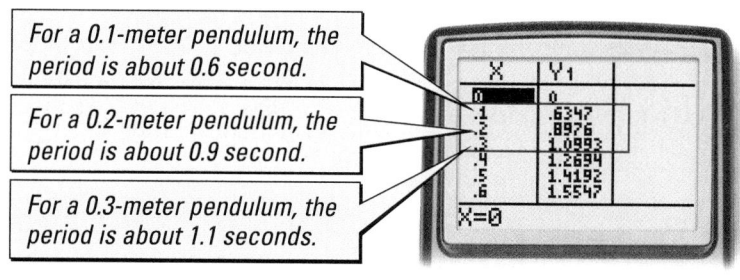

Cube-Root Functions

The **cube root** of a number, $\sqrt[3]{x}$, is a number that when multiplied by itself 3 times produces the given number, x. Recall from Lesson 2.2 that the expressions $\sqrt[3]{-8}$ and $\sqrt[3]{8}$ are both defined.

$$(-2)(-2)(-2) = -8 \text{ and } \sqrt[3]{-8} = -2$$

$$(2)(2)(2) = 8 \text{ and } \sqrt[3]{8} = 2$$

The domain of $f(x) = \sqrt[3]{x}$ is all real numbers, and the range of f is all real numbers, as shown in the graph at right.

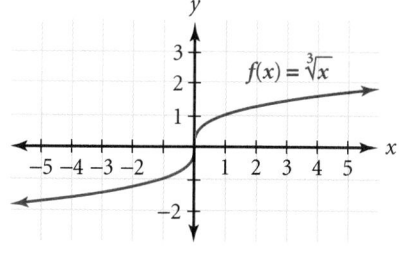

$f(x) = \sqrt[3]{x}$

E X A M P L E ⑤ Evaluate each expression.

    a. $3\sqrt[3]{27} - 5$ **b.** $2\left(\sqrt[3]{-64}\right)^2 + 7$

SOLUTION

a. $3\sqrt[3]{27} - 5$ **b.** $2\left(\sqrt[3]{-64}\right)^2 + 7$

    $= 3(3) - 5$ $3^3 = 27$ $= 2(-4)^2 + 7$ $(-4)^3 = -64$

    $= 4$ $= 39$

TRY THIS   Evaluate $-2\sqrt[3]{-125} - 10$ and $6\left(\sqrt[3]{8}\right)^2 + 2$.

A **radical function** is a function that is defined by a *radical expression*. A **radical expression** is an expression that contains at least one **radical symbol,** such as $2\pi\sqrt{\dfrac{x}{9.80}}$, $\sqrt[4]{x}$, $\sqrt[7]{x+1}$, and $\sqrt[3]{2x+5}$. In the radical expression $\sqrt[3]{2x+5}$, $2x + 5$ is the **radicand** and the number 3 is the **index.** Read the expression $\sqrt[3]{2x+5}$ as "the cube root of $2x + 5$."

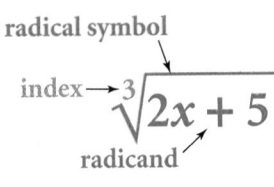

radical symbol

index → 3

radicand

Index	Root	Symbol
2	square	$\sqrt{}$
3	cube	$\sqrt[3]{}$
4	fourth	$\sqrt[4]{}$
n	nth	$\sqrt[n]{}$

> The index of the square root is usually omitted.

Recall from Lesson 2.2 that the definition of a rational exponent $\frac{1}{n}$, where n is a positive integer, is as follows: $a^{\frac{1}{n}} = \sqrt[n]{a}$. This definition is used when entering a radical expression into a calculator. For example, to evaluate $3\sqrt[3]{27} - 5$ with a calculator, enter 3 $\boxed{(}$ 27 $\boxed{\wedge}$ $\boxed{(}$ 1 $\boxed{\div}$ 3 $\boxed{)}$ $\boxed{)}$ $\boxed{-}$ 5.

The Activity below introduces two *families* of radical functions.

Activity

Comparing Radical Functions

You will need: a graphics calculator

1. Graph $y = \sqrt{x}$, $y = \sqrt[3]{x}$, $y = \sqrt[4]{x}$, $y = \sqrt[5]{x}$, $y = \sqrt[6]{x}$, and $y = \sqrt[7]{x}$ one at a time. Sketch the shape of each graph.

2. Which functions appear similar?

3. Which functions have a domain of $x \geq 0$?

4. Which functions have a domain of all real numbers?

CHECKPOINT ✔ 5. Make a conjecture about the domain and range of $y = \sqrt[n]{x}$ when n is a positive even integer and when n is a positive odd integer.

Exercises

internet connect

**Activities
Online**

Go To: **go.hrw.com**
Keyword:
MB1 RadicalGraphs

Communicate

1. Describe the transformations applied to the graph of $f(x) = \sqrt{x}$ in order to obtain the graph of $y = 3\sqrt{x-4}$.

2. How do you determine the domain of a radical function?

3. Describe the procedure for finding the inverse of $y = 4x^3 + 2$.

Guided Skills Practice

4. Find the domain of $f(x) = \sqrt{-2x+3}$. **(EXAMPLE 1)**

For each function, describe the transformations applied to $y = \sqrt{x}$.
(EXAMPLE 2)

5. $y = 2\sqrt{x-1} - 2$　　　　　　**6.** $y = \sqrt{2x+1} + 2$

7. Find the inverse of $y = 4x^2 - x$. Then graph the function and its inverse together. **(EXAMPLE 3)**

APPLICATION

8. PHYSICS The vibration period of a mass on a spring is the time required for the mass to make a complete cycle in its motion. The relationship between the vibration period, T, (in seconds) of a certain spring and its mass, m, (in kilograms) is represented by $T(m) = 2\pi\sqrt{\dfrac{m}{200}}$. Find the period for a spring with masses of 1.0, 1.5, and 2.0 kilograms. Give answers to the nearest tenth. **(EXAMPLE 4)**

Evaluate each expression. (EXAMPLE 5)

9. $4\sqrt[3]{-8} + 3$　　　　　　**10.** $-2\left(\sqrt[3]{64}\right)^2 - 3$

Practice and Apply

internet connect

**Homework
Help Online**

Go To: **go.hrw.com**
Keyword:
MB1 Homework Help
for Exercises 11–24

Find the domain of each radical function.

11. $f(x) = \sqrt{12x+24}$　　　　　　**12.** $f(x) = \sqrt{3x-2}$

13. $f(x) = \sqrt{3(x-2)}$　　　　　　**14.** $f(x) = \sqrt{3(x+2)} - 1$

15. $f(x) = \sqrt{2 - 3(x+1)}$　　　　　**16.** $f(x) = \sqrt{3 - 3(x-4)}$

17. $f(x) = \sqrt{x^2 - 25}$　　　　　　**18.** $f(x) = \sqrt{9x^2 - 16}$

19. $f(x) = \sqrt{x^2 + 5x + 6}$　　　　**20.** $f(x) = \sqrt{x^2 + 10x - 25}$

21. $f(x) = \sqrt{2x^2 + 5x - 12}$　　　**22.** $f(x) = \sqrt{3x^2 + 7x + 2}$

23. $f(x) = \sqrt{6x^2 - 13x + 5}$　　　**24.** $f(x) = \sqrt{8x^2 - 10x - 3}$

Find the inverse of each quadratic function. Then graph the function and its inverse in the same coordinate plane.

25. $y = x^2 - 1$

26. $y = x^2 + 3$

27. $y = 3x^2 + x$

28. $y = x^2 + 2x$

29. $y = x^2 + 4x + 4$

30. $y = x^2 + 6x + 9$

31. $y = x^2 - 2x + 1$

32. $y = x^2 - 7x + 12$

33. $y = 4 - x^2 + 3x$

34. $y = 2x + x^2 - 8$

35. $y = x + 2x^2 - 1$

36. $y = 3 + x - 2x^2$

Evaluate each expression.

37. $\frac{1}{2}\left(\sqrt[3]{8}\right)^6$

38. $2\left(\sqrt[4]{625}\right)^2$

39. $\frac{1}{2}\sqrt[3]{-8} + 3$

40. $-\frac{2}{5}\sqrt[3]{-125} - 3$

41. $\frac{1}{8}\left(\sqrt[3]{-8^3}\right)^2$

42. $2\left(\sqrt[3]{8}\right)^2 - 3$

43. $-2\sqrt[3]{216} - 3$

44. $3\sqrt[3]{343} + 1$

45. $10\left(\sqrt[3]{1000}\right)^3 - 1$

46. $\frac{1}{6}\left(\sqrt[3]{\frac{54}{4}}\right)^3 + 5$

47. $\frac{1}{2}\left(\sqrt[3]{-216}\right)^4$

48. $2\left(\sqrt[3]{-343}\right)^2$

49. $\frac{1}{2}\sqrt[3]{216}$

50. $\left(\sqrt[4]{81} - 1\right)^2$

51. $-\frac{1}{3}\left(\sqrt[4]{1296}\right)^2$

CHALLENGES

52. State the domain of $y = \sqrt{\dfrac{1}{x^2 + 1}}$. Graph the function to check.

53. Let $f(x) = ax^2 + bx + c$, where $a \neq 0$. Find an equation for the axis of symmetry for the graph of the inverse of f.

CONNECTIONS

TRANSFORMATIONS For each function, describe the transformations applied to $f(x) = \sqrt{x}$. Then graph each transformed function.

54. $g(x) = \sqrt{x} - 4$

55. $h(x) = \sqrt{x - 4}$

56. $p(x) = 3\sqrt{x - 4}$

57. $r(x) = -\frac{1}{5}\sqrt{x - 4}$

58. $s(x) = -2\sqrt{x - 4}$

59. $g(x) = \sqrt{x + 2} + 5$

60. $h(x) = 2\sqrt{x + 3} - 1$

61. $p(x) = 2(\sqrt{x + 3} - 1)$

62. $k(x) = \frac{1}{2}\sqrt{x - 1} + 4$

63. $m(x) = \frac{1}{3}\sqrt{x + 2} + 3$

64. GEOMETRY The volume, V, of a sphere with a radius of r is given by $V = \frac{4}{3}\pi r^3$.

   a. Solve this equation for r in terms of V.

   b. Show that if V increases, then r must increase.

   c. A spherical hot-air balloon has a volume of 12,000 cubic feet. Find the approximate radius of the balloon by using the equation you wrote in part **a** and a table. Give your answer to the nearest tenth of a foot.

65. PHYSICS If E represents the elevation in meters above sea level and T represents the boiling point of water in degrees Celsius at that elevation, then E and T are related by the equation below.

$$E \approx 1000(100 - T) + 580(100 - T)^2$$

a. Solve the equation above for T. (Hint: Begin by substituting x for $100 - T$. Then solve for x.)

b. What is the approximate boiling point of water at an elevation of 1600 meters?

66. PHYSICS In the 1840s, a French physiologist, Jean Marie Poiseuville, found a relationship between the flow rate, f, of a liquid flowing through a cylinder whose length is L and whose radius is r. The flow rate also depends on the pressure, p, exerted on the liquid and the coefficient of viscosity, N, of the liquid. (*Viscosity* is a measure of the resistance of a fluid to flow.)

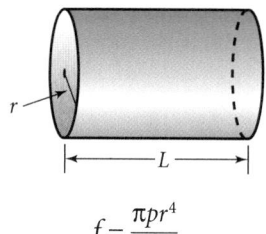

$$f = \frac{\pi p r^4}{8LN}$$

a. Solve the equation at right above for r in terms of the other variables. How does r vary as f, given that p, L, and N are constant?

b. Assume that r, L, and N are constant. How does f vary as p? How does f change if p is doubled?

c. Assume that p, L, and N are constant. How does f vary as r? How does f change if r is doubled?

Alaskan oil pipeline

 Look Back

Simplify each expression. Assume that no variable equals zero.
(LESSON 2.2)

67. $(-2y^3y^5)^2$ **68.** $2a^4(-3ab^2)^3$ **69.** $(5x^{-2}y^4)^{-1}$

70. $\left(\dfrac{-3xy^3}{x^{-4}y^5}\right)^3$ **71.** $\left(\dfrac{-4m^4n^3}{m^2n^3}\right)^{-1}$ **72.** $\left(\dfrac{3m^4n^{-2}}{2m^0n^3}\right)^{-2}$

Perform the indicated addition or subtraction. *(LESSON 5.6)*

73. $2i - (4 - 5i)$ **74.** $(-2 + 4i) + (-1 - i)$ **75.** $(-4 + i) - (3 - 2i)$

Write each expression as a sum or difference of logarithms.
(LESSON 6.4)

76. $\log(6 \cdot 3)$ **77.** $\log 2x$ **78.** $\log\left(\dfrac{17}{8}\right)$ **79.** $\log\left(\dfrac{xz}{y}\right)$

Look Beyond

80. COORDINATE GEOMETRY Let $x^2 + y^2 = 1$. Solve for y. Graph the two resulting equations together. Describe the shape that the pair of graphs creates.

Simplifying Radical Expressions

Objectives

- Add, subtract, multiply, divide, and simplify radical expressions.

- Rationalize a denominator.

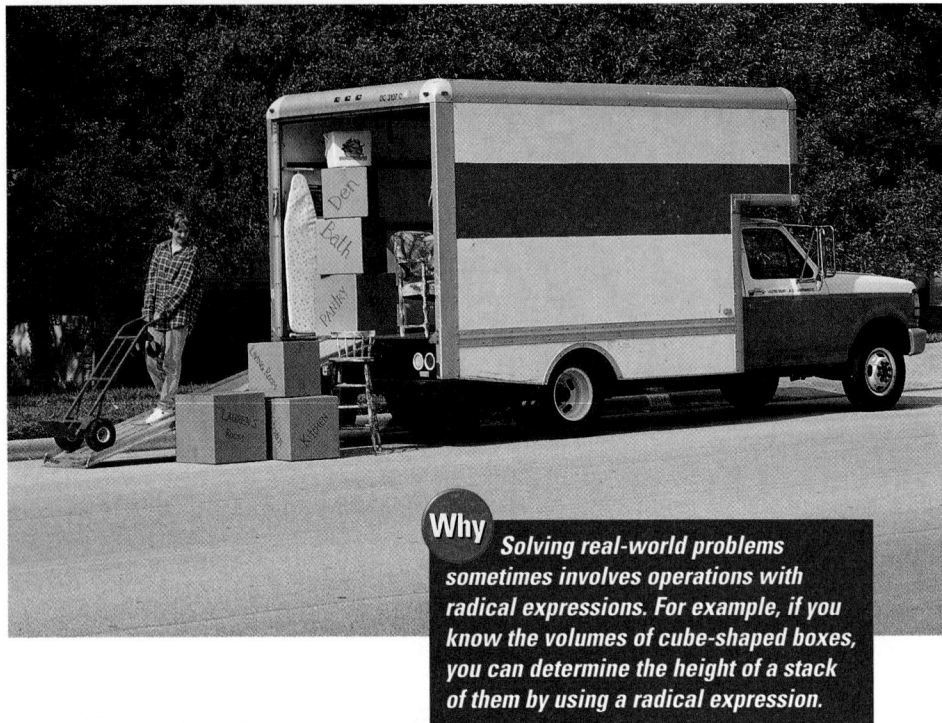

Why *Solving real-world problems sometimes involves operations with radical expressions. For example, if you know the volumes of cube-shaped boxes, you can determine the height of a stack of them by using a radical expression.*

APPLICATION
PACKAGING

Danielle is loading moving boxes onto a truck. She has three large cube-shaped boxes whose volumes are 54 cubic feet, 128 cubic feet, and 250 cubic feet. If she stacks them on top of one another, how tall will the stack be? Answering this question involves working with radical expressions. *You will answer this question in Example 3.*

In the Activity below, you will investigate some properties of radicals.

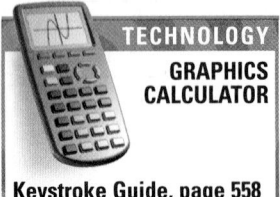

TECHNOLOGY
GRAPHICS CALCULATOR

Keystroke Guide, page 558

Activity
Exploring Properties of Radicals

You will need: a graphics calculator

Complete the following steps, using the fact that $\sqrt[n]{x} = x^{\frac{1}{n}}$:

1. Graph $y = \sqrt{x^2}$. What function does the graph represent?

PROBLEM SOLVING

2. **Guess and check.** Use your work from Step 1 to predict the appearance of the graph of $y = \sqrt[4]{x^4}$. Verify your response.

CHECKPOINT ✔
3. Predict the appearance of the graph of $y = \sqrt[n]{x^n}$, where n is a positive even integer. Then illustrate your prediction.

4. Graph $y = \sqrt[3]{x^3}$. What function does the graph represent?

5. Use your work from Step 4 to predict the appearance of the graph of $y = \sqrt[5]{x^5}$. Verify your response.

CHECKPOINT ✔
6. Predict the appearance of the graph of $y = \sqrt[n]{x^n}$, where n is a positive odd integer. Then illustrate your prediction, and explain your reasoning.

Just as there are Properties of Exponents that you can use to simplify exponential expressions, there are *Properties of Radicals* that are used to simplify radical expressions.

Properties of Radicals

For any real number a,
$$\sqrt[n]{a^n} = |a| \text{ if } n \text{ is a positive even integer, and}$$
$$\sqrt[n]{a^n} = a \text{ if } n \text{ is a positive odd integer.}$$

For example, $\sqrt{(-3)^2} = |-3| = 3$ and $\sqrt[3]{(-3)^3} = -3$.

E X A M P L E ❶ **Simplify each expression by using the Properties of Radicals.**

a. $\sqrt{49x^2y^5z^6}$

b. $\sqrt[3]{-27x^7y^3z^2}$

● **SOLUTION**

a. $\sqrt{49x^2y^5z^6} = \sqrt{7^2x^2y^4z^6}$
$$= 7|x|y^2|z^3|\sqrt{y}$$

b. $\sqrt[3]{-27x^7y^3z^2} = \sqrt[3]{(-3)^3x^6xy^3z^2}$
$$= -3x^2y\sqrt[3]{xz^2}$$

TRY THIS Simplify each expression by using the Properties of Radicals.

a. $\sqrt{64a^4bc^3}$

b. $\sqrt[5]{-32f^6g^5h^2}$

Recall from Lesson 2.2 that $a^{\frac{m}{n}} = \left(a^{\frac{1}{n}}\right)^m = \left(\sqrt[n]{a}\right)^m$ and that $a^{\frac{m}{n}} = (a^m)^{\frac{1}{n}} = \sqrt[n]{a^m}$.

You can write an expression with a rational exponent in *radical form*.	You can write an expression with a radical in *exponential form*.

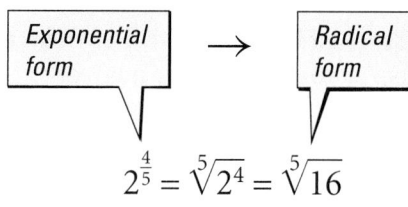

$$2^{\frac{4}{5}} = \sqrt[5]{2^4} = \sqrt[5]{16}$$

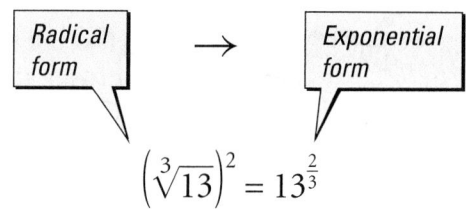

$$\left(\sqrt[3]{13}\right)^2 = 13^{\frac{2}{3}}$$

CHECKPOINT ✔ Write $2^{\frac{3}{5}}$ in radical form.

You can use the *Product and Quotient Properties of Radicals* to multiply, divide, and simplify radical expressions.

Product and Quotient Properties of Radicals

For $a \geq 0$, $b \geq 0$, and a positive integer n:
$$\sqrt[n]{ab} = \sqrt[n]{a} \cdot \sqrt[n]{b} \quad \text{and} \quad \sqrt[n]{\frac{a}{b}} = \frac{\sqrt[n]{a}}{\sqrt[n]{b}} \; (b \neq 0)$$

E X A M P L E ❷ Simplify each expression. Assume that the value of each variable is positive.

a. $(27ab^3)^{\frac{1}{3}} \cdot \sqrt[3]{5a^4b}$

b. $\dfrac{8(54x^5)^{\frac{1}{2}}}{4\sqrt{3x^3}}$

● **SOLUTION**

a. $(27ab^3)^{\frac{1}{3}} \cdot \sqrt[3]{5a^4b}$

$= \sqrt[3]{27ab^3} \cdot \sqrt[3]{5a^4b}$

$= \sqrt[3]{(27ab^3)(5a^4b)}$

$= \sqrt[3]{(3^3ab^3)(5a^4b)}$

$= \sqrt[3]{3^3a^3b^3 \cdot 5^1a^2b^1}$ *Associative Property*

$= \sqrt[3]{3^3} \cdot \sqrt[3]{a^3} \cdot \sqrt[3]{b^3} \cdot \sqrt[3]{5a^2b}$

$= 3ab\sqrt[3]{5a^2b}$

b. $\dfrac{8(54x^5)^{\frac{1}{2}}}{4\sqrt{3x^3}}$

$= \dfrac{8\sqrt{54x^5}}{4\sqrt{3x^3}}$

$= 2\sqrt{\dfrac{54x^5}{3x^3}}$

$= 2\sqrt{18x^2}$

$= 2\sqrt{3^2 \cdot x^2 \cdot 2}$ *Associative Property*

$= 2 \cdot 3 \cdot |x|\sqrt{2}$

$= 6x\sqrt{2}$ *Assume x is positive.*

TRY THIS Simplify each expression. Assume that the value of each variable is positive.

a. $\sqrt[3]{3r^2s^3} \cdot (9r^3s^4)^{\frac{1}{3}}$

b. $\dfrac{\sqrt{54x^3y^3}}{(3xy^2)^{\frac{1}{2}}}$

Operations With Radical Expressions

When you add or subtract radical expressions, it is helpful to write your answers in *simplest radical form*. The expression $\sqrt{a}$ is in **simplest radical form** if no factor of a is a perfect square.

E X A M P L E ❸ Refer to the cube-shaped boxes described at the beginning of the lesson. The volumes are 54 cubic feet, 128 cubic feet, and 250 cubic feet.

A P P L I C A T I O N
PACKAGING

How tall will the stack of boxes be? Give both an exact answer and an answer rounded to the nearest hundredth of a foot.

● **SOLUTION**

The formula for the volume, V, of a cube is $V = e^3$. The length of one edge is given by the radical expression $e = \sqrt[3]{V}$. The height of the stack is the sum of all three edge lengths.

$\sqrt[3]{54} + \sqrt[3]{128} + \sqrt[3]{250} = \sqrt[3]{3^3 \cdot 2} + \sqrt[3]{4^3 \cdot 2} + \sqrt[3]{5^3 \cdot 2}$

$= 3\sqrt[3]{2} + 4\sqrt[3]{2} + 5\sqrt[3]{2}$

$= 12\sqrt[3]{2}$

The stack of boxes will be $12\sqrt[3]{2}$, or about 15.12, feet tall.

E X A M P L E **4** Simplify each sum or difference.

    a. $\left(6 + \sqrt{12}\right) + \left(-7 + \sqrt{75}\right)$ **b.** $\left(-5 - \sqrt{18}\right) - \left(6 + \sqrt{50}\right)$

SOLUTION

   a. $\left(6 + \sqrt{12}\right) + \left(-7 + \sqrt{75}\right)$

      $= \left(6 + \sqrt{2^2 \cdot 3}\right) + \left(-7 + \sqrt{5^2 \cdot 3}\right)$

      $= \left(6 + 2\sqrt{3}\right) + \left(-7 + 5\sqrt{3}\right)$

      $= 6 - 7 + 2\sqrt{3} + 5\sqrt{3}$ *Simplify.*

      $= -1 + 7\sqrt{3}$ *Combine like terms.*

   b. $\left(-5 - \sqrt{18}\right) - \left(6 + \sqrt{50}\right)$

      $= \left(-5 - \sqrt{3^2 \cdot 2}\right) - \left(6 + \sqrt{5^2 \cdot 2}\right)$

      $= \left(-5 - 3\sqrt{2}\right) - \left(6 + 5\sqrt{2}\right)$

      $= -5 - 6 - 3\sqrt{2} - 5\sqrt{2}$ *Simplify.*

      $= -11 - 8\sqrt{2}$ *Combine like terms.*

TRY THIS   Simplify each sum or difference.

    a. $\left(-3 + \sqrt{32}\right) + \left(6 + \sqrt{98}\right)$ **b.** $\left(8 - \sqrt{45}\right) - \left(-2 + \sqrt{20}\right)$

CHECKPOINT ✔ Since $\sqrt{3}$ is between $\sqrt{1} = 1$ and $\sqrt{4} = 2$, you can estimate that the value of $-1 + 7\sqrt{3}$ is between $-1 + 7\sqrt{1} = 6$ and $-1 + 7\sqrt{4} = 13$. Use this method of estimation to show that $-1 + 7\sqrt{3}$ is a reasonable answer for the sum $\left(6 + \sqrt{12}\right) + \left(-7 + \sqrt{75}\right)$ in part **a** of Example 4.

E X A M P L E **5** Simplify each product.

    a. $\left(-3 + 5\sqrt{2}\right)\left(4 + 2\sqrt{2}\right)$ **b.** $\left(4 - \sqrt{3}\right)\left(2\sqrt{3} + 5\right)$

SOLUTION

   a. $\left(-3 + 5\sqrt{2}\right)\left(4 + 2\sqrt{2}\right)$

      $= (-3)(4) + (-3)\left(2\sqrt{2}\right) + \left(5\sqrt{2}\right)(4) + \left(5\sqrt{2}\right)\left(2\sqrt{2}\right)$ *Distributive Property*

      $= -12 - 6\sqrt{2} + 20\sqrt{2} + 20$ *Simplify.*

      $= 8 + 14\sqrt{2}$

   b. $\left(4 - \sqrt{3}\right)\left(2\sqrt{3} + 5\right)$

      $= (4)\left(2\sqrt{3}\right) + (4)(5) + \left(-\sqrt{3}\right)\left(2\sqrt{3}\right) + \left(-\sqrt{3}\right)(5)$ *Distributive Property*

      $= 8\sqrt{3} + 20 - 6 - 5\sqrt{3}$ *Simplify.*

      $= 14 + 3\sqrt{3}$

TRY THIS   Simplify each product.

    a. $\left(3 - 5\sqrt{5}\right)\left(-4 + 6\sqrt{5}\right)$ **b.** $\left(-4\sqrt{6} + 1\right)\left(5 - 3\sqrt{6}\right)$

CRITICAL THINKING   Show that $\left(a + b\sqrt{2}\right)\left(a - b\sqrt{2}\right) = a^2 - 2b^2$ is true.

Rationalizing a denominator is a procedure for transforming a quotient with a radical in the denominator into an expression with no radical in the denominator. Use this procedure so that your answers are in the same form as the answers in this textbook.

E X A M P L E **6** Write each expression with a rational denominator.

a. $\dfrac{1}{\sqrt{3}}$ **b.** $\dfrac{2}{1 + \sqrt{3}}$

● **SOLUTION**

a. $\dfrac{1}{\sqrt{3}} = \dfrac{1}{\sqrt{3}}\left(\dfrac{\sqrt{3}}{\sqrt{3}}\right)$ *Multiply by 1.*

$= \dfrac{\sqrt{3}}{\sqrt{3} \cdot \sqrt{3}}$

$= \dfrac{\sqrt{3}}{3}$

b. $\dfrac{2}{1 + \sqrt{3}} = \dfrac{2}{1 + \sqrt{3}}\left(\dfrac{1 - \sqrt{3}}{1 - \sqrt{3}}\right)$ *Use the conjugate of $1 + \sqrt{3}$ to multiply by 1.*

$= \dfrac{2 - 2\sqrt{3}}{1 - \sqrt{3} + \sqrt{3} - 3}$

$= \dfrac{2 - 2\sqrt{3}}{-2}$

$= -1 + \sqrt{3}$

TRY THIS Write each expression with a rational denominator.

a. $\dfrac{3}{\sqrt{5}}$ **b.** $\dfrac{-14}{3 - \sqrt{2}}$

CRITICAL THINKING Let a and b represent nonzero integers. Write $\dfrac{1}{a + b\sqrt{2}}$ as an expression with a rational denominator.

Exercises

● Communicate

1. Explain how to simplify $(1 + 2\sqrt{2})(2 - 3\sqrt{2})$. Include a description about how the Distributive Property is applied.

2. Explain how to simplify the radical expression $\sqrt{4x^3}$.

3. Explain how to rationalize the denominator of $\dfrac{5 + 3\sqrt{2}}{4 + 7\sqrt{2}}$.

● Guided Skills Practice

Simplify each expression by using the Properties of Radicals. (EXAMPLE 1)

4. $\sqrt{128ab^2c^5}$ **5.** $\sqrt[3]{-54x^5y^9}$

Simplify each expression. Assume that the value of each variable is positive. *(EXAMPLE 2)*

6. $\sqrt[3]{27a^4b^3}(81a^2b)^{\frac{1}{3}}$

7. $\dfrac{12\sqrt{15x^3}}{6(3x)^{\frac{1}{2}}}$

APPLICATION

8. BUSINESS How tall is a stack of three cube-shaped boxes, one on top of the other, given that their volumes are 24 cubic inches, 81 cubic inches, and 375 cubic inches? Give both an exact answer and an answer rounded to the nearest hundredth of an inch. *(EXAMPLE 3)*

Simplify each sum or difference.
(EXAMPLE 4)

9. $\left(-3 + \sqrt{32}\right) + \left(3 + 2\sqrt{98}\right)$

10. $\left(16 + \sqrt{75}\right) - \left(-4 + 10\sqrt{3}\right)$

11. Simplify the product $\left(-2 + 3\sqrt{5}\right)\left(3 - 6\sqrt{5}\right)$.
(EXAMPLE 5)

Write each expression with a rational denominator. *(EXAMPLE 6)*

12. $\dfrac{2}{\sqrt{7}}$

13. $\dfrac{-3}{5 - \sqrt{3}}$

Practice and Apply

Simplify each radical expression by using the Properties of *n*th Roots.

14. $\sqrt{50}$

15. $\sqrt{128}$

16. $\sqrt[3]{-54}$

17. $-32\sqrt[3]{-48}$

18. $\sqrt{32x^3}$

19. $\sqrt{18x^3}$

20. $\sqrt[3]{-27x^5}$

21. $\sqrt[3]{-81x^7}$

22. $\sqrt{27b^3c^4}$

23. $\sqrt{50a^3b^4}$

24. $\sqrt[3]{24x^5y^3z^9}$

25. $\sqrt[3]{250r^7s^2t^3}$

26. $\sqrt{98x^8y^3z}$

27. $(16x^6)^{\frac{1}{4}}$

28. $(40a^7)^{\frac{1}{3}}$

Simplify each product or quotient. Assume that the value of each variable is positive.

29. $\sqrt{2x^3} \cdot \sqrt{4x^3}$

30. $\sqrt[3]{3y^3} \cdot \sqrt[3]{9y^2}$

31. $\sqrt[4]{25x^2} \cdot (25x^2)^{\frac{1}{4}}$

32. $(16x^2)^{\frac{1}{3}} \cdot \sqrt[3]{4x}$

33. $(24rs)^{\frac{1}{2}} \cdot \sqrt{6r^3s^4} \cdot \sqrt{rs^2}$

34. $\sqrt[3]{3a^2b^4} \cdot (a^3b^5)^{\frac{1}{3}} \cdot \sqrt[3]{ab}$

35. $\dfrac{(64y^7)^{\frac{1}{3}}}{\sqrt[3]{y^3}}$

36. $\dfrac{(42a^4)^{\frac{1}{2}}}{\sqrt{8a^5}}$

37. $\dfrac{\sqrt{24x^5}}{(6x^3)^{\frac{1}{2}}}$

38. $\dfrac{\sqrt[3]{32x^7}}{(4x^2)^{\frac{1}{3}}}$

39. $\dfrac{(64x^7)^{\frac{1}{4}}}{\sqrt[4]{x}}$

40. $\dfrac{(24x^5z^2)^{\frac{1}{2}}}{\sqrt{12x^2z^2}}$

41. $(21x^2y^3)^{\frac{1}{2}}\sqrt{3x^4y^8}$

42. $(81d^4f^4)^{\frac{1}{2}}\sqrt{5d^2f^8}\sqrt{d^2f^2}$

43. $\sqrt[3]{64y^7c^3t^5}(yct)^{-\frac{2}{3}}$

44. $\sqrt[3]{162a^7b^3c^5}(54abc)^{-\frac{1}{3}}$

Find each sum, difference, or product. Give your answer in simplest radical form.

45. $(3 + \sqrt{3}) + (3 + \sqrt{3})$

46. $(4 + \sqrt{7}) - (-3 + 2\sqrt{7})$

47. $(3 + \sqrt{18}) + (-1 - 4\sqrt{2})$

48. $(-6 - \sqrt{6}) - (-1 - 3\sqrt{24})$

49. $(3 + \sqrt{32}) - (4 + 2\sqrt{98})$

50. $(5 + \sqrt{125}) + (-10 + 10\sqrt{5})$

51. $(\sqrt{12} - 4) - (8 + \sqrt{27})$

52. $(-3\sqrt{5} + 2) - (3 + 2\sqrt{20})$

53. $(2 + \sqrt{3})(-1 + \sqrt{3})$

54. $(\sqrt{5} - 8)(-1 + 3\sqrt{5})$

55. $(8 + \sqrt{12})(3 - \sqrt{12})$

56. $(-6 + \sqrt{5})(-4 + 2\sqrt{5})$

57. $(3 + \sqrt{2})(3 + \sqrt{2})$

58. $(2 + 3\sqrt{7})(2 - 3\sqrt{7})$

59. $(\sqrt{100} - 6)(-4 + \sqrt{12})$

60. $(5 + \sqrt{18})(-\sqrt{16} - 3)$

61. $(4 - 2\sqrt{27})(1 + \sqrt{75})$

62. $(-3 + 2\sqrt{8})(\sqrt{20} - 5)$

63. $(13 + \sqrt{2}) - (-3 + 2\sqrt{2}) + 3\sqrt{2}$

64. $(1 + \sqrt{75}) + (-2 + \sqrt{125}) - 7\sqrt{3}$

65. $(3 - 5\sqrt{2}) - (-4 + \sqrt{2})$

66. $(4 + 3\sqrt{7}) - (5 + 3\sqrt{7})$

67. $2\sqrt{6}(\sqrt{24} - 7)$

68. $3\sqrt{5}(-\sqrt{20} + 2)$

69. $(\sqrt{75} - 8)\sqrt{12}$

70. $(3\sqrt{12} + 4)\sqrt{27}$

71. $4\sqrt{2}(\sqrt{12} - 3\sqrt{2} + 4\sqrt{8})$

72. $2\sqrt{3}(7\sqrt{3} - \sqrt{8} + 2\sqrt{5})$

Write each expression with a rational denominator and in simplest form.

73. $\dfrac{2}{\sqrt{5}}$

74. $\dfrac{1}{\sqrt{2}}$

75. $\dfrac{4}{\sqrt{6}}$

76. $\dfrac{5}{\sqrt{15}}$

77. $\dfrac{6}{\sqrt{12}}$

78. $\dfrac{15}{\sqrt{18}}$

79. $\dfrac{\sqrt{5}}{\sqrt{75}}$

80. $\dfrac{\sqrt{3}}{\sqrt{27}}$

81. $\dfrac{\sqrt{24}}{\sqrt{6}}$

82. $\dfrac{\sqrt{60}}{\sqrt{5}}$

83. $\dfrac{\sqrt{18}}{\sqrt{12}}$

84. $\dfrac{1}{\sqrt{3} + 3}$

85. $\dfrac{8}{\sqrt{2} + 4}$

86. $\dfrac{12}{\sqrt{5} - 1}$

87. $\dfrac{3}{2 + \sqrt{3}}$

88. $\dfrac{14}{\sqrt{5} + \sqrt{3}}$

89. $\dfrac{10}{\sqrt{7} + \sqrt{2}}$

90. $\dfrac{14}{\sqrt{3} - \sqrt{2}}$

internet connect

**Homework
Help Online**

Go To: **go.hrw.com**
Keyword:
MB1 Homework Help
  for Exercises 84–90

CHALLENGE

Simplify.

91. $\dfrac{x}{3 - 5\sqrt{2}} - (2 + 3\sqrt{2})$

92. $\dfrac{x}{4 + \sqrt{2}} - (-1 + 3\sqrt{2})$

CONNECTIONS

93. GEOMETRY Refer to the figure at right. Find the length of the red path from point A to point B to point C. Give an exact answer and an answer rounded to the nearest hundredth.

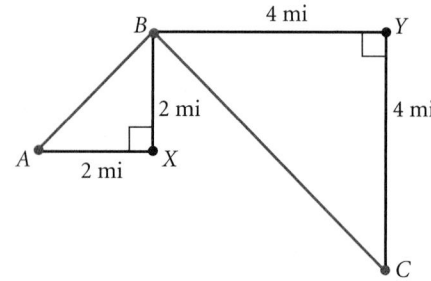

94. GEOMETRY Refer to the figure at right. Find the length of the red path from point A to point B to point C if $AX = BX = a$ and $BY = CY = 2a$, where $a > 0$. Give your answer in simplest radical form.

Coefficients of Friction

	concrete	tar
wet	$f = 0.4$	$f = 0.5$
dry	$f = 0.8$	$f = 1.0$

95. TRANSPORTATION Accident investigators can usually estimate a motorist's speed, s, in miles per hour by examining the length, d, in feet of the skid marks on the highway. The estimate of the speed also depends on the road surface and weather conditions. If f represents the coefficient of friction between rubber and concrete or tar, then $s = \sqrt{30fd}$ gives an estimate of the motorist's speed in miles per hour.

a. Write a function for s in terms of d under wet conditions on a concrete road. Give an answer in simplest radical form, and give an approximation to the nearest tenth.

b. Estimate a motorist's speed under wet conditions on a concrete road if the skid marks are estimated to be 200 feet long. Give your estimate to the nearest whole number of miles per hour.

c. Compare the speed of a motorist whose skid marks are 200 feet long with that of a motorist whose skid marks are 400 feet long, both under wet conditions on a concrete road.

 Look Back

Solve each equation, giving both exact and approximate solutions. *(LESSON 5.2)*

96. $x^2 = 34$ **97.** $2x^2 - 6 = 26$ **98.** $(x - 3)^2 + 4 = 14$

Factor each expression. *(LESSON 5.3)*

99. $x^2 + 6x + 5$ **100.** $x^2 - 2x - 15$ **101.** $x^2 - 3x - 40$

Solve each equation by factoring and applying the Zero Product Property. *(LESSON 5.3)*

102. $x^2 + 3x = 28$ **103.** $x^2 - 11x = -30$ **104.** $-x^2 = 9x + 20$

Find the zeros of each quadratic function. *(LESSON 5.3)*

105. $f(x) = x^2 + 9x + 18$ **106.** $f(x) = x^2 - 2x - 8$ **107.** $f(x) = x^2 - 3x - 18$

Find the domain of each radical function. *(LESSON 8.6)*

108. $f(x) = \sqrt{3x - 1}$ **109.** $g(x) = 2\sqrt{5 - x}$ **110.** $h(x) = -\sqrt{2(3 - 5x)}$

 Look Beyond

Rationalize each denominator. (Hint: $(1 + a)(1 - a + a^2) = 1 + a^3$)

111. $\dfrac{1}{\sqrt[3]{5}}$ **112.** $\dfrac{\sqrt[3]{6}}{\sqrt[3]{3}}$ **113.** $\dfrac{2}{1 + \sqrt[3]{x}}$

Solving Radical Equations and Inequalities

Why *Sometimes solving a real-world problem involves solving a radical equation or inequality. For example, designing a bridge may involve solving a radical equation.*

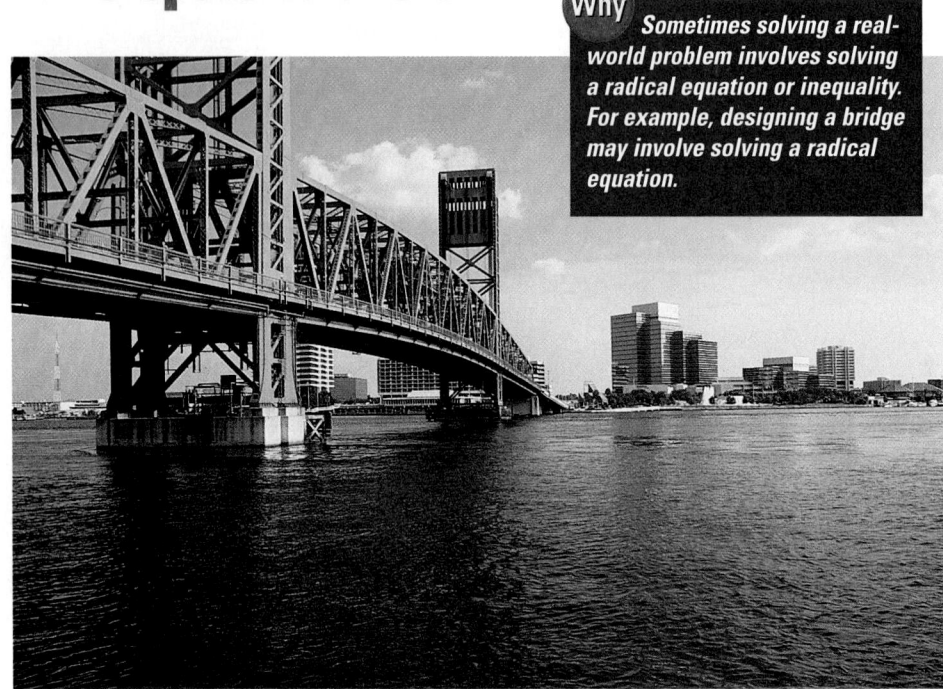

Objectives

- Solve radical equations.

- Solve radical inequalities.

APPLICATION

ENGINEERING

Engineers and town planners are proposing a new bridge to span a river. The diagram below shows a side view of the proposed bridge. The distance, d, across the river is 286 feet. Each vertical support, h, above the roadbed is 15 feet high, and there are 6 equally spaced piers below the roadbed.

The function $n = \dfrac{d}{2\sqrt{L^2 - h^2}} + 1$ relates the number of piers, n, below the roadbed to d, L, and h. What is the length, L, of each slanted support? To answer this question you need to solve a *radical equation*. *You will answer this question in Example 4.*

A **radical equation** is an equation that contains at least one radical expression with a variable under the radical symbol. To solve a radical equation, you can raise each side of the equation to the same power.

Principle of Powers

If $a = b$ and n is a positive integer, then $a^n = b^n$.

To solve a radical equation with a square root on one side, square each side of the equation. Recall from Lesson 8.5 that an extraneous solution is a solution to a resulting equation that is not a solution to the original equation. Raising the expression on each side of an equation to an even power may introduce extraneous solutions, so it is important to check your solutions.

E X A M P L E ① Solve $2\sqrt{x+5} = 8$. Check your solution.

● **SOLUTION**

$$2\sqrt{x+5} = 8$$
$$\sqrt{x+5} = 4$$
$$\left(\sqrt{x+5}\right)^2 = 4^2 \qquad \textit{Square each side of the equation.}$$
$$x + 5 = 16$$
$$x = 11$$

CHECK

$$2\sqrt{x+5} = 8$$
$$2\sqrt{(11)+5} \stackrel{?}{=} 8$$
$$2 \cdot 4 = 8 \quad \textbf{True}$$

You can also check by graphing. Graph $y = 2\sqrt{x+5}$ and $y = 8$ on the same screen. The x-coordinate of the point of intersection is 11.

The solution to $2\sqrt{x+5} = 8$ is 11.

TECHNOLOGY
GRAPHICS CALCULATOR

Keystroke Guide, page 558

TRY THIS Solve $3\sqrt{2x-1} = 6$. Check your solution.

A radical equation may contain the variable on each side of the equation, as shown in Example 2 below and Example 3 on the next page.

E X A M P L E ② Solve $\sqrt[3]{x-5} = \sqrt[3]{7-x}$. Check your solution.

● **SOLUTION**

TECHNOLOGY
GRAPHICS CALCULATOR

Keystroke Guide, page 559

Method 1 Use algebra.
$$\sqrt[3]{x-5} = \sqrt[3]{7-x}$$
$$\left(\sqrt[3]{x-5}\right)^3 = \left(\sqrt[3]{7-x}\right)^3$$
$$x - 5 = 7 - x$$
$$x = 6$$

CHECK

$$\sqrt[3]{x-5} = \sqrt[3]{7-x}$$
$$\sqrt[3]{(6)-5} \stackrel{?}{=} \sqrt[3]{7-(6)}$$
$$\sqrt[3]{1} = \sqrt[3]{1} \quad \textbf{True}$$

Method 2 Use a graph.
Graph $y = \sqrt[3]{x-5}$ and $y = \sqrt[3]{7-x}$ on the same screen, and find the x-coordinates of any points of intersection.

TRY THIS Solve $\sqrt{x+2} = \sqrt{5-2x}$. Check your solution.

E X A M P L E **3** Solve $\sqrt{x+1} + 3 = 2x$. Check your solution.

SOLUTION

$$\sqrt{x+1} + 3 = 2x$$

$$\sqrt{x+1} = 2x - 3 \qquad \textit{Isolate the radical before squaring.}$$

$$x + 1 = (2x - 3)^2 \qquad \textit{Square each side of the equation.}$$

$$x + 1 = 4x^2 - 12x + 9$$

$$4x^2 - 13x + 8 = 0 \qquad \textit{Write in standard form with a = 4, b = -13, c = 8.}$$

$$x = \frac{-(-13) \pm \sqrt{13^2 - 4(4)(8)}}{2(4)} \qquad \textit{Apply the quadratic formula.}$$

$$x = \frac{13 + \sqrt{41}}{8} \quad or \quad x = \frac{13 - \sqrt{41}}{8}$$

$$x \approx 2.43 \qquad\qquad\quad x \approx 0.82$$

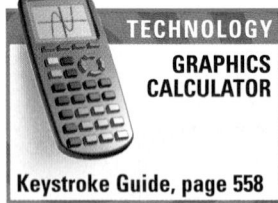

TECHNOLOGY

GRAPHICS CALCULATOR

Keystroke Guide, page 558

CHECK

Graph $y = \sqrt{x+1} + 3$ and $y = 2x$ on the same screen, and find the x-coordinates of any points of intersection. The graphs intersect at only one point, where $x \approx 2.43$.

Thus, $\frac{13 - \sqrt{41}}{8}$ is an extraneous solution; the only solution is $\frac{13 + \sqrt{41}}{8}$, or approximately 2.43.

Intersection
X=2.4253905 Y=4.8507811

TRY THIS   Solve $\sqrt{x-1} = -x + 2$. Check your solution.

E X A M P L E **4** Refer to the bridge described at the beginning of the lesson.

Find the length, L, of each slanted support.

APPLICATION

ENGINEERING

SOLUTION

Substitute 6 for n, 286 for d, and 15 for h in the function $n = \frac{d}{2\sqrt{L^2 - h^2}} + 1$ to get $6 = \frac{286}{2\sqrt{L^2 - 15^2}} + 1$. Solve for L.

Method 1 Use a graph.
Graph $y = \frac{286}{2\sqrt{L^2 - 15^2}} + 1$ and $y = 6$, and find the x-coordinates of any points of intersection.

Method 2 Use a table.
Examine the table of values for the function $y = \frac{286}{2\sqrt{L^2 - 15^2}} + 1$.

TECHNOLOGY

GRAPHICS CALCULATOR

Keystroke Guide, page 559

The x-coordinate of the point of intersection is about 32.3.

Intersection
X=32.294891 Y=6

Using an x-increment of 0.01, a solution appears to be very close to 32.3.

X	Y1
32.26	6.0069
32.27	6.0049
32.28	6.0029
32.29	6.001
32.3	5.999
32.31	5.997
32.32	5.995

Y1=6.00096579152

Thus, the length of each slanted support is about 32.3 feet.

Some radical equations have no solutions, as shown in Example 5.

E X A M P L E **5** Solve $\sqrt{x} - 1 = \sqrt{2x + 1}$. **Check your solution.**

● **SOLUTION**

$$\sqrt{x} - 1 = \sqrt{2x + 1}$$

$$\left(\sqrt{x} - 1\right)^2 = \left(\sqrt{2x + 1}\right)^2 \quad \textit{Square each side of the equation.}$$

$$x - 2\sqrt{x} + 1 = 2x + 1$$

$$-2\sqrt{x} = x \qquad\qquad \textit{Simplify.}$$

$$\left(-2\sqrt{x}\right)^2 = x^2 \qquad\qquad \textit{Square each side of the equation again.}$$

$$4x = x^2$$

$$x^2 - 4x = 0$$

$$x(x - 4) = 0$$

$$x = 0 \quad or \quad x = 4$$

CHECK

$$\sqrt{0} - 1 \overset{?}{=} \sqrt{2(0) + 1} \qquad\qquad \sqrt{4} - 1 \overset{?}{=} \sqrt{2(4) + 1}$$

$$-1 = 1 \quad \textbf{False} \qquad\qquad\qquad 1 = 3 \quad \textbf{False}$$

The equation $\sqrt{x} - 1 = \sqrt{2x + 1}$ has no real solutions.

The graphs of $y = \sqrt{x} - 1$ and $y = \sqrt{2x + 1}$ are shown on the same screen at right.

Because the graphs do not intersect, the equation $\sqrt{x} - 1 = \sqrt{2x + 1}$ has no real solutions.

TRY THIS Solve $3\sqrt{x} + 2 = \sqrt{3x}$. Check your solution.

SUMMARY
Solving Radical Equations

To solve a radical equation, follow these steps:

   1. If possible, write the equation with the radical expression isolated on one side.

   2. Raise the expression on each side of the equation to the appropriate power.

   3. Repeat Steps 1 and 2 as needed to obtain an equation with no radical expressions. Solve this equation.

   4. Check your solutions and discard extraneous solutions.

CRITICAL THINKING Describe the algebraic strategy that you would use to solve the equation $\sqrt{x - 1} = \sqrt{x + 1} - 1$.

Solving Radical Inequalities

A **radical inequality** is an inequality that contains at least one radical expression. To explore solutions to radical inequalities, complete the Activity below.

Keystroke Guide, page 559

Exploring Radical Inequalities

You will need: a graphics calculator

1. **a.** Let $f(x) = \sqrt{x}$ and $g(x) = 1$. Graph f and g on the same screen.
   b. For what values of x is $f(x) \geq g(x)$?
   c. For what values of x is $f(x) \leq g(x)$?

2. Explain why the answer to part **b** of Step 1 is not $x \leq 1$.

CHECKPOINT ✔ 3. Do $\sqrt{x} \geq a$ and $\sqrt{x} \leq a$, where $a > 0$, always have solutions? Explain.

CHECKPOINT ✔ 4. Explain how to use a graph to solve $\sqrt{x} \geq x - 2$ and $\sqrt{x} \leq x - 2$. Then state the solutions.

The fact below is helpful for solving radical inequalities.

> If $a \geq 0$, $b \geq 0$, and $a \geq b$, then $a^n \geq b^n$.

This fact allows you to square the expression on each side of an inequality, as shown in Example 6.

E X A M P L E ⑥ Solve $\sqrt{x + 1} < 2$. Check your solution.

● **SOLUTION**

Because the radicand of a radical expression cannot be negative, first solve $x + 1 \geq 0$.

$$x + 1 \geq 0$$
$$x \geq -1$$

Then solve the original inequality.

$$\sqrt{x + 1} < 2$$
$$\left(\sqrt{x + 1}\right)^2 < 2^2$$
$$x + 1 < 4$$
$$x < 3$$

It appears that the solution is $x \geq -1$ *and* $x < 3$, or $-1 \leq x < 3$.

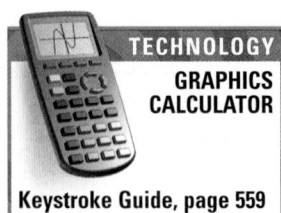

Keystroke Guide, page 559

CHECK
Graph $y = \sqrt{x + 1}$ and $y = 2$ on the same screen.

The graph verifies that the solution is $-1 \leq x < 3$.

TRY THIS Solve $\sqrt{2x - 3} < 5$. Check your solution.

EXAMPLE **7** Solve $x < 3\sqrt[3]{x+1}$ by graphing. Give the solution to the nearest tenth.

SOLUTION

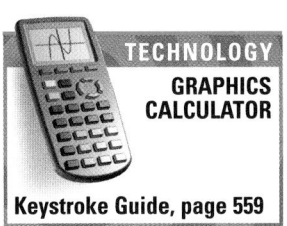

TECHNOLOGY

GRAPHICS CALCULATOR

Keystroke Guide, page 559

Graph $y = x$ and $y = 3\sqrt[3]{x+1}$ on the same screen.

The graph of $y = x$ is below that of $y = 3\sqrt[3]{x+1}$ for approximately $x < -4.6$ and for approximately $-1.0 < x < 5.6$.

Thus, the solution to $x < 3\sqrt[3]{x+1}$ is approximately $x < -4.6$ *or* $-1.0 < x < 5.6$.

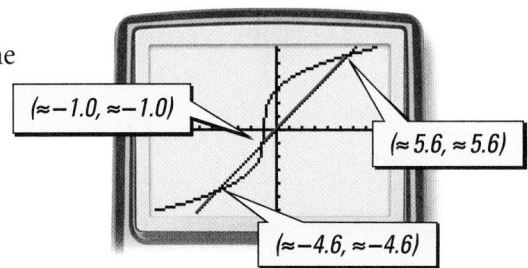

$(\approx -1.0, \approx -1.0)$

$(\approx 5.6, \approx 5.6)$

$(\approx -4.6, \approx -4.6)$

TRY THIS Solve $x - 1 < 3\sqrt[3]{2x+1}$ by graphing. Give the solution to the nearest tenth.

Exercises

internet connect

Activities Online

Go To: **go.hrw.com**
Keyword:
MB1 Relativity

Communicate

1. Briefly describe two methods discussed in the lesson for solving a radical equation or inequality such as $\sqrt{x} = 3\sqrt{x-4}$ or $\sqrt{x} \le 3\sqrt{x-4}$.

2. Explain why it is necessary to check any solutions to a radical equation that you obtain algebraically.

3. Explain how to determine that $\sqrt{x} = \sqrt{x+1}$ has no solution. Use algebra and a graph in your explanation.

Guided Skills Practice

4. Solve $3\sqrt{2x-5} = 20$. Check your solution. *(EXAMPLE 1)*

5. Solve $\sqrt[3]{3x+1} = \sqrt[3]{2x+3}$. Check your solution. *(EXAMPLE 2)*

6. Solve $\sqrt{5x+7} - 2 = x$. Check your solution. *(EXAMPLE 3)*

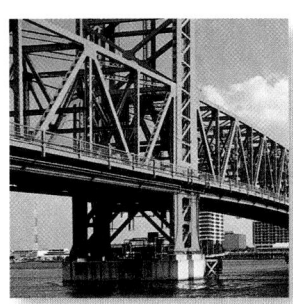

APPLICATION

7. ENGINEERING Refer to the bridge described at the beginning of the lesson. Find the length of each slanted support given that there are 6 piers below the roadbed, the distance across the river is 560 feet, and the vertical supports above the roadbed are 17 feet tall. Give your answer to the nearest tenth of a foot. *(EXAMPLE 4)*

8. Solve $2\sqrt{x+1} = \sqrt{x} - 3$. Check your solution. *(EXAMPLE 5)*

9. Solve $\sqrt{3x-2} \le 8$. Check your solution. *(EXAMPLE 6)*

10 Solve $-0.5x + 1 \le 4\sqrt[3]{3x-2}$ by graphing. Give the solution to the nearest tenth. *(EXAMPLE 7)*

Practice and Apply

internet connect

**Homework
Help Online**

Go To: **go.hrw.com**
Keyword:
MB1 Homework Help
 for Exercises 11–38

Solve each radical equation by using algebra. If the equation has no real solution, write *no solution*. Check your solution.

11. $\sqrt{x} = 4$

12. $\sqrt{x-3} = 2$

13. $5 = \sqrt{x^2 + 16}$

14. $3 = \sqrt{x^2 - 16}$

15. $\sqrt{x+2} = 4\sqrt{x}$

16. $2\sqrt{x} = 3\sqrt{x-2}$

17. $\sqrt{3x-2} = x - 2$

18. $x + 1 = \sqrt{6x-7} - 1$

19. $\sqrt[3]{x-2} = \sqrt[3]{2x+1}$

20. $\sqrt[3]{2x-3} = \sqrt[3]{2-x}$

21. $\sqrt[3]{x+2} = \sqrt[3]{x+3}$

22. $3\sqrt{2x+1} = 2\sqrt{2x} - 1$

23. $\sqrt{2x+1} = x + 1$

24. $\sqrt{3x+2} = x - 2$

Solve each radical inequality by using algebra. If the inequality has no real solution, write *no solution*. Check your solution.

25. $\sqrt{2x-1} \geq 1$

26. $\sqrt{3x+4} \geq 2$

27. $\sqrt{2x-1} \leq 1$

28. $\sqrt{3x+4} \leq 2$

29. $-\sqrt{x} \leq 2$

30. $-\sqrt{x} \geq 2$

31. $1 > 3\sqrt{3x-1}$

32. $\sqrt{2x+1} - 3 < 0$

33. $3\sqrt{3x-1} < -1$

34. $\sqrt{2x+1} + 3 < 0$

35. $\sqrt{2x+2} > \sqrt{3x}$

36. $\sqrt{9x+7} < \sqrt{14x}$

37. $x \leq \sqrt{x}$

38. $\frac{1}{8} \leq x \leq \sqrt{x}$

Solve each radical equation or inequality by using a graph. Round solutions to the nearest tenth. Check your solution by any method.

39. $\sqrt{2x-1} = x^2$

40. $(x+1)^2 = \sqrt{2x+1}$

41. $\sqrt[3]{2x+1} = x^2 + 2x$

42. $x^2 - x = \sqrt[3]{x-2}$

43. $\sqrt{x} = \sqrt[3]{x}$

44. $\sqrt[3]{x} = \sqrt[4]{x}$

45. $\sqrt{x} - 2x \geq 0$

46. $2x > \sqrt{3-x}$

47. $\sqrt[3]{x+2} > \sqrt[3]{x-2} + 2$

48. $\sqrt[3]{x} < \sqrt{x} + 3$

49. $\sqrt{x} \leq x^2 + \sqrt{x+1} - 2$

50. $0.5\sqrt[4]{x+2} > \sqrt[3]{x}$

51. $2\sqrt{x^2-1} \leq \sqrt{x+5}$

52. $2\sqrt{x^2-2} - \sqrt{3x+7} < 0$

Identify whether each statement is always true, sometimes true, or never true.

53. $\sqrt{x+3} = -12$

54. $\sqrt{x-6} = 3 + \sqrt{x}$

55. $\sqrt{3x-6} < 0$

56. $2\sqrt{2x-3} + 4 = 1$

57. $2\sqrt[4]{3x} = \sqrt[4]{3x+15}$

58. $\sqrt{x+4} + \sqrt{x-4} > 4$

59. $\sqrt{2x+5} - 7 \leq x - 2$

60. $\sqrt{x+5} - \sqrt{5x-21} \leq 4$

CHALLENGE

61. Find a value of a that makes each statement below true. Use a graph to confirm your response.

    a. The equation $\sqrt{x+a} = \sqrt{2x-a}$ has no solution.

    b. The equation $\sqrt{x+a} = \sqrt{2x-a}$ has one solution.

62. PHYSICS The function $h = -16t^2 + 128t + 50$ models the height, h, in feet above the ground of a projectile after t seconds of flight.

a. Solve for t in terms of h.

b. Graph the equation you wrote in part **a.**

c. After how many seconds will the height of the projectile above the ground be 270 feet?

63. SIGHTSEEING On a clear day, the approximate distance, d, in feet that a sightseer standing at the top of a building h feet tall can see is given by $d = 6397.2\sqrt{h}$.

a. On a clear day, what distance in feet can a sightseer see from the top of a 900-foot building? Give your answer to the nearest foot.

b. Convert your answer from part **a** to miles. (Note: 1 mile equals 5280 feet.)

c. How tall is a building from which a sightseer can see 32 miles on a clear day? Give your answer to the nearest foot.

 Look Back

Write each pair of parametric equations as a single equation in x and y. *(LESSON 3.6)*

64. $\begin{cases} x(t) = 3t \\ y(t) = t - 2 \end{cases}$

65. $\begin{cases} x(t) = t + 4 \\ y(t) = 2t + 1 \end{cases}$

66. $\begin{cases} x(t) = 3t + 1 \\ y(t) = -t \end{cases}$

Use the quadratic formula to solve each equation. Give your answers to the nearest tenth if necessary. *(LESSON 5.5)*

67. $2x^2 + 10x^2 + 12 = 0$ **68.** $2x^2 - 11x = 6$ **69.** $3x^2 + 4x = 5$

Divide by using synthetic division. *(LESSON 7.3)*

70. $(x^3 + 7x^2 - 10x - 16) \div (x - 2)$ **71.** $(x^3 - 63x - 162) \div (x + 6)$

Simplify each radical expression. Assume that the value of each variable is positive. *(LESSON 8.7)*

72. $\sqrt{28a^{16}}$

73. $4x^3y\sqrt{72x^7y^{10}}$

74. $\sqrt[3]{12s^2t} \cdot \sqrt[3]{36st^7}$

75. $\dfrac{\sqrt{30x^3}}{\sqrt{6x}}$

76. $\dfrac{\sqrt{4a^2}}{\sqrt{125b^3}}$

77. $\dfrac{\sqrt{80x^3}}{\sqrt{2x}}$

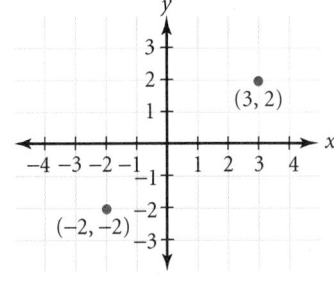 *Look Beyond*

78. Use the Pythagorean Theorem to find the distance between the two points graphed at right.

Means to an End

In problem-solving situations that are based on the calculation of an average, the choice of which average to use—arithmetic or harmonic—is critical. The results obtained from each average can be significantly different.

For any two numbers a and b, the *arithmetic mean* is $\frac{a+b}{2}$ and the *harmonic mean* is $\dfrac{2}{\frac{1}{a}+\frac{1}{b}}$.

To provide consumers with a standard to compare fuel economy for new cars, the Environmental Protection Agency (EPA) requires that estimates of fuel consumption be attached to the window of each new car.

For example, the EPA estimates that a certain car with a 1.9-liter engine and a 4-speed transmission can travel 24 miles per gallon (mpg) in the city and 34 miles per gallon on the highway.

The *Fuel Economy Guide,* published by the U.S. Department of Energy, is an aid to consumers who are considering the purchase of a new vehicle. The guide estimates the fuel consumption, in miles per gallon, for each vehicle available for the new model year. In the *Fuel Economy Guide,* the consumer is advised as follows:

Please be cautioned that simply averaging the mpg for city and highway driving and then looking up a single value in estimating may result in inaccurate estimates of the annual fuel cost.

1.9-liter engine
4-speed
CITY HWY
24   34
mpg   mpg

Activity 1

1. For the car described above, find the arithmetic mean of the fuel consumption in miles per gallon for city driving and for highway driving.

2. Find the harmonic mean for the city driving rate and highway driving rate.

3. Examine each mean. Explain why there is a warning about "simply averaging" the city rate and the highway rate when finding the annual fuel cost.

Activity 2

The number of miles that a person drives in the city may not be the same as the number of miles that the person drives on the highway. Therefore, to find the average annual fuel consumption for a car, you need to use a *weighted harmonic mean.*

Let d_1 represent the number of miles driven in the city in one year.

Let d_2 represent the number of miles driven on the highway in one year.

Then the number of gallons of fuel used per year for each type of driving is as follows:

City: $(d_1 \text{ miles})\left(\dfrac{\text{gallon}}{24 \text{ miles}}\right) = \dfrac{d_1}{24} \text{ gallons}$

Highway: $(d_2 \text{ miles})\left(\dfrac{\text{gallon}}{34 \text{ miles}}\right) = \dfrac{d_2}{34} \text{ gallons}$

A rational function, a, for the average annual fuel consumption for the car described on the previous page can be expressed in terms of the total miles driven.

$$a(d) = \frac{\text{total distance}}{\text{total number of gallons}} = \frac{d_1 + d_2}{\dfrac{d_1}{24} + \dfrac{d_2}{34}}$$

1. Suppose that you purchased this car and drove it 12,000 miles in one year—8000 miles in the city and 4000 miles on the highway. Find the average annual fuel consumption for this car.

2. Determine the total fuel cost for the year if gasoline costs $1.099 per gallon.

Activity 3

Jennifer is considering a strategy for an upcoming 2-mile bicycle race. During practice she maintains a speed of 20 miles per hour for the first mile, but fatigue reduces her speed to 10 miles per hour for the second mile.

1. Explain why Jennifer's average speed over these 2 miles is not the same as the arithmetic mean of 20 miles per hour and 10 miles per hour. Find Jennifer's average speed for these 2 miles.

2. Determine the speed at which Jennifer must travel during the second mile if she rides 20 miles per hour during the first mile and she wants her average speed for the entire 2-mile trip to be 15 miles per hour.

Chapter Review and Assessment

Key Skills & Exercises

LESSON 8.1

Key Skills

Solve problems involving inverse, joint, or combined variation.

inverse variation: $y = \frac{k}{x}$ or $xy = k$

joint variation: $y = kxz$

combined variation: $y = \frac{kz}{x}$

A variable n varies jointly as x and y and varies inversely as the cube of z.

$$n = k\frac{xy}{z^3}$$

If $n = -14$ when $x = 3$, $y = 7$, and $z = -3$, what is n when $x = 4$, $y = 5$, and $z = 3$?

First find the constant, k, by solving $n = k\frac{xy}{z^3}$ for k and using substitution.

$$n = k\frac{xy}{z^3} \quad \rightarrow \quad k = \frac{nz^3}{xy}$$

$$k = \frac{nz^3}{xy} = \frac{(-14)(-3)^3}{(3)(7)} = 18$$

Now find n when $x = 4$, $y = 5$, and $z = 3$.

$$n = k\frac{xy}{z^3} = (18)\frac{(4)(5)}{(3)^3} = \frac{40}{3}$$

Exercises

1. A variable y varies jointly as x and z. If $y = 2$ when $x = 4$ and $z = 6$, what is y when $x = 3$ and $z = 8$?

2. A variable m varies directly as a and inversely as b. If $m = 6$ when $a = 7$ and $b = 4$, what is m when $a = 9$ and $b = 12$?

3. A variable a varies directly as b and inversely as the square of c. If $a = 3$ when $b = 18$ and $c = 2$, what is a when $b = 20$ and $c = 6$?

4. A variable f varies jointly as g and the square of h and inversely as j. If $f = -14$ when $g = 5$, $h = 8$, and $j = 20$, what is f when $g = 4$, $h = 6$, and $j = 9$?

Key Skills

Identify all excluded values, asymptotes, and holes in the graph of a rational function.

$$y = \frac{4x^2 + 12x}{x^2 + x - 6} = \frac{4x(x + 3)}{(x - 2)(x + 3)}$$

The excluded values are $x = 2$ and $x = -3$.

$x + 3$ is a factor of the numerator and the denominator, so the graph has a hole when $x = -3$.

$x - 2$ is a factor of only the denominator, so the vertical asymptote is $x = 2$.

The degree of the numerator is equal to the degree of the denominator, so the horizontal asymptote is $y = \frac{4}{1} = 4$.

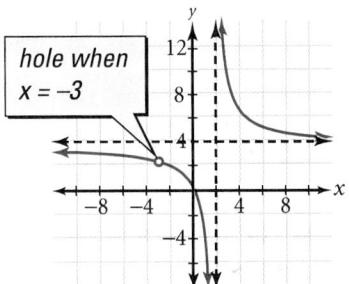
hole when x = –3

Exercises

Identify all excluded values, asymptotes, and holes in the graph of each rational function.

5. $R(x) = \dfrac{2x - 3}{x^2 - 8x + 12}$

6. $g(x) = \dfrac{3x - 5}{x^2 - 25}$

7. $f(x) = \dfrac{x^2 - x - 42}{x^2 + 5x - 14}$

8. $r(a) = \dfrac{a^2 + 4a - 12}{3a^2 - 12}$

9. $s(x) = \dfrac{x^2 - 9}{3x + 5}$

10. $M(x) = \dfrac{x^4 - 10x + 9}{3x^2 - 27}$

11. $h(y) = \dfrac{2y}{6y^4 - 18y^3}$

12. $r(t) = \dfrac{t^3 - t^2 - 4t + 4}{t^2 + t - 2}$

Key Skills

Multiply, divide, and simplify rational expressions, including complex fractions.

Simplify $\dfrac{x^2 + 2x - 3}{x^2 + 5x + 6} \div \dfrac{4x^2 - 4x}{x^2 + 3x + 2}$.

$$\frac{x^2 + 2x - 3}{x^2 + 5x + 6} \div \frac{4x^2 - 4x}{x^2 + 3x + 2}$$

$$= \frac{x^2 + 2x - 3}{x^2 + 5x + 6} \cdot \frac{x^2 + 3x + 2}{4x^2 - 4x}$$

$$= \frac{(x + 3)(x - 1)}{(x + 2)(x + 3)} \cdot \frac{(x + 1)(x + 2)}{4x(x - 1)}$$

$$= \frac{x + 1}{4x}$$

Simplify complex fractions.

$$\frac{\dfrac{x^2 - 1}{2x^2 - x - 15}}{\dfrac{4x + 4}{x^2 - 3x}} = \frac{x^2 - 1}{2x^2 - x - 15} \div \frac{4x + 4}{x^2 - 3x}$$

$$= \frac{(x + 1)(x - 1)}{(x - 3)(2x + 5)} \cdot \frac{x(x - 3)}{4(x + 1)}$$

$$= \frac{x(x - 1)}{4(2x + 5)}, \text{ or } \frac{x^2 - x}{8x + 20}$$

Exercises

Simplify each expression.

13. $\dfrac{x^2 + 6x}{10} \cdot \dfrac{4}{x^2 - 36}$

14. $\dfrac{3x^2 + 10x - 8}{3x^2 - 17x + 10} \cdot \dfrac{2x^2 + 9x - 5}{x^2 + 3x - 4}$

15. $\dfrac{4a + 8}{5a - 20} \div \dfrac{a^2 + 3a - 10}{a^2 - 4a}$

16. $\dfrac{x^2 - 9}{6} \div \dfrac{4x - 12}{x}$

17. $\dfrac{\dfrac{z}{z + 1}}{\dfrac{z + 2}{z}}$

18. $\dfrac{\dfrac{a + 1}{a^2}}{\dfrac{(a - 1)^2}{a}}$

19. $\dfrac{\dfrac{x + 1}{x}}{\dfrac{(x + 1)^2}{x + 2}}$

20. $\dfrac{\dfrac{4x^2}{6x - 3}}{\dfrac{15x}{2x - 1}}$

Key Skills

Add and subtract rational expressions.

Simplify $\dfrac{2a}{a-5} - \dfrac{5a}{3a+2}$.

$$\dfrac{2a}{a-5} - \dfrac{5a}{3a+2} = \dfrac{2a}{a-5}\left(\dfrac{3a+2}{3a+2}\right) - \dfrac{5a}{3a+2}\left(\dfrac{a-5}{a-5}\right)$$

$$= \dfrac{2a(3a+2) - 5a(a-5)}{(a-5)(3a+2)}$$

$$= \dfrac{a^2 + 29a}{3a^2 - 13a - 10}$$

Exercises

Simplify each expression.

21. $\dfrac{3y-5}{2y-6} + \dfrac{4y-2}{5y-15}$

22. $\dfrac{9y+3}{y^2-11y+18} + \dfrac{y+3}{y-9}$

23. $\dfrac{2x-3}{x^2-3x} - \dfrac{3x+1}{x-3}$

24. $\dfrac{3b-39}{b^2-7b+10} - \dfrac{3}{b-2}$

25. $\dfrac{\frac{2}{x}+\frac{5}{x}}{4 \quad 3}$

26. $\dfrac{x}{3+\frac{5}{x}} - \dfrac{4}{1+\frac{2}{x}}$

Key Skills

Solve rational equations.

Solve $\dfrac{1}{x^2} = x$.

$$\dfrac{1}{x^2} = x$$

$$1 = x^3$$

$$x^3 - 1 = 0$$

$$(x-1)(x^2 + x + 1) = 0$$

$$x = 1 \ \ or \ \ x = -\dfrac{1}{2} + \dfrac{\sqrt{3}}{2}i \ \ or \ \ x = -\dfrac{1}{2} - \dfrac{\sqrt{3}}{2}i$$

The only real solution is $x = 1$. Therefore, the only point of intersection for the graphs of $y = \dfrac{1}{x^2}$ and $y = x$ occurs when $x = 1$.

Solve rational inequalities.

Solve $\dfrac{x}{1+x} \le 2$.

$\dfrac{x}{1+x} \le 2, \ 1+x > 0 \quad or \quad \dfrac{x}{1+x} \le 2, \ 1+x < 0$

$\dfrac{x}{1+x} \le 2$	$\dfrac{x}{1+x} \le 2$
$x \le 2(1+x)$	$x \ge 2(1+x)$
$x \le 2 + 2x$	$x \ge 2 + 2x$
$-x \le 2$	$-x \ge 2$
$x \ge -2$	$x \le -2$

If $1 + x > 0$, then $x > -1$. | If $1 + x < 0$, then $x < -1$.
Thus, $x > -1$ *and* $x \ge -2$, | Thus, $x < -1$ *and* $x \le -2$,
or simply $x > -1$. | or simply $x \le -2$.

The solution is
$x > -1 \ or \ x \le -2$.

The graphs of
$y = \dfrac{x}{1+x}$ and $y = 2$
verify this solution.

Exercises

Solve each equation.

27. $\dfrac{1}{x^2+1} = \dfrac{1}{2}$

28. $\dfrac{4}{x^2+1} = 1$

29. $\dfrac{3x-1}{x^2+2x} = -1$

30. $\dfrac{2}{1-x^2} = \dfrac{x^2}{x^2+1}$

31. $\dfrac{1}{1-x^2} = -1$

32. $\dfrac{1}{x} = \dfrac{x+2}{x+1}$

Solve each inequality by using algebra.

33. $\dfrac{1}{x} < 1$

34. $\dfrac{1}{x} \ge 2$

35. $\dfrac{1}{x^2+1} < \dfrac{1}{2}$

36. $\dfrac{1}{x^2+1} \ge \dfrac{1}{3}$

37. $\dfrac{1+x}{2x+3} < 1$

38. $\dfrac{1+2x}{2x-1} < 2$

Solve each inequality by graphing.

39. $\dfrac{1}{x} \ge x$

40. $\dfrac{1}{x} < 2x$

41. $\dfrac{x^2+x+1}{x^2+3x+2} \ge x$

42. $\dfrac{x^3+2}{x^2+2x+1} \le 3x$

43. $\dfrac{1}{x^2+2x+1} > 2$

44. $\dfrac{1}{x^2-x+2} < x$

Key Skills

Find the inverse of a quadratic function.

Find the inverse of $y = x^2 - 7x + 10$. Interchange x and y, and solve for y by applying the quadratic formula.

$$x = y^2 - 7y + 10$$

$$y = \frac{-(-7) \pm \sqrt{(-7)^2 - 4(1)(10 - x)}}{2(1)}$$

$$y = \frac{7 \pm \sqrt{9 + 4x}}{2}$$

Describe the transformations applied to the square-root parent function, $f(x) = \sqrt{x}$.

Describe the transformations applied to $f(x) = \sqrt{x}$ to obtain $y = 2\sqrt{3x - 3} + 4$.

$$g(x) = 2\sqrt{3x - 3} + 4 = 2\sqrt{3(x - 1)} + 4$$

The parent function is stretched vertically by a factor of 2, compressed horizontally by a factor of $\frac{1}{3}$, translated horizontally 1 unit to the right, and translated vertically 4 units up.

Exercises

Find the inverse of each quadratic function.

45. $y = 3x + x^2$ **46.** $y = 8x + 12 + x^2$

47. $y = 3x^2 - 16x + 5$ **48.** $y = 2x^2 + 7x + 6$

For each function, describe the transformations applied to $f(x) = \sqrt{x}$.

49. $g(x) = \frac{1}{3}\sqrt{x}$ **50.** $h(x) = 3\sqrt{x} - 5$

51. $k(x) = \sqrt{2x - 3}$ **52.** $g(x) = 4\sqrt{2x + 1} + 2$

53. $h(x) = -2\sqrt{3x} - 6$ **54.** $r(x) = 5\sqrt{3(x - 1)} + 1$

Evaluate each expression.

55. $5\left(\sqrt[3]{-27}\right)^2$ **56.** $\frac{1}{2}\sqrt[3]{8} + 1$

Key Skills

Simplify expressions involving radicals.

Simplify $\dfrac{(24a^8b^5)^{\frac{1}{4}} \cdot \sqrt[4]{4a^3b^2}}{\sqrt[4]{3ab^2}}$.

$$\frac{(24a^8b^5)^{\frac{1}{4}} \cdot \sqrt[4]{4a^3b^2}}{\sqrt[4]{3ab^2}} = \frac{\sqrt[4]{24a^8b^5} \cdot \sqrt[4]{4a^3b^2}}{\sqrt[4]{3ab^2}}$$

$$= \frac{\sqrt[4]{96a^{11}b^7}}{\sqrt[4]{3ab^2}}$$

$$= \sqrt[4]{32a^{10}b^5}$$

$$= \sqrt[4]{2^4a^8b^4 \cdot 2a^2b}$$

$$= 2a^2|b|\sqrt[4]{2a^2b}$$

Rationalize the denominators of expressions.

Write $\dfrac{1}{2 + \sqrt{2}}$ with a rational denominator.

$$\frac{1}{2 + \sqrt{2}} = \frac{1}{2 + \sqrt{2}}\left(\frac{2 - \sqrt{2}}{2 - \sqrt{2}}\right) = \frac{2 - \sqrt{2}}{2}$$

Exercises

Simplify each radical expression. Assume that the value of each variable is positive.

57. $\sqrt{6x^2y^4} \cdot (3x^5y)^{\frac{1}{2}}$ **58.** $(5a^3b^5)^{\frac{1}{3}} \cdot \sqrt[3]{4a^4b}$

59. $\dfrac{\sqrt[3]{42c^4d^{17}}}{(6cd^{11})^{\frac{1}{3}}}$ **60.** $\dfrac{(45s^3t^6)^{\frac{1}{2}}}{\sqrt{3t^2}}$

61. $\dfrac{(6x^5y^7)^{\frac{1}{2}} \cdot \sqrt{3x^2y^4}}{\sqrt{2x}}$ **62.** $\dfrac{(24m^9n)^{\frac{1}{3}} \cdot \sqrt[3]{9m^3n^7}}{\sqrt[3]{3mn^2}}$

Write each expression with a rational denominator and in simplest form.

63. $\dfrac{1}{\sqrt{5}}$ **64.** $\dfrac{1}{\sqrt{7}}$

65. $\dfrac{3}{2 - \sqrt{3}}$ **66.** $\dfrac{4}{-2 + \sqrt{5}}$

67. $\dfrac{1 + \sqrt{2}}{3 - \sqrt{3}}$ **68.** $\dfrac{2 - \sqrt{3}}{3 + \sqrt{2}}$

Key Skills

Solve radical equations.

Solve $2x = \sqrt{3 - x}$.

$$2x = \sqrt{3 - x}$$
$$4x^2 = 3 - x$$
$$4x^2 + x - 3 = 0$$
$$(4x - 3)(x + 1) = 0$$
$$x = \frac{3}{4} \quad or \quad x = -1$$

Check for extraneous solutions.

$$2x = \sqrt{3 - x} \qquad\qquad 2x = \sqrt{3 - x}$$
$$2\left(\frac{3}{4}\right) \overset{?}{=} \sqrt{3 - \left(\frac{3}{4}\right)} \qquad 2(-1) \overset{?}{=} \sqrt{3 - (-1)}$$
$$\frac{3}{2} = \frac{3}{2} \quad \textbf{True} \qquad\qquad -2 = 2 \quad \textbf{False}$$

Solve radical inequalities.

To solve $\sqrt{2x - 1} \le 1$, first solve $2x - 1 \ge 0$.

$$2x - 1 \ge 0$$
$$x \ge \frac{1}{2}$$

Then solve the original inequality.

$$\sqrt{2x - 1} \le 1$$
$$\left(\sqrt{2x - 1}\right)^2 \le 1^2$$
$$2x - 1 \le 1$$
$$2x \le 2$$
$$x \le 1$$

Thus, $x \ge \frac{1}{2}$ *and* $x \le 1$, or $\frac{1}{2} \le x \le 1$. The solution can be verified by graphing.

Exercises

Solve each radical equation by using algebra. If the inequality has no real solution, write *no solution*. Check your solution.

69. $\sqrt{x + 2} = -2$ **70.** $3\sqrt{x + 7} + 8 = 6$

71. $\sqrt[3]{x + 2} = -2$ **72.** $3\sqrt[3]{x + 7} + 8 = 6$

73. $\sqrt{x} = 2x$ **74.** $\sqrt{x + 2} = 3$

75. $\sqrt{x} = \sqrt{-x + 3}$ **76.** $\sqrt{2x + 1} = \sqrt{4x - 4}$

77. $\sqrt[3]{4 - x} = \sqrt[3]{3x}$ **78.** $\sqrt[5]{2x} = \sqrt[5]{x + 3}$

79. $\sqrt{x} - 2 = \sqrt{x - 2}$ **80.** $\sqrt{3x} - 1 = \sqrt{x + 2}$

Solve each radical inequality by using algebra. Check your solution.

81. $\sqrt{x} \le 5$ **82.** $\sqrt{x - 1} < 2$

83. $\sqrt{x} \ge 5$ **84.** $\sqrt{x - 1} > 2$

85. $\sqrt[4]{x - 2} \ge 1$ **86.** $\sqrt[3]{x - 1} < 1$

87. $\sqrt{2x} + 2 > 4$ **88.** $-2\sqrt{x - 2} < -1$

89. $\sqrt{6x} < 0$ **90.** $4\sqrt{5x - 1} < 0$

Solve each radical inequality by graphing.

91 $\sqrt[3]{x - 2} \le \sqrt{x}$ **92** $\sqrt[5]{2x + 1} \ge 2$

Applications

PHYSICS The weight of an object varies inversely as the square of the distance from the object to the center of Earth, whose radius is approximately 4000 miles.

93. If an astronaut weighs 175 pounds on Earth, what will the astronaut weigh at a point 60 miles above Earth's surface?

94. If an astronaut weighs 145 pounds at a point 80 miles above the Earth's surface, how much does the astronaut weigh on Earth?

Chapter Test

1. y varies jointly as x and z. If $y = -63$ when $x = 7$ and $z = -9$, find y when $x = -15$ and $z = -\frac{1}{2}$.

2. **CONSTRUCTION** The strength of a beam varies directly with the width of a beam and inversely as the cube of the depth. If a beam 10 mm wide by 20 mm deep will support 1200 kg, how much will a beam 8 mm by 25 mm support?

Identify all excluded values, asymptotes, and holes in the graph of each rational function.

3. $f(x) = \dfrac{x - 4}{x^2 - 16}$

4. $h(x) = \dfrac{x^2 + 2x - 15}{2x^2 - 18}$

5. $g(x) = \dfrac{2x^3 - 16}{x^3 - 2x^2 - 9x + 18}$

Simplify each expression.

6. $\dfrac{x^2 - 9}{2x^2 - 8x + 6} \cdot \dfrac{4x^2 - 12x + 36}{x^3 + 27}$

7. $\dfrac{\dfrac{x^3}{3x^2 - 12}}{\dfrac{x^3 + 5x^2}{3x^2 + 9x - 30}}$

8. $\dfrac{3x}{x - 2} \div \dfrac{6x^2}{2x^2 - 8} \cdot \dfrac{5x + 1}{2x + 4}$

Simplify each expression.

9. $\dfrac{4}{x^2 - 4} + \dfrac{x + 3}{x + 2}$

10. $\dfrac{x - 37}{x^2 - 2x - 15} - \dfrac{5}{x + 3}$

11. **GEOMETRY** Find the area of the shaded region of the figure at right if the largest triangle has an area $A = x$.

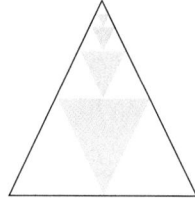

Solve each equation or inequality.

12. $\dfrac{x + 3}{x - 1} = 2$

13. $\dfrac{z - 4}{z + 2} + \dfrac{z - 5}{z - 4} = 1$

14. $\dfrac{3}{x + 4} \le 5$

15. $\dfrac{3}{x + 4} < \dfrac{5}{x + 7}$

For each function, describe the transformations applied to $f(x) = \sqrt{x}$.

16. $g(x) = \sqrt{x - 4}$

17. $h(x) = -2\sqrt{x} + 3$

Find the inverse of each quadratic function.

18. $y = x^2 + x$

19. $y = 5x^2 - 3x - 4$

Evaluate each expression.

20. $(3\sqrt[4]{81})^2 - 31$

21. $\dfrac{1}{5}\left((\sqrt{9})^3 + (\sqrt[3]{64})^2 + 2\right)$

Simplify each expression. Assume that the value of each variable is positive.

22. $5\sqrt{8x^3y^6} \cdot (2x^5y)^{\frac{1}{2}}$

23. $\dfrac{8\sqrt{5r^7s^9}}{\sqrt{25r^3s^5t}}$

24. $(5 - \sqrt{12}) - (2\sqrt{27} + 8)$

25. $(2 + \sqrt{5})(3 - 2\sqrt{5})$

Write each expression with a rational denominator and in simplest form.

26. $\dfrac{4}{\sqrt{11}}$

27. $\dfrac{1}{2 + \sqrt{5}}$

28. $\dfrac{2 - \sqrt{3}}{5 + \sqrt{7}}$

Solve each radical equation or inequality. If no solution, write no solution.

29. $\sqrt{2x + 7} = -3$

30. $\sqrt[4]{3x} = \sqrt[4]{4x - 7}$

31. $\sqrt{x - 7} < 5$

32. $\sqrt[3]{2x + 1} \ge 3$

College Entrance Exam Practice

MULTIPLE-CHOICE For Questions 1–14, write the letter that indicates the best answer.

1. Let $f(x) = 3x - 5$ and $g(x) = x^2 + 1$. Find $f \circ g$. *(LESSON 2.4)*

   a. $3x^3 - 5x^2 + 3x - 5$

   b. $9x^2 - 30x + 26$

   c. $x^2 + 3x - 4$

   d. $3x^2 - 2$

2. Which property is illustrated by the statement $x\left(\frac{1}{x}\right) = 1$, where $x \neq 0$? *(LESSON 2.1)*

   a. Identity Property of Multiplication

   b. Closure Property of Multiplication

   c. Associative Property of Multiplication

   d. Inverse Property of Multiplication

3. Solve $\log(5x - 3) + \log 2 = \log(24 - 2x)$ for x. *(LESSON 6.4)*

   a. 2.5   **b.** 3.6

   c. 1.5   **d.** 11.0

4. Solve $-5x < 10$. *(LESSON 1.7)*

   a. $x < -2$ **b.** $x > 15$

   c. $x < 15$ **d.** $x > -2$

5. Let $R(x) = \frac{1}{x^2 + 1}$. Identify all vertical asymptotes of the graph of R. *(LESSON 8.2)*

   a. no vertical asymptotes

   b. $x = 0$

   c. $x = -2$

   d. $x = 1$

6. Evaluate $\sqrt[3]{-\frac{1}{3}}$ to the nearest hundredth. *(LESSON 2.2)*

   a. -0.11 **b.** -0.69

   c. -0.04 **d.** undefined

7. If $\frac{a}{b} = \frac{c}{d}$, which of the following is *not* always true? *(LESSON 1.4)*

   a. $ad = bc$

   b. $ad = cb$

   c. $\frac{a}{d} = \frac{c}{b}$

   d. $\frac{a - b}{b} = \frac{c - d}{d}$

8. Solve $2^x = \frac{1}{64}$ for x. *(LESSON 6.3)*

   a. 32   **b.** 6

   c. -32 **d.** -6

9. Simplify $(6\sqrt{8} - 6\sqrt{2})(2\sqrt{2} + 1)$. *(LESSON 8.7)*

   a. $6\sqrt{2} - 24$

   b. $6\sqrt{2} + 24$

   c. $12\sqrt{2} - 23$

   d. $6\sqrt{2} - 23$

10. How many solutions does the system $\begin{cases} y = 3x + 2 \\ y = 3x - 2 \end{cases}$ have? *(LESSON 3.1)*

   a. 0   **b.** 1

   c. 2   **d.** infinite

11. Find the remainder when $2x^2 - 5x + 8$ is divided by $x + 4$. *(LESSON 7.3)*

   a. 60   **b.** -44

   c. 0   **d.** 20

12. Simplify $(a^3 b^{-2})^{-2}$. Assume that no variable equals zero. *(LESSON 2.2)*

   a. $\frac{b^4}{a^6}$ **b.** $\frac{1}{a^2 b}$

   c. $\frac{a^6}{b^4}$ **d.** $a^2 b$

13. Which of the following is *not* a root of
$x^3 + x^2 - 9x - 9 = 0$? *(LESSON 7.4)*
   a. -3 **b.** 3 **c.** -1 **d.** 1

14. Which would you add to $x^2 - 10x$ to complete
the square? *(LESSON 5.4)*
   a. 5 **b.** -5 **c.** 25 **d.** -25

15. Find the product $\begin{bmatrix} 3 & 6 & 1 \end{bmatrix} \begin{bmatrix} 0 & 5 \\ 1 & -2 \\ -3 & 4 \end{bmatrix}$.
(LESSON 4.2)

16. Write an equation of the line that contains the
points $(-3, 8)$ and $(9, -4)$. *(LESSON 1.3)*

17. Write the function for the graph of $f(x) = |x|$
translated 2 units to the left and 1 unit down.
(LESSON 2.7)

18. Factor $25x^2 - 60x + 36$ completely.
(LESSON 5.3)

19. Find the inverse of $f(x) = \frac{2}{3}x + 6$. *(LESSON 2.5)*

20. Simplify $\frac{1+x}{x^2 + 3x - 4} \div \frac{x^3}{x^2 + 4x}$. *(LESSON 8.3)*

21. Find x if $\log_{10} x + \log_{10} 8 = \log_{10} 16$.
(LESSON 6.4)

22. Write a polynomial function in standard form
by using the information given below.
(LESSON 7.5)
$P(0) = -12$; zeros: $-4, 3, -1$ (multiplicity 2)

23. Write the parametric equations $\begin{cases} x(t) = 3 - t^2 \\ y(t) = \frac{5}{2}t \end{cases}$
as a single equation in x and y. *(LESSON 3.6)*

24 Find the inverse, if one exists, of the matrix
$\begin{bmatrix} 2 & 4 \\ 3 & 5 \end{bmatrix}$. If the inverse does not exist, write
no inverse. *(LESSON 4.3)*

25. Write with a rational denominator $\frac{8}{5 - 3\sqrt{2}}$.
(LESSON 8.6)

26. TRAVEL An airplane travels from Hawaii to Los
Angeles at 580 miles per hour with a tailwind
and returns to Hawaii at 460 miles per hour
against a headwind. What is the average speed
of the airplane over the entire trip?
(LESSON 8.4)

27. MAXIMUM/MINIMUM At the Springfield City
Fourth of July celebration, a fireworks shell is
shot upward with an initial velocity of 250 feet
per second. Find its maximum height and the
time required to reach it. Use the formula
$h = v_0 t - 16t^2$, where v_0 is the initial velocity,
t is time in seconds, and h is the height in feet.
(LESSON 5.2)

FREE-RESPONSE GRID

The following questions may be
answered by using a free-response
grid such as that commonly used
by standardized-test services.

28. Find x if $\log_2 x = 4$.
(LESSON 6.3)

29. What is the greatest integer
x for which $-6x - 1 > 10$?
(LESSON 1.7)

30. Solve the system for z. *(LESSON 4.4)*
$\begin{cases} x - 2y - z = 2 \\ x - y + 2z = 9 \\ 2x + y + z = 3 \end{cases}$

31. Find $|7 - 24i|$. *(LESSON 5.6)*

32. Solve $2\sqrt{x - 4} = \sqrt{x + 2}$ for x. *(LESSON 8.8)*

Solve each equation. *(LESSONS 1.6 AND 1.8)*

33. $1 - 2x = 5$

34. $-5x + 3 = \frac{1}{2}x - 1$

35. Solve $\log_x 27 = -3$ for x. Give an approximate
solution to the nearest hundredth. -
(LESSON 6.7)

36. Approximate to the nearest tenth the real zero
of $f(x) = x^3 - 2x^2 + 3x - 1$. *(LESSON 7.5)*

37. Simplify $\sqrt[3]{64^{\frac{1}{2}}}$. *(LESSON 8.7)*

38. ENTERTAINMENT A rectangular stage is 20
meters wide and 38 meters long. To make
room for additional seating, two adjacent sides
of the stage are shortened by the same amount.
If this reduces the stage by 265 square meters,
by how many meters are each of the two
adjacent sides of the stage shortened?
(LESSON 5.2)

Keystroke Guide for Chapter 8

Essential keystroke sequences (using the model TI-82 or TI-83 graphics calculator) are presented below for all Activities and Examples found in this chapter that require or recommend the use of a graphics calculator.

> **internet** connect
>
> For Keystrokes of other graphing calculator models, visit the HRW web site at **go.hrw.com** and enter the keyword **MB1 CALC**.

LESSON 8.1

EXAMPLES ❶ and ❸ For Example 1, enter $y = \dfrac{60.75}{x}$, and use a table to find the
Pages 482 and 483 y-values for the given x-values.

Enter the function:

| Y= | 60.75 | ÷ | X,T,θ,n |

Make a table of values:

| 2nd | WINDOW | (TblStart=) 0 | ENTER | (△ Tbl=) 0.5 |

⇑ TI-82: (TblMin=)

| ENTER | (Indpt:) AUTO | ENTER | ▼ | (Depend:) |

| AUT | ENTER | ▼ | 2nd | GRAPH |

For Example 3, use a similar keystroke sequence. Use (TblStart=) 1.5 and (△ Tbl=) 1.

LESSON 8.2

EXAMPLE ❷ Enter $y = \dfrac{x^2 - 7x + 12}{x^2 + 9x + 20}$, and use a table of values to verify that -4 and -5 are
Page 490   not in the domain.

Enter the function:

| Y= | (| X,T,θ,n | x^2 | − | 7 | X,T,θ,n |

| + | 12 |) | ÷ | (| X,T,θ,n | x^2 |

| + | 9 | X,T,θ,n | + | 20 |) |

Make a table of values:

Use a keystroke sequence similar to that used in Example 1 of Lesson 8.1. Use (TblStart=) −8 and (△ Tbl=)1.

For Step 1, enter $y = \dfrac{1}{x-2}$, and use a table to find the y-values for the given x-values.

Page 490

Use a keystroke sequence similar to that used in Example 1 of Lesson 8.1. For part **a**, use (TblStart=) 1 and ($\triangle$ Tbl=) 0.1. For part **b**, use (TblStart=) 3 and ($\triangle$ Tbl=) −0.1.

For Step 3, use a similar keystroke sequence.

EXAMPLES 3 and 4 Graph the function, and look for asymptotes.

Pages 491–493

Use friendly viewing window [−4.7, 4.7] by [−3.1, 3.1].

Enter the function by using a keystroke sequence similar to that in Example 2 of Lesson 8.2. Then graph.

EXAMPLE 6 Enter $y = \dfrac{3x}{0.8x+25}$, and make a table of values.

Page 501

Enter the function:

| Y= | 3 | X,T,θ,n | ÷ | (| 0.8 | X,T,θ,n | + |

25 |)

Make a table of values:

Use a keystroke sequence similar to that used in Example 1 of Lesson 8.1. Use (TblStart=) 18 and ($\triangle$ Tbl=) 1.

For Steps 1 and 2, graph $y = \dfrac{\dfrac{x-3}{x+2}}{\dfrac{x-2}{x+2}}$ and $y = \dfrac{x-3}{x-2}$ on the same screen. Then

Page 501

make a table of values with the given x-values.

Use friendly viewing window [−4.7, 4.7] by [−3.1, 3.1].

Graph the functions:

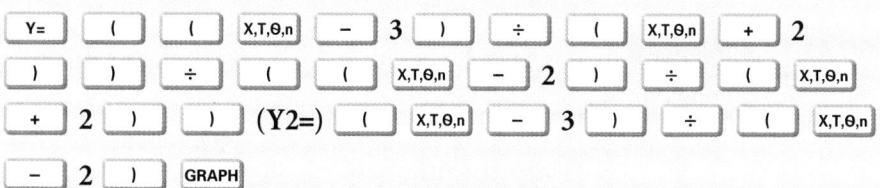

Make a table of values:

Use a keystroke sequence similar to that used in Example 1 of Lesson 8.1. Use (TblStart=) −3 and ($\triangle$ Tbl=) 1.

E X A M P L E **3** Graph $y = \dfrac{6x}{3x - 1} - \dfrac{4x}{2x + 5}$ and $y = \dfrac{34x}{6x^2 + 13x - 5}$ on the same screen.

Page 507

Use friendly viewing window $[-6, 4]$ by $[-4, 4]$.

| Y= | 6 | X,T,θ,n | ÷ | (| 3 | X,T,θ,n | − | 1 |) | − | 4 | X,T,θ,n | ÷ |

| (| 2 | X,T,θ,n | + | 5 |) | ENTER | (Y2=) | 34 | X,T,θ,n | ÷ | (| 6 | X,T,θ,n |

| x² | + | 13 | X,T,θ,n | − | 5 |) | GRAPH |

E X A M P L E **1** Graph $y = \dfrac{64x + 140}{6x(x + 5)}$ and $y = 2.5$ on the same screen, and find any points of intersection.

Pages 512 and 513

Use viewing window $[0, 5]$ by $[0, 7]$.

Graph the functions:

Intersection
X=2.7103088 Y=2.5

| Y= | (| 64 | X,T,θ,n | + | 140 |) | ÷ | (| 6 | X,T,θ,n | (| X,T,θ,n |

| + | 5 |) |) | ENTER | (Y2=) | 2.5 | GRAPH |

Find any points of intersection:

CALC

| 2nd | TRACE | 5:intersect | (First Curve?) | ENTER | (Second Curve?) | ENTER |

(Guess?) ENTER

E X A M P L E S **2** and **3** For Example 2, graph $y = \dfrac{x}{x - 6} - \dfrac{1}{x - 4}$ and find any zeros.

Pages 513 and 514

Use viewing window $[-2, 4]$ by $[-0.5, 0.5]$.

Graph the function:

Use a keystroke sequence similar to that in Example 3 of Lesson 8.4.

CALC

Find any zeros: | 2nd | TRACE | 2:intersect | (Left Bound?) | ENTER | (Right Bound?)

⇑ TI-82: 2:root

ENTER (Guess?) ENTER

For Example 3, use a similar keystroke sequence. Use friendly viewing window $[-12.4, 6.4]$ by $[-8, 8]$.

Activity

Page 515

For Step 1, graph $y = \dfrac{x + 2}{x - 4}$, and make a table of values.

Use friendly viewing window $[-6.8, 12]$ by $[-10, 10]$.

Graph the function:

| Y= | (| X,T,θ,n | + | 2 |) | ÷ | (| X,T,θ,n | − | 4 |) | GRAPH |

Make a table of values: Use a keystroke sequence similar to that used in Example 1 of Lesson 8.1. Use (TblStart=) −5 and (△ Tbl=) 1.

E X A M P L E ④ Graph $y = \dfrac{x}{2x-1}$ and $y = 1$, and find any points of intersection.

Page 515

Use friendly viewing window $[-4.7, 4.7]$ by $[-3, 3]$.

Graph the functions:

| Y= | X,T,θ,n | ÷ | (| 2 | X,T,θ,n | – | 1 |) | ENTER | (Y2=) 1 | GRAPH |

Find any points of intersection:

Use a keystroke sequence similar to that used in Example 1 of Lesson 8.5.

E X A M P L E ⑤ Graph $y = \dfrac{x-2}{2(x-3)} - \dfrac{x}{x+3}$, and find any zeros of the function. Then make a table of values.

Page 516

Use friendly viewing window $[-9.4, 9.4]$ by $[-3.1, 3.1]$.

Graph the function:

| Y= | (| X,T,θ,n | – | 2 |) | ÷ | (| 2 | (| X,T,θ,n | – | 3 |) |

⇑ TI-82: (

|) | – | X,T,θ,n | ÷ | (| X,T,θ,n | + | 3 |) | GRAPH |

⇑ TI-82: (

Find any zeros:

Use a keystroke sequence similar to that in Example 2 of Lesson 8.5.

Make a table of values:

Use a keystroke sequence similar to that in Example 1 of Lesson 8.1. Use (TblStart=) -4 and ($\triangle$ Tbl=) 1.

LESSON 8.6

E X A M P L E ① Graph $y = \sqrt{2x - 5}$.

Page 521

Use viewing window $[-1, 8]$ by $[-1, 5]$.

√ ⇓ TI-82: (

| Y= | 2nd | x^2 | 2 | X,T,θ,n | – | 5 |) | GRAPH |

E X A M P L E S ② and ③ For Example 2, part a, graph $y = \sqrt{x}$ and $y = -2\sqrt{x+1} + 4$ on the same screen, and compare the graphs.

Pages 522 and 523

Use friendly viewing window $[-2.7, 6.7]$ by $[-3, 6]$.

Graph the functions:

√ ⇓ TI-82: (

| Y= | 2nd | x^2 | X,T,θ,n |) | ENTER | (Y2=) | ◄ | ◄ | ENTER | (\Y2=) | ► | ► |

√ ⇓ TI-82: (

TI-82: omit

| (–) | 2 | 2nd | x^2 | X,T,θ,n | + | 1 |) | + | 4 | GRAPH |

For part **b** of Example 2, use a similar keystroke sequence and the same friendly viewing window.

For Example 3, use friendly viewing window $[-2.7, 6.7]$ by $[-1.6, 4.6]$.

E X A M P L E ④ Enter the function $y = 2\pi\sqrt{\dfrac{x}{9.8}}$, and make a table of values.

Page 523

Enter the function:

| Y= | 2 | 2nd | ^ (π) | 2nd | x^2 (√) | X,T,θ,n | ÷ | 9.8 |) |

Make a table of values:

Use a keystroke sequence similar to that used in Example 1 of Lesson 8.1. Use (TblStart=) 0 and (△ Tbl=) 0.1.

Activity

Page 524

For Step 1, graph each radical function.

Use viewing window [–5, 5] by [–5, 5]. Use the fact that $\sqrt[n]{x} = x^{\frac{1}{n}}$ to graph a radical function for $n > 2$. For example, graph $y = \sqrt[3]{x}$:

| Y= | X,T,θ,n | ^ | (| 1 | ÷ | 3 |) | GRAPH |

LESSON 8.7

Activity

Page 528

For Step 1, graph $y = \sqrt{x^2}$.

Use viewing window [–10, 10] by [–10, 10].

| Y= | 2nd | x^2 (√) | X,T,θ,n | x^2 |) | GRAPH |

⇑ TI-82: omit

For Step 2, graph $y = \sqrt[4]{x^4}$.

| Y= | (| X,T,θ,n | ^ | 4 |) | ^ | (| 1 | ÷ | 4 |) | GRAPH |

For Steps 3–6, use a keystroke sequence similar to that used in Step 2.

LESSON 8.8

E X A M P L E S ① and ③ For Example 1, graph $y = 2\sqrt{x + 5}$ and $y = 8$ on the same screen, and find any points of intersection.

Pages 537 and 538

Use viewing window [–5, 20] by [–2, 15].

Graph the functions:

| Y= | 2 | 2nd | x^2 (√) | X,T,θ,n | + | 5 |) | ENTER | (Y2=) 8 | GRAPH |

Find any points of intersection:

Use a keystroke sequence similar to that used in Example 1 of Lesson 8.5.

For Example 3, use a similar keystroke sequence and viewing window [–2, 10] by [–1, 10].

E X A M P L E ② Graph $y = \sqrt[3]{x-5}$ and $y = \sqrt[3]{7-x}$ on the same screen, and find any points of intersection.

Page 537

Use viewing window $[-2, 10]$ by $[-4, 4]$.

Enter the functions:

Find any points of intersection:
Use a keystroke sequence similar to that used in Example 1 of Lesson 8.5.

E X A M P L E ④ Graph $y = \dfrac{286}{2\sqrt{x^2 - 15^2}} + 1$ and $y = 6$ on the same screen, and find any points

Page 538

of intersection. Then make a table of values for $y = \dfrac{286}{2\sqrt{x^2 - 15^2}} + 1$.

Use viewing window $[-2, 50]$ by $[-1, 20]$.

Graph the functions:

Find any points of intersection:
Use a keystroke sequence similar to that used in Example 1 of Lesson 8.5.

Make a table of values:
Use a keystroke sequence similar to that used in Example 1 of Lesson 8.1.
Use (TblStart=) 32.25 and ($\triangle$ Tbl=) 0.01.

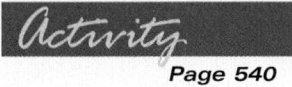

Graph $y = \sqrt{x}$ and $y = 1$ on the same screen, and find any points of intersection.

Page 540

Use viewing window $[-5, 5]$ by $[-5, 5]$.

Use a keystroke sequence similar to that used in Example 1 of Lesson 8.8.

E X A M P L E S ⑥ and **⑦** For Example 6, graph $y = \sqrt{x+1}$ and $y = 2$ on the same screen,

Pages 540 and 541

and find any points of intersection.
Use viewing window $[-3, 7]$ by $[-5, 5]$.

Use a keystroke sequence similar to that used in Example 1 of Lesson 8.8.

For Example 7, use a keystroke sequence similar to that in Example 2 of this lesson. Use viewing window $[-9.4, 9.4]$ by $[-6.2, 6.2]$.

Conic Sections

CONIC SECTIONS ARE CURVES THAT INCLUDE circles, parabolas, ellipses, and hyperbolas. Parabolas are used to describe the shape of satellite dishes. Ellipses describe the paths of planets around the Sun and of comets that return to the solar system on a regular basis, such as Halley's comet. The lens of a telescope can be either parabolic or hyperbolic. The primary mirror in the Hubble Space Telescope is parabolic.

Lessons

About the Chapter Project

In this chapter, you will study the conic sections, their equations, and some of their special properties. In the Chapter Project, *Focus on This!*, you will use an alternative method of graphing to create parabolas, ellipses, and hyperbolas based on their definitions.

After completing the Chapter Project, you will be able to do the following:

- Describe the properties of ellipses, parabolas, and hyperbolas.

- Create ellipses, parabolas, and hyperbolas by using an alternative method of graphing.

About the Portfolio Activities

Throughout the chapter, you will be given opportunities to complete Portfolio Activities that are designed to support your work on the Chapter Project.

- Using wax paper to create a parabolic conic section is included in the Portfolio Activity on page 578.

- Using wax paper to create an elliptical conic section is included in the Portfolio Activity on page 594.

- Using wax paper to create a hyperbolic conic section is included in the Portfolio Activity on page 603.

Introduction to Conic Sections

Objectives

- Classify a conic section as the intersection of a plane and a double cone.
- Use the distance and midpoint formulas.

In the diagram shown at right, a slanted line is revolved all the way around a vertical line, the axis, in three-dimensional space. Because the two lines intersect, the result is a pair of cones that have one point in common. Although the diagram cannot show it, the two cones extend indefinitely both upward and downward, forming a double-napped cone.

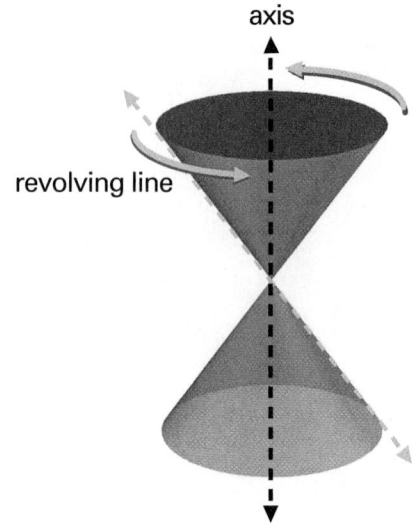

axis

revolving line

The intersection of a double cone and a plane is called a **conic section**. Three conic sections are illustrated below.

parabola

ellipse

hyperbola

A circle, a point, a line, and a pair of intersecting lines are special cases of the three conic sections shown above.

circle (ellipse)

point (ellipse)

line (hyperbola)

pair of intersecting lines (hyperbola)

Since all conic sections are plane figures, you can represent them in a coordinate plane.

E X A M P L E ❶ Graph each equation and identify the conic section.

a. $x^2 + y^2 = 25$ **b.** $x^2 - y^2 = 4$

SOLUTION

a. Solve for y.

$$x^2 + y^2 = 25$$
$$y^2 = 25 - x^2$$
$$y = \pm\sqrt{25 - x^2}$$

Graph $y = \sqrt{25 - x^2}$ and $y = -\sqrt{25 - x^2}$ together on the same screen.

> *Be sure to use a square viewing window.*

The equation $x^2 + y^2 = 25$ represents a circle.

b. Solve for y.

$$x^2 - y^2 = 4$$
$$-y^2 = 4 - x^2$$
$$y^2 = x^2 - 4$$
$$y = \pm\sqrt{x^2 - 4}$$

Graph $y = \sqrt{x^2 - 4}$ and $y = -\sqrt{x^2 - 4}$ together on the same screen.

Be sure to use a square viewing window.

The equation $x^2 - y^2 = 4$ represents a hyperbola.

TRY THIS Graph each equation and identify the conic section.

    a. $4x^2 + 9y^2 = 36$ **b.** $6x - y^2 = 0$

Using the Distance Formula

When conic sections are studied as figures in a coordinate plane, they can be described in terms of distances between points or between points and a line. The *distance formula* will play a role in the definition of each conic section studied in this chapter.

CONNECTION

COORDINATE GEOMETRY

Given points $P(-1, 4)$ and $Q(3, -2)$ in the coordinate plane, you can use the Pythagorean Theorem to find the distance, d, between them.

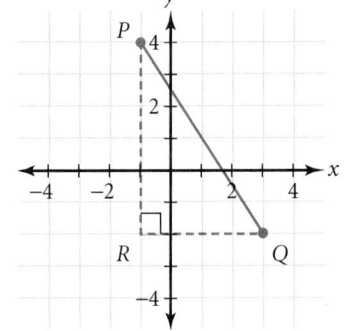

$$(PQ)^2 = (PR)^2 + (RQ)^2$$
$$d^2 = 6^2 + 4^2$$
$$d = \sqrt{52}$$
$$\approx 7.2$$

In general, given points $P(x_1, y_1)$ and $Q(x_2, y_2)$ in the coordinate plane, you can use the Pythagorean Theorem to find a formula for the distance, d, between them.

$$(PQ)^2 = (PR)^2 + (RQ)^2$$
$$d^2 = (x_2 - x_1)^2 + (y_2 - y_1)^2$$
$$d = \sqrt{(x_2 - x_1)^2 + (y_2 - y_1)^2}$$

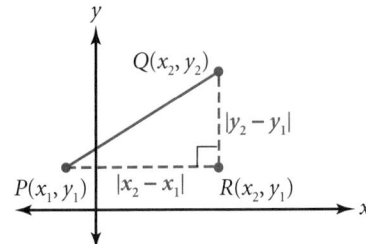

Distance Formula

The distance, d, between $P(x_1, y_1)$ and $Q(x_2, y_2)$ is

$$d = \sqrt{(x_2 - x_1)^2 + (y_2 - y_1)^2}.$$

Exploring the Distance Formula

You will need: no special materials

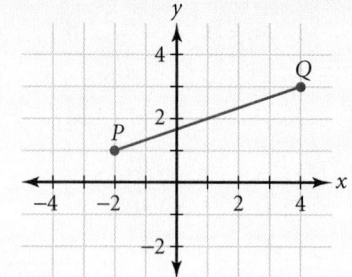

1. Let $P(x_1, y_1)$ be the point $(-2, 1)$ and $Q(x_2, y_2)$ be the point $(4, 3)$ in the graph at right. What is x_1? x_2? $(x_2 - x_1)$? $(x_2 - x_1)^2$? Use the distance formula to find PQ.

2. Let $P(x_1, y_1)$ be the point $(4, 3)$ and $Q(x_2, y_2)$ be the point $(-2, 1)$. What is x_1? x_2? $(x_2 - x_1)$? $(x_2 - x_1)^2$? Use the distance formula to find PQ.

3. Is $(x_2 - x_1)$ the same in Steps 1 and 2? Is $(x_2 - x_1)^2$ the same in Steps 1 and 2? Is PQ the same in Steps 1 and 2?

CHECKPOINT ✔ 4. What seems to happen to the distance between P and Q when you relabel points P and Q, as in Steps 1 and 2? Explain why this happens.

EXAMPLE ❷ Find the distance between $P(-1, 2)$ and $Q(6, 4)$. Give an exact answer and an approximate answer rounded to the nearest hundredth.

SOLUTION

Let (x_1, y_1) be $(-1, 2)$ and let (x_2, y_2) be $(6, 4)$.
Use the distance formula.

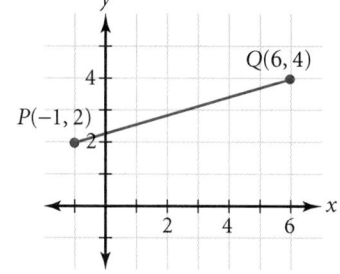

$$d = \sqrt{(x_2 - x_1)^2 + (y_2 - y_1)^2}$$
$$d = \sqrt{[(6 - (-1)]^2 + (4 - 2)^2}$$
$$d = \sqrt{53} \qquad \textit{Exact answer}$$
$$d \approx 7.28 \qquad \textit{Approximate answer}$$

Thus, the distance between P and Q is $\sqrt{53}$, or about 7.28.

TRY THIS Find the distance between $P(2, 5)$ and $Q(-3, -8)$. Give an exact answer and an approximate answer rounded to the nearest hundredth.

EXAMPLE ❸

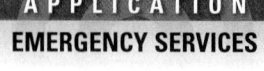
An EMS helicopter is stationed at Hospital 1, which is 4 miles west and 2 miles north of an automobile accident. Another EMS helicopter is stationed at Hospital 2, which is 3 miles east and 3 miles north of the accident.

Which helicopter is closer to the accident?

● **SOLUTION**

1. Represent the locations as points in the coordinate plane.

Since the locations of the hospitals are given with reference to the accident, place the accident at the origin. Then $A(-4, 2)$ represents the location of Hospital 1 and $B(3, 3)$ represents the location of Hospital 2.

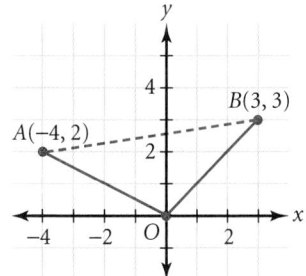

2. Find the distances OA and OB.

$$d = \sqrt{(x_2 - x_1)^2 + (y_2 - y_1)^2}$$
$$OA = \sqrt{[(-4) - 0]^2 + (2 - 0)^2}$$
$$OA = \sqrt{20} \text{ miles, or} \approx 4.47 \text{ miles}$$

$$d = \sqrt{(x_2 - x_1)^2 + (y_2 - y_1)^2}$$
$$OB = \sqrt{(3 - 0)^2 + (3 - 0)^2}$$
$$OB = \sqrt{18} \text{ miles, or} \approx 4.24 \text{ miles}$$

Since $OB < OA$, the helicopter at Hospital 2 is closer to the accident.

Using the Midpoint Formula

The coordinates of the midpoint between two points can be found by using the coordinates of the points.

Midpoint Formula

The coordinates of the midpoint, M, between two points, $P(x_1, y_1)$ and $Q(x_2, y_2)$, are $M\left(\dfrac{x_1 + x_2}{2}, \dfrac{y_1 + y_2}{2}\right)$.

Notice that the x-coordinate of M is the average of the x-coordinates of P and Q and that the y-coordinate of M is the average of the y-coordinates of P and Q. The midpoint formula is used in Example 4.

E X A M P L E ④ **Find the coordinates of the midpoint, M, of the line segment whose endpoints are $P(-4, 6)$ and $Q(5, 10)$.**

● **SOLUTION**

Let (x_1, y_1) be $(-4, 6)$ and (x_2, y_2) be $(5, 10)$.

$$\frac{x_1 + x_2}{2} = \frac{(-4) + 5}{2} = \frac{1}{2} \qquad \frac{y_1 + y_2}{2} = \frac{6 + 10}{2} = 8$$

Thus, $M\left(\dfrac{1}{2}, 8\right)$ is the midpoint.

The graph of points P, M, and Q indicates that the answer is reasonable.

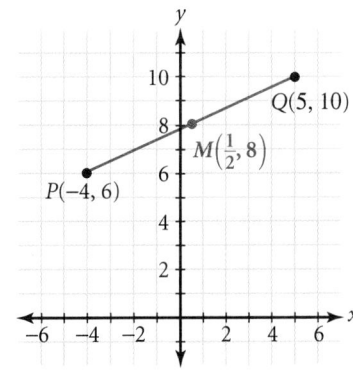

TRY THIS Find the coordinates of the midpoint, M, of the line segment whose endpoints are $A(2.5, 5.5)$ and $B(8.5, -4.5)$.

CRITICAL THINKING
A line segment has the endpoints $A(-5, -6)$ and $B(7, 4)$. Find the coordinates of points R, S, and T on segment AB such that $AR = RS = ST = TB$.

CONNECTION
GEOMETRY

Recall from geometry that a chord of a circle is a segment with endpoints on the circle. A **diameter** of a circle is a chord that contains the center. A **radius** of a circle is a segment with one endpoint at the center of the circle and the other endpoint on the circle. The length of the radius is one-half the length of the diameter.

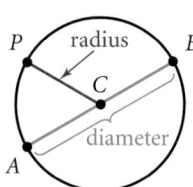

EXAMPLE 5 The endpoints of a diameter of the circle at right are $A(-2, 3)$ and $B(6, 9)$.

Find the center, circumference, and area of the circle.

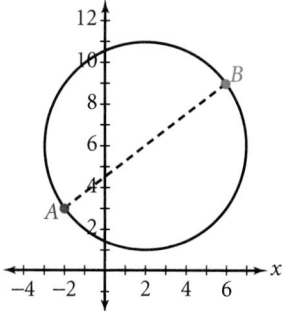

● **SOLUTION**

1. Use the midpoint formula to find the coordinates of the center, C.
$$C\left(\frac{x_1 + x_2}{2}, \frac{y_1 + y_2}{2}\right) \to C\left(\frac{-2 + 6}{2}, \frac{3 + 9}{2}\right) \to C(2, 6)$$

2. Use the distance formula to find the radius.
$$CA = \sqrt{(-2 - 2)^2 + (3 - 6)^2} = \sqrt{25} = 5$$

> You can find CA or CB to find the radius.

3. Find the circumference and area.
Circumference $= 2\pi r = 2r(5) = 10\pi$
Area $= \pi r^2 = \pi(5)^2 = 25\pi$

Thus, the center is $(2, 6)$, the circumference is 10π units, and the area is 25π square units.

TRY THIS The endpoints of a diameter of a circle are $A(-3, 2)$ and $B(5, 4)$. Find the center, circumference, and area of the circle.

Exercises

● *Communicate*

☑ internet connect

Activities
Online
Go To: **go.hrw.com**
Keyword:
MB1 Hospital

1. Illustrate and explain how a plane can intersect a double cone to produce a circle, a parabola, an ellipse, and a hyperbola.

2. Explain why it does not matter which set of coordinates you subtract from the other set when using the distance formula.

3. Explain how to find the circumference and the area of a circle if you are given the coordinates of the center and of a point on the circle.

Guided Skills Practice

Graph each equation and identify the conic section. *(EXAMPLE 1)*

4 $9x^2 - 4y^2 = 100$

5 $x^2 + y^2 = 100$

6. Find the distance between $P(-7, 12)$ and $Q(6, 5)$. Give an exact answer and an approximate answer rounded to the nearest hundredth. *(EXAMPLE 2)*

7. EMERGENCY SERVICES If a fire station is 3 miles east and 2 miles south of a fire and the trucks can travel along a straight route to the fire from the station, how long is their route? *(EXAMPLE 3)*

8. Find the coordinates of the midpoint, *M,* of the line segment whose endpoints are $P(-3, 10)$ and $Q(6, -12)$. *(EXAMPLE 4)*

9. The endpoints of a diameter of a circle are $A(-5, 2)$ and $B(3, 4)$. Find the center, circumference, and area of the circle. *(EXAMPLE 5)*

Practice and Apply

Graph each equation and identify the conic section.

10 $x^2 + y^2 = 36$

11 $x^2 + y^2 = 121$

12 $x^2 - y^2 = 36$

13 $4x^2 - 9y^2 = 36$

14 $5x^2 + 9y^2 = 45$

15 $36x^2 + 5y^2 = 180$

16 $x^2 - 4y = 0$

17 $y^2 + 4x = 0$

18 $y^2 - 4x = 0$

19 $x^2 + y^2 = 1$

20 $x^2 + 9y^2 = 9$

21 $25x^2 - 9y^2 = 225$

■ internet connect

Homework Help Online
Go To: **go.hrw.com**
Keyword:
MB1 Homework Help
for Exercises 22–37

Find the distance between *P* and *Q* and the coordinates of *M*, the midpoint of $\overline{PQ}$. Give exact answers and approximate answers to the nearest hundredth when appropriate.

22. $P(-3, -2)$ and $Q(5, -2)$

23. $P(-5, -2)$ and $Q(-5, 5)$

24. $P(7, 0)$ and $Q(8, 0)$

25. $P(-3, -4)$ and $Q(5, -5)$

26. $P(7, -2)$ and $Q(-5, -1)$

27. $P(\frac{5}{2}, 3)$ and $Q(-\frac{3}{2}, 2)$

28. $P(10, 7)$ and $Q(1, 8)$

29. $P(10, 2)$ and $Q(8, 0)$

30. $P(7.6, 10.1)$ and $Q(4.6, 3.1)$

31. $P(2\sqrt{2}, 5)$ and $Q(\sqrt{2}, 0)$

32. $P(\frac{1}{2}, \frac{7}{8})$ and $Q(3, -\frac{3}{8})$

33. $P(\frac{3}{2}, \frac{1}{4})$ and $Q(-6, \frac{3}{4})$

34. $P(5, 5\sqrt{2})$ and $Q(6, \sqrt{2})$

35. $P(2\sqrt{2}, \sqrt{7})$ and $Q(\sqrt{2}, 5\sqrt{7})$

36. $P(0, 0)$ and $Q(a, 2a + 1)$

37. $P(2a, a)$ and $Q(a, -3a)$

Find the center, circumference, and area of each circle described below.

38. diameter with endpoints $P(-4, -3)$ and $Q(-10, 5)$

39. diameter with endpoints $P(2, 4)$ and $Q(-3, 16)$

40. diameter with endpoints $P(0, 0)$ and $Q(50, 50)$

41. diameter with endpoints $P(-12, -8)$ and $Q(0, 0)$

42. diameter with endpoints $P(-2, 2)$ and $Q(4, 6)$

43. diameter with endpoints $P(8, -3)$ and $Q(-2, 1)$

For $\overline{PQ}$, the coordinates of P and M, the midpoint of $\overline{PQ}$, are given. Find the coordinates of Q.

44. $P(-2, 3)$ and $M(5, 1)$ **45.** $P(2, -3)$ and $M(-5, 1)$

46. $P(3, 11)$ and $M(0, 0)$ **47.** $P(0, 0)$ and $M(-7, 7)$

Three points, A, B, and C, are collinear if they lie on the same line. If A, B, and C are collinear and B is between A and C, then $AB + BC = AC$. For each set of points A, B, and C given below, find AB, BC, and AC, and determine whether the three points are collinear.

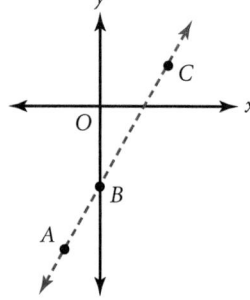

48. $A(0, 0)$, $B(2, 4)$, and $C(3, 6)$

49. $A(0, 0)$, $B(2, 4)$, and $C(3, 7)$

50. $A(-4, 5)$, $B(-2, 2)$, and $C(0, -1)$

51. $A(-3, 1)$, $B(2, 9)$, and $C(7, 17)$

CHALLENGE

52. You are given $P(-3, 2)$, $Q(3, 1)$, and $R(0, 6)$. Find the coordinates of point A such that $PA = QA = RA$, that is, $(PA)^2 = (QA)^2 = (RA)^2$.

CONNECTIONS

COORDINATE GEOMETRY **For Exercises 53–55, refer to the coordinate plane at right.**

53. a. Find AB, BC, CD, and DA.
   b. Based on your answers to part **a**, are the opposite sides of quadrilateral $ABCD$ equal in length?

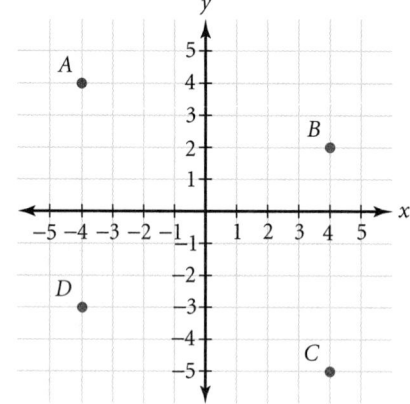

54. a. Find the coordinates of the midpoints of $\overline{AC}$ and of $\overline{BD}$.
   b. Based on your answers to part **a**, what conclusion can you draw about the diagonals of quadrilateral $ABCD$?

55. a. Find the slopes of $\overline{AB}$ and $\overline{CD}$ and of $\overline{AD}$ and $\overline{BC}$.
   b. Based on your answers to part **a**, are the opposite sides of quadrilateral $ABCD$ parallel? Explain.

56. COORDINATE GEOMETRY Determine whether the triangle with vertices at $C(-2, 3)$, $D(1, -1)$, and $E(3, 3)$ is isosceles, equilateral, or both.

57. COORDINATE GEOMETRY Determine whether the triangle with vertices at $F(7, 3)$, $H(6, 9)$, and $L(2, 3)$ is isosceles or scalene. (Hint: No two sides of a scalene triangle are equal in length.)

58. GEOMETRY A *midsegment* of a triangle is the line segment whose endpoints are the midpoints of two sides of the triangle. A triangle has vertices whose coordinates are $A(0, 0)$, $B(6, 10)$, and $C(10, 3)$. Find an equation for the line containing the midsegment formed by the midpoints of $\overline{AB}$ and $\overline{BC}$.

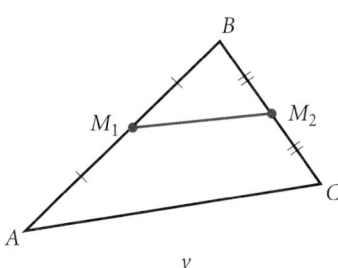

59. COORDINATE GEOMETRY The perpendicular bisector of $\overline{PQ}$ in a plane is the line, ℓ, that contains the midpoint of $\overline{PQ}$ and is perpendicular to $\overline{PQ}$. If B is on ℓ, then $BP = BQ$ and $(BP)^2 = (BQ)^2$. Write the equation in standard form for the perpendicular bisector of $\overline{PQ}$ for $P(-5, 7)$ and $Q(9, -3)$.

Look Back

Evaluate. *(LESSON 2.6)*

60. $\lceil -5.1 \rceil - \lceil -3.5 \rceil$ **61.** $\lfloor -0.33 \rfloor + \lfloor 2.99 \rfloor$ **62.** $\lceil 4.4 \rceil + \lfloor -0.5 \rfloor$

Solve by completing the square. Give exact solutions. *(LESSON 5.4)*

63. $x^2 = 8x - 15$ **64.** $x^2 - 8x = 48$ **65.** $x^2 - 6x - 20 = 0$

Solve by using the quadratic formula. *(LESSON 5.5)*

66. $x^2 - 5x = 50$ **67.** $6x^2 - 7x = -1$ **68.** $2a^2 - 7a + 6 = 0$

Divide by using synthetic division. *(LESSON 7.3)*

69. $(4x^4 - 11x^3 + 8x^2 - 3x - 2) \div (x - 2)$
70. $(5x^4 + 5x^3 + x^2 + 2x + 1) \div (x + 1)$

Let *z* vary jointly as *x* and *y*. Use the given information to find the value of *z* for the given values of *x* and *y*. *(LESSON 8.1)*

71. $z = 3$ when $x = 2$ and $y = 3$; given $x = 5$ and $y = 10$
72. $z = 8$ when $x = 1$ and $y = 4$; given $x = 6$ and $y = 8$

Look Beyond

73. Let $f(x) = x^2$. The point $(1, 1)$ is on the graph of f.
   a. Find the distance between the point $(1, 1)$ and the point $\left(0, \frac{1}{4}\right)$.

   b. Find the shortest distance between the point $(1, 1)$ and the line $y = -\frac{1}{4}$.
   c. Compare the two distances found in parts **a** and **b**.
   d. Pick another point on the graph of f. Repeat parts **a**, **b**, and **c** for your point.
   e. Make a conjecture about the relationship between points on the graph of f, the point $\left(0, \frac{1}{4}\right)$, and the line $y = -\frac{1}{4}$.

Parabolas

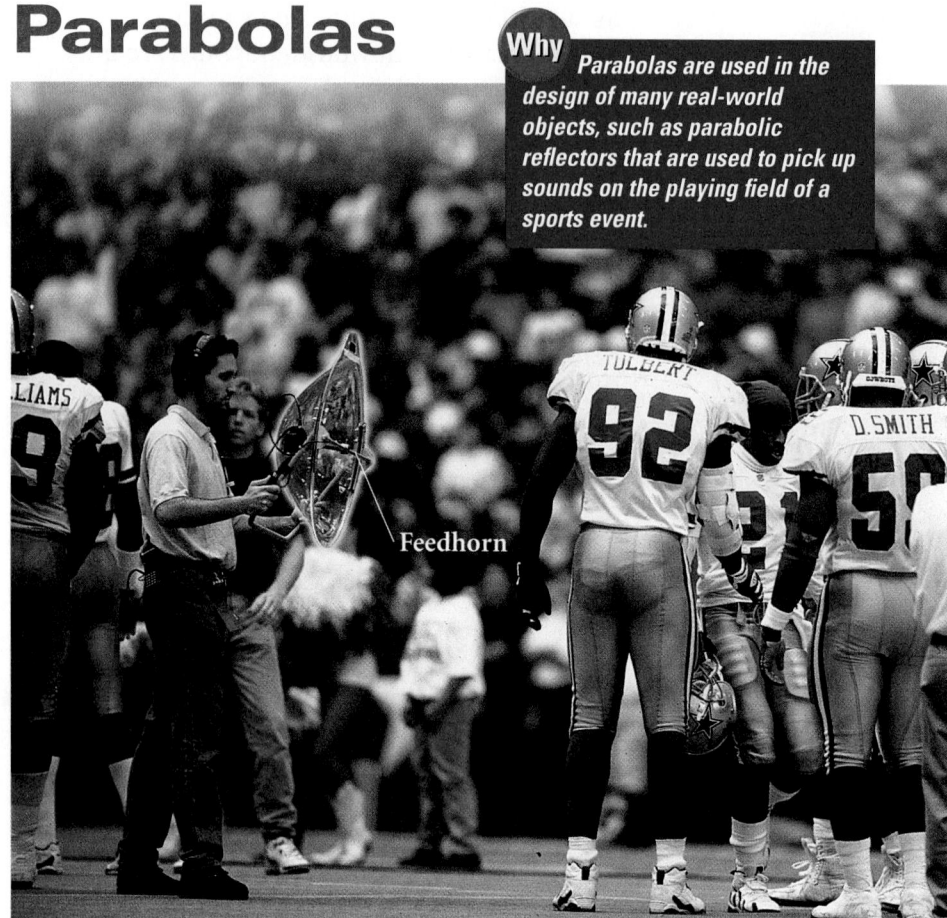

Feedhorn

Objectives

- Write and graph the standard equation of a parabola given sufficient information.

- Given an equation of a parabola, graph it and label the vertex, focus, and directrix.

APPLICATION
COMMUNICATIONS

Sports broadcast technicians often use a parabolic reflector to pick up sounds on the playing field during a sports event. The picture above shows a parabolic reflector whose feedhorn is 10 inches long. The reflector focuses the incoming sounds at the end of the feedhorn. Write the standard equation of the parabola that is a cross section of the reflector. *You will solve this problem in Example 3.*

A parabola is defined in terms of a fixed point, called the **focus**, and a fixed line, called the **directrix**.

In a parabola, the distance from any point, P, on the parabola to the focus, F, is equal to the shortest distance from P to the directrix. That is, $PF = PD$ for any point, P, on the parabola.

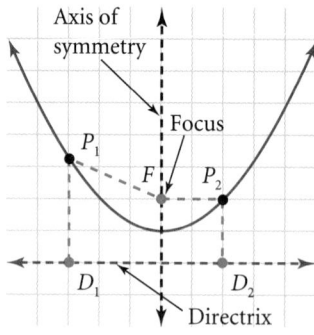

$$P_1F = P_1D_1 \text{ and } P_2F = P_2D_2$$

Definition of Parabola

A **parabola** is the set of all points $P(x, y)$ in the plane whose distance to a fixed point, called the focus, equals its distance to a fixed line, called the directrix.

If the point $F(0, 3)$ is the focus of a parabola with its vertex at the origin, then the equation for the directrix is $y = -3$. This is shown in the figure at right.

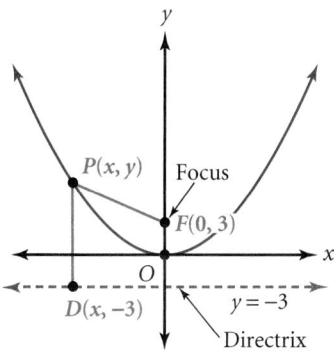

You can find an equation for this parabola by using the definition of a parabola and the distance formula, as shown below.

$$PF = PD$$
$$\sqrt{(x - 0)^2 + (y - 3)^2} = \sqrt{(x - x)^2 + (y + 3)^2}$$
$$x^2 + (y - 3)^2 = (y + 3)^2 \qquad \textit{Square each side.}$$
$$x^2 = (y + 3)^2 - (y - 3)^2$$
$$x^2 = y^2 + 6y + 9 - (y^2 - 6y + 9) \quad \textit{Expand each binomial.}$$
$$x^2 = 12y$$
$$y = \frac{1}{12}x^2$$

In general, if F is the point $(0, p)$ and the directrix is $y = -p$, then the equation of the parabola is $y = \frac{1}{4p}x^2$.

Recall from Lesson 5.1 that the **axis of symmetry** of a parabola goes through the vertex and divides the parabola into two equal parts. The axis of symmetry also contains the focus and is perpendicular to the directrix. The **vertex** of a parabola is the midpoint between the focus and the directrix.

Standard Equation of a Parabola

The standard equation of a parabola with its vertex at the origin is given below.

Horizontal directrix	**Vertical directrix**
$y = \frac{1}{4p}x^2$	$x = \frac{1}{4p}y^2$
$p > 0$: opens upward	$p > 0$: opens right
$p < 0$: opens downward	$p < 0$: opens left
focus: $(0, p)$	focus: $(p, 0)$
directrix: $y = -p$	directrix: $x = -p$
axis of symmetry: y-axis	axis of symmetry: x-axis

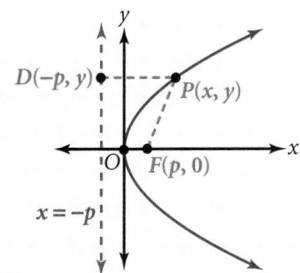

Example 1 shows how to graph a parabola from its equation.

EXAMPLE ❶ Graph $x = -\frac{1}{8}y^2$. **Label the vertex, focus, and directrix.**

● **SOLUTION**

1. Identify p. Rewrite $x = -\frac{1}{8}y^2$ as $x = \frac{1}{4(-2)}y^2$. Thus, $p = -2$.

2. Identify the vertex, focus, and directrix.

Since $p < 0$, the parabola opens to the left.

Vertex: $(0, 0)$
Focus: $(p, 0)$, or $(-2, 0)$
Directrix: $x = -p = -(-2)$, or $x = 2$

PROBLEM SOLVING

3. Use a table of values to sketch the graph.

y	-4	-2	0	2	4
x	-2	$\frac{1}{2}$	0	$\frac{1}{2}$	-2

The graph is shown at right.

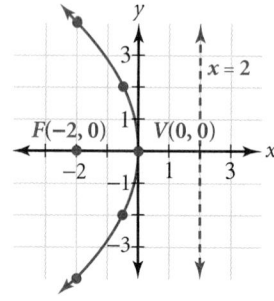

TRY THIS   Graph $y = \frac{1}{12}x^2$. Label the vertex, focus, and directrix.

When you know the locations of any two of the three main characteristics of a parabola (focus, vertex, and directrix), you can write an equation for the parabola. This is shown in Example 2.

EXAMPLE ❷ **Write the standard equation of the parabola with its vertex at the origin and with the directrix $y = 4$.**

● **SOLUTION**

PROBLEM SOLVING   **Draw a diagram.**

Because the vertex is below the directrix, the parabola opens downward. Since $y = -p$ and $y = 4$, $p = -4$.

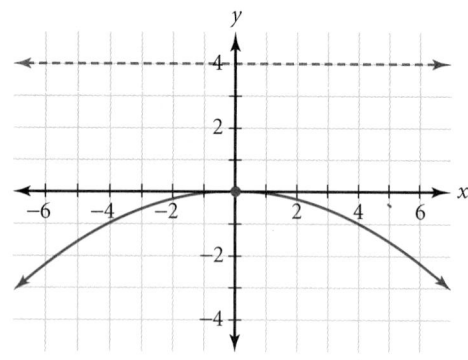

Thus, $y = \frac{1}{4(-4)}x^2$, or $y = -\frac{1}{16}x^2$, is the equation of the parabola.

TRY THIS   Write the standard equation of the parabola with its vertex at the origin and with the directrix $x = 4$.

CRITICAL THINKING   Explain how applying a vertical compression by a factor of $\frac{1}{2}$ to $x = y^2$ produces the same graph as applying a horizontal stretch by a factor of 4 to the graph of $x = y^2$.

E X A M P L E ❸ Refer to the parabolic reflector described at the beginning of the lesson.

Write the standard equation of the parabola that is a cross section of the reflector.

● **SOLUTION**

For convenience, place the vertex of the parabola at the origin. You can let the parabola open upward, downward, to the right, or to the left. If it opens to the right, then the equation is of the form $x = \frac{1}{4p}y^2$.

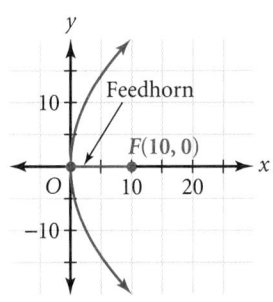

The feedhorn is 10 inches long, so the focus at the end of the feedhorn has coordinates $(10, 0)$ and $p = 10$.

$$x = \frac{1}{4p}y^2$$

$$x = \frac{1}{4(10)}y^2 \quad \text{Substitute 10 for p.}$$

$$x = \frac{1}{40}y^2$$

Thus, the equation that represents a cross section of the parabolic reflector is $x = \frac{1}{40}y^2$.

The vertex of a parabola can be anywhere in the coordinate plane. In the Activity below, you can explore some of these translations.

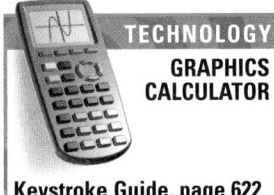

TECHNOLOGY
GRAPHICS CALCULATOR

Keystroke Guide, page 622

Activity
Exploring Translations of Parabolas

You will need: a graphics calculator

1. Graph the parabola described by the equation $y = \frac{1}{4}x^2$.

2. Solve $y - 3 = \frac{1}{4}(x - 2)^2$ for y, and graph the parabola. Find the coordinates of the vertex.

CHECKPOINT ✔ 3. Describe the translation from the graph of $y = \frac{1}{4}x^2$ in Step 1 to the graph of $y - 3 = \frac{1}{4}(x - 2)^2$ in Step 2.

4. Compare the equation $y - 5 = \frac{1}{4}(x - 4)^2$ and the coordinates of the vertex of this parabola. Describe the relationship that you observe.

CHECKPOINT ✔ 5. Predict the coordinates of the vertex of the parabola given by the equation $y + 2 = \frac{1}{4}(x - 1)^2$. Graph the parabola to verify your prediction.

Standard Equation of a Translated Parabola

The standard equation of a parabola with its vertex at (h, k) is given below.

<table>
<tr><td align="center">Horizontal Directrix</td><td align="center">Vertical Directrix</td></tr>
<tr><td align="center">$y - k = \frac{1}{4p}(x - h)^2$</td><td align="center">$x - h = \frac{1}{4p}(y - k)^2$</td></tr>
<tr><td>$p > 0$: opens upward
$p < 0$: opens downward</td><td>$p > 0$: opens right
$p < 0$: opens left</td></tr>
<tr><td>focus: $(h, k + p)$
directrix: $y = k - p$
axis of symmetry: $x = h$</td><td>focus: $(h + p, k)$
directrix: $x = h - p$
axis of symmetry: $y = k$</td></tr>
</table>

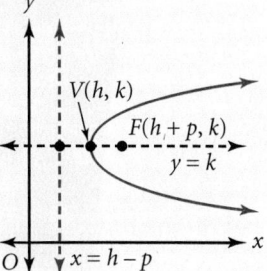

E X A M P L E 4 Write the standard equation of the parabola graphed at right.

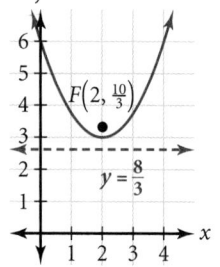

SOLUTION

The parabola opens upward, so the equation is of the form $y - k = \frac{1}{4p}(x - h)^2$ and $p > 0$.

The vertex is halfway between the focus and the directrix. Use the midpoint formula.

Vertex: $\left(2, \dfrac{\frac{10}{3} + \frac{8}{3}}{2}\right)$, or $(2, 3)$ $h = 2$ and $k = 3$

The focus is $(h, k + p)$, or $\left(2, \frac{10}{3}\right)$. Solve for p.

$$k + p = \frac{10}{3}$$
$$3 + p = \frac{10}{3}$$
$$p = \frac{1}{3}$$

Write the standard equation. $y - k = \frac{1}{4p}(x - h)^2$

$$y - 3 = \frac{1}{4\left(\frac{1}{3}\right)}(x - 2)^2$$

$$y - 3 = \frac{3}{4}(x - 2)^2$$

Thus, the standard equation of the parabola is $y - 3 = \frac{3}{4}(x - 2)^2$.

Write the standard equation of the parabola with its focus is at $(-6, 4)$ and with the directrix $x = 2$.

E X A M P L E ⑤ Graph the parabola $y^2 - 8y + 8x + 8 = 0$. Label the vertex, focus, and directrix.

● **SOLUTION**

1. Complete the square to find the standard equation.

$$y^2 - 8y + 8x + 8 = 0$$

$$y^2 - 8y = -8x - 8 \qquad \textit{Isolate the y-terms.}$$

$$y^2 - 8y + (-4)^2 = -8x - 8 + (-4)^2 \quad \textit{Complete the square.}$$

$$(y - 4)^2 = -8x + 8$$

$$(y - 4)^2 = -8(x - 1)$$

$$-\frac{1}{8}(y - 4)^2 = x - 1 \qquad \textit{Divide each side by 8.}$$

$$x - 1 = -\frac{1}{8}(y - 4)^2 \qquad \textit{Write the standard equation.}$$

2. From the standard equation, the vertex is $(1, 4)$. Find p.

$$\frac{1}{4p} = -\frac{1}{8}$$

$$-4p = 8$$

$$p = -2$$

Focus: $(h + p, k)$ | Directrix: $x = h - p$
$= (1 + (-2), 4)$ | $x = 1 - (-2)$
$= (-1, 4)$ | $x = 3$

PROBLEM SOLVING

3. Use a table of values. Choose y-values from 0 to 8.

$$x = -\frac{1}{8}(y - 4)^2 + 1$$

y	0	2	4	6	8
x	-1	$\frac{1}{2}$	1	$\frac{1}{2}$	-1

The graph is shown at right.

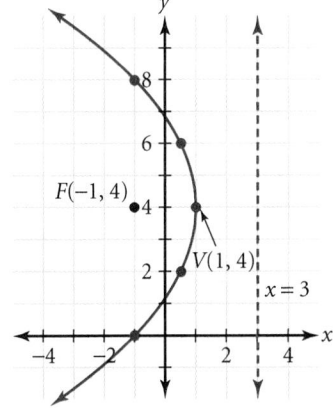

TRY THIS

Graph the parabola $x^2 - 6x + 6y + 18 = 0$. Label the vertex, focus, and directrix.

To graph the equation $x - 1 = -\frac{1}{8}(y - 4)^2$ from Example 5 on a graphics calculator, first solve for y.

$$x - 1 = -\frac{1}{8}(y - 4)^2$$

$$-8(x - 1) = (y - 4)^2$$

$$\pm\sqrt{-8(x - 1)} = y - 4$$

$$4 \pm \sqrt{-8(x - 1)} = y$$

Graph $y = 4 + \sqrt{-8(x - 1)}$ and $y = 4 - \sqrt{-8(x - 1)}$ together on the same screen.

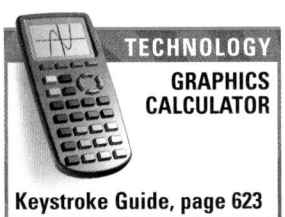

TECHNOLOGY
GRAPHICS CALCULATOR

Keystroke Guide, page 623

Exercises

● Communicate

1. Explain how to tell from the standard equation of a parabola whether the graph opens upward, downward, to the left, or to the right.

2. How can you determine from the standard equation of a parabola the locations of the focus, vertex, and directrix?

3. Explain how to graph $x = \frac{3}{4}y^2$ on a graphics calculator.

● Guided Skills Practice

4. Graph $x = y^2$. Label the vertex, focus, and directrix. **(EXAMPLE 1)**

5. Write the standard equation of the parabola with its vertex at the origin and with the directrix $x = 3$. **(EXAMPLE 2)**

APPLICATION

6. SPORTS Refer to the parabolic reflector described at the beginning of the lesson. Write the standard equation of the parabola that is a cross section of a reflector whose feedhorn is 12 inches long. **(EXAMPLE 3)**

7. Write the standard equation for the parabola with its focus at $(-2, 3)$ and with the directrix $x = 3$. **(EXAMPLE 4)**

8. Graph the parabola $x^2 + 10x + 16y - 7 = 0$. Label the vertex, focus, and directrix. **(EXAMPLE 5)**

● Practice and Apply

Write the standard equation for each parabola graphed below.

9.

10.

11.

12.

13.

14.

Graph each equation. Label the vertex, focus, and directrix.

15. $y = \frac{1}{4}x^2$
16. $y = \frac{1}{8}x^2$
17. $x = \frac{1}{20}y^2$

18. $x = \frac{1}{40}y^2$
19. $y = x^2$
20. $y = 2x^2$

21. $y + 3 = \frac{1}{8}(x + 2)^2$
22. $x - 1 = \frac{1}{12}(y + 2)^2$
23. $y - 4 = -(x - 1)^2$

24. $y - 1 = \frac{1}{4}(x - 1)^2$
25. $y = \frac{1}{8}(x - 1)^2$
26. $x - 3 = -\frac{1}{8}(y + 1)^2$

27. $y + 3 = \frac{1}{12}x^2$
28. $-12y = (x + 2)^2$
29. $x - 1 = \frac{1}{2}(y + 2)^2$

30. $x^2 + 4x - 6y = -10$
31. $x^2 - 6x + 10y = 1$
32. $x^2 - 8x - y + 20 = 0$

33. $4x + y^2 + 3y = -5$
34. $4x + y^2 - 6y = 9$
35. $-14x + 2y^2 - 8y = 20$

Write the standard equation for the parabola with the given characteristics.

36. vertex: $(0, 0)$
focus: $(-4, 0)$

37. vertex: $(0, 0)$
focus: $(0, -5)$

38. vertex: $(0, 0)$
directrix: $y = -1$

39. vertex: $(0, 0)$
directrix: $x = 4$

40. vertex: $(0, 0)$
focus: $(0, 3)$

41. vertex: $(0, 0)$
focus: $(2, 0)$

42. vertex: $(0, 0)$
directrix: $x = -3$

43. vertex: $(0, 0)$
directrix: $y = 12$

44. directrix: $y = -4$
focus: $(0, 4)$

45. focus: $(3, 0)$
directrix: $x = -3$

46. focus: $(0, -5)$
directrix: $y = 5$

47. directrix: $x = 8$
focus: $(-8, 0)$

48. TRANSFORMATIONS A parabola defined by the equation $x + 3 = \frac{1}{8}(y + 2)^2$ is translated 4 units down and 3 units to the right. Write the standard equation of the resulting parabola.

49. TRANSFORMATIONS A parabola defined by the equation $4x + y^2 - 6y = 9$ is translated 2 units up and 4 units to the left. Write the standard equation of the resulting parabola.

CHALLENGE

50. COORDINATE GEOMETRY In the diagram at right, points P, F, and Q are collinear, P and Q are on the parabola, and F is the focus of the parabola. Also, $\overline{PQ}$ is perpendicular to the axis of symmetry of the parabola. Let $y - k = \frac{1}{4p}(x - h)^2$ be an equation for the parabola. Write an equation to find PQ in terms of h, k, p, and x.

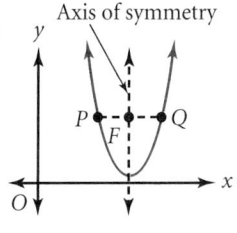

51. COMMUNICATIONS Write an equation for the cross section of a parabolic satellite dish whose focus is 1 foot from its vertex.

52. SPORTS Suppose that a golf ball travels a distance of 600 feet as measured along the ground and reaches an altitude of 200 feet. If the origin represents the tee and the ball travels along a parabolic path that opens downward, find an equation for the path of the golf ball.

53. LIGHTING The lightsource of a flashlight is $\frac{1}{2}$ inch from the vertex of the parabolic reflector and is located at the focus. Assuming that the parabolic reflector is directed upward and the vertex is at the origin, write an equation for a cross section of the reflector.

Cross section of a parabolic satellite dish

Look Back

Factor each expression. *(LESSON 5.3)*

54. $16x^2 - 1$

55. $3a^2 + 3a$

56. $6x^2y - 18xy^2$

57. $m^2n + 7m^2n^2 - 3mn$

Factor each quadratic expression. *(LESSON 5.3)*

58. $x^2 - 8x + 16$

59. $y^2 - 12y + 20$

60. $7x^2 - 16x + 4$

61. $5x^2 - 15x + 10$

62. $12w^2 - w - 6$

63. $6y^2 - 5y - 25$

Simplify each rational expression. *(LESSON 8.3)*

64. $\dfrac{x^2 - x - 2}{x^2 - 2x - 8} \cdot \dfrac{x + 2}{x^2 + 5x + 4}$

65. $\dfrac{x^2 - x - 6}{x - 1} \cdot \dfrac{x^3 - 1}{x^2 - 2x - 3}$

66. $\dfrac{x^2 - 4}{x^2 + x - 6} \div \dfrac{x + 2}{x^2 + 4x + 3}$

67. $\dfrac{x^2 + 7x + 10}{x^2 + 8x + 15} \div \dfrac{x^2 + 4x + 4}{x + 2}$

Look Beyond

internet connect

**Portfolio
Extension**

Go To: **go.hrw.com**
Keyword:
MB1 Parabola

68 Graph $y = 2(x - 3)^2 + 4$ and $x = \frac{1}{4}(y - 3)^2 + 1$ together on the same screen, and find any points of intersection.

PORTFOLIO ACTIVITY

1. Draw a straight line from one side of the patty paper, or wax paper, to the other. This will be the directrix.

2. Place the focus anywhere except on the directrix.

3. Fold the paper so that the focus lies on one end of the directrix, and crease the paper. Then unfold it.

4. Move the focus along the directrix, making folds as you go, until you come to the other end of the directrix. You should make between 15 and 25 folds.

5. Compare the parabola formed by your creases with your classmates' parabolas. Make a conjecture about how to make a

narrower or wider parabola. Verify your conjecture by folding a second parabola.

6. Fold your parabola in half along its axis of symmetry.

7. Explain how the definition of a parabola is related to your folded parabola.

WORKING ON THE CHAPTER PROJECT

You should now be able to complete Activity 1 of the Chapter Project.

Circles

Objectives

- Write an equation for a circle given sufficient information.

- Given an equation of a circle, graph it and label the radius and the center.

Why *Circles are used to describe the receiving area of radio signals.*

A radio tower is located 25 miles east and 30 miles south of Lorne's home. The radio signal is strong enough to reach homes within a 50 mile radius. Write an equation that represents all ground locations 50 miles from the radio tower. Can someone living 10 miles east and 5 miles north of Lorne receive the radio signal? This is an example of a *locus problem*. *You will solve this problem in Example 3.*

A **locus problem** involves an equation that represents a set of points that satisfy certain conditions. For example, an equation for the set of all points $P(x, y)$ in a plane that are a fixed distance, r, from $O(0, 0)$ can be obtained by using the distance formula.

$$OP = r$$
$$\sqrt{(x - 0)^2 + (y - 0)^2} = r$$
$$\sqrt{x^2 + y^2} = r$$
$$x^2 + y^2 = r^2$$

A **circle** is the set of all points in a plane that are a constant distance, called the radius, from a fixed point, called the **center.**

Standard Equation of a Circle

An equation for the circle with its center at $(0, 0)$ and a radius of r is

$$x^2 + y^2 = r^2.$$

E X A M P L E **1** Write the standard equation of the circle whose center is at the origin and whose radius is 3. Sketch the graph.

SOLUTION

$$x^2 + y^2 = r^2$$
$$x^2 + y^2 = 3^2$$

Thus, an equation for the circle is $x^2 + y^2 = 9$.

Plot the points $(3, 0)$, $(0, 3)$, $(-3, 0)$, and $(0, -3)$, and sketch a circle through these points.

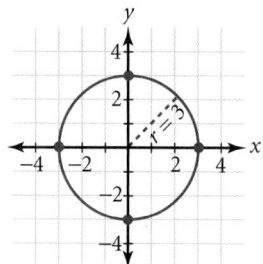

TRY THIS Write the standard equation of the circle whose center is at the origin and whose radius is 2. Sketch the graph.

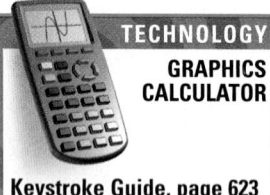

TECHNOLOGY

GRAPHICS CALCULATOR

Keystroke Guide, page 623

Recall from Lesson 9.1 that you can use a graphics calculator to graph a circle. To graph $x^2 + y^2 = 4$, solve for y and graph the two resulting equations together.

$$x^2 + y^2 = 4 \rightarrow \begin{cases} y = \sqrt{4 - x^2} \\ y = -\sqrt{4 - x^2} \end{cases}$$

Use a square viewing window.

Activity
Exploring Translations of Circles

You will need: a graphics calculator

1. Graph the circle defined by $x^2 + y^2 = 16$. Find its radius.

2. Graph the circle defined by $(x + 3)^2 + (y - 2)^2 = 16$. Find its radius, and approximate the coordinates of the center.

CHECKPOINT ✔ 3. Describe the transformation of the graph of $x^2 + y^2 = 16$ in Step 1 to the graph of $(x + 3)^2 + (y - 2)^2 = 16$ in Step 2.

4. Compare the equation of the circle $(x + 3)^2 + (y - 2)^2 = 16$ with the coordinates of its center. Describe the relationship you observe.

CHECKPOINT ✔ 5. Predict the radius and center of the circle defined by the equation $(x - 2)^2 + (y + 1)^2 = 9$. Graph the circle to support your prediction.

The standard equation for a translated circle is given below.

Standard Equation of a Translated Circle

The standard equation for a circle with its center at (h, k) and a radius of r is

$$(x - h)^2 + (y - k)^2 = r^2.$$

EXAMPLE **2** Write the standard equation for the translated circle graphed at right.

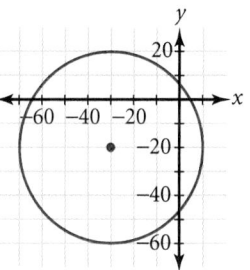

● **SOLUTION**

The center of the circle is $(-30, -20)$.
Substitute -30 for h and -20 for k.
Since the radius is 40, substitute 40 for r.

$$(x - h)^2 + (y - k)^2 = r^2$$
$$[x - (-30)]^2 + [y - (-20)]^2 = 40^2$$
$$(x + 30)^2 + (y + 20)^2 = 1600 \quad \textit{Write the standard equation.}$$

EXAMPLE **3** Refer to the radio-signal problem described at the beginning of the lesson.

APPLICATION
COMMUNICATIONS

a. Write an equation that represents all ground locations 50 miles from the radio tower, given that Lorne's home is located at $(0, 0)$.

b. Can someone who lives 10 miles east and 5 miles north of Lorne's home receive the radio signal?

● **SOLUTION**

PROBLEM SOLVING

a. **Select appropriate notation.** Since the origin represents Lorne's home, the radio tower is represented by the point $(25, -30)$. If the radio signal is strong enough to reach homes within a 50-mile radius, then $r = 50$.

Write the standard equation of a circle with its center at $(25, -30)$ and a radius of 50.

$$(x - h)^2 + (y - k)^2 = r^2$$
$$(x - 25)^2 + [y - (-30)]^2 = 50^2$$
$$(x - 25)^2 + (y + 30)^2 = 2500$$

b. The coordinates of a point that lie within the circle will satisfy the inequality $(x - 25)^2 + (y + 30)^2 < 2500$. The point $(10, 5)$ represents a location 10 miles east and 5 miles north of Lorne's home. Test $(10, 5)$ to see if it satisfies the inequality $(x - 25)^2 + (y + 30)^2 < 2500$.

$$(x - 25)^2 + (y + 30)^2 < 2500$$
$$(10 - 25)^2 + (5 + 30)^2 \overset{?}{<} 2500$$
$$1450 < 2500 \quad \textbf{True}$$

In order to listen to a radio station, you must be able to receive the radio signal.

Thus, someone who lives 10 miles east and 5 miles north of Lorne's home can receive the radio signal.

TRY THIS Tell whether $A(2, 1)$ is inside, outside, or on the circle whose center is at $(-2, 3)$ and whose radius is 4.

CRITICAL THINKING Explain how to tell whether $A(s, t)$ is inside, outside, or on the circle centered at (h, k) with a radius of r.

To write the standard equation of a translated circle, you may need to complete the square. This is shown in Example 4.

E X A M P L E **4** Write the standard equation for the circle $x^2 + y^2 + 4x - 6y - 3 = 0$. State the coordinates of its center and give its radius. Then sketch the graph.

● **SOLUTION**

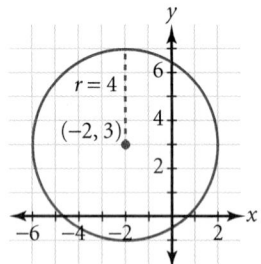

$$x^2 + y^2 + 4x - 6y - 3 = 0$$
$$x^2 + 4x + y^2 - 6y = 3$$
$$(x^2 + 4x + 4) + (y^2 - 6y + 9) = 3 + 4 + 9 \qquad \textit{Complete the squares.}$$
$$(x + 2)^2 + (y - 3)^2 = 16 \qquad \textit{Write the standard equation.}$$

Thus, the standard equation is $(x + 2)^2 + (y - 3)^2 = 16$. The center is at $(-2, 3)$ and the radius is 4.

TRY THIS Write the standard equation for the circle $x^2 + y^2 - 2x + 2y - 7 = 0$. State the coordinates of its center and give its radius. Then sketch the graph.

Exercises

● *Communicate*

1. Explain how to read the coordinates of the center of a circle and its radius from the equation $(x - 4)^2 + (y + 1)^2 = 1$.

☐ internet connect

**Activities
Online**
Go To: **go.hrw.com**
Keyword:
MB1 TV

2. How could you determine whether a given point, such as $(-1, -3)$, lies inside, outside, or on a circle whose equation is given, such as $(x - 2)^2 + (y + 1)^2 = 16$?

3. How would you determine whether the equation $x^2 + 8x + y^2 + 16 = 0$ represents a circle?

● *Guided Skills Practice*

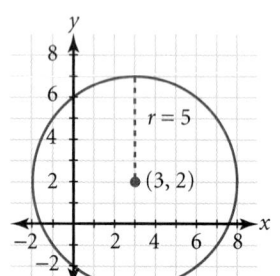

4. Write an equation for the circle whose center is at the origin and whose radius is 6. Sketch the graph. *(EXAMPLE 1)*

5. Write the standard equation for the translated circle graphed at left. *(EXAMPLE 2)*

6. **COMMUNICATIONS** Refer to the radio-signal problem posed at the beginning of the lesson. Can someone who lives 9 miles west and 5 miles south of Lorne's home receive the radio signal? *(EXAMPLE 3)*

7. Write the standard equation for the circle $x^2 + 6x + y^2 - 4y - 3 = 0$. State the coordinates of its center and give its radius. Then sketch the graph. *(EXAMPLE 4)*

● *Practice and Apply*

Write the standard equation for each circle graphed below.

8.

9.

10.

11.

12.

13.

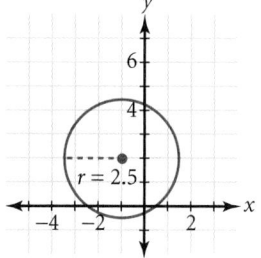

Write the standard equation of a circle with each given radius and center.

14. $r = 4$; $C(0, 0)$ **15.** $r = 5$; $C(0, 0)$

16. $r = 11$; $C(0, 0)$ **17.** $r = 7$; $C(0, 0)$

18. $r = 1$; $C(2, 3)$ **19.** $r = 12$; $C(3, 5)$

20. $r = 10$; $C(-2, -7)$ **21.** $r = 5$; $C(-5, -1)$

22. $r = 4$; $C(-2, 8)$ **23.** $r = 15$; $C(-6, 9)$

24. $r = 2$; $C(0, 12)$ **25.** $r = 3$; $C(0, 4)$

26. $r = \frac{1}{3}$; $C(-2, -2)$ **27.** $r = 2$; $C(3, 3)$

28. $r = \frac{1}{2}$; $C(2, 0)$ **29.** $r = \frac{1}{4}$; $C(1, 0)$

30. $r = 1$; $C(a, a)$, where $a > 0$ **31.** $r = 2$; $C(a, -2a)$, where $a > 0$

☑ internet connect

Homework Help Online
Go To: **go.hrw.com**
Keyword:
MB1 Homework Help
 for Exercises 32–43

Graph each equation. Label the center and the radius.

32. $x^2 + y^2 = 9$ **33.** $x^2 + y^2 = 49$

34. $(x - 2)^2 + y^2 = 4$ **35.** $(x + 5)^2 + y^2 = 36$

36. $x^2 + (y + 3)^2 = 16$ **37.** $x^2 + (y - 2)^2 = 81$

38. $(x + 1)^2 + (y + 5)^2 = 100$ **39.** $(x + 6)^2 + (y + 1)^2 = 4$

40. $(x - 2)^2 + (y + 2)^2 = 64$ **41.** $(x - 3)^2 + (y + 3)^2 = 25$

42. $(x + 4)^2 + (y - 3)^2 = 49$ **43.** $(x + 2)^2 + (y - 4)^2 = 16$

Write the standard equation for each circle. Then state the coordinates of its center and give its radius.

44. $x^2 + y^2 + 4y = 12$

45. $x^2 - 2x + y^2 = 8$

46. $x^2 + 2x + y^2 + 2y = 2$

47. $x^2 + 2x + y^2 + 6y = 6$

48. $x^2 + y^2 - 10x - 2y = 23$

49. $x^2 + y^2 - 12x + 6y = 19$

50. $x^2 + y^2 + 6x - 17 = 0$

51. $x^2 + y^2 - 20y + 19 = 0$

52. $x^2 + y^2 + x + y = 0$

53. $x^2 + y^2 - x + y = 0$

54. $x^2 + y^2 - x + 3y = 7.5$

55. $x^2 + y^2 - x + 7y = 12.5$

56. $x^2 + y^2 - 12x - 2y - 8 = 0$

57. $x^2 + y^2 - 6x - 10y - 2 = 0$

58. $x^2 + y^2 + 6x - 14y - 42 = 0$

59. $x^2 + y^2 - 10x + 6y = 0$

State whether the graph of each equation is a parabola or a circle. Justify your response.

60. $y = x^2$

61. $x^2 = 12 - y^2$

62. $y^2 = 12 - x^2$

63. $x = y^2$

64. $x^2 = 4 - (y - 2)^2$

65. $10y^2 = 5(x - 2)$

66. $4x = 8(y + 3)^2$

67. $(y + 2)^2 = 15 - (x - 2)^2$

State whether the given point is inside, outside, or on the circle whose equation is given. Justify your response.

68. $P(2, 2)$; $x^2 + y^2 = 9$

69. $P(1, 6)$; $x^2 + y^2 = 49$

70. $P(5, 1)$; $x^2 - 6x + y^2 + 8y = 24$

71. $P(2, -3)$; $x^2 - 4x + y^2 + 6y = 12$

72. $P(0, 0)$; $x^2 + 10x + y^2 + 2y = 10$

73. $P(12, 3)$; $x^2 - 12x + y^2 + 2y = 12$

74. $P(0.5, 0.5)$; $x^2 + y^2 = 1$

75. $P(1.5, 3.5)$; $x^2 + y^2 = 6$

CHALLENGE

76. Tell whether $P(a, a)$ is inside, outside, or on the circle defined by the equation $x^2 - 2ax + y^2 + 4ay = 4a^2$. Justify your response.

CONNECTIONS

77. COORDINATE GEOMETRY The figure at right shows two circles with centers at C_1 and C_2. An equation for the circle with its center at C_1 is $(x - 3)^2 + (y - 3)^2 = (r_1)^2$, and an equation with the circle for its center at C_2 is $(x - 3)^2 + (y - 1)^2 = (r_2)^2$.

  a. Find one value of r_1 and one value of r_2 such that the circle with its center at C_1 is completely enclosed by the circle with its center at C_2. Justify your response.

  b. Find one value of r_1 and one value of r_2 such that the circles intersect at two points. Justify your response.

  c. Find one value of r_1 and one value of r_2 such that the circles intersect at exactly one point. Justify your response.

78. TRANSFORMATIONS The circle defined by $(x - 1)^2 + (y + 4)^2 = 16$ is translated 3 units to the left and 2 units down. Write the standard equation for the resulting circle.

79. TRANSFORMATIONS The circle defined by $x^2 + y^2 - 8x - 4y + 9 = 0$ is translated 4 units to the right and 6 units up. Write the standard equation for the resulting circle.

80. SPACE SCIENCE A satellite in a stationary orbit rotates once each day about the Earth. Assume that the satellite is 22,300 miles above the surface of Earth and that Earth's radius is 3960 miles. Write an equation that represents the orbit of this satellite on a coordinate plane with the origin representing the center of the Earth.

81. GEOLOGY Vibrations from a certain earthquake were noticeable up to 120 miles away from the earthquake's epicenter. The center of the closest city to the earthquake's epicenter is 85 miles east and 90 miles south of the epicenter. If Alexandra was 15 miles west of this city, could she have noticed the vibrations at the time of the earthquake?

82. COMMUNICATIONS A radio program is broadcast from a van that is located 40 miles east and 30 miles north of a radio tower. The van sends the radio signal to the tower, which then transmits the signal a maximum distance of 70 miles. If Jessica is 30 miles east of the van, is she able to receive the radio program?

Many radio stations have the equipment needed to broadcast from a van.

Look Back

For each quadratic function, find the equation for the axis of symmetry and give the coordinates of the vertex. *(LESSON 5.5)*

83. $y = -11x + 28 + x^2$ **84.** $y = 2x^2 + 3x$ **85.** $y = -3x + 10 - x^2$

Solve each equation. Write the exact solution and the approximate solution to the nearest hundredth, when appropriate. *(LESSON 6.7)*

86. $7^{3x-2} + 2 = 750$ **87.** $e^{-3x} = 12$ **88.** $\log_2 7 = x$

89. $\log_a 8 = \frac{3}{2}$ **90.** $\log_3 x = 4$ **91.** $\ln(x + 1) = 2 \ln 5$

For each function, describe the transformations applied to $f(x) = \sqrt{x}$. *(LESSON 8.6)*

92. $g(x) = 4\sqrt{x - 2}$ **93.** $a(x) = \sqrt{0.5x + 4} - 3$ **94.** $b(x) = 0.5\sqrt{2x - 1} + 6$

Look Beyond

95 In this lesson you learned that the graph of $x^2 + y^2 = r^2$, where r is a positive constant, is a circle centered at the origin. Using a square viewing window, graph $4x^2 + 2y^2 = 12$, and describe the shape of the graph. Graph $8x^2 + y^2 = 24$, and describe the shape of the graph.

Ellipses

Why *Ellipses are used to describe the paths of planets around the Sun.*

Objectives

- Write the standard equation for an ellipse given sufficient information.

- Given an equation of an ellipse, graph it and label the center, vertices, co-vertices, and foci.

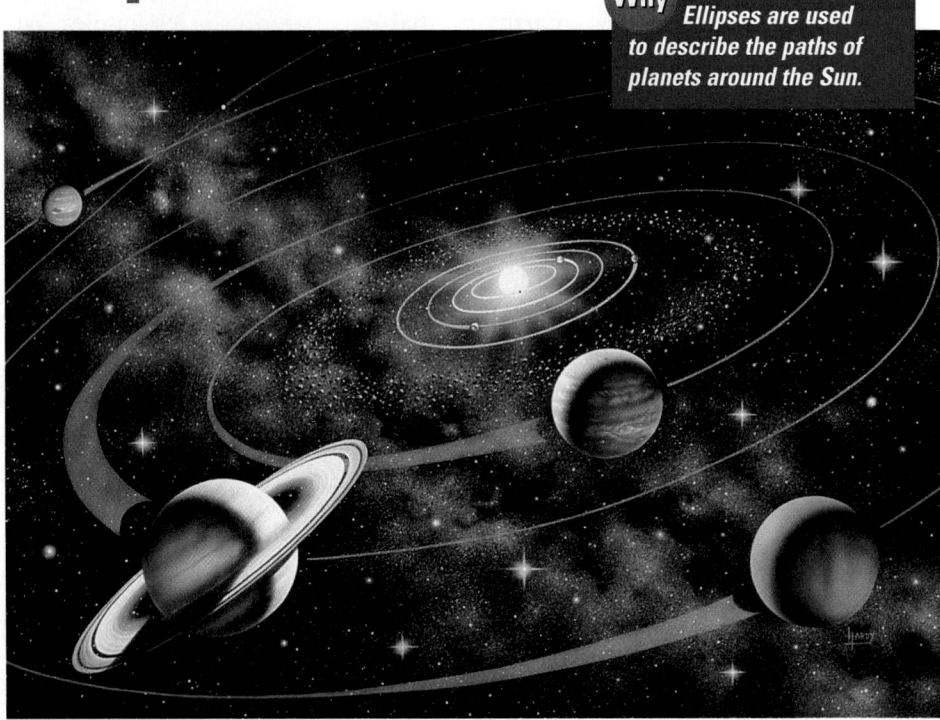

In the Activity below, you will explore the definition of an ellipse by modeling ellipses.

Modeling Ellipses

You will need: 3 pieces of corrugated cardboard at least 8 inches by 8 inches, 2 tacks, 36 inches of string, and a pencil

Draw each ellipse on a separate piece of cardboard, and write on the cardboard the length of string that was used to create the ellipse.

1. Place two tacks 4 inches apart into a piece of corrugated cardboard. Tie the ends of a 10-inch piece of string together and loop the string around the tacks. Hold the tacks down with one hand, and with the other hand, use the pencil to pull the string taut as shown above. Move your pencil along the path that keeps the string taut at all times. When you return to your starting point, the path of the pencil will have formed an ellipse.

2. Repeat Step 1 with the same locations for the tacks but a 12-inch string.

3. Repeat Step 1 with the same locations for the tacks but a 14-inch string.

CHECKPOINT ✔ 4. How does the length of the string affect the shape of the ellipse that is drawn?

Definition of Ellipse

An **ellipse** is the set of all points P in a plane such that the sum of the distances from P to two fixed points, F_1 and F_2, called the **foci**, is a constant.

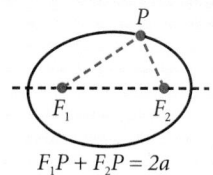

$F_1P + F_2P = 2a$

You can use the definition of an ellipse and the distance formula to write an equation for an ellipse whose foci are $F_1(-4, 0)$ and $F_2(4, 0)$ and whose constant sum is 10. Let $P(x, y)$ be any point on the ellipse.

$$F_1P + F_2P = 10$$

$$\sqrt{[x - (-4)]^2 + (y - 0)^2} + \sqrt{(x - 4)^2 + (y - 0)^2} = 10$$

$$\sqrt{(x + 4)^2 + y^2} = 10 - \sqrt{(x - 4)^2 + y^2}$$

Square each side.
$$(x + 4)^2 + y^2 = 100 - 20\sqrt{(x - 4)^2 + y^2} + [(x - 4)^2 + y^2]$$

Simplify.
$$16x - 100 = -20\sqrt{(x - 4)^2 + y^2}$$

Divide each side by 4.
$$4x - 25 = -5\sqrt{(x - 4)^2 + y^2}$$

Square each side again.
$$16x^2 - 200x + 625 = 25[(x - 4)^2 + y^2]$$

$$16x^2 - 200x + 625 = 25x^2 - 200x + 400 + 25y^2$$

$$225 = 9x^2 + 25y^2$$

Divide each side by 225.
$$1 = \frac{x^2}{25} + \frac{y^2}{9}$$

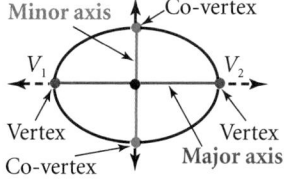

An ellipse has two axes of symmetry. The **major axis** is the longer axis of the ellipse and the **minor axis** is the shorter axis of the ellipse. The endpoints of the major axis are called the **vertices** of the ellipse. The endpoints of the minor axis are called the **co-vertices** of the ellipse. The foci are always on the major axis. The point of intersection of the major and minor axes is called the **center**.

Standard Equation of an Ellipse

The standard equation of an ellipse centered at the origin is given below.

Horizontal major axis

$$\frac{x^2}{a^2} + \frac{y^2}{b^2} = 1$$

$(0, b)$ · $V_1(-a, 0)$ · $V_2(a, 0)$ · $F_1(-c, 0)$ · $F_2(c, 0)$ · $(0, -b)$

Vertical major axis

$$\frac{x^2}{b^2} + \frac{y^2}{a^2} = 1$$

$V_2(0, a)$ · $F_2(0, c)$ · $(-b, 0)$ · $(b, 0)$ · $F_1(0, -c)$ · $V_1(0, -a)$

In each case: • $a^2 > b^2$, and $a^2 - b^2 = c^2$,
   • the length of the major axis is $2a$, and
   • the length of the minor axis is $2b$.

EXAMPLE **1** Write the standard equation for an ellipse with foci at $(0, -4)$ and $(0, 4)$ and with a minor axis of 6. Sketch the graph.

● **SOLUTION**

The coordinates of the foci are $(0, -4)$ and $(0, 4)$, so $c = 4$. The length of the minor axis is $2b$ and $2b = 6$, so $b = 3$.

Substitute 4 for c and 3 for b to find a.

$$a^2 - b^2 = c^2$$
$$a^2 - 3^2 = 4^2$$
$$a = 5$$

Substitute 5 for a and 3 for b.

$$\frac{x^2}{b^2} + \frac{y^2}{a^2} = 1 \rightarrow \frac{x^2}{9} + \frac{y^2}{25} = 1$$

To sketch the graph, plot the vertices, $(0, -5)$ and $(0, 5)$, and the co-vertices, $(-3, 0)$ and $(3, 0)$. Connect them to form an ellipse.

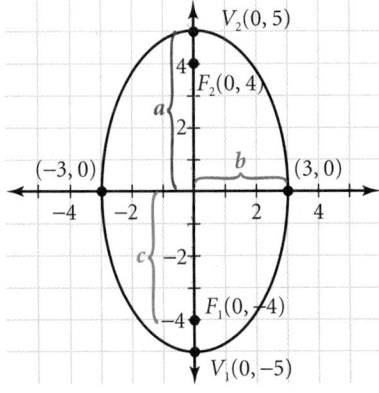

TRY THIS Write the standard equation for an ellipse with foci at $(-12, 0)$ and $(12, 0)$ and with a major axis of 26. Sketch the graph.

EXAMPLE **2** Mars orbits the Sun in an elliptical path whose minimum distance from the Sun is 129.5 million miles and whose maximum distance from the Sun is 154.4 million miles. The Sun represents one focus of the ellipse.

Write the standard equation for the elliptical orbit of Mars around the Sun, where the center of the ellipse is at the origin.

● **SOLUTION**

PROBLEM SOLVING

Draw a diagram.

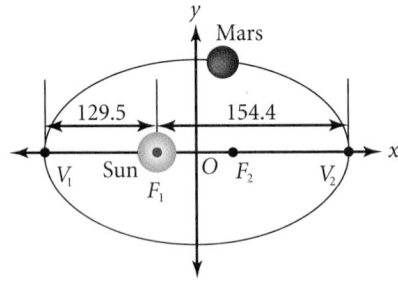

[Figure not to scale]

1. Find a^2. $V_1V_2 = 154.4 + 129.5$

$$2a = 283.9$$
$$a = 141.95$$
$$a^2 \approx 20{,}149.8$$

2. Find c. $OF_1 = OV_1 - F_1V_1$

$$c = a - 129.5$$
$$c = 141.95 - 129.5$$
$$c = 12.45$$

3. Find b^2. $a^2 - b^2 = c^2$

$$141.95^2 - b^2 = 12.45^2$$
$$19{,}994.8 = b^2$$

The standard equation for the orbit of Mars around the Sun in millions of miles is approximately $\dfrac{x^2}{20{,}149.8} + \dfrac{y^2}{19{,}994.8} = 1$.

An image of Mars, composed from 102 Viking Orbiter images

TRY THIS   Venus orbits the Sun in an elliptical path whose minimum distance from the Sun is 66.7 million miles and whose maximum distance from the Sun is 67.6 million miles. The Sun represents one focus of the ellipse. Write the standard equation for the elliptical orbit of Venus around the Sun, where the center of the ellipse is at the origin.

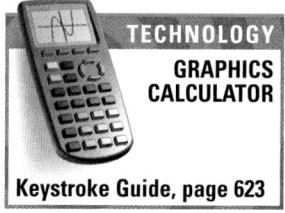

TECHNOLOGY

GRAPHICS
CALCULATOR

Keystroke Guide, page 623

You can graph ellipses with a graphics calculator. To graph $\frac{x^2}{25} + \frac{y^2}{9} = 1$, solve for y, and graph the two resulting equations together.

You may wish to simplify the equations before entering them into the graphics calculator, but this is not necessary.

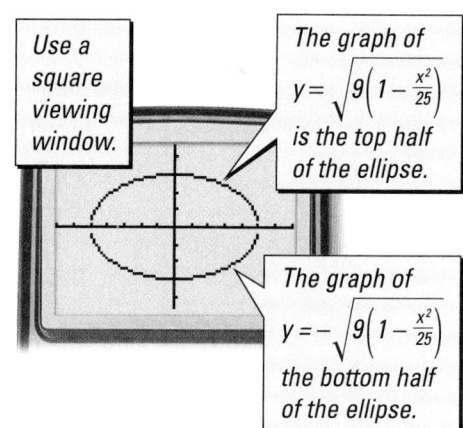

Use a square viewing window.

The graph of $y = \sqrt{9\left(1 - \frac{x^2}{25}\right)}$ is the top half of the ellipse.

The graph of $y = -\sqrt{9\left(1 - \frac{x^2}{25}\right)}$ the bottom half of the ellipse.

The center of an ellipse can be anywhere in a coordinate plane.

Standard Equation of a Translated Ellipse

The standard equation of an ellipse centered at (h, k) is given below.

Horizontal major axis

$$\frac{(x-h)^2}{a^2} + \frac{(y-k)^2}{b^2} = 1$$

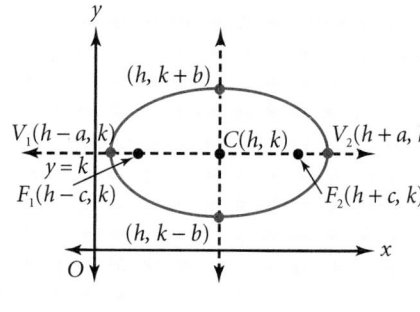

Vertical major axis

$$\frac{(x-h)^2}{b^2} + \frac{(y-k)^2}{a^2} = 1$$

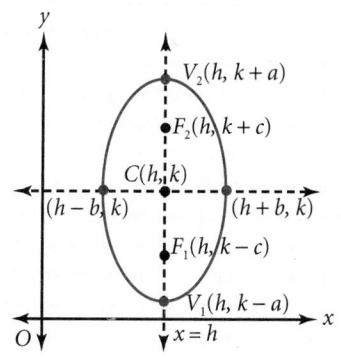

In each case: • $a^2 > b^2$, and $a^2 - b^2 = c^2$,
  • the length of the major axis is $2a$, and
  • the length of the minor axis is $2b$.

The **eccentricity** of an ellipse is a measure of how round or flat it is. The eccentricity, E, is the ratio of the distance, c, between the center and a focus to the distance, a, between the center and a vertex.

$$E = \frac{c}{a}, \text{ where } c = \sqrt{a^2 - b^2}$$

If $c = 0$, then $E = 0$ and the ellipse is a circle. As the value of c approaches the value of a, the value of E approaches 1, and the ellipse becomes flatter.

LESSON 9.4 ELLIPSES **589**

E X A M P L E **3** Write the standard equation for an ellipse with its center at (2, −4) and with a horizontal major axis of 10 and minor axis of 6. Sketch the graph.

● **SOLUTION**

The center, (h, k), is at $(2, -4)$.
The length of the major axis is $2a = 10$, so $a = 5$.
The length of the minor axis is $2b = 6$, so $b = 3$.

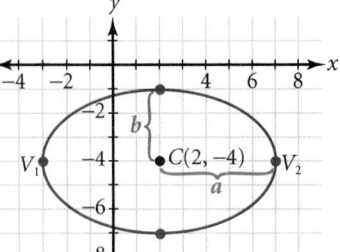

The major axis is horizontal.

$$\frac{(x - h)^2}{a^2} + \frac{(y - k)^2}{b^2} = 1$$

$$\frac{(x - 2)^2}{25} + \frac{(y + 4)^2}{9} = 1$$

Use the value of a to find the vertices, $(-3, -4)$ and $(7, -4)$.

Use the value of b to find the co-vertices, $(2, -7)$ and $(2, -1)$.

TRY THIS Write the standard equation for an ellipse with its center at $(-1, -2)$ and with a vertical major axis of 8 and minor axis of 4. Sketch the graph.

E X A M P L E **4** An ellipse is defined by $4x^2 + y^2 + 24x - 4y + 36 = 0$. Write the standard equation, and identify the coordinates of its center, vertices, co-verticcs, and foci. Sketch the graph.

● **SOLUTION**

$$4x^2 + y^2 + 24x - 4y + 36 = 0$$
$$4x^2 + 24x + y^2 - 4y = -36$$
$$4(x^2 + 6x) + (y^2 - 4y) = -36$$
$$4(x^2 + 6x + \textbf{9}) + (y^2 - 4y + \textbf{4}) = -36 + 4(\textbf{9}) + 4 \quad \textit{Complete the squares.}$$
$$4(x + 3)^2 + (y - 2)^2 = 4$$
$$\frac{(x + 3)^2}{1} + \frac{(y - 2)^2}{4} = 1 \quad \textit{Divide each side by 4.}$$

From the equation, the center is at $(-3, 2)$, $a^2 = 4$, and $b^2 = 1$. Find c.

$$a^2 - b^2 = c^2$$
$$4 - 1 = c^2$$
$$\sqrt{3} = c$$

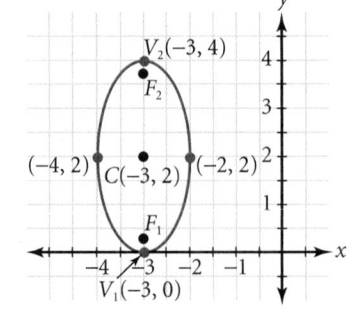

Use the value of c to find the foci.

$(-3, 2 - \sqrt{3})$ and $(-3, 2 + \sqrt{3})$

Use the value of a to find the vertices.

$(-3, 0)$ and $(-3, 4)$

Use the value of b to find the co-vertices.

$(-4, 2)$ and $(-2, 2)$

CRITICAL THINKING Identify the graph of $Ax^2 + Cy^2 + E = 0$ given that A and C are positive numbers.

Exercises

Communicate

1. Describe the information you can obtain from the standard equation of a translated ellipse, such as $\dfrac{x^2}{16} + \dfrac{(y-2)^2}{25} = 1$.

2. Describe the procedure used to write the standard equation of the ellipse defined by $9x^2 + 4y^2 + 18x - 40y + 73 = 0$.

3. Explain how to graph $\dfrac{(x-4)^2}{3^2} + \dfrac{(y-5)^2}{2^2} = 1$.

4. Describe the graph of $\dfrac{x^2}{25} + \dfrac{y^2}{25} = 1$.

Guided Skills Practice

5. Write the standard equation for an ellipse centered at the origin with foci at $(5, 0)$ and $(-5, 0)$ and with a minor axis of 8. Sketch the graph. *(EXAMPLE 1)*

APPLICATION

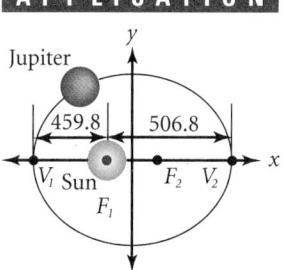

[*Not to scale*]

6. ASTRONOMY The diagram at left gives the minimum and maximum distances (in millions of miles) from Jupiter to the Sun. Write the standard equation for Jupiter's elliptical orbit around the Sun. *(EXAMPLE 2)*

7. Write the standard equation for an ellipse centered at $(1, -2)$ with a vertical major axis of 6 and a minor axis of 4. Sketch the graph. *(EXAMPLE 3)*

8. An ellipse is defined by the equation $25x^2 + 4y^2 + 50x - 8y - 71 = 0$. Write the standard equation, and identify the coordinates of the center, vertices, co-vertices, and foci. Sketch the graph. *(EXAMPLE 4)*

Jupiter as seen by Voyager 1

Practice and Apply

Find the vertices and co-vertices of each ellipse.

9. $\dfrac{x^2}{25} + \dfrac{y^2}{9} = 1$ **10.** $\dfrac{x^2}{16} + \dfrac{y^2}{49} = 1$ **11.** $\dfrac{x^2}{81} + \dfrac{y^2}{4} = 1$

12. $\dfrac{x^2}{9} + \dfrac{y^2}{36} = 1$ **13.** $\dfrac{x^2}{1} + \dfrac{y^2}{64} = 1$ **14.** $\dfrac{x^2}{1} + \dfrac{y^2}{4} = 1$

Write the standard equation of each ellipse. Find the coordinates of the center, vertices, co-vertices, and foci.

15. $3x^2 + 12y^2 = 12$ **16.** $50x^2 + 2y^2 = 50$ **17.** $3x^2 + 7y^2 = 28$

18. $5x^2 + 20y^2 = 80$ **19.** $\dfrac{x^2}{8} + \dfrac{y^2}{18} = 2$ **20.** $\dfrac{x^2}{3} + \dfrac{y^2}{12} = 3$

Write the standard equation for each ellipse.

21.

22.

23.

24.

25.

26.
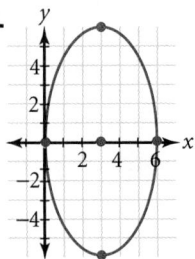

☑ **internet** connect

Homework Help Online

Go To: **go.hrw.com**
Keyword:
MB1 Homework Help
for Exercises 27–39

Sketch the graph of each ellipse. Label the center, foci, vertices, and co-vertices.

27. $\dfrac{x^2}{25} + \dfrac{y^2}{4} = 1$

28. $\dfrac{x^2}{1} + \dfrac{y^2}{9} = 1$

29. $\dfrac{x^2}{4} + \dfrac{y^2}{9} = 1$

30. $\dfrac{x^2}{16} + \dfrac{y^2}{1} = 1$

31. $\dfrac{(x+2)^2}{4} + \dfrac{(y+1)^2}{9} = 1$

32. $\dfrac{(x-2)^2}{9} + \dfrac{(y-2)^2}{4} = 1$

33. $\dfrac{x^2}{1} + \dfrac{(y+2)^2}{9} = 1$

34. $\dfrac{(x+1)^2}{4} + \dfrac{y^2}{1} = 1$

35. $\dfrac{(x-1)^2}{4} + \dfrac{(y-1)^2}{4} = 1$

36. $16(x+1)^2 + 9(y-1)^2 = 144$

37. $9(x-1)^2 + 25(y+2)^2 = 225$

38. $4x^2 + 25y^2 = 100$

39. $25x^2 + 9y^2 = 225$

Write the standard equation for the ellipse with the given characteristics.

40. foci: $(5, 0), (-5, 0)$
vertices: $(9, 0), (-9, 0)$

41. foci: $(0, 4), (0, -4)$
vertices: $(0, 8), (0, -8)$

42. foci: $(7, 0), (-7, 0)$
co-vertices: $(0, 3), (0, -3)$

43. foci: $(0, 3), (0, -3)$
co-vertices: $(1, 0), (-1, 0)$

44. co-vertices: $(0, 2), (0, -2)$
vertices: $(3, 0), (-3, 0)$

45. vertices: $(5, 0), (-5, 0)$
co-vertices: $(0, 4), (0, -4)$

State whether each equation represents a parabola, a circle, or an ellipse.

46. $\dfrac{x}{2} = \dfrac{(y-3)^2}{4}$

47. $\dfrac{y}{4} = \dfrac{(x+2)^2}{2}$

48. $\dfrac{(x-1)^2}{12} = 6 - \dfrac{(y+5)^2}{9}$

49. $\dfrac{(y+4)^2}{6} = 8 - \dfrac{(x-1)^2}{4}$

Write the standard equation for each ellipse. Identify the coordinates of the center, vertices, co-vertices, and foci.

50. $x^2 + 4y^2 + 6x - 8y = 3$

51. $16x^2 + 4y^2 + 32x - 8y = 44$

52. $x^2 + 16y^2 - 64y = 0$

53. $25x^2 + y^2 - 50x = 0$

54. $4x^2 + 9y^2 - 16x + 18y = 11$

55. $25x^2 + 9y^2 + 100x + 18y = 116$

56. $9x^2 + 16y^2 - 36x - 64y - 44 = 0$

57. $36x^2 + 25y^2 - 72x + 100y = 764$

58. TRANSFORMATIONS If the ellipse defined by the equation
$\frac{(x+5)^2}{36} + \frac{(y-1)^2}{64} = 1$ is translated 1 unit up and 5 units to the right, write the standard equation of the resulting ellipse.

59. TRANSFORMATIONS If the ellipse defined by the equation
$16x^2 + 4y^2 + 96x + 8y + 84 = 0$ is translated 4 units down and 7 units to the left, write the standard equation of the resulting ellipse.

60. Use equations to explain why the eccentricity of an ellipse cannot equal 1.

61. Describe the graph of the equation $\frac{(x+2)^2}{3} + \frac{(y-1)^2}{6} = 0$.

62. ASTRONOMY The Moon orbits Earth in an elliptical path with the center of the Earth at one focus. The major axis of the orbit is 774,000 kilometers, and the minor axis is 773,000 kilometers.

a. Using $(0, 0)$ as the center of the ellipse, write the standard equation for the orbit of the Moon around Earth.

b. How far from the center of Earth is the Moon at its closest point?

c. How far from the center of Earth is the Moon at its farthest point?

d. Find the eccentricity of the Moon's orbit around Earth.

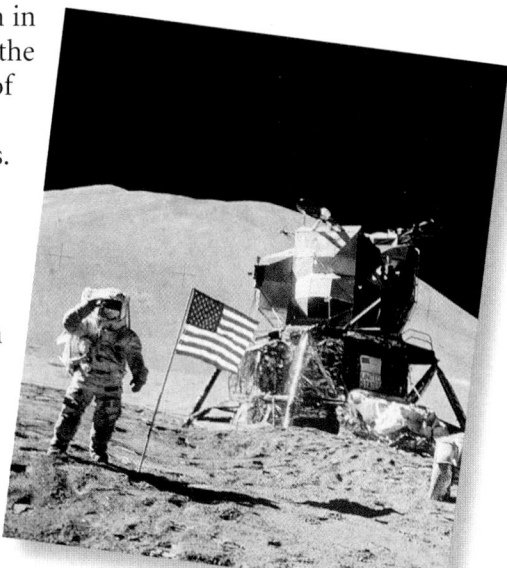

James Irwin salutes the flag during the Apollo 15 *mission to the Moon.*

63. ARCHITECTURE The ceiling of the "whispering gallery" of the Statuary Hall in the United States Capitol Building can be approximated by a *semi-ellipse*. Because of the properties of reflection, the whispering of someone standing at one focus can be clearly heard by a person standing at the other focus. It is said that John Quincy Adams used this attribute of the Statuary Hall to eavesdrop on his adversaries. Suppose that the distance between the foci is 38.5 feet and the maximum height of the ceiling above ear level is 37 feet. Find the equation of an elliptical cross section of this gallery, assuming that the center is placed at the origin.

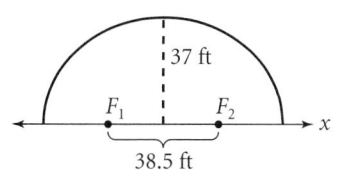

64. LIGHTING A light atop the pole represented by $\overline{PQ}$ illuminates an elliptical region at the base of the pole as shown in the illustration at left, where $PQ = 18$ feet, $CQ = 2$ feet, $AQ = 26$ feet, and $BD = 18$ feet.

a. Using the x- and y-axes shown, write an equation for the boundary of the elliptical region illuminated by the light.

b. Write an inequality in terms of x and y that represents the points in the illuminated area.

c. Describe the region that would be illuminated if the pole stood straight up at point O and the light were directed straight down.

Look Back

Simplify each expression, assuming that no variable equals zero. Write your answers with positive exponents only. *(LESSON 2.2)*

65. $(4x^3y^4)^2(2x^4y)^{-1}$ **66.** $\left(\dfrac{a^5b^{-3}}{ab^4}\right)^{-2}$ **67.** $\left(\dfrac{6xy^2z^{-5}}{5x^2y^{-2}z}\right)^2$

Solve each equation for x by using natural logarithms. Round answers to the nearest hundredth. *(LESSON 6.6)*

68. $10^x = 56$ **69.** $25^x = 123$ **70.** $0.3^{-x} = 0.81$

Write each sum or difference as a polynomial expression in standard form. *(LESSON 7.1)*

71. $(18a^3 - 5a^2 - 6a + 2) + (7a^3 - 8a + 9)$

72. $2x^4 - 3x^2 + 2 - 5x) + (4x^2 + 2x - 7x^4 + 6)$

73. $(9x^2y^2 - 5xy + 25y^2) - (5x^2y^2 + 10xy - 9y^2)$

74. $(-x^2 - y^2) - (-2x^2 + 3xy - 2y^2)$

Portfolio Extension
Go To: go.hrw.com
Keyword: **MB1 Ellipse**

 Look Beyond

75 Graph $\dfrac{x^2}{9} - \dfrac{y^2}{16} = 1$, and describe its shape. Explain why there are no real-number values of y for $-3 < x < 3$.

PORTFOLIO ACTIVITY

1. Draw a circle with a diameter of at least 4.5 inches in the middle of a piece of patty paper or wax paper.

2. Place at least 20 tick marks on the circle, approximately evenly spaced.

3. Place a point inside the circle anywhere except at the center. Fold the paper so that this inside point lies on one of the tick marks on the circle. Crease the paper, and then unfold it.

4. Repeat this procedure for each tick mark on the circle.

5. Compare the figure formed by the creases with the figures formed by your classmates. How do the figures vary? Could they all be classified as one type of conic section? If so, which one?

6. Make a conjecture about how to make a flatter or rounder figure. Verify your conjecture by repeating the process with the appropriate modification(s).

7. How does the point that you chose in Step 3 appear to be mathematically significant? Explain your reasoning.

WORKING ON THE CHAPTER PROJECT

You should now be able to complete Activity 2 of the Chapter Project.

Hyperbolas

Why *The principle of the LORAN navigation system used by ships at sea is based on the definition of a hyperbola.*

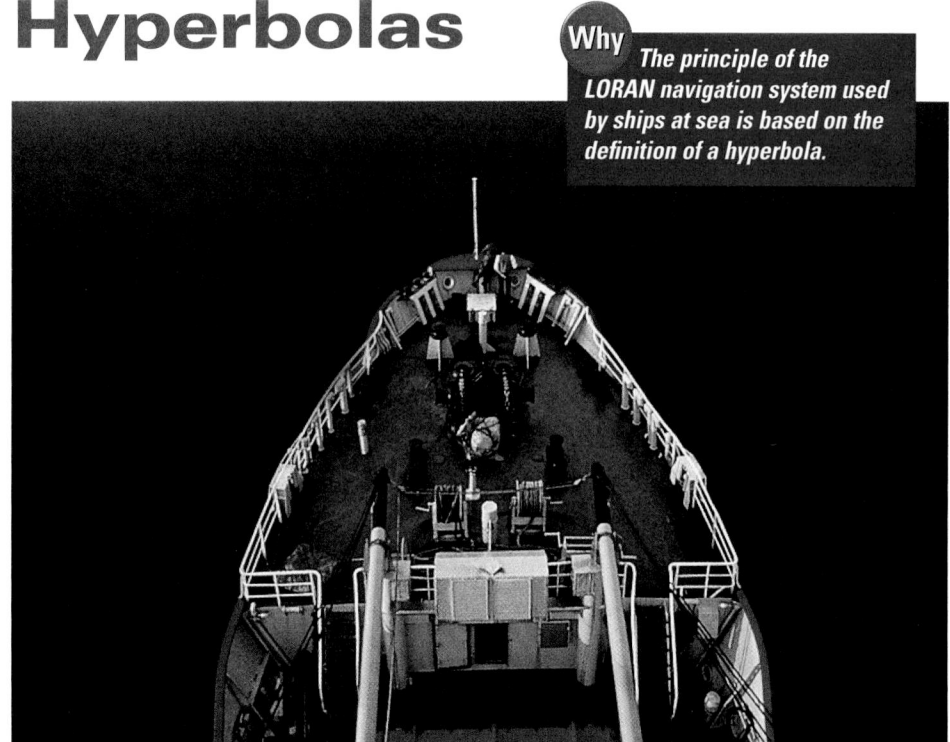

Objectives

- Write the standard equation for a hyperbola given sufficient information.

- Graph the equation of a hyperbola, and identify the center, foci, vertices, and co-vertices.

APPLICATION
RADIO NAVIGATION

Ships can navigate by using the LORAN radio navigation system, which is based on the time differences between receiving radio signals from pairs of transmitting stations that send signals at the same time.

For example, the ship at point P in the diagram at right can use the time difference $t_2 - t_1$ and the distance F_1F_2 to locate itself somewhere on the branches of the blue hyperbola. Then, using the time difference $t_3 - t_1$ and the distance F_1F_3, the ship can locate itself somewhere on the branches of the red hyperbola.

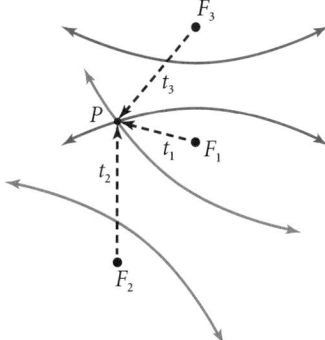

By finding the reasonable intersection of these two hyperbolas, the ship can determine its exact location.

The radio navigation system described utilizes the *definition of a hyperbola* to locate objects.

Definition of a Hyperbola

A **hyperbola** is the set of points $P(x, y)$ in a plane such that the absolute value of the difference between the distances from P to two fixed points in the plane, F_1 and F_2, called the **foci**, is a constant.

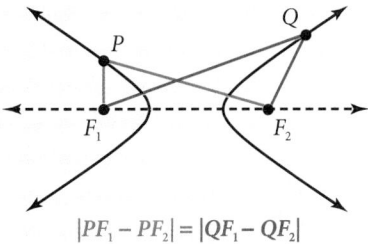

$$|PF_1 - PF_2| = |QF_1 - QF_2|$$

You can use the definition of a hyperbola and the distance formula to find an equation for the hyperbola that contains $P(x, y)$, has foci at $F_1(-5, 0)$ and $F_2(5, 0)$, and has a constant difference of 6.

$$|F_1P - F_2P| = 6$$
$$F_1P - F_2P = \pm 6$$
$$\sqrt{[x - (-5)]^2 + (y - 0)^2} - \sqrt{(x - 5)^2 + (y - 0)^2} = \pm 6$$
$$\sqrt{(x - 5)^2 + y^2} = \pm 6 + \sqrt{(x - 5)^2 + y^2}$$

Square each side.
$$(x + 5)^2 + y^2 = 36 \pm 12\sqrt{(x - 5)^2 + y^2} + (x - 5)^2 + y^2$$
$$x^2 + 10x + 25 + y^2 = 36 \pm 12\sqrt{(x - 5)^2 + y^2} + x^2 - 10x + 25 + y^2$$

Simplify.
$$20x - 36 = \pm 12\sqrt{(x - 5)^2 + y^2}$$

Divide each side by 4.
$$5x - 9 = \pm 3\sqrt{(x - 5)^2 + y^2}$$

Square each side again.
$$25x^2 - 90x + 81 = 9x^2 - 90x + 225 + 9y^2$$
$$16x^2 - 9y^2 = 144$$

Divide each side by 144.
$$\frac{x^2}{9} - \frac{y^2}{16} = 1$$

Notice that the transverse axis can be shorter than the conjugate axis.

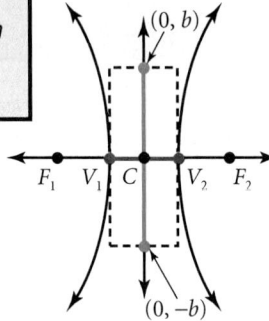

A hyperbola has two axes of symmetry. One axis contains the **transverse axis**, $\overline{V_1V_2}$, of the hyperbola, and the other axis contains the **conjugate axis**, from $(0, -b)$ to $(0, b)$, of the hyperbola. The endpoints of the transverse axis are called the **vertices** of the hyperbola. The endpoints of the conjugate axis are called the **co-vertices** of the hyperbola. The point of intersection of the transverse axis and the conjugate axis is called the **center** of the hyperbola.

Standard Equation of a Hyperbola

The standard equation of a hyperbola centered at the origin is given below.

Horizontal transverse axis

$$\frac{x^2}{a^2} - \frac{y^2}{b^2} = 1$$

Vertical transverse axis

$$\frac{y^2}{a^2} - \frac{x^2}{b^2} = 1$$

In each case: • $a^2 + b^2 = c^2$,
• the length of the transverse axis is $2a$, and
• the length of the conjugate axis is $2b$.

EXAMPLE ① Write the standard equation for the hyperbola with vertices at $(0, -4)$ and $(0, 4)$ and co-vertices at $(-3, 0)$ and $(3, 0)$. Then sketch the graph.

● **SOLUTION**

Because the vertices lie along the y-axis and the center is at the origin, the

equation is of the form $\dfrac{y^2}{a^2} - \dfrac{x^2}{b^2} = 1$.

From the coordinates of the vertices, $a = 4$. From the coordinates of the co-vertices, $b = 3$. The equation is $\dfrac{y^2}{4^2} - \dfrac{x^2}{3^2} = 1$,

or $\dfrac{y^2}{16} - \dfrac{x^2}{9} = 1$.

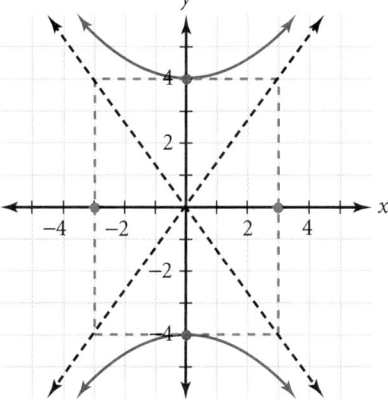

Plot the vertices and co-vertices, and draw the rectangle determined by these points. Sketch the lines containing the diagonals of this rectangle. Then sketch the branches of the hyperbola between the lines that contain the diagonals, as shown at right above.

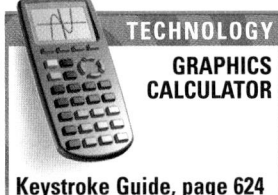
TECHNOLOGY
GRAPHICS CALCULATOR
Keystroke Guide, page 624

CHECK

To graph the hyperbola defined by $\dfrac{y^2}{16} - \dfrac{x^2}{9} = 1$, solve for y and graph the two resulting equations together.

$$\dfrac{y^2}{16} - \dfrac{x^2}{9} = 1 \ \rightarrow \ y = \pm\sqrt{16\left(1 + \dfrac{x^2}{9}\right)}$$

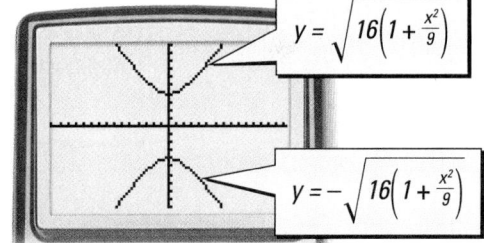

$y = \sqrt{16\left(1 + \dfrac{x^2}{9}\right)}$

$y = -\sqrt{16\left(1 + \dfrac{x^2}{9}\right)}$

TRY THIS Write the standard equation for the hyperbola with vertices at $(-7, 0)$ and $(7, 0)$ and co-vertices at $(0, -4)$ and $(0, 4)$. Then sketch the graph.

CRITICAL THINKING Write the standard equation for the hyperbola that has a horizontal transverse axis, is centered at the origin, and passes through the points $(1, 2)$ and $(5, 12)$.

Notice that the hyperbola in Example 1 above is graphed with a pair of dashed lines that contain the diagonals of the rectangle that is determined by the vertices and co-vertices. These lines are **asymptotes of the hyperbola**. In the Activity below, you will explore the equations for the asymptotes of hyperbolas.

Exploring Asymptotes of Hyperbolas

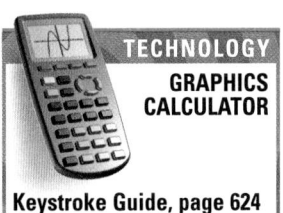
TECHNOLOGY
GRAPHICS CALCULATOR
Keystroke Guide, page 624

You will need: a graphics calculator

1. Solve $\dfrac{x^2}{2^2} - \dfrac{y^2}{3^2} = 1$ for y, and graph the resulting equations with the lines

   $y = \dfrac{3}{2}x$ and $y = -\dfrac{3}{2}x$ on the same screen. Do the branches of the

   hyperbola appear to approach these lines?

2. Copy and complete the table of values to the nearest hundredth.

x	$y = \sqrt{9\left(\frac{x^2}{4} - 1\right)}$	$y = -\sqrt{9\left(\frac{x^2}{4} - 1\right)}$	$y = \frac{3}{2}x$	$y = -\frac{3}{2}x$
10				
20				
30				
40				
50				
60				

3. Do the values in the table above suggest that the branches of this hyperbola approach the lines $y = \frac{3}{2}x$ and $y = -\frac{3}{2}x$? Explain your response.

CHECKPOINT ✔ **4.** Consider $\frac{x^2}{5^2} - \frac{y^2}{4^2} = 1$. Predict the equations for the asymptotes of this hyperbola. Use a graph and a table to check your prediction.

Given the standard equation of any hyperbola with a horizontal or vertical transverse axis and with its center at the origin, you can write equations for the asymptotes.

Asymptotes of a Hyperbola

standard equation: $\frac{x^2}{a^2} - \frac{y^2}{b^2} = 1 \rightarrow$ asymptotes: $y = \pm\frac{b}{a}x$

standard equation: $\frac{y^2}{a^2} - \frac{x^2}{b^2} = 1 \rightarrow$ asymptotes: $y = \pm\frac{a}{b}x$

E X A M P L E ② Find the equations of the asymptotes and the coordinates of the vertices for the graph of $\frac{y^2}{16} - \frac{x^2}{36} = 1$. Then sketch the graph.

● **SOLUTION**

The equation is of the form

$\frac{y^2}{a^2} - \frac{x^2}{b^2} = 1$, where $a = 4$ and $b = 6$.

The asymptotes, $y = \pm\frac{a}{b}x$, are

$y = \pm\frac{4}{6}x$, or $y = \frac{2}{3}x$ and $y = -\frac{2}{3}x$.

The vertices are $(0, -4)$ and $(0, 4)$.

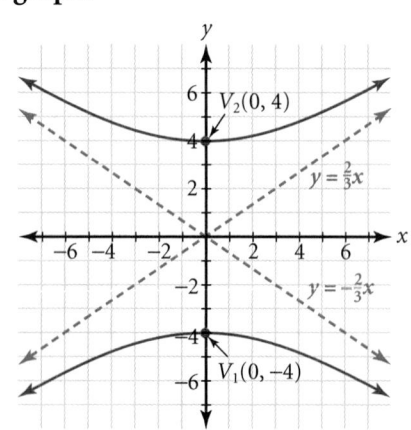

TRY THIS Find the equations of the asymptotes and the coordinates of the vertices for the graph of $\frac{x^2}{16} - \frac{y^2}{25} = 1$. Then sketch the graph.

The center of a hyperbola can be anywhere in a coordinate plane.

Standard Equation of a Translated Hyperbola

The standard equation of a hyperbola centered at (h, k) is given below.

Horizontal transverse axis

$$\frac{(x-h)^2}{a^2} - \frac{(y-k)^2}{b^2} = 1$$

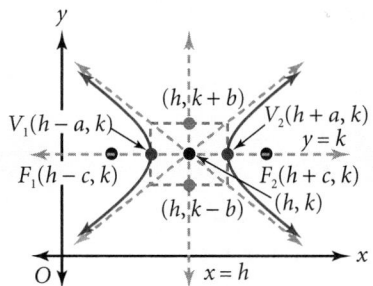

Vertical transverse axis

$$\frac{(y-k)^2}{a^2} - \frac{(x-h)^2}{b^2} = 1$$

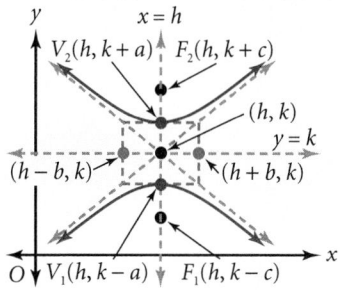

In each case: • $a^2 + b^2 = c^2$,
• the length of the transverse axis is $2a$, and
• the length of the conjugate axis is $2b$.

Given sufficient information, you can write the standard equation of a translated hyperbola.

E X A M P L E ❸ Write the standard equation of the hyperbola with foci at $(-1, 1)$ and $(5, 1)$ and vertices at $(0, 1)$ and $(4, 1)$.

● **SOLUTION**

1. To find the center, (h, k), find the midpoint of the transverse axis.

$$\frac{x_1 + x_2}{2} = \frac{0 + 4}{2} = 2 \qquad \frac{y_1 + y_2}{2} = \frac{1 + 1}{2} = 1$$

The center is at $(2, 1)$, so $h = 2$ and $k = 1$.

2. Find a, b, and c. The transverse axis is horizontal and the standard equation is of the form $\frac{(x-h)^2}{a^2} - \frac{(y-k)^2}{b^2} = 1$.

The vertex $(0, 1)$ is $(h - a, k)$, so $h - a = 0$.

$$h - a = 0$$
$$2 - a = 0$$
$$a = 2$$

The focus $(-1, 1)$ is $(h - c, k)$, so $h - c = -1$.

$$h - c = -1$$
$$2 - c = -1$$
$$c = 3$$

$$a^2 + b^2 = c^2 \quad \rightarrow \quad 2^2 + b^2 = 3^2 \quad \rightarrow \quad b^2 = 5$$

Thus, the standard equation of this hyperbola is $\frac{(x-2)^2}{4} - \frac{(y-1)^2}{5} = 1$.

TRY THIS Write the standard equation of the hyperbola with foci at $(3, -3)$ and $(3, 7)$ and vertices at $(3, -1)$ and $(3, 5)$.

E X A M P L E The equation $-2x^2 + y^2 + 4x + 6y + 3 = 0$ represents a hyperbola. Write the standard equation of this hyperbola. Give the coordinates of the center, vertices, co-vertices, and foci. Then sketch the graph.

● **SOLUTION**

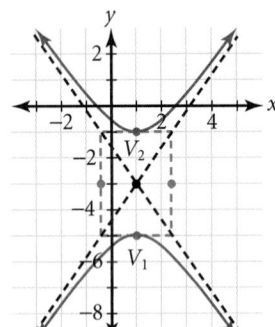

$$-2x^2 + y^2 + 4x + 6y + 3 = 0$$
$$y^2 + 6y - 2x^2 + 4x = -3$$
$$(y^2 + 6y + 9) - 2(x^2 - 2x + 1) = -3 + 9 - 2 \quad \textit{Complete the squares.}$$
$$(y + 3)^2 - 2(x - 1)^2 = 4$$
$$\frac{(y + 3)^2}{4} - \frac{(x - 1)^2}{2} = 1$$

From the equation, $h = 1$, $k = -3$, $a = 2$, and $b = \sqrt{2}$. Then $c = \sqrt{4 + 2} = \sqrt{6}$.

The center, (h, k), is at $(1, -3)$.
Use the value of a to find the vertices, $(1, -5)$ and $(1, -1)$.
Use the value of b to find the co-vertices, $\left(1 - \sqrt{2}, -3\right)$ and $\left(1 + \sqrt{2}, -3\right)$.
Use the value of c to find the foci, $\left(1, -3 - \sqrt{6}\right)$ and $\left(1, -3 + \sqrt{6}\right)$.

TRY THIS The equation $4x^2 - 25y^2 - 8x + 100y - 196 = 0$ represents a hyperbola. Write the standard equation of this hyperbola. Give the coordinates of the center, vertices, co-vertices, and foci. Then sketch the graph.

Exercises

● *Communicate*

1. Explain how to find the coordinates of the center, vertices, co-vertices, and foci when given the standard equation of a translated hyperbola.

2. Explain how to use the asymptotes and the coordinates of the vertices of a hyperbola to sketch it.

● *Guided Skills Practice*

3. Write the standard equation for the hyperbola with vertices at $(-4, 0)$ and $(4, 0)$ and co-vertices at $(0, -2)$ and $(0, 2)$. Then sketch the graph. *(EXAMPLE 1)*

4. Find the equations of the asymptotes and the coordinates of the vertices of the graph of $\dfrac{x^2}{9} - \dfrac{y^2}{25} = 1$. Then sketch the graph. *(EXAMPLE 2)*

5. Write the standard equation of the hyperbola with foci at $(0, 4)$ and $(6, 4)$ and vertices at $(1, 4)$ and $(5, 4)$. *(EXAMPLE 3)*

6. The equation $x^2 - y^2 + 2x + 4y - 2 = 12$ represents a hyperbola. Write the standard equation of this hyperbola. Give the coordinates of the center, vertices, co-vertices, and foci. Then sketch the graph. *(EXAMPLE 4)*

Write the standard equation for each hyperbola.

7.

8.

9.

10.

11.

12.

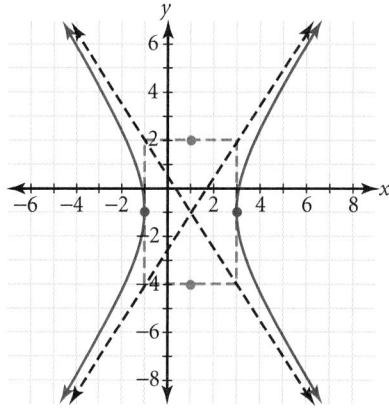

Graph each hyperbola. Label the center, vertices, co-vertices, foci, and asymptotes.

13. $x^2 - y^2 = 1$

14. $y^2 - x^2 = 1$

15. $\dfrac{y^2}{3^2} - \dfrac{x^2}{5^2} = 1$

16. $\dfrac{x^2}{2^2} - \dfrac{y^2}{3^2} = 1$

17. $x^2 - \dfrac{y^2}{2^2} = 1$

18. $y^2 - \dfrac{x^2}{3^2} = 1$

19. $\dfrac{y^2}{100} - \dfrac{x^2}{64} = 1$

20. $\dfrac{x^2}{25} - \dfrac{y^2}{36} = 1$

21. $4x^2 - 25y^2 = 100$

22. $36y^2 - 4x^2 = 144$

23. $\dfrac{(x-1)^2}{2^2} - \dfrac{(y+2)^2}{3^2} = 1$

24. $\dfrac{(x+2)^2}{3^2} - \dfrac{(y-2)^2}{4^2} = 1$

For Exercises 25–32, write the standard equation for the hyperbola with the given characteristics.

25. vertices: $(-3, 0)$ and $(3, 0)$; co-vertices: $(0, -5)$ and $(0, 5)$

26. vertices: $(0, -2)$ and $(0, 2)$; co-vertices: $(-4, 0)$ and $(4, 0)$

27. vertices: $(0, -4)$ and $(0, 4)$; foci: $(0, -5)$ and $(0, 5)$

28. vertices: $(-5, 0)$ and $(5, 0)$; foci: $(-7, 0)$ and $(7, 0)$

29. co-vertices: $(0, -2)$ and $(0, 2)$; foci: $(-3, 0)$ and $(3, 0)$

30. co-vertices: $(-1, 0)$ and $(1, 0)$; foci: $(0, -2)$ and $(0, 2)$

31. center: $(2, 3)$; vertices: $(-1, 3)$ and $(5, 3)$; co-vertices: $(2, -2)$ and $(2, 8)$

32. center: $(-1, -3)$; vertices: $(-6, -3)$ and $(4, -3)$; co-vertices: $(-1, -6)$ and $(-1, 0)$

Write the standard equation for each hyperbola. Give the coordinates of the center, vertices, co-vertices, and foci.

33. $4x^2 - 9y^2 - 8x + 54y = 113$

34. $16x^2 - 25y^2 - 32x + 100y = 484$

35. $4y^2 - 36x^2 - 72x + 8y = 176$

36. $25y^2 - 16x^2 + 64x - 50y = 439$

37. $y^2 - 9x^2 - 6y = 36 + 36x$

38. $16x^2 - 9y^2 + 64x = 89 - 18y$

39. $16x^2 + 64y - 256 = 16y^2 - 64x$

40. $25y^2 + 100x - 100y - 625 = 25x^2$

41. $3y^2 + 20x = 23 + 5x^2 + 12y$

42. $7x^2 - 5y^2 = 48 - 20y - 14x$

Write the standard equations for both hyperbolas whose asymptotes contain the diagonals of rectangle *ABCD* and whose vertices lie on the sides of the given rectangle.

43. $A(-5, 4)$, $B(5, 4)$, $C(5, -4)$, and $D(-5, -4)$

44. $A(-2, 6)$, $B(2, 6)$, $C(2, -6)$, and $D(-2, -6)$

45. $A(1, 12)$, $B(11, 12)$, $C(11, 1)$, and $D(1, 1)$

46. $A(0, 7)$, $B(6, 7)$, $C(6, 4)$, and $D(0, 4)$

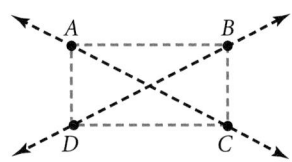

CHALLENGE

47. Let $\dfrac{x^2}{a^2} - \dfrac{y^2}{a^2} = 1$.

   a. Find the coordinates of the vertices and co-vertices.

   b. If the four points in part **a** are joined to form a quadrilateral, classify the quadrilateral.

   c. Justify your conclusion from part **b**.

CONNECTIONS

48. **TRANSFORMATIONS** If the hyperbola defined by the equation $\dfrac{(x-5)^2}{1} - \dfrac{(y-2)^2}{25} = 1$ is translated 6 units down and 3 units to the right, write the standard equation of the resulting hyperbola.

49. **TRANSFORMATIONS** Translate the hyperbola defined by the equation $9x^2 - 4y^2 + 54x + 8y + 41 = 0$ up 2 units and to the left 6 units. Write the standard equation of the resulting hyperbola.

APPLICATION

50. **LAW ENFORCEMENT** An explosion is heard by two law enforcement officers who are 1000 meters apart. One officer heard the explosion 1.5 seconds after the other officer. The speed of sound in air (at 20°C) is approximately 340 meters per second. Write an equation for the possible locations of the explosion, relative to the two law enforcement officers.

Look Back

Use substitution to solve each system of equations. *(LESSON 3.1)*

51. $\begin{cases} x = y + 1 \\ x + 4y = 11 \end{cases}$ **52.** $\begin{cases} 9m + 8n = 21 \\ 2m = 7 - n \end{cases}$ **53.** $\begin{cases} 15x + 4y = 23 \\ 10x - y = -3 \end{cases}$

Use elimination to solve each system of equations. *(LESSON 3.2)*

54. $\begin{cases} 5x - 2y = 30 \\ x + 2y = 6 \end{cases}$ **55.** $\begin{cases} 3x + 2y = 5 \\ 4x = 22 + 5y \end{cases}$ **56.** $\begin{cases} 5x - 2y = 3 \\ 2x + 7y = 9 \end{cases}$

Let $A = \begin{bmatrix} -2 \\ 1 \\ 5 \end{bmatrix}$, $B = [4 \quad 0 \quad -5]$, **and** $C = \begin{bmatrix} 2 & 4 & 1 \\ -6 & 0 & -1 \\ 3 & 2 & 9 \end{bmatrix}$. **Find each product, if it exists.** *(LESSON 4.2)*

57. AB **58.** BA **59.** BC **60.** CA
61. CB **62.** $(AB)C$ **63.** $C(AB)$ **64.** $A(BC)$

 Look Beyond

65 Consider $2x^2 + 5y^2 = 22$ and $3x^2 - y^2 = -1$.
   a. What two figures are represented by these equations?
   b. Solve both equations for y.
   c. Graph the equations from part **b** on your graphics calculator. Use a viewing window that allows you to see all points of intersection for the four graphs. Find all points of intersection.

PORTFOLIO ACTIVITY

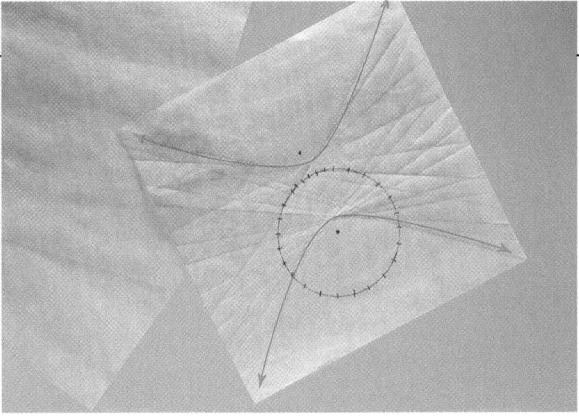

1. Draw a circle with a diameter between 2 and 4 inches on the left side of a piece of wax paper.

2. Place at least 20 tick marks on the circle, approximately evenly spaced.

3. Place a point outside and to the right of the circle. Fold the paper so that this outside point lies on one of the tick marks on the circle. Crease the paper, and then unfold it.

4. Repeat Step 3 for each tick mark on the circle.

5. Compare the figure formed by the creases with those of your classmates. How do the figures vary? Could they all be classified as one type of conic section? If so, which one?

6. Make a conjecture about how to make a flatter or more open figure. Verify your conjecture by repeating the process with the appropriate modification(s).

7. How does the point that you placed in Step 3 appear to be mathematically significant? Explain your reasoning.

WORKING ON THE CHAPTER PROJECT

You should now be able to complete Activity 3 of the Chapter Project.

WHAT'S SO FUZZY?

Time for Some Fuzzy Thinking

By Philip Elmer-Dewitt

In the pages of *Books in Print,* listed among works like *Fuzzy Bear* and *Fuzzy Wuzzy Puppy,* are some strange sounding titles: *Fuzzy Systems, Fuzzy Set Theory* and *Fuzzy Reasoning & Its Applications.* The bedtime reading of scientists gone soft in the head? No, these academic tomes are the collected output of 25 years of mostly American research in fuzzy logic, a branch of mathematics designed to help computers simulate the various kinds of vagueness and uncertainty found in everyday life. Despite a distinguished corps of devoted followers, however, fuzzy logic has been largely relegated to the back shelves of computer science—at least in the U.S.

But not, it turns out, in Japan. Suddenly the term fuzzy and products based on principles of fuzzy logic seem to be everywhere in Japan: in television documentaries, in corporate magazine ads and in novel electronic gadgets ranging from computer-controlled air conditioners to golf-swing analyzers.

What is fuzzy logic? The original concept, developed in the mid-'60s by Lofti Zadeh, a Russian-born professor of computer science at the University of California, Berkeley, is that things in the real world do not fall into neat, crisp categories defined by traditional set theory, like the set of even numbers or the set of left-handed baseball players.

[*Source:* Time, September 25, 1989]

But this on-or-off, black-or-white, 0-or-1 approach falls apart when applied to many everyday classifications, like the set of beautiful women, the set of tall men or the set of very cold days.

This mathematics turns out to be surprisingly useful for controlling robots, machine tools and various electronic systems. A conventional air conditioner, for example, recognizes only two basic states: too hot or too cold. When geared for thermostat control, the cooling system either operates at full blast or shuts off completely. A fuzzy air conditioner, by contrast, would recognize that some room temperatures are closer to the human comfort zone than others. Its cooling system would begin to slow down gradually as the room temperature approached the desired setting. Result: a more comfortable room and a smaller electric bill.

Fuzzy logic began to find applications in industry in the early '70s, when it was teamed with another form of advanced computer science called the expert system. Expert systems solve complex problems somewhat like humans experts do—by applying rules of thumb. (Example: when the oven gets very hot, turn the gas down a bit.)

Fuzzy-logic controllers create a smoother ride for passengers and use less energy than human conductors or automated systems that are based on traditional logic.

What is fuzzy logic? How can it make things work more efficiently? Does fuzzy logic resemble the way we think more than traditional logic does?

To answer questions like these, you need to explore the basis of fuzzy logic—something called *fuzzy sets*.

According to traditional logic, if someone belongs to the set of *people who are tall*, then they cannot belong to the set of *people who are not tall*. With fuzzy sets, the distinction is not so sharp, as you will see.

Traditional Logic

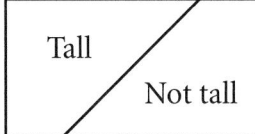

Tall

Not tall

Cooperative Learning

For Steps 1 and 2, use the data in the table at right or use the heights of 12 students from your class.

1. Before looking at fuzzy sets, examine how you might use sets in traditional logic to categorize a group of students by height.

    a. Create a 2-column table. In the left column, list the heights of the students you think are tall. List the rest in the right column.

    b. Which heights were hardest to place? Why?

    c. At what height did you draw the line between *tall* and *not tall*? Compare your response with other groups. Describe the disagreements.

    d. Why would you expect there to be disagreements?

2. Now, try using fuzzy sets.

    a. For each student letter in the table, assign a value from 0 to 1 to indicate the extent to which that person belongs to the set *tall*. For example:

        0 for someone who definitely does not belong

        0.5 for someone who *may be* tall

        0.8 for someone who is *fairly* tall

        1 for someone who definitely belongs on the *tall* list

    b. On a graph, plot the 12 values you assigned in part **a**. Draw a smooth curve through the points.

    c. How does the graph show what you think the word *tall* means?

    d. Compare your graph with the graphs of other groups. How are they a like and how are they different?

3. What sort of difficulties can you run into when you apply traditional logic to real-world situations? How can fuzzy sets help resolve those difficulties?

Student	Height
A	5' 11"
B	5' 3"
C	6' 1"
D	4' 11"
E	5' 4"
F	5' 10"
G	5' 1"
H	5' 8"
I	5' 5"
J	5' 7"
K	5' 6"
L	5' 9"

Solving Nonlinear Systems

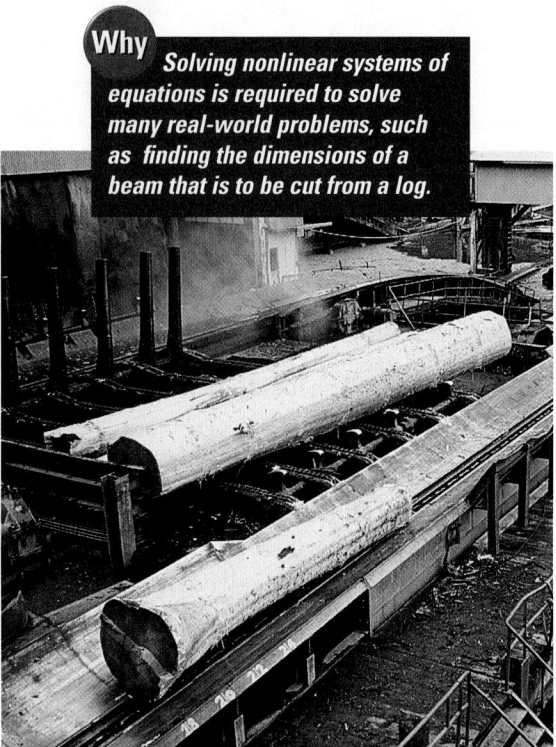

Why Solving nonlinear systems of equations is required to solve many real-world problems, such as finding the dimensions of a beam that is to be cut from a log.

Objectives

- Solve a system of equations containing first- or second-degree equations in two variables.

- Identify a conic section from its equation.

A mill operator wants to cut a rectangular beam from a cylindrical log whose circular cross section has a diameter of 10 inches. The rectangular cross section of the beam is to have a length that is twice its width.

To find the dimensions of the beam, you need to solve a *system of nonlinear equations*. *You will solve this problem in Example 2.*

A **system of nonlinear equations** is a collection of equations in which at least one equation is not linear.

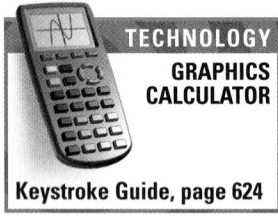

TECHNOLOGY
GRAPHICS CALCULATOR

Keystroke Guide, page 624

Activity
Exploring Nonlinear Systems

You will need: a graphics calculator

1. Graph the system of equations in part **a.** Record the number of points of intersection. Repeat this for the systems of equations in parts **b, c,** and **d.**

   a. $\begin{cases} x^2 + y^2 = 25 \\ y = 2x \end{cases}$
   b. $\begin{cases} x^2 + y^2 = 25 \\ x^2 - y^2 = 9 \end{cases}$
   c. $\begin{cases} y = x^2 \\ y = 2x + 1 \end{cases}$
   d. $\begin{cases} x^2 + y^2 = 1 \\ y = x^2 \end{cases}$

CHECKPOINT ✔ 2. The equations in part **a** of Step 1 represent a circle and a line. Consider all of the ways in which a circle and a line can intersect. Make a conjecture about the number of possible intersection points for a circle and a line, and sketch an example of each.

CHECKPOINT ✔ 3. The equations in part **b** of Step 1 represent a circle and a hyperbola. Consider all of the ways in which a circle and a hyperbola can intersect. Make a conjecture about the number of possible intersection points for a circle and a hyperbola, and sketch an example of each.

CHECKPOINT ✔ 4. The equations in part **c** of Step 1 represent a parabola and a line. Consider all of the ways in which a parabola and a line can intersect. Make a conjecture about the number of possible intersection points for a parabola and a line, and sketch an example of each.

CHECKPOINT ✔ 5. The equations in part **d** of Step 1 represent a circle and a parabola. Consider all of the ways in which a circle and a parabola can intersect. Make a conjecture about the number of possible intersection points for a circle and a parabola, and sketch an example of each.

A system of two second-degree equations in x and y can have no more than four real solutions, unless the system is dependent. This is demonstrated below for an ellipse and hyperbola.

4 real
solutions

3 real
solutions

2 real
solutions

1 real
solution

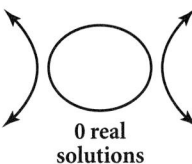
0 real
solutions

CRITICAL THINKING Give an example of a dependent system of nonlinear equations. How many solutions does it have?

Solving Systems of Nonlinear Equations

Just as you can use substitution to solve some systems of linear equations, you can use substitution to solve some systems of nonlinear equations, as shown in Example 1 below.

E X A M P L E Solve $\begin{cases} y^2 = 3x - 1 \\ x^2 + y^2 = 9 \end{cases}$ by substitution.

● **SOLUTION**

Substitute $3x - 1$ for y^2 in $x^2 + y^2 = 9$.

$$x^2 + y^2 = 9$$
$$x^2 + (3x - 1) = 9$$
$$x^2 + 3x = 10$$
$$x^2 + 3x - 10 = 0$$
$$(x - 2)(x + 5) = 0$$
$$x = 2 \quad or \quad x = -5$$

Then find the corresponding y-values.

Substitute 2 for x.
$$y^2 = 3x - 1$$
$$y^2 = 3(2) - 1$$
$$y = \pm\sqrt{5}$$

Substitute -5 for x.
$$y^2 = 3x - 1$$
$$y^2 = 3(-5) - 1$$
$$y = \pm\sqrt{-16}$$
$$y = \pm 4i$$

The real solutions are $(2, \sqrt{5})$ and $(2, -\sqrt{5})$. The nonreal solutions, $(-5, 4i)$ and $(-5, -4i)$, are meaningless in this coordinate plane.

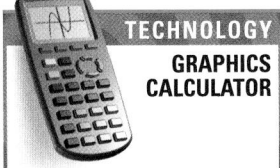
TECHNOLOGY
GRAPHICS CALCULATOR
Keystroke Guide, page 625

CHECK
Solve $y^2 = 3x - 1$ and $x^2 + y^2 = 9$ for y. Enter each of the four resulting functions separately, and graph them together in a square viewing window. From the graph, the only real solutions are $(2, \sqrt{5})$ and $(2, -\sqrt{5})$.

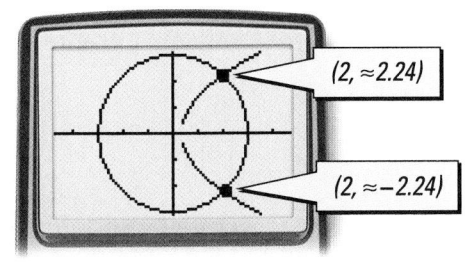
(2, ≈2.24)
(2, ≈−2.24)

TRY THIS Solve $\begin{cases} x^2 + y^2 = 25 \\ y^2 = 2x + 1 \end{cases}$ by substitution.

E X A M P L E ❷ Refer to the mill problem described at the beginning of the lesson.

Find the dimensions of the rectangular cross section of the beam to the nearest hundredth of an inch.

● **SOLUTION**

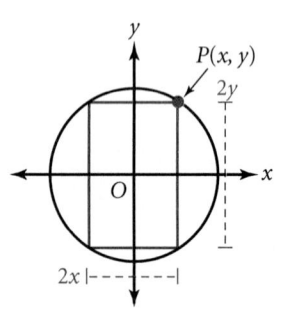

The diagram at left shows the beam inscribed in the circular cross section of the log, with the center of the circle at the origin of the coordinate plane. Since the diameter is 10, $P(x, y)$ is on a circle with a radius of 5. The equation of the circle is $x^2 + y^2 = 25$. The length of the beam is twice the width, so $y = 2x$. Solve $\begin{cases} x^2 + y^2 = 25 \\ y = 2x \end{cases}$.

$$x^2 + y^2 = 25$$
$$x^2 + (2x)^2 = 25 \quad \textit{Substitute 2x for y.}$$
$$5x^2 = 25$$
$$x^2 = 5$$
$$x = \pm\sqrt{5} \approx \pm 2.24$$

Since x represents a measurement, $\sqrt{5}$ is the only reasonable solution. The width is $2x$, or about 4.48 inches; the length is $2(2x)$, about 8.94 inches.

You can also use the elimination method to solve nonlinear systems, as shown in Example 3.

E X A M P L E ❸ **Use the elimination method to solve** $\begin{cases} 4x^2 + 25y^2 = 100 \\ x^2 + y^2 = 9 \end{cases}$. **Give your answers to the nearest hundredth.**

● **SOLUTION**

1. Multiply each side of the equation $x^2 + y^2 = 9$ by -4. Solve the resulting system by using elimination.

$$\begin{cases} 4x^2 + 25y^2 = 100 \\ x^2 + y^2 = 9 \end{cases} \rightarrow \begin{cases} 4x^2 + 25y^2 = 100 \\ -4x^2 - 4y^2 = -36 \end{cases}$$

$$\begin{aligned} 4x^2 + 25y^2 &= 100 \\ -4x^2 - 4y^2 &= -36 \\ \hline 21y^2 &= 64 \\ y &= \pm\sqrt{\frac{64}{21}} \approx \pm 1.75 \end{aligned}$$

2. Substitute $\frac{64}{21}$ for y^2 in $x^2 + y^2 = 9$.

$$x^2 + y^2 = 9$$
$$x^2 + \frac{64}{21} = 9$$
$$x = \pm\sqrt{9 - \frac{64}{21}} \approx \pm 2.44$$

The approximate solutions are $(2.44, 1.75)$, $(-2.44, 1.75)$, $(-2.44, -1.75)$, and $(2.44, -1.75)$.

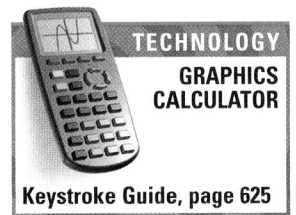

TECHNOLOGY

GRAPHICS CALCULATOR

Keystroke Guide, page 625

CHECK

Solve each equation in the system for y, and enter each of the resulting functions separately, and graph them together.

$$\begin{cases} y = \pm\sqrt{\dfrac{100 - 4x^2}{25}} \\ y = \pm\sqrt{9 - x^2} \end{cases}$$

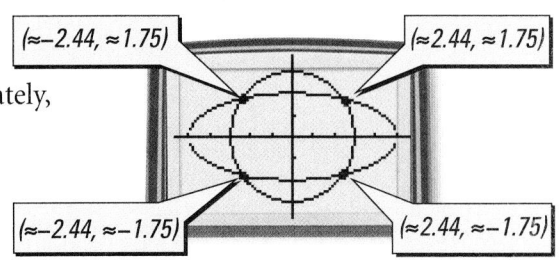

($\approx-2.44, \approx1.75$)   ($\approx2.44, \approx1.75$)

($\approx-2.44, \approx-1.75$)   ($\approx2.44, \approx-1.75$)

TRY THIS   Use the elimination method to solve $\begin{cases} 4x^2 + 9y^2 = 36 \\ 9x^2 - y^2 = 9 \end{cases}$. Give your answers to the nearest hundredth.

Classifying a Conic Section

The equation $Ax^2 + Bxy + Cy^2 + Dx + Ey + F = 0$, where A, B, and C are not all equal to zero, represents a conic section. When $B = 0$, the axes of symmetry of the conic section are parallel to the x-axis or y-axis. When $B \neq 0$, the conic sections are rotated. This book discusses only the first case, in which $B = 0$. When $B = 0$, the equation reduces to $Ax^2 + Cy^2 + Dx + Ey + F = 0$.

CLASSIFYING A CONIC SECTION $Ax^2 + Cy^2 + Dx + Ey + F = 0$	
Type of conic	**Coefficients**
ellipse (or circle)	$AC > 0$
circle	$A = C, A \neq 0, C \neq 0$
parabola	$AC = 0$
hyperbola	$AC < 0$

Using the information in the table above, you can classify an equation of the form $Ax^2 + Cy^2 + Dx + Ey + F = 0$ without completing the square.

EXAMPLE ④ **Let $4x^2 + 8x = y^2 + 6y + 13$ be the equation of a conic section.**
a. Classify the conic section defined by this equation.
b. Write the standard equation for this conic section.
c. Sketch the graph.

● **SOLUTION**

a. Rewrite $4x^2 + 8x = y^2 + 6y + 13$ in the form $Ax^2 + Cy^2 + Dx + Ey + F = 0$.
$$4x^2 - y^2 + 8x - 6y - 13 = 0, \text{ where } A = 4 \text{ and } C = -1$$
Because $4(-1) < 0$, the equation represents a hyperbola.

b.
$$4x^2 + 8x = y^2 + 6y + 13$$
$$4x^2 + 8x - y^2 - 6y = 13$$
$$4(x^2 + 2x + 4) - (y^2 + 6y + 9) = 13 + 4(4) - 9 \quad \textit{Complete the squares.}$$
$$4(x + 2)^2 - (y + 3)^2 = 20$$
$$\frac{(x + 2)^2}{5} - \frac{(y + 3)^2}{20} = 1$$

LESSON 9.6   SOLVING NONLINEAR SYSTEMS   **609**

c. center: $(-2, -3)$

vertices: $(-2 - \sqrt{5}, -3)$ and $(-2 + \sqrt{5}, -3)$

co-vertices: $(-2, -3 + \sqrt{20})$ and $(-2, -3 - \sqrt{20})$

The graph of $4x^2 + 8x = y^2 + 6y + 13$, or $\dfrac{(x+2)^2}{5} - \dfrac{(y+3)^2}{20} = 1$, is shown at right.

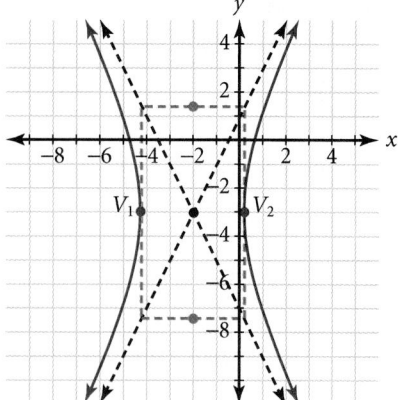

TRY THIS Let $9x^2 + 18x + 4y^2 + 8y = 23$ be the equation of a conic section. Classify the conic section defined by this equation, write the standard equation for this conic section, and sketch the graph.

Exercises

Communicate

1. Explain how to apply the substitution method to solve $\begin{cases} y = 2x \\ x^2 + y^2 = 10 \end{cases}$.

2. Explain how to apply the elimination method to solve $\begin{cases} 2x^2 - y^2 = 1 \\ x^2 + y^2 = 5 \end{cases}$.

3. Use an illustration to help describe all of the ways in which two ellipses can intersect.

4. Given the equation $Ax^2 + Cy^2 + Dx + Ey + F = 0$, what can be said about A and C if $AC > 0$? if $AC < 0$? if $AC = 0$?

Guided Skills Practice

5. Solve $\begin{cases} y^2 = 2x + 1 \\ x^2 + y^2 = 16 \end{cases}$ by substitution. **(EXAMPLE 1)**

6. **FORESTRY** Refer to the mill problem described at the beginning of the lesson. Find the dimensions of the rectangular cross section of the beam that can be cut from a log whose circular cross section has a diameter of 12 inches. **(EXAMPLE 2)**

7. Use the elimination method to solve $\begin{cases} x^2 + y^2 = 16 \\ 4x^2 - 9y^2 = 36 \end{cases}$. Give answers to the nearest hundredth. **(EXAMPLE 3)**

8. Let $4x^2 + 9y^2 + 8x + 18y - 23 = 0$ be the equation of a conic section. Classify the conic section defined by this equation, write the standard equation of this conic section, and sketch the graph. **(EXAMPLE 4)**

Practice and Apply

Use the substitution method to solve each system. If there are no real-number solutions, write *none*.

9. $\begin{cases} y = 5 \\ y = x^2 \end{cases}$
10. $\begin{cases} y = 2 \\ y = x^2 \end{cases}$
11. $\begin{cases} y = 2x \\ y = x^2 \end{cases}$
12. $\begin{cases} y = x \\ x = y^2 \end{cases}$

13. $\begin{cases} y = x \\ x^2 + y^2 = 4 \end{cases}$
14. $\begin{cases} y = 3x \\ x^2 + y^2 = 9 \end{cases}$
15. $\begin{cases} y = x \\ x^2 - y^2 = 4 \end{cases}$
16. $\begin{cases} y = x^2 \\ x^2 - y^2 = 4 \end{cases}$

17. $\begin{cases} y = x^2 \\ x^2 + y^2 = 1 \end{cases}$
18. $\begin{cases} x^2 = 4 - y^2 \\ y = x^2 \end{cases}$
19. $\begin{cases} x^2 = y \\ x^2 = 4 + y^2 \end{cases}$
20. $\begin{cases} x = y \\ 9x^2 - 4y^2 = 36 \end{cases}$

Use the elimination method to solve each system. If there are no real-number solutions, write *none*.

21. $\begin{cases} x^2 + y^2 = 1 \\ 4x^2 + y^2 = 1 \end{cases}$
22. $\begin{cases} x^2 + y^2 = 9 \\ 9x^2 + y^2 = 9 \end{cases}$
23. $\begin{cases} x^2 + y^2 = 1 \\ x^2 + y^2 = 4 \end{cases}$

24. $\begin{cases} x^2 - y^2 = 1 \\ x^2 - y^2 = 4 \end{cases}$
25. $\begin{cases} x^2 + y^2 = 25 \\ 4x^2 + 25y^2 = 100 \end{cases}$
26. $\begin{cases} x^2 + y^2 = 25 \\ 25x^2 + 4y^2 = 100 \end{cases}$

27. $\begin{cases} x^2 - y^2 = 36 \\ 4y^2 - 9x^2 = 36 \end{cases}$
28. $\begin{cases} 9x^2 + 4y^2 = 36 \\ 4x^2 + 9y^2 = 36 \end{cases}$
29. $\begin{cases} x^2 + y^2 = 36 \\ 4x^2 - 9y^2 = 36 \end{cases}$

30. $\begin{cases} 9x^2 + 4y^2 = 36 \\ 4x^2 - 9y^2 = 36 \end{cases}$
31. $\begin{cases} x^2 + y^2 = 9 \\ 4x^2 + 9y^2 = 36 \end{cases}$
32. $\begin{cases} x^2 + y^2 = 4 \\ 4x^2 - 9y^2 = 36 \end{cases}$

Use any method to solve each system. If there are no real-number solutions, write *none*.

33. $\begin{cases} y = x^2 \\ x = y^2 \end{cases}$
34. $\begin{cases} x^2 + y^2 = 16 \\ x + y = 1 \end{cases}$
35. $\begin{cases} y^2 - x^2 = 1 \\ 9x^2 - y^2 = 9 \end{cases}$

36. $\begin{cases} y = x^2 + 4 \\ x = y^2 + 4 \end{cases}$
37. $\begin{cases} x^2 - 4y^2 = 20 \\ y^2 = 4 \end{cases}$
38. $\begin{cases} y - x^2 = 0 \\ x^2 = 20 - y^2 \end{cases}$

39. $\begin{cases} 4x^2 - 25y^2 = 100 \\ 4x^2 - 9y^2 = 36 \end{cases}$
40. $\begin{cases} x^2 = y \\ x^2 = 4 - y^2 \end{cases}$
41. $\begin{cases} x = y^2 + 4 \\ y = x \end{cases}$

Solve each system by graphing. If there are no real-number solutions, write *none*.

42 $\begin{cases} x^2 + y^2 = 9 \\ 4x^2 - 4y^2 = 16 \end{cases}$
43 $\begin{cases} 4y^2 + 25x^2 = 100 \\ 5x^2 - 2y^2 = 10 \end{cases}$

44 $\begin{cases} 4x^2 + 9y^2 = 36 \\ 16x^2 + 36y^2 = 144 \end{cases}$
45 $\begin{cases} 25x^2 - 4y^2 = 9 \\ 100x^2 - 16y^2 = 36 \end{cases}$

Classify the conic section defined by each equation. Write the standard equation of the conic section, and sketch the graph.

46. $x^2 + 2x + y^2 + 6y = 15$
47. $x^2 - 2x + y^2 - 2y - 6 = 0$

48. $4x^2 + 9y^2 - 8x - 18y - 23 = 0$
49. $4x^2 + 9y^2 + 16x - 36y = -16$

50. $4y^2 - 8y - x^2 - 4x - 4 = 0$
51. $4x^2 + 8x - 9y^2 + 36y - 68 = 0$

52. $4x^2 - 75 = 50y - 25y^2$
53. $9y^2 + 18y + 9 = 24x - 4x^2$

54. $9x^2 - 3 = 18x + 4y$
55. $y^2 - 2x = 6y - 5$

56. $x^2 - 8y - 16 = 4y^2 + 4x$
57. $-18x - 4y - 109 = y^2 - x^2$

Solve each system of equations. If there are no real-number solutions, write *none*.

58. $\begin{cases} (x-1)^2 + (y-1)^2 = 4 \\ (x-1)^2 + (y+1)^2 = 9 \end{cases}$

59. $\begin{cases} (x+2)^2 + (y-2)^2 = 9 \\ (x-1)^2 + (y-2)^2 = 16 \end{cases}$

60. $\begin{cases} (x-1)^2 + y^2 = 4 \\ (x-1)^2 + y^2 = 1 \end{cases}$

61. $\begin{cases} (x+2)^2 + y^2 = 9 \\ (x+2)^2 + y^2 = 25 \end{cases}$

62. $\begin{cases} \dfrac{(x-1)^2}{9} + \dfrac{y^2}{4} = 1 \\ \dfrac{(x-1)^2}{9} + y^2 = 1 \end{cases}$

63. $\begin{cases} \dfrac{(y-1)^2}{9} - x^2 = 1 \\ \dfrac{(y-1)^2}{9} - \dfrac{x^2}{9} = 1 \end{cases}$

64. $\begin{cases} x^2 + y^2 + 2x + 6y = 15 \\ x^2 + y^2 - 2x - 6y = -1 \end{cases}$

65. $\begin{cases} x^2 + y^2 - 4x + 4y = 8 \\ x^2 + y^2 - 6x - 6y = -2 \end{cases}$

66. The graphs of two nonlinear equations in x and y are shown at right.
   a. What conic sections are graphed?
   b. Describe any solutions to the system of equations represented.
   c. Write the system of equations represented by the graphs.

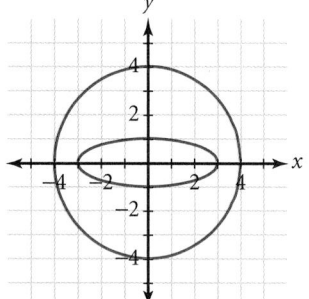

67. A positive two-digit number is represented by $10t + u$. The sum of the squares of the digits is 26. If the number is decreased by the number with its digits reversed, the result is 36. Find the two-digit number.

68. Find two negative numbers such that the sum of their squares is 170 and twice the square of the first minus 3 times the square of the second is 95.

CHALLENGES

69 You can write $\begin{cases} 4x^2 + 9y^2 = 36 \\ x^2 + y^2 = 9 \end{cases}$ as $AX = B$, where $A = \begin{bmatrix} 4 & 9 \\ 1 & 1 \end{bmatrix}$, $X = \begin{bmatrix} x^2 \\ y^2 \end{bmatrix}$, and $B = \begin{bmatrix} 36 \\ 9 \end{bmatrix}$. Use a matrix equation to find x^2 and y^2. Then find x and y.

70. Solve $\begin{cases} x^2 + y^2 < 16 \\ x^2 - 6y \le 3 \end{cases}$ by graphing.

CONNECTIONS

71. GEOMETRY Find the dimensions of a rectangle with an area of 12 square feet and a diagonal of 5 feet.

72. GEOMETRY The area of a rectangle is 48 square meters. The length of a diagonal is 10 meters. Find the perimeter of the rectangle.

73. GEOMETRY The area of a rectangle is 12 square inches. The perimeter is 24 inches. Find the dimensions of the rectangle.

APPLICATION

74. BUSINESS A company determines that its total monthly production cost, P, in thousands of dollars is defined by the equation $P = 8x + 4$. The company's monthly revenue, R, in thousands of dollars is defined by $8R - 3x^2 = 0$. In both equations, x is the number of units, in thousands, of its product manufactured and sold per month. When the cost of manufacturing the product equals the revenue obtained by selling it, the company breaks even. How many units must the company produce in order to break even?

BUSINESS The cross section of a log is circular. A mill operator wants to cut a beam from the log as shown below. Find the dimensions of each rectangular cross section described below to the nearest tenth of an inch.

75. Find the dimensions of the cross section if the circular cross section has a 16-inch diameter and the beam's height is $\frac{1}{2}$ its width.

76. Find the dimensions of the cross section if the circular cross section has an 18-inch diameter and the beam's height is $\frac{1}{2}$ its width.

77. Find the dimensions of the cross section if the circular cross section has an 18-inch diameter and the beam's width is 3 times its height.

Look Back

Find all rational zeros of each polynomial function. *(LESSON 7.5)*

78 $P(x) = x^3 - 8x^2 + 5x + 14$

79 $P(x) = x^3 + 2x^2 - x - 2$

80 $P(x) = x^4 + x^2 - 2$

81 $P(x) = x^4 + 7x^2 + 12$

Find all zeros of each polynomial function. *(LESSON 7.5)*

82 $P(x) = x^3 + 4x^2 - 17x - 60$

83 $P(x) = 2x^3 - 5x^2 + 1$

84 $P(a) = 3a^4 - 5a^3 - 5a^2 - 19a - 6$

85 $P(a) = 3a^4 - 2a^3 + 8a^2 - 6a - 3$

Simplify. *(LESSON 8.4)*

86. $\frac{x}{x+1} + \frac{1}{x^2-1}$

87. $\frac{2}{x(x-2)} - \frac{x+1}{x^2-4}$

Solve each radical equation. *(LESSON 8.8)*

88. $\sqrt{x+4} = 2$

89. $\sqrt{x-1} = 3\sqrt{x-2}$

90. $\sqrt{-x} = 4\sqrt{-x-1}$

Solve each radical inequality. *(LESSON 8.8)*

91. $\sqrt{3x+2} > 5$

92. $0 \geq 3\sqrt{x-2} - 2$

93. $-6 > 2\sqrt{x-2} - 4$

Look Beyond

Classify the conic section defined by each equation. Then graph the conic section and describe its graph.

94 $4x^2 + y^2 = 0$

95 $y^2 = 4$

96 $x^2 = 4$

97 $y^2 - x^2 = 0$

98 $(x-1)^2 = (y+1)^2$

99 $(x-2)^2 + (y+2)^2 = 0$

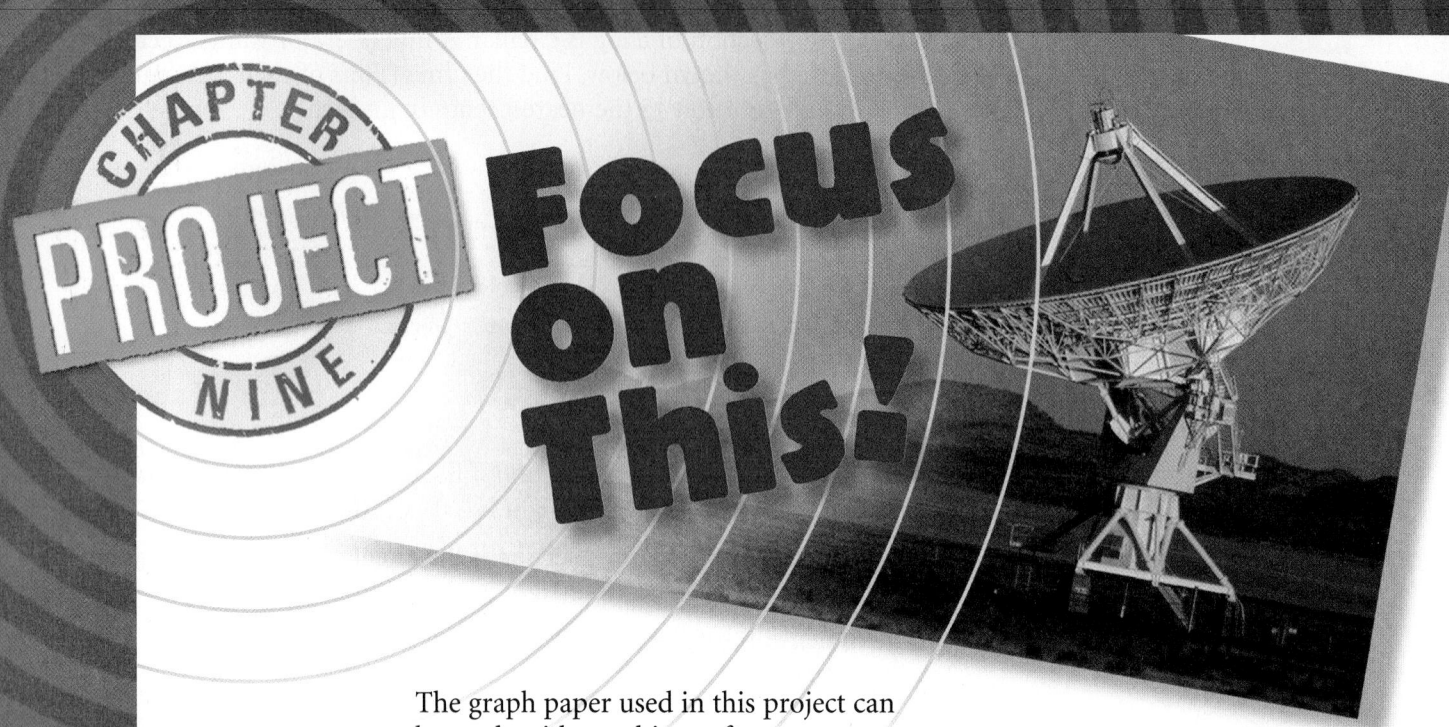

CHAPTER NINE

PROJECT

Focus on This!

The graph paper used in this project can be made with graphing software.

Parabolic radio telescope in New Mexico

 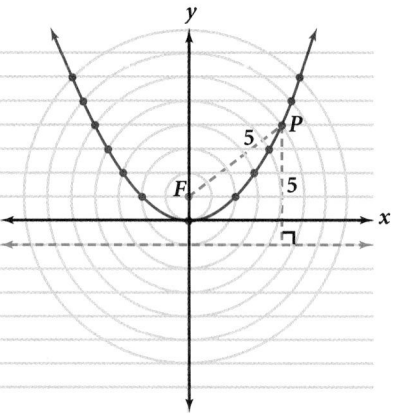

The figure at right shows a parabola with its focus at $(0, 1)$ and a directrix of $y = -1$. Equally spaced concentric circles with their center at the parabola's focus enable you to measure distances from the focus. Equally spaced horizontal lines parallel to the parabola's directrix enable you to measure vertical distances from the directrix. This type of graph paper is called focus-directrix graph paper.

Notice that P is the point of intersection of the circle centered at $(0, 1)$ with a radius of 5 and the horizontal line 5 units above the directrix. Thus, P is equidistant from the focus and directrix. Examine the figure above and note that all points on the parabola are equidistant from the focus and the directrix.

1. Create focus-directrix graph paper with the focus at $(0, 3)$ and a directrix of $y = 3$. Label the focus, directrix, x-axis, and y-axis.
   a. Plot points that are equidistant from the focus and directrix.
   b. Identify the vertex of the resulting parabola.
   c. Identify p as defined for the standard equation of a parabola.
   d. Write the equation of the parabola.

2. Repeat Step 1 with the focus at $(0, -3)$ and a directrix of $y = 3$.

3. Repeat Step 1 with the focus at $(3, 0)$ and a directrix of $x = -3$. This time the focus-directrix graph paper should have concentric circles centered at $(3, 0)$ and vertical lines parallel to the directrix, $x = -3$.

4. Repeat Step 1 with the focus at $(-3, 0)$ and a directrix of $x = 3$.

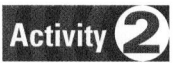 **Ellipses**

The figure at right shows an ellipse with foci at $F_1(-2, 0)$ and $F_2(2, 0)$. Equally spaced concentric circles centered at the two foci enable you to measure distances from the foci. This is called focus-focus graph paper.

Notice that P is the point of intersection of the two circles: one circle is centered at F_1 with a radius of 7, and the other circle is centered at F_2 with a radius of 5. Thus, $F_1P + F_2P = 7 + 5 = 12$. Notice that all points on the ellipse satisfy the equation $F_1P + F_2P = 12$.

1. Create focus-focus graph paper with foci at $F_1(-4, 0)$ and $F_2(4, 0)$. Label the foci, x-axis, and y-axis.
   a. Plot points that satisfy the equation $F_1P + F_2P = 10$.
   b. Identify the vertices and co-vertices of the resulting ellipse.
   c. Identify a, b, and c as defined for the standard equation of an ellipse, and find the lengths of the major and minor axes.
   d. Write the standard equation of the ellipse.

2. Repeat Step 1 with the foci at $F_1(0, -4)$ and $F_2(0, 4)$.

 Hyperbolas

The figure below shows a hyperbola with foci at $F_1(-6, 0)$ and $F_2(6, 0)$. Equally spaced concentric circles are centered at the foci. This is also called focus-focus graph paper.

Notice that P is the point of intersection of two circles: one circle is centered at $F_1(-6, 0)$ with a radius of 9, and the other circle is centered at $F_2(6, 0)$ with a radius of 5. Thus, $|F_1P - F_2P| = |9 - 5| = 4$. Notice that all points on the hyperbola satisfy the equation $|F_1P - F_2P| = 4$.

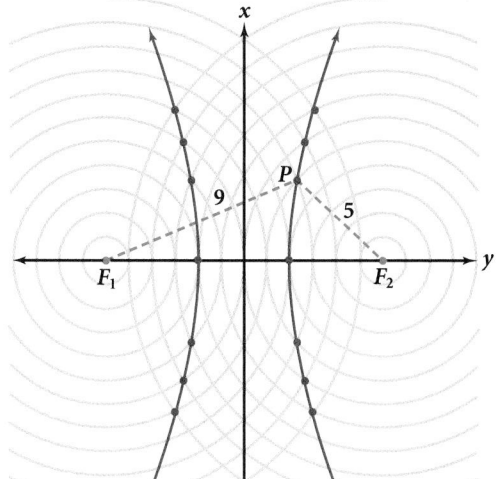

1. Create focus-focus graph paper with foci at $F_1(-5, 0)$ and $F_2(5, 0)$. Label the foci, x-axis, and y-axis.
   a. Plot points that satisfy the equation $|F_1P - F_2P| = 6$.
   b. Identify the vertices and co-vertices of the resulting hyperbola.
   c. Identify a, b, and c as defined for the standard equation of a hyperbola, and find the lengths of the transverse and conjugate axes.
   d. Write equations for the asymptotes of the hyperbola, and sketch them on your graph.
   e. Write the standard equation of the hyperbola.

Chapter Review and Assessment

Key Skills & Exercises

LESSON 9.1

Key Skills

Use the distance and midpoint formulas.

Find the distance between points $P(1, 2)$ and $Q(-3, 5)$.

$$d = \sqrt{(x_2 - x_1)^2 + (y_2 - y_1)^2}$$

$$d = \sqrt{(-3 - 1)^2 + (5 - 2)^2} = \sqrt{25} = 5$$

Find the coordinates of M, the midpoint of $P(1, 2)$ and $Q(-3, 5)$.

$$M\left(\frac{x_1 + x_2}{2}, \frac{y_1 + y_2}{2}\right) = \left(\frac{1 + (-3)}{2}, \frac{2 + 5}{2}\right) = \left(-1, \frac{7}{2}\right)$$

Exercises

Find PQ and the coordinates of M, the midpoint of PQ.

1. $P(0, 4)$ and $Q(3, 0)$
2. $P(2, 7)$ and $Q(10, 13)$
3. $P(-3, 5)$ and $Q(3, 1)$
4. $P(-1, 2)$ and $Q(-6, -8)$
5. $P(11, -9)$ and $Q(-2, -5)$

LESSON 9.2

Key Skills

Find the vertex, focus, and directrix of a parabola. Graph the parabola.

Given $y^2 - 6y - 12x + 57 = 0$, complete the square and write the standard equation of the parabola.

$$x - 4 = \frac{1}{12}(y - 3)^2$$

From the equation, $h = 4$, $k = 3$, and $p = 3$.

The vertex is at $(4, 3)$, the focus is at $(7, 3)$, and the directrix is $x = 1$.

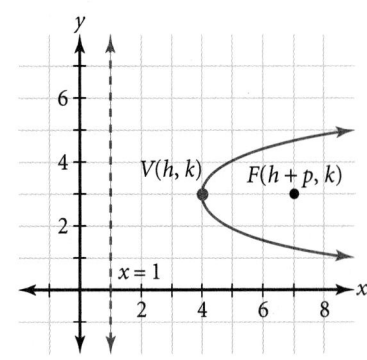

Exercises

Write the standard equation for each parabola. Find the vertex, focus, and directrix. Then sketch the graph.

6. $y = x^2 - 4x$
7. $x - 2 = y^2 - 10y$
8. $y = -2x^2 - 4x + 6$
9. $x^2 + 8x - y + 20 = 0$
10. $4y^2 - 8y - x + 1 = 0$

LESSON 9.3

Key Skills

Find the radius and center of a circle. Sketch the graph.

Given $x^2 + y^2 - 10x + 8y + 5 = 0$, complete the square and write the standard equation of the circle.

$(x - 5)^2 + (y + 4)^2 = 6^2$

The center is at $(5, -4)$, and the radius is 6.

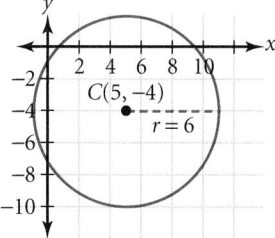

Exercises

Write the standard equation for each circle. Find the center and radius. Then sketch the graph.

11. $x^2 + y^2 = 100$

12. $3x^2 + 3y^2 = 36$

13. $(x - 1)^2 + (y - 49)^2 = 81$

14. $x^2 + y^2 - 10x + 8y + 5 = 0$

15. $x^2 + y^2 + 8y + 4x - 5 = 0$

LESSON 9.4

Key Skills

Find the coordinates of the center, vertices, co-vertices, and foci of an ellipse. Sketch the graph.

Given $16x^2 + 4y^2 - 96x + 8y + 84 = 0$, complete the square and write the standard equation.

$\dfrac{(x - 3)^2}{4} + \dfrac{(y + 1)^2}{16} = 1$

From the equation, $h = 3$, $k = -1$, $a = 4$, $b = 2$, and $c = 2\sqrt{3}$.

center: $(3, -1)$

vertices: $(3, -5)$, $(3, 3)$

co-vertices: $(1, -1)$, $(5, -1)$

foci: $(3, -1 + \sqrt{12})$, $(3, -1 - \sqrt{12})$

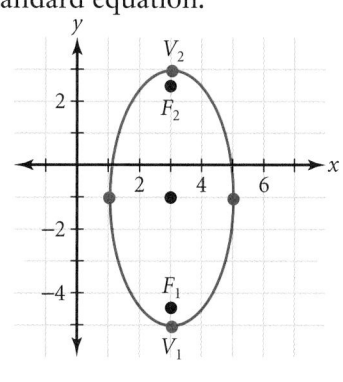

Exercises

Write the standard equation for each ellipse. Find the center, vertices, co-vertices, and foci. Then sketch the graph.

16. $\dfrac{(x + 1)^2}{16} + \dfrac{(y - 3)^2}{4} = 1$

17. $\dfrac{(x - 4)^2}{9} + \dfrac{(y + 1)^2}{25} = 1$

18. $25x^2 + 4y^2 = 100$

19. $x^2 + 4y^2 + 10x + 24y + 45 = 0$

20. $16x^2 + 4y^2 - 96x + 8y + 84 = 0$

LESSON 9.5

Key Skills

Find the center, vertices, co-vertices, and foci of a hyperbola. Sketch the graph.

Given $4x^2 - y^2 + 24x + 4y + 28 = 0$, complete the square and write the standard equation.

$\dfrac{(x + 3)^2}{1} - \dfrac{(y - 2)^2}{4} = 1$

center: $(-3, 2)$

vertices: $(-4, 2)$, $(-2, 2)$

co-vertices: $(-3, 4)$, $(-3, 0)$

foci: $(-3 + \sqrt{5}, 2)$, $(-3 - \sqrt{5}, 2)$

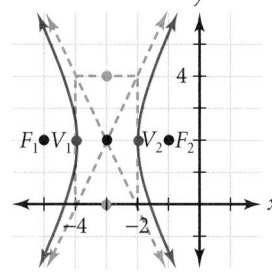

Exercises

Write the standard equation for each hyperbola. Find the center, vertices, co-vertices, and foci. Then sketch the graph.

21. $\dfrac{(x + 5)^2}{36} - \dfrac{(y - 1)^2}{64} = 1$

22. $\dfrac{(y + 5)^2}{4} - \dfrac{(x - 4)^2}{9} = 1$

23. $4y^2 - 25x^2 = 100$

24. $9x^2 - 16y^2 - 90x + 32y + 65 = 0$

25. $36y^2 - 4x^2 + 216y - 40x + 80 = 0$

Key Skills

Solve a system of nonlinear equations.

Use elimination or substitution to solve a nonlinear system algebraically. Independent systems of two conic sections can have 0, 1, 2, 3, or 4 solutions.

Identify a conic section from its equation.

$Ax^2 + Cy^2 + Dx + Ey + F = 0$ represents the following:

- a parabola if $AC = 0$
- a circle if $A = C$ ($A \neq 0$ and $C \neq 0$)
- an ellipse if $AC > 0$
- a hyperbola if $AC < 0$

Exercises

Solve each system. If there are no real-number solutions, write _none_.

26. $\begin{cases} 2x^2 + y^2 = 22 \\ x^2 + 3y^2 = 21 \end{cases}$ 27. $\begin{cases} 4x^2 + 2y^2 = 20 \\ 3x^2 - 4y^2 = 4 \end{cases}$

28. $\begin{cases} x + y = 5 \\ x^2 + y^2 = 1 \end{cases}$ 29. $\begin{cases} y - x = 5 \\ 9x^2 + 16y^2 = 144 \end{cases}$

Classify the conic section defined by each equation. Write the standard equation of the conic section, and sketch the graph.

30. $x^2 + y^2 - 2x + 8y - 8 = 0$

31. $4x^2 - 9y^2 - 24x - 18y - 9 = 0$

32. $y^2 - 8y + 4x - 8 = 0$

Applications

33. **PHYSICS** In a 220-volt electric circuit, the available power in watts, W, is given by the formula $W = 220I - 15I^2$, where I is the amount of current in amperes. Find the maximum amount of power available in the circuit.

34. **ASTRONOMY** Earth orbits the Sun in an elliptical path with the Sun at one focus of the ellipse. The closest that Earth gets to the Sun is 91.4 million miles and the farthest it gets is 94.6 million miles. Write an equation for Earth's orbit around the Sun with the center of the ellipse at the origin.

35. **BIOLOGY** To locate a whale, two microphones are placed 6000 feet apart in the ocean. One microphone picks up a whale's sound 0.5 second after the other microphone picks up the same sound. The speed of sound in water is about 5000 feet per second.
    a. Find the equation of the hyperbola that describes the possible locations of the whale.
    b. What is the shortest distance that the whale could be to either microphone?

36. **GEOLOGY** An earthquake transmits its energy in seismic waves that radiate from its underground focus in all directions. A seismograph station determines that the earthquake's epicenter (the point on the Earth's surface directly above the focus) is 100 miles from the station.
    a. Write the standard equation for the possible locations of the epicenter, using (0, 0) as the location of the seismograph station.
    b. A second station is 120 miles east and 160 miles south of the first station and 100 miles from the earthquake's epicenter. Write a second standard equation for the possible locations of the epicenter.
    c. Find the coordinates of the epicenter by solving the system formed by the equations you wrote in parts **a** and **b**.

Tail of a humpback whale near Alaska

Find the distance *PQ* and the coordinates of *M*, the midpoint of *PQ*.

1. $P(2, 5)$ and $Q(4, 9)$

2. $P(-3, 7)$ and $Q(2, -4)$

3. $P(8, -12)$ and $Q(-13, -6)$

4. CARTOGRAPHY Three cities found on a map are located at the coordinates of A(2°N, 5°W), B(8°N, 21°W), and C(17°N, 45°W). Are these three cities collinear?

Write the standard equation for the parabola with the given characteristics.

5. vertex: $(0, 0)$, focus: $(0, -2)$

6. vertex: $(0, 0)$, directrix: $y = 3$

7. focus: $(7, 0)$, directrix: $x = -7$

8. ASTRONOMY Inside a telescope the focus of a parabolic mirror 10 centimeters across in a telescope lies 2 centimeters from the vertex. Find the equation of the mirror if the vertex is at the origin.

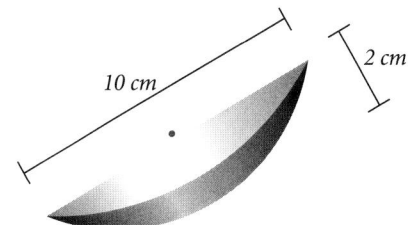

10 cm *2 cm*

Write the standard equation for each circle. Find the radius and give the coordinates for the center.

9. $x^2 + y^2 - 144 = 0$

10. $5x^2 + 5y^2 - 125 = 0$

11. $x^2 + y^2 - 14x + 8y + 1 = 0$

12. CIVIL DEFENSE A civil defense system broadcasts an emergency signal within a circular area with a radius of 250 miles. If you live a distance of 150 miles east and 195 miles north of the broadcasting tower, will you be able to receive the signal?

Find the vertices and co-vertices of each ellipse. Sketch the graph for Exercise 14.

13. $\dfrac{x^2}{36} + \dfrac{y^2}{100} = 1$

14. $\dfrac{(x - 3)^2}{25} + \dfrac{(y + 4)^2}{4} = 1$

Write the standard equation for the ellipse; identify the coordinates of the center, vertices, co-vertices, and foci.

15. $4x^2 + y^2 + 16x - 6y = -9$

For each hyperbola, find the equations of the asymptotes and the coordinates of the vertices.

16. $\dfrac{x^2}{25} - y^2 = 1$

17. $\dfrac{y^2}{9} - \dfrac{x^2}{49} = 1$

18. Find the coordinates of the center, the vertices, and the co-vertices for the graph of $\dfrac{(x-3)^2}{4} - \dfrac{(y+5)^2}{9} = 1$.

19. Sketch the graph of $\dfrac{(y + 1)^2}{1} - \dfrac{(x - 2)^2}{4} = 1$

Label the center, vertices, co-vertices, foci, and asymptotes.

Use any method to solve each system. If there are no real number solutions, write *none*.

20. $\begin{cases} y = \dfrac{4}{9}x^2 \\ x^2 + y^2 = 25 \end{cases}$

21. $\begin{cases} 4x^2 + 4y^2 = 4 \\ 4x^2 + y^2 = 1 \end{cases}$

22. $\begin{cases} 64x = 10y^2 \\ x^2 - y^2 = 36 \end{cases}$

23. $\begin{cases} 9x^2 + 4y^2 = 36 \\ 4x^2 - 9y^2 = 36 \end{cases}$

Classify the conic section defined by each equation.

24. $4x^2 + 4y^2 + 24x - 16y + 12 = 0$

25. $3x + 8y^2 - 24 = 0$

26. $16x^2 - 9y^2 + 64x + 18y - 89 = 0$

27. $9x^2 + 16y^2 - 36x - 64y - 44 = 0$

College Entrance Exam Practice

MULTIPLE-CHOICE For Questions 1–16, write the letter that indicates the best answer.

1. Solve $-\dfrac{4x}{3} = x - 1$. **(LESSON 1.4)**

  a. $x = \dfrac{3}{7}$ **b.** $x = -3$

  c. $x = \dfrac{1}{7}$ **d.** $x = 6$

2. Which of the following does *not* have a value of 8? **(LESSON 2.2)**

  a. $\left(\dfrac{1}{2}\right)^{-3}$ **b.** 4^2

  c. 2^3 **d.** $\sqrt[3]{512}$

3. Evaluate $\log_2 200$ to the nearest hundredth. **(LESSON 6.5)**

  a. 7.64
  b. 2.82
  c. 0.13
  d. −0.06

4. Identify all asymptotes and holes in the graph of $y = \dfrac{x^2 - 25}{x + 5}$. **(LESSON 8.2)**

  a. no vertical or horizontal asymptotes, hole $(x = -5)$
  b. $x = -5$, no horizontal asymptote, hole $(x = 5)$
  c. $x = -5$, $y = 2$, hole $(x = -5)$
  d. no vertical asymptote, $y = 2$, hole $(x = 5)$

5. Find the distance between $(-2, 5)$ and $(-3, 2)$ to the nearest hundredth. **(LESSON 9.1)**

  a. 8.60
  b. 3.16
  c. 4.90
  d. 4.24

6. Which polynomial function has a degree of 3? **(LESSON 7.1)**

  a. $f(x) = -1 + 6x + 5x^2$
  b. $f(x) = (5x^3 - 6x) - (x^2 + 5x^3)$
  c. $f(x) = 8x(x+1)^2$
  d. $f(x) = (-2x^2 + 3x^3) + (x^2 - 3x^3)$

7. How many solutions does an independent system of linear equations have? **(LESSON 3.1)**

  a. 0
  b. 1
  c. at least 1
  d. infinitely many

8. Which statement is true for $f(x) - 3x - 6$ and $g(x) = 12 - 6x$? **(LESSONS 2.4 AND 2.7)**

  a. $f \circ g = g \circ f$
  b. $2(f \circ g) = g \circ f$
  c. $-2(f \circ g) = g \circ f$
  d. none of these

9. Evaluate $f(x) = 2x^2 - 9x - 12$ for $x = -2$. **(LESSON 2.3)**

  a. 8
  b. 14
  c. 2
  d. −22

10. Which describes the slope of a vertical line? **(LESSON 1.2)**

  a. 0
  b. undefined
  c. negative
  d. positive

11. For matrices A and B, each with dimensions $m \times n$, which statement is always true? **(LESSONS 4.1 AND 4.2)**

  a. $A = B$
  b. $A + B = B + A$
  c. $AB = BA$
  d. $A - B = B - A$

12. Solve $7 - \sqrt{4a - 3} = 4$. *(LESSON 8.8)*
 a. 0 **b.** −3 **c.** 3 **d.** $\sqrt{3}$

13. Which equation represents $5^x = 625$ in logarithmic form? *(LESSON 6.3)*
 a. $\log_x 5 = 625$ **b.** $\log_5 625 = x$
 c. $\log_x 625 = 5$ **d.** $\log_{625} x = 5$

14. Which binomial is a factor of $x^3 - 2x^2 - 6x - 3$? *(LESSON 7.3)*
 a. $x - 3$ **b.** $x + 3$
 c. $x + 1$ **d.** $x - 1$

15. Simplify $\frac{3 + i}{1 - 3i}$. *(LESSON 5.6)*
 a. $\frac{9}{10} + i$ **b.** i
 c. $\frac{3}{10} + \frac{7}{10}i$ **d.** $\frac{3}{5} + i$

16. Which equation defines a circle with its center at $(0, -2)$ and a radius of 5? *(LESSON 9.3)*
 a. $x^2 + (y - 2)^2 = 25$
 b. $x^2 + (y - 2)^2 = 5$
 c. $x^2 + (y + 2)^2 = 25$
 d. $x^2 + (y + 2)^2 = 5$

17. Write an equation in slope-intercept form for the line that contains $(-3, 4)$ and is parallel to $y = -\frac{1}{5}x + 2$. *(LESSON 1.3)*

18. Solve the literal equation $A = p + prt$ for p. *(LESSON 1.6)*

19. Use the quadratic formula to solve $x^2 + 4x - 1 = 0$. *(LESSON 5.5)*

20. Solve $\begin{cases} 3x - y = -4 \\ 2x - 3y = 2 \end{cases}$ by graphing. *(LESSON 3.1)*

21. Graph $2y > -1$. *(LESSON 3.3)*

22. Find the determinant of $\begin{bmatrix} 4 & -2 \\ 3 & -1 \end{bmatrix}$. *(LESSON 4.3)*

23. Factor $9x^2 - 18x + 8$, if possible. *(LESSON 5.3)*

24. Write the function for the graph of $f(x) = x^2$ stretched vertically by a factor of 5 and translated 2 units up. *(LESSON 2.7)*

25. Factor $6x^3 - 15x^2 - 4x + 10$, if possible. *(LESSON 7.3)*

26. Write $(x + 2)(x^2 - 3x - 5)$ as a polynomial expression in standard form. *(LESSON 7.3)*

27. Write the standard equation for a circle with its center at $(-5, 4)$ and a radius of 6. *(LESSON 9.3)*

28. Find the domain of $h(x) = \frac{3x^2}{-5 + 2x}$. *(LESSON 8.2)*

29. Simplify $\frac{3x - 10}{x^2 - 8x + 12} - \frac{2}{x - 6}$. *(LESSON 8.4)*

30. Find the domain of $h(x) = \sqrt{5x - 7}$. *(LESSON 8.6)*

FREE RESPONSE GRID The following questions may be answered by using a free-response grid such as that commonly used by standardized-test services.

31. A truck travels 245 kilometers on 35 liters of gasoline. How many kilometers should the truck be able to travel on 100 liters? *(LESSON 1.4)*

32. Evaluate $2^{\log_2 9}$. *(LESSON 6.4)*

33. Solve $10^x = 222$ for x. Round your answer to the nearest hundredth. *(LESSON 6.3)*

34. Find the maximum value of the function $y = -2x^2 + 8x + 4$. *(LESSON 5.1)*

SPORTS A swimmer jumps from a platform that is 10 feet above the water. The vertical height of the swimmer at three different times is given in the table. *(LESSON 5.7)*

Time (s)	Vertical height (ft)
0.0	10
0.5	8
0.75	4

35. Use a quadratic function to predict the time in seconds when the swimmer enters the water.

36. Find the maximum height of the swimmer.

Keystroke Guide for Chapter 9

Essential keystroke sequences (using the model TI-82 or TI-83 graphics calculator) are presented below for all Activities and Examples found in this chapter that require or recommend the use of a graphics calculator.

internet connect

For Keystrokes of other graphing calculator models, visit the HRW web site at **go.hrw.com** and enter the keyword **MB1 CALC**.

LESSON 9.1

E X A M P L E **1** For part a, graph $y = \sqrt{25 - x^2}$ and $y = -\sqrt{25 - x^2}$ together.

Page 562

Begin with viewing window $[-10, 10]$ by $[-10, 10]$.

> *Entering {–1, 1} implements the ± sign.*

⇑ TI-82: ((

For part b, graph $y = \sqrt{x^2 - 4}$ and $y = -\sqrt{x^2 - 4}$ together.

⇑ TI-82: ((

| x^2 | – | 4 |) | ZOOM | **5: ZSquare** | ENTER |

LESSON 9.2

Activity

Page 573

For Steps 1 and 2, graph $y = \frac{1}{4}x^2$ and $y = \frac{1}{4}(x - 2)^2 + 3$ on the same screen, and find the coordinates of the vertices.

Use viewing window $[-10, 10]$ by $[-10, 10]$.

Graph the functions:

| Y= | (| 1 | ÷ | 4 |) | X,T,θ,n | x^2 | ENTER | (Y2=) | (| 1 | ÷ | 4 |

|) | (| X,T,θ,n | – | 2 |) | x^2 | + | 3 | GRAPH |

Find the vertex:

CALC

| 2nd | TRACE | **3:minimum** | ENTER | (LeftBound?) | ENTER |

(RightBound?) ENTER (Guess?) ENTER

Repeat this keystroke sequence to find the other vertex.

Graph $y = 4 + \sqrt{-8(x-1)}$ and $y = 4 - \sqrt{-8(x-1)}$ together.

Begin with viewing window $[-10, 10]$ by $[-7, 13]$.

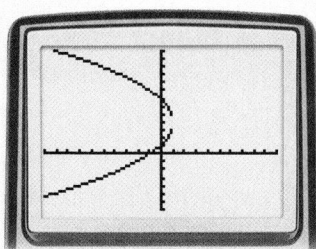

LESSON 9.3

TECHNOLOGY

Page 580

Graph $y = \sqrt{4 - x^2}$ and $y = -\sqrt{4 - x^2}$ together.

Begin with viewing window $[-5, 5]$ by $[-5, 5]$.

Activity

Page 580

Graph $x^2 + y^2 = 16$ and $(x + 3)^2 + (y - 2)^2 = 16$ on the same screen, and find the center of each.

Use friendly viewing window $[-9.4, 9.4]$ by $[-6.2, 6.2]$.

Graph the functions:

Solve for y, and use a keystroke sequence similar to that given in Example 1 of Lesson 9.1.

Find the centers:

Use the cursor keys ▲ ▼ ◄ ► to find the approximate coordinates of the center.

LESSON 9.4

TECHNOLOGY

Page 589

Graph $y = \sqrt{9\left(1 - \dfrac{x^2}{25}\right)}$ and $y = -\sqrt{9\left(1 - \dfrac{x^2}{25}\right)}$ together.

Begin with viewing window $[-7, 7]$ by $[-5, 5]$.

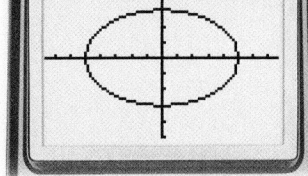

E X A M P L E **1** Graph $y = \sqrt{16\left(1 + \dfrac{x^2}{9}\right)}$ and $y = -\sqrt{16\left(1 + \dfrac{x^2}{9}\right)}$ together.

Page 597

Begin with viewing window $[-15, 15]$ by $[-10, 10]$.

Activity

Page 597

Graph $\dfrac{x^2}{2^2} - \dfrac{y^2}{3^2} = 1$, $y = \dfrac{3}{2}x$, and $y = -\dfrac{3}{2}x$ on the same screen.

Use viewing window $[-10, 10]$ by $[-10, 10]$.

Graph the functions:

Solve for y, and use a keystroke sequence similar to that given in Example 1 of this lesson.

Activity

Page 606

For part a of Step 1, graph $x^2 + y^2 = 25$ and $y = 2x$ on the same screen.

Begin with viewing window $[-10, 10]$ by $[-10, 10]$.

Solve for y, and use a keystroke sequence similar to that given in the Technology example of Lesson 9.3.

For part b of Step 1, graph $x^2 + y^2 = 25$ and $x^2 - y^2 = 9$ on the same screen.

Use viewing window $[-10, 10]$ by $[-10, 10]$.

Solve for y, and use keystroke sequences similar to those given in the Technology example of Lesson 9.3 and in Example 1 of Lesson 9.5.

For parts **c** and **d** of Step 1, use the same viewing window and similar keystroke sequences.

E X A M P L E **①** Graph $y = \sqrt{3x-1}$, $y = -\sqrt{3x-1}$, $y = \sqrt{9-x^2}$, and $y = -\sqrt{9-x^2}$ on the same screen. Find any points of intersection.

Page 607

Begin with viewing window $[-5, 5]$ by $[-5, 5]$.

> *If equations are not entered separately, it may be difficult to find the intersection points.*

Graph the functions:

⇑ TI-82: ( )

⇑ TI-82: ( )

⇑ TI-82: ( )

⇑ TI-82: ( )

Find any points of intersection:

[2nd] [TRACE] **5: intersect** (First curve?)

[ENTER] (Second curve?)

[ENTER] (Guess?) [ENTER]

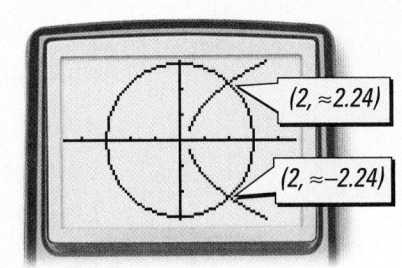

$(2, \approx 2.24)$

$(2, \approx -2.24)$

E X A M P L E **③** Graph $y = \sqrt{\dfrac{100-4x^2}{25}}$, $y = -\sqrt{\dfrac{100-4x^2}{25}}$, $y = \sqrt{9-x^2}$, and $y = -\sqrt{9-x^2}$ on the same screen. Find any points of intersection.

Page 609

Use viewing window $[-6, 6]$ by $[-4, 4]$.

Graph the functions:

⇑ TI-82: ( )

⇑ TI-82: ( )

⇑ TI-82: ( )

⇑ TI-82: ( )

[ZOOM] **5:ZSquare** [ENTER]

Find any points of intersection:

[2nd] [TRACE] **5:intersect** (First curve?)

[ENTER] (Second curve?)

[ENTER] (Guess?) [ENTER]

$(\approx -2.44, \approx 1.75)$

$(\approx 2.44, \approx 1.75)$

$(\approx -2.44, \approx -1.75)$

$(\approx 2.44, \approx -1.75)$

DISCRETE MATHEMATICS

Counting Principles and Probability

PROBABILITY IS THE RELATIVE LIKELIHOOD, or chance, that an event will occur. Some events, such as those shown here, are unlikely, or have a low probability of occurence. In this chapter, you will use the Fundamental Counting Principle to find the number of ways in which an event can occur.

Probability is used in many real-world fields, such as insurance, medical research, law enforcement, and political science.

Lessons

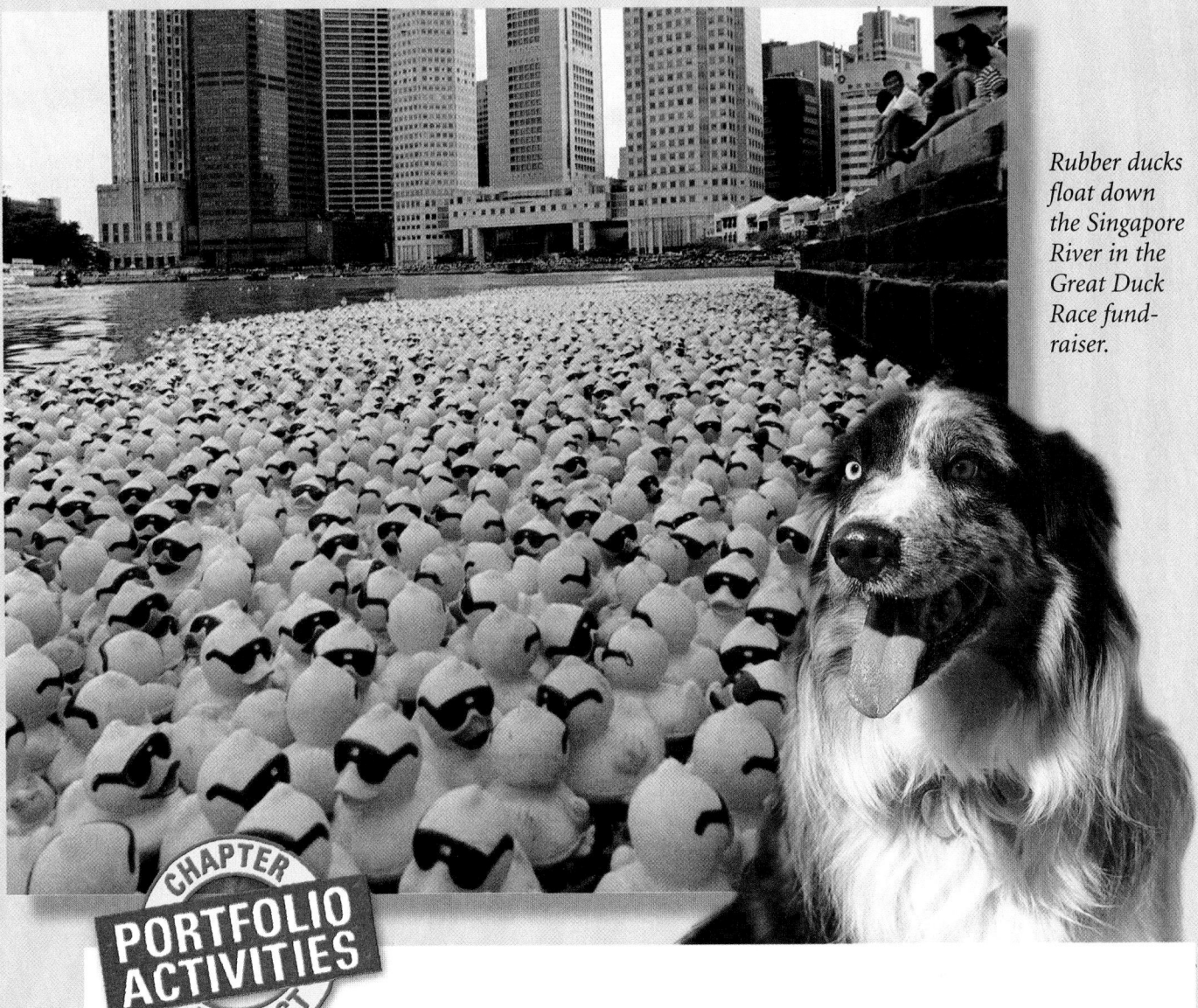

Rubber ducks float down the Singapore River in the Great Duck Race fundraiser.

PORTFOLIO ACTIVITIES
CHAPTER PROJECT

About the Chapter Project

Making reasonable predictions about random events plays an important role in decision-making strategies from the simplest problems to the most complex problems. In many situations, the probability of a random event occurring can be determined empirically by observing the number of times the event occurs. When the random event is complex, the actual observation of the event may be impossible. In these cases, simulations are used. In the Chapter Project, *Next, Please . . .*, you will simulate random events and estimate probabilities.

After completing the Chapter Project, you will be able to do the following:

- Set up models that simulate random events.

- Use data from simulations to estimate probabilities.

About the Portfolio Activities

Throughout the chapter, you will be given opportunities to complete Portfolio Activities that are designed to support your work on the Chapter Project.

- You will use a spinner to model the possible outcomes of a geometric probability problem in the Portfolio Activity on page 635.

- You will use a random-number generator to model the possible outcomes of an event in the Portfolio Activity on page 649.

- You will use a random-number generator to model two-event probabilities in the Portfolio Activity on page 658.

Introduction to Probability

Why Probability is often studied using everyday objects, such as number cubes, coins, and darts.

Objectives

- Find the theoretical probability of an event.
- Apply the Fundamental Counting Principle.

How do some businesses, such as life insurance companies and gambling establishments, make dependable profits on events that seem unpredictable? The answer is that the overall likelihood, or **probability**, of an event can be discovered by observing the results of a large number of repetitions of the situation in which the event may occur.

The terminology used to discuss probabilities is given below. An example related to rolling a number cube is given for each term.

DEFINITION	EXAMPLE
Trial: a systematic opportunity for an event to occur	rolling a number cube
Experiment: one or more trials	rolling a number cube 10 times
Sample space: the set of all possible outcomes of an event	1, 2, 3, 4, 5, 6
Event: an individual outcome or any specified combination of outcomes	rolling a 3 rolling a 3 *or* rolling a 5

Outcomes are **random** if all possible outcomes are equally likely. Although it is impossible to prove that the result of a real-world event is completely random, some outcomes are often assumed to be random. For example, the results of tossing a coin, the roll of a number cube, the outcome of a spinner, the selection of lottery numbers, and the gender of a baby are often assumed to be random.

Probability is expressed as a number from 0 to 1, inclusive. It is often written as a fraction, decimal, or percent.
- An impossible event has a probability of 0.
- An event that must occur has a probability of 1.
- The sum of the probabilities of all outcomes in a sample space is 1.

In mathematics, the probability of an event can be assigned in two ways: *experimentally* (inductively) or *theoretically* (deductively).

Experimental probability is approximated by performing trials and recording the ratio of the number of occurrences of the event to the number of trials. As the number of trials in an experiment increases, the approximation of the experimental probability improves.

Theoretical probability is based on the assumption that all outcomes in the sample space occur randomly.

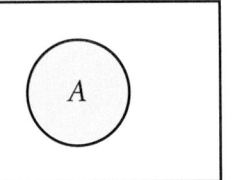
Sample space

Theoretical Probability

If all outcomes in a sample space are equally likely, then the theoretical probability of event *A*, denoted *P(A)*, is defined by

$$P(A) = \frac{\text{number of outcomes in event } A}{\text{number of outcomes in the sample space}}.$$

EXAMPLE ❶ **Find the probability of randomly selecting a red disk in one draw from a container that contains 2 red disks, 4 blue disks, and 3 yellow disks.**

● **SOLUTION**

The event is selecting *1 red disk.*

Because there are 2 red disks, the number of outcomes in the event is 2.

The sample space is the set of all disks, so the total number of outcomes in the sample space is 2 + 4 + 3, or 9.

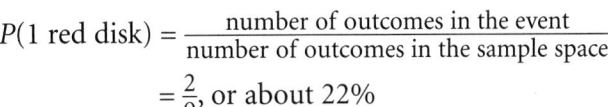

$$P(1 \text{ red disk}) = \frac{\text{number of outcomes in the event}}{\text{number of outcomes in the sample space}}$$

$$= \frac{2}{9}, \text{ or about } 22\%$$

Thus, the probability of randomly selecting a red disk in one draw is about 22%.

TRY THIS Find the probability of randomly selecting a blue disk in one draw from a container that contains 2 red disks, 4 blue disks, and 3 yellow disks.

In the next two examples, area models are used to find probabilities for situations in which the number of outcomes in the sample space is infinite, such as with area or time.

Assume that a dart will land on the dartboard and that each point on the dartboard is equally likely to be hit.

Find the probability of a dart landing in region *A*, the outer ring.

SOLUTION

The event is landing in region *A*.

The sample space consists of all points on the dartboard.

$$P(A) = \frac{\text{area of region } A}{\text{total area}} = \frac{\pi(3)^2 - \pi(2)^2}{\pi(3)^2} = \frac{5\pi}{9\pi} = \frac{5}{9} \approx 0.556$$

The probability of a dart landing in region *A* is about 55.6%.

TRY THIS Find the probability of a dart landing in region *B* of the dartboard.

Eduardo logs onto his electronic mail once during the time interval from 1:00 P.M. to 2:00 P.M.

Assuming that all times are equally likely, find the probability that he will log on during each time interval.
  a. from 1:30 P.M. to 1:40 P.M.   **b.** from 1:30 P.M. to 1:35 P.M.

SOLUTION

a. The event is the interval from 1:30 P.M. to 1:40 P.M.

The sample space is the interval from 1:00 P.M. to 2:00 P.M.

Divide the sample space into 10-minute intervals to represent the equally likely events.

The event is $\frac{1}{6}$ of the sample space. Thus, the probability is $\frac{1}{6}$, or about 16.7%.

b. The event is the interval from 1:30 P.M. to 1:35 P.M.

The sample space is the interval from 1:00 P.M. to 2:00 P.M.

Divide the sample space into 5-minute intervals to represent the equally likely events.

The event is $\frac{1}{12}$ of the sample space. Thus, the probability is $\frac{1}{12}$, or about 8.3%.

TRY THIS Janice leaves home for work sometime between 7:30 A.M. and 8:00 A.M. Assuming that all times are equally likely, find the probability that she will leave home during each time interval.
  a. from 7:30 A.M. to 7:40 A.M.   **b.** from 7:30 A.M. to 7:32 A.M.

In the Activity below, a tree diagram is used to count all possible choices of pizza toppings.

Activity
Investigating Tree Diagrams

You will need: no special tools

A pizza shop offers a special price on a 2-topping pizza. You can choose 1 topping from each of the following groups:
- provolone cheese or extra mozzarella cheese
- pepperoni, sausage, or hamburger

1. Begin a tree diagram with the two cheese choices, as shown at right.

2. From each cheese choice, extend a line for each meat choice.

3. How many possible different combinations of two toppings are possible?

CHECKPOINT ✔ 4. If the special included a third topping of either onions or green peppers, how would you extend your diagram to show the additional possibilities? How many total 3-topping combinations are there?

There are several ways to determine the size of a sample space for an event that is a combination of two or more outcomes. One way is a tree diagram.

For example, a cafe's lunch special is a hamburger meal. It comes with a choice of beverage (soda or tea) and a choice of salad (garden, potato, or bean). The tree diagram below shows that there are 2 × 3, or 6, choices.

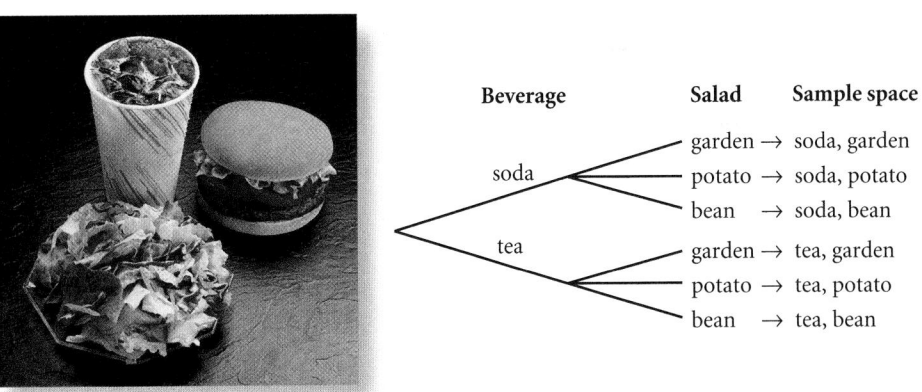

CHECKPOINT ✔ Make a tree diagram with the salad as the first choice and the beverage as the second choice. Does the order in which the choices are made affect the number of possible choices for the lunch special?

Tree diagrams illustrate the *Fundamental Counting Principle*.

Fundamental Counting Principle

If there are *m* ways that one event can occur and *n* ways that another event can occur, then there are *m* × *n* ways that both events can occur.

E X A M P L E ④ Ann is choosing a password for her access to the Internet. She decides not to use the digit 0 or the letter *O*. Each letter or number may be used more than once.

APPLICATION
COMPUTERS

How many passwords of 2 letters followed by 4 digits are possible?

● **SOLUTION**

Use the Fundamental Counting Principle. There are 25 possible letters and 9 possible digits.

1st letter		2nd letter		1st digit		2nd digit		3rd digit		4th digit
25	×	25	×	9	×	9	×	9	×	9

The number of possible passwords for Ann is $25^2 \times 9^4$, or 4,100,625.

E X A M P L E ⑤ A license plate consists of 2 letters followed by 3 digits. The letters, *A–Z*, and the numbers, 0–9, can be repeated.

APPLICATION
TRANSPORTATION

Find the probability that your new license plate contains the initials of your first and last names in their proper order.

● **SOLUTION**

1. Find the number of outcomes in the event.

	1st letter		2nd letter		1st number		2nd number		3rd number
Number of ways possible →	1	×	1	×	10	×	10	×	10

2. Find the number of outcomes in the sample space.

	1st letter		2nd letter		1st number		2nd number		3rd number
Number of ways possible →	26	×	26	×	10	×	10	×	10

3. Find the probability of this event.

$$P(A) = \frac{1 \times 1 \times 10 \times 10 \times 10}{26 \times 26 \times 10 \times 10 \times 10} = \frac{1000}{676,000} = \frac{1}{676} \approx 0.0015$$

Thus, the probability that your new license plate contains the initials of your first and last names is about 0.15%, which is more than 1 in 1000.

Exercises

● *Communicate*

1. Give three examples of an event with more than one outcome.

2. How are theoretical and experimental probabilities similar? different?

3. Explain how an area model can be used to find probabilities.

4. Find the probability of randomly selecting a red marble in one draw from a bag of 5 blue marbles, 3 red marbles, and 1 white marble. *(EXAMPLE 1)*

5. Assume that a dart will land on the dartboard and that each point on the dartboard is equally likely to be hit. Find the probability of a dart landing in region *C*, the inner ring. *(EXAMPLE 2)*

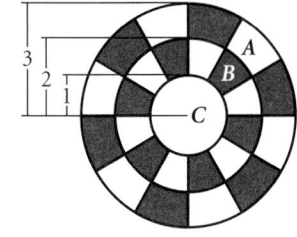

6. Sue logs onto her electronic mail once during the time interval from 7:00 A.M. to 8:00 A.M. Assuming that all times are equally likely, find the probability that she will log on during the interval from 7:30 P.M. to 7:45 P.M. *(EXAMPLE 3)*

7. John is deciding on a password for his access to the Internet. He decides not to use the digit 0 or the letter *Q*. How many possible passwords are there if he uses 2 letters followed by 3 digits? *(EXAMPLE 4)*

8. In a lottery, a 4-digit number from 0000 to 9999 is randomly selected. Find the probability that the number selected begins with 3 and ends in 2 or 0. *(EXAMPLE 5)*

● *Practice and Apply*

A bag contains 3 white cards, 2 black cards, and 5 red cards. Find the probability of each event for one draw.

9. a white card   **10.** a black card   **11.** a red card

Calculate the probability of each event for one roll of a number cube.

12. 1   **13.** 4

14. an even number   **15.** an odd number

16. a number less than 3   **17.** a number greater than 3

18. a number greater than 6   **19.** a number less than 6

A bus arrives at Jason's house anytime from 8:00 A.M. to 8:05 A.M. If all times are equally likely, find the probability that Jason will catch the bus if he begins waiting at the given times.

20. 8:04 A.M.   **21.** 8:02 A.M.   **22.** 8:01 A.M.   **23.** 8:03 A.M.

For Exercises 24 and 25, create a tree diagram that shows the sample space for each event.

24. Involvement in one of each type of extracurricular activity

        Sports: football, soccer, tennis
        Arts: music, painting
        Clubs: science, French

25. Involvement in one of each type of leisure activity

        Outdoor: biking, gardening, rappeling
        Indoor: reading, watching television, playing board games

Find the number of possible passwords (with no letters or digits excluded) for each of the following conditions:

26. 2 digits followed by 3 letters followed by 1 digit

27. 3 digits followed by 2 letters followed by 1 digit

28. 3 letters followed by 3 digits

29. 2 letters followed by 4 digits

internet connect

**Homework
Help Online**

Go To: go.hrw.com
Keyword:
MB1 Homework Help
for Exercises 30–33

The odds in favor of an event are defined as the number of ways the event can happen divided by the number of ways it can fail to happen. If the odds in favor of an event are $\frac{a}{b}$, or a to b, then the probability of the event is $\frac{a}{a+b}$. Find the probability of each event, given the odds in favor of the event.

30. 3 to 8   **31.** 4 to 5   **32.** 3 to 7   **33.** 1 to 20

GEOMETRY To the nearest tenth of a percent, find or approximate the probability that a dart thrown at the square dartboard at right will land in the regions indicated below.

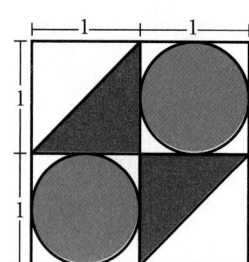

34. one of the circular regions

35. one of the red triangular regions

36. one of the white triangular regions

CHALLENGE

37. one of the white regions

APPLICATIONS

38. PUBLISHING When a book is published, it is assigned a number called an International Standard Book Number (ISBN). The number consists of 10 digits that provide information about the language in which the book is printed, the publisher of the book, the book itself, and a check digit. How many ISBN numbers are possible?

39. ACADEMICS A multiple-choice exam consists of 14 questions, each of which has 4 possible answers. How many different ways can all 14 questions on the exam be answered?

DEMOGRAPHICS The table at right shows the 1993 college enrollment statistics, in thousands, for the United States. Based on this data, find the probability that a randomly selected person enrolled in college in the United States in 1993 is in the given age group. [*Source: Statistical Abstract of the United States, 1996*]

40. 18–24   **41.** 25–29

42. 30–34   **43.** 30 or over

Age	Male	Female
14–17	83	93
18–19	1224	1416
20–21	1294	1414
22–24	1260	1263
25–29	950	1058
30–34	661	811
35 and over	955	1824

44. TRANSPORTATION How many different license plates can be made if each plate consists of 2 letters followed by 2 digits (1 through 9) followed by 3 letters?

CHALLENGE

45. SECURITY A security specialist is designing a code for a security system. The code will use only the letters *A*, *B*, and *C*. If the specialist wants the probability of guessing the code at random to be less than 0.001, how long must the code be?

 Look Back

For each function, find an equation of the inverse. Then use composition to verify that the equation you wrote is the inverse. *(LESSON 2.5)*

46. $f(x) = 3x + 10$ **47.** $g(x) = \dfrac{3x - 2}{6}$ **48.** $h(x) = \dfrac{1}{2} - 5x$

For each function, describe the transformations from $f(x) = \sqrt{x}$ to g. Graph each transformation. *(LESSON 8.6)*

49. $g(x) = \dfrac{1}{2}\sqrt{x} - 5$ **50.** $g(x) = 3\sqrt{x - 2}$ **51.** $g(x) = \sqrt{2x} + 1$

Look Beyond

 internet connect

Portfolio Extension

Go To: go.hrw.com
Keyword:
MB1 Probability

52. When Scott accesses his electronic mail, he enters a 6-symbol code that is a string of letters, numbers, or the 10 symbols which appear at the top of his keyboard (such as !, @, #).

  a. How many codes are possible if uppercase and lowercase letters (such as *B* and *b*) are considered the same?

  b. How many codes are possible if uppercase and lowercase letters are considered different?

  c. How long would it take to try all of the codes in part **b** if you could enter one code per second? Give your answer in years.

 PORTFOLIO ACTIVITY

Refer to Example 3 on page 630. Assuming that all the times are equally likely, you can perform an experiment with a spinner to model the probability that Eduardo logs onto his mail during the time interval from 1:30 P.M. to 1:40 P.M.

  1. Divide a spinner into 6 equal sections, each representing a 10-minute interval. Let region *D* represent the 10-minute interval from 1:30 P.M. to 1:40 P.M.

  2. Spin the spinner 40 times, and record the number of times that the spinner lands in region *D*.

  3. Use your results to estimate the probability that Eduardo logs onto his mail in the interval from 1:30 P.M. to 1:40 P.M.

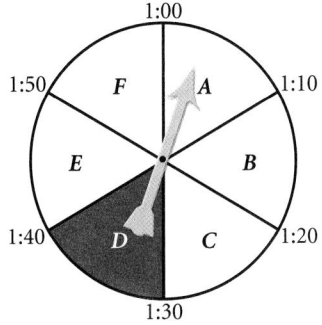

  4. Compare your estimated probability with the theoretical probability obtained in the lesson. How well do you think the spinner models this problem? Explain.

WORKING ON THE CHAPTER PROJECT
You should now be able to complete Activity 1 of the Chapter Project.

Permutations

10.2

Why There are many situations that involve an ordered arrangement, or permutation, of objects. For example, 12-tone music, developed by Arnold Schoenberg, consists of permutations of all 12 tones in an octave.

Arnold Schoenberg, 1874–1951

Objectives

- Solve problems involving linear permutations of distinct or indistinguishable objects.

- Solve problems involving circular permutations.

In 12-tone music, pioneered by Arnold Schoenberg, each note of the chromatic scale must be used exactly once before any are repeated. A set of 12 tones is called a *tone row*. How many different tone rows are possible? *You will answer this question in Example 1.*

A **permutation** is an arrangement of objects in a specific order. When objects are arranged in a row, the permutation is called a **linear permutation**. Unless otherwise noted, the term *permutation* will be used to mean *linear permutations*.

PROBLEM SOLVING

ABCD	BACD	CABD	DABC
ABDC	BADC	CADB	DACB
ACBD	BCAD	CBAD	DBAC
ACDB	BCDA	CBDA	DBCA
ADBC	BDAC	CDAB	DCAB
ADCB	BDCA	CDBA	DCBA

Make an organized list. Each of the possible permutations of the letters A, B, C, and D are listed in the table at left.

The number of different permutations, 24, can be obtained by using the Fundamental Counting Principle, as shown below.

	1st choice		2nd choice		3rd choice		4th choice		
Number of possible → choices	4	×	3	×	2	×	1	=	24

Thus, there are $4 \times 3 \times 2 \times 1$, or 24, possible arrangements. You can use *factorial notation* to abbreviate this product: $4! = 4 \times 3 \times 2 \times 1 = 24$.

If n is a positive integer, then **n factorial**, written $n!$, is defined as follows:

$$n! = n \times (n-1) \times (n-2) \times \cdots \times 2 \times 1$$

Note that the value of $0!$ is defined to be 1.

You can find the number of permutations of any number of objects by using the Fundamental Counting Principle and factorials as follows:

Permutations of *n* Objects

The number of permutations of n objects is given by $n!$.

In 12-tone music, each of the 12 notes in an octave must be used exactly once before any are repeated. A set of 12 tones is called a tone row.

How many different tone rows are possible?

● SOLUTION

Find the number of permutations of 12 notes.

$$12! = 12 \times 11 \times 10 \times 9 \times 8 \times 7 \times 6 \times 5 \times 4 \times 3 \times 2 \times 1$$
$$= 479{,}001{,}600$$

There are 479,001,600 different tone rows for 12 tones.

TRY THIS   How many different ways can the letters in the word *objects* be arranged?

The number of ways that you can listen to 3 different CDs from a selection of 10 CDs is a *permutation of 10 objects taken 3 at a time.*

	1st CD	2nd CD	3rd CD
Number of CDs available →	10 ×	9 ×	8

By the Fundamental Counting Principle, there are $10 \times 9 \times 8$, or 720, ways that you can listen to 3 different CDs from a selection of 10 CDs.

Permutations of *n* Objects Taken *r* at a Time

The number of permutations of *n* objects taken *r* at a time, denoted by $P(n, r)$ or $_nP_r$, is given by $P(n, r) = {}_nP_r = \dfrac{n!}{(n-r)!}$, where $r \le n$.

Note the use of 0! in calculating the number of permutations of *n* objects taken *n* at a time.

$$P(n, n) = {}_nP_n = \frac{n!}{(n-n)!} = \frac{n!}{0!} = n!$$

Find the number of ways to listen to 5 different CDs from a selection of 15 CDs.

● SOLUTION

Find the number of permutations of 15 objects taken 5 at a time.

$$_{15}P_5 = \frac{15!}{(15 - 5)!}$$
$$= \frac{15 \times 14 \times 13 \times 12 \times 11 \times \cancel{10!}}{\cancel{10!}}$$
$$= 15 \times 14 \times 13 \times 12 \times 11$$
$$= 360{,}360$$

TRY THIS   Find the number of ways to listen to 4 CDs from a selection of 8 CDs.

Exploring Formulas for Permutations

You will need: a calculator

1. **a.** Evaluate $_7P_3$ and $7 \times 6 \times 5$.   **b.** Evaluate $_7P_4$ and $7 \times 6 \times 5 \times 4$.
   c. Evaluate $_7P_5$ and $7 \times 6 \times 5 \times 4 \times 3$.

2. **a.** Write $_7P_r$ as a product.   **b.** Write $_nP_r$ as a product.

CHECKPOINT ✔ 3. Using your answer from part **b** of Step 2, write products to represent $_8P_4$, $_8P_5$, and $_{10}P_8$. Verify your results.

As you have seen, there are 4! permutations of the 4 letters A, B, C, and D. However, if 2 of the 4 letters are identical, as in OHIO, there will be less than 4! permutations because arrangements such as O_1HIO_2 and O_2HIO_1 are indistinguishable. To account for the 2 identical letters, divide by 2! because there are 2! ways of arranging the 2 Os.

$$\frac{4!}{2!} \begin{array}{l} \leftarrow \textit{permutation of 4 objects} \\ \leftarrow \textit{2 identical objects} \end{array}$$

Permutations With Identical Objects

The number of distinct permutations of n objects with r identical objects is given by $\frac{n!}{r!}$, where $1 \le r \le n$.

The number of distinct permutations of n objects with r_1 identical objects, r_2 identical objects of another kind, r_3 identical objects of another kind, . . . , and r_k identical objects of another kind is given by $\frac{n!}{r_1!r_2!r_3! \cdots r_k!}$

E X A M P L E ③ T'anna is planting 11 colored flowers in a line.

In how many ways can she plant 4 red flowers, 5 yellow flowers, and 2 purple flowers?

● **SOLUTION**

PROBLEM SOLVING

Use the formula for permutations with repeated objects.

$$\frac{11!}{4! \times 5! \times 2!} = \frac{11 \times 10 \times 9 \times 8 \times 7 \times 6 \times 5!}{4! \times 5! \times 2!}$$

$$= \frac{11 \times 10 \times 9 \times 8 \times 7 \times 6}{(4 \times 3 \times 2 \times 1) \times (2 \times 1)}$$

$$= \frac{11 \times 10 \times 9 \times 7}{1}$$

$$= 6930$$

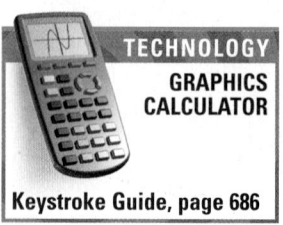

TECHNOLOGY

GRAPHICS
CALCULATOR

Keystroke Guide, page 686

There are 6930 ways that T'anna can plant the flowers in a line.

TRY THIS   In how many ways can T'anna plant 11 colored flowers if 5 are white and the remaining ones are red?

CHECKPOINT ✔ How does the formula for the number of permutations with repeated objects give the number of permutations of *n* objects when all of the objects are distinct?

CRITICAL THINKING   A row of daisies consists of *r* yellow and *s* white flowers. In terms of *r* and *s*, write a formula for the number of permutations of all of the flowers.

In how many ways can you arrange 4 objects around the edge of a circular tray? The letters *A*, *B*, *C*, and *D* are arranged in a circle, as shown below. This type of a permutation is called a **circular permutation**.

A	*B*	*C*	*D*
B	*C*	*D*	*A*
C	*D*	*A*	*B*
D	*A*	*B*	*C*

Circular permutations   Linear permutations

Notice that all 4 distinct linear permutations of the letters *A*, *B*, *C*, and *D*, give a single distinct circular permutation. Therefore, to find the number of *circular permutations* of 4 objects, divide the total number of linear permutations by 4. The result, 3!, is also $(4-1)!$, as shown below.

$$\frac{4!}{4} = \frac{4 \times 3 \times 2 \times 1}{4} = 3!$$

Circular Permutations

If *n* distinct objects are arranged around a circle, then there are $(n-1)!$ circular permutations of the *n* objects.

EXAMPLE ④ **In how many ways can 7 different appetizers be arranged on a circular tray as shown at right?**

APPLICATION
CATERING

● **SOLUTION**

PROBLEM SOLVING   **Use the formula** for circular permutations with $n = 7$.

$(n-1)! = (7-1)! = 6! = 720$

There are 720 distinct ways to arrange the appetizers on the tray.

TRY THIS   In how many ways can seats be chosen for 12 couples on a Ferris wheel that has 12 double seats?

Exercises

internet connect

**Activities
Online**

Go To: **go.hrw.com**
Keyword:
MB1 Baseball

Communicate

1. Explain how the Fundamental Counting Principle is used to find the number of permutation of 4 objects.

2. Which number of permutations of 4 letters is greater, 2 at a time or 3 at a time? Explain.

3. Explain why $_4P_4 = {_4}P_3$ is true. Is $_nP_n = {_n}P_{n-1}$ always true? Explain.

4. Does a circular permutation of 5 distinct objects always have fewer arrangements than a linear permutation of 5 distinct objects? Explain.

Guided Skills Practice

5. How many different ways can the letters in the word *orange* be arranged? *(EXAMPLE 1)*

6. Find the number of ways to watch 3 videos from a selection of 7 videos. *(EXAMPLE 2)*

7. In how many ways can 5 pennies, 2 quarters, and 3 dimes be arranged in a straight line? *(EXAMPLE 3)*

8. In how many ways can 12 different spices be arranged around a circular spice rack? *(EXAMPLE 4)*

Practice and Apply

Evaluate each expression.

9. $7! - 5!$

10. $6! - 4!$

11. $(7-5)!$

12. $(6-4)!$

13. $\dfrac{8!}{3! \times 5!}$

14. $\dfrac{10!}{4! \times 6!}$

15. $\dfrac{5! \times 0!}{(4-1)!}$

16. $\dfrac{(7-2)! \times 3!}{0!}$

17. $_{10}P_7$

18. $_7P_3$

19. $_{50}P_1$

20. $_{1000}P_1$

21. $\dfrac{_{12}P_5}{_6P_5}$

22. $\dfrac{_4P_3}{_8P_3}$

23. $_4P_2 \times {_7}P_7$

24. $_{15}P_5 \times {_5}P_5$

Find the number of permutations of the first 8 letters of the alphabet for each situation.

25. taking 5 letters at a time

26. taking 3 letters at a time

27. taking 4 letters at a time

28. taking 6 letters at a time

29. taking 1 letter at a time

30. taking all 8 letters at a time

In how many ways can 8 new employees be assigned to the following number of vacant offices?

31. 8

32. 9

33. 10

34. 15

In how many ways can a teacher arrange 6 students in the front row of a classroom with the following number of students?

35. 18   **36.** 24   **37.** 28   **38.** 30

internet connect

Homework Help Online

Go To: **go.hrw.com**
Keyword:
MB1 Homework Help
for Exercises 39–47

Find the number of permutations of the letters in each word.

39. *barley*   **40.** *pencil*   **41.** *trout*

42. *circus*   **43.** *football*   **44.** *vignette*

45. *bookkeeper*   **46.** *Mississippi*   **47.** *correspondence*

48. Five different stuffed animals are to be placed on a circular display rack in a department store. In how many ways can this be done?

49. Seven different types of sunglasses are to be displayed on one level of a circular rack. In how many ways can they be arranged?

50. Franklin High School has 4 valedictorians. In how many different ways can they give their graduation speeches?

51. Suppose that a personal identification number (PIN) consists of 4 digits from 0 through 9.
a. How many PIN numbers are possible?
b. How many PIN numbers are possible if no digit can be repeated?

52. In how many different ways can the expression $a^4b^2c^5d$ be written without exponents?

53. A spinner is divided into 8 equal regions to represent the digits 1–8. In how many ways can the digits be arranged?

CHALLENGES

54. In how many different ways can 4 blue counters and 4 red counters be placed in a circle if red and blue counters are alternated?

55. In how many ways can 3 males (Joe, Jerry, and John) and 3 females (Jamie, Jenny, and Jasmine) be seated in a row if the genders alternate down the row?

56. In how many ways can 5 seniors, 3 juniors, 4 sophomores, and 3 freshmen be seated in a row if a senior must be seated at each end? Assume that the members of each class are distinct.

CONNECTION

GEOMETRY Geometric figures are often represented by the letters that identify each vertex. Determine the number of ways that each figure below can be named with the letters *A, B, C, D, E,* and *F*. Assume that each figure is irregular.

57. triangle   **58.** quadrilateral

59. hexagon   **60.** pentagon

APPLICATIONS

61. SPORTS In a track meet, 7 runners compete for first, second, and third place. How many different ways can the runners place if there are no ties?

62. SMALL BUSINESS A caterer is arranging a row of desserts. The row will contain 8 platters of cookies, 5 trays of fruit, and 3 pies. In how many distinct ways can the cookies, fruit, and pies, be arranged in a row, if each type of dessert is of the same kind?

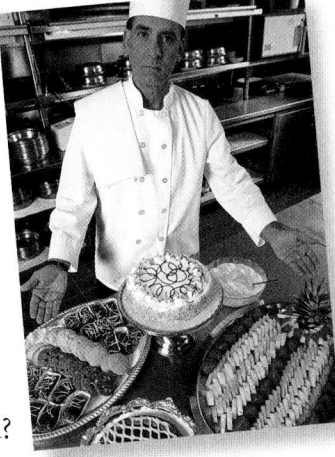

63. SPORTS A basketball team of 5 players is huddled in a circle along with their coach. In how many ways can the players and their coach be arranged in the huddle?

 Look Back

64. NUTRITION You are given the diet information below. *(LESSON 3.5)*

	Food X	Food Y	Required
Carbohydrates	2 units/ounce	3 units/ounce	at least 12 units
Fat	1 unit/ounce	2 units/ounce	at most 16 units
Protein	1 unit/ounce	3 units/ounce	at least 18 units
Cost	$0.20/ounce	$0.25/ounce	

Let x represent the required number of ounces of food X and let y represent the required number of ounces of food Y.
a. Write the set of constraints and the objective function.
b. Sketch the feasible region.
c. Find the minimum cost of a meal with foods X and Y.

Simplify each expression. *(LESSON 5.6)*

65. $(3i - 2) + (5 - 7i)$ **66.** $(-1 + 4i)(2 - i)$ **67.** $\dfrac{-1 - 8i}{2 + 5i}$

68. SMALL BUSINESS The revenue earned from selling x items is given by the revenue function $R(x) = 6x$. The cost of producing x items is given by the cost function $C(x) = -0.1x^2 + 5x + 40$. Find the number of items that must be produced and sold to generate a profit (when revenue exceeds cost). *(LESSON 5.8)*

Write each expression as a single logarithm. Then simplify, if possible. *(LESSON 6.4)*

69. $\log_b 6 + \log_b 2 - \log_b 3$ **70.** $3 \log 5^2 - 2 \log 5^3$

71. $\dfrac{1}{2} \log_2 36 - \log_2 12$ **72.** $8 \log_5 x + \log_5 4$

73 MAXIMUM/MINIMUM A rectangular piece of cardboard measures 12 inches by 16 inches. Find the maximum volume of an open-top box created by cutting squares of the same size from each corner and folding up the sides. *(LESSON 7.3)*

74. Solve the nonlinear system at right. If there is no solution, write *none*. $\begin{cases} y = x^2 + 1 \\ 3x - y = -11 \end{cases}$ *(LESSON 9.6)*

 Look Beyond

75. List all of the ways in which 2 of the letters A, B, C, D, and E can be chosen if the order in which letters are chosen is not important, that is, if AB is considered to be the same choice as BA.

76. Find the number of ways in which 2 of 26 letters can be chosen if the order in which letters are chosen is not important.

Combinations

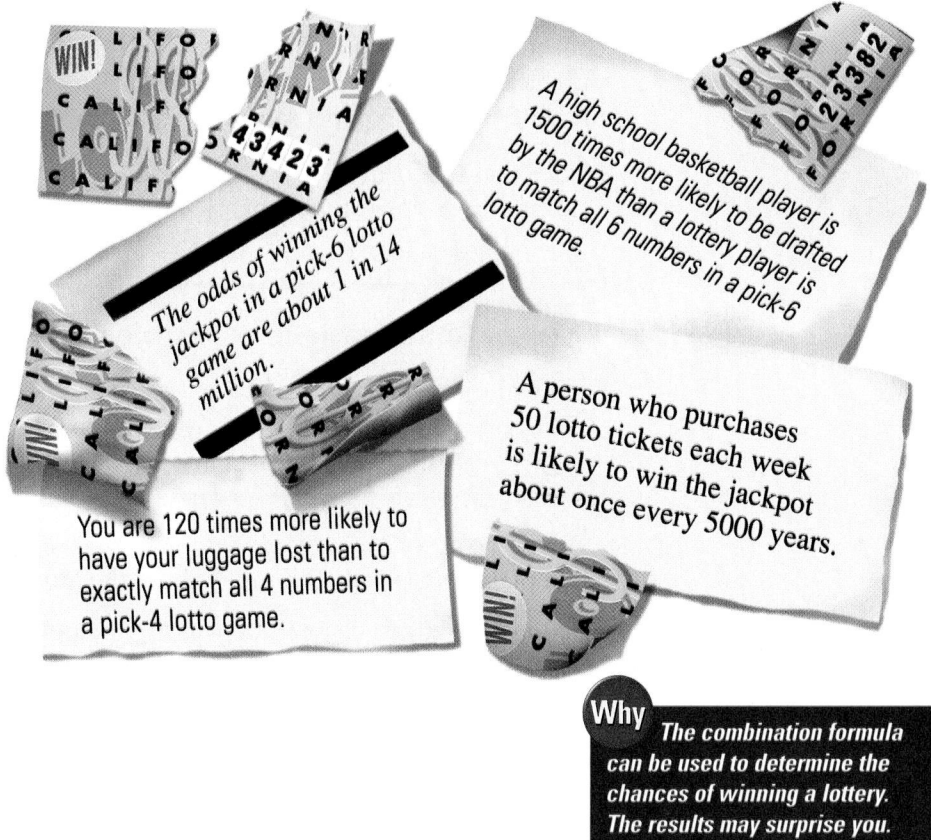

WIN! CALIFORNIA

The odds of winning the jackpot in a pick-6 lotto game are about 1 in 14 million.

A high school basketball player is 1500 times more likely to be drafted by the NBA than a lottery player is to match all 6 numbers in a pick-6 lotto game.

A person who purchases 50 lotto tickets each week is likely to win the jackpot about once every 5000 years.

You are 120 times more likely to have your luggage lost than to exactly match all 4 numbers in a pick-4 lotto game.

Objectives

● Solve problems involving combinations.

● Solve problems by distinguishing between permutations and combinations.

Why *The combination formula can be used to determine the chances of winning a lottery. The results may surprise you.*

Recall from Lesson 10.2 that a permutation is an arrangement of objects in a specific order. An arrangement of objects in which order is *not* important is called a **combination**.

In the Activity below, you can see the distinction between a permutation and a combination and learn how to count combinations.

Comparing Combinations and Permutations

APPLICATION
LOTTERY

You will need: no special tools

Consider a state lottery in which 3 numbers from 0 to 9 are selected. The numbers are not repeated. A lottery player can choose whether to play *exact match* or *any-order match*.

1. A person selects the numbers 8-4-1 and plays *exact match*. Write all of the ways that winning numbers can be drawn.

2. A person selects the numbers 8-4-1 and plays *any-order match*. Write all of the ways that winning numbers can be drawn.

3. Which has more ways to win: exact match or any-order match?

CHECKPOINT ✔ **4.** Explain why the prize is greater for winning with an exact match.

The number of ways to listen to 2 of 5 CDs is $_5P_2 = 5 \times 4 = 20$. If you want to find the number of ways to purchase 2 of 5 CDs, their order does not matter. For example, choosing to purchase CD #1 and then CD #2 is no different than choosing CD #2 and then CD #1 because they are *combined* in the total purchase. To find the number of *combinations* of 2 CDs taken from 5 CDs, divide $_5P_2$ by 2 to compensate for duplicate combinations.

Notice that the formula for $_nC_r$ below is like the formula for $_nP_r$, except that it contains the factor $r!$ to compensate for duplicate combinations.

Combinations of *n* Objects Taken *r* at a Time

The number of combinations of *n* objects taken *r* at a time, is given by

$$C(n, r) = {}_nC_r = \binom{n}{r} = \frac{n!}{r!(n-r)!}, \text{ where } 0 \leq r \leq n.$$

The notations $C(n, r)$, $_nC_r$, and $\binom{n}{r}$ have the same meaning. All are read as "*n* choose *r*." In this chapter, we will use the notation $_nC_r$.

EXAMPLE ① Find the number of ways to purchase 3 different kinds of juice from a selection of 10 different juices.

APPLICATION
SHOPPING

SOLUTION

The order in which the 3 juices are chosen is not important. Find the number of combinations of 10 objects taken 3 at a time.

$$_{10}C_3 = \frac{10!}{3!(10-3)!}$$

$$= \frac{10 \times 9 \times 8 \times 7!}{3! \times 7!}$$

$$= \frac{10 \times 9 \times 8}{3 \times 2 \times 1}$$

$$= 10 \times 3 \times 4$$

$$= 120$$

There are 120 ways to purchase 3 different kinds of juice from a selection of 10 different kinds.

TRY THIS Find the number of combinations of 9 objects taken 7 at a time.

CHECKPOINT ✔ Which is larger, $_{10}C_7$ or $_{10}P_7$? Does a given number of objects have more combinations or permutations? Explain.

When reading a problem, you need to determine whether the problem involves permutations or combinations.

EXAMPLE ②

Use a permutation or combination to answer each question.

a. How many ways are there to choose a committee of 3 people from a group of 5 people?

b. How many ways are there to choose 3 separate officeholders (chairperson, secretary, and treasurer) from a group of 5 people?

Westbrook High School
Green Team Environmental Committee
Choose 3 of the 5 nominees for the committee:
- ☐ Andrew Turner
- ☐ June Roberts
- ☐ Felipe Sanchez
- ☐ Vanessa Jackson
- ☐ Brandon Plummer

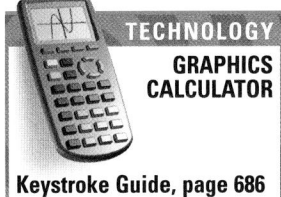

TECHNOLOGY
GRAPHICS CALCULATOR

Keystroke Guide, page 686

● **SOLUTION**

a. The members chosen for the committee will be members regardless of the order in which they are chosen. Find $_5C_3$.

$$_5C_3 = \frac{5!}{3!2!} = \frac{5 \times 4}{2} = 10$$

There are 10 ways to choose a committee of 3 people from a group of 5 people.

b. The officeholders are chosen to fulfill particular positions. Therefore, order is important. Find $_5P_3$.

$$_5P_3 = \frac{5!}{2!} = 5 \times 4 \times 3 = 60$$

There are 60 ways to choose a chairperson, a secretary, and a treasurer from a group of 5 people.

TRY THIS How many ways are there to choose a committee of 2 people from a group of 7 people? How many ways are there to choose a chairperson and a co-chairperson from a group of 7 people?

EXAMPLE ③

How many different ways are there to purchase 2 CDs, 3 cassettes, and 1 videotape if there are 7 CD titles, 5 cassette titles, and 3 videotape titles from which to choose?

● **SOLUTION**

Consider the CDs, cassettes, and videotapes separately, and apply the Fundamental Counting Principle.

Chose 1 videotape from 3 titles.

Chose 2 CDs from 7 titles.

$$_7C_2 \times {}_5C_3 \times {}_3C_1 = \frac{7!}{2!\,5!} \times \frac{5!}{3!\,2!} \times \frac{3!}{1!\,2!}$$

Chose 3 cassettes from 5 titles.

$$= 21 \times 10 \times 3$$
$$= 630$$

There are 630 different ways to make the purchase.

TRY THIS How many different ways are there to purchase 3 CDs, 4 cassettes, and 2 videotapes if there are 3 CD titles, 6 cassette titles, and 4 videotape titles from which to choose?

Using Combinations and Probability

Recall from Lesson 10.1 that you can find the probability of event A by using the following ratio:

$$P(A) = \frac{\text{number of outcomes in event } A}{\text{number of outcomes in the sample space}}$$

In many situations, you can find and evaluate the numerator and the denominator by applying the formula for combinations.

E X A M P L E **4** In a recent survey of 25 voters, 17 favor a new city regulation and 8 oppose it.

APPLICATION
SURVEYS

Find the probability that in a random sample of 6 respondents from this survey, exactly 2 favor the proposed regulation and 4 oppose it.

Survey of 25 people

17 favor	8 oppose
2 of 17	4 of 8

● **SOLUTION**

1. Find the number of outcomes in the event. Use the Fundamental Counting Principle.

$${}_{17}C_2 \times {}_8C_4$$

Choose 2 respondents of 17 respondents who favor.

Choose 4 respondents of 8 respondents who oppose.

2. Find the number of outcomes in the sample space.

$${}_{25}C_6 \quad \Longleftarrow \quad \textit{Choose 6 people from the 25 respondents.}$$

3. Find the probability.

$$\frac{\text{number of outcomes in event } A}{\text{number of outcomes in the sample space}} = \frac{{}_{17}C_2 \times {}_8C_4}{{}_{25}C_6} \approx 0.05$$

TECHNOLOGY
GRAPHICS CALCULATOR

Keystroke Guide, page 686

Thus, the probability of selecting exactly 2 respondents who favor the proposed regulation and 4 who oppose it in a randomly selected group of 6 respondents is about 0.05, or 5%.

```
(17 nCr 2)*(8 nC
r 4)/(25 nCr 6)
        .0537549407
```

TRY THIS Find the probability that in a random sample of 10 respondents from the above survey, all 10 favor the proposed regulation.

CRITICAL THINKING Sets A and B are two nonoverlapping sets. Set A contains a distinct objects and set B contains b distinct objects. You wish to choose x objects randomly from both set A and set B. Find the probability of choosing r objects from set A and s objects from set B. Are there any restrictions on r and s?

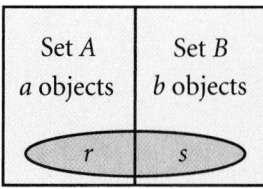

Set A a objects	Set B b objects
r	s

Exercises

Communicate

1. Describe the difference between a combination and a permutation. Give examples to illustrate your descriptions.

2. Describe the relationship between $_5P_3$ and $_5C_3$. Then explain how the formula for combinations is related to the formula for permutations.

3. Using the definition of a combination and the values for $_8C_8$ and $_8C_1$, find and describe $_nC_n$ and $_nC_1$ for any whole number n.

Guided Skills Practice

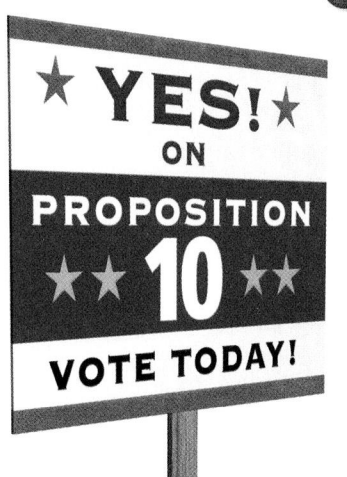

4. Find the number of ways to rent 4 comedy videos from a collection of 9 comedy videos. *(EXAMPLE 1)*

5. **Use a permutation or combination to answer each question.** *(EXAMPLE 2)*
   a. How many ways are there to choose a committee of 3 from a group of 12 people?
   b. How many ways are there to choose 3 separate officeholders (chairperson, secretary, and treasurer) from a group of 12 people?

6. How many different ways are there to purchase 3 CDs, 4 cassettes, and 2 videotapes if there are 8 CD titles, 5 cassette titles, and 5 videotape titles from which to choose? *(EXAMPLE 3)*

7. A survey of 30 people showed that 19 people favor a new city regulation and that 11 people oppose it. Find the probability that in a random sample of 8 respondents from the survey, exactly 3 favor the proposed regulation and 5 oppose it. *(EXAMPLE 4)*

Practice and Apply

Find the value of each expression.

8. $_7C_4$ **9.** $_8C_4$ **10.** $_{10}C_7$ **11.** $_9C_5$

12. $_9C_1$ **13.** $_{11}C_1$ **14.** $_{15}C_{15}$ **15.** $_{12}C_{12}$

16. $\dfrac{6!}{2!4!} \times \dfrac{5!}{4!1!}$ **17.** $\dfrac{4!}{3!1!} \times \dfrac{9!}{5!4!}$ **18.** $\dfrac{_6C_5 \times _{15}C_2}{_{21}C_7}$ **19.** $\dfrac{_{14}C_5 \times _9C_7}{_{23}C_{12}}$

Find the number of ways in which each committee can be selected.

20. 3 people from a group of 5   **21.** 7 people from a group of 8

22. 8 people from a group of 12   **23.** 6 people from a group of 10

24. How many different 12-member juries can be chosen from a pool of 32 people?

25. A test consists of 20 questions, and students are told to answer 15 of them. In how many different ways can they choose the 15 questions?

A pizza parlor offers a selection of 3 different cheeses and 9 different toppings. In how many ways can a pizza be made with the following ingredients?

26. 1 cheese and 3 toppings

27. 1 cheese and 4 toppings

28. 2 cheeses and 4 toppings

29. 2 cheeses and 3 toppings

A bag contains 5 white marbles and 3 green marbles. Find the probability of selecting each combination.

30. 1 green and 1 white

31. 2 green and 1 white

32. 2 green and 2 white

33. 3 green and 2 white

For Exercises 34–38, determine whether each situation involves a permutation or a combination.

34. Four recipes were selected for publication and 302 recipes were submitted.

35. Nine players are selected from a team of 15 to start the softball game.

36. Four out of 200 contestants were awarded prizes of $100, $75, $50, and $25.

37. A president and vice-president are elected for a class of 210 students.

38. The batting order for the 9 starting players is announced.

39. a. Find the number of different 5-card hands that can be dealt from a standard deck of 52 playing cards.
   b. Find the probability that 4 kings and a queen are randomly drawn from a standard deck of 52 playing cards.

internet connect

Homework Help Online

Go To: **go.hrw.com**
Keyword:
MB1 Homework Help
 for Exercises 34–39

CHALLENGE

40. Use the formula for $_nC_r$ to verify each statement below.
   a. $_nC_n = 1$ for all positive integer values of n
   b. $_nC_1 = n$ for all positive integer values of n
   c. $_nC_0 = 1$ for all positive integer values of n
   d. $_nC_r = {_nC_{n-r}}$ for all positive integer values of n and r, where $0 \le r \le n$
   e. Give an intuitive explanation for your answers to parts **a–d**.

41. CULTURAL CONNECTION: ASIA Around 600 B.C.E. in the Vedic period of Indian history, a writer named Sushruta found all combinations of the 6 different tastes: bitter, sour, salty, astringent, sweet, and hot. How many total combinations of the tastes are possible when taken 1 at a time, 2 at a time, etc?

APPLICATION

42. HEALTH From a group of 10 joggers and 15 nonjoggers, a university researcher will choose 5 people to participate in a study of heart disease.
   a. In how many ways can this be done if it does not matter how many of those chosen are joggers and how many are nonjoggers?
   b. In how many ways can this be done if exactly 3 joggers must be chosen?
   c. Find the probability that exactly 3 of the 5 people randomly selected from the group are joggers.

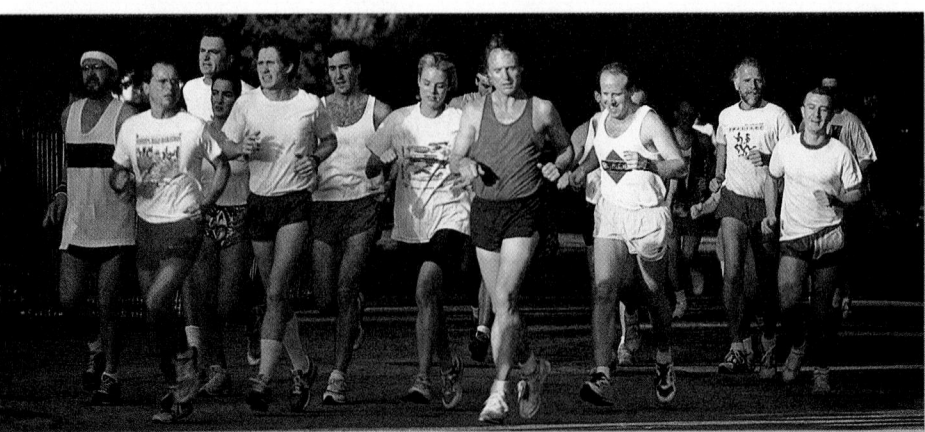

43. LOTTERY In many lotteries, contestants choose 6 out of 50 numbers (without replacement).

a. Find the probability of winning this kind of lottery with one set of numbers.

b. Determine how many times more likely than winning the lottery it is for each of the events in the table at left to occur.

Event (applies to U.S. population)	Experimental probability
Undergo an audit by the IRS this year	$\frac{1}{100}$
Being hit by lightning	$\frac{1}{9100}$
Being hit by a baseball in a major league game	$\frac{1}{300,000}$

[*Source: Les Krantz*, What the Odds Are, *Harper Perennial, 1992*]

 Look Back

BUSINESS A movie theater charges $5 for adults and $3 for children. The theater needs to sell at least $2500 worth of tickets to cover expenses. Graph the solution for each situation below. *(LESSON 3.3)*

44. The theater fails to sell at least $2500 worth of tickets.
45. The theater breaks even, selling exactly $2500 worth of tickets.
46. The theater makes a profit, selling more that $2500 worth of tickets.

Graph the solution to each inequality. *(LESSON 5.8)*

47. $y \leq x^2 - 5$ **48.** $y \geq (x + 1)^2$ **49.** $y < (x - 1)^2 + 3$

internet connect

Portfolio Extension

Go To: **go.hrw.com**
Keyword:
MB1 Combinations

 Look Beyond

50. A governor appointed 5 department heads from a group of people that consisted of 8 acquaintances and 22 others. Assuming that all choices are equally likely, find the probability of each event below.
   a. All 5 were acquaintances.
   b. Exactly 4 of the 5 were acquaintances.
   c. At least 3 of the 5 were acquaintances.

Refer to Example 4 on page 646. Assign numbers from 1 to 25 to the survey respondents. Let the numbers from 1 to 17 represent the people who favor the new city regulation, and let the numbers from 18 to 25 represent the people who oppose it.

1. Generate 6 random integers from 1 to 25 inclusive. (Refer to page 687 of the Keystroke Guide.) This represents a random sample of 6 respondents. Repeat this generation of 6 random integers for a total of 30 trials. Record the outcomes.

2. For the 30 trials, count the total number of times that exactly 2 of the 6 random integers were between 1 and 17 inclusive. Use your outcomes to approximate the probability

that exactly 2 of the 6 respondents chosen favor the proposed regulation.

3. Compare your approximate probability with the theoretical probability obtained in the lesson. How well do you think the random-number generator models this problem? Explain.

WORKING ON THE CHAPTER PROJECT
You should now be able to complete Activity 2 of the Chapter Project.

Let's Make a Deal

BY MARILYN VOS SAVANT

Ask Marilyn®

Y ou have reached the final round of a TV game show called *Let's Make a Deal*. Behind one of the three numbered doors is a new car. Behind each of the other two doors is a goat. You have chosen door number 1. The host, Monty Hall, knows what's behind each door. He opens door number 3 to show you a goat.

Behind one of these doors is a new car.

Should you stick with number 1 or switch to number 2?

Suppose you're on a game show, and you're given the choice of three doors: Behind one door is a car; behind the others, goats. You pick a door, say No. 1, and the host, who knows what's behind the doors, opens another door, say No. 3, which has a goat. He then says to you, "Do you want to pick door No. 2?" Is it to your advantage to switch your choice?

—Craig F. Whitaker, Columbus, Md.

Then he pops the question: "Do you want to change your mind?"

What would you do? Would you stick with door number 1 or switch to door number 2?

Many contestants faced such a dilemma on the show, which ran for over 25 years. In 1990, a question based on this situation was submitted to a columnist, Marilyn vos Savant, who is reported to have the highest IQ in the world.

Yes; you should switch. The first door has a one-third chance of winning, but the second door has a two-thirds chance. Here's a good way to visualize what happened. Suppose there are a million doors, and you pick door No. 1. Then the host, who knows what's behind the doors and will always avoid the one with the prize, opens them all except door #777,777. You'd switch to that door pretty fast, wouldn't you?

By permission of Parade, *copyright* ©*1990*

Nearly a year later, an article in the *New York Times* reported that Marilyn vos Savant had received about 10,000 letters in response to her answer. Most of the letters disagreed with her. Many came from mathematicians and scientists with arguments like this:

...You blew it! Let me explain: If one door is shown to be a loser, that information changes the probability of either remaining choice—neither of which has any reason to be more likely—to ½. As a professional mathematician, I'm very concerned with the general public's lack of mathematical skills. Please help by confessing your error and, in the future, being more careful...

Cooperative Learning

1. Before you analyze the problem in detail, explain which strategy you think is best and why.

2. Make three cards (two goats, one car) to model the situation. Try 10 games in which you stick with your choice. Then try 10 games in which you switch. Compare the results.

3. Make a table with the column headings shown, and complete it using all possible options. According to your table, should you switch? Explain.

4. Suppose that you wrote the response for Marilyn vos Savant's column. How would you answer the question about the game show?

Door with car	Door you choose	Door you are shown	Result if you switch	Result if you stick
1	1	2 or 3	Lose	Win
1	2	3	Win	Lose
1				
2				
⋮				

Using Addition With Probability

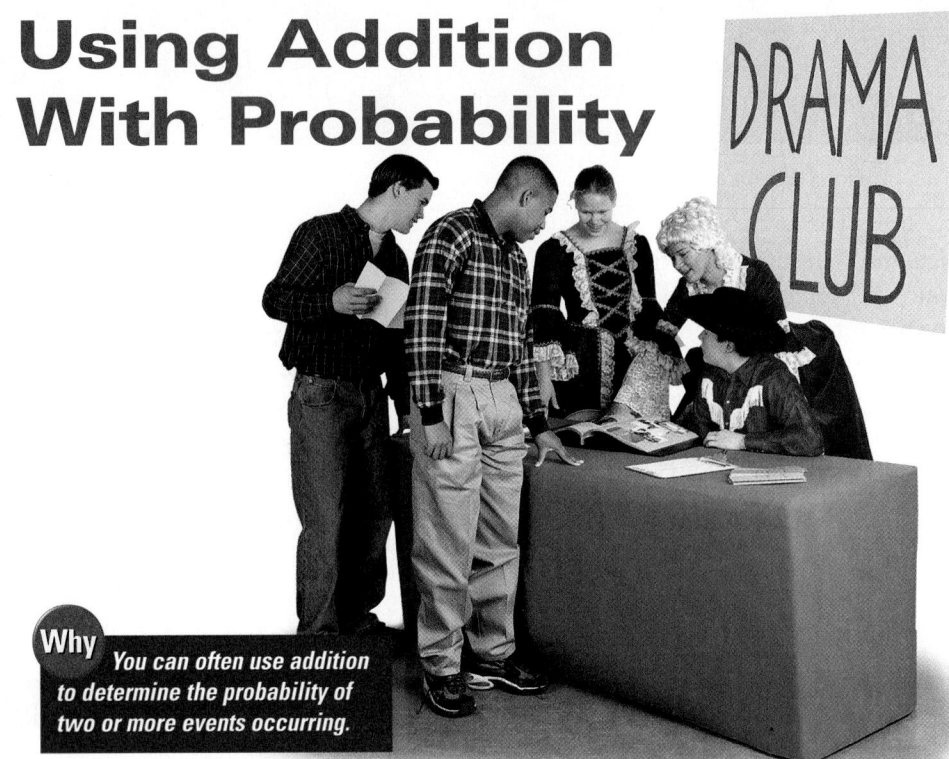

DRAMA CLUB

Objectives

● Find the probabilities of mutually exclusive events.

● Find the probabilities of inclusive events.

Why *You can often use addition to determine the probability of two or more events occurring.*

The drama, mathematics, and jazz clubs at Gloverdale High School have 32 members, 33 members, and 39 members, respectively. Some club members belong to more than one club, as indicated in the diagram at right. What is the probability that a randomly selected club member belongs to at least two clubs? *You will answer this question in Example 3.*

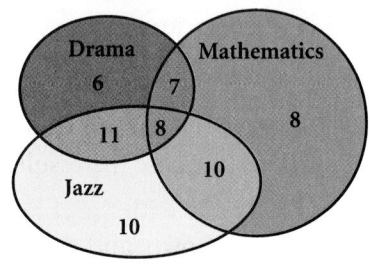

Events that can occur at the same time are called **inclusive events.** For example, a student can belong to more than one club at the same time.

Events that cannot occur at the same time are called **mutually exclusive events.** For example, if you flip a coin, you cannot get *both* heads and tails.

Activity
Exploring Two-Event Probabilities

You will need: a pair of number cubes, preferably of two different colors

1. Copy and complete the following table by rolling two number cubes 10 times:

Toss	1st cube	2nd cube	Sum	Product
1				
2				
3				
⋮				

2. Using your 10 trials, copy and complete the table of experimental probabilities for each pair of events listed below.

	a.	b.	c.
$P(A)$			
$P(B)$			
$P(A \text{ or } B)$			
$P(A) + P(B)$			

  a. Let A be the event that the first cube is a 6 and let B be the event the first cube is a 3.
  b. Let A be the event that the first cube is a 6 and let B be the event that the sum is 7.
  c. Let A be the event that the sum is less than 5 and let B be the event that the product is greater than 5.

CHECKPOINT ✔ 3. Based on your results, does $P(A \text{ or } B) = P(A) + P(B)$? When can you be sure that this statement is true?

Mutually exclusive events and inclusive events are illustrated below with a number cube.

Mutually exclusive events	**Inclusive events**

Let A represent an even number.

 $P(A) = \frac{3}{6}$

Let A represent an even number.

 $P(A) = \frac{3}{6}$

Let B represent 3.

 $P(B) = \frac{1}{6}$

Let C represent 4.

 $P(C) = \frac{1}{6}$

P(an even number *or* 3)

 $P(A \text{ or } B)$

P(an even number *or* 4)

 $P(A \text{ or } C)$

Because A and B are mutually exclusive events, you can add $P(A)$ and $P(B)$ to find $P(A \text{ or } B)$.

$$P(A \text{ or } B) = \frac{3}{6} + \frac{1}{6} = \frac{4}{6}, \text{ or } \frac{2}{3}$$

Because A and C are inclusive events, you must *subtract* $P(A \text{ and } C)$ from the sum of $P(A)$ and $P(C)$ to find $P(A \text{ or } C)$.

$$P(A \text{ or } C) = \frac{3}{6} + \frac{1}{6} - \frac{1}{6} = \frac{3}{6}, \text{ or } \frac{1}{2}$$

A or B, exclusive

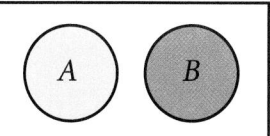

Sample space

A or B, inclusive

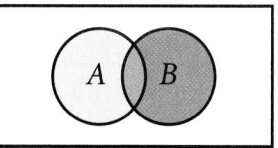

Sample space

Probability of *A or B*

Let A and B represent events in the same sample space.

If A and B are mutually exclusive events, then
$$P(A \text{ or } B) = P(A) + P(B).$$

If A and B are inclusive events, then
$$P(A \text{ or } B) = P(A) + P(B) - P(A \text{ and } B).$$

CHECKPOINT ✔ Which formula for $P(A \text{ or } B)$ can be used with any events A and B in the same sample space? Why?

EXAMPLE ❶ In a survey about a change in public policy, 100 people were asked if they favor the change, oppose the change, or have no opinion about the change. The responses are indicated at right.

APPLICATION
SURVEYS

	Men	Women	Total
Favor	18	9	27
Oppose	12	25	37
No opinion	20	16	36
Total	50	50	100

Find the probability that a randomly selected respondent to the survey opposes *or* has no opinion about the change in policy.

● **SOLUTION**

The events "oppose" and "no opinion" are mutually exclusive events.

P(oppose *or* no opinion) = P(oppose) + P(no opinion)

$$= \frac{37}{100} + \frac{36}{100}$$

$$= \frac{73}{100}, \text{ or } 73\%$$

The probability that a respondent opposes the change *or* has no opinion is 73%.

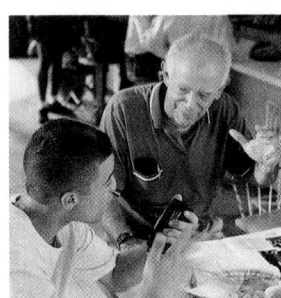

TRY THIS   Find the probability that a randomly selected respondent to this survey favors *or* has no opinion about the change in policy.

EXAMPLE ❷ Refer to the survey results given in Example 1.

Find the probability that a randomly selected respondent to the survey is a man *or* opposes the change in policy.

APPLICATION
SURVEYS

● **SOLUTION**

The events "man" and "opposes" are inclusive events.

P(man *or* opposes) = P(man) + (opposes) − P(man *and* opposes)

$$= \frac{50}{100} + \frac{37}{100} - \frac{12}{100}$$

$$= \frac{75}{100}, \text{ or } 75\%$$

The probability that a respondent is a man *or* opposes the change is 75%.

TRY THIS   Find the probability that a randomly selected respondent to this survey is a woman *or* has no opinion about the change in policy.

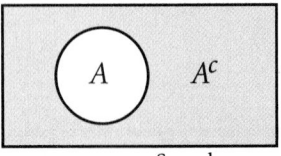

Sample space

The **complement** of event A consists of all outcomes in the sample space that are not in A and is denoted by A^c. For example, let A be the event "favor." Then the complement A^c is the event "oppose" *or* "no opinion." Conversely, if A is the event "oppose" *or* "no opinion," then A^c is the event "favor." The sum of the probabilities of all of the outcomes in a sample space is 1. Thus, $P(A) + P(A^c) = 1$.

CHECKPOINT ✔   Refer to the survey results given in Example 1. Let A be the event "favor." Verify that $P(A) + P(A^c) = 1$ is true.

Probability of the Complement of A

Let A represent an event in the sample space.

$$P(A) + P(A^c) = 1 \qquad P(A) = 1 - P(A^c) \qquad P(A^c) = 1 - P(A)$$

CRITICAL THINKING

Let A be any event in a sample space. Why is $P(A \text{ or } A^c) = P(A) + P(A^c)$ true? Explain how this equation leads to the equations in the box above.

EXAMPLE ③ The drama, mathematics, and jazz clubs have 32 members, 33 members, and 39 members, respectively.

APPLICATION
EXTRACURRICULAR
ACTIVITIES

Find the probability that a randomly selected club member belongs to at least two clubs.

● **SOLUTION**

Let A represent membership in exactly one club. Then A^c represents membership in two or three clubs.

$$P(A^c) = 1 - P(A)$$
$$P(A^c) = 1 - \frac{6 + 8 + 10}{60}$$
$$= \frac{36}{60}$$
$$= 0.6$$

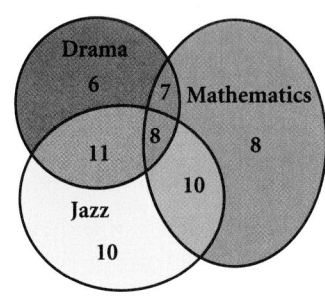

The probability that a randomly selected club member belongs to at least two clubs is 60%.

TRY THIS

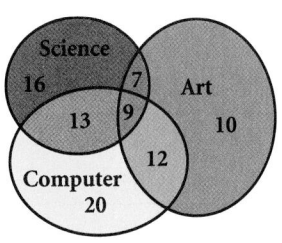

The science, art, and computer clubs have 45 members, 38 members, and 54 members, respectively. Some club members belong to more than one club, as indicated in the diagram at left. Find the probability that one of these club members selected at random will belong to more than one club.

Exercises

● *Communicate*

1. Explain the meaning of mutually exclusive events and of inclusive events. Give examples of each.

2. Describe how to find the complement of the event "rolling 1" *or* "rolling 2" on a number cube.

3. Explain how to find the probability of "rolling an odd number" *or* "rolling 3" on a number cube.

Guided Skills Practice

For Exercises 4 and 5, refer to the results of the survey about a change in public policy given on page 654.

4. Find the probability that a randomly selected respondent to the survey favors *or* opposes the change in policy. *(EXAMPLE 1)*

5. Find the probability that a randomly selected respondent to the survey is a man *or* favors the change in policy. *(EXAMPLE 2)*

APPLICATION

6. **EDUCATION** The economics, computer, and anatomy classes have 28 students, 29 students, and 24 students, respectively. Some students are taking more than one of these classes, as indicated in the diagram at right. Find the probability that a randomly selected student from these classes is taking at least two of the classes. *(EXAMPLE 3)*

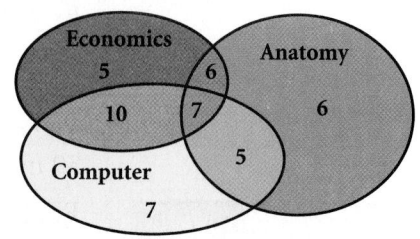

Practice and Apply

A number cube is rolled once, and the number on the top face is recorded. Find the probability of each event.

7. 5 *or* 6

8. 1 *or* 4

9. even *or* 3

10. odd *or* 2

11. less than 4 *or* 1

12. greater than 2 *or* 6

13. not 1

14. not even

15. even *or* odd

Homework Help Online

Go To: **go.hrw.com**
Keyword:
MB1 Homework Help
for Exercises 16–27

The table at right shows all of the possible outcomes of rolling two number cubes. Using the table, state whether the events in each pair below are inclusive or mutually exclusive. Then find the probability of each pair of events.

(1, 1)	(1, 2)	(1, 3)	(1, 4)	(1, 5)	(1, 6)
(2, 1)	(2, 2)	(2, 3)	(2, 4)	(2, 5)	(2, 6)
(3, 1)	(3, 2)	(3, 3)	(3, 4)	(3, 5)	(3, 6)
(4, 1)	(4, 2)	(4, 3)	(4, 4)	(4, 5)	(4, 6)
(5, 1)	(5, 2)	(5, 3)	(5, 4)	(5, 5)	(5, 6)
(6, 1)	(6, 2)	(6, 3)	(6, 4)	(6, 5)	(6, 6)

16. a sum of 2 *or* a sum of 4

17. a sum of 8 *or* a sum of 12

18. a sum of less than 3 *or* a sum of greater than 5

19. a sum of less than 7 *or* a sum of greater than 8

20. a sum of greater than 2 *or* a sum of greater than 6

21. a sum of less than 3 *or* a sum of less than 10

22. a sum of greater than 4 *or* a sum of less than 7

23. a sum of greater than 5 *or* a sum of less than 8

24. a product of greater than 8 *or* a product of less than 6

25. a product of greater than 16 *or* a product of less than 9

26. a product of greater than 6 *or* a product of less than 8

27. a product of greater than 9 *or* a product of less than 16

28. a. How many integers from 1 to 600 are divisible by 2 or by 3?
   b. Find the probability that a random integer from 1 to 600 is divisible by neither 2 nor 3.

29. a. How many integers from 1 to 3500 are divisible by 5 or by 7?
   b. Find the probability that a random integer from 1 to 3500 is divisible by neither 5 nor 7.

For Exercises 30–35, use the given probability to find $P(E^c)$.

30. $P(E) = \frac{1}{3}$ **31.** $P(E) = \frac{4}{11}$ **32.** $P(E) = 0.782$

33. $P(E) = 0.324$ **34.** $P(E) = 0$ **35.** $P(E) = 1$

Find the probability of each event.

36. 2 heads *or* 2 tails appearing in 2 tosses of a coin

37. 3 heads *or* 2 tails appearing in 3 tosses of a coin

38. at least 2 heads appearing in 3 tosses of a coin

39. at least 3 heads appearing in 4 tosses of a coin

CHALLENGE

40. A number cube is rolled 3 times. Find the probability of getting at least one 4.

41. In a group of 300 people surveyed, 46 like only cola A, 23 like only cola B, 18 like only cola C, 80 like both colas A and B, 66 like both colas A and C, 45 like both colas B and C, and 12 like all three colas. Find the probability that a randomly selected person from this survey likes none of these colas.

CONNECTION

42. GEOMETRY A circle with a radius of 3 and a 6×6 square are positioned inside a 10×10 square so that the top edge of the 6×6 square forms a diameter of the circle, as shown at right. A point inside the 10×10 square is selected at random. Find the probability of each event below.
   a. The point is within the circle.
   b. The point is within the 6×6 square.
   c. The point is within the 6×6 square *and* within the circle.
   d. The point is within the 6×6 square *or* within the circle.

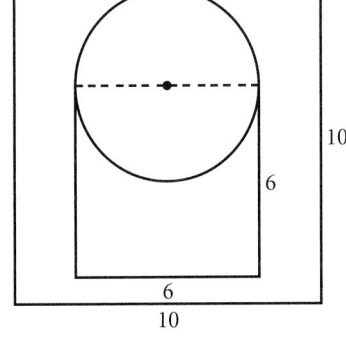

APPLICATION

POLITICS The table shows the composition of the 106th Congress of the United States (1999–2001) according to political party.

Find the probability that a randomly selected member of Congress is the following:

43. a House Democrat *or* a Senate Republican

44. a House Republican *or* a Senate Democrat

45. a Democrat *or* a Senator

46. a Republican *or* a Senator

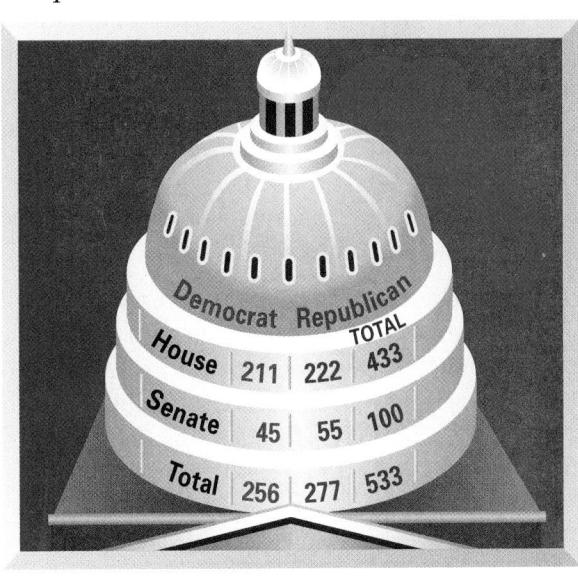

	Democrat	Republican	TOTAL
House	211	222	433
Senate	45	55	100
Total	256	277	533

47. QUALITY CONTROL A box contains 35 machine parts, 8 of which are defective. A quality control inspector randomly selects 5 of the 35 parts for testing. What is the probability that at least one part is defective?

PRODUCTION **A shipment of 20 sets of skateboard wheels contains 7 sets that have a new type of wheel surface.**

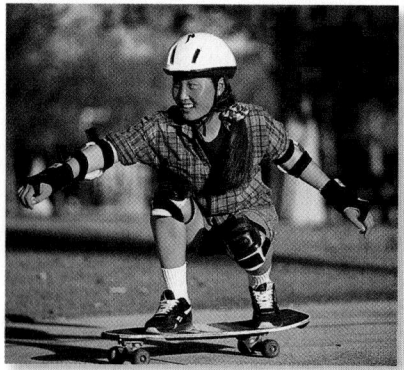

48. What is the probability that if 5 sets are chosen, at least 1 set will have the new surface?

49. What is the probability that if 5 sets are chosen, at least 2 sets will have the new surface?

 Look Back

Graph each inequality in a coordinate plane. *(LESSON 3.4)*

50. $8 > x > 3$

51. $-6 \leq x \leq -2$

52. $3 > y > -1$

Factor each quadratic trinomial. *(LESSON 5.3)*

53. $x^2 - x - 42$

54. $3x^2 - 16x - 12$

55. $81x^2 + 18x + 1$

Solve each equation. Check your solutions. *(LESSON 8.5)*

56. $\frac{x+2}{x} + 3 = \frac{x+6}{x}$

57. $\frac{3}{x-2} + x = \frac{17}{2}$

58. $\frac{2y+5}{3y-2} = \frac{4y+3}{6y-1}$

 Look Beyond

59. If a card is drawn at random from a standard 52-card deck, what is the probability that the card is an ace? If a card is drawn at random from a standard deck and you are told that the card is a spade, does the probability that it is an ace change? Explain.

 PORTFOLIO ACTIVITY

Let the sum of two random integers from 1 to 6 inclusive represent the sum of the roll of two number cubes.

1. Generate two random integers from 1 to 6 for a total of 40 trials. (Refer to the Keystroke Guide for Example 3 on page 687.) Record the outcomes.

2. Use your outcomes to estimate the probability of rolling "a sum of 7" *or* "a sum of 11." Describe how your results compare with the theoretical probability of rolling "a sum of 7" *or* "a sum of 11."

3. Perform another 40 trials for this experiment. Record the outcomes.

4. Use the outcomes of all 80 trials to estimate the probability of rolling "a sum of 7" *or* "a sum of 11." Compare your results with the theoretical probability of rolling "a sum of 7" *or* "a sum of 11." Describe what happens to your estimated probability as the number of trials increases.

WORKING ON THE CHAPTER PROJECT

You should now be able to complete the Chapter Project.

Independent Events

10.5

Objective

- Find the probability of two or more independent events.

Why *You can use the probability of independent events to find many interesting probabilities, such as the probability that two people at a party have the same birthday.*

In a group of 35 individuals, what is the probability that 2 or more individuals have the same birth month and day? *You will answer this question in Example 3.*

To answer this question, you need to know how to identify *independent* and *dependent events* and how to find probabilities of independent events. In the Activity below, you will investigate independent events.

Activity

Investigating Independent Events

You will need: no special tools

1. Let event *A* be the outcome of tossing heads on a coin. Find $P(A)$.

2. Let event *B* be the outcome of rolling a 3 on a number cube. Find $P(B)$.

3. Does event *A* have an effect on event *B*? Does event *B* have an effect on event *A*? Explain.

4. List all of the possible combinations for tossing a coin and rolling a number cube. Find the probability that both event *A and* event *B* occur, or $P(A \text{ and } B)$.

5. Find $P(A) \times P(B)$. Does $P(A \text{ and } B)$ equal $P(A) \times P(B)$?

6. Let even *C* be the outcome of rolling an odd number on a number cube. Find $P(C)$.

7. Find $P(A \text{ and } C)$ by using your list from Step 4. Does $P(A \text{ and } C)$ equal $P(A) \times P(C)$?

CHECKPOINT ✔ 8. What can you say about the probability that two events will both occur if they have no effect on one another?

Two events are **independent** if the occurrence or non-occurrence of one event has no effect on the likelihood of the occurrence of the other event. For example, tossing two coins is an example of a pair of independent events. If one event does affect the occurrence of the other event, the events are **dependent**.

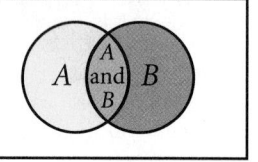
Sample space

Probability of Independent Events

Events A and B are independent events if and only if $P(A \text{ and } B) = P(A) \times P(B)$. Otherwise, A and B are dependent events.

EXAMPLE ① Bag A contains 9 red marbles and 3 green marbles. Bag B contains 9 black marbles and 6 orange marbles.

Find the probability of selecting one green marble from bag A and one black marble from bag B in one draw from each bag.

● **SOLUTION**

Bag A

$P(\text{green marble}) = \dfrac{3}{9+3} = \dfrac{3}{12} = \dfrac{1}{4}$

Bag B

$P(\text{black marble}) = \dfrac{9}{9+6} = \dfrac{9}{15} = \dfrac{3}{5}$

The events are independent.

$$P(\text{green marble } and \text{ black marble}) = \dfrac{1}{4} \times \dfrac{3}{5} = \dfrac{3}{20}$$

The probability of selecting a green marble from bag A and a black marble from bag B in one draw from each bag is 0.15, or 15%.

EXAMPLE ② Two seniors, one from each government class, are to be randomly selected to travel to Washington, D.C. John is in a class of 18 students, and Peter is in another class of 20 students.

Find the probability that both John and Peter will be selected.

● **SOLUTION**

Event A
The probability that John will be chosen is $\dfrac{1}{18}$.

Event B
The probability that Peter will be chosen is $\dfrac{1}{20}$.

Events A and B are independent events.

$$P(A \text{ and } B) = P(A) \times P(B)$$
$$= \dfrac{1}{18} \times \dfrac{1}{20} = \dfrac{1}{360},$$
$$\text{or about } 0.003$$

The probability that both John and Peter will be selected is about 0.3%.

WASHINGTON, D.C.

The formula for the probability of independent events can be extended to 3 or more events. For example, the probability of obtaining 3 heads in 3 tosses of a coin is $\frac{1}{2} \times \frac{1}{2} \times \frac{1}{2} = \frac{1}{8} = 0.125$, or 12.5%.

CRITICAL THINKING

Find the probability of obtaining 4 heads in 4 tosses of a coin. Write a formula for the probability of obtaining n heads in n tosses of a coin.

E X A M P L E ❸ Refer to the birthday problem described at the beginning of the lesson.

What is the probability that in a group of 35 people, 2 or more people have the same birth month and day?

APPLICATION
ENTERTAINMENT

● **SOLUTION**

PROBLEM SOLVING

Change your point of view. Use the complementary event, which is that all birthdays are different. Use 365 days for a year (ignoring leap years).

The first person's birthday can be any day. $\frac{365}{365}$

The second person's birthday cannot be the same day. $\frac{364}{365}$

The third person's birthday cannot be the same day as either the first or the second person's. $\frac{363}{365}$

Continue this pattern for all 35 individuals. The probability that all individuals have different birthdays is as follows:

$$P(\text{different birthday}) = \frac{365}{365} \times \frac{364}{365} \times \frac{363}{365} \times \cdots \times \frac{331}{365} \approx 0.19$$

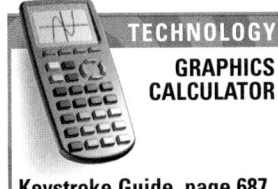
TECHNOLOGY
GRAPHICS CALCULATOR
Keystroke Guide, page 687

Find the probability that 2 or more individuals have the same birthday.
$$P(\text{same birthday}) = 1 - P(\text{different birthday})$$
$$\approx 1 - 0.19 \approx 0.81$$

The probability that 2 or more individuals have the same birth month and day is about 81%.

TRY THIS

What is the probability that in a group of 45 people, 2 or more people have the same birth month and day?

Exercises

● *Communicate*

1. Give an example of independent events and of dependent events.

2. Explain how to find the probability of two independent events occurring.

3. Explain the difference between mutually exclusive events and independent events. Give an example.

4. Bag A contains 5 black marbles and 5 white marbles. Bag B contains 1 green marble and 2 red marbles. Find the probability of selecting a black marble from bag A and a green marble from bag B in two draws. *(EXAMPLE 1)*

5. Two students, one from each science class, are to be randomly selected to attend a national science conference. Melinda is in a class of 22 students, and Seth is in another class of 19 students. Find the probability that both Melinda and Seth will be selected. *(EXAMPLE 2)*

6. What is the probability that in a group of 40 people, 2 or more people have the same birth month and day? *(EXAMPLE 3)*

• *Practice and Apply* ▬▬▬▬▬▬▬▬▬▬▬▬▬

Events *A*, *B*, *C* and *D* are independent, and *P(A)* = 0.5, *P(B)* = 0.25, *P(C)* = 0.75, and *P(D)* = 0.1. Find each probability.

7. $P(A \text{ and } B)$ **8.** $P(A \text{ and } C)$ **9.** $P(C \text{ and } B)$

10. $P(C \text{ and } D)$ **11.** $P(A \text{ and } D)$ **12.** $P(B \text{ and } D)$

Use the definition of independent events to determine whether the events below are independent or dependent.

13. the event *even* and the event *2 or 4* on one roll of a number cube

14. the event *even* and the event *1 or 4* on one roll of a number cube

15. the event *less than 5* and the event *6* on one roll of a number cube

16. the event *greater than 3* and the event *4* on one roll of a number cube

☑ internet connect

Homework Help Online

Go To: **go.hrw.com**
Keyword:
MB1 Homework Help
for Exercises 17–20

Refer to the spinner shown below in which each numbered section is exactly $\frac{1}{8}$ of the circle. Find the probability of each event in three spins of the spinner.

17. All three numbers are 3 *or* greater than 5.

18. All three numbers are 4 *or* less than 6.

19. Exactly one number is 5 *or* less than 7.

20. Exactly one number is 8 *or* greater than 3.

21. Suppose that the probability of Kevin coming to a party is 80% and the probability of Judy coming to a party is 95%. Assuming that these events are independent, what is the probability that they both will come to a party?

22. The integers 1 through 15 are written on slips of paper and placed into a box. One slip is selected at random and put back into the box, and then another slip is chosen at random.
  a. What is the probability that the number 8 is selected both times?
  b. What is the probability that the number 8 is selected exactly once? (Hint: Find the probability that an 8 is selected on the first or second draw, but not on *both* draws.)

23. TRAVEL An airline's records show that its flights from Los Angeles to Dallas arrive on schedule 92% of the time. They also show that its flights from Dallas to Miami leave on schedule 97% of the time. If you fly from Los Angeles to Miami with a connection through Dallas, what is the probability that you will arrive at Dallas and leave from Dallas at your scheduled times?

A passenger checking flight information

SECURITY Suppose that a security system consists of four components: a motion detector, a glass-break detector, magnetic door and window contacts, and a video camera. The probabilities of escaping detection by each of the four devices are 0.2, 0.3, 0.4, and 0.6, respectively. Assume that all of the components act independently.

24. What is the probability that a thief can get past the magnetic contacts and the video camera?

25. What is the probability that a thief can get past the glass-break detector and the motion detector?

26. What is the probability that a thief can get past all four components?

 Look Back

Simplify each expression. Assume that no variable equals zero. *(LESSON 2.2)*

27. $(x^{-2}y^3)^2(3xy^0)^3$

28. $(2x^2y^{-2})^{-3}(-x^2y)^3$

29. $\left(\dfrac{3x^2y^{-2}}{5x^2y}\right)^2$

30. Find the maximum and minimum values of the objective function
$C = 2x + 3y$ given the constraints $\begin{cases} y \geq x \\ y \leq 5 \\ x \geq 0 \end{cases}$. *(LESSON 3.5)*

Solve each equation for *x*. Round your answers to the nearest hundredth. *(LESSONS 6.5 AND 6.6)*

31. $e^x = 3$

32. $5^x = 11$

33. $e^{x+1} = 9$

Write the standard equation of the parabola with the given characteristics. *(LESSON 9.2)*

34. vertex: $(3, 2)$
focus: $(4, 2)$

35. vertex: $(1, 0)$
directrix: $y = 4$

36. directrix: $x = -4$
focus: $(3, 0)$

Look Beyond

37. Three coins are tossed. What is the probability of 3 heads appearing given the conditions below?
 a. All three coins are regular, fair coins.
 b. One of the three coins is a two-headed coin.
 c. Two of the three coins are two-headed coins.

Dependent Events and Conditional Probability

Why *Conditional probability applies to many real-world situations in which the probability of one event is affected by the occurrence of another event.*

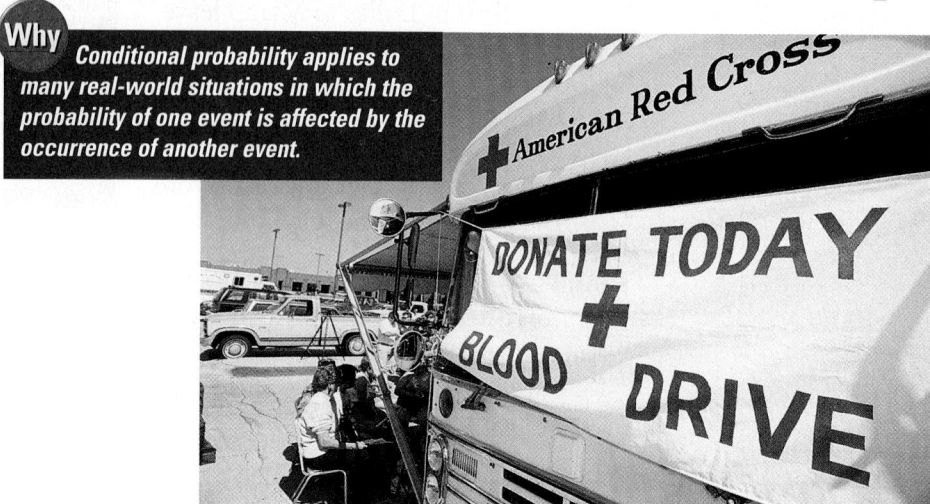

Objective

• Find conditional probabilities.

The ELISA test is used to screen donated blood for the presence of HIV antibodies. When HIV antibodies are present in the blood tested, ELISA gives a positive result 98% of the time. When HIV antibodies are not present in the blood tested, ELISA gives a positive result 7% of the time, which is called a *false positive*.

Suppose that 1 out of every 1000 units of donated blood actually contains HIV antibodies. What is the probability that a positive ELISA result is accurate? *You will answer this question in Example 4.*

To solve the problem above, you need to calculate a *conditional probability*. The Activity below will help you understand conditional probabilities.

Activity
Exploring Conditional Probability

You will need: no special materials

Suppose that you select a card at random from a standard deck of playing cards. (Note: In a standard deck of 52 playing cards, 12 cards are face cards, and 4 of the face cards are kings.)

1. Find the probability that the card drawn is a king.

2. Find the probability that the card drawn is a king if you know that the card is a face card.

3. Find the probability that the card drawn is a king if you know that 2 queens were previously removed from the deck.

4. Find the probability that the card drawn is a king if you know that 2 kings were previously removed from the deck.

CHECKPOINT ✔ 5. How does what you know in Steps 2 and 3 affect the resulting probabilities? How does what you know in Step 4 affect the resulting probability? Describe how probabilities can be affected by knowledge of a previous event.

Knowing the outcome of one event can affect the probability of another event.

EXAMPLE 1 The band at Villesdale High School has 50 members, and the student council has 20 members. Five student council members are also in the band. Suppose that a student is randomly selected from these two groups.

APPLICATION
EXTRACURRICULAR ACTIVITIES

Find the probability that the student is a member of the band if you know that he or she is on the student council.

● **SOLUTION**

Because the student is on the student council, the sample space is 20 members.

$$P(\text{band, given council}) = \frac{5}{20} = \frac{1}{4}$$

Thus, the probability that the student is also a member of the band is 25%.

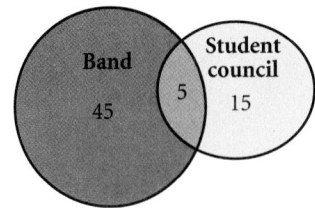

If a marble is selected from a bag of marbles and replaced and then a second marble is selected, the two selections are independent events. On the other hand, if a marble is selected from a bag of marbles and a second marble is selected *without* replacing the first marble, the second selection is a dependent event. That is, the probability of the second event changes, depending on the outcome of the first event.

EXAMPLE 2 A bag contains 9 red marbles and 3 green marbles. For each case below, find the probability of randomly selecting a red marble on the first draw and a green marble on the second draw.

  a. The first marble is replaced. **b.** The first marble is not replaced.

● **SOLUTION**

a. If the first marble is replaced before the second marble is selected, then the events are independent.

$$P(\text{red}) = \frac{9}{9+3} = \frac{9}{12} = \frac{3}{4}$$

$$P(\text{green}) = \frac{3}{9+3} = \frac{3}{12} = \frac{1}{4}$$

$$P(\text{red } and \text{ green}) = \frac{3}{4} \times \frac{1}{4} = \frac{3}{16}$$

The probability is $\frac{3}{16}$, or 18.75%.

b. If the first marble is *not* replaced before the second marble is selected, then the size of the sample space for the second event changes from 12 to 11.

$$P(\text{red}) = \frac{9}{9+3} = \frac{9}{12} = \frac{3}{4}$$

$$P(\text{green}) = \frac{3}{8+3} = \frac{3}{11}$$

$$P(\text{red } and \text{ green}) = \frac{3}{4} \times \frac{3}{11} = \frac{9}{44}$$

The probability is $\frac{9}{44}$, or about 20.5%.

The probability of event B, given that event A has happened (or will happen), is called *conditional probability*.

Conditional Probability

The **conditional probability** of event B, given event A, denoted by $P(B|A)$, is given by $P(B|A) = \frac{P(A \text{ and } B)}{P(A)}$, where $P(A) \neq 0$.

CHECKPOINT ✔ Use the conditional probability formula to verify the solution in Example 1.

Using the Multiplication Property of Equality, the conditional probability formula $P(B|A) = \frac{P(A \text{ and } B)}{P(A)}$ can be rewritten as $P(A) \times P(B|A) = P(A \text{ and } B)$. You can use this form to verify the solutions in Example 2, as shown below.

Independent Events	**Dependent Events**
The first marble is replaced.	The first marble is not replaced.
Event *A*: red first	Event *A*: red first
Event *B*: green second	Event *B*: green second
$P(A) \times P(B|A) = P(A \text{ and } B)$	$P(A) \times P(B|A) = P(A \text{ and } B)$
$\frac{3}{4} \times \frac{1}{4} = \frac{3}{16}$	$\frac{3}{4} \times \frac{3}{11} = \frac{9}{44}$

CHECKPOINT ✔ Explain why $P(B|A) = P(B)$ if *A* and *B* are independent events.

E X A M P L E ③

APPLICATION
CONTEST

In a school contest, a class (sophomore, junior, or senior) will be selected according to the probabilities listed at right. Then a student from that class will be randomly selected. The distribution of the possible contest winners is shown in the table.

$P(\text{sophomore}) = \frac{1}{4}$

$P(\text{junior}) = \frac{1}{4}$

$P(\text{senior}) = \frac{1}{2}$

Find the probability that a girl is selected.

	Girls	Boys	Total
Sophomores	10	13	23
Juniors	7	4	11
Seniors	9	5	14

● **SOLUTION**

To find the probability that a girl from any of these classes is selected, find the sum of probabilities of selecting a sophomore girl, a junior girl, and a senior girl.

Use the formula $P(A \text{ and } B) = P(A) \times P(B|A)$.

$P(\text{sophomore and girl}) = P(\text{sophomore}) \times P(\text{girl}|\text{sophomore})$
$= \frac{1}{4} \times \frac{10}{23} = \frac{5}{46}$

$P(\text{junior and girl}) = P(\text{junior}) \times P(\text{girl}|\text{junior})$
$= \frac{1}{4} \times \frac{7}{11} = \frac{7}{44}$

$P(\text{senior and girl}) = P(\text{senior}) \times P(\text{girl}|\text{senior})$
$= \frac{1}{2} \times \frac{9}{14} = \frac{9}{28}$

Then add.

$P(\text{girl}) = \frac{5}{46} + \frac{7}{44} + \frac{9}{28} = 0.589$

The probability that a girl will be selected is about 58.9%.

TRY THIS Let $P(\text{sophomore}) = \frac{1}{6}$, $P(\text{junior}) = \frac{1}{3}$, and $P(\text{senior}) = \frac{1}{2}$ and let the distribution of the possible winners remain as shown in Example 3. Find the probability that a boy is selected.

EXAMPLE **4** Refer to the donated blood problem from the beginning of the lesson.

APPLICATION
HEALTH

What is the probability that a positive ELISA result for a unit of donated blood is accurate?

● **SOLUTION**

PROBLEM SOLVING

Draw a tree diagram to show each possibility.

$$P(A) \quad \times \quad P(B|A) \ = \ P(B \text{ and } A)$$

```
                        0.98
              0.001    ELISA +  ──────→ 0.00098
              antibodies 0.02
                        ELISA −  ──────→ 0.00002
Unit of   ●
blood                   0.07
              0.999    ELISA +  ──────→ 0.06993
              no        0.93
              antibodies ELISA −  ──────→ 0.92907
                                         ─────────
                                         (Total: 1.0)
```

Use the formula for conditional probability.

$$P(\text{antibodies present}|\text{ELISA} +) = \frac{P(\text{antibodies present and ELISA} +)}{P(\text{ELISA} +)}$$

$$= \frac{0.00098}{0.00098 + 0.06993}$$

$$= 0.014$$

Thus, the probability that a positive ELISA result is accurate is only about 1.4%. This surprising result is because most positive ELISA results are *false positives*.

TRY THIS Refer to Example 4. Suppose that 75 out of every 1000 units of donated blood are contaminated, instead of 1 out of every 1000 units. What is the probability that a positive ELISA result is accurate?

CRITICAL THINKING If 1 out of every 1000 units of donated blood is contaminated, what is the probability that a negative ELISA result is accurate? Which do you feel is more important, an accurate negative result or an accurate positive result? Why?

Exercises

● *Communicate*

1. Explain what the notation $P(B|A)$ represents.

2. Describe the difference between $P(A \text{ and } B)$ and $P(B|A)$.

3. Explain why $P(B|A) = 0$ if A and B are mutually exclusive events.

Guided Skills Practice

Activities Online

Go To: go.hrw.com
Keyword:
MB1 Conditional

4. The band at Washington High School has 25 members, and the pep club has 18 members. Five students belong to both groups. Find the probability that a student randomly selected from these two groups is a member of the band if you know that he or she is in the pep club. *(EXAMPLE 1)*

A bag contains 12 blue disks and 5 green disks. For each case below, find the probability of selecting a green disk on the first draw *and* a green disk on the second draw. (EXAMPLE 2)

5. The first disk is replaced.   **6.** The first disk is *not* replaced.

7. Refer to the table on page 666 about the student body and the respective probabilities for each class. Use the method shown in Example 3 to find the probability that a boy is selected. *(EXAMPLE 3)*

APPLICATION

8. HEALTH Refer to Example 4. Suppose that 5 out of every 1000 units of donated blood are contaminated with HIV antibodies. Find the probability that a positive ELISA result for a unit of donated blood is *not* accurate. *(EXAMPLE 4)*

Practice and Apply

Homework Help Online

Go To: go.hrw.com
Keyword:
MB1 Homework Help
for Exercises 9–23

A bag contains 8 red disks, 9 yellow disks, and 5 blue disks. Two consecutive draws are made from the bag *without* replacement of the first draw. Find the probability of each event.

9. red first, red second
10. yellow first, yellow second
11. red first, blue second
12. blue first, red second
13. red first, yellow second
14. yellow first, red second
15. yellow first, blue second
16. red first, blue second

Two number cubes are rolled, and the first cube shows a 5. Find the probability of each event below for the two cubes.

17. a sum of 9   **18.** two odd numbers   **19.** a sum of 7 or 9

For one roll of a number cube, let *A* be the event "even" and let *B* be the event "2." Find each probability.

20. a. $P(A)$ **b.** $P(A \text{ and } B)$ **c.** $P(B|A)$
21. a. $P(B)$ **b.** $P(B \text{ and } A)$ **c.** $P(A|B)$

For one roll of a number cube, let *A* be the event "odd" and let *B* be the event "1 *or* 3." Find each probability.

22. a. $P(A)$ **b.** $P(A \text{ and } B)$ **c.** $(B|A)$
23. a. $P(B)$ **b.** $P(B \text{ and } A)$ **c.** $P(A|B)$

24. Given $P(A \text{ and } B) = \frac{1}{4}$ and $P(A) = \frac{1}{2}$, find $P(B|A)$.

25. Given $P(A \text{ and } B) = 0.38$ and $P(A) = 0.57$, find $P(B|A)$.

26. Given $P(B|A) = \frac{1}{3}$ and $P(A) = \frac{1}{2}$, find $P(A \text{ and } B)$.

27. Given $P(B|A) = 0.27$ and $P(A) = 0.76$, find $P(A \text{ and } B)$.

28. Given $P(B|A) = 0.87$ and $P(A \text{ and } B) = 0.75$, find $P(A)$.

29. Given $P(B|A) = \frac{3}{5}$ and $P(A \text{ and } B) = \frac{1}{2}$, find $P(A)$.

GEOMETRY A point is randomly selected in the 10×10 square at right. Find the probability of each event.

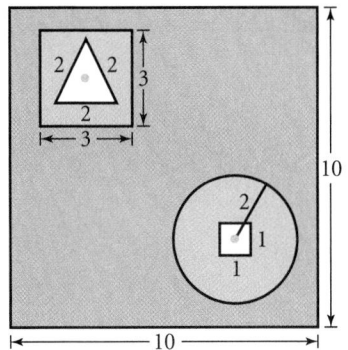

30. a. The point is inside the triangle.
   b. The point is inside the triangle, given that it is within the 3×3 square.

31. a. The point is inside the 1×1 square.
   b. The point is inside the 1×1 square, given that it is inside the circle.

DEMOGRAPHICS The table below gives data from a survey on marital status in the United States for 1995.

Age	Number of persons (in thousands)				
	Total in age group	Never married	Married	Widowed	Divorced
18 to 19	7016	6643	357	2	13
20 to 24	18,142	13,372	4407	17	347
25 to 29	19,401	8373	9913	23	1090
30 to 34	21,988	5186	14,645	80	2077
35 to 39	22,241	3649	15,664	155	2773
40 to 44	20,094	2271	14,779	205	2838
45 to 54	30,694	2173	23,465	808	4248
55 to 64	20,756	961	15,640	1680	2474
65 to 74	18,214	750	12,120	4045	1299
75 and older	13,053	561	5670	6346	473
Total	191,599	43,939	116,660	13,361	17,632

[*Source: Statistical Abstract of the United States, 1996*]

Suppose that a person were chosen at random from the population in 1995. Find the probability of each event.

32. The person is married, given that the person is 20 to 24 years old.

33. The person is married, given that the person is 20 to 29 years old.

34. The person is divorced, given that the person is 20 to 29 years old.

35. The person is divorced, given that the person is 30 to 39 years years old.

36. The person has never been married, given that the person is 20 to 29 years old.

37. The person has never been married, given that the person is 30 to 44 years old.

38. ADVERTISING Suppose that 20% of a newspaper's readers see an ad for a new product. If 9% of the readers who see the ad purchase the product, what is the probability that a newspaper reader sees the ad and purchases the product?

39. Market research indicates that 77% of all computer owners buy their computers in an electronics store as opposed to a department or general merchandise store. Furthermore, 41% of all computer owners buy their computers and software from electronics stores. If Frances purchased a computer in an electronics store and is interested in buying software, what is the probability that he will buy it in an electronics store?

40. HEALTH Suppose that for a particular test, 97% of people who have the illness test positive and 98% of people who do not have the illness test negative. If the probability of having the illness is 0.004, find each probability.
   a. that a positive test result is inaccurate
   b. that a positive test result is accurate

41. On 3 tosses of a coin, 2 were heads. What is the probability that the first toss was heads?

 Look Back

Solve each equation. *(LESSON 1.8)*

42. $|x - 4| = 9$ **43.** $|3x| - 6 = -2$ **44.** $|3 - 4x| = 21$

45. Factor $72x - 24x^2 + 2x^3$, if possible. *(LESSON 5.3)*

46. Factor $x^4 - 81$ completely. *(LESSON 5.3)*

47. Use the quadratic formula to solve $a^2 - 5a - 2 = 0$. *(LESSON 5.5)*

48. Find the zeros of the polynomial function $f(x) = x^3 - 7x^2 + 7x + 15$.
   (LESSON 7.5)

Find the domain of each radical function. *(LESSON 8.6)*

49. $f(x) = \sqrt{3x - 3}$ **50.** $f(x) = \sqrt{3(x - 3)}$ **51.** $f(x) = \sqrt{4 - 3(x + 1)}$

Find *PQ* and the coordinates of *M*, the midpoint of $\overline{PQ}$. Give exact answers and approximate answers to the nearest hundredth when appropriate. *(LESSON 9.1)*

52. $P(3, -4)$ and $Q(-2, -5)$ **53.** $P(-2, 7)$ and $Q(-8, 2)$

54. Classify the conic section defined by $16x^2 + 4y^2 - 96x + 8y + 84 = 0$. Write the standard equation for this conic section and sketch the graph. *(LESSON 9.6)*

55. VOTING A 3-person committee is to be elected from a group of 6 boys and 4 girls. If each person has an equal chance of being elected, find the probability that the elected committee consists of 2 boys and 1 girl. *(LESSON 10.3)*

 Look Beyond

56. Show that $_5C_0 + _5C_1 + _5C_2 + _5C_3 + _5C_4 + _5C_5 = 2^5$.

57. Show that $_6C_6 + _6C_5 + _6C_4 + _6C_3 + _6C_2 + _6C_1 = 2^6 - 1$.

58. Prove that $_nC_r + _nC_{r+1} = _{n+1}C_{r+1}$ is true for all integers r and n, where $0 \leq r \leq n$.

10.7

Experimental Probability and Simulation

Why *Simulations can be used to estimate probabilities. For example, you can use a simulation to estimate the probability that a family with 3 children has all boys or all girls.*

Objective

- Use simulation methods to estimate or approximate the experimental probability of an event.

Recall from Lesson 10.1 that the experimental probability of an event is approximated by performing trials and recording the ratio of the number of occurrences of the event to the number of trials.

Activity
Exploring Experimental Probability

You will need: a coin

You can model, or *simulate*, two random events with coin tosses. Let H, heads, represent a female and let T, tails, represent a male. Each trial will represent a family with three children. Assume that genders are random.

Follow the steps below to investigate *P*(all males *or* all females).

1. Toss a coin three times, and record the outcomes, such as HTH or HHH, as a single trial. Perform 10 trials for the experiment. Find the number of occurrences of the event "TTT *or* HHH." What is the ratio of this number to the total number of trials?

2. Repeat Step 1 four more times.

3. Find the total number of occurrences of the event "TTT *or* HHH" in all five experiments. What is the ratio of this number to the total number of trials in all five experiments? (Let this be called the *average ratio*.)

4. Find the theoretical probability of the event "TTT *or* HHH."

5. Compare the experimental probability ratios that you obtained in each experiment with the theoretical probability. Compare your *average ratio* from Step 3 with the theoretical probability.

CHECKPOINT ✔ 6. Which of your ratios is closest to the theoretical probability? Compare your results with those of your classmates. Make a generalization about the value of experimental probability ratios as the number of trials in an experiment increases.

Recall from Lesson 10.1 that as the number of trials in an experiment increases, the results will more closely approximate the actual probability.

One way to perform large numbers of trials is to use *simulation*. A **simulation** is a reproduction or representation of events that are likely to occur in the real world. Simulations are especially useful when actual trials would be difficult or impossible.

This lesson will concentrate on the use of *random-number generators* to perform simulations.

E X A M P L E ❶

APPLICATION
TRANSPORTATION

Traffic analysts counted the number of motorists out of 200 that went in each direction at an intersection. The results are shown in the table below.

Straight	63
Left	89
Right	48

Use a simulation to estimate the probability that 3 or more out of 5 consecutive motorists will turn right.

● **SOLUTION**

1. Copy the table, and add a third column. In the third column, write numbers from 1 to 200 according to the number of motorists recorded for each direction.

Straight	63	1–63	← *The first 63 numbers*
Left	89	64–152	← *The next 89 numbers*
Right	48	153–200	← *The last 48 numbers*

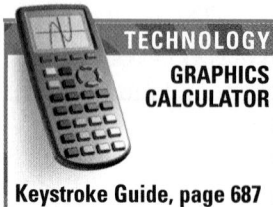

TECHNOLOGY
GRAPHICS CALCULATOR

Keystroke Guide, page 687

2. Each trial will represent 5 consecutive motorists.

Generate 5 random integers from 1 to 200 inclusive. Categorize each resulting number as a motorist who goes straight, turns left, or turns right.

randInt(1,200)
75 ← *Turns left (L)*
180 ← *Turns right (R)*
55 ← *Goes straight (S)*
85 ← *Turns left (L)*
182 ← *Turns right (R)*

Trial	Result
1	LRSLR
2	LSLLS
3	LLSRR
4	SRRLR
5	LSLRL
6	RSRRR
7	LSLLS
8	RLSLL
9	LRRRS
10	SLSSR

3. Perform 10 trials, and record your results in a table such as the one shown at right.

4. Estimate the probability.

In this experiment, there are 3 trials in which 3 or more motorists turned right.

The estimated probability is $\frac{3}{10}$.

X	P(X)
0	0.006
1	0.034
2	0.101
3	0.152
4	0.193
5	0.189
6	0.153
7	0.137
8	0.035

EXAMPLE ❷ An airline statistician made the table at right for customer arrivals per minute at a ticket counter during the time period from 11:00 A.M. to 11:10 A.M. In the table, X represents the number of customers that may arrive at the counter during a one-minute interval, and $P(X)$ represents the probability of X customers arriving during that one-minute interval. For example, the probability that 5 customers arrive during a given minute is 0.189, or 18.9%.

APPLICATION
MANAGEMENT

Find a reasonable estimate of the probability that 50 or more customers arrive at the counter between 11:00 A.M. and 11:10 A.M. inclusive.

● **SOLUTION**

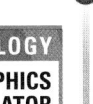
TECHNOLOGY
GRAPHICS CALCULATOR

Keystroke Guide, page 687

1. Copy the probability table and add a new column labeled *Random numbers*. In this column, write numbers from 1 to 1000 according to the given values of $P(X)$.

   For example:
   $P(X) = 0.006$: first 6 numbers, 1–6
   $P(X) = 0.034$: next 34 numbers, 7–40
   $P(X) = 0.101$: next 101 numbers, 41–141

2. Generate 10 random integers from 1 to 1000 inclusive. The results of the first trial are 684, 461, 145, 947, 832, 521, 302, 250, 947, and 926.

X	P(X)	Random numbers
0	0.006	1–6
1	0.034	7–40
2	0.101	41–141
3	0.152	142–293
4	0.193	294–486
5	0.189	487–675
6	0.153	676–828
7	0.137	829–965
8	0.035	966–1000

Use the table to find the corresponding number of customers that arrived for this trial.

$$6, 4, 3, 7, 7, 5, 4, 3, 7, 7$$

Add these numbers together to find the total number of customers for this 10-minute interval.

$$6 + 4 + 3 + 7 + 7 + 5 + 4 + 3 + 7 + 7 = 53$$

3. Perform 10 trials, and record your results as shown at left.

4. For this simulation, there were 50 or more customers in 5 out of 10 trials, so an estimate of the probability is $\frac{5}{10}$, or $\frac{1}{2}$.

Trial	Total number of customers
1	53
2	40
3	55
4	42
5	62
6	32
7	45
8	58
9	64
10	29

Using a Geometric Simulation

You can also use simulations to analyze geometric probability problems.

EXAMPLE 3

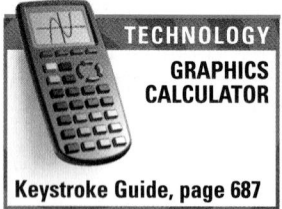

CONNECTION
GEOMETRY

Suppose that 3 darts are thrown at the dartboard at right and that any point on the board is equally likely to be hit.

Use a simulation to estimate the probability that exactly 2 of the 3 darts land in ring B.

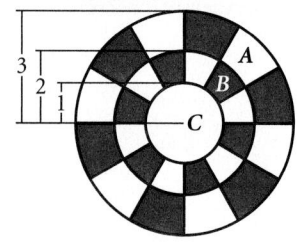

● **SOLUTION**

1. Find the probability of a dart landing in region A (the outer ring), B (the inner ring), and C (the circle).

$$P(A) = \frac{\text{area of region } A}{\text{area of dartboard}} = \frac{9\pi - 4\pi}{9\pi} = \frac{5}{9}$$

> The area of a circle is πr^2.

$$P(B) = \frac{\text{area of region } B}{\text{area of dartboard}} = \frac{4\pi - \pi}{9\pi} = \frac{3}{9} = \frac{1}{3}$$

$$P(C) = \frac{\text{area of region } C}{\text{area of dartboard}} = \frac{\pi}{9\pi} = \frac{1}{9}$$

2. Make a table of the probabilities and their respective random integers from 1 to 9 inclusive.

Probability	Random numbers
$P(A) = \frac{5}{9}$	1, 2, 3, 4, 5
$P(B) = \frac{3}{9}$	6, 7, 8
$P(C) = \frac{1}{9}$	9

TECHNOLOGY
GRAPHICS
CALCULATOR

Keystroke Guide, page 687

3. Generate a trial of 3 random integers. The results of the first trial are 1, 8, and 3. Therefore, there were 2 hits in region A (1 and 3), 1 hit in region B (8), and 0 hits in region C.

Trial	Result
1	1 in B
2	2 in B
3	0 in B
4	3 in B
5	2 in B
6	1 in B
7	2 in B
8	1 in B
9	0 in B
10	2 in B

4. Perform 10 trials, and record your results as shown in the table at right.

5. In 4 of the 10 trials, exactly 2 darts landed in region B, so an estimate of the probability is $\frac{4}{10}$, or $\frac{2}{5}$.

TRY THIS　　Refer to the dartboard in Example 3. Use a simulation to estimate the probability that exactly 2 of 3 darts land in ring A.

CRITICAL THINKING　　Calculate ${}_3C_2\left(\frac{1}{3}\right)^2\left(\frac{2}{3}\right)$, the theoretical probability of the event described in Example 3 above. Compare the experimental probability from Example 3 with the theoretical probability. How can you account for the discrepancy?

You can also use a geometric simulation to approximate π. Refer to the figure at right.

Let event R be a point in the square that is also in the circle.

$$P(R) = \frac{\text{area of circle}}{\text{area of square}} = \frac{\pi(1)^2}{2^2} = \frac{\pi}{4}$$

Make a spreadsheet that contains 20 random decimals between −1 and 1 inclusive in both columns A and B. For column C, use the following rule:

If $x^2 + y^2 \le 1$, (where x and y are the values in columns A and B), print 1, otherwise print 0.

Then compute the experimental probability:

$$P(R) = \frac{\text{number of 1s}}{20}$$

The data from one simulation gives $P(R) = 0.8$. Thus, $\frac{\pi}{4} \approx 0.8$, or $\pi \approx 3.2$. The actual value of π is 3.14159 . . .

	Workbook		
	A	**B**	**C**
1	X	Y	
2	−0.79355678	0.34678998	1
3	0.82410872	−0.92525235	0
4	0.68198496	0.38564413	1
5			
17			
18			
19	0.31884303	0.45645644	0
20	0.56456678	−0.52534556	1
21	0.25647562	0.2947445	1
22			3.2

Sheet 1 ⟨ Sheet 2 ⟨ Sheet 3

Exercises

Communicate

1. How can you use random numbers to simulate rolling a number cube?

2. For what type of event is flipping a coin an appropriate model? Explain.

3. Which experiment would generally produce better results, an experiment with 1 trial or an experiment with 100 trials? Explain.

Guided Skills Practice

APPLICATIONS

4. TRANSPORTATION Refer to the traffic data from page 672. Use a simulation with 10 trials to estimate the probability that 2 or more out of 6 consecutive motorists will go straight. *(EXAMPLE 1)*

5. MANAGEMENT Refer to the probability table for customer arrival on page 673. Use a simulation with 10 trials to estimate the probability that 30 or more customers will arrive during the given 10-minute period. *(EXAMPLE 2)*

CONNECTION

6. GEOMETRY Refer to the dartboard on page 674. Use a simulation with 10 trials to estimate the probability that exactly 1 of 4 darts land in region C. *(EXAMPLE 3)*

7. Use a simulation with 20 trials to estimate the number of coin tosses needed to obtain 2 consecutive heads. (Hint: Outcomes such as **HH**, **THH**, and **THTHTHH** meet the condition.)

8. Use a simulation with 20 trials to estimate the number of coin tosses needed to obtain heads followed by tails. (Hint: Outcomes such as **THT**, **HHT**, **TTHT**, and **THHHT** meet the condition.)

9. Use a simulation with 10 trials to estimate the number of times a 6-sided number cube must be rolled to obtain 2 consecutive numbers less than 5.

10. Use a simulation with 10 trials to estimate the number of times a 6-sided number cube must be rolled to obtain a number less than 5 followed by a 5 or 6.

◢ **internet** connect

Homework Help Online

Go To: **go.hrw.com**
Keyword:
MB1 Homework Help
for Exercises 11–14

Use the table of traffic data below and a simulation with 10 trials to estimate the probability of each event.

11. Exactly 2 out of 3 consecutive motorists turn right.

12. Exactly 3 out of 4 consecutive motorists turn left.

Straight	73
Left	53
Right	69

13. No more than 2 out of 5 consecutive motorists go straight.

14. At least 3 out of 5 consecutive motorists go straight.

A restaurant chain is giving away 1 of 4 different prizes with each purchase of a dinner. Assume that each prize is equally likely to be awarded.

15. Use a simulation with 10 trials to estimate the probability that you will have all 4 prizes after 5 dinner purchases.

16. Use a simulation with 10 trials to estimate the probability that you will have all 4 prizes after 8 dinner purchases.

17. Use a simulation with 10 trials to estimate how many dinners you must purchase to collect all 4 prizes.

A multiple-choice test consists of 10 questions. Use the number of possible answers given below, and assume that each answer is a guess.

18. Suppose that each question has 4 possible answers. Use a simulation to find the probability of answering at least 6 questions correctly.

19. Suppose that each question has 3 possible answers. Use a simulation to find the probability of answering at least 6 questions correctly.

20. Suppose that each question has only 2 possible answers, true or false. Use a simulation to find the probability of answering at least 6 questions correctly.

Use a simulation to estimate the indicated area.

21. the area of the ellipse $\frac{x^2}{4} + \frac{y^2}{9} = 1$

22. the area under the curve $y = e^x$ from $x = 0$ to $x = 5$

23. the area under the curve $y = x^2 - 2x + 3$ from $x = 0$ to $x = 5$

24. GEOMETRY A toothpick has a length of ℓ units. Parallel lines are drawn at a distance of d units apart, where $\ell < d$. When the toothpick is dropped above the parallel lines, it either intersects one of the lines or rests between them. What is the probability that the toothpick will intersect one of the lines?

a. Obtain a toothpick and paper. Perform a simulation with 20 trials to estimate the probability.

b. Compare your answer with French naturalist Compte de Buffon's theoretical value of $\frac{2\ell}{\pi d}$.

SPORTS A baseball player's batting statistics are given in the table at right. Use a simulation with 10 trials to find an approximate answer for each question below.

Batting Statistics

Outcome	Probability
Single	0.198
Double	0.061
Triple	0.020
Home run	0.032
Walk	0.118
Ground out	0.264
Fly out	0.187
Strike out	0.120
Total	**1.000**

25. How many times will the player bat before he gets a hit (a single, double, triple, or home run)?

26. How many times will the player bat before he makes a ground out, fly out, or strike out?

27. How many times will the player bat before he makes a ground out or fly out?

 Look Back

Solve each system of linear equations. *(LESSONS 3.1 AND 3.2)*

28. $\begin{cases} 21x + 2y = 3 \\ 3x + 4y = 5 \end{cases}$

29. $\begin{cases} -3x + y = -2 \\ 2x - y = 3 \end{cases}$

30. $\begin{cases} 7x - 3y = 1 \\ 2x + 5y = 2 \end{cases}$

Solve each nonlinear system of equations. *(LESSON 9.6)*

31. $\begin{cases} x^2 + y^2 = 4 \\ 3x - y = 0 \end{cases}$

32. $\begin{cases} 2x + y = 0 \\ x^2 + y^2 = 9 \end{cases}$

33. $\begin{cases} 2x^2 + \dfrac{y^2}{8} = 1 \\ x^2 + y^2 = 4 \end{cases}$

34. How many 5-digit zip codes are possible? Assume that 00000 is not a valid zip code. *(LESSON 10.1)*

A bag contains 4 red marbles, 7 white marbles, and 14 black marbles. Find the probability of each event for one random selection. *(LESSON 10.4)*

35. red *or* white

36. red *or* black

37. black *or* white

Look Beyond

38. Find the next two terms in each sequence of numbers.
 a. 1, 5, 9, 13, 17, . . .   **b.** 20, 10, 5, 2.5, . . .

Next, Please . . . .

A customer arrives at the ticket counter of an airline. A delay at the counter caused by a long line might result in the customer missing a flight or might cause the airline to delay the departure time so that the customer does not miss the flight. Both events are undesireable for the airline. Therefore, the airline is greatly concerned about its customer's arrival time and processing time in order to minimize delays.

Suppose that an airline is going to start operations in a new terminal. The airline must develop a strategy for providing the optimum number of check-in counters and service staff. Trial-and-error methods in this situation could be very expensive. Instead the airline decides to use a probability experiment.

Activity 1

Airline statisticians want to analyze the time that it takes to process customers who arrive at the ticket counter between 1:00 P.M. and 1:10 P.M. To do this, they begin by researching the time it takes to process each of 50 customers. As a result of this research, the following table of probabilities is generated:

Process Times (in seconds)

Processing time, t	10	20	30	40	50	60
Probability, $P(t)$	0.052	0.132	0.158	0.135	0.123	0.104

Processing time, t	70	80	90	100	110	120
Probability, $P(t)$	0.058	0.034	0.116	0.050	0.026	0.012

Another term for a waiting line is a queue. In real-world situations, queues can vary considerably. They grow for a while, then disappear, and then occur again.

In the table, t represents the processing time to the nearest 10 seconds, and $P(t)$ represents the probability that processing a customer will take t seconds. The probabilities in the table are given to the nearest thousandth.

In order to set up a random-number simulation, first group numbers, N, from 1 to 1000 according to the given probabilities. For example, the first 52 numbers (1–52) correspond to $t = 10$. The next 132 numbers (53–184) correspond to $t = 20$, the next 158 numbers (185–342) correspond to $t = 30$, and so on. Complete the table in this manner.

Table for Processing Time Simulations

t	$P(t)$	N
0	0	000
10	0.052	001–052
20	0.132	053–184
30	0.158	185–342
⋮	⋮	⋮

Activity 2

Perform a simulation for 50 customers who arrive at the counter between 1:00 P.M. and 1:10 P.M.

1. Using a random-number generator, generate 50 random numbers between 1 and 1000 inclusive.

2. Create a table like the one shown at right, and record your random numbers in the *Number* column. Each random number represents a customer.

3. Refer to the table you created in Activity 1. For each random number that you generated, write the corresponding value of t in the *Time* column. The corresponding value of t represents the time it takes to process that customer. For example, if the first random number generated is 179, then the corresponding value of t is 20. This simulates a processing time of 20 seconds for the first customer.

Simulated Processing Time for 50 Consecutive Customers

Customer	Number, N	Time, t
1		
2		
3		
⋮		
49		
50		

Activity 3

1. Perform 10 trials of the simulation for 50 customers who arrive at the counter between 1:00 P.M. and 1:10 P.M. Estimate the probability that processing 50 customers takes longer than 50 minutes.

2. From the activities that you have completed in this project, you can see that efficient handling of customers, particularly in high-volume situations, is complicated and is not an exact science. From your own experiences, what are some situations in which these simulation techniques might be used to estimate probabilities? Describe how simulations might be designed for these situations.

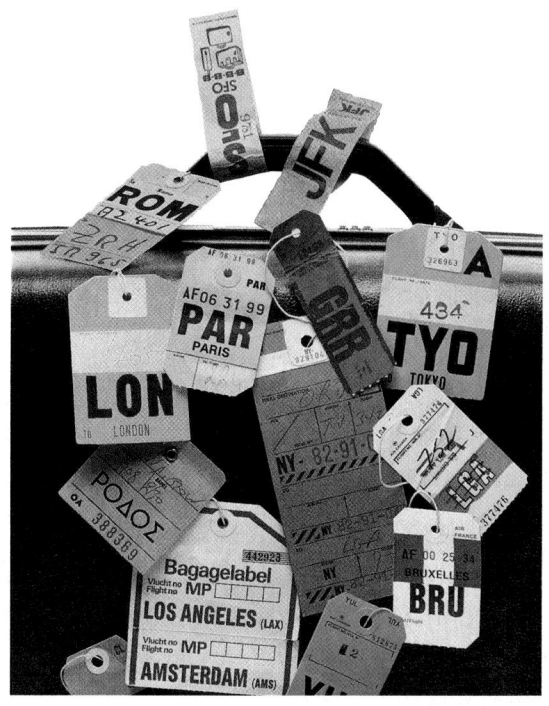

Chapter Review and Assessment

Key Skills & Exercises

LESSON 10.1

Key Skills

Find the theoretical probability of an event.

A bag contains 2 green marbles and 11 red marbles. The theoretical probability of drawing a green marble is $P(\text{green}) = \frac{2}{13}$, or about 15%.

A rehearsal is to begin at some time between 3:00 P.M. and 3:15 P.M. Assuming that all times are equally likely, find the probability that the rehearsal begins in the interval from 3:00 P.M. to 3:03 P.M.

Divide the 15-minute interval into 5 equal parts. The 3-minute interval from 3:00 P.M. to 3:03 P.M. is $\frac{1}{5}$ of the total interval. Thus, the probability is $\frac{1}{5}$.

Apply the Fundamental Counting Principle.

At a cafe, there are 5 choices of entrees and 4 choices of side dishes. By the Fundamental Counting Principle, there are 5×4, or 20, ways to choose an entree and a side dish.

Exercises

Find the probability of each event.

1. drawing a red marble from a bag that contains 3 red marbles and 5 purple marbles

2. drawing a red marble from a bag that contains 4 red marbles and 10 black marbles

A party is to begin at some time between 8:00 P.M. and 8:30 P.M. Assuming that all times are equally likely, find the probability that the first guest arrives during each given time interval.

3. from 8:00 P.M. to 8:05 P.M.

4. from 8:12 P.M. to 8:18 P.M.

5. from 8:21 P.M. to 8:24 P.M.

6. If repetition is *not* allowed, how many 4-letter codes can be formed from only 5 letters of the alphabet?

7. If repetition is allowed, how many 4-letter codes can be formed from 5 letters of the alphabet?

LESSON 10.2

Key Skills

Find the number of linear permutations.

Five books on a shelf can be arranged $_5P_5 = 5! = 5 \times 4 \times 3 \times 2 \times 1 = 120$ different ways.

Two of the five books can be chosen and arranged in $_5P_2 = \frac{5!}{(5-2)!} = 20$ different ways.

Exercises

8. In how many ways can the letters in the word *pencil* be arranged?

Find the number of ways that a coach can assign each number of basketball players to 5 distinct positions.

9. 8   10. 10   11. 12

The letters in the word *hollow* can be arranged in $\frac{6!}{2!2!} = \frac{6!}{4} = 180$ different ways.

Find the number of circular permutations.

Five objects can be arranged around a circle in $(5-1)! = 4!$, or 24, different ways.

12. How many arrangements of the letters in the word *tomorrow* are possible?

13. In how many ways can 5 children be positioned around a merry-go-round?

14. In how many ways can 8 employees be seated at a circular conference table?

LESSON 10.3

Key Skills

Find the number of combinations.

Find the number of ways to purchase 2 games from a display of 7 games.

$$_7C_2 = \frac{7!}{2!(7-2)!} = \frac{7 \times 6 \times 5!}{2!5!} = 21$$

Exercises

15. Find the number of ways to choose 2 books from a set of 10 books.

16. In how many ways can 2 of 27 ice cream flavors be chosen?

17. In how many ways can 3 student representatives be chosen from 100 students?

LESSON 10.4

Key Skills

Find the probability of event *A or B*.

For one roll of a number cube:

Mutually exclusive events: Find $P(2 \text{ or } 3)$.

$$P(A \text{ or } B) = P(A) + P(B)$$

$$P(2 \text{ or } 3) = \frac{1}{6} + \frac{1}{6} = \frac{2}{6} = \frac{1}{3}$$

Inclusive events: Find $P(\text{even or multiple of 3})$.

$$P(A \text{ or } B) = P(A) + P(B) - P(A \text{ and } B)$$

$$P(\text{even or multiple of 3}) = \frac{1}{2} + \frac{1}{3} - \frac{1}{6} = \frac{4}{6} = \frac{2}{3}$$

Use the complement of an event to find a probability.

$$P(A) = 1 - P(A^c)$$

$$P(\text{less than 6}) = 1 - P(6)$$

$$= 1 - \frac{1}{6} = \frac{5}{6}$$

Find the probability of each event for one roll of a number cube.

18. 4 *or* 7

19. 1 *or* 6

20. an odd number *or* a number greater than 4

21. an even number *or* a number less than 4

22. greater than 1

23. greater than 2

LESSON 10.5

Key Skills

Find the probability of independent events.

For 2 rolls of a number cube:

$$P(A \text{ and } B) = P(A) \times P(B)$$

$$P(6 \text{ first and even second}) = \frac{1}{6} \times \frac{3}{6} = \frac{3}{36} = \frac{1}{12}$$

Exercises

Find the probability of each event.

24. 3 heads on 3 tosses of a fair coin

25. 2 even numbers on 2 rolls of a number cube

Key Skills

Find conditional probabilities.

For 1 roll of a number cube, find the probability that the number 2 is rolled if you know that the number is even.

$$P(2|\text{even}) = \frac{P(\text{even } and\ 2)}{P(\text{even})} = \frac{\frac{1}{6}}{\frac{1}{2}} = \frac{1}{3}$$

Exercises

Find the probability of each event for one roll of a number cube.

26. 5, given that it is an odd number

27. 1, given that it is *not* an odd number

28. 2, given that it is less than or equal to 5

Key Skills

Use simulations to estimate probabilities.

The probability table gives the probabilities of the number of traffic tickets written by one officer between 3:00 A.M. and 4:00 A.M.

X	P(X)
0	0.20
1	0.30
2	0.35
3	0.15

Use a simulation with 10 trials to estimate the probability that the officer writes less than 2 tickets during this time.

Add a column, N, as shown below. Generate 10 random integers.

X	P(X)	N	Random integers
0	0.20	1–20	14
1	0.30	21–50	38, 34, 23, 28
2	0.35	51–85	72, 57, 73
3	0.15	86–100	95, 97

In this experiment, less than 2 traffic tickets occurred 5 out of 10 times, so the probability is estimated to be $\frac{1}{2}$, or 50%.

Exercises

29. The table at right gives the probabilities, $P(X)$, of the number, X, of drinks ordered at a fast-food restaurant during a 1-minute interval between 3:00 P.M. and 3:20 P.M.

X	P(X)
0	0.18
1	0.37
2	0.22
3	0.10
4	0.07
5	0.06

Use a simulation with 10 trials to estimate the probability that more than 6 drinks are ordered between 3:00 P.M. and 3:20 P.M. inclusive.

30. The table below gives the number of customers out of 100 that went up, down, or stayed on the same level after entering a mall.

Use a simulation with 10 trials to estimate the probability that 3 or more out of 5 consecutive customers go up.

Up	36
Down	20
Same	44

Applications

31. HEALTH A test of 100 adults showed that 40 of them consumed on average more than the recommended maximum of 2400 milligrams of sodium per day. Of those with the high sodium consumption, 50% had higher-than-normal blood pressure. Of the 60 adults whose sodium intake was at or below 2400 milligrams per day, only 15% had higher-than-normal blood pressure. Using this data as a sample of the general population, find the probability that a person with higher-than-normal blood pressure has a daily intake of more than 2400 milligrams of sodium.

10 Chapter Test

Find the probability of each event.

1. drawing a jack from a playing card deck of 52 cards

2. drawing a green marble from a bag that contains 8 green marbles and 6 red marbles

3. rolling an odd number on one roll of a number cube

4. **LICENSING** A fishing license identification number consists of 2 letters and 8 numbers. How many possible license numbers are available?

Evaluate the following expressions.

5. $12! - 7!$

6. $(12 - 7)!$

7. $_8P_3$

8. $_5P_3 \times _8P_5$

9. How many different ways can a president, vice president, and secretary be chosen from a group of 24 individuals?

10. Find the number of permutations of the letters in the word *probability*.

11. **SPORTS** The Indianapolis 500 race has a field of 32 cars. In how many different ways can the first three finishers be placed?

Evaluate each expression.

12. $_8C_3$

13. $_8C_8$

14. $\dfrac{_8C_5}{_5C_2 \times _5C_3}$

15. $\dfrac{8!}{4!6!} \times \dfrac{5!}{3!4!}$

16. **SMALL BUSINESS** At a deli, a sub sandwich can be ordered with any of 7 different condiments. In how many different ways can a sandwich with exactly 3 condiments be ordered?

17. **POLITICS** How many ways can a Senate committee of 12 members choose a subcommittee of 5 senators?

Find the probability of each event for one roll of a 12-sided number cube labeled with the numbers 1–12.

18. a 7 *or* an even number

19. a prime number *or* a multiple of 4

20. an odd number *or* a multiple of 3

21. a number greater than 8 *or* a multiple of 5

22. an even number *or* a number less than 6

Find the probability of each event.

23. heads on a coin and 5 on a 6-sided number cube, on one toss of a coin and one roll of a number cube

24. a 7 and a face card with the draw of two cards at random from two different decks

25. A time is chosen at random during the week to send off the next space shuttle. Find the probability of the liftoff time being on Tuesday between 5 A.M. and 6 A.M.

Find the probability of each event for one draw of a card from a playing card deck of 52 cards.

26. a queen, given that it is a face card

27. a diamond, given that it is a red card

28. a jack, given that it is a red card

29. a ten of clubs, given that it is a black card

30. Given $P(A) = \frac{1}{3}$ and $P(B|A) = \frac{2}{3}$, what is $P(A$ and $B)$?

31. Given $P(A$ and $B) = \frac{1}{6}$ and $P(A) = \frac{2}{5}$, what is $P(B|A)$?

32. An ordinary thumbtack was dropped 100 times with the results shown in the table below. Use a simulation with 20 trials to estimate the probability the thumbtack lands with the point up.

point up	point down
68	32

MULTIPLE-CHOICE For Questions 1–17, write the letter that indicates the best answer.

1. Solve $5 + \frac{1}{2}x = 6(x + 1)$. **(LESSON 1.6)**

 a. $x = \frac{4}{11}$ **b.** $x = -\frac{2}{11}$

 c. $x = \frac{8}{11}$ **d.** $x = -\frac{11}{2}$

2. Solve $10^x = 12$ for x. Round your answer to the nearest hundredth. **(LESSON 6.3)**

 a. 1.20   **b.** 1.08

 c. 0.08   **d.** 2.08

3. Which of the following systems has no solution? **(LESSON 3.1)**

 a. $\begin{cases} y = 3 - \frac{3}{2}x \\ 6x + 4\,y = 12 \end{cases}$

 b. $\begin{cases} 2x - y = 1 \\ 6x - y = 13 \end{cases}$

 c. $\begin{cases} -\frac{1}{2}x + y = 4 \\ 2x + 4y = 16 \end{cases}$

 b. $\begin{cases} y = -3x + 4 \\ y + 3x = -3 \end{cases}$

4. Determine the number of real solutions for $3x^2 - 2x + 1 = 0$. **(LESSON 5.6)**

 a. 2   **b.** 0

 c. 1   **d.** undefined

5. Let $f(x) = 2x - 1$. Find $f^{-1}(2)$. **(LESSON 2.5)**

 a. $\frac{3}{2}$ **b.** 3

 c. -3 **d.** $\frac{1}{3}$

6. Which of the following is a solution of the system $\begin{cases} 2y + x \le 6 \\ y - 3x \ge 4 \end{cases}$? **(LESSON 3.4)**

 a. $(0, 5)$ **b.** $(-1, 2)$

 c. $(1, -1)$ **d.** $(0, 0)$

7. Solve $2(x + 2) - 7 < 8x + 15$. **(LESSON 1.7)**

 a. $x > -3$ **b.** $x < -3$

 c. $x > 2$ **d.** $x < 2$

8. Which value would you add to $x^2 - 10x$ to complete the square? **(LESSON 5.4)**

 a. 5   **b.** -5

 c. 25   **d.** -25

9. Simplify $\left(-\frac{1}{125}\right)^{-\frac{2}{3}}$. **(LESSON 2.2)**

 a. $\frac{1}{25}$ **b.** $-\frac{1}{25}$

 c. 25   **d.** -25

10. If $f(x) = 2x - 6$ and $g(x) = 12 - 6x$, which statement is true? **(LESSON 2.4)**

 a. $f \circ g = g \circ f$ **b.** $2(f \circ g) = g \circ f$

 c. $-2(f \circ g) = g \circ f$ **d.** none of these

11. Which of the following describes the relationship between the lines $y = \frac{1}{2}x$ and $y = -2x - 3$? **(LESSON 1.3)**

 a. horizontal   **b.** vertical
 c. perpendicular   **d.** parallel

12. Solve $4y^2 + 7 = 0$. **(LESSON 5.6)**

 a. $y = \frac{7i}{2}$

 b. $y = \frac{-\sqrt{7}}{4}$

 c. $y = \frac{\sqrt{7}}{4}$

 d. $y = \pm\frac{i\sqrt{7}}{2}$

13. Find the coordinates of the midpoint of the segment with endpoints at $(-4, -1)$ and $(2, -7)$. *(LESSON 9.1)*

   a. $(-1, -3)$ **b.** $(-3, 3)$

   c. $(-1, -4)$ **d.** $(-3, -3)$

14. Which expression is not equivalent to the others? *(LESSON 6.4)*

   a. $2 \log_b \frac{5}{3}$ **b.** $\log_b \sqrt[3]{5^2}$

   c. $\frac{1}{3} \log_b 25$ **d.** $\frac{2}{3} \log_b 5$

15. Write $(5x^3 - 2x^2 + x - 10) + (2x^3 - 3x - 1)$ in standard form. *(LESSON 7.1)*

   a. $3x^3 - 2x^2 - 4x - 9$
   b. $3x^3 + 2x^2 + 4x - 9$
   c. $7x^3 - 2x^2 - 2x - 9$
   d. $7x^3 - 2x^2 - 2x - 11$

16. Simplify $\frac{a^2 + 3a - 4}{a^2} \cdot \frac{a^2 - 2a}{2a + 8}$. *(LESSON 8.3)*

   a. $-(a - 4)$ **b.** $\frac{(a-1)(a-2)}{2a}$

   c. $\frac{(a+4)(a-2)}{2a}$ **d.** $\frac{(a+4)(a-1)}{a}$

17. Find the coordinates of the center of the circle defined by $x^2 + y^2 - 2x - 8y = 8$. *(LESSON 9.6)*

   a. $(-1, -4)$ **b.** $(1, 2)$

   c. $(1, 4)$ **d.** $(-1, -8)$

18. Write an equation in slope-intercept form for the line containing the points $(3, -4)$ and $(2, 7)$. *(LESSON 1.3)*

19. Find the zeros of $f(x) = x^2 - 8x + 12$. *(LESSON 5.3)*

20. Find the product $-2\begin{bmatrix} 7 & -6 & 0 \\ -3 & 5 & 1 \end{bmatrix}$, if it exists. *(LESSON 4.1)*

21. Factor $5x^2 + 10x - 40$, if possible. *(LESSON 5.3)*

22. Find the inverse of $\{(2, -1), (4, 3), (6, 0), (3, 1)\}$. *(LESSON 2.5)*

23. Simplify $(1 - 2i) - (3 - 4i)$. *(LESSON 5.6)*

24. Factor $8x^3 + 64$. *(LESSON 7.3)*

25. Describe the end behavior of $P(x) = -2x^3 + x^2 - 11x + 4$. *(LESSON 7.2)*

26. Simplify $\left(\sqrt{-36x^4}\right)^2$. *(LESSON 8.7)*

27. Write equations for all vertical and horizontal asymptotes in the graph of $f(x) = \frac{(x+2)^2}{3x}$. *(LESSON 8.2)*

28. Write the standard equation for $x^2 + y^2 + 6x - 4y = 12$. *(LESSON 9.6)*

29. Factor $6x^2 + 8x - 15x - 20$, if possible. *(LESSON 7.3)*

30. Simplify $\dfrac{\frac{x+4}{9x^3}}{\frac{x-6}{3x^4}}$. *(LESSON 8.3)*

FREE-RESPONSE GRID

The following questions may be answered by using a free-response grid such as that commonly used by standardized-test services.

31. Find the slope, m, of the line $y = 8$. *(LESSON 1.2)*

32. Find the determinant of $\begin{bmatrix} -3 & 5 \\ -1 & 6 \end{bmatrix}$. *(LESSON 4.3)*

33. Solve $\frac{6x+2}{3x} = 6$. *(LESSON 8.5)*

34. Solve $3^x = 9^5$. *(LESSON 6.7)*

35. What value would you add to $x^2 + 8x$ to complete the square? *(LESSON 5.4)*

36. Find the value of v in $v = \log_{10} \frac{1}{1000}$. *(LESSON 6.3)*

EXTRACURRICULAR ACTIVITIES The Outdoors Club has 12 students—5 girls and 7 boys. *(LESSON 10.5)*

37. How many different committees of 6 students can be formed if at least 3 are girls?

38. How many different committees of 6 students can be formed if at least 3 are boys?

39. How many different committees of 6 students can be formed if no more than 3 are boys?

Keystroke Guide for Chapter 10

Essential keystroke sequences (using the model TI-82 or TI-83 graphics calculator) are presented below for all Activities and Examples found in this chapter that require or recommend the use of a graphics calculator.

internet connect

For Keystrokes of other graphing calculator models, visit the HRW web site at **go.hrw.com** and enter the keyword **MB1 CALC**.

LESSON 10.2

EXAMPLE ③ Evaluate $\dfrac{11!}{4!5!2!}$.

Page 638

11 [MATH] [PRB] [4:!] [ENTER] [÷]

[(] 4 [MATH] [PRB] [4:!] [ENTER]

[×] 5 [MATH] [PRB] [4:!] [ENTER]

[×] 2 [MATH] [PRB] [4:!] [ENTER] [)] [ENTER]

```
11!/(4!*5!*2!)
              6930
```

LESSON 10.3

EXAMPLE ② Evaluate $_5C_3$ and $_5P_3$.

Page 645

5 [MATH] [PRB] [3:nCr] [ENTER] 3 [ENTER]

5 [MATH] [PRB] [2:nPr] [ENTER] 3 [ENTER]

```
5 nCr 3
              10
5 nPr 3
              60
```

EXAMPLE ④ Evaluate $\dfrac{_{17}C_2 \times {_8}C_4}{_{25}C_6}$.

Page 646

[(] 17 [MATH] [PRB] [3:nCr] [ENTER] 2 [)]

[×] [(] 8 [MATH] [PRB] [3:nCr] [ENTER] 4

[)] [÷] [(] 25 [MATH] [PRB] [3:nCr]

[ENTER] 6 [)] [ENTER]

```
(17 nCr 2)*(8 nC
r 4)/(25 nCr 6)
        .0537549407
```

E X A M P L E **3** Evaluate $\frac{365}{365} \times \frac{364}{365} \times \frac{363}{365} \times \ldots \times \frac{361}{365}$.

Page 661

(365 [MATH] [PRB] [2:nPr] [ENTER] 35)

÷ (365 ^ 35) [ENTER]

```
(365 nPr 35)/(36
5^35)
          .1856167611
```

E X A M P L E **1** Generate 5 random integers from 1 to 200 inclusive.

Page 672

[MATH] [PRB] [5:randInt] [ENTER] 1 , 200

) [ENTER] [ENTER] [ENTER] [ENTER] [ENTER]

For TI-82: [MATH] [NUM] [4:int] [ENTER] ([MATH] [PRB] [1:rand]

[ENTER] X 200 + 1) [ENTER] [ENTER] [ENTER] [ENTER] [ENTER]

```
randInt(1,200)
              75
             180
              55
              85
             182
```

E X A M P L E **2** Generate 10 random integers from 1 to 1000 inclusive.

Page 673

[MATH] [PRB] [5:randInt] [ENTER] 1 , 1000)

For TI-82: [MATH] [NUM] [4:int] [ENTER] ([MATH] [PRB] [1:rand]

[ENTER] X 1000 + 1)

Press [ENTER] 10 times to generate the 10 random integers.

```
randInt(1,1000)
             684
             461
             145
             947
             832
             521
```

E X A M P L E **3** Generate 3 random integers from 1 to 9 for each of 10 trials.

Page 674

1st trial:

[MATH] [PRB] [5:randInt] [ENTER] 1 , 9)

[ENTER] [ENTER] [ENTER]

For TI-82: [MATH] [NUM] [4:int] [ENTER] ([MATH] [PRB] [1:rand]

[ENTER] X 9 + 1) [ENTER] [ENTER] [ENTER]

2nd trial:

ENTRY
[2nd] [ENTER] [ENTER] [ENTER] [ENTER]

Simulate additional trials by continuing to use the entry command followed by [ENTER].

```
randInt(1,9)
              1
              8
              3
```

11

DISCRETE MATHEMATICS
Series and Patterns

DISCOVERING PATTERNS AND REPRESENT-
ing them in sequences of numbers is
an important mathematical skill. In
this chapter, you will investigate
different types of sequences,
including the Fibonacci sequence.
The Fibonacci sequence is used to
describe a wide variety of structures in
nature. For example, the spiral formed
by a nautilus shell and the spiral pattern of
sunflower seeds are both related to the
Fibonacci sequence.

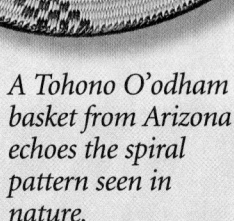

*A Tohono O'odham
basket from Arizona
echoes the spiral
pattern seen in
nature.*

Lessons

A logarithmic spiral is evident in a chambered nautilus shell.

![PORTFOLIO ACTIVITIES PROJECT / CHAPTER]

About the Chapter Project

In this chapter, you will use series and sequences to model real-world situations.

In the Chapter Project, *Over the Edge,* you will investigate centers of gravity and perform experiments to develop a model involving sequences and series that you will use to determine whether a stack of objects will remain balanced.

After completing the Chapter Project, you will be able to do the following:

- Experimentally determine the center of gravity of an object.

- Model data from your experiments with a sequence or series.

- Determine whether your model gives predictions that are consistent with observations.

About the Portfolio Activities

Throughout the chapter, you will be given opportunities to complete Portfolio Activities that are designed to support your work on the Chapter Project.

- Finding the center of gravity of an object is included in the Portfolio Activity on page 706.

- Experimenting to determine some relationships that govern center of gravity is included inthe Portfolio Activity on page 727.

- Experimenting to determine the limits involved in keeping an object balanced is included in the Portfolio Activity on page 734.

Sequences and Series

CULTURAL CONNECTION: EUROPE In the eighteenth century, German astronomers Johann Daniel Titius and Johann Elert Bode wrote a sequence of numbers to model the distances between the Sun and the planets.

They began with the number sequence below, in which each number (except 3) is double the preceding number.

$$0, 3, 6, 12, 24, 48, \ldots$$

From this sequence of numbers, Titius and Bode wrote a new sequence, called *Bode's sequence*, defined by adding 4 to each number in the original sequence and then dividing the result by 10.

Planet	Original number	Bode number
1st: Mercury	0	$\frac{0+4}{10} = 0.4$
2nd: Venus	3	$\frac{3+4}{10} = 0.7$
3rd: Earth	6	$\frac{6+4}{10} = 1.0$
4th: Mars	12	$\frac{12+4}{10} = 1.6$

Bode's law gives the distance from Earth to the Sun as 1 unit; each number in Bode's sequence represents the distance from a planet to the Sun in relation to that unit. Based on Bode's sequence, astronomers looked for a planet at the distance corresponding to the fifth Bode number, between Mars and Jupiter. The astronomers discovered Ceres, which turned out to be the largest member of the asteroid belt between Mars and Jupiter.

Sequences

In mathematics, a **sequence** is an ordered list of numbers, called **terms**. The terms of a sequence are often arranged in a pattern. Some examples are shown below.

$$2, 4, 6, 8, 10, \ldots \qquad 2, 4, 8, 16, 32, \ldots$$
$$5, 2, -1, -4, -7, \ldots \qquad 3, -9, 27, -81, 243, \ldots$$

The three dots, called an ellipsis, indicate that a sequence is an **infinite sequence,** which continues without end. A **finite sequence** has a last term.

An infinite sequence can be defined by a function whose domain is the set of all natural numbers $\{1, 2, 3, \ldots, n, \ldots\}$ and a finite sequence can be defined by a function whose domain is the first n natural numbers $\{1, 2, 3, \ldots, n\}$. The range for both functions is the set of all real numbers. For example, the sequence $2, 4, 6, 8, 10, 12, \ldots$ can be defined by the function t, shown below.

$t(n) = 2n$, where $n = 1, 2, 3, \ldots$

n	1	2	3	4	5	6	←*domain*
$t(n)$	2	4	6	8	10	12	←*range*

Each member of the range of a sequence is a term of the sequence. The terms of a sequence are often represented by the letter t with a subscript, as shown below.

$$t_1, t_2, t_3, \ldots, t_{n-1}, t_n$$

A formula that defines the nth term, or general term, of a sequence is called an **explicit formula.** With an explicit formula, each term of the sequence can be found by substituting the number of the term for n. This is shown in Example 1 below.

E X A M P L E ① Write the first six terms of the sequence defined by the explicit formula $t_n = -2n + 3$.

● SOLUTION

Evaluate $t_n = -2n + 3$ for n-values of 1, 2, 3, 4, 5, and 6.

n	1	2	3	4	5	6
t_n	1	-1	-3	-5	-7	-9

The first six terms of this sequence are $1, -1, -3, -5, -7$, and -9.

TRY THIS Write the first six terms of the sequence defined by the explicit formula $t_n = 2n^2 - 1$.

A sequence can also be defined by a *recursive formula*. With a **recursive formula,** one or more previous terms are used to generate the next term. For example, the recursive formula for Example 1 is $t_1 = 1$ and $t_n = t_{n-1} - 2$, where $n \geq 2$.

$$t_n = t_{n-1} - 2 \text{ and } t_1 = 1$$
$$t_2 = t_1 - 2 = 1 - 2 = -1$$
$$t_3 = t_2 - 2 = -1 - 2 = -3$$
$$t_4 = t_3 - 2 = -3 - 2 = -5$$

EXAMPLE 2 Write the first six terms of the sequence defined by the recursive formula $t_1 = 4$ and $t_n = 3t_{n-1} + 5$, where $n \geq 2$.

● SOLUTION

$$t_n = 3t_{n-1} + 5 \text{ and } t_1 = 4$$
$$t_2 = 3t_1 + 5 = 3(4) + 5 = 17$$
$$t_3 = 3t_2 + 5 = 3(17) + 5 = 56$$
$$t_4 = 3t_3 + 5 = 3(56) + 5 = 173$$
$$t_5 = 3t_4 + 5 = 3(173) + 5 = 524$$
$$t_6 = 3t_5 + 5 = 3(524) + 5 = 1577$$

The first six terms of this sequence are 4, 17, 56, 173, 524, and 1577.

TRY THIS Write the first six terms of the sequence defined by the recursive formula $t_1 = 1$ and $t_n = 3t_{n-1} - 1$, where $n \geq 2$.

EXAMPLE 3 **Refer to Bode's law, described at the beginning of the lesson.**

a. Find the next four terms of Bode's sequence, given the next four terms of the original sequence.

APPLICATION
ASTRONOMY

5th: Ceres	24
6th: Jupiter	48
7th: Saturn	96
8th: Uranus	192

b. Using Bode's law and 1.495×10^8 kilometers as the distance between Earth and the Sun, write the approximate distances in kilometers between the Sun and Ceres, Jupiter, Saturn, and Uranus.

● SOLUTION

a.

Planet	Original number	Bode number
5th: Ceres	24	$\frac{24+4}{10} = 2.8$
6th: Jupiter	48	$\frac{48+4}{10} = 5.2$
7th: Saturn	96	$\frac{96+4}{10} = 10.0$
8th: Uranus	192	$\frac{192+4}{10} = 19.6$

b.

Planet	Bode number	Distance from planet to Sun
5th: Ceres	2.8	$2.8(1.495 \times 10^8) = 4.186 \times 10^8$
6th: Jupiter	5.2	$5.2(1.495 \times 10^8) = 7.774 \times 10^8$
7th: Saturn	10.0	$10.0(1.495 \times 10^8) = 1.495 \times 10^9$
8th: Uranus	19.6	$19.6(1.495 \times 10^8) = 2.9302 \times 10^9$

CRITICAL THINKING Write a recursive formula for the sequence of Bode numbers, beginning with the second term.

Another famous sequence is the *Fibonacci sequence*. It is defined recursively as $a_1 = 1$, $a_2 = 1$, and $a_n = a_{n-2} + a_{n-1}$, where $n \geq 3$. The sequence is

$$1 \quad , \quad 1 \quad , \quad 2 \quad , \quad 3 \quad , \quad 5 \quad , \quad 8 \quad , \quad 13 \quad , \quad 21 \quad , \quad \ldots$$

CHECKPOINT ✔ Write the next four terms of the Fibonacci sequence.

The Fibonacci sequence, also called the *golden spiral*, has been used to study animal populations, relationships between elements in works of art, and various patterns in plants, such as the sunflower.

The seeds of a sunflower are arranged in spiral curves. The number of clockwise spirals and the number of counterclockwise spirals are always successive terms in the Fibonacci sequence.

Series

A **series** is an expression that indicates the sum of terms of a sequence. For example, if you add the terms of the sequence 2, 4, 6, 8, and 10, the resulting expression is the series $2 + 4 + 6 + 8 + 10$.

Summation notation, which uses the Greek letter **sigma, Σ,** is a way to express a series in abbreviated form. For example, the series $2 + 4 + 6 + 8 + 10$ can be represented as $\sum_{n=1}^{5} 2n$, which is read "the sum of $2n$ for values of n from 1 to 5."

Values of n from 1 to 5 are called the index. $\longrightarrow \sum_{n=1}^{5} 2n \longleftarrow$ Explicit formula for the general term of the related sequence

EXAMPLE ④ Write the terms of each series. Then evaluate.

a. $\displaystyle\sum_{k=1}^{4} 5k$ **b.** $\displaystyle 5\sum_{k=1}^{4} k$

● **SOLUTION**

a. $\displaystyle\sum_{k=1}^{4} 5k = 5(1) + 5(2) + 5(3) + 5(4)$
$= 5 + 10 + 15 + 20$
$= 50$

b. $\displaystyle 5\sum_{k=1}^{4} k = 5(1 + 2 + 3 + 4)$
$= 5(10)$
$= 50$

TRY THIS Write the terms of each series. Then evaluate.

a. $\displaystyle\sum_{k=1}^{5} 4k$ **b.** $\displaystyle \frac{1}{2}\sum_{k=1}^{4} k$

Exploring Summation Properties

You will need: no special materials

1. Evaluate $\sum_{k=1}^{4}(2k + k^2)$ and $\sum_{k=1}^{4}2k + \sum_{k=1}^{4}k^2$.

CHECKPOINT ✔ 2. Are the two results from Step 1 the same? Explain.

3. Evaluate $\sum_{k=1}^{5}2$, $\sum_{k=1}^{5}3$, and $\sum_{k=1}^{5}4$. (Hint: $\sum_{k=1}^{5}1 = 1 + 1 + 1 + 1 + 1 = 5$)

CHECKPOINT ✔ 4. Find the pattern in the results from Step 3, and write a formula for $\sum_{k=1}^{n}c$.

Two summation properties are illustrated below.

$$\sum_{n=1}^{3}4n^2 = 4 \cdot 1^2 + 4 \cdot 2^2 + 4 \cdot 3^2 \qquad \sum_{n=1}^{3}(n + n^2) = (1 + 1^2) + (2 + 2^2) + (3 + 3^2)$$

$$= 4(1^2 + 2^2 + 3^2) \qquad\qquad\qquad = (1 + 2 + 3) + (1^2 + 2^2 + 3^2)$$

$$= 4\sum_{n=1}^{3}n^2 \qquad\qquad\qquad\qquad = \sum_{n=1}^{3} + \sum_{n=1}^{3}n^2$$

These summation properties do not have names. Notice, however, the properties of real-number operations that are used in the illustrations. In the first case, the Distributive Property is used. In the second case, both the Associative and Commutative Properties are used.

Summation Properties

For sequences a_k and b_k and positive integer n:

1. $\sum_{k=1}^{n}ca_k = c\sum_{k=1}^{n}a_k$ 2. $\sum_{k=1}^{n}(a_k + b_k) = \sum_{k=1}^{n}a_k + \sum_{k=1}^{n}b_k$

Series such as $\sum_{k=1}^{5}2$ and $\sum_{k=1}^{5}3$ are called *constant series*. The general term of a series may be defined by a constant, linear, or quadratic expression. The formulas below are used to find the sums of these series.

Summation Formulas

For all positive integers n:

Constant Series

$$\sum_{k=1}^{n}c = nc$$

Linear Series

$$\sum_{k=1}^{n}k = \frac{n(n + 1)}{2}$$

Quadratic Series

$$\sum_{k=1}^{n}k^2 = \frac{n(n + 1)(2n + 1)}{6}$$

CHECKPOINT ✔ Verify the formulas for the sums of constant, linear, and quadratic series by using the series $2 + 2 + 2$, $1 + 2 + 3$, and $1 + 4 + 9$, respectively.

E X A M P L E ⑤ Evaluate $\displaystyle\sum_{m=1}^{5}(2m^2 + 3m + 2)$.

● **SOLUTION**

$$\sum_{m=1}^{5}(2m^2 + 3m + 2) = \sum_{m=1}^{5}2m^2 + \sum_{m=1}^{5}3m + \sum_{m=1}^{5}2$$

$$= 2\sum_{m=1}^{5}m^2 + 3\sum_{m=1}^{5}m + \sum_{m=1}^{5}2$$

$$= 2\left[\frac{5(6)(11)}{6}\right] + 3\left[\frac{5(6)}{2}\right] + 5 \cdot 2$$

$$= 110 + 45 + 10$$

$$= 165$$

TRY THIS Evaluate $\displaystyle\sum_{j=1}^{5}(-j^2 + 2j + 5)$.

Exercises

Communicate

internet connect

**Activities
Online**
Go To: **go.hrw.com**
Keyword:
MB1 Fibonacci

1. Explain the difference between a sequence and a series. Include examples in your response.

2. Explain the differences between the explicit formula $t_n = 2n + 1$ and the recursive formula $t_n = 2t_{n-1} + 1$.

3. Explain the difference between $\displaystyle\sum_{i=1}^{3}(i + 10)$ and $\displaystyle\sum_{i=1}^{3}i + 10$.

Guided Skills Practice

4. Write the first six terms of the sequence defined by the explicit formula $t_n = 3n - 2$. **(EXAMPLE 1)**

5. Write the first six terms of the sequence defined by the recursive formula below. **(EXAMPLE 2)**
$$t_1 = 1 \text{ and } t_n = 3t_{n-1} + 1, \text{ where } n \geq 2$$

6. The first five terms of a sequence are 3, 5, 7, 9, and 11. **(EXAMPLE 3)**
   a. Write the next five terms.
   b. Write a recursive formula for the sequence.

Write the terms of each series. Then evaluate. *(EXAMPLE 4)*

7. $\displaystyle\sum_{k=1}^{3}4k$

8. $5\displaystyle\sum_{k=1}^{4}k$

9. Evaluate $\displaystyle\sum_{k=1}^{4}(3k^2 + 2k + 4)$. **(EXAMPLE 5)**

Practice and Apply

Write the first four terms of each sequence defined by the given explicit formula.

10. $t_n = 2n + 3$

11. $t_n = 4n + 1$

12. $t_n = -2n + 1$

13. $t_n = -4n - 1$

14. $t_n = 6n + 2$

15. $t_n = 5n - 1$

16. $t_n = -7n + 3$

17. $t_n = -4n + 8$

18. $t_n = 4n + 2$

19. $t_n = \frac{1}{2}n + 1$

20. $t_n = \frac{1}{4}n + 2$

21. $t_n = 8.75n + 3.67$

22. $t_n = 3.76n + 2.5$

23. $t_n = n^3$

24. $t_n = (-1)^n$

25. $t_n = -2n^2$

Write the first six terms of each sequence defined by the given recursive formula.

26. $t_1 = 1$
$t_n = t_{n-1} + 3$

27. $t_1 = 2$
$t_n = t_{n-1} + 2$

28. $t_1 = 0$
$t_n = t_{n-1} - 4$

29. $t_1 = -6$
$t_n = -2t_{n-1} + 3$

30. $t_1 = 7$
$t_n = 4t_{n-1} + 1$

31. $t_1 = 10$
$t_n = 5t_{n-1} + 1$

32. $t_1 = 10$
$t_n = 3t_{n-1} + 1$

33. $t_1 = 8$
$t_n = 3t_{n-1} - 2$

34. $t_1 = -2.24$
$t_n = 1.2t_{n-1} + 2.2$

35. $t_1 = 3.34$
$t_n = 2.2t_{n-1} - 1$

36. $t_1 = \frac{1}{3}$
$t_n = \frac{1}{2}t_{n-1} + 2$

37. $t_1 = \frac{5}{7}$
$t_n = \frac{1}{5}t_{n-1} + \frac{1}{3}$

internet connect

Homework Help Online
Go To: **go.hrw.com**
Keyword:
MB1 Homework Help
for Exercises 38–41

For each sequence below, write a recursive formula and find the next three terms.

38. $1, 5, 9, 13, \ldots$

39. $3, 9, 15, 21, \ldots$

40. $5, 9, 17, 33, \ldots$

41. $3, 7, 15, 31, \ldots$

Write the terms of each series. Then evaluate.

42. $\sum\limits_{k=1}^{3} 4$

43. $\sum\limits_{k=1}^{4} 10$

44. $\sum\limits_{j=1}^{4} 3j$

45. $\sum\limits_{k=1}^{3} 4k$

46. $\sum\limits_{k=1}^{5} -2k$

47. $\sum\limits_{k=1}^{4} -5k$

48. $\sum\limits_{k=1}^{3} \frac{1}{2}k^2$

49. $\sum\limits_{k=1}^{5} \frac{1}{3}k^2$

50. $\sum\limits_{m=1}^{5} -\frac{1}{3}m^2 - m$

51. $\sum\limits_{n=1}^{3} -\frac{1}{4}n^2 + n$

52. $\sum\limits_{j=1}^{4} (2j + 3)$

53. $\sum\limits_{k=1}^{3} (-3k + 1)$

54. $\sum\limits_{m=1}^{4} (5m^2 + 1)$

55. $\sum\limits_{k=1}^{3} (k^2 + k + 1)$

56. $\sum\limits_{k=1}^{3} (2k^2 + 3k + 2)$

Evaluate the sum.

57. $\displaystyle\sum_{k=1}^{4} 3$

58. $\displaystyle\sum_{k=1}^{4} 2$

59. $\displaystyle\sum_{j=1}^{6} 4j$

60. $\displaystyle\sum_{k=1}^{7} 3k$

61. $\displaystyle\sum_{m=1}^{3} (5m + 4)$

62. $\displaystyle\sum_{n=1}^{4} (2n + 3)$

63. $\displaystyle\sum_{k=1}^{3} (4k + 5)$

64. $\displaystyle\sum_{m=1}^{5} (2m^2 + 3m + 2)$

65. $\displaystyle\sum_{j=1}^{4} (4j^2 + 4j + 1)$

66. $\displaystyle\sum_{m=1}^{4} (-5m^2 + 2m + 4)$

67. $\displaystyle\sum_{n=1}^{4} (3 - n)^2$

68. $\displaystyle\sum_{k=1}^{6} (k + 2)^2$

69. $\displaystyle\sum_{n=1}^{3} \left(-\frac{2}{3}n^2 + \frac{1}{2}n + \frac{5}{7}\right)$

70. $\displaystyle\sum_{j=1}^{6} \left(\frac{1}{3}j^2 + \frac{1}{5}j + 2\right)$

71. $\displaystyle\sum_{m=1}^{4} (\pi m^2 + 2\pi m + 2)$

72. $\displaystyle\sum_{n=1}^{6} (\pi n^2 + \pi n + 4)$

73. $\displaystyle\sum_{k=1}^{5} (0.7k^2 + 1.3k + 2)$

74. $\displaystyle\sum_{j=1}^{5} (8.7j^2 + 8.6j + 7.5)$

CHALLENGES

75. Find an explicit formula for the nth term of Bode's sequence.

76. A certain sequence is defined recursively by $t_1 = 1$, $t_2 = 2$, $t_{2n} = 2t_{2n-2}$, and $t_{2n+1} = 3t_{2n-1}$. Find the first eight terms of the sequence.

CONNECTION

GEOMETRY The measure of each interior angle of a regular n-sided polygon is $\dfrac{180(n-2)}{n}$ degrees. For example, the interior angle measure of a regular (equilateral) triangle is $\dfrac{180(3-2)}{3} = 60°$.

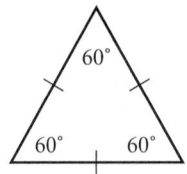

77. Find the interior angle measure of a square.

78. Find the interior angle measure of a regular pentagon.

79. Find the interior angle measure of a regular hexagon.

80. Does the interior angle measure of a regular n-sided polygon increase or decrease as n increases?

APPLICATIONS

81. INCOME Alan, a first-semester freshman, tutors in an afterschool program and earns $7.00 an hour. Each semester, Alan gets a $0.30 per hour raise. If he continues tutoring through his senior year, how much will he earn per hour in each semester of high school? Write an explicit formula to solve this problem.

82. BIOLOGY A single bacterium divides into 2 bacteria every 10 minutes. Assume that the same rate of division continues for 3 hours. Write a sequence that gives the number of bacteria after each 10-minute period.

A spherical bacterium in the process of cell division

83. RECREATION Anya is making paper flowers for the school prom. As she works, her speed increases. The first hour, she makes 12 flowers. During each additional hour that she works, she is able to make 4 more flowers than the hour before. If she works for 7 hours, how many flowers will she have made in total? Use sigma notation to model and solve this problem. (Hint: Start the index at 0.)

 Look Back

Write an equation in slope-intercept form for the line that contains the given point and is parallel to the given line. *(LESSON 1.3)*

84. $(-2, 5)$, $y = \frac{3}{4}x - 1$ 　　　　　　　　　**85.** $(-4, 2)$, $2x - 3y = 1$

Find the discriminant, and determine the number of real solutions. Then solve. *(LESSON 5.6)*

86. $x^2 - 6x + 12 = 0$ 　　　**87.** $4x^2 - 4x + 1 = 0$ 　　　**88.** $x^2 - 6x + 8 = 0$

Solve each nonlinear system of equations and check your answers. *(LESSON 9.6)*

89. $\begin{cases} 2x + y = 1 \\ 4x^2 + 9y^2 = 1 \end{cases}$ 　　**90.** $\begin{cases} 2y^2 = x \\ x - 2y = 12 \end{cases}$ 　　**91.** $\begin{cases} y^2 + 2x = 17 \\ x + 4y = -8 \end{cases}$

Calculate each permutation and combination below. *(LESSONS 10.2 AND 10.3)*

92. $_8P_3$ 　　　　　**93.** $_9P_2$ 　　　　　**94.** $_{10}C_3$ 　　　　　**95.** $_8C_4$

 Look Beyond

96. Find the next three terms of the sequence 5, 8, 11, 14, 17, . . . Then find an explicit formula for t_n, the nth term of the sequence.

Graph each sequence below. What pattern do you see in the graphs?

97.

n	1	2	3	4	5
t_n	-4	-1	2	5	8

98.

n	1	2	3	4	5
t_n	8	4	0	-4	-8

Arithmetic Sequences

Objectives

- Recognize arithmetic sequences, and find the indicated term of an arithmetic sequence.

- Find arithmetic means between two numbers.

Why *Arithmetic sequences can be used to model real-world events such as the depreciation of a watering system.*

APPLICATION

DEPRECIATION

A new garden-watering system costs $389.95. As time goes on, the value of the watering system depreciates. Its value decreases by $42.50 per year. What is the value of the system after 9 years? To answer this question, you can use an arithmetic sequence. *You will answer this question in Example 2.*

Two examples of arithmetic sequences are shown below.

$$1, \quad 4, \quad 7, \quad 10, \quad 13, \dots$$
$$+3 \quad +3 \quad +3 \quad +3$$

The common difference is 3.

$$5, \quad 3, \quad 1, \quad -1, \quad -3, \dots$$
$$-2 \quad -2 \quad -2 \quad -2$$

The common difference is −2.

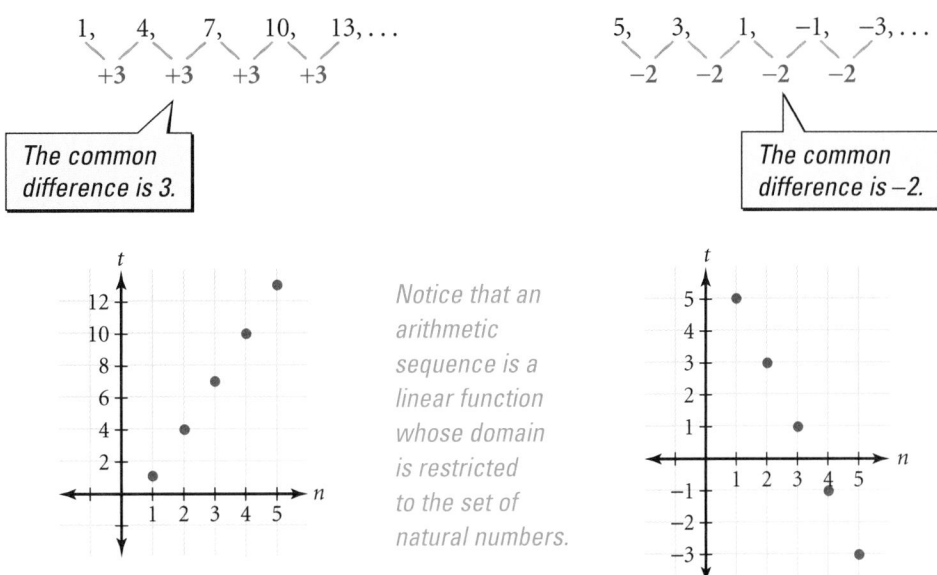

Notice that an arithmetic sequence is a linear function whose domain is restricted to the set of natural numbers.

CHECKPOINT ✔ How does the common difference of an arithmetic sequence compare with the slope of the corresponding linear function?

An **arithmetic sequence** is a sequence whose successive terms differ by the same number, d, called the **common difference**. That is, if t_n, where $n \geq 2$, is any term in an arithmetic sequence, then the statement below is true.

$$t_n - t_{n-1} = d \quad \text{or} \quad t_n = t_{n-1} + d$$

The formula $t_n = t_{n-1} + d$, where $n \geq 2$, is a recursive formula because it gives the nth term of a sequence in relation to the previous term and d.

PROBLEM SOLVING **Look for a pattern.** A pattern can be seen in the recursive formula for the arithmetic sequence defined by $t_1 = 3$ and $t_n = t_{n-1} + 4$, where $n \geq 2$.

Recursive formula	Pattern
$t_1 = 3$	$t_1 = 3 + (0)4$
$t_2 = 3 + 4$	$t_2 = 3 + (1)4$
$t_3 = (3 + 4) + 4$	$t_3 = 3 + (2)4$
$t_4 = [(3 + 4) + 4] + 4$	$t_4 = 3 + (3)4$

The pattern formed by the recursive formula gives the information needed to write an explicit formula for the same sequence.

$$t_n = 3 + (n - 1)4, \text{ where } n \geq 1$$

---

*n*th Term of an Arithmetic Sequence

The general term, t_n, of an arithmetic sequence whose first term is t_1 and whose common difference is d is given by the explicit formula $t_n = t_1 + (n - 1)d$.

If you know the first term of an arithmetic sequence and its common difference, you can use the explicit formula to find any term of the sequence. This is shown in Example 1.

E X A M P L E **1** **Find the fifth term of the sequence defined by the recursive formula $t_1 = -4$ and $t_n = t_{n-1} + 3$.**

SOLUTION

The sequence is arithmetic, in which $t_1 = -4$ and $d = 3$. Use the explicit formula for the general term of an arithmetic sequence.

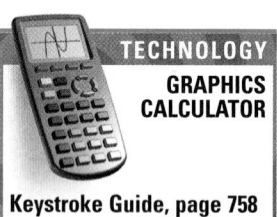

TECHNOLOGY
GRAPHICS
CALCULATOR
Keystroke Guide, page 758

$$t_n = t_1 + (n - 1)d$$
$$t_5 = -4 + (5 - 1)3$$
$$t_5 = 8$$

Thus, the fifth term of the sequence is 8.

CHECK

← 1st term
← 2nd term
← 3rd term
← 4th term
← 5th term

TRY THIS Find the seventh term of the sequence defined by the recursive formula $t_1 = 2.5$ and $t_n = t_{n-1} - 3$.

Refer to the watering system described at the beginning of the lesson.
a. Use a recursive formula to find the value of the system after 4 years.
b. Use the explicit formula for the *n*th term of an arithmetic sequence to find the value of the watering system after 9 years.

APPLICATION
DEPRECIATION

● **SOLUTION**

a. Initial value (year 0): 389.95
year 1: $389.95 - 42.5 = 347.45$
year 2: $347.45 - 42.5 = 304.95$
year 3: $304.95 - 42.5 = 262.45$
year 4: $262.45 - 42.5 = 219.95$

CHECK

The value of the system after 4 years of use is $219.95.

b. At year 9, $n = 10$. Find t_{10}.

$$t_n = t_1 + (n - 1)d$$
$$t_{10} = 389.95 + (10 - 1)(-42.5)$$
$$t_{10} = 7.45$$

The value of the system after 9 years of use is $7.45.

TECHNOLOGY
GRAPHICS CALCULATOR

Keystroke Guide, page 758

CHECKPOINT ✔ Explain why you need to find the 10th term of the arithmetic sequence in Example 2 in order to find the value after 9 years.

TRY THIS A new washing machine costs $352.65. It depreciates $48.60 each year. Find the value of the washing machine after 7 years.

E X A M P L E ③ **Find the 10th term of the arithmetic sequence in which $t_3 = -5$ and $t_6 = 16$.**

● **SOLUTION**

1. Find the common difference, *d*.

n	3	4	5	6
t_n	-5	?	?	16

$\rightarrow \quad -5 + 3d = 16$
$\qquad d = 7$

2. Find t_1. Use $d = 7$ and either $t_3 = -5$ or $t_6 = 16$.

$t_n = t_1 + (n - 1)d$ $t_n = t_1 + (n - 1)d$
$-5 = t_1 + (3 - 1)7$ *Use $t_3 = -5$.* $16 = t_1 + (6 - 1)7$ *Use $t_6 = 16$.*
$-19 = t_1$ $-19 = t_1$

3. Find the 10th term.

$$t_n = t_1 + (n - 1)d$$
$$t_{10} = -19 + (10 - 1)(7)$$
$$t_{10} = 44$$

CHECK

Thus, the 10th term of this arithmetic sequence is 44.

TECHNOLOGY
GRAPHICS CALCULATOR

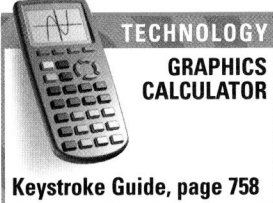

Keystroke Guide, page 758

TRY THIS Find the 12th term of the arithmetic sequence in which $t_3 = 8$ and $t_7 = 20$.

In an arithmetic sequence, you are given consecutive terms t_i and t_j. Explain how to find d, and write an explicit formula for t_n, where n is any positive integer. Assume that $i < j$.

Activity

Investigating Sequences

You will need: a graphics calculator or graph paper

1. Graph each sequence for n-values from 1 to 6.

    a. $t_n = 5 + 2n$ **b.** $t_n = 8 - 0.5n$ **c.** $t_n = 2^n$

    d. $t_n = \dfrac{1}{n}$ **e.** $t_n = 3(0.1)^n$ **f.** $t_n = n^2$

2. Which of the sequences in Step 1 are arithmetic?

CHECKPOINT ✔

3. Classify the graph of each sequence in Step 1 as linear, quadratic, exponential, or reciprocal (restricted to the domain of natural numbers).

The terms between any two nonconsecutive terms of an arithmetic sequence are called the **arithmetic means** between the two nonconsecutive terms. For example, in the sequence 5, **11, 17, 23**, 29, 35, . . . , the three arithmetic means between 5 and 29 are **11, 17**, and **23**. In the past, you have learned that an arithmetic mean is the average of two numbers. That definition still holds because each number in the sequence is the average of the numbers on each side.

E X A M P L E **4** **Find the four arithmetic means between 10 and −30.**

● **SOLUTION**

PROBLEM SOLVING

Draw a diagram. Let $t_1 = 10$ and $t_6 = -30$.

$$t_1 \qquad\qquad\qquad\qquad\qquad t_6$$
$$10, \underline{\ ?\ }, \underline{\ ?\ }, \underline{\ ?\ }, \underline{\ ?\ }, -30$$

Find the common difference, d.

$$t_n = t_1 + (n - 1)d$$
$$-30 = 10 + (6 - 1)d \quad \textit{Because } t_6 = -30, n = 6 \text{ and } t_n = -30.$$
$$-40 = 5d$$
$$\frac{-40}{5} = d$$
$$-8 = d$$

Use $d = -8$ to find the arithmetic means.

$$10 - 8 = 2$$
$$2 - 8 = -6$$
$$-6 - 8 = -14$$
$$-14 - 8 = -22$$

The four arithmetic means are 2, −6, −14, and −22.

TRY THIS Find the four arithmetic means between 24 and 39.

Exercises

Communicate

1. Explain how to write an explicit formula for the general term of the sequence −4, 2, 8, 14, . . .

2. Explain why $(n - 1)d$ instead of nd is used to find the nth term of an arithmetic sequence.

3. Describe how the arithmetic mean of 4 and 20 and the three arithmetic means between 4 and 20 are related.

Guided Skills Practice

4. Find the fourth term of the sequence defined by $t_1 = -4$ and $t_n = t_{n-1} + 2$. *(EXAMPLE 1)*

APPLICATION

5. DEPRECIATION Sheryl purchased a sewing machine for her tailoring service. If the machine cost $1425.65 and depreciates at the rate of $85 per year, what will its value be after 10 years? *(EXAMPLE 2)*

6. Find the eighth term of the arithmetic sequence in which $t_4 = 2$ and $t_7 = 6$. *(EXAMPLE 3)*

7. Find the four arithmetic means between 6 and 26. *(EXAMPLE 4)*

Practice and Apply

internet connect

Homework Help Online

Go To: **go.hrw.com**
Keyword:
MB1 Homework Help
for Exercises 8–29

Based on the terms given, state whether or not each sequence is arithmetic. If it is, identify the common difference, *d*.

8. 6, 10, 14, 18, 22, . . .

9. 2, 4, 6, 8, 10, . . .

10. 8, 5, 2, −1, −4, . . .

11. −3, 0, 3, 6, 9, . . .

12. 5, −5, 5, −5, 5, . . .

13. 1, 2, 4, 8, . . .

14. 9, 7, 5, 3, 1, . . .

15. 0, −6, −12, −18, −24, . . .

16. 3, 6, 12, 24, . . .

17. 3, 7, 12, 18, 25, . . .

18. −1, 1, −1, 1, . . .

19. 1, −3, 5, −7, . . .

20. $0, \frac{1}{2}, 1, \frac{3}{2}, 2, \ldots$

21. $\frac{1}{3}, \frac{2}{3}, 1, \frac{4}{3}, \frac{5}{3}, \ldots$

22. $\frac{2}{7}, \frac{4}{7}, 1\frac{11}{7}, \frac{16}{7}, \ldots$

23. $\frac{2}{5}, \frac{5}{6}, \frac{6}{7}, \frac{7}{8}, \frac{8}{9}, \ldots$

24. −2.8, 3.9, 5.0, 6.1, 12.2, . . .

25. 4.23, 5.67, 6.01, . . .

26. $\frac{\sqrt{2}}{\sqrt{3}}, \frac{2}{3}, \frac{4}{9}, \frac{16}{81}, \ldots$

27. 0.1, 0.01, 0.001, 0.0001, . . .

28. $\pi, 2\pi, 3\pi, 4\pi, 5\pi, \ldots$

29. $\pi, \pi^2, \pi^3, \pi^4, \pi^5, \ldots$

Use the recursive formula given to find the first four terms of each arithmetic sequence.

30. $t_1 = 5$
$t_n = t_{n-1} + 2$

31. $t_1 = 18$
$t_n = t_{n-1} - 3$

32. $t_1 = 0$
$t_n = t_{n-1} + 0.1$

33. $t_1 = 1$
$t_n = t_{n-1} + 2$

34. $t_1 = -5$
$t_n = t_{n-1} + 4$

35. $t_1 = -4$
$t_n = t_{n-1} + 3$

36. $t_1 = 3$
$t_n = t_{n-1} + 3$

37. $t_1 = 7$
$t_n = t_{n-1} + 1$

38. $t_1 = 6$
$t_n = t_{n-1} + 4$

List the first four terms of each arithmetic sequence.

39. $t_n = 4 + (n - 1)(3)$

40. $t_n = -2 + (n - 1)(4)$

41. $t_n = 3n - 4$

42. $t_n = -2n + 5$

43. $t_n = -5n + 2$

44. $t_n = 4n - 2$

45. $t_n = -3 + (n - 1)(5)$

46. $t_n = 4 + (n - 1)(-2)$

47. $t_n = \frac{1}{3} + \frac{1}{3}n$

48. $t_n = \frac{1}{5}n + \frac{4}{5}$

49. $t_n = \pi n + 4$

50. $t_n = \pi n + 5$

Find the indicated term given two other terms.

51. 5th term; $t_3 = 10$ and $t_7 = 26$

52. 5th term; $t_2 = -5$ and $t_6 = 7$

53. 10th term; $t_1 = 2.1$ and $t_4 = 1.83$

54. 10th term; $t_1 = 2.1$ and $t_6 = -2.85$

55. 1st term; $t_6 = -\frac{5}{6}$ and $t_8 = -\frac{3}{2}$

56. 1st term; $t_2 = -\frac{13}{12}$ and $t_6 = -\frac{7}{4}$

Write an explicit formula for the *n*th term of each arithmetic sequence.

57. $6, 8, 10, 12, 14, \ldots$

58. $11, 15, 19, 23, 27, \ldots$

59. $1, -6, -13, -20, -27, \ldots$

60. $14, 9, 4, -1, -6, \ldots$

61. $23, 31, 39, 47, 55, \ldots$

62. $17, 22, 27, 32, 37, \ldots$

63. $20, 15, 10, 5, 0, \ldots$

64. $33, 24, 15, 6, -3, \ldots$

65. $100, 105, 110, 115, 120, \ldots$

66. $500, 520, 540, 560, 580, \ldots$

67. $-50, -45, -40, -35, -30, \ldots$

68. $-80, -76, -72, -68, -64, \ldots$

Find the indicated arithmetic means.

69. Find the three arithmetic means between 5 and 17.

70. Find the four arithmetic means between 40 and 10.

71. Find the three arithmetic means between 18 and −10.

72. Find the five arithmetic means between −40 and −10.

73. Find the two arithmetic means between 5.26 and 6.34.

74. Find the three arithmetic means between 8.24 and 2.8.

75. Find the five arithmetic means between 12 and −6.

76. Find the six arithmetic means between −23 and 5.

77. Examine the pattern of dots below. How many dots will there be in the 14th figure?

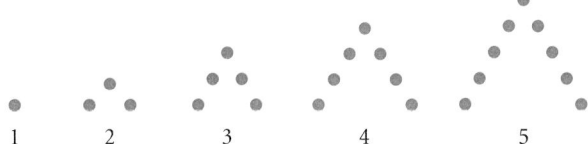

1   2   3   4   5

CHALLENGE

78. In a parking lot, each row has 3 more parking spaces than the previous row. If the 1st row has 20 spaces, how many spaces will the 15th row have?

CONNECTION

79. GEOMETRY The lengths of the sides of a certain right triangle form an arithmetic sequence. Show that the triangle is similar to a right triangle with side lengths of 3, 4 and 5.

APPLICATIONS

80. DEPRECIATION A machine that puts labels on bottles is bought by a small company for $10,000. The machine depreciates at the beginning of each year at a rate of $1429 per year.
  a. Write a formula for an arithmetic sequence that gives the value of the machine after n years.
  b. Find the value of the machine at the beginning of the second, third, and sixth year.

81. INCOME The starting salary for a teacher in one school district is $30,000. The salary increases by $800 each year.
  a. Write a formula for an arithmetic sequence that gives the salary in the nth year.
  b. Find the salary for the 10th year.

82. HEALTH Amanda is beginning a fitness program. During the first week, she will do 25 abdominal exercises each day. Each week she will increase the number of daily exercises by 3.
  a. Write a formula for an arithmetic sequence that gives the number of daily exercises done in the nth week.
  b. How many daily exercises will Amanda do after 20 weeks?

Look Back

Complete the square for each quadratic expression to form a perfect square trinomial. Then write the new expression as a binomial squared. *(LESSON 5.4)*

83. $x^2 + 6x$ **84.** $x^2 + 20x$ **85.** $x^2 + 14x$

Solve each inequality. Check your solution. *(LESSON 8.5)*

86. $\dfrac{-4}{2x+5} > 0$ **87.** $\dfrac{x-1}{x-4} \geq 2$

88. $\dfrac{(x-4)}{(x+2)} \leq 4$ **89.** $\dfrac{x^2-3}{x^2+3} < -\dfrac{1}{2}$

Write the standard equation for each circle. Then state the coordinates for its center and give its radius. *(LESSON 9.3)*

90. $x^2 - 2x + y^2 = 0$

91. $x^2 + 4x + y^2 - 10y + 13 = 0$

Write the standard equation for each ellipse. *(LESSON 9.4)*

92. foci: $(0, 6), (0, -6)$
vertices: $(0, 8), (0, -8)$

93. foci: $(4, 2), (-4, 2)$
co-vertices: $(0, 5), (0, 1)$

Representing a male child with *M* and a female child with *F*, a sample space for families with 2 children can be written as {*MM, MF, FM, FF*}. Assume that each family below has 2 children. List each event below with the same notation as above. Then find the theoretical probability of each event. *(LESSON 10.1)*

94. A family has exactly two girls.

95. A family has at least one girl.

96. A family has at most one girl.

97. A family has exactly one girl.

 Look Beyond

98. Find the sum of the first eight terms of the given arithmetic sequence.

$$\begin{cases} t_1 = 5 \\ t_n = t_{n-1} + 2 \end{cases}$$

PORTFOLIO ACTIVITY

Place a wooden 12-inch ruler on a desk so that one end of the ruler is aligned with the edge of the desk. Slowly slide the ruler over the edge of the desk as far as possible without the ruler falling off. The location on the ruler that is at the edge of the desk at this time is the ruler's center of gravity. Record the ruler's center of gravity.

All of the weight of an object can be considered to be concentrated at a single point called the center of gravity. Balancing an object is one way to locate an object's center of gravity.

WORKING ON THE CHAPTER PROJECT

You should now be able to complete Activity 1 of the Chapter Project.

Arithmetic Series

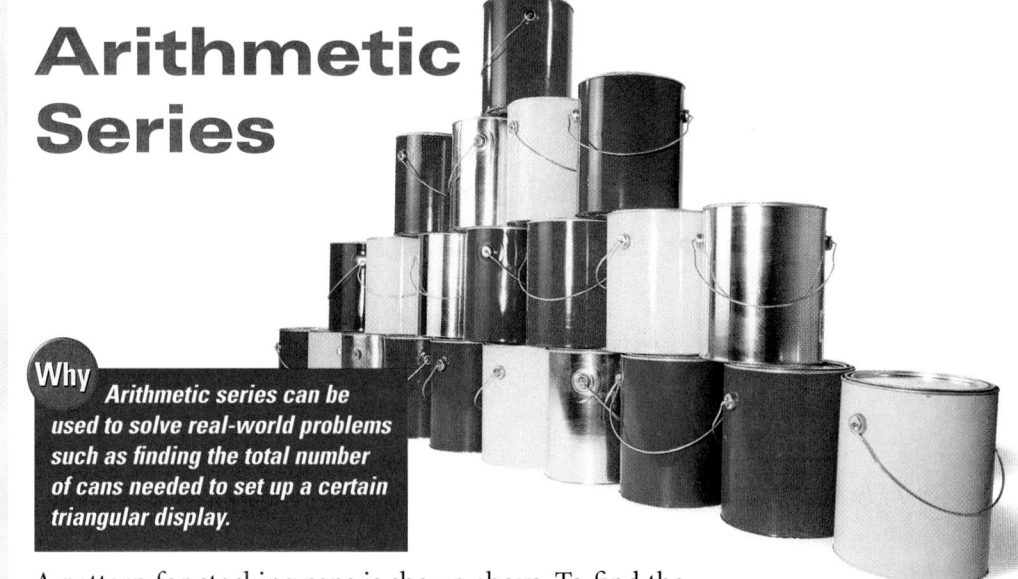

11.3

Why Arithmetic series can be used to solve real-world problems such as finding the total number of cans needed to set up a certain triangular display.

Objective

- Find the sum of the first *n* terms of an arithmetic series.

A pattern for stacking cans is shown above. To find the number of cans in a triangular display of 15 rows stacked in this pattern, you can use the sum of an *arithmetic series*. *You will solve this problem in Example 1.*

CONNECTION

PATTERNS IN DATA

Activity

Exploring Arithmetic Series

You will need: graph paper

The sum $1 + 2 + 3$ can be represented on graph paper as shown in Figure 1. Twice the sum can be represented as shown in Figure 2.

Figure 1

CHECKPOINT ✔

1. Explain how Figure 1 suggests the following:
$$1 + 2 + 3 = \frac{3(4)}{2} = \frac{3(1 + 3)}{2}$$

Figure 2

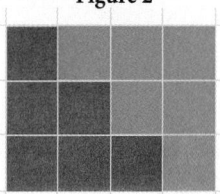

2. Draw a similar figure to represent twice the sum $1 + 2 + 3 + 4 + 5 + 6$, and write a similar equation for it.

3. Repeat Step 2 for twice the sum $1 + 2 + 3 + 4 + 5 + \cdots + 10$.

An **arithmetic series** is the indicated sum of the terms of an arithmetic sequence. Consider the sequence $1, 2, 3, \ldots$ The sum of the first six terms of this sequence is denoted by S_6.

$$S_6 = 1 + 2 + 3 + 4 + 5 + 6 = 21$$

You can derive a formula for the sum of the first *n* terms of an arithmetic series by using the Addition Property of Equality, as shown below.

$$S_n = t_1 + (t_1 + d) + (t_1 + 2d) + \cdots + (t_n - d) + t_n \longleftarrow \boxed{\text{Because } t_n - t_{n-1} = d, \\ t_{n-1} = t_n - d.}$$

$$\underline{S_n = t_n + (t_n - d) + (t_n - 2d) + \cdots + (t_1 + d) + t_1}$$

$$2S_n = (t_1 + t_n) + (t_1 + t_n) + (t_1 + t_n) + \cdots + (t_1 + t_n) + (t_1 + t_n)$$

$(t_1 + t_n)$ is added n times

$$2S_n = n(t_1 + t_n)$$

$$S_n = \frac{n(t_1 + t_n)}{2}$$

Sum of the First n Terms of an Arithmetic Series

The sum, S_n, of the first n terms of an arithmetic series with first term t_1 and nth term t_n is given by $S_n = n\left(\dfrac{t_1 + t_n}{2}\right)$.

CHECKPOINT ✔ Using the sequence 1, 2, 3, . . . , find S_6 by following the procedure used in the derivation of S_n.

EXAMPLE ① Refer to the pattern for stacking cans described at the beginning of the lesson.

How many cans are in a 15-row display of cans stacked in this pattern?

CONNECTION

PATTERNS IN DATA

SOLUTION

1. Begin with the formula for the sum of the first n terms of an arithmetic series.

$$S_n = n\left(\frac{t_1 + t_n}{2}\right)$$

$$S_{15} = 15\left(\frac{1 + t_{15}}{2}\right) \qquad \textit{Substitute 1 for } t_1 \textit{ and 15 for n.}$$

2. Find t_{15}, using the recursive formula.

$$t_n = t_1 + (n - 1)d$$
$$t_{15} = 1 + (15 - 1)3 \qquad \textit{Notice from the pattern that d = 3.}$$
$$t_{15} = 43$$

3. Substitute 43 for t_{15} in the formula.

$$S_{15} = 15\left(\frac{1 + t_{15}}{2}\right)$$

$$S_{15} = 15\left(\frac{1 + 43}{2}\right)$$

$$S_{15} = 330$$

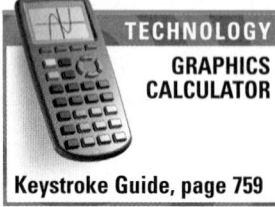

TECHNOLOGY

GRAPHICS CALCULATOR

Keystroke Guide, page 759

CHECK

Use the summation and the sequence commands of a graphics calculator. On this calculator, the summation command tells the calculator to add the items in parentheses, and the sequence command inside the parentheses describes the related sequence.

Thus, the 15-row display contains 330 cans.

The formula $S_n = n\left(\dfrac{t_1 + t_n}{2}\right)$ gives S_n in terms of n, t_1, and t_n. Notice that the sum is the number of terms, n, times the average term, $\dfrac{t_1 + t_n}{2}$. By substituting $t_1 + (n - 1)d$ for t_n in the formula for S_n, you can write a formula that can be used when the last term of the series is not known.

$$S_n = n\left(\frac{t_1 + t_n}{2}\right)$$

$$S_n = n\left[\frac{t_1 + t_1 + (n - 1)d}{2}\right]$$

$$S_n = n\left[\frac{2t_1 + (n - 1)d}{2}\right]$$

E X A M P L E ❷ Given $3 + 12 + 21 + 30 + \cdots$, find S_{25}.

● **SOLUTION**

Substitute 3 for t_1, 9 for d, and 25 for n.

Method 1 Use $S_n = n\left(\dfrac{t_1 + t_n}{2}\right)$.

First find t_{25}.
$$t_n = t_1 + (n - 1)d$$
$$t_{25} = 3 + (25 - 1)9$$
$$t_{25} = 219$$

Then find S_{25}.
$$S_{25} = 25\left(\frac{3 + 219}{2}\right) = 2775$$

Method 2 Use $S_n = n\left[\dfrac{2t_1 + (n - 1)d}{2}\right]$.

$$S_n = n\left[\frac{2t_1 + (n - 1)d}{2}\right]$$
$$S_{25} = 25\left[\frac{2(3) + (25 - 1)9}{2}\right]$$
$$S_{25} = 2775$$

CHECK

Use the summation and the sequence commands on a graphics calculator.

Thus, $S_{25} = 2775$.

```
sum(seq(3+(X-1)9
,X,1,25,1))
              2775
```

TECHNOLOGY
GRAPHICS CALCULATOR

Keystroke Guide, page 759

TRY THIS Given $(-16) + (-12) + (-8) + (-4) + \cdots$, find S_{20}.

E X A M P L E ❸ Evaluate $\displaystyle\sum_{k=1}^{12} (6 - 2k)$.

● **SOLUTION**

Method 1
This summation notation describes the summation of the first 12 terms of the arithmetic series that begins $4 + 2 + 0 + (-2) + \cdots$, in which $t_1 = 4$ and $d = -2$.

First find t_{12}.
$$t_{12} = 4 + (12 - 1)(-2) = -18$$

Then find S_{12}.
$$S_{12} = 12\left[\frac{4 + (-18)}{2}\right] = -84$$

Method 2
You can use the properties of series and the formulas for constant and linear series to find the sum.

$$\sum_{k=1}^{12}(6 - 2k) = \sum_{k=1}^{12}6 + \sum_{k=1}^{12}-2k$$
$$= 12 \cdot 6 - 2\sum_{k=1}^{12}k$$
$$= 72 - 2\left[\frac{12(1 + 12)}{2}\right]$$
$$= 72 - 156$$
$$= -84$$

CHECK

Use the sum and sequence commands on a graphics calculator. The sequence is given by $t_n = 6 - 2n$.

Thus, $\displaystyle\sum_{k=1}^{12}(6 - 2k) = -84$.

```
sum(seq(6-2X,X,1
,12,1))
               -84
```

TECHNOLOGY
GRAPHICS CALCULATOR

Keystroke Guide, page 759

Evaluate $\displaystyle\sum_{k=1}^{15}(22-7k)$.

CRITICAL THINKING   If an arithmetic sequence has a nonzero constant difference, can any sum of terms in the corresponding arithmetic series be 0? Justify your response with examples.

Exercises

● Communicate

1. What information about an arithmetic series is needed to find its sum?

2. Explain how to use summation notation to express the following series:
   $$2 + 4 + 6 + 8 + 10 + 12$$

3. In how many different ways can you represent the series $2 + 4 + 6 + 8$? Explain.

● Guided Skills Practice

APPLICATION

4. **MERCHANDISING** Refer to the pattern for stacking cans described at the beginning of the lesson. How many cans are in an 18-row triangular display of cans stacked in this pattern? *(EXAMPLE 1)*

5. Given $5 + 12 + 19 + 26 + \cdots$, find S_{26}. *(EXAMPLE 2)*

6. Evaluate $\displaystyle\sum_{k=1}^{10}(20-3k)$. *(EXAMPLE 3)*

● Practice and Apply

☑ internet connect

**Homework
Help Online**
Go To: **go.hrw.com**
Keyword:
MB1 Homework Help

Use the formula for an arithmetic series to find each sum.

7. $2 + 4 + 6 + 8 + 10$

8. $5 + 10 + 15 + 20$

9. $5 + 13 + 21 + 29$

10. $13 + 17 + 21 + 25$

11. $-100 + (-96) + (-92) + (-88)$

12. $-50 + (-47) + (-44) + (-41)$

13. $1 + 2 + 3 + 4 + \cdots + 11$

14. $15 + 21 + 27 + 33 + \cdots + 63$

15. $-4 + (-13) + (-22) + \cdots + (-76)$

16. $10 + 8 + 6 + 4 + 2 + \cdots + (-4)$

17. Find the sum of the first 300 natural numbers.

18. Find the sum of all even numbers from 2 to 200 inclusive.

19. Find the sum of the multiples of 3 from 3 to 99 inclusive.

20. Find the sum of the multiples of 9 from 9 to 657 inclusive.

For each arithmetic series, find S_{25}.

21. $3 + 7 + 11 + 15 + \cdots$

22. $25 + 24 + 23 + 22 + \cdots$

23. $4 + 14 + 24 + 34 + \cdots$

24. $6 + 2 + (-2) + (-6) + \cdots$

25. $5 + 10 + 15 + 20 + \cdots$

26. $3 + 6 + 9 + 12 + \cdots$

27. $-12 + (-6) + 0 + 6 + \cdots$

28. $-17 + (-12) + (-7) + (-2) + 3 + \cdots$

29. $10 + 20 + 30 + 40 + 50 + \cdots$

30. $100 + 200 + 300 + 400 + 500 + \cdots$

31. $-10 + (-15) + (-20) + (-25) + (-30) + \cdots$

32. $-20 + (-22) + (-24) + (-26) + (-28) + \cdots$

33. $\sqrt{2} + 2\sqrt{2} + 3\sqrt{2} + 4\sqrt{2} + 5\sqrt{2} + \cdots$

34. $5\sqrt{3} + 10\sqrt{3} + 15\sqrt{3} + 20\sqrt{3} + \cdots$

35. $2\pi + 3\pi + 4\pi + 5\pi + 6\pi + \cdots$

Evaluate.

36. $\displaystyle\sum_{m=1}^{5} (15 - 2m)$

37. $\displaystyle\sum_{j=1}^{8} (30 - 2j)$

38. $\displaystyle\sum_{k=1}^{6} (10 + k)$

39. $\displaystyle\sum_{m=1}^{4} (5 + m)$

40. $\displaystyle\sum_{n=1}^{5} (100 - 5n)$

41. $\displaystyle\sum_{n=1}^{5} (60 - 4n)$

42. $\displaystyle\sum_{j=1}^{6} (1000 + 25j)$

43. $\displaystyle\sum_{j=1}^{5} (500 + 2j)$

44. $\displaystyle\sum_{k=1}^{10} (40 - 2k)$

45. $\displaystyle\sum_{m=1}^{10} (600 - 10m)$

46. $\displaystyle\sum_{n=1}^{50} (500 + 20n)$

47. $\displaystyle\sum_{k=1}^{10} \left(\frac{2}{5} + \frac{1}{5}k\right)$

48. $\displaystyle\sum_{j=1}^{12} \left(\frac{1}{3} + \frac{1}{6}j\right)$

49. $\displaystyle\sum_{k=1}^{20} (2.2 + 3.1k)$

50. $\displaystyle\sum_{k=1}^{10} (1.2 - 4.1k)$

CHALLENGES

51. For a certain arithmetic series, $S_4 = 50$ and $S_5 = 75$. Find the first five terms.

52. Find the number of and values of the arithmetic means that should be inserted between 1 and 50 in order to make the sum of the resulting series equal to 459.

APPLICATION

53. INVENTORY Pipes are stacked as shown at right.
   a. Find the number of pipes in a stack of 6 rows if the bottom row contains 9 pipes.
   b. Find the number of pipes in a stack of 7 rows if the bottom row contains 10 pipes.

54. MERCHANDISING A pattern for stacking cans is shown at right.
  a. How many cans are in a 7-row display?
  b. If 66 cans are to be stacked in this pattern, how many rows will the display have?

55. ENTERTAINMENT A marching band formation consists of 8 rows. The first row has 5 musicians, the second has 7, the third has 9, and so on. How many musicians are in the last row? How many musicians are there in all?

Look Back

Write each pair of parametric equations as a single equation in *x* and *y*. *(LESSON 3.6)*

56. $\begin{cases} x(t) = -3t \\ y(t) = t - 6 \end{cases}$ **57.** $\begin{cases} x(t) = t + 2 \\ y(t) = |t - 2| \end{cases}$ **58.** $\begin{cases} x(t) = 2t - 1 \\ y(t) = 3t + 1 \end{cases}$

Write each product as a polynomial expression in standard form. *(LESSON 7.3)*

59. $2x(3x^2 - 5x^3 + 2x - 6)$ **60.** $(x - 3)^2(x^2 - 2x + 5)$

Write an equation to represent each relationship. Use *k* as the constant of variation. *(LESSON 8.1)*

61. y varies jointly as x and z and inversely as the square of m.
62. y varies directly as x^2 and inversely as z^3.

Find the domain for each radical function. *(LESSON 8.6)*

63. $f(x) = 2\sqrt{x^2 + 36}$ **64.** $f(x) = \sqrt{2(x - 3)} + 1$

65. In how many ways can you choose 6 objects from a collection of 30 distinct objects, if order does not matter? *(LESSON 10.3)*

66. Two number cubes are rolled. The sum of the numbers appearing on the top faces is recorded. What is the probability that the number rolled on one cube is 4 given that the sum of the numbers is 6? *(LESSON 10.6)*

Look Beyond

67. The first term of a certain sequence is 2. Each successive term is formed by doubling the previous term. Write the first eight terms of the sequence.

Graph each sequence, and describe the graph.

68.

x	1	2	3	4	5
t_n	3	6	12	24	48

69.

x	1	2	3	4	5
t_n	-4	-2	-1	$-\frac{1}{2}$	$-\frac{1}{4}$

Geometric Sequences

Why Geometric sequences can be used to model real-world events such as the depreciation of an automobile.

Objectives

● Recognize geometric sequences, and find the indicated term of a geometric sequence.

● Find the geometric means between two numbers.

APPLICATION

DEPRECIATION

An automobile that cost $12,500 depreciates, and its value at the end of a given year is 80% of its value at the end of the preceding year. What is it worth after 10 years? You can answer this question by using a *geometric sequence*.
You will answer this question in Example 2.

Two examples of geometric sequences and their graphs are shown below.

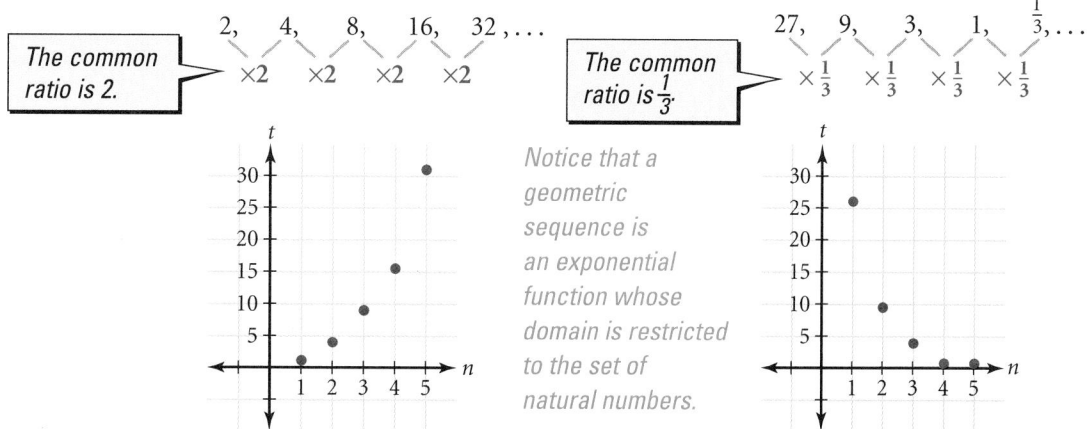

The common ratio is 2.

2,   4,   8,   16,   32 , ...
   ×2   ×2   ×2   ×2

The common ratio is $\frac{1}{3}$.

27,   9,   3,   1, $\frac{1}{3}$, ...
   ×$\frac{1}{3}$ ×$\frac{1}{3}$ ×$\frac{1}{3}$ ×$\frac{1}{3}$

Notice that a geometric sequence is an exponential function whose domain is restricted to the set of natural numbers.

A **geometric sequence** is a sequence in which the ratio of successive terms is the same number, r, called the **common ratio**. That is, if t_n is any term in a geometric sequence, then the following is true:

$$\frac{t_n}{t_{n-1}} = r, \text{ or } t_n = rt_{n-1}, \text{ where } n \geq 2$$

The formula for the general term, $t_n = rt_{n-1}$, where $n \geq 2$, is a recursive formula because it gives the nth term of a sequence in relation to the previous term and r. You can also write an explicit formula for the nth term of a sequence by using the first term and r.

Look for a pattern in the recursive formula for the geometric sequence defined by $t_1 = 3$ and $t_n = 4t_{n-1}$, where $n \geq 2$.

Recursive formula	Pattern
$t_1 = 3$	$t_1 = 4^0 \cdot 3$
$t_2 = 4 \cdot 3$	$t_2 = 4^1 \cdot 3$
$t_3 = 4(4 \cdot 3)$	$t_3 = 4^2 \cdot 3$
$t_4 = 4(4 \cdot 4 \cdot 3)$	$t_4 = 4^3 \cdot 3$

From the pattern, the explicit formula is $t_n = 4^{n-1} \cdot 3$, where $n \geq 1$.

---

*n*th Term of a Geometric Sequence

The nth term, t_n, of a geometric sequence whose first term is t_1 and whose common ratio is r is given by the explicit formula $t_n = t_1 r^{n-1}$, where $n \geq 1$.

E X A M P L E ❶ **Find the fifth term of the sequence defined by the recursive formula $t_1 = 8$ and $t_n = 3t_{n-1}$.**

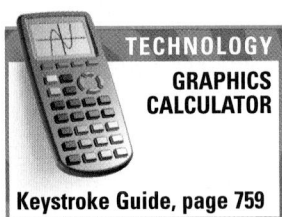

● **SOLUTION**

This is a geometric sequence in which $t_1 = 8$ and $r = 3$. Use the explicit formula for the nth term of a geometric sequence to find the fifth term.

$$t_n = t_1 r^{n-1}$$
$$t_5 = 8(3)^{5-1}$$
$$t_5 = 648$$

The fifth term of the sequence is 648.

CHECK

← 1st term
← 2nd term
← 3rd term
← 4th term
← 5th term

TRY THIS Find the eighth term of the sequence defined by $t_1 = 2.5$ and $t_n = -4t_{n-1}$.

E X A M P L E ❷ **Refer to the automobile described at the beginning of the lesson.**
   a. Use a recursive formula to find the value of the automobile after 4 years.
   b. Use the explicit formula for the nth term of a geometric sequence to find the value of the automobile after 10 years.

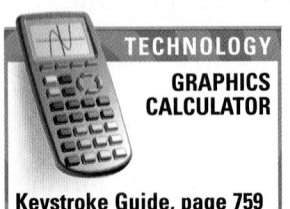

● **SOLUTION**

a. Initial value (year 0): 12,500

year 1: 12,500(0.80) = 10,000
year 2: 10,000(0.80) = 8000
year 3: 8000(0.80) = 6400
year 4: 6400(0.80) = 5120

The automobile's value after 4 years is $5120.

CHECK

← 1 year
← 2 years
← 3 years
← 4 years

b. At year 10, $n = 11$. Find t_{11}.

$$t_n = t_1 r^{n-1}$$
$$t_{11} = 12{,}500(0.8^{11-1})$$
$$t_{11} \approx 1342.18$$

The automobile's value after 10 years is $1342.18.

TRY THIS

An automobile that costs $12,500 depreciates such that its value at the end of a given year is 76% of its value at the end of the preceding year. Use the explicit formula for the nth term of a geometric sequence to find the automobile's value after 10 years.

If you know any two terms of a geometric sequence, you can often write all of the terms. However, Example 3 shows that it is possible for two geometric sequences to share terms.

EXAMPLE ③ Find the eighth term of the geometric sequence in which $t_3 = 36$ and $t_5 = 324$.

● **SOLUTION**

1. Find the common ratio, r.

n	3	4	5
t_n	36	?	324

$\rightarrow 36r^2 = 324$

$r = \pm\sqrt{\dfrac{324}{36}}$

$r = \pm 3$

2. Find t_1 for both r-values. Because $t_5 = 324$, $n = 5$ and $t_n = 324$.

For $r = 3$:

$$t_n = t_1 r^{n-1}$$
$$324 = t_1(3)^{5-1}$$
$$\frac{324}{3^4} = t_1$$
$$4 = t_1$$

For $r = -3$:

$$t_n = t_1 r^{n-1}$$
$$324 = t_1(-3)^{5-1}$$
$$\frac{324}{(-3)^4} = t_1$$
$$4 = t_1$$

3. Find the eighth term.

For $r = 3$:

$$t_n = t_1 r^{n-1}$$
$$t_8 = 4(3)^{8-1}$$
$$t_8 = 8748$$

For $r = -3$:

$$t_n = t_1 r^{n-1}$$
$$t_8 = 4(-3)^{8-1}$$
$$t_8 = -8748$$

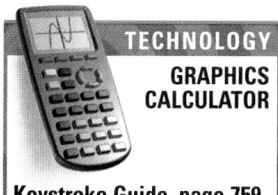
TECHNOLOGY
GRAPHICS CALCULATOR
Keystroke Guide, page 759

CHECK

CHECK

Thus, the eighth term of this geometric sequence is 8748 or −8748.

TRY THIS

Find the 12th term of the geometric sequence in which $t_2 = 240$ and $t_5 = 30$.

The terms between any two nonconsecutive terms of a geometric sequence are called the **geometric means** between the two nonconsecutive terms. For example, in the sequence 5, −10, 20, −40, 80, −160, . . . , the three geometric means between 5 and 80 are −10, 20, and −40.

E X A M P L E ❹ **Find three geometric means between 6 and 96.**

● SOLUTION

PROBLEM SOLVING   **Draw a diagram.** Let $t_1 = 6$ and $t_5 = 96$.

$$t_1 \qquad\qquad\qquad\qquad t_5$$
$$6, \underline{\ ?\ }, \underline{\ ?\ }, \underline{\ ?\ }, 96$$

Find the common ratio, r.

$$t_n = t_1 r^{n-1}$$
$$96 = 6r^{5-1} \quad \textit{Because } t_5 = 96, n = 5 \text{ and } t_n = 96.$$
$$16 = r^4$$
$$\pm 2 = r$$

Use $r = 2$ and $r = -2$ to find the two possible sets of geometric means.

$r = 2$:

$r = -2$:

TECHNOLOGY

GRAPHICS CALCULATOR

Keystroke Guide, page 759

The three geometric means are 12, 24, and 48 or −12, 24, and −48.

TRY THIS   Find three geometric means between 64 and 4.

CHECKPOINT ✔ How many sets of two geometric means are possible between $t_3 = -40$ and $t_6 = 5$? Explain.

CRITICAL THINKING   In Example 4, there are two possible common ratios. If a geometric sequence were defined to include complex numbers, what two other common ratios would be possible?

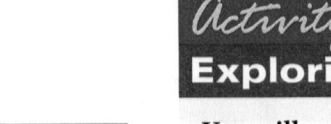

Exploring Geometric Sequences

TECHNOLOGY

GRAPHICS CALCULATOR

Keystroke Guide, page 760

You will need: a graphics calculator

1. Write the first 5 terms of each geometric sequence below.
   a. $t_1 = 1, r = 10$ **b.** $t_1 = 1, r = 2$ **c.** $t_1 = 0.1, r = 1.1$
   d. $t_1 = 1, r = 1.01$ **e.** $t_1 = 1, r = 0.1$ **f.** $t_1 = 1, r = 0.9$

2. Which sequence from Step 1 has the largest 5th term? the smallest 5th term?

CHECKPOINT ✔
3. Describe how the value of r affects the terms of the sequence when $0 < r < 1$. Describe how the value of r affects the terms of the series when $r > 1$.

Exercises

internet connect

Activities Online

Go To: **go.hrw.com**
Keyword:
MB1 College

Communicate

1. Describe how to find the nth term of $1, 3, 9, 27, \ldots$

2. Explain what happens to the terms of a geometric sequence when the common ratio, r, is doubled. Justify your answer.

3. Explain what happens to the terms of a geometric sequence when the first term, t_1, is doubled.

Guided Skills Practice

4. Find the fifth term of the sequence defined by $t_1 = 2$ and $t_n = 2t_{n-1}$. **(EXAMPLE 1)**

APPLICATION

5. DEPRECIATION A new automobile costs \$14,000 and retains 85% of its value each year. Find the value of the automobile after 10 years. **(EXAMPLE 2)**

6. Find the fifth term of the geometric sequence in which $t_4 = 768$ and $t_6 = 192$. **(EXAMPLE 3)**

7. Find three geometric means between 160 and 10. **(EXAMPLE 4)**

Practice and Apply

Determine whether each sequence is a geometric sequence. If so, identify the common ratio, r, and give the next three terms.

8. $3, 6, 12, 24, \ldots$ **9.** $20, 40, 80, 160, \ldots$ **10.** $2, 4, 6, 8, \ldots$

11. $1, 3, 5, 7, \ldots$ **12.** $10, 2, \frac{2}{5}, \frac{2}{25}, \ldots$ **13.** $2, 10, 50, 250, \ldots$

14. $2, 4, 8, 16, \ldots$ **15.** $2, 6, 18, 54, \ldots$ **16.** $1, -4, 16, -64, \ldots$

17. $2, -5, 25, \ldots$ **18.** $6, 42, 294, \ldots$ **19.** $2, 18, 162, \ldots$

20. $5, \frac{5}{2}, \frac{5}{4}, \frac{5}{8}, \ldots$ **21.** $9, 3, 1, \frac{1}{3}, \ldots$ **22.** $9, 0.9, 0.09, 0.009, \ldots$

23. $12, 3, \frac{3}{4}, \frac{3}{16}, \ldots$ **24.** $2, 3, 4.5, 6.75, \ldots$ **25.** $16, 20, 25, 31.25, \ldots$

List the first four terms of each geometric sequence.

26. $t_1 = 3$
$t_n = 2t_{n-1}$

27. $t_1 = -2$
$t_n = 4t_{n-1}$

28. $t_1 = 5$
$t_n = -2t_{n-1}$

29. $t_1 = 4$
$t_n = -3t_{n-1}$

30. $t_1 = 1$
$t_n = 4t_{n-1}$

31. $t_1 = -1$
$t_n = -0.2t_{n-1}$

32. $t_1 = -3$
$t_n = -2.2t_{n-1}$

33. $t_1 = 3$
$t_n = 3.37t_{n-1}$

34. $t_1 = 3$
$t_n = -4.88t_{n-1}$

35. In a geometric sequence, $t_1 = 6$ and $r = 4$. Find t_7.

36. In a geometric sequence, $t_1 = 5$ and $r = -2$. Find t_7.

37. In a geometric sequence, $t_1 = 3$ and $r = \frac{1}{10}$. Find t_{20}.

38. In a geometric sequence, $t_1 = 3$ and $r = -\frac{1}{10}$. Find t_{20}.

internet connect

Homework Help Online

Go To: **go.hrw.com**
Keyword:
MB1 Homework Help
for Exercises 26–56

Find the sixth term in the geometric sequence that includes each pair of terms.

39. $t_3 = 150$; $t_5 = 3750$

40. $t_4 = 189$; $t_9 = 45{,}927$

41. $t_4 = 36$; $t_8 = 2916$

42. $t_3 = 444$; $t_7 = 7104$

43. $t_5 = 24$; $t_8 = 3$

44. $t_7 = 10{,}935$; $t_{11} = 135$

45. $t_3 = -24$; $t_5 = -54$

46. $t_7 = 4$; $t_{12} = 972$

47. $t_3 = 12\frac{1}{2}$; $t_9 = \frac{25}{128}$

48. $t_2 = 25$; $t_4 = 2\frac{7}{9}$

Write an explicit formula for the nth term of each geometric sequence.

49. $2, 4, 8, 16, \ldots$

50. $1, 3, 9, 27, \ldots$

51. $1, \frac{1}{2}, \frac{1}{4}, \frac{1}{8}, \ldots$

52. $1, \frac{1}{3}, \frac{1}{9}, \frac{1}{27}, \ldots$

53. $30, 10, 3\frac{1}{3}, 1\frac{1}{9}, \ldots$

54. $40, 10, 2\frac{1}{2}, \frac{5}{8}, \ldots$

55. $\sqrt{2}, 2, 2\sqrt{2}, 4, \ldots$

56. $\sqrt{3}, 3, 3\sqrt{3}, 9, \ldots$

Find the indicated geometric means.

57. Find two geometric means between 5 and 135.

58. Find two geometric means between 4 and 13.5.

59. Find two geometric means between 5 and 16.875.

60. Find three geometric means between 1 and 81.

61. Find three geometric means between -2 and $-\frac{1}{8}$.

62. Find three geometric means between -6 and $-\frac{3}{8}$.

63. Find three geometric means between 486 and 6.

64. Find three geometric means between -40.5 and -8.

65. Find two geometric means between $41\frac{2}{3}$ and 1125.

List the first four terms of each sequence. Tell whether it is arithmetic, geometric, or neither.

66. $t_n = 4(2)^n$

67. $t_n = 4(3)^n$

68. $t_n = 20\left(\frac{1}{2}\right)^n$

69. $t_n = 9\left(\frac{2}{5}\right)^n$

70. $t_n = 3 + 10^n$

71. $t_n = 2 + 5^n$

72. $t_n = -10(3)^n$

73. $t_n = -100(4)^n$

74. $t_n = 30(-5)^n$

APPLICATION

REAL ESTATE An office building purchased for \$1,200,000 is appreciating because of rising property values in the city. At the end of each year its value is 105% of its value at the end of the previous year.

75. Use a recursive formula to determine what the value of the building will be 7 years after it is purchased.

76. Use an explicit formula to find the value of the building 4 years after it is purchased.

CHALLENGE

77. During the eighth year, the building begins to decrease in value at a rate of 8% per year. What would its value be after the 15th year?

78. MUSIC A piano keyboard has 88 equally spaced musical notes. The first, and lowest, note is assigned the letter A, and it has a frequency of 27.5 hertz (Hz). The 13th note is also assigned the letter A, and it has a frequency twice that of the preceding A note, as does each of the subsequent A notes.

27.5 Hz

a. Write an explicit formula for the frequencies of all of the A notes.

b. Find the frequency of the seventh A note in the sequence defined in part **a.**

c. Find the frequencies of the 11 equally spaced notes between the first A note and the second A note. Round your answers to the nearest hundredth.

Look Back

Write an equation in slope-intercept form for the line containing the indicated points. *(LESSON 1.3)*

79. $(-2, 5)$ and $(0, -1)$ **80.** $(9, -4)$ and $(-5, 3)$

Let $A = \begin{bmatrix} 1 & 0.5 \\ 2.4 & 3.8 \end{bmatrix}$, $B = \begin{bmatrix} 1.7 \\ 3.2 \end{bmatrix}$, **and** $C = [3.2 \quad 4.8]$. **Find each product, if it exists.** *(LESSON 4.2)*

81. AB **82.** CA **83.** BC **84.** CB

85. SPORTS Liam plans to spend a certain amount of time every day training for the school track team. He wants to run 3 miles and ride his bicycle for 6 miles. If he rides his bicycle an average of 12 miles per hour faster than he runs, at what rate must he run and bike in order to complete his training workout in one hour? *(LESSON 8.5)*

Simplify. Write each expression with a rational denominator. *(LESSON 8.7)*

86. $\sqrt{8} + \sqrt{98}$ **87.** $\dfrac{\sqrt{30} + \sqrt{14}}{\sqrt{2}}$ **88.** $\sqrt{6x} + \dfrac{\sqrt{2x}}{\sqrt{3}} - \sqrt{\dfrac{3x}{2}}$

Find the number of permutations of the letters in each word below. *(LESSON 10.2)*

89. *roommate*   **90.** *apple*   **91.** *apogee*

Look Beyond

92. Consider the geometric sequence 0.3, 0.03, 0.003, 0.0003, . . .

     a. Find the sum of the first 4 terms and the sum of the first 10 terms.

     b. What value are the sums approaching?

Geometric Series and Mathematical Induction

Objectives

● Find the sum of the first n terms of a geometric series.

● Use mathematical induction to prove statements about natural numbers.

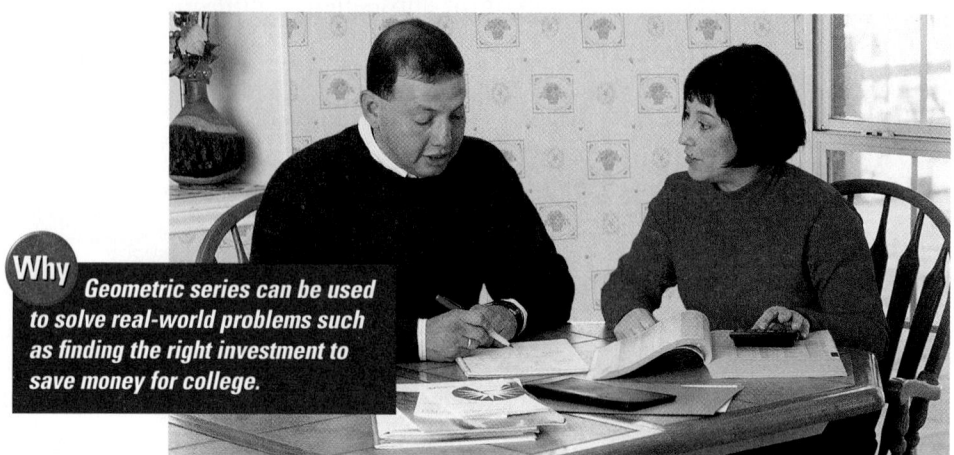

Why *Geometric series can be used to solve real-world problems such as finding the right investment to save money for college.*

Mr. and Mrs. Sanchez want to invest money for their child's college education. They have decided to invest $2000 at the beginning of every year for the next 10 years. If the investment is in an account that earns 8% annual interest, compounded once per year, how much will their investment be worth at the end of the 10th year? *You will solve this in Example 2.*

Geometric Series

A **geometric series** is the indicated sum of the terms of a geometric sequence. Consider the sequence 2, 4, 8, 16, 32, . . . The sum of the first five terms, denoted by S_5, is $S_5 = 2 + 4 + 8 + 16 + 32 = 62$.

You can derive a formula for the sum of a geometric series by using the Subtraction Property of Equality, as shown below.

$$S_n = t_1 + t_1r + t_1r^2 + \cdots + t_nr^{n-2} + t_nr^{n-1}$$

> *Each side is multiplied by the common ratio, r.*

$$rS_n = t_1r + t_1r^2 + \cdots + t_nr^{n-2} + t_nr^{n-1} + t_nr^n$$

$$S_n - rS_n = t_1 + 0 + 0 + \cdots + 0 + 0 - t_nr^n$$

$$S_n(1 - r) = t_1 - t_1r^n$$

> *To divide both sides of the equation by $1 - r$, r cannot equal 1.*

$$S_n = \frac{t_1(1 - r^n)}{1 - r}, \text{ or } t_1\left(\frac{1 - r^n}{1 - r}\right)$$

Notice that S_n is undefined when $r = 1$.

CHECKPOINT ✔ Using the sequence 2, 4, 8, . . . , find S_5 by following the procedure used in the derivation of S_n.

Sum of the First n Terms of a Geometric Series

The sum, S_n, of the first n terms of a geometric series is given by

$S_n = t_1\left(\frac{1 - r^n}{1 - r}\right)$, where t_1 is the first term, r is the common ratio, and $r \neq 1$.

Activity
Exploring Geometric Series

You will need: no special materials

Consider the geometric series $S_n = 1 + 2 + 4 + 8 + \cdots + 2^{n-1}$.

1. Copy and complete the table.

2. Compare each sum with 2^n.

n	1	2	3	4	5	6	7	8
S_n	1	3	7	15	?	?	?	?

3. Predict the sum of the first 10 terms. Check your prediction.

CHECKPOINT ✔ **4.** Compare your answer from Step 3 with the formula for S_n when $t_1 = 1$ and $r = 2$.

E X A M P L E **1** **Given the series $3 + 4.5 + 6.75 + 10.125 + \cdots$, find S_{10} to the nearest tenth.**

● **SOLUTION**

1. Find the common ratio, r. $\qquad r = \frac{4.5}{3} = \frac{6.75}{4.5} = 1.5$

2. Substitute 3 for t_1, 1.5 for r, and 10 for n in $S_n = t_1\left(\dfrac{1 - r^n}{1 - r}\right)$.

$$S_{10} = 3\left[\frac{1 - (1.5)^{10}}{1 - 1.5}\right] \approx 340.0$$

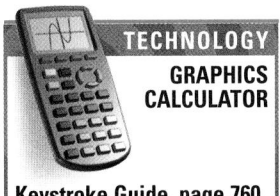

TECHNOLOGY
GRAPHICS CALCULATOR

Keystroke Guide, page 760

CHECK

Define the geometric sequence involved.

$$t_n = t_1 r^{n-1}$$
$$t_n = 3 \times 1.5^{n-1}$$

Then use the summation and sequence commands. Thus, $S_{10} \approx 340.0$.

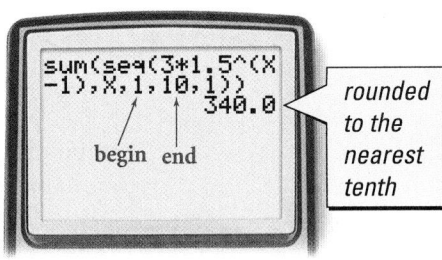

sum(seq(3*1.5^(X
−1),X,1,10,1))
                340.0

begin end

rounded to the nearest tenth

TRY THIS Given the series $400 + 300 + 225 + 168.75 + \dots$, find S_{16} to the nearest tenth.

E X A M P L E **2** Refer to the investment situation described at the beginning of the lesson. **How much money will be in the account at the end of the 10th year?**

APPLICATION
INVESTMENTS

● **SOLUTION**

After year 1 → $\quad S_1 = 2000(1.08)$

After year 2 → $\quad S_2 = 2000(1.08) + 2000(1.08)^2$

After year 3 → $\quad S_3 = 2000(1.08) + 2000(1.08)^2 + 2000(1.08)^3$
$\qquad\qquad\qquad\vdots$

After year 10 → $\quad S_{10} = 2000(1.08) + 2000(1.08)^2 + \cdots + 2000(1.08)^{10}$

This is a geometric series in which $t_1 = 2000(1.08) = 2160$, $r = 1.08$, and $n = 10$.

$$S_{10} = 2160\left[\frac{1 - (1.08)^{10}}{1 - 1.08}\right] \approx 31{,}290.97$$

At the end of the 10th year, the account will contain $31,290.97.

EXAMPLE ③ Evaluate $\sum_{k=1}^{6} 2(3^{k-1})$.

SOLUTION

TECHNOLOGY
GRAPHICS CALCULATOR

Keystroke Guide, page 760

This summation notation indicates the sum of the first six terms of the geometric series in which $t_1 = 2$ and $r = 3$.

$$S_n = t_1\left(\frac{1 - r^n}{1 - r}\right)$$

$$S_6 = 2\left(\frac{1 - 3^6}{1 - 3}\right)$$

$$S_6 = 728$$

CHECK

```
sum(seq(2*3^(X-1
),X,1,6,1))
            728
```

TRY THIS   Evaluate $\sum_{k=1}^{5} 1.5[(-2)^{k-1}]$.

CRITICAL THINKING   Evaluate $\sum_{k=1}^{6} (3^{k-1})$. Compare the result with the result in Example 3. Make a hypothesis about how a series is affected if each term of the corresponding sequence is multiplied by a constant number, c.

Mathematical Induction

How can you determine whether a general statement, such as $1 + 2 + 3 + \cdots + n = \frac{n(n + 1)}{2}$, is true for every natural number? Because it is impossible to test every natural number, n, you can use a type of proof called *mathematical induction*.

The principle of mathematical induction is like a line of dominoes that fall over one by one after the first domino is pushed. If you can show that the statement is true for one natural number, then induction will prove it to be true for the next natural number and the next natural number and so on.

Mathematical Induction

To prove that a statement is true for all natural numbers n:

Basis Step: Show that the statement is true for $n = 1$.

Induction Step: Assume the statement is true for a natural number, k. Then prove that it is true for the natural number $k + 1$.

Prove the following statement:

For every natural number n, $1 + 2 + 3 + \cdots + n = \dfrac{n(n+1)}{2}$.

● **SOLUTION**

1. Basis Step

Show that $1 + 2 + 3 + \cdots + n = \dfrac{n(n+1)}{2}$ is true for $n = 1$.

$$S_n = \frac{n(n+1)}{2}$$

$$1 \overset{?}{=} \frac{1(1+1)}{2}$$

$$1 = 1 \quad \textbf{True}$$

2. Induction Step

Assume the statement is true for a natural number, k.

$$S_k: 1 + 2 + 3 + \cdots + k = \frac{k(k+1)}{2}$$

Then prove that it is true for the next natural number, $k + 1$.

• Determine the statement to be proved, S_{k+1}:

Add $k + 1$ to the left side, and substitute $k + 1$ for k on the right.

$$S_k: 1 + 2 + 3 + \cdots + k = \frac{k(k+1)}{2}$$

$$S_{k+1}: 1 + 2 + 3 + \cdots + k + (k+1) = \frac{(k+1)[(k+1)+1]}{2}$$

> This is the statement to be proved.

$$1 + 2 + 3 + \cdots + k + (k+1) = \frac{(k+1)(k+2)}{2} \quad \textit{Simplify.}$$

• Begin with the statement assumed to be true, S_k, and use properties of equality to prove the statement that you want to prove, S_{k+1}:

$$S_k: 1 + 2 + 3 + \cdots + k = \frac{k(k+1)}{2}$$

$$1 + 2 + 3 + \cdots + k + (k+1) = \frac{k(k+1)}{2} + (k+1) \quad \textit{Addition Property of Equality}$$

$$= \frac{k(k+1)}{2} + \frac{2(k+1)}{2} \quad \textit{Common denominators}$$

$$= \frac{k^2 + k + 2k + 2}{2} \quad \textit{Add fractions.}$$

$$= \frac{k^2 + 3k + 2}{2} \quad \textit{Combine like terms.}$$

$$= \frac{(k+1)(k+2)}{2} \quad \textit{Factor.}$$

CHECK

Substitute any two consecutive natural numbers for k and $k + 1$.

$$\frac{k(k+1)}{2} + (k+1) = \frac{k(k+1)}{2} + \frac{2(k+1)}{2}$$

$$\frac{3(4)}{2} + 4 \overset{?}{=} \frac{3(4)}{2} + \frac{2(4)}{2}$$

$$10 = 10 \quad \textbf{True}$$

TRY THIS   Prove the following statement:

For every natural number n, $4 + 8 + 12 + \cdots + 4n = 2n(n+1)$.

Communicate

1. How is a geometric series different from an arithmetic series?

2. How would you use summation notation to express the series $2 + 4 + 8 + 16 + 32$? Show three different ways to do this.

3. Explain how to check the results of an induction proof.

4. If you use $n = 3$ for the basis step in an induction proof, is your general proof necessarily true for $n = 1$ and $n = 2$? Explain.

Guided Skills Practice

5. Given the series $2 + 5 + 12.5 + 31.25 + \cdots$, find S_{10} to the nearest tenth. *(EXAMPLE 1)*

APPLICATION

6. **INVESTMENTS** If a family deposits $2500 at the beginning of each year into an account earning 12% interest, compounded annually, how much would be in the account at the end of the 8th year? *(EXAMPLE 2)*

7. Evaluate $\sum_{k=1}^{6} 3(2^{k-1})$. *(EXAMPLE 3)*

8. Prove the following statement: *(EXAMPLE 4)*

   For every natural number n, $\dfrac{1}{1(2)} + \dfrac{1}{2(3)} + \cdots + \dfrac{1}{n(n+1)} = \dfrac{n}{n+1}$.

Practice and Apply

Find each indicated sum of the geometric series $1 + 2 + 4 + 8 + \cdots$

9. S_3 10. S_5 11. S_8 12. S_{11}

Find each indicated sum of the geometric series $2 + (-6) + 18 + (-54) + \cdots$

13. S_4 14. S_6 15. S_{15} 16. S_{20}

Find each indicated sum of the geometric series $4 + 6 + 9 + 13.5 + \cdots$ Give answers to the nearest tenth, if necessary.

17. S_2 18. S_3 19. S_6 20. S_7

21. S_{10} 22. S_{11} 23. S_{20} 24. S_{21}

Use the formula for the sum of the first n terms of a geometric series to find each sum. Give answers to the nearest tenth, if necessary.

25. $2 + 4 + 8 + 16 + 32$

26. $3 + 9 + 27 + 81 + 243$

27. $-1 + 2 + (-4) + 8$

28. $-5 + 15 + (-45) + 135$

29. $1 + 1.2 + 1.44 + 1.728$

30. $2 + 4.6 + 10.58 + 24.334$

31. $1 + \dfrac{2}{5} + \dfrac{4}{25} + \dfrac{8}{125}$

32. $\dfrac{2}{3} + \dfrac{1}{3} + \dfrac{1}{6} + \dfrac{1}{12} + \dfrac{1}{24}$

For Exercises 33–36, refer to the series $12 + 3 + \frac{3}{4} + \frac{3}{16} + \cdots$

33. Find t_{10}. **34.** Find t_{20}. **35.** Find S_{10}. **36.** Find S_{20}.

Identify t_1, r, and t_n, and evaluate the sum of each series.

37. $\displaystyle\sum_{k=1}^{10} 5^k$

38. $\displaystyle\sum_{k=1}^{12} (3 \cdot 2^k)$

39. $\displaystyle\sum_{j=1}^{12} \left(\frac{1}{11}\right)^{j-1}$

40. $\displaystyle\sum_{m=1}^{6} \left(\frac{1}{4}\right)^{m-1}$

41. $\displaystyle\sum_{n=1}^{8} 2.76^n$

42. $\displaystyle\sum_{t=1}^{10} 7.65^{t-1}$

Evaluate. Round answers to the nearest tenth, if necessary.

43. $\displaystyle\sum_{k=1}^{5} 4(2^{k-1})$

44. $\displaystyle\sum_{k=1}^{10} 4(5^{k-1})$

45. $\displaystyle\sum_{k=1}^{6} \left(\frac{1}{2}\right)^{k-1}$

46. $\displaystyle\sum_{d=1}^{6} \left(\frac{1}{3}\right)^{d-1}$

47. $\displaystyle\sum_{m=1}^{7} 3(0.2^{m-1})$

48. $\displaystyle\sum_{k=1}^{6} 2(0.3)^{k-1}$

49. $\displaystyle\sum_{k=1}^{7} 5(4^{k-1})$

50. $\displaystyle\sum_{k=1}^{8} 10(3^{k-1})$

51. $\displaystyle\sum_{k=1}^{12} 6.92^{k-1}$

52. $\displaystyle\sum_{p=1}^{8} 2.87^{p-1}$

53. $\displaystyle\sum_{n=1}^{10} \left(\frac{1}{\pi}\right)^{n}$

54. $\displaystyle\sum_{k=1}^{10} \left(\frac{1}{\pi}\right)^{k-1}$

Refer to the geometric series in which $t_1 = 5$ and $r = -5$.

55. Find S_4.

56. Find S_6.

57. Given $t_n = 3125$, find n.

58. Given $t_n = 125$, find n.

Use mathematical induction to prove that each statement is true for all natural numbers, n.

59. $n < n + 1$

60. $2 \leq n + 1$

61. $1 + 3 + 5 + \cdots + (2n - 1) = n^2$

62. $2 + 4 + 6 + \cdots + 2n = n(n + 1)$

Find S_{10} for each series. Round answers to the nearest tenth.

63. $2 + \sqrt{2} + 1 + \frac{\sqrt{2}}{2} + \cdots$

64. $2 + 4\pi + 8\pi^2 + 16\pi^3 + \cdots$

65. GEOMETRY A side of a square is 8 centimeters long. A second square is inscribed in it by joining the midpoints of the sides of the first square. This process is continued as shown in the diagram at right.

  a. Write the sequence of side-lengths for the first seven squares.
  b. Write an explicit formula for the sequence from part **a.**
  c. Find the sum of the side lengths of the first seven squares.
  d. Develop a formula in terms of t_1 and n for S_n, the sum of the side lengths of the first n squares.

|← 4 cm →|← 4 cm →|

66. GEOMETRY Smaller and smaller squares are formed consecutively, as shown at right. Find the sum of the perimeters of the first nine squares if the first square is 40 inches wide.

67. GEOMETRY Find the sum of the areas of the first six squares at right if the first square is 40 inches wide.

	10 in.
	20 in.
40 in.	

68. GEOMETRY A piece of wrapping paper is 0.0025 centimeter thick. Assuming that the result after folding is twice as thick, how thick will the paper be if it is folded on top of itself 5 times?

APPLICATIONS

INVESTMENTS Find the value of each investment at the end of the year of the last deposit.

69. $3000 deposited at the beginning of every year for 10 years at 9% interest, compounded annually

70. $2000 deposited at the beginning of every year for 20 years at 8% interest, compounded annually

71. $1500 deposited at the beginning of every year for 50 years at 5% interest, compounded annually

72. DEMOGRAPHICS The population of a city of 100,000 people increases 10% each year for 10 years. What will the population be after 10 years?

73. PHYSICS A ball is dropped from a height of 8 feet. It rebounds to one-half of its original height and falls again. If the ball keeps rebounding in this manner, what is the total distance, to the nearest tenth, that the ball travels after 10 rebounds? (Hint: Draw a diagram, and notice the pattern.)

Look Back

Graph the solution to each system of linear inequalities. *(LESSON 3.4)*

74. $\begin{cases} x + y \geq 4 \\ 2x \leq y \end{cases}$

75. $\begin{cases} y < 4x + 2 \\ x \leq 2 \\ y > -1 \end{cases}$

76. $\begin{cases} y < 8 - 2x \\ x \geq 1 \\ y \geq 0 \end{cases}$

APPLICATIONS

77. DEPRECIATION Personal computers often rapidly depreciate in value due to advances in technology. Suppose that a computer which originally cost $3800 loses 10% of its value every 6 months. *(LESSON 6.2)*
  a. What is the multiplier for this exponential decay function?
  b. Write a formula for the value of the computer, $V(t)$, after t 6-month periods.
  c. What is the value of the computer after 1 year?
  d. What is the value of the computer after 18 months?

Identify all asymptotes and holes in the graph of each rational function. *(LESSON 8.2)*

78. $f(x) = \dfrac{2x + 1}{x - 3}$

79. $g(x) = \dfrac{x - 5}{3x^2}$

80. $h(x) = \dfrac{x + 4}{x^2 + 3x - 4}$

Simplify each rational function. *(LESSON 8.3)*

81. $f(x) = \dfrac{x - 3}{2x^2 - 5x - 3}$

82. $f(x) = \dfrac{x^2 - 5x + 4}{x^2 + 2x - 3}$

83. MUSIC Maria, a violinist, wants to form a string octet with friends from the school orchestra. She will need 3 more violinists, 2 violists, and 2 cellists. In the orchestra, there are 24 violinists (not including Maria), 7 violists, and 12 cellists. In how many different ways can she pick members of the octet? *(LESSON 10.3)*

Look Beyond

84. Consider the geometric sequence $\frac{1}{2}, \frac{1}{4}, \frac{1}{8}, \frac{1}{16}, \ldots$ Calculate $S_1, S_2, S_3, S_4,$ and S_5. Plot these points on a number line. Describe the behavior of S_n as n increases.

PORTFOLIO ACTIVITY

Tile A
Tile B
Tile C
Tile D

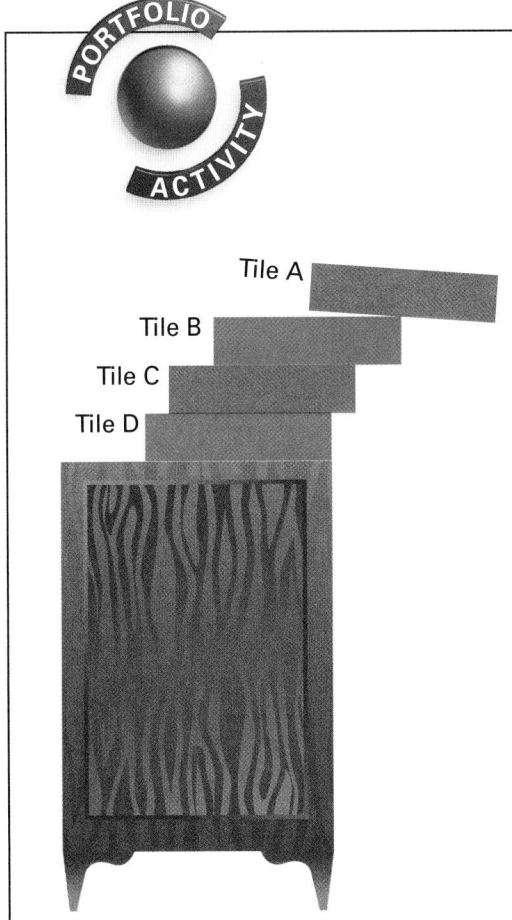

As tiles are moved over the edge of a desk, as shown at left, the center of gravity for the entire stack of tiles moves closer and closer to the edge of the desk. If the tiles are moved in such a way that the center of gravity for the entire stack is shifted beyond the edge of the desk, then the stack of tiles will fall over the edge.

Place four congruent tiles in a neat stack on your desk so that the front edge of each tile is aligned with the edge of the desk. The original center of gravity for these tiles is located half of the length of a tile from the edge of the desk.

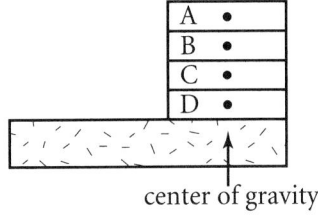

center of gravity

Extend tile A beyond tile B as far as possible while keeping the stack balanced. Keeping the position of tile A on tile B, extend tile B beyond tile C as far as possible while keeping the stack balanced. Continue this process with tiles C and D. Explain what happens to the distance that each successive tile can be extended.

WORKING ON THE CHAPTER PROJECT

You should now be able to complete Activity 2 of the Chapter Project.

Infinite Geometric Series

Objective

- Find the sum of an infinite geometric series, if one exists.

- Write repeating decimals as fractions.

Why *Infinite geometric series can be used to describe patterns such as those found in some fractal art and geometric designs.*

From *Fractals Everywhere*, ©1988 Academic Press

From *Fractals Everywhere*, ©1988 Academic Press

APPLICATION

ART

Denise is making a design using only equilateral triangles. The outer triangle is 20 inches long on each side. A second equilateral triangle is formed by joining the midpoints of the sides of the outer triangle. The process is continued. The length of the path shown in black in the figure at right can be modeled by the geometric series below.

$$20 + 10 + 5 + 2.5 + 1.25 + 0.625$$

If the path were to continue indefinitely, it could be modeled by the *infinite geometric series* below.

$$20 + 10 + 5 + 2.5 + \cdots + t_1 r^{n-1} + \cdots$$

|← 20 in. →|

An **infinite geometric series** is a geometric series with infinitely many terms. A **partial sum** of an infinite series is the sum of a given number of terms and not the sum of the entire series. Examine the table and the graph of partial sums for this infinite geometric series.

n	S_n
1	20
2	30
3	35
4	37.5
5	38.75
10	39.9609375
20	39.99996185
30	39.99999996
⋮	⋮

Notice that as n gets larger and larger, the sums get closer and closer to the number 40.

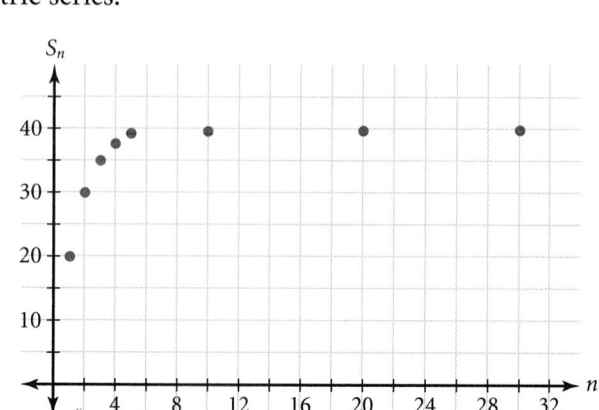

Examine the formula for the sum of a geometric series to see why this sum approaches 40.

$$S_n = t_1\left(\frac{1 - r^n}{1 - r}\right)$$

$$S_n = 20\left(\frac{1 - 0.5^n}{1 - 0.5}\right)$$

$$S_n = 20\left(\frac{1}{1 - 0.5} - \frac{0.5^n}{1 - 0.5}\right) \quad \textit{Rewrite } \frac{1 - 0.5^n}{1 - 0.5}.$$

$$S_n = \frac{20}{1 - 0.5} - \frac{20(0.5^n)}{1 - 0.5}$$

What happens to 0.5^n as n gets larger?

As n gets larger, the rational expression $\frac{20(0.5^n)}{1 - 0.5}$ gets closer and closer to 0.

Therefore, the partial sums of this geometric series get closer and closer to $\frac{20}{1 - 0.5}$, or 40.

When the partial sums of an infinite series approach a fixed number as n increases, the infinite geometric series is said to **converge**.

When the partial sums of an infinite series do not approach a fixed number as n increases, the infinite geometric series is said to **diverge.**

Exploring Convergence

TECHNOLOGY
GRAPHICS CALCULATOR

Keystroke Guide, page 760

You will need: a graphics calculator or paper and pencil

1. For each infinite geometric series indicated below, complete a table of values for n and S_n, using n-values of 1, 2, 3, 5, 10, and 100.

   a. $t_1 = -5; r = -0.25$ **b.** $t_1 = 5; r = -0.25$

   c. $t_1 = 2; r = \frac{1}{3}$ **d.** $t_1 = 2; r = -\frac{1}{3}$

2. For each infinite geometric series indicated below, complete a table of values for n and S_n, using n-values of 1, 2, 3, 5, 10, and 100.

   a. $t_1 = -5; r = -8$ **b.** $t_1 = 5; r = -8$

   c. $t_1 = 2; r = 3$ **d.** $t_1 = 2; r = -3$

3. Which of the infinite geometric series from Steps 1 and 2 converge? How are the common ratios of these series alike?

4. Which of the infinite geometric series from Steps 1 and 2 diverge? How are the common ratios of these series alike?

CHECKPOINT ✔ 5. Make a conjecture about how the common ratio of an infinite geometric series determines whether or not the series converges. Test your conjecture.

Sum of an Infinite Geometric Series

If a geometric sequence has common ratio r and $|r| < 1$, then the sum, S, of the related infinite geometric series is as follows:

$$S = \frac{t_1}{1 - r}$$

If a geometric sequence has common ratio r and $|r| > 1$, then the related infinite geometric series diverges and therefore does not have a sum. Examine the table of values and the graph of the infinite geometric series below in which $t_1 = 5$ and $r = 2$:

$$5 + 10 + 20 + 40 + \cdots + t_1 r^{n-1} + \cdots$$

n	S_n
1	5
2	15
3	35
4	75
5	155
6	315
7	635
8	1275
⋮	⋮

Notice that as n gets larger and larger, the sums also get larger and larger.

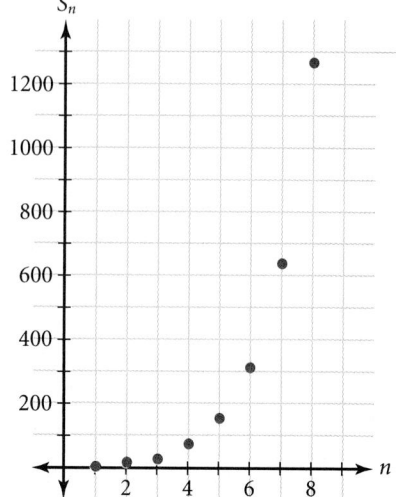

CHECKPOINT ✔ What happens to the partial sums of an infinite geometric series in which $t_1 = 5$ and $r = -2$ as n increases?

CRITICAL THINKING Examine the table and graph for S_n above. Does S_n increase exponentially? Explain.

E X A M P L E ① **Find the sum of the infinite series $3 + 1.2 + 0.48 + 0.192 + \cdots$, if it exists.**

● **SOLUTION**

1. Determine whether the infinite series is geometric.

$$\frac{t_2}{t_1} = \frac{1.2}{3} = 0.4 \qquad \frac{t_3}{t_2} = \frac{0.48}{1.2} = 0.4 \qquad \frac{t_4}{t_3} = \frac{0.192}{0.48} = 0.4$$

This is an infinite geometric series in which $t_1 = 3$ and $r = 0.4$.

2. Determine whether the series diverges or converges.

Since $|0.4| < 1$, the series converges. The sum is $S = \frac{t_1}{1 - r}$.

$$S = \frac{t_1}{1 - r} = \frac{3}{1 - 0.4} = 5$$

The sum of the series is 5. This seems reasonable because $S_4 = 4.872$.

CHECK

Graph the formula for the sum of the nth term of the geometric series in which $t_1 = 3$ and $r = 0.4$.

$$S_n = t_1\left(\frac{1 - r^n}{1 - r}\right), \text{ or } y = 3\left(\frac{1 - 0.4^x}{1 - 0.4}\right)$$

From the graph, you can see that the series converges to a sum of 5.

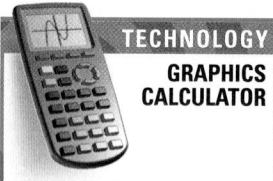

TECHNOLOGY
GRAPHICS CALCULATOR

Keystroke Guide, page 761

TRY THIS Find the sum of the infinite series $-4 + 2 + (-1) + 0.5 + \cdots$, if it exists.

The mathematical symbol for infinity is ∞. The notation $\displaystyle\sum_{k=1}^{\infty}$ indicates an infinite series.

EXAMPLE ➋ Find the sum of the infinite series $\displaystyle\sum_{k=1}^{\infty}\frac{1}{3^{k+1}}$, if it exists.

● SOLUTION

1. Determine whether the infinite series is geometric.

$$\frac{t_2}{t_1}=\frac{\frac{1}{27}}{\frac{1}{9}}=\frac{1}{3} \qquad \frac{t_3}{t_2}=\frac{\frac{1}{81}}{\frac{1}{27}}=\frac{1}{3}$$

This is a geometric series in which $t_1=\frac{1}{9}$ and $r=\frac{1}{3}$.

2. Determine whether the series diverges or converges. Because $\left|\frac{1}{3}\right|<1$, the series converges. The sum is $S=\frac{t_1}{1-r}$.

$$S=\frac{t_1}{1-r}=\frac{\frac{1}{9}}{1-\frac{1}{3}}=\frac{1}{6}$$

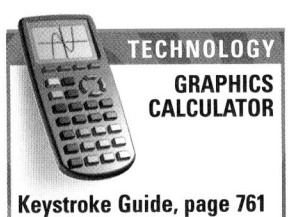
TECHNOLOGY
GRAPHICS CALCULATOR

Keystroke Guide, page 761

CHECK

Graph the formula for the sum of the nth term of the geometric series in which $t_1=\frac{1}{9}$ and $r=\frac{1}{3}$.

From the graph, you can see that the series converges to a sum of $\frac{1}{6}$.

Graph of
$$y=\frac{1}{9}\left[\frac{1-\left(\frac{1}{3}\right)^x}{1-\frac{1}{3}}\right]$$

TRY THIS Find the sum of the infinite series $\displaystyle\sum_{k=1}^{\infty}\frac{1}{2^{k+1}}$, if it exists.

Every repeating decimal is a rational number and can therefore be written in the form $\frac{p}{q}$, where p and q are integers with no common factors. Infinite series can be used to convert a repeating decimal into a fraction.

EXAMPLE ➌ Write $0.\overline{2}$ as a fraction in simplest form.

● SOLUTION

1. Write the repeating decimal as an infinite geometric series.

$$0.\overline{2}=0.222\ldots$$
$$=0.2+0.02+0.002+\cdots$$
$$=\frac{2}{10}+\frac{2}{100}+\frac{2}{1000}+\cdots$$

Notice that $0.\overline{2}$ can be written as an infinite geometric series of decimals or fractions. Thus, $t_1=0.2$, or $\frac{2}{10}$, and $r=0.1$, or $\frac{1}{10}$.

2. Because $|0.1|<1$, the series converges. The sum is $S=\frac{t_1}{1-r}$.

$$S=\frac{0.2}{1-0.1}=\frac{0.2}{0.9}=\frac{2}{9}$$

CHECK

Use a calculator: $2\div9=0.222\ldots$ Thus, $0.\overline{2}$ can be written as $\frac{2}{9}$.

TRY THIS Write $0.\overline{5}$ as a fraction in simplest form.

Exercises

● Communicate

1. Explain how to determine whether an infinite geometric series has a sum.
2. How can you tell if the series $\sum_{k=1}^{\infty}\left(\frac{1}{2}\right)^k$ and the series $\sum_{k=1}^{\infty} 2^k$ converge?
3. Explain how to write a repeating decimal as a fraction.

● Guided Skills Practice

4. Find the sum of the infinite series $3 + 2 + \frac{4}{3} + \frac{8}{9} + \cdots$, if it exists. **(EXAMPLE 1)**
5. Find the sum of the infinite series $\sum_{k=1}^{\infty} \frac{1}{4^{k+1}}$, if it exists. **(EXAMPLE 2)**
6. Write $0.\overline{3}$ as a fraction in simplest form. **(EXAMPLE 3)**

● Practice and Apply

Find the sum of each infinite geometric series, if it exists.

7. $\frac{1}{3} + \frac{1}{9} + \frac{1}{27} + \frac{1}{81} + \cdots$ 8. $1 + \frac{1}{5} + \frac{1}{25} + \frac{1}{125} + \cdots$

9. $2 + 1.5 + 1.125 + 0.84375 + \cdots$ 10. $3 + 1.2 + 0.48 + 0.192 + \cdots$

11. $1 + 2 + 4 + 8 + \cdots$ 12. $2 + 6 + 18 + 54 + \cdots$

13. $\frac{11}{15} + \frac{1}{15} + \frac{1}{165} + \frac{1}{1815} + \cdots$ 14. $\frac{9}{17} + \frac{3}{17} + \frac{1}{17} + \frac{1}{51} + \cdots$

15. $3 + 2.1 + 1.47 + 1.029 + \cdots$ 16. $4 + 3.2 + 2.56 + 2.048 + \cdots$

17. $\frac{1}{3} + \frac{4}{9} + \frac{16}{27} + \frac{64}{81} + \cdots$ 18. $\frac{2}{5} + \frac{12}{25} + \frac{72}{125} + \frac{432}{625} + \cdots$

Find the sum of each infinite geometric series, if it exists.

19. $\sum_{k=0}^{\infty}\left(\frac{1}{10}\right)^k$ 20. $\sum_{k=0}^{\infty}\left(\frac{5}{3}\right)^k$ 21. $\sum_{k=1}^{\infty}\left(\frac{1}{8}\right)^k$ 22. $\sum_{k=1}^{\infty}(-0.45)^k$

23. $\sum_{k=0}^{\infty}\frac{7}{10^k}$ 24. $\sum_{k=1}^{\infty}\frac{3}{5^{k+1}}$ 25. $\sum_{k=0}^{\infty}\left(-\frac{3}{7}\right)^k$ 26. $\sum_{j=0}^{\infty}\left(-\frac{4}{11}\right)^j$

27. $\sum_{k=1}^{\infty}2.9^k$ 28. $\sum_{k=1}^{\infty}4.6^k$ 29. $\sum_{k=1}^{\infty}0.7^k$ 30. $\sum_{k=1}^{\infty}(-0.73)^k$

31. $\sum_{n=0}^{\infty}3^n$ 32. $\sum_{m=0}^{\infty}5^m$ 33. $\sum_{k=1}^{\infty}\frac{3^{k-1}}{4^k}$ 34. $\sum_{k=1}^{\infty}\frac{4^{k+1}}{3^k}$

35. $\sum_{k=0}^{\infty}\left(\frac{1}{\sqrt{2}}\right)^k$ 36. $\sum_{j=0}^{\infty}\left(\frac{2}{\sqrt{3}}\right)^j$ 37. $\sum_{j=0}^{\infty}\left(\frac{1}{\pi}\right)^j$ 38. $\sum_{k=0}^{\infty}\left(\frac{\sqrt{2}}{\sqrt{3}}\right)^k$

Write an infinite geometric series that converges to the given number.

39. $0.191919\ldots$ **40.** $57.57575757\ldots$ **41.** $0.001001001001\ldots$

42. $0.219219219\ldots$ **43.** $0.353535\ldots$ **44.** $0.898989\ldots$

45. $0.819819819\ldots$ **46.** $0.733733733\ldots$ **47.** $0.121121121\ldots$

Write each decimal as a fraction in simplest form.

48. $0.\overline{5}$ **49.** $0.\overline{4}$ **50.** $0.\overline{72}$ **51.** $0.\overline{36}$

52. $0.\overline{43}$ **53.** $0.\overline{54}$ **54.** $0.\overline{372}$ **55.** $0.\overline{586}$

56. $0.\overline{831}$ **57.** $0.\overline{474}$ **58.** $0.\overline{626}$ **59.** $0.0\overline{31}$

60. Derive the formula for the sum of an infinite geometric series by using the examination of the formula shown on the top of page 729, in which n becomes increasingly large.

CONNECTIONS

61. GEOMETRY The midpoints of the sides of a square are joined to create a new square. This process is repeated for each new square. Find the sum of an infinite series of the areas of such squares if the side length of the original square is 10 centimeters.

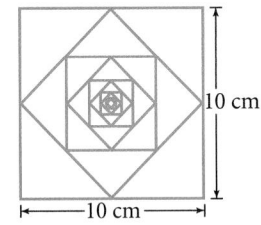

10 cm

10 cm

CHALLENGE

Step 1

Step 2

Step 3

Step 4

62. GEOMETRY A Koch curve can be constructed by taking an equilateral triangle and adding a smaller equilateral triangle along the middle third of each side (see Step 2 at left). This process is continued, or *iterated*, infinitely to form a *fractal*.

  a. Assume that the original triangle has side lengths of 9. Copy and complete the table below. Step n may contain either recursive or explicit formulas.

	Step 1	Step 2	Step 3	Step 4	...	Step n
Number of sides	3	12	48		...	
Length of each side	9	3	1		...	
Perimeter	27	36	48		...	
Number of new triangles	1	3	12		...	
New area added	$\frac{81\sqrt{3}}{4}$	$\frac{9\sqrt{3}}{4}$	$\frac{\sqrt{3}}{4}$		...	

  b. Which of the formulas in Step n describe sequences?

  c. If the formulas in Step n describe series, which are convergent and which are divergent?

  d. What is the unusual relationship between the perimeter and area of this figure?

APPLICATION

63. INVESTMENTS A *perpetuity* is an investment that pays a fixed amount of money at the end of every period forever. Perpetuities have a finite present value. For example, the present value of a perpetuity that earns 7% interest and that pays $500 at the end of every year is as follows:

$$P = 500\left(\frac{1}{1.07}\right) + 500\left(\frac{1}{1.07}\right)^2 + 500\left(\frac{1}{1.07}\right)^3 + 500\left(\frac{1}{1.07}\right)^4 + \cdots$$

  a. Find P by finding the sum of the infinite geometric series.

  b. Find the present value of a perpetuity that earns 8% interest and that pays $1000 at the end of every year forever.

64. PHYSICS A golf ball is dropped from a height of 81 inches. It rebounds to $\frac{2}{3}$ of its original height and continues rebounding in this manner. How far does it travel before coming to rest?

Look Back

65 Use a matrix equation to solve the system at right. *(LESSON 4.4)*

$$\begin{cases} -2x + y + 6z = 18 \\ 5x + 8z = -16 \\ 3x + 2y - 10z = -3 \end{cases}$$

Solve each equation for *x*. Write the exact solution and the approximate solution to the nearest hundredth, when appropriate. *(LESSONS 6.6 AND 6.7)*

66. $2^{x-2} = 23$ **67.** $3^{-x} = 19$ **68.** $8^x = 0.5$ **69.** $2^x = 7.23$

70. CONSTRUCTION A manager of a construction company is managing three projects. The probabilities that the three projects will be completed on schedule are 0.85, 0.72, and 0.94. If the events are independent, what is the probability, to the nearest hundredth, that all three projects will be completed on schedule? *(LESSON 10.5)*

Portfolio Extension
Go To: go.hrw.com
Keyword:
MB1 System COG

Look Beyond

71. a. Write out the first four terms of the infinite geometric series in which $t_1 = 0.14$ and $r_1 = 0.02$.
   b. Find the sum of the infinite series from part **a.** Simplify your answer.
   c. Write the answer as a repeating decimal with bar notation.

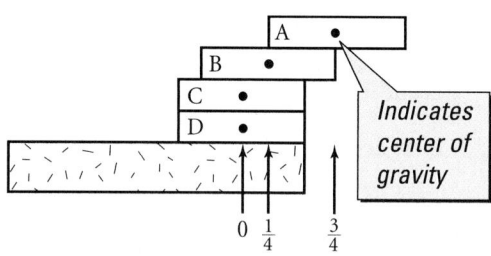

Indicates center of gravity

Refer to the diagram of tiles above. The center of gravity for tile A is $\frac{3}{4}$ of the length of a tile to the right of 0. The center of gravity for tile B is $\frac{1}{4}$ of the length of a tile to the right of 0. The centers of gravity for tiles C and D are both 0.

1. Position four tiles as shown in the diagram.

2. Keeping the position of tile A on tile B and tile B on tile C, find the maximum distance, in tile lengths, to the right of 0 that tile C can be moved without the stack of tiles falling. Record your results.

3. While keeping the position of tile A on tile B, tile B on tile C, and tile C on tile D (from Step 2), find the maximum distance to the right of 0 that tile D can be moved without the stack of tiles falling. Record your results.

WORKING ON THE CHAPTER PROJECT
You should now be able to complete Activity 3 of the Chapter Project.

Pascal's Triangle

Objectives

- Find entries in Pascal's triangle.
- Use Pascal's triangle to find combinations and probabilities.

Why *The patterns in Pascal's triangle can be used to solve real-world problems involving probability.*

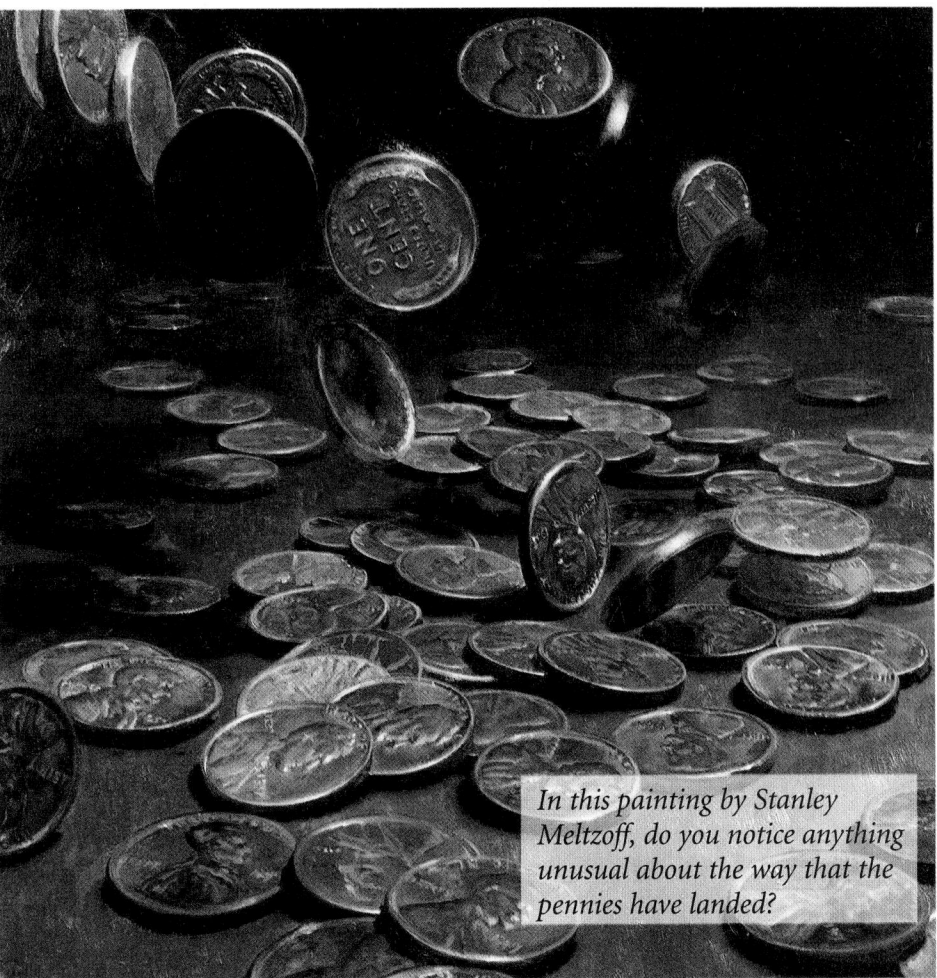

In this painting by Stanley Meltzoff, do you notice anything unusual about the way that the pennies have landed?

C O N N E C T I O N

PROBABILITY

Blaise Pascal (1623–1662)

Find the probability that exactly 3 heads or exactly 4 heads appear when a coin is tossed 7 times. *You will answer this question in Example 3.*

In this chapter you have studied the patterns in some sequences and series. A famous pattern in the form of an arithmetic triangle, called **Pascal's triangle,** is shown below.

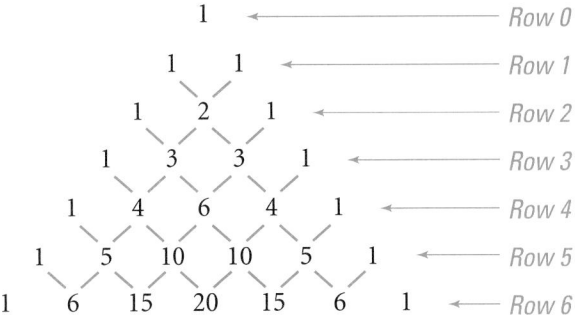

Notice that each row begins with 1 and ends with 1. Each number between the 1s is the sum of the pair of numbers above it in the previous row.

The arithmetic triangle above is called Pascal's triangle because the French mathematician and theologian Blaise Pascal analyzed the pattern extensively in the seventeenth century.

In the Activity below, you can investigate some of the many interesting patterns in Pascal's triangle.

Activity
Exploring Patterns in Pascal's Triangle

You will need: no special tools

1. Make several copies of Pascal's triangle through row 15.

2. Find the sum of the entries in each row of Pascal's triangle.

CHECKPOINT ✔ **3.** What patterns do you see in the sums from Step 2?

CHECKPOINT ✔ **4.** Notice that 5 divides all of the entries in row 5, except the first and last. Find three more rows in which the row number divides all the entries in that row (except the first and last). Find a rule to predict which rows have this property.

5. Shade all of the even numbers in the triangle.

CHECKPOINT ✔ **6.** What shape(s) do you see in the shaded numbers?

The table below shows all of the possible outcomes when a coin is tossed 4 times. It also indicates how many ways each event can occur.

0 heads	1 heads	2 heads	3 heads	4 heads
TTTT	HTTT	HHTT	HHHT	HHHH
	THTT	HTHT	HHTH	
	TTHT	HTTH	HTHH	
	TTTH	TTHH	THHH	
		THTH		
		THHT		
↓	↓	↓	↓	↓
1 way	4 ways	6 ways	4 ways	1 way

Notice that these numbers are the numbers in row 4 of Pascal's Triangle.

The number of ways that each event above can occur can be found by using combinations. For example, the number of ways that 2 heads can occur when a coin is tossed 4 times is a combination of 4 objects taken 2 at a time, or $_4C_2$.

Pascal's triangle can also be expressed in combination notation, as shown below.

$$_0C_0 \qquad \longleftarrow \text{Row 0}$$

$$\boxed{_2C_1 + _2C_2 = _3C_2} \qquad _1C_0 \quad _1C_1 \quad \longleftarrow \text{Row 1}$$

$$_2C_0 \quad _2C_1 \quad _2C_2 \quad \longleftarrow \text{Row 2}$$

$$_3C_0 \quad _3C_1 \quad _3C_2 \quad _3C_3 \quad \longleftarrow \text{Row 3}$$

$$_4C_0 \quad _4C_1 \quad _4C_2 \quad _4C_3 \quad _4C_4 \quad \longleftarrow \text{Row 4}$$

$$\boxed{_5C_0 + _5C_1 = _6C_1} \qquad _5C_0 \quad _5C_1 \quad _5C_2 \quad _5C_3 \quad _5C_4 \quad _5C_5 \quad \longleftarrow \text{Row 5}$$

$$_6C_0 \quad _6C_1 \quad _6C_2 \quad _6C_3 \quad _6C_4 \quad _6C_5 \quad _6C_6 \quad \longleftarrow \text{Row 6}$$

The patterns listed below can be found in Pascal's triangle.

Patterns in Pascal's Triangle

- Row n of Pascal's triangle contains $n + 1$ entries.
- The kth entry in row n of Pascal's triangle is $_nC_{k-1}$.
- The sum of all the entries in row n of Pascal's triangle equals 2^n.
- $_nC_{k-1} + {_nC_k} = {_{n+1}C_k}$, where $0 < k \le n$

CHECKPOINT ✔ Verify each equation below by evaluating combinations.

    a. $_7C_4 + {_7C_5} = {_8C_5}$ **b.** $_8C_1 + {_8C_2} = {_9C_2}$ **c.** $_4C_2 + {_4C_3} = {_5C_3}$

E X A M P L E ❶ **Find the 4th and 10th entries in row 12 of Pascal's triangle.**

● **SOLUTION**

The kth entry in row n of Pascal's triangle is $_nC_{k-1}$.

4th entry in row 12:

$$_nC_{k-1} = {_{12}C_3} = \frac{12!}{9!3!} = 220$$

10th entry in row 12:

$$_nC_{k-1} = {_{12}C_9} = \frac{12!}{3!9!} = 220$$

The 4th and 10th entries in row 12 of Pascal's triangle are both 220.

CHECK

TECHNOLOGY

GRAPHICS CALCULATOR

Keystroke Guide, page 761

TRY THIS Find the 2nd and 12th entries in row 11 of Pascal's triangle.

You can solve probability problems by using Pascal's triangle.

E X A M P L E ❷ **Suppose that a fair coin is tossed 7 times. In how many ways can exactly 0, 1, 2, 3, 4, 5, 6, and 7 heads appear?**

● **SOLUTION**

Because the coin is tossed 7 times, use row 7 of Pascal's triangle.

Heads	0	1	2	3	4	5	6	7
Number of ways	$_7C_0$ 1	$_7C_1$ 7	$_7C_2$ 21	$_7C_3$ 35	$_7C_4$ 35	$_7C_5$ 21	$_7C_6$ 7	$_7C_7$ 1

TRY THIS Suppose that a fair coin is tossed 8 times. In how many ways can exactly 0, 1, 2, 3, 4, 5, 6, 7, and 8 heads appear?

Row n of Pascal's triangle indicates the number of ways that each possible outcome can occur when a coin is tossed n times. The sum of all the entries in row n of Pascal's triangle, 2^n, gives the total number of possible outcomes that can occur when a coin is tossed n times.

Pascal's Triangle and Two-Outcome Experiments

If a probability experiment with 2 equally likely outcomes is repeated in n independent trials, the probability $P(A)$ of event A occurring exactly k times is given by $P(A) = \frac{{}_nC_k}{2^n}$.

E X A M P L E ③ Find the probability that exactly 3 heads or exactly 4 heads appear when a coin is tossed 7 times. Give your answer to the nearest hundredth.

CONNECTION

PROBABILITY

SOLUTION

The events "3 heads" and "4 heads" are mutually exclusive.

$P(3 \text{ heads } or\ 4 \text{ heads}) = P(3 \text{ heads}) + P(4 \text{ heads})$

$$= \frac{{}_7C_3}{2^7} + \frac{{}_7C_4}{2^7}$$

$$= \frac{35 + 35}{128}$$

$$\approx 0.55$$

The probability that exactly 3 heads or exactly 4 heads appear when a coin is tossed 7 times is about 0.55.

TECHNOLOGY

GRAPHICS CALCULATOR

Keystroke Guide, page 761

CHECK

(7 nCr 3)/(2^7)+
(7 nCr 4)/(2^7)
               .546875

TRY THIS Find the probability that exactly 4 heads or exactly 6 heads appear when a coin is tossed 8 times. Give your answer to the nearest hundredth.

Exercises

● *Communicate*

1. Describe the patterns that you see in Pascal's triangle when it is written in ${}_nC_r$ notation.

2. Describe two patterns that you see in Pascal's triangle when it is written with integer entries.

CONNECTION

3. PROBABILITY Explain how Pascal's triangle can be used to find the probability that exactly 4 tails will appear when a coin is tossed 6 times.

4. Find the third and fifth entries in row 10 of Pascal's triangle. *(EXAMPLE 1)*

5. PROBABILITY Suppose that a fair coin is tossed 6 times. In how many ways can exactly 0, 1, 2, 3, 4, 5, and 6 heads appear? *(EXAMPLE 2)*

6. PROBABILITY Find the probability that exactly 2 heads or exactly 3 heads appear when a coin is tossed 6 times. Give your answer to the nearest hundredth. *(EXAMPLE 3)*

Practice and Apply ━━━━

State the location of each entry in Pascal's triangle. Then give the value of each expression.

7. $_5C_2$ 8. $_7C_3$ 9. $_8C_5$ 10. $_7C_4$

11. $_{11}C_2$ 12. $_{12}C_4$ 13. $_{10}C_3$ 14. $_9C_2$

15. $_8C_4$ 16. $_6C_4$ 17. $_7C_2$ 18. $_9C_2$

19. $_9C_6$ 20. $_{11}C_4$ 21. $_{13}C_7$ 22. $_{12}C_8$

Find the 4th and 7th entries in the indicated row of Pascal's triangle.

23. row 7   24. row 9   25. row 11   26. row 13

internet connect

Homework Help Online
Go To: **go.hrw.com**
Keyword:
MB1 Homework Help
for Exercise 27

27. In the figure below, the sum of each diagonal is at the end of the diagonal.
   a. Find the missing sums.
   b. What is the name of the sequence formed by the sums?

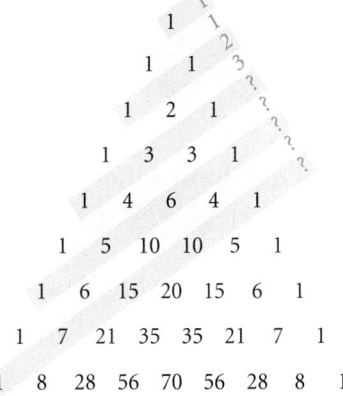

28. Evaluate 11^2, 11^3, and 11^4.
   a. How are these numbers related to Pascal's triangle?
   b. Formulate a rule for multiplying by 11 based on your answer to part a. Test your response by multiplying other numbers by 11.

PROBABILITY **Find the probability of each event.**

29. At least 4 heads appear in 6 tosses of a fair coin.
30. At least 3 heads appear in 5 tosses of a fair coin.
31. No more than 2 heads appear in 5 tosses of a fair coin.
32. No more than 3 heads appear in 6 tosses of a fair coin.
33. Either 4 *or* 5 heads appear in 8 tosses of a fair coin.
34. Either 5 *or* 6 heads appear in 7 tosses of a fair coin.

GENETICS Assume that the genders of children are equally likely. A family has 5 children. Find the probability that the children are the following:

35. exactly 3 girls   **36.** exactly 5 girls   **37.** at least 4 boys

38. at least 3 boys   **39.** at most 3 girls   **40.** at most 2 boys

ACADEMICS A student guesses the answers for 5 items on a true-false quiz. Find the probability that the indicated number of answers are correct.

41. exactly 3   **42.** exactly 4   **43.** at least 4

44. at least 3   **45.** at most 3   **46.** at most 4

47. CULTURAL CONNECTION: ASIA In 1303 the Chinese mathematician Chu Shih-Chieh published the book whose cover is shown at right. The caption reads "The Old Method Chart of the Seven Multiplying Squares."

  a. Do the numerical symbols appear to correspond to Pascal's triangle? If so, write the symbols that are equivalent to one another.

  b. How can the name of the triangle be explained? (Hint: The third row from top to bottom, 1 2 1, is labeled as the first "multiplying square.")

Look Back

Find a quadratic function that fits each list of data points. *(LESSON 5.7)*

48. $(0, 5), (1, 6), (3, 20)$ **49.** $(4, 4), (7, -2), (-3, -7)$

Solve each inequality. Graph the solution on a number line. *(LESSON 5.8)*

50. $x^2 + x - 6 > 0$ **51.** $x^2 + 7x - 18 < 0$ **52.** $6 \leq 5x + x^2$

State whether each situation involves a permutation or a combination. Then solve. *(LESSONS 10.2 AND 10.3)*

53. the number of ways to award 1st, 2nd, and 3rd prizes to a group of 10 floats entered in a homecoming parade

54. the number of ways to select a committee of 5 senators from a group of 100 senators

Look Beyond

55. Use multiplication and the Distributive Property to expand $(x + y)^4$ as a polynomial in x and y with decreasing powers of x. Compare the coefficients with Pascal's triangle. Do the entries in one of the rows agree with the coefficients in the expansion? If so, which row?

The Binomial Theorem

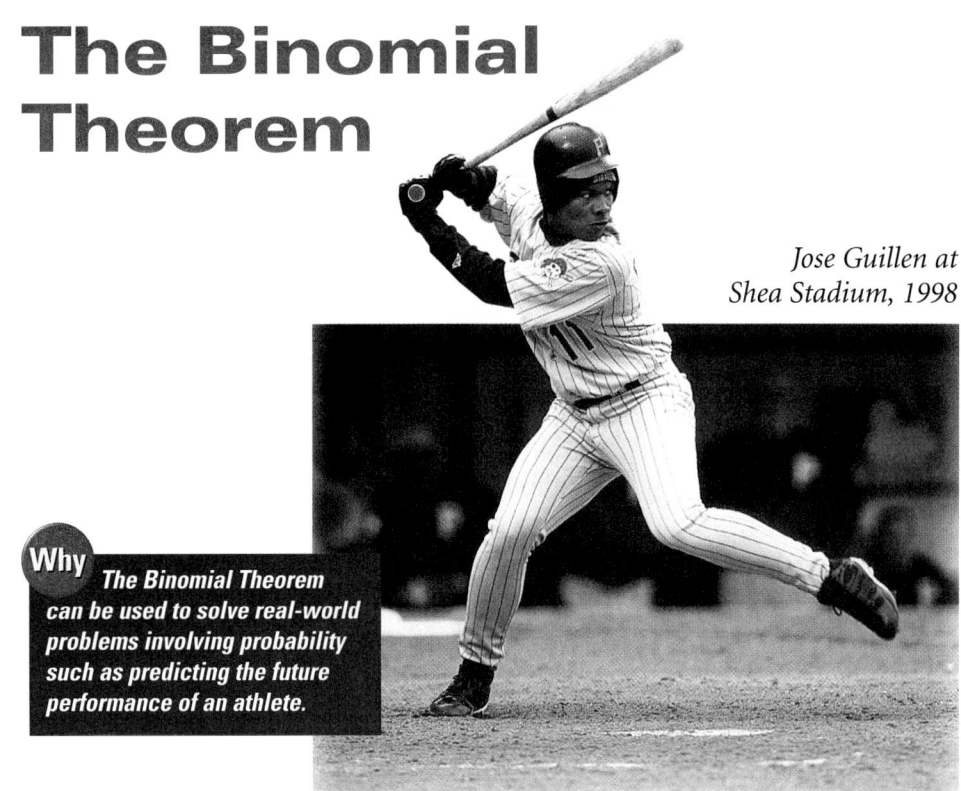

Jose Guillen at Shea Stadium, 1998

Objectives

● Use the Binomial Theorem to expand $(x + y)^n$.

● Use the Binomial Theorem to calculate a probability.

Why The Binomial Theorem can be used to solve real-world problems involving probability such as predicting the future performance of an athlete.

At one time during the 1998 season, baseball player Jose Guillen had a season batting average of 0.337. If Guillen were to maintain his 0.337 average, what is the probability that he would get exactly 4 hits in the next 5 at bats? To answer this question, you can use the *Binomial Theorem*. *You will solve this problem in Example 2.*

In Chapters 5 and 7, you worked with linear binomials in x, such as $x + 3$ and $2x - 5$. In this lesson, you will work with linear binomials in x and y, such as $x + y$ and $3x - 2y$. You can use multiplication and the Distributive Property to *expand* linear binomials in x and y that are raised to a power.

$$
\begin{aligned}
(x + y)^4 &= (x + y)^2(x + y)^2 \\
&= (x^2 + 2xy + y^2)(x^2 + 2xy + y^2) \\
&= x^2(x^2 + 2xy + y^2) + 2xy(x^2 + 2xy + y^2) + y^2(x^2 + 2xy + y^2) \\
&= x^4 + 2x^3y + x^2y^2 + 2x^3y + 4x^2y^2 + 2xy^3 + x^2y^2 + 2xy^3 + y^4 \\
&= x^4 + 4x^3y + 6x^2y^2 + 4xy^3 + y^4
\end{aligned}
$$

Exploring the Binomial Theorem

You will need: no special tools

The table below shows the expansions of the first three nonnegative integral powers of $x + y$.

1. Copy the table at right.

2. Expand $(x + y)^3$ by multiplying $(x + y)^2$ by $(x + y)$. Add a row to the bottom of the table, and write the full expansion.

Product	Expansion
$(x + y)^0 =$	1
$(x + y)^1 =$	$1x + 1y$
$(x + y)^2 =$	$1x^2 + 2xy + 1y^2$

3. Expand $(x + y)^4$ by multiplying $(x + y)^3$ by $(x + y)$. Write the full expansion below the row from Step 2.

4. Expand $(x + y)^5$ by multiplying $(x + y)^4$ by $(x + y)$. Write the full expansion below the row from Step 3.

CHECKPOINT ✔ 5. Write conjectures about the number of terms and about symmetry in the terms of the expansion in any row of the table. Verify your conjecture by filling in the row that would follow Step 4.

Notice that each row of Pascal's triangle also gives you the coefficients for the expansion of $(x + y)^n$ for positive integers n.

The Binomial Theorem stated below enables you to expand a power of a binomial. Notice that the Binomial Theorem makes use of the number of combinations of n objects taken r at a time. Recall from Lesson 10.3 that the notation $\binom{n}{k}$ indicates the combination $_nC_k$.

Binomial Theorem

Let n be a positive integer.

$$(x + y)^n = \sum_{k=0}^{n} \binom{n}{k} x^{n-k} y^k$$

$$= \binom{n}{0} x^n y^0 + \binom{n}{1} x^{n-1} y^1 + \cdots + \binom{n}{n-1} x^1 y^{n-1} + \binom{n}{n} x^0 y^n$$

E X A M P L E Expand $(x + y)^7$.

SOLUTION

Write the expansion. Then evaluate $_nC_k$ for each value of k.

$(x + y)^7$

$= \binom{7}{0} x^7 y^0 + \binom{7}{1} x^6 y^1 + \binom{7}{2} x^5 y^2 + \binom{7}{3} x^4 y^3 + \binom{7}{4} x^3 y^4 + \binom{7}{5} x^2 y^5 + \binom{7}{6} x^1 y^6 + \binom{7}{7} x^0 y^7$

$= 1x^7 y^0 + 7x^6 y^1 + 21x^5 y^2 + 35x^4 y^3 + 35x^3 y^4 + 21x^2 y^5 + 7x^1 y^6 + 1x^0 y^7$

Thus, $(x + y)^7 = x^7 + 7x^6 y + 21x^5 y^2 + 35x^4 y^3 + 35x^3 y^4 + 21x^2 y^5 + 7xy^6 + y^7$.

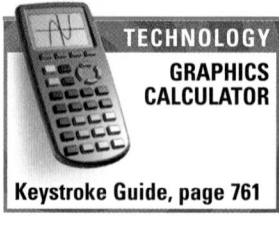
TECHNOLOGY
GRAPHICS CALCULATOR
Keystroke Guide, page 761

CHECK
Use the sequence command of a graphics calculator to check the coefficients of your answer. Use the right arrow button to view all of the coefficients. Note that $_nC_r$ notation is used.

```
seq(7 nCr X,X,0,
7,1)
{1 7 21 35 35 2...
```

TRY THIS Expand $(m + n)^6$.

CHECKPOINT ✔ Write the power of the binomial $m + n$ given by the expansion
$m^8 + 8m^7n + 28m^6n^2 + 56m^5n^3 + 70m^4n^4 + 56m^3n^5 + 28m^2n^6 + 8mn^7 + n^8$.

E X A M P L E ② Refer to the batting situation described at the beginning of the lesson.

APPLICATION
SPORTS

If Jose Guillen were to maintain his 0.337 average, what is the probability that Jose Guillen would get exactly 4 hits in the next 5 at bats?

● **SOLUTION**

$$P(\text{getting a hit}) = 0.337 \qquad P(\text{not getting a hit}) = 0.663$$

Use the Binomial Theorem because there are only two possible outcomes.

Substitute 0.337 for x and 0.663 for y in $(x + y)^n$. The number of times at bat, 5, is the exponent.

$$(0.337 + 0.663)^5 = \binom{5}{0}(0.337)^5 + \binom{5}{1}(\mathbf{0.337})^4(0.663) + \binom{5}{2}(0.337)^3(0.663)^2 +$$

$$\binom{5}{3}(0.337)^2(0.663)^3 + \binom{5}{4}(0.337)(0.663)^4 + \binom{5}{5}(0.663)^5$$

Because you are looking for the probability of 4 *hits*, evaluate the term in which $(\mathbf{0.337})^4$ appears.

$$\binom{5}{1}(0.337)^4(0.663) \approx 0.04$$

Thus, if Jose Guillen maintains his 0.337 batting average in the current season, he has approximately a 4% chance of getting exactly 4 hits in the next 5 at bats.

TRY THIS What is the probability that Jose Guillen will get exactly 2 hits in the next 4 at bats?

E X A M P L E ③ **Find the fifth term in the expansion of $(x + y)^{10}$.**

● **SOLUTION**

1. Use $(x + y)^n = \displaystyle\sum_{k=0}^{n} \binom{n}{k} x^{n-k} y^k$ to identify n and k.

For the expansion of $(x + y)^{10}$, $n = 10$.

For the fifth term, $k = 4$ because k begins at 0.

2. Evaluate $\binom{n}{k} x^{n-k} y^k$ for $n = 10$ and $k = 4$.

$$\binom{n}{k} x^{n-k} y^k = \binom{10}{4} x^{10-4} y^4$$

$$= 210 x^6 y^4$$

Thus, the fifth term in the expansion of $(x + y)^{10}$ is $210 x^6 y^4$.

TRY THIS Find the sixth term in the expansion of $(r + s)^8$.

CHECKPOINT ✔ Explain why the expansion of $(x + y)^{12}$ cannot have a term containing $x^6 y^7$.
Explain why $24a^4b^5$ cannot be a term in the expansion of $(a + b)^9$.

You can apply the Binomial Theorem to the expansion of a sum or difference of two monomials, as shown in Example 4.

E X A M P L E ④ Expand $(2x - 3y)^4$.

● **SOLUTION**

Write $(2x - 3y)^4$ as $[2x + (-3y)]^4$.

$[2x + (-3y)]^4$

$= \binom{4}{0}(2x)^4(-3y)^0 + \binom{4}{1}(2x)^3(-3y)^1 + \binom{4}{2}(2x)^2(-3y)^2 + \binom{4}{3}(2x)^1(-3y)^3 + \binom{4}{4}(2x)^0(-3y)^4$

$= 1(2x)^4(-3y)^0 + 4(2x)^3(-3y)^1 + 6(2x)^2(-3y)^2 + 4(2x)^1(-3y)^3 + 1(2x)^0(-3y)^4$

$= 1(16x^4)(1) + 4(8x^3)(-3y) + 6(4x^2)(9y^2) + 4(2x)(-27y^3) + 1(1)(81y^4)$

$= 16x^4 - 96x^3y + 216x^2y^2 - 216xy^3 + 81y^4$

TRY THIS   Expand $(x - 2y)^5$.

CRITICAL THINKING   Can you apply the Binomial Theorem to $\left(\dfrac{1}{a} + \dfrac{1}{b}\right)^4$? What is the result?

E X A M P L E ⑤ A cube has dimensions of $s \cdot s \cdot s$.

Describe all of the pieces that need to be added in order to increase the cube's length, width, and height by 0.1 unit each.

CONNECTION

GEOMETRY

● **SOLUTION**

The expansion of $(s + 0.1)^3$ is shown below.

$$(s + 0.1)^3 = 1s^3(0.1)^0 + 3s^2(0.1)^1 + 3s^1(0.1)^2 + 1s^0(0.1)^3$$

The pieces indicated by this expansion are listed below:

$1s^3(0.1)^0$: 1 piece with dimensions of $s \cdot s \cdot s$ (the original cube)

$3s^2(0.1)^1$: 3 pieces with dimensions of $s \cdot s \cdot (0.1)$

$3s^1(0.1)^2$: 3 pieces with dimensions of $s \cdot (0.1) \cdot (0.1)$

$1s^0(0.1)^3$: 1 piece with dimensions of $(0.1) \cdot (0.1) \cdot (0.1)$

Thus, 7 pieces need to be added to the original cube.

Exercises

Communicate

1. Describe the connection between Pascal's triangle and the Binomial Theorem.

2. Explain how to use the Binomial Theorem to find the fourth term in the expansion of $(x + y)^6$.

3. Explain how to use a binomial expansion to find the probability of exactly 7 heads appearing in a total of 10 coin tosses.

Guided Skills Practice

4. Expand $(a + b)^5$. *(EXAMPLE 1)*

APPLICATION

5. METEOROLOGY If there is a 0.30 probability of rain for each of the next 5 days, what is the probability of it raining exactly 3 out of the 5 days? *(EXAMPLE 2)*

6. Find the fourth term in the expansion of $(a + b)^{10}$. *(EXAMPLE 3)*

7. Expand $(3x - 2y)^5$. *(EXAMPLE 4)*

CONNECTION

8. GEOMETRY Refer to Example 5. Describe all of the pieces that need to be added to the cube in order to increase the length, width, and height by 0.2 unit each. *(EXAMPLE 5)*

Practice and Apply

Expand each binomial raised to a power.

9. $(a + b)^5$ **10.** $(p + q)^6$ **11.** $(a + b)^8$

12. $(p + q)^7$ **13.** $(x + y)^4$ **14.** $(x + y)^5$

15. $(2 + x)^5$ **16.** $(y + 3)^4$ **17.** $(y + 4)^9$

18. $(6 + x)^6$ **19.** $(x - y)^4$ **20.** $(x - y)^5$

Write each summation as a binomial raised to a power. Then write it in expanded form.

21. $\displaystyle\sum_{k=0}^{4} \binom{4}{k} a^{4-k} b^k$ **22.** $\displaystyle\sum_{k=0}^{6} \binom{6}{k} a^{6-k} b^k$

23. $\displaystyle\sum_{k=0}^{5} \binom{5}{k} a^{5-k} b^k$ **24.** $\displaystyle\sum_{k=0}^{8} \binom{8}{k} a^{8-k} b^k$

25. $\displaystyle\sum_{k=0}^{9} \binom{9}{k} x^{9-k} y^k$ **26.** $\displaystyle\sum_{k=0}^{7} \binom{7}{k} x^{7-k} y^k$

For the expansion of $(r + s)^9$, find the indicated term.

27. third term

28. fifth term

29. sixth term

30. second term

For the expansion of $(x + 4)^8$, find the indicated term.

31. fourth term

32. sixth term

33. seventh term

34. fifth term

For the expansion of $(x - y)^7$, find the indicated term.

35. fifth term

36. fourth term

37. sixth term

38. third term

internet connect

Homework Help Online

Go To: **go.hrw.com**
Keyword:
MB1 Homework Help
for Exercises 39–50

Expand each binomial.

39. $(4a + 3b)^5$

40. $(a + 2b)^4$

41. $(x - 2y)^4$

42. $(2x - y)^5$

43. $(2x + 3)^4$

44. $(x + 3y)^4$

45. $(3x + 2y)^5$

46. $(-x + 2y)^4$

47. $\left(\frac{1}{2}x + \frac{1}{3}y\right)^3$

48. $\left(\frac{2}{3}x + \frac{1}{2}y\right)^4$

49. $(0.7 + x)^4$

50. $(y + 1.2)^5$

51. Find the eighth term in the expansion of $(p + q)^{14}$.

52. How many terms are in the expansion of $(x + y)^{18}$?

53. In the expansion of $(a + b)^{10}$, a certain term contains b^3. What is the exponent of a in this term? What is the term?

54. In the expansion of $(x + y)^{15}$, a certain term contains x^{10}. What is the exponent of y in this term? What is the term?

55. The term $36a^7b^2$ appears in the expansion of $(a + b)^n$. What is the value of n?

56. The value $\binom{10}{7}$ appears as a coefficient of two different terms in the expansion of $(a + b)^{10}$. What are the two terms?

CHALLENGE

57. Let $a + bi = (1 + i)^{11}$, where $i = \sqrt{-1}$. Find a and b by using the Binomial Theorem.

CONNECTION

58. GEOMETRY The side length of a cube is a. Describe the pieces that need to be added in order to increase its length, width, and height by 0.3 unit each.

APPLICATION

59. SPORTS Refer to the batting problem in Example 2.
  a. The probability that Guillen will get at most 3 hits in the next 5 at bats is given by the sum of the last four terms of the expansion of $(0.337 + 0.663)^5$. Find this probability to the nearest hundredth.

  b. Find the probability that Guillen will get at least 3 hits in the next 5 at bats.

SPORTS If Guillen goes into a slump and his batting average drops to 0.285, what would be the probability of each event below?

60. exactly 3 hits in the next 6 at bats

61. at least 3 hits in the next 6 at bats

METEOROLOGY If there is a 20% probability of rain for each of the next 7 days, what is the probability of each event below?

62. It will rain exactly 1 of the next 7 days.

63. It will rain at least 1 of the next 7 days.

64. It will rain each of the next 7 days.

65. It will not rain each of the next 7 days.

Look Back

66. ENTERTAINMENT Ricardo won a $100 gift certificate to a movie theater. The gift certificate can be used for movie tickets. Tickets for evening shows cost $7.50 and tickets for matinees cost $4. *(LESSON 3.3)*

    a. Write an inequality that describes the total value of x tickets at $7.50 and y tickets at $4 that Ricardo could purchase with his gift certificate.
    b. Graph the inequality.
    c. Describe the values of the variables that are meaningful for this situation.
    d. What is the maximum number of $7.50 tickets he can buy?
    e. What is the maximum number of $4 tickets he can buy?
    f. Identify three reasonable solutions of the inequality.

MAXIMUM/MINIMUM Maximize and minimize each objective function within the given constraints. *(LESSON 3.5)*

67. $S = 10x + 3y$

$$\begin{cases} 0 \le x \le 10 \\ y \ge 5 \\ y \le -0.3x + 10 \end{cases}$$

68. $I = 100m + 160n$

$$\begin{cases} m + n \le 100 \\ 4m + 6n \le 500 \\ 20m + 10n \le 1600 \\ m \ge 0 \\ n \ge 0 \end{cases}$$

Classify the conic section defined by each equation, and sketch its graph. *(LESSONS 9.2, 9.3, 9.4, AND 9.5)*

69. $4x^2 + 9y^2 = 36$

70. $\dfrac{x^2}{100} + \dfrac{y^2}{36} = 1$

71. $x = y^2 - 6y + 5$

72. $y = -x^2 + 5x + 6$

73. $(x + 2)^2 + (y - 5)^2 = 10$

74. $3x^2 - 2y^2 = 30$

Look Beyond

75. Expand the expression $(x + y + z)^3$.

OVER THE EDGE

Notice the stack of 4 congruent tiles on the desk shown at right. What do you think is the maximum distance that each tile can be extended beyond the tile beneath it without falling over?

Activity ①

All of the weight of an object can be considered to be concentrated at a single point called the *center of gravity*. The Portfolio Activity on page 706 involved slowly sliding a 12-inch ruler over the edge of a desk to find its center of gravity, or balance point, which is located at the 6-inch mark. Use a 12-inch wooden ruler and a quarter for this activity.

1. Tape a quarter to the ruler at the locations described in the table below. Determine the center of gravity for the ruler with the quarter taped at each location. Record your results.

Location of the quarter	none	1 in.	2 in.	3 in.	4 in.	5 in.	6 in.
Location of the center of gravity	6 in.						

2. Let n represent the location of the quarter, and let c represent the location of the center of gravity for the ruler with the quarter. Write a recursive formula and an explicit formula for the sequence that models the relationship between the location of the quarter and the location of the center of gravity for the ruler with the quarter.

Activity ②

1. Place all of the tiles in a stack that is aligned with the edge of the desk so that the center of gravity is above 0. Extend tile A beyond the edge of tile B so that $\frac{1}{2}$ of its length is hanging over the edge of tile B. Now the center of gravity for tile A is located $\frac{1}{2}$ of a tile length to the right of 0.

center of gravity

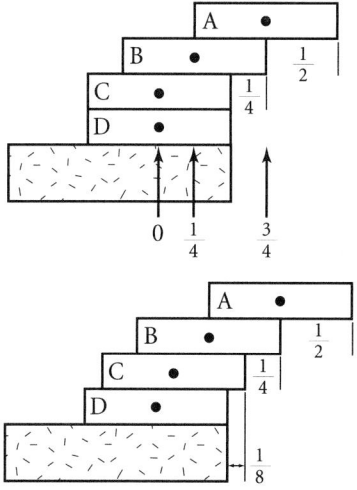

2. While keeping the same position of tile A on tile B, extend tile B so that $\frac{1}{4}$ of its length is hanging over the edge of tile C. The center of gravity for tile A is now $\frac{1}{4} + \frac{1}{2}$, or $\frac{3}{4}$, of a tile length to the right of 0, and the center of gravity for tile B is $\frac{1}{4}$ of a tile length to the right of 0.

3. While keeping the same position of tile A on tile B and tile B on tile C, extend tile C so that $\frac{1}{8}$ of its length is hanging over the edge of tile D. What is the center of gravity for tile A in this position? for tile B? for tile C?

4. Using summation notation, write a geometric series that models the shift in the center of gravity for tile A as each of these extensions is made.

Activity ③

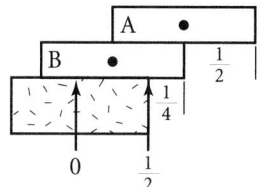

The center of gravity for an entire stack of tiles is the average of the centers of gravity for each tile in the stack. For example, the center of gravity for the 2-tile stack shown at left is to the right of 0 by the following fraction of a tile length:

$$\frac{\left(\frac{1}{2} + \frac{1}{4}\right) + \frac{1}{4}}{2} = \frac{1}{2}$$

The edge of the desk is $\frac{1}{2}$ of a tile length to the right of 0. If the center of gravity for a stack of tiles is less than or equal to $\frac{1}{2}$ of a tile length to the right of 0, then the stack will remain balanced. Since $\frac{1}{2} \leq \frac{1}{2}$, the 2-tile stack remains balanced.

Let n represent the tile number, where $n = 1$ represents the top tile (A), $n = 2$ represents the next tile (B), and so on. Let x represent the fraction of a tile length that the tile extends beyond the tile directly below it. Then the equation $x = \frac{1}{2n}$ models the pattern of tile extensions.

1. Find x for n-values of 1, 2, and 3.

2. Show that the 3-tile stack described by your results in Step 1 remains balanced. Is each stack extended the maximum distance while maintaining the stack's balance?

3. Find x for n-values of 4, 5, and 6.

4. Show that the 6-tile stack described by your results from Steps 1 and 3 remains balanced. Is each tile extended the maximum distance while maintaining the stack's balance?

5. Using summation notation, write a series that models the shift in the center of gravity for the top tile as each of the extensions described in Steps 1 and 3 are made.

6. Place 6 tiles in the position described by your results above. Does the 6-tile stack remain balanced? Describe the relationship between the mathematical results and your experimental results.

Chapter Review and Assessment

Key Skills & Exercises

LESSON 11.1

Key Skills

Find the terms of a sequence.

You can represent a sequence as follows:

- ordered pairs in a table

n	1	2	3	$\cdots$
t_n	2	5	8	$\cdots$

- a list $\{2, 5, 8, \ldots\}$
- an explicit formula $t_n = 3n - 1$
- a recursive formula $t_1 = 2, t_n = t_{n-1} + 3,$ where $n > 2$

Write the first three terms of the sequence defined by the explicit formula $t_n = 2n + 1$.

$$t_1 = 2(1) + 1 = 3$$
$$t_2 = 2(2) + 1 = 5$$
$$t_3 = 2(3) + 1 = 7$$

Write the first three terms of the sequence defined by the recursive formula $t_1 = 4$ and $t_n = 3t_{n-1} - 1$.

$$t_1 = 4$$
$$t_2 = 3(4) - 1 = 11$$
$$t_3 = 3(11) - 1 = 32$$

Evaluate the sum of a series expressed in sigma notation.

Evaluate $\displaystyle\sum_{k=1}^{8} (k^2 + 3k + 1)$.

$$\sum_{k=1}^{8}(k^2 + 3k + 1) = \sum_{k=1}^{8} k^2 + 3\sum_{k=1}^{8} k + \sum_{k=1}^{8} 1$$

$$= \frac{8 \cdot 9 \cdot 17}{6} + 3\left(\frac{8 \cdot 9}{2}\right) + 8$$

$$= 204 + 108 + 8 = 320$$

Exercises

Write the first five terms of each sequence.

1. $t_n = 2n + 3$

2. $t_n = 3n - 4$

3. $t_n = -0.2n + 0.1$

4. $t_n = -2.22n + 1.3$

5. $t_1 = 1, t_n = 2t_{n-1} + 2$

6. $t_1 = 1, t_n = 5t_{n-1} - 2$

7. $t_1 = 3, t_n = -3t_{n-1} + 1$

8. $t_1 = 2, t_n = -4t_{n-1} - 3$

Evaluate.

9. $\displaystyle\sum_{k=1}^{5} 6$

10. $\displaystyle\sum_{m=1}^{10} -5$

11. $\displaystyle\sum_{k=1}^{8} -3k$

12. $\displaystyle\sum_{k=1}^{6} 2k$

13. $\displaystyle\sum_{k=1}^{6} (2k^2 + k + 2)$

14. $\displaystyle\sum_{k=1}^{7} (3k^2 + 4k + 2)$

Key Skills

Find the indicated term of an arithmetic sequence.

Find the fifth term of the arithmetic sequence in which $t_1 = 2$ and $t_n = t_{n-1} + 3$.

$$t_n = t_1 + (n-1)d$$
$$t_5 = 2 + (5-1)3 \quad \text{$n = 5$, $t_1 = 2$, and $d = 3$}$$
$$t_5 = 14$$

Find arithmetic means between two nonconsecutive terms.

Find three arithmetic means between 10 and 18.

$$10, \underline{\ ?\ }, \underline{\ ?\ }, \underline{\ ?\ }, 18$$

Substitute 10 for t_1, 18 for t_n, and 5 for n.

$$t_n = t_1 + (n-1)d$$
$$18 = 10 + (5-1)d$$
$$d = 2$$

The three arithmetic means are 12, 14, and 16.

Exercises

Find the indicated term.

15. the sixth term of the arithmetic sequence in which $t_1 = 2$ and $t_n = t_{n-1} + 4$

16. the seventh term of the arithmetic sequence in which $t_1 = 1$ and $t_n = t_{n-1} - 2$

17. the fifth term of the arithmetic sequence in which $t_1 = -3$ and $t_n = t_{n-1} - 4$

18. the 10th term of the arithmetic sequence in which $t_1 = 3$ and $t_4 = -9$

Find the indicated arithmetic means.

19. two arithmetic means between 20 and 50

20. three arithmetic means between 100 and 180

21. four arithmetic means between −10 and −35

22. three arithmetic means between −8 and 12

Key Skills

Find the sum of the first *n* terms of an arithmetic series.

For the series $6 + 11 + 16 + 21 + \cdots$, find S_8.

Method 1:
First find t_8.

$$t_n = t_1 + (n-1)d$$
$$t_8 = 6 + (8-1)5$$
$$t_8 = 41$$

Then find S_8.

$$S_n = n\left(\frac{t_1 + t_n}{2}\right)$$
$$S_8 = 8\left(\frac{6 + 41}{2}\right)$$
$$S_8 = 188$$

Method 2:

$$S_n = n\left[\frac{2t_1 + (n-1)d}{2}\right]$$
$$S_8 = 8\left[\frac{12 + (8-1)5}{2}\right]$$
$$S_8 = 188$$

Exercises

For the series $2 + 5 + 8 + 11 + \cdots$, find the indicated sum.

23. S_5 24. S_{10}

25. S_{12} 26. S_{15}

For each arithmetic series, find S_{20}.

27. $8 + 16 + 24 + 32 + \cdots$

28. $14 + 16 + 18 + 20 + 22 + \cdots$

29. $-6 + (-12) + (-18) + (-24) + (-30) + \cdots$

30. $-7 + (-5) + (-3) + (-1) + \cdots$

Evaluate.

31. $\displaystyle\sum_{k=1}^{5} 6k$ 32. $\displaystyle\sum_{j=3}^{7} (2j - 5)$

33. $\displaystyle\sum_{k=0}^{4} (5 - 2k)$ 34. $\displaystyle\sum_{n=1}^{30} (7 - n)$

Key Skills

Find the indicated term of a geometric sequence.

Find the sixth term of the geometric sequence in which $t_1 = 4$ and $t_n = 2t_{n-1}$.

$$t_n = t_1 r^{n-1}$$
$$t_6 = 4 \cdot 2^{6-1}$$
$$t_6 = 128$$

Find geometric means between two nonconsecutive terms.

Find three geometric means between 10 and 2560.

$$10, \underline{?}, \underline{?}, \underline{?}, 2560$$

Substitute 10 for t_1 and 2560 for t_5.

$$t_n = t_1 r^{n-1}$$
$$2560 = 10 \cdot r^{5-1}$$
$$r = \pm 4$$

The three geometric means are 40, 160, and 640 or −40, 160, and −640.

Exercises

Find the indicated term.

35. the sixth term of the sequence in which $t_1 = -4$ and $t_n = 5t_{n-1}$

36. the fifth term of the sequence in which $t_1 = 8$ and $t_n = -3t_{n-1}$

37. the 10th term of the sequence in which $t_1 = \frac{1}{3}$ and $t_n = \frac{1}{2}t_{n-1}$

Find the indicated geometric means.

38. two geometric means between 10 and 1250

39. three geometric means between 5 and 100

40. three geometric means between 20 and 30

Key Skills

Find the sum of the first *n* terms of a geometric series.

Find the sum of the first eight terms in the series $1 + 2 + 4 + 8 + \cdots$

Substitute 2 for r, 1 for t_1, and 8 for n.

$$S_n = t_1\left(\frac{1-r^n}{1-r}\right)$$
$$S_8 = 1\left(\frac{1-2^8}{1-2}\right) = 255$$

Use mathematical induction to prove statements about the natural numbers.

To prove that a statement about natural numbers is true for all natural numbers, use the principle of mathematical induction stated below.

1. Show that the statement is true for $n = 1$.

2. Assume that the statement is true for a natural number k. Then prove that it is true for the natural number $k + 1$.

Exercises

For the series $1 + 1.5 + 2.25 + 3.375 + \cdots$, find each indicated sum to the nearest tenth.

41. S_4 **42.** S_5 **43.** S_{12} **44.** S_{15}

Use the formula for the first *n* terms of a geometric series to find the sum of each geometric series. Give answers to the nearest tenth, if necessary.

45. $-1 + 10 + (-100) + 1000 + (-10{,}000)$

46. $0.4 + 4 + 40 + 400 + 4000$

47. $3 + (-6) + 12 + (-24) + 48 + (-96)$

Evaluate. Give answers to the nearest hundredth, if necessary.

48. $\displaystyle\sum_{p=1}^{4} \frac{1}{6}(3)^p$ **49.** $\displaystyle\sum_{k=5}^{8}(0.2)^{k-4}$

Use mathematical induction to prove each statement for all natural numbers, *n*.

50. $n - 1 < n$

51. $7 + 9 + 11 + \cdots + (2n + 5) = n(n + 6)$

Key Skills

Find the sum of an infinite geometric series, if one exists.

Find the sum of the series $\sum_{k=0}^{\infty} \dfrac{2}{5^{k+2}}$, if it exists.

$$r = \dfrac{\frac{2}{125}}{\frac{2}{25}} = \dfrac{1}{5}$$

If a geometric sequence has common ratio r and $|r| < 1$, then the related infinite geometric series converges and has a sum.

The series converges because $|r| = \left|\dfrac{1}{5}\right| < 1$.

$$\sum_{k=0}^{\infty} \dfrac{2}{5^{k+2}} = \dfrac{t_1}{1-r}$$
$$= \dfrac{\frac{2}{25}}{1 - \frac{1}{5}}$$
$$= \dfrac{1}{10}$$

Exercises

Find the sum of each infinite geometric series, if it exists.

52. $5 + \dfrac{5}{3} + \dfrac{5}{9} + \dfrac{5}{27} + \cdots$

53. $8 + 4 + 2 + 1 + \cdots$

54. $\dfrac{1}{2} + \left(-\dfrac{1}{4}\right) + \dfrac{1}{8} + \left(-\dfrac{1}{16}\right) + \cdots$

55. $0.5 + 0.05 + 0.005 + 0.0005 + \cdots$

56. $\sum_{k=1}^{\infty} \left(\dfrac{1}{3}\right)^k$ **57.** $\sum_{k=1}^{\infty} \left(\dfrac{1}{6}\right)^k$ **58.** $\sum_{k=1}^{\infty} 4^k$

59. $\sum_{k=0}^{\infty} \left(\dfrac{3}{7}\right)^k$ **60.** $\sum_{k=0}^{\infty} \left(\dfrac{5}{6}\right)^k$ **61.** $\sum_{k=0}^{\infty} \left(\dfrac{5}{4}\right)^k$

Write each decimal as a fraction in simplest form.

62. $0.\overline{620}$ **63.** $0.0\overline{32}$

Key Skills

Find entries in Pascal's triangle.

Find the seventh entry in row 11 of Pascal's triangle.

The kth entry in the nth row is ${}_nC_{k-1}$.

$${}_{11}C_{7-1} = {}_{11}C_6$$
$$= \dfrac{11!}{5!6!}$$
$$= 462$$

Use Pascal's triangle to find probabilities.

Find the probability that exactly 1 heads *or* exactly 2 heads appears when a coin is tossed 5 times.

Number of possible outcomes $= 2^5$

Probability of exactly 1 heads $= \dfrac{{}_5C_1}{2^5}$

Probability of exactly 2 heads $= \dfrac{{}_5C_2}{2^5}$

$P(1 \text{ heads } or \text{ 2 heads}) = \dfrac{{}_5C_1}{2^5} + \dfrac{{}_5C_2}{2^5}$

≈ 0.47

Exercises

Find each entry of Pascal's triangle.

64. sixth entry of row 9

65. eighth entry of row 10

66. fifth entry of row 8

67. fourth entry of row 6

Find the probability of each event.

68. exactly 4 heads when a coin is tossed 4 times

69. exactly 3 tails when a coin is tossed 8 times

70. more than 6 tails when a coin is tossed 8 times

71. exactly 2 *or* exactly 4 heads when a coin is tossed 6 times

Key Skills

Use the Binomial Theorem to expand a binomial raised to a power.

Expand $(a + b)^4$.

$$(a + b)^n = \sum_{k=0}^{n} \binom{n}{k} a^{n-k} b^k$$

$$(a + b)^4 = \binom{4}{0} a^4 b^0 + \binom{4}{1} a^3 b^1 + \binom{4}{2} a^2 b^2 +$$

$$\binom{4}{3} a^1 b^3 + \binom{4}{4} a^0 b^4$$

$$= a^4 b^0 + 4a^3 b^1 + 6a^2 b^2 + 4a^1 b^3 + a^0 b^4$$

Find a term in a binomial expansion.

Find the seventh term in the expansion of $(a + b)^9$.

For the expansion of $(a + b)^9$, $n = 9$.

For the seventh term, $k = 6$.

$$\binom{n}{k} x^{n-k} y^k = \binom{9}{6} a^3 b^6 = 84a^3 b^6$$

Exercises

Expand each binomial raised to a power.

72. $(5 + y)^4$ **73.** $(a + 3)^5$

74. $(2x - 2y)^5$ **75.** $(3x - y)^6$

76. Find the sixth term in the expansion of $(x + y)^7$.

77. Find the eighth term in the expansion of $(a + b)^{10}$.

Write each summation as a binomial raised to a power. Then write it in expanded form.

78. $\displaystyle\sum_{k=0}^{5} \binom{5}{k} a^{5-k} b^k$ **79.** $\displaystyle\sum_{k=0}^{6} \binom{6}{k} a^{6-k} b^k$

Applications

80. INVESTMENTS Yolanda deposits $1000 in a bank at the beginning of every year for 8 years. Her account earns 8% interest compounded annually. How much is in the account after the last year?

81. PHYSICS A ball is dropped from a height of 12 meters. Each time it bounces, it rebounds $\frac{2}{3}$ of the distance it has fallen.
   a. How far will it rebound after the third bounce?
   b. Theoretically, what is the vertical distance that the ball will travel before coming to rest?

82. MERCHANDISING Boxes are stacked in a display of 21 rows with 2 boxes in the top row, 5 boxes in the second row, 8 boxes in the third row, and so on. How many boxes are there?

83. ENTERTAINMENT A theater has 18 seats in the front row. Each succeeding row has 4 more seats than the row ahead of it. How many seats are there in the first 12 rows? 20 rows?

84. REAL ESTATE A 5-year lease for an apartment calls for a rent of $500 per month the first year with an increase of 6% for each remaining year of the lease. What will be the monthly rent during the last year of the lease?

Chapter Test

Write the first five terms of each sequence.

1. $t_n = 5n + 7$

2. $t_n = -3.14n + 1.6$

3. $t_1 = 7$

   $t_n = 3t_{n-1} + 2$

Evaluate the sum.

4. $\displaystyle\sum_{k=1}^{7}(k - 3)^2$ **5.** $\displaystyle\sum_{k=1}^{5}(2k^2 - 3k + 4)$

6. COMMUNICATION A telemarketing service uses a master computer to set up a chain of activating computers. The master computer links to 2 computers and activates them. Then the activated computers each link with 2 additional computers to activate them. At each step the activation process takes 10 minutes. After an hour how many computers have been activated?

Find the indicated term.

7. 8th term; given $t_1 = 7$ and $t_n = t_{n-1} + 7$

8. 5th term; given $t_1 = -27$ and $t_n = t_{n-1} + 12$

Find the indicated arithmetic means.

9. Find the three arithmetic means between 144 and 188.

10. Find the four arithmetic means between -12 and 18.

For each arithmetic series, find S_{18}.

11. $3 + 10 + 17 + 24 + 31 + \cdots$

12. $5 + (-1) + (-7) + (-13) + (-19) + \cdots$

Evaluate.

13. $\displaystyle\sum_{k=1}^{15} -4k$ **14.** $\displaystyle\sum_{k=1}^{5}(2k - 9)$

Find the indicated geometric means.

15. Find the three geometric means between 2 and 1250.

16. Write an explicit formula for the nth term of the geometric sequence.

   $$3, 6, 12, 24\ldots$$

17. TECHNOLOGY A new laser printer costs $1800. Each year it loses 12% of its value from the previous year. Find its value after 8 years.

Evaluate. Round to the nearest tenth.

18. $\displaystyle\sum_{k=1}^{5}3(2^{k-1})$ **19.** $\displaystyle\sum_{k=1}^{6}\frac{1}{2}(4)^{k-1}$

20. Refer to the geometric series in which $t_1 = 3$ and $r = 4$. Find S_6.

21. BIOLOGY A bacterium reproduces by dividing into two bacteria. Find the number of bacteria after 10 such divisions.

Find the sum of each infinite geometric series, if it exists.

22. $0.9 + 0.09 + 0.009 + 0.0009 + \cdots$

23. $\dfrac{1}{3} + \dfrac{1}{9} + \dfrac{1}{27} + \dfrac{1}{81} + \cdots$

24. $\displaystyle\sum_{k=0}^{\infty}(1.001)^k$ **25.** $\displaystyle\sum_{k=0}^{\infty}\left(\frac{5}{9}\right)^k$

Find each entry in Pascal's triangle.

26. fifth entry in the fifth row

27. ninth entry in the twelfth row

Find the probability of each event.

28. 4 girls in a family of 6 children

29. 8 right when randomly guessing on a true/false test with 12 questions

Expand each binomial.

30. $(x + y)^4$ **31.** $(2a - 3b)^6$

32. Find the fifth term in the expansion of $(r - 3t)^8$.

MULTIPLE-CHOICE For Questions 1–18, write the letter that indicates the best answer.

1. Let $f(x) = x - 5$ and $g(x) = 3x$. Find $(f \circ g)(3)$. **(LESSON 2.4)**

a. 4   b. −6

c. −18   d. 7

2. Find the value of $_{10}C_2$. **(LESSON 10.3)**

a. 90   b. 11

c. 45   d. 0

3. Simplify $6i \cdot 7i$. **(LESSON 5.6)**

a. 42

b. −42

c. −42i

d. 42i

4. Calculate the probability of rolling an odd number on one roll of a six-sided number cube. **(LESSON 10.1)**

a. $\frac{2}{3}$ b. $\frac{1}{3}$

c. $\frac{1}{2}$ d. $\frac{1}{12}$

5. Which ordered pair is the solution of the system? $\begin{cases} 2x + 3y = 21 \\ x - 2y = -7 \end{cases}$ **(LESSON 3.1)**

a. $(3, 5)$

b. $(-3, 5)$

c. $(9, 8)$

d. $(-6, 11)$

6. Which function represents the graph of $f(x) = |x|$ translated 3 units to the right? **(LESSON 2.7)**

a. $g(x) = |x - 3|$
b. $g(x) = |x + 3|$
c. $g(x) = |x| - 3$
d. $g(x) = |x| + 3$

7. Solve $|4t - 7| = 5t + 2$. **(LESSON 1.8)**

a. 9   b. −9

c. $\frac{5}{9}$ d. $9, -\frac{5}{9}$

8. Evaluate $-5^3 - 2 \cdot 3^2 \div 6$. **(LESSON 2.1)**

a. 122   b. −128

c. −122   d. −23

9. What are the coordinates of the vertex of the graph of $y = -x^2 + 2$? **(LESSON 5.1)**

a. $(-1, 2)$ b. $(0, -2)$
c. $(-1, -2)$ d. $(0, 2)$

10. Find the slope of the line that contains $(-2, 5)$ and $(-5, -4)$. **(LESSON 1.2)**

a. $\frac{1}{3}$ b. −3

c. 3   d. $-\frac{1}{3}$

11. Which single equation represents the pair of parametric equations $\begin{cases} x(t) = 2 + t \\ y(t) = 3 + t \end{cases}$? **(LESSON 3.6)**

a. $y = x - 1$
b. $y = -x - 1$
c. $y = x + 1$
d. $y = -x + 1$

12. What is the domain of $g(x) = -\frac{1}{2}x^2 - 4$? **(LESSON 2.3)**

a. $x > 0$
b. all real numbers
c. $x > -4$
d. $x < -4$

13. Which is the greatest monomial factor of $2(6x^2 - 14x)$? **(LESSON 5.3)**

a. 2   b. 4

c. $2x$ d. $4x$

14. The graph of which ellipse has x-intercepts of 2 and -2 and y-intercepts of 5 and -5? *(LESSON 9.4)*

a. $\dfrac{x^2}{4} + \dfrac{y^2}{4} = 1$ **b.** $\dfrac{x^2}{4} - \dfrac{y^2}{25} = 1$

c. $\dfrac{x^2}{4} + \dfrac{y^2}{25} = 1$ **d.** $\dfrac{y^2}{25} - \dfrac{x^2}{4} = 1$

15. Which binomial is a factor of $x^3 - 3x^2 - 2x + 6$? *(LESSON 7.3)*
   a. $x^2 - 2$ **b.** $x^2 + 2$
   c. $x + 3$ **d.** $x + 1$

16. Which equation represents $\log_2 \dfrac{1}{32} = -5$ in exponential form? *(LESSON 6.3)*

   a. $2^{-5} = \dfrac{1}{32}$ **b.** $2^{-5} = -32$

   c. $2^{-5} = 32$ **d.** $2^{-5} = -\dfrac{1}{32}$

17. If y varies jointly as the cube of m and the square of n and inversely as p, which equation represents this relationship? *(LESSON 8.1)*

   a. $y = \dfrac{p}{m^3 n^2}$ **b.** $y = \dfrac{km^3 n^2}{p}$

   c. $y = m^3 n^2 p$ **d.** $y = km^3 n^2 p$

18. Which polynomial equation has -2 and $5i$ as roots? *(LESSON 7.4)*
   a. $x^3 - 2x^2 + 25x - 50 = 0$
   b. $x^3 + 2x^2 - 5x - 10 = 0$
   c. $x^3 + 2x^2 + 25x + 50 = 0$
   d. $x^3 - 2x^2 + 5x - 10 = 0$

19. Find the slope, m, of $x = -5$. *(LESSON 1.2)*

20. Write the equation in slope-intercept form for the line that has a slope of $-\dfrac{3}{5}$ and contains the point $(-2, -5)$. *(LESSON 1.3)*

21. Find the inverse of $\{(-1, -1), (-2, 2), (-3, 1), (0, 0)\}$. *(LESSON 2.5)*

22. Find the zeros of $f(x) = 12x^2 - 8x - 15$. *(LESSON 5.3)*

23. Graph $2y + x \le 6$. *(LESSON 3.3)*

24. Find the product $\begin{bmatrix} -1 & 2 & 3 \\ 4 & -2 & 3 \end{bmatrix} \begin{bmatrix} 2 & 1 & 3 \\ -1 & -2 & -3 \\ 4 & 1 & -2 \end{bmatrix}$, if it exists. *(LESSON 4.2)*

25. Solve $10^{-3x} = 125$ to the nearest hundredth. *(LESSON 6.7)*

26. Factor $6x^2 - 28x - 10$, if possible. *(LESSON 5.3)*

27. Find the 100th term of the sequence $-11, -5, 1, \ldots$ *(LESSON 11.2)*

28. Simplify $\dfrac{1 - 2i}{2 + i} + 3i$. *(LESSON 5.6)*

29. Graph $y \ge x^2 - 3x + 5$. *(LESSON 5.8)*

30. Solve $\begin{cases} 2x - 5y = 15 \\ 3x - 7y = 22 \end{cases}$ by using a matrix equation. *(LESSON 4.4)*

31. Write $(x - 1)^2(x^2 + 2x + 5)$ as a polynomial expression in standard form. *(LESSON 7.3)*

32. Simplify $\dfrac{x^2 + 3x - 18}{2x^2 - 5x - 3} \cdot \dfrac{1 - 4x^2}{x^2 - 36}$. *(LESSON 8.3)*

33. Use substitution to solve $\begin{cases} x + y = 18 \\ 4x - 4y = 5 \end{cases}$. *(LESSON 3.1)*

FREE-RESPONSE GRID The following questions may be answered by using a free-response grid such as that commonly used by standardized-test services.

34. Solve $\sqrt{2x - 3} = \sqrt{5x - 21}$. *(LESSON 8.8)*

35. Evaluate $\log_{\frac{1}{3}} 27 + 3^{\log_3 5}$ *(LESSON 6.4)*

36. Find the value of v in $-1 = \log_{10} v$. *(LESSON 6.3)*

37. Find the perimeter, to the nearest hundredth, of a triangle whose vertices have the coordinates $(2, 0)$, $(0, 0)$, and $(0, -4)$. *(LESSON 9.1)*

38. How many 4 letter arrangements can be made with the letters in *meet*? *(LESSON 10.2)*

PHYSICS A ball is dropped from a height of 12 meters. Each time it bounces on the ground, it rebounds to $\dfrac{2}{3}$ the distance it has fallen.

39. How many meters will it rebound after the third bounce? *(LESSON 11.4)*

40. Theoretically, how many meters will the ball travel before coming to rest? *(LESSON 11.6)*

Keystroke Guide for Chapter 11

Essential keystroke sequences (using the model TI-82 or TI-83 graphics calculator) are presented below for all Activities and Examples found in this chapter that require or recommend the use of a graphics calculator.

> **internet** connect
>
> For Keystrokes of other graphing calculator models, visit the HRW web site at **go.hrw.com** and enter the keyword **MB1 CALC**.

LESSON 11.2

EXAMPLE **1**

Page 700

Find the fifth term of the sequence defined by $t_1 = -4$ and $t_n = t_{n-1} + 3$.

[(-)] [4] [ENTER] [+] [3] [ENTER] [ENTER] [ENTER]

[ENTER]

EXAMPLES **2** and **3**

Page 701

For Example 2, find the fifth term of the sequence defined by $t_1 = 389.95$ and $t_n = t_{n-1} - 42.50$.

[389.95] [ENTER] [−] [42.5] [ENTER] [ENTER] [ENTER]

[ENTER]

Use a similar keystroke sequence for Example 3.

Activity

Page 702

For Step 1, part a, use sequence mode to graph the sequence $t_n = 5 + 2n$ for n-values from 1 to 6.

Put the calculator in sequence and dot modes:

[MODE] [Seq] [ENTER] [Dot] [ENTER] [2nd] [MODE (QUIT)]

Set the viewing window:

[WINDOW] (nMin=) 1 [ENTER] (nMax=) 6 [ENTER] (PlotStart=) 1 [ENTER] (PlotStep=) 1 [ENTER] (Xmin=) 0 [ENTER] (Xmax=) 7 [ENTER] (Xscl=) 1 [ENTER] (Ymin=) 0 [ENTER] (Ymax=) 20 [ENTER] (Yscl=) 4

TI-82:

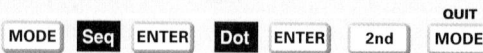

[WINDOW] [ENTER] (UnStart=) 7 [ENTER] [ENTER] (nStart=) 1 [ENTER] (nMin=) 1 [ENTER] (nMax=) 6 [ENTER] (Xmin=) 0 [ENTER] (Xmax=) 7 [ENTER] (Xsc1=) 1 [ENTER] (Ymin=) 0 [ENTER] (Ymax=) 20 [ENTER] (Ysc1=) 4

Graph the sequence:

Y= (u(*n*)=) 5 [+] 2 [X,T,Θ,n] [ENTER] (u(*n*Min)=) 7 [GRAPH]

⇑TI-82: [2nd] [ⁿ/₉] [GRAPH]

For part **b**, use the same viewing window. Use *n*Min = 1 and u(*n*Min) = 7.5.

For part **c**, change to Ymax = 40 in the viewing window. Graph the sequence by using *n*Min = 1 and u(*n*Min) = 2.

For part **d**, use Ymax = 2, Yscl = 0.5, *n*Min = 1, and u(*n*Min) = 1.

For part **e**, use Ymax = 0.4, Yscl = 0.05, *n*Min = 1, and u(*n*Min) = 0.3.

For part **f**, use Ymax = 40, Yscl = 4, *n*Min = 1, and u(*n*Min) = 1.

LESSON 11.3

EXAMPLES ① and ② Find S_{15} for the series in which $t_1 = 1$ and $d = 3$.

Pages 708 and 709

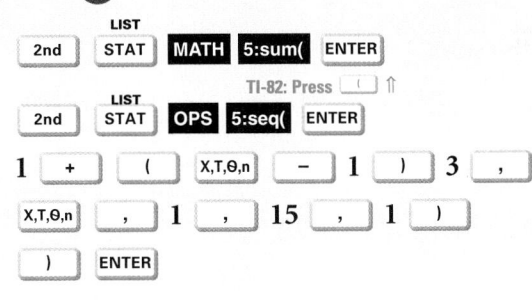

LIST
[2nd] [STAT] **MATH** **5:sum(** [ENTER]

TI-82: Press [◁] ⇑

LIST
[2nd] [STAT] **OPS** **5:seq(** [ENTER]

1 [+] [( ] [X,T,Θ,n] [−] 1 [ )] 3 [,]

[X,T,Θ,n] [,] 1 [,] 15 [,] 1 [ )]

[ )] [ENTER]

```
sum(seq(1+(X-1)3
,X,1,15,1))
                330
```

Use a similar keystroke sequence for Example 2.

EXAMPLE ③ Evaluate $\displaystyle\sum_{k=1}^{12} (6 - 2k)$.

Page 709

LIST
[2nd] [STAT] **MATH** **5:sum(** [ENTER] [2nd] [STAT]

LIST

TI-82: Press [◁] ⇑

OPS **5:seq(** [ENTER] 6 [−] 2 [X,T,Θ,n] [,]

[X,T,Θ,n] [,] 1 [,] 12 [,] 1 [ )]

[ )] [ENTER]

```
sum(seq(6-2X,X,1
,12,1))
                -84
```

LESSON 11.4

EXAMPLES ①, ②, ③, and ④ For Example 1, find the fifth term of the sequence defined by $t_1 = 8$ and $r = 3$.

Pages 714–716

8 [ENTER] [×] 3 [ENTER] [ENTER] [ENTER] [ENTER]

Use a similar keystroke sequence for Examples 2, 3, and 4.

```
8
               8
Ans*3
              24
              72
             216
             648
```

Activity
Page 716

For Step 1, part a, find the first 5 terms of the geometric sequence defined by $t_1 = 1$ and $r = 10$.

`1` `ENTER` `X` `10` `ENTER`

Press `ENTER` 18 more times to generate the rest of the terms.

Use a similar keystroke sequence for parts **b–f**.

LESSON 11.5

E X A M P L E **1** Find S_{10} to the nearest tenth for the series defined by $t_1 = 3$ and $r = 1.5$.

Page 721

Set the calculator to round answers to the nearest tenth:

`MODE` `FLOAT` `►` `►` `1` `ENTER` `ENTER`

Find the sum:

`2nd` `STAT`(LIST) `MATH` `5:sum(` `ENTER` `2nd` `STAT`(LIST) `OPS` `5:seq(` `ENTER`

TI-82: Press `(` ⇑

`3` `X` `1.5` `^` `(` `X,T,θ,n` `−` `1` `)` `,` `X,T,θ,n` `,` `1` `,`

`10` `,` `1` `)` `)` `ENTER`

E X A M P L E **3** Evaluate $\sum_{k=1}^{6} 2(3^{k-1})$.

Page 722

> Be sure that your calculator is returned to the floating decimal mode setting.

`2nd` `STAT`(LIST) `MATH` `5:sum(` `ENTER` `2nd` `STAT`(LIST) `OPS` `5:seq(` `ENTER`

TI-82: Press `(` ⇑

`2` `X` `3` `^` `(` `X,T,θ,n` `−` `1` `)` `,` `X,T,θ,n` `,` `1` `,`

`6` `,` `1` `)` `)` `ENTER`

LESSON 11.6

Activity
Page 729

For Step 1, part a, create a table of values for n and S_n for the infinite geometric series defined by $t_1 = -5$ and $r = -0.25$. Use n-values of 1, 2, 3, 5, 10, and 100.

> First clear old data from Lists 1 and 2.

`STAT` `EDIT` `1:Edit` `L1` `1` `ENTER` `2` `ENTER` `3` `ENTER` `5` `ENTER` `10`

`ENTER` `100` `ENTER` `►` `▲` `(L2)` `ENTER` `(−)` `5` `(` `1` `−` `(−)` `.25`

`^` `2nd` `1`(L1) `)` `D` `(` `1` `−` `(−)` `.25` `)` `ENTER`

Use a similar keystroke sequence for Step 1, parts **b–d**, and for Step 2.

E X A M P L E S ❶ and ❷ For Example 1, graph the formula for the sum of *n* terms of the
Pages 730 and 731 geometric series in which $t_1 = 3$ and $r = 0.4$.

Use friendly viewing window [0, 28.2] by
[0, 10].

> *Be sure that your calculator is returned to function mode.*

GRAPH TRACE ▶

Use a similar keystroke sequence for Example 2. Use friendly viewing
window [0, 28.2] by [0, 0.5].

LESSON 11.7

E X A M P L E ❶ To find the 4th and 10th entries in row 12 of Pascal's triangle, evaluate
Page 737 $_{12}C_3$ and $_{12}C_9$.

12 MATH PRB 3:nCr ENTER 3 ENTER
12 MATH PRB 3:nCr ENTER 9 ENTER

E X A M P L E ❸ Evaluate $\frac{_7C_3}{2^7} + \frac{_7C_4}{2^7}$.
Page 738

(7 MATH PRB 3:nCr ENTER 3)
D (2 ^ 7) + (
7 MATH PRB 3:nCr ENTER 4) D
(2 ^ 7) ENTER

LESSON 11.8

E X A M P L E ❶ Find the coefficients in the expansion of $(x + y)^7$.
Page 742

LIST
2nd STAT OPS 5:seq(ENTER 7 MATH
PRB 3:nCr ENTER X,T,Θ,n , X,T,Θ,n ,
0 , 7 , 1) ENTER

DISCRETE MATHEMATICS
Statistics

STATISTICS IS A BRANCH OF APPLIED MATHEMATics that involves collecting, organizing, interpreting, and making predictions from data. Statistics is categorized as descriptive or inferential. Descriptive statistics uses tables, graphs, and summary measures to describe data. Inferential statistics consists of analyzing and interpreting data to make predictions.

USA STATISTICS

Spending Habits of Teenagers

Teenagers obtain money in a variety of ways: jobs, allowances, or relatives. Teens categorized their spending habits as shown at right.

Spend most of it 12%

Save most of it 28%

Spend half and save half 60%

Source: ICR'S Teen EXCEL Survey for Merrill Lynch

Teenagers work various jobs to earn spending money.

PORTFOLIO ACTIVITIES
CHAPTER PROJECT

About the Chapter Project

To obtain information about a large group, or population, smaller parts, or samples are studied. A sample is any part of a population. A sampling method is a procedure for selecting a sample to represent the population. A sampling method is *biased* if it deliberately or unintentionally favors particular outcomes. In the Chapter Project, *That's Not Fair!*, you will design a sampling method to provide a reasonable representation of a population and use the method to conduct a survey.

After completing the Chapter Project, you will be able to do the following:

- Determine whether a sampling procedure provides a poor or a reasonable representation of the total population.

- Design a sampling method that provides a reasonable representation of the population.

- Use statistics to support conclusions made from results of a survey.

About the Portfolio Activities

Throughout the chapter, you will be given opportunities to complete Portfolio Activities that are designed to support your work on the Chapter Project.

- Comparing measures of central tendency is included in the Portfolio Activity on page 771.

- Collecting data and choosing a method of visual representation for your data is included in the Portfolio Activity on page 780.

- Collecting data and explaining what some features of a box-and-whisker plot tell you about the data is included in the Portfolio Activity on page 789.

- Explaining what the measures of dispersion tell you about data that you have collected is included in the Portfolio Activity on page 798.

Measures of Central Tendency

Objectives

- Find the mean, median, and mode of a data set.

- Find or estimate the mean from a frequency table of data.

Why *You can use measures of central tendency to analyze many real-world situations, such as the number of minutes that a commercial radio station devotes to music.*

APPLICATION

BROADCASTING

Guillermo wondered how many minutes his favorite commercial radio station actually devotes to music. He recorded the broadcast between 3:00 P.M. and 4:00 P.M. for 10 successive weekdays. Guillermo's results, in minutes, were 40, 45, 39, 40, 41, 42, 37, 41, 41, and 40.

Find *measures of central tendency* that summarize this data and compare the measures. *You will solve this problem in Example 1.*

Comparing Central Tendencies

Measures of central tendency are values that are representative of an entire data set. Three commonly used measures of central tendency are the *mean*, *median*, and *mode*.

Measures of Central Tendency

The **mean**, or arithmetic average, denoted $\overline{x}$, of a data set is the sum of all of the values in the data set divided by the number of values.

The **median** of a data set is the numerical middle value when the data values are arranged in ascending or descending order. If there are an even number of values, the median is the mean of the two middle values.

The **mode** of a data set is the value that is repeated most often in the data set. There can be one, more than one, or no mode.

EXAMPLE **1**

Refer to the radio station data given at the beginning of the lesson.

Find the measures of central tendency, and compare them.
   a. mean   **b.** median   **c.** mode

APPLICATION
BROADCASTING

● **SOLUTION**

   a. $\bar{x} = \dfrac{40 + 45 + 39 + 40 + 41 + 42 + 37 + 41 + 41 + 40}{10} = \dfrac{406}{10} = 40.6$

   The mean number of minutes devoted to music is 40.6.

PROBLEM SOLVING

   b. Make an organized list. Arrange values in the data set in ascending order.

$$37, 39, 40, 40, \mathbf{40}, \mathbf{41}, 41, 41, 42, 45$$

   The median is the mean of the fifth and sixth values, 40 and 41, which is
   $\dfrac{40 + 41}{2} = 40.5$. Thus, the median number of minutes is 40.5.

   c. The most often repeated values, 40 and 41, both appear the same number
   of times. Because there are two modes, the data set is called *bimodal.*

The mean (40.6), median (40.5), and modes (40 and 41) are all very similar.
Thus, the measures of central tendency for the number of minutes devoted to
music during this hour are all between 40 and 41, inclusive.

TRY THIS
Using the data 88, 74, 98, 76, 68, 74, 89, and 92, find the mean, median, and
mode, and compare them.

CRITICAL THINKING
What percent of the time does Guillermo's radio station play music? How
broadly can this generalization be applied? Explain.

Any of the measures of central tendency can be misleading (not truly
representative or typical) for certain data sets, as shown in Example 2.

EXAMPLE **2**

The salaries at a small business with 7 employees are as follows:
$255,000, $32,000, $30,000, $28,000, $24,000, $22,000, and $22,000.
   a. Find the mean, median, and mode of the salaries.
   b. Explain which measures best represent a typical employee's salary.

APPLICATION
BUSINESS

● **SOLUTION**

   a. mean: $\bar{x} = \dfrac{255,000 + 32,000 + 30,000 + 28,000 + 24,000 + 22,000 + 22,000}{7}$

            $= \dfrac{413,000}{7} = 59,000$

   median: The middle value is $28,000.

   mode: $22,000

   b. The mean, $59,000, does not represent
   a typical salary because all except the
   top salary are much lower. The mode,
   $22,000, is a better representation of a
   typical salary than the mean, but it is
   still not the best representation because
   it is the lowest salary. The median,
   $28,000, is the best representation of
   the typical salary. ˈ

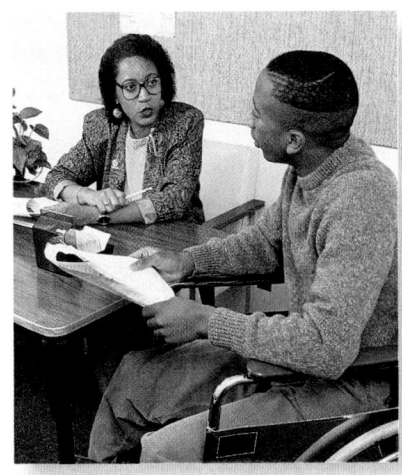

TRY THIS The yearly bonuses for five managers are $90,000, $85,000, $100,000, $0, and $80,000. Find the mean, median, and mode, and explain which measures are most representative.

CHECKPOINT ✔ Suppose that the number of employees in Example 2 increases by 6, and these employees all receive the same salary, $30,000. Does the one large salary of $255,000 have as much influence on the new mean as it did on the original mean? Why?

In the Activity below you can explore how the mean, median, and mode are influenced by various changes to the data set.

Activity
Exploring Measures of Central Tendency

You will need: 2 number cubes

1. Roll both number cubes and record their sum for 20 trials. Find the mean, median, and mode(s) of the sums.

2. Add 3 to each sum. Find the new mean, median, and mode(s), and describe how the measures have changed.

3. Double each sum from Step 1. Find the new mean, median, and mode, and describe how the measures have changed.

4. Take half of each sum from Step 1, and then subtract 1 from each value. Find the new mean, median, and mode(s), and describe how the measures have changed.

CHECKPOINT ✔ 5. Make a conjecture about what happens to the mean, median, and mode when you add, subtract, multiply, or divide each data value.

CHECKPOINT ✔ 6. Each value in Example 2 ends with three zeros. How can you use your conjecture to find the mean for the values in Example 2 by performing calculations without the final three zeros? Explain.

Frequency Tables

APPLICATION
ECOLOGY

The number of chirps that a cricket makes is related to the temperature according to the following relationship:

$$\frac{\text{number of chirps}}{\text{in 15 seconds}} + 40 = \frac{\text{temperature in}}{\text{degrees Fahrenheit}}$$

To verify this relationship, a class of 24 students counted cricket chirps for 15 seconds with the following results:

30	32	30	30	30	30	32	31
30	32	32	30	32	30	32	32
30	30	31	32	31	30	32	31

This *raw data* of cricket chirps can be organized into a **frequency table** that lists the number of times, or frequency, that each data value appears.

To make a frequency table, first list each distinct value. Then make a mark for each value in the data set. Finally, count the number of marks to get the respective frequency for each value, as shown below.

Number of chirps	Tally	Frequency
30	⫬⫬⫬ ⫬⫬⫬ ⫬	11
31	⫬⫬⫬⫬	4
32	⫬⫬⫬ ⫬⫬⫬⫬	9
	Total	24

Example 3 demonstrates how to find the mean of a data set that is organized in a frequency table.

EXAMPLE ❸ **Find the mean number of cricket chirps from the frequency table above. Then estimate the temperature at the time the chirps were counted.**

APPLICATION
ECOLOGY

● **SOLUTION**

Multiply each number of chirps by its corresponding frequency.

Frequency Table for Cricket Chirps

Number of chirps	Frequency	Product
30	11	330
31	4	124
32	9	288
Total	24	742

Add the products, and divide by the total number of values.

$$\overline{x} = \frac{742}{24} \approx 30.9$$

The mean number of cricket chirps during the 15 seconds was 30.9. Thus, according to the given relationship, the temperature should have been $30.9 + 40 = 70.9$, or about 71°F.

CHECKPOINT ✔ Would you obtain the same mean in Example 3 if you added each of the 24 values and then divided this sum by 24? Explain. Would you obtain the same mean if you calculated $\frac{30 + 31 + 32}{3}$? Explain.

TRY THIS Suppose that 9 students counted 30 chirps, 5 students counted 31 chirps, and 10 students counted 32 chirps. Find the mean number of chirps by using a frequency table. Then find the corresponding temperature.

When there are many different values, a *grouped* frequency table is used. In a **grouped frequency table**, the values are grouped into *classes* that contain a range of values. Example 4 shows the procedure for estimating the mean from a grouped frequency table.

E X A M P L E ④ The grouped frequency table at right lists the results of a survey of 80 musicians who were asked how many hours per week they spend practicing.

A P P L I C A T I O N
MUSIC

Estimate the mean number of hours that these musicians practice each week.

● SOLUTION

First find the *class mean*, or midpoint value, for each class. Then multiply each class mean by its corresponding frequency. Add the products, and divide by the total number of musicians surveyed.

$$\overline{x} = \frac{1450}{80} = 18.125$$

Hours	Frequency
1–5	13
6–10	9
11–15	9
16–20	14
21–25	16
26–30	8
31–35	8
36–40	3
Total	**80**

Hours	Class mean	Frequency	Product
1–5	3	13	39
6–10	8	9	72
11–15	13	9	117
16–20	18	14	252
21–25	23	16	368
26–30	28	8	224
31–35	33	8	264
36–40	38	3	114
Total		**80**	**1450**

Thus, a reasonable estimate of the mean number of hours that these musicians practice each week is 18 hours.

CRITICAL THINKING   Explain why the mean of the values in a grouped frequency table is an estimate.

Exercises

● *Communicate*

1. Which measure is the easiest to determine: mean, median, or mode? Which measure is the most difficult? Why?

2. Suppose that the largest and smallest value in a data set are omitted. Will the median change? Will the mean change? Explain.

3. Describe a data set for which the mean is not as representative as the mode or median.

Guided Skills Practice

4. Find the mean, median, and mode for the hourly wages below and then compare the measures. *(EXAMPLE 1)*
  $5.25, $5.00, $6.50, $6.00, $5.00, $6.75, $6.50, $5.00

5. The hours worked in one week by 10 cashiers at a grocery store were 36, 40, 34, 38, 33, 0, 40, 32, 35, and 37. *(EXAMPLE 2)*
  a. Find the mean, median, and mode of the hours worked that week.
  b. Explain which measures best represent the number of the hours worked by a typical cashier in that week.

6. Find the mean of the data set given in the horizontal frequency table at right. *(EXAMPLE 3)*

Value	3	4	5	Total
Frequency	6	11	13	30

7. **MARKETING** Thirty people were asked how many magazines they read in one month. A grouped frequency table for the responses is shown at right. Estimate the mean number of magazines read in one month. *(EXAMPLE 4)*

Number	Frequency
0–2	10
3–5	12
6–8	4
9–11	4
Total	30

Practice and Apply

internet connect

Homework Help Online
Go To: **go.hrw.com**
Keyword:
MB1 Homework Help
  for Exercises 8–21

Find the mean, median, and mode of each data set. Give answers to the nearest thousandth, when necessary.

8. 1, 3, 4, 8, 1, 7, 1, 5

9. 2, 5, 3, 6, 3, 1, 3, 4

10. 18, 13, 16, 20, 21, 13, 19

11. 14, 16, 19, 14, 12, 15, 13

12. $-5, -1, 2, -6, -2,$

13. $-12, -10, -13, -9, -11$

14. 2.1, 3.4, 3.7, 2.2, 2.1, 2.2

15. 1.7, 1.6, 3.8, 5.1, 1.6, 3.8

16. 0.33, 1.24, 2.71, 7.42, 6.21

17. 4.82, 5.22, 8.32, 3.22, 1.56

18. $\frac{1}{2}, \frac{3}{4}, \frac{5}{8}, \frac{7}{8}$

19. $\frac{1}{3}, \frac{1}{9}, \frac{5}{6}, \frac{5}{9}$

Find the mean, median, and mode of each data set, and compare them.

20. the price of haircuts (rounded to nearest half-dollar):
  $6.50, $7.50, $8, $8, $10, $10, $12.50, $14, $16, $16, $20, $24

21. the cost for a gallon of unleaded gasoline (rounded to the nearest cent):
  $1.20, $1.23, $1.25, $1.16, $1.32, $1.24, $1.33, $1.23, $1.21, $1.30, $1.20, $1.20, $1.21, $1.28

Make a frequency table for each data set, and find the mean.

22. the number of days students in 4th period were absent:
  1, 0, 3, 4, 1, 0, 2, 0, 3, 4, 1, 3, 4, 1, 2, 0, 1, 2, 0, 4, 3, 1, 2, 2, 2, 1, 3, 1, 1, 2

23. the number of pets that students in a class have:
  3, 4, 0, 1, 2, 3, 2, 0, 4, 0, 1, 0, 1, 2, 0, 1, 0, 4, 2, 0, 1, 1, 4, 2, 3, 3, 4, 2, 1, 0

Make a grouped frequency table for each data set, and estimate the mean.

24. test scores of a class: 66, 75, 74, 78, 88, 99, 75, 88, 76, 74, 66, 89, 82, 92, 67, 89, 88, 84, 92, 65, 75, 85, 78, 79, 84, 94, 91, 81, 61, 79

25. the miles per gallon for cars driven to school: 30, 21, 18, 19, 23, 24, 26, 32, 30, 22, 12, 15, 21, 28, 27, 18, 16, 19, 23, 29, 24, 25, 16

For each situation described below, decide whether you would represent the data in a frequency table or a grouped frequency table. Explain your choice.

26. the number of pencils carried by each student to class

27. the dollar value of sales recorded by the school store for one month

28. the number of points scored by a basketball team in each game for a season, which vary from 38 to 75

29. the number of brothers and sisters of each student in a class

Survey about 15 students in your class about the topics below, and find the mean, median, and mode of the responses. Then describe which measures are most representative.

30. the distance that students live from school (to the nearest tenth of a mile)

31. the estimated number of movies that students saw last year

32. the time spent sleeping the previous night

33. the time spent studying the previous day

34. BUSINESS A vending company claims that one of its beverage machines dispenses about 8 fluid ounces into each cup. To verify this claim, they measured the amount dispensed into 40 cups. The results are listed below.

7.8	7.9	7.6	8.0	7.8	8.0	7.9	7.6	8.0	8.0	7.5	7.9	7.8	7.9
7.8	8.0	8.2	7.9	7.6	8.0	7.6	8.1	8.1	7.9	7.5	8.0	7.8	7.8
8.0	8.2	7.9	8.1	8.1	7.9	7.5	8.0	7.8	7.8	8.0	8.2		

a. Find the mean, median, and mode, and compare them.
b. Do the results from part **a** support the company's claim?

35. INVENTORY The manager of the women's shoe department recorded the following sizes of shoes sold in one day:

$$5, 6, 5\frac{1}{2}, 7, 9, 6, 5, 7\frac{1}{2}, 7, 5, 8, 6\frac{1}{2}, 7, 8, 6, 4, 6\frac{1}{2}, 10, 7$$

a. Find the mean, median, and mode of the shoe sizes sold.
b. Explain which measure of central tendency is the most helpful for the manager.

36. WORKFORCE The distribution of ages in the workforce of the United States is shown in the table at right.
a. Make three grouped frequency tables, one for each year.
b. Find the estimated mean age of a worker for each year. Use 60 for the class mean of the 55+ class.
c. Compare the estimated means from part **b**. What do they indicate about the workforce?

Percent of the Labor Force by Age

Age	1979	1992	2005
16–24	24%	16%	16%
25–34	27%	28%	21%
35–44	19%	27%	25%
45–54	16%	18%	24%
55+	14%	12%	14%

[*Source: Bureau of Labor Statistics*]

APPLICATIONS

37. ACADEMICS A student's test scores are 86, 72, 85, and 90. What is the lowest score that the student can get on the next test and still have a test average (mean) of at least 80?

CHALLENGE

38. ACCOUNTING The record of Jacob's gasoline purchases on a recent vacation is given in the table below. What is the average cost per gallon of gasoline for the entire trip?

Price per gallon	$1.18	$1.04	$1.29	$1.12	$1.21
Number of gallons purchased	21	17	16	19	11

 Look Back

39. Given $f(x) = x^3$ and $g(x) = x^3 + 2x - 3$, find $f + g$ and $f - g$. *(LESSON 2.4)*

Write each equation in logarithmic form. *(LESSON 6.3)*

40. $16^{\frac{1}{2}} = 4$ **41.** $5^4 = 625$ **42.** $\left(\frac{1}{3}\right)^2 = \frac{1}{9}$ **43.** $2^{-3} = \frac{1}{8}$

Write each equation in exponential form. *(LESSON 6.3)*

44. $\log_5 125 = 3$ **45.** $4 = \log_5 625$ **46.** $-4 = \log_3 \frac{1}{81}$

Factor each polynomial expression. *(LESSON 7.3)*

47. $x^3 + 125$ **48.** $x^3 - 27$

 Look Beyond

Create a data set with at least 5 values for each description below.

49. The mean, median, and mode are all equal.

50. The mean is 4, the median is 5, and the mode is 4.

51. When one data value is deleted, the mean increases by 10.

**Portfolio
Extension**
Go To: **go.hrw.com**
Keyword:
MB1 Central

47	71	75	70	59	78
88	82	89	72	70	74
95	91	74	85	92	62
93	85	98	73	75	97

The scores in Allison's world history class are given above. Allison's score was 78.

1. Find the mean and the median score for this class.

2. Should Allison use the mean or the median to compare her score

with the rest of the class when she reports her grade to her parents? Explain.

3. Choose a score that is greater than the median and raise it by 10 points. Find the new mean and median. Explain what happens to each measure.

4. Choose a score that is less than the median and lower it by 10 points. Find the new mean and median. Explain what happens to each measure.

Stem-and-Leaf Plots, Histograms, and Circle Graphs

73	24	5	72
64	38	66	70
20	41	55	67
8	25	12	37
21	58	54	42
61	45	19	6
19	36	42	14

Objectives

- Make a stem-and-leaf plot, a histogram, or a circle graph for a data set.

- Find and use relative frequencies to solve probability problems.

APPLICATION
MARKETING

An Internet site recorded the number of "hits" between 4 P.M. and 6 P.M. on 28 randomly selected weekdays. The results are listed above.

Stem-and-Leaf Plots

Stem	Leaf	$4\|1 = 41$
0	5, 6, 8	
1	2, 4, 9, 9	
2	0, 1, 4, 5	
3	2, 6, 8	
4	1, 2, 2, 5	
5	4, 5, 8	
6	1, 4, 6, 7	
7	0, 2, 3	

This is an ordered stem-and-leaf plot because the leaves of each stem are listed in order.

A *stem-and-leaf plot* of the Internet data is shown at left. A **stem-and-leaf plot** is a quick way to arrange a set of data and view its shape, or general distribution.

In a stem-and-leaf plot, each data value is split into two parts: a *stem* and a *leaf*. The stems and leaves are chosen so that the data is represented in the most informative way.

A key, shown in the upper right corner of a stem-and-leaf plot, explains what the stems and leaves represent. For example, the key at left tells you that the stem 4 and the leaf 1 represent the data value 41.

From the stem-and-leaf plot above, you can easily see that the maximum number of "hits" is 73 and the minimum is 5. You can also see that the data values are fairly evenly distributed, with 3 or 4 leaves in each stem.

CHECKPOINT ✔ Suppose that you want to make a stem-and-leaf plot for values ranging from 105 to 162. What stems would you use? Why? What stems would you use if the values range from 12.4 to 19.3? Why?

CRITICAL THINKING Describe what the fairly even distribution of data values indicates about the Internet site.

You can also find the median and the mode(s) of a data set from a stem-and-leaf plot, as shown in Example 1.

E X A M P L E ❶ **Rosa is planning the annual Degollado family reunion. She has collected the ages of family members who plan to attend.**

32	32	34	91	38
12	17	62	22	51
27	34	43	44	44
8	30	30	31	40
34	37	38	38	78
50	26	54	28	29
19	6	45		

a. Make a stem-and-leaf plot of the ages.
b. Find the median and mode of the ages.
c. How can the stem-and-leaf plot be used to plan the reunion?

● **SOLUTION**

a. Choose digits in the tens place for the stems, as shown at right.

b. Because there are 33 values, the median is the 17th value, 34. The modes are 34 and 38.

c. The stem-and-leaf plot organizes the ages so that events can be planned for different age groups. For example, you can see that 3 members are 12 or younger, 2 members are teenagers, and 3 members are 60 or older. You can also see that the ages *cluster* around the 30s, forming a *mound-shaped* distribution.

Stem	Leaf	$5\|2 = 52$
0	6, 8	
1	2, 7, 9	
2	2, 6, 7, 8, 9	
3	0, 0, 1, 2, 2, 4, 4, 4, 7, 8, 8, 8	
4	0, 3, 4, 4, 5	
5	0, 1, 4	
6	2	
7	8	
8		
9	1	

TRY THIS Make a stem-and-leaf plot for the data at right. Find the median and mode of the data. How many values are between 5.0 and 6.0? Describe the shape of the distribution.

3.3	5.5	5.3	7.7	4.2	2.5	6.5	9.2	5.6
4.2	6.9	2.3	9.1	5.6	4.5	7.0	7.2	4.5
5.1	7.2	5.4	2.3	3.2	6.2	3.2	6.2	2.3

CHECKPOINT ✔ Use the stem-and-leaf plot at right to answer the questions below.

a. How can you find the number of values in the data set?
b. How can you find the maximum, minimum, median, and mode(s)?
c. In what order are the values in the stem-and-leaf plot arranged?

Stem	Leaf	$1\|0 = 10$
0	1, 1, 3, 7, 8	
1	0, 0, 5, 6, 9	
2	1, 2, 3, 5	
3	2	
4	2, 5, 6	

Histograms

A **histogram** is a bar graph that gives the frequency of each value.

In a histogram, the horizontal axis is like a number line divided into equal widths. Each width represents a data value or range of data values. The height of each bar indicates the frequency of that data value or range of data values.

E X A M P L E **2** Isaac manages a canoe rental business. He recorded the number of hours that each of 30 customers rented canoes.

Make a frequency table and a histogram for the canoe rental data below.

1	4	5	2	2	2	3	2	3	3
2	3	7	2	3	3	2	6	4	2
1	1	3	5	5	4	4	2	8	2

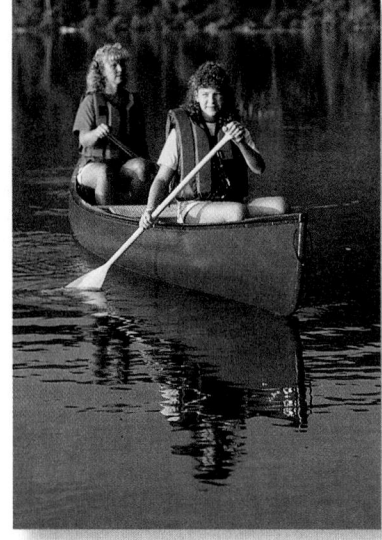

● **SOLUTION**

PROBLEM SOLVING

Make a table. Organize the data in a frequency table. Make the histogram by measuring 8 equal widths for the number of hours the canoes were rented. Draw vertical bars to the height of the corresponding frequencies.

TECHNOLOGY
GRAPHICS CALCULATOR

Keystroke Guide, page 822

Hours	Frequency
1	3
2	10
3	7
4	4
5	3
6	1
7	1
8	1

You can also make histograms on your graphics calculator by entering the frequency data into lists.

TRY THIS Make a frequency table and histogram for the data below.

| 11 | 12 | 16 | 16 | 12 | 16 | 15 | 11 | 15 | 14 | 13 | 12 |
| 17 | 15 | 17 | 13 | 14 | 13 | 11 | 13 | 12 | 15 | 13 | 15 |

CHECKPOINT ✔ Given a histogram, how can you make a frequency table for the data?

CRITICAL THINKING Describe the histogram for a set of data that has no mode.

Relative frequency tables are frequency tables that include a column that displays how frequently a value appears *relative* to the entire data set. The *relative frequency* column is the percent frequency, or probability. A relative frequency table and histogram are shown below for the canoe rental data.

Relative Frequency Table

Hours	Frequency	Relative frequency
1	3	$\frac{3}{30} = 0.10$, or 10%
2	10	$\frac{10}{30} = 0.\overline{3}$, or 33.3%
3	7	$\frac{7}{30} = 0.2\overline{3}$, or 23.3%
4	4	$\frac{4}{30} = 0.1\overline{3}$, or 13.3%
5	3	$\frac{3}{30} = 0.10$, or 10%
6	1	$\frac{1}{30} = 0.0\overline{3}$, or 3.3%
7	1	$\frac{1}{30} = 0.0\overline{3}$, or 3.3%
8	1	$\frac{1}{30} = 0.0\overline{3}$, or 3.3%
Total	30	$\frac{30}{30} = 1.00$, or 100%

Relative Frequency Histogram

There is a 0.0$\overline{3}$ probability that a randomly selected customer will rent a canoe for 8 hours.

EXAMPLE ③ Use the relative frequencies given above to estimate the probability that a randomly selected customer will rent a canoe for 5 or more hours.

CONNECTION
PROBABILITY

SOLUTION

Let event A = 5 hours, event B = 6 hours, event C = 7 hours, and event D = 8 hours. Assume that events A, B, C and D are mutually exclusive.

$$P(A \text{ or } B \text{ or } C \text{ or } D) = P(A) + P(B) + P(C) + P(D)$$
$$= 0.10 + 0.0\overline{3} + 0.0\overline{3} + 0.0\overline{3}$$
$$\approx 0.20$$

Thus, the probability that a randomly selected customer will rent a canoe for 5 or more hours is approximately 0.20, or about 20%.

TRY THIS Estimate the probability that a randomly selected customer will rent a canoe for less than 4 hours?

Exploring the Shapes of Histograms

You will need: coins and a pair of number cubes

1. Roll a number cube and record the result. Repeat this procedure for a total of 20 trials. Make a histogram with the number rolled (1–6) on the horizontal axis.

2. Toss a coin 6 times and record the number of heads that appear. Repeat this procedure for a total of 20 trials. Make a histogram with the number of heads out of 6 tosses on the horizontal axis.

CHECKPOINT ✔ 3. Compare the shape of the histogram for Step 1 with the one for Step 2. Which is flatter? Which is more mound-shaped?

4. Suppose that a pair of number cubes are rolled and the sum is recorded for 20 trials. What shape would you expect for the histogram of this data? Explain.

CHECKPOINT ✔ **5.** Roll a pair of number cubes as described in Step 4 and record the results. Make a histogram and describe its shape. Is the histogram different from the shape you expected? Explain.

Circle Graphs

You can use a **circle graph** to display the distribution of non-overlapping *parts* of a *whole*, as shown in Example 4.

E X A M P L E **4** **The causes of 1200 fires are listed at right.**

a. Make a circle graph to represent this data.

b. Find the probability that a given fire was caused by smoking, children, or cooking.

APPLICATION
PUBLIC SAFETY

● **SOLUTION**

a. Find the relative frequency, or percent, for each cause. Multiply this percent by 360° to obtain the corresponding central angle.

Cause	Number
Cooking	264
Electrical	312
Unknown	216
Children	60
Open flames	60
Smoking	120
Arson	168
Total	**1200**

Cause	Relative Frequency	Central Angle
Cooking	$\frac{264}{1200} = 0.22$	$0.22 \times 360° \approx 79°$
Electrical	$\frac{312}{1200} = 0.26$	$0.26 \times 360° \approx 94°$
Unknown	$\frac{216}{1200} = 0.18$	$0.18 \times 360° \approx 65°$
Children	$\frac{60}{1200} = 0.05$	$0.05 \times 360° = 18°$
Open flames	$\frac{60}{1200} = 0.05$	$0.05 \times 360° = 18°$
Smoking	$\frac{120}{1200} = 0.10$	$0.10 \times 360° = 36°$
Arson	$\frac{168}{1200} = 0.14$	$0.14 \times 360° \approx 50°$
Total	$\frac{1200}{1200} = 1.00$	$1.00 \times 360° = 360°$

Use a protractor to measure the central angle for each category.

b. Let each event be the cause of a given fire: event A = smoking, event B = children, and event C = cooking. Assume that events A, B, and C are mutually exclusive.

$$P(A \text{ or } B \text{ or } C) = P(A) + P(B) + P(C)$$
$$= 0.10 + 0.05 + 0.22$$
$$= 0.37$$

Thus, the probability that a fire was caused by smoking, children, or cooking is 0.37, or 37%.

SUMMARY OF DISPLAYS FOR DATA	
Name	**When useful**
stem-and-leaf plot	• to quickly arrange raw data • to show distribution and retain actual values for analysis
histogram	• to show frequency or probability distributions
circle graph	• to show how parts relate to a whole

Exercises

Communicate

1. Describe the different shapes of distributions discussed in the lesson.

2. Which contains more information, a stem-and-leaf plot or a histogram? When is each representation preferred?

3. Explain why the relative frequencies for a data set may also be probabilities.

4. Circle graphs are also called pie charts. Describe the characteristics of a circle graph that are implied by the name *pie chart*.

Guided Skills Practice

APPLICATION

5. BUSINESS The number of calls for customer service during 24 randomly selected days are listed below. *(EXAMPLE 1)*

22	32	25	42	48	42	36	51	42	53	53	29
31	38	52	51	48	24	39	37	71	51	39	21

a. Make a stem-and-leaf plot of the calls received.
b. Find the median and mode of the number of calls.
c. How could a stem-and-leaf plot of the number of calls be used?

*College campus in
New York*

6. LAW ENFORCEMENT The number of calls that a police department responded to during 24 randomly selected days are listed below. *(EXAMPLE 2)*

| 5 | 7 | 8 | 4 | 9 | 4 | 5 | 6 | 7 | 4 | 6 | 3 |
| 6 | 7 | 6 | 8 | 5 | 4 | 6 | 8 | 3 | 7 | 5 | 5 |

Make a frequency table and a histogram for the number of responses.

7. BUSINESS Refer to the relative frequency table on page 775. Find the probability that a randomly selected customer rents a canoe for 5 hours or less. *(EXAMPLE 3)*

8. EDUCATION The table at right lists the majors of students at a small college. *(EXAMPLE 4)*
  a. Make a circle graph to represent this data.
  b. Find the probability that a randomly selected student is a liberal arts major or undecided.

Major	Number
Liberal arts	891
Natural sciences	627
Undecided	235
Other	122

Practice and Apply

Make a stem-and-leaf plot for each data set. Then find the median and the mode, and describe the distribution of the data.

9. 8.9, 8.8, 7.2, 7.5, 9.2, 7.9, 8.2, 9.1, 8.7, 8.2, 8.5, 8.6, 9.5, 7.5

10. 27.2, 26.3, 30.1, 26.8, 27.3, 28.7, 28.3, 29.8, 29.4, 28.4, 29.1, 28.1, 27.6

11. 359, 357, 348, 347, 337, 347, 340, 335, 338, 348, 339, 356, 336, 358

12. 6.15, 8.55, 7.85, 9.65, 7.85, 8.45, 7.35, 6.35, 8.45, 9.65, 7.85, 9.75, 6.35

internet connect

**Homework
Help Online**
Go To: **go.hrw.com**
Keyword:
MB1 Homework Help
for Exercises 13–20

Make a frequency table and histogram for each data set.

13. 5, 4, 6, 7, 9, 2, 3, 9, 6, 9, 3, 2, 8, 10, 10

14. 3, 5, 7, 9, 2, 4, 6, 10, 7, 8, 2, 3, 9, 7, 6

15. 1.0, 0.5, 1.5, 2.0, 2.5, 1.0, 1.5, 2.0, 0.5, 1.5, 2.5, 3.0, 2.0, 1.5, 1.0

16. 0.8, 0.4, 0.6, 0.4, 0.2, 0.2, 0.6, 0.6, 0.4, 0.2, 0.4, 0.4, 0.4, 0.8, 0.6

Make a relative frequency table and relative frequency histogram for each data set.

17. 1, 3, 1, 4, 3, 2, 7, 5, 8, 3, 7, 1, 4, 8, 5, 7, 4, 2, 3, 4, 7, 3, 8, 1

18. 40, 60, 80, 30, 70, 80, 80, 60, 60, 40, 30, 40, 70, 100, 60, 70, 30, 40

19. 0.1, 0.3, 0.1, 0.2, 0.4, 0.2, 0.1, 0.5, 0.3, 0.1, 0.1, 0.2, 0.1, 0.3, 0.2

20. 8.1, 8.5, 7.6, 7.9, 8.0, 7.8, 7.9, 8.1, 8.0, 8.1, 8.3, 8.1, 7.9, 7.5, 8.0

Make a histogram with the following intervals for each data set:
$0 \le x < 1$, $1 \le x < 2$, $2 \le x < 3$, $3 \le x < 4$, $4 \le x < 5$, and $5 \le x < 6$.

21. 0.2, 1.3, 5.4, 4.3, 2.2, 4.3, 4.6, 3.5, 5.1, 4.8, 1.5, 3.7, 5.4, 4.0, 4.2, 5.2

22. 2.2, 4.6, 3.2, 1.2, 2.8, 3.8, 4.2, 1.2, 2.2, 1.5, 0.5, 2.9, 3.6, 0.9, 1.0

23. 3.4, 4.8, 1.2, 2.5, 3.6, 5.2, 5.0, 4.1, 3.8, 3.5, 4.2, 5.1, 4.8, 4.4, 4.9

24. 0.2, 1.9, 1.2, 0.7, 2.3, 3.1, 2.5, 1.8, 1.6, 1.4, 0.8, 1.3, 0.9, 2.2, 1.7

25. PATTERNS IN DATA Survey at least 20 students in your class about how they travel to school (walk, bus, car, bike, subway, . . .). Organize your data into a table and make a circle graph. Explain what your graph illustrates.

26. BUSINESS The dollar amount of the total purchases from a vending machine in an office over a 3-month period is shown below for 21 randomly selected individuals.

$10	$43	$5	$18	$8	$63	$10	$6	$30	$22	
$27	$25	$14	$18	$30	$41	$27	$22	$31	$32	$42

a. Make a stem-and-leaf plot of the dollar amounts. Describe the distribution.
b. Find the median and mode of the dollar amounts.
c. Find the probability that a randomly selected individual spent $20 or less on vending machine purchases.

27. INCOME The percent distribution by income of all households in the United States is listed in the table below for 1994.

Under $14,999	$15,000– $24,999	$25,000– $34,999	$35,000– $49,999	$50,000– $74,999	Over $75,000
22.7%	16.7%	14.2%	16.3%	16.5%	13.6%

[*Source: U.S. Bureau of the Census*]

a. Explain whether a histogram or circle graph would best display the data in the table and draw the display.
b. Interpret your display by describing what it illustrates.
c. Find the probability that a randomly selected household in the United States has an income of $50,000 or more.

28. ARMED FORCES The table below lists the location and number of the active-duty military personnel from the United States worldwide.

Location	Number
U.S., U.S. Territories, and special locations	1,397,083
Western and Southern Europe	166,249
East Asia and Pacific	99,022
North Africa, Middle East, and South Asia	11,490
Sub-Saharan Africa	6864
Other Western Hemisphere	17,758

[*Source: The World Almanac and Book of Facts, 1995*]

a. Display this information in your choice of a stem-and-leaf plot, histogram, or circle graph. Justify your choice.
b. Find the probability that a randomly selected active-duty military person from the United States is not located in the United States.

29. MARKETING A taste test of three sodas, labeled A, B, and C, included 175 participants. In the test, soda B was selected by twice as many people as soda A, and soda C was selected by twice as many people as soda B. Represent these results in a circle graph.

Look Back

Solve each proportion for x. (LESSON 1.4)

30. $\frac{3x-2}{4} = \frac{x}{9}$

31. $\frac{-4x}{7} = x + 2$

32. $\frac{20x}{-6} = \frac{x-4}{3}$

Factor each expression. (LESSON 5.3)

33. $x^2 + 16x + 64$

34. $x^2 - 10x + 25$

35. $3(2x - 5) - x(2x - 5)$

36. $25a^2 - 49b^2$

Divide by using synthetic division. (LESSON 7.3)

37. $(x^3 + x^2 - 20) \div (x + 2)$

38. $(2x^3 + 10x^2 - 2x + 8) \div (x - 3)$

Use a graph, synthetic division, and factoring to find all of the roots of each equation. (LESSON 7.4)

39 $x^3 - 2x^2 - 4x + 8 = 0$

40 $x^3 + x^2 - x - 1 = 0$

41 $c^3 + 5c^2 + 8c + 4 = 0$

42 $y^3 - 4y^2 + 4y = 0$

CONNECTION

43. TRANSFORMATIONS Translate the ellipse defined by the equation $25x^2 + 16y^2 = 100$ down 2 units and to the right 4 units. Write the standard equation of the resulting ellipse. *(LESSON 9.4)*

A coin is tossed 3 times. Use a tree diagram to find the probability that 2 of the 3 tosses land tails up, given that each event below occurs. (LESSON 10.6)

44. The first coin lands tails up.

45. The first coin lands heads up.

Look Beyond

46. A trick coin with a 0.75 probability of heads is tossed 3 times. What is the probability of getting 2 heads in 3 tosses?

Collect data from the National Weather Service about the average number of days per year that different cities have snowfall. Choose one city in each of the 50 states, including the city in which you reside. Represent the data in a stem-and-leaf plot, a histogram, and a circle graph. Then answer the questions below.

1. How does your city compare with the other cities? Which display— a stem-and-leaf plot, a histogram, or a circle graph—best compares this information? Why?

2. How many cities have the same average number of days of snowfall per year as your city? Which display—a stem-and-leaf plot, a histogram, or a circle graph—best illustrates this information? Why?

3. Which display—a stem-and-leaf plot, a histogram, or a circle graph— do you prefer for this data? Why?

WORKING ON THE CHAPTER PROJECT

You should now be able to complete Activity 1 of the Chapter Project.

Box-and-Whisker Plots

Hollywood Hill, Los Angeles, California

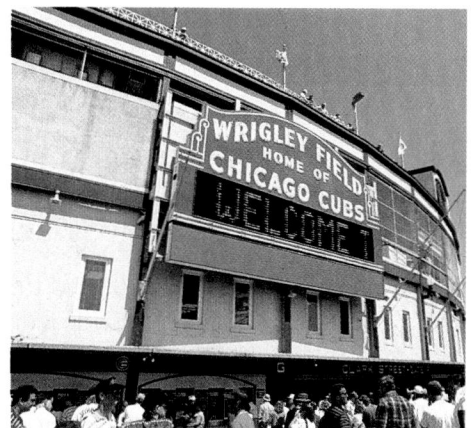
Wrigley Field, home of the Chicago Cubs

Objectives

- Find the range, quartiles, and interquartile range for a data set.

- Make a box-and-whisker plot for a data set.

APPLICATION
CLIMATE

Why *You can use box-and-whisker plots to compare the distributions of two sets of similar data, such as the monthly mean temperatures for two cities.*

The mean monthly temperatures for Los Angeles, California, and Chicago, Illinois, are listed at right. Construct a box-and-whisker plot for the temperatures in each city and compare them. *You will solve the problem in Example 2.*

Los Angeles (1961–1990) Monthly Mean Temperatures (°F)	
Jan.	55.9
Feb.	57.0
Mar.	58.3
Apr.	60.8
May	63.3
June	66.7
July	70.9
Aug.	71.8
Sep.	70.5
Oct.	66.6
Nov.	62.1
Dec.	57.6

[*Source: U.S. NOAA*]

Chicago (1961–1990) Monthly Mean Temperatures (°F)	
Jan.	21.0
Feb.	25.5
Mar.	37.0
Apr.	48.6
May	58.8
June	68.5
July	73.0
Aug.	71.6
Sep.	64.4
Oct.	52.7
Nov.	39.9
Dec.	26.6

[*Source: U.S. NOAA*]

Quartiles

Exploring Quartiles

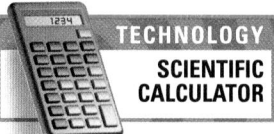
TECHNOLOGY
SCIENTIFIC CALCULATOR

You will need: a calculator and graph paper

The table below gives the mean monthly precipitation (1961–1990) in inches for Dallas–Fort Worth, Texas. [*Source: U.S. NOAA*]

Jan.	Feb.	Mar.	Apr.	May	Jun.	Jul.	Aug.	Sep.	Oct.	Nov.	Dec.
1.9	2.2	2.8	3.5	4.9	3.0	2.3	2.2	3.4	3.5	2.3	1.8

1. Find the median of the monthly precipitation data. What percent of the data values are *below* the median? *above* the median?

2. Find the median of the lower half of the values. What percent of data values are below this "lower" median?

3. Find the median of the upper half of the values. What percent of data values are above this "upper" median?

CHECKPOINT ✔ **4.** Draw a number line and plot each of the medians you calculated in Steps 1–3 along with the highest and lowest values. Write the percent of data values that are between each plotted value.

Related to the median, which divides a data set into halves, are **quartiles** which divide a data set into quarters. The second quartile, Q_2, is the median that divides the lower half of the data values from the upper half. The lower quartile, Q_1, is the median of the lower half of the data values, and the upper quartile, Q_3, is the median of the upper half of the data values.

These five measures are often called the five-point summary of a data set.

The difference between the maximum value and the minimum value is called the **range**. The difference between the upper and lower quartiles, $Q_3 - Q_1$, is called the **interquartile range**, denoted IQR. When a data value is less than $Q_1 - 1.5(\text{IQR})$ or greater than $Q_3 + 1.5(\text{IQR})$, the data value may be called an **outlier**.

EXAMPLE ①

APPLICATION
SOCIAL SERVICES

The number of calls received by a crisis hotline during 17 randomly selected days is listed at right.

50	57	77	66
53	72	51	88
82	70	112	107
69	88	98	65
155			

a. Find the minimum and maximum values, quartiles, range, and interquartile range for the data.

b. Identify any outliers.

● **SOLUTION**

a. Arrange the values in order. The median is the ninth value, 72. Then find the median of the lower half, $Q_1 = \frac{57 + 65}{2} = 61$, and the median of the upper half, $Q_3 = \frac{88 + 98}{2} = 93$.

50 51 53 57 65 66 69 70 72 77 82 88 88 98 107 112 155

Minimum value $Q_1 = 61$ $Q_2 = 72$ Median $Q_3 = 93$ Maximum value

range = maximum − minimum
      = 155 − 50 = 105

All data values lie within the range.

IQR = $Q_3 - Q_1$
    = 93 − 61 = 32

The middle half of the values lie within the interquartile range.

b. Find any possible outliers below Q_1. | Find any possible outliers above Q_3.

$Q_1 - 1.5(\text{IQR}) = 61 - 1.5(32) = 13$ | $Q_3 + 1.5(\text{IQR}) = 93 + 1.5(32) = 141$

There are no values less than or equal to 13. Because the data value 155 is greater than 141, 155 is a possible outlier.

TRY THIS Find the minimum and maximum values, quartiles, range, and interquartile range for the set of data below. Identify any possible outliers.

4	7	9	31	34	2	35	37	24	34	31	50
11	33	36	2	8	13	52	57	60	69	78	83

CRITICAL THINKING What could the possible outlier in Example 1 indicate for the crisis hotline?

Box-and-Whisker Plots

A **box-and-whisker plot** displays how data values are distributed. A box-and-whisker plot is shown below for the crisis-hotline data from Example 1.

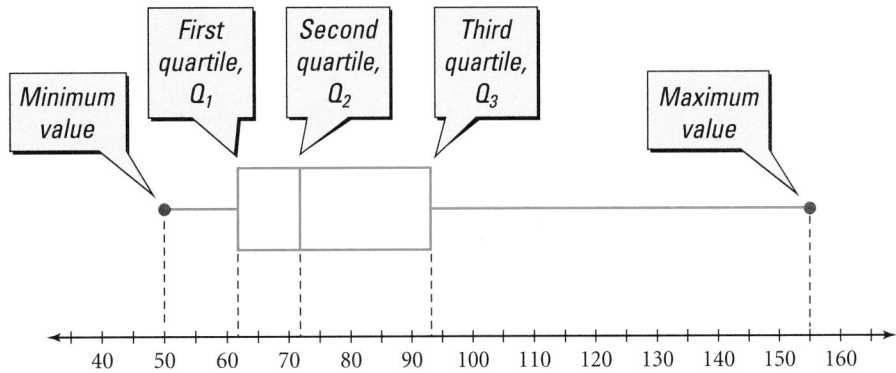

Notice that five measures define a box-and-whisker plot: the minimum value, the maximum value, Q_1, Q_2, and Q_3.

CHECKPOINT ✔ What part of the box-and-whisker plot represents the middle half of the values?

MAKING A BOX-AND-WHISKER PLOT

Step 1. Arrange the values in increasing order and compute Q_1, Q_2, and Q_3.

Step 2. Draw a number line that includes the minimum and maximum values.

Step 3. Make a box whose left end is at Q_1 and whose right end is at Q_3.

Step 4. Draw a vertical line segment to divide the box at, Q_2, the median.

Step 5. Draw a line segment from Q_1 to the minimum value and another line segment from Q_3 to the maximum value for the left and right whiskers.

EXAMPLE 2

APPLICATION
CLIMATE

TECHNOLOGY
GRAPHICS CALCULATOR
Keystroke Guide, page 822

Refer to the temperature data at the beginning of the lesson.

a. Make a box-and-whisker plot for the temperatures in each city.

b. Compare the box-and-whisker plots.

● **SOLUTION**

a. Method 1

Calculate the five measures that define the box-and-whisker plot for each city's temperatures.

	Chicago	LA
minimum	21.0	55.9
Q_1	31.8	57.95
median, Q_2	50.65	62.7
Q_3	66.45	68.6
maximum	73.0	71.8

Then draw both plots as shown below.

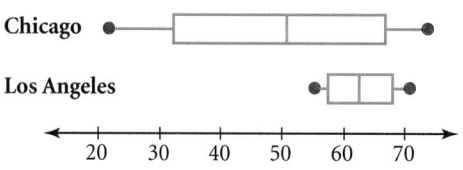

Method 2

Use a graphics calculator. First enter the temperatures for each city into separate lists. Then select box-and-whisker plots for each list of data.

Use the trace feature to identify the maximum, minimum, and quartiles that define each box-and-whisker plot.

b. The longer box and longer whiskers for Chicago indicate that the temperature in Chicago varies much more than the temperature in Los Angeles. Over one-half of Chicago's months had an average temperature less than that of any month in Los Angeles. The maximum average monthly temperature in Chicago was also slightly greater than any average monthly temperature in Los Angeles.

CHECKPOINT ✔ Calculate the IQR for Chicago and for Los Angeles in Example 2. What do your results tell you? What can you conjecture about the temperature variation in New York City, which has an IQR of 35.5?

CRITICAL THINKING Can a box-and-whisker plot have only one whisker? no whiskers? Explain.

APPLICATION
SPORTS

The regular-season batting averages for the top 10 players with at least 175 at bats are displayed at right for the teams in the 1997 World Series.

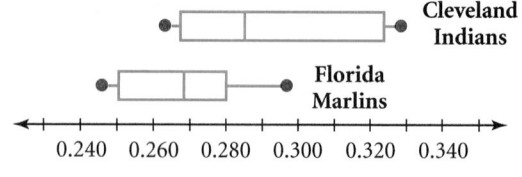

CHECKPOINT ✔ Compare the two box-and-whisker plots above.

Although the graphs show that Cleveland's players had higher batting averages, they lost the 1997 World Series to Florida. Regular-season batting averages are clearly not the only factor to consider when predicting who will win.

Exercises

Communicate

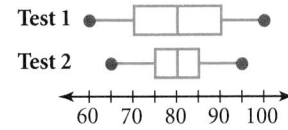

1. Explain how finding the quartiles for a data set with 20 values is different from finding the quartiles for a data set with 15 values.

2. The box-and-whisker plots at right show the test scores for a history class. Explain what the plots indicate about the class performance on the tests.

3. What does a box-and-whisker plot tell you about the data set that it represents?

4. Construct two data sets that have the following quartiles: $Q_1 = 5$, $Q_2 = 7$, and $Q_3 = 11$. Explain why you cannot determine from the quartiles what the actual data values are.

Guided Skills Practice

APPLICATIONS

5. **ECOLOGY** The lengths (in centimeters) of 24 American burying beetles are given in the table below. *(EXAMPLE 1)*

Lengths of American Burying Beetles (cm)

2.5	2.8	3.1	3.6	3.4	3.8	3.0	2.8	3.5	3.3	2.6	3.0
2.9	2.7	3.4	3.2	3.7	2.5	3.1	2.9	2.5	3.1	3.8	2.9

a. Find the minimum and maximum values, quartiles, range, and interquartile range for the data.
b. Identify any possible outliers.

6. **CLIMATE** Refer to the temperature data below. *(EXAMPLE 2)*
a. Make a box-and-whisker plot for the temperatures in each city.
b. Compare the box-and-whisker plots.

Honolulu (1961–1990)
Monthly Mean Temperatures (°F)

Jan.	71.8
Feb.	71.8
Mar.	72.5
Apr.	73.9
May	75.7
June	77.5
July	78.6
Aug.	79.3
Sep.	79.2
Oct.	77.9
Nov.	75.6
Dec.	73.2

[*Source: U.S. NOAA*]

Phoenix (1961–1990)
Monthly Mean Temperatures (°F)

Jan.	51.6
Feb.	55.8
Mar.	61.0
Apr.	68.4
May	76.5
June	85.8
July	91.0
Aug.	89.2
Sep.	83.5
Oct.	72.0
Nov.	59.9
Dec.	52.7

[*Source: U.S. NOAA*]

Practice and Apply

internet connect

Homework Help Online

Go To: **go.hrw.com**
Keyword:
MB1 Homework Help
for Exercises 7–14

Find the minimum and maximum values, quartiles, range, and interquartile range for each data set. Then make a box-and-whisker plot for each data set.

7. 42, 45, 56, 48, 59, 60, 51, 54, 44, 51, 50, 44, 42, 49, 56

8. 2, 16, 4, 11, 14, 8, 17, 19, 13, 19, 9, 15, 8, 13, 17

9. 102, 120, 154, 130, 130, 180, 190, 175, 125, 130

10. 525, 575, 580, 585, 590, 530, 545, 569, 595, 580

11. 22, 50, 78, 22, 77, 93, 27, 86, 14

12. 12, 73, 11, 96, 45, 21, 16, 98, 13

13. 3.2, 4.8, 7.8, 2.2, 7.7, 2.3, 2.7, 8.8, 4.8, 6.5

14. 6.2, 5.1, 4.5, 3.2, 3.5, 5.2, 3.2, 4.8, 8.7, 5.3

Three classes took the same test. Use the box-and-whisker plots below for the scores of each class to answer each question.

15. Which class had the highest score?

16. Which class had the greatest range?

17. Which class had the highest median?

18. Which class had the highest Q_1?

19. Which class had the greatest IQR?

Class 1, Class 2, Class 3

50 60 70 80 90 100

20. In which class do the middle half of the scores have the smallest range?

21. What percent of scores are greater than Q_1 for each class?

CHALLENGE

22. Colleges report the SAT I scores of the entering freshman class. Instead of a median score, many schools give a range of scores to represent the middle 50% of the class, such as a range from 520 to 610 for math scores. Explain what this range describes as well as the advantages of using it rather than a median score.

CONNECTION

23. **PATTERNS IN DATA** Research the mean monthly temperatures for your city. Find the quartiles and make a box-and-whisker plot. How does the plot for your city compare with those for Chicago and Los Angeles given at the beginning of the lesson?

APPLICATION

A woman in Japan seeds oysters for pearls.

24. **DEMOGRAPHICS** The table at right gives the percent of women in the labor force of eight major countries for the years 1980 and 1992. [*Source: Information Please: Almanac, Atlas, and Yearbook, 1996*]

  a. Find Q_1, Q_2, and Q_3 for both years.
  b. Make box-and-whisker plots for the data from 1980 and from 1992.
  c. Compare the two box-and-whisker plots.

Females as a Percent of the Total Labor Force

Country	1980	1992
Australia	36.4	42.1
Canada	39.7	45.5
France	39.5	43.8
Germany	38.0	42.0
Japan	38.4	40.5
Sweden	45.2	48.3
United Kingdom	40.4	44.9
United States	42.4	45.7

DEMOGRAPHICS The table below gives the life expectancy at birth for selected countries in North, Central, and South America for 1994.

Life Expectancy at Birth (years)

Country	Both genders	Male	Female
Brazil	62	57	67
Canada	78	75	82
Chile	75	72	78
Costa Rica	78	76	80
Ecuador	70	67	73
Guatemala	64	62	67
Mexico	73	69	77
Panama	75	72	78
Peru	66	63	68
Trinidad and Tobago	71	68	73
United States	76	73	79
Uruguay	74	71	77
Venezuela	73	70	76

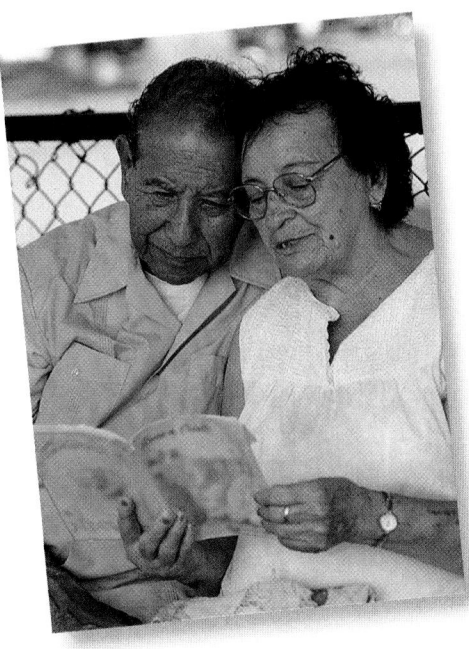

[*Source: Information Please: Almanac, Atlas, and Yearbook, 1996*]

25. a. Find the minimum and maximum values, Q_1, Q_2, and Q_3 for both genders.
   b. Make a box-and-whisker plot of the life expectancy for both genders.

26. a. Find the minimum and maximum values, Q_1, Q_2, and Q_3 for males and for females.
   b. Using the same number line as in Exercise 25, make a box-and-whisker plot of the life expectancy for males and for females. Then compare them.

27 **GEOGRAPHY** The table below gives the area for each of the 50 states.

Area of States in Square Miles

AL	52,423	HI	10,932	ME	35,387	NJ	8722	SD	77,121
AK	656,424	IA	56,276	MI	96,705	NM	121,598	TN	42,146
AR	53,182	ID	83,574	MN	86,943	NV	110,567	TX	268,601
AZ	114,006	IL	57,918	MO	69,709	NY	54,471	UT	84,904
CA	163,707	IN	36,420	MS	48,434	OH	44,828	VA	42,777
CO	104,100	KS	82,282	MT	147,046	OK	69,903	VT	9615
CT	5544	KY	40,411	NC	53,821	OR	98,386	WA	71,302
DE	2489	LA	51,843	ND	70,704	PA	46,058	WI	65,499
FL	65,756	MA	10,555	NE	77,358	RI	1545	WV	24,231
GA	59,441	MD	12,407	NH	9351	SC	32,008	WY	97,818

[*Source: The World Almanac and Book of Facts, 1996*]

   a. Find the minimum and maximum values, Q_1, Q_2, and Q_3 for this data.
   b. Make a box-and-whisker plot with the values from part **a.**
   c. Identify any possible outliers by naming the corresponding states.

APPLICATION

GOVERNMENT The table below lists the presidents and their ages at inauguration.

John F. Kennedy was 43 years old at inauguration.

Age of the Presidents of the United States at Inauguration

Name	Age	Name	Age
1. Washington	57	22. Cleveland	47
2. J. Adams	61	23. B. Harrison	55
3. Jefferson	57	24. Cleveland	55
4. Madison	57	25. McKinley	54
5. Monroe	58	26. T. Roosevelt	42
6. J. Q. Adams	57	27. Taft	51
7. Jackson	61	28. Wilson	56
8. Van Buren	54	29. Harding	55
9. W. H. Harrison	68	30. Coolidge	51
10. Tyler	51	31. Hoover	54
11. Polk	49	32. F. D. Roosevelt	51
12. Taylor	64	33. Truman	60
13. Filmore	50	34. Eisenhower	62
14. Pierce	48	35. Kennedy	43
15. Buchanan	65	36. L. B. Johnson	55
16. Lincoln	52	37. Nixon	56
17. A. Johnson	56	38. Ford	61
18. Grant	46	39. Carter	52
19. Hayes	54	40. Reagan	69
20. Garfield	49	41. Bush	64
21. Arthur	50	42. Clinton	46

[*Source: Information Please: Almanac, Atlas, and Yearbook, 1996*]

28. a. Find the minimum and maximum values, Q_1, Q_2, and Q_3 for the ages of the presidents at inauguration. Are there any possible outliers?
   b. Make a box-and-whisker plot for ages of the presidents at inauguration.

29. a. Using the same number line, make a box-and-whisker plot for the first 21 presidents and another box-and-whisker plot for the last 21 presidents.
   b. Compare the box-and-whisker plots. What do they indicate?

 Look Back

Tell whether each function represents exponential growth or decay.
(LESSON 6.2)

30. $f(x) = 0.7^x$ **31.** $f(x) = 0.7^{-x}$ **32.** $f(x) = 7^x$ **33.** $f(x) = 7^{-x}$

34. Write an exponential function that models 8% annual growth with a y-value of 1000 at $x = 0$. **(LESSON 6.2)**

Describe the end behavior of each function. **(LESSON 7.2)**

35. $P(x) = x^3 + 2x^2 - x + 1$ **36.** $P(x) = -2x^3 - 5x + 4$

Find the constant of variation, and write the equation for the relationship. *(LESSON 8.1)*

37. y varies directly as x, and $y = 12$ when $x = 3$.

38. y varies inversely as x, and $y = 20$ when $x = 3$.

39. y varies as the square of x, and $y = 2$ when $x = 3$.

Write the standard equation for each parabola with the given characteristics. *(LESSON 9.2)*

40. vertex: $(0, 0)$; focus: $(3, 0)$ **41.** directrix: $x = 4$; focus: $(-1, 2)$

Write the center, vertices, and co-vertices of each ellipse. *(LESSON 9.4)*

42. $\dfrac{(x-1)^2}{4} + \dfrac{(y+5)^2}{144} = 1$ **43.** $x^2 + 4x + 9y^2 - 21 = 0$

APPLICATION

44. SECURITY A certain type of blank key has 6 possible notches, each of which can be cut to 4 different heights (including no cut at all). How many different keys can be made from this type of blank key? *(LESSON 10.1)*

45. In a group of 7 balloons, 2 are red, 3 are blue, and the rest are white. In how many distinct ways can the balloons be arranged in a row? *(LESSON 10.2)*

46. Find the next three terms of the arithmetic sequence $2, 3.5, 5, 6.5, \ldots$ *(LESSON 11.2)*

47. Find the next three terms of the geometric sequence $5, 6, 7.2, 8.64, \ldots$ *(LESSON 11.4)*

 Look Beyond

48. The table at left shows the points scored by two basketball players in the first five games of the season.
  a. Calculate each player's mean points per game.
  b. Which player is more consistent, based on this data? Justify your response. Did the player's mean score from part **a** help you to decide which player is more consistent? Why or why not?

Lewis	Adams
15	20
25	20
30	18
10	22
20	20

Obtain the weekly television ratings from the A. C. Nielsen Company. Explain what the ratings represent. Then make a box-and-whisker plot of the data and answer the questions below.

  1. What percent of the ratings are below the median, below the lower quartile, above the upper quartile, in the box, and in the whiskers?

  2. Is one whisker longer than the other? If so, what does this indicate? If not, what does this indicate?

  3. Is the median centered in the box? If so, what does this indicate? If not, what does this indicate?

WORKING ON THE CHAPTER PROJECT

You should now be able to complete Activity 2 of the Chapter Project.

Is it RANDOM?

The Quest for True Randomness Finally Appears Successful
by James Gleick

One of the strangest quests of modern computer science seems to be reaching its goal; mathematicians believe they have found a process for making perfectly random strings of numbers.

Sequences of truly patternless, truly unpredictable digits have become a perversely valuable commodity, in demand for a wide variety applications in science and industry. Randomness is a tool for insuring fairness in statistical studies or jury selection, for designing safe cryptographic schemes and for helping scientists simulate complex behavior.

Yet random numbers—as unbiased and disorganized as the result of millions of imaginary coin tosses—have long proved extremely hard to make, either with electronic computers or mechanical devices. Consumers of randomness have had to settle for numbers that fall short, always hiding some subtle pattern.

Random number generators are sold for every kind of computer. Every generator now in use has some kind of flaw, though often the flaw can be hard to detect. Furthermore, in a way, the idea of using a predictable electronic machine to create true randomness is nonsense. No string of numbers is really random if it can be produced by a simple computer process. But in a more practical sense, a string is random if there is no way to distinguish it from a string of coin flips.

Several theorists presented details of the apparent breakthrough in random-number generation. The technique will now be subjected to batteries of statistical tests, meant to see whether it performs as well as the theorists believe it will. The way people perceive randomness in the world around them differs sharply from the way mathematicians understand it and test for it.

The need for randomness in human institutions seems to begin at whatever age "eeny-meeny-miny-moe" becomes a practical decision-making procedure: randomness is meant to insure fairness. Like "eeny-meeny-miny-moe," most such procedures prove far from random. Even the most carefully designed mechanical randomness-makers break down under scrutiny.

One such failure, on a dramatic scale, struck the national draft lottery in 1969, its first year. Military officials wrote all the possible birthdays on 366 pieces of paper and put them into 366 capsules. Then they poured the January capsules into a box and mixed them. Then they added the February capsules and mixed again—and so on.

At a public ceremony, the capsules were drawn from the box by hand. Only later did statisticians establish that the procedure had been far from random; people born toward the end of the year had a far greater chance of being drafted than people born in the early months. In general, the problem of mixing or stirring or shuffling things to insure randomness is more complicated than most experts assume.

An expert in exposing the flaws in pseudorandom-number generators, George Marsaglia of Florida State University, has begun to test the new technique. Dr. Marsaglia judges sequences (of numbers) not just by uniformity—a good distribution of numbers in a sequence —but also by "independence." No number or string of numbers should change the probability of the number or numbers that follow, any more than flipping a coin and getting 10 straight tails changes the likelihood of getting heads on the 11th flip.

[*Source:* New York Times, *April 19, 1988*]

How hard can it be to write a bunch of random numbers? Do you think you can write a sequence of 0s and 1s that looks like it came from coin flips? Do you think you could fool a psychologist or mathematician?

To find out, start by writing down a sequence of 120 zeros and ones in an order that you think looks random.

Before you put your made-up sequence to the test, you need to find out how to check for randomness. One way is by breaking the sequence into smaller sequences, such as sets of 3 digits. Then you can see whether some sets occur too often or not enough.

You can visualize these sets of digits by plotting them as points. Think of the first 3 digits in your sequence as an *ordered triple*, the *x*, *y*, and *z* coordinates of a point in space. Using the digits 0 and 1 to model heads and tails, respectively, there are 8 possible ordered triples, as shown.

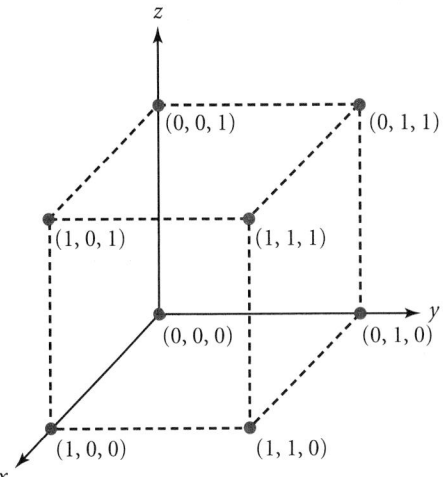

Cooperative Learning

Now you can see whether your classmates are able to distinguish your made-up sequence from an actual sequence.

1. Generate a random sequence of 120 zeros and ones by tossing a coin (heads = 0, tails = 1) or by using a random-number table (even numbers = 0, odd numbers = 1.)

   Exchange this actual sequence and your made-up sequences with another group. (Be sure to mark the sequences so that only you know which one is made up.)

2. Test each sequence you are given by following these steps:
   a. Separate the sequence into 40 ordered triples, as shown here:
   b. Count the number of times the triples **000** and **111** appear. Record your results in a chart.

	Sequence A	Sequence B	Sequence C
0 0 0			
1 1 1			

3. If you flip a coin 3 times, what is the probability of getting 3 heads? 3 tails? Explain.

4. In each new sequence you test, about how many of the 40 triples would you expect to be 000? 111?

5. How might you use your answer to Step 4 to distinguish real random sequences from fake ones?

6. Use your answer to Step 5 to tell which sequence is the fake one. Then find out whether you are correct.

7. Do you think the test would work better if you used sequences of 1200 zeros and ones instead of 120? Why?

8. Write a definition for *random numbers*.

Measures of Dispersion

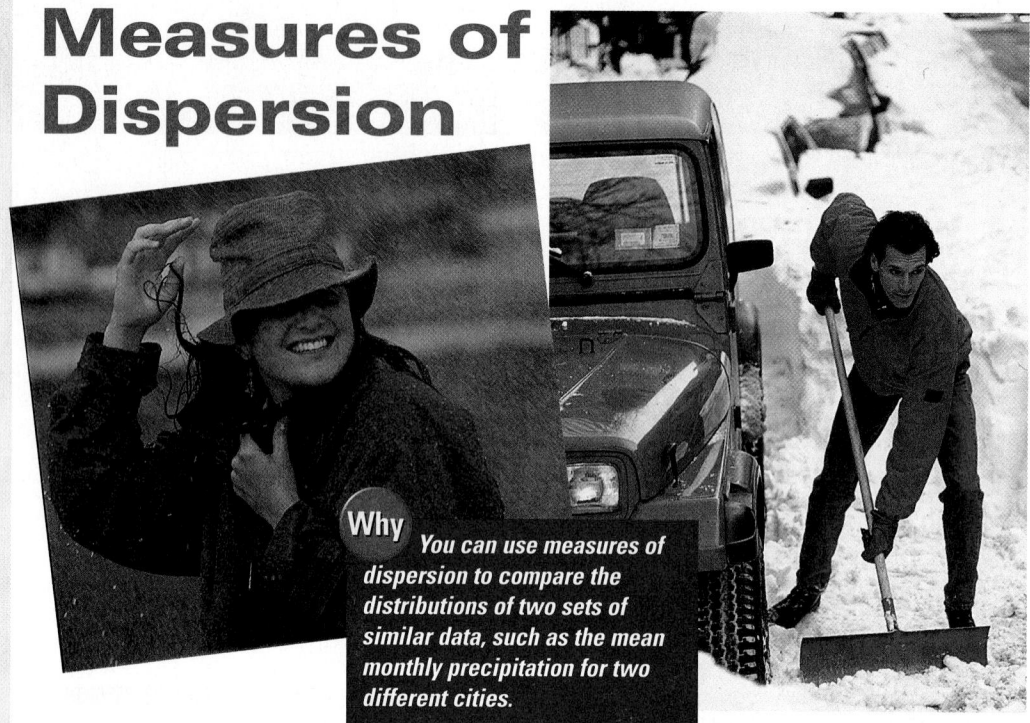

Objective

● Calculate and use measures of dispersion, such as range, mean deviation, variance, and standard deviation.

Why *You can use measures of dispersion to compare the distributions of two sets of similar data, such as the mean monthly precipitation for two different cities.*

Pittsburgh, Pennsylvania, and Kansas City, Missouri, receive similar amounts of annual precipitation (36.5 and 37.6 inches on average, respectively). However, how the precipitation is spread out, or dispersed, over the year is dramatically different. This is illustrated by the box-and-whisker plots below.

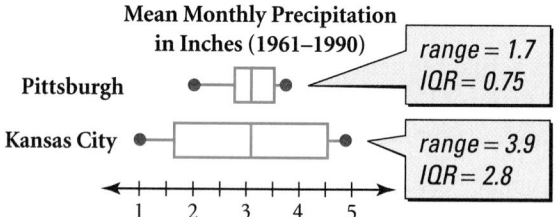

The range and the interquartile range are *measures of dispersion* because they indicate how the monthly precipitation values are *spread* out. **Measures of dispersion** indicate the extent to which values are spread around a central value such as the mean.

As a measure of dispersion, the range is not very reliable because it depends on only two data values, the maximum and the minimum. Likewise, the interquartile range depends on only two values, the first and third quartiles.

Another measure of dispersion, which depends on each data value, is the *mean deviation*. The mean deviation gives the average (mean) amount that the values in a data set differ from the mean.

Mean Deviation

The **mean deviation** of $x_1, x_2, \ldots, x_n$ is the mean of the absolute values of the differences between the data values and the mean, $\bar{x}$.

$$\text{mean deviation} = \frac{1}{n}\sum_{i=1}^{n} |x_i - \bar{x}|$$

E X A M P L E ❶ **The number of miles, in thousands, obtained in five tests of two different tires is listed in the table below.**

Tire A	66	43	37	50	54
Tire B	54	49	47	48	52

a. Find the range and the mean deviation of the number of miles for each tire.

b. Describe what these measures indicate about each tire.

● **SOLUTION**

a. Tire A

range: $66 - 37 = 29$
The range is 29,000 miles.

To find the mean deviation, first find the mean.

$$\bar{x} = \frac{66 + 43 + 37 + 50 + 54}{5} = \frac{250}{5} = 50$$

PROBLEM SOLVING

Make a table to find the absolute values of the differences from the mean. Then find the sum of the absolute values.

x_i	$|x_i - \bar{x}|$
66	16
43	7
37	13
50	0
54	4
Total	40

Divide the total by n.
$$\frac{40}{5} = 8$$
The mean deviation is 8000 miles.

Tire B

range: $54 - 47 = 7$
The range is 7000 miles.

To find the mean deviation, first find the mean.

$$\bar{x} = \frac{54 + 49 + 47 + 48 + 52}{5} = \frac{250}{5} = 50$$

Make a table to find the absolute values of the differences from the mean. Then find the sum of the absolute values.

x_i	$|x_i - \bar{x}|$
54	4
49	1
47	3
48	2
52	2
Total	12

Divide the total by n.
$$\frac{12}{5} = 2.4$$
The mean deviation is 2400 miles.

b. Because tire B has a smaller mean deviation than tire A ($2400 < 8000$), the individual values for tire B deviate less from the mean. This indicates that the mean for tire B is a more reliable measure of its central tendency. Thus, the expected mileage for tire B is more predictable.

TRY THIS Find the range and the mean deviation for the data on tire C below. Then compare these measures with those for tires A and B.

Tire C	64	52	50	49	35

CHECKPOINT ✔ Can two data sets have the same range and different mean deviations? Justify your answer with a sample set of data.

The variance and standard deviation are two more measures of dispersion that are commonly used in comparing and analyzing data.

Variance and Standard Deviation

If a data set has n data values $x_1, x_2, \ldots, x_n$ and mean $\bar{x}$, then the **variance** and **standard deviation** of the data are defined as follows:

$$\text{Variance: } \sigma^2 = \frac{1}{n}\sum_{i=1}^{n}(x_i - \bar{x})^2$$

$$\text{Standard deviation: } \sigma = \sqrt{\sigma^2}$$

E X A M P L E ② Find the standard deviation for the tire data in Example 1.

APPLICATION
MANUFACTURING

PROBLEM SOLVING

● SOLUTION

Tire A

$$\bar{x} = \frac{66 + 43 + 37 + 50 + 54}{5} = 50$$

Make a table to organize your calculations.

x_i	$x_i - \bar{x}$	$(x_i - \bar{x})^2$
66	16	256
43	−7	49
37	−13	169
50	0	0
54	4	16
Total	0	490

variance: $\sigma^2 = \frac{490}{5} = 98$

standard deviation: $\sigma = \sqrt{98} \approx 9.9$

The standard deviation is 9900 miles.

Tire B

$$\bar{x} = \frac{54 + 49 + 47 + 48 + 52}{5} = 50$$

Make a table to organize your calculations.

x_i	$x_i - \bar{x}$	$(x_i - \bar{x})^2$
54	4	16
49	−1	1
47	−3	9
48	−2	4
52	2	4
Total	0	34

variance: $\sigma^2 = \frac{34}{5} = 6.8$

standard deviation: $\sigma = \sqrt{6.8} \approx 2.6$

The standard deviation is 2600 miles.

As expected from the results in Example 1, tire B has a lower standard deviation than tire A, which indicates a greater consistency in its individual test scores.

TRY THIS Find the standard deviation for the data on tire C given in the Try This after Example 1.

CHECKPOINT ✔ Suppose that you are given a standard deviation of 1500 miles for tire D. What does this tell you about tire D relative to tires A and B in Example 2?

CRITICAL THINKING Which measure do you think is used most, the variance or the standard deviation? Why?

Investigating Standard Deviation

CONNECTION
TRANSFORMATIONS

You will need: a calculator

1. Find the standard deviation for the following data: 0, 5, 10, 15, 20.

2. Add a constant to each data value in Step 1. Find the new standard deviation, and describe how it changed.

3. Multiply each data value in Step 1 by a positive constant. Find the new standard deviation, and describe how it changed.

4. Divide each data value in Step 1 by 2, and then subtract 5. Find the new standard deviation, and describe how it changed.

CHECKPOINT ✔ 5. Make a conjecture about what happens to the standard deviation when you add, subtract, multiply, or divide each data value by a constant.

CHECKPOINT ✔ 6. Suppose that a basketball player has a mean of 12 points per game with a standard deviation of 2 points. What is a comparable standard deviation for a basketball player who has a mean of 24 points per game? 30 points per game? Explain.

The precipitation data for the box-and-whisker plots from the beginning of the lesson are shown below.

Mean Monthly Precipitation in Inches (1961–1990)

	Jan.	Feb.	Mar.	Apr.	May	Jun.
Pittsburgh	2.0	2.2	2.9	3.1	3.5	3.7
Kansas City	1.1	1.1	2.5	3.1	5.0	4.7

	Jul.	Aug.	Sep.	Oct.	Nov.	Dec.
Pittsburgh	3.5	3.4	3.4	2.5	3.2	3.1
Kansas City	4.4	4.0	4.9	3.3	1.9	1.6

[*Source: U.S. NOAA*]

You can use a graphics calculator to find the standard deviation for the precipitation of each city by entering the data into lists. Then select the appropriate statistical feature.

Pittsburgh, Pennsylvania　　　　**Kansas City, Missouri**

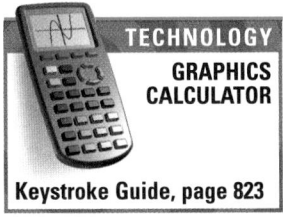

TECHNOLOGY
GRAPHICS CALCULATOR

Keystroke Guide, page 823

standard deviation

The means are within 0.1 of an inch of each other, but the standard deviations are about 0.5 inches for Pittsburgh and 1.4 inches for Kansas City. Thus, Kansas City's monthly precipitation varies much more than Pittsburgh's monthly precipitation.

Exercises

Communicate

1. Explain why the mean deviation and the standard deviation of a set of data are always nonnegative.

2. Describe the relationship between variance and standard deviation. Is the standard deviation always less than the variance? Explain.

3. Explain why the mean deviation and standard deviation are more reliable measures of dispersion than the range or interquartile range.

Guided Skills Practice

APPLICATION

4. **EDUCATION** The table at right lists five test scores for two students. *(EXAMPLE 1)*

   a. Find the range and the mean deviation of the scores for each student.

   b. Describe what these measures indicate about each student's test scores.

5. Find the standard deviation of the scores for each student in Exercise 4. *(EXAMPLE 2)*

Tricia	Morgan
81	98
84	68
88	99
82	59
85	96

Practice and Apply

Find the range and mean deviation for each data set.

6. 8, 10, 3, 9, 10

7. 1, 2, 4, 2, 6

8. 31, 103, 34, 98, 107, 23

9. 32, 23, 68, 74, 26, 93

10. 13.2, 9.4, 7.3, 12.3, 8.6, 7.6

11. 11.1, 14.2, 8.4, 12.2, 15.2, 10.9

12. −1.22, 4.35, −2.42, 2.33, 4.66

13. 8.72, 7.43, −2.92, −3.56, 5.78

internet connect

Homework Help Online
Go To: go.hrw.com
Keyword:
MB1 Homework Help
for Exercises 14–24

Find the variance and standard deviation for each data set.

14. 9, 10, 10, 8, 7, 11, 12, 9

15. 12, 8, 13, 9, 13, 11, 12, 11, 9

16. 8.1, 10.3, 3.4, 9.8, 10.7

17. 19.2, 12.3, 4.8, 22.4, 26

18. 2.42, 7.46, 4.97, 4.22, 6.44

19. 1.34, 2.56, 4.78, 11.89, 8.92

20. −3, 2, −5, 4, −2, 8, 9, −1

21. 2, 4, −8, 8, 7, −2, −4, 3, 7

Find the mean deviation and standard deviation for each data set. Which measure of variation is less affected by an extreme value?

22. 20, 30, 40, 500

23. 0, 500, 510, 520

CHALLENGES

24. Create two data sets with the same range and the same interquartile range, but different standard deviations.

25. Can the standard deviation of a data set be 0? If so, under what conditions? Use sample data sets in your explanation.

26. TRANSFORMATIONS What happens to the standard deviation of a set of data if a constant, c, is added to each value in the data set? What happens to the standard deviation for a data set if each value is multiplied by the same constant, c?

SURVEYS In a survey, 30 people were asked to rank a new soda on a scale from 1 to 10. The results are shown in the table at right.

5	7	9	6	8	10
7	8	8	9	7	8
10	8	7	9	6	8
8	10	9	8	10	10
7	9	8	7	7	9

27. Find the range and the mean deviation of the rankings.

28. Find the standard deviation of the rankings.

MANUFACTURING The table below lists the diameters in millimeters of the ball bearings produced by a certain machine.

5.001	4.9998	4.999	5.002	4.999	5.001	5.002	4.998
4.999	5.000	5.001	4.999	5.000	4.998	4.999	5.003
4.998	4.999	5.001	5.002	5.001	4.999	4.997	5.001
5.001	5.002	5.001	4.998	4.999	5.001	5.002	4.997

29. Find the range and mean deviation.

30. Find the standard deviation.

BUSINESS The tables below list the number of customers for two fast-food locations.

Location 1

12,375	13,890	13,202
12,825	11,982	12,098
11,829	13,234	12,025
12,502	12,654	11,723

Location 2

13,245	13,543	12,983
12,825	12,925	11,924
12,645	11,982	11,728
12,987	13,125	12,887

31. Find the range and the mean deviation of the data for each location. Describe what these measures indicate about each location.

32. Find the standard deviation of the data for each location. Describe what these measures indicate about each location.

SPORTS The winning times (in minutes:seconds.hundredths of a second) for the men's and women's 1500-meter speed-skating competition in several Olympics are shown below.

	1976	1980	1984	1988	1992	1994	1998
Men	1:59.38	1:55.44	1:58.36	1:52.06	1:54.81	1:51.29	1:47.87
Women	2:16.58	2:10.95	2:03.42	2:00.68	2:05.87	2:02.19	1:57.58

33. Find the mean and median winning times for men and for women.

34. Find the range and the mean deviation for men and for women. Describe what these measures indicate about the men's and women's times.

35. Find the standard deviation for men and for women. Describe what these measures indicate about men's and women's times.

Look Back

Solve each system by using a matrix equation. *(LESSON 4.4)*

36 $\begin{cases} 2.3x + 3.2y = 16.1 \\ 4.2x - 4.6y = 12.3 \end{cases}$

37 $\begin{cases} 7.2x + 10.2y = 20.1 \\ 3.8x + 9.5y = 25.6 \end{cases}$

Use the quadratic formula to solve each equation. Give answers to the nearest tenth if their solutions are irrational. *(LESSON 5.5)*

38. $3x^2 + 10x + 1 = 0$

39. $2x^2 + 12x - 4 = 0$

Find each value. *(LESSONS 10.2 AND 10.3)*

40. $_8C_3$

41. $_{10}C_3$

42. $_{17}P_3$

43. $_{21}P_3$

Find the sum of each infinite geometric series, if it exists.
(LESSON 11.6)

44. $\displaystyle\sum_{k=1}^{\infty} 0.765^k$

45. $\displaystyle\sum_{k=1}^{\infty} 0.45^k$

46. $\displaystyle\sum_{k=1}^{\infty} \left(\frac{3}{2}\right)^k$

47. $\displaystyle\sum_{k=1}^{\infty} 2.7^k$

 Look Beyond

48. A sample is often used to make predictions about a larger population. To estimate the mean of a larger population, the mean of the sample is used. However, to estimate the variance or standard deviation of a population, the *sample variance*, denoted S^2, is calculated. The formula for the sample variance is $S^2 = \dfrac{1}{n-1} \displaystyle\sum_{i=1}^{n} (x_i - \bar{x})^2$. This formula differs from the formula for variance, σ^2, in that the sum is divided by $n - 1$ instead of n.

  a. Find the sample variance, S^2, and sample standard deviation, S, for the following sample of a larger population: 15, 18, 7, 16, 5, 12.

  b. A random survey of 10 households in a certain city revealed the following numbers of automobiles: 2, 3, 2, 1, 1, 4, 2, 1, 3, 4. Use this sample to estimate the mean number of automobiles per household and the sample standard deviation of the data for the entire city.

☑ internet connect

Portfolio Extension

Go To: **go.hrw.com**
Keyword:
MB1 Simpson

 PORTFOLIO ACTIVITY

Find the mean and the standard deviation for each of the data sets that you collected for the Portfolio Activities on pages 780 and 789. Explain what these measures tell you about the dispersion of each of the data sets.

Binomial Distributions

12.5

Objective

- Find the probability of r successes in n trials of a binomial experiment.

Why *You can use a binomial experiment to find probabilities of real-world events, such as the probability that enough ambulances will be available for emergencies.*

A medical center has 8 ambulances. Given the ambulance's current condition, regular maintenance, and restocking of medical supplies, the probability of an ambulance being operational is 0.96. Find the probability that at least 6 of the 8 ambulances are operational. *You will solve this problem in Example 2.*

The ambulance problem above is an example of a *binomial experiment*.

Binomial Experiment

A probability experiment is a **binomial experiment** if both of the following conditions are met:

- The experiment consists of n trials whose outcomes are either successes (the outcome *is* the event in question) or failures (the outcome is *not* the event in question).

- The trials are identical and independent with a constant probability of success, p, and a constant probability of failure, $1 - p$.

Activity
Exploring Binomial Probability

You will need: a 6-sided number cube

Let a roll of 1 on the number cube be considered a success, S, and the roll of any other number be considered a failure, F.

1. Write a fraction for the probability of a success, $P(S)$, and for the probability of a failure, $P(F)$, in 1 roll of a number cube.

2. For each arrangement of outcomes in 5 rolls of a number cube, write the probability as a product of fractions. Use exponents in your products.
   a. S F F F F   **b.** F F S F F   **c.** S S F F F   **d.** S F F S F

CHECKPOINT ✔ **3.** Using combination notation, how many ways can you obtain exactly 1 success in 5 rolls of a number cube? exactly 2 successes?

4. Using your answers from Steps 2 and 3, write each probability below as a product, using combination notation and fractions with exponents.
   a. P(exactly 1 success)   **b.** P(exactly 2 successes)

CHECKPOINT ✔ **5.** Find the probability of exactly 3 successes in 5 rolls of a number cube.

In the preceding Activity, *a roll of 1* on a 6-sided number cube is considered a success and *a roll of not 1* is considered a failure. In 5 rolls of the number cube, the probability of 2 successes followed by 3 failures is as follows:

$$\frac{1}{6} \times \frac{1}{6} \times \frac{5}{6} \times \frac{5}{6} \times \frac{5}{6} = \left(\frac{1}{6}\right)^2 \left(\frac{5}{6}\right)^3$$

Roll number   1   2   3   4   5

However, this probability accounts for only one way in which 2 successes in 5 rolls can occur. All of the ways in which 2 successes can occur is the combination $_5C_2$. Thus, the probability of exactly 2 successes in 5 rolls of a number cube is $_5C_2 \left(\frac{1}{6}\right)^2 \left(\frac{5}{6}\right)^3$, or approximately 0.16.

To find the theoretical probability that exactly r successes will occur in n trials of a binomial experiment, you can use the formula below.

Binomial Probability

In a binomial experiment consisting of n trials, the probability, P, of r successes (where $0 \le r \le n$, p is the probability of success, and $1 - p$ is the probability of failure) is given by the following formula:

$$P = {_nC_r}\, p^r\, (1 - p)^{n-r}$$

E X A M P L E **1** Suppose that the probability a seed will germinate is 80%.

What is the probability that 7 of these seeds will germinate when 10 are planted?

APPLICATION
GARDENING

SOLUTION

$n = 10$, $r = 7$, $p = 0.8$, and $1 - p = 1 - 0.8$

$P = {_nC_r}\, p^r\, (1 - p)^{n-r}$

$= {_{10}C_7}\, (0.8)^7\, (1 - 0.8)^{10-7}$

≈ 0.201

```
10 nCr 7*.8^7*.2
^3
        .201326592
```

TECHNOLOGY
GRAPHICS CALCULATOR

Thus, the probability that 7 of these seeds will germinate when 10 are planted is about 0.201, or 20.1%.

Keystroke Guide, page 823

TRY THIS Suppose that the probability a seed will germinate is 85%. What is the probability that 7 of these seeds will germinate when 10 are planted?

CHECKPOINT ✔ Refer to Example 1. Find the probability that all 10 of these seeds will germinate when 10 are planted. Then find the probability that none of these seeds will germinate when 10 are planted. What happens to the binomial probability formula when $r = n$? when $r = 0$?

In a binomial experiment, the events r *successes* and s *successes* are mutually exclusive. Thus, you can find the probability of exactly r successes or exactly s successes by adding the probabilities.

$$P(r \text{ successes } \textbf{\textit{or}} \text{ } s \text{ successes}) = P(r \text{ successes}) + P(s \text{ successes})$$

E X A M P L E **2** Refer to the ambulance problem posed at the beginning of the lesson.

APPLICATION
EMERGENCY SERVICES

Find the probability that at least 6 of the 8 ambulances are operational. Round to the nearest tenth of a percent.

● **SOLUTION**

At least 6 ambulances are operational when exactly 6, 7, or 8 ambulances are operational.

Find $P(\text{exactly } 6) + P(\text{exactly } 7) + P(\text{exactly } 8)$.

Use $n = 8$, $p = 0.96$, and $1 - p = 1 - 0.96$.

$$P(\text{exactly } 6) = {}_8C_6(0.96)^6(1 - 0.96)^{8-6}$$
$$\approx 0.0351$$

$$P(\text{exactly } 7) = {}_8C_7(0.96)^7(1 - 0.96)^{8-7}$$
$$\approx 0.2405$$

$$P(\text{exactly } 8) = {}_8C_8(0.96)^8(1 - 0.96)^{8-8}$$
$$\approx 0.7214$$

$$P(\text{exactly } 6) + P(\text{exactly } 7) + P(\text{exactly } 8) \approx 0.0351 + 0.2405 + 0.7214$$
$$\approx 0.997$$

Thus, the probability is about 99.7%.

TECHNOLOGY
GRAPHICS CALCULATOR

Keystroke Guide, page 823

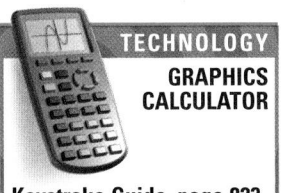

CHECK
You can check your answer by using a calculator with a built-in binomial probability feature. In the display at right, the command **binompdf** is used for 6, 7, and 8 successes. The sum gives the desired probability.

```
binompdf(8,.96,6
)+binompdf(8,.96
,7)+binompdf(8,.
96,8)
          .996920321
```

TRY THIS Find the probability that at least 7 of 8 ambulances are operational, given that the probability of an ambulance being operational is 0.95. Round to the nearest tenth of a percent.

In the binomial experiment of tossing a coin 6 times, success is heads, $n = 6$, $p = 0.5$, and r ranges from 0 heads to 6 heads. The probabilities of tossing each possible number of successes are organized in the table and the relative frequency histogram below.

Heads, r	P(heads), $P = {}_6C_r(0.5)^r(0.5)^{6-r}$
0	≈ 0.016
1	≈ 0.094
2	≈ 0.234
3	≈ 0.312
4	≈ 0.234
5	≈ 0.094
6	≈ 0.016

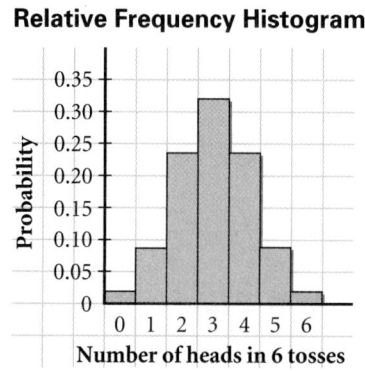

Relative Frequency Histogram

Notice that the distribution of successes is symmetric about the mode because the probabilities of success and failure are equal.

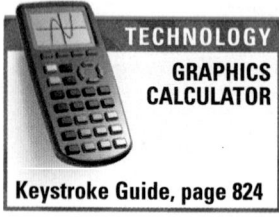

TECHNOLOGY

GRAPHICS CALCULATOR

Keystroke Guide, page 824

You can use a graphics calculator to generate simulations of tossing a coin 6 times. By graphing the experimental results in a histogram, you can compare the distributions obtained experimentally with the distribution obtained theoretically. Each calculator display below shows the distribution of the results of 100 simulations.

CHECKPOINT ✔ How are the distributions alike and how are they different?

When the probabilities of success and of failure are *not* equal, the binomial distribution obtained by theoretical probability will not be symmetric.

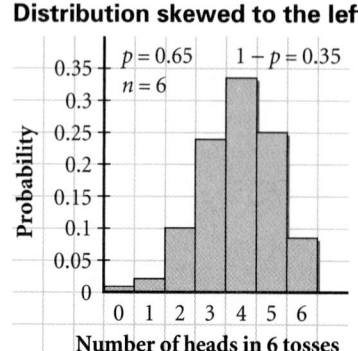

Distribution skewed to the left

$p = 0.65$ $1 - p = 0.35$
$n = 6$

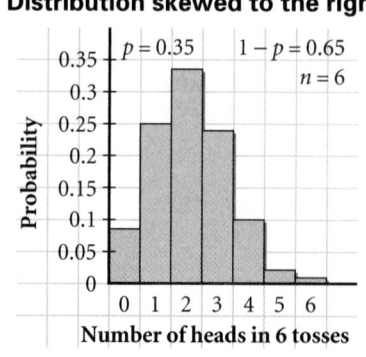

Distribution skewed to the right

$p = 0.35$ $1 - p = 0.65$
$n = 6$

CRITICAL THINKING   Explain why the distribution is skewed to the left when $p > 0.5$ and to the right when $p < 0.5$.

Exercises

Communicate

1. Describe the conditions that an experiment must satisfy in order to be a binomial experiment.

2. Explain why $_nC_r$ appears in the formula for the probability of a binomial experiment, $P = {_nC_r}p^r(1 - p)^{n-r}$.

3. A person randomly selects answers to all 12 questions of a multiple-choice test. Each question has 1 correct and 4 incorrect responses. Describe what n, r, and p represent when finding the binomial probability of 9 answers being correct.

4. Explain the conditions under which a binomial distribution is symmetric and the conditions under which it is skewed.

Guided Skills Practice

APPLICATIONS

5. VETERINARY MEDICINE Suppose that the probability of a sick animal recovering within a week is 70%. What is the probability that 4 out of 6 sick animals will recover within a week? *(EXAMPLE 1)*

6. PUBLIC SAFETY The probability that a driver is not wearing a seat belt is 0.18. Find the probability that at least 2 of 10 drivers are not wearing seat belts. *(EXAMPLE 2)*

Practice and Apply

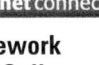

internet connect

Homework Help Online
Go To: **go.hrw.com**
Keyword:
MB1 Homework Help
for Exercises 7–14

A coin is flipped 8 times. Find the probability of each event.

7. exactly 5 heads

8. exactly 3 heads

9. exactly 2 heads

10. exactly 6 heads

11. exactly 0 heads

12. exactly 8 heads

A family has 4 children. Find the probability of each event, assuming that the probability of a male equals the probability of a female.

13. exactly 2 males

14. exactly 1 male

15. 1 female and 3 males

16. all females

Suppose that 70% of the adults in a certain city are registered voters. In a group of 10 randomly selected adults in the city, find the probability that the indicated number are registered voters.

17. exactly 5

18. exactly 8

19. at least 6

20. at least 8

21. at most 5

22. at most 6

23. 2 are not registered voters

24. 4 are not registered voters

A person randomly selects answers to all 10 questions on a multiple-choice quiz. Each question has 1 correct answer and 3 incorrect answers. Find the probability that the indicated number of answers are correct.

25. exactly 6   **26.** exactly 7   **27.** at least 8

28. at least 5   **29.** at most 3   **30.** at most 4

Find the probability that a batter with each batting average given below will get at least 3 hits in the next 5 at bats.

31. 0.200   **32.** 0.250   **33.** 0.300   **34.** 0.350

Find the probability that a batter with each batting average given below will get at most 3 hits in the next 5 at bats.

35. 0.200   **36.** 0.250   **37.** 0.300   **38.** 0.350

APPLICATIONS

HOSPITAL STATISTICS Suppose that a hospital found an 8.5% probability that the birth of a baby will require the presence of more than one doctor.

39. Find the probability that 2 of the next 20 babies born at the hospital will require the presence of more than one doctor.

40. Find the probability that 3 of the next 20 babies born at the hospital will require the presence of more than one doctor.

SURVEYS In a 1998 survey, 54% of U.S. men and 36% of U.S. women consider themselves basketball fans. [*Source: Bruskin-Goldring Research*]

41. Find the probability that 5 men randomly selected from a group of 10 U.S. men consider themselves basketball fans.

42. Find the probability that 3 women randomly selected from a group of 10 U.S. women consider themselves basketball fans.

SURVEYS In 1997, 40% of U.S. households owned at least one cellular or wireless phone. [*Source: The Wirthin Report*]

43. What is the probability that 2 in 10 U.S. households owned a cellular or wireless phone?

44. What is the probability that at least 2 in 10 U.S. households owned a cellular or wireless phone?

45. What is the probability that at least 2 in 8 U.S. households owned a cellular or wireless phone?

AWARDS Three different prizes are placed in cereal boxes, with no more than 1 prize per box. Prize A is in 10% of the cereal boxes, prize B is in 20%, and prize C is in 30%. Find the probability of each event.

46. 1 prize in 1 box

47. exactly 1 prize in 2 boxes

48. 3 different prizes in 3 boxes

49. at least 2 prizes in 3 boxes

50. AVIATION A certain twin-engine airplane can fly with only one engine. The probability of engine failure for each of this airplane's engines is 0.002. Determine whether each airplane described below is more likely than this twin-engine airplane to crash due to engine failure.

a. a single-engine airplane with an engine whose probability of failure is 0.001

b. an experimental 3-engine airplane that can fly with only 2 engines, equipped with engines whose probability of failure is 0.001

c. an airplane with 4 engines that can fly with only 2 engines, equipped with engines whose probability of failure is 0.0008.

CHALLENGE

d. Find p such that a single-engine airplane with p probability of engine failure is as safe as the 4-engine airplane described in part **c**.

Look Back

A number cube is rolled once. Find each probability. *(LESSON 10.4)*

51. $P(2 \ or \ 3)$ **52.** $P(1 \ or \ 2 \ or \ 6)$ **53.** $P(\text{even } or \ 6)$

54. $P(\text{not } 6 \ or < 2)$ **55.** $P(< 5)$ **56.** $P(> 2 \ or \ 4)$

57. Construct an arithmetic sequence with a common difference of 6. *(LESSON 11.2)*

58. Construct a geometric sequence with a common ratio of 6. *(LESSON 11.4)*

APPLICATION

59. EDUCATION Refer to the data below. *(LESSON 12.4)*

Percent of Recent High School Graduates Enrolled in College

	1988	1989	1990	1991	1992	1993	1994
Male	57.0	57.6	57.8	57.6	59.6	59.7	60.6
Female	60.8	61.6	62.0	67.1	63.8	65.4	63.2

[Source: U.S. Department of Education Statistics]

a. Find the range and mean deviation for the percent enrollments of males and females.

b. Find the standard deviation for the percent enrollments of males and of females.

c. Describe what the measures indicate about the percent enrollments of males and females.

Look Beyond

60. The standard deviation for a binomial distribution is given by $\sigma = \sqrt{np(1 - p)}$, where n is the number of trials and p is the probability of a particular event occurring. A number cube is rolled 1000 times. Find the mean ($\bar{x} = np$) and the standard deviation for the event of rolling a 5.

Normal Distributions

Why *You can use the characteristics of a normal distribution to find probabilities of many real-world events, such as the number of deaths caused by lightning each month.*

Objectives

- Find the probability of an event given that the data is normally distributed and its mean and standard deviation are known.

- Use *z*-scores to find probabilities.

The histogram at right shows that deaths caused by lightning occur much more frequently in the summer months. In fact, about 70% of the deaths occurred in June, July, or August. [*Source: NOAA*]

Because this distribution is nearly symmetric about July, you can say that this data represents a *normal distribution*.

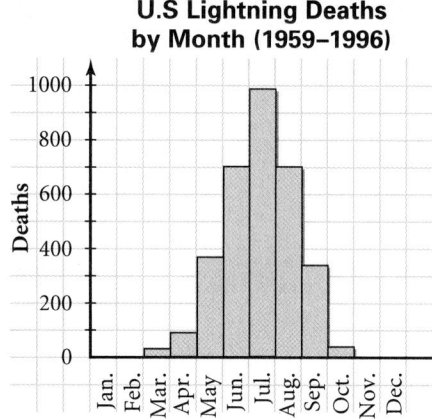

U.S Lightning Deaths by Month (1959–1996)

A **normal distribution** of data varies randomly from the mean, creating a mound-shaped pattern that is symmetric about the mean when graphed. Some examples of normally distributed data are human heights and weights.

The model obtained by drawing a curve through the midpoints of the tops of the bars in a histogram of normally distributed data is called a **normal curve.** A normal curve is defined by the mean and the standard deviation. A **standard normal curve** is a normal curve with mean of 0 and standard deviation of 1.

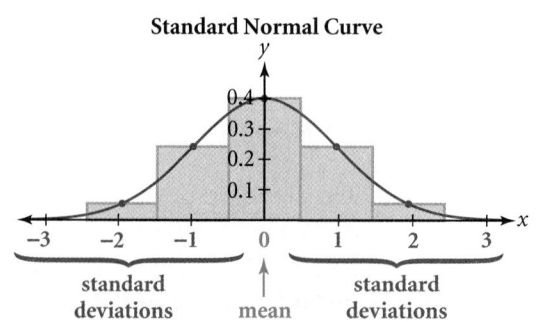

Standard Normal Curve

Recall from 12.2 that relative frequency histograms give probabilities. You can use the area under a normal curve (and above the *x*-axis) to approximate probabilities.

The total area under a normal curve is 1, with an area of 0.5 of the total to the right of the mean and an area of 0.5 of the total to the left of the mean.

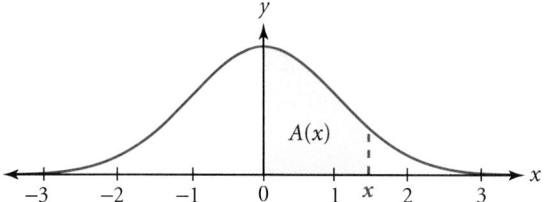

A table of approximate areas, $A(x)$, under the standard normal curve between the mean, 0, and the number of standard deviations, *x*, is given below.

Standard Normal Curve Areas

x	0	0.2	0.4	0.6	0.8	1.0	1.2	1.4	1.6	1.8	2.0
$A(x)$	0.0000	0.0793	0.1554	0.2257	0.2881	0.3413	0.3849	0.4192	0.4452	0.4641	0.4772

E X A M P L E ① **Approximate each probability by using the area table for a standard normal curve.**

a. $P(x \geq 1.6)$ **b.** $P(-2.0 \leq x \leq 0.4)$

● **SOLUTION**

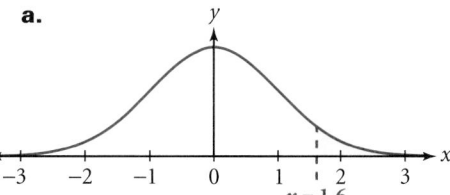

a.

$P(x \geq 1.6) = 0.5 - P(0 \leq x \leq 1.6)$
$\approx 0.5 - 0.4452$
≈ 0.0548

b.

$P(-2.0 \leq x \leq 0.4)$
$= P(-2.0 \leq x \leq 0) + P(0 \leq x \leq 0.4)$
$= P(0 \leq x \leq 2.0) + P(0 \leq x \leq 0.4)$
$\approx 0.4772 + 0.1554$
≈ 0.6326

TECHNOLOGY

GRAPHICS CALCULATOR

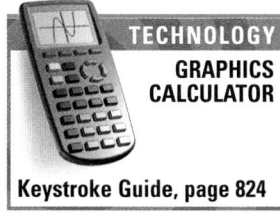

Keystroke Guide, page 824

CHECK
You can use a graphics calculator to check the probabilities.

TRY THIS Find each probability by using the area table for a standard normal curve.
a. $P(x \leq -0.8)$ **b.** $P(-1.2 \leq x \leq 1.6)$

CHECKPOINT ✔ Using the area table for a standard normal curve, describe the trend for $A(x)$ as *x* increases.

CRITICAL THINKING Why is 10^99 entered in the graphics calculator for the upper bound in part **a** of Example 1? What would you enter to find $P(x \leq 1.6)$?

Exploring the Standard Normal Curve

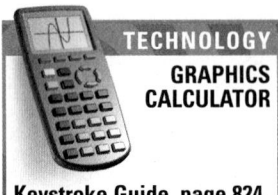
You will need: a graphics calculator

1. Graph $f(x) = \dfrac{1}{\sqrt{2\pi}} e^{\frac{-x^2}{2}}$.

2. Use the trace feature to verify that the graph is symmetric about the y-axis and that the x-axis is a horizontal asymptote.

3. Use the $\int f(x)\,dx$ feature to find the area under the curve (and above the x-axis) from $x = 0$ to $x = 1$ and from $x = -1$ to $x = 0$.

CHECKPOINT ✔ 4. What area represents 1 standard deviation on either side of the mean $(x = 0)$?

5. Repeat Step 3 for values from $x = 0$ to $x = 2$ and from $x = -2$ to $x = 0$.

CHECKPOINT ✔ 6. What area represents 2 standard deviations on either side of $x = 0$?

7. Repeat Step 3 for values from $x = 0$ to $x = 3$ and from $x = -3$ to $x = 0$.

CHECKPOINT ✔ 8. What area represents 3 standard deviations on either side of $x = 0$?

9. Find the areas corresponding to values less than $x = -3$ and to values greater than $x = 3$.

CHECKPOINT ✔ 10. What probability is represented by the total area under the curve?

All normal distributions have the properties listed below.

Properties of Normal Distributions

- The curve is symmetric about the mean, $\bar{x}$.

- The total area under the curve is 1.

- The mean, median, and mode are about equal.

- About 68% of the area is within 1 standard deviation (σ) of the mean.

- About 95% of the area is within 2 standard deviations (2σ) of the mean.

- About 99% of the area is within 3 standard deviations (3σ) of the mean.

CHECKPOINT ✔ Examine the two normal curves graphed below. How are the standard deviations different? How does the size of the standard deviation of a normal distribution affect the graph?

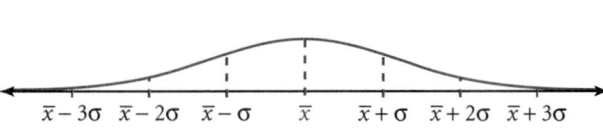

Normal distributions occur in many large data sets. For example, standardized test scores are usually normally distributed, as shown in Example 2.

EXAMPLE ② Scores for a certain professional exam are approximately normally distributed with a mean of 650 and a standard deviation of 100.

a. What is the probability that a randomly selected test score is between 450 and 850?

b. Out of 1000 randomly selected test scores, how many would you expect to be between 450 and 850?

● **SOLUTION**

a. Because $\bar{x} = 650$ and $\sigma = 100$, the interval from 450 to 850 is $650 - 2\sigma \le \bar{x} \le 650 + 2\sigma$.

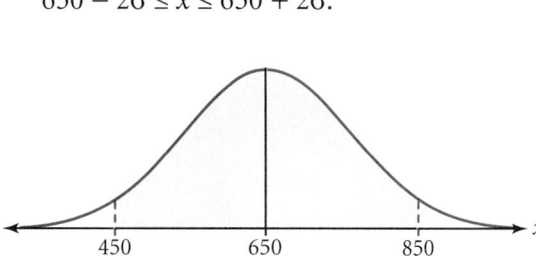

Thus, the probability that a randomly selected test score is between 450 and 850 is about 95%.

b. 95% of 1000 = $0.95 \times 1000 = 950$

Thus, you could expect about 950 out of 1000 randomly selected test scores to be between 450 and 850.

TRY THIS Refer to Example 2 above. Out of 2300 randomly selected scores, how many would you expect to be between 650 and 950?

Using z-Scores

A measure called a *z-score* tells how far a data value is from the mean in terms of standard deviations. For example, if a data set has a mean of 50 and a standard deviation of 10, then a data value of 70 has a *z*-score of 2 because it is 2 standard deviations above the mean. Similarly, a score of 20 has a *z*-score of −3 because it is 3 standard deviations below the mean.

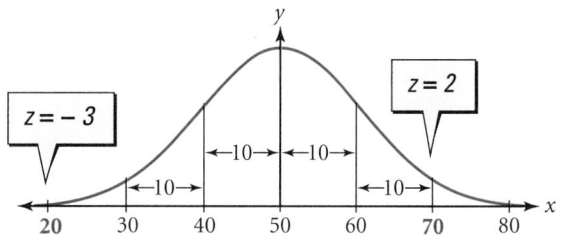

z-Score

If a data set is normally distributed with a mean of $\bar{x}$ and a standard deviation of σ, then the z-score for any data value, x, in that data set is given by $z = \dfrac{x - \bar{x}}{\sigma}$.

E X A M P L E ❸ An airline finds that the travel times between two cities have a mean of 85 minutes and a standard deviation of 7 minutes. Assume that the travel times are normally distributed.

Find the probability that a flight from the first city to the second city will take between 75 minutes and 90 minutes.

● **SOLUTION**

Method 1
Find the area between 75 and 90 under a normal curve with a mean of 85 and a standard deviation of 7.

The area is about 0.686.

Method 2
Find the z-scores for $x_1 = 75$ and $x_2 = 90$.

$$z_1 = \frac{x_1 - \bar{x}}{\sigma} = \frac{75 - 85}{7} \approx -1.43 \qquad z_2 = \frac{x_2 - \bar{x}}{\sigma} = \frac{90 - 85}{7} \approx 0.71$$

Find the area between $z_1 \approx -1.43$ and $z_2 \approx 0.71$ under the standard normal curve.

The area is about 0.685.

Thus, there is about a 69% probability that the flight will take between 75 minutes and 90 minutes.

CHECKPOINT ✔ Find the flight times that correspond to $\bar{x} - \sigma$ and $\bar{x} + \sigma$. How do your answers confirm that the solution in Example 3 is reasonable?

TRY THIS Find the probability that a flight from the first city to the second city will take between 82 minutes and 95 minutes.

Exercises

internet connect

**Activities
Online**

Go To: **go.hrw.com**
Keyword:
MB1 Distribution

Communicate

1. Describe the characteristics of the normal curve, including the measures that define it.

2. Explain how to find the area between 25 and 50 under a normal curve with a mean of 30 and a standard deviation of 10.

3. Sketch three normal curves that have the same mean but different standard deviations. Explain how the standard deviation affects the shape of the normal curve.

Guided Skills Practice

Find each probability by using the area table for a standard normal curve given on page 807. *(EXAMPLE 1)*

4. $P(-0.6 \leq x \leq 1.4)$

5. $P(0.2 \leq x \leq 1.8)$

APPLICATIONS
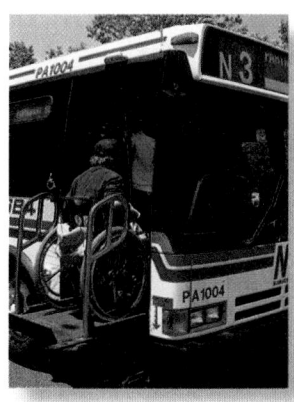

6. MANUFACTURING The lengths of a certain bolt are normally distributed with a mean of 8 centimeters and a standard deviation of 0.01 centimeter. *(EXAMPLE 2)*

  a. What is the probability that a randomly selected bolt is within 0.03 centimeter of 8 centimeters?

  b. Out of 1000 randomly selected bolts, how many can the manufacturer expect to be within 0.03 centimeter of 8 centimeters?

7. TRANSPORTATION A bus route takes a mean of 40 minutes to complete, with a standard deviation of 5 minutes. Assume that completion times for the route are normally distributed. Find the probability that it takes between 30 minutes and 45 minutes to complete the route. *(EXAMPLE 3)*

Practice and Apply

Let x be a random variable with a standard normal distribution. Use the area table for a standard normal curve, given on page 807, to find each probability.

8. $P(x \geq 0.8)$	**9.** $P(x \geq 0.4)$	**10.** $P(1.0 \leq x \leq 1.6)$
11. $P(0.2 \leq x \leq 1.8)$	**12.** $P(x \geq 1)$	**13.** $P(x \geq 2)$
14. $P(x \leq -0.2)$	**15.** $P(x \leq -1.4)$	**16.** $P(-0.4 \leq x \leq 0.4)$
17. $P(-0.2 \leq x \leq 0.2)$	**18.** $P(x \geq -1.6)$	**19.** $P(x \geq -0.8)$

Let x be a random variable with a standard normal distribution. Use a graphics calculator to find each probability. Round answers to the nearest ten-thousandth.

20 $P(0.653 \leq x)$	**21** $P(1.456 \leq x)$	**22** $P(1.254 \leq x)$
23 $P(1.457 \leq x)$	**24** $P(0.842 \leq x \leq 1.233)$	**25** $P(0.423 \leq x \leq 1.438)$

A city's annual rainfall is approximately normally distributed with a mean of 40 inches and a standard deviation of 6 inches. Find the probability, to the nearest ten-thousandth, for each amount of annual rainfall in the city.

26. less than 34 inches

27. greater than 46 inches

28. greater than 52 inches

29. less than 28 inches

30. between 34 and 40 inches

31. between 34 and 46 inches

Scores on a professional exam are normally distributed with a mean of 500 and a standard deviation of 50. Out of 28,000 randomly selected exams, find the number of exams that could be expected to have each score.

32. greater than 500

33. greater than 550

34. less than 600

35. less than 400

36. between 450 and 550

37. between 400 and 600

internet connect

**Homework
Help Online**

Go To: **go.hrw.com**
Keyword:
MB1 Homework Help
for Exercises 38–43

A survey of male shoe sizes is approximately normally distributed with a mean size of 9 and a standard deviation of 1.5. Use z-scores to find each probability to the nearest ten-thousandth.

38 $P(9 \leq x \leq 10)$

39 $P(10 \leq x \leq 11)$

40 $P(7 \leq x \leq 11)$

41 $P(7 \leq x \leq 13)$

42 $P(7 \leq x \leq 12)$

43 $P(5 \leq x)$

APPLICATIONS

TRANSPORTATION Tests show that a certain model of a new car averages 36 miles per gallon on the highway with a standard deviation of 3 miles per gallon. Assuming that the distribution is normal, find the probability, to the nearest ten-thousandth, that a car of this model gets the indicated mileage.

44. more than 40 miles per gallon

45. less than 32 miles per gallon

46. between 34 and 38 miles per gallon

MORTGAGE Mortgage statistics indicate that the number of years that a new homeowner will occupy a house before moving or selling is normally distributed with a mean of 6.3 years and a standard deviation of 2.3 years. Find the probability, to the nearest ten-thousandth, of each event.

47. A homeowner will sell or move within 3 years of buying the house.

48. A homeowner will sell or move after 10 years of buying the house.

49. A homeowner will sell or move after 6 to 8 years of buying the house.

50. QUALITY CONTROL A machine fills containers with perfume. When the machine is adjusted properly, it fills the containers with 4 fluid ounces, in a normal distribution, with a standard deviation of 0.1 fluid ounce. If 400 randomly selected containers are tested, how many containers with less than 3.8 fluid ounces of perfume should the Quality Control Manager reasonably expect to find?

51. QUALITY CONTROL The lengths of a mechanical component are normally distributed with a mean of 30.0 inches and standard deviation of 0.2 inch. All components not within 0.4 inch of 30.0 inches are rejected.
  a. What percent of the components are acceptable?
  b. If one of the *acceptable* components is randomly selected, what is the probability, to the nearest percent, that its length is within 0.1 inch of 30.0 inches?

 Look Back

Write an equation in slope-intercept form for the line that contains the given point and is parallel to the given line. *(LESSON 1.3)*

52. $(9, -4), y = -12x + 3$ **53.** $(1, -4), y = 100x + 12$

Write an equation in slope-intercept form for the line that contains the given point and is perpendicular to the given line. *(LESSON 1.3)*

54. $(6, -3), y = -2x + 18$ **55.** $(-2, 7), 6x - 7y = 8$

Simplify each expression. *(LESSON 8.4)*

56. $\frac{1}{x} + \frac{1}{x+2}$ **57.** $\frac{1}{x+1} + \frac{1}{x+2}$ **58.** $\frac{x}{1+x} + \frac{x^2+x}{x}$ **59.** $\frac{1}{x} + \frac{x+1}{x+2}$

Write each expression with a rational denominator and in simplest form. *(LESSON 8.7)*

60. $\frac{1}{\sqrt{3}}$ **61.** $\frac{1}{\sqrt{5}}$ **62.** $\frac{1}{\sqrt{2}-1}$ **63.** $\frac{1}{1-\sqrt{3}}$

64. EDUCATION The table at right shows the final exam scores for each student in an economics class. *(LESSON 10.4)*

72	88	96	75	85
98	80	87	78	90
80	87	82	88	93
92	84	97	98	83

  a. Find the range and the mean deviation of the scores.
  b. Find the variance and the standard deviation of the scores.

Find the indicated sum of the arithmetic series $5 + 7 + 9 + 11 + \cdots$ *(LESSON 11.3)*

65. S_3 **66.** S_4 **67.** S_{10} **68.** S_{15}

Find the indicated sum of the geometric series $1 + \frac{3}{2} + \frac{9}{4} + \frac{27}{8} + \cdots$ *(LESSON 11.5)*

69. S_3 **70.** S_4 **71.** S_{10} **72.** S_{15}

 Look Beyond

73 *Exponential distributions* are widely used to model lifetimes of electronic components which are generally not affected by how long they have already been operated. Suppose that the lifetime (in months) of a certain fuse can be modeled by the exponential density function

$$f(x) = \frac{1}{100}e^{\frac{-x}{100}} \text{ for } x \geq 0.$$ Graph f and describe its general shape.

That's NOT Fair!

Several weeks prior to an election, a poll can be taken to predict the percent of the votes that each candidate will receive on election day. Since contacting every eligible voter would be impractical, a subset, or *sample*, of all eligible voters is polled. This sample should represent the total population of voters as accurately as possible.

A certain city with 80,000 eligible voters can be divided into four areas that roughly correspond to the annual family incomes shown in the table below.

Area	Number of voters	Family income
Rolling Hills	400	over $100,000
South Park	40,600	$75,000–$100,000
West Side	27,000	$35,000–$74,999
North End	12,000	under $35,000

The sampling methods below will not give a good representation of the total population of voters in this city for the reasons given.

1. **Every home in Rolling Hills** The Rolling Hills area has families with the highest income level. Voters from this area might tend to vote for a candidate who will represent their interests by promising to lower taxes, to provide services based on property and home values, and so on.

2. **100 homes in each of the four areas** The 80,000 eligible voters in the city are not divided equally among the four areas. South Park and West Side would be *under* represented in the sample while Rolling Hills and North End would be *over* represented.

3. **Every 10th person entering the terminal building at the local commercial airport that serves this city** The frequency of airline trips is not a characteristic that is equally distributed among the total population of the city. Business people tend to fly more often than many other people.

In contrast to the faulty sampling methods discussed above, there are efficient methods that provide a more representative sample of a given population. Two examples are:

• Telephone every nth person listed in the telephone book.

• Mail a questionnaire with a stamped return envelope to every nth person in the telephone book. Notice that even these methods are not truly representative. For example, some people don't have telephones, some have unlisted numbers, some might not return their questionnaires, and so on. Still, for a specific city or area, these methods often give a fairly representative sample.

Activity 1

Tell whether each sampling procedure below provides a poor or a reasonable representation of the total population. Justify your answers.

1. To determine the mean (average) weight of all 20-year-old males, find the weight of all 20-year-old males in the U.S. Naval Academy.

2. To determine the majority opinion on whether a city should treat its water supply with fluoride, publish a ballot in the city's newspaper and ask the public to vote and mail the ballot to the newspaper's office.

3. To determine the majority opinion on a very controversial topic, have television viewers telephone in a "yes" or "no" response.

4. To determine the average number of chocolate chips per cookie in a bag of cookies, find the average number in every fifth cookie.

5. To determine the quality of a given model of automobile, test the last one assembled on every Friday of the model year.

6. To estimate the average brightness of the stars in the summer sky, an astronomer measures the brightness of all the stars that she can see and computes the average brightness.

7. To determine whether the effectiveness of a herbicide was less than advertised, a researcher samples a group of 50 randomly selected users of the herbicide for their opinion about its effectiveness.

Activity 2

1. Design a survey to conduct among a sample of your classmates that represents the student population at your school. Describe what you think the results of your survey will reveal. Explain why you think your sample is a reasonable and fair representation of the entire student population.

2. Conduct your survey. Then represent the data in two of the following formats: a stem-and-leaf plot, histogram, circle graph, or box-and-whisker plot. Explain why you chose these two formats to represent your data.

3. What conclusions can you make about the results of your survey? How do statistical measures and graphs support your conclusions? Are the results what you expected?

Chapter Review and Assessment

Key Skills & Exercises

LESSON 12.1

Key Skills

Find the mean, median, and mode.

For the data set 8, 7, 4, 5, 9, 4, 5, 4, 2, 3:
mean
$$\overline{x} = \frac{2 + 3 + 4 + 4 + 4 + 5 + 5 + 7 + 8 + 9}{10} = 5.1$$

median
2, 3, 4, 4, 4, 5, 5, 7, 8, 9
The middle numbers are 4 and 5, so the median is 4.5.

mode
The mode is 4.

Exercises

Find the mean, median, and mode of each data set.

1. 7, 9, 2, 9, 0, 2, 8, 9, 1

2. −3, 8, 2, 3, 2, 4, 3, 2

Make a frequency table for each data set, and find the mean.

3. 5, 4, 6, 5, 4, 6, 6, 5, 4, 7, 4, 5, 6

4. 9, 10, 11, 8, 10, 10, 11, 9, 8, 10

LESSON 12.2

Key Skills

Make a stem-and-leaf plot.

Data: 4, 4, 28, 3, 29, 15, 12, 16, 17, 24, 16, 28, 5, 28, 29

Stems	Leaves				1|2 = 12
0	3,	4,	4,	5	
1	2,	5,	6,	6,	7
2	4,	8,	8,	8,	9,	9

Make a histogram.

Data: 5, 2, 3, 3, 6, 1, 3, 4, 2, 3, 1, 5, 5, 2, 4

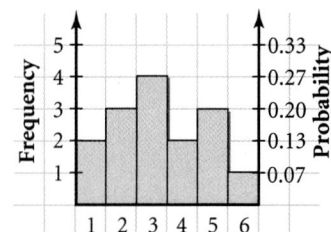

Exercises

Make a stem-and-leaf plot for each data set.

5. 35, 38, 45, 49, 45, 53, 57, 58

6. 67, 87, 82, 73, 81, 78, 79, 69

Make a histogram for each data set.

7. 4, 3, 2, 5, 4, 5, 6, 1, 2, 4, 3, 1

8. 24, 28, 30, 30, 22, 21, 29, 29, 30, 27, 26, 28, 22, 23, 25, 27, 28, 28, 24

Make a relative frequency histogram for each data set.

9. 1, 1, 3, 3, 5, 2, 5, 3

10. 10, 14, 14, 11, 15, 13, 12

Make a circle graph.

For	98
Against	67
Undecided	20

Divide each category in the table by the total, 185, to find its percent. Then multiply its percent by 360° to find the measure of the central angle.

(circle graph: For 53%, Against 36%, Undecided 11%)

11. The table below lists the number of people who selected each brand. Make a circle graph of the results.

Brand X	53
Brand Y	32
Brand Z	89

LESSON 12.3

Key Skills

Find the minimum and maximum values, range, quartiles, and interquartile range for a data set.

Data: 5, 6, 9, 2, 3, 7, 2, 9, 8
Arrange the data set in ascending order.
    2 2 3 5 6 7 8 9 9

$$Q_1 = \frac{2+3}{2} = 2.5 \quad Q_2 = 6 \quad Q_3 = \frac{8+9}{2} = 8.5$$

$$\text{range} = 9 - 2 = 7 \quad \text{IQR} = 8.5 - 2.5 = 6$$

Make a box-and-whisker plot.

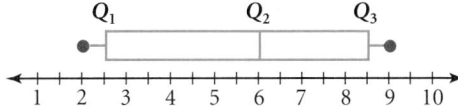

Exercises

Find the quartiles of each data set.

12. 12, 18, 13, 15, 16, 19, 17, 13, 14, 19, 17, 16

13. 23, 28, 34, 36, 34, 29, 35, 31, 45, 22, 23, 25

Make a box-and-whisker plot for each data set.

14. 5, 4, 9, 3, 1, 9, 0, 6, 3, 2

15. 22, 28, 29, 24, 25, 28, 29, 23, 23, 29

LESSON 12.4

Key Skills

Find the range, variance, mean deviation, and standard deviation of a data set.

x_i	$|x_i - x|$
3	1.167
2	2.167
3	1.167
5	0.833
7	2.833
5	0.833
Total	9

Data: 3, 2, 3, 5, 7, 5
In ascending order:
    2, 3, 3, 5, 5, 7
Range: 7 − 2 = 5
Mean:
$$\frac{2+3+3+5+5+7}{6} \approx 4.167$$

Mean deviation: $\frac{9}{6} = 1.5$

Variance: $\frac{1}{6}\sum_{i=1}^{6}(x_i - x)^2 \approx 2.8$

Standard deviation: $\sqrt{2.8} \approx 1.7$

Exercises

Find the range and mean deviation of each data set.

16. 6, 10, 12, 4, 14, 8, 11, 14

17. 20, 22, 15, 14, 13, 17

18. 3, 6, −7, 9, −3, 2

19. 4, −8, 12, 13, −22, 24, 21

Find the variance and standard deviation of each data set.

20. 10, 12, 15, 18, 11, 13, 14, 16, 19, 20

21. 100, 140, 130, 180, 80, 160

22. 8, 9, 12, 14, 7, 9, 11, 13, 14

23. 3, 4, 12, 2, 3, 4, 6, 12, 18, 20, 2

Key Skills

Find probabilities of events in a binomial experiment.

A certain trick coin has a probability of 0.75 for heads and 0.25 for tails.

The probability of 3 heads appearing in 5 tosses of the coin is found by using the formula for binomial probability, as shown below.

$$P(\text{exactly 3 heads}) = {_5C_3}(0.75)^3(0.25^{5-3})$$
$$\approx 0.26$$

Exercises

Given 10 trials of a binomial experiment with 0.6 probability of success, find each probability below.

24. $P(\text{exactly 2 successes})$

25. $P(\text{exactly 3 successes})$

26. $P(\text{at least 3 successes})$

27. Find the probability of at least 3 heads in 5 tosses of a fair coin.

Key Skills

Find probabilities by using a normal distribution.

Let x be a random variable with a standard normal distribution. To find $P(-1.6 \le x \le 0.4)$, use the area table for a standard normal curve on page 807.

$$P(-1.6 \le x \le 0.4) \approx 0.4452 + 0.1554$$
$$\approx 0.6006$$

Use *z*-scores to find probabilities.

If x is a random data value with a normally distributed data set with a mean of 6 and a standard deviation of 3, find $P(8 \le x \le 11)$.

$z_1 = \frac{8-6}{3} = \frac{2}{3} \approx 0.667$

$z_2 = \frac{11-6}{3} = \frac{5}{3} \approx 1.667$

$P(8 \le x \le 11) \approx 0.205$

Area=.204629
low=.667   lup=1.667

Exercises

Let *x* be a random variable with a standard normal distribution. Use the area table for a standard normal curve on page 807 to find each probability.

28. $P(x \le 0.4)$

29. $P(x \ge -1.8)$

30. $P(-1.6 \le x \le 1.6)$

31. $P(-0.8 \le x \le 0.8)$

Let *x* be a random data value with a normally distributed data set with a mean of 20 and a standard deviation of 2. Use *z*-scores to find each probability to the nearest percent.

32. $P(x \le -21)$

33. $P(x \le 18.6)$

34. $P(16.5 \le x \le 23.5)$

35. $P(17.2 \le x \le 22)$

Applications

36. AUTOMOBILE DISTRIBUTION The table at right gives the number of each type of vehicle on a car dealer's lot. Make a circle graph to represent this data.

Type	Number
cars (other than sports cars)	50
sports cars	20
trucks	30
sports utility vehicles	28

Chapter Test

Find the mean, median, and mode of each data set.

1. 2, 5, 8, 2, 4, 2, 8, 1, 3, 5, 2, 2, 8, 3, 2

2. 12, 10, 15, 13, 15, 16, 15, 14, 18, 12

Make a frequency table for each data set, and find the mean.

3. the number of snow days missed during the past 20 years: 1, 2, 3, 4, 4, 1, 3, 1, 3, 2, 2, 2, 4, 1, 3, 5, 3, 2, 3, 4

4. the age of students in a tennis class: 14, 18, 15, 17, 16, 16, 14, 15, 17, 15, 16, 15, 17, 16, 15, 15, 14, 15, 16, 14, 15

Make a stem-and-leaf plot for each data set.

5. 15, 20, 100, 50, 45, 37, 23, 75, 12, 25, 40, 64, 85, 20, 57, 44, 28, 60, 24, 10, 36, 30

6. 1.8, 2.4, 5.9, 4.6, 2.3, 2.8, 1.9, 3.2, 6.5, 3.4, 3.9, 2.5

Make a histogram for each data set.

7. 3, 6, 2, 4, 4, 4, 3, 5, 4, 5, 2, 3, 4, 4, 4, 3, 5

8. 13, 9, 10, 12, 11, 9, 10, 11, 8, 10, 11, 9, 8, 12, 10, 11, 11, 10, 10, 9

9. **POLITICS** The table shows the number of people voting in the last election. Represent these data with a circle graph.

Party affiliation	Number of people voting
Democrat	160
Republican	200
Independent	100
Other	40

Find the minimum and maximum values, quartiles, range, and interquartile range for each data set.

10. 18, 24, 59, 46, 23, 28, 19, 32, 65, 34, 39, 25, 27, 42, 54, 23, 34, 19, 41

11. 3, 5, 8, 9, 4, 1, 6, 5, 2, 6, 2, 8, 5, 7

Find the range and mean deviation for each data set.

12. 3, 5, 7, 9, 11, 13

13. 10, 12, 15, 18, 23, 25, 30, 33

Find the variance and standard deviation for each data set.

14. 3, 5, 7, 9, 11, 13

15. 10, 12, 15, 18, 23, 25, 30, 33

16. What can be said about a set of data if its standard deviation is 0?

Use this information for Exercises 17 and 18. The probability that a battery will fail in the cold is 8%. A new digital camcorder uses 4 of these batteries.

17. What is the probability that the camcorder will work with the supplied batteries?

18. What is the probability that exactly 2 of the batteries will fail when first used?

19. A fair coin is flipped 7 times. Find the probability of exactly 6 heads.

Let x be a random variable with a standard normal distribution. Find each probability.

20. $P(x \leq 1.6)$

21. $P(x \geq -1.2)$

22. $P(-1.4 \leq x \leq 0.8)$

23. **PSYCHOLOGY** IQ scores are normally distributed with a mean of 100 and a standard deviation of 15. If a genius has an IQ score above 127, what percentage of people can be classified as a genius?

24. **EDUCATION** Grade point averages are normally distributed with a mean of 2.5 and a standard deviation of 0.5. What percentage of students graduate with a grade point average of 3.5 or more?

1-12 College Entrance Exam Practice

MULTIPLE-CHOICE For Questions 1–18, write the letter that indicates the best answer.

1. Which equation has an x-value equal to 0? *(LESSON 1.4)*

  a. $\dfrac{x}{6} = \dfrac{2x}{5}$

  b. $\dfrac{2x-1}{3} = \dfrac{9x}{9}$

  c. $\dfrac{3x-1}{3} = \dfrac{x}{2}$

  d. $\dfrac{1-x}{3} = 3 + x$

2. Evaluate $\lceil 3.95 \rceil + \lfloor 4.95 \rfloor$. *(LESSON 2.6)*

  a. 7   **b.** 8

  c. 9   **d.** 10

3. Find the maximum value of $f(x) = -(x + 4)^2 + 3$. *(LESSON 5.4)*

  a. 3   **b.** −4

  c. −3   **d.** 4

4. Find the value of $_5P_3$. *(LESSON 10.2)*

  a. 10   **b.** 60

  c. 20   **d.** 120

5. Find the mean, median, and mode of the data set {76, 78, 71, 78, 72, 75}. *(LESSON 12.1)*

  a. 450, 75.5, 78

  b. 75, 75.5, 78

  c. 75, 74.5, 78

  d. 75, 75.5, 76

6. Solve $4(5 + 2x) = 42 - 3x$. *(LESSON 1.6)*

  a. $x = -2$ **b.** $x = 4$

  c. $x = 2$ **d.** $x = 12$

7. Which is the axis of symmetry of the graph of $y = 2x^2 - 8x - 1$? *(LESSON 5.1)*

  a. $x = 1$

  b. $x = -1$

  c. $x = 2$

  d. $x = -2$

8. Which expression gives the function rule for $f \circ g$, where $f(x) = 3 - x$ and $g(x) = 2x$? *(LESSON 2.4)*

  a. $3 - 2x$ **b.** $3 + 2x$

  c. $2(3 - x)$ **d.** $6 - 2x$

9. Simplify $\left(-\dfrac{2a^{-2}}{b^{-1}}\right)^3$. *(LESSON 2.2)*

  a. $\dfrac{8a^6}{b^3}$ **b.** $\dfrac{-8b^6}{a^3}$

  c. $\dfrac{-8b^3}{a^6}$ **d.** $-\dfrac{8a^6}{b^3}$

10. Which property is illustrated by $a + 0 = a$, where a represents a real number? *(LESSON 2.1)*

  a. Identity

  b. Inverse

  c. Reciprocal

  d. Closure

11. How many solutions does a consistent system of linear equations have? *(LESSON 3.1)*

  a. 0   **b.** 1

  c. at least 1   **d.** infinite

12. Which expression is equivalent to $|x - 2| = 6$? *(LESSON 1.8)*

  a. $x = 4$

  b. $x = 8$

  c. $x = -4 \ or \ x = 8$

  d. $x = 8 \ and \ x = -8$

13. Which best describes the roots of $3x^2 + 2x - 5 = 0$? *(LESSON 5.6)*

  a. 1 real root

  b. 2 rational roots

  c. 2 irrational roots

  d. 2 imaginary roots

14. Which function represents exponential decay? *(LESSON 6.2)*

a. $f(x) = 2.5^x$ **b.** $f(x) = 2(5)^x$
c. $f(x) = 2(0.5)^x$ **d.** $f(x) = 2x^2$

15. Evaluate $-\frac{1}{3}\sqrt[3]{27}$. *(LESSON 8.6)*

a. 3 **b.** -3 **c.** 1 **d.** -1

16. Which is the remainder when $2x^2 - 5x + 8$ is divided by $x + 4$? *(LESSON 7.3)*

a. 60 **b.** -44 **c.** 0 **d.** 20

17. Which expression is equivalent to $\log_a \frac{xy}{2}$? *(LESSON 6.4)*

a. $\log_a 2xy$ **b.** $\log_a y + 2\log_a a$
c. $\log_a xy - \log_a 2$ **d.** $\log_a xy + \log_a 2$

18. Solve $\begin{cases} 2x^2 + y^2 = 36 \\ x^2 - y^2 = 12 \end{cases}$. *(LESSON 9.6)*

a. $(2\sqrt{13}, 8), (-2\sqrt{13}, 8)$
b. $(8, 2\sqrt{13}), (-8, 2\sqrt{13})$
c. $(2, 4), (2, -4), (-2, 4), (-2, -4)$
d. $(4, 2)(-4, 2), (4, -2), (-4, -2)$

19. Write the equation in slope-intercept form for the line that has a slope of $-\frac{5}{3}$ and contains the point $(8, -3)$. *(LESSON 1.3)*

20. Write the function that represents the graph of $f(x) = |x|$ translated 2 units to the left. *(LESSON 2.7)*

21. Factor $25x^2 - 9$, if possible. *(LESSON 5.3)*

22. Graph $-2 < y \le 3$ in a coordinate plane. *(LESSON 3.4)*

Let $A = \begin{bmatrix} 1 & 4 \\ -3 & -1 \end{bmatrix}$ and $B = \begin{bmatrix} 1 & -11 \\ 6 & 15 \end{bmatrix}$. **Perform the indicated operations.** *(LESSON 4.1)*

23. AB **24.** $3BA$

25. $A + B$ **26.** $B - 2A$

27. Use elimination to solve the system. *(LESSON 3.2)* $\begin{cases} 5x + 11y = -7 \\ -3x + 2y = 30 \end{cases}$

28. Multiply $(5 - 2i)(5 - 2i)$. *(LESSON 5.6)*

29. Find the domain of $g(x) = \frac{x^2 - 1}{x - 5}$. *(LESSON 8.2)*

30. Evaluate $e^{\ln 2} + \ln e^{-7}$. *(LESSON 6.5)*

31. Describe the end behavior of $P(x) = -2x^3 + x^2 - 11x + 4$. *(LESSON 7.2)*

32. If a coin is tossed 10 times, what is the probability that it will land heads up exactly 4 times? *(LESSON 12.5)*

33. Divide by using synthetic division. $(3x^3 - 18x + 12) \div (x - 3)$ *(LESSON 7.3)*

34. Solve $x^2 + 2x - 1 \le 0$, and graph its solution. *(LESSON 5.7)*

35. Solve $\frac{3}{x^2 - 4} = \frac{-2}{5x + 10}$. *(LESSON 8.5)*

36. Find the domain of $g(x) = \sqrt{1 - 2(x + 1)}$. *(LESSON 8.6)*

37. In how many ways can a committee of 5 be chosen from a group of 8? *(LESSON 10.3)*

38. Factor $x^3 + 125$. *(LESSON 7.3)*

FREE-RESPONSE GRID The following questions may be answered by using a free-response grid such as that commonly used by standardized-test services.

39. Simplify $\sqrt{27^{\frac{2}{3}}}$. *(LESSON 8.7)*

40. Evaluate $10^{\log_{10} 1000} - \log_2 2$. *(LESSON 6.4)*

41. Find the value of v in $2 = \log_v 64$. *(LESSON 6.3)*

42. Find the sixth term of the sequence $-100, 500, -2500, \ldots$ *(LESSON 11.4)*

43. Find the distance between the points $P(-3, 2)$ and $Q(1, 5)$. *(LESSON 9.1)*

ENTERTAINMENT The top 10 movies grossed the dollar amounts (in millions) shown at right in one weekend.

44. Find the mean for this data set. *(LESSON 12.1)*

45. Find the range for this data set. *(LESSON 12.4)*

4.0	14.8
3.7	10.6
3.0	6.1
2.9	5.6
2.5	4.2

Keystroke Guide for Chapter 12

Essential keystroke sequences (using the model TI-82 or TI-83 graphics calculator) are presented below for all Activities and Examples found in this chapter that require or recommend the use of a graphics calculator.

internet connect

For Keystrokes of other graphing calculator models, visit the HRW web site at **go.hrw.com** and enter the keyword **MB1 CALC**.

LESSON 12.2

E X A M P L E **2** Make a histogram for the canoe rental data given.

Page 774

First clear old data and old equations.

Use viewing window [0, 9] by [0, 11].

Enter the data:

STAT EDIT 1:Edit ENTER L1 1 ENTER 4 ENTER 5 ENTER 2
ENTER 2 ENTER 2 ENTER 3 ENTER 2 ENTER 3 ENTER ...

Continue until all of the data values are entered into List 1.

Make a histogram:

2nd Y= (STAT PLOT) STAT PLOTS 1:Plot 1 ENTER ON
ENTER ▼ (Type:) ▮▮▮ ENTER ▼
(Xlist:) 2nd 1 (L1) ▼
  ⇑ TI-82: L1 ENTER ▼
(Freq:) 1 ENTER GRAPH
  ⇑ TI-82: 1 ENTER GRAPH

LESSON 12.3

E X A M P L E **2** Make box-and-whisker plots for the temperature data given.

Page 784

Use viewing window [10, 80] by [0, 1].

Enter the data:

STAT EDIT 1:Edit ENTER L1 21 ENTER 25.5 ENTER 37 ENTER 48.6 ENTER ...

Continue until all of the data values for Chicago are entered into List 1.

▶ L2 55.9 ENTER 57 ENTER 58.3 ENTER 60.8 ENTER 63.3 ENTER ...

Continue until all of the data values for Los Angeles are entered into List 2.

Make the box-and-whisker plots:

2nd | Y= [STAT PLOT] | [STAT PLOTS] | [1:Plot 1] | ENTER | [ON] | ENTER | ▼ (Type:) ENTER

▼ (Xlist:) | 2nd | 1 [L1] | ▼ (Freq:) 1 | ENTER | 2nd | Y= [STAT PLOT] | [STAT PLOTS] | [2:Plot 2]

⇑ TI-82: [L1] ENTER ▼   ⇑ TI-82: [1] ENTER

ENTER | [ON] | ENTER | ▼ (Type:) ENTER | ▼ (Xlist:) | 2nd | 2 [L2] | ▼

⇑ TI-82: [L2] ENTER

(Freq:) 1 | ENTER | GRAPH

⇑ TI-82: [1] ENTER

LESSON 12.4

TECHNOLOGY
Page 795

Find the standard deviations for the monthly precipitation data.

Enter the data:

Use a keystroke sequence similar to that in Example 2 of Lesson 12.3 to enter the data into Lists 1 and 2.

Find the standard deviations:

STAT | [CALC] | [1:1-Var Stats] | ENTER | 2nd | 1 [L1] | ENTER

STAT | [CALC] | [1:1-Var Stats] | ENTER | 2nd | 2 [L2] | ENTER

LESSON 12.5

E X A M P L E **1**
Page 800

Evaluate $P = {_nC_r}\, p^r\, (1 - p)^{n-r}$ for $n = 10$, $r = 7$, and $p = 0.8$.

10 | MATH | [PRB] | [3:nCr] | ENTER | 7 | × | .8 | ^

7 | × | .2 | ^ | 3 | ENTER

E X A M P L E **2**
Page 801

Find the probability of "6 successes" *or* "7 successes" *or* "8 successes" in a binomial experiment in which there are 8 possible outcomes and the probability of success is 0.96.

The TI-82 model does not have a program for finding binomial probabilities.

2nd | VARS [DISTR] | [DISTR] | [0:binompdf(] | ENTER | 8 | ,

.96 | , | 6 |) | + | 2nd | VARS [DISTR] | [DISTR]

[0:binompdf(] | ENTER | 8 | , | .96 | , | 7 |)

+ | 2nd | VARS [DISTR] | [DISTR] | [0:binompdf(] | ENTER

8 | , | .96 | , | 8 |) | ENTER

Page 802

Generate 100 simulations of tossing a coin 6 times, and display the results in a histogram.

Use viewing window [0, 6] by [0, 80].

Generate the data:

| MATH | PRB | 7:randBin(| ENTER | 6 | , | .5 | , | 100 |) | STO▶ | 2nd |

L1
| 1 | ENTER | (Wait for the calculator to finish.)

The TI-82 model does not generate random data for binomial experiments.

Display the histogram:

STAT PLOT
| 2nd | Y= | STAT PLOTS | 1:PLOT 1 | ENTER | On | ENTER | ▼ | (Type:) | ▮▮▮ | ENTER |

L1
| ▼ | (Xlist:) | 2nd | 1 | ▼ | (Freq:) 1 | ENTER | GRAPH |

LESSON 12.6

E X A M P L E **1** For part a, find $P(x \geq 1.6)$, where x is a random data value in a standard

Page 807 normal distribution.

The TI-82 model does not have a program to calculate probabilities of events in a normal distribution.

DISTR
| 2nd | VARS | DISTR | 2:normalcdf(| ENTER | 1.6 |

| , | 10 | ^ | 99 | , | 0 | , | 1 |) |

| ENTER |

Use a similar keystroke sequence for part **b**.

```
normalcdf(1.6,10
^99,0,1)
           .0547992894
normalcdf(-2,0.4
,0,1)
           .6326716351
```

Activity

Page 808

For Steps 1 and 3, graph $y = \dfrac{1}{\sqrt{2\pi}} e^{\frac{-x^2}{2}}$, and find the area under the curve above the x-axis from $x = 0$ to $x = 1$ and from $x = -1$ to $x = 0$.

Use friendly viewing window [−4.7, 4.7] by [−0.1, 0.5].

First turn off old stat plots.

Graph the function:

| Y= | (| 1 | ÷ | 2nd | x^2 | 2 | 2nd | ^ |) |) |

⇑ TI-82: (

| X | 2nd | LN | (−) | X,T,θ,n | x^2 | ÷ | 2 |) | GRAPH |

⇑ TI-82: (

The symbol $\int f(x)dx =$ indicates the area under the curve for the parameters specified.

Find the areas under the curve:

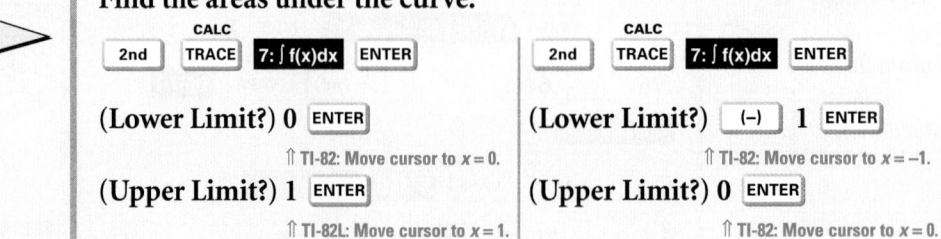

CALC
| 2nd | TRACE | 7:∫f(x)dx | ENTER |

(Lower Limit?) 0 ENTER

⇑ TI-82: Move cursor to x = 0.

(Upper Limit?) 1 ENTER

⇑ TI-82L: Move cursor to x = 1.

CALC
| 2nd | TRACE | 7:∫f(x)dx | ENTER |

(Lower Limit?) (−) 1 ENTER

⇑ TI-82: Move cursor to x = −1.

(Upper Limit?) 0 ENTER

⇑ TI-82: Move cursor to x = 0.

For Method 1, find the area between 75 and 90 under a normal curve with a mean of 85 and a standard deviation of 7.

Use viewing window [–5, 110] by [–0.02, 0.08].

To find these areas with a model TI-82, use a keystroke sequence similar to that used in the Activity for Lesson 12.6.

DISTR

| 2nd | | VARS | | DRAW | | 1:ShadeNorm(| | ENTER |

75 , 90 , 85 , 7) ENTER

For Method 2, find the area between $x \approx -1.43$ and $x \approx 0.71$ under the standard normal curve.

Use viewing window [–3, 3] by [–0.2, 0.5].

DISTR

| 2nd | | VARS | | DRAW | | 1:ShadeNorm(| | ENTER | | (–) |

1.43 , .71) ENTER

Trigonometric Functions

THE WORD TRIGONOMETRY COMES FROM THE Greek words for triangle (*trigonon*) and measure (*metria*). Trigonometry is commonly described as the study of the relationship between the angles and sides of a triangle.

Trigonometry has a wide variety of applications in physics, astronomy, architecture, engineering, and other disciplines. People's understanding and interest in triangles can be observed in the structures shown here.

Lessons

The Pyramids at Giza, Egypt

The Louvre Museum, Paris, France

About the Chapter Project

George W. G. Ferris constructed the first Ferris wheel for the World's Exposition in Chicago in 1893. In the Chapter Project, you will create a model for the altitude of a rider on the Ferris wheel at Chicago's Navy Pier, which is modeled after Ferris's original wheel.

After completing the Chapter Project, you will be able to do the following:

- Model the height of a point on a Ferris wheel as a function of time.

- Interpret the real-world meaning of each parameter in your model.

- Find the speed of a point on a given Ferris wheel.

About the Portfolio Activities

Throughout the chapter, you will be given opportunities to complete Portfolio Activities that are designed to support your work on the Chapter Project.

- Sketching a rough graph for the height of a point on the Ferris wheel (relative to the center of the wheel) as a function of the angle of rotation is included in the Portfolio Activity on page 835.

- Sketching a graph for the altitude of a rider on the Ferris wheel as a function of the angle of rotation is included in the Portfolio Activity on page 850.

- Sketching a graph for the altitude of a rider on the Ferris wheel as a function of time and finding the speed of a rider on the Ferris wheel is included in the Portfolio Activity on page 857.

- Creating and interpreting a model for the altitude of a rider on the Ferris wheel is included in the Portfolio Activity on page 866.

Rock and Roll Hall of Fame, Cleveland, Ohio

Right-Triangle Trigonometry

13.1

Objectives

- Find the trigonometric functions of acute angles.

- Solve a right triangle by using trigonometric functions.

Why *You can use right-triangle trigonometry to solve real-world problems such as finding the height of the puffins above the water.*

B — puffins

photographer

28° C

A 40 ft

15 ft

E D

APPLICATION

WILDLIFE

An ornithologist is taking pictures of puffins on the edge of a cliff. To find the height of the puffins above the water, she measures a 28° *angle of elevation* of her line of sight to the puffins. If her position is about 15 feet above the water, and about 40 feet from the cliff, how high above the water are the puffins? *You will solve this problem in Example 3.*

To find the height of the puffins, you can use *trigonometry*. **Trigonometry** can be used to find the measure of an unknown angle or an unknown side length of a right triangle.

Recall from Lesson 5.2 that the *hypotenuse* of a right triangle is the side opposite the right angle. The *legs* of a right triangle are the other two sides. Each leg is opposite one of the two *acute* angles and adjacent to the other. For example, in △*ABC*, $\overline{BC}$ is the leg *opposite* angle *A* and $\overline{AC}$ is the leg *adjacent* to angle *A*.

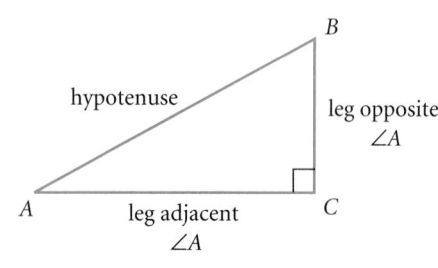

CHECKPOINT ✔ Identify the legs of △*ABC* above by their relationship to ∠*B*.

Triangle *ABC* at right shows the abbreviations for the lengths of the sides of a right triangle in terms of ∠*A*. The six trigonometric functions are defined below with these abbreviations.

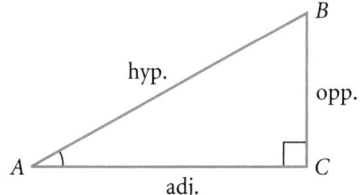

Trigonometric Functions of ∠*A*

$$\text{sine of } \angle A = \frac{\text{opp.}}{\text{hyp.}}$$

$$\text{cosine of } \angle A = \frac{\text{adj.}}{\text{hyp.}}$$

$$\text{tangent of } \angle A = \frac{\text{opp.}}{\text{adj.}}$$

$$\text{cosecant of } \angle A = \frac{\text{hyp.}}{\text{opp.}}$$

$$\text{secant of } \angle A = \frac{\text{hyp.}}{\text{adj.}}$$

$$\text{cotangent of } \angle A = \frac{\text{adj.}}{\text{opp.}}$$

The six trigonometric functions are abbreviated as sin *A*, cos *A*, tan *A*, csc *A*, sec *A*, and cot *A*.

E X A M P L E ❶ Find the values of the six trigonometric functions of ∠*X* for △*XYZ* at right. Give exact answers and answers rounded to the nearest ten-thousandth.

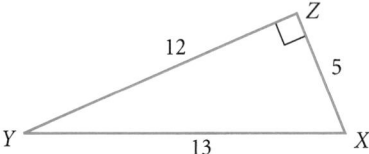

● **SOLUTION**

$$\sin X = \frac{\text{opp.}}{\text{hyp.}} = \frac{12}{13} \approx 0.9231$$

$$\cos X = \frac{\text{adj.}}{\text{hyp.}} = \frac{5}{13} \approx 0.3846$$

$$\tan X = \frac{\text{opp.}}{\text{adj.}} = \frac{12}{5} = 2.4$$

$$\csc X = \frac{\text{hyp.}}{\text{opp.}} = \frac{13}{12} \approx 1.0833$$

$$\sec X = \frac{\text{hyp.}}{\text{adj.}} = \frac{13}{5} = 2.6$$

$$\cot X = \frac{\text{adj.}}{\text{opp.}} = \frac{5}{12} \approx 0.4167$$

TRY THIS Find the values of the six trigonometric functions of ∠*Y* for △*XYZ*. Give exact answers and answers rounded to the nearest ten-thousandth.

Notice that in the solution to Example 1, the ratios for sin *X* and csc *X* are reciprocals. Likewise, the ratios for cos *X* and sec *X* are reciprocals, and the ratios for tan *X* and cot *X* are reciprocals.

The cosecant, secant, and cotangent ratios can be expressed in terms of the sine, cosine, and tangent ratios, respectively.

$$\csc A = \frac{1}{\sin A} \qquad \sec A = \frac{1}{\cos A} \qquad \cot A = \frac{1}{\tan A}$$

CHECKPOINT ✔ Show that the following statements are also true:

$$\sin A = \frac{1}{\csc A} \qquad \cos A = \frac{1}{\sec A} \qquad \tan A = \frac{1}{\cot A}$$

CRITICAL THINKING Find the number of different possible ratios of the lengths of two sides of a triangle by using permutations. Explain what your result means. Are all possible ratios given by the functions above?

Exploring Trigonometric Functions

You will need: a protractor, a centimeter ruler, and a calculator

On a sheet of paper, make a large diagram like the one shown below. Place segments $\overline{X_1Y_1}$, $\overline{X_2Y_2}$, and $\overline{X_3Y_3}$ wherever you wish, as long as they are perpendicular to $\overrightarrow{AP}$.

1. Copy and complete the table below by measuring the indicated sides and calculating sin A, cos A, and tan A.

2. Are all of the entries approximately equal in the sin A column? in the cos A column? in the tan A column?

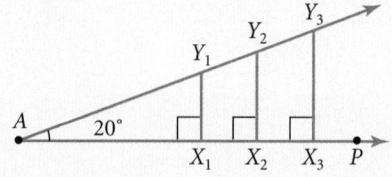

	opp. $\angle A$	adj. $\angle A$	hyp.	$\sin A = \dfrac{\text{opp.}}{\text{hyp.}}$	$\cos A = \dfrac{\text{adj.}}{\text{hyp.}}$	$\tan A = \dfrac{\text{opp.}}{\text{adj.}}$
$\triangle AY_1X_1$						
$\triangle AY_2X_2$						
$\triangle AY_3X_3$						

3. Compare your results from Step 2 with your classmates' results.

CHECKPOINT ✔ 4. What can you conjecture about the sine, cosine, and tangent functions for the measure of $\angle A$?

As the results of the Activity suggest, the ratios for the sine, cosine, and tangent of an acute angle in similar triangles does not depend on the lengths of sides. The trigonometric functions depend only on the measure of the acute angle.

For any given angle measure, you can obtain values for the sine, cosine, and tangent of the angle by using a scientific calculator in degree mode. These trigonometric function values can be used to find the unknown lengths of sides, as shown in Example 2.

E X A M P L E ② **For $\triangle ABC$ shown at right, find each side length to the nearest tenth.**

    a. AB **b.** BC

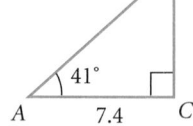

SOLUTION

From the diagram, m$\angle A = 41°$ and the length of the leg adjacent to $\angle A$ is 7.4.

a. To find AB, the length of the hypotenuse, use the cosine ratio.

$$\cos A = \frac{\text{adj.}}{\text{hyp.}}$$

$$\cos 41° = \frac{7.4}{AB}$$

$$AB = \frac{7.4}{\cos 41°}$$

$$AB \approx \frac{7.4}{0.7547} \approx 9.8$$

b. To find BC, the length of the leg opposite $\angle A$, use the tangent ratio.

$$\tan A = \frac{\text{opp.}}{\text{adj.}}$$

$$\tan 41° = \frac{BC}{7.4}$$

$$7.4 \times \tan 41° = BC$$

$$7.4 \times 0.8693 \approx BC$$

$$BC \approx 6.4$$

TRY THIS For △*KLM* shown at right, find *KL* and *LM* to the nearest tenth.

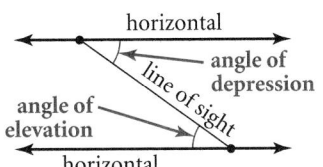

An **angle of elevation** is an angle between a horizontal line and a line of sight to a point above. An **angle of depression** is an angle between a horizontal line and a line of sight to a point below.

EXAMPLE 3

APPLICATION
WILDLIFE

Refer to the ornithologist's problem described at the beginning of the lesson.

How high above the water are the puffins? Give your answer to the nearest foot.

● **SOLUTION**

In the diagram, *BE* represents the height of the puffins above the water. Because *BE* = *BA* + *AE* and you know that *EA* is 15, you need to find *AB*. The angle of elevation is 28°.

$$\tan 28° = \frac{AB}{40}$$
$$40 \tan 28° = AB$$
$$AB \approx 21.3$$

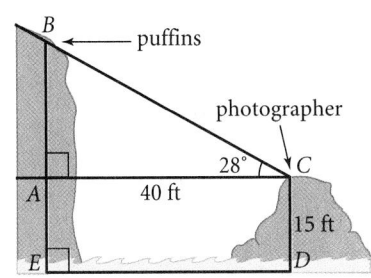

Then find *BE*.

$$BE = EA + AB$$
$$\approx 15 + 21.3$$
$$\approx 36.3$$

The puffins are about 36 feet above the water.

When you know the trigonometric ratio of an angle, you can find the measure of that angle by using the *inverse relation* of the trigonometric ratio. For example, if $\tan A$ is $\frac{4}{3}$, then the angle whose tangent is $\frac{4}{3}$ is written $\tan^{-1}\frac{4}{3}$.

$$\tan A = \frac{4}{3}$$
$$m\angle A = \tan^{-1}\frac{4}{3}$$
$$m\angle A \approx 53°$$

Most calculators have $\boxed{\text{SIN}^{-1}}$, $\boxed{\text{COS}^{-1}}$, and $\boxed{\text{TAN}^{-1}}$ keys for these inverse trigonometric relations. Note that $\sin^{-1} x$ is *not* the same as $\frac{1}{\sin x}$. These inverse relations are sometimes called the *arcsine*, *arccosine*, and *arctangent* relations.

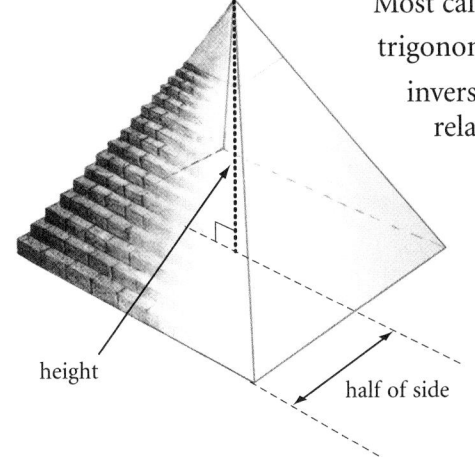

CULTURAL CONNECTION: AFRICA The Egyptians used a triangle relation called the *seked* to denote the slope of the inclined face of a pyramid.

$$seked = \frac{\text{half of the pyramid's side length in palms}}{\text{height of the pyramid in cubits, where 1 cubit equals 7 palms}}$$

Today, we use the tangent ratio, which is similar to the reciprocal of the *seked*.

Inverse trigonometric relations are often used to solve a triangle. **Solving a triangle** involves finding the measures of all of the unknown sides and angles of the triangle. A geometry fact used in solving triangles is that the sum of the measures of all the angles in a triangle is 180°. For right triangles, the sum of the measures of the two acute angles is 90°.

E X A M P L E ④ Solve △RST. Give m∠R and m∠S to the nearest degree, and give RS to the nearest tenth of a unit.

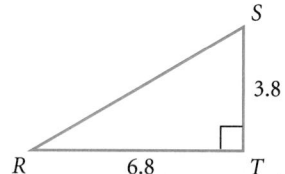

● **SOLUTION**

1. First find m∠R.

$$\tan R = \frac{3.8}{6.8}$$

$$R = \tan^{-1} \frac{3.8}{6.8} \approx 29°$$

2. Then find m∠S.

$R + S + T = 180°$	or	$R + S = 90°$
$29° + S + 90° \approx 180°$		$29° + S \approx 90°$
$S \approx 61°$		$S \approx 61°$

3. Use the Pythagorean Theorem to find RS.

$$(RS)^2 = (6.8)^2 + (3.8)^2$$
$$RS = \sqrt{(6.8)^2 + (3.8)^2}$$
$$RS \approx 7.8$$

Thus, m∠R ≈ 29°, m∠S ≈ 61°, and RS ≈ 7.8.

TRY THIS   Solve △KLM. Give m∠K and m∠L to the nearest degree and LM to the nearest tenth of a unit.

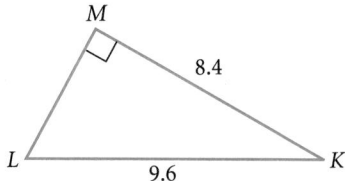

CHECKPOINT ✔ Explain how to solve △RST in Example 4 by finding RS first and then using the sine or cosine to find m∠R.

Exercises

● *Communicate*

1. Explain how to find the values of the six trigonometric functions of ∠A at right.

2. Explain how to find the measures of ∠A and ∠B in △ABC at right.

3. Explain how the expressions $\frac{1}{\sin A}$ and $\sin^{-1} A$ are different.

4. Find the values of the six trigonometric functions of ∠X in △XYZ at right. Give exact answers and answers rounded to the nearest ten-thousandth. *(EXAMPLE 1)*

5. For △ABC at left, find AC and BA to the nearest tenth. *(EXAMPLE 2)*

APPLICATION

6. SURVEYING An engineer stands 50 feet away from a building and sights the top of the building with a surveying device mounted on a tripod. If the surveying device is 5 feet above the ground and the angle of elevation is 50°, how tall is the building? *(EXAMPLE 3)*

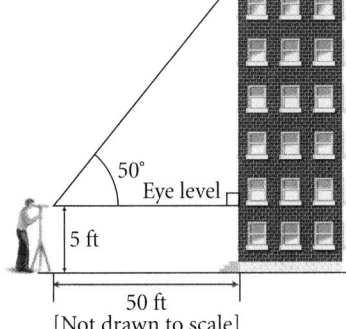

7. Solve △ABC shown below. Give m∠A and m∠B to the nearest degree, and give AB to the nearest tenth of a unit. *(EXAMPLE 4)*

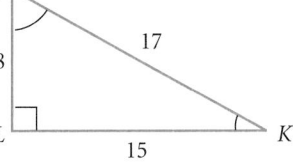

Practice and Apply

Refer to △JKL below to find each value listed. Give exact answers and answers rounded to the nearest ten-thousandth.

8. sin K **9.** sin J **10.** cos J

11. cos K **12.** tan K **13.** tan J

14. csc J **15.** csc K **16.** sec K

17. sec J **18.** cot J **19.** cot K

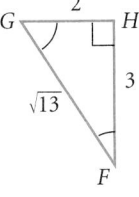

Refer to △FGH below to find each value listed. Give exact answers and answers rounded to the nearest ten-thousandth.

20. sin G **21.** sin F **22.** cos G

23. cos F **24.** tan G **25.** tan F

26. csc G **27.** csc F **28.** sec G

29. sec F **30.** cot G **31.** cot F

internet connect

Homework Help Online
Go To: **go.hrw.com**
Keyword:
MB1 Homework Help
for Exercises 32–37

Find m∠A by using inverse trigonometric functions.

32.   **33.**   **34.**

35.   **36.**   **37.**

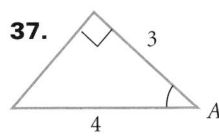

Solve each triangle. Give angle measures to the nearest degree and side lengths to the nearest tenth.

38.

39.

40.

41.

42.

43.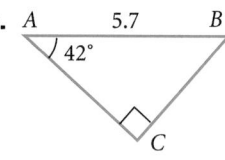

44. Show that $\tan A = \dfrac{\sin A}{\cos A}$ is true.

CONNECTION

45. GEOMETRY Quadrilateral *ABCD* at right is a rectangle. Find *AD* and *AC* to the nearest tenth of a foot.

APPLICATIONS

46. HOME IMPROVEMENT Mary and Chris want to build a right-triangular deck behind their house. They would like the hypotenuse of the deck to be 20 feet long, and they would like the other two sides of the deck to be equal in length.

  a. Find the length of the sides of the deck.

  b. Find the area of the deck.

AVIATION A commercial airline pilot is flying at an altitude of 6.5 miles. To make a gentle descent for landing, the pilot begins descending toward the airport when still fairly far away.

47. If the pilot begins descending 186 miles from the airport (measured on the ground), what angle will the plane's path make with the runway (without further adjustment)?

48. If the plane's path is to make an angle of 5° with the runway (without further adjustment), how far from the airport (measured on the ground) must the pilot begin descending?

CHALLENGE

49. CONSTRUCTION The city park manager would like to build a gazebo in the shape of a regular hexagon with sides 10 feet long. (A regular hexagon is a 6-sided polygon with all sides equal in length and all angles equal in measure.) Paving costs $15 per square foot. Use trigonometric ratios to find the cost of paving the hexagonal area.

Look Back

Determine the degree of each polynomial function. *(LESSON 7.1)*

50. $f(x) = 3x^5 - 5x^8 + 4x^3 + 2$ **51.** $f(x) = (x^2 - 9)(x^3 + 4)$

Write each polynomial in factored form. *(LESSON 7.3)*

52. $2x^3 - 18x$ **53.** $3x^3 - 7x^2 + 2x$

Write each expression with a rational denominator in simplest form.
(LESSON 8.7)

54. $\dfrac{3}{\sqrt{2}}$ **55.** $\dfrac{1}{\sqrt{3}}$ **56.** $\dfrac{5}{1 - \sqrt{2}}$ **57.** $\dfrac{-2}{\sqrt{2} + \sqrt{3}}$

Find the minimum and maximum values, Q_1, Q_2, and Q_3, and make a box-and-whisker plot for each set of data. *(LESSON 12.3)*

58. 102, 107, 122, 99, 103, 121, 113, 100, 78, 130, 125, 119, 110

59. 12, 34, 18, 25, 53, 46, 17, 14, 25, 36, 24, 19, 17, 28, 26, 22

**Portfolio
Extension**
Go To: **go.hrw.com**
Keyword:
MB1 Ferris

 Look Beyond

60. GEOMETRY A 360° angle of rotation creates a circle. What angle of rotation creates a semicircle? a quarter circle?

The world's largest Ferris wheel, as of 1998, is the Cosmoclock 21 in Yokohama City, Japan. Its center is 344.5 feet above the ground and it has a diameter of 328 feet.
[*Source: Guinness Book of World Records, 1998*]

The center of the Cosmoclock 21 is located at the origin of the coordinate plane at right. Assume that a point, P, begins its rotation at $(164, 0)$ and that it rotates in a counterclockwise direction.

   1. Identify the coordinates of Q, R, and S.

   2. Copy and complete the table below.

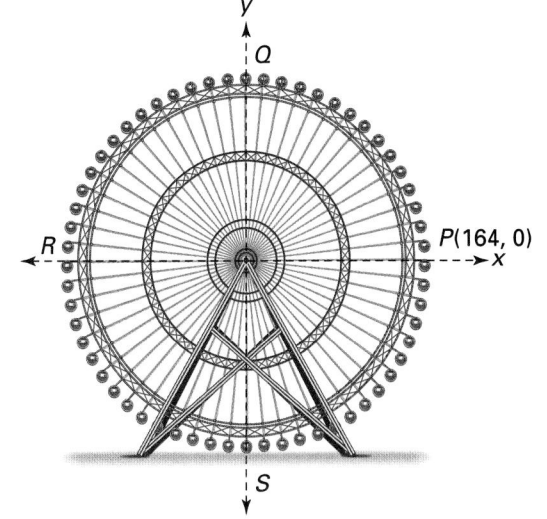

3. Plot the points from your table in a new coordinate plane. Sketch a *smooth curve* through the points.

4. Does your graph appear to be linear, quadratic, exponential, logarithmic, or none of these?

WORKING ON THE CHAPTER PROJECT
You should now be able to complete Activity 1 of the Chapter Project.

Rotation (degrees)	0°	90°	180°	270°	...	810°
Height of P relative to the x-axis (feet)	0	164		−164	...	

Angles of Rotation

Objectives

- Find coterminal and reference angles.

- Find the trigonometric function values of angles in standard position.

Why *You can use angles of rotation to describe the rate at which an airplane propeller rotates.*

The propeller of an airplane rotates 1100 times per minute. Through how many degrees will a point on the propeller rotate in 1 second? *You will solve this problem in Example 1.*

In geometry, an angle is defined by two rays that have a common endpoint. In trigonometry, an angle is defined by a ray that is rotated around its endpoint. Each position of the rotated ray, relative to its starting position, creates an **angle of rotation.** The Greek letter *theta*, θ, is commonly used to name an angle of rotation.

The initial position of the ray is called the **initial side** of the angle, and the final position is called the **terminal side** of the angle. When the initial side lies along the positive *x*-axis and its endpoint is at the origin, the angle is said to be in **standard position.**

If the direction of rotation is counterclockwise, the angle has a **positive measure.** If the direction of rotation is clockwise, the angle has a **negative measure.**

The most common unit for angle measure is the **degree.** A complete rotation of a ray is assigned a measure of 360°. Thus, a measure of 1° is $\frac{1}{360}$ of a complete rotation.

Standard position of θ

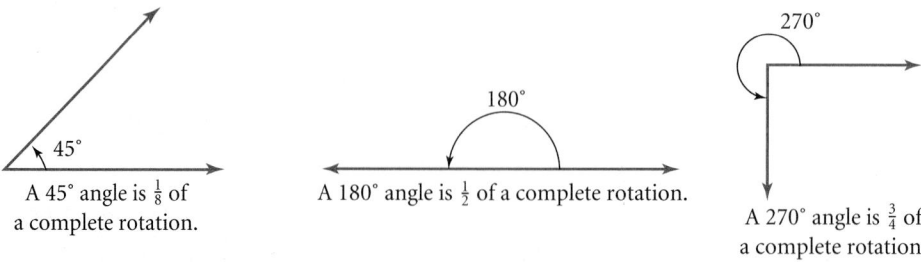

A 45° angle is $\frac{1}{8}$ of a complete rotation.

A 180° angle is $\frac{1}{2}$ of a complete rotation.

A 270° angle is $\frac{3}{4}$ of a complete rotation.

CHECKPOINT ✔ What direction of rotation generates an angle with a measure of −90°? of 120°? What portion of a complete rotation is −90°? 120°?

EXAMPLE ① Refer to the propeller problem at the beginning of the lesson.

Find the number of degrees through which a point on the propeller rotates in 1 second.

APPLICATION
AVIATION

SOLUTION

The propeller rotates 1100 times per minute. The number of degrees through which a point rotates in 1 minute is $1100 \times 360° = 396{,}000°$. The number of degrees through which a point rotates in 1 second is $\frac{396{,}000°}{60} = 6600°$.

TRY THIS   A record player makes 33.3 revolutions in 1 minute. Find the number of degrees through which a point on the record rotates in 1 second.

Angles in standard position are **coterminal** if they have the same terminal side.

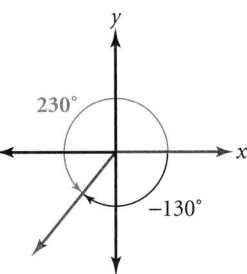

A 230° angle and a −130°
angle are coterminal.

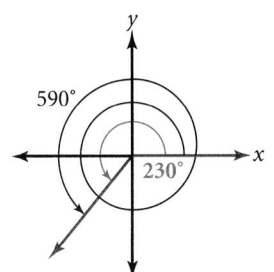

A 230° angle and a 590°
angle are coterminal.

You can find coterminal angles by adding or subtracting integer multiples of 360°. This is shown in Example 2.

EXAMPLE ② **Find the coterminal angle, θ, for each angle below such that $-360° < \theta < 360°$.**
a. 180°   **b.** −27°

SOLUTION

Add and subtract 360° from each given angle. Discard answers that are not in the given range, $-360° < \theta < 360°$.

a. $\theta = \cancel{180° + 360° = 540°}$ **b.** $\theta = -27 + 360° = 333°$
$\theta = 180° - 360° = -180°$ $\theta = \cancel{-27 - 360° = 387°}$
The coterminal angle is −180°.   The coterminal angle is 333°.

TRY THIS   Find the coterminal angle, θ, for 123° and for −185° such that $-360° < \theta < 360°$.

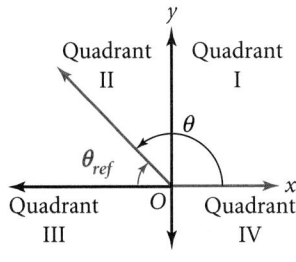

In Lesson 13.3 you will learn how to find trigonometric values for angles in standard position that are larger than 90° (or smaller than 0°). In order to do this, you will need to know how to find the measures of *reference angles*.

For an angle θ in standard position, the **reference angle,** θ_{ref}, is the positive acute angle formed by the terminal side of θ and the nearest part (positive or negative) of the x-axis. Use the positive x-axis for angles in Quadrants I and IV, and use the negative x-axis for angles in Quadrants II and III.

E X A M P L E ③ **Find the reference angle, θ_{ref}, for each angle.**

    a. $\theta = 94°$ **b.** $\theta = 245°$ **c.** $\theta = 290°$ **d.** $\theta = -110°$

● **SOLUTION**

a. $\theta = 94°$ is in Quadrant II.
Use the negative x-axis.

$$\theta_{ref} = |180° - \theta|$$

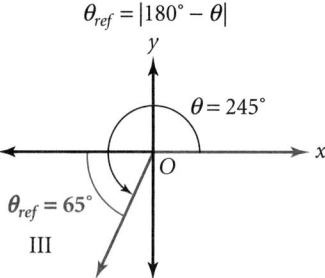

$$\theta_{ref} = |180° - 94°| = 86°$$

b. $\theta = 245°$ is in Quadrant III.
Use the negative x-axis.

$$\theta_{ref} = |180° - \theta|$$

$$\theta_{ref} = |180° - 245°| = 65°$$

c. $\theta = 290°$ is in Quadrant IV.
Use the positive x-axis.

$$\theta_{ref} = |360° - \theta|$$

$$\theta_{ref} = |360° - 290°| = 70°$$

d. $\theta = -110°$ is in Quadrant III.
Use the negative x-axis.

$$\theta_{ref} = |180° - \theta|$$

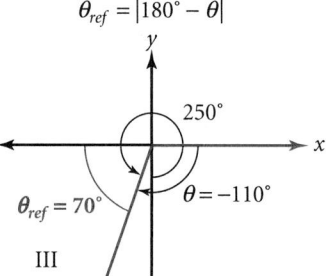

The positive coterminal angle
for $-110°$ is $250°$.

$$\theta_{ref} = |180° - 250°| = 70°$$

TRY THIS   Find the reference angle, θ_{ref}, for $\theta = 315°$ and $\theta = -235°$.

CRITICAL THINKING   How many angles in standard position between $0°$ and $360°$ have the same reference angle?

If you think of x and y as the coordinates of a point on the terminal side of an angle in standard position, you will be able to determine the correct sign of the values for the trigonometric functions.

Trigonometric Functions of θ

Let $P(x, y)$ be a point on the terminal side of θ in standard position. The distance from the origin to P is given by $r = \sqrt{x^2 + y^2}$.

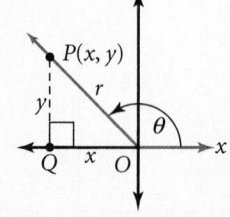

$$\sin \theta = \frac{y}{r} \qquad \cos \theta = \frac{x}{r} \qquad \tan \theta = \frac{y}{x}, x \neq 0$$

$$\csc \theta = \frac{r}{y}, y \neq 0 \qquad \sec \theta = \frac{r}{x}, x \neq 0 \qquad \cot \theta = \frac{x}{y}, y \neq 0$$

E X A M P L E ❹ Let $P(-2, -3)$ be a point on the terminal side of θ in standard position. Find the exact values of the six trigonometric functions of θ.

SOLUTION

PROBLEM SOLVING **Draw a diagram.** You know that $x = -2$ and $y = -3$. Find r.

$$r = \sqrt{x^2 + y^2}$$

$$r = \sqrt{(-2)^2 + (-3)^2} = \sqrt{13}$$

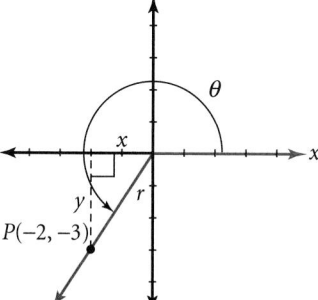

$$\sin\theta = \frac{y}{r} \qquad \cos\theta = \frac{x}{r} \qquad \tan\theta = \frac{y}{x}$$

$$= \frac{-3}{\sqrt{13}} \qquad\quad = \frac{-2}{\sqrt{13}} \qquad\quad = \frac{-3}{-2}$$

$$= -\frac{3\sqrt{13}}{13} \qquad = -\frac{2\sqrt{13}}{13} \qquad = \frac{3}{2}$$

To find $\csc\theta$, $\sec\theta$, and $\cot\theta$, use reciprocals.

$$\csc\theta = -\frac{\sqrt{13}}{3} \qquad \sec\theta = -\frac{\sqrt{13}}{2} \qquad \cot\theta = \frac{2}{3}$$

TRY THIS Let $P(3, -5)$ be a point on the terminal side of θ in standard position. Find the exact values of the six trigonometric functions of θ.

Investigating the Signs in Each Quadrant

You will need: no special materials

1. Copy and complete the table below with the signs of the trigonometric functions of θ in standard position for each quadrant.

	Quadrant			
Trig value	**I**	**II**	**III**	**IV**
$\sin\theta$ and $\csc\theta$	+			
$\cos\theta$ and $\sec\theta$				
$\tan\theta$ and $\cot\theta$				

Quadrant II $(-, +)$ Quadrant I $(+, +)$
Quadrant III $(-, -)$ Quadrant IV $(+, -)$

2. In what quadrant is the terminal side of θ if $\sin\theta = -\frac{2}{7}$? if $\cos\theta = -\frac{2}{7}$? if $\tan\theta = -\frac{1}{5}$? Give all possible answers.

CHECKPOINT ✔ 3. Does the value of r affect the sign of any of the trigonometric values? Explain.

CHECKPOINT ✔ 4. Which coordinate, x or y, determines the sign of $\sin\theta$ and $\csc\theta$? of $\cos\theta$ and $\sec\theta$? of $\tan\theta$ and $\cot\theta$?

In each quadrant at right are listed the trigonometric function values that are positive for any angle θ in that quadrant. For example, for any angle θ in Quadrant II, $\sin\theta$ and $\csc\theta$ are positive while all other trigonometric function values are negative. This occurs because the sign of $\sin\theta$ and $\csc\theta$ both depend on y, which is positive in Quadrant II.

Quadrant II $\sin\theta$ $\csc\theta$ Quadrant I all
Quadrant III $\tan\theta$ $\cot\theta$ Quadrant IV $\cos\theta$ $\sec\theta$

If you know which quadrant contains the terminal side of θ in standard position and the exact value of one trigonometric function of θ, you can find the values of the other trigonometric functions of θ. This is shown in Example 5.

EXAMPLE ⑤ The terminal side of θ in standard position is in Quadrant II, and $\cos\theta = -\dfrac{3}{5}$. Find the exact values of the six trigonometric functions of θ.

● **SOLUTION**

PROBLEM SOLVING

Draw a diagram and find the x- and y-coordinates of P.

$$\cos\theta = \frac{x}{r} = -\frac{3}{5}$$

In Quadrant II, x is negative. Thus, $x = -3$ and $r = 5$.

Use the Pythagorean Theorem to find y.

$$5^2 = (-3)^2 + y^2$$
$$y^2 = 25 - 9$$
$$y = \pm\sqrt{16}$$
$$y = 4 \quad \textit{Because P is in Quadrant II, y is positive.}$$

$$\sin\theta = \frac{y}{r} = \frac{4}{5} \qquad\qquad \cos\theta = \frac{x}{r} = \frac{-3}{5} \qquad\qquad \tan\theta = \frac{y}{x} = \frac{4}{-3}$$

$$\csc\theta = \frac{r}{y} = \frac{5}{4} \qquad\qquad \sec\theta = \frac{r}{x} = \frac{5}{-3} \qquad\qquad \cot\theta = \frac{x}{y} = \frac{-3}{4}$$

TRY THIS The terminal side of θ in standard position is in Quadrant III, and $\sin\theta = -\dfrac{4}{5}$. Find the exact values of the six trigonometric functions of θ.

If the terminal side of an angle, θ, in standard position coincides with a coordinate axis (such that x or y is 0), some trigonometric functions of θ will be undefined. For example $\csc 0°$, $\sec 90°$, $\tan 180°$, and $\cot 270°$ are all undefined because they involve division by zero. These angle measures are excluded values in the domain of the respective functions.

CHECKPOINT ✔ Find the exact values of the six trigonometric functions for $\theta = 90°$.

Exercises

● *Communicate*

1. Describe the differences between angles in right triangles and angles of rotation.

2. Describe the difference that may exist between the trigonometric functions of an angle and those of its reference angle. Explain the reason for this difference.

3. Do you need to know the measure of an angle in order to find the exact values of its trigonometric functions? Explain.

Guided Skills Practice

4. AVIATION The main rotor of a helicopter rotates 430 times per minute. Find the number of degrees through which a point on the main rotor rotates in 1 second. *(EXAMPLE 1)*

5. Find the coterminal angle, θ, for 271° such that $-360° < \theta < 360°$. *(EXAMPLE 2)*

6. Find the reference angle for 93°, 280°, and −36°. *(EXAMPLE 3)*

7. Let $P(3, -2)$ be a point on the terminal side of θ in standard position. Find the exact values of the six trigonometric functions of θ. *(EXAMPLE 4)*

8. The terminal side of θ in standard position is in Quadrant III, and $\sin \theta = -\frac{12}{13}$. Find the exact values of the six trigonometric functions of θ. *(EXAMPLE 5)*

Practice and Apply

Sketch each angle in standard position.

9. 115°   **10.** 280°   **11.** −300°   **12.** −130°

For each angle below, find all coterminal angles such that $-360° < \theta < 360°$. Then find the corresponding reference angle, if it exists.

13. 35°	**14.** 23°	**15.** 112°	**16.** 160°
17. 612°	**18.** 478°	**19.** −135°	**20.** −315°
21. 90°	**22.** −180°	**23.** −450°	**24.** −485°
25. 540°	**26.** 270°	**27.** 225°	**28.** 195°
29. 410°	**30.** 560°	**31.** −120°	**32.** −280°
33. −175°	**34.** −295°	**35.** −395°	**36.** −540°

Find the exact values of the six trigonometric functions of θ.

37.   **38.**   **39.**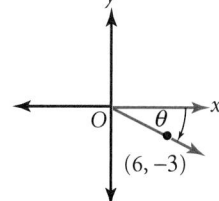

Find the exact values of the six trigonometric functions of θ given each point on the terminal side of θ in standard position.

40. $(3, 4)$ **41.** $(5, 2)$ **42.** $(-4, 2)$ **43.** $(-4, 6)$

44. $(\sqrt{3}, -3)$ **45.** $(2\sqrt{5}, -1)$ **46.** $(-4, -3)$ **47.** $(-1, -8)$

Given the quadrant of θ in standard position and a trigonometric function value of θ, find exact values for the indicated functions.

48. I, $\cos \theta = 0.25$; $\tan \theta$ **49.** III, $\cos \theta = -\frac{1}{2}$; $\tan \theta$

50. IV, $\tan \theta = -1$; $\csc \theta$ **51.** I, $\tan \theta = 2$; $\csc \theta$

52. III, $\sin \theta = -\frac{1}{2}$; $\sec \theta$ **53.** II, $\sin \theta = 0.4$; $\sec \theta$

54. IV, $\cot \theta = -1.2$; $\cos \theta$ **55.** II, $\cot \theta = -1.75$; $\cos \theta$

Find the number of rotations or the fraction of a rotation represented by each angle below. Indicate whether the rotation is clockwise or counterclockwise.

56. $45°$ **57.** $90°$ **58.** $-180°$ -   **59.** $-270°$

60. $450°$ **61.** $720°$ **62.** $-420°$ **63.** $-640°$

64. Find $\cos\theta$ if $\sin\theta = 0.375$ and $\tan\theta$ is less than 0.

65. Find $\tan\theta$ if $\cos\theta = 0.809$ and $\sin\theta$ is less than 0.

66. PROBABILITY An angle of rotation of 120° is colored red on a circular spinner at a school fair. If the spinner lands anywhere in the red space, the contestant wins. What is the probability of a contestant winning?

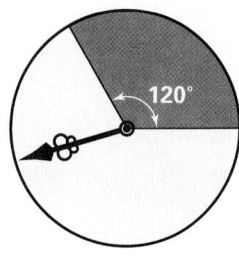

67. ENGINEERING The flywheel of an engine rotates 900 times per minute. Through how many degrees does a point on the flywheel rotate in 1 second?

68. NAVIGATION Airline pilots and sea captains both use *nautical miles* to measure distance. A nautical mile is approximately equal to the arc length intercepted on the surface of the Earth by a central angle measure of 1 *minute* (there are 60 minutes in 1 degree). The diameter of the Earth at the equator is approximately 7926.41 miles.

   a. How many minutes are there in the circumference of the Earth?
   b. Find the approximate circumference of the Earth in miles.
   c. Approximately how many miles are equal to one nautical mile?

 Look Back

69. Solve $x^2 - 8 = 188$ for x. *(LESSONS 5.5 AND 5.6)* ±14

Graph each number and its conjugate in the complex plane. *(LESSON 5.6)*

70. $-6 + 4i$ **71.** $5i$ **72.** -1 **73.** $-3 - 4i$

Evaluate. *(LESSON 5.6)*

74. $|1 + i|$ **75.** $|2 + 3i|$ **76.** $\left|\dfrac{\sqrt{2}}{2} + \dfrac{\sqrt{2}}{2}i\right|$ **77.** $\left|\dfrac{\sqrt{3}}{3} + \dfrac{\sqrt{6}}{3}i\right|$

78. Find the standard equation for the hyperbola centered at $(1, 4)$ with vertices at $(-4, 4)$ and $(6, 4)$ and co-vertices at $(1, -5)$ and $(1, 13)$. Graph the equation. *(LESSON 9.5)*

79. How many ways are there to choose a committee of 4 from a group of 10 people? *(LESSON 10.3)*

 Look Beyond

Find the exact values of the six trigonometric functions of θ given each point on the terminal side of θ in standard position.

80. $\left(\dfrac{\sqrt{3}}{2}, \dfrac{1}{2}\right)$ **81.** $\left(\dfrac{\sqrt{2}}{2}, \dfrac{\sqrt{2}}{2}\right)$ **82.** $\left(\dfrac{1}{2}, \dfrac{\sqrt{3}}{2}\right)$

Trigonometric Functions of Any Angle

Objective

- Find exact values for trigonometric functions of special angles and their multiples.

- Find approximate values for trigonometric functions of any angle.

APPLICATION
ROBOTICS

Steve is programming a 2-meter long robotic arm. The arm grasps an object at point *A*, located directly to the right of the pivot point, *O*. The arm swings through an angle of 140° and releases the object at point *B*. What is the new position of the object relative to the pivot point? *You will solve this problem in Example 3.*

There are certain angles whose exact trigonometric function values can be found without a calculator. You will explore these angles in the Activity below.

CONNECTION
GEOMETRY

Activity
Exploring Special Triangles

You will need: no special materials

1. When a square is bisected along a diagonal, two 45-45-90 triangles are formed, as shown below.

   Find the length of *c* in terms of *a* by using the Pythagorean Theorem.

2. An equilateral triangle has three 60° angles. When one angle is bisected, two 30-60-90 triangles are formed, as shown below.

   Find the length of *c* in terms of *a* by using the Pythagorean Theorem.

CHECKPOINT ✔ 3. State the relationship between the sides of a 45-45-90 triangle and the relationship between the sides of a 30-60-90 triangle.

In the Activity, you found that the lengths of the sides of a 45-45-90 triangle have a ratio of 1 to 1 to $\sqrt{2}$, and the lengths of the sides of a 30-60-90 triangle have a ratio of 1 to $\sqrt{3}$ to 2. You can use these relationships to find the exact values of the sine, cosine, and tangent of 30°, 45°, and 60° angles.

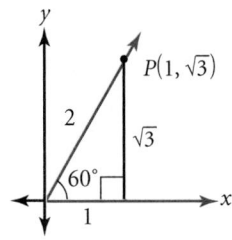

$$\sin 30° = \frac{1}{2}$$
$$\cos 30° = \frac{\sqrt{3}}{2}$$
$$\tan 30° = \frac{1}{\sqrt{3}}, \text{ or } \frac{\sqrt{3}}{3}$$

$$\sin 45° = \frac{1}{\sqrt{2}}, \text{ or } \frac{\sqrt{2}}{2}$$
$$\cos 45° = \frac{1}{\sqrt{2}}, \text{ or } \frac{\sqrt{2}}{2}$$
$$\tan 45° = 1$$

$$\sin 60° = \frac{\sqrt{3}}{2}$$
$$\cos 60° = \frac{1}{2}$$
$$\tan 60° = \sqrt{3}$$

Throughout this chapter it will be helpful to be familiar with the exact values of the sine, cosine, and tangent of 30°, 45°, and 60° angles, given above.

CHECKPOINT ✔ Make a table of the exact values and the decimal approximations of the sine, cosine, and tangent of 30°, 45°, and 60°.

You can use the exact values of the sine, cosine, and tangent given above to evaluate any angle whose reference angle is 30°, 45°, or 60°. This is shown in Example 1.

E X A M P L E ❶ **Find exact values of sin 315°, cos 315°, and tan 315°.**

● **SOLUTION**

PROBLEM SOLVING

Draw a diagram and find the reference angle.

$$\theta_{ref} = |360° − 315°| = 45°$$

Because 315° is in Quadrant IV, where y is negative, the sine and tangent are negative.

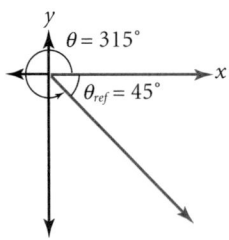

$$\sin 315° = −\sin 45°$$
$$= −\frac{1}{\sqrt{2}}, \text{ or } −\frac{\sqrt{2}}{2}$$

$$\cos 315° = \cos 45°$$
$$= \frac{1}{\sqrt{2}}, \text{ or } \frac{\sqrt{2}}{2}$$

$$\tan 315° = −\tan 45°$$
$$= −1$$

TRY THIS Find exact values of sin(−150°), cos(−150°), and tan(−150°).

In Lesson 13.2, a point on the terminal side of an angle was used to find trigonometric function values. In Example 2 on the next page, trigonometric function values are used to find the exact coordinates of a point on the terminal side of an angle.

E X A M P L E **2** Find the exact coordinates of point P, located at the intersection of a circle with a radius of 5 and the terminal side of a 150° angle in standard position.

● SOLUTION

PROBLEM SOLVING

Draw a diagram, and find the reference angle.

$$\theta_{ref} = |180° - 150°| = 30°$$

Because P is in Quadrant II, where x is negative, the cosine is negative.

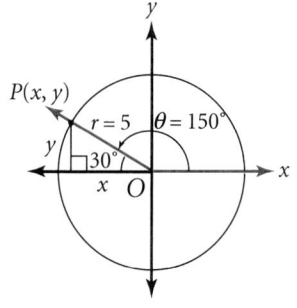

$$\cos 150° = \frac{x}{r} \qquad \sin 150° = \frac{y}{r}$$

$$-\cos 30° = \frac{x}{5} \qquad \sin 30° = \frac{y}{5}$$

$$-\frac{\sqrt{3}}{2} = \frac{x}{5} \qquad \frac{1}{2} = \frac{y}{5}$$

$$-\frac{5\sqrt{3}}{2} = x \qquad \frac{5}{2} = y$$

The exact coordinates of P are $\left(-\frac{5\sqrt{3}}{2}, \frac{5}{2}\right)$.

TRY THIS Find the exact coordinates of point P, located at the intersection of a circle with a radius of 12 and the terminal side of a 300° angle in standard position.

For any point on the terminal side of an angle in Quadrant I, $\cos \theta = \frac{x}{r}$, so $r \cos \theta = x$, and $\sin \theta = \frac{y}{r}$, so $r \sin \theta = y$. This allows you to find the coordinates of any point on a circle centered at the origin with radius r.

Coordinates of a Point on a Circle

If P lies at the intersection of the terminal side of θ in standard position and a circle with a radius of r centered at the origin, then the coordinates of P are $(r \cos \theta, r \sin \theta)$.

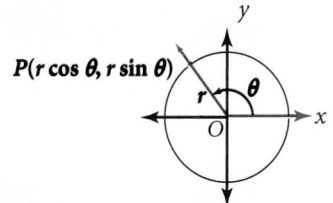

E X A M P L E **3** Refer to the robotic arm described at the beginning of the lesson.

What is the new position of the object relative to the pivot point?

● SOLUTION

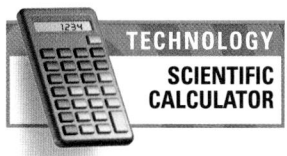
Place the pivot point at the origin. The new position at point B has the coordinates $(r \cos \theta, r \sin \theta)$. Substitute 2 for r and 140° for θ.

$$B(r \cos \theta, r \sin \theta) = B(2 \cos 140°, 2 \sin 140°)$$
$$\approx B(-1.53, 1.29) \quad \textit{Use a scientific calculator in degree mode.}$$

The object is about 1.53 meters to the left of the pivot point and about 1.29 meters above the pivot point.

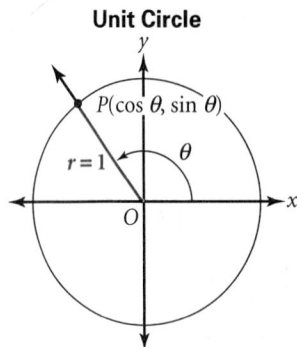

When a circle centered at the origin has a radius of 1, it is called a **unit circle**. Because *r* is 1, the coordinates of *P* are (cos *θ*, sin *θ*).

Unit circles are helpful in demonstrating the behavior of trigonometric functions. The unit circle below shows the *x*- and *y*-coordinates of *P* for special angles between 0° and 360°.

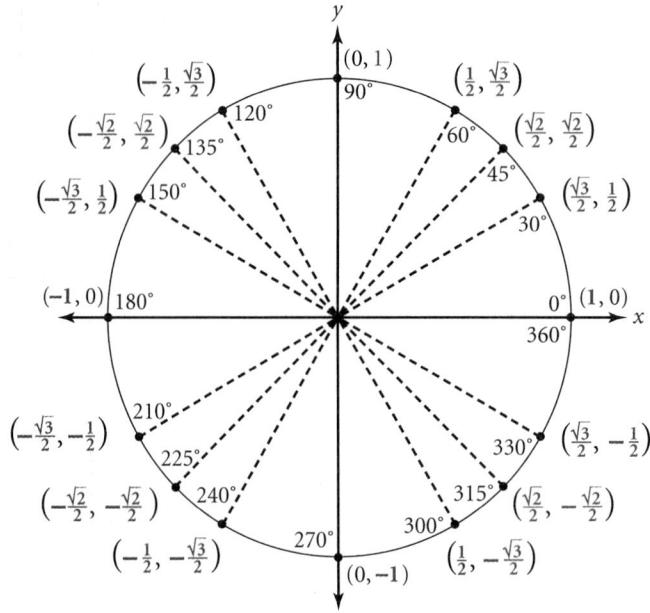

CHECKPOINT ✔ Using the coordinates on the unit circle above, find the following trigonometric function values: sin 90°, cos 60°, sin −45°, cos −30°, sin 360°, and cos 180°.

Recall from Lesson 13.2 that an angle of 90° is coterminal with angles of 450° and 810°. In fact, an angle of 90° is coterminal with any angle whose measure can be represented by 90° + *n*360°, where *n* is an integer. All coterminal angles share the same reference angle and have the same trigonometric function values. Because the values of sine and cosine repeat every 360°, they are called *periodic functions* and their *period* is 360°.

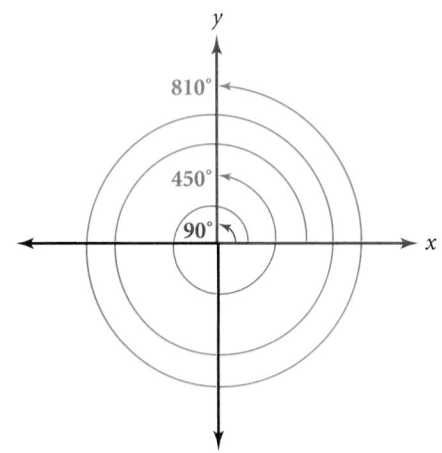

Periodic Functions

A function, *f*, is **periodic** if there is a number *p* such that $f(x + p) = f(x)$ for every *x* in the domain of *f*.

The smallest positive number *p* that satisfies the equation above is called the **period** of the function.

CRITICAL THINKING   What is the period of the tangent function?

EXAMPLE 4 **Find the exact values of the sine, cosine, and tangent of each angle.**
a. 900° **b.** −930°

● SOLUTION
Find a coterminal angle with a positive measure between 0° and 360°.

a. **b.**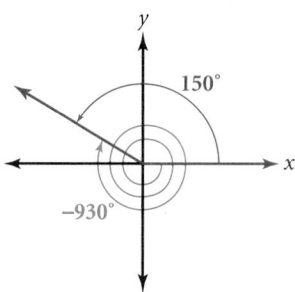

$900° - 2 \cdot 360° = 180°$
$\sin 900° = \sin 180° = 0$
$\cos 900° = \cos 180° = -1$
$\tan 900° = \tan 180° = 0$

$-930° + 3 \cdot 360° = 150°$
$\sin 930° = \sin 150° = \dfrac{1}{2}$
$\cos 930° = \cos 150° = -\dfrac{\sqrt{3}}{2}$
$\tan 930° = \tan 150° = -\dfrac{\sqrt{3}}{3}$

TRY THIS Find the exact values of the sine, cosine, and tangent of each angle.
a. 1110° **b.** −1110°

Exercises

● *Communicate*

1. Explain when it is possible to use a reference angle rather than a scientific calculator to solve a trigonometric problem.

2. Explain the relationship of the sine and cosine of θ to the coordinates of point P in the diagram at right.

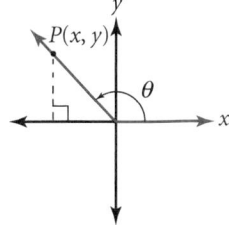

3. Describe how to find the exact value of sin 420°.

● *Guided Skills Practice*

4. Find the exact values of sin 150°, cos 150°, and tan 150°. *(EXAMPLE 1)*

5. Find the exact coordinates of a point, P, that is located at the intersection of a circle with a radius of 9 and the terminal side of a 315° angle in standard position. *(EXAMPLE 2)*

6. ROBOTICS Refer to the robotic arm described at the beginning of the lesson. Find the new position of the object relative to the pivot point after the 2-meter robotic arm swings through an angle of 110° degrees. *(EXAMPLE 3)*

7. Find the exact values of the sine, cosine, and tangent of −1200°. *(EXAMPLE 4)*

Practice and Apply

Find the exact values of the sine, cosine, and tangent of each angle.

8. 300° **9.** 210° **10.** 225° **11.** 120°

12. 135° **13.** 240° **14.** −225° **15.** −135°

16. −150° **17.** −330° **18.** −120° **19.** −210°

Point P is located at the intersection of a circle with a radius of r and the terminal side of angle θ. Find the exact coordinates of P.

20. $\theta = 60°, r = 3$ **21.** $\theta = 30°, r = 5$ **22.** $\theta = 120°, r = 8$

23. $\theta = 135°, r = 9$ **24.** $\theta = 240°, r = 50$ **25.** $\theta = 180°, r = 45$

26. $\theta = -30°, r = 6.2$ **27.** $\theta = -135°, r = 7.6$ **28.** $\theta = -330°, r = 0.9$

Point P is located at the intersection of the unit circle and the terminal side of angle θ in standard position. Find the coordinates of P to the nearest hundredth.

29. $\theta = 75°$ **30.** $\theta = 205°$ **31.** $\theta = -130°$ **32.** $\theta = -205°$

33. $\theta = 4°$ **34.** $\theta = 87°$ **35.** $\theta = -88°$ **36.** $\theta = -183°$

Find the exact values of the sine, cosine, and tangent of each angle.

37. 405° **38.** 690° **39.** 870° **40.** 855°

41. 1380° **42.** 1305° **43.** −600° **44.** −510°

45. −495° **46.** −480° **47.** −840° **48.** −1020°

Find each trigonometric function value. Give exact answers.

49. sin 135° **50.** cos 120° **51.** tan 150° **52.** sin 240°

53. cos 210° **54.** tan 225° **55.** sin 300° **56.** cos 315°

57. tan 330° **58.** sin 0° **59.** cos 0° **60.** tan 180°

61. sin 90° **62.** cos 90° **63.** tan 270° **64.** sin 180°

65. cos 180° **66.** tan 90° **67.** sin(−90°) **68.** cos(−90°)

69. tan(−180°) **70.** sin 720° **71.** cos 1080° **72.** cos 450°

73. sin 495° **74.** sin(−45°) **75.** cos(−135°) **76.** cos(−270°)

77. sin(−405°) **78.** tan(−150°) **79.** tan(−30°) **80.** sin 1125°

81. cos 810° **82.** tan 390° **83.** tan 780° **84.** csc 135°

85. sec 120° **86.** cot 150° **87.** csc(−660°) **88.** sec(−990°)

89. cot(−765°) **90.** sec 405° **91.** csc 1140° **92.** cot 1500°

93. Use the definition of a periodic function to show that the function $f(x) = x$ is not periodic.

GEOMETRY Solve each triangle.

94.

95.

96.

97.

98. ROBOTICS A robotic arm attached at point O picks up an object at point A, which is 3 meters to the right of O.

   a. The arm rotates through an angle of 212° and releases the object at point B. What is the location of the object at point B relative to O?

   b. If the arm lifts an object at A, rotates through an angle of 250°, extends to a length of 4 meters, and then places the object at point C, what is the location of the object at point C relative to O?

   c. How far must the arm be extended and through what angle must it swing in order for it to move an object from point A to a point that is located 1 meter to the right of and 2 meters below point O?

99. BICYCLE DESIGN The tires of a bicycle have a diameter of 26 inches. In the lowest gear, one complete revolution of the pedals causes the back wheel to rotate through an angle of 106°. How far, in inches, does this cause the bike to move?

100. CONSTRUCTION The Williams are building a new fence for their horse pen. The fence will have square sections with diagonal supports, as shown at right. If the height of a square fence section is 3.5 feet, find the length of a diagonal support.

Look Back

Let $f(x) = 3x + 2$ and $g(x) = 4x - 1$. Find each composite function. *(LESSON 2.4)*

101. $f \circ g$ **102.** $g \circ f$ **103.** $g \circ g$

Matrix J represents the amounts of money that Sheree and her brother Donnell had in their savings and checking accounts at the end of January. *(LESSON 4.1)*

$$\begin{array}{c c} & \text{Savings} \quad \text{Checking} \\ \begin{array}{c} \text{Sheree} \\ \text{Donnell} \end{array} & \begin{bmatrix} 325 & 512 \\ 408 & 275 \end{bmatrix} = J \end{array}$$

104. What are the dimensions of matrix J?
105. Describe the data in location j_{21}.
106. Find the total amount Sheree had in the bank at the end of January.

107. COORDINATE GEOMETRY Show that the triangle with vertices at $A(-2, 5)$, $B(4, 13)$, and $C(10, 5)$ is an isosceles triangle. *(LESSON 9.1)*

Find the mean, median, and mode of each data set. Give answers to the nearest hundredth. *(LESSON 12.1)*

108. 2, 8, 4, 11, 13, 4, 7, 8, 0   **109.** 5, 8, 3, 8, 12, 3, 16, 9, 11

Find the mean and standard deviation of each data set. Give answers to the nearest hundredth. *(LESSON 12.4)*

110. 5, 7, 38, 4, 9, 10, 11, 9, 3   **111.** 44, 43, 0, 47, 53, 54, 45, 48

Look Beyond

112. Because the whole unit circle (360°) has a circumference of 2π, an arc intercepted by angle θ will have a length ℓ given by $\ell = \dfrac{\theta}{360} \cdot 2\pi$. Find ℓ for each angle below.

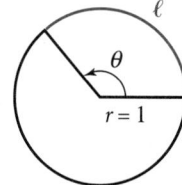

   a. $\theta = 180°$ **b.** $\theta = 90°$ **c.** $\theta = 360°$ **d.** $\theta = 45°$

Refer to the Cosmoclock 21 described in the Portfolio Activity on page 835. The center of the Ferris wheel is located at the origin of the coordinate plane at right. Assume that point P begins its rotation at (164, 0) and that it rotates counterclockwise.

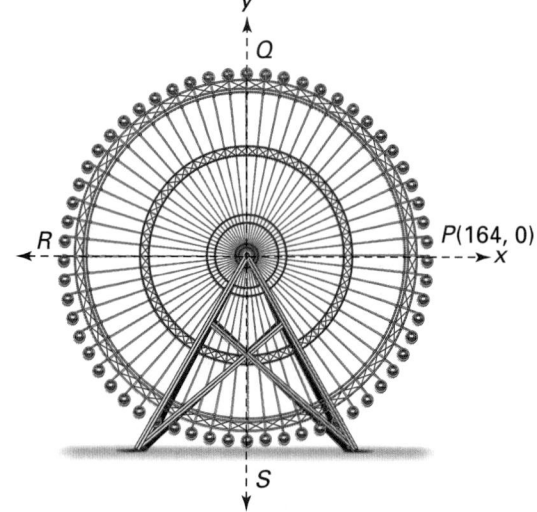

1. Find the height of P relative to the x-axis for each angle of rotation.
   a. 30°   **b.** 45°   **c.** 60°

2. Find the altitude of P, or height of P relative to the ground, for each angle of rotation given in Step 1.

3. Describe a general rule for converting from the height of P relative to the x-axis to the altitude of P.

4. Create a table of values for the altitude of P. Include all special angle measures for θ such that $0° \leq \theta \leq 360°$.

5. Plot the points from your table on graph paper. Sketch a *smooth curve* through the points.

6. Describe how the graph that you sketched in Step 5 compares with the graph that you sketched in Step 3 of the Portfolio Activity on page 835.

WORKING ON THE CHAPTER PROJECT

You should now be able to complete Activity 2 of the Chapter Project.

Radian Measure and Arc Length

Objectives

- Convert from degree measure to radian measure and vice versa.

- Find arc length.

Why *Radian measure is used to describe periodic phenomena such as seismic waves, climatic and population cycles, and the motion of circular orbiting objects such as satellites.*

APPLICATION
METEOROLOGY

A weather satellite orbits the Earth at an altitude of approximately 22,200 miles above Earth's surface. If the satellite observes a fixed region on Earth and has a period of revolution of 24 hours, what is the linear speed of the satellite? What is its angular speed? *You will answer these questions in Example 4.*

A useful angle measure other than degrees is *radian* measure. In the Activity below, you can investigate the relationship between measures in a circle, which is fundamental to the definition of radian measure.

CONNECTION
GEOMETRY

Activity
Investigating Circle Ratios

You will need: centimeter measuring tape and various cylindrical cans

1. Measure the circumference and diameter of several cylindrical objects of different sizes. Record your results in a table.

2. Plot your values as ordered pairs, with diameter on the *x*-axis.

3. Find the least-squares line for this data, and determine its slope.

CHECKPOINT ✔ 4. The slope should be approximately equal to a famous number that relates circumference and diameter. What is it? How close were you?

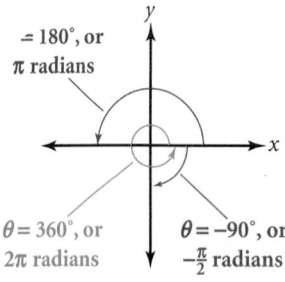

$= 180°$, or
π radians

$\theta = 360°$, or
2π radians

$\theta = -90°$, or
$-\frac{\pi}{2}$ radians

The circumference of a circle with a radius of r is $2\pi r$. Because the radius of a unit circle is 1, its circumference is 2π. The **radian** measure of an angle is equal to the length of the arc on the unit circle that is intercepted by the angle in standard position. Thus, an angle of rotation of $360°$ has a measure of 2π radians, an angle of $180°$ has a measure of π radians, and an angle of $-90°$ has a measure of $-\frac{\pi}{2}$ radians.

When the length of the arc determined by an angle of rotation equals the radius, the measure of the angle is 1 radian. Because an arc length of 1 radian represents $\frac{1}{2\pi}$ of the entire circumference, 1 radian $= \frac{1}{2\pi} \cdot 360°$, or about $57°$.

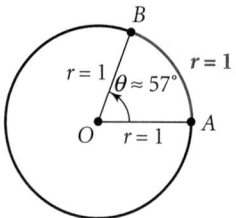

You can convert from degrees to radians, and vice versa, by using the relationship below to *multiply by 1*.

$$1 = \frac{1 \text{ rotation}}{1 \text{ rotation}} = \frac{2\pi \text{ radians}}{360° \text{ degrees}} = \frac{\pi \text{ radians}}{180° \text{ degrees}}$$

CONVERTING ANGLE MEASURES	
Degrees to radians	**Radians to degrees**
Multiply by $\dfrac{\pi \text{ radians}}{180°}$.	Multiply by $\dfrac{180°}{\pi \text{ radians}}$.

E X A M P L E ❶ **Convert from degrees to radians and from radians to degrees.**

a. $40°$ **b.** 3π radians

● **SOLUTION**

a. $40° \cdot \dfrac{\pi \text{ radians}}{180°} = \dfrac{2\pi}{9}$ radians   **b.** $3\pi \cdot \dfrac{180°}{\pi \text{ radians}} = 540°$

TRY THIS   Convert $-120°$ to radians and $-\frac{2}{3}\pi$ radians to degrees.

CHECKPOINT ✔ How many radians correspond to $1°$?

E X A M P L E ❷ **Evaluate. Give exact values.**

a. $\sin \dfrac{\pi}{3}$ **b.** $\cos \dfrac{3\pi}{4}$ **c.** $\tan \dfrac{4\pi}{3}$

● **SOLUTION**

Convert from radians to degrees. Then evaluate.

a. $\dfrac{\pi}{3} \times \dfrac{180°}{\pi} = 60°$ **b.** $\dfrac{3\pi}{4} \times \dfrac{180°}{\pi} = 135°$ **c.** $\dfrac{4\pi}{3} \times \dfrac{180°}{\pi} = 240°$

$\quad\quad \sin \dfrac{\pi}{3} = \sin 60°$ $\cos \dfrac{3\pi}{4} = \cos 135°$ $\tan \dfrac{4\pi}{3} = \tan 240°$

$\quad\quad\quad\quad = \dfrac{\sqrt{3}}{2}$ $= -\dfrac{\sqrt{2}}{2}$ $= \sqrt{3}$

TRY THIS   Evaluate $\sin \dfrac{3\pi}{2}$, $\cos \dfrac{2\pi}{3}$, and $\tan \dfrac{5\pi}{4}$. Give exact values.

CHECKPOINT ✔ Draw a unit circle and label all of the special angles in radians from 0 to 2π.

Arc Length

A circle with a radius of r and a central angle of θ, whose vertex at the center of the circle, is shown at right. You can use proportions to find a formula for the length of the intercepted arc, s, as follows:

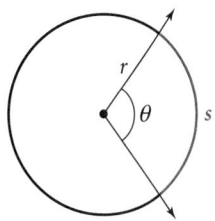

radian measure of θ $\rightarrow$ $\dfrac{\theta}{2\pi} = \dfrac{s}{2\pi r}$ $\leftarrow$ arc length of θ
radian measure of circle $\rightarrow$ $\phantom{\dfrac{\theta}{2\pi} = }$ $\leftarrow$ arc length of circle

$$\theta = \frac{s}{r} \quad \textit{Multiply each side by } 2\pi.$$

$$s = r\theta$$

Arc Length

If θ is the radian measure of a central angle in a circle with a radius of r, then the length, s, of the arc intercepted by θ is $s = r\theta$.

CRITICAL THINKING Define radian measure by using the definition of arc length. What does your definition tell you about the units for radians?

E X A M P L E ❸ A central angle in a circle with a diameter of 30 meters measures $\frac{\pi}{3}$ radians. Find the length of the arc intercepted by this angle.

⬤ **SOLUTION**

Because the diameter is 30 meters, the radius is 15 meters.

$$s = r\theta$$
$$s = 15\left(\frac{\pi}{3}\right)$$
$$s = 5\pi$$

The arc length is 5π meters, or about 15.7 meters.

TRY THIS A central angle in a circle with a radius of 1.25 feet measures 0.6 radian. Find the length of the arc intercepted by this angle.

Merry-go-round

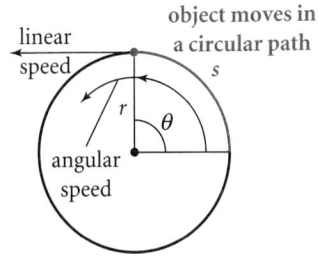

When an object is moving at a constant speed in a circular path with a radius of r, the **linear speed** of the object is a measure of how fast the position of the object changes and is given by $\frac{s}{t}$, or $\frac{r\theta}{t}$, where t is time and θ is an angle measure in radians. This is a form of the ratio $\frac{\text{distance}}{\text{time}}$.

The **angular speed** of the object is a measure of how fast the angle of rotation for the object changes and is given by $\frac{\theta}{t}$, where θ is an angle measure in radians and t is time.

Refer to the weather satellite described at the beginning of the lesson. Assume that the radius of the Earth is 3960 miles.

a. What is the linear speed of the satellite?

b. What is the angular speed of the satellite?

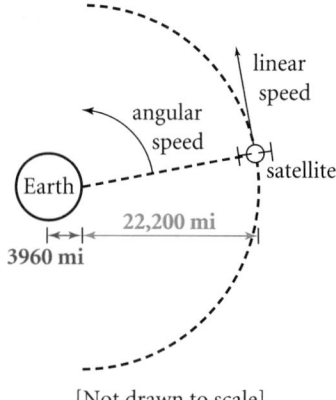

[Not drawn to scale]

SOLUTION

a. Find the radius of the satellite's orbit.

$$\begin{array}{lll} \text{radius of} & = & \text{Earth's} & + & \text{satellite's} \\ \text{orbit} & & \text{radius} & & \text{altitude} \end{array}$$

$$= 3960 + 22{,}200$$

$$= 26{,}160$$

Find the linear speed of the satellite if it makes one complete revolution (2π radians) in 24 hours.

$$\text{linear speed} = \frac{r\theta}{t}$$

$$= \frac{26{,}160 \cdot 2\pi}{24}$$

$$\approx 6848$$

The linear speed of the satellite is about 6848 miles per hour.

b. Use the formula for angular speed.

$$\text{angular speed} = \frac{\theta}{t}$$

$$= \frac{2\pi}{24}$$

$$= \frac{\pi}{12}$$

The angular speed of the satellite is $\frac{\pi}{12}$ radians per hour.

Computer enhanced image from a weather satellite

TRY THIS   Find the linear and angular speeds of a person standing on Earth, 3960 miles from its center.

Exercises

Communicate

1. Explain what the radian measure of an angle is and how it differs from degree measure.

2. Describe how to convert from radians to degrees and vice versa.

3. What happens to the length of an arc intercepted by a given central angle of a circle if the radius of the circle is doubled? Why?

4. Describe the linear and angular speeds associated with circular motion. How do they differ?

Guided Skills Practice

Convert from degrees to radians and from radians to degrees.
(EXAMPLE 1)

5. $120°$

6. $\frac{\pi}{4}$ radians

Evaluate. Give exact values. *(EXAMPLE 2)*

7. $\sin \frac{2\pi}{3}$

8. $\cos \frac{5\pi}{4}$

9. $\tan \frac{5\pi}{3}$

10. A central angle in a circle with a diameter of 90 centimeters measures $\frac{4\pi}{3}$ radians. Find the length of the arc intercepted by this angle. *(EXAMPLE 3)*

11. ENTERTAINMENT The outer 14 feet of the Space Needle Restaurant in Seattle rotates once every 58 minutes. Find the linear speed in feet per minute of a person sitting by the window of this restaurant if the diameter of the restaurant is 194.5 feet. How fast is this in miles per hour? *(EXAMPLE 4)*

Seattle's Space Needle

Practice and Apply

**Homework
Help Online**
Go To: **go.hrw.com**
Keyword:
MB1 Homework Help
for Exercises 12–35

Convert each degree measure to radian measure. Give exact answers.

12. $180°$ **13.** $90°$ **14.** $360°$ **15.** $270°$

16. $-30°$ **17.** $-120°$ **18.** $-210°$ **19.** $-240°$

20. $720°$ **21.** $930°$ **22.** $80°$ **23.** $160°$

Convert each radian measure to degree measure. Round answers to the nearest tenth of a degree.

24. 2π **25.** π **26.** $\frac{\pi}{2}$ **27.** $\frac{\pi}{4}$

28. $\frac{\pi}{3}$ **29.** $\frac{\pi}{6}$ **30.** $-\frac{\pi}{2}$ **31.** $-\frac{\pi}{4}$

32. -3.91 **33.** -9.799 **34.** 9.27 **35.** 4.96

Evaluate each expression. Give exact values.

36. $\sin \pi$ **37.** $\cos \pi$ **38.** $\cos \frac{\pi}{3}$ **39.** $\sin \frac{7\pi}{6}$

40. $\sin\left(-\frac{\pi}{6}\right)$ **41.** $\cos\left(-\frac{5\pi}{3}\right)$ **42.** $\tan \pi$ **43.** $\tan \frac{\pi}{4}$

44. $\cos \frac{2\pi}{3}$ **45.** $\cos\left(-\frac{7\pi}{4}\right)$ **46.** $\sin \frac{11\pi}{2}$ **47.** $\cos 5\pi$

48. $\tan \frac{9\pi}{4}$ **49.** $\sec \frac{\pi}{4}$ **50.** $\cot \frac{\pi}{6}$ **51.** $\csc\left(-\frac{\pi}{3}\right)$

A circle has a diameter of 10 meters. For each central angle measure below, find the length in meters of the arc intercepted by the angle.

52. 3.8 radians   **53.** 2.4 radians   **54.** 45 radians

55. 72 radians   **56.** 4.28 radians   **57.** 0.67 radians

58. $\frac{\pi}{3}$ radians   **59.** $\frac{2\pi}{3}$ radians   **60.** $\frac{\pi}{4}$ radians

61. $\frac{\pi}{2}$ radians   **62.** $\frac{7\pi}{4}$ radians   **63.** $\frac{7\pi}{6}$ radians

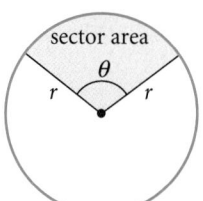

NNECTION

GEOMETRY The **area of a sector**, A, which resembles the slice of a pie, is a fraction $\left(\frac{\theta}{2\pi}\right)$ of the area of a complete circle (πr^2), so $A = \frac{\theta}{2\pi} \cdot \pi r^2 = \frac{1}{2}r^2\theta$, where θ is the measure of the central angle in radians.

64. Find the area of a sector with a central angle of $\frac{7\pi}{6}$ radians in a circle with a radius of 20 meters.

65. Find the central angle for a sector with an area of 55.5 square inches in a circle with a radius of 12 inches.

APPLICATIONS

ENGINEERING The rear windshield wiper shown below moves through an angle of $\frac{3\pi}{4}$ radians in 0.9 second at normal speed.

66. Find the approximate distances traveled by a point on the top end of the wiper and by a point on the bottom end of the wiper in one sweep of the wiper.

67. Find the approximate linear speeds in inches per second of a point at the top end of the wiper and of a point at the bottom end of the wiper. What are these speeds in miles per hour?

TECHNOLOGY A CD player rotates a CD at different speeds depending on where the laser is reading the disc. Assume that information is stored within a 6-centimeter diameter on the disc.

68. Find the linear speed of a point on the outer edge of the CD when the CD player is rotating at 200 revolutions per minute.

69. Find the linear speed of a point 2 centimeters from the outer edge of the CD when the CD player is rotating at 240 revolutions per minute.

AUTO RACING In 17.5 seconds, a car covers an arc intercepted by a central angle of 120° on a circular track with a radius of 300 meters.

70. What is the car's linear speed in meters per second?

71. What is the car's angular speed in radians per second?

72. MACHINERY The large gear shown at right rotates through angle θ_1 (measured in radians), causing the small gear to rotate through angle θ_2. Find an expression for θ_2 in terms of θ_1, r_1, and r_2.

 Look Back

Solve each inequality. Graph the solution on a number line. *(LESSON 1.8)*

73. $|x - 4| \leq -2$ **74.** $|2 - x| > 1$ **75.** $|3x + 5| < 4$

Multiply. *(LESSON 5.6)*

76. $(1 + i)(2 + 3i)$ **77.** $(1 - 2i)(-2 + i)$ **78.** $(3 + 4i)(2 - 3i)$

Solve each equation. Round your answers to the nearest hundredth. *(LESSON 6.3)*

79. $4^x = 35$ **80.** $\log x^2 = 4$ **81.** $3\log(x + 1) = 5$

Solve each rational equation algebraically. Check your solutions by any method. *(LESSON 8.5)*

82. $\dfrac{x - 3}{x + 5} = \dfrac{x}{x + 1}$ **83.** $\dfrac{x - 8}{2x} = \dfrac{x}{6}$ **84.** $\dfrac{y}{y - 4} - \dfrac{y}{y + 2} = \dfrac{5}{y^2 - 2y - 8}$

Make relative frequency table and histogram of probabilities for each set of data. *(LESSON 12.2)*

85. 3, 4, 5, 4, 5, 6, 5, 7, 4, 5, 2, 1, 3, 4, 7, 5, 3, 4, 6, 5, 4, 8, 6, 3, 3

86. 69, 74, 66, 68, 72, 74, 67, 71, 73, 67, 67, 65, 66, 67, 66, 70, 72

 Look Beyond

87 Graph $y = \sin x$ and $y = \cos x$ over the interval $-4\pi \leq x \leq 4\pi$, and compare the graphs.

Refer to the Cosmoclock 21 described in the Portfolio Activity on page 835.

1. If the Cosmoclock 21 completes 1.5 revolutions per minute, how many seconds does it take to make 1 complete revolution? $\frac{1}{4}$ of a revolution?

2. Refer to the table of values that you created in Step 4 of the Portfolio Activity on page 850. Find the corresponding time in seconds for each angle of rotation in the table.

3. Plot the altitude of P versus time on graph paper. Sketch a *smooth curve* through the points.

4. What is the period of the graph? What does the period represent?

5. Find the linear speed of a rider on the Cosmoclock 21.

WORKING ON THE CHAPTER PROJECT

You should now be able to complete Activity 3 of the Chapter Project.

Graphing Trigonometric Functions

Why *The graphs of trigonometric functions can be used to model real-world events such as the changes in air pressure that create sounds.*

Objectives

• Graph the sine, cosine, and tangent functions and their transformations.

• Use the sine function to solve problems.

APPLICATION

ACOUSTICS

Sound occurs when an object, such as a speaker, vibrates. This vibration causes small changes in air pressure, which travel away from the object in waves. The sound from an electric keyboard can be modeled by a transformed graph of a trigonometric function. *You will do this in Example 3.*

Activity
Exploring Trigonometric Graphs

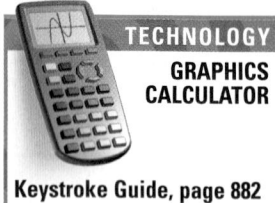

TECHNOLOGY

GRAPHICS CALCULATOR

Keystroke Guide, page 882

You will need: a graphics calculator

Using radian, parametric, and simultaneous modes, enter $x_{1t} = \cos t$ and $y_{1t} = \sin t$ to generate the unit circle, and enter $x_{2t} = t$ and $y_{2t} = \sin t$ for the function. Set a square viewing window such that t takes on values from 0 to 2π inclusive.

1. Graph the equations and watch as both curves emerge simultaneously. What is the function that you have just graphed?

CHECKPOINT ✔ 2. Describe any relationships that you see between the two curves during the graphing process. You can also use the trace feature to compare x- and y-values with t-values.

CHECKPOINT ✔ 3. **a.** What is the period of the function?

  b. Predict how the curves will change for $x_{1t} = 2 \cos t$, $y_{1t} = 2 \sin t$, $x_{2t} = t$, and $y_{2t} = 2 \sin t$. Check your prediction by graphing.

  c. Predict how the curves will differ from the original curves for $x_{1t} = \cos 3t$, $y_{1t} = \sin 3t$, $x_{2t} = t$, and $y_{2t} = \sin 3t$. Check your prediction by graphing. (Watch the graphing of the circle carefully.)

4. Repeat Steps 1–3 for $y_{2t} = \cos t$ and $y_{2t} = \tan t$.

The Sine and Cosine Functions

Recall from Lesson 13.3 that one period of the parent function $y = \sin \theta$ or $y = \cos \theta$ is 360°

The table of values at right and the graphs below show one period of the sine and cosine function over the interval $0° \le \theta \le 360°$.

The vertical line segments in the unit circle next to the graph below of $y = \sin \theta$ represent selected values of $\sin \theta$ that can be used to construct the graph.

The horizontal line segments in the unit circle next to the graph below of $y = \cos \theta$ represent selected values of $\cos \theta$ that can be used to construct the graph.

θ	$y = \sin \theta$ Exact	$y = \sin \theta$ Approx.	$y = \cos \theta$ Exact	$y = \cos \theta$ Approx.
0°	0	0.00	1	1.00
30°	$\frac{1}{2}$	0.50	$\frac{\sqrt{3}}{2}$	0.87
45°	$\frac{\sqrt{2}}{2}$	0.71	$\frac{\sqrt{2}}{2}$	0.71
60°	$\frac{\sqrt{3}}{2}$	0.87	$\frac{1}{2}$	0.50
90°	1	1.00	0	0.00
120°	$\frac{\sqrt{3}}{2}$	0.87	$-\frac{1}{2}$	−0.50
135°	$\frac{\sqrt{2}}{2}$	0.71	$-\frac{\sqrt{2}}{2}$	−0.71
150°	$\frac{1}{2}$	0.50	$-\frac{\sqrt{3}}{2}$	−0.87
180°	0	0.00	−1	−1.00
210°	$-\frac{1}{2}$	−0.50	$-\frac{\sqrt{3}}{2}$	−0.87
225°	$-\frac{\sqrt{2}}{2}$	−0.71	$-\frac{\sqrt{2}}{2}$	−0.71
240°	$-\frac{\sqrt{3}}{2}$	−0.87	$-\frac{1}{2}$	−0.50
270°	−1	−1.00	0	0.00
300°	$-\frac{\sqrt{3}}{2}$	−0.87	$\frac{1}{2}$	0.50
315°	$-\frac{\sqrt{2}}{2}$	−0.71	$\frac{\sqrt{2}}{2}$	0.71
330°	$-\frac{1}{2}$	−0.50	$\frac{\sqrt{3}}{2}$	0.87
360°	0	0.00	1	1.00

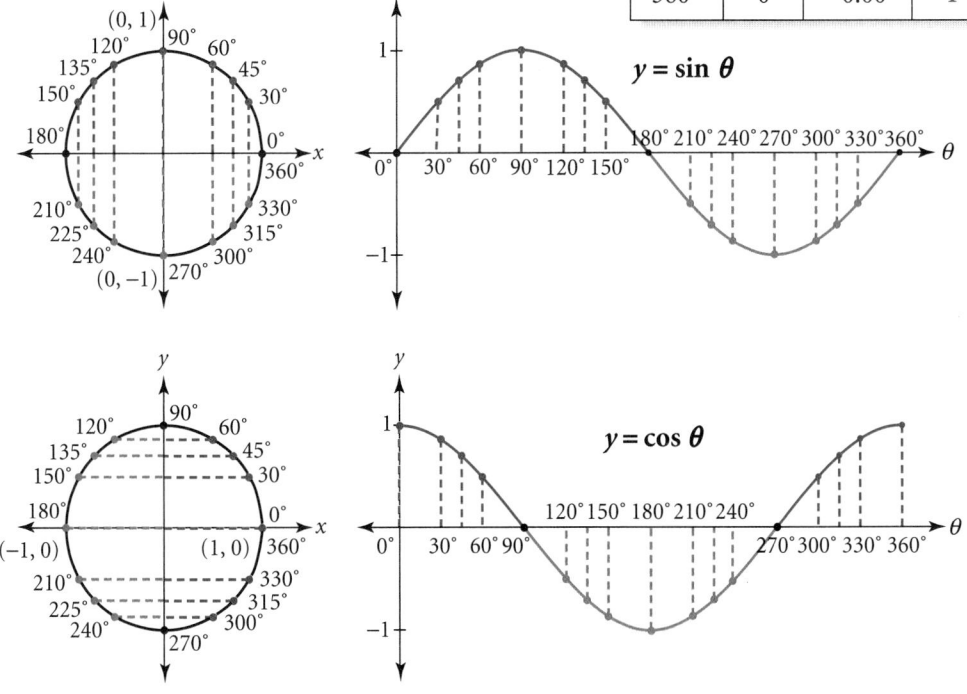

$y = \sin \theta$

$y = \cos \theta$

Stretches and Compressions

Transformations of the sine and cosine functions are quite common in real-world applications. Recall from Lesson 2.7 that the graph of the function $y = af(x)$ is a vertical stretch or compression of the graph of the parent function $y = f(x)$ by a factor of a. Similarly, the graph of $y = f(bx)$ is a horizontal stretch or compression of the graph of $y = f(x)$ by a factor of $\frac{1}{|b|}$.

EXAMPLE **Graph at least one period of each trigonometric function along with its parent function.**

CONNECTION

TRANSFORMATIONS

a. $y = 2 \sin \theta$ b. $y = \cos \frac{1}{2}\theta$

SOLUTION

a. The 2 causes the function values to be twice as big, so the graph of $y = 2 \sin \theta$ is a vertical stretch of the graph of $y = \sin \theta$ by a factor of 2. Because the zeros are the same as in the parent function, this kind of transformation is relatively easy to graph without creating a table of values.

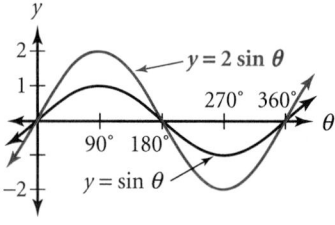

b. The values of θ are multiplied by $\frac{1}{2}$, so the curve "unfolds" half as fast, or takes twice as long to "unfold." The graph of $y = \cos \frac{1}{2}\theta$ is a horizontal stretch of the graph of $y = \cos \theta$ by a factor of 2. Note that the graph of $y = \cos \theta$ completes one period over the interval $0° \le \theta \le 360°$, while the graph of $y = \cos \frac{1}{2}\theta$ completes one period over the interval $0° \le \theta \le 720°$.

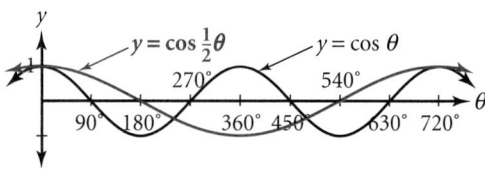

TRY THIS   Graph at least one period of each trigonometric function along with its parent function.

a. $y = \frac{1}{3} \cos \theta$ b. $y = \sin 3\theta$

The **amplitude** of a periodic function is defined as follows:

$$\text{amplitude} = \frac{1}{2}(\text{maximum value} - \text{minimum value})$$

Because $y = \sin \theta$ and $y = \cos \theta$ each have a minimum of -1 and a maximum of 1, the amplitude of each function is $\frac{1}{2}[1 - (-1)] = 1$.

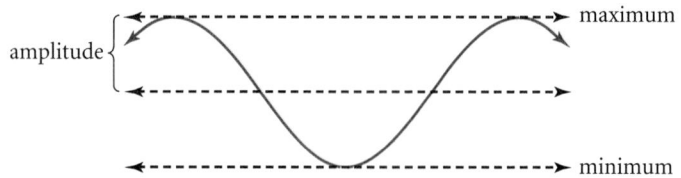

CHECKPOINT ✔ What is the amplitude of $y = 2 \sin \theta$ in Example 1? of $y = \frac{1}{4} \cos 3\theta$?

Translations

Recall from Lesson 2.7 that the graph of $y = f(x - h)$ is a horizontal translation of the graph of $y = f(x)$. The translation is h units to the right for $h > 0$ and $|h|$ units to the left for $h < 0$. A horizontal translation of a sine or cosine function is also called a **phase shift.** The graph of $y = f(x) + k$ is a vertical translation of the graph of $y = f(x)$. The translation is k units up for $k > 0$ and $|k|$ units down for $k < 0$.

E X A M P L E ❷

CONNECTION
TRANSFORMATIONS

Graph at least one period of each trigonometric function along with its parent function.

    a. $y = \sin(\theta + 45°)$ **b.** $y = \cos \theta + 1$

SOLUTION

  a. Rewrite $y = \sin(\theta + 45°)$ in the form $y = \sin(\theta - h)$.

$$y = \sin[\theta - (-45°)]$$

The graph of $y = \sin(\theta + 45°)$ is a horizontal translation 45° to the left of the graph of $y = \sin \theta$. This is reasonable because when 45° is added to the values of θ, the graph unfolds 45° *sooner.*

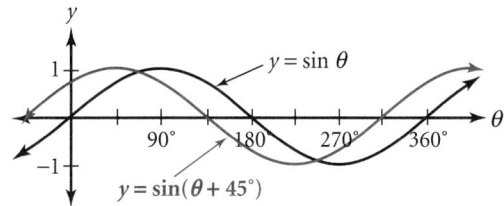

  b. The graph of $y = \cos \theta + 1$ is a vertical translation of the graph of $y = \cos \theta$ 1 unit up. This is reasonable because 1 is added to each function value.

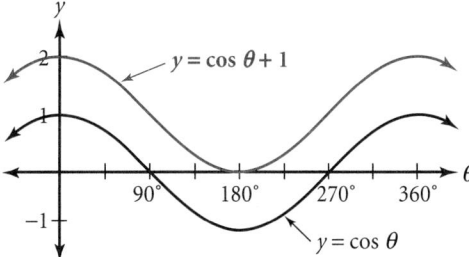

TRY THIS

Graph at least one period of each trigonometric function along with its parent function.

    a. $y = \cos(\theta - 45°)$ **b.** $y = \sin \theta - 1$

CRITICAL THINKING

Write the translated sine function and the translated cosine function represented by the graph below.

The function $y = a \sin b(t - c)$, where t is in radians and y represents relative air pressure, can represent a particular sound as follows:

- The amplitude of the graph, a, represents the relative *intensity* of the changes in air pressure. A higher intensity results in a louder sound.
- The frequency of the sound wave, measured in units called hertz (Hz), or cycles per second, determines the pitch of the sound. The value of b in the function is equal to the frequency multiplied by 2π.
- The phase shift, c, represents the change in the position of the sound wave over time.
- The period of the sound wave is the reciprocal of the frequency.

E X A M P L E ③

APPLICATION
ACOUSTICS

A particular sound has a frequency of 55 hertz and an amplitude of 3.

a. Write a transformed sine function to represent this sound.

b. Write a new function that represents a phase shift of $\frac{1}{2}$ of a period to the right of the function from part **a**. Then use a graphics calculator to graph at least one period of both functions on the same coordinate plane.

● **SOLUTION**

a. The parent function is $y = \sin t$. Write the transformed function in the form $y = a \sin b(t - c)$.

Denyce Graves singing in the opera Carmen

The amplitude is 3.	$a = 3$
The frequency is related to b.	$b = 2\pi \times 55 = 110\pi$
There is no phase shift.	$c = 0$

Thus, the transformed function is $y = 3 \sin 110\pi t$.

b. The period is the reciprocal of the frequency: $\frac{1}{55}$. One-half of the period is $\frac{1}{2} \times \frac{1}{55} = \frac{1}{110}$. Thus, a phase shift of $\frac{1}{110}$ radian to the right of the function $y = 3 \sin 110\pi t$ is given by $y = 3 \sin 110\pi\left(t - \frac{1}{110}\right)$. Graph both functions in radian mode.

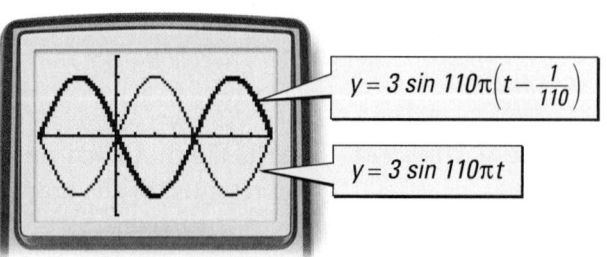

$y = 3 \sin 110\pi\left(t - \frac{1}{110}\right)$

$y = 3 \sin 110\pi t$

TRY THIS Write the function for a sound with a frequency of 120 hertz, an amplitude of 1.5, and a phase shift of $\frac{1}{3}$ of a period to the left. Graph at least one period of the function along with its parent function.

The Tangent Function

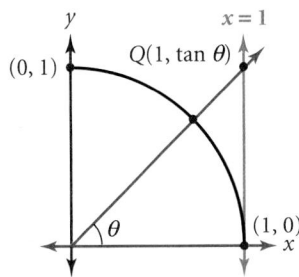

$Q(1, \tan \theta)$

$(0, 1)$

$x = 1$

$(1, 0)$

The terminal side of θ intersects the tangent line $x = 1$ at Q.

The sine and cosine functions are related to the coordinates of the points on a unit circle. The tangent function, however, relates to the points on a line *tangent* to the unit circle. Recall from geometry that a **tangent line** is perpendicular to a radius of the circle and touches the circle at only one point.

The table of values and graph for $y = \tan \theta$ below show that its period is 180°. The graph of $y = \tan \theta$ has vertical asymptotes where the function is undefined and has no amplitude because its range is all real numbers.

θ		$-90°$ $90°$	$-60°$ $120°$	$-45°$ $135°$	$-30°$ $150°$	$0°$ $180°$	$30°$ $210°$	$45°$ $225°$	$60°$ $240°$
$\tan \theta$	exact	not defined	$-\sqrt{3}$	-1	$-\frac{\sqrt{3}}{3}$	0	$\frac{\sqrt{3}}{3}$	1	$\sqrt{3}$
	approx.	not defined	-1.73	-1	-0.58	0	0.58	1	1.73

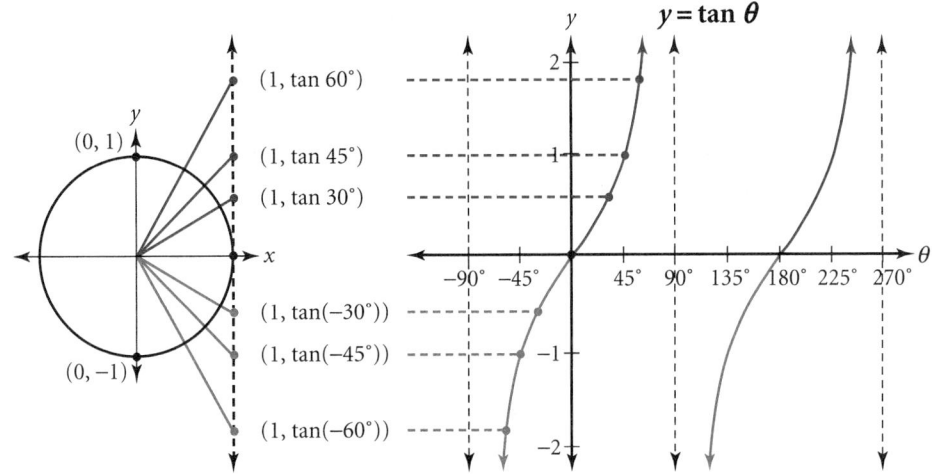

EXAMPLE ④ Graph at least one period of $y = 3 \tan \frac{\theta}{2}$ along with its parent function.

CONNECTION

TRANSFORMATIONS

SOLUTION

Make a table of approximate values. Then graph.

θ	$\frac{\theta}{2}$	$\tan \frac{\theta}{2}$	$3 \tan \frac{\theta}{2}$
$-180°$	$-90°$	not defined	not defined
$-120°$	$-60°$	-1.73	-5.20
$-90°$	$-45°$	-1	-3
$0°$	$0°$	0	0
$90°$	$45°$	1	3
$120°$	$60°$	1.73	5.20
$180°$	$90°$	not defined	not defined

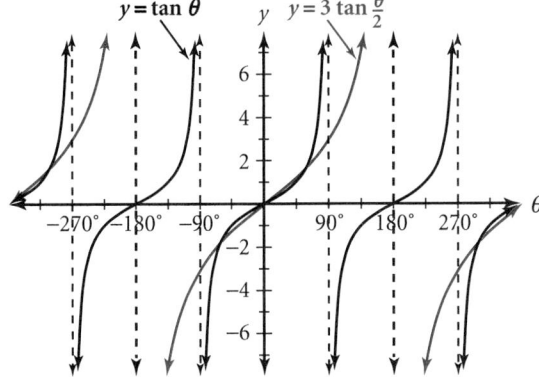

Notice that the graph of $y = 3 \tan \frac{\theta}{2}$ is a horizontal stretch of the graph of $y = \tan \theta$ by a factor of 2 and a vertical stretch by a factor of 3.

TRY THIS   Graph at least one period of $y = \frac{1}{2} \tan \theta - 3$ along with its parent function.

Exercises

Communicate

1. Compare and contrast the graph of $y = \sin \theta$ with the graph of $y = \cos \theta$.

2. Describe the shape of the graph of the tangent function.

3. Explain why the amplitude of $y = -4 \sin \theta$ is larger than that of $y = 3 \sin \theta + 2$.

4. Describe at least four ways in which the graph of $y = \tan \theta$ differs from the graph of $y = \sin \theta$.

Guided Skills Practice

Graph at least one period of each trigonometric function along with its parent function. *(EXAMPLE 1)*

5. $y = \frac{1}{3} \cos \theta$

6. $y = \sin \frac{3}{2}\theta$

Graph at least one period of each trigonometric function along with its parent function. *(EXAMPLE 2)*

7. $y = \cos(\theta - 90°)$

8. $y = \sin \theta - 1.5$

9. Write the function for a sound with a frequency of 30 hertz, an amplitude of 2, and a phase shift of $\frac{1}{4}$ of a period to the left. Graph at least one period of the function. *(EXAMPLE 3)*

10. Graph at least one period of the function $y = \frac{3}{2} \tan 3\theta$ along with its parent function. *(EXAMPLE 4)*

Practice and Apply

Identify the amplitude, if it exists, and the period of each function.

11. $y = 2.5 \sin 2\theta$

12. $y = 1.5 \sin 4\theta$

13. $y = 4.5 \tan 3\theta$

14. $y = -4 \tan 3\theta$

15. $y = -5 \cos \frac{1}{2}\theta$

16. $y = -6 \sin \frac{1}{4}\theta$

17. $y = 3 \cos(\theta + 90°)$

18. $y = -2 \sin(\theta - 30°)$

19. $y = -\sin(\theta + 45°)$

Identify the phase shift and the vertical translation of each function from its parent function.

20. $y = \sin(\theta - 90°) + 3$

21. $y = \cos(\theta - 45°) - 2$

22. $y = \cos(\theta + 30°) - 2$

23. $y = \sin(\theta + 60°) + 1$

24. $y = 3 - \sin(\theta - 45°)$

25. $y = 2 + \cos(\theta + 30°)$

26. $y = 4 \cos[3(\theta + 180°)] + 1$

27. $y = 3 \sin[2(\theta - 135°)] - 3$

Describe the transformation of each function from its parent function. Then graph at least one period of the function along with its parent function.

28. $y = 2 \cos \theta$ **29.** $y = 4 \sin \theta$

30. $y = -2 \sin \theta$ **31.** $y = -3 \cos \theta$

32. $y = \sin(\theta - 90°)$ **33.** $y = \cos(\theta + 90°)$

34. $y = 3 \cos(\theta + 90°)$ **35.** $y = 2 \sin(\theta - 90°)$

36. $y = -4 \cos \frac{1}{2}\theta$ **37.** $y = -2 \cos \frac{1}{3}\theta$

38. $y = \frac{1}{2} \sin 3\theta$ **39.** $y = \frac{1}{3} \sin 2\theta$

40. $y = 3 \tan \theta$ **41.** $y = 2 \tan \theta$

42. $y = \tan \theta + 3$ **43.** $y = \tan \theta - 2$

44. $y = \tan 2\theta$ **45.** $y = \tan 3\theta$

46. $y = 2 \tan \frac{1}{3}\theta$ **47.** $y = 3 \tan \frac{1}{2}\theta$

CHALLENGE

48. Write a function of the form $f(\theta) = a \cos[b(\theta - c)] + d$ for the graph below.

APPLICATIONS

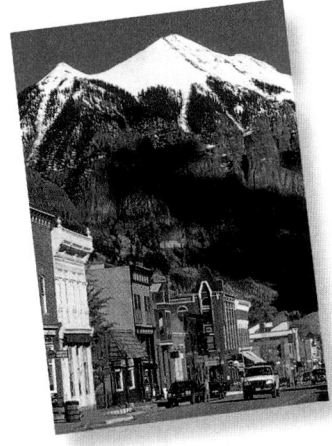

EMPLOYMENT The number of people employed in a resort town can be modeled by the function $g(x) = 1.5 \sin\left(\frac{\pi x}{6} + 1\right) + 5.2$, where x is the month of the year (beginning with 1 for January) and $g(x)$ is the number of people (in thousands) employed in the town that month.

49. What type of resort might this be? Explain.

50. About how many people are permanently employed in the town?

51. About how many people are employed in February?

52. Find two months when there are about 4500 people employed in the town.

53. If a major year-round business in the town were to close, which one of the constants in the function model would decrease?

TEMPERATURE The temperature in an air-conditioned office on a hot day can be modeled by the function $t(x) = 1.5 \cos\left(\frac{\pi x}{12}\right) + 67$, where x is the time in minutes after the air conditioner is turned on and $t(x)$ is the temperature in degrees Fahrenheit after x minutes.

54. How long does the air conditioner run after being turned on?

55. Find the maximum and minimum temperatures in the office building.

56. Find the temperature 10 minutes after the air conditioner is turned on.

57. Adjust the function to model the temperature in the office when the thermostat is set to a higher temperature.

Look Back

58. INCOME When Julie baby-sat for 4 hours and did yard work for 4 hours, she made a total of $47. When she baby-sat for 7 hours and did yard work for 2 hours, she made a total of $51. How much does Julie get paid for each type of work? *(LESSON 3.2)*

Write each pair of parametric equations as a single equation in x and y. (LESSON 3.6)

59. $\begin{cases} x(t) = 2t + 1 \\ y(t) = 2t - 3 \end{cases}$ **60.** $\begin{cases} x(t) = t - 2 \\ y(t) = 4t + 1 \end{cases}$ **61.** $\begin{cases} x(t) = 2t + 1 \\ y(t) = 8t + 13 \end{cases}$

Solve each system of equations by using a matrix equation. Give answers to the nearest hundredth. (LESSON 4.4)

62 $\begin{cases} 2.25x + 3.78y = 11.78 \\ 3.56x + 4.89y = 9.67 \end{cases}$ **63** $\begin{cases} 3.87x + 8.45y = 7.48 \\ 6.67x + 8.36y = 9.85 \end{cases}$

Find x to the nearest ten-thousandth. (LESSONS 6.3 AND 6.5)

64. $e^{2x+1} = 13$ **65.** $e^{3x-2} = 25$ **66.** $2^{2x+4} = 20$ **67.** $2^{3x-21} = 31$

 Look Beyond

68 Graph the functions $f(x) = \sin x$ and $f(x) = \dfrac{1}{\sin x}$ on the same axes. Compare their graphs. How are they alike? How are they different?

69 Graph the functions $f(x) = \cos x$ and $f(x) = \dfrac{1}{\cos x}$ on the same axes. Compare their graphs. How are they alike? How are they different?

Using the definitions from Lesson 13.1, make a table of values and graph each function.

70. $y = \sec \theta$ **71.** $y = \csc \theta$ **72.** $y = \cot \theta$

Refer to the data and the graph you created in the Portfolio Activity on page 857.

1. Find the amplitude of your graph. What does the amplitude represent in terms of the Cosmoclock 21?

2. Write an equation of the form $y = a \sin bt$ to model the data that was graphed.

3. Create a scatter plot of the data. Then graph your equation on the same coordinate axes as your scatter plot. Is the equation a good model for the data? Explain.

WORKING ON THE CHAPTER PROJECT

You should now be able to complete Activity 4 of the Chapter Project.

13.6

Inverses of Trigonometric Functions

Why *You can use inverses of trigonometric functions to solve real-world problems, such as finding the angle of depression between a supersonic aircraft and the ground.*

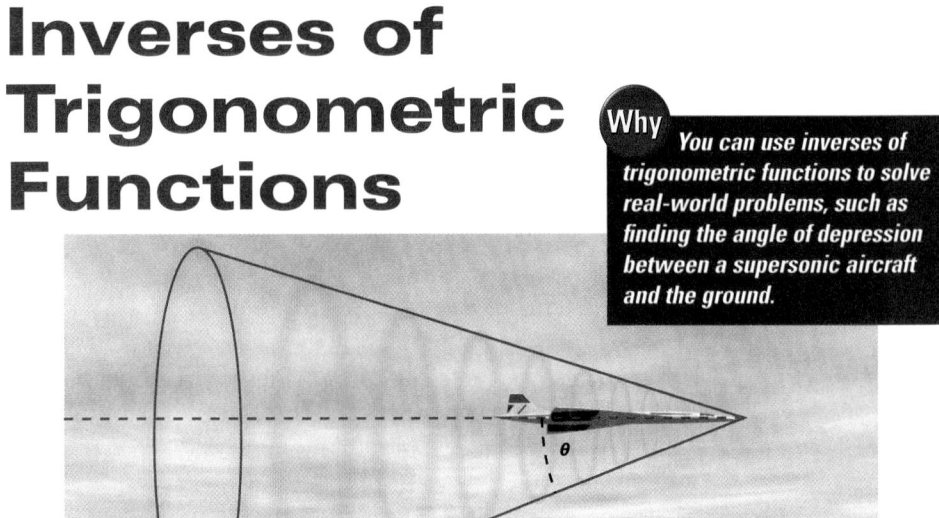

Objective

- Evaluate trigonometric expressions involving inverses.

APPLICATION

AVIATION

When an aircraft flies faster than the speed of sound, which is about 730 miles per hour, shock waves in the shape of a cone are created. When the cone passes a person on the ground, a sonic boom is heard.

The speed of an aircraft can be expressed as a *Mach number*, which gives the aircraft's speed relative to the speed of sound. For example, an aircraft flying at 1000 miles per hour has a speed of $\frac{1000}{730}$, or about Mach 1.4. If θ is the angle of depression between the aircraft and the ground, then θ depends on the speed of the aircraft in Mach numbers as follows:

$$\sin \theta = \frac{1}{\text{speed of aircraft}}$$

What is θ if the speed of the aircraft is Mach 1.3? Mach 1.8? *You will solve this problem in Example 4.*

In Lesson 2.5 you found inverse relations by interchanging the domain and range of the given relation or function. This procedure is used in the following Activity involving trigonometric functions.

Activity
Exploring the Inverse Relation of *y* = sin *x*

You will need: graph paper

1. Create a table of values and sketch the graph of $y = \sin x$ over the interval $-2\pi \le x \le 2\pi$. Use x-values of $0, \pm\frac{\pi}{2}, \pm\pi, \pm\frac{3\pi}{2}$, and $\pm 2\pi$.

2. Create a new table of ordered pairs by interchanging the x and y values in your table from Step 1. Plot the new ordered pairs on the same axes, and sketch the resulting curve, which represents $y = \sin^{-1} x$.

3. Add the line $y = x$ to your graph.

CHECKPOINT ✔ 4. Fold the graph paper along the line $y = x$. Describe what happens to the graphs of $y = \sin x$ and $y = \sin^{-1} x$ and what this result means.

CHECKPOINT ✔ 5. Describe what $y = \sin^{-1} x$ represents. Is $y = \sin^{-1} x$ a function? Explain.

Because the trigonometric functions are periodic, many values in their domains have the same function values. For example, examine the sine, cosine, and tangent of 30°, 390°, and −330° shown below.

$$\sin 30° = \frac{1}{2} \qquad \sin 390° = \frac{1}{2} \qquad \sin(-330°) = \frac{1}{2}$$

$$\cos 30° = \frac{\sqrt{3}}{2} \qquad \cos 390° = \frac{\sqrt{3}}{2} \qquad \cos(-330°) = \frac{\sqrt{3}}{2}$$

$$\tan 30° = \frac{1}{\sqrt{3}}, \text{ or } \frac{\sqrt{3}}{3} \qquad \tan 390° = \frac{1}{\sqrt{3}}, \text{ or } \frac{\sqrt{3}}{3} \qquad \tan(-330°) = \frac{1}{\sqrt{3}}, \text{ or } \frac{\sqrt{3}}{3}$$

These repeated function values are readily apparent in the graph of a trigonometric function. For example, examine the graph of $y = \sin \theta$ shown below.

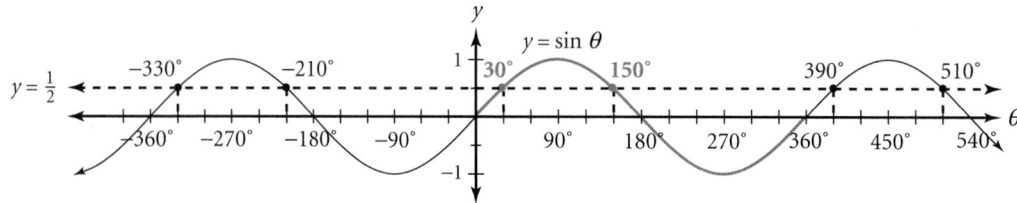

Recall from Lesson 13.1 that the inverse relations of the sine, cosine, and tangent functions are denoted as $y = \sin^{-1} x$, $y = \cos^{-1} x$, and $y = \tan^{-1} x$. To find all possible values of an inverse trigonometric function, such as $y = \sin^{-1} \frac{1}{2}$, first find all values that occur within one period. In the period between 0° and 360°, as shown above in blue, $\sin 30° = \frac{1}{2}$ and $\sin 150° = \frac{1}{2}$. Therefore, $\sin^{-1} \frac{1}{2} = 30°$ and $\sin^{-1} \frac{1}{2} = 150°$. The other values of $\sin^{-1} \frac{1}{2}$ occur at values every period before or after 30° and 150°. Thus, if n is an integer, then all possible values of $\sin^{-1} \frac{1}{2}$ occur at $30° + n360°$ and $150° + 360°$.

EXAMPLE ① Find all possible values of $\cos^{-1} \frac{1}{2}$.

SOLUTION

Find all possible values of $\cos^{-1} \frac{1}{2}$ within one period. The cosine function is positive in Quadrants I and IV.

$$\cos 60° = \frac{1}{2} \quad \textit{Quadrant I} \qquad \cos 300° = \frac{1}{2} \quad \textit{Quadrant IV}$$

Thus, all possible values of $\cos^{-1} \frac{1}{2}$ are $60° + n360°$ and $300° + n360°$.

TRY THIS Find all possible values of $\sin^{-1} \frac{\sqrt{2}}{2}$.

The graph of $y = \sin \theta$, shown above, clearly fails the horizontal-line test. Therefore, $y = \sin \theta$ is not a one-to-one function and its inverse cannot be a function. This is true for all trigonometric functions unless their domains are restricted in such a way that their inverses can be functions. The functions *Sine, Cosine,* and *Tangent* (denoted by capital letters) are defined as the sine, cosine, and tangent functions with the restricted domains defined on the next page. The restricted domains are called **principal values.**

Principal Values of Sin θ, Cos θ, and Tan θ

$$\text{Sin } \theta = \sin \theta \text{ for } -90° \leq \theta \leq 90°$$

$$\text{Cos } \theta = \cos \theta \text{ for } 0° \leq \theta \leq 180°$$

$$\text{Tan } \theta = \tan \theta \text{ for } -90° < \theta < 90°$$

The graph of $y = \sin \theta$ and the portion of the curve that represents $y = \text{Sin } \theta$ are shown below.

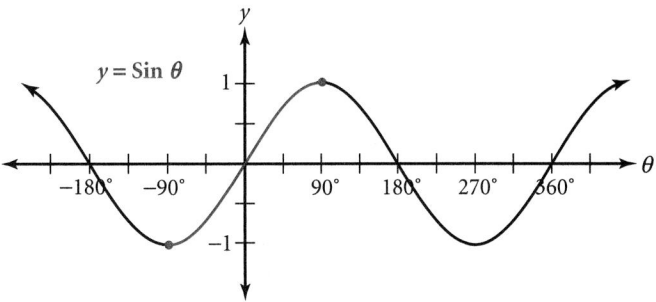

CHECKPOINT ✔ Graph $y = \cos \theta$ and $y = \tan \theta$ and indicate the portion of these curves that represent $y = \text{Cos } \theta$ and $y = \text{Tan } \theta$.

The functions $y = \text{Sin } \theta$, $y = \text{Cos } \theta$, and $y = \text{Tan } \theta$ are one-to-one functions and have inverses that are also functions. The inverse functions are denoted by $y = \text{Sin}^{-1} x$, $y = \text{Cos}^{-1} x$, and $y = \text{Tan}^{-1} x$, respectively.

Inverse Trigonometric Functions

If $y = \text{Sin } x$, then its inverse function is $y = \text{Sin}^{-1} x$.

If $y = \text{Cos } x$, then its inverse function is $y = \text{Cos}^{-1} x$.

If $y = \text{Tan } x$, then its inverse function is $y = \text{Tan}^{-1} x$.

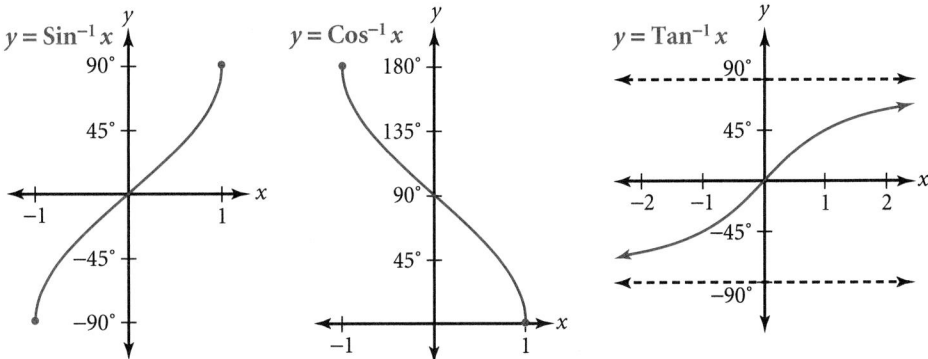

CHECKPOINT ✔ What is the range of $y = \text{Sin}^{-1} x$, of $y = \text{Cos}^{-1} x$, and of $y = \text{Tan}^{-1} x$?

M P L E **2** Evaluate each inverse trigonometric expression.

    a. $\text{Sin}^{-1} \frac{1}{2}$ **b.** $\text{Cos}^{-1}\left(-\frac{\sqrt{3}}{2}\right)$ **c.** $\text{Tan}^{-1}\left(-\frac{\sqrt{3}}{3}\right)$

● **SOLUTION**

a. Find the angle between the principal values $-90°$ and $90°$, inclusive, whose sine is $\frac{1}{2}$. Because $\sin 30° = \frac{1}{2}$, $\text{Sin}^{-1} \frac{1}{2} = 30°$.

b. Find the angle between the principal values $0°$ and $180°$, inclusive, whose cosine is $-\frac{\sqrt{3}}{2}$. Because $\cos 150° = -\frac{\sqrt{3}}{2}$, $\text{Cos}^{-1}\left(-\frac{\sqrt{3}}{2}\right) = 150°$.

c. Find the angle between the principal values $-90°$ and $90°$, inclusive, whose tangent is $-\frac{\sqrt{3}}{3}$. Because $\tan(-30°) = -\frac{\sqrt{3}}{3}$, $\text{Tan}^{-1}\left(-\frac{\sqrt{3}}{3}\right) = -30°$.

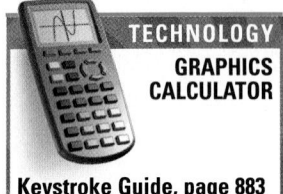
TECHNOLOGY
GRAPHICS CALCULATOR

Keystroke Guide, page 883

CHECK
A scientific or graphics calculator returns principal values for inverse trigonometric functions.

TRY THIS   Evaluate each inverse trigonometric expression.

    a. $\text{Sin}^{-1} \frac{\sqrt{3}}{2}$ **b.** $\text{Cos}^{-1}\left(-\frac{\sqrt{2}}{2}\right)$ **c.** $\text{Tan}^{-1} \sqrt{3}$

To evaluate an expression such as $\sin\left(\text{Cos}^{-1} \frac{\sqrt{3}}{2}\right)$, first evaluate the expression inside the parentheses. Then evaluate the resulting expression.

E X A M P L E **3** Evaluate each trigonometric expression.

    a. $\sin\left(\text{Cos}^{-1} \frac{\sqrt{3}}{2}\right)$ **b.** $\text{Tan}^{-1}(\cos 180°)$

● **SOLUTION**

a. Because $\cos 30° = \frac{\sqrt{3}}{2}$, substitute $30°$ for $\text{Cos}^{-1} \frac{\sqrt{3}}{2}$.

$$\sin\left(\text{Cos}^{-1} \frac{\sqrt{3}}{2}\right)$$
$$= \sin 30°$$
$$= \frac{1}{2}$$

b. First evaluate $\cos 180°$. Then use the fact that $\tan(-45°) = -1$.

$$\text{Tan}^{-1}(\cos 180°)$$
$$= \text{Tan}^{-1}(-1)$$
$$= -45°$$

TRY THIS   Evaluate each trigonometric expression.

    a. $\text{Cos}^{-1}(\sin 315°)$ **b.** $\tan\left[\text{Sin}^{-1}\left(-\frac{\sqrt{3}}{2}\right)\right]$

CRITICAL THINKING   Explain why $\text{Cos}^{-1}(\cos x) \neq x$, $\text{Sin}^{-1}(\sin x) \neq x$, and $\text{Tan}^{-1}(\tan x) \neq x$ for all values of x.

E X A M P L E ④ Refer to the aviation problem at the beginning of the lesson.

Find the angle of depression, θ, for an airplane flying at each speed.

    a. Mach 1.3   **b.** Mach 1.8

APPLICATION
AVIATION

● **SOLUTION**

a. $\sin \theta = \dfrac{1}{1.3}$

    $\theta = \text{Sin}^{-1} \dfrac{1}{1.3} \approx 50.28°$

The angle of depression is about 50.28°.

b. $\sin \theta = \dfrac{1}{1.8}$

    $\theta = \text{Sin}^{-1} \dfrac{1}{1.8} \approx 33.75°$

The angle of depression is about 33.75°.

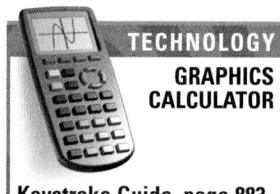

TECHNOLOGY
GRAPHICS CALCULATOR

Keystroke Guide, page 883

Exercises

Communicate

1. Describe how Sin θ, Cos θ, and Tan θ are related to sin θ, cos θ, and tan θ, respectively.

2. Describe how $\text{Sin}^{-1} x$, $\text{Cos}^{-1} x$, and $\text{Tan}^{-1} x$ are related to Sin x, Cos x, and Tan x, respectively.

3. Explain why $\text{Sin}^{-1} 5$ is not defined. Is $\text{Tan}^{-1} 5$ defined? Explain.

Guided Skills Practice

4. Find all possible values of $\cos^{-1}\left(\dfrac{\sqrt{3}}{2}\right)$. **(EXAMPLE 1)**

Evaluate each inverse trigonometric expression. (EXAMPLE 2)

5. $\text{Sin}^{-1}\left(-\dfrac{\sqrt{3}}{2}\right)$ **6.** $\text{Cos}^{-1}\left(\dfrac{1}{2}\right)$ **7.** $\text{Tan}^{-1}\left(-\sqrt{3}\right)$

Evaluate each trigonometric expression. (EXAMPLE 3)

8. $\sin\left(\text{Cos}^{-1}\dfrac{1}{2}\right)$ **9.** $\text{Cos}^{-1}(\sin 30°)$ **10.** $\text{Tan}^{-1}(\tan 150°)$

11. Find the angle of depression, θ, for an airplane flying at Mach 1.5. **(EXAMPLE 4)**

Practice and Apply

Find all possible values for each expression.

12. $\cos^{-1}\left(-\dfrac{1}{2}\right)$ **13.** $\sin^{-1}\left(-\dfrac{\sqrt{2}}{2}\right)$ **14.** $\tan^{-1}\left(-\dfrac{\sqrt{3}}{3}\right)$

15. $\tan^{-1}\sqrt{3}$ **16.** $\sin^{-1} 1$ **17.** $\cos^{-1} 0$

18. $\sin^{-1}\dfrac{\sqrt{3}}{2}$ **19.** $\cos^{-1}\dfrac{\sqrt{2}}{2}$ **20.** $\tan^{-1} 0$

Evaluate each trigonometric expression.

21. $\text{Sin}^{-1}\left(-\dfrac{1}{2}\right)$

22. $\text{Sin}^{-1}\dfrac{\sqrt{2}}{2}$

23. $\text{Cos}^{-1}\dfrac{\sqrt{2}}{2}$

24. $\text{Cos}^{-1}\left(-\dfrac{\sqrt{3}}{2}\right)$

25. $\text{Tan}^{-1}\sqrt{3}$

26. $\text{Tan}^{-1}\dfrac{\sqrt{3}}{3}$

27. $\text{Sin}^{-1}\dfrac{\sqrt{3}}{2}$

28. $\text{Sin}^{-1}1$

29. $\text{Cos}^{-1}(-1)$

30. $\text{Cos}^{-1}\dfrac{1}{2}$

31. $\text{Tan}^{-1}1$

32. $\text{Tan}^{-1}(-1)$

Evaluate each trigonometric expression.

33. $\tan\left(\text{Sin}^{-1}\dfrac{\sqrt{2}}{2}\right)$

34. $\cos\left(\text{Sin}^{-1}\dfrac{1}{2}\right)$

35. $\sin(\text{Tan}^{-1}1)$

36. $\cos\left(\text{Tan}^{-1}\dfrac{\sqrt{3}}{2}\right)$

37. $\tan\left(\text{Cos}^{-1}\dfrac{1}{2}\right)$

38. $\tan\left(\text{Cos}^{-1}\dfrac{\sqrt{2}}{2}\right)$

39. $\text{Tan}^{-1}(\sin 30°)$

40. $\text{Tan}^{-1}(\cos 135°)$

41. $\text{Cos}^{-1}(\tan 225°)$

42. $\text{Cos}^{-1}(\sin 60°)$

43. $\text{Sin}^{-1}(\cos 120°)$

44. $\text{Sin}^{-1}(\cos 300°)$

CHALLENGE

Prove each statement.

45. $\text{Sin}^{-1}(\text{Sin }\theta) = \theta$

46. $\cos(\text{Cos}^{-1}x) = x$

APPLICATIONS

47. FORESTRY A tree casts a 35-foot shadow on the ground when the angle of elevation from the edge of the shadow to the sun is about 40°. How tall is the tree? Draw a diagram to illustrate this situation.

48. ASTRONOMY Katie is setting up a new telescope in her backyard. Her neighbor's house, which is 50 feet away from the telescope, is 30 feet tall, and the eyepiece of the telescope is 5 feet above the ground. What is the minimum angle that the telescope must make with the horizon in the direction of her neighbor's house in order to see over the house?

49. CARPENTRY When using a ladder, it is recommended that the distance from the base of the ladder to the structure, x, be $\dfrac{1}{4}$ of the distance from the base of the ladder to the support for the top of the ladder, y. Find the measure of the angle formed by the ladder and the ground.

50. ARCHITECTURE A person's eyes are 6 feet above the ground and 15 feet from a building. The angle of elevation from the person's line of sight to the top of the building is 75°.
  a. How tall is the building?
  b. What would be the angle of elevation if the person were standing 50 feet from the building? 100 feet?

51. HIKING Sandra wants to find the height of a mountain. From her first location on the ground, she finds the angle of elevation to the top of the mountain to be about 35°. After moving 1000 meters closer to the mountain on level ground, she finds the angle of elevation to be 50°. Find the height of the mountain to the nearest meter. (Hint: Find two equations with two unknowns, and solve them for each unknown.)

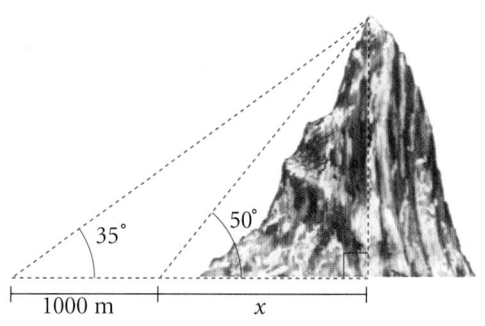

52. PUBLIC SAFETY A driver approaching an intersection sees the word *STOP* written on the road. The driver's eyes are 3.5 feet above the road and 50 feet from the nearest edge of the 8-foot long letters. What angle, θ, does the word make with the driver's eyes?

To simulate the driver's perspective, look at the page from its left edge.

Look Back

53 Solve the system of equations by using a matrix equation. *(LESSON 4.4)*

$$\begin{cases} 2x + 3y + 5z = 16 \\ -4x + 2y + 3z = -5 \\ 3x - y - z = 5 \end{cases}$$

Solve each equation for x. *(LESSON 6.7)*

54. $5e^{2x-1} = 60$

55. $2\log_3 x + \log_3 9 = 4$

56. Find the zeros of the function $f(x) = x^3 + 5x^2 - 8x - 12$. *(LESSON 7.5)*

Find the reference angle for each angle below. *(LESSON 13.2)*

57. $337°$ **58.** $-118°$ **59.** $-23°$ **60.** $520°$

Convert from radians to degrees. *(LESSON 13.4)*

61. $\frac{5\pi}{12}$ radians   **62.** $\frac{7\pi}{8}$ radians   **63.** 2.38 radians   **64.** 4.72 radians

Look Beyond

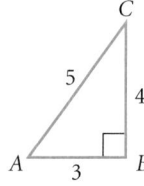

65. Evaluate $\sin^2 x + \cos^2 x$ for $x = \frac{\pi}{2}$, $x = \frac{\pi}{3}$, and $x = 0$. Then evaluate this expression for three other values of x. Make a conjecture about the value of $\sin^2 x + \cos^2 x$ for any value of x.

66. Verify that $\frac{\sin A}{4} = \frac{\sin B}{5} = \frac{\sin C}{3}$ is true for the triangle at left.

CHAPTER THIRTEEN

PROJECT

Reinventing the Wheel

Navy Pier's most visible attraction, a 150-foot Ferris wheel, is modeled after the very first Ferris wheel, which was built for Chicago's 1893 World Colombian Exposition. The Navy Pier Ferris wheel offers unparalleled views of Chicago's skyline and lakefront. With 40 gondolas that seat 6 passengers each, the Ferris wheel can accommodate up to 240 passengers at a time. In the evening, the Ferris wheel's 40 spokes, spanning a diameter of 140 feet, are illuminated by thousands of lights. The Ferris wheel takes approximately 440 seconds to make one complete revolution.

Activity ①

Graph a representation of the Navy Pier Ferris wheel on a coordinate plane with its center at the origin. Create a table of values for the distance from a point on the Ferris wheel to the x-axis..Use the following angles of counterclockwise rotation: 0°, 90°, 180°, 270°, ..., 810°. Graph the resulting ordered pairs, and sketch a *smooth curve* through the points.

George W. G. Ferris (1859–1896)

Activity ②

Create a table of values for the altitude (height above the ground) of a rider on the Ferris wheel. Let the independent variable include all common angle measures for θ such that $0° \le \theta \le 810°$. Graph the points, and sketch a *smooth curve* through the points.

Activity ③

1. Using the table of values that you created in Activity 2 and the fact that one complete revolution takes 440 seconds, convert the units of the independent variable from degrees to time in seconds. Graph the points, and sketch a *smooth curve* through the points.

2. Find the linear speed, in miles per hour, of a rider on the Ferris wheel.

Activity ④

Write an equation of the form $y = a \sin bt$ to model the altitude of a rider on the Ferris wheel as a function of time. Describe what each variable in your model represents.

Chapter Review and Assessment

<table>
<tr><td>amplitude . . . . 860</td><td>inverse trigonometric</td><td>radian . . . . 852</td></tr>
<tr><td>angle of depression . . . . . . 831</td><td>functions . . . . 869</td><td>reference angle . . . . 837</td></tr>
<tr><td>angle of elevation . . . . 831</td><td>linear speed . . . . 853</td><td>solving a triangle . . . . 832</td></tr>
<tr><td>angle of rotation . . . . 836</td><td>negative measure . . . . 836</td><td>standard position . . . . 836</td></tr>
<tr><td>angular speed . . . . 853</td><td>period . . . . 846</td><td>tangent line . . . . 863</td></tr>
<tr><td>arc length . . . . 853</td><td>periodic function . . . . 846</td><td>terminal side . . . . 836</td></tr>
<tr><td>coterminal . . . . 837</td><td>phase shift . . . . 861</td><td>trigonometric functions .. 829, 838</td></tr>
<tr><td>degree . . . . 836</td><td>positive measure . . . . 836</td><td>trigonometry . . . . 828</td></tr>
<tr><td>initial side . . . . 836</td><td>principal values . . . . 868</td><td>unit circle . . . . 846</td></tr>
</table>

Key Skills & Exercises

LESSON 13.1

Key Skills

Solve a right triangle by using trigonometric functions.

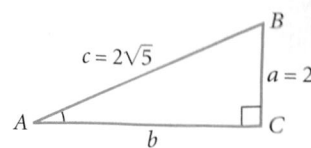

$$\sin A = \frac{2}{2\sqrt{5}}$$

$$A = \sin^{-1}\frac{2}{2\sqrt{5}}$$

$$A \approx 26.6°$$

$$2^2 + b^2 = \left(2\sqrt{5}\right)^2$$

$$b = \sqrt{\left(2\sqrt{5}\right)^2 - 2^2}$$

$$b = 4$$

$$A + B = 90°$$

$$B \approx 90° - 26.6° \approx 63.4°$$

Exercises

Solve each triangle.

1.

2.

3.

4.

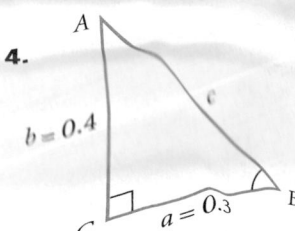

LESSON 13.2

Key Skills

Find coterminal angles and reference angles.

Coterminal angles of 480°, such that $-360° < \theta < 360°$, are found as follows:

$$480° - 360° = 120°$$
$$480° - (2)(360°) = -240°$$

$$\theta_{ref} = |180° - 120°|$$
$$= 60°$$

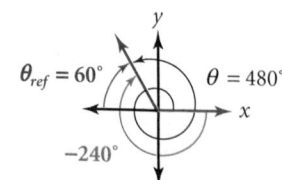

Exercises

For each angle below, find all coterminal angles such that $-360° < \theta < 360°$. Then find their corresponding reference angles.

5. 270°

6. 150°

7. −135°

8. −225°

9. 380°

10. 440°

11. 1028°

12. 973°

13. −515°

14. −612°

Find the trigonometric function values of angles in standard position.

The terminal side of θ in standard position is in Quadrant IV, and $\cos \theta = \frac{5}{13}$.

To find $\sin \theta$, find the length of the longer leg. Use the Pythagorean Theorem.

$$y = \pm\sqrt{13^2 - 5^2} = -12$$

Because P is in Quadrant IV, y is negative.

Thus, $\sin \theta = \frac{y}{r} = -\frac{12}{13}$.

Find the exact values of the six trigonometric functions of θ, given each point on the terminal side of θ in standard position.

15. $P(3, -4)$ 16. $P(-2, 5)$

17. $P(-1, -8)$ 18. $P(6, 2)$

Given the quadrant of θ in standard position and a trigonometric function value of θ, find exact values for the indicated functions.

19. III, $\sin \theta = -\frac{2}{7}$; $\tan \theta$

20. IV, $\cos \theta = \frac{1}{3}$; $\sin \theta$

21. I, $\tan \theta = 1$; $\cos \theta$

22. II, $\tan \theta = -\sqrt{3}$; $\sin \theta$

LESSON 13.3

Key Skills

Find exact values for trigonometric functions of special angles and their multiples.

$$\cos 390° = \cos(390° - 360°)$$
$$= \cos 30°$$
$$= \frac{\sqrt{3}}{2}$$

Find the coordinates of a point on a circle given an angle of rotation and the radius of the circle.

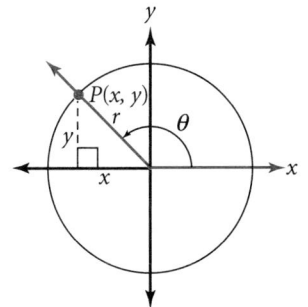

The coordinates of $P(x, y)$ shown at right are $P(r \cos \theta, r \sin \theta)$.

Exercises

Find each trigonometric function value. Give exact answers.

23. $\cos 135°$ 24. $\sin 315°$

25. $\tan 225°$ 26. $\cos 0°$

27. $\sin(-270°)$ 28. $\cos(-180°)$

29. $\tan(-90°)$ 30. $\cos 675°$

31. $\sin 600°$ 32. $\tan 765°$

Point P is located at the intersection of a circle with a radius of r and the terminal side of angle θ in standard position. Find the exact coordinates of P.

33. $\theta = 60°, r = 1$ 34. $\theta = -30°, r = 2$

35. $\theta = 240°, r = 5$ 36. $\theta = -240°, r = 3$

LESSON 13.4

Key Skills

Convert from degrees to radians and vice versa.

Multiply degrees by $\frac{\pi \text{ radians}}{180°}$.

Multiply radians by $\frac{180°}{\pi \text{ radians}}$.

Find arc length.

Use $s = r\theta$, where s is the arc length, r is the radius, and θ is the angle measure in radians.

Exercises

Convert each degree measure to radian measure, giving exact answers. Convert each radian measure to degree measure, rounding answers to the nearest tenth of a degree.

37. $78°$ 38. $334.61°$ 39. $-23°$

40. $\frac{\pi}{7}$ radians   41. $-\frac{15\pi}{16}$ radians   42. 8.87 radians

43. Find the length of the arc intercepted by a central angle of $30°$ in a circle with a radius of 4.5 meters.

Skills

ph transformations of trigonometric nctions.

For $y = a\sin(b\theta - c) + d$ and $y = a\cos(b\theta - c) + d$, $|a|$ is the amplitude; $\frac{2\pi}{|b|}$, where $b \neq 0$, is the period; $|c|$ is the phase shift (to the right for $c > 0$ and to the left for $c < 0$); and $|d|$ is the vertical shift (upward for $d > 0$ and downward for $d < 0$).

For $y = a\tan(b\theta - c) + d$, there is no amplitude, but a represents a vertical stretch or compression, and $\frac{\pi}{|b|}$, where $b \neq 0$, is the period. The phase shift and vertical shift are the same as those of sine and cosine.

Exercises

Identify the amplitude, if it exists, and the period of each trigonometric function.

44. $y = -3\sin\theta$ **45.** $y = -4\sin\theta$

46. $y = \frac{1}{2}\sin 3\theta$ **47.** $y = 2\tan\frac{1}{3}\theta$

Identify the phase shift and the vertical shift of each function from its parent function.

48. $y = 2\sin(\theta - 90°)$ **49.** $y = -4\cos(\theta + 45°)$

50. $y = \sin(\theta - 215°) + 3$ **51.** $y = \cos(\theta + 120°) - 2$

Describe the transformation of each function from its parent function. Then graph at least one period of the function along with its parent function.

52. $y = \cos 4\theta$ **53.** $y = \tan\frac{1}{2}\theta$

54. $2\sin(\theta - 45°)$ **55.** $y = 3\cos(\theta + 45°)$

LESSON 13.6
Key Skills

Evaluate trigonometric expressions involving inverses.

Find all possible values of $\sin^{-1}\frac{\sqrt{2}}{2}$.

For $0° \leq \theta < 360°$, $\sin^{-1}\frac{\sqrt{2}}{2} = 45°$ and $\sin^{-1}\frac{\sqrt{2}}{2} = 135°$.

Thus, all possible values are $45° + n360°$ and $135° + n360°$, where n is an integer.

Evaluate composite trigonometric functions.

$$\cos\left(\text{Sin}^{-1}\frac{\sqrt{3}}{2}\right) = \cos 60°$$
$$= \frac{1}{2}$$

Exercises

Find all possible values for each expression.

56. $\sin^{-1} 0$ **57.** $\cos^{-1} 1$

58. $\tan^{-1}\left(-\frac{\sqrt{3}}{3}\right)$ **59.** $\cos^{-1}\left(-\frac{\sqrt{2}}{2}\right)$

60. $\sin^{-1}\left(-\frac{\sqrt{3}}{2}\right)$ **61.** $\tan^{-1} 1$

Evaluate each trigonometric expression.

62. $\text{Sin}^{-1}\frac{1}{2}$ **63.** $\text{Cos}^{-1}\left(-\frac{\sqrt{3}}{2}\right)$

64. $\text{Tan}^{-1}\sqrt{3}$ **65.** $\text{Sin}^{-1}\left(-\frac{\sqrt{2}}{2}\right)$

66. $\tan\left(\text{Sin}^{-1}\frac{1}{2}\right)$ **67.** $\cos\left[\text{Tan}^{-1}(-\sqrt{3})\right]$

68. $\text{Tan}^{-1}(\cos 135°)$ **69.** $\text{Sin}^{-1}[\sin(-120°)]$

Applications

70. MAPMAKING A map maker is making a map of a park. She would like to find the distance across a river. She marks a point on the bank of the river at C and then walks 200 meters up the river to point A, where she measures an angle of 50° between points B and C. What is the distance from point B to point C across the river?

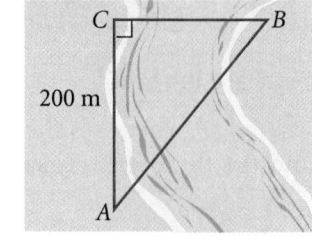

Activity ①

Graph a representation of the Navy Pier Ferris wheel on a coordinate plane with its center at the origin. Create a table of values for the distance from a point on the Ferris wheel to the *x*-axis.,Use the following angles of counterclockwise rotation: 0°, 90°, 180°, 270°, . . . , 810°. Graph the resulting ordered pairs, and sketch a *smooth curve* through the points.

George W. G. Ferris (1859–1896)

Activity ②

Create a table of values for the altitude (height above the ground) of a rider on the Ferris wheel. Let the independent variable include all common angle measures for θ such that $0° \le \theta \le 810°$. Graph the points, and sketch a *smooth curve* through the points.

Activity ③

1. Using the table of values that you created in Activity 2 and the fact that one complete revolution takes 440 seconds, convert the units of the independent variable from degrees to time in seconds. Graph the points, and sketch a *smooth curve* through the points.

2. Find the linear speed, in miles per hour, of a rider on the Ferris wheel.

Activity ④

Write an equation of the form $y = a \sin bt$ to model the altitude of a rider on the Ferris wheel as a function of time. Describe what each variable in your model represents.

13 Chapter Review and Assessment

Key Skills & Exercises

LESSON 13.1

Key Skills

Solve a right triangle by using trigonometric functions.

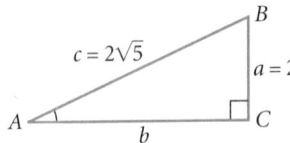

$$\sin A = \frac{2}{2\sqrt{5}}$$

$$A = \sin^{-1} \frac{2}{2\sqrt{5}}$$

$$A \approx 26.6°$$

$$2^2 + b^2 = \left(2\sqrt{5}\right)^2$$

$$b = \sqrt{\left(2\sqrt{5}\right)^2 - 2^2}$$

$$b = 4$$

$$A + B = 90°$$

$$B \approx 90° - 26.6° \approx 63.4°$$

Exercises

Solve each triangle.

1.

2.

3.

4.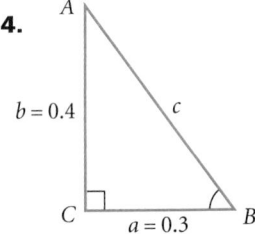

LESSON 13.2

Key Skills

Find coterminal angles and reference angles.

Coterminal angles of 480°, such that
$-360° < \theta < 360°$, are found as follows:

$$480° - 360° = 120°$$
$$480° - (2)(360°) = -240°$$

$$\theta_{ref} = \left|180° - 120°\right|$$
$$= 60°$$

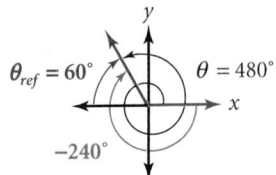

Exercises

For each angle below, find all coterminal angles such that $-360° < \theta < 360°$. Then find their corresponding reference angles.

5. 270°

6. 150°

7. −135°

8. −225°

9. 380°

10. 440°

11. 1028°

12. 973°

13. −515°

14. −612°

Find the trigonometric function values of angles in standard position.

The terminal side of θ in standard position is in Quadrant IV, and $\cos \theta = \frac{5}{13}$.

To find $\sin \theta$, find the length of the longer leg. Use the Pythagorean Theorem.

$$y = \pm\sqrt{13^2 - 5^2} = -12$$

Because P is in Quadrant IV, y is negative.

Thus, $\sin \theta = \frac{y}{r} = -\frac{12}{13}$.

Find the exact values of the six trigonometric functions of θ, given each point on the terminal side of θ in standard position.

15. $P(3, -4)$ **16.** $P(-2, 5)$

17. $P(-1, -8)$ **18.** $P(6, 2)$

Given the quadrant of θ in standard position and a trigonometric function value of θ, find exact values for the indicated functions.

19. III, $\sin \theta = -\frac{2}{7}$; $\tan \theta$

20. IV, $\cos \theta = \frac{1}{3}$; $\sin \theta$

21. I, $\tan \theta = 1$; $\cos \theta$

22. II, $\tan \theta = -\sqrt{3}$; $\sin \theta$

Key Skills

Find exact values for trigonometric functions of special angles and their multiples.

$$\cos 390° = \cos(390° - 360°)$$
$$= \cos 30°$$
$$= \frac{\sqrt{3}}{2}$$

Find the coordinates of a point on a circle given an angle of rotation and the radius of the circle.

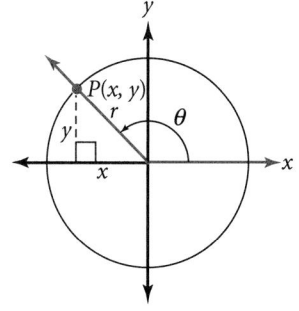

The coordinates of $P(x, y)$ shown at right are $P(r \cos \theta, r \sin \theta)$.

Exercises

Find each trigonometric function value. Give exact answers.

23. $\cos 135°$ **24.** $\sin 315°$

25. $\tan 225°$ **26.** $\cos 0°$

27. $\sin(-270°)$ **28.** $\cos(-180°)$

29. $\tan(-90°)$ **30.** $\cos 675°$

31. $\sin 600°$ **32.** $\tan 765°$

Point P is located at the intersection of a circle with a radius of r and the terminal side of angle θ in standard position. Find the exact coordinates of P.

33. $\theta = 60°, r = 1$ **34.** $\theta = -30°, r = 2$

35. $\theta = 240°, r = 5$ **36.** $\theta = -240°, r = 3$

Key Skills

Convert from degrees to radians and vice versa.

Multiply degrees by $\frac{\pi \text{ radians}}{180°}$.

Multiply radians by $\frac{180°}{\pi \text{ radians}}$.

Find arc length.

Use $s = r\theta$, where s is the arc length, r is the radius, and θ is the angle measure in radians.

Exercises

Convert each degree measure to radian measure, giving exact answers. Convert each radian measure to degree measure, rounding answers to the nearest tenth of a degree.

37. $78°$ **38.** $334.61°$ **39.** $-23°$

40. $\frac{\pi}{7}$ radians   **41.** $-\frac{15\pi}{16}$ radians   **42.** 8.87 radians

43. Find the length of the arc intercepted by a central angle of $30°$ in a circle with a radius of 4.5 meters.

Key Skills

Graph transformations of trigonometric functions.

For $y = a \sin(b\theta - c) + d$ and $y = a \cos(b\theta - c) + d$, $|a|$ is the amplitude; $\frac{2\pi}{|b|}$, where $b \neq 0$, is the period; $|c|$ is the phase shift (to the right for $c > 0$ and to the left for $c < 0$); and $|d|$ is the vertical shift (upward for $d > 0$ and downward for $d < 0$).

For $y = a \tan(b\theta - c) + d$, there is no amplitude, but a represents a vertical stretch or compression, and $\frac{\pi}{|b|}$, where $b \neq 0$, is the period. The phase shift and vertical shift are the same as those of sine and cosine.

Exercises

Identify the amplitude, if it exists, and the period of each trigonometric function.

44. $y = -3 \sin \theta$

45. $y = -4 \sin \theta$

46. $y = \frac{1}{2} \sin 3\theta$

47. $y = 2 \tan \frac{1}{3}\theta$

Identify the phase shift and the vertical shift of each function from its parent function.

48. $y = 2 \sin(\theta - 90°)$

49. $y = -4 \cos(\theta + 45°)$

50. $y = \sin(\theta - 215°) + 3$

51. $y = \cos(\theta + 120°) - 2$

Describe the transformation of each function from its parent function. Then graph at least one period of the function along with its parent function.

52. $y = \cos 4\theta$

53. $y = \tan \frac{1}{2}\theta$

54. $2 \sin(\theta - 45°)$

55. $y = 3 \cos(\theta + 45°)$

Key Skills

Evaluate trigonometric expressions involving inverses.

Find all possible values of $\sin^{-1} \frac{\sqrt{2}}{2}$.

For $0° \leq \theta < 360°$, $\sin^{-1} \frac{\sqrt{2}}{2} = 45°$ and $\sin^{-1} \frac{\sqrt{2}}{2} = 135°$.

Thus, all possible values are $45° + n360°$ and $135° + n360°$, where n is an integer.

Evaluate composite trigonometric functions.

$$\cos\left(\mathrm{Sin}^{-1} \frac{\sqrt{3}}{2}\right) = \cos 60°$$
$$= \frac{1}{2}$$

Exercises

Find all possible values for each expression.

56. $\sin^{-1} 0$

57. $\cos^{-1} 1$

58. $\tan^{-1}\left(-\frac{\sqrt{3}}{3}\right)$

59. $\cos^{-1}\left(-\frac{\sqrt{2}}{2}\right)$

60. $\sin^{-1}\left(-\frac{\sqrt{3}}{2}\right)$

61. $\tan^{-1} 1$

Evaluate each trigonometric expression.

62. $\mathrm{Sin}^{-1} \frac{1}{2}$

63. $\mathrm{Cos}^{-1}\left(-\frac{\sqrt{3}}{2}\right)$

64. $\mathrm{Tan}^{-1} \sqrt{3}$

65. $\mathrm{Sin}^{-1}\left(-\frac{\sqrt{2}}{2}\right)$

66. $\tan\left(\mathrm{Sin}^{-1} \frac{1}{2}\right)$

67. $\cos\left[\mathrm{Tan}^{-1}(-\sqrt{3})\right]$

68. $\mathrm{Tan}^{-1}(\cos 135°)$

69. $\mathrm{Sin}^{-1}[\sin(-120°)]$

Applications

70. MAPMAKING A map maker is making a map of a park. She would like to find the distance across a river. She marks a point on the bank of the river at C and then walks 200 meters up the river to point A, where she measures an angle of 50° between points B and C. What is the distance from point B to point C across the river?

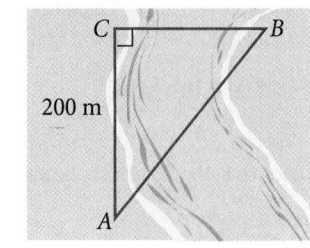

13 Chapter Test

Solve each triangle. Give angle measures to the nearest degree and side lengths to the nearest tenth.

1.

2.

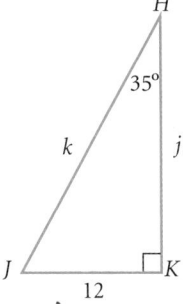

3. GEOMETRY A regular octagon is made by cutting off the corners of a square so that each triangle cut off is isosceles. What is the length of the side of an octagon made from a square of side length 10?

For each angle below, find all coterminal angles such that $-360° < \theta < 360°$. Then find the corresponding reference angle, if it exists.

4. 137°

5. 515°

6. 38°

7. 1729°

Given the quadrant of θ in standard position and a trigonometric function value of θ, find exact values for the indicated functions.

8. IV, $\cos\theta = \frac{5}{13}$; $\sin\theta$

9. II, $\tan\theta = -\frac{1}{2}$; $\sin\theta$

Find each trigonometric function value. Give exact answers.

10. $\sin 330°$

11. $\cos (-150°)$

12. $\sin 720°$

13. $\tan (-765°)$

14. $\cos 300°$

15. $\tan 270°$

Point P is located at the intersection of a circle with a radius of *r* and the terminal side of an angle θ in standard position. Find the exact coordinates of *P*.

16. $\theta = 30°, r = 5$

17. $\theta = 225°, r = 12$

18. $\theta = -150°, r = 4$

19. $\theta = 300°, r = 8$

20. CONSTRUCTION A roofline has a $\frac{7}{12}$ pitch, meaning that the roof rises 7 feet for each 12 feet of horizontal distance. What angle does the roof make with the horizontal?

Convert each degree measure to radian measure or radian measure to degree measure. Give exact answers.

21. 315°

22. $-150°$

23. 495°

24. $\frac{\pi}{12}$

25. $\frac{5\pi}{4}$

26. $\frac{-5\pi}{3}$

27. TECHNOLOGY A 12-inch LP vinyl record rotates at $33\frac{1}{3}$ rpm. When the record needle is placed 4 inches from the center of the record, what is the linear speed of the record at that point?

Identify the amplitude, if it exists, and the period of each function.

28. $y = 3 \sin 2\theta$

29. $y = \frac{2}{3} \tan 5\theta$

30. $y = 5 \sin \frac{1}{3}\theta$

31. $y = -3 \cos\left(\theta - \frac{\pi}{4}\right)$

Describe the transformations of each function from its parent function.

32. $y = \sin(\theta + 60°) + 2$

33. $y = -3 \cos(\theta - 300°)$

Find all possible values for each expression.

34. $\sin^{-1}\left(\frac{\sqrt{2}}{2}\right)$

35. $\cos^{-1}\left(\frac{1}{2}\right)$

36. $\tan^{-1}(1)$

37. $\tan^{-1}(\sqrt{3})$

Evaluate each trigonometric expression.

38. $\sin\left(\text{Cos}^{-1}\frac{1}{2}\right)$

39. $\text{Tan}^{-1}(\sin 90°)$

1-13 College Entrance Exam Practice

 internet connect

Standardized Test Prep Online
Go To: go.hrw.com
Keyword: MM1 Test Prep

MULTIPLE-CHOICE For Questions 1–17, write the letter that indicates the best answer.

1. Which expression has a value of $\frac{1}{36}$? *(LESSON 2.2)*

 a. 6^{-2}
 b. -6^2
 c. 2^{-6}
 d. $-2^2 \cdot 3^2$

2. Which value is the x-coordinate of the center of the circle whose equation is $(x + 2)^2 + y^2 = 1$? *(LESSON 9.3)*

 a. 2
 b. -2
 c. 0
 d. 1

3. If the degree of a polynomial is 2 and the polynomial is multiplied by $(3x - 2)$, find the degree of the product. *(LESSON 7.1)*

 a. 3
 b. 1
 c. 6
 d. 5

4. Convert $\frac{5\pi}{3}$ radians to degrees. *(LESSON 13.4)*

 a. $108°$
 b. $300°$
 c. $600°$
 d. $150°$

5. A music group is making a CD for an audition. In how many ways can they choose 8 songs to record from their 10 favorites? *(LESSON 10.3)*

 a. 90
 b. 20
 c. 45
 d. 73

6. Which of the following functions is denoted by $[-2.01]$? *(LESSON 2.6)*

 a. rounding-up
 b. greatest-integer
 c. absolute value
 d. inverse

7. The domain of $f(x) = \frac{2x - 3}{x + 1}$ includes all real numbers except which value? *(LESSON 8.2)*

 a. 1
 b. -1
 c. $-\frac{3}{2}$
 d. $\frac{3}{2}$

8. Which expression is not equivalent to the others? *(LESSON 6.4)*

 a. $\log_3 (2x)^{\frac{1}{4}}$
 b. $\frac{1}{4} \log_3 2x$
 c. $\log_3 \sqrt[4]{2x}$
 d. $3^{\frac{1}{4} \log_3 2x}$

9. Which represents $(2x^3 - x^4) + (3x^2 - 5) - (x^2 - x^4 + 1)$ as a polynomial in standard form? *(LESSON 7.1)*

 a. $-2x^4 + 2x^3 + 3x^2 - 6$
 b. $2x^3 + 2x^2 - 6$
 c. $2x^3 + 2x^2 - 4$
 d. $2x^3 + 3x^2 + 4$

10. Which is the value of x at the vertex of the graph of $f(x) = 2x^2 - 4x + 1$? *(LESSON 5.1)*

 a. -1
 b. 1
 c. 2
 d. $-\frac{1}{2}$

11. Which describes a number that cannot be written as the ratio of two integers? *(LESSON 2.1)*

 a. prime
 b. integer
 c. rational
 d. irrational

12. Which of the following is the complex conjugate of $3 - 2i$? *(LESSON 5.6)*

 a. $-3 + 2i$
 b. $3 + 2i$
 c. $2i - 3$
 d. $-3 - 2i$

13. Solve $|2x + 5| = 11$. *(LESSON 1.8)*

 a. $3, -3$
 b. $8, -8$
 c. $3, -8$
 d. $8, -3$

14. If y varies directly as x and y is 8 when x is 4, which of the following is the constant of variation? *(LESSON 1.4)*

    a. $\frac{1}{2}$ **b.** 2   **c.** 32   **d.** -2

15. If an entire population of 100 bacteria doubles every hour, how many bacteria are in the population after 3 hours? *(LESSON 6.1)*

    a. 200   **b.** 300   **c.** 400   **d.** 800

16. Which of the following is true of the ellipse given by $\frac{x^2}{36} + \frac{y^2}{4} = 1$? *(LESSON 9.4)*

    a. The major axis is horizontal.
    b. The major axis is vertical.
    c. The foci are $\left(0, \pm 4\sqrt{2}\right)$.
    d. The length of the major axis is 6.

17. Which equation defines the inverse of $f(x) = \frac{1}{3}x + 1$? *(LESSON 2.5)*

    a. $y = -\frac{1}{3}x + 1$ **b.** $y + 1 = \frac{1}{3}x$
    c. $y + 3 = 3x$ **d.** $y + 3x = 3$

18. Graph $y \le \frac{1}{4}x - 6$. *(LESSON 3.3)*

19. Evaluate $3\left(\sqrt{45}\right)^2$. *(LESSON 8.6)*

20. Write the function represented by the graph of $f(x) = x^2$ translated 3 units to the left. *(LESSON 2.7)*

Use the diagram below to find each value. Give exact answers. (LESSON 13.1)

21. $\sin A$

22. $\cos A$

23. $\tan B$

24. $\cot A$

25. $\sec B$

26. Use the quadratic formula to solve $5x^2 + x - 2 = 0$. *(LESSON 5.5)*

27. Write the pair of parametric equations as a single equation in only x and y. *(LESSON 3.6)*
$$\begin{cases} x(t) = 3t \\ y(t) = 5 - 2t \end{cases}$$

28. Solve $\frac{6}{x - 2} > \frac{5}{x - 3}$. *(LESSON 8.5)*

29. Write an equation in standard form for the line that contains $(-3, 4)$ and is perpendicular to $y = 3x - 5$. *(LESSON 1.3)*

30. Simplify $\frac{x}{x + 4} \div \frac{6x^2}{3x + 12}$. *(LESSON 8.3)*

31. State the domain of $f(x) = \sqrt{2 - 3x}$. *(LESSON 8.6)*

32. Factor $3y(5x + 2) - 4(5x + 2)$, if possible. *(LESSON 5.3)*

33. Find the product $\begin{bmatrix} 2 & -2 & 4 \\ -1 & 3 & 5 \end{bmatrix} \begin{bmatrix} 3 & 5 \\ 2 & -2 \\ -1 & 4 \end{bmatrix}$, if it exists. *(LESSON 4.2)*

FREE-RESPONSE GRID The following questions may be answered by using a free-response grid such as that commonly used by standardized-test services.

34. Solve $\ln(2x - 7) = \ln 13$. *(LESSON 6.7)*

35. Evaluate $\sum\limits_{n=1}^{3} 8$. *(LESSON 11.1)*

36. Evaluate $\sin\left(\cos^{-1} \frac{1}{2}\right)$. *(LESSON 13.6)*

37. Give the exact value of $\sin\left(\frac{\pi}{2}\right)$. *(LESSON 13.4)*

38. Evaluate $\log_{10} 10^5 + 7^{\log_7 6}$. *(LESSON 6.4)*

39. Find the reference angle, θ_{ref}, for $640°$. *(LESSON 13.2)*

40. Find the value of v in $\frac{1}{2} = \log_v 4$. *(LESSON 6.3)*

41. **PROBABILITY** In how many different ways can a committee chairman and vice-chairman be selected from 15 members? *(LESSON 10.2)*

42. What is the minimum value of $f(x) = 3 + 2\cos\left(x + \frac{\pi}{2}\right)$? *(LESSON 13.5)*

43. What is the 13th term of the arithmetic sequence 50, 46, 42, . . . ? *(LESSON 11.2)*

Keystroke Guide
for Chapter 13

Essential keystroke sequences (using the model TI-82 or TI-83 graphics calculator) are presented below for all Activities and Examples found in this chapter that require or recommend the use of a graphics calculator.

internet connect

For Keystrokes of other graphing calculator models, visit the HRW web site at **go.hrw.com** and enter the keyword **MB1 CALC**.

LESSON 13.5

Page 858

For Step 1, use radian, parametric, and simultaneous modes to graph the parametric equations $x_1(t) = \cos t$ and $y_1(t) = \sin t$ in order to generate the unit circle and $x_2(t) = t$ and $y_2(t) = \sin t$ in order to generate the basic sine function.

Set the modes:

| MODE | ▼ | ▼ | **Radian** | ENTER | ▼ | **Par** | ENTER | ▼ | ▼ | **Simul** |

| ENTER | 2nd | QUIT MODE |

Set the viewing window:

| WINDOW | (Tmin=) 0 | ENTER | (Tmax=) 2 | 2nd | π ^ | ENTER |

(Tstep=) | 2nd | π ^ | D | 24 | ENTER | (Xmin=) | (−) | 1 | ENTER |

(Xmax=) 2 | 2nd | π ^ | ENTER | (Xscl=) | 2nd | π ^ | D | 2 | ENTER |

(Ymin=) | (−) | 2 | ENTER | (Ymax=) 2 | ENTER | (Yscl=) 1 | 2nd | QUIT MODE |

Graph the parametric equations:

| Y= | (X_{1T}=) | COS | X,T,θ,n | ENTER | (Y_{1T}=) | SIN |

| X,T,θ,n | ENTER | (X_{2T}=) | X,T,θ,n | ENTER | (Y_{2T}=) | SIN |

| X,T,θ,n | ZOOM | **5:ZSquare** | ENTER |

For Step 2, use the trace feature to compare the x-values and y-values for various t-values.

Use TRACE and the cursor keys. The ◄ and ► keys move the cursor along the graph. The ▲ and ▼ keys move the cursor to and from corresponding points on the two curves.

For part b of Step 3, graph the parametric equations $x_1(t) = 2 \cos t$, $y_1(t) = 2 \sin t$, $x_2(t) = t$, and $y_2(t) = 2 \sin t$.
Change Xmin to −2 in the viewing window, and use a keystroke sequence similar to that for Step 1.

For part c of Step 3, graph the parametric equations $x_1(t) = 3 \cos t$, $y_1(t) = 3 \sin t$, $x_2(t) = t$, and $y_2(t) = 3 \sin t$.
Change Xmin to −3 in the viewing window, and use a keystroke sequence similar to that for Step 1.

E X A M P L E ❸ In radian, function, and sequential modes, graph $y = 3 \sin 110\pi x$ and

Page 862 $y = 3 \sin 110\pi\left(x - \dfrac{1}{110}\right)$ on the same screen.

Use a viewing window $\left[-\dfrac{1}{110}, \dfrac{2}{110}\right]$ by $[-4, 4]$ and an x-scale of $\dfrac{1}{440}$.

$\boxed{\text{Y=}}$ $\boxed{3}$ $\boxed{\text{SIN}}$ $\boxed{110}$ $\boxed{\text{2nd}}$ $\boxed{\overset{\pi}{\wedge}}$ $\boxed{\text{X,T,θ,n}}$ $\boxed{\text{ENTER}}$

$\boxed{\blacktriangleleft}$ $\boxed{\blacktriangleleft}$ $\boxed{\text{ENTER}}$ ($\searrow$ Y2=) $\boxed{\blacktriangleright}$ $\boxed{\blacktriangleright}$ $\boxed{3}$ $\boxed{\text{SIN}}$

$\boxed{110}$ $\boxed{\text{2nd}}$ $\boxed{\overset{\pi}{\wedge}}$ $\boxed{(}$ $\boxed{\text{X,T,θ,n}}$ $\boxed{-}$ $\boxed{(}$ $\boxed{1}$

⇑ TI-82: $\boxed{(}$

$\boxed{\text{D}}$ $\boxed{110}$ $\boxed{)}$ $\boxed{)}$ $\boxed{)}$ $\boxed{\text{GRAPH}}$

LESSON 13.6

E X A M P L E ❷ Evaluate $\operatorname{Sin}^{-1}\dfrac{1}{2}$, $\operatorname{Cos}^{-1}\left(-\dfrac{\sqrt{3}}{2}\right)$, and $\operatorname{Tan}^{-1}\left(-\dfrac{\sqrt{3}}{3}\right)$.

Page 870 **Set the mode:**

$\boxed{\text{MODE}}$ $\boxed{\blacktriangledown}$ $\boxed{\blacktriangledown}$ $\boxed{\text{Degree}}$ $\boxed{\text{ENTER}}$ $\boxed{\text{2nd}}$ $\overset{\text{QUIT}}{\boxed{\text{MODE}}}$

Evaluate:

$\overset{\text{SIN}^{-1}}{\boxed{\text{2nd}}}$ $\boxed{\text{SIN}}$ $\boxed{1}$ $\boxed{\text{D}}$ $\boxed{2}$ $\boxed{)}$ $\boxed{\text{ENTER}}$

⇑ TI-82: $\boxed{(}$

$\overset{\text{COS}^{-1}}{\boxed{\text{2nd}}}$ $\boxed{\text{COS}}$ $\boxed{(-)}$ $\boxed{\text{2nd}}$ $\overset{\sqrt{\ }}{\boxed{x^2}}$ $\boxed{3}$ $\boxed{)}$ $\boxed{\text{D}}$ $\boxed{2}$ $\boxed{)}$ $\boxed{\text{ENTER}}$

⇑ TI-82: $\boxed{(}$ ⇑ TI-82: $\boxed{(}$

$\overset{\text{TAN}^{-1}}{\boxed{\text{2nd}}}$ $\boxed{\text{TAN}}$ $\boxed{(-)}$ $\boxed{\text{2nd}}$ $\overset{\sqrt{\ }}{\boxed{x^2}}$ $\boxed{3}$ $\boxed{)}$ $\boxed{\text{D}}$ $\boxed{3}$ $\boxed{)}$ $\boxed{\text{ENTER}}$

⇑ TI-82: $\boxed{(}$ ⇑ TI-82: $\boxed{(}$

E X A M P L E ❹ For part a, find $\operatorname{Sin}^{-1}\dfrac{1}{1.3}$ in degrees.

Page 871 **Set the mode:**

$\boxed{\text{MODE}}$ $\boxed{\blacktriangledown}$ $\boxed{\blacktriangledown}$ $\boxed{\text{Degree}}$ $\boxed{\text{ENTER}}$ $\boxed{\text{2nd}}$ $\overset{\text{QUIT}}{\boxed{\text{MODE}}}$

Evaluate:

$\overset{\text{SIN}^{-1}}{\boxed{\text{2nd}}}$ $\boxed{\text{SIN}}$ $\boxed{1}$ $\boxed{\text{D}}$ $\boxed{1.3}$ $\boxed{)}$ $\boxed{\text{ENTER}}$

⇑ TI-82: $\boxed{(}$

Further Topics in Trigonometry

IN THIS SECOND CHAPTER ON TRIGONOMETRY, YOU will study additional uses of trigonometry and several relationships among the trigonometric functions. For example, the law of sines and the law of cosines will enable you to solve more general triangles. A classic application of trigonometry is ship navigation, which involves the instruments shown here.

The astrolabe, an astronomical instrument useful for ship navigation, consisted of circles marked with angular measurements. This brass Islamic astrolabe is from the period 1350–1450.

A present-day sextant, which is used to find the position of a ship

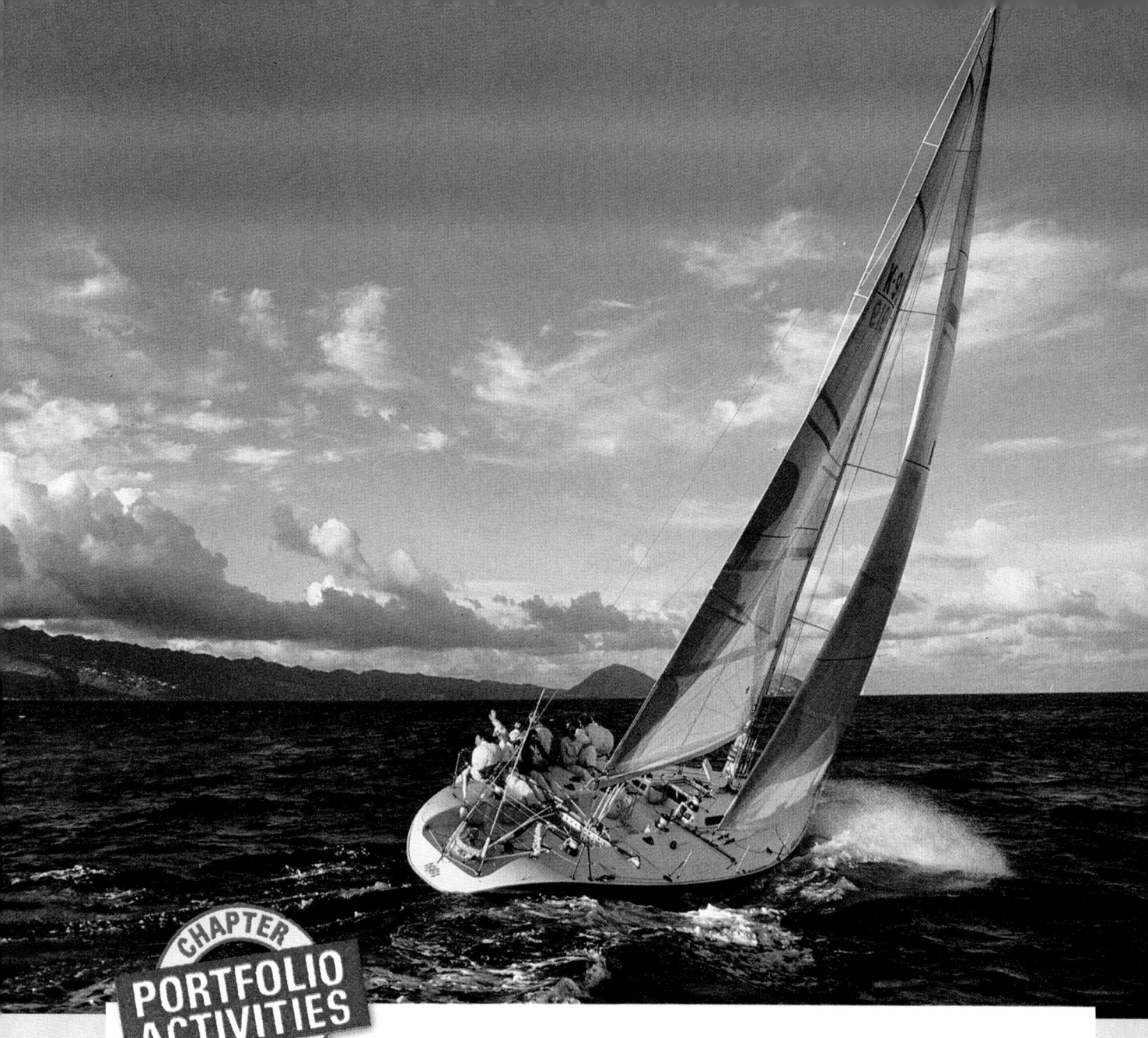

About the Chapter Project

Gear design has evolved over hundreds of years and can involve some complex mechanical engineering. The Chapter Project, *Gearing Up*, will give you some insight into the mathematics that allow gears to mesh smoothly.

After completing the Chapter Project, you will be able to:

- Determine a gear tooth profile and the spacing of gear teeth around a base circle.

- Design a gear template for a set of gears.

- Make a working model of a set of gears that mesh together smoothly.

About the Portfolio Activities

Throughout the chapter, you will be given opportunities to complete the Portfolio Activities that are designed to support your work on the Chapter Project.

- Sketching an involute gear profile and determining the radius of the curved edge of a gear tooth is included in the Portfolio Activity on page 901.

- Using rotation matrices to find the positions of gear teeth on a gear's base circle is included in the Portfolio Activity on page 916.

The Law of Sines

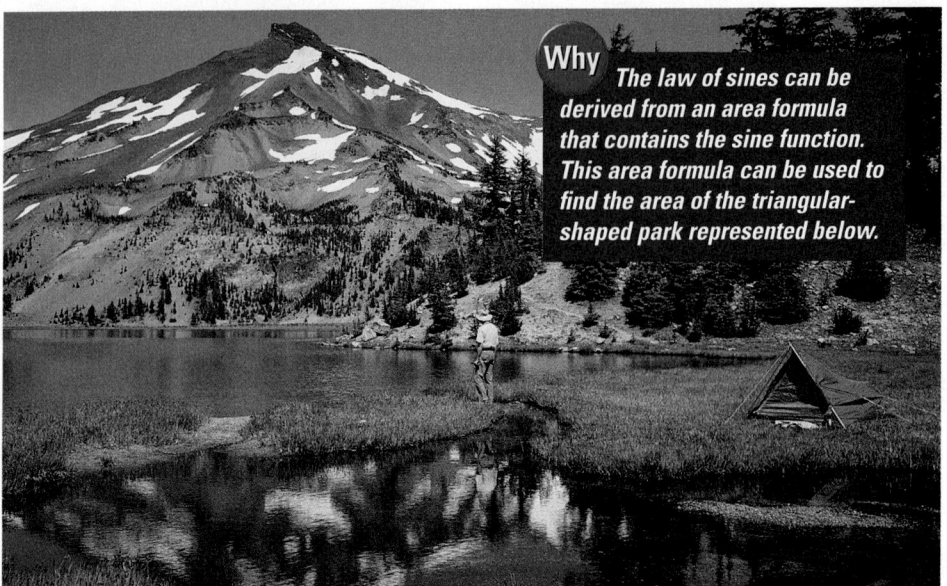

Why *The law of sines can be derived from an area formula that contains the sine function. This area formula can be used to find the area of the triangular-shaped park represented below.*

Objective

● Solve mathematical and real-world problems by using the law of sines.

The triangular piece of land represented at right will be used for a new park. What is the approximate area of the land?

Let K represent the area of $\triangle ABC$.

$$K = \tfrac{1}{2} \times \text{base} \times \text{height}$$

$$K = \tfrac{1}{2} \times AC \times \mathbf{BD}$$

$$K = \tfrac{1}{2} \times 2.5 \times (\mathbf{2 \sin 32°}) \quad \text{\textit{Because } sin 32° = \tfrac{BD}{2}, \text{\textit{substitute}} 2 \sin 32° \text{\textit{for BD.}}}$$

$$K \approx 1.3$$

The area of the triangular piece of land is about 1.3 square miles.

The information given in the park problem above includes AC, BC, and the measure of the included angle, C. This information is known as side-angle-side, or SAS, information. Given SAS information for a triangle, you can always find its area with one of the formulas below.

Area of a Triangle

The area, K, of $\triangle ABC$ is given by the equations below.

$$K = \tfrac{1}{2}bc \sin A \qquad K = \tfrac{1}{2}ac \sin B$$

$$K = \tfrac{1}{2}ab \sin C$$

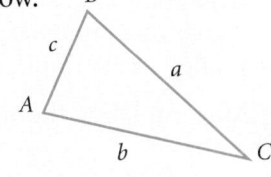

When labeling triangles, it is customary to use capital letters for the angles or angle measures, and lowercase letters for the sides or side lengths. Furthermore, an angle and the side opposite that angle are labeled with the same letter.

E X A M P L E ❶

Find the area of △*RST* to the nearest tenth of a square unit.

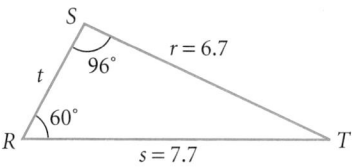

CONNECTION
GEOMETRY

● **SOLUTION**

In order to have SAS information, you need to know *T*. Recall that the sum of the angle measures of any triangle is 180°.

$$R + S + T = 180°$$

$$60° + 96° + T = 180°$$

$$T = 24°$$

With SAS information, you can use one of the area formulas from the previous page to find the area of △*RST*.

$$K = \frac{1}{2}sr \sin T$$

$$K = \frac{1}{2}(7.7)(6.7) \sin 24°$$

$$K \approx 10.5$$

Thus, the area of △*RST* is about 10.5 square units.

TRY THIS   Find the area of △*XYZ* to the nearest tenth of a square unit.

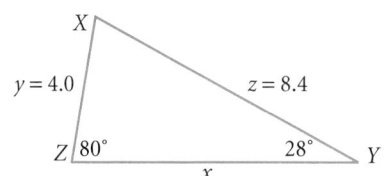

Law of Sines

Using the area formulas, you can derive the *law of sines*. Because the formulas $K = \frac{1}{2}bc \sin A$, $K = \frac{1}{2}ac \sin B$, and $K = \frac{1}{2}ab \sin C$ all represent the area of △*ABC*, they are equal.

$$\frac{1}{2}bc \sin A \;=\; \frac{1}{2}ac \sin B \;=\; \frac{1}{2}ab \sin C$$

$$bc \sin A \;=\; ac \sin B \;=\; ab \sin C$$

$$\frac{bc \sin A}{abc} \;=\; \frac{ac \sin B}{abc} \;=\; \frac{ab \sin C}{abc}$$

$$\frac{\sin A}{a} \;=\; \frac{\sin B}{b} \;=\; \frac{\sin C}{c}$$

Law of Sines

For △*ABC*, the **law of sines** states the following:

$$\frac{\sin A}{a} = \frac{\sin B}{b} = \frac{\sin C}{c}$$

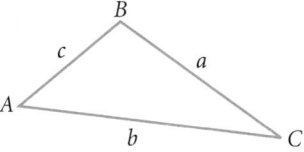

CRITICAL THINKING   Show that $\dfrac{\sin A + \sin B}{\sin B} = \dfrac{a + b}{b}$ is true for any △*ABC*.

When you are given the measures of two angles and the length of the included side in a triangle, this is called angle-side-angle (ASA) information. Given ASA information, you can use the law of sines to solve triangles, as shown in Example 2.

EXAMPLE **2** Solve △*ABC*. Give answers to the nearest tenth, if necessary.

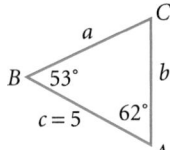

● **SOLUTION**

First find *C*.

$$A + B + C = 180°$$
$$62° + 53° + C = 180°$$
$$C = 65°$$

Now apply the law of sines to find sides *a* and *b*.

$$\frac{\sin A}{a} = \frac{\sin C}{c}$$

$$\frac{\sin 62°}{a} = \frac{\sin 65°}{5}$$

$$a = \frac{5 \sin 62°}{\sin 65°}$$

$$a \approx 4.9$$

$$\frac{\sin B}{b} = \frac{\sin C}{c}$$

$$\frac{\sin 53°}{b} = \frac{\sin 65°}{5}$$

$$b = \frac{5 \sin 53°}{\sin 65°}$$

$$b \approx 4.4$$

TRY THIS Solve △*DEF*. Give answers to the nearest tenth, if necessary.

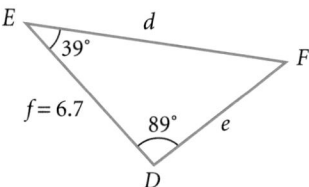

Example 3 shows how you can use the law of sines to solve a triangle for which you are given side-angle-angle (SAA) information.

EXAMPLE **3** A surveying crew needs to find the distance between two points, *A* and *B*. They cannot measure the distance directly because there is a hill between the two points. The surveyors obtain the information shown in the diagram at right.

Find *c* to the nearest foot.

● **SOLUTION**

$$\frac{\sin C}{c} = \frac{\sin A}{a}$$

$$\frac{\sin 110°}{c} = \frac{\sin 30°}{422} \qquad \textit{Substitute A = 30°, a = 422, and C = 110°.}$$

$$c = \frac{422 \sin 110°}{\sin 30°}$$

$$c \approx 793$$

Thus, the distance between points *A* and *B* is approximately 793 feet.

TRY THIS In △*KLM* at right, find *m* to the nearest whole number.

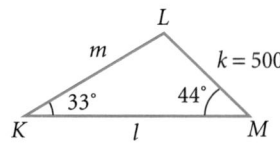

The Ambiguous Case

When you are given two side lengths and the measure of an angle that is not between the sides, the given information is called side-side-angle (SSA) information.

Activity
Exploring SSA Information

You will need: no special materials

1. The figure below illustrates SSA triangle information. Side *a* is free to pivot about *C*. How many triangles can be formed when *a* < *h*, where *h* is the altitude of the triangle? Use the illustration to explain your answer.

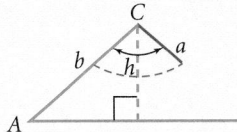

2. How many triangles can be formed when *a* = *h*? Use the illustration to explain your answer.

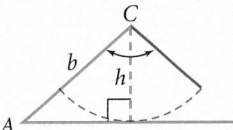

3. How many triangles can be formed when *a* > *h* and *a* < *b*? Use the illustration to explain your answer.

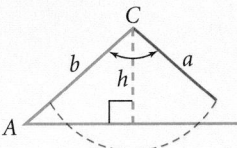

4. How many triangles may be formed when *a* > *h* and *a* > *b*? Use the illustration to explain your answer.

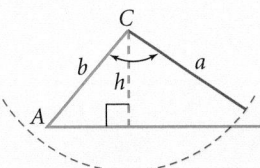

CHECKPOINT ✔ 5. Explain how you may find 0, 1, or 2 triangles, given SSA information.

CONNECTION
GEOMETRY

Recall from geometry that SSA information is not sufficient to prove triangle congruence. With SSA information, 0, 1, or 2 triangles may be possible.

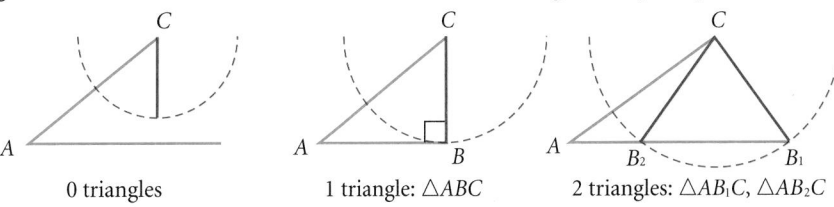

0 triangles   1 triangle: △*ABC*   2 triangles: △*AB₁C*, △*AB₂C*

Determine whether the given SSA information defines 0, 1, or 2 triangles.

a. $b = 2$, $c = 8$, and $B = 120°$　　　　**b.** $c = 10$, $a = 6$, and $A = 28°$

● **SOLUTION**

a.
$$\frac{\sin C}{c} = \frac{\sin B}{b}$$
$$\frac{\sin C}{8} = \frac{\sin 120°}{2}$$
$$\sin C = \frac{8 \sin 120°}{2}$$
$$\sin C \approx 3.4641$$

The range of $y = \sin \theta$ is $-1 \le y \le 1$. Because there is no angle whose sine is 3.4641, no triangle can be formed.

b.
$$\frac{\sin C}{c} = \frac{\sin A}{a}$$
$$\frac{\sin C}{10} = \frac{\sin 28°}{6}$$
$$\sin C = \frac{10 \sin 28°}{6}$$
$$\sin C \approx 0.7825$$

Recall from Lesson 13.3 that there are two possible values of θ between 0° and 180° for which $\sin \theta \approx 0.7825$. Thus, there are two possible triangles.

$$C \approx 51.5° \quad or \quad C \approx 180° - 51.5°$$
$$C \approx 128.5°$$

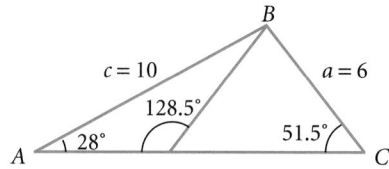

TRY THIS　　Determine whether the given SSA information defines 0, 1, or 2 triangles.
a. $a = 10$, $c = 4$, and $C = 148°$　　　**b.** $a = 2.4$, $b = 3.1$, and $A = 24°$

LAW OF SINES			
Given	**You can**	**Given**	**You can**
SAS	find the area of a triangle	SAA	solve a triangle
ASA	solve a triangle	SSA	define 0, 1, or 2 triangles

Exercises

● Communicate

1. Explain how to solve a triangle when ASA information is known.

2. Explain how to solve a triangle when SAA information is known.

3. Explain under what circumstances SSA information does *not* determine a triangle.

4. Explain how information about sides and angles may determine two different triangles.

Guided Skills Practice

5. Find the area of △*RST* to the nearest tenth of a square unit. *(EXAMPLE 1)*

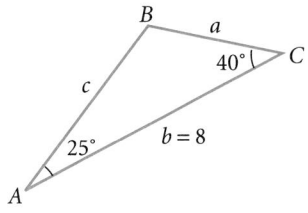

6. Solve △*ABC* at left. Give answers to the nearest tenth, if necessary. *(EXAMPLE 2)*

7. In △*XYZ* at right, find *x* to the nearest tenth. *(EXAMPLE 3)*

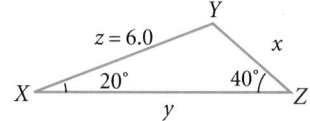

Determine whether the given SSA information defines 0, 1, or 2 triangles. *(EXAMPLE 4)*

8. $a = 12$, $b = 15$, and $A = 30°$

9. $c = 2$, $b = 20$, and $C = 150°$

Practice and Apply

Find the area of △*ABC* to the nearest tenth of a square unit.

10. $b = 5$ in., $c = 8$ in., $A = 45°$

11. $a = 10$ ft, $c = 12$ ft, $B = 30°$

12. $a = 9$ in., $b = 11$ in., $C = 60°$

13. $b = 7$ cm, $c = 10$ cm, $A = 45°$

14. $a = 6$ km, $c = 10$ km, $B = 57°$

15. $a = 25$ ft, $b = 32$ ft, $C = 67°$

16. $b = 13$ in., $c = 16$ in., $A = 110°$

17. $a = 17$ m, $c = 22$ m, $B = 121°$

18. $a = 19$ ft, $b = 8$ ft, $C = 102.32°$

19. $b = 5$ cm, $c = 8$ cm, $A = 94.75°$

20. $a = 5$ km, $c = 9$ km, $B = 67.23°$

21. $a = 87$ ft, $b = 42$ ft, $C = 73.97°$

22. $a = 7$ m, $c = 10$ m, $B = 23°$

23. $a = 33$ ft, $c = 49$ ft, $B = 63.34°$

internet connect

Homework Help Online

Go To: **go.hrw.com**
Keyword:
MB1 Homework Help
for Exercises 24–43

Use the given information to find the indicated side length in △*ABC*. Give answers to the nearest tenth.

24. Given $A = 42°$, $B = 35°$, and $a = 10$, find b.

25. Given $A = 50°$, $C = 25°$, and $a = 15$, find c.

26. Given $B = 60°$, $C = 70°$, and $c = 15$, find b.

27. Given $C = 55°$, $A = 100°$, and $c = 8$, find a.

28. Given $A = 115°$, $B = 30°$, and $c = 10$, find a.

29. Given $A = 40°$, $C = 80°$, and $b = 15$, find c.

Solve each triangle. Give answers to the nearest tenth, if necessary.

30. $A = 43°$, $B = 52°$, $b = 20$

31. $B = 27°$, $C = 52°$, $c = 6$

32. $A = 20°$, $C = 60°$, $a = 10$

33. $A = 35°$, $B = 62°$, $a = 8$

34. $A = 23°$, $B = 62°$, $c = 15$

35. $B = 80°$, $C = 20°$, $a = 10$

36. $A = 60°$, $B = 40°$, $a = 10$

37. $B = 35°$, $C = 48°$, $b = 12$

38. $B = 40°$, $C = 60°$, $b = 8$

39. $A = 37°$, $C = 42°$, $b = 20$

40. $A = 40°$, $B = 45°$, $c = 16$

41. $C = 42°$, $B = 58°$, $c = 9$

42. $B = 30°$, $C = 45°$, $a = 9$

43. $A = 45°$, $C = 23°$, $b = 11$

State the number of triangles determined by the given information. If 1 or 2 triangles are formed, solve the triangle(s). Give answers to the nearest tenth, if necessary.

44. $A = 45°, c = 10, a = 2$

45. $A = 30°, c = 2, a = 1.5$

46. $A = 45°, c = 4, a = 5$

47. $A = 60°, c = 8, a = 2$

48. $A = 30°, c = 2, a = 1$

49. $A = 45°, c = 5, a = \dfrac{5\sqrt{2}}{2}$

50. Find the length of side x in the figure at right to the nearest tenth.

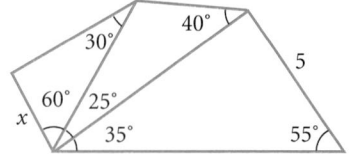

51. GEOMETRY In the figure at right, $CD = 100$ centimeters, m∠1 = 33°, m∠2 = 42°, m∠3 = m∠1 + m∠2, m∠4 = 37°, m∠5 = 78°, and m ∠6 = 50°. Find AB to the nearest centimeter.

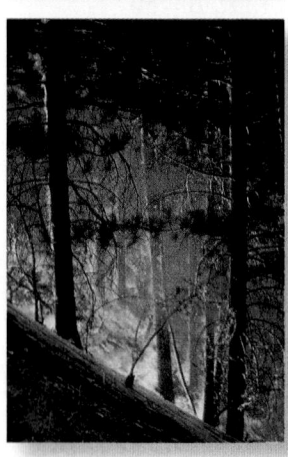

52. FIRE FIGHTING Two rangers, one at station A and one at station B, observe a fire in the forest. The angle at station A formed by the lines of sight to station B and to the fire is 65.23°. The angle at station B formed by the lines of sight to station A and to the fire is 56.47°. The stations are 10 kilometers apart.

  a. How far from station A is the fire?

  b. How far from station B is the fire?

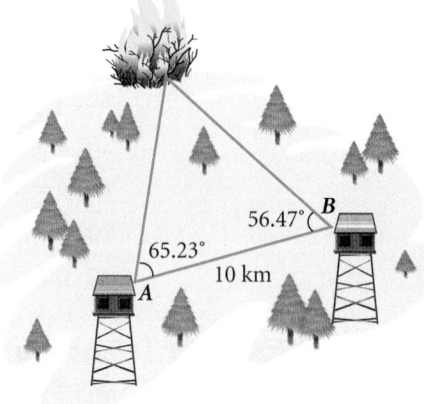

53. SURVEYING Refer to the diagram below. Find the distance from point A to point B across the river. Give your answer to the nearest meter.

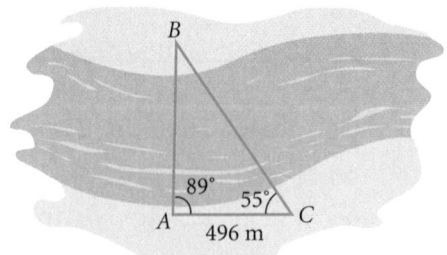

54. FORESTRY The angle of elevation between a straight path and a horizontal is 6°. A tree at the higher end of the path casts a 6.5-meter shadow down the path. The angle of elevation from the end of the shadow to the top of the tree is 32°. How tall is the tree?

The U.S. Coast Guard aids vessels in distress.

55. RESCUE A boat in distress at sea is sighted from two coast guard observation posts, *A* and *B*, on the shore. The angle at post *A* formed by the lines of sight to post *B* and to the boat is 41.67°. The angle at post *B* formed by the lines of sight to post *A* and to the boat is 36.17°. Find the distance, to the nearest tenth of a kilometer, from observation post *A* to the boat.

56. SURVEYING Surveyors made the angle and distance measurements shown at right.

 a. Find distance *c* to the nearest meter.
 b. Find distance *a* to the nearest meter.

 Look Back

57. INVESTMENTS How long does it take for an investment to double at an annual interest rate of 5% compounded continuously? *(LESSON 6.6)*

Factor each polynomial. *(LESSON 7.3)*

58. $3x^3 - 12x$

59. $2x^4 - 12x^3 + 18x^2$

60. Identify all asymptotes and holes in the graph of $f(x) = \dfrac{2x^2 + 10x}{x^2 + 2x - 15}$. *(LESSON 8.2)*

Convert each degree measure to radian measure. Give exact answers. *(LESSON 13.4)*

61. $90°$ **62.** $-180°$ **63.** $135°$ **64.** $120°$

Convert each radian measure to degree measure. Round answers to the nearest tenth of a degree. *(LESSON 13.4)*

65. $-\dfrac{\pi}{5}$ **66.** $\dfrac{3\pi}{7}$ **67.** 4.1802 **68.** -2.3221

 Look Beyond

69. For each triangle, verify that $c^2 = a^2 + b^2 - 2ab \cos C$.

 a.

 b.

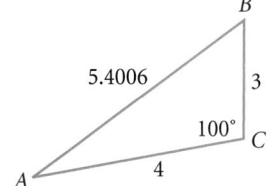

The Law of Cosines

Why *The law of cosines can be used to find distances that cannot be measured easily. For example, the law of cosines can be used to find the distance between two boats when a distress signal is sent.*

Objective

● Use the law of cosines to solve triangles.

APPLICATION

NAVIGATION

Two fishing boats, the *Tina Anna* and the *Melissa Jane*, leave the same dock at the same time. The *Tina Anna* sails at 15 nautical miles per hour and the *Melissa Jane* sails at 17 nautical miles per hour in directions that create a 115° angle between their paths.

After 3 hours, the *Tina Anna* sends a distress signal to the *Melissa Jane*. How far apart are the two boats when the distress signal is sent? As soon as the signal is sent, the *Tina Anna* stops and the *Melissa Jane* sails at 17 nautical miles per hour directly toward the *Tina Anna*. How long will it take for the *Melissa Jane* to reach the *Tina Anna*? To answer these questions, you can use the *law of cosines*. *You will solve this problem in Example 2.*

The law of cosines is used in solving triangles for which side-side-side (SSS) or side-angle-side (SAS) information is given. In these cases, the law of sines can be used only after more information is found by using the law of cosines.

To derive the law of cosines, consider $\triangle ABC$ with altitude $\overline{BD}$ whose length is h.

In $\triangle ABD$:

$$c^2 = x^2 + h^2 \text{ and } \cos A = \frac{x}{c}, \text{ or } x = c \cos A$$

In $\triangle CBD$:

$$a^2 = (b - x)^2 + h^2$$
$$a^2 = b^2 - 2bx + x^2 + h^2$$
$$a^2 = b^2 - 2bx + c^2 \qquad \textit{Substitute } c^2 \textit{ for } x^2 + h^2.$$
$$a^2 = b^2 - 2b(c \cos A) + c^2 \qquad \textit{Substitute } c \cos A \textit{ for } x.$$
$$a^2 = b^2 + c^2 - 2bc \cos A \qquad \textit{Simplify.}$$

The two other formulas for the law of cosines can be derived in a similar fashion.

Law of Cosines

In any triangle $\triangle ABC$, the law of cosines states the following:

$$a^2 = b^2 + c^2 - 2bc \cos A$$
$$b^2 = a^2 + c^2 - 2ac \cos B$$
$$c^2 = a^2 + b^2 - 2ab \cos C$$

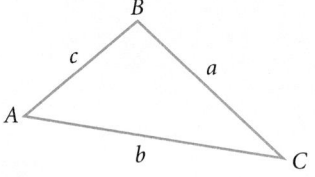

CRITICAL THINKING

Show that the Pythagorean Theorem is a special case of the law of cosines. Then show that if $c^2 = a^2 + b^2$, then $\triangle ABC$ is a right triangle in which C is the right angle.

Example 1 below shows you how to use the law of cosines in two situations to find the unknown length of a side of a triangle when given SAS information and the unknown measure of an angle when given SSS information.

E X A M P L E ❶ **Find the indicated measure to the nearest tenth for $\triangle ABC$.**

a. Given $a = 123$, $c = 97$, and $B = 22°$, find b.

b. Given $a = 11.3$, $b = 7.2$, and $c = 14.8$, find A.

● **SOLUTION**

PROBLEM SOLVING

a. Draw a diagram.

You are given SAS information. Use the law of cosines to find b.

$$b^2 = a^2 + c^2 - 2ac \cos B$$

$$b^2 = 123^2 + 97^2 - 2(123)(97) \cos 22°$$

$$b = \sqrt{123^2 + 97^2 - 2(123)(97) \cos 22°}$$

$$b \approx 49.1$$

CHECK

Note that the side opposite the smallest angle has the shortest length.

b. Draw a diagram.

You are given SSS information. Use the law of cosines to find A.

$$a^2 = b^2 + c^2 - 2bc \cos A$$

$$11.3^2 = 7.2^2 + 14.8^2 - 2(7.2)(14.8) \cos A$$

$$\cos A = \frac{11.3^2 - 7.2^2 - 14.8^2}{-2(7.2)(14.8)}$$

$$\cos A \approx 0.6719$$

$$A \approx \cos^{-1}(0.6719)$$

$$A \approx 47.8°$$

TRY THIS

Find the indicated measure, to the nearest tenth, for $\triangle XYZ$.
a. Given $x = 82$, $z = 63.2$, and $Y = 114°$, find y.
b. Given $x = 2.47$, $y = 3.80$, and $z = 4.24$, find X.

EXAMPLE ② Refer to the two fishing boats described at the beginning of the lesson. The boats leave the dock at the same time, and after 3 hours the *Tina Anna* sends a distress signal to the *Melissa Jane*.

APPLICATION
NAVIGATION

a. How far apart are the two boats when the distress signal is sent? Give your answer to the nearest tenth of a nautical mile.

b. If the *Tina Anna* stops and the *Melissa Jane* sails at 17 nautical miles per hour toward the *Tina Anna*, about how long will it take for the *Melissa Jane* to reach the *Tina Anna*?

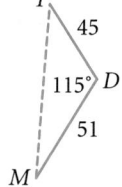

Tina Anna

15 nautical miles per hour

115° D

17 nautical miles per hour

Melissa Jane

● **SOLUTION**

PROBLEM SOLVING

a. Draw a diagram. Use the formula *distance = rate × time* to find *TD* and *MD*.

$$TD = 15(3) = 45$$
$$MD = 17(3) = 51$$

T
45
115° D
51
M

Use the law of cosines to find *MT*.

$$(MT)^2 = (TD)^2 + (MD)^2 - 2(TD)(MD) \cos D$$
$$(MT)^2 = (45)^2 + (51)^2 - 2(45)(51) \cos 115°$$
$$MT = \sqrt{(45)^2 + (51)^2 - 2(45)(51) \cos 115°}$$
$$MT \approx 81.0$$

The boats are about 81.0 nautical miles apart.

b. To find the time, use the formula *distance = rate × time*.

$$d = rt$$
$$81.0 = 17t$$
$$t = \frac{81.0}{17}$$
$$t \approx 4.8$$

It will take the *Melissa Jane* about 4.8 hours, or 4 hours and 48 minutes, to reach the *Tina Anna*.

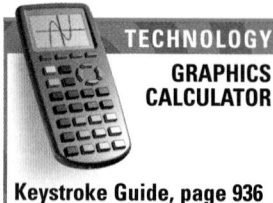

TECHNOLOGY
GRAPHICS CALCULATOR

Keystroke Guide, page 936

Activity
Using Graphs to Explore Solutions

You will need: a graphics calculator or graph paper

1. Graph $y = \sin \theta$ for $0° \leq \theta \leq 180°$.

2. How many times does $\sin \theta = \frac{1}{2}$ on this interval?

CHECKPOINT ✔ 3. What is the maximum number of solutions that are possible when finding an angle of a triangle by using the law of sines? Explain.

4. Graph $y = \cos \theta$ for $0° \leq \theta \leq 180°$.

5. How many times does $\cos \theta = \frac{1}{2}$ on this interval?

CHECKPOINT ✔ 6. What is the maximum number of solutions that are possible when finding an angle of a triangle by using the law of cosines? Explain.

Example 3 below shows you how to use the law of cosines and the law of sines with SAS information to solve a triangle.

E X A M P L E **③** **Solve △DFG at right. Give answers to the nearest tenth.**

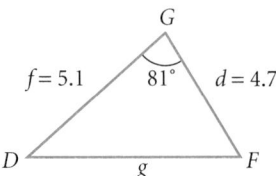

● SOLUTION

1. Use the law of cosines to find g.

$$g^2 = d^2 + f^2 - 2df \cos G$$
$$g^2 = (4.7)^2 + (5.1)^2 - 2(4.7)(5.1) \cos 81°$$
$$g = \sqrt{(4.7)^2 + (5.1)^2 - 2(4.7)(5.1) \cos 81°}$$
$$g \approx 6.4$$

2. Then use the law of sines to find a second angle. Find D.

$$\frac{\sin D}{d} = \frac{\sin G}{g}$$
$$\frac{\sin D}{4.7} = \frac{\sin 81°}{6.4}$$
$$\sin D = \frac{4.7 \sin 81°}{6.4}$$
$$\sin D = 0.7253$$
$$D \approx 46.5° \quad or \quad D \approx 133.5°$$

If $d < g$, then $D < G$. Therefore, $D \approx 46.5°$.

> *Remember to consider both possible angle measures when using the law of sines.*

3. Find G.

$$D + G + F = 180°$$
$$F \approx 180° - 81° - 46.5°$$
$$F \approx 52.5°$$

Thus, $g \approx 6.4$, $D \approx 46°$, and $F \approx 53°$.

TRY THIS   Solve △XYZ at right. Give answers to the nearest tenth.

Example 4 below shows you how to use the law of cosines and the law of sines with SSS information to solve a triangle.

E X A M P L E **④** **Solve △ABC at right. Give answers to the nearest tenth.**

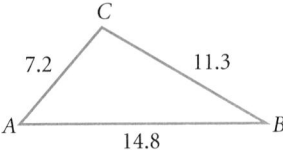

● SOLUTION

The angle opposite the largest side can be either obtuse or acute. If you begin by using the law of cosines to find this angle, then you can use the law of sines to find the next angle without having to consider the ambiguous case.

1.
$$c^2 = a^2 + b^2 - 2ab \cos C$$
$$(14.8)^2 = (11.3)^2 + (7.2)^2 - 2(11.3)(7.2) \cos C$$
$$(14.8)^2 - (11.3)^2 - (7.2)^2 = -2(11.3)(7.2) \cos C$$
$$\cos C = \frac{(14.8)^2 - (11.3)^2 - (7.2)^2}{-2(11.3)(7.2)}$$
$$\cos C \approx -0.2428$$
$$C \approx 104.1°$$

Identify the wanted, given, and needed information. You could continue to use the law of cosines to find the measure of the second angle, but the law of sines is the easier method to use. Because C is obtuse, you know that the other angles are acute, so there will be no guessing involved when using the law of sines.

2. Find the measure of one of the other angles.

$$\frac{\sin B}{b} = \frac{\sin C}{c}$$

$$\frac{\sin B}{7.2} = \frac{\sin 104.1°}{14.8}$$

$$\sin B = \frac{7.2 \sin 104.1°}{14.8}$$

$$\sin B = 0.4718$$

$$B \approx 28.2°$$

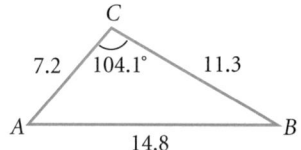

3. Find the measure of the remaining angle.

$$A + B + C = 180°$$
$$A + 28.2 + 104.1 \approx 180°$$
$$A \approx 180° - 28.2° - 104.1°$$
$$A \approx 47.7°$$

SOLVING A TRIANGLE	
Given:	**Use:**
SSS	law of cosines, then law of sines
SSA	law of sines (ambiguous)
SAA	law of sines
ASA	law of sines
SAS	law of cosines, then law of sines
AAA	not possible

Exercises

Communicate

1. What variables appear in each of the three versions of the law of cosines, and what do these variables represent?

2. Explain how to solve a triangle by using the law of cosines if the lengths of the three sides of the triangle are known.

3. Explain how to solve a triangle by using the law of cosines if the lengths of two sides and the measure of the angle between them are known.

4. GEOMETRY Explain why it is not possible to solve a triangle by using AAA information.

Guided Skills Practice

5. Find the indicated measure to the nearest tenth for △*ABC*.
(EXAMPLE 1)
   a. Given *a* = 65, *c* = 52, and *B* = 31°, find *b*.
   b. Given *a* = 8, *b* = 12.1, and *c* = 9.4, find *A*.

APPLICATION

6. NAVIGATION Refer to the two boats described at the beginning of the lesson and continued in Example 2. Assume that *D* = 128°, the *Tina Anna* sails at 21 nautical miles per hour and the *Melissa Jane* sails at 18.5 nautical miles per hour. How far apart are the boats when the distress signal is sent? How long will it take the *Melissa Jane* to reach the *Tina Anna*? **(EXAMPLE 2)**

7. Solve △*DEF*. Give answers to the nearest tenth.
(EXAMPLE 3)

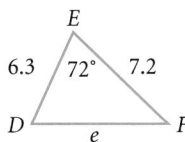

8. Solve △*ABC* at right. Give answers to the nearest tenth. **(EXAMPLE 4)**

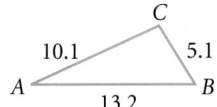

Practice and Apply

Classify the type of information given, and then find the measure of *A* in each triangle. Give answers to the nearest tenth.

9.

10.

11.

12.

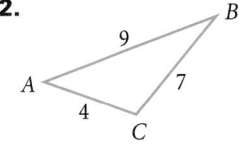

☑ internet connect

Homework Help Online
Go To: **go.hrw.com**
Keyword:
MB1 Homework Help
for Exercises 13–42

Classify the type of information given, and then use the law of cosines to find the missing side length of △*ABC* to the nearest tenth.

13. *a* = 10, *b* = 15, *C* = 24°

14. *b* = 20, *c* = 14, *A* = 21°

15. *a* = 24.4, *c* = 16.2, *B* = 112°

16. *a* = 47.5, *b* = 58.0, *C* = 74°

17. *A* = 78°, *b* = 2, *c* = 4

18. *B* = 108°, *a* = 7, *b* = 10

Solve each triangle. Give answers to the nearest tenth.

19. *a* = 35, *b* = 49, *c* = 45

20. *a* = 8, *b* = 9, *c* = 33

21. *a* = 12.3, *b* = 14.0, *c* = 15.7

22. *a* = 18.1, *b* = 21.0, *c* = 23.7

23. *a* = 0.7, *b* = 0.9, *c* = 1.2

24. *a* = 8.4, *b* = 9.6, *c* = 11.4

Classify the type of information given, and then solve △ABC. Give answers to the nearest tenth. If no such triangle exists, write *not possible*.

25. $a = 30, b = 25, c = 22$

26. $a = 10, b = 20, c = 15$

27. $a = 123, c = 97, B = 22°$

28. $b = 123, c = 63.2, A = 114°$

29. $B = 30°, a = 4, c = 6$

30. $B = 45°, a = 3, c = 5$

31. $a = 7, b = 9, c = 18$

32. $a = 8, b = 12, c = 21$

33. $C = 60°, a = 7, b = 5$

34. $C = 30°, a = 4, b = 10$

35. $a = 6, b = 3, c = 5$

36. $a = 8, b = 7, c = 6$

37. $A = 58°, a = 10, b = 8$

38. $A = 42°, a = 9, b = 12$

39. $a = 9, b = 15, c = 5$

40. $a = 4, b = 8, c = 13$

41. $a = 11, b = 13, c = 12$

42. $a = 29, b = 25, c = 23$

CHALLENGE

43. Find x in the figure at right.

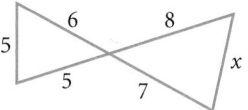

CONNECTIONS

44. GEOMETRY In parallelogram $ABCD$, $AC = 8.4$, $BD = 5.6$, and m$\angle CED = 80°$. Find the length of the sides of parallelogram $ABCD$ to the nearest tenth.

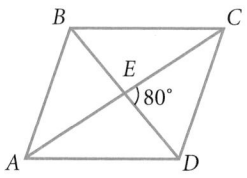

45. GEOMETRY Find all of the angle measures in an isosceles triangle whose base is $\frac{1}{3}$ as long as its legs.

MAXIMUM/MINIMUM A TV antenna is to be installed on a roof that has a pitch of 5 in 12, or a rise of 5 feet for every 12 feet of run, as shown below. The manufacturer's instructions state that the angle that each of the two guy wires make with the pole should be no less than 30°.

46. What is the minimum length of each guy wire that could be used? Round your answer to the nearest foot.

47. What is the height to the nearest tenth of a foot of the longest antenna pole that could fit on the roof shown at right if the roof attachment point can vary? What is the length to the nearest foot of the guy wire that will be required for an antenna pole of this length?

48. Is it possible for the guy wire to make a 40° angle with a 13-foot antenna pole?

49. SURVEYING A surveying crew needs to find the distance between two points, *A* and *B*, but a boulder blocks the path. The surveyors obtain the information shown in the diagram at right. Find *AB*. Give your answer to the nearest foot.

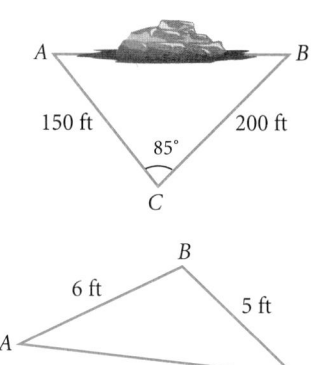

50. MANUFACTURING A piece of sheet metal is to be cut using a blowtorch so that it forms a triangle with the side lengths shown at right. Find the measures of angles *A*, *B*, and *C*.

Look Back

Graph each pair of parametric equations for the given interval of *t*.
(LESSON 3.6)

51. $\begin{cases} x(t) = 4t \\ y(t) = 2 - t \end{cases}$ for $2 \le t \le 6$

52. $\begin{cases} x(t) = 2t - 1 \\ y(t) = \frac{1}{2}t \end{cases}$ for $-4 \le t \le 4$

Use the quadratic formula to solve each equation. Give exact answers.
(LESSON 5.5)

53. $y = 6x^2 - x - 12$

54. $y = 2x^2 + 5x + 2$

55. $y = x^2 + 3x - 2$

56. $y = 2x^2 + 3x$

Look Beyond

57. Graph the function $y = \sin^2 x + \cos^2 x$ for *x*-values from 0 to 2π. Describe the graph.

Gear-Tooth Design Gear makers often shape the sides of gear teeth so that they curve toward each other. This gear design allows gears to mesh smoothly without seizing up or jamming.

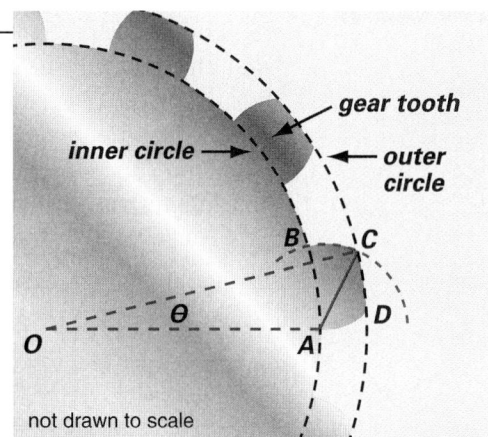

not drawn to scale

On gear tooth *ABCD*, $\overset{\frown}{BC}$ is the arc of a circle with its center at *A* and radius *AC*. In the diagram, $\theta = 13.5°$. The radius of the gear's base circle is 6 centimeters and the radius of the outer circle is 7 centimeters.

1. Make a sketch like the gear tooth above by using the given lengths and angle measures.

2. Use the law of cosines to find *AC*, the radius of the circle that generates $\overset{\frown}{BC}$.

WORKING ON THE CHAPTER PROJECT

You should now be able to complete Activity 1 of the Chapter Project.

14.3

Fundamental Trigonometric Identities

Objectives

- Prove fundamental trigonometric identities.

- Use fundamental trigonometric identities to rewrite expressions.

Why *Fundamental trigonometric identities can be used to rewrite a trigonometric expression as a single trigonometric function. This lets you solve real-world problems such as finding the angle of incline where rubber on concrete starts to slip.*

The coefficients of friction between rubber and concrete keeps this runner from slipping.

APPLICATION
PHYSICS

A block of rubber rests on a concrete platform. One end of the platform is slowly elevated. At what angle, θ, will the block of rubber begin to slide down the concrete platform? This angle is used to find the *coefficient of static friction, μ_s* (read "*mu* sub *s*"), between the rubber block and the cement. For a rubber block on concrete, this number is $\mu_s = 1.4$.

The force of friction that prevents the block from sliding is equal to $\mu_s mg \cos \theta$, where m is the mass of the block and g is the acceleration due to gravity. The force that causes the block to slide is $mg \sin \theta$. At the instant that the block begins to slide, both forces are equal, as shown below.

$$mg \sin \theta = 1.4 mg \cos \theta$$

Use this equation to find the angle, θ, at which the block begins to slide. *You will solve this problem in Example 5.*

Trigonometric identities are equations that are true for all values of the variables for which the expressions on each side of the equation are defined. Recall from Chapter 13 that if $P(x, y)$ is a point on the terminal side of θ in standard position, then $\tan \theta = \frac{x}{y}$ and $P(x, y) = P(r \cos \theta, r \sin \theta)$. You can use these definitions to prove the identity $\tan \theta = \frac{\sin \theta}{\cos \theta}$.

EXAMPLE ❶ Prove the identity $\tan \theta = \frac{\sin \theta}{\cos \theta}$.

● **SOLUTION**

$\tan \theta = \frac{y}{x}$ *Use the definition of tan θ.*

$\tan \theta = \frac{r \sin \theta}{r \cos \theta}$ *Use substitution.*

$\tan \theta = \frac{\sin \theta}{\cos \theta}$

CHECK

In degree mode, graph $y = \tan x$ and $y = \frac{\sin x}{\cos x}$ on the same screen. The graphs appear to be the same. Note that this does not prove the identity, it only verifies it.

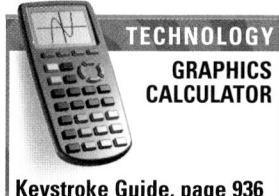
TECHNOLOGY
GRAPHICS CALCULATOR

Keystroke Guide, page 936

TRY THIS   Prove the identity $\cot \theta = \frac{\cos \theta}{\sin \theta}$.

You can use a procedure similar to that shown in Example 1 to prove *ratio identities* and *reciprocal identities*. You can use the Pythagorean Theorem and the definitions of the trigonometric functions to prove the *Pythagorean identities*.

Fundamental Identities

Ratio identities	Reciprocal identities	Pythagorean identities
$\tan \theta = \frac{\sin \theta}{\cos \theta}$	$\csc \theta = \frac{1}{\sin \theta}$	$\cos^2 \theta + \sin^2 \theta = 1$
		$\sin^2 \theta = 1 - \cos^2 \theta$
	$\sec \theta = \frac{1}{\cos \theta}$	$\cos^2 \theta = 1 - \sin^2 \theta$
$\cot \theta = \frac{\cos \theta}{\sin \theta}$		$\tan^2 \theta + 1 = \sec^2 \theta$
	$\cot \theta = \frac{1}{\tan \theta}$	$1 + \cot^2 \theta = \csc^2 \theta$

Note that the square of $\sin \theta$ is written as $\sin^2 \theta$. This form is used for all trigonometric functions.

EXAMPLE ❷ Prove the identity $\cos^2 \theta + \sin^2 \theta = 1$.

● **SOLUTION**

$\cos^2 \theta + \sin^2 \theta = \left(\frac{x}{r}\right)^2 + \left(\frac{y}{r}\right)^2$ *Use definitions of cos θ and sin θ.*

$\cos^2 \theta + \sin^2 \theta = \frac{x^2 + y^2}{r^2}$

$\cos^2 \theta + \sin^2 \theta = \frac{r^2}{r^2}$ *By the Pythagorean Theorem, $x^2 + y^2 = r^2$.*

$\cos^2 \theta + \sin^2 \theta = 1$

TRY THIS   Prove the identity $\tan^2 \theta + 1 = \sec^2 \theta$.

You can use the fundamental identities to rewrite trigonometric expressions in terms of a single trigonometric function.

E X A M P L E **3** Write $\dfrac{\sin^2 \theta}{1 - \cos \theta}$ in terms of a single trigonometric function.

● **SOLUTION**

$$\frac{\sin^2 \theta}{1 - \cos \theta} = \frac{1 - \cos^2 \theta}{1 - \cos \theta} \qquad \textit{Use } \sin^2 \theta = 1 - \cos^2 \theta.$$

$$= \frac{(1 + \cos \theta)(1 - \cos \theta)}{1 - \cos \theta} \qquad \textit{Factor the difference of two squares.}$$

$$= \frac{(1 + \cos \theta)\cancel{(1 - \cos \theta)}}{\cancel{1 - \cos \theta}}$$

$$= 1 + \cos \theta$$

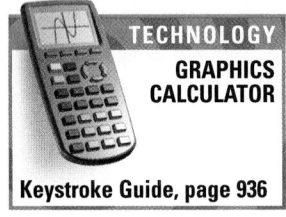

TECHNOLOGY

GRAPHICS CALCULATOR

Keystroke Guide, page 936

CHECK

Graph $y = \dfrac{\sin^2 \theta}{1 - \cos \theta}$ and $y = 1 + \cos \theta$ on the same screen. The graphs appear to coincide.

TRY THIS

Write $\dfrac{\cos^2 \theta}{1 - \sin \theta}$ in terms of a single trigonometric function.

Activity
Exploring Graphing Methods

TECHNOLOGY

GRAPHICS CALCULATOR

Keystroke Guide, page 937

You will need: a graphics calculator

1. Graph $y = (\csc \theta)(1 - \cos \theta)(1 + \cos \theta)$.
2. Write a simple function involving only $\sin \theta$ or $\cos \theta$ for the graph in Step 1.
3. Show algebraically that setting your function rule from Step 2 equal to $(\csc \theta)(1 - \cos \theta)(1 + \cos \theta)$ results in an identity.
4. Repeat Steps 1–3, using $y = \tan \theta (\csc \theta - \tan \theta \cos \theta)$.

CHECKPOINT ✔ 5. Describe one advantage to graphing the related function for a trigonometric expression to help simplify the expression.

6. Use your own example to illustrate how a graph can help you simplify a trigonometric expression.

C O N N E C T I O N

TRANSFORMATIONS

You can use a graphics calculator to get hints on the outcome of rewriting a trigonometric expression. For example, you can graph $y = \dfrac{\sin^2 \theta}{1 - \cos \theta}$ from Example 3 before rewriting the expression to see that it appears to be the graph of $y = \cos \theta$ translated 1 unit up.

CHECKPOINT ✔ Graph $y = \tan^2 \theta - \sec^2 \theta$. What does it suggest to you about the result of rewriting the expression $\tan^2 \theta - \sec^2 \theta$?

Write $\sec \theta - \tan \theta \sin \theta$ in terms of $\cos \theta$.

TECHNOLOGY

GRAPHICS CALCULATOR

Keystroke Guide, page 937

● **SOLUTION**

Graph $y = \sec \theta - \tan \theta \sin \theta$.

Notice that the graph appears to be the same as $y = \cos \theta$.

Use algebra to verify this.

$$\sec \theta - \tan \theta \sin \theta = \frac{1}{\cos \theta} - \left(\frac{\sin \theta}{\cos \theta}\right)(\sin \theta) \qquad \text{\textit{Use reciprocal and ratio identities.}}$$

$$= \frac{1}{\cos \theta} - \frac{\sin^2 \theta}{\cos \theta}$$

$$= \frac{1 - \sin^2 \theta}{\cos \theta}$$

$$= \frac{\cos^2 \theta}{\cos \theta} \qquad \text{\textit{Use a Pythagorean identity.}}$$

$$= \cos \theta$$

TRY THIS   Write $\dfrac{1}{\sec^2 \theta}$ in terms of $\sin \theta$.

CRITICAL THINKING   Write $\tan \theta$ in terms of $\sin \theta$.

Example 5 uses substitution of equivalent trigonometric expressions to solve problems.

E X A M P L E   5 Refer to the friction problem at the beginning of the lesson.

APPLICATION

PHYSICS

Use the equation $mg \sin \theta = \mu_s mg \cos \theta$ to determine the angle at which each material begins to slide.

a. rubber block on cement: $\mu_s = 1.4$

b. glass block on lubricated metal: $\mu_s = 0.25$

● **SOLUTION**

a. $mg \sin \theta = \mu_s mg \cos \theta$

    $mg \sin \theta = \mathbf{1.4}mg \cos \theta$

      $\sin \theta = 1.4 \cos \theta$

      $\dfrac{\sin \theta}{\cos \theta} = 1.4$

      $\tan \theta = 1.4$

        $\theta \approx 54.5°$

Thus, rubber will begin to slide on cement at an angle of about 54.5°.

b. $mg \sin \theta = \mu_s mg \cos \theta$

    $mg \sin \theta = \mathbf{0.25}mg \cos \theta$

      $\sin \theta = 0.25 \cos \theta$

      $\dfrac{\sin \theta}{\cos \theta} = 0.25$

      $\tan \theta = 0.25$

        $\theta \approx 14.4°$

Thus, glass will begin to slide on lubricated metal at an angle of about 14.4°.

TRY THIS   The coefficient of static friction for a certain type of leather on metal is $\mu_s = 0.8$. At what angle will a block of this type of leather begin to slide on a metal platform?

Exercises

⬤ Communicate

1. How is the tangent function related to the sine and cosine functions?

2. Describe two strategies that can be used to rewrite trigonometric expressions.

CONNECTION

3. **GEOMETRY** Explain how the trigonometric Pythagorean identity $\sin^2 \theta + \cos^2 \theta = 1$ is related to the Pythagorean Theorem.

⬤ Guided Skills Practice

4. Prove the identity $\sec \theta = \dfrac{1}{\cos \theta}$, for $\cos \theta \neq 0$. *(EXAMPLE 1)*

5. Prove the identity $\sin^2 \theta = 1 - \cos^2 \theta$. *(EXAMPLE 2)*

6. Write $\dfrac{\cos^2 \theta}{1 + \sin \theta}$ in terms of a single trigonometric function. *(EXAMPLE 3)*

7. Write $\cot^2 \theta$ in terms of $\sin \theta$. *(EXAMPLE 4)*

APPLICATION

8. **PHYSICS** The coefficient of static friction for a certain type of rubber on concrete is $\mu_s = 1.2$. At what angle will a block of this type of rubber begin to slide on a concrete platform? *(EXAMPLE 5)*

⬤ Practice and Apply

Use definitions to prove each identity.

9. $\cot \theta = \dfrac{1}{\tan \theta}$, $\tan \theta \neq 0$

10. $\csc \theta = \dfrac{1}{\sin \theta}$, $\sin \theta \neq 0$

11. $\cos^2 \theta = 1 - \sin^2 \theta$

12. $1 + \cot^2 \theta = \csc^2 \theta$

Write each expression in terms of a single trigonometric function.

13. $\cot \theta \sin \theta$

14. $\tan \theta \cos \theta$

15. $\tan \theta \csc \theta$

16. $\tan \theta \sec \theta \sin \theta$

17. $\csc \theta \sin^2 \theta$

18. $\sec \theta \cos^2 \theta$

19. $\left(\dfrac{\sin^2 \theta}{\cos \theta}\right)(\csc \theta)$

20. $\left(\dfrac{\cos^3 \theta}{\sin \theta}\right)(\sec^2 \theta)$

21. $\dfrac{\sin \theta}{\tan \theta}$

22. $\dfrac{\cos \theta}{\cot \theta}$

23. $\dfrac{\csc^2 \theta}{\cot^2 \theta}$

24. $\dfrac{\sec^2 \theta}{\tan^2 \theta}$

25. $\left(\dfrac{\sin \theta}{\cot \theta}\right)(\cos \theta)$

26. $\left(\dfrac{\cos \theta}{\tan \theta}\right)(\sin \theta)$

Write each expression in terms of cos θ.

27. $2 \sin^2 \theta - 1$

28. $(1 - \sin^2 \theta)(1 + \sec^2 \theta)$

29. $(1 - \cot^2 \theta)(\cot^2 \theta + 1)$

30. $\dfrac{\tan \theta}{\sin \theta}$

Write each expression in terms of sin θ.

31. $\cot \theta \cos \theta$

32. $\cot^2 \theta$

33. $\tan^2 \theta \cos^2 \theta + \csc \theta$

34. $\dfrac{1}{\sec^2 \theta}$

Use identities to verify that each statement is true.

internet connect

Homework Help Online

Go To: **go.hrw.com**
Keyword:
MB1 Homework Help
for Exercises 35–50

35. $\dfrac{\sec \theta}{\csc \theta} = \tan \theta$

36. $\dfrac{\csc \theta}{\sec \theta} = \cot \theta$

37. $\dfrac{\tan^2 \theta}{\sec^2 \theta} = \sin^2 \theta$

38. $\dfrac{\cot^2 \theta}{\csc^2 \theta} = \cos^2 \theta$

39. $\cot^2 \theta = \cos^2 \theta \csc^2 \theta$

40. $\tan^2 \theta = \sin^2 \theta \sec^2 \theta$

41. $\dfrac{\sec \theta}{\cos \theta} = \sec^2 \theta$

42. $\dfrac{\csc \theta}{\sin \theta} = \csc^2 \theta$

43. $\dfrac{\cos \theta}{1 - \sin^2 \theta} = \sec \theta$

44. $\dfrac{\sin \theta}{1 - \cos^2 \theta} = \csc \theta$

45. $(\sec \theta)(1 - \sin^2 \theta) = \cos \theta$

46. $(\csc \theta)(1 - \cos^2 \theta) = \sin \theta$

47. $(\tan \theta)(\csc \theta)(\sec \theta) = \sec^2 \theta$

48. $(\cot \theta)(\csc \theta)(\sec \theta) = \csc^2 \theta$

49. Write $\tan^2 \theta - 2 \sec \theta \sin \theta$ in terms of $\sin \theta$ and $\cos \theta$.

50. Write $\tan^2 \theta - 2 \sec \theta \sin \theta$ in terms of $\tan \theta$.

Write each expression in terms of cos θ.

51. $\sin \theta$

52. $\csc \theta$

53. $\tan \theta$

54. $\cot \theta$

CHALLENGE

Write all of the trigonometric functions in terms of each given function.

55. $\sin \theta$

56. $\tan \theta$

57. $\cot \theta$

58. $\sec \theta$

APPLICATION

PHYSICS Refer to the friction problem described at the beginning of the lesson and continued in Example 5. Use the equation $mg \sin \theta = \mu_s mg \cos \theta$ to determine the angle at which each material begins to slide.

59. waxed wood on wet snow: $\mu_s = 0.14$

60. wood on wood: $\mu_s = 0.4$

61. wood on brick: $\mu_s = 0.6$

62. silk on silk: $\mu_s = 0.25$

Friction slows the motion of a skier, allowing them to turn and stop.

63 Write the matrix equation that represents the system at right and solve the system, if possible. *(LESSON 4.4)*

$$\begin{cases} 2x + y - 6z = -12 \\ -x + y + z = -7 \\ 5x - 3y + 7z = 11 \end{cases}$$

APPLICATION

GEOLOGY Recall from Lesson 6.7 that on the Richter scale, the magnitude, M, of an earthquake depends on the amount of energy, E, in ergs released by the earthquake as given by the equation $M = \frac{2}{3} \log \frac{E}{10^{11.8}}$. The list below gives information about some earthquakes that have occurred in the recent past.

Central square of Leninakan, Armenia, in 1988

Year	Location	Richter magnitude
1976	Tangshan, China	8.2
1978	Northeast Iran	7.7
1985	Mexico City, Mexico	8.1
1988	Northwest Armenia	6.8
1989	San Francisco, CA	7.1
1990	Northwest Iran	7.7
1993	South India	6.4
1994	Northridge, CA	6.8
1995	Kobe, Japan	7.2

Compare the amounts of energy released by the earthquakes listed for the indicated years. How much more energy was released by the greater earthquake? *(LESSON 6.7)*

64. 1976 and 1989

65. 1976 and 1985

66. 1978 and 1993

67. 1990 and 1993

68. 1976 and 1995

69. 1985 and 1994

70. Graph $y = 2(x - 3)^2 + 5$. Label the vertex, focus, and directrix. *(LESSON 9.2)*

71. Graph $\frac{x^2}{4} + \frac{y^2}{9} = 1$. Label the center, vertices, co-vertices, and foci. *(LESSON 9.4)*

72. In the diagram at right, $\angle BAC$ is the angle of depression. Point A represents the eyes of a person who is standing on top of a building and sees a traffic accident at C. How far from the base of the building, D, is the accident? Give your answer to the nearest foot. *(LESSON 13.1)*

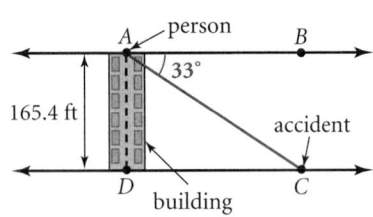

73. Carry out the procedure below by using radian measure.
   a. On the same axes, graph $y = \sin x$ and $y = x$ for $-0.3 \leq x \leq 0.3$. Does this suggest that $\sin x = x$?
   b. Repeat part **a** for $-2 \leq x \leq 2$.
   c. Draw a conclusion about using a graph to verify identities.

Sum and Difference Identities

Objectives

- Evaluate expressions by using the sum and difference identities.

- Use matrix multiplication with sum and difference identities to perform rotations.

APPLICATION

DESIGN

A design is made by rotating a rectangular figure as shown at left below. The figure on the positive x-axis has the vertices A, B, C, and D, shown at right below.

Why *You can use the sum and difference identities and matrix multiplication to create designs that are composed of multiple rotations of an image.*

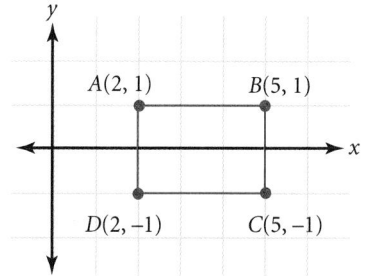

Find the coordinates of the vertices after a 30° rotation about the origin.
You will solve this problem in Example 5.

To solve the problem above, you can use a rotation matrix. The entries in the matrix are found by using the trigonometric *sum and difference identities*.

Activity
Proving the Difference Identity for Cosine

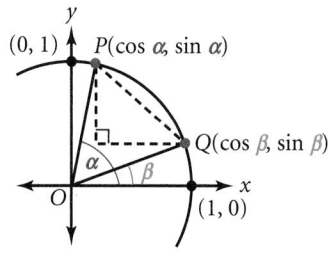

You will need: no special materials

In the diagram at left, m∠$POQ = \alpha - \beta$.

1. Using the distance formula, $d = \sqrt{(x_2 - x_1)^2 + (y_2 - y_1)^2}$, you can write the equation below.

$$(PQ)^2 = (\cos \alpha - \cos \beta)^2 + (\sin \alpha - \sin \beta)^2$$

    a. Show that the right side of the equation can be rewritten as

        $2 - 2 \cos \alpha \cos \beta - 2 \sin \alpha \sin \beta$.

    b. What identity did you use in part **a**?

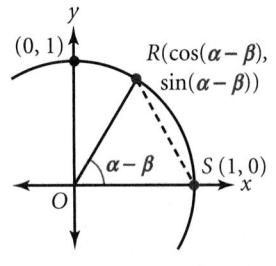

$(0, 1)$

$R(\cos(\alpha - \beta), \sin(\alpha - \beta))$

$S(1, 0)$

$\alpha - \beta$

O

In the diagram at left, m$\angle ROS = \alpha - \beta$.

2. Using the distance formula, you can write the equation below.

$$(RS)^2 = [\cos(\alpha - \beta) - 1]^2 + [\sin(\alpha - \beta) - 0]^2$$

    a. Show that the right side of the equation can be rewritten as $2 - 2\cos(\alpha - \beta)$.

    b. What identity did you use in part **a**?

CHECKPOINT ✔   **3.** Does $PQ = RS$? Explain. Does $(PQ)^2 = (RS)^2$? Explain.

CHECKPOINT ✔   **4.** Using $(PQ)^2 = (RS)^2$ and the expressions for $(PQ)^2$ and $(RS)^2$ given in Step 1**a** and 2**a**, derive an expression for $\cos(\alpha - \beta)$ that includes $\sin \alpha$, $\sin \beta$, $\cos \alpha$, and $\cos \beta$.

All of the sum and difference identities can be proved in a manner similar to that explored in the Activity.

Sum and Difference Identities

$$\sin (A + B) = \sin A \cos B + \cos A \sin B$$
$$\sin (A - B) = \sin A \cos B - \cos A \sin B$$

$$\cos (A + B) = \cos A \cos B - \sin A \sin B$$
$$\cos (A - B) = \cos A \cos B + \sin A \sin B$$

E X A M P L E **1** Find the exact value of each expression.

    a. $\sin(120° + 45°)$ **b.** $\cos(120° + 45°)$

● **SOLUTION**

    a. $\sin(120° + 45°) = (\sin 120°)(\cos 45°) + (\cos 120°)(\sin 45°)$

$$= \left(\frac{\sqrt{3}}{2}\right)\left(\frac{\sqrt{2}}{2}\right) + \left(-\frac{1}{2}\right)\left(\frac{\sqrt{2}}{2}\right)$$

$$= \frac{\sqrt{6}}{4} - \frac{\sqrt{2}}{4}$$

$$= \frac{\sqrt{6} - \sqrt{2}}{4}$$

    b. $\cos(120° + 45°) = (\cos 120°)(\cos 45°) - (\sin 120°)(\sin 45°)$

$$= \left(-\frac{1}{2}\right)\left(\frac{\sqrt{2}}{2}\right) - \left(\frac{\sqrt{3}}{2}\right)\left(\frac{\sqrt{2}}{2}\right)$$

$$= \frac{-\sqrt{2}}{4} - \frac{\sqrt{6}}{4}$$

$$= \frac{-\sqrt{2} - \sqrt{6}}{4}$$

TRY THIS   Find the exact value of each expression.

    a. $\cos(210° - 30°)$ **b.** $\sin(330° - 135°)$

You can use the difference identities to derive other identities.

EXAMPLE 2 **Prove the identity $\sin(180° − \theta) = \sin \theta$.**

● **SOLUTION**

$$\sin(180° − \theta) = (\sin 180°)(\cos \theta) − (\cos 180°)(\sin \theta)$$
$$= (0)(\cos \theta) − (−1)(\sin \theta)$$
$$= \sin \theta$$

TRY THIS Prove the identity $\sin(90° − \theta) = \cos \theta$.

A function, f, is **even** if $f(−x) = f(x)$ for all values of x in its domain. A function f is **odd** if $f(−x) = −f(x)$ for all x in its domain. You can use the difference identities to show that cosine is an even function and sine is an odd function.

$$\cos(−\theta) = \cos(0° − \theta) \qquad\qquad \sin(−\theta) = \sin(0° − \theta)$$
$$= \cos 0° \cos \theta + \sin 0° \sin \theta \qquad\qquad = \sin 0° \cos \theta − \cos 0° \sin \theta$$
$$= (1)(\cos \theta) + (0)\sin \theta \qquad\qquad = (0)(\cos \theta) − (1)(\sin \theta)$$
$$= \cos \theta \qquad\qquad\qquad\qquad = −\sin \theta$$

Thus, the cosine function is an even function and the sine function is an odd function.

CHECKPOINT ✔ Use the reciprocal identities to determine whether the secant and cosecant functions are odd or even.

EXAMPLE 3 **Find the exact value of each expression.**
a. $\sin(−165°)$ **b.** $\cos 195°$

● **SOLUTION**

a. $\sin(−165°) = −\sin 165°$
$$= −\sin(120° + 45°)$$
$$= −[(\sin 120°)(\cos 45°) + (\cos 120°)(\sin 45°)]$$
$$= −\left[\left(\frac{\sqrt{3}}{2}\right)\left(\frac{\sqrt{2}}{2}\right) + \left(−\frac{1}{2}\right)\left(\frac{\sqrt{2}}{2}\right)\right]$$
$$= −\left(\frac{\sqrt{6} − \sqrt{2}}{4}\right)$$
$$= \frac{\sqrt{2} − \sqrt{6}}{4}$$

b. $\cos 195° = \cos(150° + 45°)$
$$= (\cos 150°)(\cos 45°) − (\sin 150°)(\sin 45°)$$
$$= \left(−\frac{\sqrt{3}}{2}\right)\left(\frac{\sqrt{2}}{2}\right) − \left(\frac{1}{2}\right)\left(\frac{\sqrt{2}}{2}\right)$$
$$= \frac{−\sqrt{6} − \sqrt{2}}{4}$$

TRY THIS Find the exact value of each expression.
a. $\cos(−105°)$ **b.** $\sin 285°$

E X A M P L E **4** Graph $y = \sin(30° − \theta)$.

● **SOLUTION**

$$y = \sin(30° − \theta)$$
$$= \sin[−(\theta − 30°)]$$
$$= −\sin(\theta − 30°) \quad \textit{The sine function is odd.}$$

Graph $y = \sin \theta$.

Then translate the graph 30° to the right, and reflect the graph across the x-axis.

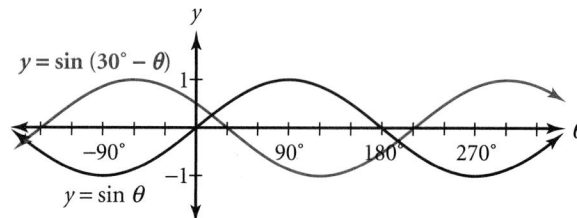

TRY THIS Graph $y = \cos(45° − \theta)$.

Rotation Matrices

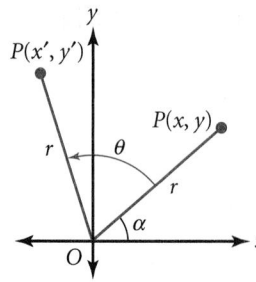

Matrix multiplication can be used in combination with sum and difference identities to determine the coordinates of points rotated on a plane about the origin. In the diagram at left, $P'(x', y')$ is the image of $P(x, y)$ after a rotation of θ degrees.

Recall from Lesson 13.3 that the coordinates of P are $(r \cos \alpha, r \sin \alpha)$. The coordinates of P' are found below.

$$x' = r \cos(\alpha + \theta) \qquad\qquad y' = r \sin(\alpha + \theta)$$
$$= r[(\cos \alpha)(\cos \theta) − (\sin \alpha)(\sin \theta)] \qquad = r[(\sin \alpha)(\cos \theta) + (\cos \alpha)(\sin \theta)]$$
$$= (r \cos \alpha)(\cos \theta) − (r \sin \alpha)(\sin \theta) \qquad = (r \sin \alpha)(\cos \theta) + (r \cos \alpha)(\sin \theta)$$
$$= x(\cos \theta) − y(\sin \theta) \qquad\qquad = y(\cos \theta) + x(\sin \theta)$$
$$= x \cos \theta − y \sin \theta \qquad\qquad = x \sin \theta + y \cos \theta$$

Thus, you can find the coordinates of the image point, $P'(x', y')$, by using a *rotation matrix*.

$$\begin{bmatrix} x' \\ y' \end{bmatrix} = \begin{bmatrix} x \cos \theta − y \sin \theta \\ x \sin \theta + y \cos \theta \end{bmatrix}$$
$$= \begin{bmatrix} \cos \theta & −\sin \theta \\ \sin \theta & \cos \theta \end{bmatrix} \begin{bmatrix} x \\ y \end{bmatrix}$$

Rotation Matrix

If $P(x, y)$ is any point in a plane, then the coordinates of the image of point $P'(x', y')$ after a rotation of θ degrees about the origin can be found by using a *rotation matrix* as follows:

$$\begin{bmatrix} \cos \theta & −\sin \theta \\ \sin \theta & \cos \theta \end{bmatrix} \begin{bmatrix} x \\ y \end{bmatrix} = \begin{bmatrix} x' \\ y' \end{bmatrix}$$

Write the rotation matrix for each angle of rotation.

    a. 90°   **b.** 180°   **c.** 270°

E X A M P L E ❺ Refer to the rectangular figure described at the beginning of the lesson.

APPLICATION
DESIGN

**Find the coordinates to the nearest hundredth of the vertices after a 30°
rotation about the origin.**

● **SOLUTION**

The rectangular figure has vertices at $A(2, 1)$, $B(5, 1)$, $C(5, -1)$, and $D(2, -1)$.

Write matrices for a 30° rotation and for the vertices of figure $ABCD$.

$$R_{30°} = \begin{bmatrix} \cos 30° & -\sin 30° \\ \sin 30° & \cos 30° \end{bmatrix} \qquad S = \begin{bmatrix} 2 & 5 & 5 & 2 \\ 1 & 1 & -1 & -1 \end{bmatrix}$$

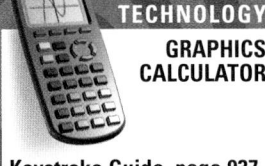

TECHNOLOGY
**GRAPHICS
CALCULATOR**

Keystroke Guide, page 937

Find the matrix product.

$$R_{30°} \times S = \begin{bmatrix} \cos 30° & -\sin 30° \\ \sin 30° & \cos 30° \end{bmatrix} \begin{bmatrix} 2 & 5 & 5 & 2 \\ 1 & 1 & -1 & -1 \end{bmatrix}$$

$$\approx \begin{bmatrix} 1.23 & 3.83 & 4.83 & 2.23 \\ 1.87 & 3.37 & 1.63 & 0.13 \end{bmatrix}$$

The approximate coordinates of the vertices for the image of figure $ABCD$ are
$A'(1.23, 1.87)$, $B'(3.83, 3.37)$, $C'(4.83, 1.63)$, and $D'(2.23, 0.13)$.

TRY THIS Given the figure described in Example 5, find the coordinates of the vertices
for the image of this figure after a 60° rotation about the origin.

CRITICAL THINKING Show that a 90° rotation about the origin is the same as a 60° rotation about
the origin followed by a 30° rotation.

Exercises

● *Communicate*

1. Explain how to use sum or difference
identities to find the exact value of cos 75°.

2. Explain how to use sum or difference
identities to find the exact value of sin(−15°).

3. Explain how a matrix can be used to rotate
the point $P(2, 3)$ at right 45° about the
origin.

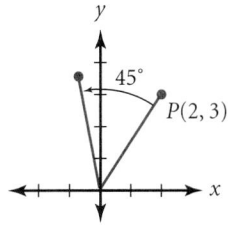

Guided Skills Practice

Find the exact value of each expression. *(EXAMPLE 1)*

4. $\sin(135° + 60°)$ **5.** $\cos(60° − 45°)$

6. Prove the identity $−\cos(\theta + 180°) = \cos\theta$. *(EXAMPLE 2)*

Find the exact value of each expression. *(EXAMPLE 3)*

7. $\cos(−270°)$ **8.** $\sin(−240°)$

CONNECTION

9. TRANSFORMATIONS Graph $y = \sin(45° − \theta)$. *(EXAMPLE 4)*

APPLICATION

10. DESIGN Refer to the design problem described at the beginning of the lesson. Find the coordinates to the nearest hundredth of the vertices after a 120° rotation about the origin. *(EXAMPLE 5)*

Practice and Apply

Find the exact value of each expression.

11. $\sin(30° + 45°)$ **12.** $\sin(30° + 135°)$ **13.** $\cos(30° + 135°)$

14. $\cos(30° + 45°)$ **15.** $\sin(135° + 180°)$ **16.** $\sin(135° − 180°)$

17. $\cos(120° − 45°)$ **18.** $\cos(150° − 45°)$ **19.** $\sin(210° − 315°)$

20. $\sin(240° − 315°)$ **21.** $\cos(225° − 330°)$ **22.** $\cos(135° − 330°)$

Prove each identity.

23. $\sin(90° − \theta) = \cos\theta$ **24.** $\cos(90° − \theta) = \sin\theta$

25. $\cos(90° + \theta) = −\sin\theta$ **26.** $\sin(270° + \theta) = −\cos\theta$

27. $\sin(180° − \theta) = \sin\theta$ **28.** $\cos(180° − \theta) = −\cos\theta$

Use substitution to verify each statement.

29. $\sin(A + B) \neq \sin A + \sin B$ **30.** $\cos(A + B) \neq \cos A + \cos B$

31. $\sin(A − B) \neq \sin A − \sin B$ **32.** $\sin(A − B) \neq \cos A − \cos B$

Find the exact value of each expression.

33. $\sin 105°$ **34.** $\sin 165°$ **35.** $\cos 195°$

36. $\cos 225°$ **37.** $\sin 15°$ **38.** $\sin 75°$

39. $\cos 165°$ **40.** $\cos 285°$ **41.** $\sin(−135°)$

42. $\sin(−210°)$ **43.** $\cos(−225°)$ **44.** $\cos(−15°)$

Find the rotation matrix for each angle of rotation. Round entries to the nearest hundredth, if necessary.

45. $45°$ **46.** $60°$ **47.** $320°$ **48.** $224°$

49. $−120°$ **50.** $−200°$ **51.** $−135°$ **52.** $−320°$

Graph each function.

53. $y = \sin(\theta − 60°)$ **54.** $y = \sin(\theta − 45°)$ **55.** $y = \cos(30° − \theta)$

56. $y = \cos(180° − \theta)$ **57.** $y = \sin(120° − \theta)$ **58.** $y = \cos(135° − \theta)$

Find the coordinates of the image of each point after a 135° rotation.

59. $P(2, 3)$ **60.** $P(1, 5)$ **61.** $P(-3, 2)$ **62.** $P(4, -5)$

Find the coordinates of the image of each point after a −30° rotation.

63. $P(-1, 2)$ **64.** $P(2, -3)$ **65.** $P(10, 23)$ **66.** $P(7, 35)$

CHALLENGES

67. Use the sum and difference identities for the sine function to show that $\sin(A + B) + \sin(A - B) = 2 \sin A \cos B$ is true.

68. Use the definition of an inverse matrix to verify that the rotation matrix for θ degrees and the rotation matrix for $-\theta$ degrees are inverse matrices.

CONNECTION

TRANSFORMATIONS A rectangular figure has vertices at $W(3, 0)$, $X(3, 2)$, $Y(6, 2)$, and $Z(6, 0)$. Find the coordinates, to the nearest hundredth, of the vertices after the indicated rotation.

69. 60° counterclockwise   **70.** 120° counterclockwise

71. 30° clockwise   **72.** 150° clockwise

73. 225° clockwise   **74.** 330° clockwise

75. 270° counterclockwise   **76.** 240° counterclockwise

APPLICATIONS

77. PHYSICS The function $f(t) = a \cos(At + B)$ represents simple harmonic motion, where t is time, a is the amplitude of the motion, A is the angular frequency in radians, and B is the phase shift in radians. Show that f can be expressed in terms of a difference of the cosine and sine functions when $a = 3$, $A = 1$, and $B = \frac{\pi}{4}$.

78 PHYSICS The *superposition principle* states that if two or more waves are traveling in the same medium (air, water, and so on) the resulting wave is found by adding together the displacements of the individual waves. For instance, for waves f and g, the resulting wave is $y = f(x) + g(x)$.
  a. Graph $f(x) = \cos 2x$ and $g(x) = \cos(2x - 1)$ over the interval $0 \leq x \leq 2\pi$. How do the graphs of f and g differ?
  b. Graph $h(x) = f(x) + g(x)$ in the same screen as f and g. Describe the behavior of the graph of h.
  c. Compare the periods of f, g, and h.
  d. The identity $\cos x + \cos y = 2 \cos \frac{1}{2}(x + y) \cos \frac{1}{2}(x - y)$ can be derived from the identities of this lesson. Use this identity to simplify h.

The up-and-down motion of a pogo stick spring can illustrate simple harmonic motion.

Ocean waves generally pass through one another without being altered. However, a momentary combination of waves can result in an unusually tall wave.

Look Back

79. Find an equation for the inverse of $f(x) = -3x + 7$. Then use composition to verify that the equation you wrote is the inverse. **(LESSON 2.5)**

APPLICATION

80. LAW ENFORCEMENT An explosion is heard by two law enforcement officers who are 2000 meters apart. Electronic equipment allows them to determine that one officer heard the explosion 1.8 seconds after the other officer. The speed of sound in air (at 20°C) is approximately 340 meters per second. Write an equation for the possible locations of the explosions relative to the two law enforcement officers. **(LESSON 9.5)**

81. Solve $\triangle ABC$ given that $a = 2.96$, $b = 3.78$, and $c = 4.54$. **(LESSON 14.2)**

Look Beyond

82. Is $\sin \frac{A}{2} = \frac{\sin A}{2}$ true for all angle measures A? Justify your response.

83. Is $\sin 2A = 2 \sin A$ true for all angle measures A? Justify your response.

PROGRAMMING A machine-tool operator needs to program a gear-cutting machine to cut a gear with 12 teeth. The teeth are to be positioned at 30° intervals. The coordinates for the vertices of the gear-tooth profile are $A(8.00, 0.00)$, $B(7.52, 2.74)$, $C(9.72, 2.33)$, and $D(9.94, 1.13)$.

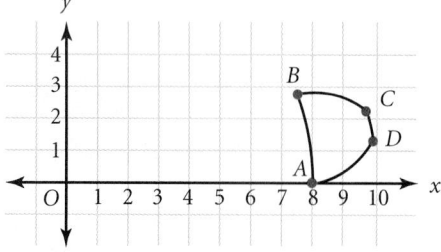

1. Find the coordinates for the image of the gear-tooth profile after a 30° rotation about the origin.
  a. Write matrices for a 30° rotation and for the vertices of the gear-tooth profile.
  b. Find the matrix product.

2. Find the coordinates to the nearest hundredth for the image of the gear-tooth profile after a 60° rotation about the origin.

WORKING ON THE CHAPTER PROJECT

You should now be able to complete Activity 2 of the Chapter project.

Double-Angle and Half-Angle Identities

Why *You can use double- and half-angle identities to evaluate and simplify trigonometric expressions. The half-angle identities are derived from properties of an isosceles triangle.*

U.S. Supreme Court, Washington, D.C.

Objective

● Evaluate and simplify expressions by using double-angle and half-angle identities.

An isosceles roof system, such as the one shown above, is represented at right. The width, *s*, can be written in terms of *a* and θ as follows:

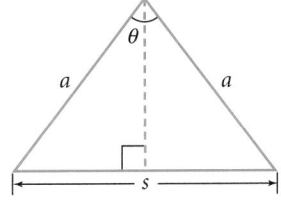

$$\sin \frac{\theta}{2} = \frac{\left(\frac{s}{2}\right)}{a}$$

$$s = 2a \sin \frac{\theta}{2}$$

Another expression for *s* can be derived from the law of cosines.

$$s^2 = a^2 + a^2 - 2aa \cos \theta$$
$$s^2 = 2a^2 - 2a^2 \cos \theta$$
$$s^2 = a^2(2 - 2 \cos \theta)$$
$$s = a\sqrt{2 - 2 \cos \theta}$$

By equating these two expressions for *s*, you can write what is called a *half-angle identity* for the sine function. *This is shown on page 919.*

Double-Angle Identities

You can use sum identities to prove the *double-angle identities* for the sine and cosine functions.

$$\begin{aligned}\sin 2\theta &= \sin(\theta + \theta)\\ &= \sin \theta \cos \theta + \cos \theta \sin \theta\\ &= 2 \sin \theta \cos \theta\end{aligned}$$

$$\begin{aligned}\cos 2\theta &= \cos(\theta + \theta)\\ &= \cos \theta \cos \theta - \sin \theta \sin \theta\\ &= \cos^2 \theta - \sin^2 \theta\end{aligned}$$

Double-Angle Identities

$$\sin 2\theta = 2 \sin \theta \cos \theta \qquad\qquad \cos 2\theta = \cos^2 \theta - \sin^2 \theta$$

You can use double-angle identities to simplify a trigonometric expression, as shown in Example 1.

E X A M P L E ❶ Simplify $(\cos\theta + \sin\theta)^2$.

● **SOLUTION**

$$\begin{aligned}(\cos\theta + \sin\theta)^2 &= \cos^2\theta + 2\cos\theta\sin\theta + \sin^2\theta && \textit{Expand.}\\ &= \cos^2\theta + \sin^2\theta + 2\sin\theta\cos\theta && \textit{Rearrange terms.}\\ &= 1 + \sin 2\theta && \textit{Use substitution.}\end{aligned}$$

CRITICAL THINKING   Use a double-angle identity to write $\sin 3\theta$ in terms of $\sin\theta$ and $\cos\theta$.

You can use double-angle identities to find the exact value of a double-angle given certain information.

E X A M P L E ❷ Given $90° \le \theta \le 180°$ and $\cos\theta = -\frac{3}{4}$, find the exact value of $\cos 2\theta$.

● **SOLUTION**

PROBLEM SOLVING   **Draw a diagram** and find the exact value of $\sin\theta$.

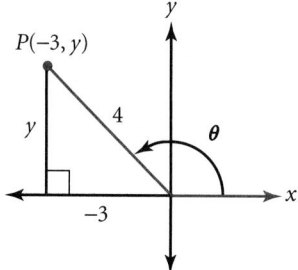

$$\begin{aligned}x^2 + y^2 &= r^2\\ (-3)^2 + y^2 &= 4^2\\ y &= \pm\sqrt{4^2 - (-3)^2}\\ y &= \sqrt{7} && \textit{y is positive in Quadrant II.}\end{aligned}$$

Thus, $\sin\theta = \dfrac{y}{r} = \dfrac{\sqrt{7}}{4}$.

Use the double-angle identity.

$$\begin{aligned}\cos 2\theta &= \cos^2\theta - \sin^2\theta\\ &= \left(-\frac{3}{4}\right)^2 - \left(\frac{\sqrt{7}}{4}\right)^2\\ &= \frac{2}{16}, \text{ or } \frac{1}{8}\end{aligned}$$

TRY THIS   Given $270° \le \theta \le 360°$ and $\cos\theta = \frac{1}{4}$, find the exact value of $\sin 2\theta$.

You can use the identity $\cos^2\theta = 1 - \sin^2\theta$ or $\sin^2\theta = 1 - \cos^2\theta$ to write alternative identities for $\cos 2\theta$.

$$\begin{aligned}\cos 2\theta &= \cos^2\theta - \sin^2\theta\\ &= (1 - \sin^2\theta) - \sin^2\theta\\ &= 1 - 2\sin^2\theta\end{aligned} \qquad \begin{aligned}\cos 2\theta &= \cos^2\theta - \sin^2\theta\\ &= \cos^2\theta - (1 - \cos^2\theta)\\ &= 2\cos^2\theta - 1\end{aligned}$$

Alternative Double-Angle Identities for Cosine

$$\cos 2\theta = 1 - 2\sin^2\theta \qquad\qquad \cos 2\theta = 2\cos^2\theta - 1$$

CHECKPOINT ✔   Solve the problem in Example 2 by using each of the alternative double-angle identities for cosine.

Half-Angle Identities

Refer to the isosceles triangle described at the beginning of the lesson. A half-angle identity for the sine function can be found by solving the two expressions for s that relate $\sin\frac{\theta}{2}$ and $\cos\theta$.

$$2a\sin\frac{\theta}{2} = a\sqrt{2-2\cos\theta} \quad (0° < \theta < 180° \text{ and } a > 0)$$

$$\sin\frac{\theta}{2} = \frac{\sqrt{2-2\cos\theta}}{2}$$

$$\sin\frac{\theta}{2} = \sqrt{\frac{2-2\cos\theta}{4}}$$

$$\sin\frac{\theta}{2} = \sqrt{\frac{1-\cos\theta}{2}}$$

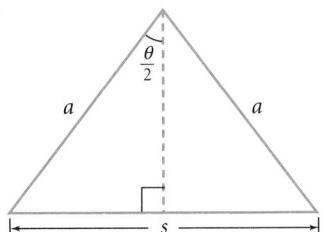

The *half-angle identities* for the sine and cosine of any angle are given below.

Half-Angle Identities

$$\sin\frac{\theta}{2} = \pm\sqrt{\frac{1-\cos\theta}{2}} \qquad\qquad \cos\frac{\theta}{2} = \pm\sqrt{\frac{1+\cos\theta}{2}}$$

Choose $+$ or $-$ depending on the sign of the value for $\sin\frac{\theta}{2}$ or $\cos\frac{\theta}{2}$.

E X A M P L E **③** Given $180° \le \theta \le 270°$ and $\sin\theta = -\frac{2}{3}$, find the exact value of $\cos\frac{\theta}{2}$.

● **SOLUTION**

PROBLEM SOLVING

Draw a diagram and find the exact value of $\cos\theta$.

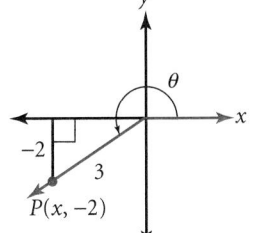

$$x^2 + y^2 = r^2$$
$$x^2 + (-2)^2 = 3^2$$
$$x = \pm\sqrt{3^2 - (-2)^2}$$
$$x = -\sqrt{5} \qquad \textit{x is negative in Quadrant III.}$$

Thus, $\cos\theta = \frac{x}{r} = \frac{-\sqrt{5}}{3}$.

Use the half-angle identity for cosine. If $180° \le \theta \le 270°$, then $\frac{180°}{2} \le \frac{\theta}{2} \le \frac{270°}{2}$, or $90° \le \theta \le 135°$. Therefore, the sign of the value for $\cos\frac{\theta}{2}$ will be negative.

$$\cos\frac{\theta}{2} = -\sqrt{\frac{1+\cos\theta}{2}}$$

$$= -\sqrt{\frac{1+\left(\frac{-\sqrt{5}}{3}\right)}{2}}$$

$$= -\sqrt{\frac{1}{2}\left(1-\frac{\sqrt{5}}{3}\right)}$$

$$= -\sqrt{\frac{1}{2} - \frac{\sqrt{5}}{6}}$$

TRY THIS Given $90° \le \theta \le 180°$ and $\cos\theta = -\frac{1}{3}$, find the exact value of $\sin\frac{\theta}{2}$.

CULTURAL CONNECTION: AFRICA Ptolemy was an astronomer who lived and worked in the North African city of Alexandria during the second century C.E. Ptolemy wrote the most authoritative work on trigonometry of that time, called the *Almagest*, which included the double-angle identities for the sine of an angle.

CRITICAL THINKING Use identities to show that $\cos 2\left(\frac{\theta}{2}\right) = 2\cos^2\frac{\theta}{2} - 1$

can be rewritten as the identity $\cos\frac{\theta}{2} = \pm\sqrt{\frac{1 + \cos\theta}{2}}$.

Ptolemy, a second century astronomer

Exercises

Communicate

internet connect

Activities Online

Go To: **go.hrw.com**
Keyword:
MB1 Archimedes

1. Use the range of $y = \sin\theta$ to explain why $\sin 2\theta$ is not, in general, equivalent to $2\sin\theta$.

2. Describe how to determine the sign of the value of $\sin\frac{\theta}{2}$ or $\cos\frac{\theta}{2}$ if you are given $0° < \theta < 360°$ and the quadrant in which θ terminates.

Guided Skills Practice

3. Simplify $\cos^4\theta - \sin^4\theta$. *(EXAMPLE 1)*

Given $0° \leq \theta \leq 90°$ and $\sin\theta = \frac{2}{5}$, find the exact value of each expression.
(EXAMPLES 2 AND 3)

4. $\cos 2\theta$ **5.** $\sin 2\theta$ **6.** $\cos\frac{\theta}{2}$ **7.** $\sin\frac{\theta}{2}$

Practice and Apply

internet connect

Homework Help Online

Go To: **go.hrw.com**
Keyword:
MB1 Homework Help
for Exercises 8–14

Simplify.

8. $\dfrac{\sin 2\theta}{\cos\theta}$ **9.** $\cos 2\theta + 1$ **10.** $\cos 2\theta + 2\sin^2\theta$

11. $\dfrac{\cos\theta\sin 2\theta}{1 + \cos 2\theta}$ **12.** $\dfrac{\cos 2\theta}{\cos\theta + \sin\theta}$ **13.** $\dfrac{\cos 2\theta}{\cos\theta - \sin\theta} - \sin\theta$

Write each expression in terms of trigonometric functions of θ rather than multiples of θ.

14. $\sin^2 2\theta$ **15.** $\sin 4\theta$ **16.** $\cos^2 2\theta$

17. $\cos 4\theta$ **18.** $\sin 2\theta - 1 + \cos^2\theta$ **19.** $\dfrac{\sin^2\theta}{\sin 2\theta}$

Write each expression in terms of a single trigonometric function.

20. $\sin\theta\cos\theta$ **21.** $2\cos^2\theta - 2\sin^2\theta$ **22.** $2\cos^2\theta - \sin^2\theta$

CHALLENGE

23. Find the exact value of $\sin 7.5°$.

Use the information given to find the exact value of sin 2θ and cos 2θ.

24. $90° \leq \theta \leq 180°$; $\cos \theta = -\frac{3}{5}$

25. $90° \leq \theta \leq 180°$; $\sin \theta = \frac{3}{5}$

26. $270° \leq \theta \leq 360°$; $\cos \theta = \frac{2}{5}$

27. $270° \leq \theta \leq 360°$; $\sin \theta = -\frac{2}{5}$

28. $0° \leq \theta \leq 90°$; $\sin \theta = \frac{1}{4}$

29. $0° \leq \theta \leq 90°$; $\cos \theta = \frac{1}{4}$

30. $180° \leq \theta \leq 270°$; $\sin \theta = -\frac{\sqrt{5}}{4}$

31. $180° \leq \theta \leq 270°$; $\cos \theta = -\frac{\sqrt{5}}{4}$

Use the information given to find the exact value of sin $\frac{\theta}{2}$ and cos $\frac{\theta}{2}$.

32. $0° \leq \theta \leq 90°$; $\sin \theta = \frac{1}{5}$

33. $0° \leq \theta \leq 90°$; $\cos \theta = \frac{1}{5}$

34. $90° \leq \theta \leq 180°$; $\cos \theta = -\frac{5}{6}$

35. $90° \leq \theta \leq 180°$; $\sin \theta = \frac{5}{6}$

36. $180° \leq \theta \leq 270°$; $\sin \theta = -\frac{\sqrt{5}}{3}$

37. $180° \leq \theta \leq 270°$; $\cos \theta = -\frac{\sqrt{5}}{3}$

38. $270° \leq \theta \leq 360°$; $\cos \theta = \frac{3}{8}$

39. $270° \leq \theta \leq 360°$; $\sin \theta = -\frac{3}{8}$

APPLICATION

SPORTS A golf ball is struck with an initial velocity of v_0, in feet per second, and leaves the ground at angle x. The distance that the ball travels is given by the function $d(x) = \frac{(v_0)^2 \sin x \cos x}{16}$.

40. Write the function, d, in terms of the double angle, $2x$.

41. At what angle must a golf ball be hit in order to achieve the maximum possible distance for a given initial velocity? Explain.

Tiger Woods, 1997

 Look Back

State whether each relation represents a function. *(LESSON 2.3)*

42. $\{(-1, 6), (0, 3), (1, 3), (2, 6)\}$

43. $\{(1, 2), (2, 3), (2, 4), (3, 5)\}$

Evaluate. *(LESSONS 10.2 AND 10.3)*

44. $\frac{5!}{2!}$

45. $0!$

46. $_{12}C_4$

47. $_{13}C_3$

48. $_{10}P_4$

49. $_{15}P_3$

50. $\binom{7}{3}$

51. $\binom{10}{2}$

CONNECTION

52. TRANSFORMATIONS For the function $f(\theta) = 3 \sin(2\theta - 60°)$, describe the transformation from its parent function. Then graph at least one period of the function along with the parent function. *(LESSON 13.5)*

 Look Beyond

53. Consider the equation $\sin^2 \theta + 2 \sin \theta - 3 = 0$. Substitute x for $\sin \theta$, and solve the resulting equation for x. Then solve for θ given that $0° \leq \theta \leq 360°$.

Solving Trigonometric Equations

Objectives

- Solve trigonometric equations algebraically and graphically.

- Solve real-world problems by using trigonometric equations.

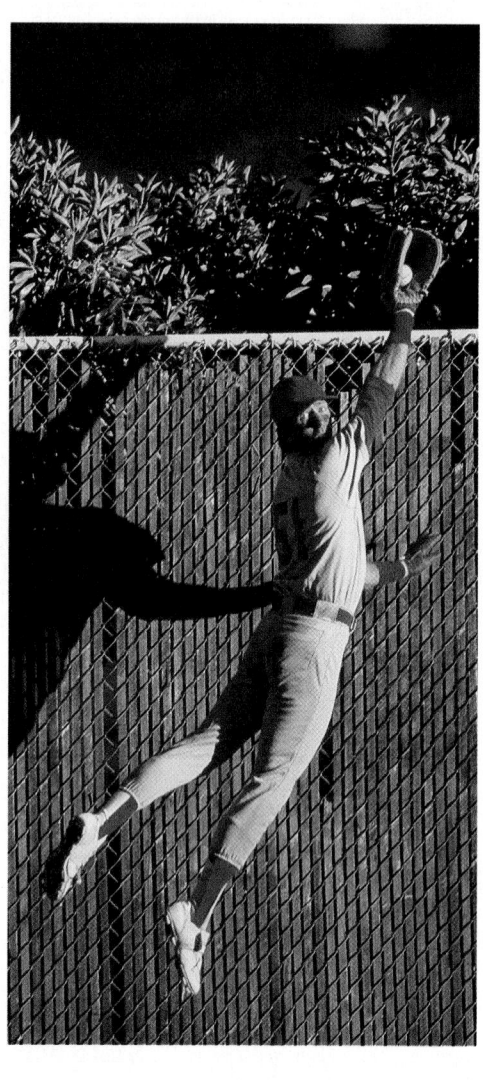

Why *Trigonometric equations can be used to solve real-world problems such as finding the angle at which a batter hits a ball.*

APPLICATION
SPORTS

When a batter hits a baseball, the ball travels in a parabolic path. For a certain hit, the path of the ball in terms of time, t, in seconds is represented by the parametric equations below.

$$\begin{cases} x(t) = 122t \cos \theta & \text{\textit{x(t) is the distance in feet.}} \\ y(t) = 122t \sin \theta - 16t^2 & \text{\textit{y(t) is the height in feet.}} \end{cases}$$

At what angle is the ball hit if it has a height of 15 feet after 3 seconds? *You will answer this question in Example 4.*

Notice that each of the parametric equations is a trigonometric equation. A **trigonometric equation** is an equation that contains at least one trigonometric function. Each of the equations below are trigonometric equations.

$$\cos \theta = 0.5 \qquad \sin^2\left(2x - \frac{\pi}{3}\right) = \frac{\sqrt{3}}{2} \qquad \cos^2 x - 2 \cos x + 3 = 0$$

A solution to a trigonometric equation is any value of the variable for which the equation is true.

Exploring Trigonometric Equations

You will need: a graphics calculator in degree mode

1. Graph $y = \sin \theta$ for the interval $0° \le \theta < 360°$. Over this range, how many values of θ satisfy $\sin \theta = 1$? What are these values?

2. Graph $y = \sin \theta$ for the interval $0° \le \theta < 720°$. Over this range, how many values of θ satisfy $\sin \theta = 0.5$? What are these values?

3. Copy and complete the table below. Based on the table, write a complete solution to $\sin \theta = 1$ in general terms.

Interval	$0° \le \theta < 360°$	$0° \le \theta < 720°$	$0° \le \theta < 1080°$	$0° \le \theta < 1440°$
Number of solutions				
Solutions				

CHECKPOINT ✔

4. Let $\sin \theta = a$, where θ is any real number and a is a fixed real number. Find one value of a for which $\sin \theta = a$ has no solution.

5. Is there a value of a for which there is exactly one solution to $\sin \theta = a$? Justify your response.

6. If $\sin \theta = a$ has at least one solution, must it have infinitely many solutions? Explain your response.

Trigonometric equations are true only for certain values of the variables, unlike trigonometric identities, which are true for all values of the variables. Example 1 shows you how to find all possible solutions of a trigonometric equation.

E X A M P L E **Find all solutions of $\cos \theta = \sqrt{3} - \cos \theta$.**

● **SOLUTION**

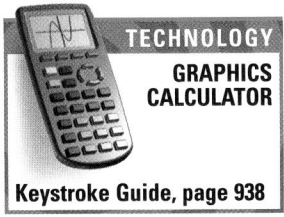
Method 1 Use algebra.

First solve for $0° \le \theta < 360°$.

$$\cos \theta = \sqrt{3} - \cos \theta$$
$$2 \cos \theta = \sqrt{3}$$
$$\cos \theta = \frac{\sqrt{3}}{2}$$
$$\theta = 30° \text{ or } \theta = 330°$$

Method 2 Use a graph.

Graph $y = \cos \theta$ and $y = \sqrt{3} - \cos \theta$ on the same screen over the interval $0° \le \theta < 360°$, and find any points of intersection.

The graphs intersect at $\theta = 30°$ and at $\theta = 330°$.

Thus, $\theta = 30° + n360° \text{ or } \theta = 330° + n360°$.

TRY THIS Find all solutions of $1 - 2 \sin \theta = 0$.

A trigonometric equation may also be solved by using methods for solving quadratic equations.

EXAMPLE ② Find the exact solutions of $\sin^2 \theta - 2 \sin \theta - 3 = 0$ for $0° \leq \theta < 360°$.

● **SOLUTION**

$$\sin^2 \theta - 2 \sin \theta - 3 = 0$$
$$(\sin \theta)^2 - 2(\sin \theta) - 3 = 0$$
$$u^2 - 2u - 3 = 0 \qquad \textit{Substitute u for sin θ.}$$
$$(u + 1)(u - 3) = 0 \qquad \textit{Factor the quadratic expression.}$$
$$(\sin \theta + 1)(\sin \theta - 3) = 0 \qquad \textit{Substitute sin θ for u.}$$
$$\sin \theta = -1 \textit{ or } \sin \theta = 3 \qquad \textit{Apply the Zero-Product Property.}$$

For $\sin \theta = -1$, $\theta = 270°$. The equation $\sin \theta = 3$ has no solution.

Thus, the solution for $0° \leq \theta < 360°$ is $\theta = 270°$.

TRY THIS   Find the exact solutions of $\cos^2 \theta - \sqrt{2} \cos \theta + \frac{1}{2} = 0$ for $0° \leq \theta < 360°$.

CRITICAL THINKING   Use substitution to find the exact solutions of $\sin 3\theta = \frac{1}{2}$ for $0° \leq \theta < 360°$.

A trigonometric equation may contain two trigonometric functions. You can often use trigonometric identities to write the equation in terms of only one of the functions. This is shown in Example 3.

EXAMPLE ③ Solve $2 \cos^2 \theta = \sin \theta + 1$ for $0° \leq \theta < 360°$.

● **SOLUTION**

$$2 \cos^2 \theta = \sin \theta + 1$$
$$2(1 - \sin^2 \theta) = \sin \theta + 1 \qquad \textit{Substitute 1 − sin² θ for cos² θ = 1.}$$
$$2 - 2\sin^2 \theta = \sin \theta + 1$$
$$2 \sin^2 \theta + \sin \theta - 1 = 0$$
$$2u^2 + u - 1 = 0 \qquad \textit{Substitute u for sin θ.}$$
$$(u + 1)(2u - 1) = 0 \qquad \textit{Factor.}$$
$$(\sin \theta + 1)(2 \sin \theta - 1) = 0$$

$$\sin \theta = -1 \qquad \textit{or} \qquad \sin \theta = \frac{1}{2}$$
$$\theta = 270° \quad \textit{or} \quad \theta = 30° \quad \textit{or} \quad \theta = 150°$$

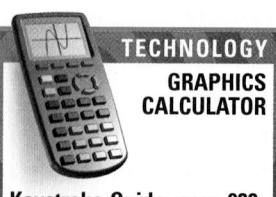

TECHNOLOGY
GRAPHICS CALCULATOR
Keystroke Guide, page 938

CHECK
Graph $y = 2 \cos^2 x$ and $y = \sin x + 1$ on the same screen for $0° \leq x < 360°$, and find any points of intersection.

The graph shows intersections at $x = 30°$, $x = 150°$, and $x = 270°$.

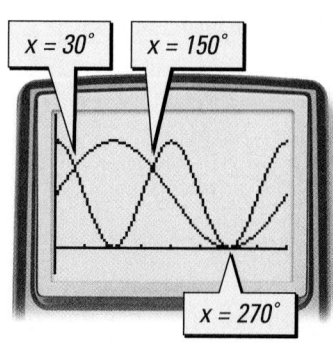

$x = 30°$ $x = 150°$ $x = 270°$

TRY THIS   Solve $1 + \tan^2 \theta + \sec \theta = 0$ for $0° \leq \theta < 360°$.

E X A M P L E ④ Refer to the baseball problem at the beginning of the lesson.

At what angle is the ball hit if it has a height of 15 feet after 3 seconds?

SOLUTION

Substitute 15 for $y(t)$ and 3 for t in the equation for the height.

$$y(t) = 122t \sin \theta - 16t^2$$
$$15 = 122(3) \sin \theta - 16(3)^2$$
$$15 = 366 \sin \theta - 144$$
$$\sin \theta = \frac{15 + 144}{366}$$
$$\theta \approx \sin^{-1}(0.4344)$$
$$\approx 25.7°$$

CHECK

Graph $y = 366 \sin x - 144$ and $y = 15$ on the same screen, and look for any points of intersection.

The graph shows an intersection at $\theta \approx 25.7°$.

Intersection
X=25.74879   Y=15

TECHNOLOGY
GRAPHICS CALCULATOR

Keystroke Guide, page 939

CHECKPOINT ✔ What distance has the ball traveled if it has a height of 15 feet after 3 seconds? Is the hit a home run if the fence is 325 feet from home plate and 15 feet tall?

Exercises

Communicate

1. Describe how trigonometric equations differ from trigonometric identities.

2. Give the number of solutions to $\sin x = -1$ and $\cos x = 2$, and explain why they differ.

3. Summarize the different methods used to solve trigonometric equations in Examples 1, 2, and 3.

Guided Skills Practice

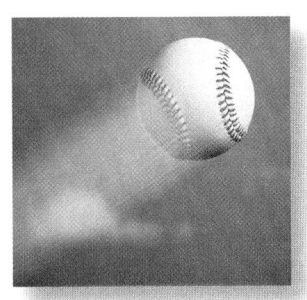

4. Find all solutions of $4 \cos \theta + 1 = 3$. *(EXAMPLE 1)*

5. Find the exact solutions of $\cos^2 \theta - \cos \theta - 2 = 0$ for $0 \le \theta < 360°$. *(EXAMPLE 2)*

6. Solve $1 - 2 \cos \theta + \cos^2 \theta = \sin^2 \theta$ for $0 \le \theta < 360°$. *(EXAMPLE 3)*

7. SPORTS Refer to the baseball problem at the beginning of the lesson. At what angle is the ball hit if it has a height of 20 feet after 3 seconds? *(EXAMPLE 4)*

Practice and Apply

Find all solutions of each equation.

8. $2 \sin \theta - 1 = 0$

9. $2 \cos \theta + 1 = 0$

10. $4 \sin \theta + 2\sqrt{3} = 0$

11. $4 \cos \theta - 2 = 0$

12. $\sin \theta = \sqrt{2} - \sin \theta$

13. $1 - \sin \theta = \sin \theta$

14. $2 - 3 \cos \theta = \cos \theta + 2$

15. $1 + 5 \cos \theta = 2 \cos \theta - 2$

16. $\tan \theta - \sqrt{3} = 0$

17. $\cot \theta + 1 = 0$

18. $6 \cos \theta - 1 = 3 + 4 \cos \theta$

19. $1 - 2 \sin \theta = \sin \theta - \sqrt{3}$

Find the exact solutions of each equation for $0° \le \theta < 360°$.

20. $2 \cos^2 \theta - \cos \theta = 1$

21. $2 \sin^2 \theta = 1 - \sin \theta$

22. $2 \sin^2 \theta - 5 \sin \theta = -2$

23. $2 \cos^2 \theta - 3 \cos \theta = 2$

24. $3 \cos \theta + 2 = -\cos^2 \theta$

25. $3 - \sin \theta = -\sin^2 \theta$

26. $\sin \theta + \sin \theta \cos \theta = 0$

27. $\cos^2 \theta + \cos \theta = 0$

28. $6 \sin^2 \theta - 3 \sin \theta = 0$

29. $2 \cos^2 \theta + \sqrt{3} \cos \theta = 0$

30. $\cos^2 \theta + 2 \cos \theta = -2$

31. $25 \sin^2 \theta + 8 \sin \theta = -8$

32. $2 \cos^2 \theta = \sin^2 \theta + 2$

33. $\cos^2 \theta = \sin^2 \theta + 1$

34. $\cos \theta \tan \theta = -1$

35. $\sec \theta \cos^2 \theta - 1 = 0$

36. $2 \tan^2 \theta = \sec^2 \theta$

37. $\sec^2 \theta + 2 \cot^2 \theta = 3$

38. $\cos \theta - \sin^2 \theta = 1$

39. $3 + 3 \sin \theta = \cos^2 \theta$

40. $2 \cos^2 \theta = \sin \theta + 1$

41. $-\cos \theta - \sin^2 \theta = 1$

42. $2 \cos^2 \theta - 2 \cos \theta = -\sin^2 \theta$

43. $1 - \cos^2 \theta = \cos^2 \theta + 2 \cos \theta + 1$

Solve each equation to the nearest tenth of a degree for $0° \le \theta < 360°$.

44 $2 \cos^2 \theta - \sin \theta - 1 = 0$

45 $\tan^2 \theta + \cot^2 \theta + 2 = 0$

46 $\cos 2\theta - \sin \theta = 0$

47 $\sin 2\theta + \sin \theta = 0$

48 $\cos^2 \theta + 5 \cos \theta + 2 = 0$

49 $4 \sin^2 \theta - 3 \sin \theta - 2 = 0$

CHALLENGE

50. Solve $|\sin \theta| = \sin \theta$ and $|\cos \theta| = \cos \theta$ over the interval $-360° \le \theta < 360°$.

CONNECTION

51. GEOMETRY A circular cap is formed by subtracting the area of the triangle (with legs of length r and angle θ in radians) from the area of the sector, as shown in the figure at right. The area of a circular cap is given by the formula $A = \frac{1}{2}r^2(\theta - \sin \theta)$. A circular sector with a radius of 5 and angle θ has a circular cap whose area is 20. What is the measure of angle θ in radians?

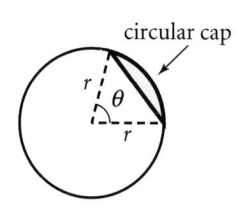
circular cap

APPLICATION

PHYSICS The position of a weight attached to an oscillating spring is given by $y = 5 \cos \pi t$, where t is time in seconds and y is vertical distance in centimeters. Rest position is at the point where $y = 0$.

52. Find the times at which the weight is 5 centimeters above its rest position.

53. Find the times at which the weight is 4 centimeters above its rest position.

PHYSICS When light travels from one medium to another, the path of the light ray changes direction. Snell's law states that a light ray traveling from air to water changes direction according to the equation $\dfrac{\sin \theta_{air}}{\sin \theta_{water}} = n_{water}$, where θ_{air} and θ_{water} are the angles shown in the diagram below, and n_{water} is a constant called the *index of refraction*.

For example, when looking at a fish underwater, a bird hovering in the air perceives the fish to be nearer to the water's surface than it actually is. Conversely, the fish perceives the bird in the air to be farther away from the water's surface than it actually is.

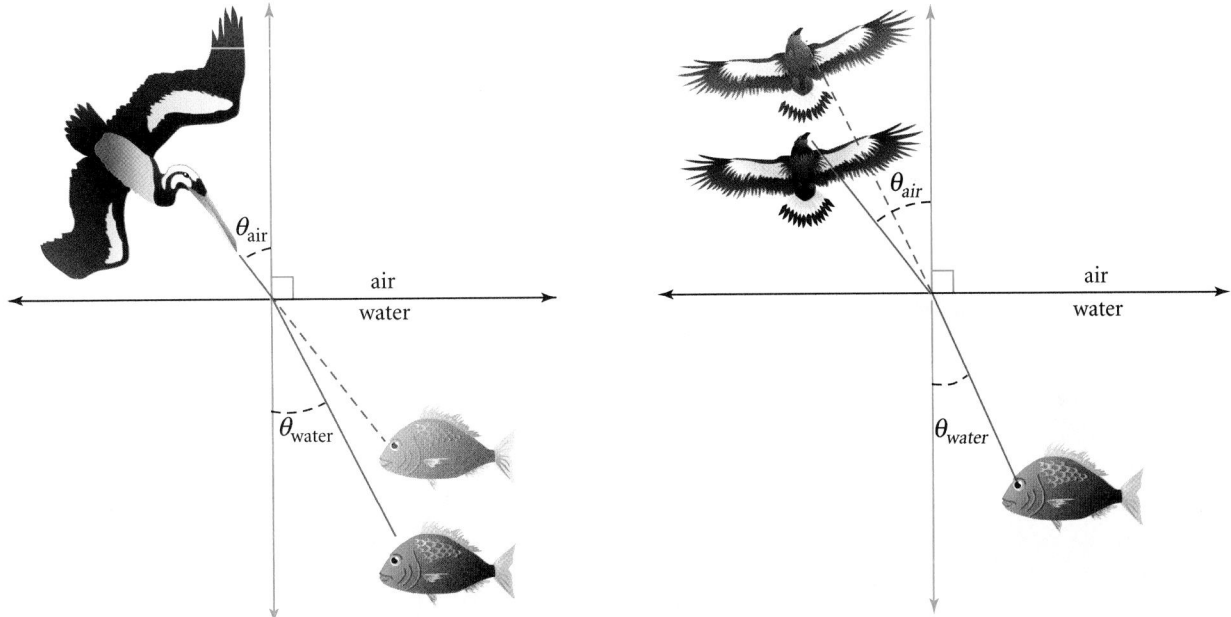

Given the index of refraction for water, n_{water}, is approximately 1.33, find each indicated angle.

54. θ_{air} if θ_{water} is 30°.

55. θ_{water} if θ_{air} is 60°.

56. θ_{water} if θ_{air} is 42°.

57. θ_{air} if θ_{water} is 25°.

Look Back

Let $A = \begin{bmatrix} 5 & -4 \\ 7 & 3 \end{bmatrix}$, $B = \begin{bmatrix} 3 \\ -5 \end{bmatrix}$, and $C = \begin{bmatrix} 7 \\ -3 \end{bmatrix}$. **Find each product. If the product does not exist, write *none*. (LESSON 4.2)**

58. AC

59. BA

60. BC

61. Solve $\triangle ABC$ given that $a = 12.7$, $c = 10.4$, and $B = 26.5°$. Give answers to the nearest tenth. *(LESSON 14.2)*

A pencil in a glass of water appears bent or broken because of the bending of light, or refraction.

Look Beyond

62. In calculus, it can be proved that $\sin x = x - \dfrac{x^3}{3!} + \dfrac{x^5}{5!} - \dfrac{x^7}{7!} + \cdots$ and $\cos x = 1 - \dfrac{x^2}{2!} + \dfrac{x^4}{4!} - \dfrac{x^6}{6!} + \cdots$ (where x is expressed in radians) are true. Use the first five terms of these series, called the *Taylor series*, to approximate the value of $\sin \dfrac{\pi}{6}$ and $\cos \pi$. Compare your answers with the exact values.

GEARING UP

Much of the activity in today's world depends on electricity. This modern technology is in turn equally dependent on a much older technology that you will study in this Chapter Project. Electricity flows into our homes because turbines turn, and the smooth and efficient transfer of this mechanical energy to electricity often depends on systems of gears.

A gear is usually classified as a "simple machine"—a wheel with teeth. But what size and shape should the teeth be so that a system of gears will mesh together properly? It turns out that this is not a simple question to answer.

In this project, you will design a template for a set of gears that will mesh together smoothly. Then you will make the gears to see if they work properly.

Activity 1

You may lay out your gear template on a sheet of centimeter graph paper or on an unlined sheet of white paper. In both cases, orient the paper horizontally rather than vertically.

1. Mark and label point O in the center of the graph paper, and draw the x-axis and y-axis.

2. Use a compass to draw a *base circle* centered at point O with a radius of 8 centimeters and an *outer circle* centered at point O with a radius of 10 centimeters. Mark and label point $A(8, 0)$. If you are using unlined paper, place point A anywhere on the base circle.

3. Set a compass to draw a radius of 2.8 centimeters. Put the compass point on A and draw an arc that passes through the base circle and the outer circle. Mark and label point B, the arc's intersection with the base circle, and point C, the arc's intersection with the outer circle.

4. With the compass point on B and the pencil point on A, draw an arc that passes through the outer circle, and label the point of intersection D. Quadrilateral $ABCD$ constitutes the *gear tooth profile*.

5. Use the Law of Cosines to determine the measure of arc AB on the base circle to the nearest degree.

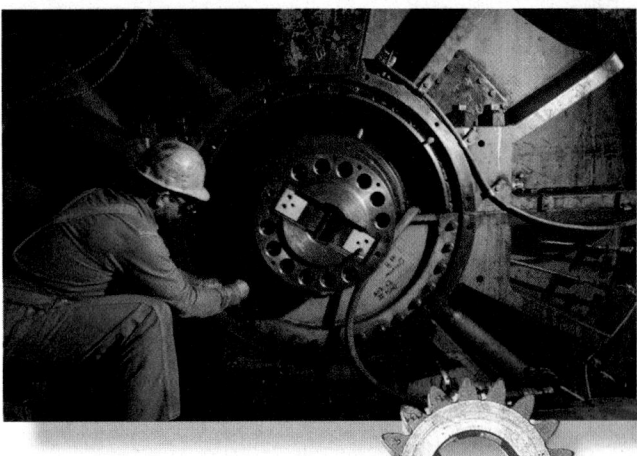

Activity 2

In this activity you will complete the gear template you began in Activity 1.

1. Use the coordinates from the Portfolio Activity on page 916 for the images of the original gear tooth profile under a 30° and a 60° rotation about the origin. Carefully plot these coordinates on the base circle and on the outer circle.

2. Use matrix multiplication to determine the coordinates for the images of the original gear tooth profile under rotations of 90°, 120°, 150°, 180°, 210°, 240°, 270°, 300°, and 330° about the origin. Carefully plot these coordinates on the base circle and on the outer circle. Note: Plot the points as carefully as you can. Rounding error and the precision of the centimeter grid will often make your vertices fall just above or below the base circle and the outer circle. Use these circles as guides for positioning the vertices of the gear teeth.

3. Use a compass to draw arcs for the curved sides of each gear tooth. (See Steps 3 and 4 in Activity 1.)

Activity 3

Make working models of the gears.

1. Cut out the gear template that you completed in Activity 3.

2. Pin the gear template to cardboard or fiberboard, and carefully trace around it. Then outline a second gear.

3. Cut out the gears. Position them on a piece of cardboard so that their teeth mesh, and pin them at their centers to keep them in place. The gears should turn smoothly in opposite directions. Observe how the curved surfaces touch each other when the gear teeth engage.

Chapter Review and Assessment

Key Skills & Exercises

LESSON 14.1

Key Skills

Use the law of sines to solve triangles.

Solve triangle $\triangle ABC$ given that $A = 42°$, $B = 52°$, and $a = 10$.

$$\frac{\sin A}{a} = \frac{\sin B}{b}$$
$$\frac{\sin 42°}{10} = \frac{\sin 52°}{b}$$
$$b = \frac{10 \sin 52°}{\sin 42°} \approx 11.8$$

Determine whether the given SSA information defines 0, 1, or 2 triangles.

SSA information: $c = 12$, $a = 8$, and $A = 30°$

$$\frac{\sin A}{a} = \frac{\sin C}{c}$$
$$\frac{\sin 30°}{8} = \frac{\sin C}{12}$$
$$\sin C \approx 0.75$$
$$C \approx 48.6° \text{ or } C \approx 131.4°$$

There are 2 possible triangles.

Exercises

Solve each triangle. Give answers to the nearest tenth, if necessary.

1. $A = 35°$, $B = 45°$, $a = 12$

2. $B = 27°$, $C = 40°$, $b = 20$

3. $A = 30°$, $c = 10$, $B = 50°$

4. $B = 42°$, $a = 14$, $C = 57°$

State the number of triangles determined by the given information. If 1 or 2 triangles are formed, solve the triangle(s). Give answers to the nearest tenth, if necessary.

5. $A = 40°$, $c = 20$, $a = 5$

6. $A = 60°$, $c = 10$, $a = 5\sqrt{3}$

7. $B = 30°$, $b = 3$, $c = 5$

8. $B = 75°$, $c = 9$, $b = 3$

LESSON 14.2

Key Skills

Use the law of cosines to solve triangles.

$$a^2 = b^2 + c^2 - 2bc \cos A$$
$$b^2 = a^2 + c^2 - 2ac \cos B$$
$$c^2 = a^2 + b^2 - 2ab \cos C$$

Given:	Use:
SSS	law of cosines, then law of sines
SSA	law of sines (ambiguous)
SAA	law of sines
ASA	law of sines
SAS	law of cosines, then law of sines
AAA	not possible

Exercises

Classify the type of information given, and then solve $\triangle ABC$ to the nearest tenth.

9. $A = 37°$, $b = 10$, $c = 14$

10. $B = 63°$, $a = 12$, $c = 15$

11. $a = 6$, $b = 3$, $c = 5$

12. $a = 9$, $b = 4$, $c = 12$

13. $A = 35°$, $c = 30$, $a = 20$

Key Skills

Use fundamental trigonometric identities to rewrite expressions.

Verify the identity $(\tan \theta) \dfrac{\cos \theta}{\sin^2 \theta} = \csc \theta$.

$$(\tan \theta) \dfrac{\cos \theta}{\sin^2 \theta} = \dfrac{\sin \theta}{\cos \theta} \cdot \dfrac{\cos \theta}{\sin^2 \theta} = \dfrac{1}{\sin \theta} = \csc \theta$$

Exercises

Write each expression in terms of a single trigonometric function.

14. $(\sec \theta)(\cos^2 \theta)$ **15.** $(\csc \theta)(\tan \theta)$

16. $\dfrac{2 \cos^2 \theta}{1 - \sin^2 \theta}$ **17.** $\dfrac{-3 \tan^2 \theta}{1 + \sec^2 \theta}$

Key Skills

Use the sum and difference identities.

Find the exact value of $\sin(30° - 45°)$.

$\sin(30° - 45°)$
$= (\sin 30°)(\cos 45°) - (\cos 30°)(\sin 45°)$
$= \left(\dfrac{1}{2}\right)\left(\dfrac{\sqrt{2}}{2}\right) - \left(\dfrac{\sqrt{3}}{2}\right)\left(\dfrac{\sqrt{2}}{2}\right) = \dfrac{\sqrt{2} - \sqrt{6}}{4}$

Use rotation matrices.

Find the coordinates of the image of $P(-3, 4)$ after a 20° rotation about the origin.

$$\begin{bmatrix} \cos 20° & -\sin 20° \\ \sin 20° & \cos 20° \end{bmatrix} \begin{bmatrix} -3 \\ 4 \end{bmatrix} \approx \begin{bmatrix} -4.2 \\ 2.7 \end{bmatrix}$$

Exercises

Find the exact value of each expression.

18. $\sin(45° - 210°)$ **19.** $\sin(60° + 270°)$

20. $\cos(90° + 60°)$ **21.** $\cos(120° - 135°)$

22. $\sin 195°$ **23.** $\cos 75°$

24. $\cos(-210°)$ **25.** $\sin(-15°)$

Find the coordinates of the image of each point after a 120° rotation.

26. $(3, -5)$ **27.** $(-2, 7)$

Key Skills

Use the double- and half-angle identities.

$\sin 2\theta = 2 \sin \theta \cos \theta$ $\sin \dfrac{\theta}{2} = \pm \sqrt{\dfrac{1 - \cos \theta}{2}}$

$\cos 2\theta = \cos^2 \theta - \sin^2 \theta$ $\cos \dfrac{\theta}{2} = \pm \sqrt{\dfrac{1 + \cos \theta}{2}}$

Given $180° \le \theta \le 270°$ and $\sin \theta = -\dfrac{4}{7}$, find the exact value of $\cos \dfrac{\theta}{2}$.

Find $\cos \theta$: $x^2 + y^2 = r^2$
$\qquad\qquad x^2 + (-4)^2 = 7^2$
$\qquad\qquad\qquad x = -\sqrt{33} \quad \leftarrow \textit{Quadrant III}$

$\cos \theta = \dfrac{-\sqrt{33}}{7}$

$\cos \dfrac{\theta}{2} = \pm \sqrt{\dfrac{1 + \cos \theta}{2}}$

$\qquad = -\sqrt{\dfrac{1 + \left(-\dfrac{\sqrt{33}}{7}\right)}{2}} \quad \leftarrow \textit{90°} \le \dfrac{\theta}{2} \le \textit{135°}$

$\qquad = -\sqrt{\dfrac{1}{2} - \dfrac{\sqrt{33}}{14}}$

Exercises

Given $0° \le \theta \le 90°$ and $\cos \theta = \dfrac{1}{8}$, find the exact value of each expression.

28. $\cos 2\theta$ **29.** $\sin 2\theta$

30. $\cos \dfrac{\theta}{2}$ **31.** $\sin \dfrac{\theta}{2}$

Given $270° \le \theta \le 360°$ and $\sin \theta = -\dfrac{5}{8}$, find the exact value of each expression.

32. $\sin 2\theta$ **33.** $\cos 2\theta$

34. $\sin \dfrac{\theta}{2}$ **35.** $\cos \dfrac{\theta}{2}$

Write each expression in terms of trigonometric functions of θ rather than multiples of θ.

36. $\sin 2\theta + \cos 2\theta$ **37.** $\cos 4\theta$

Key Skills

Solve trigonometric equations.

Find the exact solutions of $-\cos^2\theta = 1 + 5\sin\theta$ for $0° \le \theta < 360°$.

$$-2\cos^2\theta = 1 + 5\sin\theta$$
$$-2(1 - \sin^2\theta) = 1 + 5\sin\theta$$
$$2\sin^2\theta - 5\sin\theta - 3 = 0$$
$$(2\sin\theta + 1)(\sin\theta - 3) = 0$$
$$\sin\theta = -\frac{1}{2} \quad or \quad \sin\theta = 3$$

For $\sin\theta = -\frac{1}{2}$, $\theta = 225°$ or $\theta = 315°$. For $\sin\theta = 3$, there is no solution.

Exercises

Find the exact solutions of each equation for $0° \le \theta < 360°$.

38. $2\cos\theta - \sqrt{2} = 0$

39. $\sin^2\theta + \sin\theta = 2$

40. $2\cos^2\theta - \cos\theta - 1 = 0$

41. $\cos^2\theta - \sin^2\theta + 1 = 0$

42. $4\sin^2\theta + 4\cos\theta - 1 = 0$

43. $4\sin^2\theta - 2(\sqrt{2} + 1)\sin\theta + \sqrt{2} = 0$

Applications

44. SURVEYING A map maker makes the measurements shown in the diagram at right. Find the distance across the river from B to C.

RECREATION At a distance of 3000 yards from the base of a mountain, the angle of elevation to the top is 20°. At a distance of 1000 yards from the base of the mountain, a tram ride goes to the top of the mountain at an inclination of 35°.

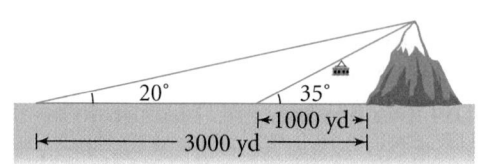

45. What is the height of the mountain, to the nearest yard?

46. What is the length of the tram ride to the nearest yard?

47. REAL ESTATE A triangular lot has sides of 215 feet, 185 feet, and 125 feet. Find the measures of the angles at its corners.

48. SURVEYING A tunnel from point A to point B runs through a mountain. From point C, both ends of the tunnel can be observed. If $AC = 165$ meters, $BC = 115$ meters, and $C = 74°$, find AB, the length of the tunnel.

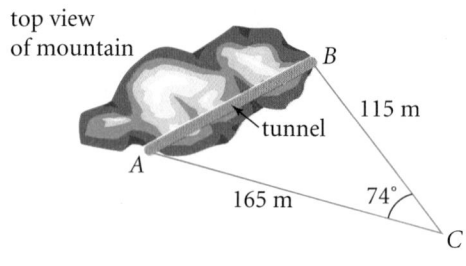

top view of mountain

49. SPACE SCIENCE Two space-monitoring stations are located at two different points, A and B, on Earth's surface. The inscribed angle at the Earth's center is $C = 110°$. The radius of the Earth is about 3960 miles. Find the straight-line distance, AB, between the two stations.

Chapter Test

Solve each triangle. Give answers to the nearest tenth.

1. $B = 18°$, $C = 65°$, $b = 9$

2. $A = 23°$, $C = 57°$, $c = 45$

3. PIONEERING Two hikers leave a campsite, walking at a constant rate of 2.4 miles per hour. One follows a northeast path 37° north of the east-west line. The other is on a southeast path 57° south of the east-west line. How far apart are they after 3 hours?

State the number of triangles determined by the given information. If one or two are formed, solve the triangle(s). Give answers to the nearest tenth.

4. $A = 60°$, $c = 12$, $a = 3$

5. $A = 30°$, $a = 24$, $c = 36$

Find the area of $\triangle ABC$ to the nearest tenth of a square unit.

6. $b = 15$, $c = 8$, $A = 35°$

7. $a = 15$, $c = 13$, $B = 70°$

Classify the type of information given, then solve each triangle to the nearest tenth.

8. $A = 35°$, $b = 8$, $c = 7$

9. $a = 15$, $b = 18$, $C = 105°$

10. AIR TRAFFIC CONTROL An airplane is spotted on radar at a line of sight distance of 75 miles east at an angle 16° above the horizon. A second airplane is spotted west at an angle of 24° above the horizon with a line of sight distance of 36 miles. Find the line of sight distance between the two planes.

Write each expression in terms of a single trigonometric function.

11. $\dfrac{\sec\theta}{\cos\theta} - \sec\theta$

12. $\csc\theta - \cot\theta\cos\theta$

13. $\dfrac{1}{\cos^2\theta} - \tan^2\theta - \sin^2\theta$

Find the exact value of each expression.

14. $\sin(330° - 225°)$

15. $\cos(45° - 60°)$

16. $\cos 105°$

Find the coordinates of the image of each point after the given rotation.

17. $(5, 8)$; $30°$

18. $(-2, 6)$; $-60°$

19. $(8, -1)$; $60°$

Given $0° \leq \theta \leq 90°$ and $\cos\theta = \dfrac{2}{3}$, find the exact value of each expression.

20. $\cos 2\theta$

21. $\sin 2\theta$

22. $\sin\dfrac{\theta}{2}$

23. $\cos\dfrac{\theta}{2}$

Write each expression below in terms of trigonometric functions of θ rather than multiples of θ.

24. $\dfrac{2\sin^2\theta}{\sin 2\theta}$

25. $\dfrac{\cos 2\theta}{\cos\theta - \sin\theta}$

26. $\dfrac{1 + \sin 2\theta}{\sin\theta + \cos\theta}$

27. The minute hand on a clock face is 3 inches long. How far does the minute hand travel in 5 minutes?

Find the exact solution of each equation for $0° \leq \theta < 360°$.

28. $2\sin^2\theta = -\sqrt{3}\sin\theta$

29. $2\sin^2\theta = -\sin\theta + 4$

30. $2\cos^2\theta = -\sqrt{2}\cos\theta$

31. $\cos 2\theta - \sin\theta + 2\sin^2\theta = 0$

1-14 College Entrance Exam Practice

MULTIPLE-CHOICE For Questions 1–17, write the letter that indicates the best answer.

1. Identify the period of $f(\theta) = -3 \sin \frac{\theta}{2}$.
(LESSON 13.5)

  a. π **b.** 4π

  c. 3π **d.** $\frac{\pi}{4}$

2. Evaluate $\sum\limits_{n=1}^{5} 4n$. **(LESSON 11.1)**

  a. 60   **b.** 1364

  c. 80   **d.** 122,880

3. What are the roots of the quadratic equation $2x^2 - 3x - 3 = 0$? **(LESSON 5.6)**

  a. $\dfrac{3 \pm \sqrt{33}}{4}$ **b.** $\dfrac{3 \pm i\sqrt{3}}{4}$

  c. $\dfrac{3 \pm \sqrt{15}}{4}$ **d.** $\dfrac{3 \pm i\sqrt{15}}{4}$

4. Which expression is equivalent to x?
(LESSON 6.6)

  a. e^x **b.** $\log x$

  c. $\ln x$ **d.** $\ln e^x$

5. Which set of data has a mean, median, and mode that are all equal? **(LESSON 12.1)**
  a. 14, 12, 19, 14, 12, 15, 12
  b. 2, 3, 4, 3, 3
  c. −6, 4, 4, 5, 6, 7, 8
  d. −12, −10, −13, −9, −11

6. Which of the following has the least slope?
(LESSON 1.2)
  a. $3x + 2y = 6$
  b. $-2x - 4y = 8$
  c. $\frac{1}{2}x + 2y = -4$
  d. $-3x + y = -5$

7. Which word describes the number $\frac{1}{12}$?
(LESSON 2.1)
  a. prime   **b.** integer
  c. rational   **d.** irrational

8. Simplify $(x^3 - 8x^2 + 17x - 6) \div (x^2 - 5x + 2)$.
(LESSON 7.3)
  a. $x + 3$ **b.** $x - 3$
  c. $x + 1$ **d.** $x - 1$

9. Which equation below has a graph that opens downward? **(LESSON 5.1)**
  a. $y = 5x^2$
  b. $y = 5 - x^2$
  c. $y - x^2 = 5$
  d. $y = x^2 - 5$

10. Which equation represents the line that has a slope of $\frac{1}{2}$ and contains the point $P(2, -2)$?
(LESSON 1.3)
  a. $y + 2 = \frac{1}{2}(x - 2)$
  b. $y - 2 = \frac{1}{2}(x - 2)$
  c. $y - 2 = \frac{1}{2}(x + 2)$
  d. $y + 2 = \frac{1}{2}(x + 2)$

11. Which expression represents $(a^3 - 1) - (a^3 - a^2 + 5)$ in standard form?
(LESSON 7.1)
  a. $2a^3 + a^2 - 6$ **b.** $-a^2 + 6$
  c. $a^2 - 6$ **d.** $-2a^3 + 4$

12. What is the amplitude of $y = 3 \sin(2\theta - 5)$?
(LESSON 13.5)
  a. 1   **b.** 3
  c. 2   **d.** 5

13. Simplify $(4 - 5i) + (-7 - 5i)$. **(LESSON 5.6)**
  a. $-(7 + i)$ **b.** $-3 - 10i$
  c. $-3 + i$ **d.** -3

14. Which ellipse has a horizontal major axis that is 18 units long? *(LESSON 9.4)*

a. $\dfrac{x^2}{4} + \dfrac{y^2}{81} = 1$

b. $\dfrac{x^2}{9} + \dfrac{y^2}{4} = 1$

c. $4x^2 + 81y^2 = 324$

d. $81x^2 + 4y^2 = 324$

15. A committee of 3 is selected from 8 eligible members. How many different committees are possible? *(LESSON 10.3)*

a. $8!$ b. $3!$

c. $\dfrac{8!}{5!}$ d. $\dfrac{8!}{3!5!}$

16. Find A in $\triangle ABC$ if $a = 6$, $b = 9$, and $C = 30°$. *(LESSON 14.2)*

a. $\approx 68.3°$ b. $\approx 38.3°$

c. $\approx 111.7°$ d. $60°$

17. Which expression is not equivalent to the others? *(LESSON 6.4)*

a. $3 \log_5 2x$ b. $\log_5 2x^3$

c. $\log_5 (2x)^3$ d. $\log_5 8x^3$

For Items 18–19, state the property that is illustrated in each statement. All variables represent real numbers. *(LESSON 2.1)*

18. $3(x^2 - 1) = 3x^2 - 3$

19. $-4 + 4 = 0$

20. Simplify $\dfrac{-9x - 3}{x^2 - 11x + 18} + \dfrac{x + 3}{x - 9}$. *(LESSON 8.4)*

21. Find the area of $\triangle ABC$ to the nearest tenth of a square unit if $a = 4.5$, $c = 8.3$, and $B = 55°$. *(LESSON 14.1)*

22. Find the inverse of $f(x) = -\dfrac{1}{4}x + 2$. *(LESSON 2.5)*

23. Solve the literal equation $R = \dfrac{S + F + P}{S + P}$ for S. *(LESSON 1.6)*

24. Solve $\begin{cases} 3x - 4y = -14 \\ 3x + 2y = 16 \end{cases}$. *(LESSON 3.2)*

25. Use the quadratic formula to solve $x^2 - 2x + 4 = 0$. *(LESSON 5.6)*

26. Graph the solution of $\begin{cases} x < 2 \\ y \le 3x - 4 \end{cases}$. *(LESSON 3.4)*

27. Simplify the complex fraction $\dfrac{\frac{3x}{5}}{\frac{x}{2}}$. *(LESSON 8.3)*

28. Factor $4x^4 - 17x^2 + 4$ completely. *(LESSON 7.3)*

29. Find the domain of $f(x) = \dfrac{x^2 - 4}{x - 2}$. *(LESSON 8.2)*

FREE-RESPONSE GRID The following questions may be answered by using a free-response grid such as that commonly used by standardized-test services.

30. Solve $\dfrac{3x}{4} - 12 = \dfrac{3(x - 12)}{5}$. *(LESSON 8.5)*

31. A coin is flipped 10 times. Find the probability of exactly 4 heads appearing. *(LESSON 11.7)*

32. Find the coterminal angle, θ, for $255°$ such that $-360° < \theta < 360°$. *(LESSON 13.2)*

33. Find the value of v if $v = \log_3 1$. *(LESSON 6.3)*

34. Convert $\dfrac{3\pi}{5}$ radians to degrees. *(LESSON 13.4)*

35. Find the final amount of a $1000 investment earning 5% interest compounded annually for 10 years. Round answer to the nearest dollar. *(LESSON 6.2)*

36. Evaluate $\cos^{-1}(\sin 30°)$. *(LESSON 13.6)*

37. Evaluate $\log_5 73.25$ to the nearest hundredth. *(LESSON 6.4)*

38. Evaluate $\displaystyle\sum_{n=1}^{4} (8 - 5n)$. *(LESSON 11.3)*

39. PROBABILITY A 6-sided number cube is rolled once. Find the probability of getting an even number *or* 1. *(LESSON 10.4)*

40. PROBABILITY A coin is flipped 5 times. Find the probability of exactly 3 heads appearing. *(LESSON 12.5)*

Keystroke Guide for Chapter 14

Essential keystroke sequences (using the model TI-82 or TI-83 graphics calculator) are presented below for all Activities and Examples found in this chapter that require or recommend the use of a graphics calculator.

📓 **internet** connect

For Keystrokes of other graphing calculator models, visit the HRW web site at **go.hrw.com** and enter the keyword **MB1 CALC**.

LESSON 14.2

Activity
Page 896

For Steps 1 and 2, graph $y = \sin x$ and $y = \frac{1}{2}$ on the same screen for $0° \leq x \leq 180°$.

Use viewing window [0, 180] by [−2, 2] in degree mode.

| Y= | SIN | X,T,θ,n | ENTER | (Y2=) 1 | ÷ | 2 GRAPH |

Use a similar keystroke sequence for Steps 4 and 5.

LESSON 14.3

EXAMPLE ❶ Graph $y = \tan x$ and $y = \frac{\sin x}{\cos x}$ on the same screen.

Page 903

Use viewing window [−360, 360] by [−10, 10] in degree mode.

| Y= | TAN | X,T,θ,n | ENTER | (Y2=) | SIN |

| X,T,θ,n |) | ÷ | COS | X,T,θ,n |) | GRAPH |

⇑ TI-82: (⇑ TI-82: (

EXAMPLE ❸ Graph $y = \frac{\sin^2 x}{1 - \cos x}$ and $y = 1 + \cos x$ on the same screen.

Page 904

Use viewing window [−720, 720] by [−3, 3] in degree mode.

| Y= | (| SIN | X,T,θ,n |) |) | x^2 |

⇑ TI-82: (

| ÷ | (| 1 | − | COS | X,T,θ,n |) |

|) | ENTER | (Y2=) 1 | + | COS | X,T,θ,n |

| GRAPH |

Activity

Page 904

For Step 1, graph $y = (\csc x)(1 - \cos x)(1 + \cos x)$.

Use viewing window $[-360, 360]$ by $[-3, 3]$ in degree mode.

For Step 3, use the same viewing window and a similar keystroke sequence.

E X A M P L E ④ Graph $y = \sec x - \tan x \sin x$.

Page 905

Use viewing window $[-360, 360]$ by $[-3, 3]$ in degree mode.

LESSON 14.4

E X A M P L E ⑤ Find the product $\begin{bmatrix} \cos 30° & -\sin 30° \\ \sin 30° & \cos 30° \end{bmatrix}\begin{bmatrix} 2 & 5 & 5 & 2 \\ 1 & 1 & -1 & -1 \end{bmatrix}$.

Page 913

Set the mode:

MODE ▼ 2 ENTER 2nd MODE (QUIT)

For TI-83 Plus, press
2nd x^{-1} (MATRX) to access the matrix menu.

Enter the matrices:

MATRX EDIT 1:[A] ENTER (Matrix[A]) 2 ENTER 2 ENTER COS 30) ENTER ⇑ TI-82: (

(−) SIN 30) ENTER SIN 30) ENTER COS 30) ENTER
⇑ TI-82: (⇑ TI-82: (⇑ TI-82: (

MATRX EDIT 2:[B] ENTER (Matrix[B]) 2 ENTER 4 ENTER 2 ENTER 5 ENTER 5 ENTER
QUIT
2 ENTER 1 ENTER 1 ENTER (−) 1 ENTER (−) 1 ENTER 2nd MODE

Multiply the matrices:

MATRX NAMES 1:[A] ENTER × MATRX
NAMES 2:[B] ENTER ENTER

Activity
Page 923

Graph $y = \sin x$ and $y = 1$ on the same screen.

Use viewing window $[0, 360]$ by $[-3, 3]$ in degree mode.

| Y= | SIN | X,T,Θ,n | ENTER | (Y2=) 1 | GRAPH |

For Step 2 use viewing window $[0, 720]$ by $[-3, 3]$.

E X A M P L E ❶
Page 923

Graph $y = \cos x$ and $y = \sqrt{3} - \cos x$ on the same screen, and find any points of intersection.

Use viewing window $[0, 360]$ by $[-2, 3]$ in degree mode.

Graph the functions:

| Y= | COS | X,T,Θ,n | ENTER | (Y2=) | 2nd | $\sqrt{}$ x^2 | 3 |) | − |

| COS | X,T,Θ,n | GRAPH |

Find any points of intersection:

| 2nd | TRACE CALC | 5:intersect | (First curve?) | ENTER |
(Second curve?) ENTER (Guess?) ENTER

E X A M P L E ❸
Page 924

Graph $y = 2 \cos^2 x$ and $y = \sin x + 1$ on the same screen, and find any points of intersection.

Use viewing window $[0, 360]$ by $[-0.5, 2.5]$ in degree mode.

Graph the functions:

| Y= | 2 | (| COS | X,T,Θ,n |) |) | x^2 | ENTER | (Y2=) | SIN | X,T,Θ,n |
⇑ TI-82: ☐   ⇑ TI-82: ☐

|) | + | 1 | GRAPH |

Find any points of intersection:

| 2nd | TRACE CALC | 5:intersect | (First curve?) | ENTER |
(Second curve?) ENTER (Guess?) ENTER

The calculator may return an error message when looking for the intersection point (270°, 0).

EXAMPLE **4**

Page 925

Graph *y* = 366 sin *x* − 144 and *y* = 15 on the same screen, and find any points of intersection.

Use viewing window [−15, 90] by [−75, 250] in degree mode.

Graph the functions:

Y= 366 SIN X,T,Θ,n − 144 ENTER (Y2=) 15 GRAPH

Find any points of intersection:

CALC

2nd TRACE 5:intersect (First curve?) ENTER

(Second curve?) ENTER (Guess?) ENTER

Intersection
X=25.74879   Y=15

Info Bank

Extra Practice

Chapter 1

LESSON 1.1

State whether each equation is a linear equation.

1. $y = 2x$ **2.** $y = -3x - 1$ **3.** $y = x + 3$ **4.** $y = \frac{3}{4}x + 1$

5. $y = 10 - x$ **6.** $y = \frac{4x}{5}$ **7.** $y = 7 + x^2$ **8.** $y = 2 - x^3$

Determine whether each table represents a linear relationship between *x* and *y*. If the relationship is linear, write the next ordered pair that would appear in the table.

9.

x	0	1	2	3
y	1	6	11	16

10.

x	−2	−1	0	1
y	4	1	0	1

11.

x	2	4	6	8
y	7	13	19	25

For each graph, make a table of values to represent the points. Does the table represent a linear relationship? Explain.

12.

13.

14.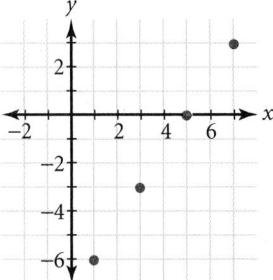

LESSON 1.2

Write an equation in slope-intercept form for the line that has the indicated slope, *m*, and *y*-intercept, *b*.

1. $m = -3, b = 6$ **2.** $m = -2, b = 0$ **3.** $m = 0, b = \frac{1}{2}$ **4.** $m = \frac{4}{5}, b = 1$

Find the slope of the line containing the indicated points.

5. $(0, 0)$ and $(-2, -8)$ **6.** $(1, 2)$ and $(2, 6)$ **7.** $(-4, 5)$ and $(1, 5)$

Identify the slope, *m*, and the *y*-intercept, *b*, for each line. Then graph.

8. $x = 1.5$ **9.** $-2x + y = 1$ **10.** $3x - y = 2$ **11.** $y = -3$

Write an equation in slope-intercept form for each line.

12.

13.

14.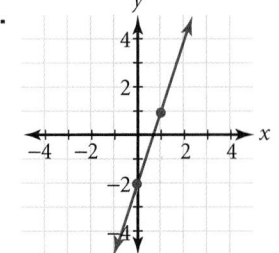

LESSON 1.3

Write an equation in slope-intercept form for the line containing the indicated points.

1. $(4, -7)$ and $(9, 3)$

2. $(3, 10)$ and $(-8, -12)$

3. $(8, -11)$ and $(13, -11)$

4. $(3, -17)$ and $(-4, 18)$

5. $(-7, -1)$ and $(5, 7)$

6. $(0, 13)$ and $(4, -11)$

Write an equation in slope-intercept form for the line that has the indicated slope, m, and that contains the given point.

7. $m = -8; (-1, -2)$

8. $m = -\frac{1}{2}; (4, 6)$

9. $m = -13; (5, 1)$

10. $m = \frac{5}{6}; (-12, 8)$

Write an equation in slope-intercept form for the line that contains the given point and is parallel to the given line.

11. $(0, 7); y = 5x - 3$

12. $(-11, 8); y = -x + 5$

13. $\left(4\frac{1}{2}, 9\right); y = -2x + 15$

14. $(9, 7); y = \frac{2}{3}x - 1$

15. $(-2, -3); 3x + 4y = 9$

16. $(-7, 2); -x + 3y = 1$

Write an equation in slope-intercept form for the line that contains the given point and is perpendicular to the given line.

17. $(3, -6); y = \frac{1}{2}x + 7$

18. $(4, 5); y = -\frac{1}{8}x + 17$

19. $(-3, 9); y = 5x + \frac{1}{4}$

20. $(0, 7); x - 4y = 3$

21. $(3, -3); 5x + 2y = 1$

22. $(6, -4); 3x - y = 0.5$

LESSON 1.4

In Exercises 1–6, y varies directly as x. Find the constant of variation, and write an equation of direct variation that relates the two variables.

1. $y = 32$ when $x = 8$

2. $y = -12$ when $x = -4$

3. $y = 4.2$ when $x = 0.7$

4. $y = 65$ when $x = 13$

5. $y = -3$ when $x = 11$

6. $y = \frac{1}{4}$ when $x = \frac{1}{2}$

Solve each proportion for the indicated variable. Check your answers.

7. $\frac{5}{32} = \frac{10}{x}$

8. $\frac{w}{14} = \frac{14}{49}$

9. $\frac{0.7}{10} = \frac{21}{k}$

10. $\frac{4}{5} = \frac{t}{8}$

11. $\frac{n+1}{7} = \frac{3}{5}$

12. $\frac{3y+4}{10} = \frac{y}{5}$

13. $\frac{z+2}{7} = \frac{z}{6}$

14. $\frac{m-2}{15} = \frac{m+2}{6}$

15. $\frac{5x-3}{7} = \frac{2x}{3}$

Determine whether the values in each table are related by a direct variation. If so, write an equation for the variation. If not, explain.

16.

x	1	2	3	4	5
y	1.5	3	4.5	6	7.5

17.

x	1	2	3	4	6
y	24	12	8	6	4

18.

x	5	6	7	8	9
y	6	7.2	8.4	9.6	10.8

19.

x	-2	-1	1	2
y	14	7	-7	-14

LESSON 1.5

Create a scatter plot of the data in each table. Describe the correlation.
Then find an equation for the least-squares line.

1.

x	5	8	4	9	7	6	3	2	6	6	4	3	3	9
y	17	20	12	28	17	15	6	8	11	18	14	10	8	24

2.

x	1	2	2	3	4	5	6	7	8	8	4	8	9	9
y	70	55	75	72	66	58	38	45	17	19	52	15	15	10

The table lists the total weight lifted by the winners in eight weight
classes of the 1996 Women's National Weightlifting Championship.

Weight class (kg)	46	50	54	59	64	70	76	83
Total lifted (kg)	140.0	127.5	167.5	167.5	192.5	185.0	197.5	200.0

3 Let x represent weight class, and let y represent the total weight lifted.
Enter the data into a graphics calculator, and find an equation of the
least-squares line.

4 Find the correlation coefficient, r, to the nearest tenth.

5 Suppose that there were a 68-kilogram weight class. Predict the total
weight lifted by the winner.

LESSON 1.6

Solve each equation.

1. $x - 9 = -23$

2. $\frac{1}{2}x - 3 = 11$

3. $3x - 2 = 13$

4. $-3x + 5 = 19$

5. $12 - 5x = -8$

6. $\frac{3}{4}x + \frac{1}{4} = 9$

7. $\frac{9}{10}x - 17 = 19$

8. $\frac{16}{15}x + 78 = 14$

9. $\frac{5}{12}x - 12 = 48$

10. $7x + 8 = 11x$

11. $4x + 12 = 7x$

12. $9x - 42 = 3x$

13. $4x + 5 = x - 3$

14. $7x - 22 = 3x + 18$

15. $\frac{x+3}{2} = x - 4$

16. $8\left(\frac{3}{4}x + \frac{1}{2}\right) = 5x$

17. $8x = 6x - 11$

18. $\frac{2}{3}x - 7 = 3$

19. $-3x + 5 = 5x - 3$

20. $18 = 6x + 8$

21. $x + \frac{15}{8} = \frac{3x}{2}$

22. $0.7x + 0.3x = 2x - 4$

23. $\frac{1}{2}x + 6 = x - 4$

24. $x - 7 = 3\frac{1}{2} + 2x$

Solve each literal equation for the indicated variable.

25. $S = 180(n - 2)$ for n

26. $A = \frac{1}{2}pr$ for p

27. $V = \frac{1}{3}Bh$ for h

28. $m = \frac{1}{2}(a - b)$ for a

29. $m = \frac{1}{2}(a - b)$ for b

30. $\frac{x}{a} + \frac{y}{b} = 1$ for a

31. $m = \frac{y_2 - y_1}{x_2 - x_1}$ for x_1

32. $F = \frac{W}{d}$ for d

33. $E = IR$ for R

34. $t = -0.55\left(\frac{a}{1000}\right)$ for a

35. $R = \frac{s^2}{A}$ for A

36. $S = \frac{1}{2}(a + b + c)$ for b

37. Given the equation $x = 4 + y$, use substitution to solve $3y - x = -14$ for y.

38. Given the equation $x - 2y = 8$, use substitution to solve $6y = -3x$ for x.

LESSON 1.7

Write an inequality that describes each graph.

1.

2.

3.

4.

5.

6.

Solve each inequality, and graph the solution on a number line.

7. $8x < 64$

8. $14x \leq -42$

9. $x + 15 > 7$

10. $-3x > -21$

11. $x - 9 \geq 1$

12. $3x - 2 \leq 13$

13. $11 - x < 7$

14. $6 - 7x \geq -8$

15. $-\frac{x}{4} \geq 3$

16. $7x - 2 < 3x + 4$

17. $4 - 2(x + 1) \leq -3$

18. $3(x - 2) + 5 \geq 7 + x$

Graph the solution of each compound inequality on a number line.

19. $x \geq -5 \ and \ x < 3$

20. $2x + 1 \leq 7 \ and \ -3x + 1 < -5$

21. $x + 5 \geq 2 \ and \ x - 3 < 2$

22. $7 - x < 4 \ or \ 2x + 1 < -2$

23. $4x < -20 \ or \ 5x - 2 \geq 3$

24. $3x - 6 < 12 \ and \ 1 - 2x \leq 17$

25. $\frac{1}{3}(x + 9) \geq 4 \ or \ 3 < -2x - 5$

26. $\frac{3}{4}(12 - 2x) \leq 0 \ or \ 8 - x > 3$

LESSON 1.8

Match each statement on the left with a statement on the right.

1. $|x - 3| = -4$

2. $|x - 3| \leq 4$

3. $|x - 3| \geq -4$

4. $|x - 3| = 4$

5. $|x - 3| \geq 4$

6. $|x - 3| \leq -4$

a. $x = -1 \ or \ x = 7$

b. $x \geq -1 \ and \ x \leq 7$

c. $x \leq -1 \ or \ x \geq 7$

d. There is no solution.

e. All real numbers are solutions.

Solve each absolute-value equation. If the equation has no solution, write *no solution*.

7. $|x - 1| = 3$

8. $|x + 9| = 13$

9. $|x - 6| = 9$

10. $|7 + x| = 13$

11. $|2x - 2| = 5$

12. $|4x + 1| = 10$

13. $|3x| = -14$

14. $|3x - 5| + 7 = 4$

15. $|10x + 5| - 7 = 8$

16. $3 = \left|\frac{1}{5}(2 - x)\right|$

17. $\left|\frac{2}{3}x\right| = \frac{1}{12}$

18. $|1 - x| = 8$

Solve each absolute-value inequality. Graph the solution on a number line.

19. $|2x| < 8$

20. $|x - 1| \geq 4$

21. $|2 - x| \leq 6$

22. $|3x + 5| > 2$

23. $|5x - 10| > 0$

24. $|6x + 3| \leq -7$

25. $|6 - 12x| \leq -7$

26. $|4x + 3| > 5$

27. $|6 - 3x| \leq 2$

28. $|2x - 6| < 4$

29. $|3x - 7| \geq 2$

30. $|4x + 3| - 2 > 4$

Chapter 2

Extra Practice

Classify each number in as many ways as possible.

1. 47   **2.** 12.86   **3.** $\sqrt{7}$ **4.** $-\sqrt{100}$

5. $\dfrac{7}{9}$ **6.** $0.\overline{456}$ **7.** $123.45678\ldots$ **8.** $12.888888\ldots$

State the property that is illustrated in each statement. All variables represent real numbers.

9. $z + 1.09 = 1.09 + z$ **10.** $152 + 0 = 152$

11. $23(x + 34) = 23x + 23(34)$ **12.** $-7 + (19 + 2) = (-7 + 19) + 2$

13. $-42y = y(-42)$ **14.** $\dfrac{12}{y} \cdot \dfrac{y}{12} = 1$, where $y \neq 0$

15. $1 \cdot 77 = 77$ **16.** $422 + (-422) = 0$

Evaluate each expression by using the order of operations.

17. $24 \div 8 + 4$ **18.** $2 + 7^2$ **19.** $3(11 + 2^2) + 1$

20. $(29 + 7) + 12 \div 6$ **21.** $8 + 2 \times 5 + 7$ **22.** $1 + 2 \times 7 - 5$

23. $\dfrac{15 + 10}{5} - 16 \div 4$ **24.** $\dfrac{7^2 - 1}{3 + 5}$ **25.** $16 \times 2 \div (1 - 5)$

26. $1 - \dfrac{4}{2 \cdot 7 + 4}$ **27.** $\dfrac{13 - 2 \cdot 6}{5 + 2 \cdot 3}$ **28.** $3 + \dfrac{4(3 - 1)}{8}$

29. $\dfrac{5}{8} + \dfrac{6}{2(7 + 1)}$ **30.** $\dfrac{2(7 - 3)}{3(4 + 5)}$ **31.** $20 \cdot 9 + \dfrac{8 - 3}{5}$

Evaluate each expression.

1. 12^1 **2.** $(-27)^0$ **3.** 5^{-1}

4. $\left(\dfrac{4}{5}\right)^{-2}$ **5.** $\left(\dfrac{1}{3}\right)^{-2}$ **6.** $\left(\dfrac{2}{3}\right)^{-4}$

7. $8^{\frac{1}{3}}$ **8.** $\left(\dfrac{1}{8}\right)^{-3}$ **9.** $81^{\frac{3}{4}}$

10. $27^{\frac{2}{3}}$ **11.** $\left(100^{\frac{2}{3}}\right)^{\frac{3}{4}}$ **12.** $125^{\frac{1}{3}}$

Simplify each expression, assuming that no variable equals zero. Write your answer with positive exponents only.

13. $z^5 z^{-3}$ **14.** $\left(\dfrac{a^{\frac{-2}{3}}}{b^8}\right)^{-2}$ **15.** $3b^3 \cdot b^4 \cdot b^{-2}$

16. $\left(\dfrac{9z^4}{16w^8}\right)^{-2}$ **17.** $2xy(-3x^2y^3)$ **18.** $(-6ab^2c^5)^2$

19. $\dfrac{k^7}{k^5}$ **20.** $\dfrac{n^{-3}}{n^4}$ **21.** $\left(\dfrac{3x^{-4}}{y^3}\right)^2$

22. $(x^{-1}y^{-2}z^3)^{-2}(x^2y^{-4}z^6)$ **23.** $(a^{-3}b^{-4})^{-2}(a^9b^{-7})^0$ **24.** $\left(\dfrac{24x^4y^{-5}}{-4x^{-2}y^{-1}}\right)^{-3}$

25. $\dfrac{(x^3y^2)^{-2}}{x^2y^4}$ **26.** $\left(\dfrac{a^{-3}}{b^{-5}}\right)^{-2}\left(\dfrac{b^3}{a^2}\right)^{-1}$ **27.** $\left(\dfrac{5c^{-2}}{z^3}\right)^2\left(\dfrac{c^3z^3}{x}\right)^{-2}$

State whether each relation represents a function. Explain.

1.

2.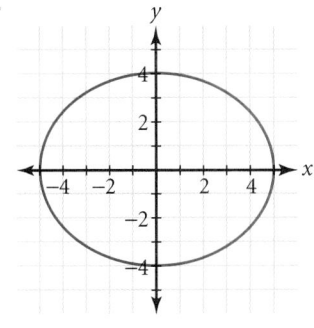

3.

x	y
−2	8
−2	7
−1	6
0	5

4. {(32, 1), (48, 15), (56, 19)} **5.** {(−8, 25), (−8, 24), (−8, 23)} **6.** {(7, 8), (9, 10), (11, 12)}

State the domain and range of each function.

7. {(−2, 8), (3, 13)}

8. {(0, 1), (1, 4), (2, 7), (3, 10)}

9. {(−4, 16), (0, 0), (2, 4)(4, 16)}

10. {(1.1, 5), (2.2, 10), (3.3, 15), (4.4, 20)}

Evaluate each function for the given values of x.

11. $f(x) = 1 - 2x$ for $x = -3$ and $x = 1$

12. $f(x) = \frac{x-1}{4}$ for $x = 7$ and $x = -3$

13. $f(x) = 10x - 7$ for $x = -1$ and $x = 0$

14. $f(x) = x^2 + 2x + 1$ for $x = 3$ and $x = 4$

15. $f(x) = -\frac{3x}{5}$ for $x = 10$ and $x = -2$

16. $f(x) = -2x^2 - x$ for $x = -3$ and $x = \frac{1}{4}$

Let $f(x) = x^2$ and $g(x) = 2x - 1$. Find each new function, and state any domain restrictions.

1. $f + g$

2. $f - g$

3. $g - f$

4. $f \cdot g$

5. $\frac{f}{g}$

6. $\frac{g}{f}$

Let $f(x) = -2x^2$ and $g(x) = x + 1$. Find each new function, and state any domain restrictions.

7. $f + g$

8. $f - g$

9. $g - f$

10. $f \cdot g$

11. $\frac{f}{g}$

12. $\frac{g}{f}$

Find $f \circ g$ and $g \circ f$.

13. $f(x) = 4x$ and $g(x) = x^2 - 2$

14. $f(x) = x^2 - 3x$ and $g(x) = 2x$

15. $f(x) = -3x$ and $g(x) = 2x^2 - 3x$

16. $f(x) = \frac{1}{3}x$ and $g(x) = -9x^2$

Let $f(x) = 3x$, $g(x) = -2x^2$, and $h(x) = x^2 - 1$. Evaluate each composite function.

17. $(f \circ g)(3)$

18. $(f \circ h)(2)$

19. $(g \circ f)(1)$

20. $(h \circ f)(0)$

21. $(f \circ f)(1)$

22. $(h \circ g)(-2)$

Extra Practice

Find the inverse of each relation. State whether the relation is a function. State whether the inverse is a function.

1. $\{(1, 2), (2, 2), (3, 2), (4, 2)\}$

2. $\{(1, 0), (1, 2), (4, 3), (4, -2)\}$

3. $\{(1, 6), (2, 9), (3, 12), (4, 19)\}$

4. $\{(-2, 9), (-1, 8), (0, 7), (1, 6)\}$

For each function, find an equation for the inverse. Then use composition to verify that the equation you wrote is the inverse.

5. $f(x) = 10x - 6$

6. $g(x) = -6x + 5$

7. $h(x) = 0.5x + 2.5$

8. $g(x) = 9.5 - x$

9. $h(x) = \dfrac{x-2}{6}$

10. $f(x) = 14.4x$

Graph each function, and use the horizontal-line test to determine whether the inverse is a function.

11 $f(x) = 10x - 6$

12 $h(x) = 1 - 2x^2$

13 $g(x) = \frac{1}{2}x + 4$

14 $g(x) = x^3 + 1$

15 $f(x) = \frac{1}{x}$

16 $f(x) = \frac{1}{x^2}$

Graph each function.

1. $g(x) = \begin{cases} x & \text{if } x \le 0 \\ -x & \text{if } x > 0 \end{cases}$

2. $f(x) = \begin{cases} -2x + 1 & \text{if } x \le 2 \\ 4x + 1 & \text{if } x > 2 \end{cases}$

3. $h(x) = \begin{cases} 9 & \text{if } x < -3 \\ x^2 & \text{if } -3 \le x \le 3 \\ 9 & \text{if } x > 3 \end{cases}$

4. $g(x) = |x| - 2$

5. $f(x) = \lceil x \rceil + 1$

6. $g(x) = -[x]$

Write the piecewise function represented by each graph.

7.

8.

9.

10.

11.

12.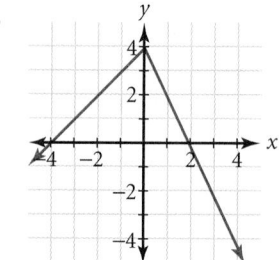

Evaluate.

13. $\lceil 14.07 \rceil$

14. $[14.07]$

15. $\lceil -8.65 \rceil$

16. $[72.4] + |-6|$

17. $\lceil 23.4 \rceil + [23.4]$

18. $[12.6] - [9.2]$

19. $|-12| + |12|$

20. $\lceil -7 \rceil - |-7|$

LESSON 2.7

Identify each transformation from the parent function $f(x) = x^4$ to g.

1. $g(x) = 8x^4$

2. $g(x) = (x + 11)^4$

3. $g(x) = -x^4$

4. $g(x) = (-6x)^4$

5. $g(x) = x^4 - 16$

6. $g(x) = x^4 + 5$

7. $g(x) = (-x)^4 + 13$

8. $g(x) = 7(x - 4)^4$

9. $g(x) = 2(x + 3)^4$

Identify each transformation from the parent function $f(x) = |x|$ to g.

10. $g(x) = |34x|$

11. $g(x) = |x - 19|$

12. $g(x) = |x| - 19$

13. $g(x) = 2|3x|$

14. $g(x) = \left|\frac{1}{3}x\right|$

15. $g(x) = 24|x| + 9$

Write a function, g, for the graph described.

16. the graph of $f(x) = x^2$ translated 18 units down

17. the graph of $f(x) = |x|$ vertically stretched by a factor of 10

18. the graph of $f(x) = \sqrt{x}$ reflected across the x-axis

19. the graph of $f(x) = 21x + 17$ reflected across the y-axis

20. the graph of $f(x) = x^2$ horizontally stretched by a factor of 6

21. the graph of $f(x) = x^2$ translated 3.5 units to the left

22. the graph of $f(x) = x^3$ translated 11 units up

23. the graph of $f(x) = |x|$ horizontally compressed by a factor of $\frac{1}{3}$

Chapter 3

LESSON 3.1

Graph and classify each system. Then find the solution from the graph.

1. $\begin{cases} y = 7x + 8 \\ y = 3x \end{cases}$

2. $\begin{cases} 3x - 2y = 9 \\ 2y - 3x = 6 \end{cases}$

3. $\begin{cases} 2x + y = -1 \\ 2y = -4x - 2 \end{cases}$

4. $\begin{cases} 4x + 5y = 2 \\ x + y = 1 \end{cases}$

5. $\begin{cases} x - 2y = 1 \\ 2x - 5y = -1 \end{cases}$

6. $\begin{cases} 4x - y = 5 \\ y = 4x + 3 \end{cases}$

7. $\begin{cases} 5x + 2y = 6 \\ x - y = -3 \end{cases}$

8. $\begin{cases} 3x - 2y = -2 \\ x + 2y = -6 \end{cases}$

9. $\begin{cases} 2x - y = 5 \\ 3x + 2y = 4 \end{cases}$

10. $\begin{cases} y - x = 1 \\ 2x + y = -5 \end{cases}$

11. $\begin{cases} y - 2x = -1 \\ x + 3y = 4 \end{cases}$

12. $\begin{cases} 2x + 3y = -4 \\ y = \frac{1}{2}x + 1 \end{cases}$

Use substitution to solve each system.

13. $\begin{cases} y = x - 13 \\ 2x + 3y = 1 \end{cases}$

14. $\begin{cases} x + y = 12 \\ x - y = 8 \end{cases}$

15. $\begin{cases} y = 2x - 7 \\ x + y = 5 \end{cases}$

16. $\begin{cases} y = \frac{1}{2}x - 3 \\ x = y + 1 \end{cases}$

17. $\begin{cases} 6x - 2y = 0 \\ x - y = 12 \end{cases}$

18. $\begin{cases} \frac{2}{3}x + \frac{1}{2}y = 2 \\ x - y = 10 \end{cases}$

19. $\begin{cases} y = 4x - 9 \\ y = 3x + 5 \end{cases}$

20. $\begin{cases} 2x - y = -1 \\ x + y = -17 \end{cases}$

21. $\begin{cases} x + 3y = 12 \\ x - 2y = -8 \end{cases}$

22. $\begin{cases} 2x + 5y + z = -4 \\ 4y + z = 0 \\ z = 8 \end{cases}$

23. $\begin{cases} x - 2y + 3z = 9 \\ x + y = -3 \\ x = -2 \end{cases}$

24. $\begin{cases} x + y + z = 10 \\ x + z = 8 \\ z = 5 \end{cases}$

LESSON 3.2

Use elimination to solve each system. Check your solution.

1. $\begin{cases} 13x - 2y = 10 \\ 8x + y = 24 \end{cases}$

2. $\begin{cases} 7x - y = 5 \\ 3x + y = 15 \end{cases}$

3. $\begin{cases} -2x - y = 7 \\ x - 3y = 14 \end{cases}$

4. $\begin{cases} 3x - 4y = 12 \\ 8y - 6x = -24 \end{cases}$

5. $\begin{cases} \frac{1}{2}x - y = 5 \\ x + 2y = -2 \end{cases}$

6. $\begin{cases} 7x - 4y = -9 \\ 3x + 2y = -15 \end{cases}$

7. $\begin{cases} 7x - 3y = 5 \\ 3y - 7x = 8 \end{cases}$

8. $\begin{cases} \frac{3}{4}x + \frac{1}{2}y = 11 \\ 3x - y = 14 \end{cases}$

9. $\begin{cases} 2x + 11y = 18 \\ 5x + 3y = -4 \end{cases}$

Use any method to solve each system. Check your solution.

10. $\begin{cases} y = 12x - 3 \\ 4x - y = -1 \end{cases}$

11. $\begin{cases} 2x + 5y = 43 \\ 7x - y = -16 \end{cases}$

12. $\begin{cases} 2x + y = -3 \\ 2x - y = -17 \end{cases}$

13. $\begin{cases} -3x + 2y = 1 \\ 4y - 6x = 2 \end{cases}$

14. $\begin{cases} y = 4x - 2 \\ y = 2x + 8 \end{cases}$

15. $\begin{cases} \frac{3}{4}x - y = 2 \\ 3x - 4y = 3 \end{cases}$

16. $\begin{cases} 9x + 3y = -3 \\ y - x = 11 \end{cases}$

17. $\begin{cases} 5y - 7x = -13 \\ 2x + 3y = 17 \end{cases}$

18. $\begin{cases} 17 - 5y = 3x \\ x + y = 5 \end{cases}$

LESSON 3.3

Graph each linear inequality.

1. $y < 2x - 4$

2. $y \geq -x + 3$

3. $y \leq 4x - 1$

4. $y > 4x + 4$

5. $-y \geq -3x$

6. $-y < 3x$

7. $x + 2y \leq 5$

8. $2x + y > -1$

9. $x + 4y < 8$

10. $3x + 2y \leq 6$

11. $5x - y > 6$

12. $\frac{2}{3}x + y \geq -2$

13. $x \geq -3$

14. $y < 0$

15. $x > 2$

16. $x + 5 < 0$

17. $-\frac{1}{2}y \leq 3$

18. $-\frac{2}{3}y \leq -4$

Write an inequality for each graph.

19.

20.

21.

22.

23.

24.
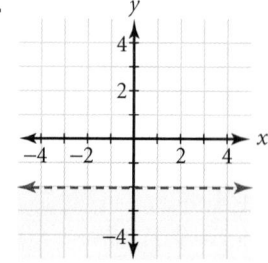

LESSON 3.4

Graph each compound inequality in a coordinate plane.

1. $-3 \leq x \leq 0$ **2.** $-4 < x < -1$ **3.** $-6 < y < -1$

4. $-2 \leq y \leq 4$ **5.** $2 \leq x < 5$ **6.** $1 < y \leq 4$

Graph each system of linear inequalities.

7. $\begin{cases} y < 3 \\ y \geq 2x - 1 \end{cases}$ **8.** $\begin{cases} x \leq 2 \\ y > x \end{cases}$ **9.** $\begin{cases} y < 5 - x \\ y > 2x + 1 \end{cases}$

10. $\begin{cases} x > 1 \\ y \leq 4 \\ y < 2x + 1 \end{cases}$ **11.** $\begin{cases} x > 0 \\ y < -x + 5 \\ y > x - 5 \end{cases}$ **12.** $\begin{cases} x \geq 2 \\ y \geq 0 \\ y \geq -x + 3 \\ y \leq x + 1 \end{cases}$

Write the system of inequalities whose solution is graphed. Assume that each vertex has integer coordinates.

13.

14.

15.
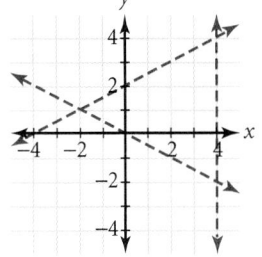

LESSON 3.5

Graph the feasible region for each set of constraints.

1. $\begin{cases} x + y \leq 5 \\ 2x + y \leq 9 \\ x \geq 0 \\ y \geq 0 \end{cases}$ **2.** $\begin{cases} 2x + 3y \leq 15 \\ x - y \leq 4 \\ x \geq 0 \\ y \geq 0 \end{cases}$ **3.** $\begin{cases} y \leq \frac{1}{2}x + 4 \\ y \geq \frac{1}{2}x - 2 \\ 0 \leq x < 6 \end{cases}$

The feasible region for a set of constraints has vertices at (0, 0), (60, 0), (60, 30), and (10, 50). Given this feasible region, find the maximum and minimum values of each objective function.

4. $C = 100x + 25y$ **5.** $P = 40x + 65y$

Find the maximum and minimum values, if they exist, of each objective function for the given constraints.

6. $P = 5x + 2y$
Constraints:
$\begin{cases} x + y \leq 7 \\ x - y \leq 5 \\ x \geq 0 \\ y \geq 0 \end{cases}$

7. $P = 10x + y$
Constraints:
$\begin{cases} 5x + 2y \leq 20 \\ x - y \leq 4 \\ x \geq 0 \\ y \geq 0 \end{cases}$

8. $E = 4x + 5y$
Constraints:
$\begin{cases} x + 2y \geq 6 \\ x + 2y \leq 12 \\ x \geq 0 \\ y \geq 0 \end{cases}$

LESSON 3.6

Graph each pair of parametric equations for the given interval of *t*.

1. $\begin{cases} x(t) = t + 4 \\ y(t) = t - 3 \end{cases}$ for $-4 \le t \le 4$

2. $\begin{cases} x(t) = -4t \\ y(t) = t + 2 \end{cases}$ for $-3 \le t \le 3$

3. $\begin{cases} x(t) = 2t + 1 \\ y(t) = t - 4 \end{cases}$ for $-3 \le t \le 3$

4. $\begin{cases} x(t) = 2 - t \\ y(t) = \frac{1}{2}t + 1 \end{cases}$ for $-4 \le t \le 4$

Write each pair of parametric equations as a single equation in *x* and *y*.

5. $\begin{cases} x(t) = 2 - t \\ y(t) = 3 + t \end{cases}$

6. $\begin{cases} x(t) = t + 4 \\ y(t) = 1 - 2t \end{cases}$

7. $\begin{cases} x(t) = 4 - t \\ y(t) = t + 1 \end{cases}$

8. $\begin{cases} x(t) = 4t \\ y(t) = 3t - 1 \end{cases}$

9. $\begin{cases} x(t) = 2t \\ y(t) = \frac{t}{3} \end{cases}$

10. $\begin{cases} x(t) = 3t \\ y(t) = t^2 \end{cases}$

Graph the function represented by each pair of parametric equations. Then graph its inverse in the same coordinate plane.

11. $\begin{cases} x(t) = t^2 - 4 \\ y(t) = t \end{cases}$

12. $\begin{cases} x(t) = t^2 \\ y(t) = t - 4 \end{cases}$

13. $\begin{cases} x(t) = t^2 + 2 \\ y(t) = 1 - t \end{cases}$

14. $\begin{cases} x(t) = 2 - t^2 \\ y(t) = t + 1 \end{cases}$

15. $\begin{cases} x(t) = t^2 + 3t - 1 \\ y(t) = t + 2 \end{cases}$

16. $\begin{cases} x(t) = t^2 - 4t + 2 \\ y(t) = 1 - t \end{cases}$

Chapter 4

LESSON 4.1

For Exercises 1–14, let $A = \begin{bmatrix} 2 & 3 & -2 \\ 1 & 4 & 5 \\ 0 & 1 & 7 \end{bmatrix}$, $B = \begin{bmatrix} -3 & -2 & 1 \\ 0 & 5 & 5 \\ 1 & 2 & -1 \end{bmatrix}$, and $C = \begin{bmatrix} 8 & 0 & 1 \\ -6 & 4 & 3 \end{bmatrix}$.

Give the dimensions of each matrix.

1. A 　　　　　　2. B 　　　　　　3. C

Give the entry at the indicated address in matrix *A*, *B*, or *C*.

4. a_{13} 　　　　　　5. c_{21} 　　　　　　6. b_{31}

Perform the indicated matrix operations. If it is not possible, explain why.

7. $-A$ 　　8. $A + B$ 　　9. $-2C$ 　　10. $B - A$

11. $A + C$ 　　12. $2A - B$ 　　13. $2B + A$ 　　14. $4C$

Solve for *x* and *y*.

15. $\begin{bmatrix} x + 3 & -3 \\ 2 & 3y + 1 \end{bmatrix} = \begin{bmatrix} 10 & -3 \\ 2 & 10 \end{bmatrix}$

16. $\begin{bmatrix} -4 & 21 \\ -4y - 3 & 1 \end{bmatrix} = \begin{bmatrix} -4 & -2x + 5 \\ -19 & 1 \end{bmatrix}$

17. Quadrilateral $ABCD$ has vertices at $A(0, 0)$, $B(1, 4)$, $C(4, 2)$, and $D(2, 0)$.
   a. Represent quadrilateral $ABCD$ in a matrix called Q.
   b. Find $-2Q$.
   c. Sketch quadrilateral $ABCD$ and its image, $A'B'C'D'$, represented by $-2Q$. Describe the transformation.

LESSON 4.2

Find each product, if it exists.

1. $[2 \quad 4 \quad 3]\begin{bmatrix} -4 \\ 0 \\ 6 \end{bmatrix}$

2. $\begin{bmatrix} -2 & -1 \\ 0 & 4 \\ 0 & -4 \end{bmatrix}\begin{bmatrix} 8 \\ 0 \\ 12 \end{bmatrix}$

3. $\begin{bmatrix} -6 & 2 \\ 4 & 0 \end{bmatrix}\begin{bmatrix} 3 & 2 \\ 1 & -1 \end{bmatrix}$

4. $\begin{bmatrix} -7 & 2 \\ 2 & 3 \end{bmatrix}\begin{bmatrix} 8 & -1 & 2 \\ 3 & 2 & 4 \\ -3 & 5 & 1 \end{bmatrix}$

5. $[-3 \quad -3 \quad 7]\begin{bmatrix} 9 & 1 \\ 0 & 3 \\ 3 & 5 \end{bmatrix}$

6. $[2 \quad 1 \quad 0 \quad 3]\begin{bmatrix} -5 & 4 \\ 4 & 9 \\ 2 & 7 \\ -3 & -6 \end{bmatrix}$

7. $\begin{bmatrix} 1 & 4 \\ 2 & 3 \\ -3 & -3 \end{bmatrix}\begin{bmatrix} -5 & 3 & 4 \\ 1 & 1 & 0 \end{bmatrix}$

8. $\begin{bmatrix} 1 & 0 & 4 \\ -2 & 2 & 3 \end{bmatrix}\begin{bmatrix} 6 \\ 2 \\ 5 \end{bmatrix}$

9. $[9 \quad 4 \quad 1]\begin{bmatrix} -5 & 1 \\ 0.5 & 4 \\ 2 & 1 \end{bmatrix}$

10. Triangle DEF has vertices at $D(-2, 4)$, $E(4, 0)$, and $F(0, -4)$.
 a. Represent $\triangle DEF$ in a matrix called T.
 b. Multiply T by the transformation matrix $S = \begin{bmatrix} \frac{3}{4} & 0 \\ 0 & \frac{3}{4} \end{bmatrix}$.
 c. Sketch $\triangle DEF$ and its image, $\triangle D'E'F'$, represented by ST. Describe the transformation.

LESSON 4.3

Determine whether each pair of matrices are inverses of each other.

1. $\begin{bmatrix} 5 & -4 \\ 1 & 6 \end{bmatrix}$ and $\begin{bmatrix} -5 & 4 \\ -1 & 6 \end{bmatrix}$

2. $\begin{bmatrix} 2 & 4 \\ 0 & -3 \end{bmatrix}$ and $\begin{bmatrix} \frac{1}{2} & \frac{2}{3} \\ 0 & -\frac{1}{3} \end{bmatrix}$

3. $\begin{bmatrix} 2 & -3 \\ -1 & 2 \end{bmatrix}$ and $\begin{bmatrix} 2 & 3 \\ 1 & 2 \end{bmatrix}$

4. $\begin{bmatrix} 3 & 2 \\ 5 & 4 \end{bmatrix}$ and $\begin{bmatrix} 2 & -1 \\ -2.5 & 1.5 \end{bmatrix}$

Find the determinant, and state whether each matrix has an inverse.

5. $\begin{bmatrix} 5 & 3 \\ 2 & 1 \end{bmatrix}$

6. $\begin{bmatrix} 4 & 2 \\ 3 & 2 \end{bmatrix}$

7. $\begin{bmatrix} 4 & 2 \\ 6 & 3 \end{bmatrix}$

8. $\begin{bmatrix} -3 & 1 \\ 7 & 4 \end{bmatrix}$

9. $\begin{bmatrix} \frac{1}{2} & -\frac{1}{4} \\ \frac{3}{4} & \frac{5}{2} \end{bmatrix}$

10. $\begin{bmatrix} \frac{2}{3} & -\frac{3}{4} \\ \frac{1}{3} & -5 \end{bmatrix}$

Find the inverse matrix, if it exists. Round entries to the nearest hundredth, if necessary. If the inverse matrix does not exist, write *no inverse*.

11. $\begin{bmatrix} 5 & 8 \\ 2 & 3 \end{bmatrix}$

12. $\begin{bmatrix} 2.5 & 5 \\ 2 & 4 \end{bmatrix}$

13. $\begin{bmatrix} 8 & 3 \\ 4 & 2 \end{bmatrix}$

14. $\begin{bmatrix} 12 & 9 \\ 4 & 3 \end{bmatrix}$

15. $\begin{bmatrix} 3 & 2 \\ 13 & 8 \end{bmatrix}$

16. $\begin{bmatrix} 3 & 8 \\ 4 & 12 \end{bmatrix}$

17. $\begin{bmatrix} 4 & -2 & 1 \\ 1 & 1 & 3 \\ 1 & -1 & 1 \end{bmatrix}$

18. $\begin{bmatrix} 6 & 1 & -7 \\ -2 & 0 & 4 \\ 4 & 5 & -3 \end{bmatrix}$

19. $\begin{bmatrix} \frac{1}{3} & \frac{2}{3} & 0 \\ -\frac{1}{2} & 3 & -1 \\ 4 & -\frac{1}{4} & 3 \end{bmatrix}$

LESSON 4.4

Write the matrix equation that represents each system.

1. $\begin{cases} 2x + y = 2 \\ 5x - 3y = -17 \end{cases}$

2. $\begin{cases} 8x + 2y = 10 \\ 5x + y = 7 \end{cases}$

3. $\begin{cases} 3x - 2y = 4 \\ x - 4y = 15 \end{cases}$

4. $\begin{cases} 2x + y + z = 1 \\ x + 3y - 4z = 19 \\ 4x - 2y + 3z = -9 \end{cases}$

5. $\begin{cases} 2x - 3y + z = 3 \\ x - 5y + 2z = 4 \\ 4x - y - z = -1 \end{cases}$

6. $\begin{cases} 3x - y + 2z = 3 \\ 2x + 5y - 3z = -12 \\ x - 3y + 4z = 8 \end{cases}$

Write the system of equations represented by each matrix equation.

7. $\begin{bmatrix} -2 & 1 & -1 \\ 5 & -1 & 2 \\ 3 & 4 & 1 \end{bmatrix} \begin{bmatrix} x \\ y \\ z \end{bmatrix} = \begin{bmatrix} 4 \\ -6 \\ 10 \end{bmatrix}$

8. $\begin{bmatrix} 0.5 & -2 & -1 \\ 3 & -6 & 2 \\ 1 & 1 & -5 \end{bmatrix} \begin{bmatrix} x \\ y \\ z \end{bmatrix} = \begin{bmatrix} -1 \\ 8 \\ 0 \end{bmatrix}$

Write the matrix equation that represents each system, and solve the system, if possible, by using a matrix equation.

9. $\begin{cases} 15x - 7y = 9 \\ 11x + 5y = 37 \end{cases}$

10. $\begin{cases} x + y - z = 2 \\ 2x - y + z = 7 \\ x + y = 10 \end{cases}$

11. $\begin{cases} 2x + y + z = 5 \\ x - y + 3z = -11 \\ y + z = 1 \end{cases}$

12. $\begin{cases} x - 2y + 3z = -6 \\ 2x + y - 4z = -7 \\ 5x + 3y - 2z = 10 \end{cases}$

13. $\begin{cases} 4x - 3y + z = 9 \\ 2x + y - 3z = -7 \\ 3x + 2y + z = 12 \end{cases}$

14. $\begin{cases} x + y - z = 15 \\ 2x - y + z = 0 \\ 3x + 2y - 3z = 38 \end{cases}$

LESSON 4.5

Write the augmented matrix for each system of equations.

1. $\begin{cases} 4x - 3y = 7 \\ 2x - y = 5 \end{cases}$

2. $\begin{cases} 11x - 5y + z = 9 \\ 3x + 7y - z = 3 \\ x - y + 4z = 8 \end{cases}$

3. $\begin{cases} 6x - y + z = 6 \\ 3x + 4y - z = 3 \\ 9x - 3y + 2z = 9 \end{cases}$

Find the reduced row-echelon form of each matrix.

4. $\begin{bmatrix} 2 & 1 & -1 & \vdots & -1 \\ 1 & -1 & 3 & \vdots & 8 \\ 1 & 1 & 1 & \vdots & 2 \end{bmatrix}$

5. $\begin{bmatrix} 1 & 1 & 2 & \vdots & 2 \\ 1 & 0 & 2 & \vdots & -3 \\ -1 & 0 & 3 & \vdots & 5 \end{bmatrix}$

6. $\begin{bmatrix} -1 & -2 & 0 & \vdots & -4 \\ 1 & 2 & 1 & \vdots & 7 \\ 3 & 6 & 3 & \vdots & 21 \end{bmatrix}$

Solve each system of equations by using the row-reduction method. Show each step.

7. $\begin{cases} 8x - 5y = -6 \\ 4x + 3y = 8 \end{cases}$

8. $\begin{cases} 2x - 5y = 4 \\ 5x - 7y = -1 \end{cases}$

9. $\begin{cases} 7x - 3y = 29 \\ 10x + 3y = 5 \end{cases}$

10. $\begin{cases} 2x - y + 3z = -7 \\ x + 4y - 2z = 17 \\ 3x + y + 2z = 2 \end{cases}$

11. $\begin{cases} x + 5y - 3z = 14 \\ 2x + y - z = 10 \\ x - 2y + z = 0 \end{cases}$

12. $\begin{cases} -x - 3y + 2z = -10 \\ 2x + y + z = 5 \\ 3x - 2y + 3z = -5 \end{cases}$

Classify each system as inconsistent, dependent, or independent.

13. $\begin{cases} -y - z = -1 \\ x + y + z = -2 \\ 2x - y - z = -7 \end{cases}$

14. $\begin{cases} x - 2y + 3z = 13 \\ 2x + 5y - 3z = -19 \\ x + 4y - 5z = -21 \end{cases}$

15. $\begin{cases} x - y + z = 4 \\ -2x + y - 2z = -7 \\ x + z = 6 \end{cases}$

Chapter 5

LESSON 5.1

Show that each function is a quadratic function by writing it in the form $f(x) = ax^2 + bx + c$ and identifying a, b, and c.

1. $f(x) = (x + 1)(x - 7)$

2. $f(x) = (x - 11)(x + 2)$

3. $f(x) = (2x + 1)(x - 4)$

4. $f(x) = (12 - x)(1 + x)$

5. $f(x) = (2x + 7)(x - 5)$

6. $f(x) = (x - 2)^2 + 9$

Identify whether each function is a quadratic function. Use a graph to check your answers.

7. $g(x) = 5 - 2x + x^2$

8. $h(x) = (x - 1)(x^2 + 1)$

9. $f(x) = x^2 - (x + 1)^2$

10. $g(x) = 3x(-x + 4)$

State whether each parabola opens up or down and whether the y-coordinate of the vertex is the minimum value or the maximum value of the function.

11. $f(x) = 16 - x^2$

12. $h(x) = x^2 - x - 12$

13. $g(x) = (4 - x)(6 - x)$

14. $f(x) = (x - 4)^2 - 2x^2$

Graph each function and give the approximate coordinates of the vertex.

15 $f(x) = 4 + 2x + x^2$

16 $h(x) = 3x^2 + x - 3$

17 $k(x) = \frac{1}{2}x^2 + 5$

18 $g(x) = (x - 3)^2$

19 $f(x) = 0.5x + x^2$

20 $h(x) = -(x - 2)(x - 3)$

LESSON 5.2

Solve each equation. Give exact solutions. Then approximate each solution to the nearest hundredth, if necessary.

1. $x^2 = 51$

2. $16x^2 = 49$

3. $3x^2 = 39$

4. $x^2 - 44 = 0$

5. $7x^2 + 3 = 29$

6. $(x - 4)^2 = 19$

Find the unknown length in each triangle. Give answers to the nearest tenth.

7.

8.

9.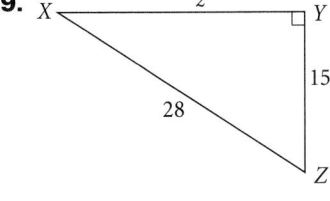

Find the missing side length in right triangle *ABC*. Round answers to the nearest tenth, if necessary.

10. $a = 17$ and $b = 8$

11. $a = 20$ and $c = 32$

12. $b = 7.2$ and $c = 13$

13. $b = 4.5$ and $c = 16$

14. $c = \sqrt{102}$ and $a = 6$

15. $a = 9$ and $b = 11$

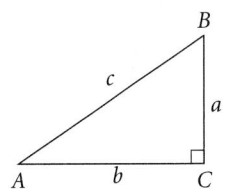

LESSON 5.3

Factor each expression.

1. $7x + 49$

2. $36x + 108x^2$

3. $4x^2 - 28x$

4. $-9x^2 + 3x$

5. $14(3 - x^2) + x(3 - x^2)$

6. $3x(x - 8) + 7(x - 8)$

7. $-3x^3 - 12x^2$

8. $(9 - 2x)3x - 8(9 - 2x)$

Factor each quadratic expression.

9. $x^2 + 14x + 49$

10. $x^2 - 13x + 30$

11. $x^2 + 17x + 42$

12. $x^2 - 7x - 60$

13. $3x^2 + 8x + 4$

14. $2x^2 - 7x + 6$

15. $5x - 2x^2 - 3$

16. $x + 2 - 6x^2$

Solve each equation by factoring and applying the Zero-Product Property.

17. $x^2 - 144 = 0$

18. $x^2 - 18x + 81 = 0$

19. $16x^2 - 25 = 0$

20. $x^2 + 3x - 4 = 0$

21. $9x^2 - 6x + 1 = 0$

22. $x^2 + 10x + 25 = 0$

Use factoring and the Zero-Product Property to find the zeros of each quadratic function.

23. $h(x) = x^2 - 12x$

24. $k(x) = x^2 - 4x - 21$

25. $g(x) = 2x^2 + 17x - 9$

26. $f(x) = x^2 + 16x + 55$

27. $h(x) = x^2 - 12x + 35$

28. $a(x) = 2x^2 + 9x - 5$

LESSON 5.4

Complete the square for each quadratic expression in order to form a perfect-square trinomial. Then write the new expression as a binomial squared.

1. $x^2 + x$

2. $x^2 + 18x$

3. $x^2 - 10x$

4. $x^2 + 26x$

5. $x^2 - 9x$

6. $x^2 + 3x$

7. $x^2 - 22x$

8. $x^2 + 17x$

9. $x^2 - 0.5x$

Solve each equation by completing the square. Give exact solutions.

10. $x^2 - 10x + 4 = 0$

11. $x^2 + 2x - 7 = 0$

12. $x^2 - 12x = 20$

13. $x^2 = 8x + 12$

14. $0 = x^2 - 14x + 2$

15. $21 = x^2 - 16x$

16. $x^2 + 5x = 7$

17. $x^2 + 3x + 6 = 17$

18. $x^2 - 7x = 15 - x$

19. $2x^2 - 15 = 8x$

20. $4x^2 + 12x = 14$

21. $x^2 + x - 3 = 0$

Write each quadratic function in vertex form. Give the coordinates of the vertex and the equation of the axis of symmetry.

22. $f(x) = 9x^2$

23. $f(x) = x^2 - 3$

24. $f(x) = -x^2 + 12$

25. $f(x) = x^2 + 4x$

26. $f(x) = -x^2 + 3x + 1$

27. $f(x) = x^2 + 6x + 5$

28. $f(x) = x^2 + 12x + 42$

29. $f(x) = 2x^2 + 4x - 3$

30. $f(x) = -x^2 - 3x + 7$

LESSON 5.5

Use the quadratic formula to solve each equation. Give exact solutions.

1. $x^2 - 8x + 15 = 0$ **2.** $x^2 + 14x = 0$ **3.** $x^2 - 5x + 1 = 0$

4. $x^2 - x = 12$ **5.** $x^2 - 10x + 14 = 5$ **6.** $x^2 + 5x + 3 = 0$

7. $x^2 - 7 = 2x$ **8.** $2x^2 + 3x - 1 = 0$ **9.** $(x - 3)(x + 4) = 5$

10. $3x^2 - 2x - 5 = 0$ **11.** $7x^2 - 2x - 8 = 0$ **12.** $-2x^2 + 3x + 1 = 0$

13. $4x + x^2 - 9 = 0$ **14.** $4x^2 = x + 6$ **15.** $x^2 - 14 = x$

For each quadratic function, write the equation for the axis of symmetry and find the coordinates of the vertex.

16. $y = 3x^2 + 6x - 2$ **17.** $y = x^2 + 4x - 11$ **18.** $y = -x^2 + 8x + 12$

19. $y = 2x^2 + 3x - 5$ **20.** $y = 6 + 2x - x^2$ **21.** $y = x^2 + x - 9$

22. $y = -3x^2 + 2x + 8$ **23.** $y = -3x^2 - 4x + 2$ **24.** $y = 5x^2 + 10x + 3$

25. $y = 4x^2 + 2x - 1$ **26.** $y = -7 + 6x + x^2$ **27.** $y = 3x^2 - 9x + 5$

28. $y = -x^2 + 8x - 16$ **29.** $y = 4x^2 - 3x - 5$ **30.** $y = -5x^2 - 4x + 7$

LESSON 5.6

Find the discriminant and determine the number of real solutions. Then solve.

1. $x^2 - 3x - 5 = 0$ **2.** $2x^2 - 4x + 3 = 0$ **3.** $x^2 - 7x + 17 = 0$

4. $3x^2 - 5x + 8 = 0$ **5.** $4x - 8x^2 = 3$ **6.** $x^2 - 5x + 10 = 0$

7. $4x^2 + 9 = 2x$ **8.** $x - x^2 = 11$ **9.** $-3x^2 = 6x - 2$

Write the conjugate of each complex number.

10. -2 **11.** $13 - 5i$ **12.** $7 + 2i$

13. $-3i + 4$ **14.** $i - 1$ **15.** $3i$

Simplify.

16. $(6 + 5i) + (13 - 4i)$ **17.** $(-2 + 14i) - (-7 + 12i)$ **18.** $(17 + 8i) + (-4 + i)$

19. $(6i + 2) + (3i - 1)$ **20.** $(3i - 1) - (-2i + 1)$ **21.** $(-5 - 3i) + (2i - 6)$

22. $(20 - 16i) - (9 + 2i)$ **23.** $(15 - 6i) + (15 + 6i)$ **24.** $(14 + 3i) - (3 + i)$

25. $3(-9 + 12i)$ **26.** $2i(-4 - 8i)$ **27.** $(7 + 3i)(2 - 5i)$

28. $(2 - 4i)(7 + i)$ **29.** $(-3i + 2)(4 - i)$ **30.** $(3 + 5i)(-2i - 4)$

31. $\dfrac{5 - i}{3 + i}$ **32.** $\dfrac{4 - 7i}{-1 + i}$ **33.** $\dfrac{6 - 2i}{-4 + i}$

34. $\dfrac{5 + i}{i}$ **35.** $\dfrac{4 + 3i}{2i}$ **36.** $\dfrac{2i + 5}{-3i}$

37. $(2i - 9)^2$ **38.** $(-3 + 10i)^2$ **39.** $(4 - 5i)^2$

Graph each number and its conjugate in the complex plane.

40. $4 + i$ **41.** $4i$ **42.** 4

43. $i + 2$ **44.** $-i - 3$ **45.** -6

LESSON 5.7

Solve a system of equations in order to find a quadratic function that fits each set of data points exactly.

1. $(-7, 51)$, $(5, 27)$, $(-4, 18)$ **2.** $(-2, 9)$, $(6, -47)$, $(-1, 9)$

3. $(-4, -13)$, $(-2, -11)$, $(2, 17)$ **4.** $(-3, 14)$, $(2, 19)$, $(4, 49)$

5. $(0, 6)$, $(1, 8)$, $(3, 18)$ **6.** $(-5, 19)$, $(-3, 7)$, $(6, 52)$

7. $(-3, 4)$, $(-2, -19)$, $(9, -140)$ **8.** $(-6, -114)$, $(-5, -81)$, $(4, -54)$

9. $(2, 7)$, $(4, 19)$, $(-6, -1)$ **10.** $(3, 47)$, $(-1, 13)$, $(0, 1)$

11. $(4, 0)$, $(6, -12)$, $(-2, -12)$ **12.** $(1, 4)$, $(2, -20)$, $(-1, -8)$

13. $(4, 3)$, $(-4, 7)$, $(2, 1)$ **14.** $(-3, 51)$, $(3, 27)$, $(0, 3)$

15. $(-8, -28)$, $(6, 0)$, $(3, 10.5)$ **16.** $(-5, 17)$, $(5, 47)$, $(3, 25)$

Randall plays baseball for his high school team. The table shows the height, y, of the ball x seconds after Randall hit it.

17. Find a quadratic function that fits the data by solving a system.

18. Find the height of the ball 2.5 seconds after it was hit.

19. After how many seconds did the ball hit the ground?

Time (seconds)	Height (feet)
1	48
2	60
3	40

LESSON 5.8

Solve each inequality. Graph the solution on a number line.

1. $x^2 - 9 < 0$ **2.** $x^2 - 25 \geq 0$

3. $x^2 + 11x + 18 \leq 0$ **4.** $x^2 - 11x + 30 < 0$

5. $x^2 + x - 12 > 0$ **6.** $x^2 - 5x + 4 \geq 0$

7. $x^2 - 8x + 16 \leq 0$ **8.** $x^2 - 6x + 9 \leq 0$

9. $x^2 - 6x - 7 > 0$ **10.** $x^2 + 4x - 1 > 0$

11. $x^2 - 3x - 5 \leq 0$ **12.** $x^2 + 2x + \frac{1}{2} < 0$

Sketch the graph of each inequality. Then decide which of the given points are in the solution region.

13. $y < (x + 2)^2 - 3$ $A(-3, -1)$ $B(-3, -2)$ $C(-3, -4)$

14. $y \leq -(x + 1)^2 + 4$ $A(1, 2)$ $B(1, -2)$ $C(1, -5)$

15. $y > -(x - 4)^2 + 3$ $A(3, 2)$ $B(4, -3)$ $C(7, -5)$

Graph each inequality and shade the solution region.

16. $y \geq (x - 3)^2$ **17.** $y \leq (x - 1)^2$

18. $y > -x^2 + 2x - 1$ **19.** $y \leq x^2 + 4x + 3$

20. $y \geq x^2 + 5x + 4$ **21.** $y \leq (x + 2)^2 + 2$

22. $y > x^2 + 2x - 4$ **23.** $y < 2x^2 + 2x - 2$

24. $y > -(x + 4)^2$ **25.** $y < (x - 4)^2 - 1$

26. $y \geq 2x^2 + 6x + 9$ **27.** $y < x^2 + 4x + 1$

Chapter 6

LESSON 6.1

Find the multiplier for each rate of exponential growth or decay.

1. 3% growth

2. 2.4% growth

3. 10% decay

4. 4% decay

5. 0.7% growth

6. 1.4% growth

7. 18% growth

8. 9% decay

9. 0.04% growth

10. 7.2% decay

11. 1.15% growth

12. 0.7% decay

Evaluate each expression to the nearest thousandth for the given value of x.

13. 2^x for $x = 1.5$

14. $40(2)^{2x}$ for $x = 2.5$

15. $30(0.5)^x$ for $x = 3$

16. $20(2)^{x+1}$ for $x = 0.5$

17. 2^{3x} for $x = 0.8$

18. $50(0.5)^{2x}$ for $x = 0.75$

19. $3(0.5)^x$ for $x = 5$

20. $10(2)^x$ for $x = 2.4$

21. A physician gives a patient 250 milligrams of an antibiotic that is eliminated from the bloodstream at a rate of 15% per hour. Predict the number of milligrams remaining after 3 hours.

22. A lab sample contains 400 bacteria that double every 15 minutes. Predict the number of bacteria after 3 hours.

23. The population of a city was approximately 450,000 in the year 2000 and was projected to grow at an annual rate of 2.3%. Predict the population, to the nearest ten thousand, for the year 2006.

LESSON 6.2

Identify each function as linear, quadratic, or exponential.

1. $f(x) = x^2 - 12$

2. $g(x) = 2x - 12$

3. $h(x) = (x + 3)^2$

4. $k(x) = \left(\frac{5}{4}\right)^{2x}$

5. $p(x) = 3x + 2^2$

6. $q(x) = 3^{x+2}$

Tell whether each function represents exponential growth or decay.

7. $b(x) = 40(3.8)^x$

8. $f(x) = 100(0.18)^x$

9. $g(x) = \left(\frac{1}{5}\right)^x$

10. $w(x) = 3.5(1.01)^x$

11. $z(x) = 0.4^x$

12. $m(x) = 450(2.04)^x$

13. $k(x) = 500(0.99)^x$

14. $h(x) = 20(1.75)^x$

15. $f(x) = 17(4)^{-x}$

Find the final amount for each investment.

16. $1200 earning 5% interest compounded annually for 10 years

17. $900 earning 6% interest compounded annually for 15 years

18. $5000 earning 6.5% interest compounded semiannually for 12 years

19. $500 earning 5.5% interest compounded semiannually for 3 years

20. $8000 earning 8% interest compounded quarterly for 5 years

21. $600 earning 7.5% interest compounded quarterly for 2 years

22. $10,000 earning 8% interest compounded daily for 1 year

23. $4000 earning 5.25% interest compounded daily for 2 years

Write each equation in logarithmic form.

1. $3^4 = 81$

2. $4^3 = 64$

3. $\left(\dfrac{1}{2}\right)^7 = \dfrac{1}{128}$

4. $\left(\dfrac{1}{4}\right)^3 = \dfrac{1}{64}$

5. $\left(\dfrac{1}{3}\right)^{-4} = 81$

6. $\left(\dfrac{1}{15}\right)^{-2} = 225$

7. $5^{-3} = \dfrac{1}{125}$

8. $10^{-2} = 0.01$

9. $9^{-2} = \dfrac{1}{81}$

Write each equation in exponential form.

10. $\log_{14} 196 = 2$

11. $\log_7 2401 = 4$

12. $\log_8 \dfrac{1}{512} = -3$

13. $\log_6 \dfrac{1}{1296} = -4$

14. $\log_3 81 = 4$

15. $\log_2 256 = 8$

16. $\log_{17} 289 = 2$

17. $\log_{10} 0.0001 = -4$

18. $\log_{10} 10{,}000 = 4$

Solve each equation for x. Round your answers to the nearest hundredth.

19. $10^x = 15$

20. $10^x = 72$

21. $10^x = 4.5$

22. $10^x = 7.8$

23. $10^x = 1042$

24. $10^x = 2509$

25. $10^x = 0.835$

26. $10^x = 0.007$

27. $10^x = 14.2$

Find the value of v in each equation.

28. $v = \log_4 1024$

29. $v = \log_{13} 1$

30. $\log_6 \dfrac{1}{36} = v$

31. $4 = \log_5 v$

32. $\log_4 v = -3$

33. $-6 = \log_2 v$

34. $-3 = \log_v \dfrac{1}{27}$

35. $\log_v \dfrac{1}{625} = -4$

36. $7 = \log_v 128$

Write each expression as a sum or difference of logarithms. Then simplify, if possible.

1. $\log_3 9x$

2. $\log_3 27x$

3. $\log_4 (2 \cdot 3 \cdot 4)$

4. $\log_2 \dfrac{16}{y}$

5. $\log_5 \dfrac{4}{5}$

6. $\log_{10} \dfrac{xy}{10}$

Write each expression as a single logarithm. Then simplify, if possible.

7. $\log_2 3 + \log_2 7$

8. $\log_6 12 + \log_6 15 - \log_6 5$

9. $2 \log_4 5 - \log_4 6$

10. $\log_9 x - 3 \log_9 y$

11. $3 \log_5 3 - \log_5 5.4$

12. $\dfrac{1}{2} \log_b 25 + 3 \log_b z$

Evaluate each expression.

13. $\log_3 3^4 - \log_8 8^4$

14. $\log_7 7^5 + \log_6 6^3$

15. $4^{\log_4 87} + \log_5 25$

16. $8^{\log_8 9} - \log_4 16$

17. $\log_3 \dfrac{1}{81} + \log_4 64$

18. $\log_2 64 - 7^{\log_7 1}$

Solve for x, and check your answers. If the equation has no solution, write *no solution*.

19. $\log_8 (x + 1) = \log_8 (2x - 2)$

20. $\log_3 (3x - 4) = \log_3 (8 - 5x)$

21. $\log_7 (6x + 4) = \log_7 (-3x - 5)$

22. $\log_{10} (6x + 3) = \log_{10} 3x$

23. $\log_2 x + \log_2 (x - 4) = 5$

24. $\log_8 (3x + 1) + \log_8 (x - 1) = 2$

25. $2 \log_b x = \log_b 2 + \log_b (2x - 2)$

26. $2 \log_b x = \log_b (x - 1) + \log_b 4$

LESSON 6.5

Evaluate each logarithmic expression to the nearest hundredth.

1. $\log_2 51$ **2.** $\log_5 64$ **3.** $\log_6 0.5$

4. $\log_4 9$ **5.** $\log_9 14$ **6.** $\log_7 32$

7. $\log_8 0.23$ **8.** $\log_{\frac{1}{2}} 15$ **9.** $\log_2 0.72$

10. $\log_{\frac{1}{4}} 16$ **11.** $2 - \log_5 7$ **12.** $\log_9 10$

13. $\log_6 \frac{2}{3}$ **14.** $\log_8 50$ **15.** $3 + \log_3 22$

16. $\log_7 \frac{3}{4}$ **17.** $\log_8 \frac{1}{3}$ **18.** $\log_7 8$

19. $10 + \log_4 25$ **20.** $\log_{15} 40$ **21.** $\log_9 \frac{3}{4}$

Solve each equation. Round your answers to the nearest hundredth.

22. $5^x = 24$ **23.** $6^x = 44$ **24.** $8^x = 0.9$

25. $2^x = 3.5$ **26.** $9^x = 17$ **27.** $3^x = 41$

28. $8^{-x} = 0.25$ **29.** $4^x = 22$ **30.** $9^x = 2$

31. $2.5^x = 17$ **32.** $7^x = 3$ **33.** $12^x = 140$

34. $1 + 3^x = 14$ **35.** $3^{-x} = 0.9$ **36.** $4^{x+1} = 64$

37. $5^{2x} = 114$ **38.** $7 - 2^x = 1$ **39.** $4 + 4^x = 14$

40. $5^{x-2} = 70$ **41.** $5^x = 20.5$ **42.** $7^x = 22$

LESSON 6.6

Evaluate each expression, if possible, to the nearest thousandth.

1. e^3 **2.** e^{-2} **3.** $e^{4.5}$ **4.** $e^{0.6}$

5. $e^{\sqrt{3}}$ **6.** $\ln 17$ **7.** $\ln \sqrt{7}$ **8.** $\ln 45$

9. $\ln(-12)$ **10.** $\ln(-5)$ **11.** $\ln 0.8$ **12.** $\ln \sqrt{3}$

Write an equivalent logarithmic or exponential equation.

13. $e^{3.22} \approx 25.03$ **14.** $e^5 \approx 148.41$ **15.** $\ln 50 \approx 3.91$

16. $\ln 3.6 \approx 1.28$ **17.** $e^{3.4} \approx 29.96$ **18.** $\ln 5 \approx 1.61$

19. $\ln 25 \approx 3.22$ **20.** $e^{\frac{1}{2}} \approx 1.65$ **21.** $e^{\frac{2}{3}} \approx 1.95$

22. $e^{-7} \approx 0.000912$ **23.** $\ln\left(\frac{1}{4}\right) \approx -1.39$ **24.** $\ln\left(\frac{3}{4}\right) \approx -0.29$

Solve each equation for x by using the natural logarithm function. Round your answers to the nearest hundredth.

25. $15^x = 27$ **26.** $4.2^x = 15$ **27.** $7^{-x} = 120$

28. $0.5^x = 11$ **29.** $8^{\frac{-x}{2}} = 21$ **30.** $9^{-x} = 0.2$

31. $\left(\frac{1}{3}\right)^{-2x} = 125$ **32.** $\left(\frac{2}{3}\right)^x = 12$ **33.** $1.5^{3x} = 1500$

34. $2.3^x = 15$ **35.** $7^x = 14{,}000$ **36.** $11^{-2x} = 15{,}000$

37. An investor puts \$5000 in an account that earns 6.5% annual interest which is compounded continuously. Find the amount that will be in the account at the end of 5 years if no deposits or withdrawals are made.

Solve each equation for *x*. Write the exact solution and the approximate solution to the nearest hundredth, when appropriate.

1. $2^x = 2^5$

2. $\log_6 216 = x$

3. $3^{x-1} = 3^4$

4. $\log x = 2.1$

5. $x = \log_3 27$

6. $\log_9 x = 2$

7. $5 = \log_x 32$

8. $\log_x \frac{1}{4} = -1$

9. $3^x = 4$

10. $\log_4(x - 2) = 2$

11. $10^{x-1} = 121$

12. $e^{x+1} = 14$

13. $e^{2x-1} = 9$

14. $\ln(x + 1) = \ln 7$

15. $\ln(x - 5) = \ln(3x + 1)$

16. $2\ln\left(x + \frac{1}{2}\right) = \ln\frac{1}{4}$

17. $e^{-3x+4} = 22$

18. $2\ln x = \ln(2x - 1)$

In Exercises 19 and 20, use the equation $M = \frac{2}{3}\log\frac{E}{10^{11.8}}$.

19. On October 15, 1997, an earthquake with a magnitude of 6.8 struck parts of Chile and Argentina. Find the amount of energy released by the earthquake.

20. From December 1811 to early 1812, a series of earthquakes shook the Mississippi Valley near New Madrid, Missouri. One of the earthquakes released about 2.5×10^{24} ergs of energy. Find the earthquake's magnitude on the Richter scale. Round your answer to the nearest tenth.

Chapter 7

Determine whether each expression is a polynomial. If so, classify the polynomial by degree and by number of terms.

1. $12x^3 - 2x^2 + \frac{1}{2}$

2. $\frac{x^3}{11} + \frac{x^2}{8}$

3. $\frac{11}{x^3} + \frac{8}{x^2}$

4. $4x - 2^{2x} + 3^{5x}$

5. $0.66x^4 - 1$

6. $10x^3 + 6x^7 - 15x$

Evaluate each polynomial expression for the indicated value of *x*.

7. $x^3 - 3x^2 + 4x$ for $x = -2$

8. $4 - 2x + 3x^2 - x^4$ for $x = -1$

9. $\frac{3}{4}x^4 + \frac{1}{2}x^2 - \frac{1}{4}x + \frac{1}{2}$ for $x = 2$

10. $-x^4 - x^3 - x^2 + 12$ for $x = 5$

11. $0.5x^4 + 2.5x^3 - x^2$ for $x = 4$

12. $x^4 - 3x^3 + 3x^2 - 9$ for $x = 3$

Write each sum or difference as a polynomial expression in standard form. Then classify the polynomial by degree and by number of terms.

13. $(-2x^3 + 5x^2 - 3x + 7) + (5x^3 + x^2 + 9)$

14. $(7x^4 - 3x^3 + 5x) - (2x^4 + x^3 + x^2 + 3x - 2)$

15. $(4.1x^3 + 3.5x - 6x^2 - 11) - (3x^2 - 4x^3 + 9)$

16. $(5x^3 - 2x^4 + 3x - 6) + (x^4 - 7x^2 + 3x - 9)$

17. $(3x^5 - 4x^2 + 2x^3) - (4x^4 + 3x^3 - 9x^2 - 7)$

18. $(7.5x^3 + 3.2x^4 + 5.1x^2 + x) + (x^4 - 7x^2 - 3x)$

Graph each function. Describe the general shape of the graph.

19 $f(x) = x^3 - x^2 - x + 1$

20 $g(x) = -2x^3 + 3x - 1$

21 $k(x) = x^4 - x^3 - 3x^2 + 1$

22 $h(x) = 0.5x^4 - 3x^2$

LESSON 7.2

Graph each function. Approximate any local maxima or minima to the nearest tenth.

1 $P(x) = 10x - 8x^2$

2 $P(x) = x^2 - 3x - 2$

3 $P(x) = x^4 - x^3 - x^2$

4 $P(x) = 5x - x^3 + 1$

Graph each function. Approximate any local maxima or minima to the nearest tenth. Find the intervals over which the function is increasing and decreasing.

5 $P(x) = x^3 + x^2; -6 \le x \le 6$

6 $P(x) = 0.5x^4 + x^2 - 3; -5 \le x \le 5$

7 $P(x) = -2x^4 + 3x^3 + 2x^2; -4 \le x \le 4$

8 $P(x) = x^3 - 4x^2 + 1; -5 \le x \le 5$

9 $P(x) = 0.2x^3 - 6x + 4; -6 \le x \le 6$

10 $P(x) = 3x^4 - 8x^2 - 2; -2 \le x \le 2$

Describe the end behavior of each function.

11. $P(x) = 17x^2 - 8x^3 - 6$

12. $P(x) = 9 - 2x - x^2 + 5x^3$

13. $P(x) = 4x^4 - 6x^3 + 2x^2 - x$

14. $P(x) = -8 + x^3 - 5x^4$

15 The number (in thousands) of federal employees in the United States is given in the table below. Find a quartic regression model for the data by using $x = 0$ for 1982. [*Source: U.S. Bureau of the Census*]

1982	1983	1984	1985	1986	1987	1988	1989
15,841	16,034	16,436	16,690	16,933	17,212	17,588	18,369

LESSON 7.3

Write each product as a polynomial in standard form.

1. $2x^3(-5x^4 + 3x^3 - 2x - 6)$

2. $(4x - 7)(3x + 4)$

3. $(x - 6)(x^2 + 3x - 5)$

4. $(2x - 3)(x + 4)^2$

5. $(2x - 1)^3$

6. $(x + 7)(2x^2 - 3x - 4)$

Use substitution to determine whether the given linear expression is a factor of the polynomial.

7. $2x^3 + 7x^2 - 15x; x + 5$

8. $x^3 - 4x^2 - 20x - 7; x - 7$

9. $2x^3 + 15x^2 - 9x - 10; x + 8$

Divide by using long division.

10. $(2x^3 + 3x^2 - 6x - 3) \div (2x - 3)$

11. $(x^3 + 3x + 4) \div (x + 1)$

12. $(x^2 - 27x + x^3 + 28) \div (x - 4)$

13. $\left(\frac{1}{2}x^2 - 5x + 3x^3 + 2\right) \div \left(x - \frac{1}{2}\right)$

Divide by using synthetic division.

14. $(x^2 + 9x - 36) \div (x - 3)$

15. $(x^3 - 5x^2 - 2x + 24) \div (x - 3)$

16. $(x^3 + 8) \div (x - 4)$

17. $(9x - 17x^2 - 9 + 5x^3) \div (x - 3)$

For each function, use both synthetic division and substitution to find the indicated value.

18. $P(x) = x^4 + 3x^3 - 2x + 1; P(2)$

19. $P(x) = x^3 - 8; P(-2)$

20. $P(x) = 5x^2 - 4x + 3; P(-1)$

21. $P(x) = -3x^3 + 4 - x^2; P(3)$

Use factoring to solve each equation.

1. $x^3 + 3x^2 - 10x = 0$
2. $x^3 - 64x = 0$
3. $x^3 + 49x = 14x^2$
4. $2x^3 - 22x^2 + 56x = 0$
5. $3x^3 + 3x^2 = 6x$
6. $x^3 - 77x + 4x^2 = 0$

Use a graph, synthetic division, and factoring to find all of the roots of each equation.

7 $x^3 - 2x^2 - 4x + 8 = 0$
8 $x^3 - 3x^2 - x + 3 = 0$
9 $x^3 - 2x^2 - 13x - 10 = 0$
10 $x^3 + 5x^2 = x + 5$
11 $x^3 + x + 6 = 4x^2$
12 $x^3 - 9x^2 + 15x - 7 = 0$

Use variable substitution and factoring to find all of the roots of each equation.

13. $x^4 - 14x^2 + 45 = 0$
14. $x^4 - 16x^2 + 15 = 0$
15. $x^4 + 12 = 13x^2$
16. $x^4 - 25x^2 + 144 = 0$
17. $x^4 + 33 = 14x^2$
18. $x^4 - 8x^2 + 7 = 0$

Use a graph and the Location Principle to find the real zeros of each function. Give approximate values to the nearest hundredth, if necessary.

19 $g(x) = x^3 - 5x^2 + 7x$
20 $b(x) = 0.8x^4 - 2x^2 + 1$
21 $f(x) = x^3 - 4x + 2$

Find all of the rational roots of each polynomial equation.

1. $3x^2 - 14x + 8 = 0$
2. $2x^2 - 5x - 3 = 0$
3. $10x^3 - 31x^2 + 25x - 6 = 0$
4. $2x^3 - 9x^2 + 7x + 6 = 0$
5. $4x^3 - 9x^2 - x + 6 = 0$
6. $15x^3 - 47x^2 + 38x - 8 = 0$

Find all zeros of each polynomial function.

7 $M(x) = x^3 - x^2 - 7x + 3$
8 $H(x) = x^3 - 3x^2 - 5x + 15$
9 $J(x) = x^3 - 2x^2 + 7x - 14$
10 $R(x) = x^4 - 3x^3 - x^2 - 9x - 12$
11 $F(x) = x^4 - 5x^2 - 24$
12 $H(x) = x^4 + 5x^3 + x^2 - 20x - 20$

Find all real values of x for which the functions are equal. Give your answers to the nearest hundredth.

13 $P(x) = x^4 + 3x^2 + 2x$ and $Q(x) = x + 2$
14 $P(x) = -x^2 + 6x - 2$ and $Q(x) = 0.2x^4 + x^3 - 3$
15 $P(x) = x^4 - 3x^2$ and $Q(x) = x^2 + 3x - 5$
16 $P(x) = x^4 - x^3 + 1$ and $Q(x) = x^2 - 2x + 3$

Write a polynomial function, P, in factored form and in standard form by using the given information.

17. P is of degree 3; $P(0) = 2$; zeros: $-1, 1, 2$
18. P is of degree 4; $P(0) = 6$; zeros: $2, -3, \frac{1}{2}, -\frac{1}{2}$
19. P is of degree 4; $P(0) = -9$; zeros: $\frac{1}{2}$ (multiplicity 2), $\frac{3}{2}, -\frac{3}{2}$
20. P is of degree 3; $P(0) = -1$; zeros: $\frac{1}{2}, \frac{1}{3}$ (multiplicity 2)
21. P is of degree 3; $P(0) = -36$; zeros: $2, 3i$
22. P is of degree 4; $P(0) = 24$; zeros: $2, 3, i$

Chapter 8

For Exercises 1–4, *y* varies inversely as *x*. Write the appropriate inverse-variation equation, and find *y* for the given values of *x*.

1. $y = 18$ when $x = 8$; $x = 4, 9, 15$, and 20

2. $y = 7.5$ when $x = 8$; $x = 4, 5, 6$, and 18

3. $y = 0.32$ when $x = 5$; $x = 0.1, 0.2, 4$, and 8

4. $y = 9.5$ when $x = 4$; $x = 1.9, 5, 6$, and 20

For Exercises 5–8, *y* varies jointly as *x* and *z*. Write the appropriate joint-variation equation, and find *y* for the given values of *x* and *z*.

5. $y = 18$ when $x = 4$ and $z = 3$; $x = 4.5$ and $z = 6$

6. $y = 375$ when $x = 6$ and $z = 5$; $x = 0.4$ and $z = 30$

7. $y = 24$ when $x = 2$ and $z = -4$; $x = -3$ and $z = 0.8$

8. $y = 1.5$ when $x = 1.5$ and $z = 6$; $x = 8$ and $z = 0.4$

For Exercises 9–12, *z* varies jointly as *x* and *y* and inversely as *w*. Write the appropriate inverse-variation equation, and find *z* for the given values of *x*, *y*, and *w*.

9. $z = 82.5$ when $x = 12$, $y = 5$, and $w = 4$; $x = 8$, $y = 4.5$, and $w = 10$

10. $z = 19.2$ when $x = 20$, $y = 4.2$, and $w = 3.5$; $x = 16$, $y = 9$, and $w = 5$

11. $z = 6$ when $x = 12$, $y = -2$, and $w = 5$; $x = 7$, $y = 0.2$, and $w = 14$

12. $z = 2.5$ when $x = -6$, $y = 5$, and $w = 4$; $x = 3$, $y = -0.6$, and $w = 2$

13. The time, *t*, that it takes to travel a given distance, *d*, varies inversely as *r*, the rate of speed. A certain trip can be made in 7.5 hours at a rate of 60 miles per hour. Find the constant of variation, and write an inverse-variation equation. Find *t* to the nearest tenth when *r* is 40, 45, 50, and 55.

Determine whether each function is a rational function. If so, find the domain. If not, explain.

1. $f(x) = \dfrac{x - 0.5}{(x + 2)(x + 5)}$ **2.** $g(x) = \dfrac{2^{x+1}}{x^2 + 1}$ **3.** $h(x) = \dfrac{x^2 + 3x + 1}{x^2 - 9}$

Identify all asymptotes and holes in the graph of each rational function.

4. $b(x) = \dfrac{x + 6}{2x - 1}$ **5.** $m(x) = \dfrac{x - 5}{x^2 - 3}$ **6.** $k(x) = \dfrac{2x}{x^2 - x - 2}$

7. $f(x) = \dfrac{2x^3 + 6x^2}{x^2 - x - 12}$ **8.** $f(x) = \dfrac{-x^3 + x^2}{x^2 + x - 2}$ **9.** $f(x) = \dfrac{x^2 + 2x - 15}{x - 3}$

10. $f(x) = \dfrac{x^2 - 2x - 3}{x + 1}$ **11.** $f(x) = \dfrac{x^2 - 4}{2x^2 - 5x + 2}$ **12.** $f(x) = \dfrac{3x^2 + x - 4}{x^2 + 2x - 3}$

Find the domain of each rational function. Identify all asymptotes and holes in the graph of each function. Then graph.

13. $h(x) = \dfrac{x + 4}{x - 4}$ **14.** $f(x) = \dfrac{x}{3x(x - 1)}$ **15.** $g(x) = \dfrac{x + 3}{x^2 + 8x + 15}$

16. $f(x) = \dfrac{1}{x + 2}$ **17.** $b(x) = \dfrac{x - 1}{x + 2}$ **18.** $d(x) = \dfrac{x - 1}{x^2 - 5x + 4}$

LESSON 8.3

Simplify each rational expression.

1. $\dfrac{7x(12x^5)}{3x^2(28x^2)}$

2. $\dfrac{x^2 + 8x - 9}{x^2 - 81}$

3. $\dfrac{x^2 + 10x + 24}{x^2 + x - 12}$

4. $\dfrac{x^2 + 4x - 12}{3x^2 - 12x + 12}$

5. $\dfrac{x^2 - 8x - 20}{12x - x^2 - 20}$

6. $\dfrac{x^2 - 25}{2x^2 - 7x - 15}$

Simplify each product or quotient.

7. $\dfrac{2x^2 - x - 1}{3x^2 - 2x - 1} \cdot \dfrac{15x^3 + 5x^2}{4x^2 - 1}$

8. $\dfrac{x^2 - 2x - 3}{x^2 + x - 20} \div \dfrac{x^2 + 2x + 1}{x^2 + 6x + 5}$

9. $\dfrac{4x + 8}{5x - 20} \div \dfrac{10 + 3x - x^2}{x^2 - 4x}$

10. $\dfrac{2x^2 - 12x - 14}{x^3 - 16x} \cdot \dfrac{-16 - 4x}{6x - 42}$

11. $\dfrac{3x^2 + 10x - 8}{3x^2 - 17x + 10} \cdot \dfrac{5 + 9x - 2x^2}{x^2 + 3x - 4}$

12. $\dfrac{3x^2 + 14x - 5}{x^2 + 2x - 15} \div \dfrac{3x^2 - 25x + 8}{8 + 15x - 2x^2}$

Simplify each complex fraction.

13. $\dfrac{\dfrac{x^2 - 49}{x^2 - 100}}{\dfrac{x - 7}{x + 10}}$

14. $\dfrac{\dfrac{(x + 7)^2}{(2x - 3)^2}}{\dfrac{x^2 - 49}{2x^2 - 17x + 21}}$

15. $\dfrac{\dfrac{x^2 + 8x - 33}{x^2 - x - 6}}{\dfrac{x^2 + 10x - 11}{x^2 + 9x + 14}}$

Simplify each product or quotient involving complex fractions.

16. $\dfrac{\dfrac{1}{x + 1}}{\dfrac{x}{x^2 - 1}} \cdot \dfrac{x}{x - 1}$

17. $\dfrac{x - 3}{x - 4} \cdot \dfrac{\dfrac{2x - 8}{x^2 - 9}}{\dfrac{x + 5}{x + 3}}$

18. $\dfrac{x + 4}{x^2 - 9} \div \dfrac{\dfrac{x^2 + 4x}{x + 3}}{\dfrac{x - 3}{x}}$

19. $\dfrac{\dfrac{-2x - 5}{x^2 - 1}}{\dfrac{x + 1}{x - 3}} \cdot \dfrac{x^2 - 1}{2x^2 - x - 15}$

20. $\dfrac{x}{x + 4} \cdot \dfrac{\dfrac{x^2 + 6x + 8}{x + 10}}{\dfrac{x^2}{2x + 20}}$

21. $\dfrac{\dfrac{x^2 + 4x - 32}{x^2 - 12x + 35}}{\dfrac{16x - 4x^2}{x^2 - 4x - 21}} \cdot \dfrac{x^2 - 10x}{x^2 + 11x + 24}$

LESSON 8.4

Simplify each sum or difference.

1. $\dfrac{3x}{2x + 5} - \dfrac{2x}{2x + 5}$

2. $\dfrac{2x + 1}{3x - 4} + \dfrac{x - 1}{3x - 4}$

3. $\dfrac{3x^2 + x}{12} - \dfrac{x^2 + 1}{4}$

4. $\dfrac{5x - 15}{x^2 - 9} - \dfrac{2}{x + 3}$

5. $\dfrac{2x - 1}{x + 8} + \dfrac{34x}{x^2 - 64}$

6. $\dfrac{2}{x - 8} + \dfrac{1}{x + 2}$

7. $\dfrac{3x - 10}{x^2 + 4x - 12} - \dfrac{2}{x + 6}$

8. $\dfrac{-2x - 3}{x^2 - 3x} - \dfrac{-x}{x - 3}$

9. $\dfrac{2x + 1}{5 - x} + \dfrac{1}{3x + 2}$

Simplify each sum or difference involving complex fractions.

10. $\dfrac{5}{\dfrac{x}{3x + 1}} - \dfrac{7x^2 + 3x}{x}$

11. $\dfrac{\dfrac{3}{2x - 1}}{\dfrac{6x}{2x - 1}} + \dfrac{3}{x}$

12. $\dfrac{\dfrac{x + 1}{x - 2}}{\dfrac{x + 2}{2}} - \dfrac{x}{x^2 - 4}$

13. $\dfrac{\dfrac{7x}{x^2 - 4}}{\dfrac{6}{x - 2}} - \dfrac{\dfrac{2x - 6}{x + 2}}{\dfrac{x - 3}{2x}}$

14. $\dfrac{\dfrac{2}{x + 5}}{\dfrac{x - 5}{x}} + \dfrac{\dfrac{5x - 10}{x - 5}}{\dfrac{x^2 + 3x - 10}{2}}$

15. $\dfrac{\dfrac{2}{x^2 + 2x - 3}}{\dfrac{x - 4}{x^3 - x^2}} + \dfrac{\dfrac{6}{x^2 + 5x + 6}}{\dfrac{x - 4}{x + 2}}$

Write each expression as a single rational expression in simplest form.

16. $\dfrac{3}{x + 7} - \dfrac{2x + 8}{x + 7} + \dfrac{4x + 19}{x + 7}$

17. $\dfrac{8x - 5}{2x + 3} + \dfrac{x + 4}{2x + 3} - \dfrac{3x - 10}{2x + 3}$

18. $\dfrac{3x}{x + 2} - \dfrac{3x}{x + 5} + \dfrac{18}{x^2 + 7x + 10}$

19. $\dfrac{2x - 1}{x + 5} + \dfrac{x}{x - 2} - \dfrac{5x + 4}{x^2 + 3x - 10}$

LESSON 8.5

Solve each equation. Check your solution.

1. $\dfrac{x-3}{x-1} = \dfrac{x}{x+4}$

2. $\dfrac{x+1}{x-2} = \dfrac{x+3}{x-1}$

3. $\dfrac{x-7}{x+3} = \dfrac{x-9}{x-3}$

4. $\dfrac{1}{x} - \dfrac{5}{6x} = \dfrac{2}{3}$

5. $\dfrac{3}{2} - \dfrac{3}{x} = \dfrac{9}{2x}$

6. $\dfrac{x-7}{x+1} - \dfrac{x-4}{3x-2} = 0$

7. $\dfrac{3}{x-2} + \dfrac{5}{x+2} = \dfrac{4x^2}{x^2-4}$

8. $\dfrac{3}{x-1} - \dfrac{1}{x+1} = \dfrac{3}{x^2-1}$

9. $5 - \dfrac{26}{x+2} = \dfrac{27}{x^2-4}$

10. $\dfrac{2x-3}{4} + 2 = \dfrac{2x+1}{3}$

11. $\dfrac{3x}{4} - \dfrac{2x-1}{2} = \dfrac{x-7}{6}$

12. $\dfrac{x+1}{x-3} = \dfrac{3}{x} + \dfrac{12}{x^2-3x}$

13. $\dfrac{4}{x^2-8x+12} = \dfrac{x}{x-2} + \dfrac{1}{x-6}$

14. $\dfrac{2x-3}{x-5} = \dfrac{x}{x+4} + \dfrac{20x-37}{x^2-x-20}$

15. $\dfrac{x-2}{x+1} = \dfrac{x-3}{x^2-5x-6} - \dfrac{2x-7}{x-6}$

Solve each inequality. Check your solution.

16. $\dfrac{x-2}{x+6} > 4$

17. $\dfrac{3x+2}{2x} < 1$

18. $\dfrac{3x+3}{2x} > 1$

19. $\dfrac{4x}{3x-2} > \dfrac{1}{2}$

20. $\dfrac{x-2}{x+2} < 3$

21. $\dfrac{3x+5}{2x-3} < 6$

Use a graphics calculator to solve each rational inequality. Round answers to the nearest tenth.

22 $\dfrac{3x+5}{2x-3} < 0$

23 $\dfrac{2}{x} > x^2 + 1$

24 $\dfrac{3}{2x} < x^2 + 2$

25 $\dfrac{x+4}{x-2} < x$

26 $\dfrac{x+3}{x+1} > 2x$

27 $x^2 - 3 \geq \dfrac{1}{x^2}$

28 $\dfrac{x+5}{x-2} < \dfrac{36}{x^2-4}$

29 $\dfrac{x+1}{6-x} \leq \dfrac{2-x}{x+1}$

30 $\dfrac{x}{x+1} + \dfrac{2x}{x-1} > \dfrac{2}{x^2-1}$

LESSON 8.6

Evaluate each expression.

1. $\dfrac{3}{5}\sqrt[3]{-27}$

2. $0.25\sqrt[4]{16}$

3. $3\left(\sqrt[3]{-512}\right)^2$

4. $\dfrac{3}{2}\left(\sqrt[3]{-1000}\right)^2$

5. $\dfrac{1}{3}\left(\sqrt[3]{64}\right)^2$

6. $5\left(\sqrt{81}\right)^{-2}$

7. $\dfrac{1}{2}\left(\sqrt[3]{-512}\right)^{-1}$

8. $\left(\sqrt[4]{1296} - 2\right)^{\frac{1}{2}}$

9. $3\left(\sqrt[4]{625} + 3\right)^{\frac{1}{3}}$

10. $\dfrac{1}{3}\left(\sqrt[5]{-243}\right)^2 - 3$

11. $\dfrac{2}{3}\left(\sqrt[4]{\dfrac{21}{8}}\right)^4 + \dfrac{1}{4}$

12. $\dfrac{3}{5}\left(\sqrt[4]{\dfrac{35}{9}}\right)^4 + \dfrac{2}{3}$

Find the domain of each radical function.

13. $f(x) = \sqrt{x^2 - 16}$

14. $f(x) = \sqrt{3x + 6}$

15. $f(x) = \sqrt{4(x-1)}$

16. $f(x) = \sqrt{4x^2 - 9}$

17. $f(x) = \sqrt{x^2 + 2x + 1}$

18. $f(x) = \sqrt{x^2 + 7x + 12}$

Find the inverse of each quadratic function. Then graph the function and its inverse in the same coordinate plane.

19. $y = x^2 + 4$

20. $y = x^2 - 3$

21. $y = x^2 + 4x$

22. $y = x^2 - 8x + 16$

23. $y = x^2 - 6x + 9$

24. $y = x^2 - 4x + 1$

25. The speed of an ocean wave depends on the depth of the water in which it travels. A wave's speed, in miles per hour, in water that is x feet deep is given by the function $f(x) = \sqrt{21.92x}$. Find the speed of a wave in water that is 25, 50, and 100 feet deep. Round your answers to the nearest tenth.

LESSON 8.7

Simplify each radical expression by using the Properties of *n*th Roots.

1. $\sqrt{125}$

2. $\sqrt[3]{162x^6y^3}$

3. $\sqrt[4]{80x^8z^{10}}$

4. $\sqrt[3]{-56x^4y^4z^3}$

5. $\left(75x^2y^3z\right)^{\frac{1}{2}}$

6. $\left(54x^5\right)^{\frac{1}{3}}$

Simplify each product or quotient. Assume that the value of each variable is positive.

7. $\sqrt[3]{9x^2} \cdot \sqrt[3]{3x}$

8. $\sqrt[3]{4x^5} \cdot \sqrt[3]{54xy^2}$

9. $\sqrt{8x^3} \cdot \left(2xz^5\right)^{\frac{1}{2}} \cdot \sqrt{4x^3z^4}$

10. $\dfrac{\left(81y^5\right)^{\frac{1}{4}}}{\sqrt[4]{x^4y}}$

11. $\dfrac{\sqrt[3]{48x^2y^4z^4}}{\sqrt[3]{6x}}$

12. $\dfrac{\sqrt{15x^9y^3}}{\sqrt{5x^5y}}$

13. $\sqrt[4]{8x^5} \cdot \sqrt[4]{4x^7}$

14. $\dfrac{\sqrt{9b^7}}{\left(12b^5\right)^{\frac{1}{2}}}$

15. $\dfrac{\sqrt[4]{8x^5}}{\left(20x^2\right)^{-\frac{1}{4}}}$

Find each sum, difference, or product. Give your answer in simplest radical form.

16. $\left(12 - \sqrt{2}\right) + \left(15 + \sqrt{2}\right)$

17. $\left(9 + 2\sqrt{5}\right) - \left(1 + \sqrt{45}\right)$

18. $\left(7 - 2\sqrt{6}\right)\left(7 + 2\sqrt{6}\right)$

19. $\left(3 - \sqrt{8}\right)\left(5 + \sqrt{2}\right)$

20. $\left(4 + \sqrt{3}\right)\left(-2 + \sqrt{2}\right)$

21. $6\sqrt{3}\left(2\sqrt{5} + 4\sqrt{6}\right)$

22. $7\sqrt{20} + 8\sqrt{5} - 2\sqrt{45}$

23. $6\sqrt{8} - \left(\sqrt{24} - 3\sqrt{72} + \sqrt{54}\right)$

24. $4\sqrt{2}\left(\sqrt{12} - 3\sqrt{2} + 4\sqrt{8}\right)$

25. $\left(4\sqrt{2} - 2\sqrt{3}\right)\left(5\sqrt{2} - \sqrt{3}\right)$

Write each expression with a rational denominator and in simplest form.

26. $\dfrac{3}{\sqrt{15}}$

27. $\dfrac{\sqrt{135}}{\sqrt{15}}$

28. $\dfrac{5}{1 - \sqrt{6}}$

29. $\dfrac{-3}{\sqrt{6} - \sqrt{2}}$

30. $\dfrac{14}{\sqrt{5} + \sqrt{3}}$

31. $\dfrac{\sqrt{3} - \sqrt{2}}{\sqrt{3} + \sqrt{2}}$

32. $\dfrac{2\sqrt{5} - \sqrt{3}}{\sqrt{5} + \sqrt{3}}$

33. $\dfrac{2\sqrt{x}}{3\sqrt{x} - 4\sqrt{y}}$

LESSON 8.8

Solve each radical equation by using algebra. If the equation has no real solution, write *no solution*. Check your solutions.

1. $\sqrt{x - 5} = 3$

2. $\sqrt{x^2 - 15} = 7$

3. $\sqrt{x - 4} = \sqrt{x + 4}$

4. $\sqrt{2x - 5} + 4 = 3$

5. $\sqrt{3x - 5} = 5$

6. $\sqrt{5x - 11} = x - 1$

7. $\sqrt{2x - 1} = x$

8. $\sqrt[3]{x + 5} = \sqrt[3]{3x - 2}$

9. $\sqrt{x^2 - 4x - 5} = \sqrt{5x - x^2}$

Solve each radical inequality by using algebra. If the inequality has no real solution, write *no solution*. Check your solution.

10. $\sqrt{x - 3} \geq 2$

11. $3 > \sqrt{2x}$

12. $\sqrt{4x - 1} > 2$

13. $3 \geq \sqrt{x^2 - 4x + 4}$

14. $\sqrt{1 - x} > 3$

15. $\sqrt{3x - 2} \leq 2$

16. $4 \leq \sqrt{7 - x}$

17. $\sqrt{5x - 6} > 12$

18. $\sqrt{4x + 1} \geq 5$

***Solve* each radical equation or inequality *by graphing*. Round solutions to the nearest tenth. Check your solutions by any method.**

19. $2\sqrt{x} \leq 3x - 4$

20. $3\sqrt{x + 2} \geq \sqrt{x^2 + 4}$

21. $0.25\sqrt{3x - 1} < x + 2$

22. $\sqrt[3]{x^2 + 1} = x$

23. $\sqrt[3]{x + 2} = \sqrt{x}$

24. $\sqrt[3]{2x - 1} > 2\sqrt{x - 4}$

Chapter 9

LESSON 9.1

Graph each equation and identify the conic section.

1 $x^2 + y^2 = 4$

2 $y^2 - 9x = 0$

3 $9x^2 - 4y^2 = 25$

4 $x^2 + 4y^2 = 16$

5 $x^2 - y^2 = 16$

6 $4x^2 - y = 0$

7 $16x^2 + y^2 = 81$

8 $x^2 + y^2 = 144$

9 $9x^2 - 16y^2 = 144$

Find the distance between *P* and *Q* and the coordinates of *M*, the midpoint of $\overline{PQ}$. Give exact answers and approximate answers to the nearest hundredth when appropriate.

10. $P(-6, 4)$ and $Q(2, -2)$

11. $P(6, -2)$ and $Q(2, 4)$

12. $P(8, -4)$ and $Q(6, 0)$

13. $P(0, 1)$ and $Q(4, 7)$

14. $P(-2, 3)$ and $Q(5, 4)$

15. $P(\sqrt{2}, 4)$ and $Q(3\sqrt{2}, 0)$

Find the center, circumference, and area of a circle whose diameter has the given endpoints.

16. $P(12, -8)$ and $Q(6, 0)$

17. $P(3, 4)$ and $Q(10, -20)$

18. $P(0, 10)$ and $Q(2, -6)$

19. $P(14, 8)$ and $Q(-2, -8)$

20. $P(4, -5)$ and $Q(8, 3)$

21. $P(24, 16)$ and $Q(-2, 18)$

LESSON 9.2

Write the standard equation for each parabola below.

1.

2.

3.
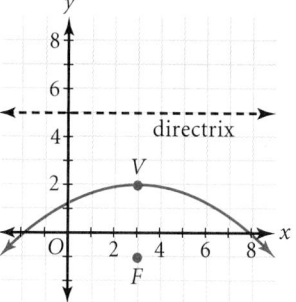

Graph each equation. Label the vertex, focus, and directrix.

4. $y = \frac{1}{2}x^2$

5. $x = -\frac{1}{4}y^2$

6. $y = -\frac{1}{12}x^2$

7. $y - 2 = (x - 2)^2$

8. $x + 3 = \frac{1}{8}(y - 1)^2$

9. $y - x^2 + 6x = 0$

10. $y - x^2 + 2x = 0$

11. $y - x^2 - 10x = 27$

12. $x^2 + 2x - 3y = 5$

Write the standard equation for a parabola with the given characteristics.

13. vertex: $(0, 0)$
directrix: $x = -15$

14. focus: $(-2, 3)$
directrix: $x = 2$

15. vertex: $(0, 2)$
directrix: $y = -4$

16. vertex: $(2, 0)$
focus: $(6, 0)$

17. focus: $(1, 1)$
directrix: $y = 0$

18. vertex: $(3, 2)$
focus: $(6, 2)$

19. The parabola defined by the equation $y = -2x^2 + 12x - 13$ is translated 3 units up and 2 units to the left. Write the standard equation of the resulting parabola.

LESSON 9.3

Write the standard equation for each circle below.

1.

2.

3.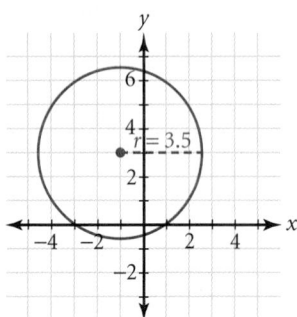

Write the standard equation of a circle with each given radius and center.

4. $r = 5$; $C(0, 4)$

5. $r = 4.5$; $C(0, 0)$

6. $r = 1.5$; $C(-3, -5)$

Write the standard equation for each circle. Then state the coordinates of its center and give its radius.

7. $x^2 + y^2 - 16x + 4y = -43$

8. $x^2 - 8x + y^2 = 33$

9. $x^2 + y^2 - 20x - 10y + 61 = 0$

Graph each equation. Label the center and the radius.

10. $\left(x - \frac{5}{2}\right)^2 + y^2 = \frac{25}{4}$

11. $(x - 5)^2 + (y - 9)^2 = 100$

12. $x^2 + (y - 7)^2 = \frac{49}{4}$

13. State whether $C(-1, 3)$ is inside, outside, or on the circle whose equation is $x^2 + y^2 - 12x - 2y = 8$.

LESSON 9.4

Write the standard equation for each ellipse below.

1.

2.

3.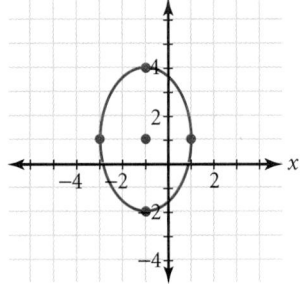

Write the standard equation of each ellipse. Find the coordinates of its center, vertices, co-vertices, and foci.

4. $25x^2 + 9y^2 = 225$

5. $49x^2 + y^2 = 49$

6. $x^2 + 4y^2 = 64$

7. $x^2 - 2x + 9y^2 - 8 = 0$

8. $x^2 + 4y^2 - 18x - 8y + 81 = 0$

9. $9x^2 + 4y^2 - 144x - 8y = -544$

Write the standard equation for an ellipse with the given characteristics.

10. foci: $(-2, 0)$, $(2, 0)$; vertices: $(-6, 0)$, $(6, 0)$

11. foci: $(0, -3)$, $(0, 3)$; vertices: $(0, -4)$, $(0, 4)$

Graph each ellipse. Label the center, foci, vertices, and co-vertices.

12. $\frac{x^2}{100} + \frac{y^2}{25} = 1$

13. $\frac{x^2}{4} + \frac{y^2}{25} = 1$

14. $\frac{(x - 2)^2}{16} + \frac{(y - 1)^2}{25} = 1$

LESSON 9.5

Write the standard equation for each hyperbola below.

1.

2.

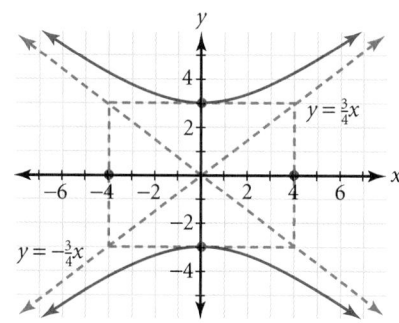

Write the standard equation for each hyperbola. Give the coordinates of the center, vertices, co-vertices, and foci.

3. $x^2 - 100y^2 = 100$

4. $25y^2 - 100y + 100 - x^2 = 25$

5. $9x^2 - 4y^2 - 18x + 8y = 31$

Write the standard equation for a hyperbola with the given characteristics.

6. vertices: $(-6, 0)$ and $(6, 0)$; foci: $(-8, 0)$ and $(8, 0)$

7. vertices: $(0, -12)$ and $(0, 12)$; co-vertices: $(-11, 0)$ and $(11, 0)$

Graph each hyperbola. Label the center, vertices, co-vertices, foci, and asymptotes.

8. $\dfrac{x^2}{9} - \dfrac{y^2}{4} = 1$

9. $\dfrac{y^2}{36} - \dfrac{x^2}{9} = 1$

10. $\dfrac{(x-2)^2}{4} - (y-1)^2 = 1$

11. The hyperbola defined by the equation $25x^2 - 36y^2 = 900$ is translated 4 units up and 3 units to the right. Write the standard equation of the resulting hyperbola.

LESSON 9.6

Use the substitution method to solve each system. If there are no real solutions, write *none*.

1. $\begin{cases} y = 7 - x \\ y = x^2 + 1 \end{cases}$

2. $\begin{cases} y = 12 - 6x \\ x^2 + y = 4 \end{cases}$

3. $\begin{cases} x = 12y - 4 \\ x^2 - 16y^2 = 16 \end{cases}$

Use the elimination method to solve each system. If there are no real solutions, write *none*.

4. $\begin{cases} 4x^2 + y^2 = 20 \\ x^2 + 4y^2 = 20 \end{cases}$

5. $\begin{cases} x^2 + y^2 = 36 \\ 9x^2 + 4y^2 = 16 \end{cases}$

6. $\begin{cases} 16x^2 + 9y^2 = 144 \\ -48x^2 + y^2 = 144 \end{cases}$

Solve each system by graphing. Round answers to the nearest hundredth, if necessary. If there are no real solutions, write *none*.

7. $\begin{cases} x^2 + y^2 = 16 \\ 2x^2 - y^2 = -4 \end{cases}$

8. $\begin{cases} 3y^2 - 4x^2 = 1 \\ x^2 + y^2 = 9 \end{cases}$

9. $\begin{cases} 9x^2 + 16y^2 = 144 \\ 3x^2 - 2y^2 = 6 \end{cases}$

Classify the conic section defined by each equation. Write the standard equation of the conic section, and sketch the graph.

10. $x^2 - 8x + y = -2$

11. $x^2 + y^2 - 6x - 10y = 2$

12. $x^2 + 10x - 8y = -73$

13. $9x^2 + 4y^2 - 72x - 32y = -172$

14. $9x^2 - 4y^2 + 54x + 8y + 41 = 0$

15. $4x^2 + 25y^2 + 16x + 50y - 59 = 0$

Chapter 10

LESSON 10.1

Find the probability of each event.

1. A yellow marble is drawn at random from a bag containing 3 white, 2 yellow, 1 green, and 4 blue marbles.

2. Arden arrives at home at 10:07 P.M. and is there to receive a package that was expected at any time between 10:00 P.M. and 10:15 P.M.

3. When a number cube is rolled, a number less than 5 appears.

4. A card chosen at random from a standard deck is red.

5. When an 8-sided number die is rolled, a multiple of 3 appears.

6. A card chosen at random from a standard deck is a jack, queen, king, or ace.

A spinner is divided into three colored regions. The results of 125 spins are recorded in the table at right. Find the probability of each event.

7. red   8. blue   9. yellow

red	53
blue	32
yellow	40

Find the number of possible passwords (with no letters or digits excluded) for each of the following conditions:

10. 2 letters followed by 3 digits, with no letters or digits excluded

11. 3 letters followed by 3 digits, with only vowels and even digits allowed (Consider *y* a consonant.)

12. 2 letters followed by 2 digits followed by 3 letters, with no letters or digits excluded

13. In a 5-digit U.S. zip code, the last 2 digits identify the local delivery area. How many local delivery areas can be designated if any digit can be used?

14. For a given telephone area code, how many 7-digit telephone numbers are possible if the first digit cannot be 0?

LESSON 10.2

A city recreation program has one summer job available at each of its 6 parks. In how many ways can the 6 jobs be assigned if the given number of employees are available?

1. 6   2. 10   3. 12   4. 15

Find the number of permutations of the digits 1–5 for each situation.

5. using all 5 digits   6. taking 3 digits at a time

7. taking 4 digits at a time   8. taking 2 digits at a time

Find the number of permutations of the letters in each word.

9. *heptagon*   10. *pentagon*   11. *circle*   12. *textbook*

13. The United Nations Security Council has 15 member nations. In how many ways can the representatives be seated around a circular table if each nation has one representative?

14. The 8 winning entries in a school art contest are to be displayed in a row. In how many different orders can the entries be displayed?

15. A shoe store has 6 different models of running shoes on sale. In how many ways can a rotating display of the models be arranged?

LESSON 10.3

Find the number of ways in which each committee can be selected.

1. 2 people from a group of 5 people **2.** 4 people from a group of 7 people
3. 3 people from a group of 8 people **4.** 1 person from a group of 9 people

A take-out restaurant offers a selection of 5 main dishes, 4 vegetables, and 3 desserts. In how many ways can a family choose a meal consisting of the following?

5. 2 different main dishes, 3 different vegetables, and 1 dessert
6. 3 different main dishes, 2 different vegetables, and 3 different desserts
7. 5 different main dishes, 4 different vegetables, and 3 different desserts

Four marbles are chosen at random (without replacement) from a bag containing 4 white marbles and 6 green marbles. Find the probability of selecting each combination.

8. 4 green **9.** 2 white *and* 2 green **10.** 1 white *and* 3 green

Fifteen students are entered in a public-speaking contest. Determine whether each situation involves a permutation or a combination.

11. The order in which the contestants speak must be chosen.
12. First, second, and third prizes are awarded.
13. Two of the 15 represent the school in a regional contest.

14. In a survey of 50 voters, 33 favor a policy change, and 17 oppose it or have no opinion. Find the probability that in a random sample of 10 respondents from this survey, exactly 8 favor the proposed regulation and 2 oppose it or have no opinion.

LESSON 10.4

A card is drawn at random from a standard deck of playing cards. State whether the events *A* and *B* are inclusive or mutually exclusive. Then find *P(A or B)*. (Note: A standard deck of 52 cards has 12 face cards, 4 of which are kings. Also, exactly half of the cards are red, including 6 of the face cards and 2 of the kings.)

1. *A*: The card is a queen. **2.** *A*: The card is red.
  B: The card is a king.   *B*: The card is a king.

3. *A*: The card is red. **4.** *A*: The card is a face card.
  B: The card is not a king.   *B*: The card is not a king.

5. *A*: The card is red. **6.** *A*: The card is a face card.
  B: The card is not red.   *B*: The card is a king.

A number cube is rolled once, and the number on the top face is recorded. Find the probability of each pair of events.

7. The number is even *or* greater than 5. **8.** The number is 5 *or* a multiple of 3.
9. The number is odd *or* greater than 4. **10.** The number is greater than 2 *or* less than 5.

Each of the digits from 0 to 9 is written on a card. The cards are placed in a sack, and one is drawn at random. Find the probability of each pair of events.

11. digit is odd *or* a multiple of 3 **12.** digit is less than 2 *or* greater than 8
13. digit is odd *or* less than 5 **14.** digit is greater than 7 *or* even

A coin is tossed 3 times. Find the probability of each event.

1. All 3 tosses are heads.

2. The first toss is heads, but the second and the third are tails.

Events *Q*, *R*, and *S* are independent, and *P(Q)* = 0.2, *P(R)* = 0.4, and *P(S)* = 0.1. Find each probability.

3. $P(Q \text{ and } R)$ **4.** $P(Q \text{ and } S)$ **5.** $P(R \text{ and } S)$

A red number cube and a green number cube are rolled. Find the probability of each event.

6. The red cube is a 3, *and* the green cube is greater than 3.

7. The red cube is greater than 1, *and* the green cube is less than 6.

8. The red cube is less than or equal to 4, *and* the green cube is greater than or equal to 5.

9. The green cube is less than or equal to 6, *and* the red cube is greater than or equal to 1.

A bag contains 3 red, 2 green, and 5 blue marbles. A marble is picked at random and is replaced. A second marble is picked at random. Find the probability of each event.

10. Both marbles are red.   **11.** The first marble is green, *and* the second is blue.

12. Neither marble is green.   **13.** The first marble is blue, *and* the second is not blue.

A number cube is rolled twice. On each roll, the number on the top face of the cube is recorded. Find the probability of each event.

14. The first number is even, *and* the second number is greater than 3.

15. The first number is greater than 4, *and* the second number is less than 3.

A bag contains 5 red, 7 blue, and 4 white marbles. Two consecutive draws are made from the bag without replacement of the first draw. Find each probability.

1. red first *and* blue second   **2.** red first *and* white second

3. blue first *and* red second   **4.** white first *and* white second

Two number cubes are rolled, and the first cube shows a 3. Find the probability of each event below.

5. a sum of 8   **6.** one even number *and* one odd number

7. a sum of less than 6   **8.** a sum of greater than 5 *and* less than 9

For one roll of a number cube, let *A* be the event "even" and let *B* be the event "4". Find each probability.

9. $P(A)$ **10.** $P(B)$ **11.** $P(A \text{ and } B)$ **12.** $P(A \text{ or } B)$ **13.** $P(A \mid B)$ **14.** $P(B \mid A)$

For one roll of a number cube, let *A* be the event "less than 4" and let *B* be the event "1 *or* 2". Find each probability.

15. $P(A)$ **16.** $P(B)$ **17.** $P(A \text{ and } B)$ **18.** $P(A \text{ or } B)$ **19.** $P(A \mid B)$ **20.** $P(B \mid A)$

21. Given that $P(A \text{ and } B) = 0.2$ and $P(A) = 0.5$, find $P(B \mid A)$.

22. Given that $P(B \mid A) = 0.8$ and $P(A \text{ and } B) = 0.6$, find $P(A)$.

LESSON 10.7

Use a simulation with 20 trials to estimate each probability. Simulation results may vary.

1. In 3 tosses of a coin, 2 consecutive heads will appear.

2. In 4 tosses of a coin, tails will appear exactly once.

3. In 3 rolls of a number cube, the number 3 will appear exactly twice.

4. In 5 rolls of a number cube, the number 4 will appear exactly 3 times.

5. In 6 rolls of a number cube, the number 1 will not appear.

Of 150 motorists observed at an intersection, 47 turned left, 72 went straight, and 31 turned right. Use a simulation with 10 trials to estimate the probability of each event.

6. At least 2 out of every 5 consecutive motorists go straight.

7. More than 1 out of every 5 consecutive motorists turn left.

8. Less than 3 out of every 5 consecutive motorists turn right.

9. At least 3 out of every 5 consecutive motorists do not go straight.

10. No more than 1 out of every 5 consecutive motorists goes left.

11. Assume that a person who is learning to play darts has acquired enough skill to hit the target but is just as likely to hit any one spot on the target as any other. Use a simulation with 10 trials to estimate the probability that exactly 3 out of 5 darts that land on the square target shown at right land inside the circle.

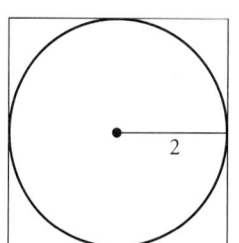

Chapter 11

LESSON 11.1

Write the first five terms of each sequence.

1. $t_n = -3n + 8$

2. $t_n = 4n - 12$

3. $t_n = 2n^2$

4. $t_1 = 1$
   $t_n = t_{n-1} + 5$

5. $t_1 = 16$
   $t_n = t_{n-1} - 6$

6. $t_1 = 3$
   $t_n = 2t_{n-1}$

Write a recursive formula for each sequence and find the next three terms.

7. $1, 10, 19, 28, \ldots$

8. $2, 7, 12, 17, \ldots$

9. $4, 9, 19, 34, \ldots$

Write the terms of each series and then evaluate the sum.

10. $\sum_{n=1}^{6} (12n + 1)$

11. $\sum_{j=1}^{5} (j - 1)^2$

12. $\sum_{k=1}^{4} (3k^2 + 4k)$

Evaluate.

13. $\sum_{m=1}^{6} 5m$

14. $\sum_{n=1}^{5} (10n - 3)$

15. $\sum_{j=1}^{4} (2j^2 - 3j + 1)$

LESSON 11.2

Based on the terms given, state whether each sequence is arithmetic. If it is, identify the common difference, *d*.

1. $5, 7, 10, 14, 19, \ldots$

2. $-8, -5, -2, 1, 4, \ldots$

3. $1, 8, 27, 64, 125, \ldots$

4. $0.1, 0.2, 0.3, 0.4, 0.5, \ldots$

5. $4.4, 5.5, 6.6, 7.7, \ldots$

6. $1.2, 3.4, 5.6, 7.8, \ldots$

Write an explicit formula for the *n*th term of each arithmetic sequence.

7. $5, 8, 11, 14, 17, \ldots$

8. $7, 3, -1, -5, -9, \ldots$

9. $10, 16, 22, 28, 34, \ldots$

10. $30, 37, 44, 51, 58, \ldots$

11. $-12, -8, -4, 0, 4, \ldots$

12. $40, 33, 26, 19, 12, \ldots$

List the first four terms of each arithmetic sequence.

13. $t_1 = 5, \ t_n = t_{n-1} + 11$

14. $t_1 = -13, \ t_n = t_{n-1} + 10$

15. $t_1 = 0, \ t_n = t_{n-1} + 20$

16. $t_n = 5n - 8$

17. $t_n = -8n - 4$

18. $t_n = 6n - 10$

Find the indicated number of arithmetic means between the two given numbers.

19. three arithmetic means between 5 and 29

20. four arithmetic means between -12 and 28

21. two arithmetic means between 6.5 and 15.8

22. three arithmetic means between -6 and 4

LESSON 11.3

Use the formula for an arithmetic series to find each sum.

1. $3 + 6 + 9 + 12 + 15$

2. $-8 + (-15) + (-22) + (-29) + (-36)$

3. $40 + 42 + 44 + \cdots + 68$

4. $-45 + (-40) + (-35) + (-30) + \cdots + 25$

5. Find the sum of the first 175 natural numbers.

6. Find the sum of the multiples of 6 from 18 to 120 inclusive.

7. Find the sum of the multiples of 8 from 40 to 480 inclusive.

For each arithmetic series, find S_{20}.

8. $4, 8, 12, 16, 20, 24, \ldots$

9. $3, 8, 13, 18, 23, \ldots$

10. $-15, -12, -9, -6, -3, \ldots$

11. $-20, -40, -60, -80, -100, \ldots$

12. $\pi, 3\pi, 5\pi, 7\pi, 9\pi, \ldots$

13. $\sqrt{7}, 4\sqrt{7}, 7\sqrt{7}, 10\sqrt{7}, \ldots$

Evaluate.

14. $\displaystyle\sum_{j=1}^{5} (24 - 3j)$

15. $\displaystyle\sum_{n=1}^{8} (15n - 1)$

16. $\displaystyle\sum_{k=1}^{10} (3k + 50)$

17. $\displaystyle\sum_{m=1}^{20} (120 - 10m)$

18. $\displaystyle\sum_{n=1}^{12} (25n + 4)$

19. $\displaystyle\sum_{k=1}^{15} (10 + 20k)$

Determine whether each sequence is a geometric sequence. If so, identify the common ratio, r, and give the next three terms.

1. $12, 6, 3, \frac{3}{2}, \ldots$

2. $11, 22, 44, 88, \ldots$

3. $-2, -6, -18, -54, \ldots$

4. $27, 9, 3, 1, \ldots$

5. $25, 36, 49, 64, \ldots$

6. $25, 2.5, 0.25, 0.025, \ldots$

List the first four terms of each geometric sequence.

7. $t_1 = 5$
$t_n = 0.2t_{n-1}$

8. $t_1 = 4$
$t_n = 10t_{n-1}$

9. $t_1 = -2$
$t_n = -4.5t_{n-1}$

Find the fifth term in the geometric sequence that includes the given terms.

10. $t_2 = 48; t_3 = 144$

11. $t_2 = 224; t_4 = 14$

12. $t_3 = 75; t_8 = 234{,}375$

Write an explicit formula for the nth term of each geometric sequence.

13. $0.04, 0.2, 1, 5, \ldots$

14. $16, 8, 4, 2, \ldots$

15. $\sqrt{6}, 6, 6\sqrt{6}, 36, \ldots$

Find the indicated number of geometric means between the two given numbers.

16. two geometric means between 12 and 324

17. two geometric means between 6.4 and 21.6

18. three geometric means between 16 and 81

19. three geometric means between 8 and 312.5

Find each sum. Round answers to the nearest tenth, if necessary.

1. S_{10} for the geometric series $3 + 6 + 12 + 24 + \cdots$

2. S_8 for the geometric series $-32 + 16 + (-8) + 4 + (-2) + \cdots$

3. $\frac{3}{4} + \frac{3}{8} + \frac{3}{16} + \frac{3}{32} + \frac{3}{64} + \frac{3}{128}$

4. $-0.48 + 2.4 - 12 + 60 - 300$

For Exercises 5–8, refer to the series $0.2 + 0.6 + 1.8 + 5.4 + \cdots$

5. Find t_8.

6. Find t_{16}.

7. Find S_8.

8. Find S_{16}.

Evaluate. Round answers to the nearest tenth, if necessary.

9. $\displaystyle\sum_{k=1}^{8} 2(3^k - 1)$

10. $\displaystyle\sum_{n=1}^{6} 4(0.5^n)$

11. $\displaystyle\sum_{k=1}^{10} 3.5^{k-1}$

12. $\displaystyle\sum_{k=1}^{20} 0.5(2^{k-1})$

Use mathematical induction to prove that each statement is true for every natural number, n.

13. $\frac{1}{2} + \frac{1}{2^2} + \frac{1}{2^3} + \cdots + \frac{1}{2^n} = 1 - \frac{1}{2^n}$

14. $1^3 + 3^3 + 5^3 + \cdots + (2n-1)^3 = n^2(2n^2 - 1)$

LESSON 11.6

Find the sum of each infinite geometric series, if it exists.

1. $\frac{1}{5} + \frac{1}{25} + \frac{1}{125} + \frac{1}{625} + \cdots$

2. $20 + 12 + 7.2 + 4.32 + \cdots$

3. $0.2 + 0.4 + 0.8 + 1 + \cdots$

4. $5 + \frac{5}{7} + \frac{5}{49} + \frac{5}{343} + \cdots$

Find the sum of each infinite geometric series, if it exists.

5. $\sum_{n=0}^{\infty} 4^n$

6. $\sum_{k=1}^{\infty} \frac{3}{5^k}$

7. $\sum_{n=1}^{\infty} 0.4^n - 1$

8. $\sum_{k=0}^{\infty} (-0.25)^k$

Write each decimal as a fraction in simplest form.

9. $0.\overline{7}$

10. $0.\overline{23}$

11. $0.3\overline{21}$

12. $0.\overline{726}$

Write an infinite geometric series that converges to the given number.

13. $0.3131313131\ldots$

14. $0.4747474747\ldots$

15. $0.357357357\ldots$

LESSON 11.7

State the location of each entry in Pascal's triangle. Then give the value of each expression.

1. $_4C_2$

2. $_9C_5$

3. $_8C_3$

4. $_6C_5$

5. $_{10}C_7$

6. $_{15}C_7$

7. $_{11}C_8$

8. $_{20}C_{10}$

Find the fifth and eighth entries in the indicated row of Pascal's triangle.

9. row 8

10. row 10

11. row 13

12. row 16

Find the probability of each event.

13. exactly 3 heads in 4 tosses of a fair coin

14. 3 *or* 4 heads in 8 tosses of a fair coin

15. no more than 3 heads in 7 tosses of a fair coin

16. no fewer than 4 heads in 9 tosses of a fair coin

17. 3 *or* 4 *or* 5 heads in 10 tosses of a fair coin

A student guesses the answers for 8 items on a true-false quiz. Find the probability that the indicated number of answers is correct.

18. exactly 6

19. at least 5

20. at most 4

Expand each binomial.

1. $(a + b)^4$ **2.** $(w + z)^5$ **3.** $(c + d)^6$

4. $(1 + x)^3$ **5.** $(y + 2)^5$ **6.** $(z + 1)^4$

For Exercises 7–8, refer to the expansion of $(x + y)^{12}$.

7. How many terms are in the expansion?

8. What is the exponent of x in the term containing y^7? What is the term?

Expand each binomial.

9. $(2x + y)^5$ **10.** $(3z - 2)^4$ **11.** $(x - 2y)^4$

12. $(3y - 2z)^5$ **13.** $\left(\frac{1}{2}x + 2y\right)^3$ **14.** $\left(\frac{2}{3}x - y\right)^3$

Use the Binomial Theorem to find each theoretical probability for a baseball player with a batting average of 0.250.

15. exactly 4 hits in 5 at bats

16. no more than 3 hits in 5 at bats

17. exactly 2 hits in 6 at bats

18. no more than 3 hits in 6 at bats

Chapter 12

Find the mean, median, and mode of each data set. Round answers to the nearest thousandth, if necessary.

1. 12, 16, 22, 45, 30, 58, 11, 21, 29, 37   **2.** 92, 90, 88, 88, 99, 70, 55, 85, 92, 93, 90

3. 12.6, 8.5, 7.7, 9.9, 12.8, 12.6, 12.5, 13.2   **4.** 5, 5, 6, 16, 24, 32, 5, 66, 7, 10, 22, 6

Find the mean, median, and mode of each data set and compare the three measures.

5. minimum starting salaries (in dollars per year) in selected professional specialties: 35,700; 24,700; 34,100; 35,700; 22,900; 29,300; 28,300

6. number of people (in millions) viewing prime-time television in a given week: 94.5, 93.2, 85.2, 88.8, 79.2, 77.6, 92.8

Make a frequency table for each data set and find the mean.

7. workers' sick days in one year: 0, 5, 2, 1, 3, 5, 5, 10, 22, 0, 0, 4, 3, 2, 0, 0, 1, 1, 1, 8

8. the number of bicycles in students' families: 1, 4, 3, 3, 6, 2, 4, 4, 3, 1, 1, 1, 2, 2, 2, 3, 5, 4, 4, 3

Make a grouped frequency table for each data set and estimate the mean.

9. class test scores: 88, 72, 65, 58, 90, 71, 66, 82, 76, 75, 77, 91, 56, 70, 92, 80, 66, 86, 84, 75

10. the number of hours worked per week: 40, 32, 30, 44, 40, 52, 30, 25, 20, 42, 46, 38, 35, 27, 55, 51

LESSON 12.2

Make a stem-and-leaf plot for each data set. Then find the median and the mode, and describe the distribution of the data.

1. 16, 22, 26, 43, 30, 12, 15, 40, 47, 25, 46, 33, 32, 12

2. 55, 87, 92, 50, 54, 58, 57, 72, 88, 96, 90, 78, 74, 55, 60, 61, 76

Make a frequency table and a histogram for each data set.

3. 3, 5, 7, 2, 2, 3, 5, 5, 6, 6, 6, 2, 3, 4, 1, 5, 7, 5, 4, 6, 7, 7, 2, 1, 2, 7, 5, 3

4. 13, 16, 15, 12, 12, 15, 18, 20, 17, 16, 15, 16, 12, 13, 17, 19, 20, 15, 15, 14

Make a relative frequency table and a histogram of probabilities for each data set.

5. 20, 22, 25, 21, 24, 22, 25, 23, 23, 20, 21, 25, 22, 21, 24, 21, 22, 23, 25, 22

6. 5, 4, 8, 5, 8, 4, 6, 8, 4, 5, 8, 8, 4, 8, 4, 8, 6, 5, 5, 5, 7, 6, 5, 7, 5

The table below lists the number of United States military personnel by branch.

United States Military Personnel, 1996

Army	Air Force	Navy	Marine Corps
493,330	389,400	436,608	172,287

7a. Make a circle graph to represent this data set.

b. Find the probability that a randomly selected person in the U.S. military is in the marines or the navy.

LESSON 12.3

Find the minimum and maximum values, quartiles, range, and interquartile range for each data set. Then make a box-and-whisker plot for each data set.

1. 12, 35, 22, 18, 16, 21, 19, 33, 7, 10, 14, 28, 27, 16, 13

2. 5.4, 7.8, 1.1, 9.2, 12.6, 15.5, 18.0, 16.2, 18.8, 12.1, 13.2, 13.2, 15.0, 16.3, 20.2

3. 210, 185, 340, 715, 224, 290, 168, 312, 272, 300

4. 47, 40, 31, 22, 62, 50, 43, 28, 47, 35, 32, 44, 29, 28, 56, 50, 52, 54, 36, 20, 22

5. 5.0, 6.5, 8.0, 3.2, 8.1, 7.4, 6.7, 6.2, 5.0, 12.3, 5.7, 6.3, 6.8, 5.7, 7.2, 8.4

The box-and-whisker plots below compare the state per capita personal incomes in dollars for 1990 and 1995. Refer to the box-and-whisker plots for Exercises 6–8.

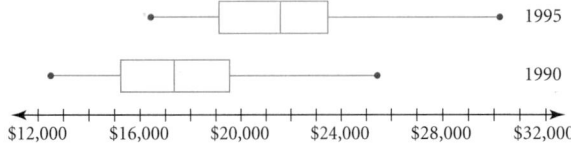

6. Which data set has the greater range?

7. Compare the interquartile ranges for the two data sets.

8. Q_1 for the 1995 data and Q_3 for the 1990 data are about the same. Describe what this means in terms of the distribution of the data.

LESSON 12.4

Find the range and the mean deviation for each data set.

1. 6, 5, 3, 2, 4, 6, 8, 6
2. 20, 22, 20, 21, 23, 26

3. 5, 8, 10, 16, 9, 12
4. 28, 40, 20, 32, 30, 54

5. −12, 25, 17, −8, 15
6. 3.5, 4.0, 2.8, 3.8, 7.2, 7.5

Find the variance and the standard deviation for each data set.

7. 52, 61, 54, 48, 72
8. 115, 120, 132, 140, 113

9. 61, 20, 93, 72, 30, 24
10. 0.4, 1.1, 6.9, 9.8, 6.3

11. 9, 7, 3, 1, 2, 8
12. 59, 60, 7, 37, 69

The table below shows the number of free throws made by the 15 best free-throw shooters in the National Basketball Association for the 1995–1996 season. Refer to the table for Exercises 13–14.

146	259	338	130	167	425	430	132
125	342	137	146	135	247	172	

13. Find the range and the mean deviation of the data.

14. Find the standard deviation of the data.

LESSON 12.5

A coin is flipped 5 times. Find the probability of each event.

1. exactly 3 heads
2. exactly 2 heads

3. at least 4 heads
4. at most 4 heads

5. at most 1 heads
6. at least 2 heads

A spinner is divided into 6 congruent segments, each labeled with one of the letters *A–F*. Find each of the following probabilities:

7. exactly 3 *A*s in 5 spins

8. exactly 2 *D*s in 4 spins

9. more than 2 *B*s in 5 spins

10. no more than 2 *C*s in 4 spins

Find the probability that a batter will get *exactly* 3 hits in her next 6 at bats given each batting average below.

11. 0.300
12. 0.280
13. 0.312

Find the probability that a batter will get *at least* 3 hits in his next 6 at bats given each batting average below.

14. 0.290
15. 0.285
16. 0.315

Let *x* be a random variable with a standard normal distribution. Use the area table for a standard normal curve, given on page 807, to find each probability.

1. $P(x \le 0.4)$

2. $P(x \ge 0.6)$

3. $P(1.4 \le x \le 1.8)$

4. $P(x \le -0.8)$

5. $P(-0.2 \le x \le 1.4)$

6. $P(x \ge -0.6)$

At one university, the ages of first-year students are approximately normally distributed with a mean of 19 and a standard deviation of 1. A first-year student is chosen at random. Find the probability that the student is

7. not less than 21 years old.

8. 19 or younger.

9. between 18 and 20 inclusive.

10. between 19 and 21 inclusive.

On an assembly line, the time required to perform a certain task is approximately normally distributed with a mean of 140 seconds and a standard deviation of 10 seconds. Of 1000 separate tasks, how many can be expected to take the given number of seconds?

11. more than 150 seconds

12. less than 150 seconds

13. between 120 and 150 seconds

14. more than 160 seconds

Chapter 13

Refer to $\triangle XYZ$ at right in order to find each value below. Give exact answers and answers rounded to the nearest ten-thousandth.

1. $\sin Y$

2. $\sin X$

3. $\cos Y$

4. $\cos X$

5. $\tan Y$

6. $\tan X$

7. $\csc Y$

8. $\csc X$

9. $\sec Y$

10. $\sec X$

11. $\cot Y$

12. $\cot X$

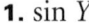

Solve each triangle. Round angle measures to the nearest degree and side lengths to the nearest tenth.

13.

14.

15.

16.

17.

18.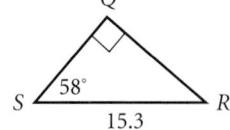

For each angle below, find all coterminal angles such that −360° < θ < 360°.

1. $114°$ **2.** $22°$ **3.** $-53°$

4. $-272°$ **5.** $512°$ **6.** $-495°$

Find the reference angle for each angle below.

7. $117°$ **8.** $-78°$ **9.** $1024°$

10. $-512°$ **11.** $245°$ **12.** $311°$

Given each point on the terminal side of θ in standard position, find the exact values of the six trigonometric functions of θ.

13. $(3, 6)$ **14.** $(-4, 5)$ **15.** $(3, -8)$

16. $(2, -\sqrt{2})$ **17.** $(-4, -3)$ **18.** $(6, 5)$

Given the quadrant of θ in standard position and a trigonometric function value of θ, find the exact values for the indicated function.

19. I, $\tan \theta = \sqrt{3}$; $\cos \theta$ **20.** III, $\sin \theta = -\frac{5}{13}$; $\cos \theta$ **21.** IV, $\csc \theta = -\frac{4}{3}$; $\tan \theta$

Point P is located at the intersection of a circle with a radius of r and the terminal side of angle θ in standard position. Find the exact coordinates of P.

1. $\theta = -60°, r = 10$ **2.** $\theta = 120°, r = 6$ **3.** $\theta = 45°, r = 100$

4. $\theta = 300°, r = 2$ **5.** $\theta = 135°, r = 20$ **6.** $\theta = 330°, r = 50$

Point P is located at the intersection of a unit circle and the terminal side of angle θ in standard position. Find the coordinates of P to the nearest hundredth.

7. $\theta = 50°$ **8.** $\theta = -95°$ **9.** $\theta = 345°$

Find the exact values of the sine, cosine, and tangent of each angle.

10. $-300°$ **11.** $405°$ **12.** $-420°$ **13.** $1380°$

14. $495°$ **15.** $330°$ **16.** $-1800°$ **17.** $930°$

Find each trigonometric value. Give exact answers.

18. $\cos 495°$ **19.** $\tan 870°$ **20.** $\sin 780°$

21. $\sin 330°$ **22.** $\cos 405°$ **23.** $\sin 570°$

24. $\tan 405°$ **25.** $\cos 660°$ **26.** $\tan 420°$

27. $\tan 1395°$ **28.** $\sin(-1485°)$ **29.** $\cos 660°$

30. $\sin 1110°$ **31.** $\sec 780°$ **32.** $\cot 300°$

33. $\sin 390°$ **34.** $\csc(-765°)$ **35.** $\cot(-210°)$

LESSON 13.4

Convert each degree measure to radian measure. Give exact answers.

1. $30°$

2. $-90°$

3. $20°$

4. $400°$

5. $1080°$

6. $50°$

Convert each radian measure to degree measure. Round answers to the nearest tenth of a degree, if necessary.

7. $\frac{2\pi}{3}$ radians

8. $-\frac{\pi}{9}$ radian

9. 3π radians

10. $-\frac{3\pi}{4}$ radians

11. 3.245 radians

12. -6.122 radians

Evaluate each expression. Give the values.

13. $\sin\frac{3\pi}{4}$

14. $\csc\frac{\pi}{6}$

15. $\tan(-2\pi)$

16. $\cos\frac{5\pi}{6}$

17. $\cos\frac{\pi}{3}$

18. $\tan\left(-\frac{3\pi}{4}\right)$

19. $\cot\frac{\pi}{4}$

20. $\cos\left(-\frac{11\pi}{6}\right)$

A circle has a diameter of 8 meters. For each central angle measure below, find the length in meters of the arc intercepted by the angle.

21. $\frac{5\pi}{6}$ radians

22. $\frac{\pi}{12}$ radians

23. 2.5 radians

24. 1.2 radians

LESSON 13.5

Identify the amplitude, if it exists, and the period of each function.

1. $y = 3.5\sin 4\theta$

2. $y = 8\tan x$

3. $y = -6\cos(-x)$

4. $y = 7\cos\frac{1}{2}\theta$

5. $y = \frac{2}{3}\sin 3\theta$

6. $y = -\frac{1}{2}\tan 6\theta$

Identify the phase shift and vertical translation of each function from its parent function.

7. $y = \cos(\theta + 45°) + 1$

8. $y = \sin(\theta + 180°) - 3$

9. $y = \tan(\theta - 90°)$

10. $y = 3\cos(\theta - 30°) - 1$

11. $y = 3 + \sin(\theta - 45°)$

12. $y = 2 - \tan(\theta + 30°)$

Describe the transformation of each function from its parent function. Then graph at least one period of the given function and its parent function.

13. $y = 5\sin\theta$

14. $y = \cos(\theta + 90°)$

15. $y = \tan 2\theta$

16. The sales of a seasonal product are modeled by the function $s(x) = 40\sin\frac{\pi}{6}x + 74$, where s is thousands of units and x is time in months (beginning with 1 for January). Identify the amplitude, period, and phase shift of the function. Sketch a graph of the function for at least one period. What month shows the greatest number of units sold?

LESSON 13.6

Find all possible values for each expression.

1. $\sin^{-1}\frac{\sqrt{3}}{2}$

2. $\cos^{-1}\frac{1}{2}$

3. $\cos^{-1}\left(-\frac{\sqrt{2}}{2}\right)$

4. $\tan^{-1} 1$

5. $\tan^{-1} -1$

6. $\sin^{-1} 0$

Evaluate each trigonometric expression.

7. $\text{Cos}^{-1} 0$

8. $\text{Sin}^{-1}\left(-\frac{1}{2}\right)$

9. $\text{Cos}^{-1}\frac{\sqrt{3}}{2}$

10. $\text{Tan}^{-1}\left(-\sqrt{3}\right)$

11. $\text{Sin}^{-1}\left(-\frac{\sqrt{2}}{2}\right)$

12. $\text{Tan}^{-1} 0$

Evaluate each trigonometric expression.

13. $\tan\left(\text{Sin}^{-1}\frac{\sqrt{3}}{2}\right)$

14. $\cos(\text{Tan}^{-1} 1)$

15. $\sin\left[\text{Cos}^{-1}\left(-\frac{\sqrt{2}}{2}\right)\right]$

16. $\text{Sin}^{-1}(\cos 45°)$

17. $\text{Tan}^{-1}(\cos 90°)$

18. $\text{Sin}^{-1}(\cos 30°)$

19. At one point in the day, a 15-foot flagpole casts a 19.5-foot shadow. Find the angle of elevation between the sun and the far end of the shadow.

Chapter 14

LESSON 14.1

Find the area of $\triangle ABC$ to the nearest tenth of a square unit.

1. $b = 18$ in., $c = 24$ in., $A = 42°$

2. $a = 4$ m, $c = 9$ m, $B = 67°$

3. $c = 20$ cm, $a = 10$ cm, $B = 110°$

4. $b = 5$ in., $c = 4$ in., $A = 120°$

Use the given information to find the indicated side length of $\triangle ABC$. Round answers to the nearest tenth, if necessary.

5. Given $A = 38°$, $B = 50°$, and $a = 7$, find b.

6. Given $B = 120°$, $C = 42°$, and $b = 70$, find c.

7. Given $A = 52°$, $C = 88°$, and $a = 6$, find c.

8. Given $C = 59°$, $B = 63°$, and $c = 15$, find b.

Solve each triangle. Round answers to the nearest tenth, if necessary.

9. $A = 65°$, $C = 20°$, $b = 9$

10. $C = 37°$, $B = 20°$, $a = 40$

11. $A = 21°$, $C = 104°$, $b = 10$

12. $B = 50°$, $C = 32°$, $a = 35$

13. $A = 50°$, $C = 44°$, $a = 12$

14. $A = 65°$, $C = 70°$, $b = 15$

State the number of triangles determined by the given information. If 1 or 2 triangles are fomed, solve the triangle(s). Round the angle measures and sides lengths to the nearest tenth.

15. $A = 117°$, $b = 40$, $a = 28$

16. $B = 39°$, $a = 4$, $b = 3$

17. A surveyor marks the corners of a triangular lot and labels them as A, B, and C. If $AC = 110$ feet, $BC = 158$ feet, and the measure of the angle between $\overline{AC}$ and $\overline{BC}$ is $65°$, find the area of the park to the nearest hundredth of a square foot.

Classify the type of information given, and then use the law of cosines to find the missing side length of △ABC to the nearest tenth.

1. $b = 64, c = 80, A = 80°$

2. $a = 5, b = 12, C = 46°$

3. $a = 7, c = 9, B = 100°$

4. $b = 42, c = 30, A = 56°$

5. $b = 90, c = 120, A = 55°$

6. $a = 4, b = 6, C = 130°$

Solve each triangle. Round answers to the nearest tenth.

7. $a = 13, b = 15, c = 9$

8. $a = 8, b = 12, c = 7$

9. $a = 20, b = 24, c = 32$

10. $a = 24, b = 22, c = 30$

11. $a = 40, b = 50, c = 80$

12. $a = 10, b = 12, c = 20$

Classify the type of information given, and then solve △ABC, if possible. Round answers to the nearest tenth. If no such triangle exists, write *not possible*.

13. $a = 5.8, b = 6.4, c = 7.5$

14. $A = 39°, b = 42, a = 16$

15. $B = 72°, a = 8.2, b = 10$

16. $C = 50°, a = 102, b = 95$

17. $A = 40°, a = 5, b = 20$

18. $A = 70°, a = 6, b = 2$

19. A piece of gold cord 42 inches long will be used to trim the edges of a banner in the shape of an isosceles triangle. If the base of the triangle is 20 inches, find the measure of each angle of the triangle to the nearest tenth of a degree.

Use definitions to prove each identity.

1. $(\sec \theta)(\sin \theta) = \tan \theta$

2. $\sin^2 \theta + \cos^2 \theta = \sec^2 \theta - \tan^2 \theta$

3. $\tan \theta = \dfrac{1}{\cot \theta}$

4. $1 + \cot^2 \theta = \csc^2 \theta$

Write each expression in terms of a single trigonometric function, if possible.

5. $(\cos \theta)(\sec \theta) - \cos^2 \theta$

6. $\dfrac{\tan \theta}{\sin \theta}$

7. $\dfrac{(\sin \theta)(\sec \theta)}{\tan \theta}$

8. $(\csc \theta)(\cos \theta)(\sin \theta)$

9. $\sec^2 \theta - \tan^2 \theta + \cot^2 \theta$

10. $\dfrac{\tan \theta + 1}{\tan \theta}$

Write each expression in terms of only one trigonometric function. Then simplify, if possible.

11. $\dfrac{\sec \theta - \cos \theta}{\tan \theta}$

12. $\sec^2 \theta - \tan^2 \theta$

13. $(\cot \theta)(1 - \sin \theta) + \cos \theta$

14. $(\sec \theta)(\sec \theta - \cos \theta)$

15. $\dfrac{\sin \theta + \tan \theta}{1 + \sec \theta}$

16. $\dfrac{1 + \cot^2 \theta}{1 + \tan^2 \theta}$

LESSON 14.4

Find the exact value of each expression.

1. $\sin(45° - 30°)$
2. $\sin(225° + 60°)$

3. $\cos(120° + 45°)$
4. $\cos(150° - 135°)$

5. $\sin(90° - 120°)$
6. $\cos(30° + 120°)$

7. $\sin 210°$
8. $\cos 105°$

9. $\sin 285°$
10. $\cos 75°$

11. $\cos 15°$
12. $\sin 195°$

Find the rotation matrix for each angle of rotation.

13. $30°$
14. $-45°$
15. $80°$

16. A rectangle has vertices at $(4, 2)$, $(4, 8)$, $(10, 8)$, and $(10, 2)$. Find the coordinates, to the nearest hundredth, of the vertices for the image of the rectangle after a $45°$ rotation about the origin.

LESSON 14.5

Write each expression in terms of trigonometric functions of θ rather than multiples of θ.

1. $\cos 4\theta$
2. $\dfrac{1 - \cos 2\theta}{2}$
3. $\cos 2\theta + \sin^2 \theta$

Write each expression in terms of a single trigonometric function.

4. $\dfrac{\sin^2 \theta}{\sin 2\theta}$
5. $\dfrac{\cos 2\theta}{\cos \theta + \sin \theta} + \sin \theta$
6. $\dfrac{\sin 2\theta}{1 - \cos 2\theta}$

Use the information given to find the exact value of $\sin 2\theta$ and $\cos 2\theta$.

7. $0° \leq \theta \leq 360°$; $\cos\theta = \dfrac{4}{5}$
8. $90° \leq \theta \leq 180°$; $\sin \theta = \dfrac{1}{4}$

Use the information given to find the exact value of $\sin \frac{1}{2}\theta$ and $\cos \frac{1}{2}\theta$.

9. $0° \leq \theta \leq 180°$; $\tan\theta = \dfrac{4}{3}$
10. $180° \leq \theta \leq 270°$; $\cos\theta = -\dfrac{3}{8}$

LESSON 14.6

Find all solutions of each equation.

1. $2 \sin \theta + \sqrt{2} = 0$
2. $6 \sin \theta + 3 = 0$
3. $\sqrt{3} - \sin \theta = \sin \theta$

Find the exact solutions of each equation for $0° \leq \theta < 360°$.

4. $\sec^2 \theta - 4 = 0$
5. $\sin 2\theta = \sin \theta$

6. $\sec^2 \theta + 2 \sec \theta = 0$
7. $\cos 2\theta = 3 \cos \theta + 1$

8. $2 \cos^2 \theta - \cos \theta - 1 = 0$
9. $2 \sin \theta \cos \theta = \tan \theta$

Solve each equation to the nearest tenth of a degree for $0° \leq \theta < 360°$.

10 $4 \cos \theta - 5 \sin \theta = 0$
11 $3 \sin^2 \theta - 2 \sin \theta - 1 = 0$

Parent Functions and Their Graphs

The simplest form of any function is called the parent function. Each parent function has a distinctive graph. These two pages summarize the basic graphs of some parent functions.

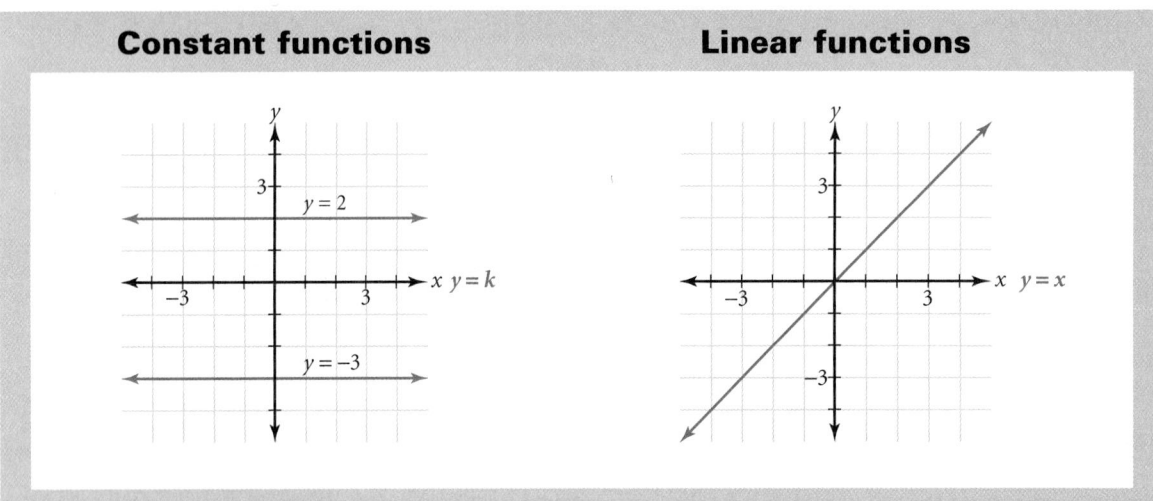

Constant functions

$y = 2$

$y = k$

$y = -3$

Linear functions

$y = x$

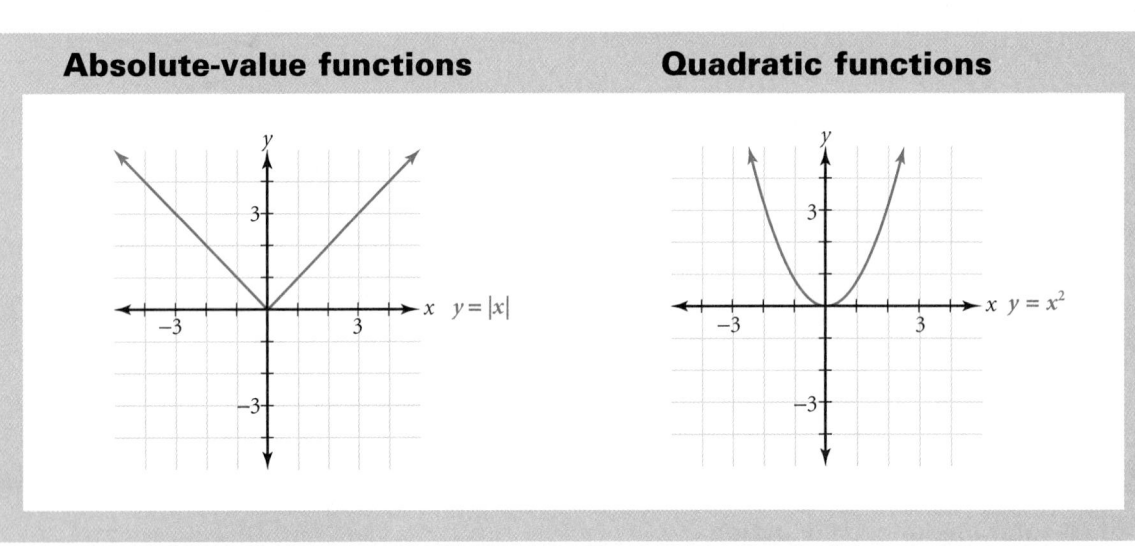

Absolute-value functions

$y = |x|$

Quadratic functions

$y = x^2$

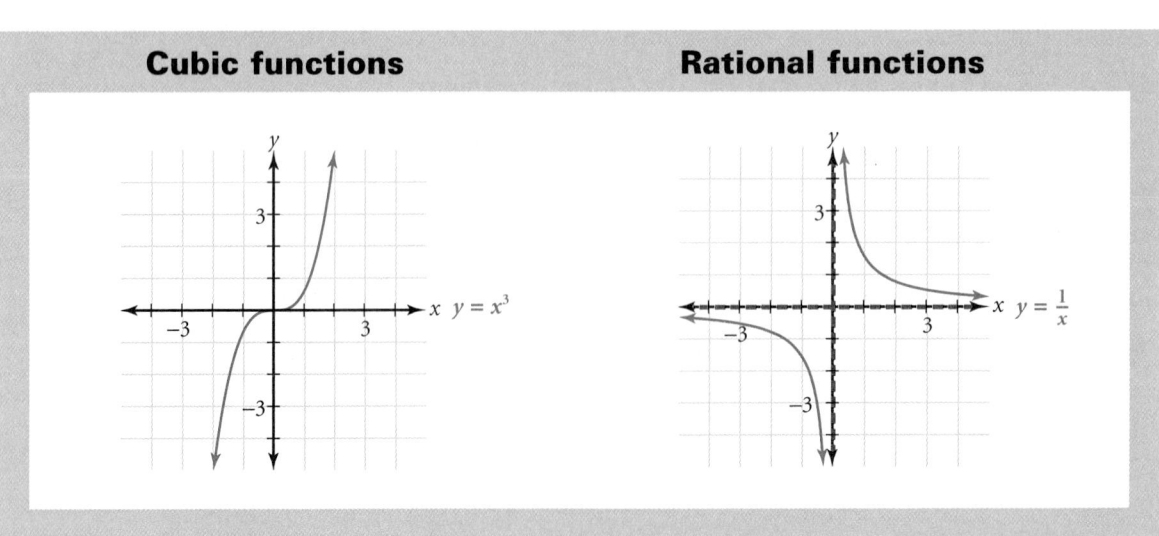

Cubic functions

$y = x^3$

Rational functions

$y = \frac{1}{x}$

Radical functions

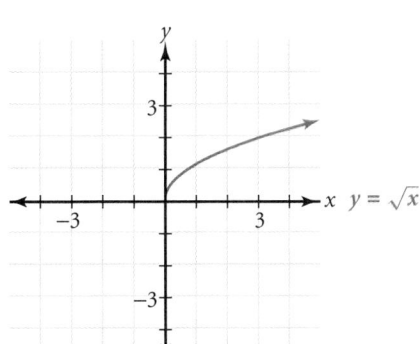

$y = \sqrt{x}$

Exponential functions

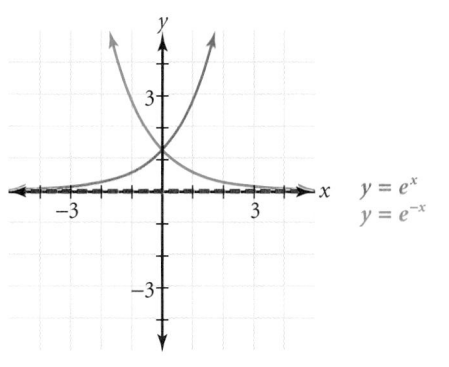

$y = e^x$
$y = e^{-x}$

Logarithmic functions

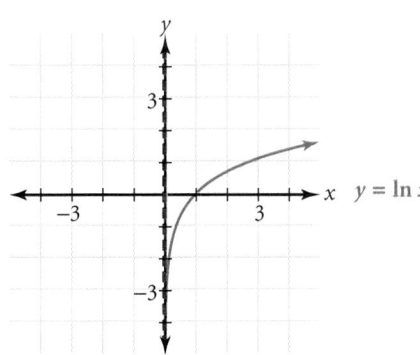

$y = \ln x$

Sine functions

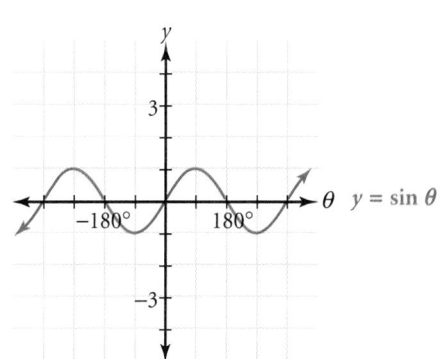

$y = \sin \theta$

Cosine functions

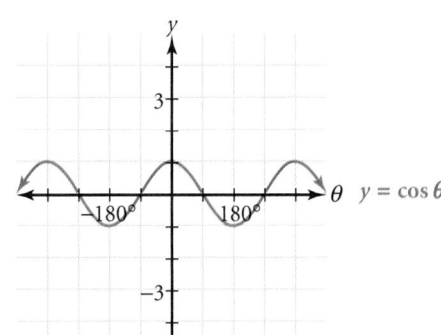

$y = \cos \theta$

Tangent functions

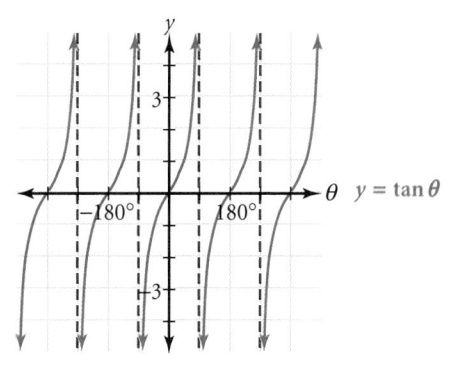

$y = \tan \theta$

Transformations of Parent Functions

A transformation of a parent function is an alteration of its function rule that results in an alteration of its graph. The new graph retains the distinctive features of the graph of the parent function. These two pages summarize transformations.

Translations

Vertical

If , then gives a vertical translation of the graph of f. The translation is k units up for and units down for .

Horizontal

If , then gives a horizontal translation of the graph of f. The translation is h units to the right for and units to the left for .

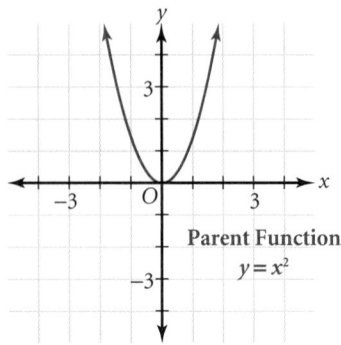

Parent Function
$y = x^2$

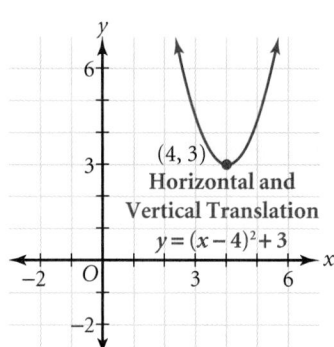

$(4, 3)$
Horizontal and
Vertical Translation
$y = (x - 4)^2 + 3$

Vertical Stretches and Compressions

If , then gives a vertical stretch or vertical compression of the graph of f.

    If , the graph is stretched vertically by a factor of a.
    If , the graph is compressed vertically by a factor of a.

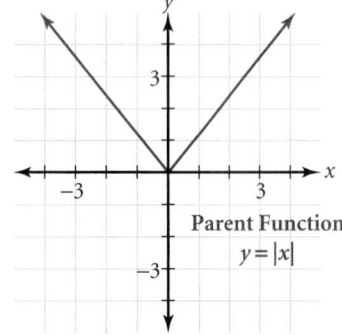

Parent Function
$y = |x|$

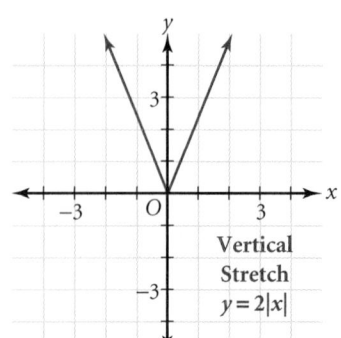

Vertical
Stretch
$y = 2|x|$

Horizontal Stretches and Compressions

If , then gives a horizontal stretch or horizontal compression of the graph of f.

   If , the graph is compressed horizontally by a factor of .

   If , the graph is stretched horizontally by a factor of .

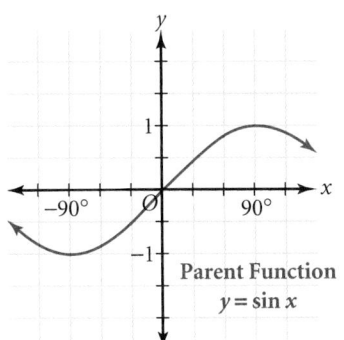

Parent Function
$y = \sin x$

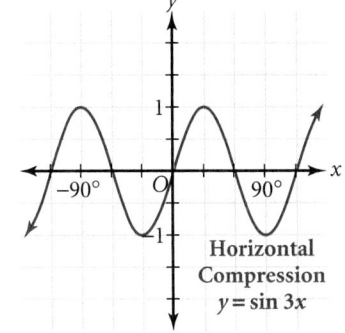

Horizontal
Compression
$y = \sin 3x$

Reflections

If , then gives a reflection of the graph of f across the x-axis.

If , then gives a reflection of the graph of f across the y-axis.

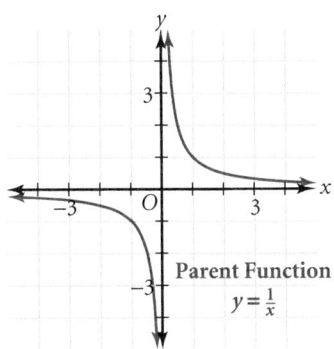

Parent Function
$y = \frac{1}{x}$

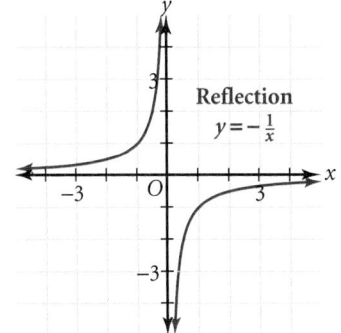

Reflection
$y = -\frac{1}{x}$

Combining Transformations

Any number of the above transformations can be combined. For example, the graph at right represents . It is a vertical stretch, a horizontal and vertical translation, and a reflection of the graph of the parent function,.

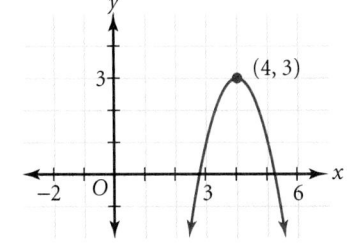

(4, 3)

Table of Random Digits

Column	(1)	(2)	(3)	(4)	(5)	(6)	(7)	(8)	(9)	(10)	(11)	(12)	(13)	(14)
Line														
1	10480	15011	01536	02011	81647	91646	69179	14194	62590	36207	20969	99570	91291	90700
2	22368	46573	25595	85393	30995	89198	27982	53402	93965	34095	52666	19174	39615	99505
3	24130	48360	22527	97265	76393	64809	15179	24830	49340	32081	30680	19655	63348	58629
4	42167	93093	06243	61680	07856	16376	39440	53537	71341	57004	00849	74917	97758	16379
5	37570	39975	81837	16656	06121	91782	60468	81305	49684	60672	14110	06927	01263	54613
6	77921	06907	11008	42751	27756	53498	18602	70659	90655	15053	21916	81825	44394	42880
7	99562	72905	56420	69994	98872	31016	71194	18738	44013	48840	63213	21069	10634	12952
8	96301	91977	05463	07972	18876	20922	94595	56869	69014	60045	18425	84903	42508	32307
9	89579	14342	63661	10281	17453	18103	57740	84378	25331	12566	58678	44947	05585	56941
10	85475	36857	53342	53988	53060	59533	38867	62300	08158	17983	16439	11458	18593	64952
11	28918	69578	88231	33276	70997	79936	56865	05859	90106	31595	01547	85590	91610	78188
12	63553	40961	48235	03427	49626	69445	18663	72695	52180	20847	12234	90511	33703	90322
13	09429	93969	52636	92737	88974	33488	36320	17617	30015	08272	84115	27156	30613	74952
14	10365	61129	87529	85689	48237	52267	67689	93394	01511	26358	85104	20285	29975	89868
15	07119	97336	71048	08178	77233	13916	47564	81056	97735	85977	29372	74461	28551	90707
16	51085	12765	51821	51259	77452	16308	60756	92144	49442	53900	70960	63990	75601	40719
17	02368	21382	52404	60268	89368	19885	55322	44819	01188	65225	64835	44919	05944	55157
18	01011	54092	33362	94904	31273	04146	18594	29852	71585	85030	51132	01915	92747	64951
19	52162	53916	46369	58586	23216	14513	83149	98736	23495	64350	94738	17752	35156	35749
20	07056	97628	33787	09998	42698	06691	76988	13602	51851	46104	88916	19509	25625	58104
21	48663	91245	85828	14346	09172	30168	90229	04734	59193	22178	30421	61666	99904	32812
22	54164	58492	22421	74103	47070	25306	76468	26384	58151	06646	21524	15227	96909	44592
23	32639	32363	05597	24200	13363	38005	94342	28728	35806	06912	17012	64161	18296	22851
24	29334	27001	87637	87308	58731	00256	45834	15398	46557	41135	10367	07684	36188	18510
25	02488	33062	28834	07351	19731	92420	60952	61280	50001	67658	32586	86679	50720	94953
26	81525	72295	04839	96423	24878	82651	66566	14778	76797	14780	13300	87074	79666	95725
27	29676	20591	68086	26432	46901	20849	89768	81536	86645	12659	92259	57102	80428	25280
28	00742	57392	39064	66432	84673	40027	32832	61362	98947	96067	64760	64584	96096	98253
29	05366	04213	25669	26422	44407	44048	37937	63904	45766	66134	75470	66520	34693	90449
30	91921	26418	64117	94305	26766	25940	39972	22209	71500	64568	91402	42416	07844	69618
31	00582	04711	87917	77341	42206	35126	74087	99547	81817	42607	43808	76655	62028	76630
32	00725	69884	62797	56170	86324	88072	76222	36086	84637	93161	76038	65855	77919	88006
33	69011	65795	95876	55293	18988	27354	26575	08625	40801	59920	29841	80150	12777	48501
34	25976	57948	29888	88604	67917	48708	18912	82271	65424	69774	33611	54262	85963	03547
35	09763	83473	73577	12908	30883	18317	28290	35797	05998	41688	34952	37888	38917	88050
36	91567	42595	27958	30134	04024	86385	29880	99730	55536	84855	29080	09250	79656	73211
37	17955	56349	90999	49127	20044	59931	06115	20542	18059	02008	73708	83517	36103	42791
38	46503	18584	18845	49618	02304	51038	20655	58727	28168	15475	56942	53389	20562	87338
39	92157	89634	94824	78171	84610	82834	09922	25417	44137	48413	25555	21246	35509	20468
40	14577	62765	35605	81263	39667	47358	56873	56307	61607	49518	89656	20103	77490	18062
41	98427	07523	33362	64270	01638	92477	66969	98420	04880	45585	46565	04102	46880	45709
42	34914	63976	88720	82765	34476	17032	87589	40836	32427	70002	70663	88863	77775	69348
43	70060	28277	39475	46473	23219	53416	94970	25832	69975	94884	19661	72828	00102	66794
44	53976	54914	06990	67245	68350	82948	11398	42878	80287	88267	47363	46634	06541	97809
45	76072	29515	40980	07391	58745	25774	22987	80059	39911	96189	41151	14222	60697	59583
46	90725	52210	83974	29992	65831	38857	50490	83765	55657	14361	31720	57375	56228	41546
47	64364	67412	33339	31926	14883	24413	59744	92351	97473	89286	35931	04110	23726	51900
48	08962	00358	31662	25388	61642	34072	81249	35648	56891	69352	48373	45578	78547	81788
49	95012	68379	93526	70765	10592	04542	76463	54328	02349	17247	28865	14777	62730	92277
50	15664	10493	20492	38391	91132	21999	59516	81652	27195	48223	46751	22923	32261	85653

Standard Normal Curve Areas

The table below gives the area under the standard normal curve between the mean, 0, and the desired number of standard deviations, z.

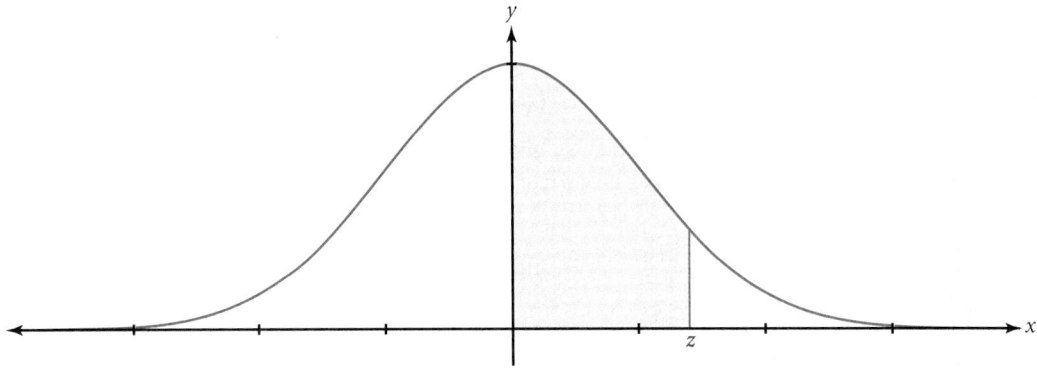

P(x < a) for a ≥ 0

a	0	1	2	3	4	5	6	7	8	9
0.0	.0000	.0040	.0080	.0120	.0160	.0199	.0239	.0279	.0319	.0359
0.1	.0398	.0438	.0478	.0517	.0557	.0596	.0636	.0675	.0714	.0753
0.2	.0793	.0832	.0871	.0910	.0948	.0987	.1026	.1064	.1103	.1141
0.3	.1179	.1217	.1255	.1293	.1331	.1368	.1406	.1443	.1480	.1517
0.4	.1554	.1591	.1628	.1664	.1700	.1736	.1772	.1808	.1844	.1879
0.5	.1915	.1950	.1985	.2019	.2054	.2088	.2123	.2157	.2190	.2224
0.6	.2257	.2291	.2324	.2357	.2389	.2422	.2454	.2486	.2518	.2549
0.7	.2580	.2612	.2642	.2673	.2704	.2734	.2764	.2794	.2823	.2852
0.8	.2881	.2910	.2939	.2967	.2995	.3023	.3051	.3078	.3106	.3133
0.9	.3159	.3186	.3212	.3238	.3264	.3289	.3315	.3340	.3365	.3389
1.0	.3413	.3438	.3461	.3485	.3508	.3531	.3554	.3577	.3599	.3621
1.1	.3643	.3665	.3686	.3708	.3729	.3749	.3770	.3790	.3810	.3830
1.2	.3849	.3869	.3888	.3907	.3925	.3944	.3962	.3980	.3997	.4015
1.3	.4032	.4049	.4066	.4082	.4099	.4115	.4131	.4147	.4162	.4177
1.4	.4192	.4207	.4222	.4236	.4251	.4265	.4279	.4292	.4306	.4319
1.5	.4332	.4345	.4357	.4370	.4382	.4394	.4406	.4418	.4429	.4441
1.6	.4452	.4463	.4474	.4484	.4495	.4505	.4515	.4525	.4535	.4545
1.7	.4554	.4564	.4573	.4582	.4591	.4599	.4608	.4616	.4625	.4633
1.8	.4641	.4649	.4656	.4664	.4671	.4678	.4686	.4693	.4699	.4706
1.9	.4713	.4719	.4726	.4732	.4738	.4744	.4750	.4756	.4761	.4767
2.0	.4772	.4778	.4783	.4788	.4793	.4798	.4803	.4808	.4812	.4817
2.1	.4821	.4826	.4830	.4834	.4838	.4842	.4846	.4850	.4854	.4857
2.2	.4861	.4864	.4868	.4871	.4875	.4878	.4881	.4884	.4887	.4890
2.3	.4893	.4896	.4898	.4901	.4904	.4906	.4909	.4911	.4913	.4916
2.4	.4918	.4920	.4922	.4925	.4927	.4929	.4931	.4932	.4934	.4936
2.5	.4938	.4940	.4941	.4943	.4945	.4946	.4948	.4949	.4951	.4952
2.6	.4953	.4955	.4956	.4957	.4959	.4960	.4961	.4962	.4963	.4964
2.7	.4965	.4966	.4967	.4968	.4969	.4970	.4971	.4972	.4973	.4974
2.8	.4974	.4975	.4976	.4977	.4977	.4978	.4979	.4979	.4980	.4981
2.9	.4981	.4982	.4982	.4983	.4984	.4984	.4985	.4985	.4986	.4986
3.0	.4986	.4987	.4987	.4988	.4988	.4989	.4989	.4989	.4990	.4990

Glossary

absolute value For any real number x, $|x| = x$ if $x \geq 0$ and $|x| = -x$ if $x < 0$. On a number line, $|x|$ is the distance from x to 0. (62)

absolute value of a complex number The distance of the complex number $a + bi$ from the origin in the complex plane, denoted $|a + bi| = \sqrt{a^2 + b^2}$. (318)

absolute-value function A function described by $f(x) = |x|$. (127)

additive inverse matrix The scalar product of a matrix and -1. (219)

adjacency matrix A representation of a network that indicates how many one-stage (direct) paths are possible from one vertex to another. (228)

amplitude The amplitude of a periodic function is one-half of the difference between the maximum and minimum function values and is always positive. (860)

angle of depression The angle formed by a horizontal line and a line of sight to a point below. (831)

angle of elevation The angle formed by a horizontal line and a line of sight to a point above. (831)

angle of rotation The angle formed by a ray that is rotated around its endpoint. (836)

arc length The length of the arc intercepted by a central angle with a radian measure of θ in a circle with a radius of r is given by the equation $s = r\theta$. (853)

arithmetic means The terms between any two nonconsecutive terms of an arithmetic sequence. (702)

arithmetic sequence A sequence whose successive terms differ by the same number, d, called the common difference. (700)

arithmetic series The indicated sum of the terms of an arithmetic sequence. (707)

asymptote A line that a curve approaches (but does not reach) as its x- or y-values become very large or very small. (362)

asymptotes of a hyperbola The diagonals of the rectangle that is determined by the vertices and co-vertices. (597)

augmented matrix A matrix that consists of the coefficients and the constant terms in a system of linear equations. (251)

axis of symmetry of a parabola A line that divides the parabola into two parts that are mirror images of each other. (276, 310)

base In an exponential expression of the form b^x, b is the base. (94, 362)

binomial A polynomial with exactly two terms. (425)

binomial experiment A probability experiment that meets the following conditions: The experiment consists of n trials whose outcomes are either successes or failures, and the trials are identical and independent with a constant probability of success, p, and a constant probability of failure, $1 - p$. (799)

binomial probability In a binomial experiment consisting of n trials, the probability, P, of r successes (where $0 \leq r \leq n$, p is the probability is of success, and $1 - p$ is the probability of failure) is given by the equation $P = {}_nC_r\, p^5(1 - p)^{n-r}$. (800)

Binomial Theorem A theorem that tells how to expand a positive integer power of a binomial. (742)

box-and-whisker plot A summary display of how values are distributed within a data set. (783)

center A fixed point that is used to define a circle, ellipse, or hyperbola. (579, 587, 596)

change-of-base formula For any positive real numbers $a \neq 1$, $b \neq 1$, and $x > 0$, $\log_b x = \dfrac{\log_a x}{\log_a b}$. (388)

circle graph A display of the distribution of non-overlapping parts of a whole by using sectors of a circle. (776)

circle The set of all points in a plane that are at a constant distance, called the radius, from a fixed point, called the center. (579)

circular permutation An arrangement of distinct objects in a specified order around a circle. (639)

coefficient The numerical factor of a monomial. (425)

combination An arrangement of a group of objects in which order is *not* important. (643)

combined variation A relationship containing both direct and inverse variation. (484)

common difference The number by which successive terms of an arithmetic sequence differ. (700)

common logarithm A logarithm whose base is 10. (385)

common ratio The ratio by which successive terms of a geometric sequence differ. (713)

complement The complement of event A consists of all outcomes in the sample space that are not in A, denoted A^c. (654)

completing the square A process used to form a perfect-square trinomial. (300)

Complex Conjugate Root Theorem If P is a polynomial function with real-number coefficients and $a + bi$ (where $b \neq 0$) is a root of $P(x) = 0$, then $a - bi$ is also a root of $P(x) = 0$. (461)

complex fraction A quotient that contains one or more fractions in the numerator, the denominator, or both. (500)

complex number Any number that can be written as $a + bi$, where a and b are real numbers and $i = \sqrt{-1}$. (316)

complex plane A set of coordinates axes in which the horizontal axis is the real axis and the vertical axis is the imaginary axis; used to graph complex numbers. (318)

composition of functions The composition of functions f and g, $(f \circ g)(x)$, is defined as $(f(g(x))$. The domain of f must include the range of g. (113)

compound inequalities A pair of inequalities combined by the words *and* or *or*. (56)

conditional probability The probability of event B, given that event A has happened (or will occur), denoted $P(B|A)$. (665)

conic section A plane figure formed by the intersection of a double cone and a plane. (562)

conjugate axis The axis of symmetry of a hyperbola that is perpendicular to the transverse axis. (596)

conjugate of a complex number The conjugate of a complex number $a + bi$ is $a - bi$, denoted $\overline{a + bi}$. (318)

consistent system A system of equations or inequalities that has at least one solution. (157)

constant A monomial with no variables. (425)

constant function A constant function is a function of the form $f(x) = k$. (125)

constant of variation The constant k in an inverse-, joint-, or combined-variation equation. (480)

constraints The inequalities that form the feasible region in a linear-programming problem. (187)

continuous compounding formula If P dollars are invested at an interest rate, r, that is compounded continuously, then the amount, A, of the investment at time t is given by $A = Pe^{rt}$. (393)

continuous function A function whose graph is an unbroken line or smooth curve. (105, 434)

converge Describes a infinite series whose partial sums approach a fixed number as n increases. (729)

Corner-Point Principle A principle in linear programming that identifies the maximum and minimum values of the objective function as occurring at one of the vertices of the feasible region. (189)

correlation coefficient A number represented by the variable r, where $-1 \leq r \leq 1$, that describes how closely points in a scatter plot cluster around the least-squares line. (39)

coterminal angle Describes angles that have the same terminal side when in standard position. (837)

co-vertices The endpoints of the minor axis of an ellipse; the endpoints of the conjugate axis of a hyperbola. (587, 596)

cube root A number, $\sqrt[3]{x}$, that when multiplied by itself three times produces the given number, x. (523)

decreasing function For a function f and any numbers x_1 and x_2 in the domain of f, the function f is decreasing over an open interval if for every $x_1 < x_2$ in the interval, $f(x_1) > f(x_2)$. (433)

degree of a monomial The sum of the exponents of the variables in the monomial. (425)

degree of a polynomial The degree of the monomial with the highest degree after simplification. (425)

degree The most common unit for angle measure; one degree, $1°$, is defined as $\frac{1}{360}$ of a complete rotation of a ray. (836)

dependent events Two events are dependent if the occurrence of one event affects the occurrence of the other, or if the events are not independent. (660)

dependent system A system of equations that has infinitely many solutions. (157)

dependent variable The output of a function. For $y = f(x)$, $f(x)$ is the dependent variable. (106)

determinant A real number associated with a square matrix. (238)

diameter A chord of a circle that contains the center of the circle. (566)

dimensions of a matrix A matrix of m horizontal rows and n vertical columns has the dimension $m \times n$. (216)

direct variation The equation $y = kx$ describes a direct variation, where y varies directly as x, k is the constant of variation, and $k \neq 0$. (29)

directrix A fixed line used to define a parabola. (570)

discontinuous function A function whose graph has breaks or holes in it. (434)

discrete function A function whose graph consists of points that are not connected. (105)

discriminant The discriminant of a quadratic equation $ax^2 + bx + c = 0$ is $b^2 - 4ac$. (314)

distance formula The distance, d, between $P(x_1, y_1)$ and $Q(x_2, y_2)$ is $d = \sqrt{(x_2 - x_1)^2 + (y_2 - y_1)^2}$. (563)

diverge Describes a infinite series whose partial sums do not approach a fixed number as n increases. (729)

domain The set of possible values for the first coordinate of a function. (102, 104)

double root For a quadratic equation, if $b^2 - 4ac = 0$, the equation has only one solution, called a double root. (314)

effective yield The annually compounded interest rate that yields the final amount of an investment. (365)

elementary row operations Operations performed on a matrix that result in an equivalent matrix. (252)

elimination method A method of solving a system of equations by multiplying and combining the equations in the system in order to eliminate a variable. (164)

ellipse The set of all points P in a plane such that the sum of the distances from P to two fixed points, F_1 and F_2, called the foci, is a constant. (587)

end behavior What happens to a polynomial function as its domain values get very small and very large. (435)

entry Each value in a matrix; also called an element. (216)

equation A statement of equality between two expressions that may be true or false. (45)

equivalent equations Equations that have the same solution set. (48)

even function A function f for which $f(-x) = f(x)$ for all values of x in its domain. (911)

event An individual outcome or any specified combination of outcomes. (628)

excluded values Real numbers for which a rational function is not defined. (491)

experimental probability A probability approximated by performing trials and recording the ratio of the number of occurrences of the event to the number of trials. (629)

explicit formula A formula that defines the nth term, or general term, of a sequence. (691)

exponential expression An algebraic expression in which the exponent is a variable and the base is a fixed number. (355)

exponential function A function of the form $f(x) = b^x$, where b is a positive real number other than 1 and x is any real number. (362)

exponential growth and decay Represented by a function of the form $f(x) = b^x$, where $b > 1$ or $0 < b < 1$, respectively. (363)

Exponential-Logarithmic Inverse Property For $b > 0$ and $b \neq 0$, $\log_b b^x = x$ and $b^{\log_b x} = x$ for $x > 0$. (380)

extraneous solution A solution to a derived equation that is not a solution to the original equation. (514)

Factor Theorem For a polynomial $P(x)$, if and only if $P(r) = 0$, then $x - r$ is a factor $P(x)$. (442)

factorial If n is a positive integer, then n factorial, written $n!$, is given by $n \times (n-1) \times (n-2) \times \cdots \times 2 \times 1$. (636)

factoring The process that allows a sum to be written as a product. (290)

feasible region The solution set of a linear-programming problem. (187)

finite sequence A sequence that ends and therefore has a last term. (691)

foci Fixed points that are used to define an ellipse or hyperbola. (587, 595)

focus A fixed point used to define a parabola. (570)

frequency table A table that lists the number of times, or frequency, that each data value appears. (767)

function A relation in which, for each first coordinate, there is exactly *one* corresponding second coordinate. (102)

function notation A function is usually defined in terms of x and y, where $y = f(x)$, x is the independent variable, and $f(x)$ is the dependent variable. (106)

Fundamental Counting Principle If there are m ways that one event can occur and n ways that another event can occur, then there are $m \times n$ ways that both events can occur. (631)

Fundamental Theorem of Algebra Every polynomial function with degree $n \geq 1$ has at least one complex zero. Corollary: Every polynomial function with degree $n \geq 1$ has exactly n complex zeros, counting multiplicities. (462)

geometric means The terms between any two nonconsecutive terms of a geometric sequence. (716)

geometric sequence A sequence in which the ratio of successive terms is the same number, r, called the common ratio. (713)

geometric series The indicated sum of the terms of a geometric sequence. (720)

greatest-integer function A function denoted by $f(x) = [x]$ that converts a real number, x, into the largest integer that is less than or equal to x. (125)

grouped frequency table A frequency table in which the values are grouped into classes that contain a range of data values. (767)

histogram A bar graph that gives the frequency of each value in a data set. (774)

hole in the graph If the factor $x - b$ is a factor of both the numerator and denominator of a rational function, then a hole occurs in the graph of the rational function when $x = b$. (494)

horizontal line A line with slope of 0. (16)

horizontal-line test If a horizontal line crosses the graph of a function in more than one point, the inverse of the function is not a function. (120)

hyperbola The set of all points P in a plane such that the absolute value of the difference between the distances from P to two fixed points in the plane, F_1 and F_2, called the foci, is a constant. (595)

identity function A linear function defined by $I(x) = x$. (120)

identity matrix for multiplication An $n \times n$ matrix with 1s along the main diagonal (upper left entry to lower right entry) and 0s elsewhere. (235)

imaginary axis The vertical axis in the complex plane. (318)

imaginary part of a complex number For a complex number $a + bi$, b is the imaginary part. (316)

imaginary unit The imaginary unit i is defined as $i = \sqrt{-1}$ and $i^2 = -1$. (315)

inclusive events Events which can occur at the same time. (652)

inconsistent system A system of equations or inequalities that has no solution. (157)

increasing function For a function f and any numbers x_1 and x_2 in the domain of f, the function f is increasing over an open interval if for every $x_1 < x_2$ in the interval, $f(x_1) < f(x_2)$. (433)

independent events Two events are independent if the occurrence (or non-occurrence) of one event has no effect on the likelihood of the occurrence of the other event. (660)

independent system A system of equations that has exactly one solution. (157)

independent variable The input of a function. For $y = f(x)$, x is the independent variable. (106)

inequality A mathematical sentence that contains $>, <, \geq, \leq$, or $\neq$. (54)

infinite geometric series A geometric series with infinitely many terms. (729)

infinite sequence A sequence that continues without end. (691)

initial side The initial position of a rotated ray. (836)

interquartile range (IQR) The difference between the upper and lower quartiles of a data set. (782)

inverse of a matrix If A is an $n \times n$ matrix with an inverse, then A^{-1} is its inverse matrix, and $AA^{-1} = A^{-1}A = I$. (235)

inverse of a relation The inverse of a relation consisting of the ordered pairs (x, y) is the set of all ordered pairs (y, x). (118)

inverse variation Two variables, x and y, have an inverse-variation relationship if there is a nonzero number k such that $xy = k$, or $y = \frac{k}{x}$. (480)

irrational number A number whose decimal part does not terminate or repeat. (86)

joint variation If $y = kxz$ where k is a nonzero constant, then y varies jointly as x and z ($x \neq 0$ and $z \neq 0$). (482)

law of cosines For $\triangle ABC$, $a^2 = b^2 + c^2 - 2bc \cos A$, $b^2 = a^2 + c^2 - 2ac \cos B$, $c^2 = a^2 + b^2 - 2ab \cos C$. (895)

law of sines For $\triangle ABC$, $\frac{\sin A}{a} = \frac{\sin B}{b} = \frac{\sin C}{c}$. (887)

leading coefficient The coefficient of the term with the highest degree. (435)

least-squares line A linear model that fits a data set. (38)

like terms Two or more monomials that can only differ in their coefficients. (46)

linear equation An equation whose graph is a line. (5)

linear permutation A arrangement of objects in a specified order in a straight line. (636)

linear programming A method of finding a maximum or a minimum value that satisfies all of the given conditions of a particular situation. (187)

linearly related A relationship in which a constant difference in consecutive x-values results in a constant difference in consecutive y-values. (5)

literal equation An equation that contains two or more variables. (47)

local maximum For a function f, $f(a)$ is a local maximum if there is an interval around a such that $f(a) > f(x)$ for all values of x in the interval, where $x \neq a$. (433)

local minimum For a function f, $f(a)$ is a local minimum if there is an interval around a such that $f(a) < f(x)$ for all values of x in the interval, where $x \neq a$. (433)

Location Principle If P is a polynomial function and $P(x_1)$ and $P(x_2)$ have opposite signs, then there is a real number r between x_1 and x_2 that is a zero of P, that is $P(r) = 0$. (450)

logarithmic function A function of the form $y = \log_b x$ with base b, or $x = b^y$, which is the inverse of the exponential function $y = b^x$, where $b \neq 1$ and $b > 0$. (372)

major axis The longer axis of an ellipse. (587)

mathematical induction A type of mathematical proof that uses the following two steps to prove a statement for all natural numbers n: the basis step, which shows that the statement is true for $n = 1$, and the induction step, which assumes that the statement is true for a natural number, k, and proves that the statement is true for the natural number $k + 1$. (722)

matrix Any rectangular array of numbers enclosed in a single set of brackets. (216)

matrix equation An equation of the form $AX = B$, where A is the coefficient matrix, X is the variable matrix, and B is the constant matrix. (244)

matrix multiplication If matrix A has dimension $m \times n$ and matrix B has dimensions $n \times r$, then the product AB has dimensions $m \times r$. (226)

mean The sum of all of the values in a data set divided by the number of values; also called arithmetic average. (764)

mean deviation The average amount that the values in a data set differ from the mean. (792)

median The middle value, denoted Q_2, in a data set that is arranged in ascending or descending order. If there are an even number of data values, the median is the mean of the two middle values. (764)

midpoint formula The coordinates of the midpoint, M, between two points $P(x_1, y_1)$ and $Q(x_2, y_2)$ are $M\left(\frac{x_1 + x_2}{2}, \frac{y_1 + y_2}{2}\right)$. (565)

minor axis The shorter axis of an ellipse. (587)

mode The value in a data set that occurs most often. There can be one, more than one, or no mode. (764)

monomial A numeral, variable, or product of a numeral and one or more variables. (425)

multiplicity The number of times that a factor is repeated in the factorization of a polynomial expression. (449)

multiplier The base of an exponential expression. (355)

mutually exclusive events Events that cannot occur at the same time. (652)

natural base The irrational number e, which is approximately equal to 2.71828... (393)

natural exponential function An exponential function with base e; $f(x) = e^x$. (393)

natural logarithmic function The function $y = \log_e x$, the inverse of the natural exponential function. (394)

normal distribution Data that varies randomly from the mean, creating a bell-shaped pattern that is symmetric about the mean when graphed. (806)

objective function The function to be maximized or minimized in a linear-programming problem. (187)

odd function A function f for which $f(-x) = -f(x)$ for all values of x in its domain. (911)

one-to-one A one-to-one function can be intersected by a horizontal line at no more than one point. The inverse of a one-to-one function is also a function. (120)

One-to-One Property of Exponents If $b^x = b^y$, then $x = y$. (372)

One-to-One Property of Logarithms If $\log_b x = \log_b y$, then $x = y$. (380)

outlier A data value that is less than $Q_1 - 1.5(IQR)$ or greater than $Q_3 + 1.5(IQR)$. (782)

parabola The graph of a quadratic function. (276) The set of all points $P(x, y)$ in the plane whose distance to a point, called the focus, equals the distance to a fixed line, called the directrix. (570)

parallel lines Two lines (in the same plane) that have the same slope. All vertical lines are parallel and all horizontal lines are parallel. (23)

parametric equations A pair of continuous functions that define the x- and y-coordinates of a point in a coordinate plane in terms of a third variable. (196)

99 BANK

partial sum The sum of a specified number of terms of an infinite geometric series. (728)

Pascal's triangle A triangular pattern formed by the coefficients of binomial expansion. (735)

period The smallest positive number p that satisfies the equation in the definition of a periodic function. (846)

periodic function Describes functions for which there is a number p such that $f(x + p) = f(x)$ for every x in the domain of f. (846)

permutation An arrangement of objects in a specified order. (636)

perpendicular lines Two lines whose slopes are negative reciprocals of one another. All vertical and horizontal lines are perpendicular. (24)

phase shift A horizontal translation of a sine or cosine function. (861)

piecewise function A function that consists of different function rules for different parts of the domain. (124)

point-slope form The point-slope form of a line is $y - y_1 = m(x - x_1)$, where m is the slope and (x_1, y_1) is the coordinates of a point on the line. (22)

polynomial A monomial or a sum of terms that are monomials. (425)

polynomial function A function that is defined by a polynomial. (427)

power An expression of the form a^n. (94)

Power Property of Logarithms For $m > 0$, $b > 0$, $b \neq 1$, and any real number p, $\log_b m^p = p \log_b m$. (379)

Principle of Powers If $a = b$ and n is a positive integer, then $a^n = b^n$. (536)

principal square root The positive square root of a number a, denoted $\sqrt{a}$. (281)

principal values The restricted domains of the Sine, Cosine, and Tangent functions. (868)

probability The overall likelihood of the occurrence of an event. (628)

Product Property of Logarithms For $m > 0$, $n > 0$, and $b \neq 1$, $\log_b(mn) = \log_b m + \log_b n$. (378)

Product Property of Radicals For $a \geq 0$. $b \geq 0$, and a positive integer n, $\sqrt[n]{ab} = \sqrt[n]{a} \cdot \sqrt[n]{b}$ (529)

Product Property of Square Roots If $a \geq 0$ and $b \geq 0$, then $\sqrt{ab} = \sqrt{a} \cdot \sqrt{b}$. (281)

Properties of nth Roots For any real number a, $\sqrt[n]{a^n} = |a|$ if n is a positive even integer, and $\sqrt[n]{a^n} = a$ if n is a positive odd integer. (529)

proportion An equation that states that two ratios are equal. (31)

Pythagorean Theorem If $\triangle ABC$ is a right triangle with the right angle at C, the $a^2 + b^2 = c^2$. (284)

quadratic expression An expression of the form $ax^2 + bx + c$, where $a \neq 0$. (275)

quadratic formula The quadratic formula, $\dfrac{-b \pm \sqrt{b^2 - 4ac}}{2a}$, gives the solutions of the quadratic equation $ax^2 + bx + c = 0$ and $a \neq 0$. (308)

quadratic function Any function that can be written in the form $f(x) = ax^2 + bx + c$, where $a \neq 0$. (275)

quadratic inequality in two variables An inequality that can be written in one of the following forms, where a, b, and c are real numbers and $a \neq 0$: $y \geq ax^2 + bx + c$, $y > ax^2 + bx + c$, $y \leq ax^2 + bx + c$, and $y < ax^2 + bx + c$. (333)

quartiles Two values that, along with the median (Q_2), divide a data set into quarters; there is a lower quartile, Q_1, and an upper quartile, Q_3. (782)

Quotient Property of Logarithms For $m > 0$, $n > 0$, and $b \neq 1$, $\log_b \frac{m}{n} = \log_b m - \log_b n$. (378)

Quotient Property of Radicals For $a \geq 0$. $b \geq 0$, and a positive integer n, $\sqrt[n]{\frac{a}{b}} = \frac{\sqrt[n]{a}}{\sqrt[n]{b}}$, where $b \neq 0$. (529)

Quotient Property of Square Roots If $a \geq 0$ and $b \geq 0$, then $\sqrt{\frac{a}{b}} = \frac{\sqrt{a}}{\sqrt{b}}$. (281)

radian A unit of angle measure that is equal to $\frac{1}{2\pi}$ of the circumference of the unit circle; 1 radian is equal to approximately 57°. (852)

radical equation An equation that contains at least one radical expression with a variable in the radicand. (536)

radical expression An expression that contains at least one radical symbol. (524)

radical function A function that contains at least one radical expression. (524)

radical inequality An inequality that contains at least one radical expression. (540)

radical symbol The symbol $\sqrt{\ }$ in a radical expression. (524)

radicand The number or expression under a radical symbol. (524)

radius A segment with one endpoint at the center of the circle and the other endpoint on the circle. (566)

random Describes outcomes whose occurrences are all equally likely. (628)

range The set of possible values for the second coordinate of a function. (102, 104) The absolute value of the difference between the largest value and the smallest value of a data set. (782)

rational equation An equation that contains at least one rational expression. (512)

rational expression The quotient of two polynomials. (489)

rational function A function defined by a rational expression. (489)

rational inequality An inequality that contains at least one rational expression. (515)

rational number A number that can be expressed as the quotient of two integers, where the denominator is not equal to zero. (86)

Rational Root Theorem Let P be a polynomial function with integers coefficients in standard form. If $\frac{p}{q}$ (in lowest terms) is a root of $P(x) = 0$, then p is a factor of the constant term of P and q is a factor of the leading coefficient of P. (458)

rationalizing the denominator The process of removing an imaginary number from the denominator of a quotient. (318) A procedure that involves transforming a quotient with a radical in the denominator into an expression with no radical in the denominator. (532)

real axis The horizontal axis in the complex plane. (318)

real number Any rational or irrational number. (86)

real part of a complex number For a complex number $a + bi$, a is the real part. (316)

recursive formula A formula for a sequence in which one or more previous terms are used to generate the next term. (691)

reduced row-echelon form An augmented matrix is in this form if the coefficient columns form an identity matrix. (252)

reference angle For an angle in standard position, the reference angle, θ_{ref}, is the positive acute angle formed by the terminal side of θ and the nearest part (positive or negative) of the x-axis. (837)

relation Any set of ordered pairs. (104)

relative frequency table A frequency table that includes a column showing how frequently each value appears relative to the entire data set. (775)

Remainder Theorem If the polynomial expression that defines the function P is divided by $x - a$, then the remainder is the number $P(a)$. (444)

roots Solutions to an equation. (449)

rounding-up function The function, denoted $f(x) = \lceil x \rceil$, that converts a real number, x, into the smallest integer greater than or equal to x. (125)

row-reduction method The process of performing elementary row operations on an augmented matrix to solve a system of equations and determine whether the system is independent, dependent, or inconsistent. (251)

sample space The set of all possible outcomes of an event. (628)

scalar multiplication Multiplication of each entry in a matrix by the same real number. (218)

scatter plot The graph of the ordered pairs that describe a relationship between two sets of data. (37)

sequence An ordered list of numbers. (691)

series The indicated sum of the terms of a sequence. (693)

sigma The Greek letter Σ, used to denote a series. (693)

simplest radical form The expression $\sqrt{a}$ is in simplest radical form if no factor of a is a perfect square. (530)

simulation A representation of events that are likely to occur in the real world that can be used to find experimental probabilities. (672)

slope-intercept form A linear equation in the form $y = mx + b$, where m represents the slope and b represents the y-intercept. (14)

slope of a line The ratio of the change in vertical direction to the corresponding change in the horizontal direction. (13)

solution A value that can replace a variable that makes an equation or inequality true. (45, 55)

solving a triangle Finding the measures of all of the unknown sides and angles of the triangle. (832)

square matrix A matrix that has the same number of columns and rows. (234)

square root A number, $\sqrt{x}$, that when multiplied by itself produces the given number, x. (520)

standard deviation A measure of dispersion for a data set, given by the formula $\sigma = \sqrt{\sigma^2}$. (794)

standard form The standard form of a linear equation is $Ax + By = C$, where A and B are not both 0. (15)

standard form of a quadratic equation A quadratic equation of the form $ax^2 + bx + c = 0$. (294)

standard normal curve A normal curve with a mean of 0 and a standard deviation of 1. (806)

standard position An angle is in standard position when its initial side lies along the x-axis and its endpoint is at the origin. (836)

stem-and-leaf plot A way of displaying a data set in which each data value is split into two parts, a stem and a leaf. (772)

step function A function whose graph looks like a series of steps. (125)

Substitution Property If $a = b$, then a may replace b in any statement containing a and the resulting statement will be true. (46)

summation notation A way to express a series in an abbreviated form by using the Greek letter sigma, Σ. (693)

synthetic division A method of division of a polynomial by a binomial in which only coefficients are used. (442)

system of equations A set of equations in the same variables. (156)

system of linear inequalities A set of linear inequalities in the same variables. (179)

system of nonlinear equations A set of equations in which at least one equation is nonlinear. (606)

tangent line A line that is perpendicular to a radius of a circle and that touches the circle at only one point. (863)

terminal side The final position of a rotated ray. (836)

terms Parts of an algebraic expression separated by addition or subtraction signs. (46) The numbers in a sequence. (691)

theoretical probability The theoretical probability of event A is defined by
$P(A) = \dfrac{\text{number of outcomes in event } A}{\text{number of outcomes in the sample space}}$. (629)

transformation An alteration in the function rule and its graph. (133)

transverse axis The axis of symmetry of a hyperbola that contains vertices and foci. (596)

trial A systematic opportunity for an event to occur. (628)

trigonometric equation An equation that includes at least one trigonometric function. (922)

trigonometric functions A function that uses one of the six trigonometric ratios to assign values to the measures of the acute angles of a right triangle, or angles of rotation. (829, 838)

trigonometric identity An equation that includes trigonometric functions and that is true for all values of the variables for which the expressions on each side of the equation are defined. (902)

trinomial A polynomial with three terms. (425)

turning points The points on the graph of a polynomial function that correspond to local maxima and minima. (433)

unit circle A circle centered at the origin with a radius of 1. (846)

variable A symbol used to represent one or many different numbers. (45)

variance A measure of dispersion for a data set, given by the formula $\sigma^2 = \dfrac{1}{n} \sum_{i=1}^{n} (x_i - \bar{x})^2$ where n is the number of values in the data set and $\bar{x}$ is the mean. (794)

vertex A point in a finite set of connected points called a network. (228)

vertex form of a parabola If the coordinates of the vertex of the graph of $y = ax^2 + bx + c$, where $a \neq 0$, are (h, k), then the parabola can be represented in vertex form as $y = a(x - h)^2 + k$. (302)

vertex of a parabola Either the lowest point on the graph or the highest point on the graph. (276) The midpoint between the focus and directrix. (571)

vertical-line test If a vertical line crosses the graph of a relation in more than one point, the relation is not a function. (103)

vertical line A line that has an undefined slope. (16)

vertices The endpoints of the major axis of an ellipse; the endpoints of the transverse axis of a hyperbola. (587, 596)

x-intercept The x-coordinate of the point where the graph crosses the x-axis. (15)

y-intercept The y-coordinate of the point where the graph of a line crosses the y-axis. (14)

zero of a function Any number r such that $f(r) = 0$. (294, 434)

Zero-Product Property If $pq = 0$, then $p = 0$ or $q = 0$. (294)

z-score A measure of how far a value is from the mean in terms of the standard deviation. (809)

Selected Answers

Chapter 1

LESSON 1.1

TRY THIS (p. 5)

a.

Time (min)	1	2	3	4
Volume (gal)	64	73	82	91

b.

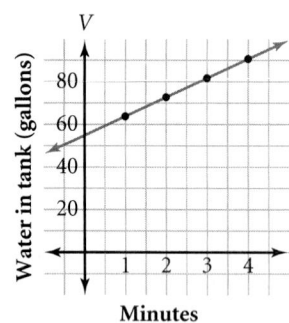

c. $V = 9t + 55$, where V is volume in gallons and t is time in minutes.
d. 235 gallons

TRY THIS (p. 6)

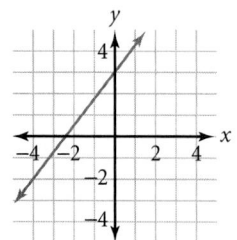

TRY THIS (p. 7)
The relationship is not linear because there is not a constant difference in the y-values.

Exercises

4a.

Weekly sales, x	Weekly income, y
100	$50 + (0.15)(100) = 65$
200	$50 + (0.15)(200) = 80$
300	$50 + (0.15)(300) = 95$
400	$50 + (0.15)(400) = 110$
x	$50 + (0.15)x = 0.15x + 50$

b.

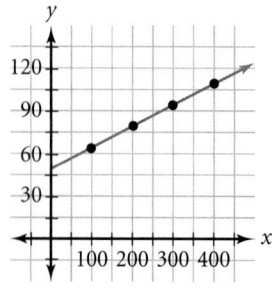

c. $y = 0.15x + 50$
d. $230

5.

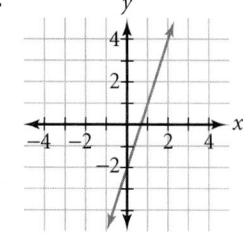

6. yes; $(26, 49)$ **7.** linear **9.** linear **11.** linear
13. not linear **15.** not linear **17.** linear

19.

21.

23.

25.

27.

29.

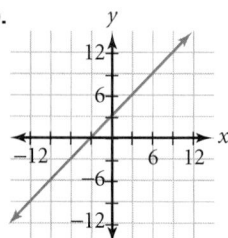

31. linear; $(4, 58)$ **33.** not linear **35.** linear; $(0, 4)$
37. not linear

39.

x	y
0	0
2	3
4	6
6	9

This is a linear relationship, because there is a constant difference of 2 in consecutive x-values and a constant difference of 3 in consecutive y-values.

41.

x	y
0	1
1	3
2	7

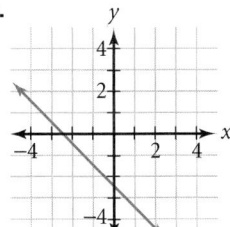

The point $(2, 6)$ is not on the line because $x = 2$ is paired with $y = 7$ in the table. The point $(2, 6)$ also does not make the equation true. Finally, the point $(2, 6)$ is not a point on the graph of $y = 4x - 1$.

43. **45.**

47.

49a.

x	y
0	6
1	9
2	12
3	15

b. $51 **c.** 7 videos
d. The answers to parts **b** and **c** could also be found by continuing the table and the graph until the desired ordered pairs are found.

51a.

Half-hours	Total charge ($)
0	$2 + (1)(0) = 2$
1	$2 + (1)(1) = 3$
2	$2 + (1)(2) = 4$
3	$2 + (1)(3) = 5$
10	$2 + (1)(10) = 12$

b.

c. $c = 2 + h$
d. 144; $146

53a.

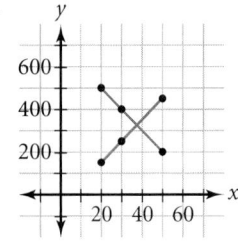

b. about $37; about $350 **c.** When the price is higher, supply is greater than demand. When the price is lower, supply is less than demand.

55. $a = 9$, $b = 4$ **57.** $a = 41$, $b = 2$ **59.** $a = 8$, $b = 16$
61. $a = 16$, $b = 3$ **63.** $\frac{2}{7}$ **65.** 2 **67.** 8 **69.** 24

LESSON 1.2

TRY THIS (p. 13)
$-\frac{7}{8}$

TRY THIS (p. 15, Ex. 2)

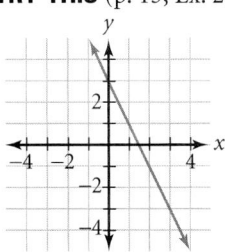

TRY THIS (p. 15, Ex. 3)
$y = x + 3$

TRY THIS (p. 16)

Exercises

5. $-\frac{7}{10}$

6.

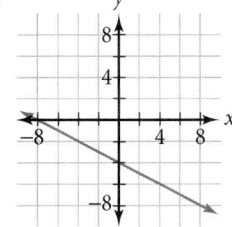

7. $y = \frac{1}{2}x - 3$

8.

9.

10.
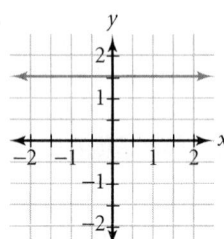

11. $y = 2x + 0.75$ **13.** $y = -3$ **15.** $y = -3x + 7$

17. $y = \frac{1}{4}x - \frac{3}{4}$ **19.** 10   **21.** 7   **23.** $\frac{7}{3}$ **25.** 1

27. $m = -2; b = 0$ **29.** $m = \frac{1}{3}; b = -7$

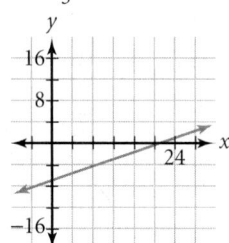

31. $m = 1; b = 0$ **33.** $m = 0.6; b = -4$

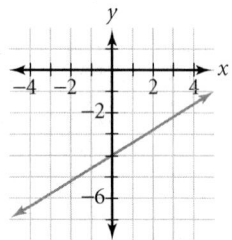

35. m is undefined; there is no y-intercept.

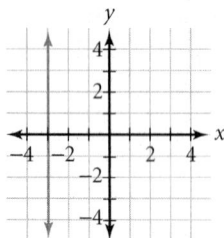

37. $y = \frac{3}{2}x - 1$ **39.** $y = -3x + 2$

41.

43.

45.

47.

49.

51.
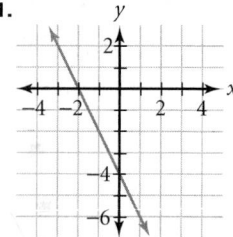

53. Slope is undefined.   **55.** slope = 0

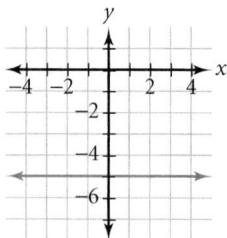

57. Slope is undefined.   **59.** slope = 0

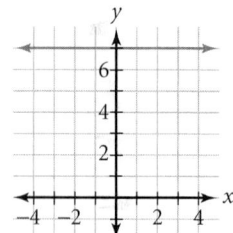

61. Slope is undefined.   **63.** slope = 0

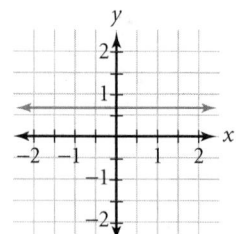

65a. $m = -600$ **b.** $b = 3600$ **c.** $y = -600x + 3600$, where $0 \le x \le 6$ **d.** $y = 900$

67a. Answers may vary. sample answer:
$50°F = 10°C$, $32°F = 0°C$

b.
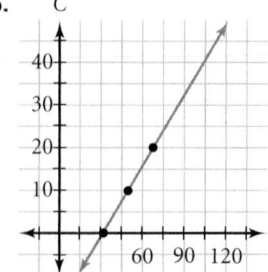

c. $m = \frac{5}{9}; b = -\frac{160}{9}$

d. $C = \frac{5}{9}F - \frac{160}{9}$

69a.

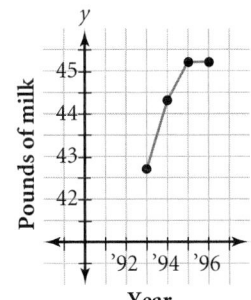

b. 1993–1994; 1.6 pounds per day **c.** 1995–1996; 0 pounds per day

71. \$160 **73.** Yes; there is a constant difference of 3 in the x-values and a constant difference of -2 in the y-values; $(10, -3)$.

LESSON 1.3

TRY THIS (p. 24)
$y = -4x - 16$

TRY THIS (p. 25)
$y = \frac{1}{4}x + \frac{21}{4}$

Exercises

5. $y = \frac{1}{2}x + \frac{3}{2}$ **6.** $y = 3x - 5$ **7.** 20 miles

8. $y = \frac{2}{5}x - \frac{37}{5}$ **9.** $y = \frac{5}{2}x + \frac{41}{2}$ **11.** $y = -x - 2$

13. $y = \frac{1}{7}x - \frac{18}{7}$ **15.** $x = -2$ **17.** $y = -\frac{3}{8}x$ **19.** $y = x - \frac{7}{2}$

21. $x = -5$ **23.** $y = -\frac{2}{3}x - 1$ **25.** $y = 5x + 2$ **27.** $y = 8$

29. $y = 3x + 21$ **31.** $y = -\frac{2}{3}x - \frac{2}{3}$ **33.** $y = 2.5x + 4$; slope represents average cost in dollars per item.

35. $y = -3x - 3$ **37.** $y = \frac{1}{2}x - 4$ **39.** $y = -\frac{2}{5}x - \frac{17}{5}$

41. $y = \frac{1}{2}x - \frac{3}{2}$ **43.** $y = \frac{1}{2}x + 6$ **45.** $y = x - 3$

47. $y = \frac{1}{3}x + \frac{13}{3}$ **49.** $y = -6x - 8$ **51.** $y = \frac{5}{2}x + 3$, or $5x - 2y = -6$ **53.** ℓ_1 is parallel to ℓ_2. **55.** ℓ_1 is perpendicular to ℓ_3. **57.** ℓ_2 is not perpendicular to ℓ_4.

59. $m_1 = \frac{4-1}{2-4} = \frac{3}{-2}$ $m_2 = \frac{0-(-3)}{-4-(-2)} = \frac{3}{-2}$

$m_3 = \frac{4-0}{2-(-4)} = \frac{2}{3}$ $m_4 = \frac{1-(-3)}{4-(-2)} = \frac{2}{3}$

There are two pairs of parallel sides, so the quadrilateral is a parallelogram.

61. slope of $D_1 = \frac{a-0}{0-a} = -1$; slope of $D_2 = \frac{a-0}{a-0} = 1$; the slopes are negative reciprocals of each other, so the diagonals are perpendicular.

63a. $y = \frac{3}{4}x + 30$ **b.** 64 **c.** 72

	Fraction	Decimal	Percent
65.	$\frac{1}{3}$	$0.0\overline{3}$	$33\frac{1}{3}\%$
67.	$\frac{1}{50}$	0.02	2%
69.	$\frac{1}{8}$	0.125	$12\frac{1}{2}\%$
71.	$\frac{1}{6}$	$0.1\overline{6}$	$16\frac{2}{3}\%$
73.	$\frac{4}{5}$	0.80	80%
75.	$\frac{9}{20}$	0.45	45%

77. 200 meters

LESSON 1.4

TRY THIS (p. 29)
$k = 5$; $y = 5x$

TRY THIS (p. 30)
72 minutes

TRY THIS (p. 32)
$x = 4$

Exercises

8. $k = 5$; $y = 5x$ **9.** 8375 feet **10a.** 20 **b.** $y = 6.35x$; the constant of variation is the hourly wage.

11. $x = 2$ **12.** $x = -3$ **13.** $x = 4$ **15.** $k = 2$; $y = 2x$

17. $k = 3$; $y = 3x$ **19.** $k = \frac{5}{3}$; $y = \frac{5}{3}x$

21. $k = -50$; $y = -50x$ **23.** $k = -0.4$; $y = -0.4x$

25. $k = 48$; $y = 48x$ **27.** $k = 20$; $y = 20x$ **29.** $k = -0.3$; $y = -0.3x$ **31.** $a = kb$ **33.** $b = 60$ **35.** $a = \frac{1}{2}$ **37.** $w = 3\frac{1}{3}$

39. $x = 12\frac{1}{2}$ **41.** $x = -2\frac{1}{10}$ **43.** $x = 9\frac{1}{3}$ **45.** $x = 5$

47. $x = -2$ **49.** $x = 8$ **51.** $x = 3$ **53.** yes; $y = 0.02x$

55. yes; $y = -\frac{1}{2}x$ **57.** No; there is no value of k such that $y = kx$ for every x in the table. **59.** If a varies directly as c, then $a = k_1c$ for some nonzero constant, k_1. If b varies directly as c, then $b = k_2c$ for some nonzero constant, k_2. Add each side of these equations together in order to get $a + b = (k_1 + k_2)c$. Because $k_1 + k_2$ is a nonzero constant, $a + b$ varies directly as c. **61.** $k = 0.11$; $m = 0.11g$ **63.** 35.2 grams **65.** 35 kilometers, 30 kilometers **67.** 10 amperes **69.** 0.29 ampere **71a.** 0.1875; $s = 0.1875w$; the constant represents the "stretchiness" of the spring as compared with that of other springs. **b.** 16 pounds **c.** 7.5 inches **73.** $2^2 \cdot 5 \cdot 43$ **75.** $2^2 \cdot 3^2 \cdot 5$

77. $2 \cdot 5 \cdot 7^2$ **79.** $\frac{2}{3}$ **81.** $-\frac{5}{14}$

LESSON 1.5

TRY THIS (p. 40)
about 13.66 minutes, or about 13:39.93

Exercises

9. strong negative correlation; $y \approx -0.8x + 9.2$
10. fairly strong positive correlation; $y \approx 0.83x + 1.1$
11. No reliable correlation; the calculator gives a least-squares line with equation $y \approx 0.8x + 1.4$, but the correlation coefficient is about -0.1. **12.** 112.58
13. fairly strong positive correlation; $y \approx 0.8x + 1.36$
15. $r = -1$ **17.** $r = 1$ **19.** $r \approx 0.63$ **21.** *Interpolate*—to estimate values (of a function) between two known values. *Extrapolate*—to predict by projecting past known data. **23a.** $y \approx 0.17x - 2.97$
b. $y \approx 0.52x - 26.91$

c. $r \approx 0.3$ for women; $r \approx 0.9$ for men; the data set for men is almost linear and has most of its data points clustered around the least-squares line. The data set for women is not very linear and has many of its data points away from the least-squares line. **d.** about a size 7.5 shoe **e.** about $11\frac{1}{2}$ **f.** about 6 feet and 3 inches **g.** about 5 feet and 5 inches **25a.** $y \approx -0.57x + 77.12$ **b.** $y \approx -0.94x + 111.97$ **c.** $r \approx -0.89$ for women; $r \approx -0.95$ for men; the data set for men is more linear than the data for women. **d.** about 32% **e.** about 46% **f.** about 1966 **g.** about 1996 **27.** $0.\overline{3}$ **29.** 4.25 **31.** 0.35 **33.** 25 **35.** $m = -1.6$

LESSON 1.6

TRY THIS (p. 47, Ex. 2)   **TRY THIS** (p. 47, Ex. 3)
$x = \frac{3}{2}$ $x \approx 1.25$

Exercises

6. $x = 2$ **7.** $x = 5$ **8.** $x = -1$ **9.** $x = 2$ **10.** $x \approx -1.28$
11. $y = -\frac{A}{B}x + \frac{C}{B}$ **13.** $x = -8$ **15.** $x = \frac{8}{3}$ **17.** $x = 3$
19. $x = -3$ **21.** $x = -8$ **23.** $x = \frac{5}{9}$ **25.** $x = -2$

27. $x = -5$ **29.** $x = 3$ **31.** $x = \frac{40}{3}$ **33.** $x = 3$ **35.** $x = \frac{12}{11}$
37. $x = \frac{78}{7}$ **39.** $x = \frac{2}{3}$ **41.** $x \approx 1.12$ **43.** $x \approx 10.75$
45. $x \approx 11.08$ **47.** $b = \frac{2A}{h}$ **49.** $r_2 = -\frac{r_1 R}{R - r_1}$, or $\frac{R r_1}{r_1 - R}$

51. $h = \frac{2A}{b_1 + b_2}$ **53.** $x = -\frac{b - d}{a - c}$, or $\frac{d - b}{a - c}$ **55.** $r = \frac{I - P}{Pt}$
57. $v = \frac{x}{t}$ **59.** $v = \frac{2y}{x}$ **61.** $x = 13$ **63.** $s = \frac{A - \pi r^2}{\pi r}$
65. 7 years **67.** 30 pairs of shoes **69.** 8 hours

71. about 35 hours

73. slope $= -\frac{3}{4}$;
y-intercept $= \frac{9}{4}$

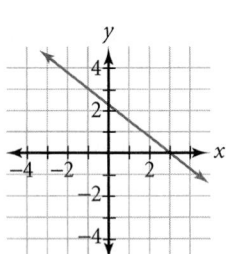

75. 57,360 **77.** 46,720,000 **79.** 2.5×10^4
81. 2.6007×10^2 **83.** 5×10^{-2}

LESSON 1.7

TRY THIS (p. 55, Ex. 1)
$x < \frac{11}{3}$
TRY THIS (p. 55, Ex. 2)
$t < -1$

TRY THIS (p. 57, Ex. 4)
$x \le 1$ *and* $x > -7$

TRY THIS (p. 57, Ex. 5)
$x \le \frac{5}{2}$ *or* $x > 5$

Exercises

5. $x < 4$

6. $q > 5$

7. $t \ge 76$

8. $x \ge -2$ *and* $x < 6$

9. $x \ge -7$ *or* $x > 5$

11. $x > -1$ **13.** $x \ge -1$ **15.** $x \le 5$ **17.** $x \ge 2$ **19.** $x < 3$

21. $x > 2$

23. $x < -2$

25. $x < 2$

27. $y < -8$

29. $x \ge 11$

31. $x \le 150$

33. $x \ge -6$

35. $x < -15$

37. $x \le 9$

39. $t > -64$

41. $x \le \frac{1}{4}$

$$\begin{array}{ccccccccccccc} \hline -6 & -5 & -4 & -3 & -2 & -1 & 0 & 1 & 2 & 3 & 4 & 5 & 6 \end{array}$$

43. $a < 5$

$$\begin{array}{ccccccccccccc} \hline -6 & -5 & -4 & -3 & -2 & -1 & 0 & 1 & 2 & 3 & 4 & 5 & 6 \end{array}$$

45. $x \ge 15$

$$\begin{array}{ccccc} \hline -30 & -15 & 0 & 15 & 30 \end{array}$$

47. $x \ge -4$

$$\begin{array}{ccccccccccccc} \hline -6 & -5 & -4 & -3 & -2 & -1 & 0 & 1 & 2 & 3 & 4 & 5 & 6 \end{array}$$

49. $x \le -\frac{6}{19}$

$$\begin{array}{ccccccccccccc} \hline -6 & -5 & -4 & -3 & -2 & -1 & 0 & 1 & 2 & 3 & 4 & 5 & 6 \end{array}$$

51a. $x < -4$

$$\begin{array}{ccccccccccccc} \hline -6 & -5 & -4 & -3 & -2 & -1 & 0 & 1 & 2 & 3 & 4 & 5 & 6 \end{array}$$

b. no solution

c. $x < 2$

$$\begin{array}{ccccccccccccc} \hline -6 & -5 & -4 & -3 & -2 & -1 & 0 & 1 & 2 & 3 & 4 & 5 & 6 \end{array}$$

d. $x < -4$ or $x > 2$

$$\begin{array}{ccccccccccccc} \hline -6 & -5 & -4 & -3 & -2 & -1 & 0 & 1 & 2 & 3 & 4 & 5 & 6 \end{array}$$

53. $y < 6$ and $y > 3$

$$\begin{array}{ccccccccccccc} \hline -6 & -5 & -4 & -3 & -2 & -1 & 0 & 1 & 2 & 3 & 4 & 5 & 6 \end{array}$$

55. $x < -3$ or $x > 4$

$$\begin{array}{ccccccccccccc} \hline -6 & -5 & -4 & -3 & -2 & -1 & 0 & 1 & 2 & 3 & 4 & 5 & 6 \end{array}$$

57. $y \ge 3$ and $y \ge -6$

$$\begin{array}{ccccccccccccc} \hline -6 & -5 & -4 & -3 & -2 & -1 & 0 & 1 & 2 & 3 & 4 & 5 & 6 \end{array}$$

59. $x \le -4$ or $x \ge 3$

$$\begin{array}{ccccccccccccc} \hline -6 & -5 & -4 & -3 & -2 & -1 & 0 & 1 & 2 & 3 & 4 & 5 & 6 \end{array}$$

61. $t > 2$ and $t < 4$

$$\begin{array}{ccccccccccccc} \hline -6 & -5 & -4 & -3 & -2 & -1 & 0 & 1 & 2 & 3 & 4 & 5 & 6 \end{array}$$

63. $d > -8$ and $d < 1$

$$\begin{array}{ccccccccccc} \hline -10 & -8 & -6 & -4 & -2 & 0 & 2 & 4 & 6 & 8 & 10 & 12 \end{array}$$

65. $x \ge 4$ or $x \le -3$

$$\begin{array}{ccccccccccccc} \hline -6 & -5 & -4 & -3 & -2 & -1 & 0 & 1 & 2 & 3 & 4 & 5 & 6 \end{array}$$

67. $x > -4$ or $x \le -5$

$$\begin{array}{ccccccccccccc} \hline -6 & -5 & -4 & -3 & -2 & -1 & 0 & 1 & 2 & 3 & 4 & 5 & 6 \end{array}$$

69. $m > -\frac{9}{4}$ and $m \le -\frac{5}{2}$; no solution

71. $x > -5$ or $x \le 4$; all real numbers

$$\begin{array}{ccccccccccccc} \hline -6 & -5 & -4 & -3 & -2 & -1 & 0 & 1 & 2 & 3 & 4 & 5 & 6 \end{array}$$

73. $60 or greater **75.** less than 370 fat calories

77. slope $= -2$ **79.** slope $= \frac{1}{3}$ **81.** $y = -\frac{3}{2}x + \frac{7}{2}$

83. $y = -\frac{8}{3}x - \frac{26}{3}$ **85.** 60,000 voters **87.** $t = \frac{A - p}{pr}$

LESSON 1.8

TRY THIS (p. 63)

$x = -4$ or $x = \frac{2}{3}$

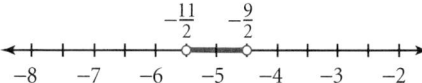

$$\begin{array}{ccccccccccccc} \hline -6 & -5 & -4 & -3 & -2 & -1 & 0 & 1 & 2 & 3 & 4 & 5 & 6 \end{array}$$

TRY THIS (p. 64)

$x = \frac{3}{2}$

TRY THIS (p. 65, Ex. 3)

$x \le -\frac{4}{3}$ or $x \ge \frac{2}{5}$

$$\begin{array}{ccccccccccccc} \hline -6 & -5 & -4 & -3 & -2 & -1 & 0 & 1 & 2 & 3 & 4 & 5 & 6 \end{array}$$

TRY THIS (p. 65, Ex. 4)

$x \ge -\frac{4}{3}$ and $x \le \frac{2}{5}$, or $-\frac{4}{3} \le x \le \frac{2}{5}$

$$\begin{array}{ccccccccccccc} \hline -6 & -5 & -4 & -3 & -2 & -1 & 0 & 1 & 2 & 3 & 4 & 5 & 6 \end{array}$$

TRY THIS (p. 66)

$|t - 12.00| \le 0.01$

Exercises

6. $x = 14$ or $x = 6$ **7.** $x = 4$ or $x = 1$ **8.** $x = -1$ or $x = \frac{17}{3}$

9. $x = -1$ **10.** $x = 8$ or $x = 0$ **11.** no solution

12. $x < 2$ or $x > 6$

$$\begin{array}{ccccccccccccc} \hline -4 & -3 & -2 & -1 & 0 & 1 & 2 & 3 & 4 & 5 & 6 & 7 & 8 \end{array}$$

13. $x \le -3$ or $x \ge 2$

$$\begin{array}{ccccccccccccc} \hline -6 & -5 & -4 & -3 & -2 & -1 & 0 & 1 & 2 & 3 & 4 & 5 & 6 \end{array}$$

14. $-\frac{11}{2} < x < -\frac{9}{2}$

$$\begin{array}{ccccccc} \hline -8 & -7 & -6 & -5 & -4 & -3 & -2 \end{array}$$

15. $x \le -1$ or $x \ge 1$

$$\begin{array}{ccccccccccccc} \hline -6 & -5 & -4 & -3 & -2 & -1 & 0 & 1 & 2 & 3 & 4 & 5 & 6 \end{array}$$

16. $x \ge -\frac{3}{2}$

$$\begin{array}{ccccccccccccc} \hline -6 & -5 & -4 & -3 & -2 & -1 & 0 & 1 & 2 & 3 & 4 & 5 & 6 \end{array}$$

17. all real numbers

$$\begin{array}{ccccccccccccc} \hline -6 & -5 & -4 & -3 & -2 & -1 & 0 & 1 & 2 & 3 & 4 & 5 & 6 \end{array}$$

18a. $|x - 25| \le 2$ or $|25 - x| \le 2$ **b.** $23 \le x \le 27$

18 19 20 21 22 23 24 25 26 27 28 29 30

19. b   **21.** d   **23.** c   **25.** $x = 4$ or $x = -12$

27. $x = 8$ or $x = -12$ **29.** $x = -7$ or $x = 11$ **31.** $x = 2$ or $x = 13$ **33.** $x = -4\frac{1}{2}$ or $x = 9\frac{1}{2}$ **35.** $x = \frac{4}{5}$ or $x = \frac{8}{5}$

37. $x = -\frac{4}{5}$ or $x = \frac{2}{5}$ **39.** no solution

41. $x \ge -12$ and $x \le 2$

-12-10-8 -6 -4 -2 0 2 4 6 8 10 12

43. $x \ge -6$ and $x \le 6$

-6 -5 -4 -3 -2 -1 0 1 2 3 4 5 6

45. all real numbers

-6 -5 -4 -3 -2 -1 0 1 2 3 4 5 6

47. $x > -4$ and $x < 7$

-12-10-8 -6 -4 -2 0 2 4 6 8 10 12

49. $x > -9$ and $x < 6$

-12-10-8 -6 -4 -2 0 2 4 6 8 10 12

51. all real numbers

-6 -5 -4 -3 -2 -1 0 1 2 3 4 5 6

53. no solution

55. $x \le -\frac{3}{4}$ or $x \ge \frac{1}{4}$

-6 -5 -4 -3 -2 -1 0 1 2 3 4 5 6

57. no solution

59. The distance between x and 4 is less than 1.

-4 -3 -2 -1 0 1 2 3 4 5 6 7 8

61. $x \ge -\frac{3}{2}$ **63.** He is either 7.25 or 12.75 feet away from the end of the rope.   **65.** 65%; 71%

67. 6 runs   **69.** $x = 6$ **71.** $h = \frac{2A}{b}$

73. $x < \frac{9}{2}$

-6 -5 -4 -3 -2 -1 0 1 2 3 4 5 6

75. $-1 < x < 5$

-4 -3 -2 -1 0 1 2 3 4 5 6 7 8

77. $x \le -2$ or $x > 4$

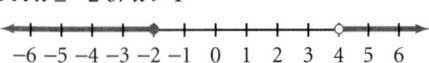

-6 -5 -4 -3 -2 -1 0 1 2 3 4 5 6

1. not linear   **3.** linear; (35, 25)

5.

Mental age	IQ
10	67
14	94
15	100
19	127
25	167
m	$\frac{100}{15}m$

$$y = \frac{100}{15}m$$

7.

9.

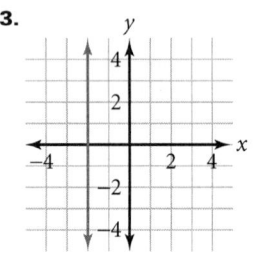

11.

13.

15. $y = 100x + 398$ **17.** $y = 4$ **19.** $x = -2$

21. $y = -1.25x + 10.5$ **23.** $y = \frac{1}{3}x - 1$ **25.** $x = 4$

27. $k = 0.005$; $y = 0.005x$ **29.** 50 millimeters

31. The correlation is negative.   **33.** $t = h + 15$

35. $C = \frac{5}{9}F - \frac{160}{9}$ **37.** $f = \frac{f_1 f_2}{f_1 + f_2}$

39. $2(10) + 2l \le 140$; $l \le 60$ meters

-60   -40   -20   0   20   40   60

41. $x < 8$ and $x > 3$

-12-10-8 -6 -4 -2 0 2 4 6 8 10 12

43. $x < 8$ or $x > 3$

-6 -5 -4 -3 -2 -1 0 1 2 3 4 5 6

45. $x = -40$ or $x = 40$

-60-50-40-30-20-10 0 10 20 30 40 50 60

47. $x = -4.5$ or $x = 4.5$

-6 -5 -4 -3 -2 -1 0 1 2 3 4 5 6

49. $x < -40$ or $x > 40$

-60   -40   -20   0   20   40   60

Selected Answers

51. all real numbers

53. $k = 2$; $h = 2s$ **55.** $2850 < \frac{1}{10}I$, where $I > 0$; $I > 28,500$

Chapter 2

LESSON 2.1

TRY THIS (p. 88, Ex. 2)

$(a + b)(c - d) = a(c - d) + b(c - d)$

　　　　　　　Distributive Property

$= ac - ad + bc - bd$

　　　　　　　Distributive Property

or

$(a + b)(c - d) = (a + b)c - (a + b)d$

　　　　　　　Distributive Property

$= ac + bc - (ad + bd)$

　　　　　　　Distributive Property

$= ac + bc - ad - bd$

　　　　　　　Distributive Property

TRY THIS (p. 88, Ex. 3)

$T = c + 0.06c$

$T = 1c + 0.06c$　　Use the Identity Property.

$T = (1 + 0.06)c$　　Use the Distributive Property.

$T = 1.06c$　　Add.

TRY THIS (p. 89)

$\frac{4}{3}$

Exercises

4. $\frac{3}{2}$ is a rational and real number; $-2.101001000\ldots$ is an irrational and real number. **5.** $2b + 2d$ **6.** 0 **7.** 15 **8.** 2 **9.** 5 **10.** $-20t^2$

11. $m = \frac{p}{12} + \frac{0.06p}{12}$

$m = \frac{1p}{12} + \frac{0.06p}{12}$　Use the Identity Property.

$m = \frac{(1 + 0.06)p}{12}$　Use the Distributive Property.

$m = \frac{1.06p}{12}$　Add.

12. 25 **13.** -4 **14.** $\frac{35}{6}$ **15.** -122 **17.** -5.1 is a rational and real number. **19.** $\sqrt{2}$ is an irrational and real number. **21.** $\frac{3}{9}$ is a rational and real number. **23.** $-1.0\overline{63}$ is a rational and real number. **25.** $\sqrt{25}$, or 5, is a natural number, a whole number, an integer, a rational number, and a real number. **27.** 1 is a natural number, a whole number, an integer, a rational number, and a real number. **29.** $-\pi$ is an irrational and real number. **31.** $\sqrt{28}$ is an irrational and real number.

33.

35.

37.

39. Associative Property of Multiplication **41.** Commutative Property of Addition **43.** Associative Property of Addition **45.** Inverse Property of Multiplication **47.** Inverse Property of Addition **49.** Identity Property of Multiplication **51.** Identity Property of Addition **53.** Distributive Property **55.** Commutative Property of Multiplication **57.** 4 **59.** 15 **61.** 5 **63.** 26 **65.** 7 **67.** 6 **69.** 5 **71a.** Answers may vary. **b.** In general, whole, rational, and real numbers are represented. Sometimes negative integers are also represented. **c.** Answers may vary. sample answers: integers: 0 through 10 on the phone, 0 on a scale; rational: 3.5-ounce bag of microwave popcorn, $\frac{1}{4}$-cup marking on a measuring cup **73a.** No; Ron calculated $8 + 10 + 14 + \frac{16}{4}$, not $\frac{8 + 10 + 14 + 16}{4}$. **b.** Ron should have entered $(8 + 10 + 14 + 16) \div 4$, which would have given an answer of 12. **75.** The annual premium is $5376. **77.** $\frac{14.6}{1000} = \frac{146}{10,000}$, which is rational. **79.** 13%; $\frac{13}{100}$; rational; real **81.** $m = -3$ **83.** $m = \frac{3}{4}$ **85.** $m = \frac{3}{4}$ **87.** $x = \frac{19}{3}$ **89.** $x = -\frac{17}{4}$ **91.** $x = \frac{12}{5}$ or $x = -\frac{12}{5}$

93. $x < -1$ or $x > \frac{1}{3}$

LESSON 2.2

TRY THIS (p. 95)

9.5 feet per second squared

TRY THIS (p. 96, Ex. 2)

$\frac{30x^2}{z^2}$

TRY THIS (p. 96, Ex. 3)

$\frac{-27c^9}{b^{15}}$

TRY THIS (p. 97)

4; 216

TRY THIS (p. 98)

about 1.8 square meters

Exercises

5. 140 feet per second squared **6.** x^6 **7.** z^6 **8.** y^{18}
9. $a^{12}b^{28}$ **10.** y^{12} **11.** $\dfrac{4y^2}{25x^8}$ **12.** $\dfrac{b^6}{a^{10}}$ **13.** $\dfrac{y^3}{x}$ **14.** 10
15. 27 **16.** 3 **17.** 16 **18.** 1.60 square meters **19.** 1
21. 1 **23.** $\dfrac{1}{6}$ **25.** $\dfrac{81}{625}$ **27.** 4 **29.** −27 **31.** 7 **33.** 256
35. 216 **37.** −16 **39.** y^7 **41.** $-10xy^7$ **43.** m^4 **45.** $\dfrac{1}{x^7}$
47. $8x^{12}y^3$ **49.** $25w^8v^{10}$ **51.** $-\dfrac{128z^{14}}{x^{21}}$ **53.** $-\dfrac{8p^{15}}{q^{21}}$
55. $243x^{20}y^{10}$ **57.** $\dfrac{1}{5r^2s}$ **59.** $\dfrac{1}{5xy}$ **61.** $\dfrac{b^{10}}{16a^8}$ **63.** $\dfrac{y}{x^3}$
65. $\dfrac{1}{ab^8}$ **67.** $\dfrac{8x^{47}y^{18}z^{11}}{3}$ **69.** $\dfrac{b^{30}}{a^9c^6}$ **71.** 3,382,159.1
73. 1.1 **75.** 68.1 **77.** For all values of a and b,
$-(a-b) = b - a$; therefore, $y^{a-b} = y^{-(b-a)} = \dfrac{1}{y^{b-a}}$
79a. 11.9 centimeters **b.** $\dfrac{3V}{\pi r^2}$ **81a.** 2,633,744.9
b. $\dfrac{2l}{3r^4}$ **83.** 99.7% **85.** 97.2% **87.** 12.4 pounds per square inch
89. $x > -3$ and $x < 1$

91. all real numbers

93. 9.373737… is a rational and real number.
95. 5.38388388838888… is an irrational and real number. **97.** 5 **99.** 63

LESSON 2.3

TRY THIS (p. 104)
A customer with checking and savings accounts has at least one account number, so the correspondence is a relation. Some customers may have both a checking account number and a savings account number, so the relation is not a function.

TRY THIS (p. 105)
a. domain: {−4, −3, −1, 2, 3, 5}; range: {−3, 0, 1, 2}
b. domain: $x \geq -2$; range: $y \geq -1$

Exercises

5. no; (5, 3) and (5, 7) **6.** yes **7.** yes **8.** no; (2, 2) and (2, 1) **9.** yes **10.** No; for example, the y-axis crosses the graph at two points. **11.** A registered automobile has at least one license plate number. Thus, the correspondence is a relation. Each registered automobile may not have more than one license plate number, so the relation is also a function. **12.** domain: $x \geq -3$; range: $y \leq 4$
13. domain: {−3, −1, 1, 3}; range: {−2, −1, 0, 1}
14. $f(3) = 14$; $f(1.5) = 4.25$
15a. $w(h) = 24.00h + 20.00$ **b.** For 5.5 hours of work, the plumber earns $152.00. **17.** yes **19.** yes

21. yes **23.** yes **25.** No; for the first coordinate, −1, there is more than one second coordinate, 8 and 7.
27. yes **29.** yes **31.** yes **33.** No; for example, the points (−2, −1) and (−2, 2) are on the graph. For the first coordinate, −2, there is more than one second coordinate, −1 and 2. **35.** yes **37.** domain: {0, 3}; range: {2, 4} **39.** domain: {7, 8, 9}; range: {−1, −2, −3} **41.** domain: {4, 5, 6}; range: {−6, −5, −4} **43.** $f(1) = -4$; $f(3) = 0$ **45.** $g(-1) = -1$; $g(1) = \dfrac{1}{3}$ **47.** $f(3) = 9$; $f(-2.5) = 20$ **49.** $f(-1) = \dfrac{1}{3}$; $f\left(\dfrac{3}{4}\right) = \dfrac{3}{16}$ **51.** domain: all real numbers; range: all real numbers **53.** domain: all real numbers; range: $y \geq 0$ **55.** domain: all real numbers; range: $y = 4$ **57.** domain: all real numbers; range: all real numbers
59. Answers may vary.
sample answer:

61. $f(\sqrt{2}) = -1$ **63.** $f(a + \sqrt{2}) = a^2 + (2\sqrt{2})a - 1$
65. $A(3) = 3^2 = 9$ square meters **67.** $S(P) = 0.7P$
69. The sale price of the items was $36.40.
71. $y = -3x + 13$ **73.** $y = -\dfrac{2}{3}x - \dfrac{25}{3}$ **75.** $y = x + 2$
77. $y = \dfrac{4}{7}x - \dfrac{27}{7}$ **79.** $y = 2x + 13$ **81.** 15,625

LESSON 2.4

TRY THIS (p. 112, Ex. 1)
$(f + g)(x) = 12x - 2.5$; $(f - g)(x) = -14x^2 + 12x + 7.5$
TRY THIS (p. 112, Ex. 2)
$(f \cdot g)(x) = 15x^3 - 6x^2 + 5x - 2$; $\left(\dfrac{f}{g}\right)(x) = \dfrac{3x^2 + 1}{5x - 2}$, where $x \neq \dfrac{2}{5}$
TRY THIS (p. 113)
$(f \circ g)(x) = -8x^2 + 3$; $(g \circ f)(x) = 4x^2 - 6$

Exercises

4. $(f + g)(x) = \dfrac{7}{2}x + 1$ **5.** $(f - g)(x) = -\dfrac{5}{2}x - 1$
6. $(f \cdot g)(x) = \dfrac{3}{2}x^2 + \dfrac{x}{2}$ **7.** $\left(\dfrac{f}{g}\right)(x) = \dfrac{x}{2(3x + 1)}$, where $x \neq -\dfrac{1}{3}$ **8.** $(f \circ g)(x) = \dfrac{3x + 1}{2}$ **9.** $(g \circ f)(x) = \dfrac{3}{2}x + 1$

10. Let x be the total cost of the meal.

$R(x) = x - 5$ and $T(x) = x + 0.15x = 1.15x$

$(R \circ T)(x) = R(T(x)) = R(1.15x)$
$\qquad\qquad\qquad\qquad = 1.15x - 5$

$(T \circ R)(x) = (T(R(x))) = T(x - 5)$
$\qquad\qquad\qquad\qquad = 1.15(x - 5)$
$\qquad\qquad\qquad\qquad = 1.15x - 5.75$

$(R \circ T)(x)$ represents the total cost of the meal, plus the tip, minus \$5. $(T \circ R)(x)$ represents the total cost of the meal, plus the tip, minus \$5.75. $(R \circ T)(x)$ represents the conditions of the coupon.

11. $(f + g)(x) = 4x + 8$; $(f - g)(x) = 4x - 2$
13. $(f + g)(x) = x^2 + 5x - 6$; $(f - g)(x) = x^2 - x + 4$
15. $(f + g)(x) = -3x^2 + x + 2$; $(f - g)(x) = 3x^2 + x - 6$
17. $(f \bullet g)(x) = 3x^3 - 24x^2$; $\left(\frac{f}{g}\right)(x) = \frac{3x^2}{x - 8}, x \neq 8$
19. $(f \bullet g)(x) = -3x^3$; $\left(\frac{f}{g}\right)(x) = -\frac{x}{3}, x \neq 0$
21. $(f \bullet g)(x) = 14x^2 - 2x^3$; $\left(\frac{f}{g}\right)(x) = \frac{2x^2}{7 - x}, x \neq 7$
23. $(f \bullet g)(x) = 3x^3 - 14x^2 - 5x$; $\left(\frac{f}{g}\right)(x) = \frac{-3x^2 - x}{5 - x}, x \neq 5$
25. $(f + g)(x) = f(x) + g(x)$
$\qquad = (x^2 - 1) + (2x - 3)$ Substitution
$\qquad = x^2 - 1 + 2x - 3$ Commutative
$\qquad\qquad\qquad\qquad$ Property
$\qquad = x^2 + 2x - 4$ Combine like terms.
27. $(g - f)(x) = g(x) - f(x)$
$\qquad = (2x - 3) - (x^2 - 1)$ Substitution
$\qquad = 2x - 3 - x^2 + 1$ Distributive
$\qquad\qquad\qquad\qquad$ Property
$\qquad = -x^2 + 2x - 2$ Combine like terms.
29. $\left(\frac{f}{g}\right)(x) = \frac{f(x)}{g(x)} = \frac{x^2 - 1}{2x - 3}$, where $x \neq \frac{3}{2}$ (Substitution)
31. $(f - g)(x) = f(x) - g(x)$
$\qquad = (x - 3) - (x^2 - 9)$ Substitution
$\qquad = x - 3 - x^2 + 9$ Distributive
$\qquad\qquad\qquad\qquad$ Property
$\qquad = -x^2 + x + 6$ Combine like terms.
33. $(f \bullet g)(x) = f(x) \bullet g(x)$
$\qquad = (x - 3)(x^2 - 9)$ Substitution
$\qquad = x^3 - 9x - 3x^2 + 27$ Distributive
$\qquad\qquad\qquad\qquad$ Property
$\qquad = x^3 - 3x^2 - 9x + 27$ Combine like terms.
35. $(f \circ g)(x) = 2x + 1$; $(g + f)(x) = 2x + 2$
37. $(f \circ g)(x) = 3x + 4$; $(g + f)(x) = 3x$
39. $(f \circ g)(x) = -75x^2 - 1$; $(g \circ f)(x) = 15x^2 + 5$
41. $(f \circ g)(x) = -28$; $(g + f)(x) = 3$ **43.** $(f \circ g)(2) = -16$
45. $(f \circ f)(2) = 2$ **47.** $(g \circ g)(2) = -16$
49. $(g \circ f)(0) = -16$ **51.** $(f \circ g)(x) = 2x^2 + 4$
53. $(f \circ h)(x) = -8x + 6$ **55.** $(f \circ f)(x) = 4x$

57. $(h \circ (h \circ g))(x) = 16x^2 + 23$ **59.** Answers may vary. Sample answer: Let $f(x) = x - 9$ and $g(x) = x^2$. Then $f \circ g = h$. **61a.** $C(t) = 360t + 850$ **b.** \$2650 **c.** 450 **63a.** $C(n) = 0.10n + 125.00$ **b.** $I(n) = 0.25n$ **c.** $P(n) = 0.15n - 125.00$ **d.** 1500 buttons
65. $y = -\frac{1}{2}x - \frac{1}{2}$ **67.** almost no correlation
69. weak positive correlation **71.** domain: all real numbers; range: all real numbers

LESSON 2.5

TRY THIS (p. 119)
$y = \frac{1}{4}x + \frac{5}{4}$
TRY THIS (p. 121)

$(f \circ g)(x) = f(g(x))$ $\qquad$ $(g \circ f)(x) = g(f(x))$
$\qquad = f\left(-\frac{1}{5}x + \frac{7}{5}\right)$ $\qquad = g(-5x + 7)$
$\qquad = -5\left(-\frac{1}{5}x + \frac{7}{5}\right) + 7$ $\qquad = -\frac{1}{5}(-5x + 7) + \frac{7}{5}$
$\qquad = x - 7 + 7$ $\qquad\qquad = x - \frac{7}{5} + \frac{7}{5}$
$\qquad = x$ $\qquad\qquad\qquad = x$

Exercises

5. $F = \frac{9}{5}(K - 273) + 32$ **6.** Inverse: $\{(3, 8), (2, 2),$ $(3, 4)\}$; the relation is a function; the inverse is not a function. **7.** Inverse: $\{(2, 3), (5, 9), (3, 2), (7, 4)\}$; the relation is a function; the inverse is a function.
8. $y = \frac{1}{3}x - 3$ **9.** $y = -\frac{1}{3}x + \frac{5}{3}$
10. $(f \circ g)(x) = f\left(\frac{1}{6}x + \frac{5}{6}\right)$ $\qquad$ $(g \circ f)(x) = g(6x - 5)$
$\qquad\qquad = 6\left(\frac{1}{6}x + \frac{5}{6}\right) - 5$ $\qquad = \frac{1}{6}(6x - 5) + \frac{5}{6}$
$\qquad\qquad = (x + 5) - 5$ $\qquad\qquad = \left(x - \frac{5}{6}\right) + \frac{5}{6}$
$(f \circ g)(x) = x$ $\qquad\qquad$ $(g \circ f)(x) = x$
Thus, f and g are inverses.
11. $\{(5, 3), (10, 6), (15, 9)\}$; yes; yes **13.** $\{(2, 5),$ $(3, 4), (4, 3), (5, 2)\}$; yes; yes **15.** $\{(-6, -3), (2, -1),$ $(2, 1), (6, 3)\}$; yes; no **17.** $\{(2, 1), (4, 3), (4, -3),$ $(2, -1)\}$; yes; no **19.** $\{(0, -1), (1, 2), (3, 4), (4, 3)\}$; yes **21.** $\{(2, 1), (3, 2), (2, 3), (1, 4)\}$; no
23. $\{(2, 5), (3, 4), (5, 3), (3, 2)\}$; no **25.** $\{(2, 0), (3, 2),$ $(4, 3), (1, 1)\}$; yes **27.** The inverse is a function.
29. $f^{-1}(x) = \frac{1}{5}x - \frac{1}{5}$ **31.** $h^{-1}(x) = -2x + 6$
33. $h^{-1}(x) = 3x - 8$ **35.** $f^{-1}(x) = \frac{4x + 3}{2}$
37. $g^{-1}(x) = \frac{4}{5}x$ **39.** $g^{-1}(x) = 2(x + 3) - 2$, or
$g^{-1}(x) = 2x + 4$ **41.** No, the inverse is not a function.
43. Yes, the inverse is a function. **45.** No, the inverse is not a function. **47.** No, the inverse is not a function. **49.** Yes, the inverse is a function.
51a. $c = 17.50s + 50$ **b.** $s = \frac{c - 50}{17.50}$ **c.** 82 square yards of carpeting can be installed for \$1485.

53. Let a be your age and g be the guess. Then the guess, g, can be represented by the function $g = \frac{2(a+4)-6}{2}$. Now solve for a:

$$g = \frac{2(a+4)-6}{2}$$
$$2g = 2(a+4)-6$$
$$2g+6 = 2(a+4)$$
$$g+3 = a+4$$
$$g-1 = a$$

In other words, your age is found by subtracting 1 from the guess.

55. 256 **57.** 729 **59.** $(f \cdot g)(x) = 15x^2 - 4x - 4$
61. 143

LESSON 2.6

TRY THIS (p. 125)

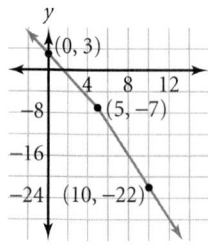

TRY THIS (p. 126, Ex. 2)

$0.32; $0.78

TRY THIS (p. 126, Ex. 3)

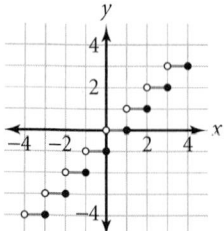

TRY THIS (p. 127)

x	$f(x) = \frac{1}{2}|x| + 1$
-2	2
-1	1.5
0	1
1	1.5
2	2

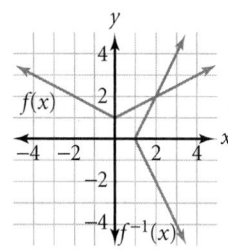

TRY THIS (p. 128)

The relative error is about 0.00125, or 0.125%.

Exercises

5.

6.

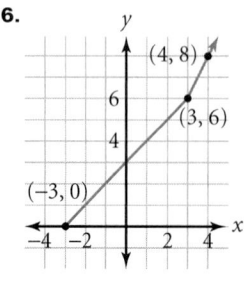

7. $3.08 **8.** $1.40 **9.** $4.76 **10.** $0.14

11.

Interval of x	$f(x) = 3\lceil x \rceil$
$-4 < x \le -3$	$3(-3) = -9$
$-3 < x \le -2$	$3(-2) = -6$
$-2 < x \le -1$	$3(-1) = -3$
$-1 < x \le 0$	$3(0) = 0$
$0 < x \le 1$	$3(1) = 3$
$1 < x \le 2$	$3(2) - 6$
$2 < x \le 3$	$3(3) = 9$

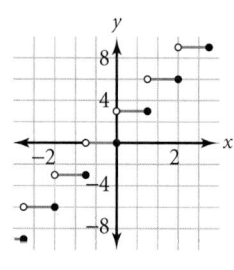

12.

Interval of x	$g(x) = -4[x]$
$-3 \le x < -2$	$-4(-3) = 12$
$-2 \le x < -1$	$-4(-2) = 8$
$-1 \le x < 0$	$-4(-1) = 4$
$0 \le x < 1$	$-4(0) = 0$
$1 \le x < 2$	$-4(1) = -4$
$2 \le x < 3$	$-4(2) = -8$
$3 \le x < 4$	$-4(3) = -12$

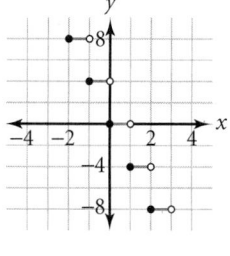

13.

x	$f(x) = |x| + 2$
-3	$|-3| + 2 = 5$
-2	$|-2| + 2 = 4$
-1	$|-1| + 2 = 3$
0	$|0| + 2 = 2$
1	$|1| + 2 = 3$
2	$|2| + 2 = 4$
3	$|3| + 2 = 5$

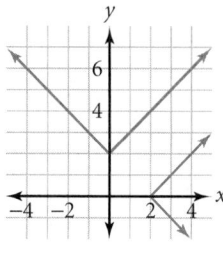

14.

x	$g(x) = 2|x| - 1$
-3	$2|-3| - 1 = 5$
-2	$2|-2| - 1 = 3$
-1	$2|-1| - 1 = 1$
0	$2|0| - 1 = -1$
1	$2|1| - 1 = 1$
2	$2|2| - 1 = 3$
3	$2|3| - 1 = 5$

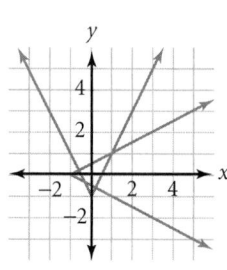

15. 0.002, or 0.2%

17.

19.

21.

23.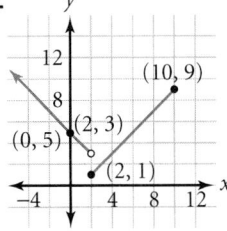

25. $g(x) = \begin{cases} \frac{5}{4} + 2 & \text{if } -4 < x \le 0 \\ -\frac{1}{2}x & \text{if } 0 < x \le 4 \end{cases}$

27. $g(x) = \begin{cases} -x & \text{if } -3 < x \le 2 \\ -x + 5 & \text{if } x > 2 \end{cases}$

29. -7 **31.** -6 **33.** 2 **35.** 4 **37.** -1 **39.** -4 **41.** -10
43. -2 **45.** 1 **47.** 4.8 **49.** -2 **51.** 3.33

53.   **55.**

57.   **59.**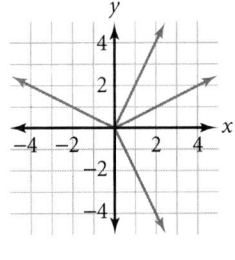

61. false; for example: $|(-1) + 1| = |0| = 0$ and
$|-1| + |1| = 1 + 1 = 2$ **63.** true for all values of x and y

65.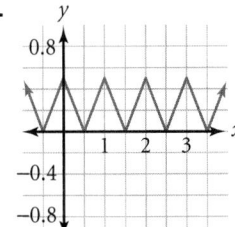

The shape of the graph is a sawtooth.

67. $f(x) = \frac{1}{10}\lceil 10x \rceil$ will round x up to the nearest
tenth. $g(x) = \frac{1}{100}\lfloor 100x \rfloor$ will round x down to the
nearest hundredth. **69.** 0.6% **71.** 2.5%

73a.

Coffee (lb)	Cost ($)
1	9.89
2	19.78
3	29.67
4	39.56
5	49.45
6	57.43
7	65.41
8	73.39
9	81.37
10	89.35

b.

c. $c(x) = \begin{cases} 9.89x & \text{if } x \le 5 \\ 49.45 + 7.98(x - 5) & \text{if } x > 5 \end{cases}$ **d.** $\$53.44$

75a.

Labor hours	Repair charges
0.5	45
1.0	45
1.5	65
2.0	85
2.5	105
3.0	125
3.5	145
4.0	165
4.5	185
5.0	205

b.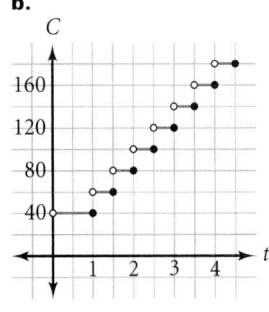

c. $C(t) = \begin{cases} 45 & \text{if } 0 < t \le 1 \\ 45 + 20\lceil 2(t - 1) \rceil & \text{if } 1 < t \le 5 \end{cases}$

d. $\$165$ **77a.** $c(x) = 2.00 + 1.50x$ **b.** $\$7.25$
79. $(g \circ f)(x) = 3x + 6$ **81.** $(g \circ g)(x) = 9x$
83. $(f + g)(x) = 4x + 2$ **85.** $\left(\frac{f}{g}\right) = \frac{x + 2}{3x}, x \ne 0$
87. $a^{-1}(x) = \frac{4}{3}x + 2$ **89.** $g^{-1}(x) = 8 - x$

LESSON 2.7

TRY THIS (p. 134)
a. vertical translation 2 units down
b. horizontal translation 3 units to the right

TRY THIS (p. 135)
a. vertical stretch by a factor of 3
b. vertical compression by a factor of $\frac{1}{3}$

TRY THIS (p. 136)
a. horizontal compression by a factor of $\frac{1}{3}$
b. horizontal stretch by a factor of 4

TRY THIS (p. 137)
a. reflection across the x-axis
b. reflection across the y-axis

TRY THIS (p. 138)

a. translation 1 unit to the right; vertical stretch by a factor of 3

b. vertical compression by a factor of $\frac{1}{2}$; vertical translation 2 units down

Exercises

6. vertical translation 3 units down **7.** vertical stretch by a factor of $\frac{4}{3}$ **8.** horizontal compression by a factor of $\frac{1}{2}$ **9.** reflection across the *y*-axis **10.** horizontal translation 3 units to the right and vertical translation 1 unit up **11.** vertical stretch by a factor of 4 **13.** horizontal compression by a factor of $\frac{1}{4}$ **15.** vertical compression by a factor of $\frac{1}{2}$ and reflection across the *x*-axis **17.** vertical translation 2 units down **19.** horizontal translation 2 units to the right **21.** horizontal compression by a factor of $\frac{1}{5}$, vertical translation 2 units up, and reflection across the *y*-axis **23.** vertical compression by a factor of $\frac{1}{3}$ and vertical translation 1 unit down

25. horizontal translation 4 units to the left, vertical stretch by a factor of 2, reflection across the *x*-axis, and vertical translation 1 unit up **27.** vertical stretch by a factor of 4 **29.** vertical compression by a factor of $\frac{1}{4}$ and reflection across the *x*-axis **31.** horizontal compression by a factor of $\frac{1}{4}$ and reflection across the *y*-axis **33.** vertical translation 4 units up **35.** horizontal translation 4 units to the left **37.** horizontal compression by a factor of $\frac{1}{2}$, reflection across the *y*-axis, and vertical translation 1 unit up **39.** horizontal translation 4 units to the right, reflection across the *x*-axis, and vertical translation 3 units up **41.** reflection across the *x*-axis and reflection across the *y*-axis **43.** $g(x) = (x - 2)^2$

45. $g(x) = x^2 - 6$ **47.** $g(x) = \frac{1}{3}\sqrt{x}$ **49.** $g(x) = \sqrt{\frac{1}{4}x}$

51. $g(x) = 2(-x) - 1$ **53.** $g(x) = -|3x| - 3$

55. $g(x) = x^2 + 5$ **57.** $g(x) = \left(-\frac{1}{2}x\right)^2$ **59.** Answers may vary. Consider the vertical compression of the graph of $f(x) = x^2$ given by $\frac{1}{4}f(x) = \frac{1}{4}x^2$ and the horizontal stretch given by $f\left(\frac{1}{2}x\right) = \left(\frac{1}{2}x\right)^2$. Because $\left(\frac{1}{2}x\right)^2 = \left(\frac{1}{2}\right)^2 x^2 = \frac{1}{4}x^2$, the effect of the vertical compression by a factor of $\frac{1}{4}$ and the horizontal stretch by a factor of 2 are identical.

61.

63.

65.

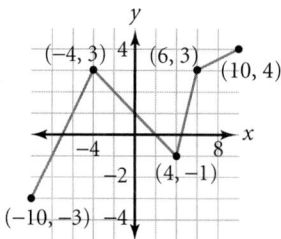

67. $y = 2x + 10$ **69.** $s = \dfrac{4D}{\pi b^2 n}$ **71.** 14.393939... is a rational and real number.

73. The relation is a function; the inverse, {(100, 1), (200, 2), (300, 3), (400, 4)}, is a function because each domain value is paired with exactly one range value.

75.

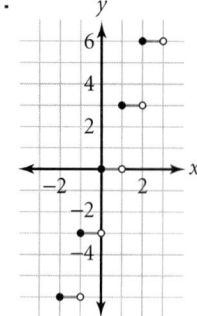

CHAPTER REVIEW AND ASSESSMENT

1. Commutative Property of Multiplication **3.** Inverse Property of Multiplication **5.** Identity Property of Addition **7.** Commutative Property of Addition **9.** -75 **11.** $-\frac{10}{9}$ **13.** $9x^6$ **15.** $u^6 v$ **17.** $\frac{8x^9}{27y^2}$ **19.** yes **21.** no **23.** domain: $\{-1, 0, 2, 4\}$; range: $\{2, 6, 7, -7\}$ **25.** $g(1) = 9; g(-1) = -13$ **27.** $h(1) = -1;$ $h(-1) = 5$ **29.** $(f - g)(x) = \frac{5x}{2} + 1$

31. $(f \circ g)(x) = \frac{3x^2}{2} - 17x + 20$

33. $\left(\frac{g}{f}\right)(x) = \dfrac{\frac{x}{2} - 5}{3x - 4}, x \neq \frac{4}{3}$ **35.** $(g \circ f)(x) = -2x + 2$

37. $(g \circ g)(x) = x$ **39.** -45 **41.** $\{(0, -2), (1, -1),$ $(0, 0), (1, 1), (0, 2)\}$ **43.** $f^{-1}(x) = -\frac{3}{2}x + 6$ **45.** Yes, the inverse is a function. **47.** Yes, the inverse is a function.

49.

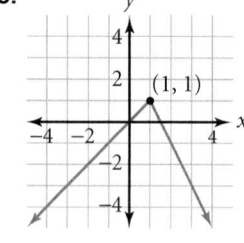

51.

53. -78 **55.** 4 **57.** 8 **59.** horizontal translation 2 units to the right **61.** horizontal translation 3 units to the left and reflection across the *x*-axis **63.** vertical stretch by a factor of 9.8, reflection across the *x*-axis, and vertical translation 1.5 units up

Chapter 3

LESSON 3.1

TRY THIS (p. 157)
The system is consistent and independent. The solution is $x = 0$ and $y = 4$.

TRY THIS (p. 158)
$(-1, 11)$

TRY THIS (p. 159)
approximately 167 milliliters of the 7% solution and 333 milliliters of the 4% solution

TRY THIS (p. 160)
$(5, 3, -3)$

Exercises

5. This is a consistent, independent system with the unique solution $(1, 5)$. **6.** This is a dependent system, so there are infinitely many solutions.
7. $(-12, 32)$ **8.** 480 pounds of $2.00 candy; 520 pounds of $0.75 candy **9.** $(1, 1, -3)$ **11.** dependent; infinitely many solutions **13.** dependent; infinitely many solutions **15.** independent; $(3, 5)$
17. inconsistent; no solution **19.** independent; $(0, 4)$
21. independent; $(2, -3)$ **23.** inconsistent; no solution **25.** $(7, 10)$ **27.** $(4, 2)$
29. $(4, 2)$ **31.** $\left(\frac{11}{3}, \frac{2}{3}\right)$ **33.** $(4, 2)$ **35.** $(42, 17)$
37. $\left(-\frac{7}{3}, -\frac{13}{15}\right)$ **39.** independent; $\left(-\frac{1}{6}, -\frac{3}{2}\right)$
41. $(5, -2, 4)$ **43.** $(-2, 3, -1)$ **45.** $\left(-2, \frac{3}{5}, 2\right)$
47. independent; $(0.29, 4.17)$ **49.** independent; $(0.67, 0.17)$ **51.** independent; $(4.15, 5.86)$
53. $x = \frac{c - be}{a + bd}$, $y = d\frac{c - be}{a + bd} + e$; $(3, 5)$ **55.** 750 square yards **57.** The two options will be equal for 2 hours of parking, and the cost will be $11. If Armando stays less than 2 hours, the second option is less expensive; for more than 2 hours, the first option is less expensive. **59.** 7 2-point baskets and 3 3-point baskets **61.** $-3 \le x \le 7$ **63.** Distributive Property
65. Additive Inverse **67.** 5 **69.** $\frac{1}{5}$ **71.** $4x^{10}$ **73.** $-\frac{1}{2ab}$
75. $\{(4, 1), (4, -3), (0, 2)\}$; not a function
77. $\{(4, 3), (3, 4), (-1, 3), (-3, 11)\}$; function

LESSON 3.2

TRY THIS (p. 165)
$r = 1$ and $s = -3$, or $(1, -3)$

TRY THIS (p. 166)
90 small frames and 100 large frames

TRY THIS (p. 167)
$0 = 2$; the statement is false, so the system is inconsistent. There is no solution.

TRY THIS (p. 168)
The resulting statement, $0 = 0$, is true, so the system is dependent. There are infinitely many solutions.

Exercises

5. $(2, 1)$ **6.** 85 small picture frames and 60 large ones **7.** no solution **8.** all points on the graph of either equation **9.** $(6, -4)$ **11.** $(4, -2)$ **13.** $(-9, -8)$
15. $(3, 1)$ **17.** $(-2, -1)$ **19.** $(3, 2)$ **21.** no solution
23. all points on the graph of either equation
25. $\left(\frac{2}{3}, \frac{3}{4}\right)$ **27.** all points on the graph of either equation **29.** $(-4, 3)$ **31.** $(2, 0)$ **33.** $(4, -3)$
35. $\left(-\frac{5}{7}, -\frac{73}{84}\right)$ **37.** no solution **39.** $\frac{25}{2}$, or 12.5, acres of good land and $\frac{175}{2}$, or 87.5, acres of bad land
41. $3875 at 5% and $625 at 9% **43.** 7 packages under 3 pounds and 5 packages weighing 3 pounds or more **45.** approximately 5.4 units of whole-wheat flour and 0.5 unit of whole milk **47.** $124.80
49. positive correlation **51.** $x = -\frac{15}{2}$
53. $x > \frac{3}{2}$

55. $x \ge -10$

57. $-6 \le y \le 2$

59. all real numbers

61. -25

LESSON 3.3

TRY THIS (p. 173, Ex. 1)

a. **b.**
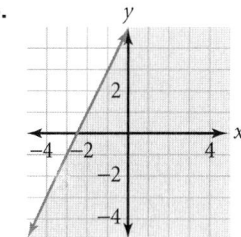

TRY THIS (p. 173, Ex. 2)

TRY THIS (p. 174)

Exercises

4.

5.

6.

7.
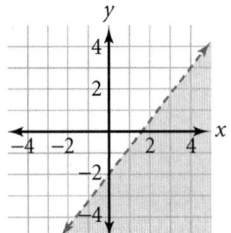

8. Yes, (25, 400) is in the solution region.

9.

10.

11.

13.

15.

17.

19.

21.

23.

25.

27.
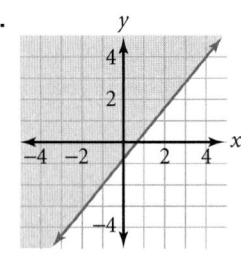

29. $y < 3x + 2$

31. $x \leq -1$

33.

35.

37.

39.

41.

43.
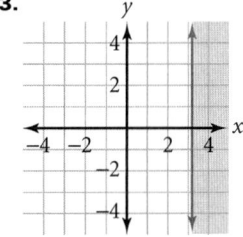

45. $x < n$, where $n = 1, 2, 3$, and 4, is a series of half-planes that lie to the left of the dashed vertical lines $x = 1$, $x = 2$, $x = 3$, and $x = 4$. **47.** $ny \le 2x$, where $n = 1, 2, 3$, and 4, or $y \le \frac{2}{n}x$, where $n = 1, 2, 3$, and 4, is the series of half-planes below the successive solid lines $y = 2x$, $y = x$, $y = \frac{2}{3}x$, and $y = \frac{1}{2}x$.

49. $2x + 3y < 24$, where x and y are nonnegative integers

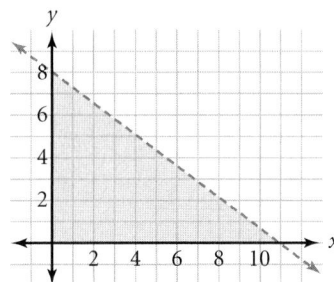

51. $2x + 3y > 24$ or $2x + 3y \ge 25$, where x and y are nonnegative integers

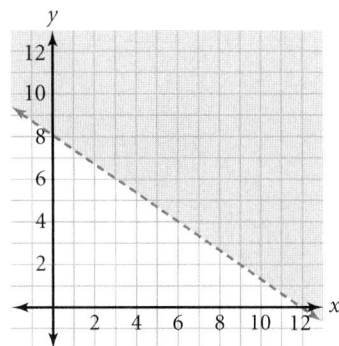

53a. $3x + 2y \le 60$, where x and y are nonnegative integers

b.

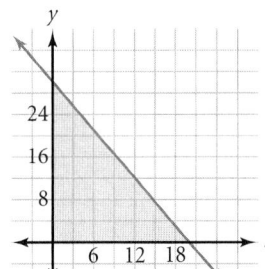

c. 20 pounds
d. 30 pounds

55a. $0.95x + 1.25y \le 5.75$, where x and y are nonnegative integers **b.** $y \le -0.76x + 4.6$

c.

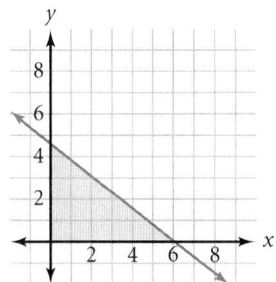

57. $k = 8$; $y = 8x$ **59.** $k = -270$; $y = -270x$ **61.** $x = \frac{4}{9}$

63. independent; $(1, -1)$ **65.** independent; $(4, 5)$

67. $(1, 7)$ **69.** $\left(\frac{3}{2}, 2\right)$ **71.** $(3, 1)$

LESSON 3.4

TRY THIS (p. 180, Ex. 1)

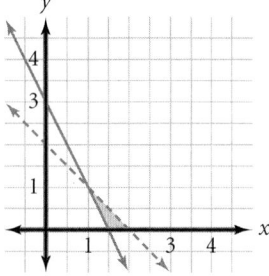

TRY THIS (p. 180, Ex. 2)

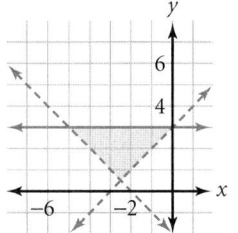

TRY THIS (p. 181)

a.

b.

Exercises

4.

5.

6.

7.

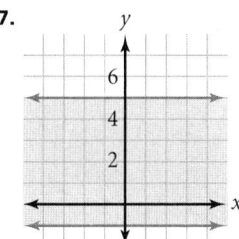

8. $\begin{cases} x \geq 0 \\ y \geq 0 \\ y \leq \frac{2}{5}x + 2 \\ y \leq -4x + 24 \end{cases}$

9.

11.

13.

15.

17.

19.

21.

23.

25.

27.

29.

31.

33. $\begin{cases} y > -2 \\ y \leq 2x \\ y \leq -2x + 4 \end{cases}$

35. $\begin{cases} x \leq 1 \\ y < -3x + 3 \\ y \leq 2x + 3 \\ y \geq -3 \end{cases}$

37.

39.

41.

43.

45.

47. The figure is an isosceles right triangle.

49a. $\begin{cases} 9 \leq x \leq 10 \\ 5 \leq y \leq 5\frac{1}{2} \end{cases}$

b.
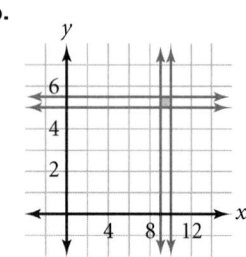

51a. $\begin{cases} x + y \leq 5000 \\ x \leq 3000 \\ y \leq 4000 \\ x \geq 0, y \geq 0 \end{cases}$

b.

c. The change increases the number of possible combinations.

53.

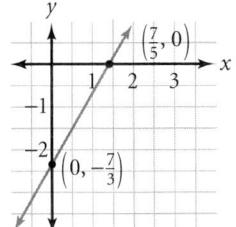

55. $x = \frac{5}{6}$ **57.** $x = -\frac{37}{9}$ **59.** $x = \frac{13}{9}$

61. $(f - g)(x) = 4x - 3$ **63.** $\left(\frac{f}{g}\right)(x) = \frac{3x + 2}{5 - x}, x \neq 5$

65. $\left(\frac{2}{15}, -\frac{5}{13}\right)$; independent **67.** infinitely many

solutions; dependent

LESSON 3.5

Exercises

4. Let x be the number of acres of corn and y be
the number of acres of soybeans. The constraints are
$\begin{cases} x + y \leq 150 \\ 40 \leq x \leq 120 \\ 0 \leq y \leq 100 \end{cases}$.

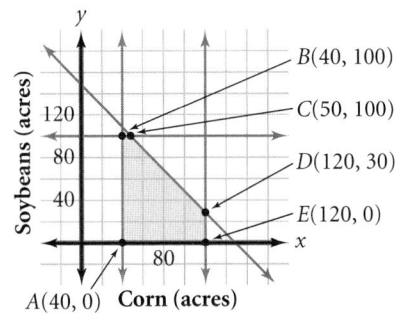

The objective function is $R = 357.525x + 237.32y$.

5. Let x be the number of acres of wheat and
y be the number of acres of soybeans. The

constraints are $\begin{cases} x + y \leq 220 \\ 100 \leq x \leq 200 \\ 0 \leq y \leq 75 \end{cases}$.

The objective function is $R = 159.31x + 237.32y$.
6. 120 acres of corn and 30 acres of soybeans **7.** 145
acres of wheat and 75 acres of soybeans
8. maximum value = 48, minimum value = 23
9. no maximum value, minimum value = 34

11.

13.

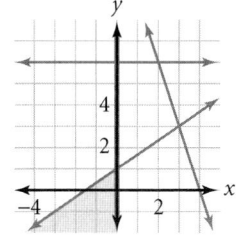

15. (0, 2), (0, 6), and (2, 3) **17.** (0, 1)
19. maximum value = 6, minimum value = −2
21. maximum value = 23, minimum value = −6
23. maximum value = 12, minimum value = 3
25. maximum value = 36, minimum value = 2
27. no maximum value, minimum value = 2
29. maximum value = 10, minimum value = −5
31. Answers may vary. Sample answers are given.
a. The objective function, $P = 2x + 3y$, has its
maximum value, 6, at (0, 2) and at $\left(\frac{6}{5}, \frac{6}{5}\right)$.

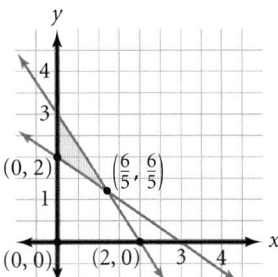

b. The objective function, $P = 2x + 3y$, has its
minimum value, 6, at $\left(\frac{6}{5}, \frac{6}{5}\right)$ and at (3, 0).

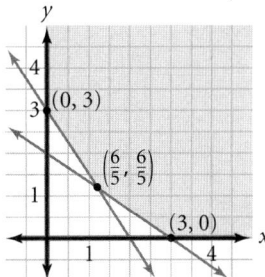

33a. $\begin{cases} 10{,}000x + 20{,}000y \leq 100{,}000 \\ 100x + 75y \leq 500 \\ x \geq 0, y \geq 0 \end{cases}$

b.

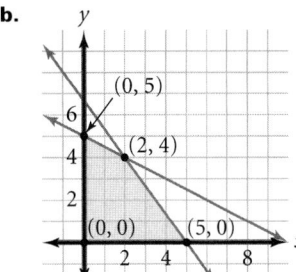

c. The objective
function is
$P = 7x + 15y$.
The maximum
number of
passengers is 75.

35a. $\begin{cases} 45x + 9y \geq 45 \\ 10x + 6y \geq 20 \\ x \geq 0, y \geq 0 \end{cases}$

b.

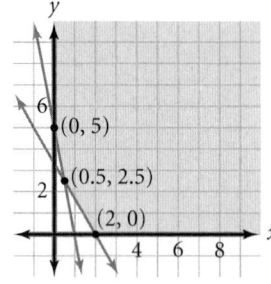

c. The objective function is $M = 4x + 2y$. The minimum number of fat grams is 7.

37a. $\begin{cases} 6x + 2y \leq 24 \\ x \geq 2 \\ y \geq 2 \end{cases}$

b.

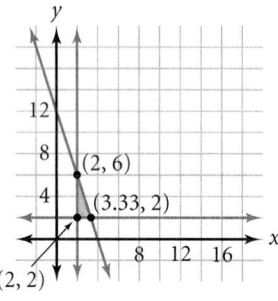

c. The objective function is $P = 50x + 20y$. The maximum profit is \$220. **39.** linear; $(-5, 10)$

41.

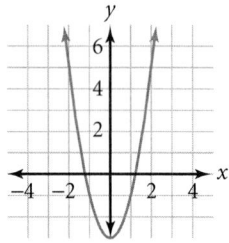

domain: all real numbers; range: $g(x) \geq -3$

43. $g^{-1}(x) = -\frac{1}{2}x + \frac{1}{8}$ **45.** $g^{-1}(x) = 4x + 24$

LESSON 3.6

TRY THIS (p. 196)

$\begin{cases} x(t) = -2t + 2 \\ y(t) = -t - 2 \end{cases}$ for $-4 \leq t \leq 4$

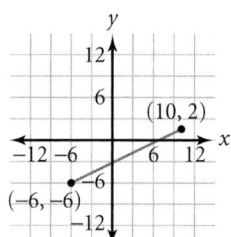

TRY THIS (p. 197)

$y = -\frac{3}{2}x - 10$

TRY THIS (p. 198)

a. after about 0.95 seconds **b.** no

Exercises

4.

5.

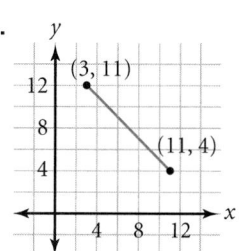

6. $y = \frac{3}{5}x + \frac{23}{5}$ **7.** $y = -x + 8$ **8a.** approximately 2.6 seconds **b.** yes

9.

11.

13.

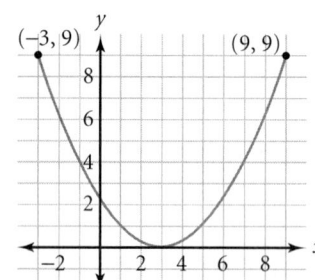

15. $y = \frac{1}{2}x - 1$ **17.** $y = \frac{1}{2}x + \frac{9}{2}$ **19.** $y = 1 - \frac{1}{3}x$

21. $y = \frac{1}{4}x^2 - 1$ **23.** $y = 9x^2$ **25.** $x = 5 - \frac{4}{9}y^2$

27. inverse parametric equations: $\begin{cases} x(t) = t \\ y(t) = t^2 - 2 \end{cases}$

29. inverse parametric equations: $\begin{cases} x(t) = 6 - t^2 \\ y(t) = t \end{cases}$

31. inverse parametric equations: $\begin{cases} x(t) = t + 1 \\ y(t) = t^2 + 5t - 1 \end{cases}$

33. $x(t) = t, y(t) = 3t - 17$ **35a.** 31.5 feet high after 1.25 seconds **b.** The ball hits the ground 159.2 feet away after 2.65 seconds. **37a.** $x(t) = 160t$, $y(t) = 2000 - 15t$ **b.** about 133 seconds **c.** about 21,300 feet **39.** $(f \circ g)(x) = 3 - x$ **41.** $(f \circ f)(x) = x + 4$ **43.** a vertical stretch by a factor of 12 followed by a vertical translation 3 units up **45.** a horizontal stretch by a factor of 2, a reflection across the x-axis, and then a vertical translation 4 units up **47.** $g(x) = |x - 2|$ **49.** $g(x) = \frac{1}{5}x^2$

CHAPTER REVIEW AND ASSESSMENT

1. independent; $(4, 2)$ **3.** dependent; infinitely many solutions **5.** independent; $(4, -1)$ **7.** $x = 2$ and $y = 0$ **9.** $x = \frac{1}{6}$ and $y = \frac{1}{12}$ **11.** $x = 0$ and $y = 3$ **13.** $x = -2$ and $y = -1$ **15.** $x = -4$ and $y = 4$ **17.** infinitely many solutions **19.** no solution

21.   **23.**

25.   **27.**

29.   **31.**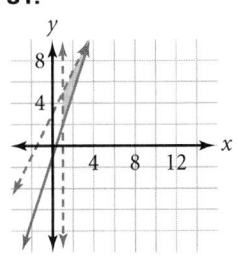

33. 13.5 minutes **35.** $y = 3x - 10$ **37.** $y = 4x - 23$

39. $\begin{cases} 5x + 12y \le 1000 \\ 8x + 12y \le 1500 \end{cases}$

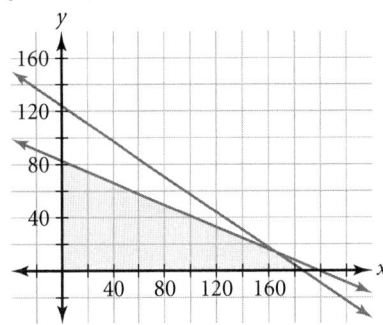

Chapter 4

LESSON 4.1

TRY THIS (p. 216)

	Small	Large
Picnic tables	15	20
Barbecue grills	18	24

$d_{21} = 18$; in June, 18 small barbecue grills were delivered.

TRY THIS (p. 217, Ex. 2)

$x = 6$ and $y = 5$

TRY THIS (p. 217, Ex. 3)

a. $\begin{bmatrix} 10 & -5 \\ 4 & -3 \\ 4 & -8 \end{bmatrix}$ **b.** $\begin{bmatrix} -10 & 5 \\ 4 & 5 \\ -10 & -2 \end{bmatrix}$

TRY THIS (p. 218)

$\begin{bmatrix} -1 & 9 \\ 0 & -9 \end{bmatrix}$

TRY THIS (p. 220)

a.   **b.**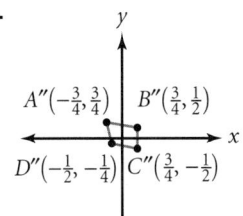

Exercises

5. $M = \begin{bmatrix} 12 & 28 & 17 \\ 15 & 32 & 45 \\ 6 & 20 & 30 \end{bmatrix}$, there are 45 large T-shirts in the inventory. **6.** $x = 3$ and $y = -4$

7a. $\begin{bmatrix} 11 & -7 \\ -7 & 5 \\ 0 & 6 \end{bmatrix}$ **b.** $\begin{bmatrix} -5 & 11 \\ -3 & -7 \\ -14 & 12 \end{bmatrix}$ **8.** $\begin{bmatrix} -3 & -9 & -9 \\ -12 & -1 & 15 \end{bmatrix}$

9. $\begin{bmatrix} \frac{1}{2} & 0 & -4 \\ -3 & 2 & -\frac{5}{2} \end{bmatrix}$ **10.** $Q = \begin{bmatrix} -3 & 2 & 1 & -4 \\ 3 & 3 & -3 & -3 \end{bmatrix}$

11a.   **b.**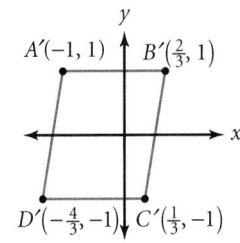

13. 4×3 **15.** 8 **17.** 6 **19.** $\begin{bmatrix} -28 \\ -8 \\ -24 \end{bmatrix}$ **21.** $\begin{bmatrix} -8 & 5 & -2 \\ 1 & -4 & 2 \\ 0 & 5 & -3 \\ -5 & -7 & 6 \end{bmatrix}$

23. $\begin{bmatrix} 4 & -\frac{5}{2} & 1 \\ -\frac{1}{2} & 2 & -1 \\ 0 & -\frac{5}{2} & \frac{3}{2} \\ \frac{5}{2} & \frac{7}{2} & -3 \end{bmatrix}$ **25.** $x = -7$ and $y = -18$

27. $x = 9$ and $y = 8$ **29.** $x = 4$ and $y = 3$

31. $\begin{bmatrix} 1 & 3 & -12 & 8 \\ 3 & 6 & 8 & -13 \end{bmatrix}$ **33.** $\begin{bmatrix} -18 & 0 & -33 & 9 \\ 15 & -6 & 24 & -27 \end{bmatrix}$

35. $\begin{bmatrix} 6 & 0 & 11 & -3 \\ -5 & 2 & -8 & 9 \end{bmatrix}$ **37.** $\begin{bmatrix} 20 & 6 & 9 & 7 \\ -9 & 18 & -8 & 1 \end{bmatrix}$

39. $\begin{bmatrix} 27 & 9 & 8 & 12 \\ -11 & 26 & -8 & -3 \end{bmatrix}$

41. $\begin{bmatrix} -46 & -12 & -29 & -11 \\ 23 & -38 & 24 & -11 \end{bmatrix}$

43. $\begin{bmatrix} 32 & 6 & 31 & 1 \\ -19 & 22 & -24 & 19 \end{bmatrix}$

45. $\begin{bmatrix} \frac{98}{3} & 14 & -\frac{14}{3} & \frac{70}{3} \\ -\frac{28}{3} & \frac{112}{3} & 0 & -\frac{56}{3} \end{bmatrix}$ **47a.** $\begin{bmatrix} -2 & 3 & 0 \\ 3 & 4 & 0 \end{bmatrix}$

b.

c.

d.

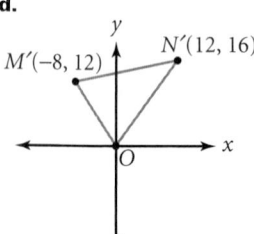

49a. $\begin{bmatrix} 0 & -3 & -3 \\ 0 & -3 & 0 \end{bmatrix}$

b.

c. **d.**

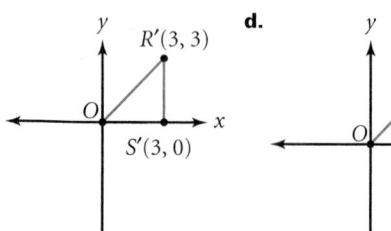

51. $m_{42} = 5$; there are 5 maps of Africa from the 1970s.
53. 23 **55.** $P = \begin{bmatrix} 27 & 31 & 24 & 18 \\ 48 & 72 & 61 & 25 \end{bmatrix}$ **57.** p_{21}, which
represents the number of squash Jane sold **59.** 3×5
61. 6 **63.** Answers may vary. sample answer: records:
10 country, 15 jazz, 5 rock, 8 blues, 3 classical; tapes:

5 country, 9 jazz, 1 rock, 13 blues, 6 classical;
compact discs: 3 country, 1 jazz, 9 rock, 5 blues, 10
classical **65.** Answers may vary. In matrix M above,
$m_{23} = 1$ rock tape. **67.** $y = 4x - 37$

69. $y = \frac{x+1}{2}$ **71.** $y = -3x + 15$, or $x = 5 - \frac{1}{3}y$

LESSON 4.2

TRY THIS (p. 226)

a. $\begin{bmatrix} -2 & -21 \\ 20 & 35 \\ -10 & 0 \end{bmatrix}$ **b.** does not exist

Exercises

4a. $[-15]$ **b.** $\begin{bmatrix} 4 & -12 & -20 \\ -2 & 6 & 10 \\ 5 & -15 & -25 \end{bmatrix}$

5a. $\begin{bmatrix} 4 & 3 & 2 \\ 2 & 3 & 4 \end{bmatrix}$ **b.** $\begin{bmatrix} 52 & 69 & 86 \\ 302 & 258 & 214 \\ 108 & 159 & 210 \end{bmatrix}$

c. The trail mix has the most protein. The sport mix
has the most carbohydrates.

6.
$$\begin{array}{c} \quad X \quad Y \quad Z \\ \begin{array}{c} X \\ Y \\ Z \end{array} \begin{bmatrix} 1 & 1 & 1 \\ 1 & 0 & 1 \\ 2 & 1 & 0 \end{bmatrix} = M \end{array}$$

a. $\begin{bmatrix} 4 & 2 & 2 \\ 3 & 2 & 1 \\ 3 & 2 & 3 \end{bmatrix}$ **b.** $m_{22} = 2$, which is the number of
two-stage paths from Y to Y: $Y \rightarrow Z \rightarrow Y$ and
$Y \rightarrow X \rightarrow Y$.

7. $\begin{bmatrix} 2 & -6 & 8 \\ 0 & 0 & 0 \\ 6 & -18 & 24 \end{bmatrix}$ **9.** $\begin{bmatrix} 20 & 13 & 4 \\ 0 & 1 & 3 \end{bmatrix}$ **11.** $\begin{bmatrix} 30 & 27 \\ 13 & -3 \end{bmatrix}$

13. $\begin{bmatrix} 19 & 18 & -3 \\ -1 & 30 & 9 \end{bmatrix}$ **15.** $\begin{bmatrix} -12 & 62 \\ 6 & 13 \\ -16 & 0 \\ -10 & 77 \end{bmatrix}$

17. does not exist **19.** $\begin{bmatrix} -188 & 222 \\ 12 & 794 \\ 60 & -142 \end{bmatrix}$

21a. $A'(-1, 0), B'\left(\frac{3}{2}, 0\right), C'(0, -2)$

b.

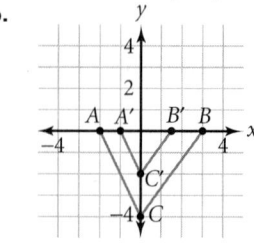

c. This transformation
is the same as mul-
tiplying the original
matrix by a scalar
factor of $\frac{1}{2}$.

23a. $\begin{bmatrix} -3 & 3 & 3 & -2 \\ -3 & -2 & 2 & 1 \end{bmatrix}$ **b.**

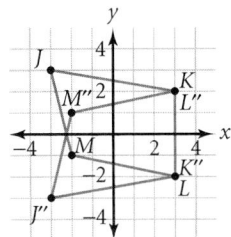

c. Answers may vary. Sample answer: The geometric figure is reflected across the x-axis.

25a. $\begin{bmatrix} 17 \\ 37 \\ 28 \\ 40 \end{bmatrix}$; 28; 122 **b.** 9 points; second game

c. 9 rows and 1 column

27a. $\left[833\frac{1}{3} \quad 1166\frac{2}{3} \right]$; 833 cars in NY and 1167 cars in LA **b.** $\left[805\frac{5}{9} \quad 1194\frac{4}{9} \right]$; 806 cars in NY and 1194 cars in LA **c.** 800 cars in NY and 1200 cars in LA; 4 months have passed.

29a.

$$\begin{array}{c c} & \begin{array}{ccc} R & S & T \end{array} \\ \begin{array}{c} R \\ S \\ T \end{array} & \begin{bmatrix} 3 & 2 & 0 \\ 1 & 2 & 1 \\ 1 & 3 & 2 \end{bmatrix} \end{array}$$

b. 15 two-stage paths **c.** R to S to R, R to T to R, R to T to R, R to S to S, R to T to S, S to S to R, S to S to S, S to R to S, S to R to T, T to S to R, T to S to S, T to R to S, T to R to S, T to R to R, and T to R to T
31. undefined; no y-intercept **33.** -18; 0 **35.** true
37. true **39.** $10x + 13$ **41.** 59

LESSON 4.3

TRY THIS (p. 238)
a. -19; has an inverse **b.** 0; has no inverse

Exercises

5. $\begin{bmatrix} 2 & 1 \\ 1 & 1 \end{bmatrix} \begin{bmatrix} 1 & -1 \\ -1 & 2 \end{bmatrix} = \begin{bmatrix} 1 & 0 \\ 0 & 1 \end{bmatrix}$

$\begin{bmatrix} 1 & -1 \\ -1 & 2 \end{bmatrix} \begin{bmatrix} 2 & 1 \\ 1 & 1 \end{bmatrix} = \begin{bmatrix} 1 & 0 \\ 0 & 1 \end{bmatrix}$ **6.** $\begin{bmatrix} 4 & -5 \\ -7 & 9 \end{bmatrix}$

7. WAY TO GO **8.** 0; no **9.** 4; yes **11.** yes
13. 1; yes **15.** 0; no **17.** 0; no **19.** 2; yes
21. $\begin{bmatrix} 4 & -2 & 3 \\ 8 & -3 & 5 \\ 7 & -2 & 4 \end{bmatrix}$ **23.** no inverse **25.** $\begin{bmatrix} \frac{1}{2} & -\frac{1}{6} \\ 0 & \frac{1}{3} \end{bmatrix}$

27. $\begin{bmatrix} \frac{10}{33} & -\frac{1}{11} \\ -\frac{3}{11} & \frac{2}{11} \end{bmatrix}$ **29.** $\begin{bmatrix} 5 & -7 \\ -2 & 3 \end{bmatrix}$ **31.** $\begin{bmatrix} 1 & -1 \\ -1 & 2 \end{bmatrix}$

33. $\begin{bmatrix} 3 & 7 \\ 2 & 5 \end{bmatrix}$ **35.** $\begin{bmatrix} 8 & -2 \\ -10 & 4 \end{bmatrix}$ **37.** $\begin{bmatrix} 2 & 0 \\ -8 & 4 \end{bmatrix}$

39. $\begin{bmatrix} -0.86 & 2.57 \\ 2.57 & -1.71 \end{bmatrix}$ **41.** $\begin{bmatrix} -0.54 & 0.23 & -0.08 \\ 0.77 & -0.62 & 0.54 \\ 0.69 & -0.15 & 0.38 \end{bmatrix}$

43. $\begin{bmatrix} 0.27 & -0.05 & 0.10 \\ 0.02 & 0.13 & -0.10 \\ -0.12 & 0.12 & 0.12 \end{bmatrix}$ **45a.** 10 **b.** 0 **c.** 59

47. $A^{-1} = \begin{bmatrix} \frac{1}{2} & 0 \\ 0 & 1 \end{bmatrix}$; $\begin{bmatrix} \frac{1}{2} & 0 \\ 0 & 1 \end{bmatrix} \begin{bmatrix} 2 & 2 & -2 & -2 \\ 2 & -2 & -2 & 2 \end{bmatrix} = \begin{bmatrix} 1 & 1 & -1 & -1 \\ 2 & -2 & -2 & 2 \end{bmatrix}$

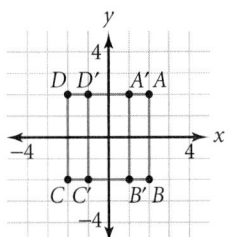

49. $\begin{bmatrix} 82 & 70 & 59 & 80 & 24 \\ 52 & 45 & 39 & 52 & 16 \end{bmatrix}$, or

82 | 70 | 59 | 80 | 24 | 52 | 45 | 39 | 52 | 16

51. $\begin{bmatrix} 15 & 43 & 32 & 149 & 40 \\ 9 & 27 & 21 & 93 & 25 \end{bmatrix}$, or

15 | 43 | 32 | 149 | 40 | 9 | 27 | 21 | 93 | 25
53. MAN DOWN **55.** CHARGE AT NOON
57. $y = \frac{9}{2}x + 3$ **59.** $-\frac{1}{2} = x$ **61.** $x = 1.5$
63. $x = 3$ **65.** $x = \frac{35}{6}$ and $y = \frac{17}{42}$
67.

LESSON 4.4

TRY THIS (p. 245)
$33,333.33 at 5% and $16,666.67 at 14%

TRY THIS (p. 246)
$(1, -1, -3)$

TRY THIS (p. 247)
no inverse; dependent

Exercises

7. $2500 at 6% and $7500 at 8%
8. $x = -7$ and $y = 15$ **9.** inconsistent **10.** inconsistent
11. $\begin{bmatrix} 3 & -5 \\ 2 & 1 \end{bmatrix} \begin{bmatrix} x \\ y \end{bmatrix} = \begin{bmatrix} 1 \\ -2 \end{bmatrix}$ **13.** $\begin{bmatrix} 2 & 4 \\ 1 & -1 \end{bmatrix} \begin{bmatrix} a \\ b \end{bmatrix} = \begin{bmatrix} -3 \\ 9 \end{bmatrix}$

15. $\begin{bmatrix} 0 & 1 & 5 \\ -2 & 3 & -1 \\ 6 & 0 & -3 \end{bmatrix} \begin{bmatrix} x \\ y \\ z \end{bmatrix} = \begin{bmatrix} -14 \\ 2 \\ 21 \end{bmatrix}$

17. $\begin{cases} 2x - y + 3z = 4 \\ -3x - z = 1 \\ x - 3y + z = 5 \end{cases}$ **19.** $x = 4, y = 3,$ and $z = -7$

21. $x = 3, y = 0,$ and $z = 0$ **23.** $x = 1.4, y = -2.4,$ and $z = 1.6$ **25.** not possible **27.** $x = -2, y = 0,$ and $z = 1$ **29.** $x = 1, y = 2, z = 3,$ and $w = 4$ **31.** Answers may vary. sample answers:

$\begin{bmatrix} 1 & 0 \\ 0 & -1 \end{bmatrix}$, $\begin{bmatrix} 0 & -1 \\ -1 & 0 \end{bmatrix}$, or $\begin{bmatrix} 0 & 1 \\ 1 & 0 \end{bmatrix}$ **33.** 70

children, 35 adults, and 15 seniors **35.** 1 liter of 4% acid and 2 liters of 7% acid **37.** domain: all real numbers; range: all real numbers ≥ 2

39. $4x^2 + 6x + 1$ **41.**

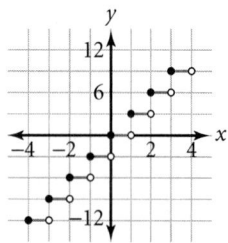

LESSON 4.5

TRY THIS (p. 254)

$(8z - 28, 18 - 5z, z)$; dependent

TRY THIS (p. 255)

no solution; inconsistent

Exercises

5a. $\begin{cases} x + y = 120 \\ 200x + 50y = 12{,}750 \end{cases}$ **b.** 45 leather jackets and

75 imitation leather jackets **6.** no solution; inconsistent **7.** $(6, -3, -2)$; independent

9. $\begin{bmatrix} -1 & 2 & -5 & \vdots & 23 \\ 2 & 0 & 7 & \vdots & 19 \\ 5 & -2 & 1 & \vdots & -10 \end{bmatrix}$

11. $R_2 = [0 \quad 13 \quad -17 \quad \vdots \quad 15]$ **13.** $\begin{bmatrix} 1 & 0 & \vdots & 2 \\ 0 & 1 & \vdots & 3 \end{bmatrix}$

15. $\begin{bmatrix} 1 & 0 & \vdots & 4 \\ 0 & 1 & \vdots & 4 \end{bmatrix}$ **17.** $\begin{bmatrix} 1 & 0 & 0 & \vdots & -2 \\ 0 & 1 & 0 & \vdots & 2 \\ 0 & 0 & 1 & \vdots & 2 \end{bmatrix}$

19. $x = 1, y = -1$ **21.** $x = 1, y = -1$ **23.** $x = -3, y = 5,$ $z = -1$ **25.** $x = -\frac{5}{7}, y = \frac{27}{7}, z = -\frac{1}{7}$ **27.** $x = 0, y = 0,$ $z = 1$ **29.** $x = \frac{2}{3}, y = -\frac{4}{3}, z = \frac{10}{3}$ **31.** dependent

33. independent **35.** dependent **37a.** $E = \begin{bmatrix} 2 & 0 \\ 0 & 1 \end{bmatrix}$;

$EA = \begin{bmatrix} 2 & 4 \\ 3 & 4 \end{bmatrix}$ **b.** $E = \begin{bmatrix} 0 & 1 \\ 1 & 0 \end{bmatrix}$; $EA = \begin{bmatrix} 3 & 4 \\ 1 & 2 \end{bmatrix}$

c. $E = \begin{bmatrix} 1 & 0 \\ 2 & 1 \end{bmatrix}$; $EA = \begin{bmatrix} 1 & 2 \\ 5 & 8 \end{bmatrix}$ **39.** $p_1 = \frac{2}{3}, p_2 = \frac{1}{6},$ and

$p_3 = \frac{1}{6}$ **41.** 3 days in Peru, 2 days in Bolivia, and 5 days in Chile **43.** not linear **45.** function

47. function

49.

51.

53a. $\begin{bmatrix} -4 & 3 & 15 \\ 17 & 5 & -13 \\ 8 & -4 & -9 \end{bmatrix}$ **b.** $\begin{bmatrix} 8 & 9 & 11 \\ -7 & 0 & 0 \\ 17 & 1 & -16 \end{bmatrix}$ **c.** no

CHAPTER REVIEW AND ASSESSMENT

1. $\begin{bmatrix} 5 & -7 & 5 \\ 1 & 5 & 10 \end{bmatrix}$ **3.** $\begin{bmatrix} 0 & 0 & 0 \\ 0 & 0 & 0 \end{bmatrix}$

5. $\begin{bmatrix} 0 & -11 & -22 \\ 22 & 44 & 77 \end{bmatrix}$ **7.** $\begin{bmatrix} 3 & -7 & -5 \\ 2 & -11 & -2 \end{bmatrix}$

9. $\begin{bmatrix} -12 & 19 & -6 \\ -4 & -4 & -21 \end{bmatrix}$ **11.** not possible

13. $\begin{bmatrix} -16 & 13 \\ 22 & -3 \\ -27 & 6 \end{bmatrix}$ **15.** not possible

17. -15; $\begin{bmatrix} 0 & 0.2 \\ 0.\overline{3} & 0.1\overline{3} \end{bmatrix}$ **19.** 0; no inverse

21. 24; $\begin{bmatrix} 0.208\overline{3} & 0.041\overline{6} \\ 0.041\overline{6} & 0.208\overline{3} \end{bmatrix}$ **23.** 5; $\begin{bmatrix} -0.6 & 0.8 \\ 0.2 & -0.6 \end{bmatrix}$

25. 0; no inverse **27.** not possible

29. $x = 0, y = 1, z = -5$ **31.** $x = 0, y = 1, z = -5$

33. $(0, 1, -3)$; independent **35.** no solution; inconsistent **37.** $(0, 0, 0)$; independent **39.** 70 regular tickets, 110 student tickets, and 30 child tickets

Chapter 5

LESSON 5.1

TRY THIS (p. 275)
$g(x) = 2x^2 - 9x + 10$ has the form $g(x) = ax^2 + bx + c$, where $a = 2$, $b = -9$, and $c = 10$.

TRY THIS (p. 276)
maximum; $(-1, 3)$

Exercises
4. $f(x) = x^2 - 6x - 7$; $a = 1$, $b = -6$, and $c = -7$
5. $g(x) = x^2 + 7x + 10$; $a = 1$, $b = 7$, and $c = 10$
6. $f(x)$ $6x^2 + 17x + 5$; $a = 6$, $b = 17$, and $c = 5$
7. minimum; $x = 1.5$, $y = 2.75$ **8.** maximum; $x = -1.5$ and $y = 4.25$ **9.** minimum; $x = -2.5$ and $y = -3.25$ **10.** opens up; minimum **11.** opens down; maximum **12.** opens down; maximum
13. $f(x) = x^2 + 5x - 24$; $a = 1$, $b = 5$, $c = -24$
15. $g(x) = -x^2 - 3x + 28$; $a = -1$, $b = -3$, $c = 28$
17. $g(x) = -x^2 - 4x + 12$; $a = -1$, $b = -4$, $c = 12$
19. $f(x) = 3x^2 - 3x - 6$; $a = 3$, $b = -3$, $c = -6$
21. $h(x) = x^2 - 3x$; $a = 1$, $b = -3$, $c = 0$
23. $g(x) = -2x^2 + 5x + 12$; $a = -2$, $b = 5$, $c = 12$
25. $h(x) = x^2 - 16$; $a = 1$, $b = 0$, $c = -16$
27. quadratic **29.** quadratic **31.** not quadratic
33. opens down; maximum **35.** opens down; maximum **37.** opens down; maximum **39.** opens down; maximum **41.** $x = 0.5$, $y = 8.75$ **43.** $x = 0.25$, $y = 1.75$ **45.** $x = 2$, $y = -1$ **47.** The axis of symmetry of the parabola will lie midway between the values of a and $-a$. Therefore, the vertex will occur when $x = 0$ and $y = f(0) = -a^2$.

49a.

Width (yd)	Length (yd)	Area (yd²)
3	14	42
4	12	48
x	$20 - 2x$	$20x - 2x^2$

b. $0 < x < 10$ **c.** $l(x) = 20 - 2x$, where $0 < x < 10$
d. $A(x) = -2x^2 + 20x$ **e.** domain: $0 < x < 10$; range: $0 < A(x) < 50$ **f.** Maximum area will be 50 square yards when the width is 5 yards and the length is 10 yards. **51.** slope $= -4$ **53.** $y = 11$

LESSON 5.2

TRY THIS (p. 282, Ex. 1)
$x = \pm 5\sqrt{2} \approx \pm 7.07$

TRY THIS (p. 282, Ex. 2)
$x = -\frac{11}{2}$ or $x = \frac{3}{2}$

TRY THIS (p. 283)
about 1.5 seconds

TRY THIS (p. 285, Ex. 4)
a. about 8.1 units
b. about 9.3 units

TRY THIS (p. 285, Ex. 5)
$PQ \approx 1207$ meters

Exercises
4. $\pm\sqrt{29} \approx \pm 5.39$ **5.** $\pm\sqrt{11} \approx \pm 3.32$ **6.** $-4, 2$
7. $2 \pm \sqrt{7}$; $-0.65, 4.65$ **8.** $\pm\sqrt{10} \approx \pm 3.16$
9. $\pm\sqrt{24} \approx \pm 2\sqrt{6} \approx \pm 4.90$ **10.** about 2.6 seconds **11.** $e \approx 3.7$
12. $n \approx 17.7$ **13.** 107.6 meters **15.** $\pm\sqrt{32} \approx \pm 4\sqrt{2} \approx \pm 5.66$
17. $\pm\sqrt{5} \approx \pm 2.24$ **19.** $\pm\sqrt{12} \approx \pm 2\sqrt{3} \approx \pm 3.46$ **21.** ± 6
23. $\pm\sqrt{\frac{11}{2}}$; ± 2.35 **25.** $\pm\sqrt{2}$; ± 1.41 **27.** 1, 9
29. $\pm\sqrt{126} \approx \pm 3\sqrt{14} \approx \pm 11.22$ **31.** $-1 \pm \sqrt{5}$; $-3.24, 1.24$
33. $t \approx 2.2$ **35.** $d \approx 5.3$ **37.** $v \approx 24.2$ **39.** $c \approx 8.9$
41. $a = 2$ **43.** $b = 5$ **45.** $x^2 - 17 = 0$ **47.** about 4.47 inches **49a.** $a \approx 4.24$ feet **b.** $b \approx 5.20$ feet **51.** 1.43 seconds **53.** 127.28 feet **55.** 120.93 feet **57.** 19.49 feet **59.** 14 feet **61.** linear; $(9, 15)$ **63.** $m = \frac{4}{9}$; $y = \frac{4}{9}x + \frac{11}{3}$ **65.** $\frac{1}{25}$ **67.** domain: all real numbers; range: all real numbers ≥ -7 **69.** domain: all real numbers; range: all real numbers ≥ 0

LESSON 5.3

TRY THIS (p. 290)
a. $5x(x + 3)$
b. $(2x - 1)(4 + x)$

TRY THIS (p. 292, Ex. 2)
$(x + 4)(x + 5)$

TRY THIS (p. 292, Ex. 3)
$(x + 1)(x - 11)$

TRY THIS (p. 293, Ex. 4)
$(3x + 4)(x - 5)$

TRY THIS (p. 293, Ex. 5)
$9x^2 - 49 = (3x + 7)(3x - 7)$
$3x^2 + 6x + 3 = 3(x + 1)^2$

TRY THIS (p. 294)
a. $x = 0$ or $x = -4$
b. $x = -7$ or $x = 3$

Exercises
4. $2x(x - 4)$ **5.** $2y(y - 3)$ **6.** $5ax(x - 3a)$
7. $(4x - 7)(x + 3)$ **8.** $(4r + 7)(3 - 2r)$
9. $(9s - 5)(8s + 3)$ **10.** $(x + 3)(x + 2)$
11. $(x + 7)(x + 1)$ **12.** $(y - 4)(y - 1)$
13. $(x + 2)(x - 6)$ **14.** $(y + 3)(y - 12)$
15. $(x + 12)(x - 2)$ **16.** $(2x + 5)(x + 2)$
17. $(3x + 2)(x + 1)$ **18.** $(x + 3)(5x - 2)$
19. $2(4x - 7)(x + 3)$ **20.** $(3r - 2)(4r + 7)$
21. $4(2s - 1)(9s - 7)$ **22.** $(x^2 + 9)(x + 3)(x - 3)$
23. $2(x + 2)(x - 2)$ **24.** $(4x + 5)(4x - 5)$ **25.** $(x + 4)^2$
26. $x = 0$ or $x = -7$ **27.** $x = -3$ **28.** $t = -5$ or $t = 2$
29. 9 points **31.** $3(x^2 + 6)$ **33.** $x(1 - 4x)$
35. $-3y(y + 5)$ **37.** $(x + 3)(2x + 7)$ **39.** $2ab(2b - 3a)$
41. $(x + 4)^2$ **43.** $(x + 8)(x - 4)$ **45.** $(x - 12)(x + 2)$
47. $(x + 6)(x - 4)$ **49.** $-(x + 4)(x - 14)$
51. $-(x + 2)(x - 12)$ **53.** $(2x + 1)(x + 2)$
55. $(3x + 1)(x + 2)$ **57.** $(3x + 1)(x - 2)$
59. $x = -\frac{1}{3}$ or $x = 2$ **61.** $x = \frac{1}{3}$ or $x = 3$
63. $x = \frac{4}{3}$ or $x = \frac{3}{2}$ **65.** $t = -3$ or $t = 3$

67. $x = -1$ or $x = 1$ **69.** $x = -\frac{4}{5}$ or $x = \frac{4}{5}$ **71.** $x = -2$

73. $x = \frac{1}{2}$ **75.** $x = -\frac{5}{4}$ **77.** $x = 3$ **79.** $t = -3$ or $t = 5$

81. $x = -\frac{3}{2}$ or $x = 1$ **83.** $x = 8$ or $x = 7$ **85.** $x = -5$

or $x = 8$ **87.** $x = \frac{3}{2}$ or $x = \frac{1}{2}$ **89.** $t = -2$ or $t = 6$

91. $x = -4$ or $x = -2$ **93.** $x = -0.5$ or $x = 6$

95. $(x^n + 1)(x^n - 1)$ **97.** 7 centimeters **99.** 6 inches

101. 4 seconds

103. $x < -5\frac{1}{3}$

105. $x \le -1\frac{1}{19}$

107a. $\begin{cases} 40{,}000x + 25{,}000y \le 1{,}270{,}000 \\ x + y \ge 40 \\ x \ge 0 \\ y \ge 0 \end{cases}$

b.

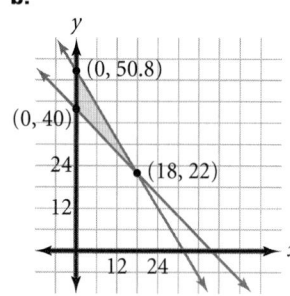

c. Answers may vary. Sample answer: The point $(18, 22)$ is a solution to the system. This point represents buying 18 commercials in the \$40,000 time slot and 22 commercials in the \$25,000 time slot.

109. $\begin{bmatrix} 0 & -1 & -4 \\ -\frac{1}{2} & -2 & -\frac{3}{2} \\ 1 & 0 & \frac{1}{2} \end{bmatrix}$ **111.** $\begin{bmatrix} -3 & 5 & 16 \\ 4 & 14 & 2 \\ 1 & -2 & -1 \end{bmatrix}$

113. $8x^2 - 50x + 63$

LESSON 5.4

TRY THIS (p. 300)

a. $x^2 - 7x + \left(\frac{7}{2}\right)^2 = \left(x - \frac{7}{2}\right)^2$ **b.** $x^2 + 16x + 8^2 = (x + 8)^2$

TRY THIS (p. 301, Ex. 2)

$x = -12$ or $x = 2$

TRY THIS (p. 301, Ex. 3)

$x = \frac{-5 \pm \sqrt{37}}{2} \approx 0.54$ or -5.54

TRY THIS (p. 302)

$g(x) = 3\left(x - \frac{3}{2}\right)^2 + \left(-\frac{35}{4}\right)$; $\left(\frac{3}{2}, -\frac{35}{4}\right)$; $x = \frac{3}{2}$. g is f stretched by a factor of 3, translated $\frac{35}{4}$ units down and $\frac{3}{2}$ units to the right.

Exercises

5. $x^2 - 12x + 36 = (x - 6)^2$ **6.** $x^2 + 5x + \frac{25}{4} = \left(x + \frac{5}{2}\right)^2$

7. $x = -3$ or $x = 7$ **8.** $x = -3$ or $x = \frac{1}{2}$

9. $g(x) = [x - (-6)]^2 + (-16)$; vertex: $(-6, -16)$; axis of symmetry: $x = -6$. The graph of g is the graph of f translated 16 units down and 6 units to the left.

10. $h(t) = -16(t - 1)^2 + 21$; 21 feet

11. $x^2 + 10x + 25 = (x + 5)^2$ **13.** $x^2 - 8x + 16 = (x - 4)^2$

15. $x^2 + 13x + \frac{169}{4} = \left(x + \frac{13}{2}\right)^2$ **17.** $x = 4 \pm \sqrt{19}$

19. $x = 1 \pm \sqrt{6}$ **21.** $x = \frac{-7}{2} \pm \sqrt{\frac{153}{4}}$

23. $x = -5$ or $x = -2$ **25.** $x = -5$ or $x = 6$

27. $x = -3$ or $x = 10$ **29.** $x = 2$ or $x = 6$

31. $x = -5 \pm \sqrt{29}$ **33.** $x = \frac{-7}{2} \pm \sqrt{\frac{41}{4}}$ **35.** $x = \frac{11}{2} \pm \sqrt{\frac{99}{4}}$

37. $x = \frac{3}{4} \pm \sqrt{\frac{105}{16}}$

39. $g(x) = -(x - 0)^2 + 2$; $(0, 2)$; $x = 0$; g is f reflected across the y-axis and translated up 2 units.

41. $g(x) = [x - (-4)]^2 + (-5)$; $(-4, -5)$; $x = -4$; g is f horizontally translated 4 units left and vertically translated down 5 units. **43.** $g(x) = -(x - 2)^2 + 6$; $(2, 6)$; $x = 2$; g is f reflected across the y-axis, translated right 2 units and translated up 6 units.

45. $g(x) = -3(x - 1)^2 + (-6)$; $(1, -6)$; $x = 1$; g is f reflected across the y-axis, stretched by a factor of 3, translated 1 unit right and 6 units down.

47. Answers may vary. sample answers:
$f(x) = (x - 2)^2 + 5 = x^2 - 4x + 9$
$g(x) = -2(x - 2)^2 + 5 = -2x^2 + 8x - 3$
$h(x) = 5(x - 2)^2 + 5 = 5x^2 - 20x + 25$

49. $-2 + \sqrt{30} \approx 3.5$ centimeters **51a.** 6:00 A.M.

b. 174 megawatts **c.** 3rd hour (between 2:00 and 3:00 A.M.) and 10th hour (between 9:00 and 10:00 A.M.)

53. $x = 5$ **55.** $x = 5$ **57.** function **59.** function

61. $g(2) = -1$; $g(-3) = 19$ **63.** $g(x) = x^2 - 6$

65. $g(x) = -|3x|$

LESSON 5.5

TRY THIS (p. 308, Ex. 1)   **TRY THIS** (p. 308, Ex. 2)

$x = 1$ or $x = 6$ $x = \frac{3 \pm \sqrt{3}}{2}$; $x \approx -0.6$ or $x \approx 2.4$

TRY THIS (p. 309)   **TRY THIS** (p. 310)

7.9 feet $x = 2$; $(2, -3)$

Exercises

4. $x = 1$ or $x = 4$ **5.** $x = -\frac{1}{2}$ or $x = 3$ **6.** $x = \frac{3 \pm \sqrt{57}}{6}$; $x \approx -0.8$ or $x \approx 1.8$ **7.** 10.7 feet **8.** $x = \frac{1}{2}$; $\left(\frac{1}{2}, -\frac{9}{4}\right)$

9. $x = 3$; $(3, -7)$ **11.** $x = -6$ or $x = 0$

13. $x = \frac{-1 \pm \sqrt{109}}{2}$ **15.** $x = \frac{3 \pm \sqrt{13}}{2}$ **17.** $x = -3$ or $x = 8$

19. $x = -\frac{3}{2}$ or $x = -\frac{1}{2}$ **21.** $x = \frac{-5 \pm \sqrt{33}}{2}$

23. $x = -5 \pm \sqrt{30}$ **25.** $x = -\frac{3}{5}$ or $x = 1$ **27.** $x = \frac{3 \pm \sqrt{13}}{-2}$

29. $x = -\frac{9}{2}; \left(-\frac{9}{2}, -\frac{25}{4}\right)$ **31.** $x = -\frac{3}{2}; \left(-\frac{3}{2}, -\frac{85}{4}\right)$

33. $x = 2; (2, 22)$ **35.** $x = -3; (-3, 11)$ **37.** $x = \frac{3}{4}; \left(\frac{3}{4}, \frac{1}{8}\right)$

39. $x = 2; (2, 21)$ **41.** $x = \frac{1}{3}; \left(\frac{1}{3}, -\frac{7}{3}\right)$ **43.** $x = -1;$

$(-1, -3)$ **45.** $x = 0; (0, 9)$ **47.** $x = -\frac{1}{5}; \left(-\frac{1}{5}, -\frac{16}{5}\right)$

49. 6 seconds **51.** Answers may vary. Sample answer:
The pyrotechnician should begin firing after
$6 - 2.5$, or 3.5, seconds. **53.** 3 inches **55.** $2687.50

57. $30.35 < x < 219.65$ **59a.** $a = \frac{b \pm b\sqrt{5}}{2}$ **b.** ≈ 1.62

61. $y = -\frac{1}{2}x - 4$ **63.** $y = -5x - 22$

65. $x > -2$ and $x < 8$

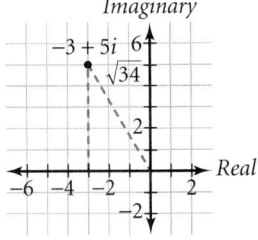

67. $x \le 1$ or $x \ge 7$

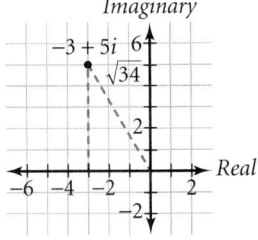

69. $\begin{bmatrix} 0.28 & 0.32 \\ 0.16 & 0.04 \end{bmatrix}$ **71.** $x = 2\sqrt{2}$ or $x = -2\sqrt{2}$

73. $x = -3\sqrt{2}$ or $x = 3\sqrt{2}$

LESSON 5.6

TRY THIS (p. 315)

$216 > 0$, so there are 2 real solutions.

TRY THIS (p. 316, Ex. 2)

$x = \frac{5}{8} + \frac{i\sqrt{23}}{8}$ or $x = \frac{5}{8} - \frac{i\sqrt{23}}{8}$

TRY THIS (p. 316, Ex. 3) **TRY THIS** (p. 317)

$x = -4$ and $y = \frac{10}{3}$ $\qquad 14 - 44i$

TRY THIS (p. 318)

$\frac{2}{5} - \frac{11}{5}i$

TRY THIS (p. 319)

$\sqrt{34}$

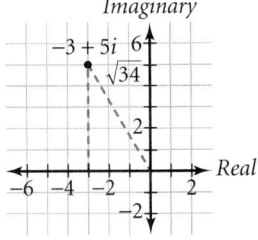

Exercises

4. 1 real solution **5.** no real solutions **6.** 2 real

solutions **7.** $x = -\frac{5}{4} \pm \frac{i\sqrt{7}}{4}$ **8.** $x = -1$ and $y = 2$

9. $6 + 10i$ **10.** $5 + 2i$ **11.** $-11 + 2i$ **12.** $\frac{10}{13} + \frac{11}{13}i$

13. 5

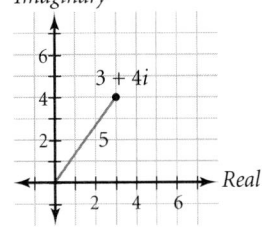

15. 2 is the real part, and 1 is the imaginary part.

17. 0 is the real part, and 4 is the imaginary part.

19. $10i$ **21.** $i\sqrt{17}$ **23.** -49 **25.** -23; no real solutions;

$x = \frac{5}{6} \pm \frac{i\sqrt{23}}{6}$ **27.** -15; no real solutions; $x = \frac{1}{2} \pm \frac{i\sqrt{15}}{10}$

29. 37; 2 real solutions; $x = \frac{3}{2} \pm \frac{\sqrt{37}}{2}$ **31.** -4; no real

solutions; $x = \frac{3}{2} \pm \frac{i}{2}$ **33.** 9; 2 real solutions; $x = 0$ or

$x = -\frac{3}{2}$ **35.** -12; no real solutions; $x = -\frac{1}{2} \pm \frac{i\sqrt{3}}{2}$

37. 0; 1 real solution; $x = 7$ **39.** -39; no real

solutions; $x = -\frac{5}{16} \pm \frac{i\sqrt{39}}{16}$ **41.** 0; 1 real solution; $x = \frac{1}{3}$

43. $x = \frac{4}{3}$ and $y = -1$ **45.** $-3 - i$ **47.** $1 + \frac{1}{5}i$ **49.** $9 - i$

51. $-1 + 2i$ **53.** $12 - 8i$ **55.** $-13 - 84i$ **57.** $-4 - 2i\sqrt{5}$

59. $-14 - 12i\sqrt{2}$ **61.** 8 **63.** $8 + 3i$ **65.** $\frac{17}{26} + \frac{7}{26}i$

67. $\frac{132}{25} - \frac{24}{25}i$ **69.** 1 **71.** $\frac{30}{17} + \frac{18}{17}i$ **73.** -4 **75.** i

77.

79.

81.

83.

85.

87.

89. 1

91. $\sqrt{1.0001}$

93. $\sqrt{13}$

95. 1

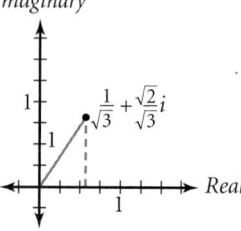

97. (3, 1), (−2, −4), (−3, 3)

99. rectangle

101.

103.

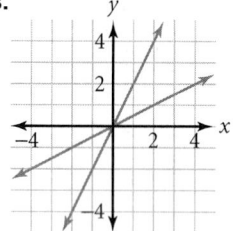

105. $(f \circ f^{-1})(x) = x$ **107.** 5 framed prints

LESSON 5.7

TRY THIS (p. 323)

$f(x) = -x^2 + 9x - 17$

Exercises

3. $f(x) \approx 2x^2 - 11x + 6$

4a.

Number of people, n	Number of handshakes, h
2	1
3	3
4	6
5	10
6	15

The first differences for the number of handshakes are 2, 3, 4, and 5; the second differences are all equal to 1, indicating a quadratic relationship.

b. $h(n) = 0.5n^2 - 0.5n$ **c.** 45 handshakes

5a. 400

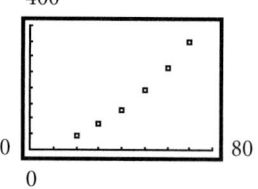

b. yes; $d \approx 0.06x^2 + 1.10x + 0.06$

7. $y = x^2 + 3x - 5$ **9.** $y = -x^2 + 6x + 10$
11. $y = 3x^2 - 2x + 4$ **13.** $y = 2x^2 - 9x + 15$
15. $y = 2x^2 - 18x + 49$ **17.** $y = -0.5x^2 + 4x + 7$
19. $y = 0.5x^2 - 0.5x + 4$ **21.** $y = 2x^2 - 5x + 7$
23. $h(t) = -6t^2 + 20t + 5$ **25.** $1\frac{2}{3}$ seconds **27.** about
3.57 seconds **29.** 0.69 second, 2.64 seconds
31. $h(t) \approx -15.11t^2 + 15.19t + 1.65$
33. yes **35.** yes **37.** yes **39.** −4 **41.** 8; yes
43. $-\frac{1}{12}$; yes

LESSON 5.8

TRY THIS (p. 331)

$2 \leq x \leq 6$

TRY THIS (p. 332)

no solution

TRY THIS (p. 333)

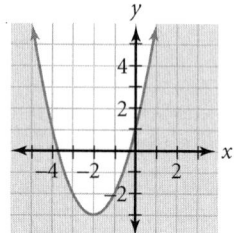

Exercises

6. $x \leq 3$ or $x \geq 4$

7. 5, 6, and 7 **8.** no solution **9.** all real numbers
except 5 **10.** no solution

11.

13. $2 < x < 3$

15. $-1 < x < 5$

17. $x < 5 \ or \ x > 10$

19. $-3 \le x \le 4$

21. $x < -2 \ or \ x > 6$

23. $-3 \le x \le 2$

25. $1 \le x \le 6$

27. $-10 \le x \le 1$

29. $x < -6 \ or \ x > 3$

31. $x \le -7 \ or \ x \ge 1$

33. $x < \dfrac{3}{2} - \dfrac{\sqrt{33}}{2} \ or \ x > \dfrac{3}{2} + \dfrac{\sqrt{33}}{2}$

35. $-\dfrac{1}{2} - \dfrac{\sqrt{29}}{2} < x < -\dfrac{1}{2} + \dfrac{\sqrt{29}}{2}$

37.

C

39.

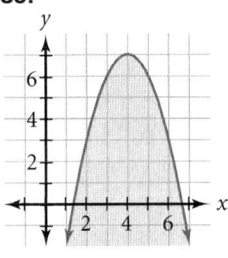

$A \ and \ B$

41.

43.

45.

47.

49.

51.

53.

55.

57.

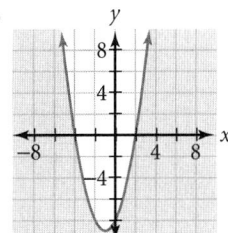

59. $x^2 - 10x + 21 > 0$ **61.** $0.2 \le t \le 1.3$ seconds
63a. from 0 to 33,000 **b.** 20,000 **c.** No; the cost increases as the number of backpacks increases.

d.

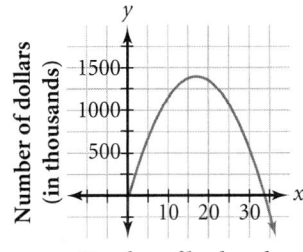

Number of dollars (in thousands)

Number of backpacks (in thousands)

e. from 1000 to 33,000; same as part **a**
f. 17,000; yes
g. after 33,000

65. approximately $0 \le t < 2.48$ **67.** about 2.32 seconds **69.** between 16 and 159 pairs, inclusive **71.** yes **73.** yes **75.** $x = \pm\sqrt{8}$ **77.** $x = \pm\sqrt{18}$ **79.** $-1 + 4i$ **81.** $6 + i$

CHAPTER REVIEW AND ASSESSMENT

1. $f(x) = -x^2 + 3x + 4$; $a = -1$, $b = 3$, and $c = 4$
3. $(1.5, 1.25)$ **5.** opens down; maximum
7. $x = \pm\sqrt{8}$; $x \approx \pm 2.83$ **9.** $x \approx \pm 7$ **11.** $x = -5 \ or \ x = 11$
13. $x = -1 \pm \frac{\sqrt{54}}{7}$; $x \approx -3.78 \ or \ x \approx 1.78$ **15.** $c \approx 6.4$
17. $a \approx 9.7$ **19.** $a \approx 24.5$ **21.** $b \approx 0.7$ **23.** $7x(x-3)$
25. $(x+5)(x+2)$ **27.** $(t+3)(t-8)$
29. $(x+2)(x-10)$ **31.** $(x+5)(x-4)$
33. $(3y+2)(y-1)$ **35.** $(4+3x)(4-3x)$ **37.** $(x-8)^2$
39. $x = 4 \ or \ x = 6$ **41.** $t = -\frac{5}{2} \ or \ t = \frac{2}{3}$
43. $x = \frac{1}{5} \pm \frac{\sqrt{6}}{5}$ **45.** $x = -12 \ or \ x = 7$
47. $x = -4 \ or \ x = \frac{1}{2}$ **49.** $x = -\frac{4}{3} \ or \ x = 2$
51. $y = -3(x+1)^2 - 4$; $(-1, -4)$
53. $y = 4\left(x - \frac{9}{8}\right)^2 - \frac{49}{16}$; $\left(\frac{9}{8}, -\frac{49}{16}\right)$ **55.** $x = -\frac{3}{5} \pm \frac{\sqrt{76}}{10}$
57. $x = -4 \ or \ x = -2$ **59.** $x = \frac{1}{12} \pm \frac{\sqrt{73}}{12}$
61. $x = -\frac{1}{2} \pm \frac{\sqrt{5}}{2}$ **63.** $\left(\frac{1}{2}, -\frac{49}{4}\right)$ **65.** $(-6, -31)$
67. 2 real solutions **69.** no real solutions
71. $x = -5 - 3i \ or \ x = -5 + 3i$ **73.** $x = 3 \pm \frac{i\sqrt{8}}{2}$
75. $x = \frac{1}{3} \pm \frac{i\sqrt{20}}{6}$ **77.** $1 - 7i$ **79.** $-1 + 8i$ **81.** $6 - 9i$
83. $2 - 4i$

85. $\sqrt{10}$

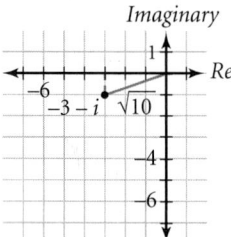

87. $\sqrt{2}$

89. $f(x) = 5x^2 + 2x - 9$ **91.** $f(x) = -5x^2 - x + 6$
93. $f(x) = 3x^2 - 3x - 3$ **95.** $f(x) = 7x^2 - 1$
97. $f(x) \approx -0.7x^2 + 1.5x - 3.1$
99. $x < 2 \ or \ x > 6$

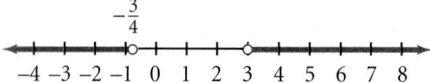

101. $x \le -5 \ or \ x \ge -2$

103. $x < -\frac{3}{4} \ or \ x > 3$

105. $0 \le x \le \frac{5}{2}$

107.

109.

111.

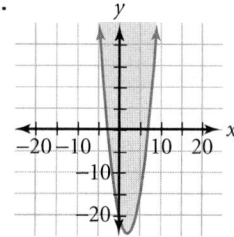

113. about 2.8 seconds

Chapter 6

LESSON 6.1

TRY THIS (p. 356)
188,700,000; 194,400,000

TRY THIS (p. 357)
192 milligrams, 62.9 milligrams

Exercises
5. 1.055 **6.** 1.0025 **7.** 0.97 **8.** 0.995 **9.** 8 **10.** 1350
11. 0.512 **12.** 42.1875 **13.** 31,400,000 **14.** 31.0 milligrams and 27.3 milligrams **15.** 1.07 **17.** 0.94
19. 1.065 **21.** 0.9995 **23.** 1.00075 **25.** 1.9
27. 1,638,400 **29.** 37.9 **31.** 394.0 **33.** 941,013.7
35. 32.6 **37a.** 8000 bacteria **b.** 32,000 bacteria
39a. 1200 bacteria **b.** 4800 bacteria **41a.** 6975 bacteria **b.** 62,775 bacteria **43.** exponential
45. linear **47.** 278,700,000 **49.** 1,359,600,000 and 1,399,800,000 **51a.** 1,002,600,000 and 1,140,800,000
b. 13.79% **c.** 1,107,500,000
53. 310,000 gallons **55.** 2 **57.** 7 **59.** $\frac{m^3}{n^{15}}$ **61.** $\frac{1}{12xy^2}$
63. reflection across y-axis and horizontal compression by a factor of $\frac{1}{2}$ **65.** reflection across x-axis, horizontal stretch by a factor of 2, and vertical translation 3 units up **67.** reflection across x-axis, vertical stretch by a factor of 5, horizontal translation 2 units to the right, and vertical translation 4 units down **69.** opens down; maximum value

LESSON 6.2

TRY THIS (p. 364)   **TRY THIS** (p. 366)
a. exponential growth; $\frac{1}{3}$ 7.2%
b. exponential decay; $\frac{1}{4}$

Exercises

5. exponential decay; 1 **6.** exponential growth; 3
7. exponential decay; 5 **8.** $334.56, $336.71, and
$337.46 **9.** 4.7% **11.** quadratic **13.** exponential
15. quadratic **17.** growth **19.** decay **21.** decay
23. decay **25.** d **27.** b **29.** $3207.14 **31.** $2013.80
33. $2132.45 **35a.** $h(x) = 8^x$; $f(x) = 2^x$ **b.** 1
c. Both functions have a domain of all real numbers
and a range of all positive real numbers. **37.** when
$a = 0$ or when $b = 1$ **39.** g is f compressed vertically
by a factor of $\frac{1}{2}$. **41.** g is f stretched vertically by a
factor of 2 and translated vertically 3 units down.
43. g is f translated 1 unit to the right and stretched
vertically by a factor of 5. **45.** g is f stretched
vertically by a factor of 2. **47.** 3.8% **49.** 1.3%
51. $2615.16 **53a.** Final amount is doubled:
$114,674. **b.** Final amount is more than 10 times
larger: $586,954.26. **c.** Final amount is more than
11 times larger: $657,506.29. **d.** doubling the
investment period **55.** {(2, 7), (−1, 3), (2, 2), (0, 0)};
not a function **57.** $y = \pm\frac{\sqrt{3x}}{3}$; not a function
59. $y = \pm\sqrt{-x}$; not a function

61.

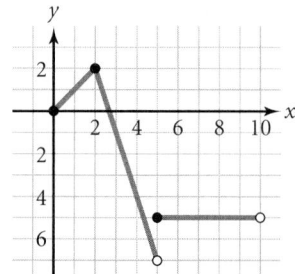

63. does not exist **65.** $\begin{bmatrix} -2 & 40 & -38 \\ 51 & 52 & -9 \end{bmatrix}$

67. $\begin{bmatrix} -32 & 14 \\ -27 & 12 \end{bmatrix}$ **69.** $y = 3x^2 - 2x + 4$

LESSON 6.3

TRY THIS (p. 371, Ex. 1)

Exponential form	Logarithmic form
$2^5 = 32$	$\log_2 32 = 5$
$10^3 = 1000$	$\log_{10} 1000 = 3$
$3^{-2} = \frac{1}{9}$	$\log_3 \frac{1}{9} = -2$
$16^{\frac{1}{2}} = 4$	$\log_{16} 4 = \frac{1}{2}$

TRY THIS (p. 371, Ex. 2) **TRY THIS** (p. 373, Ex. 3)
−2.037
                    a. $v = 3$ **b.** $v = 5$
                    c. $v = 729$

TRY THIS (p. 373, Ex. 4)
$[H^+] \approx 0.00018$ moles per liter

Exercises

4. $\log_4 16 = 2$ **5.** $5^2 = 25$ **6.** 2.754 **7.** −2.699 **8.** 2
9. 12 **10.** 16 **11.** 10^{-5}, or 0.00001
13. $\log_5 625 = 4$ **15.** $\log_6 216 = 3$ **17.** $\log_7 \frac{1}{49} = -2$
19. $\log_{16} 2 = \frac{1}{4}$ **21.** $\log_{\frac{1}{9}} 81 = -2$ **23.** $\log_{\frac{1}{2}} \frac{1}{8} = 3$
25. $10^3 = 1000$ **27.** $10^{-1} = 0.1$ **29.** $7^3 = 343$
31. $2^{-5} = \frac{1}{32}$ **33.** $3^{-3} = \frac{1}{27}$ **35.** $144^{\frac{1}{2}} = 12$ **37.** 2 **39.** 4
41. 0 **43.** −4 **45.** 1.08 **47.** 3.55 **49.** 0.28 **51.** −1.46
53. −3.04 **55.** −1.35 **57.** 3 **59.** 2 **61.** 1 **63.** −2
65. −2 **67.** 0 **69.** 49 **71.** 3 **73.** 2 **75.** $\frac{1}{64}$ **77.** 1 **79.** 5
81. 64 **83.** 2 **85.** 3

87.

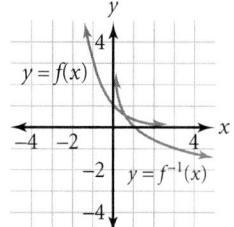

Tables may vary. Sample tables provided.

x	$f(x) = 3^{-x}$
−3	27
−2	9
−1	3
0	1
1	$\frac{1}{3}$
2	$\frac{1}{9}$
3	$\frac{1}{27}$

x	$f^{-1}(x) = \log_{\frac{1}{3}} x$
27	−3
9	−2
3	−1
1	0
$\frac{1}{3}$	1
$\frac{1}{9}$	2
$\frac{1}{27}$	3

89. 4.5 **91.** stretched vertically by a factor of 3
93. compressed vertically by a factor of $\frac{1}{2}$ and
translated 1 unit up **95.** reflected across the x-axis
and translated 2 units to the right **97.** 10^{-10} moles
per liter **99.** 3.98×10^{-8} moles per liter **101.** 5261.1
feet **103.** Identity Property of Multiplication
105. Commutative Property of Multiplication
107. Inverse Property of Multiplication
109. $A^{-1} \approx \begin{bmatrix} 0.364 & 0.273 \\ 0.091 & -0.182 \end{bmatrix}$ **111.** $\pm i$

LESSON 6.4

TRY THIS (p. 379, Ex. 1) **TRY THIS** (p. 379, Ex. 2)
a. 4.17 **b.** −0.4150   **a.** $\log_4 3$ **b.** $\log_b \frac{4x}{3}$
TRY THIS (p. 380, Ex. 3) **TRY THIS** (p. 380, Ex. 4)
300   **a.** 7 **b.** 13

Exercises

5. 3.5424 **6.** −0.7712 **7.** $\log_3 \frac{xz}{y}$ **8.** $\log_2 \frac{9}{5}$ **9.** 16

10. 12 **11.** 3 **12.** $x = 4$ **13.** $\log_8 5 + 1$
15. $\log_3 x - 2$ **17.** 1.9535 **19.** 4.8074 **21.** 2.9535
23. 2.9191 **25.** −0.3685 **27.** 0.1610 **29.** $\log_2 35$
31. $\log_3 5$ **33.** $\log_2 \frac{x}{2}$ **35.** $\log_7 2y$ **37.** $\log_2 \frac{m^5}{n^2}$
39. $\log_b \frac{m^4 n^{\frac{1}{2}}}{8p^3}$ **41.** $\log_7 \frac{7}{x^2}$ **43.** 8 **45.** 5 **47.** 12 **49.** 8
51. 5 **53.** −5 **55.** $x = 3$ or $x = 4$ **57.** $x = 8$ **59.** $x = 3$
61. $x = 3$ **63.** always **65.** always **67.** never
69. always **71.** sometimes **73.** $x = 243$
75. 1.83 times greater **77.** 12

79. $\begin{bmatrix} 3 & 2 & -1 \\ 5 & 3 & -2 \\ 2 & 3 & -1 \end{bmatrix} \begin{bmatrix} x \\ y \\ z \end{bmatrix} = \begin{bmatrix} 7 \\ -12 \\ -5 \end{bmatrix}$ **81.** $\begin{bmatrix} -3 & 2 & 11 \\ 4 & 1 & 5 \end{bmatrix}$

83. $\begin{bmatrix} 0.5 & 0.3 & 0 & 2.2 \\ 0 & -8.5 & 1.2 & -24.4 \\ 1.3 & 0 & 3.3 & 29 \end{bmatrix}$

85. $802.35; $866.99; $936.49

LESSON 6.5

TRY THIS (p. 387)   **TRY THIS** (p. 388)
$x \approx 3.21$ 1.72

Exercises
4. 18.75 **5.** 10^{13} times louder **6.** 0.67 **7.** 3.08 **8.** 5.52
9. 0.43 **11.** 5.61 **13.** 2.64 **15.** 2.05 **17.** −1.23
19. 1.96 **21.** 0.16 **23.** 10 **25.** 4.81 **27.** 3.66 **29.** 2.49
31. 2.46 **33.** 0.43 **35.** 0.53 **37.** 0.16 **39.** −3
41. −2.01 **43.** −0.89 **45.** 7 **47.** 105 decibels
49. $10^{11.5}$ times louder **51.** 30 decibels **53.** $10^{12.8}$
times louder **55.** $10^{-14} < [H^+] < 10^{-7}$ **57.** ≈1.3
59. ≈10.5 **61.** (5, 2) **63.** (−3, 2)
65. $g(x) = 2x^2 - 8x - 10$ **67.** $f(x) = -3x^2 - 2x + 1$
69. −5 or 3 **71.** exponential growth **73.** exponential
growth

LESSON 6.6

TRY THIS (p. 393)   **TRY THIS** (p. 394)
403.429; 0.717 $716.66

TRY THIS (p. 395)
about 15.26 years

Exercises
5. 20.086 **6.** 33.115 **7.** $2250.88; $2260.23 **8.** 1.609
9. 0.916 **10.** about 9.24 years **11.** about 20,066 years
old **13.** 8103.084 **15.** 29.964 **17.** 3.154
19. 2.320 **21.** 1.284 **23.** 1.946 **25.** 11.513
27. −0.006 **29.** 0.805 **31.** undefined **33.** $\ln \frac{1}{2}$, $\ln 1$,
e^0, e **35.** $\log 1.3$, $\ln 1.3$, $e^{1.3}$, $10^{1.3}$ **37.** always true
39. sometimes true **41.** 5 **43.** 25 **45.** 4 **47.** 8
49. $\ln 1 = x$ **51.** $5 \approx e^{1.61}$ **53.** $\ln 1.99 \approx 0.69$
55. 7.93 **57.** 0.42 **59.** −9.97 **61.** vertical stretch by
a factor of 6 and vertical translation 1 unit up

---

63. horizontal translation 1 unit to the left,
horizontal compression by a factor of $\frac{1}{4}$, and vertical
compression by a factor of 0.25 **65.** vertical stretch
by a factor of 3 and vertical translation 1 unit to the
left **67.** horizontal compression by a factor of $\frac{1}{5}$,
vertical compression by a factor of 0.5, and vertical
translation of 2 units down **69.** f to h: reflection
across the y-axis and horizontal compression by a
factor of $\frac{1}{2}$; g to h: reflection across the y-axis; i to h:
horizontal compression by a factor of $\frac{1}{2}$ **71.** The
only changes are the following: **a.** no changes
b. x-intercept: changes **c.** x-intercept: changes
d. domain: real numbers greater than the value of
the translation; asymptotes: x is the value of the
translation; x-intercept: value of the translation plus
1 **73a.** $285,000,000 **b.** during 1999 **75.** No;
according to the tests, the chest is only about 700 years
old. **77.** almost 11 years and 7 months **79.** 18.7%
81. $x \geq 5$ or $x \leq -5$

83. $x \geq 6$ or $x \leq -\frac{22}{3}$

85.   **87.**

      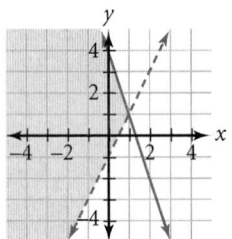

89.   **91.** $3(x - 1)^2$

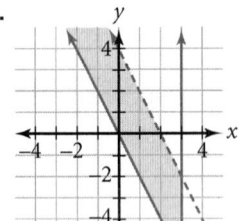

LESSON 6.7

TRY THIS (p. 404)
Method 1
$$\log(x + 48) + \log x = 2$$
$$\log[x(x + 48)] = 2$$
$$x(x + 48) = 10^2$$
$$x^2 + 48x - 100 = 0$$
$$(x + 50)(x - 2) = 0$$
$$x = -50 \text{ or } x = 2$$

Check: Let $x = -50$.

$\log(x + 48) + \log x = 2$

$\log(-2) + \log(-50) = 2$ Undefined

Let $x = 2$.

$\log(x + 48) + \log x = 2$

$\log 50 + \log 2 = 2$

$2 = 2$ True

The solution is 2.

Method 2

Graph $y = \log(x + 48) + \log x$ and $y = 2$, and find the point of intersection. The solution is 2.

Exercises

4. 2.82×10^{22} ergs **5.** $x = 100$ **6.** $x \approx 54.78$
7a. $T(t) = 70 + 100e^{-0.7133t}$, or $T(t) = 70 + 100(0.7)^{2t}$
b. 119°F **c.** about 2.26 hours, or about 2 hours and
16 minutes **9.** 2 **11.** -3 **13.** 4 **15.** $\frac{\ln 20}{2} \approx 1.50$
17. 12 **19.** $\frac{\log 75}{2} \approx 0.94$ **21.** 2 **23.** $e^{-\frac{1}{2}} \approx 0.61$
25. $10^{-\frac{2}{3}} \approx 0.22$ **27.** 1; $10^{-\sqrt{3}} \approx 0.02$; $10^{\sqrt{3}} \approx 53.96$
29. 5.4 **31.** about 31.6 times **33a.** $P(t) = 10,000e^{0.46t}$
b. 2,500,000 bacteria **c.** 623,000,000 bacteria
35a. $0.40N_0 = N_0 e^{-0.00012t}$ **b.** 7636 years old
37.

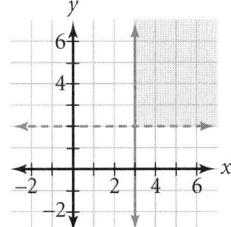

39. $x = 7$ or $x = -7$ **41.** $x = 5$ **43.** $x = \frac{1}{2}$ and $x = 2$
45. ≈ 13.86 years **47.** 21.7%

CHAPTER REVIEW AND ASSESSMENT

1. $12,000(1.08)^t$; about \$38,066 **3.** exponential decay
5. exponential growth **7.** \$4070.12 **9.** \$4118.28
11. $3^3 = 27$ **13.** 2 **15.** 144 **17.** $\frac{1}{8}$ **19.** 7 **21.** 1.9563
23. 1.8271 **25.** $\log 98$ **27.** 3 **29.** 100,000,000.00
31. no solution **33.** 2.77 **35.** 2.40 **37.** -2.58
39. $10^{-2.5}$ **41.** 0.007 **43.** -2.996 **45.** 2 **47.** -1
49. about 2 days **51.** 85 decibels

Chapter 7

LESSON 7.1

TRY THIS (p. 425)
  a. cubic polynomial
  b. quintic trinomial

TRY THIS (p. 425, Ex. 2)
17.6875

TRY THIS (p. 425, Ex. 3)
$4x^3 - 7x^2 + 13x - 12$

TRY THIS (p. 427)
$3x^3 - 11x^2 - 10x - 7$

TRY THIS (p. 428)
a. The graph of this cubic function is S-shaped and has 2 turns.
b. The graph of this quartic function is W-shaped and has 3 turns.

Exercises

4. quartic trinomial **5.** quintic polynomial **6.** 15
7. $2x^3 + 3x + 7$ **8.** $3x^3 - 3x^2 + 7x + 5$ **9.** S-shaped
with 2 turns **10.** W-shaped with 3 turns
11. $5x^3 + 2x^2 + 4x + 1$ **13.** $3.3x^8 + 2.7x^3 + 4.1x^2$
15. $\frac{x^9}{7} + \frac{x^7}{13} - \frac{2}{3}$ **17.** yes; quintic polynomial **19.** no
21. yes; quartic trinomial **23.** no **25.** yes; trinomial
of degree 6 **27.** no **29.** -17 **31.** -138 **33.** 414
35. $8\frac{5}{8}$ **37.** -39.625
39. $3x^3 + 4x^2 + 2x + 4$; cubic polynomial
41. $-2x^4 - 4x^3 + 10x^2 - 5x + 1$; quartic polynomial
43. $4x^3 + 8x^2 - 7x + 8$; cubic polynomial
45. $-2x^3 + 5x^2 + 4$; cubic trinomial
47. $\frac{2}{3}x^3 + \frac{1}{3}x^2 + x + \frac{5}{3}$; cubic polynomial
49. $2.5x^4 + 7.6x^3 - 3.2x^2 + 7.8x$; quartic polynomial
51. S-shaped with 2 turns **53.** W-shaped with 3 turns
55. S-shaped with 2 turns **57.** W-shaped with 3 turns
59. $a = -2, b = 4, c = 7, d = -7$ **61.** $28x^2 + 54x$
63. \$23,996,445 **65.** $\begin{bmatrix} -2 & 5 \\ 5 & 1 \end{bmatrix}$ **67.** $\begin{bmatrix} -2 & 8 \\ 10 & 6 \end{bmatrix}$
69. $\begin{bmatrix} -1 & 9 \\ 5 & 1 \end{bmatrix}$ **71.** $\begin{bmatrix} -4 & 7 \\ 5 & -3 \end{bmatrix}$ **73.** $x = -3$ or $x = 5$
75. $x = -9$ or $x = -8$ **77.** $x = -2$ or $x = -\frac{1}{3}$
79. $x = \frac{-1 - i\sqrt{19}}{5}$ or $x = \frac{-1 + i\sqrt{19}}{5}$

LESSON 7.2

TRY THIS (p. 434)
a. maximum of 6.6
   minimum of 3.9
b. decreases for all values of x except over the interval of approximately $-0.2 < x < 1.5$, where it increases

TRY THIS (p. 436)
a. falls on the left and rises on the right
b. rises on the left and the right

TRY THIS (p. 437)
$y \approx -0.10x^4 + 2.74x^3 - 26.16x^2 + 100.55x - 112.79$

Exercises

5. maximum of 2.1, minimum of -0.6; increases for all values of x except over the interval of approximately $-1.2 < x < 0.5$, where it decreases
6. rises on the left and the right **7.** rises on the left and falls on the right

8. $f(x) \approx 0.125x^4 - 0.917x^3 + 1.375x^2 + 1.417x$
9. maximum of 3.1, minimum of −3.1 **11.** maximum of 3.2, minimum of −1.2 **13.** no maximum, minimum of 2.0 **15.** maximum of 2.0, minima of −4.3 and −4.3 **17.** maximum of 4.3, minima of 1.9 and 1.0 **19.** maximum of 3.1, minimum of −3.1; increases for all values of x except over the interval of approximately $-1.2 < x < 1.2$, where it decreases **21.** maximum of 2.0, minima of 1.0 and 1.0; decreases for $-\infty < x < -1.0$ and $0.0 < x < 1.0$, increases for $-1.0 < x < 0.0$ and $1.0 < x < \infty$
23. maximum of 3.0, no minimum; increases for $-\infty < x < 2.0$, decreases for $2.0 < x < \infty$ **25.** maximum of 4.3, minima of 1.9 and 1.0; decreases for $-\infty < x < -0.5$ and $0.7 < x < 2.1$, increases for $-0.5 < x < 0.7$ and $2.1 < x < \infty$ **27.** maximum of 5.0, minimum of 1.0; increases for all values of x except over the interval of approximately $-1.0 < x < 1.0$, where it decreases **29.** falls on the left and rises on the right **31.** falls on the left and the right **33.** falls on the left and rises on the right **35.** rises on the left and falls on the right **37.** The end behavior of the graph should be rising on the left and the right. The graph shown falls to the left. A more appropriate window may be [−20, 10] by [−3000, 1000].
39. $f(x) \approx 1.17x^4 - 14.33x^3 + 60.83x^2 - 102.67x + 56$
41. $f(x) \approx 0.12x^4 - 2.89x^3 + 23.51x^2 - 76.96x + 84$
43. $f(x) \approx 0.176x^4 - 8.677x^3 + 156.139x^2 - 1199.023x + 3662.963$ **45.** no inverse **47.** $\begin{bmatrix} 5.5 & -2.5 \\ -2 & 1 \end{bmatrix}$
49. $x = -5\sqrt{2}$ or $x = 5\sqrt{2}$ **51.** $x = -1$ or $x = 3$
53. $x = 2$ **55.** $x > 0$

LESSON 7.3

TRY THIS (p. 441, Ex. 1)
$2x^5 - 6x^4 + 4x^3 - 12x^2$

TRY THIS (p. 441, Ex. 2)
$x^3 - 9x = x(x + 3)(x - 3)$;
$x^3 - x^2 + 2x - 2 = (x - 1)(x^2 + 2)$

TRY THIS (p. 441, Ex. 3)
$x^3 + 1000 = (x + 10)(x^2 - 10x + 100)$;
$x^3 - 125 = (x - 5)(x^2 + 5x + 25)$

TRY THIS (p. 442)
$(-3)^3 - 3(-3)^2 - 6(-3) + 8 = -28$, so $x + 3$ is not a factor.

TRY THIS (p. 443)
$x + 5$

TRY THIS (p. 444, Ex. 6)
$(x + 3)(x - 4)(x + 1)$

TRY THIS (p. 444, Ex. 7)
$P(3) = 94$

Exercises
4. $P(x) = -x^3 + 8x^2 + 20x$ **5.** $x(x - 2)(x - 3)$
6. $(x^2 + 3)(x + 5)$ **7.** $(x - 6)(x^2 + 6x + 36)$
8. $f(-2) = (-2)^3 + 4(-2)^2 + 5(-2) + 2 = 0$; yes
9. $x + 3$ **10.** $(x + 3)(x^2 - 3x - 5)$
11. $(x + 3)(x^2 - 3x - 5)$ **12.** 37 **13.** 37
15. $8x^6 - 4x^5 + 2x^4 + 6x^3$ **17.** $5x^2 + 32x - 21$
19. $2x^4 + 9x^3 + 9x^2 + x + 3$ **21.** $2x^3 - 7x^2 - 10x - 3$
23. $-3x^4 + 15x^3 - 4x^2 + 19x + 5$
25. $-2x^3 + 7x^2 + 3x - 18$ **27.** $2x^3 - 6x - 4$
29. $27x^3 + 54x^2 + 36x + 8$ **31.** $-3x^4 - 7x^3 - 3x^2 + 3x + 2$
33. $\frac{2}{3}x^3 + \frac{1}{6}x^2 + \frac{7}{12}x - \frac{1}{6}$ **35.** $x(x + 2)(x + 4)$
37. $x(x + 3)(x - 1)$ **39.** $x(x - 3)(x + 1)$ **41.** $2x(3x - 5)^2$
43. $(x^2 + 4)(x - 3)$ **45.** $(x^2 - 5)(x - 2)$
47. $(1 + x^2)(1 - x)$ **49.** $(x^2 + 2)(x + 1)$
51. $(x + 10)(x^2 - 10x + 100)$ **53.** $(x^2 + 3)(x^4 - 3x^2 + 9)$
55. $(x - 6)(x^2 + 6x + 36)$ **57.** $(3x - 5)(9x^2 + 15x + 25)$
59. $(4 - x)(16 + 4x + x^2)$ **61.** not a factor **63.** factor
65. factor **67.** factor **69.** factor **71.** $x + 2$
73. $x^2 - x - 6$ **75.** $x - 1$ **77.** $x - 6$ **79.** $x + \frac{1}{3}$
81. $x^2 - \frac{12}{x - 4}$ **83.** $x^2 - 9$ **85.** $x^2 + 2x - 6$
87. $x^2 + x + 1 + \frac{4}{x - 1}$ **89.** $x^3 + 4x^2 + 8x + 13 + \frac{20}{x - 2}$
91. 2 **93.** 6 **95.** 33 **97.** 392 **99.** $k = -18$
101a. $4x^3 - 92x^2 + 448x$ **b.** 560 cubic inches
103. $3 \leq x$

105. $5(a + b)(a - b)$ **107.** $(n + 4)(n - 3)$
109. $(2x + 1)^2$ **111.** $x \approx 1.51$ **113.** $x \approx 1.61$

LESSON 7.4

TRY THIS (p. 449, Ex. 1)
$x(2x - 3)(x + 2) = 0$
$x = 0$ or $x = \frac{3}{2}$ or $x = -2$

TRY THIS (p. 449, Ex. 2)

```
2| 1   2   -4   -8
      2    8    8
   ─────────────────
   1   4    4 | 0
```

The quotient is $x^2 + 4x + 4 = (x + 2)^2$.
$x^3 + 2x^2 - 4x - 8 = (x - 2)(x + 2)^2$

TRY THIS (p. 450)
$x = \pm\sqrt{7}$ and $x = \pm\sqrt{2}$

Exercises
4. $x = 0$ or $x = 4$ or $x = -3$ **5.** $y = 0$ or $y = -6$ or $y = -9$
6. $x = 0, x = \frac{5 + \sqrt{13}}{2}, x = \frac{5 - \sqrt{13}}{2}$
7. $x = 2, x = -1, x = -1$ **8.** $x = \pm 2$ **9.** $x = \pm 1$
10. 4.9 feet **11.** $x = 0, x = 5, x = -7$
13. $y = 0, y = -3, y = 9$ **15.** $x = 0, x = 5, x = 8$

17. $x = 0, x = 5, x = -5$ **19.** $x = 0, x = -5, x = 10$
21. $y = 0, y = -9, y = 6$ **23.** $x = 0, x = -11, x = 5$
25. $a = 0, a = \frac{7}{3}, a = -4$ **27.** $a = 3, a = -1$
29. $x = 1, x = -3$ **31.** $b = 0, b = -4$
33. $x = 2, x = -1$ **35.** $x = -3, x = 2, x = 3$
37. $n = 2, n = -2$ **39.** $x = \pm\sqrt{2}$ **41.** $y = \pm 3$
43. $x = \pm 3$ or $x = \pm 2$ **45.** $x = \pm 2\sqrt{2}$ or $x = \pm 1$ or $x = 0$
47. $x = \pm\sqrt{6}$ **49.** $h = \pm\sqrt{3}$ or $h = \pm 2$ **51.** There are
zeros of f between 8 and 9 (about 8.97) and between
1 and 2 (about 1.45). **53.** There are zeros of f at
$a = -3$ and $a = 2$. **55.** There is a zero of m at $n = 2$.
57. There are zeros of g between -2 and -1 (about
-1.49) and between 0 and 1 (about 0.44). **59.** There
are zeros of f at $x = 0$, between -1 and 0 (about
-0.68), and between 0 and 1 (about 0.88).
61. $0 < c < 5$ **63.** 2 feet by 6 feet by 3 feet **65.** $x = 9$ or
$x = -7$ **67.** $x = 4$ or $x = 5$ **69.** $9i$ **71.** $6 + 2i$ **73.** 5
75.

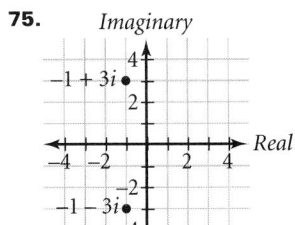
Imaginary

77. $-1 \pm i\sqrt{6}$ **79.** $\frac{3}{2} \pm \frac{3\sqrt{3}}{2}i$

LESSON 7.5

TRY THIS (p. 459)
one rational root, $\frac{5}{3}$

TRY THIS (p. 460, Ex. 2)
The zeros are 2, $2 + \sqrt{5}$,
and $2 - \sqrt{5}$.

TRY THIS (p. 460, Ex. 3)
The zeros are 5, $2 + 5i$, and $2 - 5i$.

TRY THIS (p. 463)
$P(x) = -2(x - 1)(x^2 - 6x + 25)$
$= -2x^3 + 14x^2 - 62x + 50$

Exercises

5. 5, $-\frac{5}{2}$, and $\frac{1}{6}$ **6.** 2, $-\frac{5}{2} + \frac{\sqrt{17}}{2}$, and $-\frac{5}{2} - \frac{\sqrt{17}}{2}$
7. 3, $-\frac{1}{2} + \frac{1}{2}i$, and $-\frac{1}{2} - \frac{1}{2}i$ **8.** $x = 2$
9. $P(x) = -\frac{2}{75}(x - 3)^2(x^2 - 6x + 25)$
$= -\frac{2}{75}x^4 + \frac{8}{25}x^3 - \frac{28}{15}x^2 + \frac{136}{25}x - 6$
11. 6, $-\frac{3}{2}$, and $\frac{1}{3}$ **13.** -2, 2, and $\frac{2}{3}$ **15.** -1
17. -7, $-\frac{2}{5}$, and $\frac{1}{2}$ **19.** $-\frac{3}{5}$, $-\frac{1}{2}$, and $\frac{2}{5}$
21. 3, 6, $-\frac{1}{5}$, and $\frac{3}{2}$ **23.** $\frac{1}{3}$, $-2\sqrt{2}$, and $2\sqrt{2}$
25. -8, $\frac{\sqrt{5}}{3}$, and $-\frac{\sqrt{5}}{3}$ **27.** 5, $12i$, and $-12i$
29. 5, $3i$, and $-3i$ **31.** 3, $2i\sqrt{3}$, and $-2i\sqrt{3}$
33. -5, 1, $2i$, and $-2i$ **35.** $x = 2$ **37.** $x = 0, x = -1.65$

39. $x = -2.14, x = -0.66, x = 0.66, x = 2.14$
41. $P(x) = 2(x - 2)(x - 3)$
$= 2x^2 - 10x + 12$
43. $P(x) = 5(x + 2)(x - 1)(x - 2)$
$= 5x^3 - 5x^2 - 20x + 20$
45. $P(x) = \frac{1}{4}(x - 1)^2(x - 2)^2$
$= \frac{1}{4}x^4 - \frac{3}{2}x^3 + \frac{13}{4}x^2 - 3x + 1$
47. $P(x) = (x - 1)(x - i)(x + i)$
$= x^3 - x^2 + x - 1$
49. $P(x) = \frac{3}{50}(x - 1)(x - 2)(x - 5i)(x + 5i)$
$= \frac{3}{50}x^4 - \frac{9}{50}x^3 + \frac{81}{50}x^2 - \frac{9}{2}x + 3$
51. Because $P(\sqrt{3}) = (\sqrt{3})^2 - 3 = 3 - 3 = 0$, $\sqrt{3}$ is a
root of P. By the Rational Root Theorem, if $\sqrt{3} = \frac{p}{q}$,
where p and q are integers, then p is a factor of -3
and q is a factor of 1. However, the only possible
values of $\frac{p}{q}$ are ± 3 and ± 1. Therefore, $\sqrt{3}$ is
irrational. **53.** about 143 seconds **55.** $-2 - 5x$
57. 24 **59.** 29 **61.** axis of symmetry: $x = -\frac{5}{4}$; vertex:
$\left(-\frac{5}{4}, -\frac{9}{8}\right)$ **63.** The graph of f falls on the left and rises
on the right. **65.** $3x^3 + 3x^2 - x + 1$

CHAPTER REVIEW AND ASSESSMENT

1. cubic polynomial **3.** quartic polynomial **5.** 6; 3
7. -6; -21 **9.** $14x^3 - 6x^2 + 10x - 2$; cubic polynomial
11. The leading coefficient is negative and the degree
is even, so the graph falls on both sides. **13.** The
leading coefficient is positive and the degree is even,
so the graph rises on both sides.
15. The graph of f has a local minimum of 8 at $x = 1$,
is decreasing when $x < 1$, and is increasing when
$x > 1$. **17.** The graph of f has a local maximum of
about 3.6 at $a = -1\frac{2}{3}$ and a local minimum of -1 at
$a = 0$. The graph is increasing when $a < -1\frac{2}{3}$ and
when $a > 0$. The graph is decreasing when
$-1\frac{2}{3} < a < 0$. **19.** $-10x^7 + 2x^6 - 2x^5 + 6x^4 + 12x^3$
21. $x(x + 5)(x - 1)$ **23.** $(x - 5)(x^2 + 5x + 25)$
25. factor **27.** $x^2 + 8x + 15$ **29.** $x^2 + 6x - 16$
31. $x = \pm 2$ **33.** $x = \pm 1$ or $x = \pm 3$ **35.** $x = \pm\sqrt{6}$ or $x = 1$
37. $x = 1$ or $x = -2$ **39.** -2 **41.** 2 and 5 **43.** $-\frac{2}{5}$ and $\frac{1}{3}$
45. 2
47. $P(x) = (x - 2)(x + 1)^2(x - 3)$
$= x^4 - 3x^3 - 3x^2 + 7x + 6$
49. $P(x) = -(x - 3)^2[x - (2 + i)][x - (2 - i)]$
$= -x^4 + 10x^3 - 38x^2 + 66x - 45$ **51.** $\approx 8.3\%$

Chapter 8

LESSON 8.1

TRY THIS (p. 482)

$k = 780$; $y = \frac{780}{x}$; 520; 173.3$\overline{3}$; 97.5; 62.4; $\approx$55.7

TRY THIS (p. 483, Ex. 2)

a. $V = 12wh$; volume varies jointly as the width, w, and the height, h; $k = 12$ **b.** 96 cubic inches

TRY THIS (p. 483, Ex. 3)

a. $A = \pi r^2$; area varies directly as the square of r; $k = \pi$ **b.** $\approx$7.07, $\approx$19.63, $\approx$38.48, and $\approx$63.62 sq units

TRY THIS (p. 484)

about 8.5 miles per hour

Exercises

7. $k = 1980$; $y = \frac{1980}{x}$; 1320, 990, 792, 660, $\approx$565.71
8. $V = 2.5\ell h$; volume varies jointly as length, ℓ, and height, h; $k = 2.5$ **9.** 40 cubic centimeters
10. $A = 3x^2$; area varies directly as the square of the side, x; $k = 3$ **11.** 6.75, 18.75, 36.75, 60.75, 90.75, and 126.75 sq units **12.** about 20.8 miles per hour.
13. $y = \frac{324}{x}$; 108, 81, 64.8, 54, $\approx$46.3 **15.** $y = \frac{4}{x}$; 0.8, 1, $\approx$1.3, 2, 4 **17.** $y = \frac{112}{x}$; 11.2, $\approx$7.47, 5.6 **19.** $y = \frac{200}{x}$; 2, 0.2, 0.02 **21.** $y = 9xz$; -108 **23.** $y = \frac{10}{9}xz$; 60
25. $y = \frac{3}{4}xz$; 283.5 **27.** $y = 10xz$; 10^8 **29.** $z = \frac{2xy}{w}$; -21
31. $z = \frac{6xy}{w}$; 216 **33.** $z = \frac{2xy}{7w}$; $\frac{8}{9} \approx 0.89$ **35.** $x = 9.6$
37. $y = 2.5$ **39.** $y = 6$ or $y = -6$ **41.** If $x_1 y_1 = k$ and $x_2 y_2 = k$, then by substitution, $x_1 y_1 = x_2 y_2$. Divide both sides by $x_2 y_1$, which results in $\frac{x_1}{x_2} = \frac{y_2}{y_1}$. Multiply both sides by y_1, which results in $y_2 = y_1 \left(\frac{x_1}{x_2} \right)$ **43.** The distance remains the same, 6 feet. **45.** 5625 calories
47. $\frac{1}{x}$ **49.** $\frac{y^2}{x^2}$ **51.** $\frac{1}{x^{18}}$ **53.** vertex: $(-1, -4)$; axis of symmetry: $x = -1$ **55.** vertex: $(0, 2)$; axis of symmetry: $x = 0$ **57.** vertex: $\left(\frac{3}{4}, \frac{7}{8} \right)$; axis of symmetry: $t = \frac{3}{4}$ **59.** 3 **61.** The graph rises on the left and the right.

LESSON 8.2

TRY THIS (p. 490)

all real numbers except -3 and 1

TRY THIS (p. 491)

$x = -2$ and $x = -3$

TRY THIS (p. 493)

$x = -3$ and $x = 4$; $y = 2$

TRY THIS (p. 494)

hole when $x = -3$; vertical asymptote: $x = 1$; no horizontal asymptote

Exercises

5. $C(x) = \frac{13.5}{90 + x}$; 5.6% **6.** all real numbers except $x = 3$ and $x = 4$ **7.** no holes; vertical asymptotes: $x = -\frac{3}{2}$ and $x = \frac{3}{2}$; horizontal asymptote: $y = 0$
8. no holes; vertical asymptotes: $x = -3$ and $x = 3$; horizontal asymptote: $y = 2$ **9.** hole when $x = 3$; vertical asymptote: $x = 2$; horizontal asymptote: $y = 1$
10.

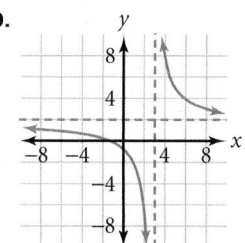

11. a rational function; all real numbers except $x = \frac{7}{2}$

13. not a rational function because the numerator is not a polynomial **15.** not a rational function because the numerator is not a polynomial
17. no holes; vertical asymptote at $x = 2$; horizontal asymptote at $y = 3$ **19.** vertical asymptote at $x = 2$; horizontal asymptote at $y = 1$ **21.** hole when $x = 4$; vertical asymptote $x = 1$; horizontal asymptote: $y = 1$
23. domain of all real numbers except $x = -1$; vertical asymptote: $x = -1$; horizontal asymptote: $y = 1$; no holes

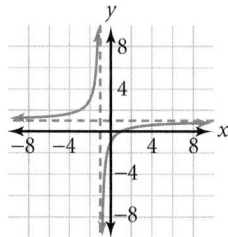

25. domain of all real numbers except $x = -2$; no vertical asymptote; no horizontal asymptote; hole when $x = -2$

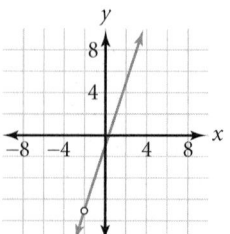

27. domain of all real numbers except $x = -2$ and $x = 2$; vertical asymptotes: $x = -2$ and $x = 2$; horizontal asymptote: $y = 0$; no holes

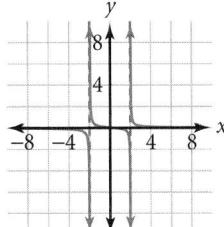

29. domain of all real numbers; no vertical asymptotes; horizontal asymptote: $y = 0$; no holes

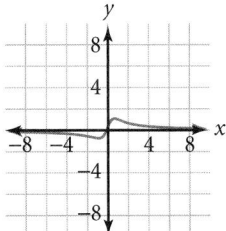

31. domain of all real numbers except $x = 1$ and $x = 6$; vertical asymptotes: $x = 1$ and $x = 6$; no horizontal asymptote; no holes

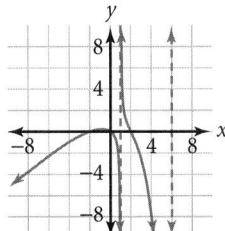

33. domain of all real numbers except $x = 0$ and $x = 4$; vertical asymptote: $x = 4$; horizontal asymptote: $y = 0$; hole when $x = 0$

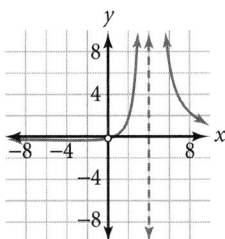

35. $f(x) = \dfrac{3x}{x - 2}$ **37.** $f(x) = \dfrac{3x^3}{2x^3 - 2x}$ **39.** $f(x) = \dfrac{x^3 - 2x^2}{x^2 - 2x}$

41a. $c > \frac{9}{4}$; if there are no vertical asymptotes, then $x^2 - 3x + c = 0$ has no solutions and $b^2 - 4ac < 0$, $9 - 4c < 0$. **b.** $c = \frac{9}{4}$; if there is 1 vertical asymptote, then $x^2 - 3x + c = 0$ has 1 solution and $b^2 - 4ac = 0$, $9 - 4c = 0$. **c.** $c < \frac{9}{4}$; if there are 2 vertical asymptotes, then $x^2 - 3x + c = 0$ has 2 solutions and $b^2 - 4ac > 0$, $9 - 4c > 0$. **43a.** $R(x) = \frac{2}{x}$ **b.** all real numbers greater than 0; all real numbers greater than 0; all real numbers greater than 0

45a. $T(x) = 11.45x + 250$

b. $C(x) = \dfrac{T(x)}{x} = \dfrac{11.45x + 250}{x}$ **47.** $x < \frac{4}{5}$ or $x > \frac{8}{5}$

49. $-\frac{4}{5} \leq x \leq 2$ **51.** $-36x^2 + 24x$ **53.** $-5x^2 + 49x - 36$

55. $9x^2 - 16$ **57.** $3x(x - 2)$ **59.** $(3x + 7)(3x - 7)$

61. $(x + 6)^2$

LESSON 8.3

TRY THIS (p. 498)

$\dfrac{b + 7}{b - 1}$

TRY THIS (p. 499, Ex. 2)

$\dfrac{4}{49a^2}$

TRY THIS (p. 499, Ex. 3)

$\dfrac{x^2 - 3x - 10}{x^2 - 6x + 9}$

TRY THIS (p. 500)

$x + 3$

TRY THIS (p. 501)

$\dfrac{x^2 - x - 6}{x - 2}$

Exercises

4. $\dfrac{x + 5}{x - 5}$ **5.** $8x$ **6.** $\dfrac{x + 2}{x - 3}$ **7.** $\dfrac{x - 1}{x + 4}$ **8.** $\dfrac{2x^2 + 2}{x^2 + 8x + 15}$

9. $4x + 4$ **11.** $5x^2$ **13.** $\dfrac{x - 9}{x + 3}$ **15.** $\dfrac{5}{2x^5}$ **17.** $\dfrac{x + 1}{x - 1}$

19. $\dfrac{2x^2 - 2x}{x^2 - x - 6}$ **21.** $\dfrac{x^2 + 2x + 1}{x^2 + 2x - 3}$ **23.** $\dfrac{8x^2 - 18}{3x + 2}$

25. $\dfrac{a - b}{a + b}$ **27.** $3y$ **29.** $\dfrac{(x + 2)^3}{(x + 3)^3}$ **31.** $\dfrac{x^2 - 4x + 4}{x^2 - 2x + 1}$

33. $\dfrac{x^2}{x + 1}$ **35.** 3 **37.** $\dfrac{x + 3}{x}$ **39.** 1 **41.** $\dfrac{x - 9}{x - 2}$ **43.** $\dfrac{x - y}{x + y}$

45a. $V = \ell \times w \times h$; $V = (20 - 2x)(16 - 2x)x$; $V = x(20 - 2x)(16 - 2x)$

b. Total Area $A = (20 - 2x)(16 - 2x) + 2x(20 - 2x) + 2x(16 - 2x) = 320 - 40x - 32x + 4x^2 + 40x - 4x^2 + 32x - 4x^2 = 320 - 4x^2$ **c.** $R(x) = \dfrac{x^3 - 18x^2 + 80x}{80 - x^2}$

d. $R(x)$ increases **47a.** $a = \dfrac{d_2 t_1 - d_1 t_2}{t_1 t_2 (t_2 - t_1)}$

b. feet per second per second **49.** $y = -5x + 20$

51.

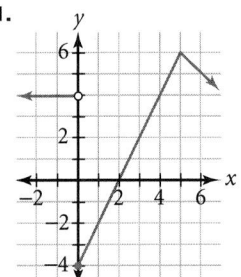

53. $3(4x^2 - x + 2)$ **55.** $\frac{8}{13} - \frac{1}{13}i$ **57.** $\frac{1}{2} - \frac{1}{2}i$

59. $3x^4 - 7x^3 - 4x^2 + 12x$ **61.** $(x - 1)(x^2 + x + 1)$

63. $x(x^2 - 6x - 8)$ **65.** $\frac{4}{x}$ **67.** $\frac{11}{6x}$

LESSON 8.4

TRY THIS (p. 505)

a. $\dfrac{5x+4}{2x-1}$ **b.** 2

TRY THIS (p. 506)

$\dfrac{x^2-5x-5}{(x+5)(x-5)} = \dfrac{x^2-5x-5}{x^2-25}$

TRY THIS (p. 507, Ex. 3)

$\dfrac{5x+12}{x(x-2)(x+2)} = \dfrac{5x+12}{x^3-4x}$

TRY THIS (p. 507, Ex. 4)

$\dfrac{2a^2}{(a+1)(a-1)(a^2+1)} = \dfrac{2a^2}{a^4-1}$

Exercises

4. $\dfrac{3x+2}{x-1}$ **5.** 2 **6.** $\dfrac{4x+8}{(x+1)(x-1)} = \dfrac{4x+8}{x^2-1}$

7. $\dfrac{-3x^2}{(2x-1)(x-1)} = \dfrac{-3x^2}{2x^2-3x+1}$ **8.** $\dfrac{t}{t-1}$ **9.** 43.9 mph

11. 4 **13.** $\dfrac{-x+20}{9}$ **15.** $\dfrac{2x^2+5x+3}{(x+3)^2} = \dfrac{2x^2+5x+3}{x^2+6x+9}$

17. $\dfrac{-4x-16}{(x+2)(x-2)} = \dfrac{-4x-16}{x^2-4}$

19. $\dfrac{37x-11}{(3x-5)(2x+3)} = \dfrac{37x-11}{6x^2-x-15}$

21. $\dfrac{-3x^2+3x-2}{(2x-1)(x-1)} = \dfrac{-3x^2+3x-2}{2x^2-3x+1}$

23. $\dfrac{x^2-2x+3}{(x-1)^2} = \dfrac{x^2-2x+3}{x^2-2x+1}$

25. $\dfrac{3x}{2x-1}$ **27.** $\dfrac{2x+1}{x-1}$ **29.** $\dfrac{x^2+4x+1}{(x-1)(x+1)} = \dfrac{x^2+4x+1}{x^2-1}$

31. x **33.** $\dfrac{b-a}{b+a}$ **35.** $\dfrac{6}{x-1}$

37. $\dfrac{x^2+x+16}{(x-3)(x+4)} = \dfrac{x^2+x+16}{x^2+x-12}$

39. $\dfrac{4ab}{(a-b)^2(a+b)^2} = \dfrac{4ab}{a^4-2a^2b^2+b^4}$

41. $\dfrac{2r^2+5rs+2s^2}{(2r-s)(2r+s)} = \dfrac{2r^2+5rs+2s}{4r^2-s^2}$ **43.** $B = 1$ and $D = -2$

45. $A = \dfrac{1}{6}$, $C = \dfrac{5}{6}$, and $D = -\dfrac{7}{3}$ **47a.** ≈2.45 ohms

b. $R_T = \dfrac{R_A R_B R_C}{R_B R_C + R_A R_C + R_A R_B}$ **49.** ≈48.8 mph

51. Distributive Property **53.** −7; 0; $x = \dfrac{3}{2} \pm \dfrac{i\sqrt{7}}{2}$

55. 121; 2; $x = \dfrac{3}{2}$ or $x = -4$ **57.** $\log_2 \dfrac{32}{8}$, or $\log_2 4$; 2

59. $x = -1$ or $x = 3$ or $x = 4$

61. $x = 2$ or $x = -1$ or $x = -3$

LESSON 8.5

TRY THIS (p. 513)

$x = -1$ or $x = 3$

TRY THIS (p. 514)

$x = -\dfrac{1}{2}$

TRY THIS (p. 515)

$x > -2$ or $x < -\dfrac{7}{2}$

TRY THIS (p. 516)

$x < 1$

Exercises

4. Rachel must swim at about 3.6 miles per hour, bicycle at about 6(3.6), or 21.6, miles per hour, and run at about 5 + 3.6, or 8.6, miles per hour.

5. $x = -1$ or $x = 1$ **6.** no solution **7.** $x < 0$

8. $-3 < x < -2$ **9.** $x = 12$ **11.** $n = 0$ **13.** $z = 8$

15. $y = -7$ **17.** $x = 2$ **19.** $x = -\dfrac{1}{10} \pm \dfrac{\sqrt{41}}{10}$

21. $x = 3 \pm \sqrt{17}$ **23.** no solution **25.** $b = -2$ **27.** no solution **29.** $0 < x < \dfrac{2}{3}$ **31.** $0 < x < \dfrac{1}{2}$ **33.** $2 < x < \dfrac{9}{2}$

35. $-2 \le x < 0$ **37.** $-\dfrac{2}{3} < x < 4$ **39.** $x < 0$ or $x \ge 1.3$

41. $-2.1 \le x < 0$ or $0 < x \le 2.1$

43. $-1.3 \le t < -1$ or $1 < t \le 2.3$

45. $a < -3$ or $-2 \le a < 0$ or $a \ge 5$ **47.** always

49. never **51.** sometimes **53.** all real numbers except $x = 1$ **55.** $2.5 \le w \le 10$ and $\ell = w + 5$; thus, $7.5 \le \ell \le 15$. **57.** about 4530 km **59.** 1 **61.** 3

63. $\{(-4, -1), (-3, -2), (-2, -3), (-1, 0)\}$; function

65. $h^{-1}(x) = 5 - 2x$; function **67.** a horizontal translation of 2 units to the right **69.** a vertical stretch by a factor of 3 and then a vertical translation of 5 units down **71.** a horizontal translation 4 units to the right, a reflection across the y-axis, a vertical stretch by a factor of 2, and a vertical translation 6 units down

LESSON 8.6

TRY THIS (p. 521)

$x \ge -\dfrac{18}{5}$ or $x \ge -3.6$

TRY THIS (p. 522)

a. a vertical stretch by a factor of 3, a vertical translation 2 units down, and a horizontal translation 1 unit to the right **b.** a horizontal compression by a factor of $\dfrac{1}{2}$, a vertical translation 3 units up, and a horizontal translation $\dfrac{1}{2}$ unit to the left

TRY THIS (p. 523)

Interchange the roles of x and y.

$y = x^2 + 3x - 4 \rightarrow x = y^2 + 3y - 4$

$y = \dfrac{-3 \pm \sqrt{25 + 4x}}{2}$

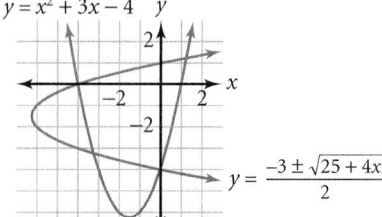

TRY THIS (p. 524)

0, 26

Exercises

4. $x \le \frac{3}{2}$ **5.** a horizontal translation 1 unit to the right, a vertical stretch by a factor of 2, and a vertical translation 2 units down **6.** a horizontal translation $\frac{1}{2}$ unit to the left, a horizontal compression by a factor of $\frac{1}{2}$, and a vertical translation 2 units up

7. $y = \dfrac{1 \pm \sqrt{1 + 16x}}{8}$

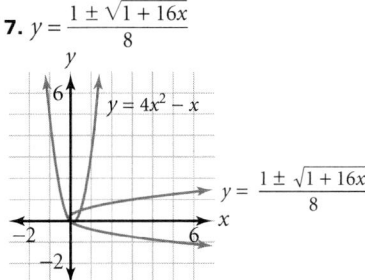

8. 0.4 second; 0.5 second; 0.6 second **9.** -5 **10.** -35
11. $x \ge -2$ **13.** $x \ge 2$ **15.** $x \le -\frac{1}{3}$ **17.** $x \le -5 \ or \ x \ge 5$
19. $x \le -3 \ or \ x \ge -2$ **21.** $x \le -4 \ or \ x \ge \frac{3}{2}$
23. $x \le \frac{1}{2} \ or \ x \ge \frac{5}{3}$
25. $y = \pm\sqrt{x + 1}$

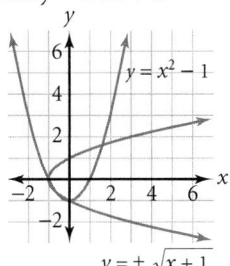

27. $y = \dfrac{-1 \pm \sqrt{1 + 12x}}{6}$

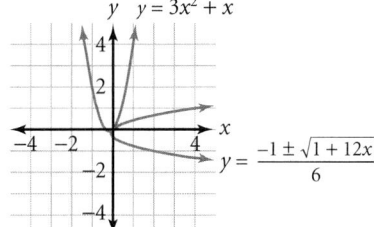

29. $y = -2 \pm \sqrt{x}$

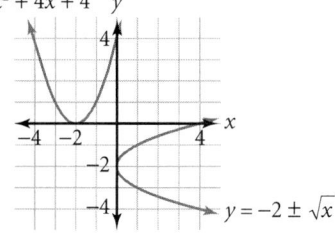

31. $y = 1 \pm \sqrt{x}$

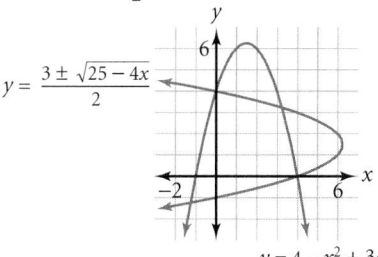

33. $y = \dfrac{3 \pm \sqrt{25 - 4x}}{2}$

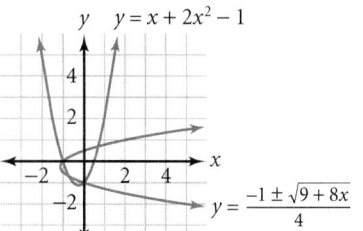

35. $y = \dfrac{-1 \pm \sqrt{9 + 8x}}{4}$

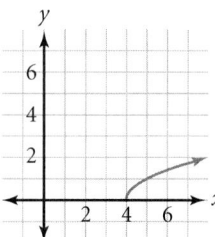

37. 32 **39.** 2 **41.** 8 **43.** -15 **45.** 9999 **47.** 648 **49.** 3
51. -12 **53.** $y = -\dfrac{b}{2a}$
55. a horizontal translation 4 units to the right

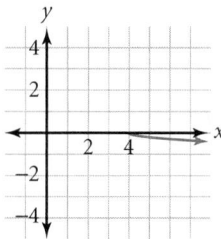

57. a horizontal translation 4 units to the right, a vertical compression by a factor of $\frac{1}{5}$, and a reflection across the x-axis

59. a horizontal translation 2 units to the left and a vertical translation 5 units up

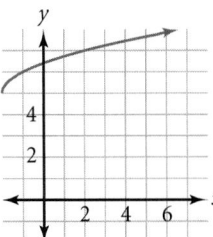

61. a horizontal translation 3 units to the left, a vertical translation 2 units down, and a vertical stretch by a factor of 2

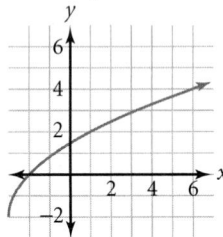

63. a horizontal translation 2 units to the left, a vertical compression by a factor of $\frac{1}{3}$, and a vertical translation 3 units up

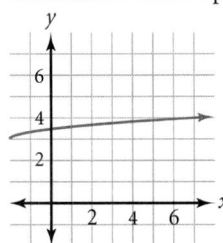

65a. $T \approx \dfrac{29{,}250 \pm \sqrt{5(12{,}500 + 29E)}}{290}$ **b.** 99°C or 103°C; choose 99°C because the boiling point is lower at higher elevations.   **67.** $4y^{16}$ **69.** $5^{-1}x^2y^{-4}$ or $\dfrac{x^2}{5y^4}$ **71.** $-\dfrac{1}{4m^2}$ **73.** $-4 + 7i$ **75.** $-7 + 3i$ **77.** $\log 2 + \log x$ **79.** $\log x + \log z - \log y$

LESSON 8.7

TRY THIS (p. 529)
a. $8a^2|c|\sqrt{bc}$ **b.** $-2fg\sqrt[5]{fh^2}$
TRY THIS (p. 530)
a. $3rs^2\sqrt[3]{r^2s}$ **b.** $3x\sqrt{2y}$
TRY THIS (p. 531, Ex. 1)
$\left(\sqrt[5]{2}\right)^3 = \sqrt[5]{2^3} = \sqrt[5]{8}$
a. $3 + 11\sqrt{2}$ **b.** $10 - 5\sqrt{5}$
TRY THIS (p. 531, Ex. 2)
a. $-162 + 38\sqrt{5}$ **b.** $77 - 23\sqrt{6}$
TRY THIS (p. 532)
a. $\dfrac{3\sqrt{5}}{5}$ **b.** $-6 - 2\sqrt{2}$

Exercises

4. $8|b|c^2\sqrt{2ac}$ **5.** $-3xy^3\sqrt[3]{2x^2}$ **6.** $9a^2b\sqrt[3]{3b}$ **7.** $2|x|\sqrt{5}$
8. $10\sqrt[3]{3}$, or about 14.42 feet   **9.** $18\sqrt{2}$ **10.** $20 - 5\sqrt{3}$
11. $-96 + 21\sqrt{5}$ **12.** $\dfrac{2\sqrt{7}}{7}$ **13.** $\dfrac{-15 - 3\sqrt{3}}{22}$ **15.** $8\sqrt{2}$
17. $-2\sqrt[3]{6}$ **19.** $3|x|\sqrt{2x}$ **21.** $-3x^2\sqrt[3]{3x}$ **23.** $5|a|b^2\sqrt{2a}$
25. $5r^2t\sqrt[3]{2rs^2}$ **27.** $2|x|\sqrt[4]{x^2}$ **29.** $2x^3\sqrt{2}$ **31.** $5x$
33. $12r^2s^3\sqrt[3]{rs}$ **35.** $4y^3\sqrt[3]{y}$ **37.** $2x$ **39.** $2x\sqrt[4]{4x^2}$, or $2x\sqrt{2x}$ **41.** $3x^3y^5\sqrt[3]{7y}$ **43.** $4yt\sqrt[3]{y^2c}$ **45.** $6 + 2\sqrt{3}$
47. $2 - \sqrt{2}$ **49.** $-1 - 10\sqrt{2}$ **51.** $-12 - \sqrt{3}$ **53.** $1 + \sqrt{3}$
55. $12 - 10\sqrt{3}$ **57.** $11 + 6\sqrt{2}$ **59.** $-16 + 8\sqrt{3}$
61. $-86 + 14\sqrt{3}$ **63.** $16 + 2\sqrt{2}$ **65.** $7 - 6\sqrt{2}$
67. $24 - 14\sqrt{6}$ **69.** $30 - 16\sqrt{3}$ **71.** $40 - 8\sqrt{6}$
73. $\dfrac{2\sqrt{5}}{5}$ **75.** $\dfrac{2\sqrt{6}}{3}$ **77.** $\sqrt{3}$ **79.** $\dfrac{\sqrt{15}}{15}$ **81.** 2 **83.** $\dfrac{\sqrt{6}}{2}$
85. $\dfrac{16 - 4\sqrt{2}}{7}$ **87.** $6 - 3\sqrt{3}$ **89.** $2\sqrt{7} - 2\sqrt{2}$
91. $-\dfrac{3x + 5x\sqrt{2} + 82 + 123\sqrt{2}}{41}$ **93.** $6\sqrt{2}$, or about 8.49
miles   **95a.** $s = 2\sqrt{3d}$, or $\approx 3.5\sqrt{d}$ mph   **b.** about 49
mph   **c.** The speed is not double; ≈ 69 mph.
97. $x = \pm 4$ **99.** $(x + 5)(x + 1)$ **101.** $(x + 5)(x - 8)$
103. $x = 5$ or $x = 6$ **105.** $x = -6$ or $x = -3$
107. $x = -3$ or $x = 6$ **109.** $x \le 5$ **113.** $\dfrac{2 - 2\sqrt[3]{x} + 2\sqrt[3]{x^2}}{1 + x}$

LESSON 8.8

TRY THIS (p. 537, Ex. 1)
$x = \dfrac{5}{2}$
TRY THIS (p. 537, Ex. 2)
$x = 1$
TRY THIS (p. 538)
$x = \dfrac{5 - \sqrt{5}}{2}$, or ≈ 1.38
TRY THIS (p. 539)
no real solutions
TRY THIS (p. 540)
Square both sides of the equation, isolate the radical expression, and then square both sides again. Check answers for extraneous solutions.
$\dfrac{3}{2} \le x < 14$
TRY THIS (p. 541)
$x < -5.4$ or $-0.6 < x < 9.0$

Exercises

4. $x = \dfrac{445}{18}$, or $24\dfrac{13}{18}$ **5.** $x = 2$ **6.** $x = \dfrac{1 \pm \sqrt{13}}{2}$, or $x \approx 2.30$
or $x \approx -1.30$ **7.** about 58.5 feet   **8.** no solution
9. $\dfrac{2}{3} \le x \le 22$ **10.** $x \ge 0.7$ **11.** $x = 16$ **13.** $x = \pm 3$
15. $x = \dfrac{2}{15}$ **17.** $x = 6$ **19.** $x = -3$ **21.** no solution
23. $x = 0$ **25.** $x \ge 1$ **27.** $\dfrac{1}{2} \le x \le 1$ **29.** $x \ge 0$
31. $\dfrac{1}{3} \le x < \dfrac{10}{27}$ **33.** no solution   **35.** $0 \le x < 2$
37. $0 \le x \le 1$ **39.** $x \approx 0.5$ or $x = 1$
41. $x = -1$ or $x \approx 0.5$ **43.** $x = 0$ or $x = 1$
45. $0 \le x \le 0.3$ **47.** $x \approx -1.9$ or $x \approx 1.9$ **49.** $x \ge 1.3$

51. $-1.4 \le x \le -1$ *or* $1 \le x \le -1.6$ **53.** never **55.** never
57. sometimes **59.** always **61a.** $a < 0$
b. $a \ge 0$ **63a.** 191,916 feet **b.** 36.3 miles
c. 698 feet **65.** $y = 2x - 7$ **67.** $x = -2$ *or* $x = -3$
69. $x = 0.8$ *or* $x = -2.1$ **71.** $x^2 - 6x - 27$
73. $24x^6y^6\sqrt{2x}$ **75.** $x\sqrt{5}$ **77.** $2x\sqrt{10}$

CHAPTER 8 REVIEW

1. $y = 2$ **3.** $a = \frac{10}{27}$ **5.** excluded values: $x = 2$ and $x = 6$;
no holes; vertical asymptotes: $x = 2$ and $x = 6$;
horizontal asymptote: $y = 0$ **7.** excluded values:
$x = -7$ and $x = 2$; no holes; vertical asymptotes:
$x = -7$ and $x = 2$; horizontal asymptote: $y = 1$
9. excluded value: $x = -\frac{5}{3}$; no holes; vertical
asymptote: $x = -\frac{5}{3}$; no horizontal asymptote
11. excluded values: $y = 0$ and $y = 3$; hole when
$y = 0$; vertical asymptote: $y = 3$; horizontal
asymptote: $h = 0$
13. $\frac{2x}{5x - 30}$ **15.** $\frac{4a^2 + 8a}{5a^2 + 15a - 50}$ **17.** $\frac{z^2}{z^2 + 3z + 2}$ **19.** $\frac{x + 2}{x^2 + x}$
21. $\frac{23y - 29}{10y - 30}$ **23.** $\frac{-3x^2 + x - 3}{x^2 - 3x}$ **25.** $\frac{23}{x}$ **27.** $x = \pm 1$
29. $x = \frac{-5 \pm \sqrt{29}}{2}$ **31.** $x = \pm\sqrt{2}$ **33.** $x > 1$ or $x < 0$
35. $x < -1$ or $x > 1$ **37.** $x < -2$ or $x > -\frac{3}{2}$
39. $x \le -1$ or $0 < x \le 1$ **41.** $x < -2$ or $-1 < x \le 0.5$
43. $-1.7 < x < -1$ *or* $-1 < x < -0.3$
45. $y = \frac{-3 \pm \sqrt{9 + 4x}}{2}$ **47.** $y = \frac{8 \pm \sqrt{49 + 3x}}{3}$
49. The parent function is vertically compressed by a
factor of $\frac{1}{3}$. **51.** The parent function is horizontally
translated $\frac{3}{2}$ units to the right and horizontally
compressed by a factor of $\frac{1}{2}$. **53.** The parent
function is horizontally compressed by a factor of $\frac{1}{3}$,
vertically stretched by a factor 2, reflected across the
x-axis, and vertically translated 6 units down. **55.** 45
57. $3x^3y^2\sqrt{2xy}$ **59.** $cd^2\sqrt[3]{7}$ **61.** $3x^3y^5\sqrt{y}$ **63.** $\frac{\sqrt{5}}{5}$
65. $6 + 3\sqrt{3}$ **67.** $\frac{3 + \sqrt{6} + \sqrt{3} + 3\sqrt{2}}{6}$ **69.** no solution
71. $x = -10$ **73.** $x = 0$ or $x = \frac{1}{4}$ **75.** $x = \frac{3}{2}$ **77.** $x = 1$
79. no solution **81.** $0 \le x \le 25$ **83.** $x \ge 25$ **85.** $x \ge 3$
87. $x > 2$ **89.** no solution **91.** $x \ge 0$ **93.** ≈ 169.9
pounds

Chapter 9

LESSON 9.1

TRY THIS (p. 563)
a. ellipse $\left(y = \pm\frac{1}{3}\sqrt{36 - 4x^2}\right)$
b. parabola $\left(y = \pm\sqrt{6x}\right)$

TRY THIS (p. 564)
$\sqrt{194}$, or about 13.93

TRY THIS (p. 565)
$(5.5, 0.5)$

TRY THIS (p. 566)
center: $(1, 3)$; $C = 2\sqrt{17}\pi$; $A = 17\pi$

Exercises

4. hyperbola **5.** circle **6.** $\sqrt{218} \approx 14.76$
7. $\sqrt{13} \approx 3.61$ miles **8.** $M\left(\frac{3}{2}, -1\right)$ **9.** $(-1, 3)$;
$C = 2\pi\sqrt{17}$; $A = 17\pi$ **11.** circle **13.** hyperbola
15. ellipse **17.** parabola **19.** circle **21.** hyperbola
23. 7; $M\left(-5, \frac{3}{2}\right)$ **25.** $\sqrt{65} \approx 8.06$; $M\left(1, -\frac{9}{2}\right)$
27. $\sqrt{17} \approx 4.12$; $M\left(\frac{1}{2}, \frac{5}{2}\right)$ **29.** $2\sqrt{2} \approx 2.83$; $M(9, 1)$
31. $3\sqrt{3} \approx 5.20$; $M\left(\frac{3\sqrt{2}}{2}, \frac{5}{2}\right) \approx M(2.12, 2.5)$
33. $\sqrt{\frac{113}{2}} \approx 7.52$; $M\left(-\frac{9}{4}, \frac{1}{2}\right)$ **35.** $\sqrt{114} \approx 10.68$;
$M\left(\frac{3\sqrt{2}}{2}, 3\sqrt{7}\right) \approx M(2.12, 7.94)$ **37.** $|a|\sqrt{17} \approx 4.12|a|$;
$M\left(\frac{3a}{2}, -a\right)$ **39.** $\left(-\frac{1}{2}, 10\right)$; $C = 13\pi$; $A = \frac{169\pi}{4}$
41. $(-6, -4)$; $C = 4\pi\sqrt{13}$; $A = 52\pi$
43. $(3, -1)$; $C = 2\pi\sqrt{29}$; $A = 29\pi$ **45.** $(-12, 5)$
47. $(-14, 14)$ **49.** $AB = 2\sqrt{5}$; $BC = \sqrt{10}$; $AC = \sqrt{58}$;
not collinear **51.** $AB = \sqrt{89}$; $BC = \sqrt{89}$; $AC = 2\sqrt{89}$;
collinear **53a.** $AB = 2\sqrt{17}$; $BC = 7$; $CD = 2\sqrt{17}$;
$DA = 7$ **b.** yes **55a.** $\overline{AB}$: $m = -\frac{1}{4}$; $\overline{CD}$: $m = -\frac{1}{4}$; the
slopes of $\overline{AD}$ and $\overline{BC}$ are undefined. **b.** Yes, because
$\overline{AB}$ and $\overline{CD}$ have the same slope, and $\overline{AD}$ and $\overline{BC}$ are
both vertical. **57.** scalene **59.** $y = \frac{7}{5}x - \frac{4}{5}$ **61.** 1
63. $x = 3$ or $x = 5$ **65.** $x = 3 \pm \sqrt{29}$ **67.** $x = \frac{1}{6}$ or $x = 1$
69. $4x^3 - 3x^2 + 2x + 1$ **71.** 25

LESSON 9.2

TRY THIS (p. 572, Ex. 1)

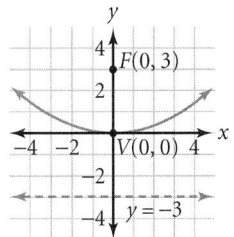

TRY THIS (p. 572, Ex. 2)
$x = -\frac{1}{16}y^2$
TRY THIS (p. 575, Ex. 4)
$x + 2 = -\frac{1}{16}(y - 4)^2$

TRY THIS (p. 575, Ex. 5)

Exercises

4.

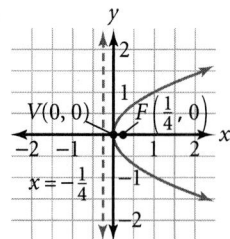

5. $x = -\frac{1}{12}y^2$ **6.** $x = \frac{1}{48}y^2$ **7.** $x - \frac{1}{2} = -\frac{1}{10}(y-3)^2$

8.

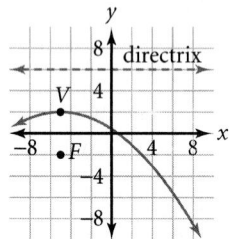

vertex: $(-5, 2)$; focus: $(-5, -2)$; directrix: $y = 6$

9. $y = -\frac{1}{4}x^2$ **11.** $x = -\frac{1}{8}y^2$ **13.** $x - 1 = -\frac{1}{8}(y-2)^2$

15.

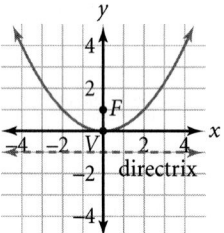

vertex: $(0, 1)$; focus: $(0, 0)$; directrix: $y = -1$

17.

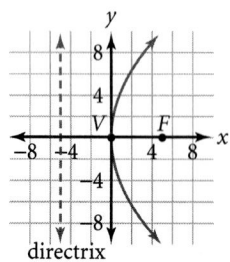

vertex: $(0, 0)$; focus: $(5, 0)$; directrix: $x = -5$

19.

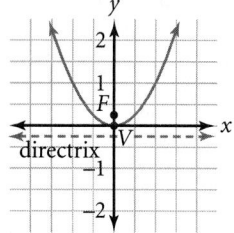

vertex: $(0, 0)$; focus: $\left(0, \frac{1}{4}\right)$; directrix: $y = -\frac{1}{4}$

21.

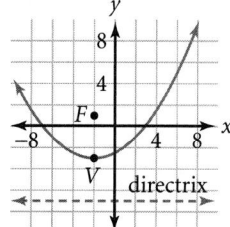

vertex: $(-2, -3)$; focus: $(-2, 1)$; directrix: $y = -7$

23.

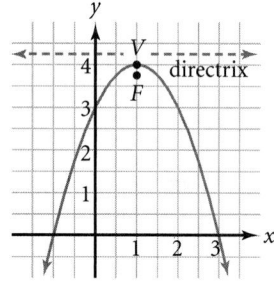

vertex: $(1, 4)$; focus: $\left(1, \frac{15}{4}\right)$; directrix: $y = \frac{17}{4}$

25.

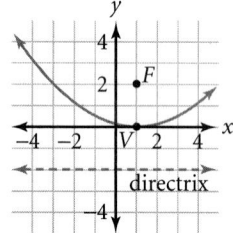

vertex: $(1, 0)$; focus: $(1, 2)$; directrix: $y = -2$

27.

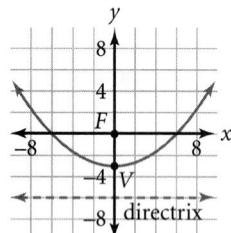

vertex: $(0, -3)$; focus: $(0, 0)$; directrix: $y = -6$

29.

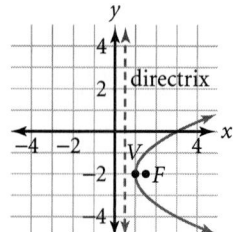

vertex: $(1, -2)$; focus: $\left(\frac{3}{2}, -2\right)$; directrix: $x = \frac{1}{2}$

31.

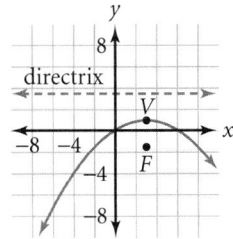

vertex: (3, 1); focus: $\left(3, -\frac{3}{2}\right)$; directrix: $y = \frac{7}{2}$

33.

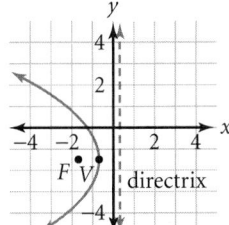

vertex: $\left(-\frac{11}{16}, -\frac{3}{2}\right)$; focus: $\left(-\frac{27}{16}, -\frac{3}{2}\right)$; directrix: $x = \frac{5}{16}$

35.

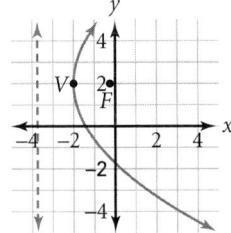

vertex: (−2, 2); focus: $\left(-\frac{1}{4}, 2\right)$; directrix: $x = -\frac{15}{4}$

37. $y = -\frac{1}{20}x^2$ **39.** $x = -\frac{1}{16}y^2$ **41.** $x = \frac{1}{8}y^2$

43. $y = -\frac{1}{48}x^2$ **45.** $x = \frac{1}{12}y^2$ **47.** $x = -\frac{1}{32}y^2$

49. $x - \frac{1}{2} = -\frac{1}{4}(y - 5)^2$ **51.** If the parabola opens to the right and has its vertex at the origin, the equation is $x = \frac{1}{4}y^2$. **53.** $y = \frac{1}{2}x^2$ **55.** $3a(a + 1)$

57. $mn(m + 7mn - 3)$ **59.** $(y - 2)(y - 10)$

61. $5(x - 2)(x - 1)$ **63.** $(3y + 5)(2y - 5)$

65. $\frac{x^3 + 3x^2 + 3x + 2}{x + 1}$ **67.** $\frac{1}{x + 3}$

LESSON 9.3

TRY THIS (p. 580)

$x^2 + y^2 = 4$

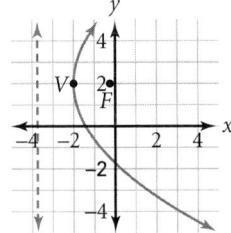

TRY THIS (p. 581)

outside

TRY THIS (p. 582)

$(x - 1)^2 + (y + 1)^2 = 9$; center: (1, −1); $r = 3$

Exercises

4. $x^2 + y^2 = 36$

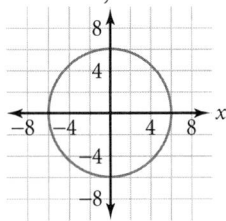

5. $(x - 3)^2 + (y - 2)^2 = 25$ **6.** yes

7. $(x + 3)^2 + (y - 2)^2 = 16$; $C(-3, 2)$; $r = 4$

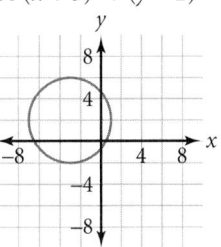

9. $x^2 + y^2 = 1$ **11.** $(x + 2)^2 + (y + 4)^2 = 9$

13. $(x + 1)^2 + (y - 2)^2 = 6.25$ **15.** $x^2 + y^2 = 25$

17. $x^2 + y^2 = 49$ **19.** $(x - 3)^2 + (y - 5)^2 = 144$

21. $(x + 5)^2 + (y + 1)^2 = 25$

23. $(x + 6)^2 + (y - 9)^2 = 225$ **25.** $x^2 + (y - 4)^2 = 9$

27. $(x - 3)^2 + (y - 3)^2 = 4$ **29.** $(x - 1)^2 + y^2 = \frac{1}{16}$

31. $(x - a)^2 + (y + 2a)^2 = 4$

33.

35.

37.

39.

41.

43.

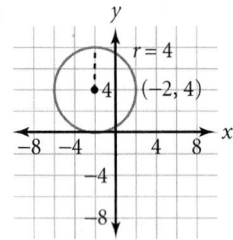

45. $(x-1)^2 + y^2 = 9$; $C(1, 0)$; $r = 3$

47. $(x+1)^2 + (y+3)^2 = 16$; $C(-1, -3)$; $r = 4$

49. $(x-6)^2 + (y+3)^2 = 64$; $C(6, -3)$; $r = 8$

51. $x^2 + (y-10)^2 = 81$; $C(0, 10)$; $r = 9$

53. $\left(x-\frac{1}{2}\right)^2 + \left(y+\frac{1}{2}\right)^2 = \frac{1}{2}$; $C\left(\frac{1}{2}, -\frac{1}{2}\right)$; $r = \frac{\sqrt{2}}{2} \approx 0.71$

55. $(x-0.5)^2 + (y+3.5)^2 = 25$; $C(0.5, -3.5)$; $r = 5$

57. $(x-3)^2 + (y-5)^2 = 36$; $C(3, 5)$; $r = 6$

59. $(x-5)^2 + (y+3)^2 = 34$; $C(5, -3)$; $r = \sqrt{34} \approx 5.83$

61. Circle; the equation can be written as $x^2 + y^2 = 12$, which has the form $x^2 + y^2 = r^2$, where $r = \sqrt{12} = 2\sqrt{3}$. **63.** Parabola; the equation has the form $x = \frac{1}{4p}y^2$, where $p = \frac{1}{4}$. **65.** Parabola; the equation can be written as $x - 2 = 2y^2$, which has the form $(x - h) = \frac{1}{4p}(y - k)^2$, where $h = 2$, $k = 0$, and $p = \frac{1}{8}$. **67.** Circle; the equation can be written as $(x-2)^2 + (y+2)^2 = 15$, which has the form $(x-h)^2 + (y-k)^2 = r^2$, where $h = 2$, $k = -2$, and $r = \sqrt{15}$. **69.** Inside; because $1^2 + 6^2 = 37$, $1^2 + 6^2 < 49$. **71.** Inside; the equation can be written as $(x-2)^2 + (y+3)^2 = 25$. $P(2, -3)$ is the center of the circle, so it is inside the circle.

73. Outside; the equation can be written as $(x-6)^2 + (y+1)^2 = 49$. Because $(12-6)^2 + (3+1)^2 = 52$, $(12-6)^2 + (3+1)^2 > 49$.

75. Outside; because $1.5^2 + 3.5^2 = 14.5$, $1.5^2 + 3.5^2 > 6$. **77a.** Answers may vary. Sample answer: The centers of the circles are at $(3, 3)$ and $(3, 1)$, which are 2 units apart. C_1 will be completely enclosed by C_2 if $r_2 - r_1 > 2$. For example, let $r_1 = 4$ and $r_2 = 1$. **b.** Answers may vary. Sample answer: If

$r_1 = \sqrt{2}$ and $r_2 = \sqrt{2}$, the ...s intersect at $(2, 2)$ and $(4, 2)$. **c.** If $r_1 + r_2 = 2$, then the circles will intersect at one point. For example, if $r_1 = 1$ and $r_2 = 1$, then the circles will intersect at $(3, 2)$.

79. $(x-8)^2 + (y-8)^2 = 11$ **81.** yes **83.** $x = \frac{11}{2}$; $\left(\frac{11}{2}, -\frac{9}{4}\right)$ **85.** $x = -\frac{3}{2}$; $\left(-\frac{3}{2}, \frac{49}{4}\right)$ **87.** $x = \frac{\ln 12}{-3} \approx 0.83$ **89.** $a = 4$ **91.** $x = 24$ **93.** Translate the graph 4 units to the left, stretch it horizontally by a factor of 2, and then translate it 3 units down.

LESSON 9.4

TRY THIS (p. 588)

$$\frac{x^2}{169} + \frac{y^2}{25} = 1$$

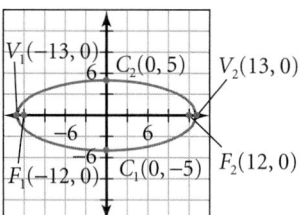

TRY THIS (p. 589)

$$\frac{x^2}{4509.1} + \frac{y^2}{4508.9} = 1$$

TRY THIS (p. 590)

$$\frac{(x+1)^2}{4} + \frac{(y+2)^2}{16} = 1$$

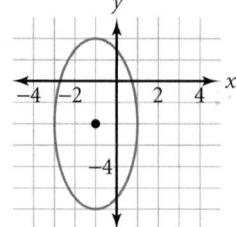

Exercises

5. $\frac{x^2}{41} + \frac{y^2}{16} = 1$

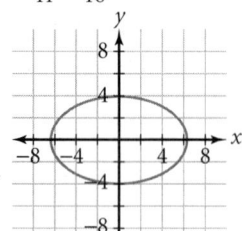

6. $\frac{x^2}{233,578.89} + \frac{y^2}{233,026.64} = 1$

7. $\dfrac{(x-1)^2}{4} + \dfrac{(y+2)^2}{9} = 1$

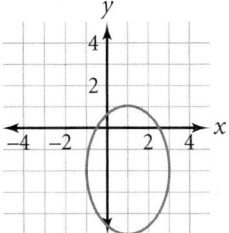

8. $\dfrac{(x+1)^2}{4} + \dfrac{(y-1)^2}{25} = 1$; center: $(-1, 1)$; vertices: $(-1, -4)$ and $(-1, 6)$; co-vertices: $(-3, 1)$ and $(1, 1)$; foci: $\left(-1, 1 - \sqrt{21}\right)$ and $\left(-1, 1 + \sqrt{21}\right)$

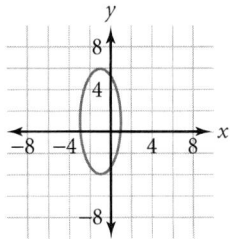

9. vertices: $(-5, 0)$ and $(5, 0)$; co-vertices: $(0, -3)$ and $(0, 3)$ **11.** vertices: $(-9, 0)$ and $(9, 0)$; co-vertices: $(0, -2)$ and $(0, 2)$ **13.** vertices: $(0, -8)$ and $(0, 8)$; co-vertices: $(-1, 0)$ and $(1, 0)$ **15.** $\dfrac{x^2}{4} + \dfrac{y^2}{1} = 1$; center: $(0, 0)$; vertices: $(-2, 0)$ and $(2, 0)$; co-vertices: $(0, -1)$ and $(0, 1)$; foci: $\left(-\sqrt{3}, 0\right)$ and $\left(\sqrt{3}, 0\right)$

17. $\dfrac{x^2}{\frac{28}{3}} + \dfrac{y^2}{4} = 1$; center: $(0, 0)$; vertices: $\left(-\dfrac{2\sqrt{21}}{3}, 0\right)$ and $\left(\dfrac{2\sqrt{21}}{3}, 0\right)$; co-vertices: $(0, -2)$ and $(0, 2)$; foci: $\left(-\dfrac{4\sqrt{3}}{3}, 0\right)$ and $\left(\dfrac{4\sqrt{3}}{3}, 0\right)$ **19.** $\dfrac{x^2}{16} + \dfrac{y^2}{36} = 1$; center: $(0, 0)$; vertices: $(0, -6)$ and $(0, 6)$; co-vertices: $(-4, 0)$ and $(4, 0)$; foci: $\left(0, -2\sqrt{5}\right)$ and $\left(0, 2\sqrt{5}\right)$

21. $\dfrac{x^2}{36} + \dfrac{y^2}{25} = 1$ **23.** $\dfrac{(x-3)^2}{16} + \dfrac{(y-3)^2}{9} = 1$

25. $\dfrac{(x+2)^2}{4} + \dfrac{(y-2)^2}{9} = 1$

27. center: $(0, 0)$; vertices: $(-5, 0)$ and $(5, 0)$; co-vertices: $(0, -2)$ and $(0, 2)$; foci: $\left(-\sqrt{21}, 0\right)$ and $\left(\sqrt{21}, 0\right)$

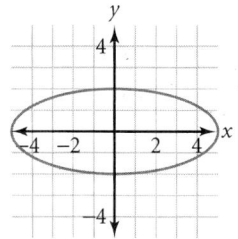

29. center: $(0, 0)$; vertices: $(0, -3)$ and $(0, 3)$; co-vertices: $(-2, 0)$ and $(2, 0)$; foci: $\left(0, -\sqrt{5}\right)$, $\left(0, \sqrt{5}\right)$

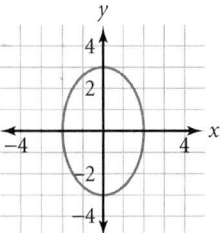

31. center: $(-2, -1)$; vertices: $(-2, -4)$ and $(-2, 2)$; co-vertices: $(-4, -1)$ and $(0, -1)$; foci: $\left(-2, -1 - \sqrt{5}\right)$ and $\left(-2, -1 + \sqrt{5}\right)$

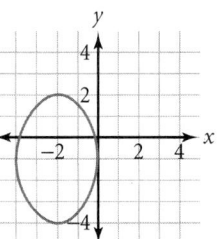

33. center: $(0, -2)$; vertices: $(0, -5)$ and $(0, 1)$; co-vertices: $(-1, -2)$ and $(1, -2)$; foci: $\left(0, -2 - 2\sqrt{2}\right)$ and $\left(0, -2 + 2\sqrt{2}\right)$

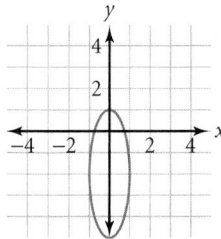

35. The graph is a circle with its center at $(1, 1)$ and a radius of 2.

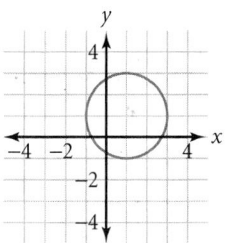

37. center: $(1, -2)$; vertices: $(-4, -2)$ and $(6, -2)$; co-vertices: $(1, -5)$ and $(1, 1)$; foci: $(-3, -2)$ and $(5, -2)$

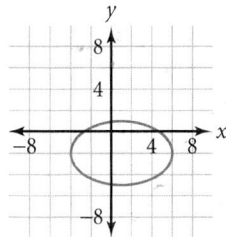

39. center: $(0, 0)$; vertices: $(0, -5)$ and $(0, 5)$;
co-vertices: $(-3, 0)$ and $(3, 0)$; foci: $(0, -4)$ and $(0, 4)$

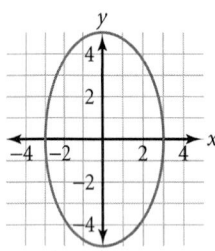

41. $\dfrac{x^2}{48} + \dfrac{y^2}{64} = 1$ **43.** $\dfrac{x^2}{1} + \dfrac{y^2}{10} = 1$ **45.** $\dfrac{x^2}{25} + \dfrac{y^2}{16} = 1$

47. parabola **49.** ellipse **51.** $\dfrac{(x + 1)^2}{4} + \dfrac{(y - 1)^2}{16} = 1$;
center: $(-1, 1)$; vertices: $(-1, -3)$ and $(-1, 5)$;
co-vertices: $(-3, 1)$ and $(1, 1)$; foci: $\left(-1, 1 - 2\sqrt{3}\right)$ and
$\left(-1, 1 + 2\sqrt{3}\right)$ **53.** $\dfrac{(x - 1)^2}{1} + \dfrac{y^2}{25} = 1$; center: $(1, 0)$;
vertices: $(1, -5)$ and $(1, 5)$; co-vertices: $(0, 0)$ and
$(2, 0)$; foci: $\left(1, -2\sqrt{6}\right)$ and $\left(1, 2\sqrt{6}\right)$

55. $\dfrac{(x + 2)^2}{9} + \dfrac{(y + 1)^2}{25} = 1$; center: $(-2, -1)$; vertices:
$(-2, -6)$ and $(-2, 4)$; co-vertices: $(-5, -1)$ and
$(1, -1)$; foci: $(-2, -5)$ and $(-2, 3)$

57. $\dfrac{(x - 1)^2}{25} + \dfrac{(y + 2)^2}{36} = 1$; center: $(1, -2)$; vertices:
$(1, -8)$ and $(1, 4)$; co-vertices: $(-4, -2)$ and $(6, -2)$;
foci: $\left(1, -2 - \sqrt{11}\right)$ and $\left(1, -2 + \sqrt{11}\right)$

59. $\dfrac{(x + 10)^2}{4} + \dfrac{(y + 5)^2}{16} = 1$ **61.** the point $(-2, 1)$

63. $\dfrac{x^2}{1739.6} + \dfrac{y^2}{1369} = 1$ **65.** $8x^2y^7$ **67.** $\dfrac{36y^8}{25x^2z^{12}}$

69. $x \approx 1.50$ **71.** $25a^3 - 5a^2 - 14a + 11$

73. $4x^2y^2 - 15xy + 34y^2$

LESSON 9.5

TRY THIS (p. 597)
$\dfrac{x^2}{49} - \dfrac{y^2}{16} = 1$

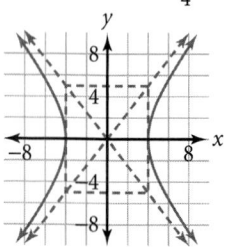

TRY THIS (p. 598)
asymptotes: $y = \pm\dfrac{5}{4}x$; vertices: $(-4, 0)$ and $(4, 0)$

TRY THIS (p. 599)
$\dfrac{(y - 2)^2}{9} - \dfrac{(x - 3)^2}{16} = 1$

TRY THIS (p. 600)
$\dfrac{(x - 1)^2}{25} - \dfrac{(y - 2)^2}{4} = 1$; center: $(1, 2)$; vertices: $(-4, 2)$
and $(6, 2)$; co-vertices: $(1, 0)$ and $(1, 4)$;
foci: $\left(1 - \sqrt{29}, 2\right)$ and $\left(1 + \sqrt{29}, 2\right)$

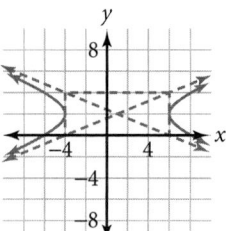

Exercises

3. $\dfrac{x^2}{16} - \dfrac{y^2}{4} = 1$

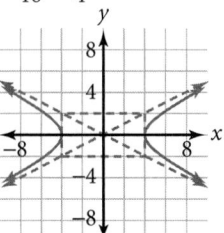

4. asymptotes: $y = \dfrac{5}{3}x$ and $y = -\dfrac{5}{3}x$; vertices: $(-3, 0)$
and $(3, 0)$

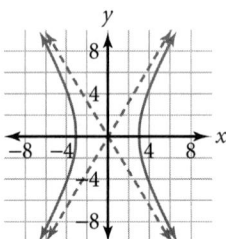

5. $\dfrac{(x - 3)^2}{4} - \dfrac{(y - 4)^2}{5} = 1$ **6.** $\dfrac{(x + 1)^2}{11} - \dfrac{(y - 2)^2}{11} = 1$;
center: $(-1, 2)$; vertices: $\left(-1 - \sqrt{11}, 2\right)$ and
$\left(-1 + \sqrt{11}, 2\right)$; co-vertices: $\left(-1, 2 - \sqrt{11}\right)$ and
$\left(-1, 2 + \sqrt{11}\right)$; foci: $\left(-1 - 2\sqrt{11}, 2\right)$ and $\left(-1 + 2\sqrt{11}, 2\right)$

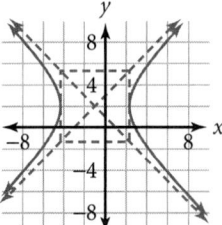

7. $\dfrac{x^2}{9} - \dfrac{y^2}{25} = 1$ **9.** $\dfrac{y^2}{1} - \dfrac{(x + 1)^2}{9} = 1$ **11.** $\dfrac{y^2}{4} - \dfrac{x^2}{9} = 1$

13. center: $(0, 0)$; vertices: $(-1, 0)$ and $(1, 0)$; co-vertices: $(0, -1)$ and $(0, 1)$; foci: $\left(-\sqrt{2}, 0\right)$ and $\left(\sqrt{2}, 0\right)$; asymptotes: $y = -x$ and $y = x$

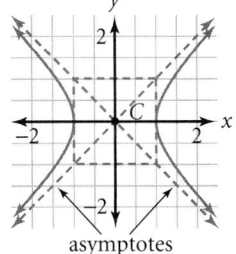

asymptotes

15. center: $(0, 0)$; vertices: $(0, -3)$ and $(0, 3)$; co-vertices: $(-5, 0)$ and $(5, 0)$; foci: $\left(0, -\sqrt{34}\right)$ and $\left(0, \sqrt{34}\right)$; asymptotes: $y = -\frac{3x}{5}$ and $y = \frac{3x}{5}$

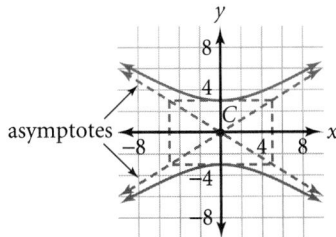

asymptotes

17. center: $(0, 0)$; vertices: $(-1, 0)$ and $(1, 0)$; co-vertices: $(0, -2)$ and $(0, 2)$; foci: $\left(-\sqrt{5}, 0\right)$ and $\left(\sqrt{5}, 0\right)$; asymptotes: $y = -2x$ and $y = 2x$

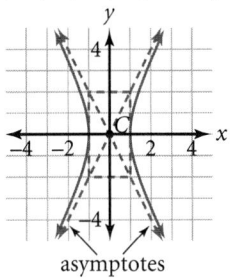

asymptotes

19. center: $(0, 0)$; vertices: $(0, -10)$ and $(0, 10)$; co-vertices: $(-8, 0)$ and $(8, 0)$; foci: $\left(0, -2\sqrt{41}\right)$ and $\left(0, 2\sqrt{41}\right)$; asymptotes: $y = -\frac{5x}{4}$ and $y = \frac{5x}{4}$

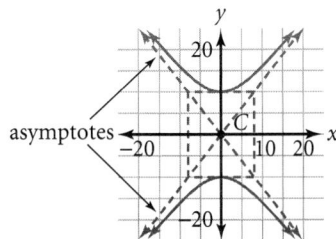

asymptotes

21. center: $(0, 0)$; vertices: $(-5, 0)$ and $(5, 0)$; co-vertices: $(0, -2)$ and $(0, 2)$; foci: $\left(-\sqrt{29}, 0\right)$ and $\left(\sqrt{29}, 0\right)$; asymptotes: $y = -\frac{2x}{5}$ and $y = \frac{2x}{5}$

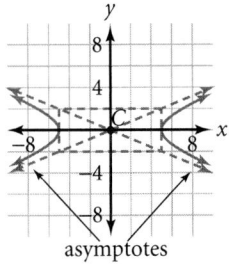

asymptotes

23. center: $(1, -2)$; vertices: $(-1, -2)$ and $(3, -2)$; co-vertices: $(1, -5)$ and $(1, 1)$; foci: $\left(1 - \sqrt{13}, -2\right)$ and $\left(1 + \sqrt{13}, -2\right)$; asymptotes: $y = -\frac{3x}{2} - \frac{1}{2}$ and $y = \frac{3x}{2} - \frac{7}{2}$

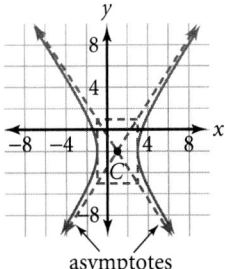

asymptotes

25. $\frac{x^2}{9} - \frac{y^2}{25} = 1$ **27.** $\frac{y^2}{16} - \frac{x^2}{9} = 1$ **29.** $\frac{x^2}{5} - \frac{y^2}{4} = 1$

31. $\frac{(x-2)^2}{9} - \frac{(y-3)^2}{25} = 1$ **33.** $\frac{(x-1)^2}{9} - \frac{(y-3)^2}{4} = 1$; center: $(1, 3)$; vertices: $(-2, 3)$ and $(4, 3)$; co-vertices: $(1, 1)$ and $(1, 5)$; foci: $\left(1 - \sqrt{13}, 3\right)$ and $\left(1 + \sqrt{13}, 3\right)$

35. $\frac{(y+1)^2}{36} - \frac{(x+1)^2}{4} = 1$; center: $(-1, -1)$; vertices: $(-1, -7)$ and $(-1, 5)$; co-vertices: $(-3, -1)$ and $(1, -1)$; foci: $\left(-1, -1 - 2\sqrt{10}\right)$ and $\left(-1, -1 + 2\sqrt{10}\right)$

37. $\frac{(y-3)^2}{9} - \frac{(x+2)^2}{1} = 1$; center: $(-2, 3)$; vertices: $(-2, 0)$ and $(-2, 6)$; co-vertices: $(-3, 3)$ and $(-1, 3)$; foci: $\left(-2, 3 - \sqrt{10}\right)$ and $\left(-2, 3 + \sqrt{10}\right)$

39. $\frac{(x+2)^2}{16} - \frac{(y-2)^2}{16} = 1$; center: $(-2, 2)$; vertices: $(-6, 2)$ and $(2, 2)$; co-vertices: $(-2, -2)$ and $(-2, 6)$; foci: $\left(-2 - 4\sqrt{2}, 2\right)$ and $\left(-2 + 4\sqrt{2}, 2\right)$

41. $\frac{(y-2)^2}{5} - \frac{(x-2)^2}{3} = 1$; center: $(2, 2)$; vertices: $\left(2, 2 - \sqrt{5}\right)$ and $\left(2, 2 + \sqrt{5}\right)$; co-vertices: $\left(2 - \sqrt{3}, 2\right)$ and $\left(2 + \sqrt{3}, 2\right)$; foci: $\left(2, 2 - 2\sqrt{2}\right)$ and $\left(2, 2 + 2\sqrt{2}\right)$

43. $\frac{x^2}{25} - \frac{y^2}{16} = 1$ or $\frac{y^2}{16} - \frac{x^2}{25} = 1$

45. $\frac{(x-6)^2}{25} - \frac{\left(y - \frac{13}{2}\right)^2}{\frac{121}{4}} = 1$ or

$\frac{\left(y - \frac{13}{2}\right)^2}{\frac{121}{4}} - \frac{(x-6)^2}{25} = 1$

47a. vertices: $V_1(-a, 0)$ and $V_2(a, 0)$; co-vertices: $C_1(0, -a)$ and $C_2(0, a)$

b. square **c.** Answers may vary. Sample answer:

Side	Length	Slope
$\overline{V_1C_1}$	$\sqrt{[0-(-a)]^2 + (-a-0)^2} = \sqrt{2a^2} = a\sqrt{2}$	$\frac{-a-0}{0-(-a)} = -1$
$\overline{C_1V_2}$	$\sqrt{(a-0)^2 + [0-(-a)]^2} = \sqrt{2a^2} = a\sqrt{2}$	$\frac{0-(-a)}{a-0} = 1$
$\overline{V_2C_2}$	$\sqrt{(0-a)^2 + (a-0)^2} = \sqrt{2a^2} = a\sqrt{2}$	$\frac{a-0}{0-a} = -1$
$\overline{C_2V_1}$	$\sqrt{(-a-0)^2 + (0-a)^2} = \sqrt{2a^2} = a\sqrt{2}$	$\frac{0-a}{-a-0} = 1$

The table shows that the sides all have the same length and that the sides meet at right angles because the slopes of adjacent sides are negative reciprocals. Therefore, quadrilateral $V_1C_1V_2C_2$ is a square.

49. $\frac{(x+9)^2}{4} - \frac{(y-3)^2}{9} = 1$ **51.** $(3, 2)$ **53.** $\left(\frac{1}{5}, 5\right)$

55. $(3, -2)$ **57.** $\begin{bmatrix} -8 & 0 & 10 \\ 4 & 0 & -5 \\ 20 & 0 & -25 \end{bmatrix}$ **59.** $[-7 \quad 6 \quad -41]$

61. does not exist **63.** does not exist

LESSON 9.6

TRY THIS (p. 608)

$(4, 3), (4, -3), (-6, \sqrt{11}i), (-6, -\sqrt{11}i)$

TRY THIS (p. 609)

4 solutions: $\left(\pm 3\sqrt{\frac{13}{85}}, \pm 12\sqrt{\frac{2}{85}}\right)$, or approximately $(\pm 1.17, \pm 1.84)$

TRY THIS (p. 610)

a. ellipse

b. $\frac{(x+1)^2}{4} + \frac{(y+1)^2}{9} = 1$

c.

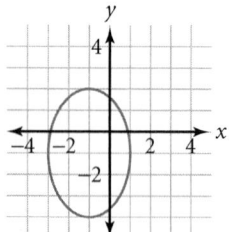

Exercises

5. $(-5, \pm 3i)$ and $\left(3, \pm\sqrt{7}\right)$ **6.** width: $\frac{12\sqrt{5}}{5} \approx 5.37$ inches; length: $\frac{24\sqrt{5}}{5} \approx 10.73$ inches

7. $\left(\pm\frac{6\sqrt{65}}{13}, \pm\frac{2\sqrt{91}}{13}\right)$ or $(\pm 3.72, \pm 1.47)$

8. ellipse; $\frac{(x+1)^2}{9} + \frac{(y+1)^2}{4} = 1$

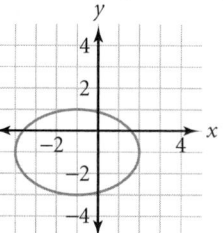

9. $\left(\pm\sqrt{5}, 5\right)$ **11.** $(0, 0)$ and $(2, 4)$ **13.** $\left(-\sqrt{2}, -\sqrt{2}\right)$ and $\left(\sqrt{2}, \sqrt{2}\right)$ **15.** none **17.** $\left(\pm\sqrt{-\frac{1}{2} + \frac{\sqrt{5}}{2}}, -\frac{1}{2} + \frac{\sqrt{5}}{2}\right)$

19. none **21.** $(0, \pm 1)$ **23.** none **25.** $(\pm 5, 0)$

27. none **29.** 4 solutions: $\left(\pm\frac{6\sqrt{130}}{13}, \pm\frac{6\sqrt{39}}{13}\right)$

31. $(\pm 3, 0)$ **33.** $(0, 0), (1, 1)$ **35.** 4 solutions: $\left(\pm\frac{\sqrt{5}}{2}, \pm\frac{3}{2}\right)$ **37.** 4 solutions: $(\pm 6, \pm 2)$ **39.** none

41. none **43.** 4 approximate solutions: $(\pm 1.85, \pm 1.89)$

45. infinitely many solutions:

47. circle; $(x-1)^2 + (y-1)^2 = 8$

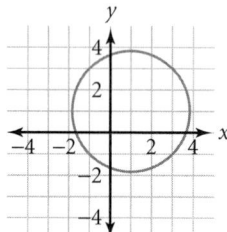

49. ellipse; $\frac{(x+2)^2}{9} + \frac{(y-2)^2}{4} = 1$

51. hyperbola; $\frac{(x+1)^2}{9} - \frac{(y-2)^2}{4} = 1$

53. ellipse; $\frac{(x-3)^2}{9} + \frac{(y+1)^2}{4} = 1$

55. parabola; $x + 2 = \frac{1}{2}(y - 3)^2$

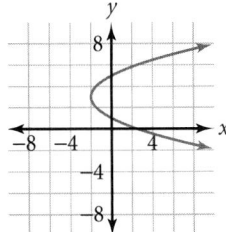

57. hyperbola; $\frac{x^2}{123} - \frac{(y+2)^2}{123} = 1$

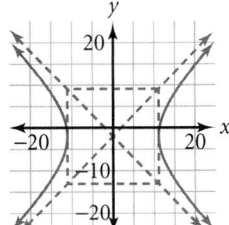

59. $\left(-\frac{5}{3}, 2 \pm \frac{4\sqrt{5}}{3}\right)$ **61.** none **63.** $(0, -2)$ and $(0, 4)$

65. $\left(\frac{5}{2} + \frac{5\sqrt{247}}{26}, \frac{1}{2} - \frac{\sqrt{247}}{25}\right)$ and

$\left(\frac{5}{2} - \frac{5\sqrt{247}}{26}, \frac{1}{2} + \frac{\sqrt{247}}{26}\right)$, or about $(5.52, -0.10)$ and

$(-0.52, 1.10)$ **67.** 51 **69.** $x^2 = 9$, $y^2 = 0$; $x = \pm 3$, $y = 0$

71. 3 feet by 4 feet **73.** $6 - 2\sqrt{6}$ inches by $6 + 2\sqrt{6}$

inches, or about 1.10 inches by 10.90 inches

75. $\frac{32\sqrt{5}}{5}$ inches by $\frac{16\sqrt{5}}{5}$ inches, or about 14.31

inches by 7.16 inches **77.** $\frac{27\sqrt{10}}{5}$ inches by $\frac{9\sqrt{10}}{5}$

inches, or about 17.08 inches by 5.69 inches

79. $-2, -1$, and 1 **81.** no rational zeros

83. $\frac{1}{2}, 1 - \sqrt{2}$, and $1 + \sqrt{2}$ **85.** $-\frac{1}{3}, 1, i\sqrt{3}, -i\sqrt{3}$

87. $\frac{x^2 + 3x + 4}{x^3 - 4x}$ **89.** $x = \frac{17}{8}$ **91.** $x > \frac{23}{3}$

93. no solution

CHAPTER REVIEW AND ASSESSMENT

1. 5; $M\left(\frac{3}{2}, 2\right)$ **3.** $PQ = 2\sqrt{13} \approx 7.21$; $M(0, 3)$

5. $PQ = \sqrt{185} \approx 13.60$; $M\left(\frac{9}{2}, -7\right)$

7. $x + 23 = (y - 5)^2$; vertex: $(-23, 5)$; focus: $\left(-\frac{91}{4}, 5\right)$;

directrix: $x = -\frac{93}{4}$

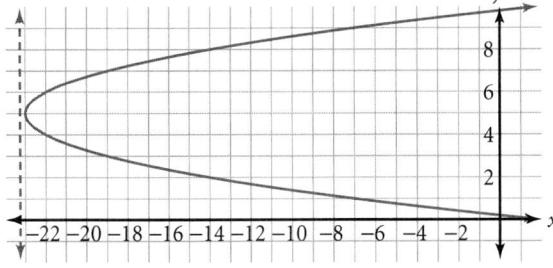

9. $y - 4 = (x + 4)^2$; vertex: $(-4, 4)$; focus: $\left(-4, \frac{17}{4}\right)$;

directrix: $y = \frac{15}{4}$

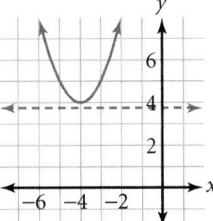

11. $x^2 + y^2 = 100$; $C(0, 0)$; $r = 10$

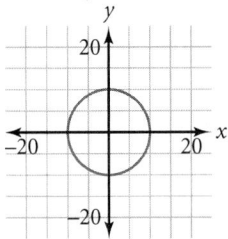

13. $(x - 1)^2 + (y - 49)^2 = 81$; $C(1, 49)$; $r = 9$

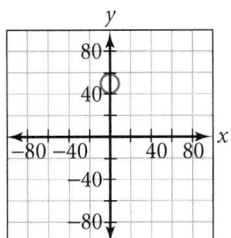

15. $(x + 2)^2 + (y + 4)^2 = 25$; $C(-2, -4)$; $r = 5$

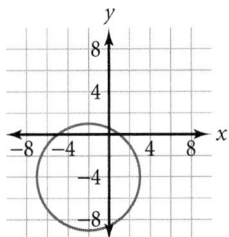

17. $\frac{(x-4)^2}{9} + \frac{(y+1)^2}{25} = 1$; center: $(4, -1)$; vertices:

$(4, -6)$ and $(4, 4)$; co-vertices: $(1, -1)$ and $(7, -1)$;

foci: $(4, -5)$ and $(4, 3)$

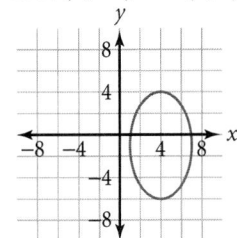

19. $\frac{(x+5)^2}{16} + \frac{(y+3)^2}{4} = 1$; center: $(-5, -3)$; vertices: $(-9, -3)$ and $(-1, -3)$; co-vertices: $(-5, -5)$ and $(-5, -1)$; foci: $\left(-5 - 2\sqrt{3}, -3\right)$ and $\left(-5 + 2\sqrt{3}, -3\right)$

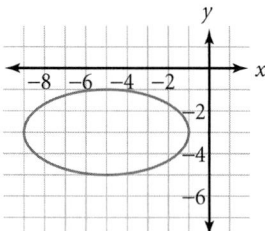

21. $\frac{(x+5)^2}{36} - \frac{(y-1)^2}{64} = 1$; center: $(-5, 1)$; vertices: $(-11, 1)$ and $(1, 1)$; co-vertices: $(-5, -7)$ and $(-5, 9)$; foci: $(-15, 1)$ and $(5, 1)$

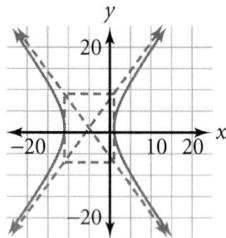

23. $\frac{y^2}{25} - \frac{x^2}{4} = 1$; center: $(0, 0)$; vertices: $(0, -5)$ and $(0, 5)$; co-vertices: $(-2, 0)$ and $(2, 0)$; foci: $\left(0, -\sqrt{29}\right)$ and $\left(0, \sqrt{29}\right)$

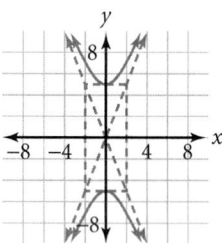

25. $\frac{(y+3)^2}{4} - \frac{(x+5)^2}{36} = 1$; center: $(-5, -3)$; vertices: $(-5, -5)$ and $(-5, -1)$; co-vertices: $(-11, -3)$ and $(1, -3)$; foci: $\left(-5, -3 - 2\sqrt{10}\right)$ and $\left(-5, -3 + 2\sqrt{10}\right)$

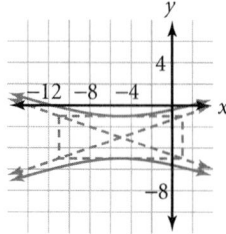

27. 4 solutions: $\left(\pm 2, \pm\sqrt{2}\right)$, or about $(\pm 2, \pm 1.41)$

29. $\left(-\frac{16}{5}, \frac{9}{5}\right)$ **31.** hyperbola; $\frac{(x-3)^2}{9} - \frac{(y+1)^2}{4} = 1$

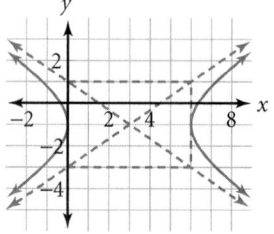

33. $\frac{2420}{3}$ watts, or about 806.7 watts **35a.** Answers may vary. Sample answer: Assuming that distances are measured in feet and that the microphones are located on the x-axis, $\frac{x^2}{1,562,500} - \frac{y^2}{7,437,500} = 1$.
b. 1750 feet

Chapter 10

LESSON 10.1

TRY THIS (p. 629)
$\frac{4}{9}$, or $\approx 44\%$

TRY THIS (p. 630, Ex. 2)
$\frac{1}{3}$, or $\approx 33.3\%$

TRY THIS (p. 630, Ex. 3)
a. $\frac{1}{3}$, or $\approx 33.3\%$

b. $\frac{1}{15}$, or $\approx 6.7\%$

Exercises
4. $\frac{3}{9}$, or $\approx 33.3\%$ **5.** $\frac{1}{9}$, or $\approx 11.1\%$ **6.** $\frac{1}{4}$, or 25%
7. 455,625 **8.** $\frac{1}{50}$, or 2% **9.** $\frac{3}{10}$, or 30% **11.** $\frac{1}{2}$, or 50%
13. $\frac{1}{6}$, or $\approx 16.7\%$ **15.** $\frac{1}{2}$, or 50% **17.** $\frac{1}{2}$, or 50%
19. $\frac{5}{6}$, or $\approx 83.3\%$ **21.** $\frac{3}{5}$, or 60% **23.** $\frac{2}{5}$, or 40%

25.

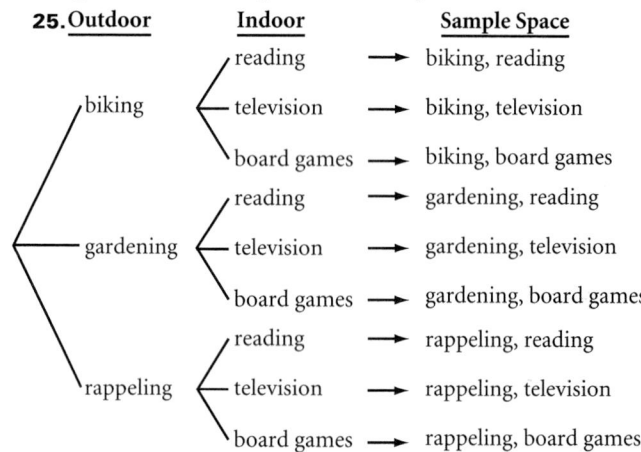

Outdoor	Indoor	Sample Space
biking	reading	biking, reading
	television	biking, television
	board games	biking, board games
gardening	reading	gardening, reading
	television	gardening, television
	board games	gardening, board games
rappeling	reading	rappeling, reading
	television	rappeling, television
	board games	rappeling, board games

27. 6,760,000 **29.** 6,760,000 **31.** $\frac{4}{9}$, or $\approx 44.4\%$
33. $\frac{1}{21}$, or $\approx 4.8\%$ **35.** 25% **37.** 35.7%
39. 268,435,456 **41.** $\approx 14.0\%$ **43.** $\approx 29.7\%$
45. at least 7 letters long **47.** $g^{-1}(x) = \frac{6x+2}{3}$

49. a vertical compression by a factor of $\frac{1}{2}$ and a vertical translation 5 units down **51.** a horizontal compression by a factor of $\frac{1}{2}$ and a vertical translation 1 unit up

LESSON 10.2

TRY THIS (p. 637, Ex. 1)
There are 5040 ways to arrange the letters.

TRY THIS (p. 637, Ex. 2)

There are 1680 ways to listen to 4 out of 8 CDs.

TRY THIS (p. 639, Ex. 3)

There are 462 ways to plant the flowers.

TRY THIS (p. 639, Ex. 4)

There are 39,916,800 ways to choose the seats.

Exercises

5. 720 **6.** 210 **7.** 2520 **8.** 39,916,800 **9.** 4920 **11.** 2
13. 56 **15.** 20 **17.** 604,800 **19.** 50 **21.** 132
23. 60,480 **25.** 6720 **27.** 1680 **29.** 8 **31.** 40,320
33. 1,814,400 **35.** 13,366,080 **37.** 271,252,800
39. 720 **41.** 60 **43.** 10,080 **45.** 151,200
47. 908,107,200 **49.** 720 **51a.** 10,000 **b.** 5040
53. 5040 **55.** 72 **57.** 120 **59.** 720 **61.** 210 **63.** 120
65. $3 - 4i$ **67.** $-\frac{42}{29} - \frac{11}{29}i$ **69.** $\log_b 4$ **71.** -1
73. ≈ 194.1 cubic inches

LESSON 10.3

TRY THIS (p. 644)

36

TRY THIS (p. 645, Ex. 2)

21; 42

TRY THIS (p. 645, Ex. 3)

90

TRY THIS (p. 646)

$\approx 0.6\%$

Exercises

4. 126 **5a.** 220 **b.** 1320 **6.** 2800 **7.** $\approx 7.6\%$ **9.** 70
11. 126 **13.** 11 **15.** 1 **17.** 504 **19.** ≈ 0.053 **21.** 8
23. 210 **25.** 15,504 **27.** 378 **29.** 252 **31.** $\approx 26.8\%$
33. $\approx 17.9\%$ **35.** combination **37.** permutation
39a. 2,598,960 **b.** $\frac{1}{649,740} \approx 0.00000154\%$
41. $_6C_1 = 6$; $_6C_2 = 15$; $_6C_3 = 20$; $_6C_4 = 15$; $_6C_5 = 6$;
$_6C_6 = 1$ **43a.** $\frac{1}{15,890,700} \approx 0.0000000629$
b. Undergoing an audit this year is about 158,907
times more likely, being hit by lightning is about
1746 times more likely, and being hit by a baseball in
a major league game is about 53 times more likely
than winning the lottery.

45. **47.**

49.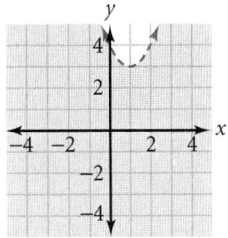

LESSON 10.4

TRY THIS (p. 654, Ex. 1)

63%

TRY THIS (p. 654, Ex. 2)

70%

TRY THIS (p. 655)

$\approx 47\%$

Exercises

4. 64% **5.** 59% **6.** $\approx 60.9\%$ **7.** $\frac{1}{3}$ **9.** $\frac{2}{3}$ **11.** $\frac{1}{2}$ **13.** $\frac{5}{6}$
15. 1 **17.** mutually exclusive; $\frac{1}{6}$ **19.** mutually
exclusive; $\frac{25}{36}$ **21.** inclusive; $\frac{5}{6}$ **23.** inclusive; 1
25. mutually exclusive; $\frac{13}{18}$ **27.** inclusive; 1
29a. 1100 **b.** $\frac{24}{35}$ **31.** $\frac{7}{11}$ **33.** 0.676 **35.** 0 **37.** $\frac{1}{2}$
39. $\frac{5}{16}$ **41.** $\approx 3.3\%$ **43.** $\approx 49.9\%$ **45.** $\approx 60.2\%$
47. $\approx 75.1\%$ **49.** $\approx 59.4\%$

51.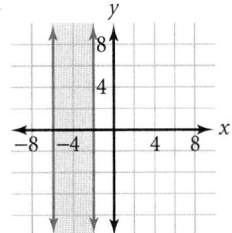

53. $(x + 6)(x - 7)$ **55.** $(9x + 1)^2$ **57.** $x = \frac{5}{2}$ or $x = 8$

LESSON 10.5

TRY THIS (p. 661)

$\approx 94.1\%$

Exercises

4. $\frac{1}{6}$ **5.** $\frac{1}{418}$, or $\approx 0.24\%$ **6.** $\approx 89\%$ **7.** 0.125 **9.** 0.1875
11. 0.05 **13.** dependent **15.** dependent **17.** $\frac{1}{8}$, or
12.5% **19.** $\frac{9}{64}$, or $\approx 14.1\%$ **21.** 76% **23.** 89.24%
25. 0.06 **27.** $\frac{27y^6}{x}$ **29.** $\frac{9}{25y^6}$ **31.** ≈ 1.10 **33.** ≈ 1.20
35. $y = -\frac{1}{16}(x - 1)^2$

LESSON 10.6

TRY THIS (p. 666)

≈39.4%

TRY THIS (p. 667)

≈53.2%

Exercises

4. $\frac{5}{18}$, or ≈27.8% **5.** $\frac{25}{289}$, or ≈8.7% **6.** $\frac{5}{68}$, or ≈7.4%
7. ≈41.1% **8.** ≈93.4% **9.** $\frac{4}{33}$, or ≈12.1% **11.** $\frac{20}{231}$, or
≈8.6% **13.** $\frac{12}{77}$, or ≈15.6% **15.** $\frac{15}{154}$, or ≈9.7%
17. $\frac{1}{6}$, or ≈16.7% **19.** $\frac{1}{3}$, or ≈33.3% **21a.** $\frac{1}{6}$ **b.** $\frac{1}{6}$
c. 1 **23a.** $\frac{1}{3}$ **b.** $\frac{1}{3}$ **c.** 1 **25.** $\frac{2}{3}$ **27.** 0.205 **29.** $\frac{5}{6}$
31a. $\frac{1}{100}$, or 1% **b.** $\frac{1}{4\pi}$, or ≈8.0% **33.** $\frac{14,320}{37,543}$,
or ≈38.1% **35.** $\frac{4850}{44,229}$, or ≈11.0% **37.** $\frac{11,106}{64,323}$,
or ≈17.3% **39.** 53.2% **41.** $\frac{2}{3}$ **43.** $x = -\frac{4}{3}$ or $x = \frac{4}{3}$
45. $2x(x-6)^2$ **47.** $a = \frac{5 \pm \sqrt{33}}{2}$ **49.** $x \geq 1$
51. $x \leq \frac{1}{3}$ **53.** $M(-5, 4.5)$ **55.** $\frac{1}{2}$, or 50%

LESSON 10.7

TRY THIS (p. 674)

Answers may vary. The estimated probability should
be close to 0.4.

Exercises

For Exercises 4–6, answers may vary but should be
close to those given below.
4. about 60% **5.** about 99% **6.** about 30%

For Exercises 7–27, answers may vary but should be
close to those given below.
7. on average about 6 tosses **9.** on average about 4
rolls **11.** about 24% **13.** about 73% **15.** about 25%
17. on average about 8 **19.** about 8% **21.** about 19
square units **23.** about 32 square units **25.** about 3
times **27.** about 2 times **29.** $(-1, -5)$
31. $\left(\frac{\sqrt{10}}{5}, \frac{3\sqrt{10}}{5}\right), \left(-\frac{\sqrt{10}}{5}, -\frac{3\sqrt{10}}{5}\right)$
33. $\left(\frac{2\sqrt{15}}{15}, \frac{2\sqrt{210}}{15}\right), \left(-\frac{2\sqrt{15}}{15}, \frac{2\sqrt{210}}{15}\right),$
$\left(\frac{2\sqrt{15}}{15}, -\frac{2\sqrt{210}}{15}\right), \left(-\frac{2\sqrt{15}}{15}, -\frac{2\sqrt{210}}{15}\right)$ **35.** $\frac{11}{25}$ **37.** $\frac{21}{25}$

CHAPTER REVIEW AND ASSESSMENT

1. $\frac{3}{8}$ **3.** $\frac{1}{6}$ **5.** $\frac{1}{10}$ **7.** 625 **9.** 6720 **11.** 95,040 **13.** 24
15. 45 **17.** 161,700 **19.** $\frac{1}{3}$ **21.** $\frac{5}{6}$ **23.** $\frac{2}{3}$ **25.** $\frac{1}{4}$ **27.** 0
29. Answers may vary but should be close to 1 or
100%. **31.** ≈69%

Chapter 11

LESSON 11.1

TRY THIS (p. 693)

n	1	2	3	4	5	6
t_n	1	7	17	31	49	71

TRY THIS (p. 694)

1, 2, 5, 14, 41, 122

TRY THIS (p. 693)

a. $\sum_{k=1}^{5} 4k = 4 + 8 + 12 + 16 + 20$
$= 60$

b. $\frac{1}{2}\sum_{k=1}^{4} k = \frac{1}{2}(1 + 2 + 3 + 4)$
$= 5$

TRY THIS (p. 695)

$\sum_{j=1}^{5} (-j^2 + 2j + 5) = 0$

Exercises

4. 1, 4, 7, 10, 13, 16 **5.** 1, 4, 13, 40, 121, 364 **6a.** 13,
15, 17, 19, 21 **b.** $t_1 = 3, t_n = t_{n-1} + 2$ **7.** 24 **8.** 50
9. 126 **11.** 5, 9, 13, 17 **13.** −5, −9, −13, −17 **15.** 4, 9,
14, 19 **17.** 4, 0, −4, −8 **19.** $\frac{3}{2}, 2, \frac{5}{2}, 3$ **21.** 12.42,
21.17, 29.92, 38.67 **23.** 1, 8, 27, 64 **25.** −2, −8, −18,
−32 **27.** 2, 4, 6, 8, 10, 12 **29.** −6, 15, −27, 57, −111,
225 **31.** 10, 51, 256, 1281, 6406, 32,031 **33.** 8, 22, 64,
190, 568, 1702 **35.** 3.34, 6.348, 12.9656, 27.52432,
59.553504, 130.0177088 **37.** $\frac{5}{7}, \frac{10}{21}, \frac{3}{7}, \frac{44}{105}, \frac{73}{175}, \frac{1094}{2625}$
39. $t_1 = 3, t_n = t_{n-1} + 6$; 27, 33, 39 **41.** $t_1 = 3,$
$t_n = 2t_{n-1} + 1$; 63, 127, 255
43. $10 + 10 + 10 + 10 = 40$ **45.** $4 + 8 + 12 = 24$
47. $-5 - 10 - 15 - 20 = -50$
49. $\frac{1}{3} + \frac{4}{3} + \frac{9}{3} + \frac{16}{3} + \frac{25}{3} = \frac{55}{3}$ **51.** $\frac{3}{4} + 1 + \frac{3}{4} = \frac{5}{2}$
53. $-2 - 5 - 8 = -15$ **55.** $3 + 7 + 13 = 23$ **57.** 12
59. 84 **61.** 42 **63.** 39 **65.** 164 **67.** 6 **69.** $-\frac{88}{21}$
71. $50\pi + 8$ **73.** 68 **75.** $t_1 = 0.4, t_n = 0.3(2^{n-2}) + 0.4$,
or $t_n = \frac{3(2^{n-2}) + 4}{10}$, where $n \geq 2$ **77.** 90° **79.** 120°
81. 7.00, 7.30, 7.60, 7.90, 8.20, 8.50, 8.80, 9.10;
$t_n = 7.00 + 0.30(n-1)$ **83.** $\sum_{n=0}^{6} 12 + 4n = 168$ flowers
85. $y = \frac{2}{3}x + \frac{14}{3}$ **87.** 0; 1 real solution; $\frac{1}{2}$
89. $\left(\frac{2}{5}, \frac{1}{5}\right)$ and $\left(\frac{1}{2}, 0\right)$ **91.** $(4, -3)$ and $(-52, 11)$
93. 72 **95.** 70

LESSON 11.2

TRY THIS (p. 700)

−15.5

TRY THIS (p. 701, Ex. 2)

$12.45

TRY THIS (p. 701, Ex. 3)   **TRY THIS** (p. 702)
35   27, 30, 33, 36

Exercises
4. $t_4 = 2$ **5.** \$575.65 **6.** $\frac{22}{3}$ **7.** 10, 14, 18, and 22
9. yes; $d = 2$ **11.** yes; $d = 3$ **13.** no **15.** yes; $d = -6$
17. no **19.** no **21.** yes; $d = \frac{1}{3}$ **23.** no **25.** no **27.** no
29. no **31.** 18; 15; 12; 9 **33.** 1; 3; 5; 7
35. -4; -1; 2; 5 **37.** 7, 8, 9, 10 **39.** 4, 7, 10, 13
41. -1, 2, 5, 8 **43.** -3, -8, -13, -18 **45.** -3, 2, 7, 12
47. $\frac{2}{3}$, 1, $\frac{4}{3}$, $\frac{5}{3}$ **49.** $\pi + 4$, $2\pi + 4$, $3\pi + 4$, $4\pi + 4$
51. $t_5 = 18$ **53.** $t_{10} = 1.29$ **55.** $t_1 = \frac{5}{6}$
57. $t_n = 6 + (n-1)(2)$ **59.** $t_n = 1 + (n-1)(-7)$
61. $t_n = 23 + (n-1)(8)$ **63.** $t_n = 20 + (n-1)(-5)$
65. $t_n = 100 + (n-1)(5)$ **67.** $t_n = -50 + (n-1)(5)$
69. 8, 11, and 14 **71.** 11, 4, and -3 **73.** 5.62 and 5.98
75. 9, 6, 3, 0 and -3 **77.** 27 dots **79.** Let a, b, and c
represent the sides of a triangle. $a = a$; $b = a + d$;
$c = a + 2d$; Let $a = 3$ and $d = 1$. $b = a + d = 3 + 1 = 4$;
$c = a + 2d = 3 + 2 = 5$
81a. $t_n = 30{,}000 + (n-1)(800)$ **b.** \$37,200
83. $(x + 3)^2$ **85.** $(x + 7)^2$ **87.** $4 < x \le 7$ **89.** $-1 < x < 1$
91. $(x + 2)^2 + (y - 5)^2 = 16$; $C(-2, 5)$; $r = 4$
93. $\frac{x^2}{25} + \frac{(y-2)^2}{9} = 1$ **95.** $\{MF, FM, FF\}$; $\frac{3}{4}$
97. $\{MF, FM\}$; $\frac{1}{2}$

LESSON 11.3

TRY THIS (p. 709)   **TRY THIS** (p. 710)
440   -510

Exercises
4. 477 cans **5.** 2405 **6.** 35 **7.** 30 **9.** 68 **11.** -376
13. 66 **15.** -360 **17.** 45,150 **19.** 1683 **21.** 1275
23. 3100 **25.** 1625 **27.** 1500 **29.** 3250 **31.** -1750
33. $325\sqrt{2}$ **35.** 350π **37.** 168 **39.** 30 **41.** 240
43. 2530 **45.** 5450 **47.** 15 **49.** 695
51. 5, 10, 15, 20, 25 **53a.** 39 pipes **b.** 49 pipes
55. 19 musicians; 96 musicians **57.** $y = |x - 4|$
59. $-10x^4 + 6x^3 + 4x^2 - 12x$ **61.** $y = k\frac{xz}{m^2}$ **63.** all real
numbers **65.** 593,775

LESSON 11.4

TRY THIS (p. 714)   **TRY THIS** (p. 715, Ex. 2)
$-40{,}960$ \$803.61

TRY THIS (p. 715, Ex. 3)   **TRY THIS** (p. 716)
$\frac{15}{64}$ 32, 16, and 8 or -32, 16,
                              and -8

Exercises
4. 32 **5.** \$2756.24 **6.** ± 384 **7.** 80, 40, and 20 or -80,
40, and -20 **9.** yes; $r = 2$; 320, 640, 1280 **11.** no
13. yes; $r = 5$; 1250, 6250, 31,250 **15.** yes; $r = 3$; 162,
486, 1458 **17.** no **19.** yes; $r = 9$; 1458, 13,122,
118,098 **21.** yes; $r = \frac{1}{3}, \frac{1}{9}, \frac{1}{27}, \frac{1}{81}$ **23.** yes; $r = \frac{1}{4}, \frac{3}{64}$,
$\frac{3}{256}, \frac{3}{1024}$ **25.** yes; $r = 1.25$; 39.0625, 48.828125,
61.03515625 **27.** -2, -8, -32, -128 **29.** 4, -12, 36,
-108 **31.** -1, 0.2, -0.04, 0.008 **33.** 3, 10.11, 34.0707,
114.818259 **35.** 24,576
37. $\dfrac{3}{10{,}000{,}000{,}000{,}000{,}000{,}000} = 3.0 \times 10^{-19}$
39. 18,750 or $-18{,}750$ **41.** 324 **43.** 12 **45.** -81
47. $\frac{25}{16}$ or $-\frac{25}{16}$ **49.** $t_n = 2(2)^{n-1}$ or $t_n = 2^n$
51. $t_n = \left(\frac{1}{2}\right)^{n-1}$ **53.** $t_n = 30\left(\frac{1}{3}\right)^{n-1}$
55. $t_n = \sqrt{2}(\sqrt{2})^{n-1}$ or $t_n = (\sqrt{2})^n$ **57.** 15 and 45
59. 7.5 and 11.25 **61.** -1, $-\frac{1}{2}$, and $-\frac{1}{4}$ or 1, $-\frac{1}{2}$, and $\frac{1}{4}$
63. 162, 54, and 18 or -162, 54, and -18
65. 125 and 375 **67.** 12, 36, 108, 324; geometric
69. $\frac{18}{5}, \frac{36}{25}, \frac{72}{125}, \frac{144}{625}$; geometric
71. 7, 27, 127, 627; neither
73. -400, -1600, -6400, $-25{,}600$; geometric
75. \$1,688,520.51 **77.** \$866,580.59 **79.** $y = -3x - 1$
81. $\begin{bmatrix} 3.3 \\ 16.24 \end{bmatrix}$ **83.** $\begin{bmatrix} 5.44 & 8.16 \\ 10.24 & 15.36 \end{bmatrix}$
85. run: 4.68 mph; bike: 16.68 mph **87.** $\sqrt{15} + \sqrt{7}$
89. 10,080 **91.** 360

LESSON 11.5

TRY THIS (p. 721)   **TRY THIS** (p. 722)
1584.0   16.5

TRY THIS (p. 723)
Basis Step
Show that $4 + 8 + 12 + \cdots + 4n = 2n(n + 1)$ is true
for $n = 1$.
$4 = 2(1)(2)$ True
Induction Step
Assume the statement is true for a natural number k.
$4 + 8 + 12 + \cdots + 4k = 2k(k + 1)$
Determine the statement to be proved: Add $4(k + 1)$
to the left side, and substitute $k + 1$ for k on the right.
$$4 + 8 + 12 + \cdots + 4k = 2k(k + 1)$$
$$4 + 8 + 12 + \cdots + 4k + 4(k + 1) = 2(k + 1)[(k + 1) + 1]$$
$$4 + 8 + 12 + \cdots + 4k + 4(k + 1) = 2(k + 1)(k + 2)$$
Rewrite the left-hand side by using the statement
assumed to be true.
$$4 + 8 + 12 + \cdots + 4k + 4(k + 1) = 2k(k + 1) + 4(k + 1)$$
$$= (k + 1)(2k + 4)$$
$$= (k + 1)2(k + 2)$$
$$= 2(k + 1)(k + 2)$$
True

Exercises

5. 12,714.3 **6.** $34,439.14 **7.** 189

8. Basis Step

Show that $\dfrac{1}{1\cdot 2}+\dfrac{1}{2\cdot 3}+\cdots+\dfrac{1}{n(n+1)}=\dfrac{n}{n+1}$ is true

for $n=1$.

$\dfrac{1}{1\cdot 2}=\dfrac{1}{1+1}$ True

Induction Step

Assume the statement is true for a natural number k.

$\dfrac{1}{1\cdot 2}+\dfrac{1}{2\cdot 3}+\cdots+\dfrac{1}{k(k+1)}=\dfrac{k}{k+1}$

Determine the statement to be proved: Add

$\dfrac{1}{(k+1)(k+2)}$ to the left side, and substitute $k+1$ for k

on the right.

$\dfrac{1}{1\cdot 2}+\dfrac{1}{2\cdot 3}+\cdots+\dfrac{1}{k(k+1)}+\dfrac{1}{(k+1)(k+2)}=\dfrac{k+1}{[(k+1)+1]}$

$\dfrac{1}{1\cdot 2}+\dfrac{1}{2\cdot 3}+\cdots+\dfrac{1}{k(k+1)}+\dfrac{1}{(k+1)(k+2)}=\dfrac{k+1}{k+2}$

Rewrite the left side by using the statement assumed
to be true.

$\dfrac{1}{1\cdot 2}+\dfrac{1}{2\cdot 3}+\cdots+\dfrac{1}{k(k+1)}+\dfrac{1}{(k+1)(k+2)}$

$=\dfrac{k}{k+1}+\dfrac{1}{(k+1)(k+2)}$

$=\dfrac{k}{k+1}\left(\dfrac{k+2}{k+2}\right)+\dfrac{1}{(k+1)(k+2)}$

$=\dfrac{k(k+2)+1}{(k+1)(k+2)}$

$=\dfrac{k^2+2k+1}{(k+1)(k+2)}$

$=\dfrac{(k+1)^2}{(k+1)(k+2)}$

$=\dfrac{k+1}{k+2}$ True

9. 7 **11.** 255 **13.** −40 **15.** 7,174,454 **17.** 10 **19.** 83.1

21. 453.3 **23.** 26,594.1 **25.** 62 **27.** 5 **29.** 5.4 **31.** $\dfrac{203}{125}$

33. $\dfrac{3}{65,536}\approx 4.58\times 10^{-5}$ **35.** $\dfrac{1,048,575}{65,536}\approx 16.0$

37. $t_1=5; r=5; t_{10}=9{,}765{,}625; S_{10}=12{,}207{,}030$

39. $t_1=1; r=\dfrac{\frac{1}{121}}{\frac{1}{11}}=\dfrac{1}{11}; t_{12}=\dfrac{1}{285{,}311{,}670{,}611}; S_{12}=\dfrac{11}{10}$

41. $t_1=2.76; r=2.76; t_8=3367.23; S_8=5278.86$

43. 124 **45.** $\dfrac{63}{32}$ **47.** 3.8 **49.** 27,305

51. 2,036,814,259 **53.** 0.5 **55.** −520 **57.** $n=5$

59. $n<n+1$

Basis Step

Show that $n<n+1$ is true for $n=1$.

$1<1+1$ True

Induction Step

Assume the statement is true for a natural number k.

$k<k+1$

Determine the statement to be proved.

$k+1<k+2$

Rewrite the inequality by using the statement
assumed to be true.

$k+1<k+2$

$(k)+1<(k+1)+1$ True

61. $1+3+5+\cdots+(2n-1)=n^2$

Basis Step

Show that $1+3+5+\cdots+(2n-1)=n^2$ is true for

$n=1$.

$1=1^2$ True

Induction Step

Assume the statement is true for a natural number k.

$1+3+5+\cdots+(2k-1)=k^2$

Determine the statement to be proved: Add $2(k+1)-1$
to the left side and substitute $k+1$ for k on the
right side.

$1+3+5+\cdots+(2k-1)+[2(k+1)-1]=(k+1)^2$

$1+3+5+\cdots+(2k-1)+(2k+1)=(k+1)^2$

Rewrite the left side by using the statement assumed
to be true.

$1+3+5+\cdots+(2k-1)+(2k+1)=k^2+(2k+1)$

$=k^2+2k+1$

$=(k+1)^2$ True

63. 6.6 **65a.** $8, 4\sqrt{2}, 4, 2\sqrt{2}, 2, \sqrt{2}, 1$

b. $t_n=8\left(\dfrac{\sqrt{2}}{2}\right)^{n-1}$ **c.** $S_7=15+7\sqrt{2}\approx 24.90$

d. $S_n=\displaystyle\sum_{k=1}^{n}8\left(\dfrac{\sqrt{2}}{2}\right)^{k-1}$, or $S_n=8\left(\dfrac{1-\left(\frac{\sqrt{2}}{2}\right)^n}{1-\frac{\sqrt{2}}{2}}\right)$

67. 2132.8125 in.^{2} **69.** $49,680.88 **71.** $329,723.09

73. about 24.0 feet

75.

77a. 0.9 **b.** $V(t)=3800(0.9)^t$ **c.** $3078 **d.** $2770.20

79. vertical asymptote: $x=0$; horizontal asymptote:
$y=0$; no holes **81.** $\dfrac{1}{2x+1}$ **83.** 2,805,264 ways

LESSON 11.6

TRY THIS (p. 730)
$-\dfrac{8}{3}$

TRY THIS (p. 731)
$\dfrac{1}{2}$

TRY THIS (p. 732)
$\dfrac{5}{9}$

Exercises

4. 9 **5.** $\dfrac{1}{12}$ **6.** $\dfrac{1}{3}$ **7.** $\dfrac{1}{2}$ **9.** 8 **11.** does not converge

13. $\dfrac{121}{150}$ **15.** 10 **17.** does not converge **19.** $\dfrac{10}{9}$ **21.** $\dfrac{1}{7}$

23. $\dfrac{70}{9}$, or $7.\overline{7}$ **25.** $\dfrac{7}{10}$ **27.** does not converge **29.** $\dfrac{7}{3}$

31. does not converge **33.** 1 **35.** $2 + \sqrt{2}$, or about

3.4142 **37.** $\frac{\pi}{\pi-1}$, or about 1.4669 **39.** $\sum_{k=1}^{\infty} 19\left(\frac{1}{100}\right)^k$

41. $\sum_{k=1}^{\infty} \left(\frac{1}{1000}\right)^k$ **43.** $\sum_{k=1}^{\infty} 35\left(\frac{1}{100}\right)^k$ **45.** $\sum_{k=1}^{\infty} 819\left(\frac{1}{1000}\right)^k$

47. $\sum_{k=1}^{\infty} 121\left(\frac{1}{1000}\right)^k$ **49.** $\frac{4}{9}$ **51.** $\frac{4}{11}$ **53.** $\frac{6}{11}$ **55.** $\frac{586}{999}$

57. $\frac{158}{333}$ **59.** $\frac{31}{999}$ **61.** 200 square centimeters

63a. \$7142.86 **b.** \$12,500 **65.** $x = -4, y = 7$, and

$z = 0.5$ **67.** $x = \frac{\ln 19}{\ln 3}, x \approx -2.68$

69. $x = \frac{\ln 7.23}{\ln 2}, x \approx 2.85$

LESSON 11.7

TRY THIS (p. 737, Ex. 1)   **TRY THIS** (p. 737, Ex. 2)
11, 1   1, 8, 28, 56, 70, 56, 28,
                               8, 1

TRY THIS (p. 738)
0.38

Exercises

4. $_{10}C_2 = 45$ and $_{10}C_4 = 210$ **5.** $_6C_0 = 1, _6C_1 = 6,$

$_6C_2 = 15, _6C_3 = 20, _6C_4 = 15, _6C_5 = 6, _6C_6 = 1$

6. 0.55 **7.** $_5C_2$ is the third entry in the fifth row;

$_5C_2 = 10.$ **9.** $_8C_5$ is the sixth entry in the eighth row;

$_8C_5 = 56.$ **11.** $_{11}C_2$ is the third entry in the 11th row;

$_{11}C_2 = 55.$ **13.** $_{10}C_3$ is the fourth entry in the tenth

row; $_{10}C_3 = 120.$ **15.** $_8C_4$ is the fifth entry in the

eighth row; $_8C_4 = 70.$ **17.** $_7C_2$ is the third entry in the

seventh row; $_7C_2 = 21.$ **19.** $_9C_6$ is the seventh entry in

the ninth row; $_9C_6 = 84.$ **21.** $_{13}C_7$ is the eighth entry

in the 13th row; $_{13}C_7 = 1716.$ **23.** 35; 7 **25.** 165; 462

27a. 5, 8, 13, 21, 34 **b.** a Fibonacci sequence

29. ≈ 0.34 **31.** 0.5 **33.** ≈ 0.49 **35.** ≈ 0.31 **37.** ≈ 0.19

39. ≈ 0.81 **41.** ≈ 0.31 **43.** ≈ 0.19 **45.** ≈ 0.81

47a. yes;   −1, =2, ≡3, ≣4, ≣5, ⊢6, ⊨7,
               ⊫8, ⚎10, ⦀15, ⚏20, ⊥21, ⚌28,
                   ⚏35, ⦀56, ⚐70

b. Answers may vary. Sample answer: The sums of the

rows are multiples of 2. **49.** $f(x) = -\frac{5}{14}x^2 + \frac{27}{14}x + 2$

51. $-9 < x < 2$

$\longleftarrow\!\!\circ\!+\!\!+\!\!+\!\!+\!\!+\!\!+\!\!+\!\!+\!\!+\!\!+\!\!\circ\!+\!\longrightarrow$
   −9 −8 −7 −6 −5 −4 −3 −2 −1 0 1 2 3

53. permutations; $_{10}P_3 = 720$

LESSON 11.8

TRY THIS (p. 741)
$m^6 + 6m^5n + 15m^4n^2 + 20m^3n^3 + 15m^2n^4 + 6mn^5 + n^6$

TRY THIS (p. 742, Ex. 2)
$\binom{4}{2}(0.337)^2(0.663)^2 \approx 0.30$

TRY THIS (p. 742, Ex. 3)
$\binom{8}{5}r^{8-5}s^5 = 56r^3s^5$

TRY THIS (p. 744)
$x^5 - 10x^4y + 40x^3y^2 - 80x^2y^3 + 80xy^4 - 32y^5$

Exercises

4. $a^5 + 5a^4b + 10a^3b^2 + 10a^2b^3 + 5ab^4 + b^5$

5. $\binom{5}{2}(0.30)^3(0.70)^2 \approx 0.13$ **6.** $120a^7b^3$

7. $243x^5 - 810x^4y + 1080x^3y^2 - 720x^2y^3$
   $+ 240xy^4 - 32y^5$

8. 7 pieces need to be added: 3 pieces with

dimensions $s \cdot s \cdot (0.2)$, 3 pieces with dimensions

$s \cdot (0.2) \cdot (0.2)$, and 1 piece with dimensions

$(0.2) \cdot (0.2) \cdot (0.2).$

9. $a^5 + 5a^4b + 10a^3b^2 + 10a^2b^3 + 5ab^4 + b^5$

11. $a^8 + 8a^7b + 28a^6b^2 + 56a^5b^3 + 70a^4b^4$
   $+ 56a^3b^5 + 28a^2b^6 + 8ab^7 + b^8$

13. $x^4 + 4x^3y + 6x^2y^2 + 4xy^3 + y^4$

15. $32 + 80x + 80x^2 + 40x^3 + 10x^4 + x^5$

17. $y^9 + 36y^8 + 576y^7 + 5376y^6 + 32{,}256y^5 + 129{,}024y^4$
   $+ 344{,}064y^3 + 589{,}824y^2 + 589{,}824y + 262{,}144$

19. $x^4 - 4x^3y + 6x^2y^2 - 4xy^3 + y^4$

21. $(a + b)^4 = a^4 + 4a^3b + 6a^2b^2 + 4ab^3 + b^4$

23. $(a + b)^5 = a^5 + 5a^4b + 10a^3b^2 + 10a^2b^3 + 5ab^4 + b^5$

25. $(x + y)^9 = x^9 + 9x^8y + 36x^7y^2 + 84x^6y^3$
   $+ 126x^5y^4 + 126x^4y^5 + 84x^3y^6$
   $+ 36x^2y^7 + 9xy^8 + y^9$

27. $36r^7s^2$ **29.** $126r^4s^5$ **31.** $3584x^5$ **33.** $114{,}688x^2$

35. $35x^3y^4$ **37.** $-21x^2y^5$

39. $1024a^5 + 3840a^4b + 5760a^3b^2 + 4320a^2b^3$
   $+ 1620ab^4 + 243b^5$

41. $x^4 - 8x^3y + 24x^2y^2 - 32xy^3 + 16y^4$

43. $16x^4 + 96x^3 + 216x^2 + 216x + 81$

45. $243x^5 + 810x^4y + 1080x^3y^2 + 720x^2y^3$
   $+ 240xy^4 + 32y^5$

47. $\frac{1}{8}x^3 + \frac{1}{4}x^2y + \frac{1}{6}xy^2 + \frac{1}{27}y^3$

49. $0.2401 + 1.372x + 2.94x^2 + 2.8x^3 + x^4$

51. $3432p^7q^7$ **53.** 7; $120a^7b^3$ **55.** $n = 9$

57. $a = -32$ and $b = 32$ **59a.** 0.95 **b.** 0.22

61. 0.23 **63.** 0.79 **65.** 0.21

67.

121; 15

69.

ellipse

71.

parabola

73.

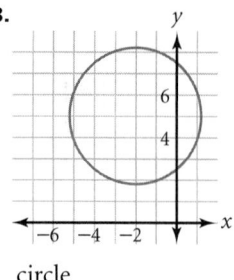

circle

CHAPTER REVIEW AND ASSESSMENT

1. 5, 7, 9, 11, 13 **3.** −0.1, −0.3, −0.5, −0.7, −0.9
5. 1, 4, 10, 22, 46 **7.** 3, −8, 25, −74, 223 **9.** 30
11. −108 **13.** 215 **15.** 22 **17.** −19 **19.** 30 and 40
21. −15, −20, −25, and −30 **23.** 40 **25.** 222
27. 1680 **29.** −1260 **31.** 90 **33.** 5 **35.** −12,500
37. $\frac{1}{1536}$ **39.** $5(20)^{\frac{1}{4}}$, $5(20)^{\frac{1}{2}}$, and $5(20)^{\frac{3}{4}}$ or $-5(20)^{\frac{1}{4}}$,
$5(20)^{\frac{1}{2}}$, and $-5(20)^{\frac{3}{4}}$ **41.** 8.1 **43.** 257.5 **45.** −9091
47. −63 **49.** 0.2
51. <u>Basis Step</u>
Show that $7 + 9 + 11 + \cdots + (2n + 5) = n(n + 6)$ is
true for $n = 1$.
$7 = 1(1 + 6) = 7$ <u>True</u>
<u>Induction Step</u>
Assume the statement is true for a natural number k.
$7 + 9 + 11 + \cdots + (2k + 5) = k(k + 6)$
Then prove that it is true for the next natural
number, $k + 1$.
Determine the statement to be proved.
$7 + 9 + 11 + \cdots + [2(k + 1) + 5] = (k + 1)[(k + 1) + 6]$
$\quad 7 + 9 + 11 + \ldots + (2k + 7) = (k + 1)(k + 7)$
Begin with the statement assumed to be true and use
properties of equality.
$7 + 9 + 11 + \cdots + (2k + 5) + (2k + 7) = (k + 1)(k + 7)$
$\quad\quad\quad\quad k(k + 6) + (2k + 7) = (k + 1)(k + 7)$
$\quad\quad\quad\quad\quad\quad k^2 + 8k + 7 = (k + 1)(k + 7)$
$\quad\quad\quad\quad (k + 1)(k + 7) = (k + 1)(k + 7)$ True
53. 16 **55.** $\frac{5}{9}$ **57.** $\frac{1}{5}$ **59.** $\frac{7}{4}$ **61.** does not converge
63. $\frac{32}{999}$ **65.** 120 **67.** 20 **69.** 0.22 **71.** 0.47
73. $a^5 + 15a^4 + 90a^3 + 270a^2 + 405a + 243$
75. $729x^6 - 1458x^5y + 1215x^4y^2 - 540x^3y^3$
$\quad\quad + 135x^2y^4 - 18xy^5 + y^6$
77. $120a^3b^7$
79. $(a + b)^6 = a^6 + 6a^5b + 15a^4b^2 + 20a^3b^3$
$\quad\quad + 15a^2b^4 + 6ab^5 + b^6$
81a. ≈3.6 meters **b.** 60 meters **83.** 480 seats;
1120 seats

Chapter 12

LESSON 12.1

TRY THIS (p. 765)
$\bar{x} = 82.375$, median = 82, mode = 74; the mean and
median are very close, but the mode is lower than
the others.

TRY THIS (p. 766)
$\bar{x} = \$71,000$, median = \$85,000, no mode; the median
is the best measure because the mean is below every
value except \$0.

TRY THIS (p. 767)
$\bar{x} \approx 31.0$, temperature ≈ 71.0°F

Exercises

4. $\bar{x} = \$5.75$; median = \$5.625; mode = \$5.00; the
mean and median are close, but the mode is the
smallest value in the data set. **5a.** $\bar{x} = 32.5$ hours;
median = 35.5 hours; mode = 40 hours **b.** The
median best represents the data because mean is
more influenced by the extreme value, 0. The mode
is the largest value, which happens to occur twice.
6. $\bar{x} \approx 4.23$ **7.** $x = 4.2$ magazines per month
9. $\bar{x} = 3.375$; median = 3; mode = 3 **11.** $\bar{x} \approx 14.714$;
median = 14; mode = 14 **13.** $\bar{x} = -11$; median = −11;
no mode **15.** $\bar{x} \approx 2.933$; median = 2.75; modes = 1.6
and 3.8 **17.** $\bar{x} = 4.628$; median = 4.82; no mode
19. $\bar{x} = \frac{11}{24} \approx 0.458$; median = $\frac{4}{9} \approx 0.444$; no mode
21. $\bar{x} = \$1.24$; median = \$1.23; mode = \$1.20; all
three measures are similar and seem to be good
measures of central tendency.

23.

Number of pets	Frequency
0	8
1	7
2	6
3	4
4	5
Total	30

$\bar{x} = 1.7$ pets
25. Answers may vary due to arrangement of groups.
sample answers:

Miles per gallon	Class mean	Frequency
10−14	12	1
15−19	17	7
20−24	22	7
25−29	27	5
30−35	32	3
	Total	23

Estimate of the mean is 22 miles per gallon.

27. Grouped frequency table; there will be many different values that can be grouped into classes. **29.** Frequency table; number of brothers and sisters should be from about 0 to 6. **31 and 33.** Answers will vary. Find the following measures:

$$\text{mean} = \frac{\text{sum of data values}}{\text{number of values}},\ \text{median} = \text{numerical}$$

middle value, or average of the two middle values if there are an even number of values, and mode = the value or values repeated most often. The most representative measures will depend on the data collected. **35a.** $\bar{x} = 6.632$; median $= 6\frac{1}{2}$; mode $= 7$; the mean and median are similar, but the mode is a bit higher. **b.** The mode will be the most helpful because the manager should stock the most of this size. **37.** 67 **39.** $2x^3 + 2x - 3; -2x + 3$

41. $\log_5 625 = 4$ **43.** $\log_2 \frac{1}{8} = -3$ **45.** $5^4 = 625$

47. $(x + 5)(x^2 - 5x + 25)$ **49 and 51.** Answers may vary. Sample answers are given. **49.** 2, 2, 2, 2, 2 or 2, 3, 3, 3, 4 **51.** $-10, 20, 30, 40, 70; \bar{x} = 30$; 20, 30, 40, 70; $\bar{x} = 40$

LESSON 12.2

TRY THIS (p. 773)

Stem	Leaf 2|3 = 2.3
2	3, 3, 3, 5
3	2, 2, 3
4	2, 2, 5, 5
5	1, 3, 4, 5, 6, 6
6	2, 2, 5, 9
7	0, 2, 2, 7
8	
9	1, 2

median = 5.4; mode = 2.3; there are 6 data values between 5.0 and 6.0; the graph is slightly mound-shaped with a gap between 7.7 and 9.1.

TRY THIS (p. 774)

Data	Frequency
11	3
12	4
13	5
14	2
15	5
16	3
17	2

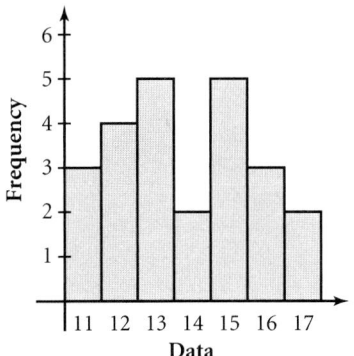

TRY THIS (p. 775)
about 66.7%

Exercises

5a.

Stem	Leaf 2|1 = 21
2	1, 2, 4, 5, 9
3	1, 2, 6, 7, 8, 9, 9
4	2, 2, 2, 8, 8
5	1, 1, 1, 2, 3, 3
6	
7	1

b. median = 40.5; modes = 42 and 51 **c.** possible answer: to determine how many people should be available to answer calls

6a.

Responses	Frequency
3	2
4	4
5	5
6	5
7	4
8	3
9	1

7. 0.9

8a.

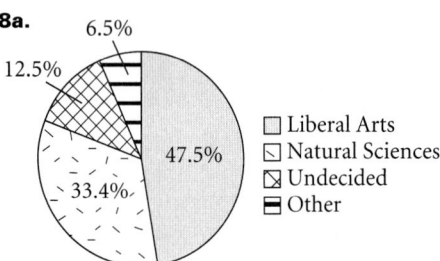

b. 0.6

9.

Stem	Leaf 7|2 = 7.2
7	2, 5, 5, 9
8	2, 2, 5, 6, 7, 8, 9
9	1, 2, 5

median = 8.55; modes = 7.5 and 8.2; mound-shaped

11.

Stem	Leaf 33|5 = 335
33	5, 6, 7, 8, 9
34	0, 7, 7, 8, 8
35	6, 7, 8, 9

median = 347; modes = 347 and 348; flat-shaped

13.

Data	Frequency
2	2
3	2
4	1
5	1
6	2
7	1
8	1
9	3
10	2

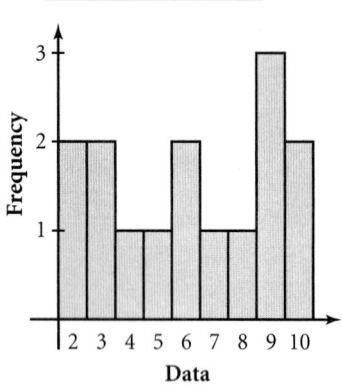

15.

Data	Frequency
0.5	2
1.0	3
1.5	4
2.0	3
2.5	2
3.0	1

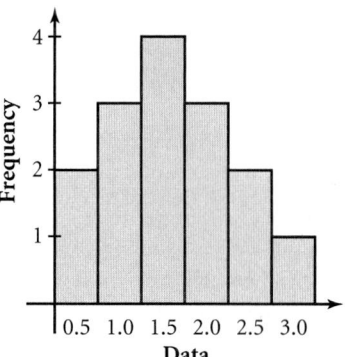

17.

Data	Frequency	Relative Frequency
1	4	$\frac{4}{24} = 0.1\overline{6}$
2	2	$\frac{2}{24} = 0.08\overline{3}$
3	5	$\frac{5}{24} = 0.208\overline{3}$
4	4	$\frac{4}{24} = 0.1\overline{6}$
5	2	$\frac{2}{24} = 0.08\overline{3}$
6	0	$\frac{0}{24} = 0$
7	4	$\frac{4}{24} = 0.1\overline{6}$
8	3	$\frac{3}{24} = 0.125$
Total	24	1

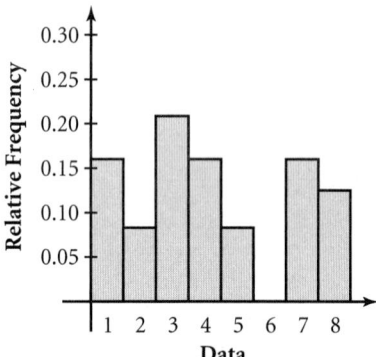

19.

Data	Frequency	Relative Frequency
0.1	6	$\frac{6}{15} = 0.4$
0.2	4	$\frac{4}{15} = 0.2\overline{6}$
0.3	3	$\frac{3}{15} = 0.2$
0.4	1	$\frac{1}{15} = 0.0\overline{6}$
0.5	1	$\frac{1}{15} = 0.0\overline{6}$
Total	15	1

21.

23.

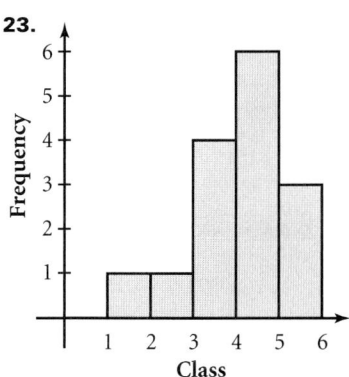

25. Answers may vary. **27a.** Answers may vary. Sample answers: A histogram most effectively shows how the incomes are divided into fairly even percents. Alternatively, a circle graph best illustrates that the incomes represent the entire United States and have fairly even parts that represent the percent in each income.

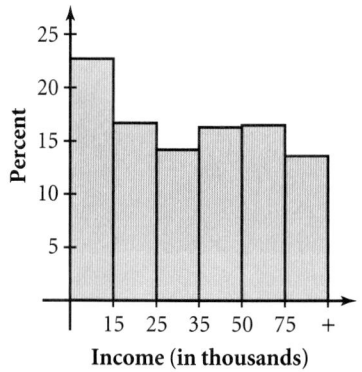

b. Distribution is fairly even.
c. 30.1%

29.

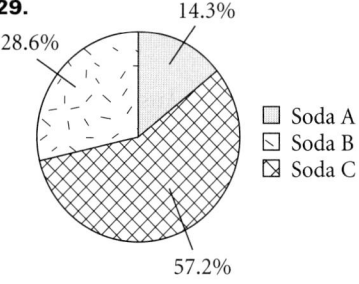

31. $-\frac{14}{11}$ **33.** $(x+8)^2$ **35.** $(3-x)(2x-5)$

37. $x^2 - x + 2 - \frac{24}{x+2}$ **39.** $-2, 2$ **41.** $-2, -1$

43. $\frac{(x-4)^2}{4} + \frac{(y-2)^2}{6.25} = 1$ **45.** $\frac{1}{4}$

LESSON 12.3

TRY THIS (p. 783)
minimum = 2; maximum = 83; $Q_1 = 10$; $Q_2 = 33.5$; $Q_3 = 51$; range = 81; IQR = 41; no possible outliers

Exercises
5a. minimum = 2.5; $Q_1 = 2.8$; $Q_2 = 3.05$; $Q_3 = 3.4$; maximum = 3.8; range = 1.3; IQR = 0.6 **b.** no outliers

6a.

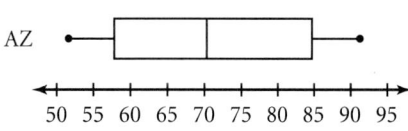

b. Hawaii's median temperature is higher than Arizona's. Arizona's temperature is more variable than Hawaii's.
7. minimum = 42; $Q_1 = 44$; $Q_2 = 50$; $Q_3 = 56$; maximum = 60; range = 18; IQR = 12

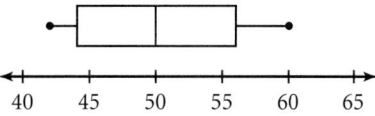

9. minimum = 102; $Q_1 = 125$; $Q_2 = 130$; $Q_3 = 175$; maximum = 190; range = 88; IQR = 50

11. minimum = 14; $Q_1 = 22$; $Q_2 = 50$; $Q_3 = 82$; maximum = 93; range = 79; IQR = 60

13. minimum = 2.2; Q_1 = 2.7; Q_2 = 4.8; Q_3 = 7.7; maximum = 8.8; range = 6.6; IQR = 5.0

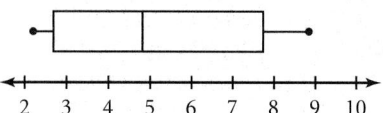

15. class 2 **17.** class 3 **19.** class 3 **21.** 75%
23. Answers may vary. **25a.** minimum = 62; Q_1 = 68; Q_2 = 73; Q_3 = 75.5; maximum = 78
b.

Both sexes

27a. minimum value = 1545; Q_1 = 36,420; Q_2 = 57,097; Q_3 = 84,904; maximum value = 656,424
b.

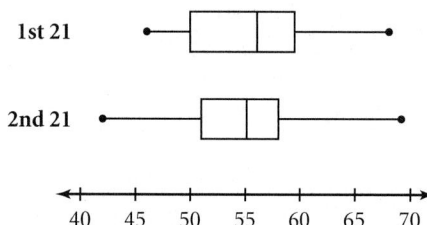

c. yes; Alaska, California, and Texas
29a.

1st 21

2nd 21

b. The distributions of the ages of the presidents at inauguration are all fairly similar. The perception of how old a president should be has not changed much over the last 200 years. **31.** growth **33.** decay **35.** falls to the left and rises to the right **37.** k = 4; y = 4x **39.** $k = \frac{2}{9}$; $y = \frac{2}{9}x^2$ **41.** $x - \frac{3}{2} = -\frac{1}{10}(y - 2)^2$
43. C(−2, 0); vertices: (−7, 0) and (3, 0); co-vertices: $\left(-2, -\frac{5}{3}\right)$ and $\left(-2, \frac{5}{3}\right)$ **45.** 210 ways
47. 10.368, 12.4416, 14.92992

LESSON 12.4

TRY THIS (p. 793)
range = 29,000 miles; mean deviation = 6400 miles; The range for tire C is the same as the range for tire A, which is larger than the range for tire B. The mean deviation for tire C is larger than the mean deviation for tire B and smaller than the mean deviation for tire A.

TRY THIS (p. 794)
$\sigma \approx 9230$ miles

Exercises

4a. Tricia: range = 7; mean deviation = 2
Morgan: range = 40; mean deviation = 16.4
b. Tricia's scores are less variable (more consistent) than those of Morgan. **5.** Tricia: $\sigma \approx 2.45$; Morgan: $\sigma \approx 17.01$ **7.** range = 5; mean deviation = 1.6 **9.** range = 70; mean deviation ≈ 25.7
11. range = 6.8; mean deviation ≈ 1.87
13. range = 12.28; mean deviation = 5.064
15. $\sigma^2 \approx 2.99$; $\sigma \approx 1.73$ **17.** $\sigma^2 \approx 57.18$; $\sigma \approx 7.56$
19. $\sigma^2 \approx 15.64$; $\sigma \approx 3.95$ **21.** $\sigma^2 \approx 26.99$; $\sigma \approx 5.19$
23. mean deviation = 191.25; standard deviation ≈ 220.95; mean deviation is slightly less affected. **25.** yes; if all the data values are the same
27. range = 5; mean deviation ≈ 1.02
29. range = 0.006 mm; mean deviation ≈ 0.0014 mm
31. location 1: range = 2167 customers, mean deviation ≈ 527.3 customers; location 2: range = 1815 customers, mean deviation ≈ 442.3 customers; the sales at location 1 are more variable, or less consistent, than those at location 2.
33. men: $\bar{x}$ = 1:54.17, median = 1:54.81; women: $\bar{x}$ = 2:05.32, median = 2:03.42
35. men: σ = 3.7637; women: σ = 6.0194; the men's times are more consistent, and the women's times are more variable. **37.** (≈−2.37, ≈3.64)
39. x ≈ −6.3 or x ≈ 0.3 **41.** 120 **43.** 7980
45. $\frac{9}{11} = 0.\overline{81}$ **47.** does not exist

LESSON 12.5

TRY THIS (p. 800)   **TRY THIS** (p. 801)
about 0.130, or 13.0%   about 0.943, or 94.3%

Exercises

5. about 0.324, or 32.4% **6.** about 0.561, or 56.1%
7. ≈0.219 **9.** ≈0.109 **11.** ≈0.004 **13.** 0.375 **15.** 0.25
17. ≈0.103 **19.** ≈0.849 **21.** ≈0.151 **23.** ≈0.233
25. ≈0.016 **27.** ≈0.0004 **29.** ≈0.776 **31.** ≈0.058
33. ≈0.163 **35.** ≈0.993 **37.** ≈0.969 **39.** ≈0.277
41. ≈0.238 **43.** ≈0.121 **45.** ≈0.894 **47.** 0.48
49. 0.648 **51.** $\frac{1}{3}$ **53.** $\frac{1}{2}$ **55.** $\frac{2}{3}$ **57.** Answers may vary. sample answer: −3, 3, 9, 15, . . . **59a.** male: range = 3.6, mean deviation ≈ 1.21; female: range = 6.3, mean deviation ≈ 1.73 **b.** male: $\sigma \approx 1.276$; female: $\sigma \approx 2.065$ **c.** The percent of female enrollment is more variable than that of the male enrollment.

LESSON 12.6

TRY THIS (p. 807)   **TRY THIS** (p. 809)
a. 0.2119   about 1140
b. 0.8301

TRY THIS (p. 810)
about 59% of the time

Exercises

4. 0.6449 **5.** 0.3848 **6a.** about 0.99 **b.** about 990

7. 0.8185 **9.** 0.3446 **11.** 0.3848 **13.** 0.0228

15. 0.0808 **17.** 0.1586 **19.** 0.7881 **21.** 0.0727

23. 0.0726 **25.** 0.2609 **27.** 0.1587 **29.** 0.0228

31. 0.6826 **33.** 4444 **35.** 638 **37.** 26,723 **39.** 0.1596

41. 0.9044 **43.** 0.9962 **45.** 0.0918 **47.** 0.0764

49. 0.3221 **51a.** 95% **b.** 40% **53.** $y = 100x - 104$

55. $y = -\frac{7}{6}x + \frac{14}{3}$ **57.** $\frac{2x+3}{x^2+3x+2}$ **59.** $\frac{x^2+2x+2}{x^2+2x}$

61. $\frac{\sqrt{5}}{5}$ **63.** $-\frac{1+\sqrt{3}}{2}$ **65.** 21 **67.** 140

69. $\frac{19}{4} \approx 4.75$ **71.** $\frac{58,025}{512} \approx 113.33$

CHAPTER REVIEW AND ASSESSMENT

1. mean = $5.\overline{2}$; median = 7; mode = 9

3.

Data	Frequency
4	4
5	4
6	4
7	1
Total	13

mean = 5.15

5.

Stems	Leaves 3|5 = 35
3	5 8
4	5 5 9
5	3 7 8

7.

9.

11.

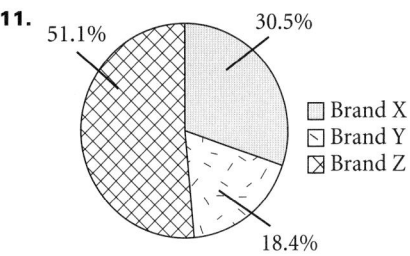

51.1%　30.5%　18.4%
□ Brand X
◫ Brand Y
▨ Brand Z

13. $Q_1 = 24$; $Q_2 = 30$; $Q_3 = 34.5$

15.

17. range = 9; mean deviation ≈ 2.83 **19.** range = 46;
mean deviation ≈ 12.82 **21.** $\sigma^2 \approx 1147.22$; $\sigma \approx 33.87$
23. $\sigma^2 \approx 39.42$; $\sigma \approx 6.28$ **25.** ≈0.0425 **27.** 0.5
29. 0.9641 **31.** 0.5762 **33.** 0.2420 **35.** 0.7606

Chapter 13

LESSON 13.1

TRY THIS (p. 828)

$\sin Y = \frac{5}{13} \approx 0.3846$ 　　 $\csc Y = \frac{13}{5} \approx 2.6$

$\cos Y = \frac{12}{13} \approx 0.9231$ 　　 $\sec Y = \frac{13}{12} = 1.0833$

$\tan Y = \frac{5}{12} \approx 0.4167$ 　　 $\cot Y = \frac{12}{5} = 2.4$

TRY THIS (p. 831)　　**TRY THIS** (p. 832)
$KL \approx 14.1$ 　　 m∠K ≈ 29°
$LM \approx 9.5$ 　　 m∠L ≈ 61°
　　　　　　　　$LM = 4.6$

Exercises

4. $\sin x = \frac{3}{5} = 0.6$; $\cos x = \frac{4}{5} = 0.8$; $\tan x = \frac{3}{4} = 0.75$;
$\csc x = \frac{5}{3} \approx 1.6667$; $\sec x = \frac{5}{4} = 1.25$; $\cot x = \frac{4}{5} \approx 1.3333$

5. $BA \approx 10.6$; $AC \approx 5.8$ **6.** about 64.6 feet

7. m∠A ≈ 47°; m∠B ≈ 43°; $AB \approx 7.3$ **9.** $\frac{15}{17} \approx 0.8824$

11. $\frac{15}{17} \approx 0.8824$ **13.** $\frac{15}{8} = 1.875$ **15.** $\frac{17}{8} = 2.125$

17. $\frac{17}{8} = 2.125$ **19.** $\frac{15}{8} = 1.875$ **21.** $\frac{2}{\sqrt{13}} \approx 0.5547$

23. $\frac{3}{\sqrt{13}} \approx 0.8321$ **25.** $\frac{2}{3} \approx 0.6667$ **27.** $\frac{\sqrt{13}}{2} \approx 1.8028$

29. $\frac{\sqrt{13}}{3} \approx 1.2019$ **31.** $\frac{3}{2} = 1.5$ **33.** 30° **35.** 20.6°

37. 41.4° **39.** m∠R ≈ 32°; m∠S ≈ 58°; $ST \approx 2.1$

41. m∠S ≈ 50°; $RS \approx 11.4$; $RT \approx 8.7$ **43.** m∠B = 48°;
$BC \approx 3.8$; $AC \approx 4.2$ **45.** $AD \approx 687.9$ ft; $AC \approx 829.8$ ft

47. 2° **49.** \$3897 **51.** 5 **53.** $x(3x - 1)(x - 2)$ **55.** $\frac{\sqrt{3}}{3}$

57. $2\sqrt{2} - 2\sqrt{3}$

59. $Q_1 = 17.5$; $Q_2 = 24.5$; $Q_3 = 31$; range = 41; IQR = 12.5

LESSON 13.2

TRY THIS (p. 837, Ex. 1)   **TRY THIS** (p. 837, Ex. 2)
199.8° in 1 second   −237°; 175°

TRY THIS (p. 837, Ex. 3)
45°; 55°

TRY THIS (p. 837, Ex. 4)

$\sin \theta = -\frac{5\sqrt{34}}{34}$ $\csc \theta = -\frac{\sqrt{34}}{5}$

$\cos \theta = \frac{3\sqrt{34}}{34}$ $\sec \theta = \frac{\sqrt{34}}{3}$

$\tan \theta = -\frac{5}{3}$ $\cot \theta = -\frac{3}{5}$

TRY THIS (p. 840)

$\sin \theta = -\frac{4}{5}$ $\csc \theta = -\frac{5}{4}$

$\cos \theta = -\frac{3}{5}$ $\sec \theta = -\frac{5}{3}$

$\tan \theta = \frac{4}{3}$ $\cot \theta = \frac{3}{4}$

Exercises

4. 2580°/s **5.** −89° **6.** 87°; 80°; 36°

7. $\sin \theta = -\frac{2\sqrt{13}}{13}$; $\cos \theta = \frac{3\sqrt{13}}{13}$; $\tan \theta = -\frac{2}{3}$;

$\csc \theta = -\frac{\sqrt{13}}{2}$; $\sec \theta = \frac{\sqrt{13}}{3}$; $\cot \theta = -\frac{3}{2}$ **8.** $\sin \theta = -\frac{12}{13}$;

$\cos \theta = -\frac{5}{13}$; $\tan \theta = \frac{12}{5}$; $\csc \theta = -\frac{13}{12}$; $\sec \theta = -\frac{13}{5}$;

$\cot \theta = \frac{5}{12}$

9.

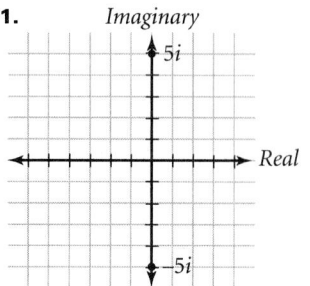

11.

13. −325°; $\theta_{ref} = 35°$ **15.** −248°; $\theta_{ref} = 68°$ **17.** 252°;
−108°; $\theta_{ref} = 72°$ **19.** 225°; $\theta_{ref} = 45°$ **21.** −270°;
$\theta_{ref} = 90°$ **23.** −90°; 270°; $\theta_{ref} = 90°$ **25.** 180°; −180°;
$\theta_{ref} = 0°$ **27.** −135°; $\theta_{ref} = 45°$ **29.** 50°; −310°;
$\theta_{ref} = 50°$ **31.** 240°; $\theta_{ref} = 60°$ **33.** 185°; $\theta_{ref} = 5°$
35. −35°; 325°; $\theta_{ref} = 35°$ **37.** $\sin \theta = \frac{1}{\sqrt{17}} = \frac{\sqrt{17}}{17}$;

$\cos \theta = -\frac{4}{\sqrt{17}} = -\frac{4\sqrt{17}}{17}$; $\tan \theta = -\frac{1}{4}$; $\csc \theta = \sqrt{17}$;

$\sec \theta = -\frac{\sqrt{17}}{4}$; $\cot \theta = -4$ **39.** $\sin \theta = -\frac{1}{\sqrt{5}} = -\frac{\sqrt{5}}{5}$;

$\cos \theta = \frac{2}{\sqrt{5}} = \frac{2\sqrt{5}}{5}$; $\tan \theta = -\frac{1}{2}$; $\csc \theta = -\sqrt{5}$;

$\sec \theta = \frac{\sqrt{5}}{2}$; $\cot \theta = -2$ **41.** $\sin \theta = \frac{2\sqrt{29}}{29}$; $\cos \theta = \frac{5\sqrt{29}}{29}$;

$\tan \theta = \frac{2}{5}$; $\csc \theta = \frac{\sqrt{29}}{2}$; $\sec \theta = \frac{\sqrt{29}}{5}$; $\cot \theta = \frac{5}{2}$

43. $\sin \theta = \frac{3\sqrt{13}}{13}$; $\cos \theta = -\frac{2\sqrt{13}}{13}$; $\tan \theta = -\frac{3}{2}$;

$\csc \theta = \frac{\sqrt{13}}{3}$; $\sec \theta = -\frac{\sqrt{13}}{2}$; $\cot \theta = -\frac{2}{3}$

45. $\sin \theta = -\frac{\sqrt{21}}{21}$; $\cos \theta = \frac{2\sqrt{105}}{21}$; $\tan \theta = -\frac{\sqrt{5}}{10}$;

$\csc \theta = -\sqrt{21}$; $\sec \theta = \frac{\sqrt{105}}{10}$; $\cot \theta = -2\sqrt{5}$

47. $\sin \theta = -\frac{8\sqrt{65}}{65}$; $\cos \theta = -\frac{\sqrt{65}}{65}$; $\tan \theta = 8$;

$\csc \theta = -\frac{\sqrt{65}}{8}$; $\sec \theta = -\sqrt{65}$; $\cot \theta = \frac{1}{8}$ **49.** $\sqrt{3}$

51. $\frac{\sqrt{5}}{2}$ **53.** $-\frac{5\sqrt{21}}{21}$ **55.** $-\frac{7\sqrt{65}}{65}$ **57.** $\frac{1}{4}$ rotation

counterclockwise **59.** $\frac{3}{4}$ rotation clockwise

61. 2 rotations counterclockwise **63.** $1\frac{7}{9}$ rotations

clockwise **65.** ≈−0.7266 **67.** 5400°/s **69.** ±14

71.

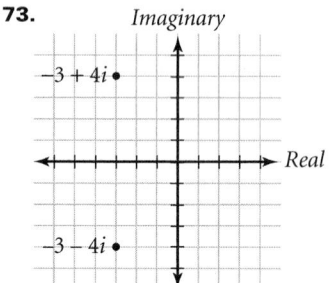

73.

75. $\sqrt{13}$ **77.** 1 **79.** 210

LESSON 13.3

TRY THIS (p. 844)   **TRY THIS** (p. 845)

$\sin(-150°) = -\frac{1}{2}$ $(6, -6\sqrt{3})$

$\cos(-150°) = -\frac{\sqrt{3}}{2}$

$\tan(-150°) = \frac{\sqrt{3}}{3}$

TRY THIS (p. 847)

a. $\sin 1110° = \frac{1}{2}$ **b.** $\sin(-1110°) = -\frac{1}{2}$

$\cos 1110° = \frac{\sqrt{3}}{2}$ $\cos(-1110°) = \frac{\sqrt{3}}{2}$

$\tan 1110° = \frac{\sqrt{3}}{3}$ $\tan(-1110°) = -\frac{\sqrt{3}}{3}$

Exercises

4. $\sin 150° = \frac{1}{2}$; $\cos 150° = -\frac{\sqrt{3}}{2}$; $\tan 150° = -\frac{\sqrt{3}}{3}$

5. $\left(\frac{9\sqrt{2}}{2}, -\frac{9\sqrt{2}}{2}\right)$ **6.** $(-0.68, 1.88)$

7. $\sin(-1200°) = -\frac{\sqrt{3}}{2}$; $\cos(-1200°) = -\frac{1}{2}$; $\tan(-1200°) = \sqrt{3}$ **9.** $\sin 210° = -\frac{1}{2}$; $\cos 210° = -\frac{\sqrt{3}}{2}$; $\tan 210° = \frac{\sqrt{3}}{3}$ **11.** $\sin 120° = \frac{\sqrt{3}}{2}$; $\cos 120° = -\frac{1}{2}$; $\tan 120° = -\sqrt{3}$ **13.** $\sin 240° = -\frac{\sqrt{3}}{2}$; $\cos 240° = -\frac{1}{2}$; $\tan 240° = \sqrt{3}$ **15.** $\sin(-135°) = -\frac{\sqrt{2}}{2}$; $\cos(-135°) = -\frac{\sqrt{2}}{2}$; $\tan(-135°) = 1$ **17.** $\sin(-330°) = \frac{1}{2}$; $\cos(-330°) = \frac{\sqrt{3}}{2}$; $\tan(-330°) = \frac{\sqrt{3}}{3}$ **19.** $\sin(-210°) = \frac{1}{2}$; $\cos(-210°) = -\frac{\sqrt{3}}{2}$; $\tan(-210°) = -\frac{\sqrt{3}}{3}$ **21.** $P\left(\frac{5\sqrt{3}}{2}, \frac{5}{2}\right)$

23. $P\left(-\frac{9\sqrt{2}}{2}, \frac{9\sqrt{2}}{2}\right)$ **25.** $P(-45, 0)$

27. $P(-3.8\sqrt{2}, -3.8\sqrt{2})$ **29.** $P(0.26, 0.97)$

31. $P(-0.64, -0.77)$ **33.** $P(1.00, 0.07)$

35. $P(0.03, -1.00)$ **37.** $\sin 405° = \frac{\sqrt{2}}{2}$; $\cos 405° = \frac{\sqrt{2}}{2}$; $\tan 405° = 1$ **39.** $\sin 870° = \frac{1}{2}$; $\cos 870° = -\frac{\sqrt{3}}{2}$; $\tan 870° = -\frac{\sqrt{3}}{3}$ **41.** $\sin 1380° = -\frac{\sqrt{3}}{2}$; $\cos 1380° = \frac{1}{2}$; $\tan 1380° = -\sqrt{3}$ **43.** $\sin(-600°) = \frac{\sqrt{3}}{2}$; $\cos(-600°) = -\frac{1}{2}$; $\tan(-600°) = -\sqrt{3}$

45. $\sin(-495°) = -\frac{\sqrt{2}}{2}$; $\cos(-495°) = -\frac{\sqrt{2}}{2}$; $\tan(-495°) = 1$

47. $\sin(-840°) = -\frac{\sqrt{3}}{2}$; $\cos(-840°) = -\frac{1}{2}$; $\tan(-840°) = \sqrt{3}$ **49.** $\frac{\sqrt{2}}{2}$ **51.** $-\frac{\sqrt{3}}{3}$ **53.** $-\frac{\sqrt{3}}{2}$ **55.** $-\frac{\sqrt{3}}{2}$

57. $-\frac{\sqrt{3}}{3}$ **59.** 1 **61.** 1 **63.** undefined **65.** -1 **67.** -1

69. 0 **71.** 1 **73.** $\frac{\sqrt{2}}{2}$ **75.** $-\frac{\sqrt{2}}{2}$ **77.** $-\frac{\sqrt{2}}{2}$ **79.** $-\frac{\sqrt{3}}{3}$

81. 0 **83.** $\sqrt{3}$ **85.** -2 **87.** $\frac{2\sqrt{3}}{3}$ **89.** -1 **91.** $\frac{2\sqrt{3}}{3}$

93. If f is periodic, then there is a function f such that $f(x + p) = f(x)$. Then for the function $f(x) = x$, $f(x + p) = x + p$ and $x + p = x$ for some p, which is not possible unless $p = 0$. **95.** $JL = 15$ cm; $KL = 15\sqrt{3}$ cm; m∠$K = 30°$ **97.** $PR = 12$ in.; $PQ = 12\sqrt{2}$ in.; m∠$Q = 45°$ **99.** ≈ 24 in. **101.** $12x - 1$ **103.** $16x - 5$ **105.** 2nd row, 1st column; the amount that Donnell has in his savings account, $408 **107.** $AB = BC$, therefore triangle ABC is isosceles.

109. mean $= 8\frac{1}{3}$; median $= 8$; modes = 3 and 8

111. mean $= 41.75$; standard deviation ≈ 16.22

LESSON 13.4

TRY THIS (p. 852, Ex. 1)
$-120° = -\frac{2\pi}{3}$ radians
$-\frac{2}{3}\pi$ radians $= -120°$

TRY THIS (p. 852, Ex. 2)
$\sin \frac{3\pi}{2} = -1$
$\cos \frac{2\pi}{3} = -0.5$
$\tan \frac{5\pi}{4} = 1$

TRY THIS (p. 853)
0.75 feet

TRY THIS (p. 854)
linear speed ≈ 1037 miles per hour; angular speed $\approx \frac{\pi}{12}$ radians per hour

Exercises

5. $\frac{2\pi}{3}$ radians **6.** 45° **7.** $\frac{\sqrt{3}}{2}$ **8.** $-\frac{\sqrt{2}}{2}$ **9.** $-\sqrt{3}$ **10.** 60π, or 188.5 cm **11.** $10.54 \frac{ft}{min}$; $0.12 \frac{mi}{hr}$ **13.** $\frac{\pi}{2}$ radians

15. $\frac{3\pi}{2}$ radians **17.** $-\frac{2\pi}{3}$ radians **19.** $-\frac{4\pi}{3}$ radians

21. $\frac{31\pi}{6}$ radians **23.** $\frac{8\pi}{9}$ radians **25.** 180° **27.** 45°

29. 30° **31.** $-45°$ **33.** $-561.4°$ **35.** $284.2°$ **37.** -1

39. $-\frac{1}{2}$ **41.** $\frac{1}{2}$ **43.** 1 **45.** $\frac{\sqrt{2}}{2}$ **47.** -1 **49.** $\sqrt{2}$

51. $-\frac{2\sqrt{3}}{3}$ **53.** 12 m **55.** 360 m **57.** 3.35 m **59.** $\frac{10\pi}{3}$ m

61. $\frac{5\pi}{2}$ m **63.** $\frac{35\pi}{6}$ m **65.** $\frac{37}{48}$ rad **67.** top: 60.2 in./s;

bottom: 23.6 in./s; $3.42 \frac{mi}{hr}$; $1.34 \frac{mi}{hr}$ **69.** 480π, or ≈ 1508 cm/min **71.** 0.12 rad/s

73. no solution

75. $-3 < x < -\frac{1}{3}$

$-6\ -5\ -4\ -3\ -2\ -1\ \ 0\ \ 1\ \ 2\ \ 3\ \ 4\ \ 5\ \ 6$

77. $5i$ **79.** 2.56 **81.** 45.42 **83.** $x = \frac{3 \pm i\sqrt{87}}{2}$

85.

Data	Frequency	Relative Frequency
1	1	$\frac{1}{25} = 0.04$, or 4%
2	1	$\frac{1}{25} = 0.04$, or 4%
3	5	$\frac{5}{25} = 0.20$, or 20%
4	6	$\frac{6}{25} = 0.24$, or 24%
5	6	$\frac{6}{25} = 0.24$, or 24%
6	3	$\frac{3}{25} = 0.12$, or 12%
7	2	$\frac{2}{25} = 0.08$, or 8%
8	1	$\frac{1}{25} = 0.04$, or 4%
Total	25	1, or 100%

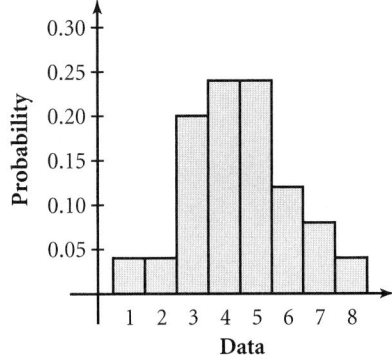

TRY THIS (p. 860)

a.

$y = \frac{1}{3}\cos\theta$

b.

$y = \sin 3\theta$

TRY THIS (p. 861)

a.

$y = \cos(\theta - 45°)$

b.

$y = \sin\theta - 1$

TRY THIS (p. 862)

$y = 1.5\sin 240\pi\left(t + \frac{1}{360}\right)$

TRY THIS (p. 863)

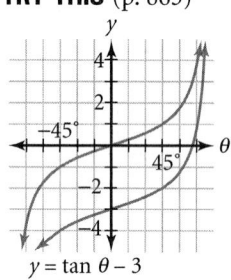
$y = \tan\theta - 3$

Exercises

5.

$y = \frac{1}{3}\cos\theta$

6.

$y = \sin\frac{3}{2}\theta$

7.

$y = \cos\theta$
$y = \cos(\theta - 90°)$

8.

$y = \sin\theta - 1.5$

9. $y = 2\sin 60\pi\left(t + \frac{1}{120}\right)$

10.
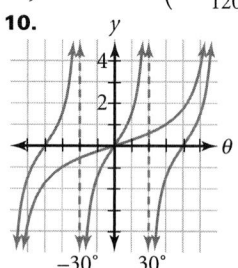

11. amplitude: 2.5; period: π **13.** amplitude: none; period: $\frac{\pi}{3}$ **15.** amplitude: 5; period: 4π

17. amplitude: 3; period: 2π **19.** amplitude: 1; period: 2π **21.** phase shift: 45° to the right; vertical translation: 2 units down **23.** phase shift: 60° to the left; vertical translation: 1 unit up **25.** phase shift: 30° to the left; vertical translation: 2 units up

27. phase shift: 135° to the right; vertical translation: 3 units down

29. stretched vertically by a factor of 4

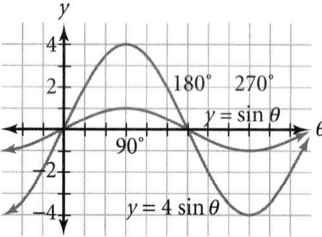
$y = \sin\theta$
$y = 4\sin\theta$

31. reflected across θ-axis and stretched vertically by a factor of 3

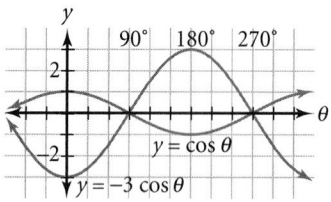
$y = \cos\theta$
$y = -3\cos\theta$

33. translated 90° to the left

35. stretched vertically by a factor of 2 and translated 90° to the right

37. reflected across the θ-axis, stretched vertically by a factor of 2, and stretched horizontally by a factor of 3

39. compressed vertically by a factor of $\frac{1}{3}$ and compressed horizontally by a factor of $\frac{1}{2}$

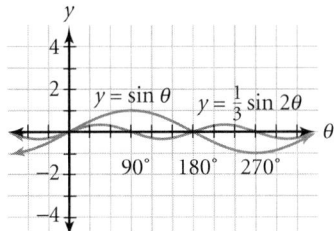

41. stretched vertically by a factor of 2

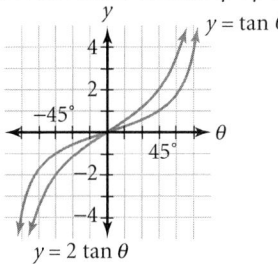

43. translated down 2 units

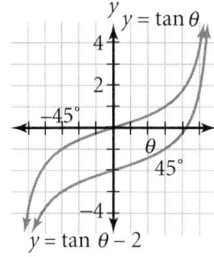

45. compressed horizontally by a factor of $\frac{1}{3}$

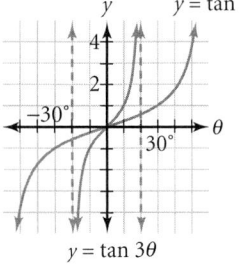

47. stretched vertically by a factor of 3 and stretched horizontally by a factor of 2

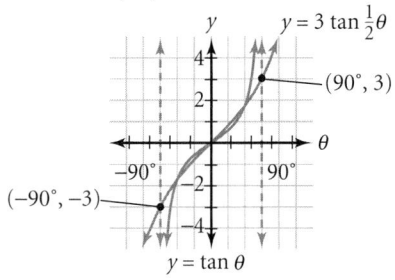

49. a ski resort or a tropical resort because the population of the town is highest in January
51. ≈6533 **53.** 5.2 **55.** max: 68.5°F; min: 65.5°F
57. Answers may vary, but the number 67 should be increased. **59.** $x - y = 4$ **61.** $4x - y = -9$
63. (0.86, 0.49) **65.** $x \approx 1.7396$ **67.** $x \approx 8.6514$

LESSON 13.6

TRY THIS (p. 868)
45° + n360° and 135° + n360, where n is an integer

TRY THIS (p. 870, Ex. 2)   **TRY THIS** (p. 870, Ex. 3)
a. $\text{Sin}^{-1} \frac{\sqrt{3}}{2} = 60°$ **a.** $\text{Cos}^{-1}(\sin 315°) = 135°$
b. $\text{Cos}^{-1} -\frac{\sqrt{2}}{2} = 135°$ **b.** $\tan\left[\text{Sin}^{-1}\left(-\frac{\sqrt{3}}{2}\right)\right] = -\sqrt{3}$
c. $\text{Tan}^{-1} \sqrt{3} = 60°$

Exercises
4. 30° + n360° and 330° + n360°, where n is an integer
5. −60° **6.** 60° **7.** −60° **8.** $\frac{\sqrt{3}}{2}$ **9.** 60° **10.** −30°
11. 41.81° **13.** 225° + n360° and 315° + n360°, where n is an integer **15.** 60° + n360° and 240° + n360°, where n is an integer **17.** 90° + n360° and 270° + n360°, where n is an integer **19.** 45° + n360° and 315° + n360°, where n is an integer **21.** −30°
23. 45° **25.** 60° **27.** 60° **29.** 180° **31.** 45° **33.** 1
35. $\frac{\sqrt{2}}{2}$ **37.** $\sqrt{3}$ **39.** 26.57° **41.** 0° **43.** −30°
45. Let $f(\theta) = \text{Sin } \theta$. $(f^{-1} \circ f)(\theta) = (f \circ f^{-1})(\theta) = \theta$
Definition of inverse functions;
$(\text{Sin}^{-1} \circ \text{Sin } \theta)(\theta) = (\text{Sin} \circ \text{Sin } \theta^{-1})(\theta) = \theta$ Substitute Sin for f. $(\text{Sin}^{-1} \circ \text{Sin } \theta)(\theta) = \theta$

47. Let x be the height of the tree.

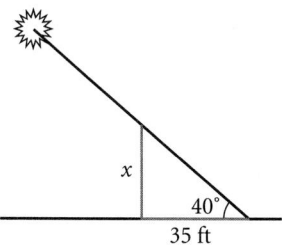

≈ 29.4 feet

49. $\approx 75.5°$ **51.** ≈ 1698 meters **53.** $(3, 5, -1)$ **55.** 3
57. 23° **59.** 23° **61.** 75° **63.** $\approx 136.4°$

CHAPTER REVIEW AND ASSESSMENT

1. $a = \sqrt{5}$; $A \approx 48.2°$; $B \approx 41.8°$ **3.** $b \approx 8.2°$; $a \approx 21.5$;
$A = 69°$ **5.** $-90°$; $90°$ **7.** $225°$; $45°$ **9.** $20°$ and $-340°$;
$20°$ **11.** $308°$ and $-52°$; $52°$ **13.** $205°$ and $-155°$; $25°$
15. $\sin \theta = -\frac{4}{5}$; $\cos \theta = \frac{3}{5}$; $\tan \theta = -\frac{4}{3}$; $\csc \theta = -\frac{5}{4}$;
$\sec \theta = \frac{5}{3}$; $\cot \theta = -\frac{3}{4}$ **17.** $\sin \theta = -\frac{8\sqrt{65}}{65}$;
$\cos \theta = -\frac{\sqrt{65}}{65}$; $\tan \theta = 8$; $\csc \theta = -\frac{\sqrt{65}}{8}$; $\sec \theta = -\sqrt{65}$;
$\cot \theta = \frac{1}{8}$ **19.** $\tan \theta = \frac{2\sqrt{5}}{15}$ **21.** $\cos \theta = \frac{\sqrt{2}}{2}$ **23.** $-\frac{\sqrt{2}}{2}$
25. 1 **27.** 1 **29.** undefined **31.** $-\frac{\sqrt{3}}{2}$ **33.** $\left(\frac{1}{2}, \frac{\sqrt{3}}{2}\right)$
35. $\left(-\frac{5}{2}, -\frac{5\sqrt{3}}{2}\right)$ **37.** $\frac{13\pi}{30}$ radians **39.** $-\frac{23\pi}{180}$ radians
41. $-168.8°$ **43.** ≈ 2.36 meters **45.** $4; 2\pi$ **47.**
amplitude does not exist; 3π **49.** $45°$ to the left; no
vertical translation
51. $120°$ to the left; 2 units down
52. $y = \cos 4\theta$ is $y = \cos \theta$ compressed horizontally
by a factor of $\frac{1}{4}$.

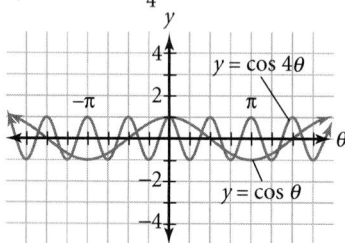

53. $y = \tan \frac{1}{2}\theta$ is $\tan \theta$ stretched horizontally by a
factor of 2.

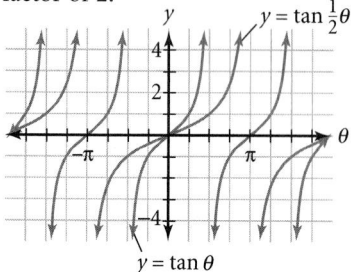

54. $y = 2 \sin(\theta - 45°)$ is $y = \sin \theta$ stretched vertically
by a factor of 2 and translated $45°$ to the right.

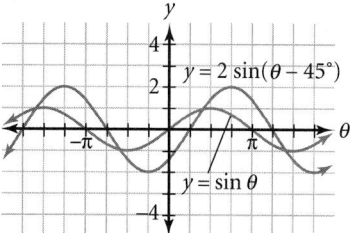

55. $y = 3 \cos(\theta + 45°)$ is $y = \cos \theta$ stretched vertically
by a factor of 3 and translated $45°$ to the left.

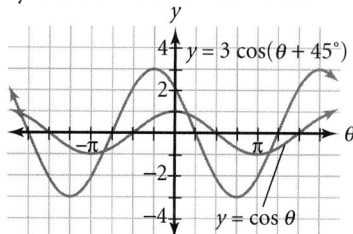

56. $n180°$ (or $0° + n360°$ and $180° + n360°$), where n
is an integer **57.** $n360°$, where n is an integer
58. $150° + n360°$ and $330° + n360°$, where n is an
integer **59.** $135° + n360°$ and $225° + n360°$, where n
is an integer **60.** $240° + n360°$ and $300° + n360°$,
where n is an integer **61.** $45° + n360°$ and
$225° + n360°$, where n is an integer **62.** $30°$ **63.** $150°$
64. $60°$ **65.** $-45°$ **66.** $\frac{\sqrt{3}}{3}$ **67.** $\frac{1}{2}$ **68.** $\approx -35.26°$
69. $-60°$ **70.** ≈ 238.4 meters

Chapter 14

LESSON 14.1

TRY THIS (p. 887)   **TRY THIS** (p. 888, Ex. 2)
$K \approx 16.0$ square units $F = 52°$, $d \approx 8.5$, $e \approx 5.4$

TRY THIS (p. 888, Ex. 3)   **TRY THIS** (p. 890)
$m \approx 638$ **a.** 0 triangles
                               b. 2 triangles

Exercises
5. 29.6 square units **6.** $B = 115°$; $a \approx 3.7$; $c \approx 5.7$
7. $x \approx 3.2$ **8.** 2 possible triangles **9.** 0 possible
triangles **11.** 30 ft^2 **13.** 24.7 cm^2 **15.** 368.2 ft^2
17. 160.3 m^2 **19.** 19.9 cm^2 **21.** 1756.0 ft^2
23. 722.5 ft^2 **25.** 8.3 **27.** 9.6 **29.** 17.1 **31.** $A = 101°$;
$b \approx 3.5$; $a \approx 7.5$ **33.** $C = 83°$; $b \approx 12.3$; $c \approx 13.8$
35. $A = 80°$; $b = 10$; $c \approx 3.5$ **37.** $A = 97°$; $a \approx 20.8$;
$c \approx 15.5$ **39.** $B = 101°$; $a \approx 12.3$; $c \approx 13.6$ **41.** $A = 80°$;
$a \approx 13.2$; $b \approx 11.4$ **43.** $B = 112°$; $a \approx 8.4$; $c \approx 4.6$
45. 2 possible triangles: $A = 30°$, $B = 108.2°$,
$C = 41.8°$, $a = 1.5$, $b = 2.8$, $c = 2$ and $A = 30°$,
$B = 11.8°$, $C = 138.2°$, $a = 1.5$, $b = 0.6$, $c = 2$
47. 0 possible triangles

49. 1 possible triangle: $A = 45°$, $B = 45°$, $C = 90°$, $a = \frac{5\sqrt{2}}{2}$, $b = 3.5$, $c = 5$ **51.** 73 cm **53.** 691 meters
55. 14.5 km **57.** about 14 years **59.** $2x^2(x-3)^2$
61. $\frac{\pi}{2}$ **63.** $\frac{3\pi}{4}$ **65.** $-36°$ **67.** $239.5°$

LESSON 14.2

TRY THIS (p. 895)   **TRY THIS** (p. 897)
a. $y \approx 122.2$ $y \approx 8.5$, $X \approx 22.4°$,
b. $X \approx 35.2°$ $Z \approx 21.6°$

Exercises
5a. 33.7 **b.** 41.3° **6.** about 106.6 nautical miles apart; about 5.8 hours, or 5 hours and 48 minutes
7. $e \approx 8.0$; $D \approx 59°$; $F \approx 49°$ **8.** $A = 20.2°$; $B \approx 43.1°$; $C \approx 116.7°$ **9.** SAS; $A \approx 52.5$ **11.** SSS; $A \approx 88.0°$
13. SAS; $c \approx 7.1$ **15.** SAS; $b \approx 34.0$ **17.** SAS; $a \approx 4.1$
19. $A \approx 43.5°$; $B \approx 74.4°$; $C \approx 62.1°$ **21.** $A \approx 48.5°$; $B \approx 58.5°$; $C \approx 73.0°$ **23.** $A \approx 35.4°$; $B \approx 48.2°$; $C \approx 96.4°$ **25.** SSS; $A \approx 79.0°$, $B \approx 54.9°$, $C \approx 46.1°$
27. SAS; $b \approx 49.1$, $A \approx 110.3°$, $C \approx 47.7°$ **29.** SAS; $b \approx 3.2$, $A \approx 38.7°$, $C \approx 111.3°$ **31.** SSS; not possible
33. SAS; $c \approx 6.2$, $A \approx 77.9°$, $B \approx 42.1°$ **35.** SSS; $A \approx 93.8°$, $B \approx 29.9°$, $C \approx 56.3°$ **37.** SSA; $B \approx 42.7°$, $C \approx 79.3°$, $c \approx 11.6°$ **39.** SSS; not possible **41.** SSS; $A \approx 52.0°$, $B \approx 68.6°$, $C \approx 59.4°$ **43.** $x \approx 6.8$ **45.** 19.2°, 80.4°, 80.4° **47.** The longest pole is 15.8 feet. The guy wire should be 24.0 feet. **49.** 239 feet

51.
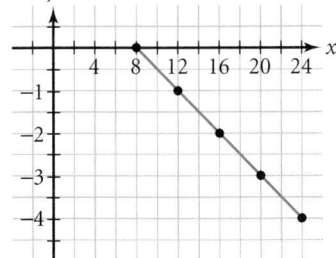

53. $x = -\frac{4}{3}$ or $x = \frac{3}{2}$ **55.** $x = \frac{-3 - \sqrt{17}}{2}$ or $x = \frac{-3 + \sqrt{17}}{2}$

LESSON 14.3

TRY THIS (p. 903, Ex. 1)

$\cot \theta = \frac{y}{x}$ Definition of $\cot \theta$

$\cot \theta = \frac{r \cos \theta}{r \sin \theta}$ Substitution

$\cot \theta = \frac{\cos \theta}{\sin \theta}$ Simplify.

TRY THIS (p. 903, Ex. 2)

$\tan^2 \theta + 1 = \left(\frac{x}{y}\right)^2 + 1$ Definition of $\tan \theta$

$\tan^2 \theta + 1 = \frac{x^2 + y^2}{y^2}$

$\tan^2 \theta + 1 = \frac{r^2}{y^2}$ Substitution

$\tan^2 \theta + 1 = \left(\frac{r}{y}\right)^2$

$\tan^2 \theta + 1 = \sec^2 \theta$

TRY THIS (p. 904)   **TRY THIS** (p. 905, Ex. 4)
$1 + \sin \theta$ $1 - \sin^2 \theta$

TRY THIS (p. 905, Ex. 5)
38.7°

Exercises
4. $\sec \theta = \frac{r}{x}$ (by definition of $\sec \theta$) $= \frac{1}{\frac{x}{r}} = \frac{1}{\cos \theta}$

5. $\sin^2 \theta = \left(\frac{y}{r}\right)^2 = \frac{y^2}{r^2} = \frac{r^2 - x^2}{r^2} = \frac{r^2}{r^2} - \frac{x^2}{r^2} = 1 - \left(\frac{x}{r}\right)^2$
$\qquad = 1 - \cos^2 \theta$

6. $1 - \sin \theta$ **7.** $\frac{1 - \sin^2 \theta}{\sin^2 \theta}$ **8.** 50.2° **9.** $\cot \theta = \frac{x}{y}$
(by definition of $\cot \theta$) $= \frac{1}{\frac{y}{x}} = \frac{1}{\tan \theta}$, $\tan \theta \neq 0$

11. $\cos^2 \theta = \left(\frac{x}{r}\right)^2 = \frac{x^2}{r^2} = \frac{r^2 - y^2}{r^2} = \frac{r^2}{r^2} - \frac{y^2}{r^2} = 1 - \left(\frac{y}{r}\right)^2$
$\qquad = 1 - \sin^2 \theta$

13. $\cos \theta$ **15.** $\sec \theta$ **17.** $\sin \theta$ **19.** $\tan \theta$ **21.** $\cos \theta$
23. $\sec^2 \theta$ **25.** $\sin^2 \theta$ **27.** $1 - 2 \cos^2 \theta$

29. $\frac{1 - 2 \cos^2 \theta}{(1 - \cos^2 \theta)^2}$ **31.** $\frac{1 - \sin^2 \theta}{\sin \theta}$ **33.** $\sin^2 \theta + \frac{1}{\sin \theta}$

35. $\tan \theta = \frac{\sec \theta}{\csc \theta} = \frac{\frac{1}{\cos \theta}}{\frac{1}{\sin \theta}} = \frac{\sin \theta}{\cos \theta} = \tan \theta$

37. $\sin^2 \theta = \frac{\tan^2 \theta}{\sec^2 \theta} = \frac{\frac{\sin^2 \theta}{\cos^2 \theta}}{\frac{1}{\cos^2 \theta}} = \sin^2 \theta$

39. $\cot^2 \theta = \cos^2 \theta \, \csc^2 \theta = \cos^2 \theta \left(\frac{1}{\sin^2 \theta}\right) = \frac{\cos^2 \theta}{\sin^2 \theta}$
$\qquad = \cot^2 \theta$

41. $\frac{\sec \theta}{\cos \theta} = \frac{\frac{1}{\cos \theta}}{\cos \theta} = \frac{1}{\cos^2 \theta} = \sec^2 \theta$

43. $\frac{\cos \theta}{1 - \sin^2 \theta} = \frac{\cos \theta}{\cos^2 \theta} = \frac{1}{\cos \theta} = \sec \theta$

45. $(\sec \theta)(1 - \sin^2 \theta) = \left(\frac{1}{\cos \theta}\right)(\cos^2 \theta) = \cos \theta$

47. $(\tan \theta)(\csc \theta)(\sec \theta) = \left(\frac{\sin \theta}{\cos \theta}\right)\left(\frac{1}{\sin \theta}\right)\left(\frac{1}{\cos \theta}\right)$
$\qquad\qquad = \frac{1}{\cos^2 \theta} = \sec^2 \theta$

49. $\frac{\sin^2 \theta - 2 \sin \theta \cos \theta}{\cos^2 \theta}$, or $\frac{\sin^2 \theta}{\cos^2 \theta} - \frac{2 \sin \theta}{\cos \theta}$

51. $\pm\sqrt{1 - \cos^2 \theta}$ **53.** $\pm\frac{\sqrt{1 - \cos^2 \theta}}{\cos \theta}$

55. $\cos\theta = \pm\sqrt{1-\sin^2\theta}$; $\tan\theta = \pm\dfrac{\sin\theta}{\sqrt{1-\sin^2\theta}}$;

$\csc\theta = \dfrac{1}{\sin\theta}$; $\sec\theta = \pm\dfrac{1}{\sqrt{1-\sin^2\theta}}$; $\cot\theta = \pm\dfrac{\sqrt{1-\sin^2\theta}}{\sin\theta}$

57. $\sin\theta = \pm\dfrac{1}{\cot\theta\sqrt{1+\frac{1}{\cot^2\theta}}}$; $\cos\theta = \pm\dfrac{\cot\theta}{\sqrt{1+\cot^2\theta}}$;

$\tan\theta = \dfrac{1}{\cot\theta}$; $\csc\theta = \pm\cot\theta\sqrt{1+\dfrac{1}{\cot^2\theta}}$;

$\sec\theta = \pm\dfrac{\sqrt{1+\cot^2\theta}}{\cot^2\theta}$ **59.** $8.0°$ **61.** $31.0°$

63. $\begin{bmatrix} 2 & 1 & -6 \\ -1 & 1 & 1 \\ 5 & -3 & 7 \end{bmatrix}\begin{bmatrix} x \\ y \\ z \end{bmatrix} = \begin{bmatrix} -12 \\ -7 \\ 11 \end{bmatrix}$; $\left(-\dfrac{30}{11}, -\dfrac{102}{11}, -\dfrac{5}{11}\right)$,
or about $(-2.7, -9.3, -0.5)$

65. The earthquake in 1976 released about 1.4 times more energy than the one in 1985.   **67.** The earthquake in 1990 released about 89.1 times more energy than the one in 1993.   **69.** The earthquake in 1985 released about 89.1 times more energy than the one in 1994.

71.

center: $(0, 0)$; foci: $\left(0, -\sqrt{5}\right)$ and $\left(0, \sqrt{5}\right)$; vertices: $(0, -3)$ and $(0, 3)$; co-vertices: $(-2, 0)$ and $(2, 0)$

LESSON 14.4

TRY THIS (p. 910)
a. -1 **b.** $\dfrac{\sqrt{2}-\sqrt{6}}{4}$

TRY THIS (p. 911, Ex. 2)
$\sin(90° - \theta) = \sin 90° \cos\theta - \cos 90° \sin\theta$
$\qquad\qquad = 1 \cdot \cos\theta - 0 \cdot \sin\theta$
$\qquad\qquad = \cos\theta$

TRY THIS (p. 911, Ex. 3)
a. $\dfrac{\sqrt{2}-\sqrt{6}}{4}$ **b.** $\dfrac{-\sqrt{2}-\sqrt{6}}{4}$

TRY THIS (p. 912)
$y = \cos(45° - \theta)$

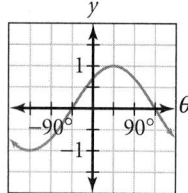

TRY THIS (p. 913)
$A'(0.13, 2.23)$; $B'(1.63, 4.83)$; $C'(3.37, 3.83)$; $D'(1.87, 1.23)$

Exercises
4. $\dfrac{\sqrt{2}-\sqrt{6}}{4}$ **5.** $\dfrac{\sqrt{2}+\sqrt{6}}{4}$

6. $-\cos(\theta + 180°) = -[\cos\theta\cos 180° - \sin\theta\sin 180°]$
$\qquad\qquad\qquad = -[\cos\theta(-1) - \sin\theta(0)]$
$\qquad\qquad\qquad = -(-\cos\theta) = \cos\theta$

7. 0 **8.** $\dfrac{\sqrt{3}}{2}$

9.

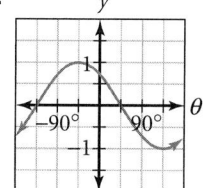

10. $A'(-1.87, 1.23)$, $B'(-3.37, 3.83)$, $C'(-1.63, 4.83)$, $D'(-0.13, 2.23)$ **11.** $\dfrac{\sqrt{2}+\sqrt{6}}{4}$ **13.** $\dfrac{-\sqrt{6}-\sqrt{2}}{4}$ **15.** $-\dfrac{\sqrt{2}}{2}$

17. $\dfrac{-\sqrt{2}+\sqrt{6}}{4}$ **19.** $\dfrac{-\sqrt{2}-\sqrt{6}}{4}$ **21.** $\dfrac{-\sqrt{6}+\sqrt{2}}{4}$

23. $\sin(90° - \theta) = \sin 90° \cos\theta - \cos 90° \sin\theta$
$\qquad\qquad = 1 \cdot \cos\theta - 0 \cdot \sin\theta = \cos\theta$

25. $\cos(90° + \theta) = \cos 90° \cos\theta - \sin 90° \sin\theta$
$\qquad\qquad = 0 \cdot \cos\theta - 1 \cdot \sin\theta = -\sin\theta$

27. $\sin(180° - \theta) = \sin 180° \cos\theta - \cos 180° \sin\theta$
$\qquad\qquad = 0 \cdot \cos\theta - (-1)\sin\theta = \sin\theta$

29. Answers may vary. Sample answer: $\sin(30° + 60°) = 1$; $\sin 30° + \sin 60° = \dfrac{1+\sqrt{3}}{2}$; So, $\sin(A + B) \neq \sin A + \sin B$.   **31.** Answers may vary. Sample answer: $\sin(60° - 30°) = \dfrac{1}{2}$; $\sin 60° - \sin 30° = \dfrac{\sqrt{3}-1}{2}$; So, $\sin(A - B) \neq \sin A - \sin B$.

33. $\dfrac{\sqrt{2}+\sqrt{6}}{4}$ **35.** $\dfrac{-\sqrt{2}-\sqrt{6}}{4}$ **37.** $\dfrac{\sqrt{6}-\sqrt{2}}{4}$ **39.** $\dfrac{-\sqrt{2}-\sqrt{6}}{4}$

41. $-\dfrac{\sqrt{2}}{2}$ **43.** $-\dfrac{\sqrt{2}}{2}$ **45.** $\begin{bmatrix} \dfrac{\sqrt{2}}{2} & -\dfrac{\sqrt{2}}{2} \\ \dfrac{\sqrt{2}}{2} & \dfrac{\sqrt{2}}{2} \end{bmatrix}$

47. $\approx \begin{bmatrix} 0.766 & 0.643 \\ -0.643 & 0.766 \end{bmatrix}$ **49.** $\begin{bmatrix} -\dfrac{1}{2} & \dfrac{\sqrt{3}}{2} \\ -\dfrac{\sqrt{3}}{2} & -\dfrac{1}{2} \end{bmatrix}$

51. $\begin{bmatrix} -\dfrac{\sqrt{2}}{2} & \dfrac{\sqrt{2}}{2} \\ -\dfrac{\sqrt{2}}{2} & -\dfrac{\sqrt{2}}{2} \end{bmatrix}$

53.

55.

57.

59. $P'\left(-\dfrac{5\sqrt{2}}{2}, -\dfrac{\sqrt{2}}{2}\right)$ **61.** $P'\left(\dfrac{\sqrt{2}}{2}, -\dfrac{5\sqrt{2}}{2}\right)$

63. $P'\left(\dfrac{-\sqrt{3}+2}{2}, \dfrac{1+2\sqrt{3}}{2}\right)$

65. $P'\left(\dfrac{10\sqrt{3}+23}{2}, \dfrac{-10+23\sqrt{3}}{2}\right)$

67. $\sin(A+B) + \sin(A-B) = \sin A \cos B +$ $\cos A \sin B + \sin A \cos B - \cos A \sin B =$ $(\sin A \cos B + \sin A \cos B) + (\cos A \sin B - \cos A \sin B) =$ $2 \sin A \cos B + 0 = 2 \sin A \cos B$ **69.** $W'(1.50, 2.60)$, $X'(-0.23, 3.60)$, $Y'(1.27, 6.20)$, $Z'(3.00, 5.20)$
71. $W'(2.60, -1.50)$, $X'(3.60, 0.23)$, $Y'(6.20, -1.27)$, $Z'(5.20, -3.00)$ **73.** $W'(-2.12, 2.12)$, $X'(-3.54, 0.71)$, $Y'(-5.66, 2.83)$, $Z'(-4.24, 4.24)$ **75.** $W'(0, -3)$, $X'(2, -3)$, $Y'(2, -6)$, $Z'(0, -6)$ **77.** $\dfrac{3\sqrt{2}}{2}(\cos t - \sin t)$
79. $f^{-1}(x) = \dfrac{7-x}{3}$ **81.** $A \approx 40.4°$, $B \approx 55.9°$, $C \approx 83.7°$

LESSON 14.5

TRY THIS (p. 918)   **TRY THIS** (p. 919)
$-\dfrac{\sqrt{15}}{8}$ $\sqrt{\dfrac{2}{3}}$

Exercises
3. $\cos^4 \theta - \sin^4 \theta = (\cos^2 \theta + \sin^2 \theta)(\cos^2 \theta - \sin^2 \theta)$
$= 1(\cos 2\theta) = \cos 2\theta$
4. $\dfrac{17}{25}$ **5.** $\dfrac{4\sqrt{21}}{25}$ **6.** $\sqrt{\dfrac{1}{2} + \dfrac{\sqrt{21}}{10}}$ **7.** $\sqrt{\dfrac{1}{2} - \dfrac{\sqrt{21}}{10}}$ **9.** $2\cos^2 \theta$
11. $\sin \theta$ **13.** $\cos \theta$
15. $4\sin \theta \cos^3 \theta - 4\sin^3 \theta \cos \theta$
17. $\cos^4 \theta - 6\sin^2 \theta \cos^2 \theta + \sin^4 \theta$ **19.** $\dfrac{\sin \theta}{2\cos \theta}$
21. $2\cos 2\theta$ **23.** $\dfrac{\sqrt{2 - \sqrt{2 + \sqrt{3}}}}{2}$ **25.** $\sin 2\theta = -\dfrac{24}{25}$;
$\cos 2\theta = \dfrac{7}{25}$ **27.** $\sin 2\theta = -\dfrac{4\sqrt{21}}{25}$; $\cos 2\theta = \dfrac{17}{25}$
29. $\sin 2\theta = \dfrac{\sqrt{15}}{8}$; $\cos 2\theta = -\dfrac{7}{8}$ **31.** $\sin 2\theta = \dfrac{\sqrt{55}}{8}$;
$\cos 2\theta = -\dfrac{3}{8}$ **33.** $\sin \dfrac{\theta}{2} = \sqrt{\dfrac{2}{5}}$; $\cos \dfrac{\theta}{2} = \sqrt{\dfrac{3}{5}}$

35. $\sin \dfrac{\theta}{2} = \sqrt{\dfrac{1}{2} + \dfrac{\sqrt{11}}{12}}$; $\cos \dfrac{\theta}{2} = \sqrt{\dfrac{1}{2} - \dfrac{\sqrt{11}}{12}}$

37. $\sin \dfrac{\theta}{2} = \sqrt{\dfrac{1}{2} + \dfrac{\sqrt{5}}{6}}$; $\cos \dfrac{\theta}{2} = \sqrt{\dfrac{1}{2} - \dfrac{\sqrt{5}}{6}}$

39. $\sin \dfrac{\theta}{2} = \sqrt{\dfrac{1}{2} - \dfrac{\sqrt{55}}{16}}$; $\cos \dfrac{\theta}{2} = -\sqrt{\dfrac{1}{2} + \dfrac{\sqrt{55}}{16}}$

41. 45°; Sample answer: The graph of the function reaches its maximum at 45°. **43.** not a function
45. 1 **47.** 286 **49.** 2730 **51.** 45

LESSON 14.6

TRY THIS (p. 923)
$\theta = 30° + n360°$ or $\theta = 150° + n360°$

TRY THIS (p. 924, Ex. 2)   **TRY THIS** (p. 924, Ex. 3)
$\theta = 45°$ or $\theta = 315°$ $\theta = 180°$

Exercises
4. $\theta = 60° + n360°$ or $\theta = 300° + n360°$ **5.** $\theta = 180°$
6. $\theta = 0°, 90°, 270°$ **7.** $\theta \approx 26.6°$ **9.** $\theta = 120° + n360°$
or $\theta = 240° + n360°$ **11.** $\theta = 60° + n360°$ or
$\theta = 300° + n360°$ **13.** $\theta = 30° + n360°$ or
$\theta = 150° + n360°$ **15.** $\theta = 180° + n360°$
17. $\theta = 135° + n360°$ or $\theta = 315° + n360°$
19. $\theta \approx 65.6° + n360°$ or $\theta \approx 114.4° + n360°$
21. $\theta = 30°, 150°, 270°$ **23.** $\theta = 120°, 240°$
25. no solution **27.** $\theta = 90°, 180°, 270°$
29. $\theta = 90°, 150°, 210°, 270°$ **31.** no solution
33. $\theta = 0°, 180°$ **35.** $\theta = 0°$ **37.** no solution
39. $\theta = 270°$ **41.** $\theta = 180°$ **43.** $\theta = 90°, 180°, 270°$
45. no solution **47.** $\theta = 0°, 120°, 180°, 240°$
49. $\theta \approx 205.2°, 334.8°$ **51.** $\theta \approx 2.33$ radians, or $\approx 133.5°$
53. $t \approx 0.2 + 2n$ or $t \approx 1.8 + 2n$ seconds
55. $\theta_{water} \approx 40.6°$ **57.** $\theta_{air} \approx 34.2°$ **59.** none
61. $b \approx 5.7$, $A \approx 83.8°$, $c \approx 69.7°$

CHAPTER REVIEW AND ASSESSMENT

1. $b \approx 14.8$, $c \approx 20.6$, $C = 100°$ **3.** $a \approx 5.1$, $b \approx 7.8$,
$C = 100°$ **5.** 0 possible triangles **7.** 2 possible
triangles: $C \approx 56.4°$, $A \approx 93.6°$, $a \approx 6.0$ or $C \approx 123.6°$,
$A \approx 26.4°$, $a \approx 2.7$ **9.** SAS; $a \approx 8.5$, $B \approx 45.0°$, $C \approx 98.0°$
11. SSS; $A \approx 93.8°$, $B \approx 29.9°$, $C \approx 56.3°$ **13.** SSA;
$B \approx 85.6°$, $C \approx 59.4°$, $b \approx 34.8$ or $B \approx 24.4°$,
$C \approx 120.6°$, $b \approx 14.4$ **15.** $\sec \theta$ **17.** $\dfrac{-3\tan^2 \theta}{2 + \tan^2 \theta}$ **19.** $-\dfrac{1}{2}$
21. $\dfrac{\sqrt{2} + \sqrt{6}}{4}$ **23.** $\dfrac{\sqrt{6} - \sqrt{2}}{4}$ **25.** $\dfrac{\sqrt{2} - \sqrt{6}}{4}$
27. $(-5.06, -5.23)$ **29.** $\dfrac{\sqrt{63}}{32}$ **31.** $\dfrac{\sqrt{7}}{4}$ **33.** $\dfrac{7}{32}$
35. $-\dfrac{\sqrt{8 + \sqrt{39}}}{4}$ **37.** $\cos^4 \theta - 6\cos^2 \theta \sin^2 \theta + \sin^4 \theta$
39. $\theta = 90°$ **41.** $\theta = 90°, 270°$ **43.** $\theta = 30°, 45°, 135°$,
150° **45.** 1516 yards **47.** 85.5°, 59.1°, 35.4°
49. 6487.7 miles

Extra Practice

CHAPTER 1

Lesson 1.1

1. linear **3.** linear **5.** linear **7.** not linear **9.** linear; (4, 21) **11.** linear; (10, 31)

13.

x	-6	-3	-1	2
y	-3	-4	-5	-6

No; there is no constant difference in the x-values.

Lesson 1.2

1. $y = -3x + 6$ **3.** $y = \frac{1}{2}$ **5.** 4 **7.** 0
9. $m = 2$; $b = 1$ **11.** $m = 0$; $b = -3$

 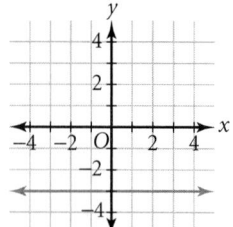

13. $y = -2x - 1$

Lesson 1.3

1. $y = 2x - 15$ **3.** $y = -11$ **5.** $y = \frac{2}{3}x + \frac{11}{3}$
7. $y = -8x - 10$ **9.** $y = -13x + 66$ **11.** $y = 5x + 7$
13. $y = -2x + 18$ **15.** $y = -\frac{3}{4}x - \frac{9}{2}$ **17.** $y = -2x$
19. $y = -\frac{1}{5}x + \frac{42}{5}$ **21.** $y = \frac{2}{5}x - \frac{21}{5}$

Lesson 1.4

1. 4; $y = 4x$ **3.** 6; $y = 6x$ **5.** $-\frac{3}{11}$; $y = -\frac{3}{11}x$ **7.** $x = 64$
9. $k = 300$ **11.** $n = \frac{16}{5}$, or 3.2 **13.** $z = 12$ **15.** $x = 9$
17. The variables are not related by a direct variation. For example, $\frac{24}{1} \neq \frac{12}{2}$. **19.** The variables are related by the direct-variation equation $y = -7x$.

Lesson 1.5

1.

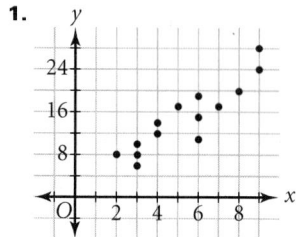

The correlation is positive; $y \approx 2.51x + 1.41$.
3. $y \approx 1.86x + 55.38$ **5.** ≈ 182 kg

Lesson 1.6

1. $x = -14$ **3.** $x = 5$ **5.** $x = 4$ **7.** $x = 40$ **9.** $x = 144$
11. $x = 4$ **13.** $x = -\frac{8}{3}$, or $-2\frac{2}{3}$ **15.** $x = 11$

17. $x = -\frac{11}{2}$, or $-5\frac{1}{2}$ **19.** $x = 1$ **21.** $x = \frac{15}{4}$, or $3\frac{3}{4}$
23. $x = 20$ **25.** $n = \frac{S}{180} + 2$ **27.** $h = \frac{3V}{B}$
29. $b = a - 2m$ **31.** $x_1 = \frac{y_1 - y_2}{m} + x_2$ **33.** $R = \frac{E}{I}$
35. $A = \frac{s^2}{R}$ **37.** $y = -5$

Lesson 1.7

1. $x < -2$ **3.** $x > -7$ **5.** $x \geq -14$

7. $x < 8$

9. $x > -8$

11. $x \geq 10$

13. $x > 4$

15. $x \leq -12$

17. $x \geq 2\frac{1}{2}$

19. $-5 \leq x < 3$

21. $-3 \leq x < 5$

23. $x < -5$ or $x \geq 1$

25. $x < -4$ or $x \geq 3$

Lesson 1.8

1. d **3.** e **5.** c **7.** $x = -2$ or $x = 4$ **9.** $x = -3$ or $x = 15$
11. $x = -1\frac{1}{2}$ or $x = 3\frac{1}{2}$ **13.** no solution **15.** $x = -2$ or $x = 1$ **17.** $x = \frac{1}{8}$ or $x = -\frac{1}{8}$
19. $-4 < x < 4$

21. $-4 \leq x \leq 8$

23. $x < 2$ or $x > 2$

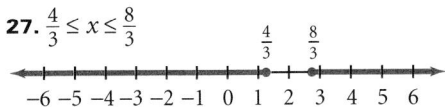

25. no solution

27. $\frac{4}{3} \le x \le \frac{8}{3}$

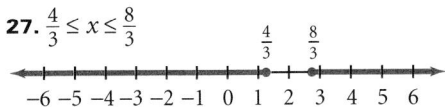

29. $x \le \frac{5}{3}$ or $x \ge 3$

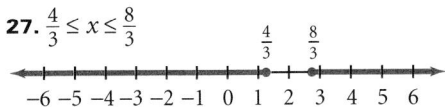

CHAPTER 2

Lesson 2.1
1. natural, whole, integer, rational, real **3.** irrational, real **5.** rational, real **7.** irrational, real
9. Commutative Property of Addition
11. Distributive Property **13.** Commutative Property of Multiplication **15.** Identity Property of Multiplication **17.** 7 **19.** 46 **21.** 25 **23.** 1 **25.** −8
27. $\frac{1}{11}$ **29.** 1 **31.** 181

Lesson 2.2
1. 12 **3.** $\frac{1}{5}$ **5.** 9 **7.** 2 **9.** 27 **11.** 10 **13.** z^2 **15.** $3b^5$
17. $-6x^3y^4$ **19.** k^2 **21.** $\frac{9}{x^8y^6}$ **23.** a^6b^8 **25.** $\frac{1}{x^8y^8}$
27. $\frac{25x^2}{c^{10}z^{12}}$

Lesson 2.3
1. Yes; no vertical line intersects the graph at more than one point. **3.** No; two different y-values are paired with the x-value −2. **5.** No; three different y-values are paired with the x-value −8.
7. domain: {−2, 3}; range: {8, 13}
9. domain: {−4, 0, 2, 4}; range: {0, 4, 16}
11. $f(-3) = 7$ and $f(1) = -1$ **13.** $f(-1) = -17$ and $f(0) = -7$ **15.** $f(10) = -6$ and $f(-2) = \frac{6}{5}$

Lesson 2.4
1. $(f + g)(x) = x^2 + 2x - 1$ **3.** $(g - f)(x) = -x^2 + 2x - 1$
5. $\left(\frac{f}{g}\right)(x) = \frac{x^2}{2x-1}, x \ne \frac{1}{2}$ **7.** $(f + g)(x) = -2x^2 + x + 1$
9. $(g - f)(x) = 2x^2 + x + 1$ **11.** $\left(\frac{f}{g}\right)(x) = -\frac{2x^2}{x+1}, x \ne -1$
13. $(f \circ g)(x) = 4x^2 - 8; (g \circ f)(x) = 16x^2 - 2$
15. $(f \circ g)(x) = -6x^2 + 9x; (g \circ f)(x) = 18x^2 + 9x$
17. −54 **19.** −18 **21.** 9

Lesson 2.5
1. {(2, 1), (2, 2), (2, 3), (2, 4)}; yes; no
3. {(6, 1), (9, 2), (12, 3), (19, 4)}; yes; yes
5. $y = \frac{x+6}{10}$ **7.** $y = 2x - 5$ **9.** $y = 6x + 2$ **11.** yes
13. yes **15.** yes

Lesson 2.6
1.

3.

5.

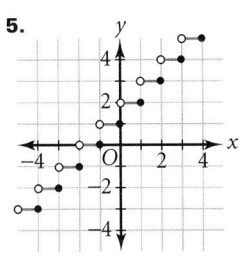

7. $f(x) = \begin{cases} -3 & \text{if } -7 \le x \le -3 \\ \frac{3}{2}x + \frac{3}{2} & \text{if } -3 < x \le 1 \end{cases}$

9. $f(x) = \begin{cases} 4 & \text{if } x < -4 \\ -x & \text{if } -4 \le x \le 4 \\ -4 & \text{if } x > -4 \end{cases}$

11. $f(x) = \begin{cases} -3 & \text{if } x < -2 \\ 3 & \text{if } -2 \le x < 2 \\ -2x + 6 & \text{if } x \ge 2 \end{cases}$

13. 15 **15.** −8 **17.** 47 **19.** 24

Lesson 2.7
1. a vertical stretch by a factor of 8 **3.** a reflection across the x-axis **5.** a vertical translation 16 units down **7.** a reflection across the y-axis and a vertical translation 13 units up **9.** a vertical stretch by a factor of 2 and a horizontal translation 3 units to the left **11.** a horizontal translation 19 units to the right
13. a horizontal compression by a factor of $\frac{1}{3}$ and a vertical stretch by a factor of 2 **15.** a vertical stretch by a factor of 24 and a vertical translation 9 units up
17. $g(x) = 10|x|$ **19.** $g(x) = 21(-x) + 17$
21. $g(x) = (x + 3.5)^2$ **23.** $g(x) = |3x|$

CHAPTER 3

Lesson 3.1

1. independent; $(-2, -6)$ **3.** dependent; infinitely many solutions **5.** independent; $(7, 3)$
7. independent; $(0, 3)$ **9.** independent; $(2, -1)$
11. independent; $(1, 1)$ **13.** $(8, -5)$ **15.** $(4, 1)$
17. $(-6, -18)$ **19.** $(14, 47)$ **21.** $(0, 4)$ **23.** $(-2, -1, 3)$

Lesson 3.2

1. $(2, 8)$ **3.** $(-1, -5)$ **5.** $(4, -3)$ **7.** no solution
9. $(-2, 2)$ **11.** $(-1, 9)$ **13.** infinitely many solutions
15. no solution **17.** $(4, 3)$

Lesson 3.3

1. **3.**

5. **7.**

9. **11.**

13. **15.**

17.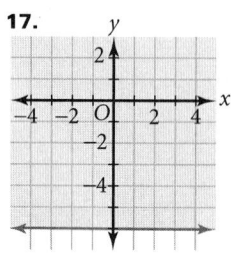

19. $y \leq -3x + 5$ **21.** $x < 4$ **23.** $y < \frac{1}{2}x + \frac{3}{2}$

Lesson 3.4

1. **3.**

5. **7.**

9. **11.**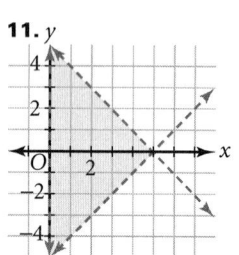

13. $\begin{cases} x \leq 3 \\ y < x + 2 \\ y > -\frac{1}{2}x - \frac{5}{2} \end{cases}$ **15.** $\begin{cases} y \leq \frac{1}{2}x + 2 \\ y > -\frac{1}{2}x \\ x < 4 \end{cases}$

Lesson 3.5

1. **3.**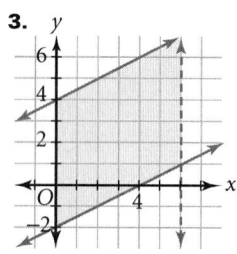

5. max = 4350; min = 0 **7.** max = 40; min = 0

Lesson 3.6

1. **3.**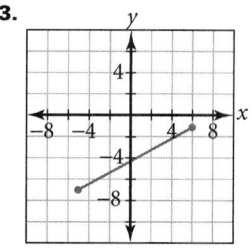

5. $y = 5 - x$ **7.** $y = 5 - x$ **9.** $y = \frac{x}{6}$

11.

13.

15.

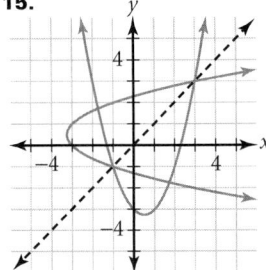

CHAPTER 4

Lesson 4.1

1. 3×3 **3.** 2×3 **5.** -6

7. $\begin{bmatrix} -2 & -3 & 2 \\ -1 & -4 & -5 \\ 0 & -1 & -7 \end{bmatrix}$ **9.** $\begin{bmatrix} -16 & 0 & -2 \\ 12 & -8 & -6 \end{bmatrix}$

11. Not possible; the matrices do not have the same dimensions.

13. $\begin{bmatrix} -4 & -1 & 0 \\ 1 & 14 & 15 \\ 2 & 5 & 5 \end{bmatrix}$ **15.** $x = 7, y = 3$

17a. $Q = \begin{bmatrix} 0 & 1 & 4 & 2 \\ 0 & 4 & 2 & 0 \end{bmatrix}$

b. $-2Q = \begin{bmatrix} 0 & -2 & -8 & -4 \\ 0 & -8 & -4 & 0 \end{bmatrix}$

c.

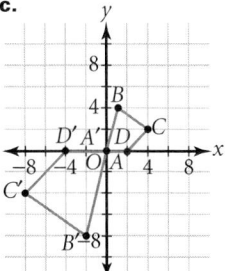

Lesson 4.2

1. $[10]$ **3.** $\begin{bmatrix} -16 & -14 \\ 12 & 8 \end{bmatrix}$ **5.** $[-6 \quad 23]$

7. $\begin{bmatrix} -1 & 7 & 4 \\ -7 & 9 & 8 \\ 12 & -12 & -12 \end{bmatrix}$ **9.** $[-41 \quad 26]$

Lesson 4.3

1. no **3.** yes **5.** -1; yes **7.** 0; no **9.** 1.4375; yes

11. $\begin{bmatrix} -3 & 8 \\ 2 & -5 \end{bmatrix}$ **13.** $\begin{bmatrix} 0.5 & -0.75 \\ -1 & 2 \end{bmatrix}$

15. $\begin{bmatrix} -4 & 1 \\ 6.5 & -1.5 \end{bmatrix}$ **17.** $\begin{bmatrix} 0.4 & 0.1 & -0.7 \\ 0.2 & 0.3 & -1.1 \\ -0.2 & 0.2 & 0.6 \end{bmatrix}$

19. $\begin{bmatrix} 7 & -1.6 & -0.53 \\ -2 & 0.8 & 0.27 \\ -9.5 & 2.2 & 1.07 \end{bmatrix}$

Lesson 4.4

1. $\begin{bmatrix} 2 & 1 \\ 5 & -3 \end{bmatrix}\begin{bmatrix} x \\ y \end{bmatrix} = \begin{bmatrix} 2 \\ -17 \end{bmatrix}$ **3.** $\begin{bmatrix} 3 & -2 \\ 1 & -4 \end{bmatrix}\begin{bmatrix} x \\ y \end{bmatrix} = \begin{bmatrix} 4 \\ 15 \end{bmatrix}$

5. $\begin{bmatrix} 2 & -3 & 1 \\ 1 & -5 & 2 \\ 4 & -1 & -1 \end{bmatrix}\begin{bmatrix} x \\ y \\ z \end{bmatrix} = \begin{bmatrix} 3 \\ 4 \\ -1 \end{bmatrix}$

7. $\begin{cases} -2x + y - z = 4 \\ 5x - y + 2z = -6 \\ 3x + 4y + z = 10 \end{cases}$ **9.** $\begin{bmatrix} 15 & -7 \\ 11 & 5 \end{bmatrix}\begin{bmatrix} x \\ y \end{bmatrix} = \begin{bmatrix} 9 \\ 37 \end{bmatrix}$; $(2, 3)$

11. $\begin{bmatrix} 2 & 1 & 1 \\ 1 & -1 & 3 \\ 0 & 1 & 1 \end{bmatrix}\begin{bmatrix} x \\ y \\ z \end{bmatrix} = \begin{bmatrix} 5 \\ -11 \\ 1 \end{bmatrix}$; $(2, 4, -3)$

13. $\begin{bmatrix} 4 & -3 & 1 \\ 2 & 1 & -3 \\ 3 & 2 & 1 \end{bmatrix}\begin{bmatrix} x \\ y \\ z \end{bmatrix} = \begin{bmatrix} 9 \\ -7 \\ 12 \end{bmatrix}$; $(2, 1, 4)$

Lesson 4.5

1. $\begin{bmatrix} 4 & -3 & \vdots & 7 \\ 2 & -1 & \vdots & 5 \end{bmatrix}$ **3.** $\begin{bmatrix} 6 & -1 & 1 & \vdots & 6 \\ 3 & 4 & -1 & \vdots & 3 \\ 9 & -3 & 2 & \vdots & 9 \end{bmatrix}$

5. $\begin{bmatrix} 1 & 0 & 2 & \vdots & -3.8 \\ 0 & 1 & 0 & \vdots & 5 \\ 0 & 0 & 1 & \vdots & 0.4 \end{bmatrix}$ **7.** $\left(\frac{1}{2}, 2\right)$ **9.** $(2, -5)$

11. $(4, 2, 0)$ **13.** dependent **15.** inconsistent

CHAPTER 5

Lesson 5.1

1. $f(x) = x^2 - 6x - 7$; $a = 1, b = -6, c = -7$
3. $f(x) = 2x^2 - 7x - 4$; $a = 2, b = -7, c = -4$
5. $f(x) = 2x^2 - 3x - 35$; $a = 2, b = -3, c = -35$
7. yes **9.** no **11.** down; maximum **13.** up; minimum **15.** $(-1, 3)$ **17.** $(0, 5)$
19. $(-0.25, -0.0625)$

Lesson 5.2

1. $\pm\sqrt{51} \approx \pm 7.14$ **3.** $\pm\sqrt{13} \approx \pm 3.61$ **5.** $\pm\dfrac{\sqrt{182}}{7} \approx \pm 1.93$

7. $q \approx 19.4$ **9.** $z \approx 23.6$ **11.** $b \approx 25.0$ **13.** $a \approx 15.4$

15. $c \approx 14.2$

Lesson 5.3

1. $7(x + 7)$ **3.** $4x(x - 7)$ **5.** $(14 + x)(3 - x^2)$

7. $-3x^2(x + 4)$ **9.** $(x + 7)^2$ **11.** $(x + 3)(x + 14)$

13. $(3x + 2)(x + 2)$ **15.** $(3 - 2x)(x - 1)$ **17.** ± 12

19. $\pm\dfrac{5}{4}$ **21.** $\dfrac{1}{3}$ **23.** 0 or 12 **25.** -9 or 0.5 **27.** 5 or 7

Lesson 5.4

1. $x^2 + x + \dfrac{1}{4}; \left(x + \dfrac{1}{2}\right)^2$ **3.** $x^2 - 10x + 25; (x - 5)^2$

5. $x^2 - 9x + \dfrac{81}{4}; \left(x - \dfrac{9}{2}\right)^2$ **7.** $x^2 - 22x + 121; (x - 11)^2$

9. $x^2 - 0.5x + 0.0625; (x - 0.25)^2$ **11.** $-1 \pm 2\sqrt{2}$

13. $4 \pm 2\sqrt{7}$ **15.** $8 \pm \sqrt{85}$ **17.** $-\dfrac{3}{2} \pm \dfrac{\sqrt{53}}{2}$ **19.** $2 \pm \dfrac{\sqrt{46}}{2}$

21. $-\dfrac{1}{2} \pm \dfrac{\sqrt{13}}{2}$ **23.** $f(x) = x^2 + (-3); (0, -3)$

25. $f(x) = [x - (-2)]^2 + (-4); (-2, -4)$

27. $f(x) = [x - (-3)]^2 + (-4); (-3, -4)$

29. $f(x) = 2[x - (-1)]^2 + (-5); (-1, -5)$

Lesson 5.5

1. 3 or 5 **3.** $\dfrac{5 \pm \sqrt{21}}{2}$ **5.** 1 or 9 **7.** $1 \pm 2\sqrt{2}$ **9.** $\dfrac{-1 \pm \sqrt{69}}{2}$

11. $\dfrac{1 \pm \sqrt{57}}{7}$ **13.** $-2 \pm \sqrt{13}$ **15.** $\dfrac{1 \pm \sqrt{57}}{2}$

17. $x = -2; (-2, -15)$ **19.** $x = -\dfrac{3}{4}; \left(-\dfrac{3}{4}, -6\dfrac{1}{8}\right)$

21. $x = -\dfrac{1}{2}; \left(-\dfrac{1}{2}, -9\dfrac{1}{4}\right)$ **23.** $x = -\dfrac{2}{3}; \left(-\dfrac{2}{3}, 3\dfrac{1}{3}\right)$

25. $x = -\dfrac{1}{4}; \left(-\dfrac{1}{4}, -1\dfrac{1}{4}\right)$ **27.** $x = \dfrac{3}{2}; \left(\dfrac{3}{2}, -1\dfrac{3}{4}\right)$

29. $x = \dfrac{3}{8}; \left(\dfrac{3}{8}, -5\dfrac{9}{16}\right)$

Lesson 5.6

1. 29; 2 solutions; $\dfrac{3}{2} \pm \dfrac{\sqrt{29}}{2}$ **3.** -19; 0 solutions;

$\dfrac{7}{2} \pm \dfrac{i\sqrt{19}}{2}$ **5.** -80; 0 solutions; $\dfrac{1}{4} \pm \dfrac{i\sqrt{5}}{4}$ **7.** -140;

0 solutions; $\dfrac{1}{4} \pm \dfrac{i\sqrt{35}}{4}$ **9.** 60; 2; $-1 \pm \dfrac{\sqrt{15}}{3}$

11. $13 + 5i$ **13.** $3i + 4$ **15.** $-3i$ **17.** $5 + 2i$ **19.** $1 + 9i$

21. $-11 - i$ **23.** 30 **25.** $-27 + 36i$ **27.** $29 - 29i$

29. $5 - 14i$ **31.** $\dfrac{7}{5} - \dfrac{4i}{5}$ **33.** $-\dfrac{26 - 2i}{17}$ **35.** $\dfrac{3}{2} - 2i$

37. $77 - 36i$ **39.** $-9 - 40i$

41. *Imaginary*

43. *Imaginary*

45. *Imaginary*

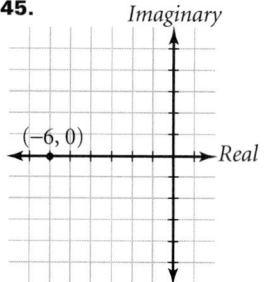

Lesson 5.7

1. $f(x) = x^2 + 2$ **3.** $f(x) = x^2 + 7x - 1$

5. $f(x) = x^2 + x + 6$ **7.** $f(x) = x^2 - 18x - 59$

9. $f(x) = 0.5x^2 + 3x - 1$ **11.** $f(x) = -x^2 + 4x$

13. $f(x) = 0.25x^2 - 0.5x + 1$ **15.** $f(x) = -0.5x^2 + x + 12$

17. $f(x) = -16x^2 + 60x + 4$ **19.** about 3.8 seconds

Lesson 5.8

1. $-3 < x < 3$

3. $-9 \le x \le -2$

5. $x < -4$ or $x > 3$

7. $x = 4$

9. $x < -1$ or $x > 7$

11. $\dfrac{3}{2} - \dfrac{\sqrt{29}}{2} \le x \le \dfrac{3}{2} + \dfrac{\sqrt{29}}{2}$

13.

C

15.

C

17.

19.

21.

23.

25.

27.

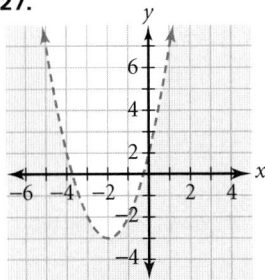

CHAPTER 6

Lesson 6.1
1. 1.03 **3.** 0.9 **5.** 1.007 **7.** 1.18 **9.** 1.0004 **11.** 1.0115
13. 2.828 **15.** 3.750 **17.** 5.278 **19.** 0.094 **21.** 153.53
milligrams **23.** 520,000

Lesson 6.2
1. quadratic **3.** quadratic **5.** linear **7.** exponential
growth **9.** exponential decay **11.** exponential decay
13. exponential decay **15.** exponential decay
17. \$2156.90 **19.** \$588.38 **21.** \$696.13 **23.** \$4442.81

Lesson 6.3
1. $\log_3 81 = 4$ **3.** $\log_{\frac{1}{2}} \frac{1}{128} = 7$ **5.** $\log_{\left(\frac{1}{3}\right)} 81 = -4$
7. $\log_5 \frac{1}{125} = -3$ **9.** $\log_9 \frac{1}{81} = -2$ **11.** $7^4 = 2401$
13. $6^{-4} = \frac{1}{1296}$ **15.** $2^8 = 256$ **17.** $10^{-4} = 0.0001$
19. $x \approx 1.18$ **21.** $x \approx 0.65$ **23.** $x \approx 3.02$ **25.** $x \approx -0.08$
27. $x \approx 1.15$ **29.** $v = 0$ **31.** $v = 625$ **33.** $v = \frac{1}{64}$
35. $v = 5$

Lesson 6.4
1. $\log_3 9 + \log_3 x = 2 + \log_3 x$
3. $\log_4 2 + \log_4 3 + \log_4 4 = 1.5 + \log_4 3$
5. $\log_5 4 - \log_5 5 = \log_5 4 - 1$ **7.** $\log_2 21$ **9.** $\log_4 \frac{25}{6}$
11. $\log_5 5 = 1$ **13.** 0 **15.** 89 **17.** -1 **19.** $x = 3$
21. no solution **23.** $x = 8$ **25.** $x = 2$

Lesson 6.5
1. 5.67 **3.** -0.39 **5.** 1.20 **7.** -0.71 **9.** -0.47 **11.** 0.79
13. -0.23 **15.** 5.81 **17.** -0.53 **19.** 12.32 **21.** -0.13
23. $x \approx 2.11$ **25.** $x \approx 1.81$ **27.** $x \approx 3.38$ **29.** $x \approx 2.23$
31. $x \approx 3.09$ **33.** $x \approx 1.99$ **35.** $x \approx 0.10$ **37.** $x \approx 1.47$
39. $x \approx 1.66$ **41.** $x \approx 1.88$

Lesson 6.6
1. 20.086 **3.** 90.017 **5.** 5.652 **7.** 0.973 **9.** not defined
11. -0.223 **13.** $\ln 25.03 \approx 3.22$ **15.** $e^{3.91} \approx 50$
17. $\ln 29.96 \approx 3.4$ **19.** $e^{3.22} \approx 25$ **21.** $\ln 1.95 \approx \frac{2}{3}$
23. $e^{-1.39} \approx \frac{1}{4}$ **25.** $x \approx 1.22$ **27.** $x \approx -2.46$
29. $x \approx -2.93$ **31.** $x \approx 2.20$ **33.** $x \approx 6.01$ **35.** $x \approx 4.91$
37. \$6920.15

Lesson 6.7

1. $x = 5$ **3.** $x = 5$ **5.** $x = 3$ **7.** $x = 2$ **9.** $x = \frac{\ln 4}{\ln 3} \approx 1.26$

11. $x = 1 + \log 121 \approx 3.08$ **13.** $x = \frac{1}{2}(1 + \ln 9) \approx 1.60$

15. no solution **17.** $x = \frac{1}{3}(4 - \ln 22) \approx 0.30$

19. 10^{22} ergs

CHAPTER 7

Lesson 7.1

1. yes; 3 **3.** no **5.** yes; 4 **7.** -28 **9.** 14 **11.** 272

13. $3x^3 + 6x^2 - 3x + 16$; cubic polynomial

15. $8.1x^3 - 9x^2 + 3.5x - 20$; cubic polynomial

17. $3x^5 - 4x^4 - x^3 + 5x^2 + 7$; quintic polynomial

19. S-shape **21.** W-shape

Lesson 7.2

1. local maximum of 3.1 **3.** local maximum of 0; local minima of -1.1 and -0.1 **5.** local maximum of 0.1; local minimum of 0; increasing for $-6 < x < -0.7$ and $0 < x < 6$, decreasing for $-0.7 < x < 0$ **7.** local maxima of 0.1 and 4.5; local minimum of 0; increasing for $-4 < x < -0.3$ and $0 < x < 1.5$, decreasing for $-0.3 < x < 0$ and $1.5 < x < 4$ **9.** local maximum of 16.6; local minimum of -8.6; increasing for $x < -3.2$ and $x > 3.2$, decreasing for $-3.2 < x < 3.2$ **11.** rises on the left, falls on the right **13.** rises on the left and the right **15.** $f(x) = 3.83x^4 - 44.15x^3 + 156.86x^2 + 112.93x + 15{,}833.87$

Lesson 7.3

1. $-10x^7 + 6x^6 - 4x^4 - 12x^3$ **3.** $x^3 - 3x^2 - 23x + 30$

5. $8x^3 - 12x^2 + 6x - 1$ **7.** yes **9.** no **11.** $x^2 - x + 4$

13. $3x^2 + 2x - 4$ **15.** $x^2 - 2x - 8$ **17.** $5x^2 - 2x + 3$

19. -16 **21.** -86

Lesson 7.4

1. $0, -5, 2$ **3.** $0, 7$ (multiplicity 2) **5.** $-2, 0, 1$ **7.** -2 and 2 (multiplicity 2) **9.** $-1, -2$, and 5 **11.** $-1, 2$, and 3 **13.** $-3, 3, -\sqrt{5}$, and $\sqrt{5}$ **15.** $-1, 1, -2\sqrt{3}$, and $2\sqrt{3}$ **17.** $-\sqrt{11}, \sqrt{11}, -\sqrt{3}$, and $\sqrt{3}$ **19.** 0 **21.** -2.21, 0.54, and 1.68

Lesson 7.5

1. $\frac{2}{3}$ and 4 **3.** $\frac{1}{2}, \frac{3}{5}$, and 2 **5.** $-\frac{3}{4}, 1$, and 2

7. $-1 - \sqrt{2}, -1 + \sqrt{2}$, and 3 **9.** $2, -i\sqrt{7}$, and $i\sqrt{7}$

11. $-2\sqrt{2}, 2\sqrt{2}, -i\sqrt{3}$, and $i\sqrt{3}$ **13.** -0.87 and 0.63

15. 0.86 and 2.07

17. $P(x) = (x + 1)(x - 1)(x - 2) = x^3 - 2x^2 - x + 2$

19. $P(x) = 16\left(x - \frac{1}{2}\right)^2\left(x - \frac{3}{2}\right)\left(x + \frac{3}{2}\right)$
$= 16x^4 - 16x^3 - 32x^2 + 36x - 9$

21. $P(x) = 2(x - 2)(x - 3i)(x + 3i)$
$= 2x^3 - 4x^2 + 18x - 36$

CHAPTER 8

Lesson 8.1

1. $y = \frac{144}{x}$; 36, 16, 9.6, 7.2 **3.** $y = \frac{1.6}{x}$; 16, 8, 0.4, 0.2

5. $y = 1.5xz$; 40.5 **7.** $y = -3xz$; 7.2 **9.** $z = \frac{5.5xy}{w}$; 19.8

11. $z = \frac{-1.25xy}{w}$; -0.125 **13.** 450; $t = \frac{450}{r}$; 11.3, 10, 9, and 8.2 hours

Lesson 8.2

1. yes; all real numbers except -2 and -5 **3.** yes; all real numbers except -3 and 3 **5.** vertical asymptotes: $x = -\sqrt{3}, x = \sqrt{3}$; horizontal asymptote: $y = 0$ **7.** vertical asymptote: $x = 4$; no horizontal asymptotes; hole when $x = -3$ **9.** no vertical asymptotes; no horizontal asymptotes; hole when $x = 3$ **11.** vertical asymptote: $x = \frac{1}{2}$; horizontal asymptote: $y = \frac{1}{2}$; hole when $x = 2$

13. all real numbers except 4; vertical asymptote: $x = 4$; horizontal asymptote: $y = 1$; no holes

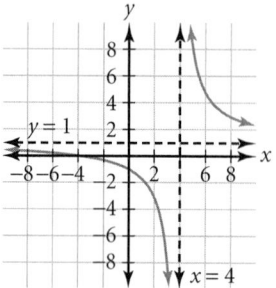

15. all real numbers except -3 and -5; vertical asymptote: $x = -5$; horizontal asymptote: $y = 0$; hole when $x = -3$

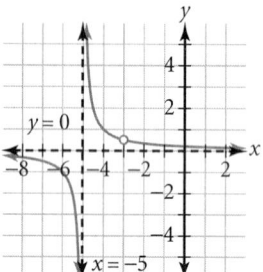

17. all real numbers except -2; vertical asymptote: $x = -2$; horizontal asymptote: $y = 1$; no holes

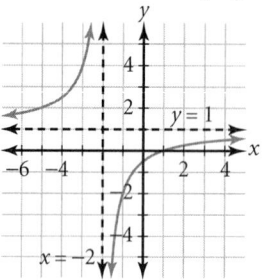

Lesson 8.3

1. x^2 **3.** $\frac{x + 6}{x - 3}$ **5.** $-\frac{x + 2}{x - 2}$ **7.** $\frac{5x^2}{2x - 1}$ **9.** $-\frac{4x}{5x - 25}$

11. $-\dfrac{2x+1}{x-1}$ **13.** $\dfrac{x+7}{x-10}$ **15.** $\dfrac{x+7}{x-1}$ **17.** $\dfrac{2}{x+5}$ **19.** $-\dfrac{1}{x+1}$

21. $-\dfrac{x-10}{4x-20}$

Lesson 8.4

1. $\dfrac{x}{2x+5}$ **3.** $\dfrac{x-3}{12}$ **5.** $\dfrac{2x+1}{x-8}$ **7.** $\dfrac{x-6}{x^2+4x-12}$

9. $-\dfrac{6x^2+6x+7}{3x^2-13x-10}$ **11.** $\dfrac{7}{2x}$ **13.** $-\dfrac{17}{6x+12}$ **15.** $\dfrac{2x^2+6}{x^2-x-12}$

17. 3 **19.** $\dfrac{3x+1}{x+5}$

Lesson 8.5

1. $x=6$ **3.** $x=12$ **5.** $x=5$ **7.** $x=1$ **9.** $\dfrac{1}{5}$ or 5 **11.** 4

13. -1 **15.** 4 or $\dfrac{2}{3}$ **17.** $-2 < x < 0$ **19.** $x < -\dfrac{2}{5}$ or $x > \dfrac{2}{3}$

21. $x < \dfrac{3}{2}$ or $x > \dfrac{23}{9}$ **23.** $0 < x < 1$ **25.** $-1 < x < 2$ or $x > 4$

27. $x \le -1.8$ or $x \ge 1.8$ **29.** $-1 < x \le 1.1$ or $x > 6$

Lesson 8.6

1. $-\dfrac{9}{5}$ **3.** 192 **5.** $\dfrac{16}{3}$ **7.** $-\dfrac{1}{16}$ **9.** 6 **11.** 2

13. $x \le -4$ or $x \ge 4$ **15.** $x \ge 1$ **17.** all real numbers

19. $y = -\sqrt{x-4},\ y = \sqrt{x-4}$

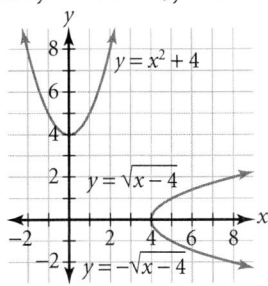

21. $y = -2 - \sqrt{x+4},\ y = -2 + \sqrt{x+4}$

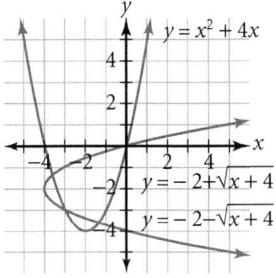

23. $y = 3 - \sqrt{x},\ y = 3 + \sqrt{x}$

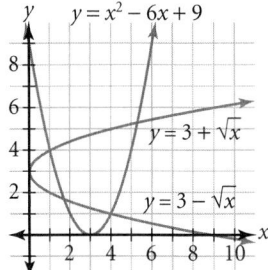

25. 23.4 mph; 33.1 mph; 46.8 mph

Lesson 8.7

1. $5\sqrt{5}$ **3.** $2x^2z^2\sqrt[4]{5z^2}$ **5.** $5|xy|\sqrt{3yz}$ **7.** $3x$ **9.** $8x^3z^4\sqrt{xz}$

11. $2yz\sqrt[3]{xyz}$ **13.** $2x^3\sqrt[4]{2}$ **15.** $2x\sqrt[4]{10x^3}$ **17.** $8 - \sqrt{5}$

19. $11 - 7\sqrt{2}$ **21.** $12\sqrt{15} + 72\sqrt{2}$ **23.** $30\sqrt{2} - 5\sqrt{6}$

25. $46 - 14\sqrt{6}$ **27.** 3 **29.** $\dfrac{-3\sqrt{6} - 3\sqrt{2}}{4}$ **31.** $5 - 2\sqrt{6}$

33. $\dfrac{6x + 8\sqrt{xy}}{9x - 16y}$

Lesson 8.8

1. $x = 14$ **3.** no solution **5.** $x = 10$ **7.** $x = 1$ **9.** 5

11. $0 \le x < 4.5$ **13.** $-1 \le x \le 5$ **15.** $\dfrac{2}{3} \le x \le 2$ **17.** $x > 30$

19. $x \ge 2.4$ **21.** $x \ge \dfrac{1}{3}$ **23.** $x = 2.9$

CHAPTER 9

Lesson 9.1

1. circle **3.** hyperbola **5.** hyperbola **7.** ellipse

9. hyperbola **11.** $2\sqrt{13} \approx 7.21;\ M(4, 1)$

13. $2\sqrt{13} \approx 7.21;\ M(2, 4)$ **15.** $2\sqrt{6} \approx 4.90;$

$M(2\sqrt{2}, 2) \approx M(2.83, 2)$ **17.** $\left(\dfrac{13}{2}, -8\right);\ 25\pi;\ 156.25\pi$

19. $(6, 0);\ 16\pi\sqrt{2};\ 128\pi$ **21.** $(11, 17);\ 2\pi\sqrt{170};\ 170\pi$

Lesson 9.2

1. $y = \dfrac{1}{2}x^2$ **3.** $y - 2 = -\dfrac{1}{12}(x - 3)^2$

5.

7.

9.

11.

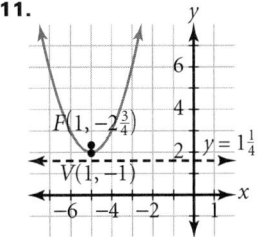

13. $x = \dfrac{1}{60}y^2$ **15.** $y - 2 = \dfrac{1}{24}x^2$ **17.** $y - \dfrac{1}{2} = \dfrac{1}{2}(x - 1)^2$

19. $y - 8 = -2(x - 1)^2$

Lesson 9.3

1. $(x - 4)^2 + (y - 2)^2 = 4$ **3.** $(x + 1)^2 + (y - 3)^2 = \dfrac{49}{4}$

5. $x^2 + y^2 = 20.25$ **7.** $(x - 8)^2 + (y + 2)^2 = 25;\ r = 5;$
$C(8, -2)$ **9.** $(x - 10)^2 + (y - 5)^2 = 64;\ r = 8;\ C(10, 5)$

11.

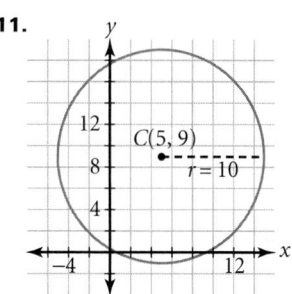

13. outside

Lesson 9.4

1. $\frac{x^2}{4} + \frac{y^2}{16} = 1$ **3.** $\frac{(x+1)^2}{4} + \frac{(y-1)^2}{9} = 1$ **5.** $x^2 + \frac{y^2}{49} = 1$; center: $(0, 0)$ vertices: $(0, -7)$ and $(0, 7)$; co-vertices: $(-1, 0)$ and $(1, 0)$; foci: $(0, -4\sqrt{3})$ and $(0, 4\sqrt{3})$

7. $\frac{(x-1)^2}{9} + y^2 = 1$; center: $(1, 0)$; vertices: $(-2, 0)$ and $(4, 0)$; co-vertices: $(1, 1)$ and $(1, -1)$; foci: $(1 - 2\sqrt{2}, 0)$ and $(1 + 2\sqrt{2}, 0)$ **9.** $\frac{(x-8)^2}{4} + \frac{(y-1)^2}{9} = 1$; center: $(8, 1)$; vertices: $(8, -2)$ and $(8, 4)$; co-vertices: $(6, 1)$ and $(10, 1)$; foci: $(8, 1 - \sqrt{5})$ and $(8, 1 + \sqrt{5})$ **11.** $\frac{x^2}{16} + \frac{y^2}{7} = 1$

13.

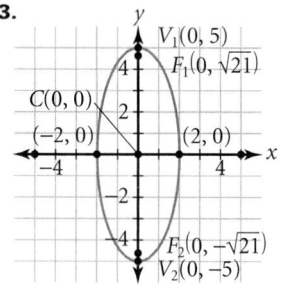

Lesson 9.5

1. $\frac{x^2}{16} - \frac{y^2}{4} = 1$ **3.** $\frac{x^2}{100} - y^2 = 1$; center: $(0, 0)$; vertices: $(-10, 0)$ and $(10, 0)$; co-vertices: $(0, -1)$ and $(0, 1)$; foci: $(\sqrt{101}, 0)$ and $(-\sqrt{101}, 0)$

5. $\frac{(x-1)^2}{4} - \frac{(y-1)^2}{9} = 1$; center: $(1, 1)$; vertices: $(-1, 1)$ and $(3, 1)$ co-vertices: $(1, -2)$ and $(1, 4)$; foci: $(1 + \sqrt{13}, 1)$ and $(1 - \sqrt{13}, 1)$ **7.** $\frac{y^2}{144} - \frac{x^2}{121} = 1$

9.

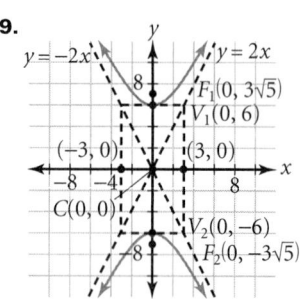

11. $\frac{(x-3)^2}{36} - \frac{(y-4)^2}{25} = 1$

Lesson 9.6

1. $(-3, 10)$ and $(2, 5)$ **3.** $(-4, 0)$ and $(5, \frac{3}{4})$ **5.** none

7. $(-2, -3.46)$, $(-2, 3.46)$, $(2, -3.46)$, and $(2, 3.46)$

9. $(-2.41, -2.39)$, $(-2.41, 2.39)$, $(2.41, -2.39)$, and $(2.41, 2.39)$

11. circle; $(x-3)^2 + (y-5)^2 = 36$

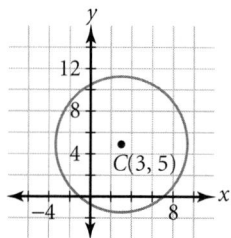

13. ellipse; $\frac{(x-4)^2}{4} + \frac{(y-4)^2}{9} = 1$

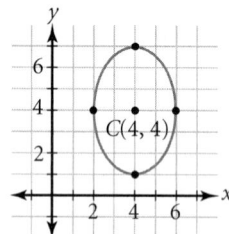

15. ellipse; $\frac{(x+2)^2}{25} + \frac{(y+1)^2}{4} = 1$

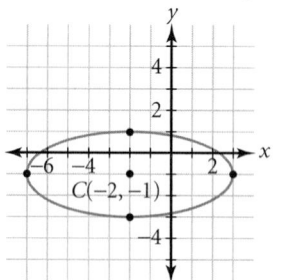

CHAPTER 10

Lesson 10.1

1. $\frac{1}{5} = 20\%$ **3.** $\frac{2}{3} \approx 67\%$ **5.** $\frac{1}{4} = 25\%$ **7.** $\frac{53}{125} = 42.4\%$
9. $\frac{8}{25} = 32\%$ **11.** 15,625 **13.** 100

Lesson 10.2

1. 720 **3.** 665,280 **5.** 120 **7.** 120 **9.** 40,320 **11.** 360
13. about 8.7×10^{10} **15.** 120

Lesson 10.3

1. 10 **3.** 56 **5.** 120 **7.** 1 **9.** about 43%
11. permutation **13.** combination

Lesson 10.4

1. mutually exclusive; $\frac{2}{13} \approx 15\%$ **3.** inclusive; $\frac{25}{26} \approx 96\%$
5. mutually exclusive; $1 = 100\%$ **7.** $\frac{1}{2} = 50\%$
9. $\frac{2}{3} \approx 67\%$ **11.** $\frac{3}{5} = 60\%$ **13.** $\frac{4}{5} = 80\%$

Lesson 10.5

1. $\frac{1}{8} = 12.5\%$ **3.** $0.08 = 8\%$ **5.** $0.04 = 4\%$
7. $\frac{25}{36} \approx 69.4\%$ **9.** $1 = 100\%$ **11.** $0.1 = 10\%$
13. $0.25 = 25\%$ **15.** $\frac{1}{9} \approx 11.1\%$

Lesson 10.6

1. $\frac{7}{48} \approx 14.6\%$ **3.** $\frac{7}{48} \approx 14.6\%$ **5.** $\frac{1}{6} \approx 17\%$ **7.** $\frac{1}{3} \approx 33\%$
9. $\frac{1}{2} = 50\%$ **11.** $\frac{1}{6} \approx 17\%$ **13.** $1 = 100\%$ **15.** $\frac{1}{2} = 50\%$
17. $\frac{1}{3} \approx 33\%$ **19.** $1 = 100\%$ **21.** $0.4 = 40\%$

Lesson 10.7

Simulation results may vary.
1. about 38% **3.** about 7% **5.** about 33%
7. about 50% **9.** about 54% **11.** about 22%

CHAPTER 11

Lesson 11.1

1. 5, 2, −1, −4, −7 **3.** 2, 8, 18, 32, 50 **5.** 16, 10, 4, −2, −8 **7.** $t_1 = 1$, $t_n = t_{n-1} + 9$; 37, 46, 55 **9.** $t_1 = 4$, $t_n = t_{n-1} + 5(n-1)$; 54, 79, 109 **11.** 0, 1, 4, 9, 16; 30
13. 105 **15.** 34

Lesson 11.2

1. no **3.** no **5.** yes; 1.1 **7.** $t_n = 3n + 2$ **9.** $t_n = 6n + 4$
11. $t_n = 4n - 16$ **13.** 5, 16, 27, 38 **15.** 0, 20, 40, 60
17. −12, −20, −28, −36 **19.** 11, 17, and 23
21. 9.6 and 12.7

Lesson 11.3

1. 45 **3.** 810 **5.** 15,400 **7.** 14,560 **9.** 1010 **11.** −4200
13. $590\sqrt{7} \approx 1561$ **15.** 532 **17.** 300 **19.** 2550

Lesson 11.4

1. yes; $\frac{1}{2}$; $\frac{3}{4}, \frac{3}{8}, \frac{3}{16}$ **3.** yes; 3; −162, −486, −1458 **5.** no **7.** 5, 1, 0.2, 0.04 **9.** −2, 9, −40.5, 182.25 **11.** 3.5
13. $t_n = 0.04 \cdot 5^{n-1}$ **15.** $t_n = 6^{\frac{n}{2}}$, or $\left(\sqrt{6}\right)^n$ **17.** 9.6 and 14.4 **19.** 20, 50, and 125 or −20, 150, and −125

Lesson 11.5

1. 3069 **3.** $\frac{189}{128} \approx 1.5$ **5.** 437.4 **7.** 656 **9.** 19,664
11. 110,341.5 **13.** $\frac{1}{2} = 1 - \frac{1}{2}$, so the statement is true for $n = 1$. Assume that the statement is true for an integer k. Then $\frac{1}{2} + \frac{1}{2^2} + \frac{1}{2^3} + \cdots + \frac{1}{2^k} = 1 - \frac{1}{2^k}$ and $\frac{1}{2} + \frac{1}{2^2} + \frac{1}{2^3} + \cdots + \frac{1}{2^k} + \frac{1}{2^{k+1}} = 1 - \frac{1}{2^k} + \frac{1}{2^{k+1}} = 1 - \left(\frac{1}{2^k} - \frac{1}{2^{k+1}}\right) = 1 - \left(\frac{2}{2^{k+1}} - \frac{1}{2^{k+1}}\right) = 1 - \frac{1}{2^{k+1}}$ and the statement is true for $k + 1$

Lesson 11.6

1. $\frac{1}{4}$ **3.** none **5.** none **7.** $-\frac{1}{3} \approx -0.33$ **9.** $\frac{7}{9}$ **11.** $\frac{107}{333}$
13. $\sum_{k=1}^{\infty} 31\left(\frac{1}{100}\right)^k$ **15.** $\sum_{k=1}^{\infty} 357\left(\frac{1}{1000}\right)^k$

Lesson 11.7

1. third entry, row 4; 6 **3.** fourth entry, row 8; 56
5. eighth entry, row 10; 120 **7.** ninth entry, row 11; 165
9. 70; 8 **11.** 715; 1716 **13.** 0.25 **15.** 0.5 **17.** about 0.57 **19.** about 0.36

Lesson 11.8

1. $a^4 + 4a^3b + 6a^2b^2 + 4ab^3 + b^4$
3. $c^6 + 6c^5d + 15c^4d^2 + 20c^3d^3 + 15c^2d^4 + 6cd^5 + d^6$
5. $y^5 + 10y^4 + 40y^3 + 80y^2 + 80y + 32$ **7.** 13 terms
9. $32x^5 + 80x^4y + 80x^3y^2 + 40x^2y^3 + 10xy^4 + y^5$
11. $x^4 - 8x^3y + 24x^2y^2 - 32xy^3 + 16y^4$
13. $\frac{1}{8}x^3 + \frac{3}{2}x^2y + 6xy^2 + 8y^3$ **15.** about 0.01
17. about 0.30

CHAPTER 12

Lesson 12.1

1. 28.1; 25.5; no mode **3.** 11.225; 12.55; 12.6
5. 30,100; 29,300; 35,700; sample answer: The mode is too high, but the mean and median are reasonable values to describe the data.

7.

Number of days	Tally	Frequency
0	THL	5
1	IIII	4
2	II	2
3	II	2
4	I	1
5	III	3
8	I	1
10	I	1
22	I	1

mean: 3.65

9.

Score	Class mean	Freq.	Product
50–59	54.5	2	109
60–69	64.5	3	193.5
70–79	74.5	7	521.5
80–89	84.5	5	422.5
90–99	94.5	3	283.5

estimated mean: 76.5

Lesson 12.2

1.

Stem	Leaf 3|0 = 30
1	2, 2, 5, 6
2	2, 5, 6
3	0, 2, 3
4	0, 3, 6, 7

28; 12; flat-shaped

3.

Number	Frequency
1	2
2	5
3	4
4	2
5	6
6	4
7	5

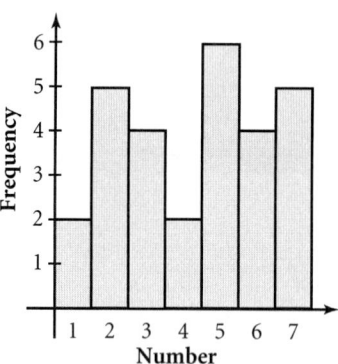

5.

Number	Frequency	Rel. Freq.
20	2	10%
21	4	20%
22	5	25%
23	3	15%
24	2	10%
25	4	20%

7a.

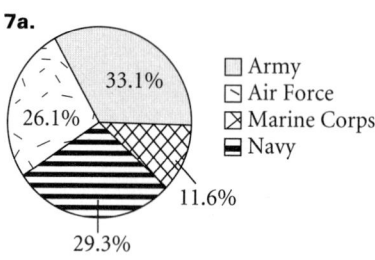

☐ Army
☐ Air Force
☒ Marine Corps
▤ Navy

33.1%
26.1%
11.6%
29.3%

b. 0.41

Lesson 12.3

1. min = 7; Q_1 = 13; Q_2 = 18; Q_3 = 27; max = 35; range = 28; IQR = 14

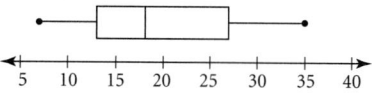

3. min = 168; Q_1 = 210; Q_2 = 281; Q_3 = 312; max = 715; range = 547; IQR = 102

5. min = 3.2; Q_1 = 5.7; Q_2 = 6.6; Q_3 = 7.7; max = 12.3; range = 9.1; IQR = 2

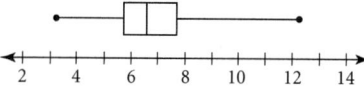

7. They are about the same.

Lesson 12.4

1. 6; 1.5 **3.** 11; 2.7 **5.** 37; 13.9 **7.** 71.04; about 8.4
9. 738.3; about 27.2 **11.** 9.7; about 3.1
13. 305; about 94.5

Lesson 12.5

1. 31.25% **3.** 18.75% **5.** 18.75% **7.** about 3.2%
9. about 3.5% **11.** about 18.5% **13.** about 19.8%
15. about 22.8%

Lesson 12.6

1. 0.6554 **3.** 0.0449 **5.** 0.4986 **7.** ≈0.02 **9.** ≈0.68
11. about 160 **13.** about 820

CHAPTER 13

Lesson 13.1

1. $\frac{20}{29}$; 0.6897 **3.** $\frac{21}{29}$; 0.7241 **5.** $\frac{20}{21}$; 0.9524 **7.** $\frac{29}{20}$; 1.45
9. $\frac{29}{21}$; 1.3810 **11.** $\frac{21}{20}$; 1.05 **13.** $m\angle G$ = 53°; GI ≈ 2.6; GH ≈ 4.4 **15.** JK ≈ 14.4; $m\angle J$ ≈ 56°; $m\angle K$ ≈ 34°
17. $m\angle M$ = 64°; MN ≈ 22.1; NO ≈ 19.9

Lesson 13.2

1. −246° **3.** 307° **5.** 152°, −208° **7.** 63° **9.** 56° **11.** 65°
13–17. Answers are given in order as follows: sin, cos, tan, csc, sec, cot.
13. $\frac{2\sqrt{5}}{5}$; $\frac{\sqrt{5}}{5}$; 2; $\frac{\sqrt{5}}{2}$; $\sqrt{5}$; $\frac{1}{2}$
15. $-\frac{8\sqrt{73}}{73}$; $\frac{3\sqrt{73}}{73}$; $-\frac{8}{3}$; $-\frac{\sqrt{73}}{8}$; $\frac{\sqrt{73}}{3}$; $-\frac{3}{8}$
17. $-\frac{3}{5}$; $-\frac{4}{5}$; $\frac{3}{4}$; $-\frac{5}{3}$; $-\frac{5}{4}$; $\frac{4}{3}$ **19.** $\frac{1}{2}$ **21.** $-\frac{3\sqrt{7}}{7}$

Lesson 13.3

1. $\left(5, -5\sqrt{3}\right)$ **3.** $\left(50\sqrt{2}, 50\sqrt{2}\right)$ **5.** $\left(-10\sqrt{2}, 10\sqrt{2}\right)$

7. (0.64, 0.77) **9.** (0.97, −0.26) **11.** $\frac{\sqrt{2}}{2}$; $\frac{\sqrt{2}}{2}$; 1

13. $-\frac{\sqrt{3}}{2}$; $\frac{1}{2}$; $-\sqrt{3}$ **15.** $-\frac{1}{2}$; $\frac{\sqrt{3}}{2}$; $-\frac{\sqrt{3}}{3}$ **17.** $-\frac{1}{2}$; $-\frac{\sqrt{3}}{2}$; $\frac{\sqrt{3}}{3}$

19. $-\frac{\sqrt{3}}{3}$ **21.** $-\frac{1}{2}$ **23.** $-\frac{1}{2}$ **25.** $\frac{1}{2}$ **27.** −1 **29.** $\frac{1}{2}$ **31.** 2

33. $\frac{1}{2}$ **35.** $-\sqrt{3}$

Lesson 13.4

1. $\frac{\pi}{6}$ radians **3.** $\frac{\pi}{9}$ radians **5.** 6π radians **7.** 120°

9. 540° **11.** 185.9° **13.** $\frac{\sqrt{2}}{2}$ **15.** 0 **17.** $\frac{1}{2}$ **19.** 1

21. ≈10.5 m **23.** 10 m

Lesson 13.5

1. 3.5; 90° **3.** 6; 360° **5.** $\frac{2}{3}$; 120° **7.** 45° left; 1 unit up

9. 90° right; no vertical translation **11.** 45° right; 3 units up

13. vertical stretch by factor of 5

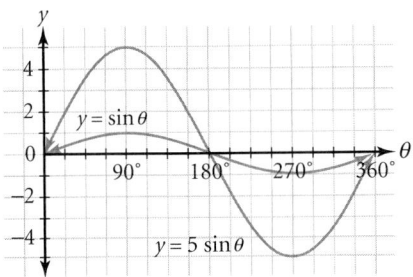

15. horizontal compression by a factor of $\frac{1}{2}$

Lesson 13.6

1. 60° + $n360°$ and 120° + $n360°$

3. 135° + $n360°$ and 225° + $n360°$

5. 135° + $n360°$ and 315° + $n360°$ **7.** 90° **9.** 30°

11. −45° **13.** $\sqrt{3}$ **15.** $\frac{\sqrt{2}}{2}$ **17.** 0° **19.** 38°

CHAPTER 14

Note: Throughout Chapter 14, answers may vary slightly due to rounding, method of calculation, or order in which solutions were found.

Lesson 14.1

1. 144.5 sq. in. **3.** 94.0 cm² **5.** 8.7 **7.** 7.6

9. $B = 95°$, $a = 8.2$, $c = 3.1$ **11.** $B = 55°$, $a = 4.4$, $c = 11.8$

13. $B = 86°$, $b = 15.6$, $c = 10.9$ **15.** 0 **17.** 7875.8 sq ft

Lesson 14.2

1. SAS, $a = 93.4$ **3.** SAS, $b = 12.3$ **5.** SAS, $a = 100.6$

7. $A = 59.5°$, $B = 83.9°$, $C = 36.6°$

9. $A = 38.6°$, $B = 48.5°$, $C = 92.9°$

11. $A \approx 24.1°$, $B = 30.8°$, $C \approx 125.1°$

13. SSS, $A = 48.5°$, $B = 55.8°$, $C = 75.7°$

15. SSA, $A = 51.2°$, $C = 56.8°$, $c \approx 8.8$

17. SSA, not possible **19.** 24.6°, 24.6°, and 130.8°

Lesson 14.3

1. $(\sec \theta)(\sin \theta) = \frac{r}{x} \cdot \frac{y}{r} = \frac{y}{x} = \tan \theta$

3. $\tan \theta = \frac{y}{x} = \frac{1}{\frac{x}{y}} = \frac{1}{\cot \theta}$

5. $\sin^2 \theta$ **7.** 1 **9.** $\cot^2 \theta$ **11.** $\dfrac{\frac{1}{\cos \theta} - \cos \theta}{\frac{\sin \theta}{\cos \theta}} = (\sin \theta)$

13. $\frac{\cos \theta}{\sin \theta}(1 - \sin \theta) + \cos \theta = \frac{\cos \theta}{\sin \theta} = \cot \theta$

15. $\dfrac{\sin \theta + \frac{\sin \theta}{\cos \theta}}{1 + \frac{1}{\cos \theta}} = \sin \theta$

Lesson 14.4

1. $\frac{\sqrt{6}}{4} - \frac{\sqrt{2}}{4}$ **3.** $-\frac{\sqrt{2}}{4} - \frac{\sqrt{6}}{4}$ **5.** $-\frac{1}{2}$ **7.** $-\frac{1}{2}$ **9.** $-\frac{\sqrt{6}}{4} - \frac{\sqrt{2}}{4}$

11. $\frac{\sqrt{6}}{4} + \frac{\sqrt{2}}{4}$ **13.** $\begin{bmatrix} 0.87 & -0.5 \\ 0.5 & 0.87 \end{bmatrix}$ **15.** $\begin{bmatrix} 0.17 & -0.98 \\ 0.98 & 0.17 \end{bmatrix}$

Lesson 14.5

1. $\cos^4 \theta - 6 \cos^2 \theta \sin^2 \theta + \sin^4 \theta$

3. $\cos^2 \theta$ **5.** $\cos \theta$ **7.** $\frac{24}{25}$, $\frac{7}{25}$ **9.** $\frac{1}{\sqrt{5}}$ or $\frac{\sqrt{5}}{5}$, $\frac{2}{\sqrt{5}}$ or $\frac{2\sqrt{5}}{5}$

Lesson 14.6

1. 225° + $n360°$ and 315° + $n360°$

3. 60° + $n360°$ and 120° + $n360°$ **5.** 0°, 60°, 180°, and 300° **7.** 120° and 240° **9.** 0°, 45°,135°, 180°, 225°, and 315° **11.** 90.0°, 199.5°, 340.5°

INDEX

Credits

Digital Stock Corp.; 663 (tr), Llewellyn/Uniphoto; 664 (t), Bob Daemmrich Photo; 667 (tr), Don Couch/ HRW Photo; 669 (br), Chip Simons/FPG International; 671 (tl), (tr), Superstock;
672 (cr), Alan Schein/The Stock Market; 673 (tc), Peter Gridley/FPG International; 678 (bl), (tr), Image Copyright © 2001 PhotoDisc, Inc.; 679 (br), Stockman/International Stock Photo. **CHAPTER ELEVEN:** Page 688 (br), Image Copyright © 2001 PhotoDisc, Inc.; 688 (cr), Arizona State Museum/University of Arizona; 689 (t), James Randklev/ Tony Stone Images; 690 (t), Mehau Kulyk/Science Photo Library/Photo Researchers; 693 (c), Runk/Schoenberger from Grant Heilman; 697 (br), Dr. Tony Brain/Science Photo Library/Photo Researchers; 698 (t), Randal Alhadeff/HRW Photo; 699 (t), Courtesy of Rainbird; 703 (tr), Mark Bolster/International Stock Photo; 705 (cr), Stephen Simpson/FPG International; 706 (br), John Langford/HRW Photo; 707 (t), 712 (tr), Don Couch/HRW Photo; 713 (t), John Langford/HRW Photo; 718 (br), Walter Bibikow/FPG International; 720 (t), John Langford/HRW Photo; 726 (cl), Globus, Holway & Lobel/The Stock Market; 727 (tr), Bob Daemmrich/ Uniphoto; 735 (bl) frame, Image Copyright © 2001 PhotoDisc, Inc.; 735 (t), Stanley Meltzoff; 740 (cr), reprinted with permission of Cambridge University Press, 1959; 741 (t), David Seelig/Allsport; 743 (tl), Courtesy of The Topps Company, Inc.; 746 (bc), (br), Image Copyright © 2001 PhotoDisc, Inc.; 747 (tr), Stephen Simpson/FPG International; 748 (tr), Christine Galida/HRW Photo; 749 (bl), Christine Galida/HRW Photo.
CHAPTER TWELVE: Page 762 (bl), David Young-Wolff/Tony Stone Images; 762 (c), Mark Scott/FPG International; 762 (tr), Novastock/PhotoEdit; 763 (tl), Janeart/The Image Bank; 764 (t), John Langford/HRW Photo; 765 (br), Robert E. Daemmrich/Tony Stone Images; 766 (bl), E.R. Degginger/Science Source/Photo Researchers; 768 (cl), Billy Hustace/Tony Stone Images; 769 (cl), David De Lossy/The Image Bank; 770 (bl), Sam Dudgeon/HRW Photo; 772 (tr), Loren Santow/Tony Stone Images; 773 (frame), Image Copyright © 2001 PhotoDisc, Inc.; 773 (tr), Rob Lewine/The Stock Market; 774 (tr), Andre Jenny/International Stock Photo; 776 (br), Charles D. Winters/Science Source/Photo Researchers; 778 (tl), Uniphoto; 779 (bl), Robert Ginn/PhotoEdit; 781 (tl), Jeff Hunter/The Image Bank; 781 (tr), John Livzey/Tony Stone Images; 784 (bl), National Baseball Hall of Fame Library & Archive; 784 (br), Milo Stewart Jr./Baseball Hall of Fame Library; 786 (bl), Grandadam/Tony Stone Images; 787 (tl), Michael Newman/PhotoEdit; 788 (tl), UPI/Corbis-Bettmann; 790 (bl), VCG/FPG International; 790 (br), Image Copyright © 2001 PhotoDisc, Inc.; 791 (br), Ron Tanaka, photo manipulation by Jun Park; 792 (tl), John Terence Turner/ FPG International; 792 (tr), David Pollack/The Stock Market; 793 (tr), Superstock; 795 (cl),

Peter Pearson/Tony Stone Images; 797 (bl), William Sallaz/The Image Bank; 798 (b), Scott Barrow/International Stock Photo; 799 (t), Yoav Levy/Phototake NYC; 801 (cr), Gabe Palmer/The Stock Market; 801 (tr), Helmut Gritscher/Peter Arnold, Inc.; 803 (cr), Renee Lynn/Science Source/Photo Researchers; 804 (bc), Randal Alhadeff/HRW Photo; 804 (bl), Corbis; 805 (tr), Matt Bradley/Uniphoto; 806 (t), Ralph H. Wetmore/Tony Stone Images; 809 (tr), Robert Essel/The Stock Market; 810 (tr), David Frazier/Tony Stone Images; 811 (cl), Gerhard Gscheidle/Peter Arnold, Inc.; 812 (bl), Sigrid Owen/ International Stock Photo; 812 (cr), Tony Freeman/PhotoEdit; 814 (bl), Scott Barrow/ International Stock Photo; 814 (c), Image Copyright © 2001 PhotoDisc, Inc.; 814 (tl), Michael Young/HRW Photo; 815 (br), (tr), Image Copyright © 2001 PhotoDisc, Inc. **CHAPTER THIRTEEN:** Page 826 (bl), F. Hidalgo/The Image Bank; 827 (bl), Superstock; 827 (C), Image Copyright © 2001 PhotoDisc, Inc.; 827 (tr), Stephen Studd/Tony Stone Images; 828 (t), S.J. Krasemann/Peter Arnold, Inc.; 833 (cl), Mark E. Gibson; 834 (br), Grant Heilman Photography; 836 (t), Joe McBride/ Tony Stone Images; 841 (tl), Neville Dawson/Check Six; 843 (tc), Tom Tracy/FPG International; 851 (t), Daily Telegraph Colour Library/International Stock Photo; 853 (bl), Roger Tully/Tony Stone Images; 854 (cr), Warren Faidley/International Stock Photo; 855 (tl), Matt Brown/Uniphoto; 858 (tr), D. Roundtree/The Image Bank; 862 (tr), Ron Scherl/Stage Image; 865 (cl), Marc Romanelli/The Image Bank; 872 (cr), Merritt Vincent/PhotoEdit; 874 (br), Peter Pearson/Tony Stone Images; 874–875 (bckgd), UPI/Corbis Bettmann; 875 (tr), Carnegie Library, Pittsburgh.
CHAPTER FOURTEEN: Page 884 (bc), David Parker/Science Photo Library/Photo Researchers; 884 (br), Spencer Jones/FPG International; 885 (t), Tony Stone Images; 886 (t), Superstock; 892 (c), VCG/FPG International; 893 (tl), Joe Towers/The Stock Market; 894 (t), Grant V. Faint/The Image Bank; 900 (br), Walter Bibicow/The Image Bank; 901 (tl), Uniphoto; 902 (t), Superstock, photo manipulation by Morgan-Cain & Associates; 905 (cr), Ben Osborne/Tony Stone Images; 906 (c), Image Copyright © 2001 PhotoDisc, Inc.; 907 (br), Superstock; 908 (cl), Francois Gohier/Photo Researchers; 909 (tl), Adam Peiperl/The Stock Market; 915 (br), Warren Bolster/Tony Stone Images; 915 (cl), Dennis Hallinan/FPG International; 916 (tr), Will Ryan/The Stock Market; 917 (t), Superstock; 920 (frame), Image Copyright © 2001 PhotoDisc, Inc.; 920 (tr), Erich Lessing/Art Resource, NY; 921 (tr), Rich Kane/SportsChrome USA; 922 (tl), Uniphoto; 922 (tr), David Madison/Tony Stone Images; 925 (bl), Henry T. Kaiser/ Uniphoto; 927 (bl), Bill Beatty/Visuals Unlimited; 928 (bl), Corbis; 928 (l), T. Shinoda/Photonica; 929 (br), Randal Alhadeff/HRW Photo; 929 (r), T. Simabukuro/Photonica; 929 (tr), Corbis.

ILLUSTRATIONS

All technical and line art by Morgan-Cain & Associates. Other art, unless otherwise noted, by Holt, Rinehart & Winston.

Abbreviated as follows: (t) top, (b) bottom, (l) left, (r) right, (c) center.
CHAPTER ONE: Page 3 (cr), Morgan-Cain & Associates; 9 (bl), Stephen Durke/ Washington-Artists' Represents; 22 (tl), Michael Morrow Design; 42 (c), Visual Sense Illustration/Margo Davies Leclair; 43 (t), Ian Phillips; 50 (cr), Leslie Kell; 51 (tl), Leslie Kell; 54 (tr), Stephen Durke/Washington-Artists' Represents; 66 (t), Michael Morrow Design. **CHAPTER TWO:** Page 88 (c), Leslie Kell; 90 (t), Stephen Durke/Washington-Artists' Represents; 92 (cl), Stephen Durke/Washington-Artists' Represents; 100 (bl), Stephen Durke/Washington-Artists' Represents; 107 (bl), Stephen Durke/Washington-Artists' Represents; 113 (tc), Stephen Durke/Washington-Artists' Represents; 118 (tr), Stephen Durke/Washington-Artists' Represents; 123 (c), Stephen Durke/Washington-Artists' Represents; 124 (tr), Leslie Kell. **CHAPTER THREE:** Page 154 (c), Morgan-Cain & Associates; 158 (tr), Stephen Durke/Washington-Artists' Represents; 172 (c), Leslie Kell; 182 (tr), Leslie Kell. **CHAPTER FOUR:** Page 214 (c), Morgan-Cain & Associates; 232 (c), Stephen Durke/Washington-Artists' Represents; 244 (tr), Leslie Kell; 249 (br), Leslie Kell; 250 (tc), Jun Park. **CHAPTER FIVE:** Page 274 (c), Stephen Durke/ Washington-Artists' Represents; 279 (cl), Stephen Durke/Washington-Artists' Represents; 283 (cr), Stephen Durke/ Washington-Artists' Represents; 289 (tr), Stephen Durke/ Washington-Artists' Represents; 290 (t), Uhl Studio Incorporated; 295 (tr), Uhl Studio Incorporated; 307 (cr), Stephen Durke/Washington-Artists' Represents; 312 (tl), Uhl Studio Incorporated; 314 (tl), Stephen Durke/Washington-Artists' Represents. **CHAPTER SIX:** Page 360 (tl), Leslie Kell; 368 (br), Martha Newbigging; 374 (cr), Stephen Durke/Washington-Artists' Represents; 383 (cr), Stephen Durke/ Washington-Artists' Represents; 391 (cr), Stephen Durke/Washington-Artists' Represents; 398 (br), Nenad Jakesevic; 405 (bl), Stephen Durke/Washington-Artists' Represents; 407 (br), Leslie Kell; 408 (tr), Jun Park. **CHAPTER SEVEN:** Page 424 (tr),

Stephen Durke/Washington-Artists' Represents; 448 (tr), Uhl Studio Incorporated; 453 (tr), Stephen Durke/Washington-Artists' Represents; 458 (tc), Leslie Kell.
CHAPTER EIGHT: Page 478 (c), Uhl Studio Incorporated; 484 (tr), Uhl Studio Incorporated; 504 (t), Stephen Durke/Washington-Artists' Represents; 510 (b), Stephen Durke/Washington-Artists' Represents; 533 (tr), Stephen Durke/Washington-Artists' Represents; 544 (c), Leslie Kell. **CHAPTER NINE:** Page 560–1 (all), Uhl Studio Incorporated; 562 (tr), Stephen Durke/Washington-Artists' Represents; 564 (br), Ortelius Design; 577 (bl), Jun Park; 586, (br), Jun Park; 593 (bl), Leslie Kell; 610 (bl), Uhl Studio Incorporated; 613 (tr), Stephen Durke/Washington-Artists' Represents.
CHAPTER TEN: Page 634 (br), Michael Herman; 643 (t), Stephen Durke/ Washington-Artists' Represents; 643 (t), Stephen Durke/Washington-Artists' Represents; 645 (cr), Leslie Kell; 647 (cl), Stephen Durke/Washington-Artists' Represents; 650 (bc), Leslie Kell; 657 (br), Leslie Kell; 662 (br), Stephen Durke/Washington-Artists' Represents; 675 (tr), Leslie Kell; 677 (tr), Leslie Kell. **CHAPTER ELEVEN:** Page 711 (br), Stephen Durke/ Washington-Artists' Represents; 719 (t), Uhl Studio Incorporated; 722 (b), Uhl Studio Incorporated; 725 (br), Michael Herman; 727 (bl), Leslie Kell; 728 (cr), Michael Herman; 744 (bl), Pronk & Associates. **CHAPTER TWELVE:** Page 762 (b), Morgan-Cain & Associates; 763 (tr), Stephen Durke/ Washington-Artists' Represents; 782 (r), Leslie Kell; 785 (cl), Bernadette Lau. **CHAPTER THIRTEEN:** Page 828 (cl), Morgan-Cain & Associates; 831 (cr), Morgan-Cain & Associates; 831 (bl), Nenad Jakesevic; 833 (tr), Terry Guyer; 834 (cr), Nenad Jakesevic; 835 (t), Terry Guyer; 837 (tr), Leslie Kell; 849 (cl), Uhl Studio Incorporated; 850 (cr), Terry Guyer; 856 (cr), Uhl Studio Incorporated; 856 (br) David Puckett; 867 (t), Stephen Durke/Washington-Artists' Represents; 872 (br), Morgan-Cain & Associates; 873 (tr), Terry Guyer; 873 (cr), Stephen Durke/Washington-Artists' Represents. **CHAPTER FOURTEEN:** Page 892 (cr), Morgan-Cain & Associates; 892 (b), Morgan-Cain & Associates; 893 (tr), Morgan-Cain & Associates; 896 (tr), Morgan-Cain & Associates; 901 (br), Leslie Kell; 927 (c), Morgan-Cain & Associates; 932 (all), Morgan-Cain & Associates.

PERMISSIONS

For permission to reprint copyrighted material, grateful acknowledgment is made to the following sources:

Carlisle & Company on behalf of James Gleick: From "The Quest for True Randomness Finally Appears Successful" by James Gleick from *The New York Times,* April 19, 1988. Copyright © 1988 by James Gleick.

The New York Times Company: From "Biggest Division a Giant Leap in Math" by Gina Kolata and "Factoring a 155 Digit Number: The Problem Solved" from *The New York Times,* June 20, 1990. Copyright © 1990 by The New York Times Company.

Marilyn vos Savant and Parade: From column "Ask Marilyn™" by Marilyn vos Savant from *PARADE,* September 9, 1990. Copyright © 1990 by Parade.

Sandusky Register, Ohio: From "Coasting to Records" from *Sandusky Register,* July 27, 1989. Copyright © 1989 by Sandusky Register.

St. Louis Mercantile Library Association: Photo caption "St. Louis Can Now Boast of the Nation's Highest Memorial" from *St. Louis Globe-Democrat,* October 29, 1965. From the collections of the St. Louis Mercantile Library at the University of Missouri–St. Louis.

Time Inc.: From "Time for Some Fuzzy Thinking" by Philip Elmer-Dewitt from *Time,* September 25, 1989. Copyright © 1989 by Time Inc.

USA Today: Excerpt from "U.S. Birth Rate at a Record Low." Copyright © 1998 by USA Today.